ENCYCLOPEDIA OF THE

VIETNAM WAR

A POLITICAL, SOCIAL, AND MILITARY HISTORY

ENCYCLOPEDIA OF THE

VOLUME TWO

VIETNAM WAR

A POLITICAL, SOCIAL, AND MILITARY HISTORY

Spencer C. Tucker, editor

Santa Barbara, California
Denver, Colorado
Oxford, England

Library of Congress Cataloging-in-Publication Data

Encyclopedia of the Vietnam War : a political, social, and military history / Spencer C. Tucker ; with a foreword by Admiral Elmo R. Zumwalt, Jr.
    p.   cm.
   Includes bibliographical references (p.) and index.
   1. Vietnamese Conflict, 1961–1975—Encyclopedias.   I. Tucker, Spencer C., 1937– .
DS557.7.E53   1998   98-4184
959.7'03—dc21   CIP

ISBN 0-87436-983-5 (alk. paper)

02   01   00   99   98   10 9 8 7 6 5 4 3 2 1

ABC-CLIO, Inc.
130 Cremona Drive, P.O. Box 1911
Santa Barbara, California 93116-1911

This book is printed on acid-free paper ∞.
Manufactured in the United States of America.

The Contributors

Betsy Alexander
Department of History
Texas Christian University
Fort Worth, Texas

Kevin Arceneaux
Department of History
Texas Christian University
Fort Worth, Texas

Lacie Ballinger
Department of History
Texas Christian University
Fort Worth, Texas

Capt. Pat Barker
U.S. Air Force Academy
Colorado Springs, Colorado

John Barcus
Department of History
Louisiana State University
Baton Rouge, Louisiana

Dr. Mark Barringer
Department of History
Texas Tech University
Lubbock, Texas

Dr. Harry Basehart
Department of Political Science
Salisbury State University
Salisbury, Maryland

Dr. John L. Bell, Jr.
Department of History
Western Carolina University
Cullowhee, North Carolina

Dr. David M. Berman
Department of Curriculum and Education
School of Education
University of Pittsburgh
Pittsburgh, Pennsylvania

Dr. Ernest C. Bolt
Mitchell-Billikopf Professor of History
University of Richmond
Richmond, Virginia

Walter Boyne
Smithsonian Institution (retired)
Ashburn, Virginia

Dr. Robert Brigham
Department of History
Vassar College
Poughkeepsie, New York

Dean Brumley
Department of History
Texas Christian University
Fort Worth, Texas

Peter Brush
Central Library
Vanderbilt University
Nashville, Tennessee

Dr. Hum Dac Bui
Redlands, California

Dr. Robert J. Bunker
Claremont, California

Dr. Paul R. Camacho
University of Massachusetts—Boston
The William Joiner Center
Boston, Massachusetts

J. Nathan Campbell
Department of History
Texas Christian University
Fort Worth, Texas

Dr. Ralph Carter
Department of Political Science
Texas Christian University
Fort Worth, Texas

Thomas R. Carver
Seymour, Texas

Rajesh H. Chauhan
Claremont, California

Dr. Edwin Clausen
Department of History
Pacific Lutheran University
Tacoma, Washington

David Coffey
Department of History
Texas Christian University
Fort Worth, Texas

Matthew Crump
Department of History
Texas Christian University
Fort Worth, Texas

Dr. Cecil B. Currey
University of South Florida
Lutz, Florida

Dr. Paul Daum
Department of History
New England College
Henniker, New Hampshire

Dr. Arthur J. Dommen
The Indochina Institute
George Mason University
Fairfax, Virginia

Timothy G. Dowling
Department of History
Louisiana State University
Baton Rouge, Louisiana

Benjamin Dubberly
Department of History
Texas Tech University
Lubbock, Texas

Dr. Joe P. Dunn
Department of History and Politics
Converse College
Spartanburg, South Carolina

Blake Dunnavent
Department of History
Lubbock Christian College
Lubbock, Texas

Dr. Bruce Elleman
History Department
Texas Christian University
Fort Worth, Texas

Dr. Mark A. Esposito
Department of History
West Virginia University
Morgantown, West Virginia

Lt. Col. Peter Faber
Department of History
U.S. Air Force Academy
Colorado Springs, Colorado

Dr. Will E. Fahey, Jr.
Haverhill, Massachusetts

Dr. Charles Fasanaro
Santa Fe, New Mexico

Dr. Arthur Thomas Frame
Lansing, Kansas

James Friguglietti
Department of History
Montana State University—Billings
Billings, Montana

Dr. Peter K. Frost
Department of History
Williams College
Williamstown, Massachusetts

1st Lt. Noel Fulton
Department of History
U.S. Air Force Academy
Colorado Springs, Colorado

George J. Gabera
Claremont, California

Charles J. Gaspar
Department of Humanities and Communi-
cation Arts
Brenau University
Gainesville, Georgia

John Gates
Department of History
Wooster College
Wooster, Ohio

Capt. Larry Gatti
Department of History
U.S. Air Force Academy
Colorado Springs, Colorado

Laurie Geist
Department of Humanities
Illinois Institute of Technology
Chicago, Illinois

Dr. Marc J. Gilbert
Department of History
North Georgia College
Dahlonega, Georgia

Dr. Mark Gilderhus
Department of History
Texas Christian University
Fort Worth, Texas

Dr. James Gilliam
Spellman College
Atlanta, Georgia

Tim Grammer
Dallas, Texas

Professor John Robert Greene
Department of History
Cazenovia College
Cazenovia, New York

Capt. John Grenier
Department of History
U.S. Air Force Academy
Colorado Springs, Colorado

Dr. Charles J. Gross
Departments of the Army and the Air
Force
National Guard Bureau
Washington, D.C.

Debra Hall
Department of History
Cazenovia College
Cazenovia, New York

Dr. Mitchell K. Hall
Department of History
Central Michigan University
Mount Pleasant, Michigan

Dr. William Head
Chief, Office of History
Warner Robins Air Logistics Center
Warner Robins, Georgia

Glenn E. Helm
Naval Historical Center
Department of the Navy
Washington Navy Yard
Washington, D.C.

Pia C. Heyn
Lexington, Kentucky

2nd Lt. Joel Higley
Department of History
U.S. Air Force Academy
Colorado Springs, Colorado

2nd Lt. Lincoln Hill
Department of History
U.S. Air Force Academy
Colorado Springs, Colorado

Anh Dieu Hô
Madison, Connecticut

Dr. Richard Hunt
Center for Military History
Washington, D.C.

Dr. Arnold Isaacs
Pasadena, Maryland

Dr. Eric Jarvis
Department of History
King's College
London, Ontario, Canada

Susan G. Kalaf

Mary Kelley
Department of History
Texas Christian University
Fort Worth, Texas

Ann Kelsey
Whippany, New Jersey

Dr. Gary Kerley
Brenau Academy
Gainesville, Georgia

Dr. Jeff Kinard
Greensboro, North Carolina

Lt. Col. Richard L. Kiper
Leavenworth, Kansas

2nd Lt. Brent Langhals
Department of History
U.S. Air Force Academy
Colorado Springs, Colorado

Capt. Alex R. Larzelere
U.S. Coast Guard, Retired
Alexandria, Virginia

Dr. Clayton D. Laurie
Conventional Warfare Studies Branch
Histories Division
United States Army Center of Military
*   History*
Washington, D.C.

Dr. William M. Leary
Department of History
University of Georgia
Athens, Georgia

Dr. Jack McCallum, M.D.
Fort Worth, Texas

Dr. Stanley McGowen
Department of History
Texas Christian University
Fort Worth, Texas

James McNabb
Claremont, California

Dr. Robert G. Mangrum
Department of History
Howard Payne University
Brownwood, Texas

Justin Marks
Department of History
Cazenovia College
Cazenovia, New York

Dr. Edward J. Marolda
Senior Historian
Naval Historical Center
Department of the Navy
Washington Navy Yard
Washington, D.C.

Dr. (Col.) Joseph Martino
U.S. Air Force, Retired
Sidney, Ohio

Jay Menzoff
Department of History
Texas Christian University
Fort Worth, Texas

Dr. Edwin E. Moise
Department of History
Clemson University
Clemson, South Carolina

Louise Mongelluzo
Department of History
Cazenovia College
Cazenovia, New York

Dr. Malcolm Muir, Jr.
Department of History
Austin Peay State University
Clarksville, Tennessee

Mike Nichols
Department of History
Texas Christian University
Fort Worth, Texas

Ngô Ngoc Trung
Institute for East Asian Studies
University of California
Berkeley, California

Nguyôn Công Luân
Santa Clara, California

Stephen R. Maynard
Denton, Texas

Dr. Long Ba Nguyen
Viet Business Publications
Toronto, Ontario, Canada

Dr. Edward McNertney
Department of Economics
Texas Christian University
Fort Worth, Texas

Cynthia Northrup
Department of History
Texas Christian University
Fort Worth, Texas

Dr. Michael G. O'Loughlin
Department of Political Science
Salisbury State University
Salisbury, Maryland

Eric Osborne
Department of History
Texas Christian University
Fort Worth, Texas

Edward Page
Department of History
Texas Christian University
Fort Worth, Texas

Greg Perdue
Department of History
University of Texas
Austin, Texas

Delia Pergande
Department of History
University of Kentucky
Lexington, Kentucky

Dr. Dùòng Cao Pham
Huntington Beach, California

Thomas Phu
Alexandria, Virginia

Dr. Charlotte A. Power
Department of History
Black River Technical College
Pochantas, Arkansas

Dr. John Clark Pratt
Department of English
Colorado State University
Fort Collins, Colorado

Dr. Michael Richards
Department of History
Sweet Briar College
Sweet Briar, Virginia

Dr. Priscilla Roberts
Department of History
University of Hong Kong
Hong Kong

Dr. John D. Root
Lewis Department of Humanities
Armour College
Illinois Institute of Technology
Chicago, Illinois

Dr. Rodney J. Ross
Harrisburg, Pennsylvania

Mr. Harve Saal
MACV, Studies and Observations Group
MACV-SOG History Project
Tumwater, Washington

Dr. David C. Saffell
Department of History and Political
Science
Ohio Northern University
Ada, Ohio

Dr. Stanley Sandler
JFK Special Warfare School
Fort Bragg
Fayetteville, North Carolina

Dr. Claude R. Sasso
Kansas City, MO

Captain Carl Otis Schuster
HQ USCINCPAC, J-22
Kailua, Hawaii

Dr. Michael Share
Department of History
The University of Hong Kong
Hong Kong

Dr. Lewis Sorley
Potomac, Maryland

Dr. James Southerland
Brenau University
Gainesville, Georgia

Dr. Phoebe Spinrad
Columbus, Ohio

Richard Starnes
Auburn, Alabama

Leslie-Rahye Strickland
Stephenville, Texas

1st Lt. Tracy Szczepaniak
Department of History
U.S. Air Force Academy
Colorado Springs, Colorado

Dr. Brenda Taylor
Department of History
Texas Wesleyan University
Fort Worth, Texas

Capt. John Terino
U.S. Air Force Academy
Colorado Springs, Colorado

Dr. Francis H. Thompson
Department of History
Western Kentucky University
Bowling Green, Kentucky

Dr. Earl H. Tilford, Jr.
Army War College
Carlisle, Pennsylvania

Dr. Vincent Transano
Naval Facilities Engineering Command
Naval Construction Battalion Center
Port Hueneme, California

Zsolt Varga
Department of History
Texas Christian University
Fort Worth, Texas

Dr. John F. Votaw
The Cantigny First Division Foundation
Wheaton, Illinois

Hieu Dinh Vu
Dallas, Texas

Wes Watters
Department of History
Texas Christian University
Fort Worth, Texas

Dr. James M. Welsh
English Department
Salisbury State University
Salisbury, Maryland

Mike Werttheimer
Naval Historical Center
Department of the Navy
Washington Navy Yard
Washington, D.C.

Donald Whaley
Department of History
Salisbury State University
Salisbury, Maryland

Lt. Col. James H. Willbanks
Department of Joint and Combined
Operations
US Army Command and General Staff
College
Fort. Leavenworth, Kansas

Professor Sandra Wittman
Library Services
Oakton Community College
Des Plaines, Illinois

Dr. Laura M. Wood
Department of Social Sciences
Tarrant County Junior College,
Northwest
Fort Worth, Texas

Lee Ann Woodall
Department of History
McMurry University
Abilene, Texas

Colonel David T. Zabecki
Freiburg, Germany

Admiral Elmo R. Zumwalt, Jr.
U.S. Navy, Retired
Arlington, Virginia

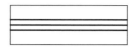

Contents

ENCYCLOPEDIA OF THE VIETNAM WAR
A Political, Social, and Military History

List of Entries

Volume I

List of Maps

PEOPLE'S REPUBLIC OF CHINA

Black River

Red River

SOCIALIST REPUBLIC OF VIETNAM

Hà Nôi

MYANMARA

LAOS

Gulf of Tonkin

20°

Hainan Island

Vientiane

Mekong River

THAILAND

16°

Bangkok

CAMBODIA

12°

Phnom Penh

HÔ CHI MINH CITY
(SÀI GON)

South China Sea

Côn Sơn

INDO-CHINA

Political   1998

International Boundaries — · — · —

Miles   200
Kms   200

100°   104°   106°

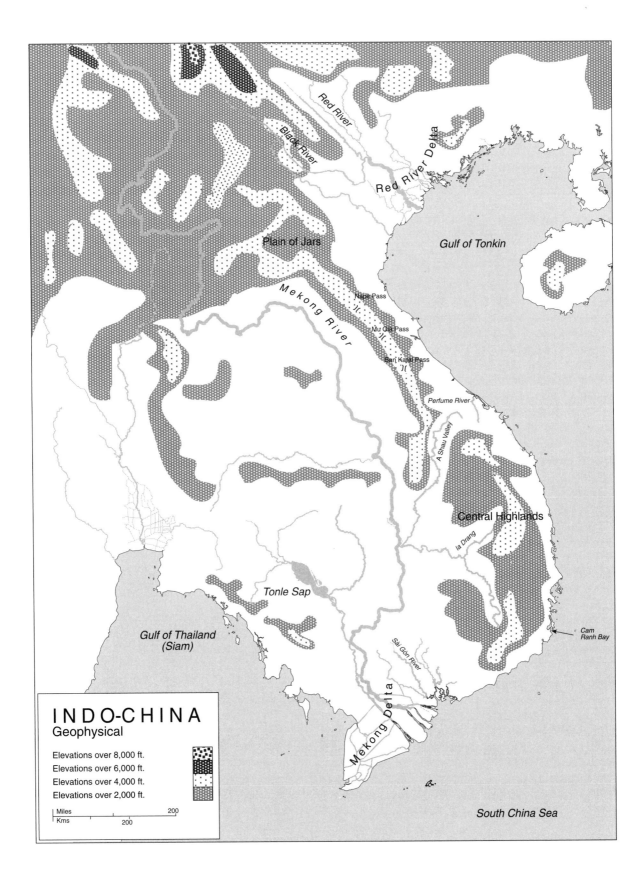

INDO-CHINA
Geophysical

Elevations over 8,000 ft.
Elevations over 6,000 ft.
Elevations over 4,000 ft.
Elevations over 2,000 ft.

Miles 200
Kms 200

Red River

Black River

Red River Delta

Gulf of Tonkin

Plain of Jars

Mekong River

Nape Pass

Mu Gia Pass

Ban Karai Pass

Perfume River

A Shau Valley

Central Highlands

Ia Drang

Tonle Sap

Gulf of Thailand
(Siam)

Sai Gon River

Cam Ranh Bay

Mekong Delta

South China Sea

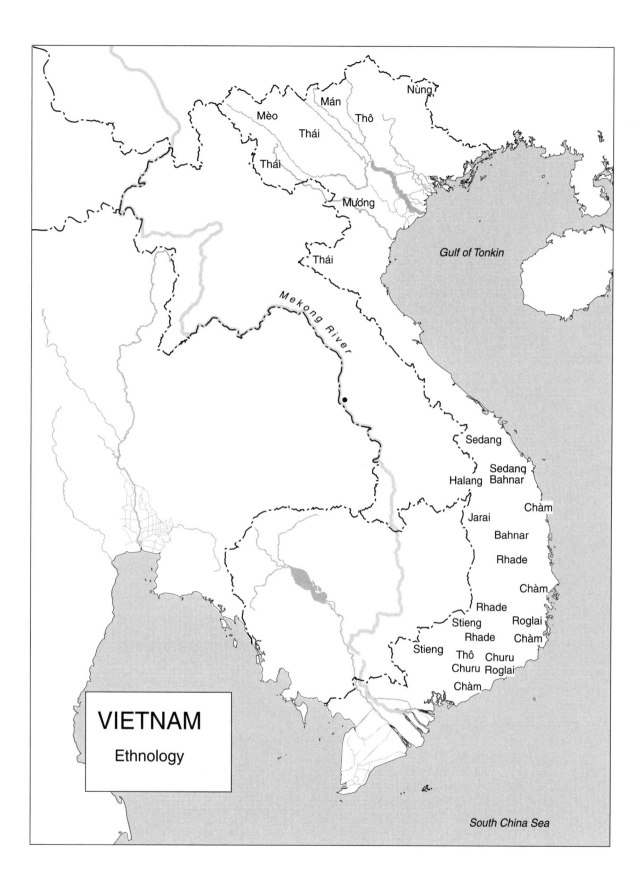

VIETNAM

Ethnology

Mèo

Mán

Nùng

Thái

Thô

Thái

Mường

Thái

Mekong River

Gulf of Tonkin

Sedang

Sedang

Halang Bahnar

Chàm

Jarai

Bahnar

Rhade

Chàm

Rhade

Stieng Roglai

Rhade Chàm

Stieng

Thô Churu

Churu Roglai

Chàm

South China Sea

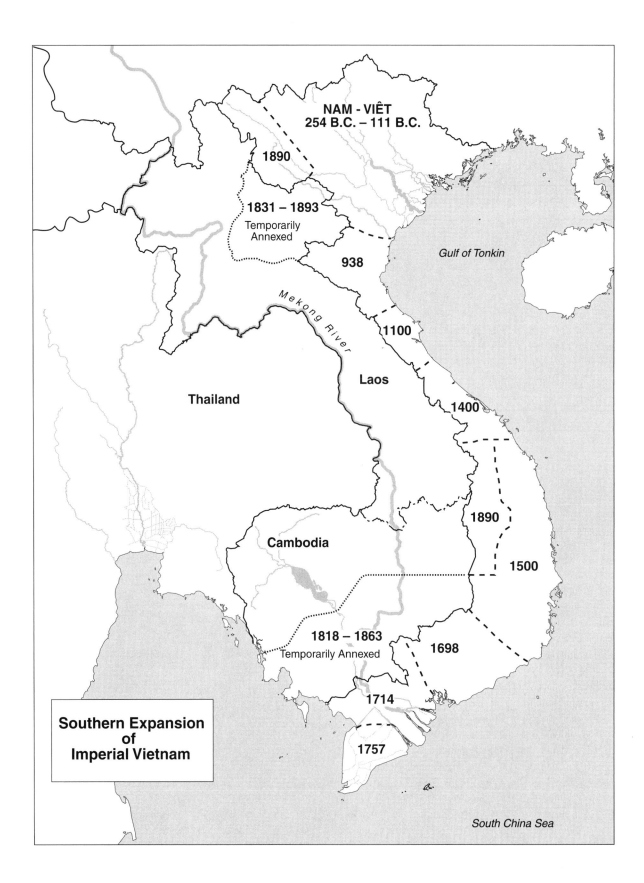

NAM - VIÊT
254 B.C. – 111 B.C.

1890

1831 – 1893
Temporarily
Annexed

938

Gulf of Tonkin

Mekong River

1100

Laos

1400

Thailand

1890

1500

Cambodia

1818 – 1863
Temporarily Annexed

1698

1714

**Southern Expansion
of
Imperial Vietnam**

1757

South China Sea

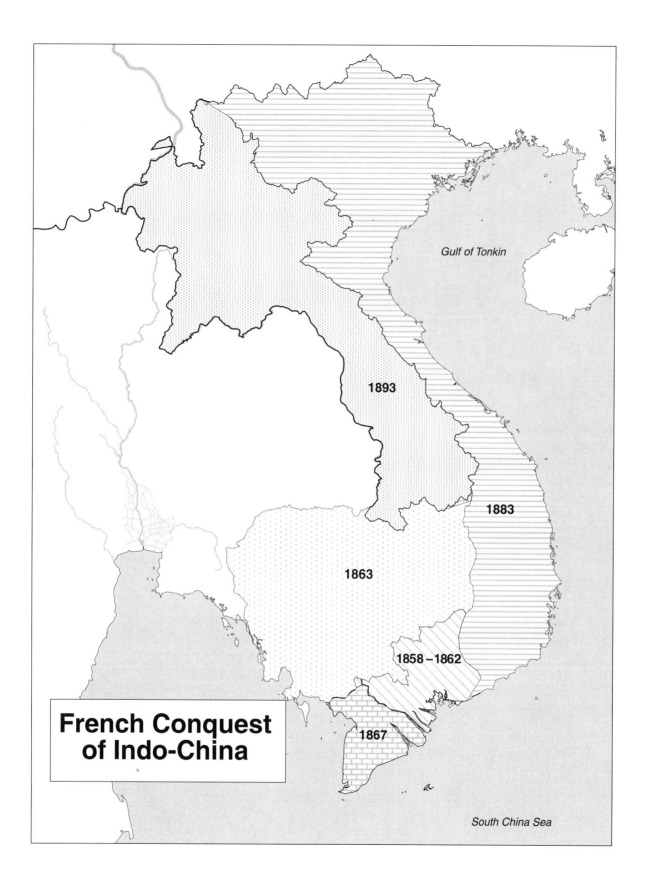

Gulf of Tonkin

1893

1883

1858–1862

1863

1867

French Conquest of Indo-China

South China Sea

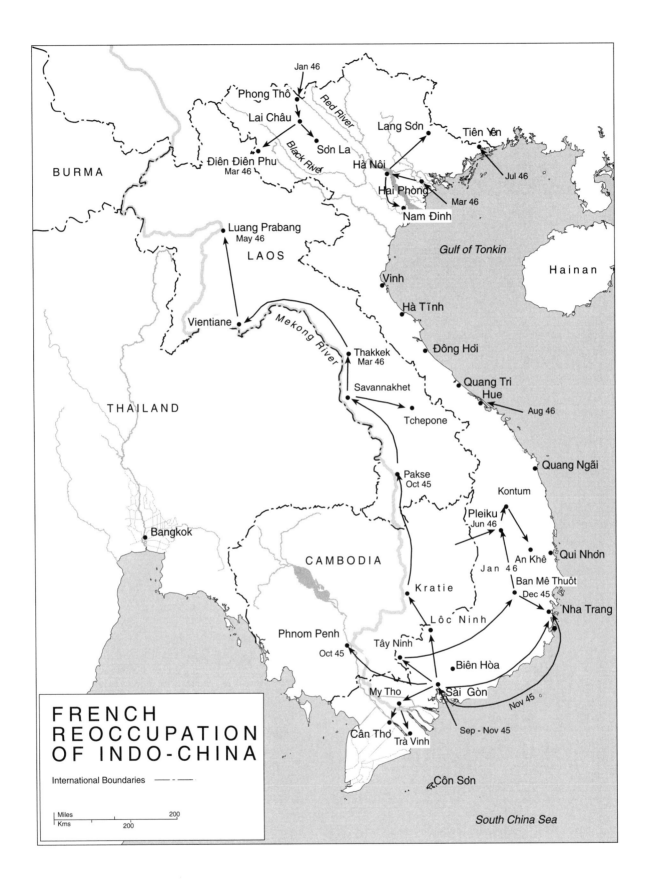

**FRENCH
REOCCUPATION
OF INDO-CHINA**

International Boundaries — · — ·

Miles 200
Kms 200

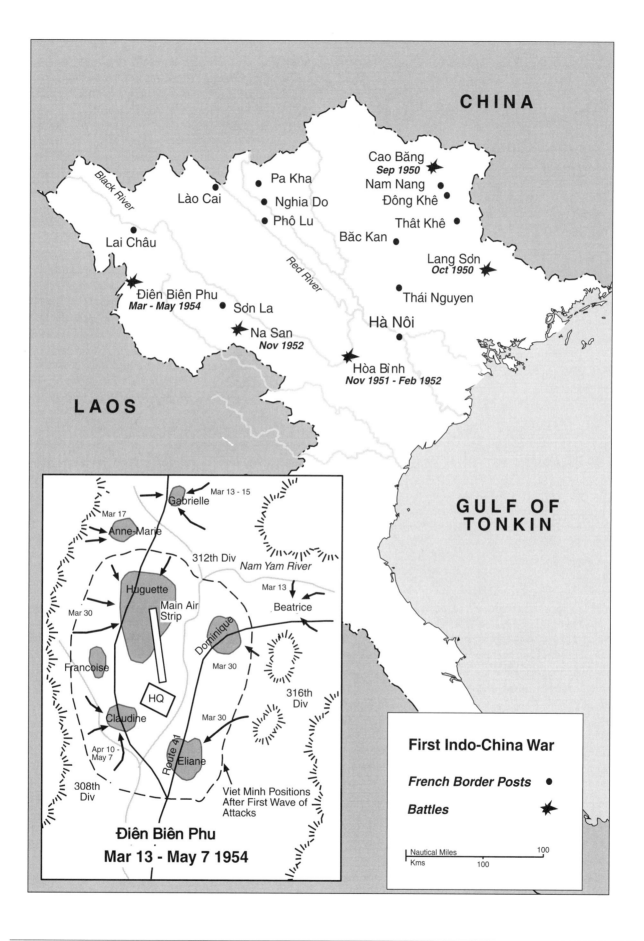

CHINA

Black River

Pa Kha
Lào Cai
Nghia Do
Phô Lu

Cao Băng
Sep 1950

Nam Nang
Đông Khê

Thât Khê

Lai Châu

Bắc Kan

Red River

Lang Sơn
Oct 1950

Điên Biên Phu
Mar - May 1954

Sơn La

Thái Nguyen

Na San
Nov 1952

Hà Nôi

LAOS

Hòa Bình
Nov 1951 - Feb 1952

GULF OF
TONKIN

Mar 13 - 15
Gabrielle

Mar 17
Anne-Marie

312th Div

Nam Yam River

Huguette

Mar 13
Beatrice

Mar 30

Main Air
Strip

Dominique

Mar 30

Francoise

316th
Div

HQ

Claudine

Mar 30

Apr 10 -
May 7

Eliane

Route 41

308th
Div

Viet Minh Positions
After First Wave of
Attacks

Điên Biên Phu

Mar 13 - May 7 1954

First Indo-China War

French Border Posts •

Battles ✦

Nautical Miles   100
Kms   100

xxvii

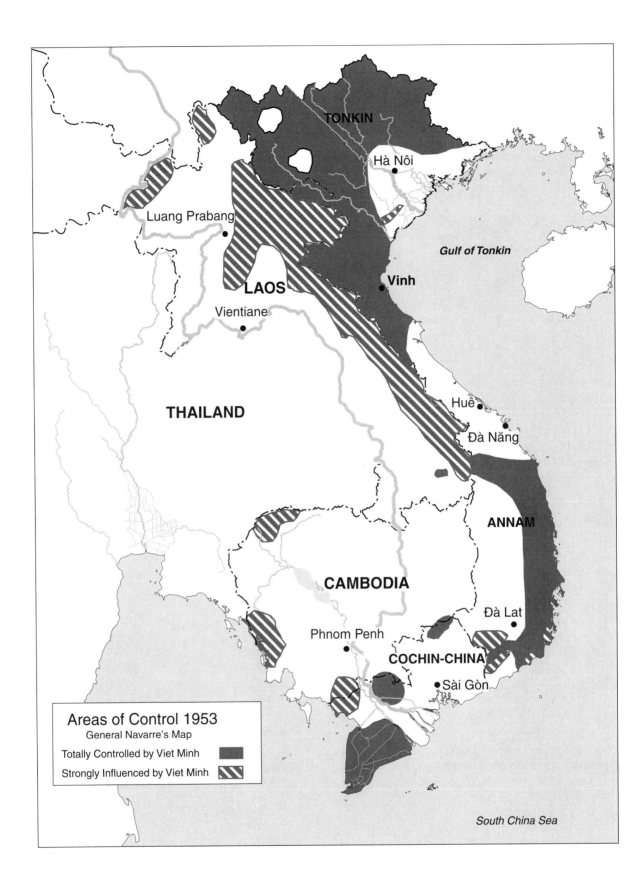

Areas of Control 1953
General Navarre's Map

| | Totally Controlled by Viet Minh |
| | Strongly Influenced by Viet Minh |

TONKIN

Hà Nôi

Luang Prabang

Gulf of Tonkin

LAOS

Vinh

Vientiane

THAILAND

Huê

Đà Nẵng

ANNAM

CAMBODIA

Đà Lat

Phnom Penh

COCHIN-CHINA

Sài Gòn

South China Sea

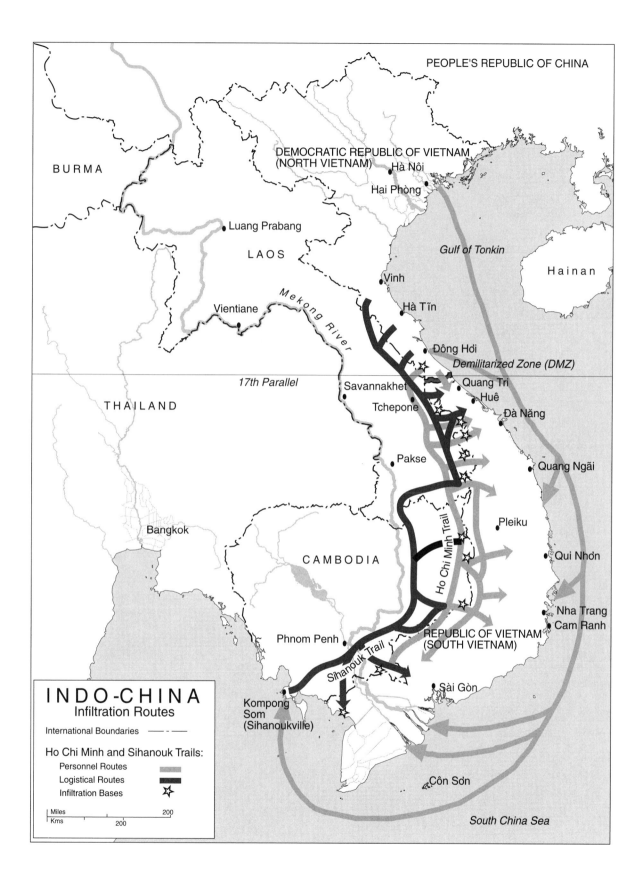

PEOPLE'S REPUBLIC OF CHINA

BURMA

DEMOCRATIC REPUBLIC OF VIETNAM
(NORTH VIETNAM) Hà Nôi

Hai Phòng

Luang Prabang

LAOS

Gulf of Tonkin

Hainan

Vinh

Vientiane

Mekong River

Hà Tĩn

Đông Hơi

Demilitarized Zone (DMZ)

17th Parallel

Savannakhet

Quang Tri
Huê

THAILAND

Tchepone

Đà Nẵng

Pakse

Quang Ngãi

Bangkok

Pleiku

CAMBODIA

Ho Chi Minh Trail

Qui Nhơn

Nha Trang
Cam Ranh

Phnom Penh

REPUBLIC OF VIETNAM
(SOUTH VIETNAM)

Sihanouk Trail

Sài Gòn

Kompong
Som
(Sihanoukville)

INDO-CHINA
Infiltration Routes

International Boundaries   — - — - —

Ho Chi Minh and Sihanouk Trails:

Personnel Routes

Logistical Routes

Infiltration Bases   ☆

| Miles | | 200 |
| Kms | 200 | |

Côn Sơn

South China Sea

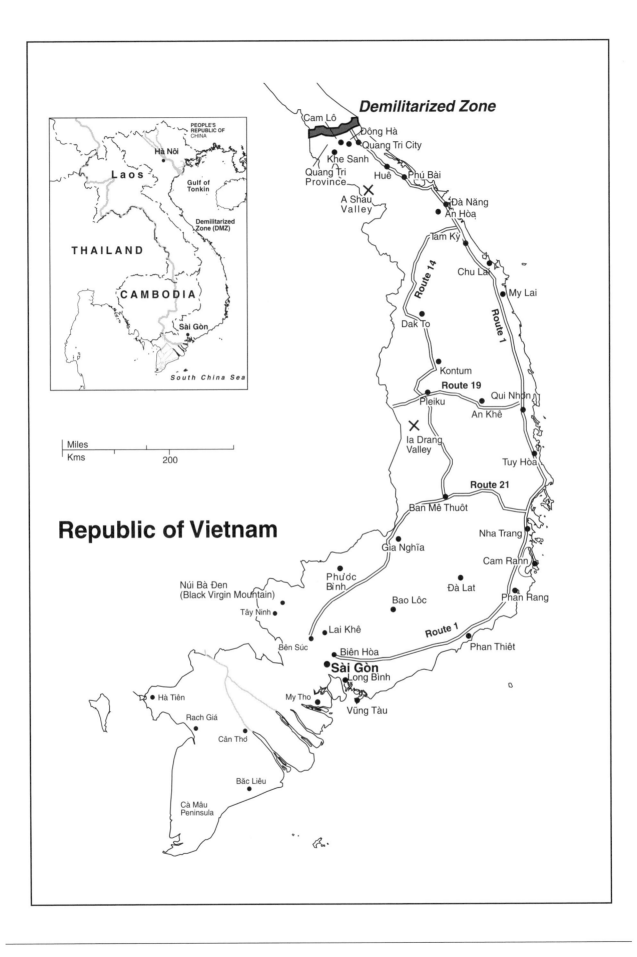

Demilitarized Zone

Republic of Vietnam

PEOPLE'S REPUBLIC OF CHINA

Laos

Gulf of Tonkin

Demilitarized Zone (DMZ)

THAILAND

CAMBODIA

South China Sea

Hà Nôi

Sài Gòn

Cam Lô
Đông Hà
Quang Tri City
Khe Sanh
Quang Tri Province
Huê
Phú Bài
A Shau Valley
Đà Nẵng
An Hòa
Tam Kỳ
Route 14
Chu Lai
My Lai
Route 1
Dak To
Kontum
Route 19
Qui Nhơn
Pleiku
An Khê
Ia Drang Valley
Tuy Hòa
Route 21
Ban Mê Thuôt
Nha Trang
Gia Nghĩa
Cam Rahn
Núi Bà Đen (Black Virgin Mountain)
Phước Bình
Đà Lat
Bao Lôc
Phan Rang
Tây Ninh
Lai Khê
Route 1
Bên Súc
Biên Hòa
Phan Thiêt
Sài Gòn
Long Bình
Hà Tiên
My Tho
Vũng Tàu
Rach Giá
Cân Thơ
Bắc Liêu
Cà Mâu Peninsula

Miles
Kms
200

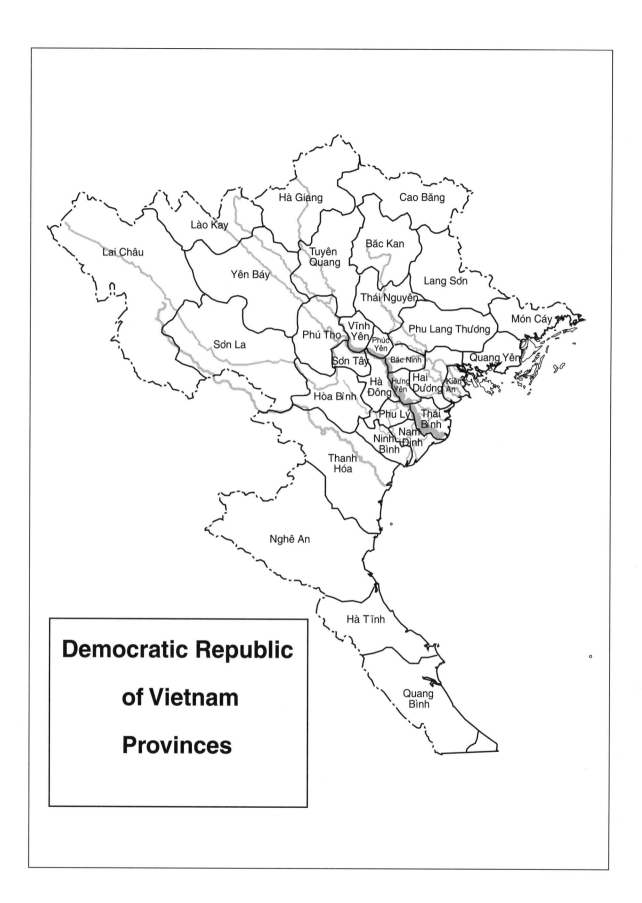

Lai Châu

Lào Kay

Hà Giang

Cao Băng

Yên Báy

Tuyên
Quang

Băc Kan

Lang Sơn

Sơn La

Thái Nguyên

Phú Tho

Vĩnh
Yên

Phúc
Yên

Phu Lang Thương

Món Cáy

Băc Ninh

Sơn Tây

Hà
Đông

Hưng
Yên

Hai
Dương

Kiên
An

Quang Yên

Hòa Bình

Phu Lý

Thái
Bình

Ninh
Bình

Nam
Định

Thanh
Hóa

Nghê An

Hà Tĩnh

Quang
Bình

Democratic Republic

of Vietnam

Provinces

Corps boundary

Province boundary

Autonomous municipality

Republic of Vietnam Provinces

Demilitarized Zone

Quang Tri

Huê

Thừa Thiên

Đà Nẵng

Quang Nam

Quang Tín

Quang Ngãi

Kontum

Bình Định

Pleiku

Phú Bổn

Phú Yên

Darlac

Khánh Hòa

Quang Đức

Tuyên Đức

Phước Long

Ninh Thuận

Bình Long

Lâm Đồng

Tây Ninh

Bình Dương

Long Khánh

Bình Tuy

Bình Thuận

Biên Hòa

Hậu Nghĩa

Gia Định

Chau Doc

Kiên Phuong

Kiên Tường

Long An

Gò Công

Phước Tuy

Kiên Giang

An Giang

Sa Đéc

Đinh Tường

VUNG TÀU

Phuong Dinh

Vĩnh Long

Kiên Hòa

Đao Phú Quôc
(Kiên Giang)

Chương Thiên

Ba Xuyên

Vĩnh Bình

Bắc Liêu

An Xuyên

Côn Sơn

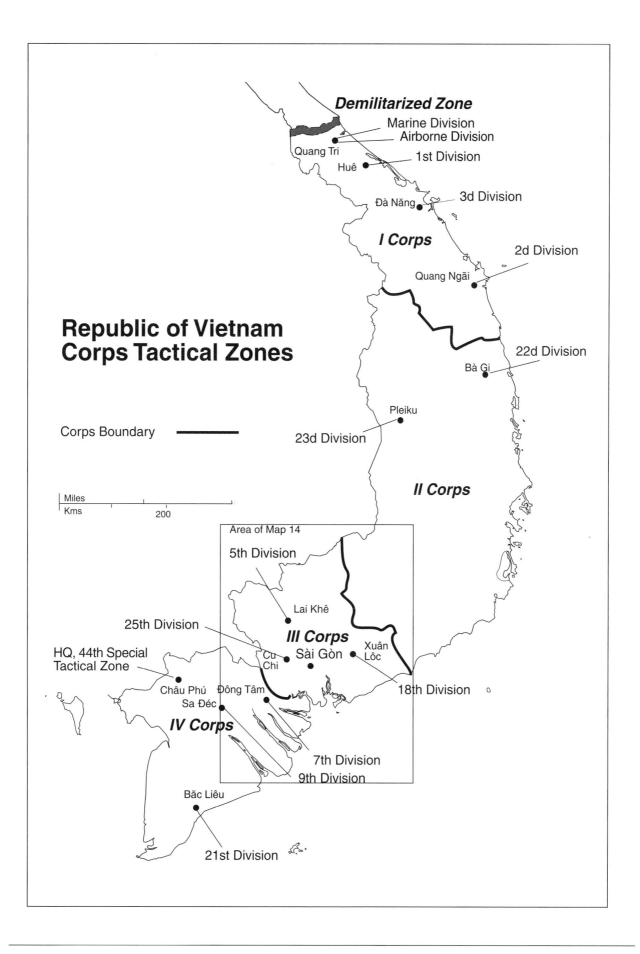

**Republic of Vietnam
Corps Tactical Zones**

Demilitarized Zone

Marine Division
Airborne Division
1st Division
3d Division
2d Division
22d Division
23d Division
5th Division
25th Division
HQ, 44th Special
Tactical Zone
18th Division
7th Division
9th Division
21st Division

Quang Tri
Huê
Đà Năng
Quang Ngãi
Bà Gi
Pleiku
Lai Khê
Cu Chi
Sài Gòn
Xuân Lôc
Châu Phú
Đông Tâm
Sa Đéc
Bắc Liêu

I Corps

II Corps

III Corps

IV Corps

Area of Map 14

Corps Boundary

Miles
Kms
200

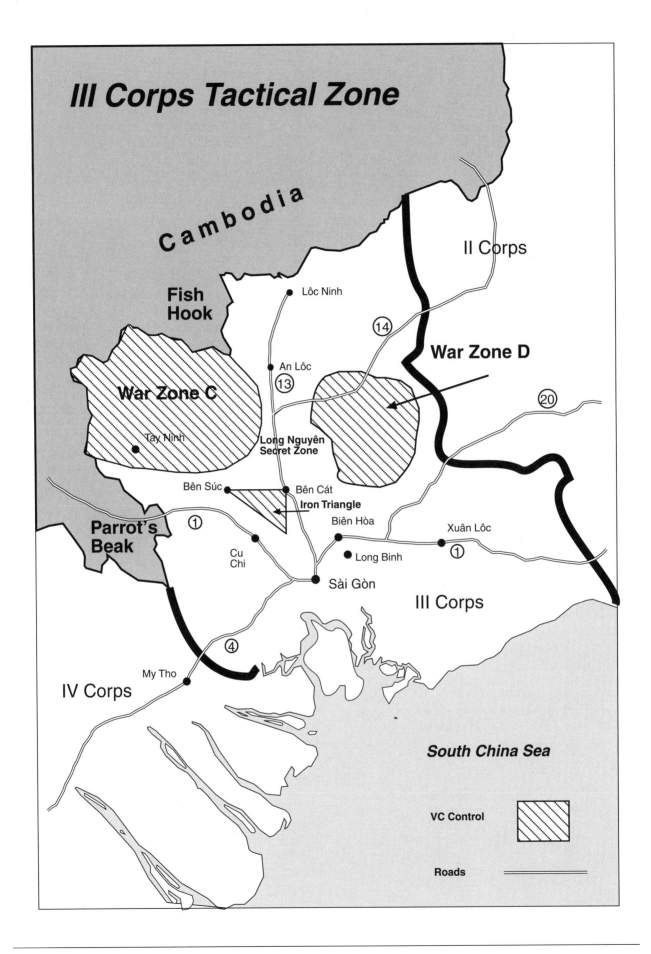

III Corps Tactical Zone

Cambodia

Fish Hook

II Corps

Lôc Ninh

⑭

War Zone D

An Lôc

⑬

War Zone C

⑳

Tây Ninh

Long Nguyên
Secret Zone

Bên Súc

Bên Cát

Iron Triangle

Parrot's
Beak

①

Biên Hòa

Xuân Lôc

Cu
Chi

Long Binh

①

Sài Gòn

III Corps

④

My Tho

IV Corps

South China Sea

VC Control

Roads

CHINA

Lào Cai

Lang Sơn

Yên Bái

Viêt Trì

Hồn Gai

Hà Nôi

Cân Pha

Hai Phòng

Barrel Roll
North

Barrel Roll
East

Barrel Roll West

Thanh Hóa

Gulf of Tonkin

LAOS

Vinh

Quang Khê

Đông Hơi

Udorn
Air Base

Steel Tiger

Yankee Station

THAILAND

U-Tapo
(B-52 Base)

CAMBODIA

Dixie Station

South China Sea

AIR WAR

LINEBACKER Strikes

Port mining

Main rail line

Main road

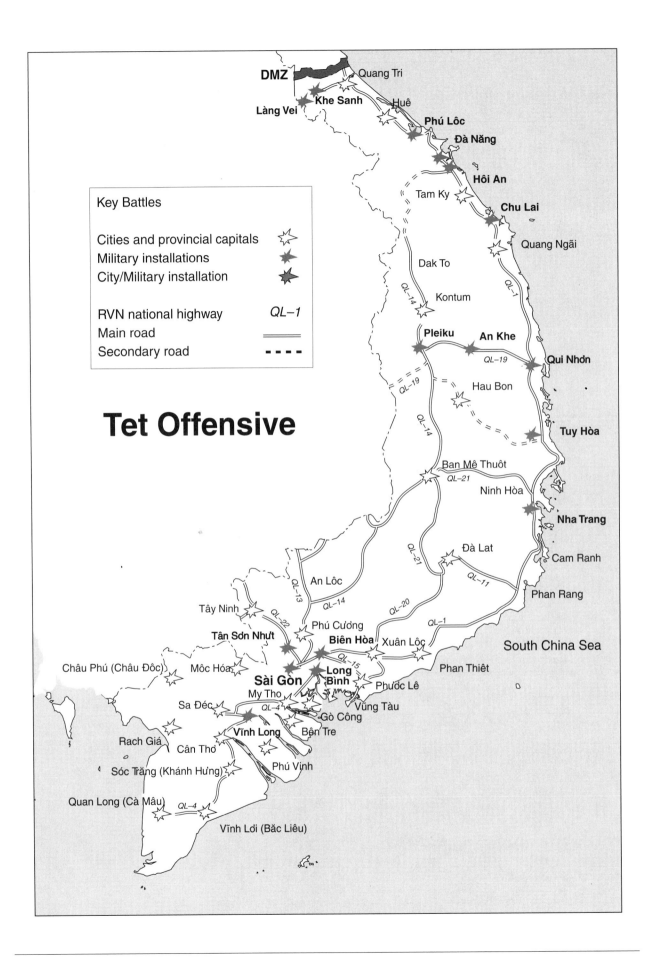

Tet Offensive

Key Battles

Cities and provincial capitals
Military installations
City/Military installation

RVN national highway — *QL–1*
Main road
Secondary road

DMZ
Quang Tri
Khe Sanh
Huê
Làng Vei
Phú Lôc
Đà Nẵng
Hôi An
Tam Ky
Chu Lai
Quang Ngãi
Dak To
Kontum
Pleiku
An Khe
Qui Nhơn
Hau Bon
Tuy Hòa
Ban Mê Thuôt
Ninh Hòa
Nha Trang
Cam Ranh
Đà Lat
Phan Rang
An Lôc
Tây Ninh
Phú Cường
Tân Sơn Nhưt
Biên Hòa
Xuân Lôc
South China Sea
Châu Phú (Châu Đôc)
Môc Hóa
Sài Gòn
Long Bình
Phan Thiêt
My Tho
Phước Lê
Sa Đéc
Vũng Tàu
Gò Công
Rach Giá
Vĩnh Long
Bên Tre
Cân Thơ
Phú Vĩnh
Sóc Trăng (Khánh Hưng)
Quan Long (Cà Mâu)
Vĩnh Lơi (Bắc Liêu)

QL–14
QL–1
QL–19
QL–14
QL–21
QL–11
QL–21
QL–20
QL–1
QL–13
QL–14
QL–22
QL–15
QL–4
QL–4

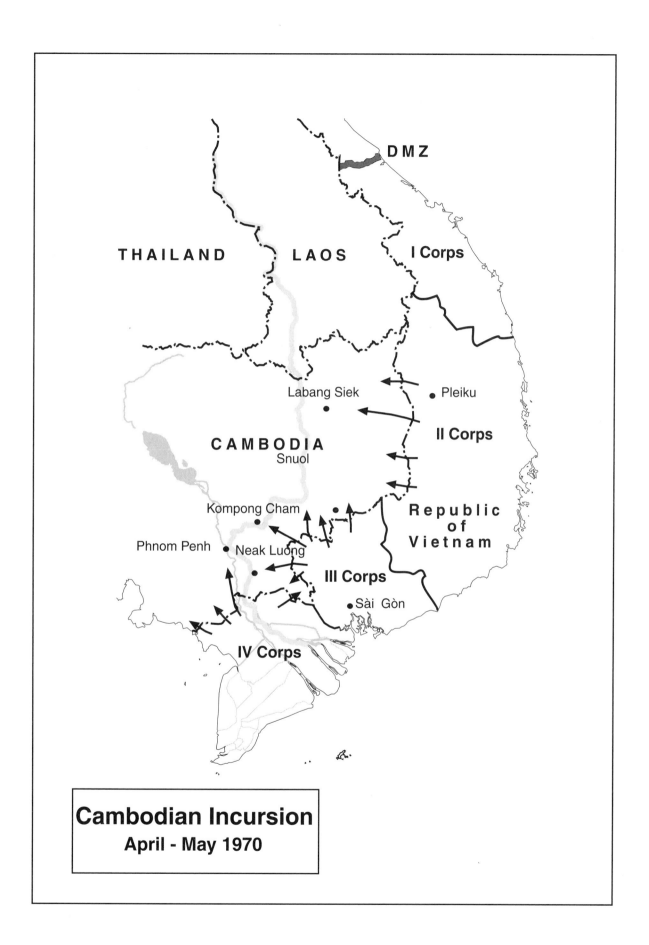

DMZ

THAILAND   LAOS   I Corps

Labang Siek   • Pleiku

CAMBODIA   II Corps

Snuol

Kompong Cham   Republic
of
Vietnam

Phnom Penh   • Neak Luong

III Corps

• Sài Gòn

IV Corps

Cambodian Incursion
April - May 1970

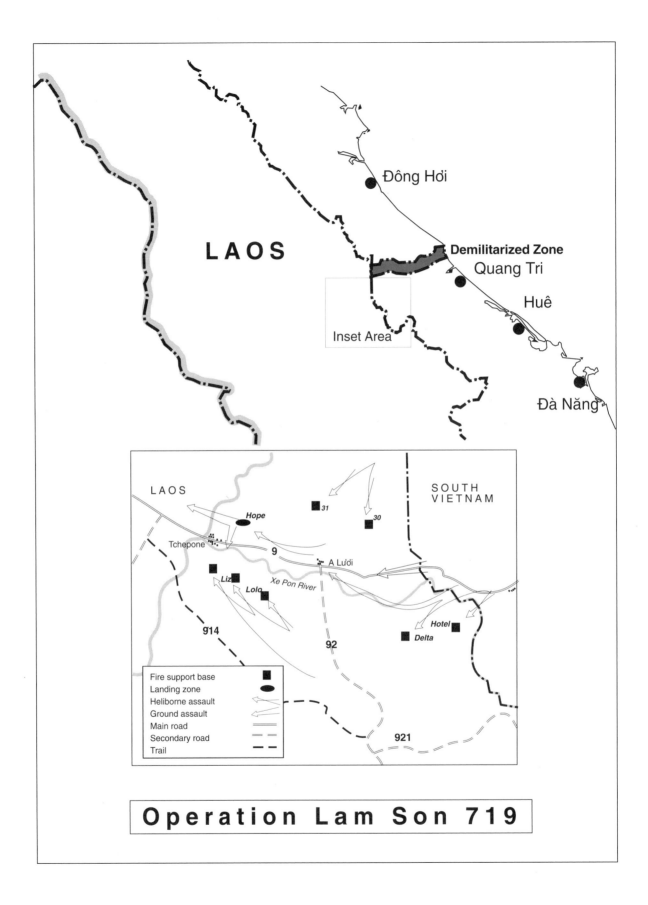

LAOS

Đông Hới

Demilitarized Zone

Quang Tri

Huê

Inset Area

Đà Năng

LAOS

SOUTH VIETNAM

Hope

31

30

Tchepone

9

A Lưới

Liz

Lolo

Xe Pon River

92

Hotel

Delta

914

921

Fire support base
Landing zone
Heliborne assault
Ground assault
Main road
Secondary road
Trail

Operation Lam Son 719

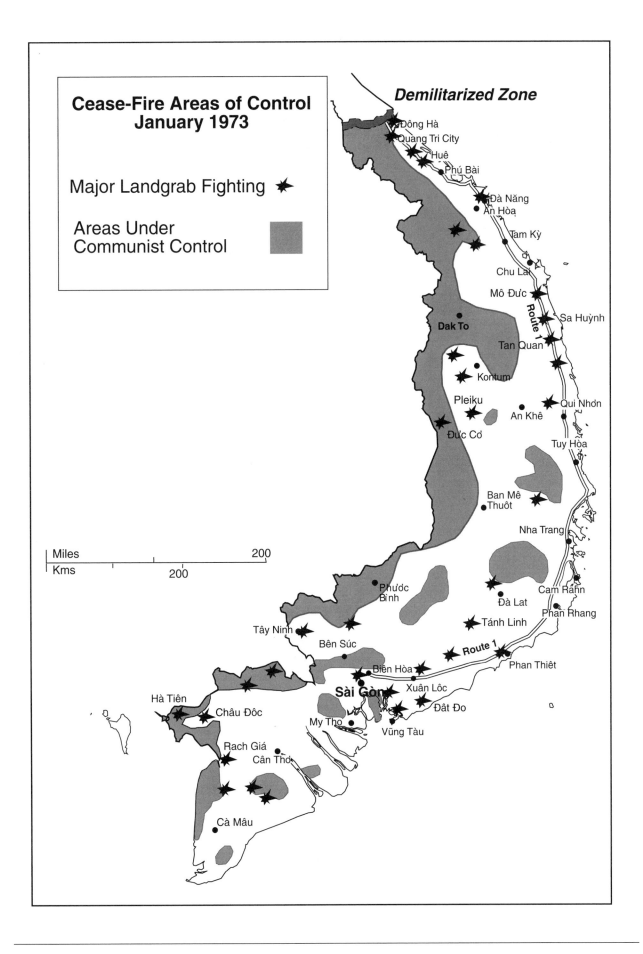

Cease-Fire Areas of Control
January 1973

Major Landgrab Fighting ✳

Areas Under
Communist Control

Demilitarized Zone

Đông Hà
Quảng Trị City
Huế
Phú Bài
Đà Nẵng
An Hòa
Tam Kỳ
Chu Lai
Mô Đức
Sa Huỳnh
Dak To
Tan Quan
Kontum
Pleiku
An Khê
Qui Nhơn
Đức Cơ
Tuy Hòa
Ban Mê
Thuột
Nha Trang
Cam Rảnh
Phước
Bình
Đà Lat
Phan Rhang
Tây Ninh
Tánh Linh
Bên Súc
Route 1
Phan Thiêt
Biên Hòa
Hà Tiên
Sài Gòn
Xuân Lộc
Châu Đốc
Đất Đo
My Tho
Rạch Giá
Vũng Tàu
Cần Thơ
Cà Mâu

Miles
Kms
200
200

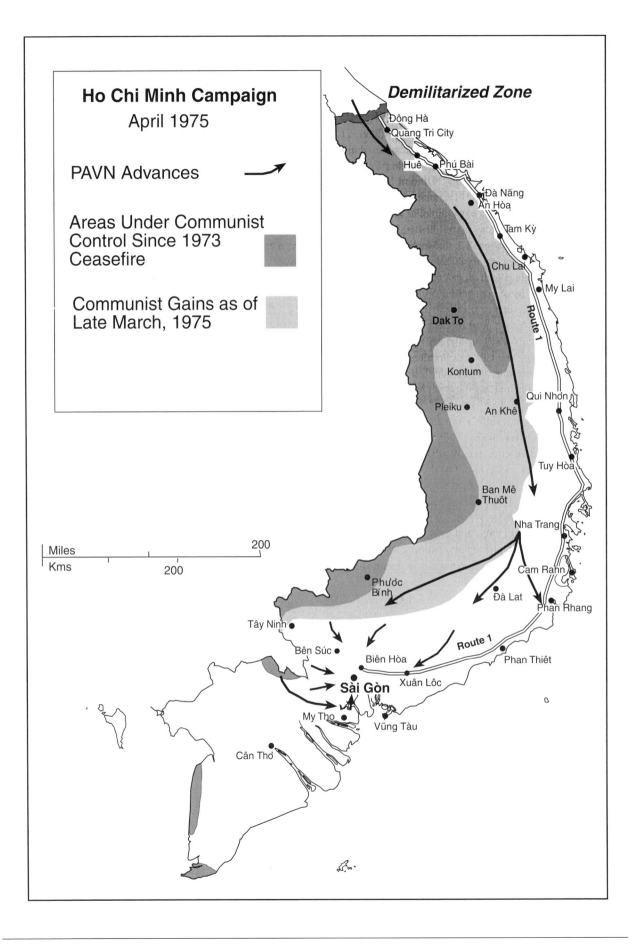

Ho Chi Minh Campaign
April 1975

PAVN Advances

Areas Under Communist
Control Since 1973
Ceasefire

Communist Gains as of
Late March, 1975

Demilitarized Zone

Đông Hà
Quảng Trị City
Huế
Phú Bài
Đà Nẵng
An Hòa
Tam Kỳ
Chu Lai
My Lai
Route 1
Dak To
Kontum
Qui Nhơn
Pleiku
An Khê
Tuy Hòa
Ban Mê Thuột
Nha Trang
Cam Ranh
Phước Bình
Đà Lạt
Phan Rhang
Tây Ninh
Route 1
Bến Súc
Biên Hòa
Phan Thiết
Xuân Lộc
Sài Gòn
My Tho
Vũng Tàu
Cân Thơ

Miles
Kms
200
200

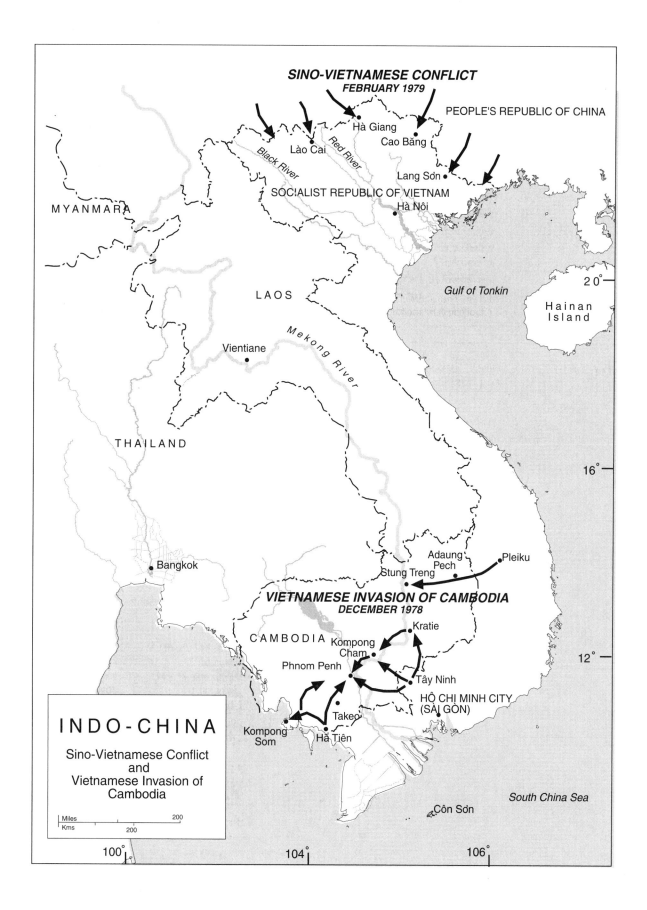

SINO-VIETNAMESE CONFLICT
FEBRUARY 1979

PEOPLE'S REPUBLIC OF CHINA

Hà Giang

Lào Cai

Cao Bằng

Red River

Black River

Lang Sơn

SOCIALIST REPUBLIC OF VIETNAM

Hà Nôi

MYANMAR

LAOS

Gulf of Tonkin

20°

Hainan
Island

Mekong River

Vientiane

THAILAND

16°

Bangkok

Adaung
Pech

Pleiku

Stung Treng

VIETNAMESE INVASION OF CAMBODIA
DECEMBER 1978

Kratie

CAMBODIA

Kompong
Cham

Phnom Penh

Tây Ninh

12°

HÔ CHI MINH CITY
(SÀI GÒN)

Takeo

Kompong
Som

Hà Tiên

South China Sea

Côn Sơn

INDO-CHINA

Sino-Vietnamese Conflict
and
Vietnamese Invasion of
Cambodia

Miles   200
Kms
      200

100°

104°

106°

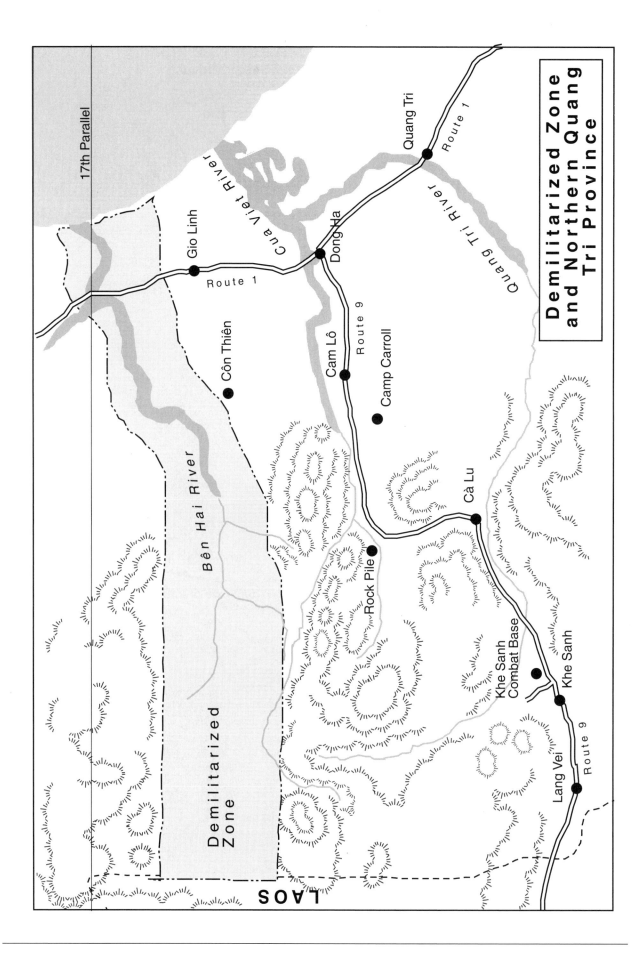

Demilitarized Zone and Northern Quang Tri Province

ENCYCLOPEDIA OF THE VOLUME TWO

VIETNAM WAR

A POLITICAL, SOCIAL, AND MILITARY HISTORY

N

Na San, Battle of
(November–December 1953)

French military operation in late 1952 that foreshadowed the Battle of Điên Biên Phu. Commander of French forces in Indo-China General Raoul Salan believed that, at the conclusion of the rainy season in August 1952, Viêt Minh commander Võ Nguyên Giáp intended to resume the offensive in the mountains of northwest Vietnam. Hoping to forestall that, Salan established a base deep inside Viêt Minh–held territory in the mountain-ringed Na San Valley. He planned this to be the meeting point for garrisons from the scattered French border posts and as a base to protect Laos and the Thai (T'ai) Highlands. The French planned to construct an airstrip at Na San, less than 50 minutes flying time from Hà Nôi. Salan hoped to tempt Giáp into frontal assaults at the base, attacks that Salan planned to smash with artillery and airpower.

Col. Jean Giles, a tough, one-eyed, paratroop officer, commanded French forces at Na San. The first phase of the operation went well. Most of the scattered French garrisons were extracted to Na San, and both the airfield and base fortifications were constructed in record time.

On 30 November and 1 December 1952 the 308th and 312th Viêt Minh Divisions attacked the French garrison but were repulsed. On 2 December the Viêt Minh attackers withdrew after suffering between 500 and 1,000 dead. On the surface, the battle seemed a great success for the French. Little noticed at the time was the loss to the Viêt Minh on 30 November of the small French post and airfield at Điên Biên Phu, then held by a Laotian infantry unit.

After putting a deception plan into effect, the French evacuated Na San by air without incident on 11 August 1953. They also removed about 1,500 Thai peasants and local officials who had cooperated with them.

The Na San operation should have demonstrated convincingly to French commanders the great difficulty of supplying a distant garrison with an inadequate airlift capacity. The French occupation of Na San also was little obstacle to Viêt Minh military operations in the area, which simply flowed through the jungle around the French base. Giáp later remarked that the Battle of Na San taught him that a fortified enemy camp supplied by air could be taken only by bringing the landing strip under heavy artillery fire.

—Spencer C. Tucker

References: Fall, Bernard. *Street without Joy.* Harrisburg, PA: Stackpole, 1961.
Roy, Jules. *The Battle of Dienbienphu.* New York: Harper & Row, 1965.
Simpson, Howard R. *Dien Bien Phu: The Epic Battle America Forgot.* Washington, DC: Brassey's, 1994.

See also: Điên Biên Phu, Battle of; LORRAINE, Operation; Salan, Raoul Albin Louis; Võ Nguyên Giáp.

Nam Đông, Battle of
(6 July 1964)

Battle at the Nam Đông Special Forces camp near the Republic of Vietnam (RVN) borders with Laos and North Vietnam. The 12 Americans, one Australian, and 311 Vietnamese soldiers who defended the camp were there to provide security and improve living conditions for about 5,000 Vietnamese civilians in the area. Capt. Roger Donlon commanded a U.S. Special Forces "A" Detachment that advised RVN Special Forces and Civilian Irregular Defense Group (CIDG) companies in the camp.

At 0226 on 6 July 1964 the camp was subjected to an intense mortar barrage followed by a ground attack by 800 to 900 Viêt Công (VC) soldiers. All camp buildings were soon destroyed along with most radios. The defenders were able to send a quick message that they were under attack, but it was not until 0400 that air support reached them. By dawn the fighting was over.

In the battle, the defenders suffered 55 killed (including 2 Americans and 1 Australian) and 65 wounded. Sixty-two VC bodies were found in and around the camp. On 5 December 1964, for his actions in the Nam Đông battle, Captain Donlon was awarded the first Medal of Honor since the Korean conflict.

—Richard L. Kiper

Reference: Donlon, Roger H. C., and Warren Rogers. *Outpost of Freedom.* New York: McGraw-Hill, 1965.
See also: Civilian Irregular Defense Group (CIDG); United States: Special Forces; Vietnam, Republic of: Special Forces (Lực Lượng Đặc Biêt [LLDB]).

NANTUCKET BEACH, Operation
See BOLD MARINER, Operation.

Napalm

One of the U.S. military's primary incendiary weapons in Vietnam; its use also attracted public protest as a weapon of terror. The napalm compound itself is gasoline thickened to a gel and named for two of its original thickening agents, aluminum naphthenate and aluminum palmitate, though the ingredients changed over time. Harvard Professor Louis Fieser directed the research that developed this petroleum gel, applying for a patent on 1 November 1943. Its advantages over unthickened fuel included longer burning time of up to several minutes and more effective spreading, which increased the probability of igniting targeted materials. The U.S. military first used napalm toward the end of

A Vietnamese man and woman carry young children from a village near Sài Gòn on 8 June 1972, following an accidental napalm bombing by Republic of Vietnam Air Force A-1 Skyraiders. The brutal effects of napalm led many antiwar activists to protest its use in Vietnam.

World War II in bombs and flamethrowers. Napalm bombs required igniting, generally by a high-explosive rod, such as TNT, surrounded by white phosphorus.

Napalm-B, the napalm used during the Vietnam War, retained the name although the composition changed. Made up of 50 percent polystyrene thickener, 25 percent benzene, and 25 percent gasoline, it is a thick, sticky liquid that was developed at Eglin Air Force Base, Florida, by the Dow Chemical Company. Napalm-B burns at a higher temperature, about 850 degrees centigrade, and burns up to 15 minutes, two to three times longer than ordinary napalm. It also doubled the coverage area to 200 meters long by 30 meters wide, making possible much greater destruction to targets. The jellied mixture sticks to virtually everything it touches and is almost impossible to remove. These characteristics led the U.S. Air Force to adopt napalm-B as its main incendiary weapon in 1966. During the Vietnam War, napalm bombs constituted roughly 10 percent, nearly 400,000 tons, of all fighter-bomber munitions. Individual bombs typically weighed between 250 and 750 pounds.

Humans caught in the open by napalm attacks have little defense. Death occurs not only by burning but from asphyxiation caused by carbon monoxide poisoning. Only those on the perimeter of the strike zone usually survive, although many suffer severe burns from heat that is hot enough to melt their flesh.

The brutal effects of napalm led many antiwar activists to protest its use in Vietnam. Dow Chemical Company was the nation's major napalm manufacturer during the war years. It faced a boycott of consumer products and an organized effort to persuade shareholders to sell their stock, as well as pickets and demonstrations at Dow offices and against campus recruiters. The protests affected Dow's image and profits and in 1969, whether deliberately or not, Dow lost the government contract for napalm to another company. The production and use of napalm, however, continued for the war's duration.

—Mitchell K. Hall

References: Dreyfus, Gilbert. "Napalm and Its Effects on Human Beings." In *Against the Crime of Silence,* edited by John Duffett. Flanders, NJ: O'Hare Books, 1968, pp. 374–381.
Stockholm International Peace Research Institute. *Incendiary Weapons.* Cambridge, MA: MIT Press, 1975.
United Nations. *Napalm and Other Incendiary Weapons and All Aspects of Their Possible Use: Report of the Secretary-General.* New York: United Nations, 1973.
See also: Air Power, Role in War; Antiwar Movement, United States; Bombs, Dumb; International War Crimes Tribunal.

Napoleon III

(1808–1873)

Emperor of France, 1852–1870. Born in Paris on 20 April 1808 and raised in Switzerland, the son of Napoleon Bonaparte's younger brother Louis, Charles Louis Napoleon made attempts to seize power in France in 1836 and 1840. Following the second attempt, he was tried and sentenced to perpetual imprisonment. In 1846 he escaped from the Fortress of Ham and fled to Britain. He returned to France following the 1848 June Days and was elected to the Constituent Assembly. In December 1849 he was elected president, largely on the magic of his name and a national vote. He seized power in a coup on 2 December 1851 and was crowned Emperor as Napoleon III on 2 December 1852.

Napoleon III used the Crimean War (1854–1856) to secure the French position in Europe and to build an alliance with Britain. When that war ended, he was determined to maintain cooperation with the British. This entailed supporting British endeavors in China, where French troops often fought alongside British soldiers. But Napoleon III also sought to secure territorial gains.

As early as 1853 the French Foreign Office had urged the acquisition of a port in Indo-China. French missionaries, who were being persecuted by Annamese Emperor Tư Đức, appealed to Napoleon III, and in 1857 he ordered the French China squadron to intervene there in hopes of obtaining a Vietnamese port in the fashion of Hong Kong and establishing a protectorate over Cochin China.

On 31 August 1857 French Adm. Rigault de Genouilly's squadron of 14 vessels and 3,000 men, including troops sent by Spain from Manila, appeared off Tourane (now Đà Nẵng). The troops soon took the Tourane forts and the port, inaugurating the first phase of the French conquest of Indo-China. Within a few months, the French were forced from Tourane, however. De Genouilly shifted operations southward to the fishing village of Sài Gòn, which fell to the French on 17 February 1859.

In 1861 Tư Đức agreed to cede to France three of the eastern provinces of Cochin China, allow the free practice of Catholic worship in the dominions, and accept a protectorate. The remainder of Cochin China was taken from An Nam between 1866 and 1867.

Napoleon III was taken prisoner by the Germans following the 1 September 1870 Battle of Sedan. Roundly condemned by his countrymen for their defeat in the Franco-German War (1870–1871), he went into unlamented exile. He died in England on 9 January 1873, having laid the groundwork for the new French dominion in the Far East.

—Michael R. Nichols

References: Bury, J. P. T. *Napoleon III and the Second Empire.* London: English Universities Press, 1964.
MacMillan, James F. *Napoleon III.* London: Longman, 1991.
Smith, W. H. C. *Napoleon III.* New York: St. Martin's Press, 1972.
See also: An Nam; Cochin China; French Indo-China; Rigault de Genouilly, Charles; Tư Đức; Vietnam: From 938 through the French Conquest.

National Assembly Law 10/59

Repressive legislation aimed at the Communists and enacted by the Republic of Vietnam (RVN) government in October 1959. The National Assembly Law was in response to Hà Nội's March 1959 decision to increase support for the insurgency in the South.

President Ngô Đình Diêm's response to this was increased military raids, acceleration of the relocation program, and anti-Communist legislative measures. Beginning in February 1959, a series of articles were published in Diêm's mouthpiece, the *Cách Mang Quôc Gia* (National Revolution) daily. These outlined a new program of intensified repression by means of an organized Viêt Công watch system and concentrated military and police raids on villages based on secret informers' reports.

As a part of Diêm's *Cách Mang Quôc Gia* plan, the RVN National Assembly passed Law 10/59 on 6 May 1959. This legislation legalized courts-martial and executions of individuals convicted of working with the Viêt Công, the name arbitrarily given about that time to anyone who opposed the regime.

Special courts were set up to be run by military personnel only. Proceedings could take place without any preliminary inquiry. A summons was served 24 hours before the court sat, if the accused "commits or intends to commit crimes with the aim of sabotage, or of infringing upon the security of the State, or of injuring the life or the property of the people." Trials lacked any formalities, with the courts preferring a straight-out denunciation, quick verdict, and immediate execution. There were only two types of punishment: death or life imprisonment. In theory, there was an appeal to President Diêm against the death sentence—there was none against life imprisonment. About half of those condemned to death were actually executed—many of these on the spot by mobile guillotines.

Apart from arming, financing, and advising these anti-Communist operations, the U.S. government provided specialized help by training Diêm police agents in the United States and sending a special mission to Sài Gòn to reorganize police methods, especially to improve the system of dossiers and control lists. Diêm ultimately closed this down after some of the specialists returned to the United States and wrote anti-Diêm articles.

In October 1959 the Assembly passed another law ordering not only Viêt Công and former Viêt Minh to be executed but also their friends, relatives, and "associates." Consequently distrust grew among South Vietnamese. Both laws reflected the determination of Diêm and his brother Ngô Đình Nhu to handle the Communist threat forcefully. The National Assembly itself was not a decision-making legislative body, but was rather a rubber stamp for the Diêm regime.

These repressive measures helped provoke popular uprisings in Quang Ngãi Province in August 1959 and another in Ban Tre in January 1960. Although Army of the Republic of Vietnam (ARVN) troops suppressed these, loyalty to the Sài Gòn government was never successfully restored in the countryside.

Although Law 10/59 imposed brutal measures, it must be understood against the background of brutal and rampant Communist terrorist activities in the remote areas between 1957 and 1959. These included blowing up bridges, schools, and dispensaries and assassinating unarmed village committee members, antimalaria spray teams, and even military dependents. At the time, there was no effective legislation to cope with this situation. After Diêm's assassination, Law 10/59 was quietly dropped.

—Zsolt J. Varga

References: Burchett, Wilfred G. *The Furtive War: The United States in Vietnam and Laos.* New York: International Publishers, 1963.

Karnow, Stanley. *Vietnam: A History.* New York: Viking Press, 1983.

Moss, George Donelson. *Vietnam: An American Ordeal.* Englewood Cliffs, NJ: Prentice-Hall, 1990.

Scigliano, Robert. *South Vietnam: Nation under Stress.* Boston: Houghton Mifflin, 1963.

Wintle, Justin. *The Vietnam Wars.* New York: St. Martin's Press, 1991.

See also: Ngô Đình Diêm; Ngô Đình Nhu; Vietnam, Republic of: 1954–1975.

National Bank of Vietnam

Name of the state banks of the Democratic Republic of Vietnam (DRV) and Republic of Vietnam (RVN). The National Bank of Vietnam was established on 31 December 1954 by Republic Ordinance Number 48. The Bank superseded the Bank of Indo-China that served the states of Vietnam, Cambodia, and Laos. After the 1954 division of Vietnam, the National Bank became the official state bank of the DRV. After 1960 all foreign currency and business profits were deposited in the National Bank, and within five years, 95 percent of North Vietnam's economy was state owned.

In South Vietnam in 1955 President Ngô Đình Diêm created another National Bank of Vietnam and named his brother Ngô Đình Nhu as chairman. To receive U.S. imports, local merchants contributed national currency called piasters into the bank's "counterpart fund." Under the Commercial Import Program, $1.9 billion in economic aid was directed to South Vietnam by 1964. Although the aid appeared to be extensive, the imports were largely luxury goods for the Sài Gòn upper class and did little to assist the South Vietnamese economy as a whole.

In 1975 after the fall of Sài Gòn, the North Vietnamese bank assumed control of South Vietnam's economy by requiring residents to exchange their piasters for dông at a 500 to 1 exchange rate. In an attempt to squelch the capitalists, every household was given a form to declare the amount of old money in its possession. Despite garnering some money for the government treasury and creating a certain amount of socioeconomic leveling, the currency exchange scheme affected most of the population in the South by causing distrust and loss of confidence in the central government, its banking system, and the value of its currency. Partly as a result of this distrust, the new currency steadily lost value and was reluctantly floated by the National Bank of Vietnam in 1989. By destroying the economic power of the moneyed class, Vietnam left no avenue for the huge amounts of government-issued money to make their way back to the central banks, which added to the already spiraling inflation.

—J. Nathan Campbell

References: Dacy, Douglas C. *The Fiscal System of Wartime Vietnam.* Arlington, VA: Institute for Defense Analysis, 1969.

Davies, S. Gethyn. *Central Banking in South and East Asia.* Hong Kong: Hong Kong University Press, 1960.

Emery, Robert F. *The Financial Institutions of Southeast Asia.* New York: Praeger, 1970.

Honey, P. J. *Communism in North Vietnam.* Cambridge, MA: MIT Press, 1962.

Lansdale, Edward Geary. *In the Midst of Wars.* New York: Harper & Row, 1972.

Ngô Vĩnh Hai. "Postwar Vietnam: Political Economy." In *Coming to Terms: Indochina, the United States, and the War,* edited by Douglas Allen and Ngô Vĩnh Long. Boulder, CO: Westview Press, 1991, pp. 65–88.

Taylor, Milton C. "South Vietnam: Lavish Aid, Limited Progress." *Pacific Affairs* 34 (1961): 242–256.

See also: Vietnam, Republic of: 1954–1975.

National Coordinating Committee to End the War in Vietnam (NCC)

First effort to build a national coalition of antiwar organizations during the Vietnam War. Organized in Washington, D.C., from discussions at the August 1965 Assembly of Unrepresented People, the original purpose of the National Coordinating Committee to End the War in Vietnam (NCC) was to help coordinate the 15–16 October International Days of Protest announced by Berkeley's Vietnam Day Committee. Delegates selected Frank Emspak as coordinator and set up offices in Madison, Wisconsin. The NCC lacked any decision-making authority for its 33 affiliated organizations, but provided a central location for receiving and distributing information about antiwar activities. Initiative for the demonstrations remained primarily with local groups. The NCC generated broad support, though some liberal groups such as SANE opposed close cooperation with radicals and rejected formal affiliation. The October protests attracted roughly 100,000 participants in 80 cities and several nations.

The first NCC convention, held 25–29 November in Washington, drew over 1,500 delegates from about 100 antiwar and civil rights organizations. Efforts to develop an ongoing antiwar program failed as the meeting degenerated into factional disputes, largely between the Communist Party and the Socialist Workers Party (SWP). Communists favored a multi-issue organization and electoral activity, while the SWP demanded immediate withdrawal from Vietnam and proposed a separate organization of independent committees against the war. For the majority of delegates, inexperienced in leftist ideological struggles, the conference proved demoralizing. The spectacle pushed some activists out of the movement, while others had doubts about cooperation with Marxists reaffirmed. The conference's only accomplishment was to set a date for demonstrations in the spring.

An NCC standing committee meeting on 8–9 January 1966 brought no resolution. Divided over whether to call for immediate withdrawal or a negotiated settlement, that Milwaukee meeting proved to be the NCC's last. The organization continued as a clearinghouse and formally sponsored the Second International Days of Protest of 25–26 March 1966, but local groups again carried the burden of planning and conducting antiwar demonstrations. The results exceeded the previous effort, attracting over 100,000 demonstrators in perhaps 100 cities and several foreign countries.

With the organization in disarray, NCC leadership resisted planning summer demonstrations. Activists dissatisfied with this hesitation bypassed the NCC staff. A series of antiwar conferences in Cleveland during 1966 produced a temporary coalition to organize protests, the 5–8 November Mobilization Committee, which was in turn succeeded by the Spring Mobilization Committee. The NCC continued to operate, but forfeited its leadership role in the antiwar movement. Within months, it declined as a national body and functioned as a local Wisconsin organization that remained active within the larger coalition.

—Mitchell K. Hall

References: DeBenedetti, Charles, and Charles Chatfield. *An American Ordeal: The Antiwar Movement of the Vietnam Era.* Syracuse, NY: Syracuse University Press, 1990.
Halstead, Fred. *Out Now! A Participant's Account of the American Movement against the Vietnam War.* New York: Monad Press, 1978.
Wells, Tom. *The War Within: America's Battle over Vietnam.* Berkeley, CA: University of California Press, 1994.
See also: Antiwar Movement, United States; Spring Mobilization to End the War in Vietnam.

National Council of National Reconciliation and Concord (NCNRC)

Organization established to implement political provisions of the 1973 Paris Peace Agreement within the Republic of Vietnam. The Paris Peace Agreement was to go into effect at midnight Greenwich mean time (GMT) on 27 January 1973. On the political side, the South Vietnamese people were to decide their future through "genuinely free and democratic elections under international supervision." The organization of the elections was to be in the hands of the National Council of National Reconciliation and Concord (NCNRC), composed of representatives of the government of the Republic of Vietnam (RVN), the Provisional Revolutionary Government (PRG), and the neutralists. It was to work on the basis of unanimity, which in effect gave each party a veto. The NCNRC was to promote observance of the agreement and the democratic liberties it guaranteed as well as national reconciliation and concord. The country was to be reunified step by step by mutual agreement; in the meantime the Demilitarized Zone (DMZ) was to be reestablished as in 1954, and relations between North and South Vietnam were to be normalized.

President Nguyên Văn Thiêu had proclaimed before the Paris Peace Agreement a national policy known as the "Four Nos": no negotiating, no Communist activity in the South, no coalition, and no surrender of territory. Thiêu objected to the tripartite NCNRC structure because he saw the neutralists as favoring the Communists and the NCNRC as a stalking horse for a coalition government, and he believed that he would be maneuvered into a position in which the RVN would be seen as blocking a peaceful solution. In fact, little came of the NCNRC, as Thiêu and the Communists opted to renew the war. Both sides strengthened and resupplied their forces and conducted sporadic attacks on the other. On 6 January 1975 Communist forces overran Phước Bình, capital city of Phước Long Province, 60 miles north of Sài Gòn. The Communists launched the attack in part to test the reaction of the U.S. government, and much to their relief, Washington did not intervene.

Leftist opposition circles continued to demand the adoption of the NCNRC up until President Thiêu's government collapsed in April 1975, but it was on the battlefield that the Vietnam War was decided.

—Ho Diêu Anh and Spencer C. Tucker

References: Isaacs, Arnold R. *Without Honor: Defeat in Vietnam and Cambodia.* Baltimore: Johns Hopkins University Press, 1983.
Le Gro, William E. *Vietnam from Ceasefire to Capitulation.* Washington, DC: U.S. Army Center of Military History, 1981.
Porter, D. Gareth. *A Peace Denied: The United States, Vietnam, and the Paris Agreement.* Bloomington, IN: Indiana University Press, 1975.
See also: Nguyên Văn Thiêu; Paris Peace Accords.

National Front for the Liberation of South Vietnam (NFLSV)

The National Front for the Liberation of South Vietnam (NFLSV), usually known as the National Liberation Front (NLF), was formed on 20 December 1960 in Tây Ninh Province in South Vietnam after the Communists concluded that a new revolutionary strategy was needed to overthrow the American-backed Sài Gòn regime. After six years of trying to unify the country through political means, the Lao Đông Party (the name then used by the Communist Party) accepted the recommendations of Central Committee member Lê Duân and approved the use of armed violence. The NFLSV-led insurgency against the Republic of Vietnam government of President Ngô Đình Diêm caused great concern in Sài Gòn and Washington.

From the birth of NFLSV in 1960, Washington policymakers claimed that Hà Nôi alone directed the armed struggle in South Vietnam. Key members of the Kennedy and Johnson administrations argued that the flow of troops and supplies from North to South kept the revolution alive. This remained the underpinning of the official explanation for U.S. involvement in the Vietnam War and provided its justification. Stop this externally supported insurgency, U.S. officials believed, and South Vietnam could be stabilized. Those who opposed U.S. intervention argued on the other hand that the insurgency was essentially a civil war. They suggested that the NFLSV was a southern organization that had risen at southern initiative in response to southern demands.

The NFLSV, known as the Viêt Công by its enemies, was a classic Communist front organization comprised of Communists and non-Communists. It was organized with the purpose of mobilizing the anti-Diêm forces in southern society. As with its predecessors, the Viêt Minh and Liên Viêt fronts, the NFLSV made temporary alliances with all elements of southern society who opposed American intervention and the Sài Gòn regime. Nguyên Hûu Tho, supposedly a non-Communist, presided over the NFLSV. But it clearly was dominated by Communist Party members.

The NFLSV's military arm was the People's Liberation Armed Forces (PLAF). PLAF attacks against U.S. Army installations at Pleiku and Quy Nhơn in February 1965 convinced President Lyndon Johnson and members of his administration that something had to be done to stop the infiltration of soldiers and supplies. It was impossible, the president concluded, to build a stable government in Sài Gòn while the Democratic Republic of Vietnam (DRV) and its Communist supporters waged a war of aggression. Johnson therefore ordered retaliatory attacks on North Vietnamese targets that paved the way for Operation ROLLING THUNDER, the sustained bombing policy that many of his advisors had long advocated. Punishing the DRV for NFLSV military

A Viêt Công (VC) prisoner awaits interrogation. Captured VCs were turned over to the Army of the Republic of Vietnam, which frequently executed them.

action in the South became standard U.S. policy. PLAF attacks also changed the scope of U.S. military requirements on the ground. In late February 1965 Military Assistance Command, Vietnam (MACV) commander General William Westmoreland requested two U.S. Marine battalions to protect the air base at Đà Năng from NFLSV reprisal attacks. President Johnson approved Westmoreland's request, and the first U.S. ground troops came ashore in Vietnam in March 1965.

Over time, the mission of the U.S. troops changed from protection of air bases to interdiction and combat against combined PLAF and People's Army of Vietnam (PAVN) forces. The U.S. strategy was based on attrition—Westmoreland hoping he could inflict a higher casualty rate among the PLAF and the PAVN than either could replace. Theoretically, the end result would be a diminishing of Communist will and a negotiated settlement.

The NFLSV reached its zenith during the 1968 Têt Offensive when the Communists launched a coordinated attack against key urban centers throughout the South. Although it suffered tremendous military losses, the NFLSV, many scholars have concluded, gained a tremendous psychological victory over the Americans and their Sài Gòn allies. The Front had demonstrated its ability to attack heavily guarded cities, long thought of as the base of sup-

port for the Sài Gòn regime. In addition, the PLAF attack on the U.S. Embassy in Sài Gòn produced political upheaval in Washington and caused many longtime supporters of the war to question the Johnson administration's optimistic predictions. Shortly after the Têt Offensive, peace talks opened in Paris and the NFLSV sent its own representatives, Nguyên Thi Bình and Trân Bửu Kiêm, to the conference.

In 1969 the NFLSV oversaw the creation of a government-in-waiting, the Provisional Revolutionary Government (PRG). The PRG hoped to come to full power in the South after the political and military struggles were concluded. As the war dragged on, PAVN conventional forces played a more active role in the southern strategy. Eventually, this created a great deal of tension between the NFLSV and northern party leaders in Hà Nôi. After the fall of Sài Gòn, only a handful of NFLSV officials were incorporated into the new national government.

—Robert K. Brigham

References: Duncanson, Dennis. *Government and Revolution in Vietnam.* New York: Oxford University Press, 1968.
Fall, Bernard. *Viet-Nam Witness, 1953–1966.* New York: Praeger, 1966.

Kahin, George McT., and John Lewis. *The United States in Vietnam.* New York: Dial Press, 1967.

Nguyen Thi Dinh. *No Other Road to Take: Memoir of Mrs. Nguyen Thi Dinh.* Ithaca, NY: Cornell Southeast Asia Studies Program, 1976.

Pike, Douglas. *Viet Cong: The Organization and Techniques of the National Liberation Front of South Vietnam.* Cambridge, MA: MIT Press, 1966.

Race, Jeffrey. *War Comes to Long An: Revolutionary Conflict in a Vietnamese Province.* Berkeley, CA: University of California Press, 1972.

Thayer, Carlyle A. *War by Other Means: National Liberation and Revolution in Viet-Nam, 1954–1960.* Sydney: Allen & Unwin, 1989.

Truong Nhu Tang. *A Viet Cong Memoir: An Inside Account of the Vietnam War and Its Aftermath.* New York: Vintage Books, 1985.

See also: Đấu Tranh; Dương Quỳnh Hoa; Lê Duân; Ngô Đình Diêm; Ngô Đình Nhu; Nguyên Cao Kỳ; Nguyên Hữu Tho; Nguyên Khánh; Nguyên Thi Bình; Nguyên Văn Thiêu; Paris Negotiations; Paris Peace Accords; Provisional Revolutionary Government of South Vietnam (PRG); ROLLING THUNDER, Operation; Tết Offensive: Overall Strategy; Tết Offensive: The Sài Gòn Circle; Trân Bửu Kiêm; United Front; Westmoreland, William Childs.

National Leadership Council

(1965–1967)

Governing political body in the Republic of Vietnam (RVN), established in June 1965. Following the overthrow of Ngô Đình Diêm in November 1963, the RVN underwent a period of chronic political instability. On 17 February 1965 a new civilian government was installed in Sài Gòn with Phan Huy Quát as premier. The military was still strongly represented, however, with three generals holding ministerial positions. The civilian government maintained an uneasy relationship with younger Army generals known as the "Young Turks," and a series of threatened or attempted coups imperiled political stability.

On 9 June Premier Phan Huy Quát turned to the Armed Forces Council to settle a dispute with Head of State Phan Khăc Sửu and was told to resign. After Quát resigned, on 12 June a triumvirate of Young Turks—Generals Nguyên Cao Kỳ, Nguyên Văn Thiêu, and Nguyên Hữu Có—announced the formation of a National Leadership Committee to rule the RVN. The youngest and least experienced government to date, it was subsequently expanded to include ten members. This body was in effect an inner circle of the 50-member Armed Forces Council, which, much to U.S. Ambassador Maxwell Taylor's chagrin, then elected Kỳ as chairman of the Central Executive Committee, or premier, charged with conducting the day-to-day government operations. Nguyên Văn Thiêu occupied the relatively powerless position of chairman of the National Leadership Committee (chief of state). Kỳ recalled in his memoirs that Thiêu, who was senior to him and the Army chief of staff, at that time declined the top post. Nonetheless, the two men were soon locked in a bitter rivalry for power.

This was the ninth RVN government in less than two years, but it proved to be the most durable since that of Diêm. In September 1966 South Vietnam elected a Constituent Assembly, which had as its task the drafting of a new constitution. This document came into effect in April 1967. On 3 September presidential and senatorial elections were held under the auspices of the new constitution. Thiêu and Kỳ were nominated by the Armed Forces Council

to run for the presidency on the same slate, with Kỳ forced to yield the top spot to Thiêu on the grounds of military seniority. This slate won only 34.8 percent of the votes, but it was sufficient for victory, as the remainder of the vote was split among ten other slates. The new government, still military dominated, then assumed power.

—Ho Diêu Anh and Spencer C. Tucker

References: FitzGerald, Frances. *Fire in the Lake: The Vietnamese and the Americans in Vietnam.* Boston: Little, Brown, 1972.

Nguyên Cao Kỳ. *Twenty Years and Twenty Days.* New York: Stein & Day, 1976.

See also: Elections (National), Republic of Vietnam: 1955, 1967, 1971; Ngô Đình Diêm; Nguyên Cao Kỳ; Nguyên Văn Thiêu; Phan Huy Quát; Taylor, Maxwell Davenport.

Naval Bombardment

(1965–1972)

Naval bombardment during the Vietnam conflict can be divided between the SEA DRAGON interdiction and harassment operations directed against the Democratic Republic of Vietnam (DRV) from 1966 to 1968 and gunnery support for friendly troops in South Vietnam. In the latter role, U.S. warships fired their first missions in 1965 and would continue to do so until the end of active U.S. naval operations in 1972. With its 1,200-mile coastline, the Republic of Vietnam (RVN) offered the U.S. Navy an ideal theater for its gunships. Cruisers, frigates, and destroyers could cover one-third of the land area of I Corps and large portions of II and III Corps.

Planning for naval gunfire support began at a joint Navy–Air Force conference in Sài Gòn on 3–5 May 1965. The Seventh Fleet tasked its gunfire support ships with delivering two types of artillery fire: unobserved saturation bombardment of preselected areas and call fire controlled by ground or aerial spotters. Targets included Communist forces opposing amphibious landings and People's Army of Vietnam (PAVN) artillery batteries that fired across the Demilitarized Zone (DMZ).

The first U.S. naval bombardment occurred in mid-May 1965, when the 8-inch gun cruiser *Canberra* and five destroyers fired at Viêt Công assembly areas, caches, and troops on the move. Operation STARLITE in August 1965 clearly demonstrated the effectiveness of naval gunfire support. By spring 1966 escorts, rocket landing ships, and the inshore fire support ship *Carronade* had joined the effort and were joined in 1968 by the battleship *New Jersey* for one tour. Ammunition expenditure increased from 90,000 rounds for all of 1965 to 40,000 rounds monthly by late 1966. In 1967 the ships fired a half-million projectiles. During the 1968 Tết Offensive, 22 gunships—2 cruisers, 18 destroyers, and 2 rocket ships—were in action at once, firing over 100,000 rounds monthly and providing key support in the defeat of Communist forces at Huê.

This aspect of the war was not totally one-sided. On occasion, the gunships came to close quarters with the Communists. For example, the destroyer *Ozbourn* was damaged by mortar fire when steaming only two miles offshore. Additionally, the large number of gunfire support missions wore on equipment, necessitating re-gunning, which was usually done at Subic Bay in the Philippines. Some of the newer pieces of ordnance also proved liable to mal-function, with the first such instance occurring in May 1965 with an in-bore five-inch gun explosion on the destroyer *Somers*. By 1969 seven additional ships suffered such accidents, some of which killed crewmen.

From its high point in the spring of 1968, the gunfire support mission decreased as the war wound down. By 1971 an average of only three ships patrolled the gunline. Ordnance expenditures fell from 454,000 rounds in 1969 to 114,000 in 1971. A last surge of activity came during the PAVN Easter Offensive, when as many as 20 ships fired against PAVN forces in Quang Tri and Thừa Thiên Provinces and were a key force in staving off attacks on Huê.

—Malcolm Muir, Jr.

References: Marolda, Edward J. *By Sea, Air, and Land: An Illustrated History of the U.S. Navy and the War in Southeast Asia.* Washington, DC: Naval Historical Center, 1994.

Muir, Malcolm, Jr. *Black Shoes and Blue Water: Surface Warfare in the United States Navy, 1945–1975.* Washington, DC: Naval Historical Center, 1996.

Shumlimson, Jack. *U.S. Marines in Vietnam: An Expanding War, 1966.* Washington, DC: U.S. Marine Corps, 1982.

See also: *New Jersey* (BB-62); SEA DRAGON, Operation; STARLITE, Operation; United States: Navy; Warships, Allied and Democratic Republic of Vietnam.

Navarre, Henri Eugène

(1898–1983)

French Army general and commander of French forces in Indo-China (1953–1954), chiefly remembered as the architect of the Điên Biên Phu debacle. Henri Navarre was born on 31 July 1898 at Villefranche de Rouergue in Aveyron; his father was a Greek scholar and dean of the Faculty of Letters at the University of Toulouse. In 1916 during the First World War, Navarre enlisted in the army to secure admittance to the French military academy of Saint-Cyr the next year. He was commissioned a second lieutenant of Hussars in November 1918.

Following the war, Navarre served in Syria, Morocco, and Germany. His years in Germany (1922–1926) led to his being regarded as a specialist in that country's affairs. Study at the Cavalry School at Saumur fostered Navarre's conviction that the future of warfare rested on mechanized forces, and he transferred to the armored branch. He fought in the 1925–1926 Riff War in Morocco, for which he received the Legion of Honor. From 1928 to 1930 he attended the Ecole Supérieur de Guerre. From 1936 to 1939 Navarre headed the German Section of the Deuxième Bureau (army intelligence). Promoted to major in October 1939, he became intelligence officer to General Maxime Weygand. In 1940 Navarre helped organize military intelligence in occupied France, and until 1942 he headed army intelligence in North Africa. He then commanded a heavy cavalry regiment, but in November 1942 he was recalled to France, where he became active in organizing Resistance intelligence operations. In late 1944 he joined Allied forces invading southern France and was promoted to

General Henri Navarre, pictured in 1953, when he was named commander in chief of the French forces in Indo-China.

colonel. In 1945 he commanded a regiment of Moroccan Spahis that helped capture Colmar and Karlsruhe.

Navarre's war record and knowledge of Germany led to his appointment as chief of staff to the French military commander in Germany. Promoted brigadier general in October 1945, he then became inspector general of French occupation forces in Germany. In 1948 he commanded a division in Algeria and, after study at the Institute of Advanced Studies for the National Defense, in 1950 he was promoted to major general and returned to Germany for two years to command the 5th Armored Division. Promoted to lieutenant general in April 1952, he served as chief of staff to Marshal Alphonse Juin, commander of the North Atlantic Treaty Organization's (NATO's) central European forces.

On 8 May 1953 the René Mayer government named Navarre to replace General Raoul Salan as commander of French Union forces in Indo-China with the task of finding an honorable way out of the war. Navarre did not receive the post of commissioner general, which the Paris government thought should go to a civilian to negotiate a peace settlement.

Navarre, who made his decisions in isolation, soon changed the French tactics from largely static defense to fluid offensive operations. Determined to take the war to the Viêt Minh, he ended up hastening the French military defeat. Navarre withdrew forces from various defensive positions to create a large mobile strike force. In July he flew to Paris to present French leaders with his plans to step up the war. These included negotiations with the Indo-Chinese states that would grant them greater independence but secure their support for a wider war. He also proposed the deployment of an additional 20,000 French troops and 108 native Indo-Chinese battalions. Navarre was quoted that, if he received the requested reinforcements, if independence was granted to the Indo-Chinese states, and if China did not step up aid to the Viêt Minh, the war could be ended in 18 months. Navarre later claimed that he never thought he could win the war and only hoped to restore the military situation in a *coup nul* (draw).

Navarre's decision to send significant military resources to occupy the remote outpost of Điên Biên Phu, as the key element of Operation CASTOR, was prompted by his desire to secure a blocking position on the main Viêt Minh invasion route into Laos. He also hoped to draw limited Viêt Minh resources into a pitched battle, where they might be destroyed. His plan rested on the assumption that the French would enjoy absolute superiority in airpower and artillery, but Điên Biên Phu was too far removed from French air bases in Hà Nôi and Hai Phòng and, in any case, French air assets were insufficient. Navarre was also guilty of seriously underestimating his enemy. General Võ Nguyên Giáp took up the challenge and committed all available resources in hope of administering a resounding defeat. The fact that Điên Biên Phu is in a valley made its French defenders vulnerable targets for heavy artillery, which Viêt Minh porters dragged over the mountains to the battlefield, something Navarre had thought impossible.

An embittered Navarre retired from the army in 1956 to run a brick factory and write his memoirs (*Agonie de Indochine*) free from military censorship. Although Navarre took responsibility for Điên Biên Phu, he blamed the politicians, who "entangled France in the Geneva Conference," for the ultimate French defeat in Indo-China. He died in Paris on 21 June 1983.

—Spencer C. Tucker

References: Fall, Bernard. *Hell in a Very Small Place: The Siege of Dien Bien Phu*. Philadelphia, PA: J. B. Lippincott, 1967.
Navarre, Gén. Henri. *Agonie de Indochine*. Paris: Plon, 1956.
_____. *Le Temps des Vérités*. Paris: Plon, 1979.
Roy, Jules. *The Battle of Dienbienphu*. New York: Harper & Row, 1965.
See also: CASTOR, Operation; Điên Biên Phu, Battle of; Indo-China War; Navarre Plan; Salan, Raoul Albin Louis; Võ Nguyên Giáp.

Navarre Plan

Plan developed by French commander in Indo-China Lt. Gen. Henri Navarre to find an honorable way for France out of the Indo-China War. After his May 1953 appointment to command in Indo-China, Navarre and his deputy, Maj. Gen. René Cogny, developed the so-called Navarre Plan.

Navarre, who made his decisions in isolation, changed French tactics from what had been a largely static defense to fluid offensive operations and withdrew forces from various defensive positions in order to create a mobile strike force. In July he flew to Paris to present to French leaders with his plans to step up the war.

The Navarre Plan included negotiations with the Indo-China states that would grant them greater independence in exchange for their support for a wider war. He also proposed deploying an additional 20,000 French troops and raising 108 native Indo-Chinese battalions. Navarre was quoted as telling the Paris press that, if he received the requested reinforcements, if the Indo-Chinese states were granted independence, and if China did not increase its aid to the Viêt Minh, the war could be ended in 18 months. Navarre later claimed that he did not think he could win the war, but only hoped to restore the military situation and secure a *coup nul* (draw).

The U.S. government supported the Navarre Plan in 1953 with nearly $400 million in assistance. Secretary of State John Foster Dulles described the plan to a Senate committee as designed to "break the organized body of Communist aggression by the end of the 1955 fighting season."

Navarre's decision to send significant military resources to occupy the remote outpost of Điên Biên Phu as the key element of Operation CASTOR was prompted by his desire to secure a blocking position on the main Viêt Minh invasion route into Laos. CASTOR led to the most important battle of the war and hastened the French defeat in Indo-China.

—Spencer C. Tucker

References: Fall, Bernard. *Hell in a Very Small Place: The Siege of Dien Bien Phu*. Philadelphia, PA: J. B. Lippincott, 1967.
Navarre, Gén. Henri. *Agonie de Indochine*. Paris: Plon, 1956.
Roy, Jules. *The Battle of Dienbienphu*. New York: Harper & Row, 1965.
Simpson, Howard R. *Dien Bien Phu: The Epic Battle America Forgot*. Washington, DC: Brassey's, 1994.
See also: CASTOR, Operation; Điên Biên Phu, Battle of; Dulles, John Foster; Indo-China War; Navarre, Henri Eugène.

Neutrality

Under international law, regimes declaring themselves neutral in wartime are required to live up to that pledge. The 1907 Hague Convention states: "A neutral country has the obligation not to allow its territory to be used by a belligerent. If the neutral country is unwilling or unable to prevent this, the other belligerent has the right to take appropriate counteraction."

In the Vietnam War this "neutrality/belligerency" issue involved both Laos and Cambodia. Beginning in 1959 their neutral status was compromised as the Democratic Republic of Vietnam (DRV) began covertly using their territories for supply routes into South Vietnam. The Hô Chí Minh Trail evolved from a network of footpaths through eastern Laos and Cambodia to a major supply artery, moving personnel and arms from North to South Vietnam. By the early to mid-1960s Viêt Công and People's Army of Vietnam (PAVN) troops were using Laotian and Cambodian territories as rest, resupply, and retraining sanctuaries. As early as 1964 the North Vietnamese headquarters directing operations in South Vietnam (the Central Office for South Vietnam [COSVN]) was located in Cambodia. The fragile governments of

Laos and Cambodia were unable to prevent these violations of their neutrality.

Although covert Central Intelligence Agency (CIA) operations directed at aiding anti-Communist forces in Laos dated back to the early 1950s, covert responses by the U.S. military began with the introduction of Special Forces teams into Laos in 1959. These teams of advisors trained Hmong to attack Vietnamese moving along the Trail, but political sensitivities over the "neutral" status of Laos led to their withdrawal in 1962. Thereafter, unannounced U.S. bombing and artillery attacks began targeting Laotian portions of the Trail in 1963 and Cambodian positions by 1966. Reflecting Cambodia's growing importance to the North Vietnamese war effort in South Vietnam, some 3,600 B-52 bombing missions were flown over Cambodia from March 1969 through May 1970.

The watershed of this activity came on 28 April 1970, when U.S. and Army of the Republic of Vietnam (ARVN) troops invaded Cambodia. Militarily, the short-term impact of this operation was mixed at best. Valuable North Vietnamese intelligence documents were captured, as were stocks of military equipment. Since the North Vietnamese had withdrawn from the area prior to the invasion, however, they suffered no large personnel losses. Their forces lived to fight another day, and their equipment loss was easily resupplied by the Chinese and Soviets. The long-term military impact was somewhat more significant, as much of the ground fighting after 1970 involved PAVN/ARVN battles in Cambodia. Thus, the military scope of ground operations widened considerably.

On the other hand, the political fallout of this operation was both immediate and substantial. When President Richard Nixon revealed the "Cambodian incursion" to the nation in a televised address on 30 April 1970, domestic opposition to the war exploded over this invasion of a "neutral" country. Inside the Nixon administration, Interior Secretary Walter Hickel publicly denounced the invasion, as did 200 State Department employees in a public petition. the *New York Times* and *The Wall Street Journal*, longtime bastions of eastern elite support of U.S. foreign policy, published editorials condemning this expansion of the war. Antiwar demonstrations resulted in the deaths of four students at Kent State University and two at Jackson State University and briefly shut down over 400 college campuses. Nearly 100,000 students marched on the nation's capital. Reacting to this public outrage, the U.S. Senate passed an amendment prohibiting U.S. operations in Cambodia after 1 July 1970.

Ironically, Laotian and Cambodian neutrality had long been a myth. However, the public reaction to the Cambodian invasion dramatically increased pressures within the Nixon administration to find a negotiated peace in Vietnam. It also fostered congressional attempts to legislate an end to U.S. military involvement in Southeast Asia by prohibiting the expenditure of public funds for such purposes. In short, the violation of Cambodia's "neutrality" by U.S. forces helped speed the termination of the American phase of the war.

—Ralph G. Carter

References: Ambrose, Stephen E. *Rise to Globalism: American Foreign Policy since 1938.* 6th rev. ed. New York: Penguin Books, 1991.
Karnow, Stanley. *Vietnam: A History.* Rev. ed. New York: Penguin Books, 1991.
Lomperis, Timothy J. *The War Everyone Lost—and Won: America's Intervention in Viet Nam's Twin Struggles.* Rev. ed. Washington, DC: CQ Press, 1993.
Spanier, John, and Steven W. Hook. *American Foreign Policy since World War II.* 13th ed. Washington, DC: CQ Press, 1995.
Summers, Harry G., Jr. *On Strategy: A Critical Analysis of the Vietnam War.* New York: Dell, 1982.
See also: Antiwar Movement, United States; Cambodia; Cambodian Incursion; COSVN (Central Office for South Vietnam or Trung Ương Cuc Miên Nam); Hồ Chí Minh Trail; Kent State University; Laos; Nixon, Richard Milhous.

NEVADA EAGLE, Operation

(May 1968–February 1969)

Military operation involving the U.S. 101st Airborne (Airmobile) Division conducted during the 1968 Tết Counteroffensive. On 17 May 1968 the 101st launched NEVADA EAGLE as part of the overall Allied post–Tết Counteroffensive. The operation was one of many battalion-sized forays designed to smash Việt Công (VC) and People's Army of Vietnam (PAVN) forces throughout South Vietnam. Except for some sharp engagements during airmobile sweeps in the mountains of Thừa Thiên Province, NEVADA EAGLE made little contact with Communist units in the field.

The 101st's main mission became keeping open major road networks that protected the South Vietnamese rice harvest. The division aggressively engaged in combat and ambush patrols, road clearing sweeps, and small operations to try to bring VC/PAVN units into open battle. The Communists refused, however, to be drawn into a major conflict and used mines and booby traps to inflict a number of U.S. casualties.

NEVADA EAGLE revealed an alarming trend: the North Vietnamese ability to entice U.S. helicopter pilots into ambushes. The North Vietnamese used small groups of personnel to present an obvious target; then, as the helicopters came in low to engage, Communist troops would open fire with carefully concealed machine guns. U.S. forces responded with increased use of artillery fire in support of their aviation assets.

The one major engagement of Operation NEVADA EAGLE occurred on 21 May 1968. While most of the 101st's combat elements were dispersed on sweeps, a PAVN battalion struck the division base camp near Huế. The North Vietnamese managed to break through the outer perimeter, pushing the defending 1st Brigade back to its final defensive bunkers. Helicopter gunships and artillery, used in the direct fire mode, used "beehive" rounds to break up the attack. By dawn on 22 May what remained of the PAVN battalion broke contact and retreated. Operation NEVADA EAGLE terminated in February 1969.

—J. A. Menzoff

References: Olson, James, ed. *Dictionary of the Vietnam War.* New York: Greenwood Press, 1988.
Stanton, Shelby. *The Rise and Fall of an American Army: U.S. Ground Forces in Vietnam 1965–1973.* Novato, CA: Presidio Press, 1985.

See also: Airmobility; Artillery, Allied and People's Army of Vietnam; Helicopters, Employment of, in Vietnam; Search and Destroy; United States: Army.

New Jersey (BB-62)

The only U.S. battleship to serve in the Vietnam conflict. The battleship *New Jersey* was recommissioned to supplement the few cruisers operating in Southeast Asian waters. A Pacific Fleet gunfire support review in May 1967 concluded that certain key targets in North Vietnam such as the Thanh Hoa Bridge and the Song Giang–Kiên Giang logistic bottleneck would be vulnerable to the battleship's nine 16-inch guns that fired shells weighing up to 2,700 pounds over 22 miles. Other important advantages included the battleship's superior endurance and resistance to damage. The principal objections to returning the *New Jersey* to service were the costs of supporting a "one-of-a-kind" ship.

At the direction of Secretary of Defense Robert S. McNamara, the *New Jersey,* originally completed in 1943, underwent an "austere" modernization costing only $21.5 million, about as much as four jet fighters. Arriving in Vietnamese waters on 29 September 1968, the battleship found many of the most lucrative targets in North Vietnam removed from its reach by President Lyndon Johnson's order forbidding SEA DRAGON operations above the 19th parallel. After 1 November when SEA DRAGON was scrapped altogether, the *New Jersey* engaged in gunfire support missions south of the Demilitarized Zone (DMZ), where her performance earned accolades from hard-pressed troops ashore and won for the ship the Navy Unit Commendation "for exceptionally meritorious service."

Leaving the gun line on 31 March 1969, the battleship returned to the United States for upkeep. Although originally scheduled for a second tour, the battleship was placed in mothballs when the Nixon administration scaled down America's participation in the war.

—Malcolm Muir, Jr.

References: Muir, Malcolm, Jr. *The Iowa Class Battleships: Iowa, New Jersey, Missouri, & Wisconsin.* Poole, Dorset, United Kingdom: Blandford Press, 1987.
Stillwell, Paul. *Battleship New Jersey: An Illustrated History.* Annapolis, MD: Naval Institute Press, 1986.
Sumrall, Robert F. *Iowa Class Battleships: Their Design, Weapons & Equipment.* Annapolis, MD: Naval Institute Press, 1988.
See also: McNamara, Robert S.; Naval Bombardment; SEA DRAGON, Operation; United States: Navy; Warships, Allied and Democratic Republic of Vietnam.

New Zealand

New Zealand sent both military and nonmilitary assistance to South Vietnam. New Zealand's rationales for the aid were that the decline of British power made New Zealand's security dependent upon the United States and that communism in Southeast Asia threatened New Zealand's vital interests.

New Zealanders in Vietnam served with Australian forces. A New Zealand civic action contingent arrived in 1964 and was replaced with an artillery battery the following year that supported the Australian task force in Phước Tuy Province. In May 1967 a New Zealand rifle company was transferred from Malaysia to Vietnam. Later that year, additional infantry, reconnaissance, and engineer troops were dispatched and integrated with the Australians to form an Australian/New Zealand (ANZAC) battalion. New Zealand troop strength was 517 men, and its financial aid to the Republic of Vietnam was $350,000 annually. Nonmilitary assistance included health teams to support refugee camps, vocational experts, surgical personnel, and funding for universities in Huê and Sài Gòn.

As domestic opposition to the war in Vietnam grew in the United States, the same occurred in New Zealand. In 1970, concomitant with the American policy of Vietnamization, New Zealand proposed replacing one rifle company with a 25-man army training team. New Zealand Prime Minister Keith Holyoake, in tandem with the Australian government, announced that his nation's combat troops would be withdrawn from Vietnam by the end of 1971.

—Peter W. Brush

Reference: Larsen, Stanley R., and James L. Collins, Jr. *Allied Participation in Vietnam.* Washington, DC: Department of the Army, 1975.
See also: Australia; Civic Action; Free World Assistance Program; Order of Battle; Southeast Asia Treaty Organization (SEATO).

Ngô Đình Cân

(?–1963)

Younger brother of RVN President Ngô Đình Diêm and proconsul of northern South Vietnam. Cân was a poorly educated man—the only one of the Ngô brothers without a Western-style education. He never traveled abroad or even very far from his home and spent most of his time living reclusively in Huê with his widowed mother. Because of his family relationship with Diêm and the trust given to him by his brother, Cân came to be, in effect, the warlord of central Vietnam from Phan Thiêt Province north to the 17th parallel. Although he held no official position within the RVN government, he had great, almost untrammeled power, ruling his area as if it were a feudal satrapy. Cân had both his own army and secret police and used them to fight the Viêt Công, terrify opponents, and to enforce his will. As a result, although he personally lived simply enough, Cân became a very rich man. Among his other enterprises, he sought out lucrative American aid contracts. Allegedly he also headed a smuggling ring that shipped rice to Hà Nôi and distributed opium across Asia. Undeterred by such corruption, Diêm referred to him in matters relating to Cân's area of control. Sometimes at odds with Diêm's policies, Cân nevertheless was a staunch supporter of the Ngô regime.

Following the 1963 assassination of his brothers, Diêm and Nhu, Cân was himself seized by the new administration, tried, and executed.

—Cecil B. Currey

References: Baker, Joseph, interview with author.
Baritz, Loren. *Backfire: A History of How American Culture Led Us into Vietnam and Made Us Fight the Way We Did.* New York: William Morrow, 1985.

Conein, Lucien, interview with author.

Karnow, Stanley. *Vietnam: A History.* New York: Penguin Books, 1984.

Lansdale, Edward, interview with author.

See also: Ngô Đình Diêm; Ngô Đình Khôi; Ngô Đình Luyên; Ngô Đình Nhu; Ngô Đình Nhu, Madame (Trân Lê Xuân); Ngô Đình Thuc.

Ngô Đình Diêm

(1901–1963)

President of the Republic of Vietnam (RVN) from June 1954 to November 1963. Ngô Đình Diêm was born in Quang Bình Province on 3 January 1901. His father, Ngô Đình Kha, an official in the imperial court at Huê, rose to the rank of counselor to Emperor Thành Thái. Seventeenth-century Portuguese missionaries converted the Ngô Đình clan to Catholicism. When the French deposed the emperor in 1907, Ngô Đình Kha protested by refusing to sign the French-supported court resolution against Thành Thái and returned to his village of Phú Cam to teach and farm.

Ngô Đình Diêm was one of nine children and the third of six sons. He attended his father's private school and French Catholic schools in Huê. As a teenager, he considered becoming a priest like his older brother Ngô Đình Thuc, who later became archbishop of Huê. Instead, Diêm entered the School of Law and Public Administration in Hà Nôi, graduating four years later at the top of his class. His first assignment was to the bureaucracy in An Nam. At 25 he became a provincial governor.

Diêm was very popular, riding on horseback over the province personally to carry out land reforms and ensure justice for even the poorest peasants. In 1929 he uncovered a Communist-led uprising and crushed it. This event deeply affected Diêm, who now became an ardent anti-Communist.

In 1932 the 18-year-old Emperor Bao Đai returned from France to take the throne. Early in 1933 upon French advice, he appointed Diêm as interior minister and chief of the newly formed Commission for Administrative Reforms. Diêm soon discovered that the positions were powerless. After only three months he resigned, and French authorities stripped him of his decorations and rank and threatened to arrest him.

For the next ten years, Diêm lived in seclusion in Huê with his mother and younger brother, Ngô Đình Cân. He met regularly with nationalist comrades even though the French closely watched him. French authorities even dismissed his older brother, Ngô Đình Khôi, as governor of Quang Nam Province. In early 1942, not long after the Japanese took over in Vietnam, Diêm tried to persuade them to grant independence. Instead, the Japanese operated through the Vichy French colonial bureaucracy.

In September 1945, with the Japanese surrender, fearing that Bao Đai's puppet government might side with the powerful Viêt Minh forces of Hô Chí Minh and Võ Nguyên Giáp, Diêm set out for Hà Nôi to convince the emperor otherwise. On the way, he was kidnapped by Viêt Minh agents and taken to a remote village near the Chinese border, where he contracted malaria. When he recovered, he discovered that his brother Ngô Đình Khôi had been shot by the Viêt Minh.

After six months, Diêm was taken to Hà Nôi, where he met Hô Chí Minh, who asked him to join the Communists. Diêm refused,

President Ngô Đình Diêm in 1958. Diem used most of the massive U.S. aid for internal security and estranged himself from the peasantry. Although Lyndon Johnson had private reservations about Diêm, he publicly called Diêm the "Winston Churchill of Southeast Asia." Diêm was president of the Republic of Vietnam (RVN) from June 1954 to November 1963.

even though he expected this would cost him his life. Instead Hô released him. Later, Communist leaders realized this had been a mistake and sentenced Diêm to death in absentia. Over the next four years, Diêm traveled over Vietnam trying to gain political support. An attempt on his life in 1950 convinced him to leave the country.

In 1950 he went to the Vatican and had an audience with Pope Pius XII. The next year, he went to the United States, where he spent two years at Maryknoll Seminaries in New Jersey and New York as a novice, performing menial jobs and meditating. While in the United States, Diêm met prominent individuals such as Francis Cardinal Spellman, Justice William O. Douglas, and then Senator John F. Kennedy. Diêm effectively argued his case, declaring that he opposed both the French and Communists and represented the only real nationalist course. As a result of his devout Catholicism, he and Spellman became close friends. Spellman soon became Diêm's greatest American promoter.

In May 1953, frustrated by the Eisenhower administration's support of the French, Diêm went to a Benedictine monastery in Belgium. From there, he regularly traveled to Paris, where he met with the large community of Vietnamese exiles, including his youngest brother, Ngô Đình Luyên, a prominent engineer.

Through Luyên, Diêm finally began to gain supporters and real political power.

In 1954 delegates at the Geneva Conference settled the first Indo-China War, restoring Indo-China as three nations—Cambodia, Laos, and Vietnam. Vietnam was temporarily divided at the 17th parallel with national elections set for 1956. At this time, Bao Đai was in Cannes, fearful that his future as emperor was in jeopardy. Diêm needed Bao Đai to legitimate his rise to power, and Bao Đai needed the support of Diêm's powerful allies, including his brother Ngô Đình Nhu, who had set up the influential Front for National Salvation in Sài Gòn as an alternative to Hô Chí Minh. Because of Diêm's time in the United States and meetings with American leaders, Bao Đai believed that the U.S. government backed Diêm.

On 18 June 1954 Bao Đai summoned Diêm to his chateau in Cannes and appointed him prime minister. With growing American support, Diêm returned to Sài Gòn on 26 June, and on 7 July officially formed his new government, technically for all of Vietnam.

Fearing that the Communists would overrun this fledgling Asian "domino," U.S. President Dwight D. Eisenhower and Secretary of State John Foster Dulles began sending aid to the new regime. Unfortunately, Diêm's power base was limited to minority Catholics, rich and powerful Vietnamese, and foreigners. But his earlier trip to the United States meant that Diêm was the only non-Communist Vietnamese that U.S. officials knew. Washington dispatched Col. Edward Lansdale, the successful architect of Philippine anti-Communist counterinsurgency, to council Diêm.

After the Geneva Accords, the United States pressured France to withdraw all its remaining forces from Vietnam, the last leaving on 28 April 1956. In early 1955 Diêm moved to consolidate his power. Employing five loyal army battalions, Diêm moved against his opponents, culminating the action on 6 May 1955, when his forces defeated those of the Bình Xuyên in Sài Gòn. He also moved against the political cadres of the Viêt Minh, allowed in the South by the Geneva Convention. In 1955 Diêm ignored an effort by Bao Đai (then in France) to remove him from office; instead, Diêm called an October election for the people to choose between them. Clearly he would have won any honest election, but Diêm ignored appeals of U.S. officials for this and managed the results so that the announced vote in his favor was 98.2 percent. On 26 October 1955, using the referendum as justification, Diêm proclaimed the Republic of Vietnam with himself as president. Washington, prompted by Lansdale, officially recognized him in this position and withdrew its support of Bao Đai.

During Eisenhower's last six years as U.S. president, material aid from Washington to the RVN totaled $1.8 billion. In an effort to bolster Diêm's image, Eisenhower arranged state visits to the RVN by Dulles in 1955 and Vice-President Richard Nixon in 1956. In 1957 Diêm traveled to the United States and spoke to a joint session of Congress.

By 1960 the situation in South Vietnam was poor. The Viêt Minh had resumed guerrilla activities and, in spite of massive U.S. aid to fight communism, Diêm used eight of every ten aid dollars for internal security. Even worse, he estranged himself from the peasants. Little was done to carry out land reform, and by 1961, 75 percent of the land in the South was owned by 15 percent of the population.

When John F. Kennedy became president, he reexamined U.S. policy in Vietnam and demanded that Diêm institute domestic reforms. But, seeing no alternative to Diêm, Kennedy also sent 400 Special Operations military advisors to Vietnam to bolster America's sagging ally. He also dispatched Vice-President Lyndon Johnson to Vietnam on a fact-finding mission. Although Johnson had private reservations, he publicly called Diêm the "Winston Churchill of Southeast Asia." Less than a week after Johnson returned, Kennedy agreed to increase the size of the Army of the Republic of Vietnam (ARVN) from 170,000 to 270,000 men. ARVN forces, as a rule, did not perform well, and by October 1963 U.S. forces in Vietnam had increased to 16,732 men.

Concurrently, despite constant pleading by Lansdale, Diêm's oppression of the Buddhist majority and his political opponents grew. To U.S. officials, it seemed that internal opposition to Ngô Đình Diêm rivaled opposition to the Communists. Diêm threw hundreds of political adversaries, real or imagined, into hellish prison camps. Hundreds were tortured and assassinated. His family and friends (mostly Catholics) held all the senior government positions. Most influential were his brother Nhu and his wife Madame Nhu. Diêm himself was celibate. His oldest brother, Archbishop Thuc, controlled Catholic property in the South that included 370,000 acres of nontaxable farmland exempt from redistribution.

Nhu was particularly embarrassing. He set up the Personalist Labor Party, which used totalitarian techniques such as "self-criticism" sessions, storm troops, and mass rallies. He was also the leading advocate of the Agroville and Strategic Hamlet programs that forcibly resettled whole villages into armed compounds to "protect" them from the Viêt Công. The rampant corruption in the program soon alienated the majority of peasants from the regime.

Madame Nhu used her position as state host to enrich herself and influence her brother-in-law to violent acts against the Buddhist majority. She also undertook morality campaigns, persuading Diêm to outlaw divorce, dancing, beauty contests, gambling, fortune-telling, boxing, kung fu, cockfighting, prostitution, contraception, and adultery. The harsh punishments that accompanied these excessive rules eventually antagonized large sections of the southern population.

In the summer of 1963 Buddhist protests and rallies became more frequent and intense. On 11 June elderly Buddhist monk Thích Quang Đưc publicly burned himself alive. By November six more monks had followed suit. Madame Nhu exacerbated the crisis by calling these self-immolations "barbecues."

In late August 1963 Henry Cabot Lodge replaced Frederick Nolting as U.S. ambassador. On 24 August Lodge reported to Washington that an influential faction of South Vietnamese generals wanted to overthrow Diêm. With the president and most senior officials out of Washington, Acting Secretary of State George Ball, Acting Secretary of Defense Roswell Gilpatrick, and General Maxwell Taylor formulated a reply. After a phone consultation with Kennedy and Secretary of State Dean Rusk, they cabled

Lodge, informing him that, while they wanted to afford Diêm a reasonable time to remove the Nhus, the United States was "prepared to accept the obvious implications that we can no longer support Diêm . . . [and] to tell the appropriate military commanders we will give them direct support in any interim period of breakdown of the central government mechanism."

Lodge immediately met with senior U.S. officials in Vietnam and then cabled Washington that Diêm would never replace Nhu and that to ask him to would only alert Nhu and lead to a bloodbath, since Nhu had loyal troops in Sài Gòn. Lodge recommended going straight to the generals, bypassing Diêm, and leaving it up to them if they wanted to keep Diêm. Ball and Roger Hilsman replied, "Agree to modification proposed. . . ." Kennedy later affirmed their instructions. On 25 August Lodge immediately called another meeting. He decided to distance the United States from the proposed coup and expressed support for the generals through lower-ranking Central Intelligence Agency (CIA) officers, specifically Lt. Col. Lucien Conein, the former World War II Office of Strategic Services (OSS) agent who had a long-standing friendship with many of the conspiring generals.

By September most U.S. administration officials began to have second thoughts, especially General Taylor. At his urging, Kennedy called a meeting of the National Security Council. It was hopelessly divided, with the State Department favoring the coup and Taylor, Secretary of Defense Robert McNamara, and especially Johnson vehemently opposed. Kennedy, although coy about the matter, never acted to prevent the coup or to restrain Lodge.

On 2 October Kennedy suspended economic subsidies for South Vietnamese commercial imports, froze loans for Sài Gòn waterworks and electrical power plant projects, and cut off financial support of Nhu's Vietnamese Special Forces units. Just over an hour after midnight on 1 November 1963 (All Soul's Day for Catholics) the generals, led by Major Generals Dương Văn "Big" Minh, Military Governor of Sài Gòn Tôn Thât Đính, and Trân Văn Đôn, began their coup.

Upon learning of the coup, Diêm phoned Lodge to ask "what is the attitude of the U.S." Lodge feigned ignorance and replied, "I do not feel well enough informed to be able to tell you." He assured Diêm that he would do anything possible to guarantee Diêm's personal safety. Diêm and Nhu fled the presidential palace through a tunnel and took refuge in Chơ Lớn, the Chinese section of Sài Gòn. About 0600 the next morning, the two men agreed to surrender. The generals leading the coup guaranteed them safe passage out of the country. While negotiations for their flight dragged on, they were discovered by troops commanded by a longtime foe. The brothers were ordered into the rear of an armored personnel carrier and shot to death. Nhu's body was repeatedly stabbed. Madame Nhu was out of the country at the time, in Los Angeles.

Washington never did find a viable alternative to Ngô Đình Diêm. Certainly no subsequent leader of the Republic of Vietnam had his air of legitimacy. As a result, U.S. leaders, who had seen Diêm as an alternative to Hô Chí Minh and an agent to stop the spread of communism, soon found themselves taking direct control of the war in Vietnam.

—William Head

References: Karnow, Stanley. *Vietnam: A History.* New York: Viking Press, 1983.

U.S. Senate Committee on Foreign Relations. *U.S. Involvement in the Overthrow of Diem, 1963.* Washington, DC: U.S. Government Printing Office, 1972.

Warner, Denis. *The Last Confucian.* London: Angus & Robertson, 1964.

See also: Ball, George W.; Bao Dai; Caravelle Group; Conein, Lucien Emile; Dulles, John Foster; Dương Văn Minh; Eisenhower, Dwight David; Faure, Edgar; Fishel, Wesley Robert; Heath, Donald R.; Hilsman, Roger; Johnson, Lyndon Baines; Joint General Staff; Kennedy, John Fitzgerald; Lansdale, Edward Geary; National Assembly Law 10/59; National Bank of Vietnam; Ngô Đình Cân; Ngô Đình Diêm, Overthrow of; Ngô Đình Khôi; Ngô Đình Luyên; Ngô Đình Nhu; Ngô Đình Nhu, Madame (Trân Lê Xuân); Ngô Đình Thuc; Richardson, John H.; Spellman, Francis Joseph; Taylor, Maxwell Davenport; Taylor-McNamara Report; Tôn Thât Đính; Trân Văn Đôn; Vietnam, Republic of: National Police.

Ngô Đình Diêm, Overthrow of

(November 1963)

Ever since the Great Migration of 1954 when northerners flooded to the south, the Ngô Đình Diêm government tended to favor the newly arrived Roman Catholics over the predominately Buddhist population of South Vietnam. Catholics received lands, business favors, military and government jobs, and other special rewards. Over the years, egged on by his brother Ngô Đình Nhu, Diêm's predilection toward the Catholic citizens increased. On 8 May 1963 Buddhists gathered in Huê to honor the 2,527th birthday of Buddha. The deputy province chief, a Catholic, prohibited the Buddhists from displaying their flag. This was in accordance with a Diêm decree requiring that flags of religions, associations, and other countries be displayed outside only in company with the national flag. When the protesters gathered at the radio station, a concussion hand grenade thrown by a Regional Force soldier to break up the crowd killed several people and wounded others. Diêm blamed the situation, as he often did, on the Communists.

The Buddhists speedily organized, coordinating strikes and protests, making certain that the American news media was kept fully informed of developments. They met with U.S. officials and urged the United States to get rid of Diêm or at least force reforms from him. Ambassador Frederick Nolting urged Diêm to act more responsibly, but the president refused to modify his stance. Then on 11 June 1963, 60-year-old Thích Quang Đức, a Buddhist monk, went to one of Sài Gòn's busy intersections and committed self-immolation as a protest against Diêm and his policies. Other self-immolations by Buddhists followed and unrest grew. Meanwhile, in August, Nolting was replaced by Henry Cabot Lodge.

Now members of Diêm's own military—Generals Trân Văn Đôn, Lê Văn Kim, Dương Văn Minh, and others—began questioning whether he should be allowed to continue in office. They began secretly meeting with Central Intelligence Agency (CIA) agent Lucien Conein, supposedly serving as an advisor to the RVN's ministry of interior but in reality the conduit between the generals and Ambassador Lodge. The generals wanted assurance that American aid would continue if Diêm fell.

On 21 August the Diêm government mounted another raid on the Buddhists, this time in Sài Gòn, arresting hundreds and beating and clubbing others as they ran. More voices in the Kennedy administration began calling for Diêm to be replaced; others, just as strident, claimed that doing so would only help the Communists. Lodge supported a coup. General Paul Harkins, head of the U.S. Military Assistance and Advisory Group (USMAAG) in Vietnam, demurred and informed General Trân Văn Đôn that any coup would be a grave mistake. Đôn then told Conein that he was postponing the coup despite Conein's insistence that the US-MAAG chief did not speak for the U.S. government. President Kennedy waffled, torn by these conflicting crosscurrents. Ngô Đình Nhu, aware of the plotting, considered an accommodation with Hà Nôi as a means of blackmailing U.S. support for his brother's government.

Unwilling to give up on the struggle in Vietnam, Kennedy sent Robert McNamara and General Maxwell Taylor to Sài Gòn on a fact-finding mission. Their report did little to ease the president's mind. CIA station chief in Sài Gòn John Richardson told Lodge that he doubted General Minh could conduct a successful coup. Lodge then dismissed Richardson. Then Lodge informed Kennedy that the plotters were now ready to act. Conein told General Trân Văn Đôn that America would not stand in the way. On 29 October, during a meeting of the National Security Council, General Maxwell Taylor spoke out strongly on behalf of Diêm. At the last minute, President Kennedy sought a way to postpone any coup. He cabled Lodge to order the generals to postpone any action. Lodge never delivered the message. Inexorably the coup went ahead as scheduled, culminating on 1 November when rebels seized the radio station and police headquarters and besieged the presidential palace. Diêm telephoned Lodge asking for help. It was not forthcoming. Diêm and Nhu secretly left the palace early in the evening and sought refuge in Chơ Lớn at St. Francis Xavier Church.

Early the next morning, Diêm telephoned General Dưởng Văn Minh, asking for negotiations. The plotters had already told Lodge that Diêm's life would be spared if he and Nhu agreed to go into exile. Although Nhu would never be allowed to return, Diêm might be invited back one day to serve in some figurehead capacity. By now Minh had changed his mind and so rejected Diêm's telephoned plea. Then Diêm called General Trân Văn Đôn, offered to surrender, and revealed his hiding place. The two brothers were arrested by General Mai Hữu Xuân, who arrived at the church with an M-113 armored personnel carrier (APC) and four jeeploads of soldiers. Among his entourage, were Maj. Dưởng Hiửu Nghĩa and Capt. Nguyên Văn Nhung, General Minh's bodyguard. The captors ordered Diêm and Nhu into the APC. Nghĩa and Nhung drove them away. On the road back to Sài Gòn, they stopped near a railroad crossing and murdered their prisoners, spraying them with bullets and stabbing them. The Diêm regime had ended.

—Cecil B. Currey

References: Conein, Lucien, and Edward Lansdale, interviews with author. Karnow, Stanley. *Vietnam: A History.* New York: Viking Press, 1983.
See also: Conein, Lucien Emile; Dưởng Văn Minh; Harkins, Paul D.; Lodge, Henry Cabot, Jr.; McCone, John Alex; Military Revolutionary Council; Ngô Đình Diêm; Ngô Đình Nhu; Nolting, Frederick, Jr.; Richardson, John H.; Trân Văn Đôn.

Ngô Đình Khôi
(?–1945)
Eldest brother of Republic of Vietnam President Ngô Đình Diêm and prominent figure in the government of An Nam. Born into a mandarin family in Central Vietnam, Khôi attended the Imperial Court School in Huê. In 1910 he was assigned to the ministry of defense as a protégé of Minister Nguyên Hửu Bài, and in 1916 Khôi was promoted to chief of staff to the Regency Council.

In 1917 Khôi was appointed chief of Phù Cát District, Bình Đình Province, then chief of Tuy An in Phú Yên Province. In the same year, Nguyên Hửu Bài was promoted head of the cabinet, as minister of administration.

Khôi's advance was rapid. In 1919 he became presiding judge of Phú Yên; in 1920, financial chief of Bình Đình; in 1926, chief of Quang Ngãi Province; in 1930, governor of Quang Nam Province; and in 1933, governor in charge of the provinces south of central Vietnam. During the early 1940s Khôi reportedly had some personal disagreements with Pham Quỳnh, a famous scholar and high mandarin, and retired from the administration in 1943. In August 1945 the Communists killed Khôi as part of their plan to remove all potential rivals for power. His death was a principal factor in causing Ngô Đình Diêm to reject Hô Chí Minh's offer of a Democratic Republic of Vietnam (DRV) cabinet post in 1945.

—Ngô N. Trung

Reference: Biographical Files, Indo-China Archives, University of California at Berkeley.
See also: French Indo-China; Ngô Đình Cân; Ngô Đình Diêm; Ngô Đình Luyên; Ngô Đình Nhu; Ngô Đình Thuc.

Ngô Đình Luyên
(1914–1990)
Youngest brother of President Ngô Đình Diêm and prominent political figure in the Republic of Vietnam (RVN). Born in 1914 in Huê, from 1923 to 1926 Luyên attended Pellerin School at Huê, and from 1926 to 1931, the College of Seine et Marne. Luyên continued his study in mathematics at College Stanista from 1931 to 1933, and from 1933 to 1936 studied at the Ecole Centrale des Arts et Manufactures de Paris.

Luyên returned to Vietnam and from 1937 to 1938 worked at the Land Survey Service of Bình Đình and Quang Ngãi Provinces. In 1939 he worked as a land surveyor in Cambodia and later at the Hôi An Land Survey Service. In 1942 he became deputy chief of the Central Land Survey Directorate and the next year moved to the Land Survey Service of Phan Thiêt Province, remaining there until 1955.

After his brother Diêm became president of the Republic of Vietnam, Luyên held the important post of RVN ambassador to the United Kingdom (1955–1963). Luyên was said to be the most liberal person in Diêm's immediate family. During the early days of his administration, Diêm considered Luyên his most trusted advisor, but Luyên was supplanted by his very conservative brother, Ngô Đình Nhu.

Luyên visited the United States a few times after 1975 and met with Vietnamese emigré friends. He was the only family member who attended the 1984 funeral of Archbishop Ngô Đình Thuc in Missouri. Luyên died in London in 1990.

—Ngô N. Trung

Reference: Biographical Files, Indo-China Archives, University of California at Berkeley.
See also: Ngô Đình Diêm; Ngô Đình Nhu; Ngô Đình Thuc; Vietnam, Republic of: 1954–1975.

Ngô Đình Nhu
(1910–1963)

Younger brother of Republic of Vietnam President Ngô Đình Diêm. Ngô Đình Nhu was born in 1910 into a Catholic family near Huê in central Vietnam. He was educated at the Ecole des Chartes, a school for archivists in Paris. He then worked in the National Library in Hà Nội until he was removed from his post as punishment for his brother's nationalist activities. A capable organizer, Nhu organized the Cân Lao Nhân Vi Cách Mang Đang, or Revolutionary Personalist Labor Party, a party based on the obscure French philosophy of "personalism," conceived in the 1930s by Emmanuel Mounier. Copying Communist organizations and using the Cân Lao Party as a basis, Nhu organized a system of covert political, security, and labor groups structured in five-man cells that reported on opponents of the regime and allowed the Diêm brothers to maintain their power rather than establish democracy or build national unity. The party never held a convention and never voiced a public stand on any issue, and its controlling body never met as a group.

Nhu's appearance on the Vietnamese nationalist political scene occurred in September 1953 at Sài Gòn, when he organized demonstrations against the French and Communists and masterminded the beginning phases of the revolution in the South against Emperor Bao Đai. It was his aim, during a national congress organized as a demonstration of anti–Viêt Minh and anti-French sentiment, to support a new government headed by his brother Diêm. To do this, Nhu formed the National Union for Independence and Peace and enlisted the support of the leadership of the Cao Đài, the Hòa Hao, and the Bình Xuyên. This too-open effort to oust Bao Đai came before the time was judicious and resulted in failure.

The French defeat in the 1954 Battle of Điên Biên Phu made the anti–Viêt Minh nationalists, and even Bao Đai, realize that their future depended upon a break with the French and the formation of a new government not subject to any French control. In Sài Gòn, Nhu formed another coalition called the Front for National Salvation, comprised of the political-religious sects, the organized Catholics, the Đai Viêt, and other nationalist groups. These "Front" groups, some that Nhu and his brother would soon move to destroy, now called for Diêm to head a new regime to fight communism. Many did so believing that the task would destroy anyone who tried—a fate that they wished on Ngô Đình

Diêm. Consequently, on 16 June 1954 Bao Đai invited Diêm, the most prominent nationalist to oppose the French "Bao Đai experiment," to form a new government as prime minister.

For the new government to possibly survive, it was necessary to gain control of the army, take control of the police from the Bình Xuyên, and consolidate areas controlled by the Cao Đài and Hòa Hao sects into the national administration. With the assistance of the United States, the army was brought into line in late 1954. However, in the spring of 1955, when the Bình Xuyên and the sects refused to cooperate, it became necessary to destroy them, and Diêm took the only road open to him. Nhu believed that the only path to power was through intrigue, and, with Nhu's able assistance, Diêm maneuvered to divide the sects from the Bình Xuyên and then from each other, and then use the army to crush each one separately.

In the midst of this struggle to consolidate power, Nhu allegedly hatched the final scheme to oust Bao Đai. On 30 April 1955 a group of some 200 people, representing 18 political "parties," gathered at the Sài Gòn town hall. Constituting itself as the "General Assembly of Democratic and Revolutionary Forces of the Nation," and after the symbolic act of throwing Bao Đai's picture out a window, the gathering called for the emperor's abdication and the formation of a new government under Ngô Đình Diêm. On 7 July 1955 Diêm announced that a national referendum would be held on 23 October to decide the future form of Vietnam's government. As his brother's chief political advisor and head of all of the national secret service organizations, Nhu used his secret police to control the election, and on 26 October 1955 Diêm was declared president of the new Republic of Vietnam.

Throughout his brother's reign, Nhu used his Cân Lao Party and secret service apparatus to keep the family in power. As head of the secret police, he created 13 intelligence units and even commanded the Vietnamese Special Forces, his own personal army. Nhu helped administer the Khu Trù Mât farm communities known as Agrovilles and recommended and administered the later Strategic Hamlet program, both designed to isolate the rural population from the Communists. Both were poorly administered, hampered by corruption, and easily subverted by the Viêt Công.

Viewing internal dissent as just as dangerous as the Communists and with his control of secret police forces, Nhu thwarted several attempts to depose his brother. However, the intrigue, corruption, and brutality of the regime caught up with Nhu in 1963, when he used his forces to suppress Buddhist demonstrations against the Diêm government. Because of the brutal nature of the suppression and inflammatory statements by him and his wife, Madame Nhu, the United States demanded Nhu's removal. When Diêm refused, U.S. officials notified plotting Vietnamese generals that Washington would not oppose a coup. The coup began on 1 November 1963, and the next day Nhu and Diêm were taken in a Catholic church in Chơ Lớn and subsequently assassinated.

—Arthur T. Frame

References: Boetcher, Thomas D. *Vietnam: The Valor and the Sorrow.* Boston: Little, Brown, 1985.

Banners dominating a crowd scene in downtown Sài Gòn marked the Republic of South Vietnam government's marshaled demonstration. Included in the pro-Diệm rally are large groups from Ngô Đình Nhu's blue-uniformed Republic Youth Organization.

Buttinger, Joseph. *Vietnam: A Political History.* New York: Praeger, 1968.
Collins, Gen. J. Lawton. *Lightning Joe: An Autobiography.* Baton Rouge, LA: Louisiana State University Press, 1979.
Karnow, Stanley. *Vietnam: A History.* New York: Penguin Books, 1984.

See also: Cân Lao Nhân Vi Cách Mang Đang (Revolutionary Personalist Labor Party); Cao Đài; Collins, Joseph Lawton; Conein, Lucien Emile; Dương Văn Minh; Elections (National), Republic of Vietnam: 1955, 1967, 1971; Geneva Conference and Geneva Accords; Lodge, Henry Cabot, Jr.; National Assembly Law 10/59; National Bank of Vietnam; Ngô Đình Diêm; Ngô Đình Diêm, Overthrow of; Ngô Đình Nhu, Madame (Trân Lê Xuân); Richardson, John H.; Sheehan, Cornelius Mahoney (Neil); Taylor-McNamara Report; Thích Quang Đưc; United States: Involvement in Vietnam, 1954–1965; Vietnam, Republic of: National Police.

Ngô Đình Nhu, Madame (Trân Lê Xuân)

(1924–)

Wife of Ngô Đình Nhu. Trân Lê Xuân (Beautiful Spring) was born in 1924 in Hà Nôi, the second of three children. Although Vietnamese, her family was thoroughly Gallicized and had amassed a fortune while in service to the French colonial administration. Her father Trân Văn Chưởng earned a law degree in Paris before returning to Vietnam to practice law and marry a member of the imperial family. Madame Chưởng, a renowned beauty, entertained the French and the Frenchified Vietnamese lavishly in the family's Hà Nôi villa and is reported to have taken a series of lovers, including Ngô Đình Nhu after his return from his studies in France. Lê Xuân dropped out of the prestigious French high school in Hà Nôi, the Lycée Albert Sarraut. A mediocre student, she was fluent in French, but never learned to write her native Vietnamese.

Lê Xuân married Nhu, 14 years her senior, in 1943. When the French dismissed Nhu from his job in the National Library because of his brother Diêm's nationalist activities, the couple moved to Đà Lat. There she gave birth to their four children while he edited a newspaper and dabbled in politics. Upon Ngô Đình Diêm's ascendancy to the presidency in 1955, the Nhus moved into the presidential palace in Sài Gòn. Because Diêm never married, Madame Nhu acted as official host and became, in effect, the Republic of Vietnam's First Lady and an outspoken and powerful force in her own right.

In addition to the couple's formal and official roles in the Diêm government, Madame Nhu's father was appointed ambassador to the United States and her mother became an observer at the United Nations. Also, two of her uncles were cabinet ministers.

As official host for her bachelor brother-in-law, Madame Nhu quickly adopted an imperious manner and began to display the insensitivity and uncaring attitude toward anyone or anything outside the ruling family clique that earned her the sobriquet the "Dragon Lady." It was not long into the Diêm regime before U.S. Ambassador General J. Lawton Collins encouraged Diêm to get rid of her because she was a "troublemaker." Diêm, however, opted to keep the family together. Remembering this attempt to send her away caused Madame Nhu to heap reproach upon the United States during the following years, often claiming that Americans were aiding Vietnamese factions attempting to topple the Diêm regime.

Overlooking her own family's decadence and her brother-in-law's brutal, inept, and corrupt administration, and impervious to

The South Vietnamese presidential family in 1963. Madame Ngô Đình Nhu is second from the left. Because president Ngô Đình Diêm never married, Madame Nhu, Diêm's sister-in-law, acted as official host and became, in effect, the Republic of Vietnam's First Lady and an outspoken and powerful force in her own right.

the suffering of the Vietnamese people, Madame Nhu issued decrees backed by the force of law. Her edicts abolished divorce and banned abortions, contraceptives, prostitution, dancing, beauty contests, fortune-telling, and boxing matches. She made adultery a crime; this included being seen in public with a person of the opposite sex. Fancying herself a feminist, she lectured on women's issues and even formed her own paramilitary force, the Women's Solidarity Movement. Madame Nhu often embarrassed and infuriated her brother-in-law with provocative remarks, but he tolerated her out of family fidelity.

As the Diêm regime faced increasing dissent from within and doubt from without, Madame Nhu contributed to its decay with her vitriolic remarks. When Buddhist protests brought Nhu's brutal repressions and led to several Buddhist self-immolations, Madame Nhu accused the United States of manipulating the Buddhists. She later referred to these events as Buddhist "barbecues" and her husband followed suit by declaring that "if the Buddhists want to have another barbecue, I will be glad to supply the gasoline." These statements helped to turn American public opinion and the Kennedy administration against the Diêm regime, and even Madame Nhu's father and mother resigned their posts in response. When Diêm refused to get rid of the Nhus and their negative impact on his regime, it paved the way for the November 1963 coup that cost Diêm and Nhu their lives.

At that time, Madame Nhu was on a propaganda tour that took her to Belgrade, Rome, Paris, and the United States. When Diêm and her husband were being assassinated, she was in Los Angeles. With the death of her husband and his benefactor, Madame Nhu withdrew into exile in Rome.

—Arthur T. Frame

References: Boetcher, Thomas D. *Vietnam: The Valor and the Sorrow.* Boston: Little, Brown, 1985.
Buttinger, Joseph. *Vietnam: A Political History.* New York: Praeger, 1968.

Karnow, Stanley. *Vietnam: A History.* New York: Penguin Books, 1984.
See also: Collins, Joseph Lawton; Conein, Lucien Emile; Dương Văn Minh; Elections (National), Republic of Vietnam: 1955, 1967, 1971; Lodge, Henry Cabot, Jr.; Ngô Đình Diêm; Ngô Đình Diêm, Overthrow of; Ngô Đình Nhu; Thích Quang Đức; United States: Involvement in Vietnam, 1954–1965; Women in the War, Vietnamese.

Ngô Đình Thuc
(1897–1984)

Roman Catholic archbishop and older brother of Republic of Vietnam (RVN) President Ngô Đình Diêm. Thuc was an important bridge between Diêm and the American political circle that supported him. Born into a traditional Catholic family in 1897, Ngô Đình Thuc became a priest in 1929. In 1938 he was named bishop of Vĩnh Long Diocese in the Mekong Delta.

In October 1945 French police arrested Thuc at Biên Hòa while he was on his way to the North to attend the induction of Bishop Lê Hữu Tử. Thuc admitted that he had encouraged some young people to join the Thanh Niên Tiên Phong (Pioneer Youth League), a Communist youth organization in Vĩnh Long, but he feared increased Communist influence. Thuc wanted a truly independent Vietnamese state.

In 1950 in Sài Gòn, Thuc met Cardinal Francis Spellman of New York, Catholic chaplain of the U.S. Armed Forces. In June 1950 Thuc applied for a visa to stop in the United States on his way to Rome. Traveling with Thuc were his younger brother, Ngô Đình Diêm, and Nguyên Viêt Canh.

In August 1950 Thuc and Diêm stopped in Tokyo, Japan, where they met Prince Cường Đê to discuss the establishment of an anti-Communist Vietnamese government. Thuc and Diêm arrived in the United States in September and met with Cardinal Spellman and William S. B. Lacy, head of Philippines and Southeast Asia Affairs in the Department of State. Thuc raised the issue of building a Vietnam centered on Catholics. This idea would later be supported by the U.S. Department of State.

On 15 October 1950 Thuc and Diêm left for Europe, and Thuc returned to Vietnam at the end of that year. Diêm stayed for a while in Paris, but returned to the United States in January 1951. In mid-1954 Emperor Bao Đai named Diêm premier, so he returned to Vietnam that July to assume the post. During the first years of Diêm's government, Thuc's diocese became a training base for the cadre of the Cân Lao Nhân Vi Cách Mang Đang (Revolutionary Personalist Labor Party) headed by Ngô Đình Nhu, another younger brother of Thuc.

In 1961 Thuc became archbishop of Huê, where in 1963 he intervened to forbid display of the Buddhist flag during celebration of Buddha's birthday. This unfortunate incident began a chain of events that led to the 1 November 1963 coup d'état that overthrew Diêm; both Diêm and Nhu died in the coup.

Archbishop Thuc survived the coup, having been recalled to Rome in September 1963. He was living in France when he was excommunicated for investing priests without permission from Rome. In 1983 Thuc moved to a monastery in Missouri. He died of cancer on 13 December 1984 in Carthage, Missouri.

—Ngô N. Trung

Reference: Biographical Files, Indo-China Archives, University of California at Berkeley.
See also: Bao Đai; Buddhists; Kennedy, John Fitzgerald; Mansfield, Michael Joseph; Ngô Đình Diêm; Ngô Đình Nhu; Spellman, Francis Joseph.

Ngô Quang Trưởng
(1929–)

Army of the Republic of Vietnam (ARVN) general who commanded, successively, 1st ARVN Division, IV Corps, and I Corps. Trưởng was born 19 December 1929 in the Delta province of Kiên Hòa. After graduating from My Tho College, he attended the reserve officer school at Thu Đức, from which he was commissioned into the South Vietnamese Army in 1954. He worked his way up through battalion and regimental command in the Airborne Division and in June 1966 took command of the ARVN 1st Division. His American advisor wrote to General Harold K. Johnson that Trưởng was "dedicated, humble, imaginative and tactically sound." That assessment was validated when Trưởng and his division played a key role in the most difficult and protracted fighting of the 1968 Têt Offensive—the fight for Huê.

Trưởng's division was well regarded by American commanders in Vietnam. General Creighton Abrams reported that "the 1st ARVN Division does better in the jungle than we do. They're really better than any of the enemy they're dealing with up there—NVA [North Vietnamese Army] or VC [Viêt Công]."

Early in 1971 the austere and capable Trưởng took command of IV Corps in the Mekong Delta. There he was so successful that he voluntarily offered up forces for redeployment to other more threatened regions of the country. When the People's Army of Vietnam (PAVN) 1972 Easter Offensive erupted and initially made serious inroads in I Corps, Trưởng was brought up to assume command. With characteristic directness he began by issuing an order, broadcast throughout the region, that all military deserters who had not returned to their units within 24 hours would be shot on sight. Trưởng then went on television himself and promised that he would hold Huê and repulse the Communist thrust.

Trưởng's arrival had a remarkable effect on the I Corps staff. General Frederick Kroesen remembered: "Sober grimaces, frowns, gloom gave way to smiles, enthusiasm and a rebirth of hope. General Trưởng was back, all would be well, and the assembled soldiers were immediately ready to serve him in whatever capacity he asked." Trưởng organized and fought a stubborn defense, halting further PAVN advances. He then successfully counterattacked with three divisions against six PAVN divisions to retake Quang Tri City. Once again, Trưởng had given evidence that he was, as General Bruce Palmer, Jr. styled him in *The 25-Year War,* "probably the best field commander in South Vietnam."

Trưởng distinguished himself during the 1975 all-out Communist offensive. "General Truong had fought a tremendous fight against insuperable odds," wrote Palmer. "This fine soldier deserved a better fate." Subsequent to the final collapse of the Republic of Vietnam, General Trưởng made his way to the United States, where he has lived since 1975.

—Lewis Sorley

References: Hoang Ngoc Lung, Col. *The General Offensives of 1968–69.* Washington, DC: U.S. Army Center of Military History, 1981.

Jones, James. *Viet Journal.* New York: Delacorte Press, 1973.

Warner, Denis. *Certain Victory.* Kansas City, KS: Sheed Andrews and McMeel, 1978.

See also: Easter Offensive (Nguyên Huê Campaign); Hô Chí Minh Campaign; Huê, Battle of; Vietnam, Republic of: Army (ARVN).

Ngô Quyên
(898–944)

Vietnamese national hero whose victory over the Southern Han (Nam Hán in Vietnamese) on the Bach Dang River in 938 marked the end of 1,000 years of Chinese domination. Born in 898 to a noble family in Dường Lâm (Sơn Tây), Ngô Quyên was the son-in-law of Dường Diên Nghê (or Dường Đình Nghê), who defeated the Nam Hán army of Lý Tiên, Lý Khăc Chính, and Trân Bao in 931 and regained autonomy for Giao Châu. In 937, when Dường Diên Nghê was assassinated by Kiêu Công Tiên, Ngô Quyên was governor of Ái Châu (Thanh Hóa). To secure revenge, Quyên moved back to Tông Binh, the capital. Kiêu Công Tiên called on the Nam Hán for support, and a Chinese army led by Prince Hoăng Tháo was sent to Giao Châu. In 938, on the Bach Dang River, using the tactic of planting iron-tipped poles under the water, Ngô Quyên won a famous victory that ended the long period of Chinese rule and opened a new era in Vietnamese history.

After the victory, Ngô Quyên declared himself king and moved the capital to Cô Loa, the ancient capital of the Thuc, a Vietnamese independent dynasty that ruled the country long before the Chinese invasion (257–207 B.C.). The selection of Cô Loa as capital was to show Ngô Quyên's willingness to build a new nation completely independent from China.

Ngô Quyên died in 944 at the age of 47. The dynasty he founded did not last long. After being usurped for five years by Dường Tam Kha, Ngô Quyên's brother-in-law, the throne was regained by the hero's two sons, Ngô Xưởng Văn and Ngô Xưởng Ngâp. These younger kings, however, were unable to control the situation. In 965 Ngô Xưởng Văn was killed in a battle against a local lord, and the newly independent country fell into the hands of 12 local lords and was reunified only in 968 by Đinh Bô Linh.

—Pham Cao Dường

References: Lê Thành Khôi. *Histoire du Viet-Nam des origines à 1858.* Paris: Sudestasie, 1981.

Pham Cao Dường. *Lich Sư Dân Tôc Viêt Nam, Quyên I: Thơi Kỳ Lâp Quôc* (History of the Vietnamese People, Vol. I: The Making of the Nation). Fountain Valley, CA: Truyên Thông Viêt, 1987.

Phan Huy Lê, Trân Quôc Vưởng, Hà Văn Tân, and Lưởng Minh. *Lich Sư Viêt Nam, Tâp I.* Hà Nôi: Nhà Xuât Ban Đai Hoc Va Giáo Duc Chuyên Nghiêp, 1991.

Taylor, Keith W. *The Birth of Vietnam.* Berkeley, CA: University of California Press, 1983.

See also: Vietnam: From 938 through the French Conquest.

Nguyên Bình
(1906–1951)

Viêt Minh lieutenant general. Born in 1906 at Bân Yên Nhân, My Văn District, Hai Hưng Province, Nguyên Bình (his real name was Nguyên Phưởng Thao), joined the Viêt Nam Quôc Dân Đang (Vietnam National Party) and participated in the abortive 1930 uprising of this party. Arrested by French authorities, Bình was sentenced to five years exile on Poulo Condore (Côn Sởn) penal island.

In early 1936 Bình was freed and returned to his hometown to continue his revolutionary activities. At the beginning of 1945 he moved to Hai Phòng to prepare for an uprising against the French. In June 1945, after attacking military posts at Bi Cho and Mao Khê, Bình attempted to establish the Đông Triêu Resistance Zone under his command. In July 1945 his forces occupied Quang Yên, the capital of Quang Ninh Province. On 23 August 1945 Bình led his troops to Hà Nôi to participate in the Communist revolution.

In October 1945 Hô Chí Minh named Bình a member of the Southern Region Military Committee and commander of the southern front. Bình apparently contributed to the unification of factions in the South against the French, and in November 1947 he was promoted to lieutenant general. He was best known for his commando attack on the French ammunition depot at Thi Nghè, Sài Gòn. Tradition has it that he warned the French beforehand. On 29 September 1951 Bình was ambushed and killed by the French on his way to the North to attend a conference. There is some suggestion that this was not without the assistance of the Communist leadership.

—Ngô N. Trung

Reference: Biographical Files, Indo-China Archives, University of California at Berkeley.

See also: Hô Chí Minh; Indo-China War; Viêt Minh (Viêt Nam Đôc Lâp Đông Minh Hôi [Vietnam Independence League]).

Nguyên Cao Kỳ
(1930–)

Republic of Vietnam Air Force air vice-marshal, premier (1965–1967), and vice-president (1967–1971). Born 8 September 1930 in Sơn Tây, 25 miles northwest of Hà Nôi, Nguyên Cao Kỳ was the only son of a conservative schoolteacher father. Kỳ attended local primary school in Sơn Tây and high school in Hà Nôi. He was about to enter college when in 1951 he was drafted into the Vietnamese National Army (VNA). After six months of officer training, he was commissioned an infantry lieutenant. Kỳ then commanded a platoon at a Red River Delta outpost but within a few weeks volunteered for pilot training. He spent a year training in Morocco, two years in France learning to fly C-47s, and six months in Algeria for bombing and strafing training. In 1954 he graduated as a fully qualified pilot and returned to Vietnam.

By the time Kỳ arrived in Vietnam, the Indo-China War was over. He then flew from Hai Phòng to the South and settled there. Promotion was rapid in the infant Republic of Vietnam Air Force (RVNAF). Kỳ flew C-47s, and in 1959, as a major, he took command of the RVNAF 43d Air Transport group. In 1960 he assumed command at Tân Sơn Nhưt Air Base outside of Sài Gòn.

That same year, Kỳ began working with Central Intelligence Agency (CIA) station chief in Sài Gòn William Colby, flying agents into North Vietnam, an operation that Kỳ publicly dis-

President Lyndon Johnson and Republic of Vietnam Premier Nguyên Cao Kỳ at the Honolulu Conference in 1966. Kỳ took steps to strengthen the armed forces but also instituted needed land reforms, programs for the construction of schools and hospitals, and price controls. His government also launched a campaign to remove corrupt officials.

closed to worldwide attention in July 1964. Kỳ was involved in the November 1963 coup that led to the overthrow and assassination of President Ngô Đình Diêm; he played the key role in securing RVNAF support and was, in reward, immediately promoted to full colonel. Ten days after the coup, new chief of state General Dương Văn Minh promoted Kỳ to brigadier general and named him commander of the RVNAF, which post he held until June 1965.

Members of the Military Revolutionary Council that had carried out the coup against Diêm soon fell to quarreling among themselves. In January 1964 Kỳ supported Maj. Gen. Nguyên Khánh in another coup, this time against Minh. That year saw seven changes of government.

Khánh promoted Kỳ to major general and then named him air vice-marshal. By this time, Kỳ was the leader in a faction of young officers known as the "Young Turks" that included Army Maj. Gen. Nguyên Văn Thiêu. Disillusioned by the ineffective national government, in mid-December 1964 they overthrew the Military Revolutionary Council of older officers. In late January 1965 the new Armed Forces Council decided that Premier Trân Văn Hường would have to be replaced. Khánh, who replaced him as premier, was in turn ousted in February in a coup led by General Lâm Văn Phát. Kỳ was not involved in this coup, but his threat to bomb headquarters toppled Phát. Phan Huy Quát then became premier with Phan Khắc Sửu as chief of state.

On 8 February 1965 the flamboyant Kỳ led a flight of RVNAF planes in Operation FLAMING DART I, the reprisal air strike ordered by President Lyndon Johnson against the Đông Hời military barracks north of the Demilitarized Zone (DMZ).

In June 1965 the new Republic of Vietnam (RVN) government collapsed, and on 12 June a triumvirate of Generals Nguyên Cao Kỳ, Nguyên Văn Thiêu, and Nguyên Hữu Có announced the formation of a National Leadership Committee to rule the RVN. It was subsequently expanded to include 10 members. This body was an inner circle of the 50-member Armed Forces Council, which then elected Kỳ as chief executive of the council, or premier, charged with conducting the day-to-day government operations. Nguyên Văn Thiêu occupied the relatively powerless position of chief of state. It was the ninth government in less than two years.

When U.S. Ambassador Henry Cabot Lodge asked him about his program, Kỳ replied with the words "social justice." He took steps to strengthen the armed forces but also instituted needed land reforms, programs for the construction of schools and hospitals, and price controls. His government also launched a campaign to remove corrupt officials. But Kỳ also instituted a number of unpopular repressive actions against civilians, including a ban on newspapers.

The new government was soon embroiled in controversy with the Buddhists. The issue was over Army of the Republic of Vietnam (ARVN) I Corps commander General Nguyễn Chánh Thi. Kỳ and others in the government believed that Thi was too powerful and posed a threat to the government. In early March 1966 they had secured his agreement to resign and go into exile in the United States. Buddhist leaders seized on this and began demonstrations. On 14 March Đà Nẵng workers began a two-day general strike that seriously affected American activities. Buddhist students in Huế also began protests. Thi took advantage of this and refused to relinquish command of I Corps. He also attended rallies in Huế and Đà Nẵng to address supporters. Thi's removal was soon no longer the central issue as Buddhist leaders sought a complete change of government. The Buddhists took control of radio stations in Huế and Đà Nẵng, and it was evident that there was growing sympathy for the movement among the civil service and many ARVN units. On 3 April Kỳ announced "Đà Nẵng is in Communist hands," but it is by no means clear what role, if any, the Communists played.

Kỳ tried to control the situation by appointing General Tôn Thất Đính as the new commander of I Corps on 10 April, but Đính could not assert his authority with Thi still in Huế. After a significant military operation to suppress the Buddhists and rebel ARVN units, Thi accepted his dismissal on 24 May and, following a "reconciliation" with Kỳ, went into exile in the United States. In June, supported by U.S. forces, Kỳ's troops crushed opposition in Huế.

Kỳ's popularity and political clout were enhanced in February 1966 as a result of a two-day conference with President Lyndon Johnson in Hawaii. The two men agreed on social and economic reforms and on the need for national elections. In May 1966 a government decree set up a committee to draft election laws and procedures. In October 117 delegates met in Sài Gòn to begin drafting a constitution, which was completed in March 1967. It provided for a president with wide powers, and a premier and cabinet responsible to a two-chamber house. Local elections were held in May 1967, and elections for the lower House in October.

Tensions were high between Kỳ and Thiêu. At first the two men got on fairly well, but then both openly vied for control of the government. In his memoir, *Twenty Years and Twenty Days* (1976) Kỳ was sharply critical of Thiêu, who "wanted power and glory but he did not want to have to do the dirty work." He also accused Thiêu of corruption and involvement in heroin traffic.

Although the more senior Thiêu had stepped aside in 1965 to allow Kỳ to take the premier's post (Kỳ claimed that Thiêu had said at the time that he "did not want the responsibility"), his determination to challenge Kỳ for the highest office in the 3 September 1967 elections led the Armed Forces Council to force Kỳ and Thiêu onto a joint ticket, giving the presidential nomination to Thiêu and the vice-presidential nomination to Kỳ, simply on the basis of seniority. The Thiêu-Kỳ ticket won the election with 34.8 percent of the vote against ten other slates.

After the election, Kỳ's influence was gradually eclipsed by Thiêu's consolidation of power, though Kỳ tried to suppress Thiêu's followers in the military. In 1971 Thiêu engineered an election law to disqualify his major opponents, Kỳ and Dương Văn Minh. Although the Supreme Court said that Kỳ, who had charged Thiêu's government with corruption, could run, he chose not to. Thiêu's election made one-person rule a reality and did serious injury to the RVN government's image.

In his memoirs, Kỳ was sharply critical of Thiêu's handling of the 1975 Communist Hô Chí Minh Offensive and his abandonment of the Central Highlands. As he put it, "Thiêu's strategic error turned a tactical withdrawal into a rout and the eventual disintegration of our entire armed forces." In early April 1975 Kỳ led a well-publicized demonstration in front of the U.S. Embassy in Sài Gòn, during which he and several hundred other officers promised never to leave Vietnam. On the 29th, however, Kỳ commandeered a helicopter and flew it to the USS *Midway*.

Kỳ went to the United States, where he opened a liquor store in Los Angeles. In 1985 Kỳ filed for bankruptcy; his liabilities included the loan to buy the liquor store and a $20,000 gambling debt.

—Spencer C. Tucker

References: Nguyễn Cao Kỳ. *Twenty Years and Twenty Days.* New York: Stein & Day, 1976.
Olson, James S., ed. *Dictionary of the Vietnam War.* Westport, CT: Greenwood Press, 1988.
See also: Đà Nẵng; Dương Văn Minh; Elections (National), Republic of Vietnam: 1955, 1967, 1971; FLAMING DART, Operation; Honolulu Conference; Johnson, Lyndon Baines; Lodge, Henry Cabot, Jr.; Manila Conference; Military Revolutionary Council; Ngô Đình Diêm, Overthrow of; Nguyễn Khánh; Nguyễn Văn Thiêu; Trân Văn Hưởng; Vietnam, Republic of: 1954–1975.

Nguyễn Chánh Thi

(1923–)

Army of the Republic of Vietnam (ARVN) general and commander of I Corps, whose removal sparked countrywide Buddhist protests. Born in 1923, Nguyễn Chánh Thi was a devout Buddhist. In 1955 Thi helped Ngô Đình Diêm defeat the Bình Xuyên gangsters. Thi rose to the rank of colonel and came to command ARVN paratroops. Resenting Diêm's favoritism toward the Catholics, he participated in the November 1960 coup attempt against the Republic of Vietnam (RVN) president. Thi claimed he did not want a neutralist government but instead wanted to change the corrupt and incompetent nature of the existing central government. The coup failed after Diêm stalled for time by promising to reform his administration, while secretly bringing in reinforcements. Immediately after the coup collapse, Thi fled to Cambodia.

Following Diêm's November 1963 assassination, Thi returned to the RVN and received command of I Corps, which included the cities of Huế and Đà Nẵng. As corps commander he exercised significant control over the region. Premier Nguyễn Cao Kỳ and others in the government believed that Thi was too powerful and posed a threat to the government. Kỳ had heard rumors in March 1966 that some of the older generals were trying to form an alliance with Thi because of his strong Buddhist support, which included Thích Trí Quang, militant leader of the Central Vietnamese Buddhist movement. On 4 March Kỳ confronted Thi about this, and on 10 March convinced the National Leadership Committee in Sài Gòn to dismiss Thi from I Corps command.

At first Thi appeared to accept the decision and be willing to depart for exile in the United States. On 11 March the Armed Forces Council confirmed the decision to remove Thi from command, but it was then clear that some form of protest by the Buddhists would occur in Đà Nẵng and Sài Gòn. On 14 March workers in Đà Nẵng went on a two-day general strike that affected American activities. Buddhist students in Huế had also initiated protests. Thi sought to use the situation to his own advantage; he now refused to relinquish command of I Corps and leave for the United States. On both 17 and 18 March he spoke to his supporters in rallies in Huế and Đà Nẵng.

Buddhist leaders also took advantage of the situation to try to bring about a change of government. They seized control of radio stations in Huế and Đà Nẵng. With support for the movement growing among civil servants and the ARVN, on 3 April Kỳ announced "Đà Nẵng is in Communist hands." The Communist role in events is unclear, but the Communists certainly took advantage of the situation to try to turn public opinion against the Americans.

On 10 April Kỳ appointed General Tôn Thất Đính as commander of I Corps, but Đính was unable to take command with Thi still in Huế. After a government-mounted operation to suppress the Buddhists and the rebel ARVN units, on 24 May Thi agreed to step down. Following a "reconciliation" with Kỳ at Chu Lai on 27 May, Thi left for exile in the United States.

—Michael R. Nichols

References: Bain, Chester A. *Vietnam: The Roots of Conflict.* Englewood Cliffs, NJ: Prentice-Hall, 1967.
Duncanson, Dennis J. *Government and Revolution in Vietnam.* New York: Oxford University Press, 1968.
FitzGerald, Frances. *Fire in the Lake: The Vietnamese and the Americans in Vietnam.* Boston: Little, Brown, 1972.
Harrison, James P. *The Endless War: Vietnam's Struggle for Independence.* New York: Columbia University Press, 1989.
Smith, R. B. *An International History of the Vietnam War.* 3 vols. New York: St. Martin's Press, 1991.
See also: Buddhists; Ngô Đình Diệm; Nguyễn Cao Kỳ; Thích Trí Quang; Tôn Thất Đính.

Nguyễn Chí Thanh

(1914–1967)

Senior general in the People's Army of Vietnam (PAVN) and director of the Central Office for South Vietnam (COSVN), 1965–1967. Born on 1 January 1914 at Nghiêm Phô village, Thừa Thiên Province, Nguyễn Chí Thanh joined the Communist Party in 1937 and quickly rose through its ranks. French authorities arrested him in 1938 and again in 1939. During the early 1940s Thanh worked closely with the Youth Union.

After the formation of the Democratic Republic of Vietnam (DRV) in 1945, Thanh was given a series of party posts, including a seat in the secretariat of the important Thừa Thiên Province Central Committee and membership in the national Central Committee. In 1950 he became a member of the Military Central Committee, a move that paved his way for a leadership position with the People's Army.

After the Communist victory at Điên Biên Phu, Thanh spent a good deal of time traveling in the Communist world, one of the few PAVN leaders to do so. Trips to Czechoslovakia, Bulgaria, the Soviet Union, and North Korea highlighted his considerable political and diplomatic talents. However, Thanh was first a warrior and secondly a politician. During the Vietnam War, he advocated a battlefield victory at all costs. When some in Hà Nội suggested adopting a more pragmatic approach more in line with Moscow's thinking in the early 1960s, Thanh openly rebelled. Once a close colleague of Vietnamese Communist Party Secretary General Lê Duẩn, Thanh became a maverick in his strong opposition to the protracted war strategy adopted by the Central Committee at the Twelfth Party Plenum in December 1965. His leadership of COSVN was extremely controversial, and many scholars have suggested that Thanh's view of military matters made him a candidate for conflict with General Võ Nguyên Giáp.

The circumstances surrounding Thanh's death are mysterious. His official obituary says that he died in Hà Nội on 6 July 1967 of a heart attack, while many officers who served with Thanh in the southern theater say he died during a U.S. bombing raid.

—Robert K. Brigham

References: Duiker, William J. "Waging Revolutionary War: The Evolution of Hanoi's Strategy in the South, 1959–1965." In *The Vietnam War: Vietnamese and American Perspectives,* edited by Jayne S. Werner and Luu Doan Huynh. Armonk, NY: M. E. Sharpe, 1993.
Herring, George C. *America's Longest War: The United States and Vietnam, 1950–1975.* 2d ed. New York: Alfred A. Knopf, 1986.
Lockhart, Greg. *Nation in Arms: The Origins of the People's Army of Vietnam.* Sydney: Allen & Unwin, 1989.
Pike, Douglas. *PAVN: People's Army of Vietnam.* Novato, CA: Presidio Press, 1986.
Theis, Wallace J. *When Governments Collide: Coercion and Diplomacy in the Vietnam Conflict, 1964–1968.* Berkeley, CA: University of California Press, 1980.
See also: COSVN (Central Office for South Vietnam or Trung Ương Cuc Miên Nam); Lê Duẩn; National Front for the Liberation of South Vietnam (NFLSV); Vietnam, Democratic Republic of: Army (People's Army of Vietnam [PAVN]); Võ Nguyên Giáp.

Nguyễn Cơ Thạch

(1932–)

Vietnamese revolutionary; Democratic Republic of Vietnam (DRV) ambassador to India, 1956–1960; head of the DRV delegation to the 1962 Geneva Conference; and minister for foreign affairs for the Socialist Republic of Vietnam (SRV), 1975–1991. Born on 3 August 1932, Nguyễn Cơ Thạch was educated in Hà Nội and Moscow. He joined the Communist Party in the early 1950s and quickly rose through the DRV diplomatic corps, serving as the DRV's ambassador to India from 1956 to 1960 and as head of the DRV delegation to the 1962 Geneva Conference. In 1966 he chaired the Vietnamese delegation to the Conference to Investigate U.S. War Crimes.

During the American phase of the Vietnam War, Thach was best remembered for his role in what became known as the "Ronning Missions," secret peace initiatives spearheaded by retired Canadian diplomat Chester A. Ronning. In March 1966 Ronning spent five days in Hà Nôi, meeting with Thach, Nguyên Duy Trinh, and Pham Văn Đông. Ronning believed that he had been party to a major change in DRV policy when Pham Văn Đông assured him that, if the United States stopped the bombings, the DRV was prepared to enter into talks. The Johnson administration flatly rejected this proposal brought back by Ronning, instead calling for a reciprocal de-escalation in return for a bombing halt. Thach and Ronning met again in June 1966, but ultimately their talks produced little result.

In 1975 Thach became minister of foreign affairs. In 1976 he became a member of the Vietnamese Communist Party's Central Committee and was elected as an alternative member to the Political Bureau in 1981. During the 1986 Sixth Party Congress, Thach was instrumental in moving the party toward economic reform (đổi mới), advocating a more international outlook. Working closely with U.S. presidential emissary John W. Vessey, Jr., Thach also supervised the return of the remains of U.S. servicemen killed in action. In 1991 there was a period of backlash against đổi mới and what some party leaders called "too much cooperation with Western capitalist countries." As a result, Thach was removed from the Political Bureau and the Foreign Ministry at the Seventh Party Congress that June.

—Robert K. Brigham

References: Herring, George C., ed. The Secret Diplomacy of the Vietnam War: The Negotiating Volumes of the Pentagon Papers. Austin, TX: University of Texas Press, 1983.
Marr, David G., and Christine White, eds. Postwar Vietnam: Dilemmas in Socialist Development. Ithaca, NY: Cornell Southeast Asia Studies Program, 1988.
Nguyen Van Canh. Vietnam under Communism, 1975–1982. Stanford, CA: Hoover Institute Press, 1983.
Porter, Gareth. Vietnam: The Politics of Bureaucratic Socialism. Ithaca, NY: Cornell University Press, 1993.
Thayer, Carlyle A. "Political Reform in Viet Nam: Doi Moi and the Emergence of Civil Society." In The Development of Civil Society in Communist Systems, edited by Robert F. Miller. Sydney: Allen & Unwin, 1992.
See also: Đổi Mới; Missing in Action, Allied; Paris Negotiations; Vietnam, Socialist Republic of: 1975 to the Present.

Nguyên Duy Trinh
(1910–1988)
Member of the Lao Đông (Communist Party of Vietnam) Central Committee and foreign minister of the Democratic Republic of Vietnam (DRV), 1965–1975. Nguyên Duy Trinh was born in the village of Nghi Lôc, Nghê An Province in central Vietnam in 1910. After years of resistance work in the New Vietnam Revolutionary

Party, Trinh was arrested in 1928 for his revolutionary activities in Sài Gòn. When the French released him in 1930, Trinh joined the Indo-Chinese Communist Party and was active in the Nghê Tinh Soviet Movement between 1930 and 1931. The following year, the French arrested him again, and he remained in a colonial prison until 1945.

In 1951 Trinh was selected as a member of the Lao Đông (Communist Party) Central Committee. After the 1954 victory over the French, he became secretary of the Lao Đông's Central Committee, one of the most powerful positions within the party. In 1960 Trinh became the deputy prime minister of the DRV, a post he held until the end of the Vietnam War.

From 1965 to 1975 Trinh gained international recognition as the DRV's minister of foreign affairs. He participated in the DRV's secret contacts with the United States through third parties before the Paris peace talks began and played a key role in the ASPEN and PENNSYLVANIA peace initiatives. He also supervised the first secret contact in Paris between DRV delegate Mai Văn Bô and American Edmund Gullion, known in the west as XYZ. Perhaps Trinh is best known for his statement of 29 December 1967, in which he declared that serious peace talks "will begin" when the United States stopped bombing the North unconditionally. Earlier in the year, he had announced that substantive talks "could begin" if the United States called a bombing halt. The December statement represented a dramatic shift in Hà Nôi's negotiating stance, and some suggested that this compromise would lead to a quick settlement. In the end, Trinh's comment produced little and the war continued with few prospects for peace.

As the war dragged on, Trinh's role in the peace talks diminished. He remained an active deputy prime minister, and after the fall of Sài Gòn in 1975 he became of member of the Lao Đông's Political Bureau. Also in 1975 the second generation of Communist Party leaders began to succeed the first, and Nguyên Cơ Thach replaced the elderly Trinh as foreign minister. Trinh died in 1988.

—Robert K. Brigham

References: Herring, George. C., ed. The Secret Diplomacy of the Vietnam War: The Negotiating Volumes of the Pentagon Papers. Austin, TX: University of Texas Press, 1983.
Huynh Kim Khanh. Vietnamese Communism, 1925–1945. Ithaca, NY: Cornell University Press, 1982.
Porter, Gareth. Vietnam: The Politics of Bureaucratic Socialism. Ithaca, NY: Cornell University Press, 1993.
Thies, Wallace J. When Governments Collide: Coercion and Diplomacy in the Vietnam Conflict, 1964–1968. Berkeley, CA: University of California Press, 1980.
See also: Lao Đông Party; Nguyên Cơ Thach; Paris Negotiations; Paris Peace Accords.

Nguyên Dynasty
(1802–1945)
Ruling family in Vietnam from 1802 to 1945. In the seventeenth century, Vietnam was divided in two. The Trinh lords ruled the North, while the Nguyên lords came to control then-southern Vietnam from their fortress city of Phú Xuân (present-day Huê).

Each family hated the other and ruled in the name of the power-less Lê kings at Thăng Long (present-day Hà Nôi). The Trinh tried to conquer the South but their armies were unable to penetrate walls that the Nguyên constructed near the 17th parallel.

By 1700 the Nguyên had extended their influence in the South to include parts of Laos, Cambodia, and Thailand. In 1771, how-ever, Nguyên power came under attack in the Tây Sơn Rebellion. The Tây Sơn were on the verge of overthrowing the Nguyên alto-gether when in 1775 a Trinh army moved south and took Phú Xuân. The Tây Sơn managed to avoid being crushed between their enemies by reaching accommodation with the Trinh until the latter tired of their southern involvement and withdrew into the North.

In 1776 the Tây Sơn attacked the Nguyên stronghold in Gia Đinh Province and took Sài Côn (later Sài Gòn and present-day Hô Chí Minh City). Only one Nguyên prince, Nguyên Phúc Ánh, managed to escape; he and some supporters fled into the swamps of the western Mekong Delta. In 1783 Tây Sơn troops led by the youngest Tây Sơn brother, Nguyên Huê, again defeated Nguyên Ánh, forcing him into refuge on Phú Quôc Island. Nguyên Ánh then called in the Siamese, and in 1784 a Siamese army invaded the western Mekong Delta. In 1785 Nguyên Huê defeated the in-vaders, and the remainder of Nguyên Ánh's family fled to Siam.

Nguyên Huê succeeded in established his control over North Vietnam and then the whole country by defeating the Trinh, the Lê, and an intervening Chinese army. He then ruled the country as Emperor Quang Trung. He died in 1792, however, before he had a chance to establish his dynasty.

Nguyên Ánh had not given up. He made friends with French missionary Pigneau de Béhaine, who supported his cause and se-cured military assistance in the form of French mercenary troops from India. With Western advisors and weaponry, Nguyên Ánh launched a military campaign to establish his rule over all Viet-nam, something he accomplished in 1802. Nguyên Ánh then founded the Nguyên dynasty. He took the dynastic name Gia Long (Gia from the customary name for Sài Gòn, Gia Đinh; and Long from Thăng Long).

Gia Long moved the capital from Hà Nôi in the North to Huê in the central part of the country. He died in 1820 and was fol-lowed by Minh Mang (1820–1841), Thiêu Tri (1841–1847), Tư Đức (1847–1883), Duc Đức (July 1883), Hiêp Hòa (August–November 1883), Kiên Phúc (1883–1884), Hàm Nghi (1884–1888), Đông Khánh (1885–1888), Thành Thái (1889–1907), Duy Tân (1907–1916), Khai Đinh (1916–1925), and Bao Đai (1925–1945).

Gia Long's successors lacked his understanding of Western strengths and weaknesses. Perhaps they would have been unable to resist Western military technology in any case, but it was under them that the French conquered the country and established their authority. The Nguyên dynasty lasted in Vietnam until the 1945 abdication of Bao Đai.

—Spencer C. Tucker

References: Lê Thành Khôi. *Histoire de Viêt Nam des Origines à 1858.* Paris: Sudestasie, 1981.

Nguyên Khăc Viên. *Vietnam: A Long History.* Hà Nôi: Foreign Languages Publishing House, 1987.
See also: Bao Đai; Duy Tân; Hàm Nghi; Minh Mang; Nguyên Huê (Quang Trung); Nguyên Phúc Ánh (Gia Long); Tây Sơn Uprising; Thiêu Tri; Tư Đức.

Nguyên Hà Phan

(1933–)

Prominent leader in the Vietnamese Communist Party (VCP) and the Socialist Republic of Vietnam (SRV). Born on 2 February 1933 in Châu Hòa village, Giông Trôm District, Bên Tre Province, Nguyên Hà Phan's background is obscure, except that he was edu-cated in the North during the war. Phan was an alternate member of the VCP Central Committee at the December 1986 Sixth Party Congress. Elevated to full member at the Seventh Party Congress, he became head of the Department of Economics. In June 1991 he became secretary of the VCP Central Committee's Secretariat and in January 1994 was promoted to the political bureau of the VCP Central Committee.

Phan was also active in the government. In 1981 he was chair-man of Hâu Giang Province People's Committee. He was also a deputy to the National Assembly from that province and a mem-ber of that body's Economics, Planning, and Budget Committee. After the division of Hâu Giang Province into two provinces, he was elected as a deputy to the National Assembly from Cân Thơ Province, and in July 1992 became deputy chairman of the Na-tional Assembly. Regarded as one of the likely candidates to re-place Võ Văn Kiêt as premier, Phan in April 1996 was suddenly re-moved both from the Politburo and the National Assembly, apparently over his opposition to a more open economy. He was the highest-level party official expelled in more than a decade.

—Ngô N. Trung

Reference: Biographical Files, Indo-China Archives, University of Cali-fornia at Berkeley.
See also: Vietnam, Socialist Republic of: 1975 to the Present.

Nguyên Hai Thân

(1869–1951)

Nationalist Vietnamese leader who opposed Hô Chí Minh. Born in Đai Tư village, Thường Tín District, Hà Đông Province in 1869, Nguyên Hai Thân (real name Nguyên Văn Thăng or Vũ Hai Thu) in 1891 earned the degree of Tú Tài in the mandarin examina-tions. Around 1905 he went to China in Phan Bôi Châu's "Exodus to the East" Movement that encouraged Vietnamese to study abroad.

In China, Thân graduated from the Whampoa Military Acad-emy. Years later he became a close friend of Sun Yat-sen and was highly respected by Jiang Jieshi (Chiang Kai-shek). For a time he taught at Whampoa.

In 1942 Thân helped found the Viêt Nam Cách Mênh Đông Minh Hôi (VNCMDMH) with help from Chinese General Chang Fa Kwei. When the latter imprisoned Hô Chí Minh, Vietnamese nationalist leaders in South China, who thought of Hô as a com-patriot rather than a Communist, urged Nguyên Hai Thân to intercede with Jiang Jieshi for Hô's freedom, which he did, obtaining Hô's release. Hô then joined the VNCMDMH, of which Nguyên Thân was chairman. Hô's (new) Viêt Nam Dôc Lâp Dông Minh Hôi (VNDLDMH, or Viêt Minh) Party joined the umbrella VNCMDMH organization.

Within the VNCMDMH, Hô was assigned the task of observing the situation in Vietnam and determining the right time for the league to attempt a general uprising in which all member parties were to participate. After pledging full allegiance to the league, Hô returned to Vietnam. But in August 1945 Hô's Viêt Minh seized power. Although the other league-affiliated nationalist parties, especially the Viêt Nam Quôc Dân Dang (VNQDD), were more powerful than the Viêt Minh, they were not prepared for the imminent defeat of the Japanese.

Aware of the Viêt Minh betrayal, the nationalist parties held an emergency meeting on 18 August 1945 in Hà Nôi to decide whether they should try to drive the Viêt Minh from power. The majority concluded that, since the Viêt Minh were fighting for independence, a civil war should be avoided.

Too late Nguyên Hai Thân returned to Hà Nôi. The nationalist parties formed a front, with the major element in it the VNQDD. Nguyên Hai Thân became the front's leader. Although supported by Jiang Jieshi, Thân did not get full assistance from commander of Chinese forces in northern Vietnam General Lu' Hán, undoubtedly a consequence of Hô's having bought Lu' off with gold contributed by the people in the so-called "Gold Week."

Meanwhile Hô maneuvered skillfully to marginalize Nguyên and minimize nationalist influence, essential because the nationalist forces were more powerful than the Viêt Minh. Hô practiced every stratagem to fool Nguyên and finally went to see him at VNCMDMH headquarters to secure an agreement. They spent an entire day in discussions, with Hô warning Nguyên that, if he refused a coalition and civil war were to break out, the Vietnamese people and history would condemn him.

That was what Nguyên most feared, and so he finally agreed to accept the vice-presidency and place his supporters in cabinet posts, including foreign affairs, treasury, public health, and agriculture. Hô also offered 70 seats of 350 seats of the Parliament to parties allied with Nguyên. Of this number, the VNQDD received 50 seats, and the others shared the remaining 20. This meant that the two sides agreed to rig the 6 January 1946 elections.

After the preliminary agreement with the French on 6 March 1946, the nationalist forces were routed by an all-out surprise Viêt Minh offensive (ironically during the Great Solidarity Campaign). In many places in North Vietnam, French forces also attacked nationalist strongholds.

Nguyên Hai Thân soon left Vietnam for China. Subsequently he was blamed for the failure to overthrow the Viêt Minh when it was still possible. He stayed on in China after the defeat of the Kuomintang in 1949 and died in Nanning, southern China, in 1951.

Although Nguyên Hai Thân was a virtuous leader of unquestioned morality, he was not a talented politician, especially when faced with the likes of Hô Chí Minh.

—Nguyên Công Luân (Lu' Tuân)

Reference: Hoàng Văn Dào. *Viêt Nam Quôc Dân Dang*. Sài Gòn: Published by the author, 1970; reprinted in the United States.
See also: August Revolution; French Indo-China; Hô Chí Minh; Hô-Sainteny Agreement; Jiang Jieshi (Chiang Kai-shek).

Nguyên Huê (Quang Trung)
(1752–1792)

Also known as Vua Quang Trung (King Quang Trung) or Quang Trung Hoàng Dê (Emperor Quang Trung), the most important military strategist and national hero in Vietnamese history, who with 100,000 men successfully defeated a Chinese army of 200,000 in January 1789. Nguyên Huê was born in 1752, the youngest and most capable of the three brothers from the village of Tây Sơn in Bình Dinh Province (the others were Nguyên Nhac and Nguyên Lu'). The three revolted against the Nguyên lords in South Vietnam in the early 1770s. After 15 years they defeated both the Nguyên in the South and the Trinh in the North, and to a certain extent, reunified the country after 150 years of division.

Thanks to this success, King Hiên Tông of the Lê regained power. After the death of Hiên Tông, his grandson Chiêu Thông was unable to maintain order. This situation led Nguyên Huê to move back to the capital at Thăng Long.

Lê Chiêu Thông then fled to China and asked for assistance in regaining his throne. This request provided Chinese Emperor Càn Long (Kien Lung) an excellent opportunity to reconquer his country's former colony. To accomplish this, in 1788 Tôn Su Nghi (Sun Shiyi), governor of Kwang-tung and Kwang-si, was placed at the head of a Chinese army of 200,000 men.

Being no match for the huge Chinese army, Ngô Văn Sơ, the Tây Sơn general, decided to abandon Thăng Long and move further southward to await Nguyên Huê's orders. It was at this time that Nguyên Huê decided to proclaim himself king and prepared to move north. He left Phú Xuân (Huê) on the 22d day of the 11th month of the Mâu Thân Year (22 December 1788) and arrived in Nghê An on 26 December. There he recruited more men for his army. Before continuing his march, he ordered the army to celebrate Têt ahead of time.

Following a series of battles, that of Phú Xuyên (thirtieth day of the twelfth month), Hà Hôi (third day of the first month of the Ky Dâu Year, 1789), and Ngoc Hôi, the Tây Sơn won a decisive victory at Khu'ơng Thu'ơng. Sâm Nghi Dông, the Chinese commander, hung himself at Dông Da Hill. Tôn Sĩ Nghi and his lieutenants fled. On the fifth day of Têt, Quang Trung entered the capital. His campaign had lasted 40 days, with 35 of them in preparation and only 5 days in battle. Nguyên Huê's victory at Dông Da on the fifth day of Têt Ky Dâu became a national holiday in the official calendar of South Vietnam before 1975. It is now celebrated by overseas Vietnamese throughout the world.

Quang Trung's lightening victory over the Chinese was not his only military achievement. In 1784 Nguyên Phúc Ánh called in the Siamese to help him against the Tây Sơn, and a Siamese force of between 20,000 and 50,000 men with 300 ships invaded the western Mekong Delta area. On 19 January 1785, in one of the most important military victories in Vietnamese history, Quang Trung lured the Siamese into an ambush on the My Tho River in the Rach

Gâm–Xoài Mút area of Đinh Tưởng Province and defeated them. According to Vietnamese sources, only 2,000 Siamese escaped. The remaining Nguyên family members then fled to Siam. The battle halted Siamese expansion into southern Vietnam.

In addition to these two great military victories, Quang Trung did much domestically for Vietnam. He showed himself willing to work with capable individuals, regardless of their past loyalties. This helped attract the best men to his service. He reorganized the army and carried out fiscal reforms. He also redistributed unused lands, mainly to the peasants. He promoted the crafts and trade and pushed for reforms in education, stating that in building a country nothing was more important than educating the people.

Quang Trung also believed in the importance of studying history; he had his own tutors lecture to him on Vietnamese history and culture six times a month. He wanted to open trade with the countries of the West, and Western missionaries in Vietnam at the time noted the safe conditions in which they were able to carry out their religious activities with more freedom than before.

Quang Trung was the first Vietnamese leader to stress the importance of science, insisting it be added to requirements for the Mandarinate examinations. He also introduced a Vietnamese currency and insisted that *Chư Nôm*, the demotic writing system combining Chinese characters with Vietnamese, be used exclusively, rather than Chinese, in court documents.

Unfortunately, his reign was short. Quang Trung was not to have the "ten years" he believed necessary; he died of an unknown illness in March or April 1792. Many Vietnamese believe that had he lived a decade longer their history would have developed quite differently. His son, Quang Toan, ascended the throne, but he was then only ten years old. Within a decade Nguyên Ánh, the surviving Nguyên lord, came to power and proclaimed himself king as Gia Long, establishing the Nguyên Dynasty.

—Pham Cao Dưởng and Spencer C. Tucker

References: Hoa Bang. *Quang Trung Nguyên Huê: Anh Hùng Dân Tôc (1788–1792).* (Quang Trung Nguyen Hue, Our National Hero). Sài Gòn: Bôn Phường tái ban, 1950.
Le Thanh Khoi. *Le Viet-Nam, Histoire et Civilisation.* Paris: Editions de Minuit, 1955.
Nguyên Huyên Anh. *Viêt Nam Danh Nhân Tư Điên* (Dictionary of Vietnamese Great Men and Women). Houston: Zieleks, 1990.
Trân Trong Kim. *Viêt Nam Sư Lươc.* Sài Gòn: Bô Giáo Duc, Trung Tâm Hoc Liêu, 1971.
See also: Hà Nôi (Đông Đa), Battle of; Nguyên Dynasty; Nguyên Phúc Ánh (Gia Long); Vietnam: From 938 through the French Conquest.

Nguyên Hữu Có
(1923–?)
Army of the Republic of Vietnam (ARVN) general and Republic of Vietnam (RVN) defense minister in 1966. Nguyên Hữu Có was born on 23 February 1923 in My Tho, South Vietnam. Có's first public appearance came during the coup that overthrew Ngô Đình Diêm. As one of General Tôn Thât Đính's deputies, Có, then a colonel, was in charge of preventing Diêm loyalists in the Mekong Delta from coming to Sài Gòn to rescue the Ngô brothers, a task he successfully fulfilled.

After the coup, Có was promoted to lieutenant general, and in 1965 he became chief of ARVN Joint General Staff. In 1966 he became deputy prime minister and minister of defense. In this turbulent period in RVN politics, with five governments in three months, there was little Có could do in his position. Reportedly he was more interested in making money in real estate than he was interested in national affairs. After the 1975 Communist victory, Có stayed in Vietnam and was sent to a prison camp along with other ARVN officers. When he was released in 1990, he chose to stay instead of immigrating to the United States.

—Ho Diêu Anh

References: Stanley, Karnow. *Vietnam: A History.* New York: Viking Press, 1983.
Who's Who in Vietnam. Sài Gòn: Vietnam Press Agency, 1974.
See also: Ngô Đình Diêm, Overthrow of ; Tôn Thât Đính; Vietnam, Republic of: 1954–1975.

Nguyên Hữu Tho
(1910–1994)
Southern Vietnamese revolutionary and first president of the National Front for the Liberation of South Vietnam (NFLSV). Born on 10 July 1910 in Chơ Lớn, Tho attended law school in France and worked as a lawyer in Sài Gòn during the 1940s. In 1949 he helped organize a successful anti-French protest in Sài Gòn and caught the attention of colonial officials. In 1950 the French arrested Tho and deported him to Lai Châu (North Vietnam) where he remained until the signing of the Geneva Accords in 1954.

Tho returned to Sài Gòn in 1954 and resumed his resistance activities. He founded the Sài Gòn–Chơ Lớn Peace Movement and was elected as its vice-president in 1955. Although Tho never joined the Communist Party officially, Ngô Đình Diêm, the president of the newly created Republic of Vietnam, claimed that Tho was a party member and had him arrested. Tho served several years in southern jails before Diêm put him under house arrest in Phú Yên (central Vietnam). At the organizational meeting of the National Front for the Liberation of South Vietnam (NFLSV) on 20 December 1960, Tho was the delegates' choice as its first president. During a commando raid, southern revolutionaries liberated Tho and brought him to NFLSV headquarters in Tây Ninh Province.

From 1961 through 1968 Tho served as the president of the Presidium of the NFLSV's Central Committee. He insisted that the NFLSV was independent and autonomous from the Communists in Hà Nôi and that the Front had come into being in response to southern demands. From 1962 to 1968 he was the international spokesperson for the NFLSV, granting interviews to hundreds of reporters worldwide. In 1969 Huỳnh Tân Phát replaced Tho as the newly formed Provisional Revolutionary Government's president. Tho continued as chairman of the NFLSV's Central Committee and in 1976 was named to the purely ceremonial position of acting vice-president of the Socialist Republic of Vietnam (SRV). Tho's powerlessness after the fall of Sài Gòn became symbolic of the difficulties and tensions between northern and southern Communists after the war. Tho died in 1994.

—Robert K. Brigham

References: Kahin, George McT., and John Lewis. *The United States in Vietnam: An Analysis in Depth of the History of America's Involvement in Vietnam.* New York: Delta, 1967.
Personalities of the South Vietnam Liberation Movement. Tran Phu, Vietnam: Foreign Relations Commission of the South Vietnam National Front for Liberation, 1965.
Porter, Gareth. *Vietnam: The Politics of Bureaucratic Socialism.* Ithaca, NY: Cornell University Press, 1993.
Truong Nhu Tang. *A Viet Cong Memoir: An Inside Account of the Vietnam War and Its Aftermath.* New York: Vintage Books, 1985.
See also: Huỳnh Tân Phát; National Front for the Liberation of South Vietnam (NFLSV); Ngô Đình Diêm; Nguyên Thi Bình; Provisional Revolutionary Government of South Vietnam (PRG); Trân Bưu Kiêm; Trưởng Như Tang; Vietnam, Republic of: 1954–1975.

Nguyên Hửu Tri

(ca. 1903–1954)

Leader of the Đai Viêt Quôc Dân Đang (National Party of Greater Vietnam) and nationalist governor of northern Vietnam for the State of Vietnam during much of the Indo-China War. The date and place of Nguyên Hửu Tri's birth are uncertain; he may have been born in 1903.

When the Đai Viêt Quôc Dân Đang announced their support for former emperor Bao Đai's government in June 1949, Tri was appointed chief magistrate of North Vietnam. Initially, Tri presided only over the municipalities, since the countryside was controlled by the Viêt Minh. The nationalist cause was hurt when in 1951 French General Jean de Lattre de Tassigny ordered Tri removed from office.

Subsequently reappointed governor, Tri was considered by the American Special and Economic Technical Mission (Mutual Security Agency) in North Vietnam as the most competent of the Vietnamese administrators. He pressed the French for real independence and organized the Đông Quan pacification project south of Hà Nôi. Tri worked closely with the Americans and the French to create other pacification centers in order to protect the population from Viêt Minh infiltration in the Red River Delta. He was disappointed by the success of Viêt Minh terror and by the scant support received from the French. The pacification centers that Tri organized with U.S. funding became mostly refugee centers to accommodate the tens of thousands of Vietnamese fleeing Viêt Minh–controlled areas. He was called to Sài Gòn by the government in mid-1954 and died there under mysterious circumstances.

—Claude R. Sasso

References: Buttinger, Joseph. *Vietnam: A Dragon Embattled.* New York: Praeger, 1967.
Hendrick, James P. Papers. Harry S Truman Library, Independence, MO.
See also: Đai Viêt Quôc Dân Đang (National Party of Greater Vietnam); de Lattre de Tassigny, Jean Joseph Marie Gabriel; Đông Quan Pacification Project; United States: Involvement in Indo-China through 1954; Vietnam, Democratic Republic of: 1945–1954.

Nguyên Khánh

(1927–)

Army of the Republic of Vietnam (ARVN) general whose political ambitions led him through two coups eventually to become pre-

mier of the Republic of Vietnam (RVN). Born in 1927, Nguyên Khánh lived with his father who was a wealthy landowner and was raised by his father's lover, a popular Vietnamese singer and actor. He left his Sài Gòn school at age 16 in 1943 to join the Viêt Minh effort against the Japanese and French. Expelled by the Viêt Minh for poor discipline, he joined the French, who trained him to be an officer in the Vietnamese National Army (VNA). Khánh supported President Ngô Đình Diêm in 1954 and successfully defended the presidential palace during the attempted coup of November 1960. But as the commander of II Corps, Khánh was vital in the November 1963 coup against Diêm. In a move essential to the coup's success, principal plotters Generals Trân Văn Đôn, Dưởng Văn Minh, and Lê Văn Kim secured the support of Khánh and I Corps commander General Đô Cao Trí.

In the months following the coup, the new government leaders failed to capitalize on their initial popularity by not asserting the leadership that the nation and the situation demanded. Before General Minh could begin a reform program, Generals Khánh, Đô Mâu, and Trân Thiên Khiêm carried out a bloodless coup on 31 January 1965 on the pretext that others in the new government were preparing to institute a neutralist program. Khánh asked Minh to remain as chief of state while he became premier and chairman of the Military Revolutionary Council (MRC).

The Americans were impressed with Khánh's promises, which called for urban and rural development as well as the renewal of the Strategic Hamlet program under the new name of New Rural Life Hamlets. Khánh also vowed to institute a civilian government with a constitution. South Vietnamese were less impressed with their new premier. One of the many reasons for Khánh's unpopularity was that he had ousted the popular General Minh. Intellectuals did not like his common background (his mother had run a bar in Đà Lat) and found that, when they asked for an all-civilian cabinet, Khánh declared that the army alone could lead the country. Many were demoralized by the purge he instituted as well as the rapid turnover of chiefs at the provincial and district levels.

Most South Vietnamese Buddhist organizations and sects joined together in the United Buddhist Association (UBA). Khánh, himself a Buddhist, tried to appease the UBA by recognizing it and donating land for a national pagoda. He also removed the favored legal status of Catholics and endorsed the use of a Buddhist chaplain corps for the armed forces. Despite these moves, Buddhists still complained of repression, and many military commanders were not happy with the new chaplains. The Viêt Công took advantage of these disruptions by increasing their activities.

Thinking this an opportune moment to begin a dictatorship, Khánh declared a national emergency and instituted a new constitution, the Vung Tau Charter, giving the president nearly absolute powers. The MRC then elected Khánh president. Protests broke out in Sài Gòn, Đà Năng, and Huê as Communists infiltrated many demonstrations to aggravate the religious tension. Khánh then withdrew the charter and resigned. The MRC elected a triumvirate of Khánh, Minh, and Khiêm as an interim government to restore some order. Khánh remained commander in chief of the new government, but was ousted in February 1965 by Generals

Nguyên Cao Kỳ and Nguyên Văn Thiêu. Khánh then went to the United States and settled in Palm Beach, Florida.

—Michael R. Nichols

References: Bain, Chester A. *Vietnam: The Roots of Conflict.* Englewood Cliffs, NJ: Prentice-Hall, 1967.
Davidson, Phillip B. *Vietnam at War, the History: 1946–1975.* Novato, CA: Presidio Press, 1988.
Duncanson, Dennis J. *Government and Revolution in Vietnam.* New York: Oxford University Press, 1968.
Fishel, Wesley R., ed. *Vietnam: Anatomy of a Conflict.* Itasca, IL: Peacock, 1968.
Karnow, Stanley. *Vietnam: A History.* Rev. ed. New York: Penguin Books, 1991.
Olson, James, ed. *Dictionary of the Vietnam War.* New York: Peter Bedrick Books, 1987.
Smith, R. B. *An International History of the Vietnam War.* 3 vols. New York: St. Martin's Press, 1991.
See also: Buddhists; Đô Cao Trí; Dương Văn Minh; Lê Văn Kim; Military Revolutionary Council; National Front for the Liberation of South Vietnam (NFLSV); Ngô Đình Diêm; Ngô Đình Diêm, Overthrow of; Nguyên Cao Kỳ; Nguyên Văn Thiêu; Trân Thiên Khiêm; Trân Văn Đôn; Viêt Minh (Viêt Nam Đôc Lâp Đông Minh Hôi [Vietnam Independence League]; Vietnamese National Army (VNA).

Nguyên Khoa Nam
(1927–1975)

Army of the Republic of Vietnam (ARVN) major general. Born in Quang Nam province, Nguyên Khoa Nam graduated from high school in 1946 and later graduated from the College of Administration in Huê. Drafted into the army, he graduated from the Thu Đức Reserve Officers School in 1953.

After October 1953 Nam held a succession of Airborne posts. He graduated from the Parachutists Training Center in Pau, France, in 1953, was at Fort Bragg in 1962, and attended the Infantry Officer Advanced Course at Fort Benning in 1953. He took command of the 5th Airborne Battalion in 1965 and the 3d Airborne Brigade in 1968. In September 1969 he was promoted to brigadier general and command of the 7th Infantry Division. Nam was promoted to major general in November 1972, and after November 1974 he had command of IV Corps.

After Sài Gòn fell, General Nam committed suicide on the night of 30 April 1975 after biding good-bye to his staff and talking by telephone with General Lê Văn Hưng, who also committed suicide.

—Nguyên Công Luân (Lư Tuân)

Reference: Hà Mai Viêt. *Famous generals of the Republic of Viêt Nam Armed Forces.* Unpublished Vietnamese manuscript.
See also: Lê Văn Hưng.

Nguyên Lưởng Băng
(1904–1979)

Prominent leader in the Indo-Chinese Communist Party (ICP), Democratic Republic of Vietnam (DRV), and Socialist Republic of Vietnam (SRV). Born on 2 April 1904 in Doan Lâm village, Thanh Miên District, Hai Dưởng Province to a poor scholar's family, Băng spent his youth as a maritime worker. In 1925 Băng met Nguyên Ái Quôc (Hô Chí Minh) in Kwang Chou, China, and became active in revolutionary activities. Later Băng joined the Viêt Nam Thanh Niên Cách Mênh Đông Chí Hôi (Vietnamese Revolutionary Youth Association), predecessor of the Indo-Chinese Communist Party, and attended political training classes taught by Nguyên Ái Quôc at Kwang Chou. Băng was assigned to work in the labor movement in Hai Phòng, and later in Sài Gòn.

In 1928 Băng was sent to take part in revolutionary activities abroad and became a member of the Indo-Chinese Communist Party. During the period 1930 to 1943 he was arrested several times by the French authorities and twice escaped from prison, first from Hoa Lò, Hà Nôi in 1932 and then from Sơn La in 1943.

In 1941 Băng was president of the Viêt Minh and head of the Financial Department of the Viêt Minh. In October 1943 Băng became an alternate member of the Vietnamese Communist Party Central Committee in charge of financial affairs and military recruiting. In 1945 Băng was elected a full member of the ICP Central Committee. After the 1945 August Revolution, he held important party and state posts and was a member of the ICP Central Committee and vice-president of the DRV (1969). In 1976 he became vice-president of the Socialist Republic of Vietnam, which post he held until his death on 20 July 1979 in Hà Nôi.

—Ngô N. Trung

Reference: Biographical Files, Indo-China Archives, University of California at Berkeley.
See also: Hô Chí Minh; Lao Đông Party; Viêt Minh (Viêt Nam Đôc Lâp Đông Minh Hôi [Vietnam Independence League]; Vietnam, Democratic Republic of: 1954–1975; Vietnam, Socialist Republic of: 1975 to the Present.

Nguyên Manh Câm
(1929–)

Leader in the Vietnamese Communist Party (VCP) and minister of foreign affairs of the Socialist Republic of Vietnam (SRV). Born on 15 September 1929 at Hưng Dung village, Hưng Nguyên District, Nghê An Province, and a graduate of Hà Nôi's College of Foreign Languages, Nguyên Manh Câm joined the anti-French struggle in 1945 in his hometown area and the Indo-Chinese Communist Party in 1946. From 1947 he was assigned various tasks in Interzone IV.

On the state level, Câm joined the Democratic Republic of Vietnam (DRV) ministry of foreign affairs in 1952 and was assigned to various departments of the ministry, such as the USSR and Eastern Europe departments, Office of the Foreign Ministry, Department of General Services, and Department of Monitoring the Paris Peace Talks and Paris Agreement Implementation. Câm was in the USSR as a junior embassy official from 1952 to 1956. A Soviet specialist who studied Russian in China and the USSR, Câm returned to his Moscow station during 1962 to 1966, when he was embassy first secretary. From 1973 to 1977

Câm served as DRV ambassador to Hungary, Austria, and Iran concurrently. In 1977 he was appointed ambassador concurrently to the Federal Republic of Germany, Switzerland, and Iran. In 1981 he returned to Vietnam and became vice-minister of the ministry of foreign trade. In December 1986 Câm became an alternate member of the Vietnamese Communist Party Central Committee (VCPCC) before returning to the ministry of foreign affairs in 1987 as ambassador to Moscow. In June 1991 he was made a full member of VCPCC.

Câm became minister of foreign affairs in August 1991, a post he apparently accepted with reluctance. He was elected as a National Assembly deputy from Nghê An Province in July 1992 and then a member of Vietnam's National Defense and Security Council. In January 1994 Câm was rewarded with a Politburo post. A career diplomat with a reputation for integrity, Câm is credited with normalizing relations with the United States in July 1995.

—Ngô N. Trung

Reference: Biographical Files, Indo-China Archives, University of California at Berkeley.
See also: Lao Đông Party; Vietnam, Socialist Republic of: 1975 to the Present.

Nguyên Ngoc Loan
(1931–1998)

Republic of Vietnam Air Force (VNAF) brigadier general and director of National Police, 1966–1968. Born in 1931 in Huê, one of eleven children of a prosperous mechanical engineer, Nguyên Ngoc Loan graduated near the top of his class at the University of Huê and became a VNAF pilot. He advanced rapidly and became commander of the Light Observation Group, then assistant commander of the Tactical Operations Center. An old classmate and close friend of Nguyên Cao Kỳ, Loan served as deputy commander of the VNAF in the aftermath of the 1963 coup against Ngô Đình Diêm. In June 1967 when Kỳ became premier of the Republic of Vietnam (RVN) he appointed Loan director of the Military Security Service (MSS). A few months later Loan became director of the Central Intelligence Organization (CIO) and, in April 1966, director of the National Police. Not even under Diêm had one man directed so many police and intelligence agencies.

U.S. officials were pleased to see Loan take control of the police and intelligence services and improve stability in the South, particularly in Sài Gòn. A U.S. embassy official favorably reported that from October 1966 to January 1968 not a single terrorist incident nor a National Liberation Front (NLF) meeting

Republic of Vietnam Air Force (VNAF) brigadier general and director of the National Police from 1966 to 1968, Nguyên Ngoc Loan is best known for his cold-blooded execution of a Viêt Công suspect during the 1968 Têt Offensive. While this photo earned Associated Press photographer Eddie Adams prestigious professional awards, it undermined Loan's career and gave an unfavorable image of the Republic of Vietnam government.

was recorded in districts 7, 8, or 9 of Sài Gòn, whereas before then daytime meetings were occurring in the same areas and there were over 40 terrorist incidents a month. To finance the struggle against urban guerrillas Loan revived the Bình Xuyên formula of systematic and large-scale corruption. Traffic in opium, which he oversaw, was an important source of cash rewards for agents reporting on NLF activities.

Loan had always been known for his ability to deal by extralegal means with political rivals; once he marched armed guards into the National Assembly to break a legislative logjam. But Loan received international attention when during the 1968 Têt Offensive, on 1 February he shot a Viêt Công suspect in the head with a revolver on a Sài Gòn street. The slain man was reportedly a member of a death squad that had killed the family of one of his deputy commanders. AP photographer Eddie Adams recorded the event and his photograph undermined Loan's career and presented an unfavorable image abroad of the RVN government. In *Twenty Years and Twenty Days* Kỳ bitterly remarks that Loan's act was wrongly taken as a war crime and that it was simply "an isolated incident of the cruelty of war." Nonetheless the execution drew immediate rebukes from U.S. officials.

On 5 May 1968 Loan was severely wounded while leading an attack on a Viêt Công hideout in a suburb north of Sài Gòn. He was forced to resign his posts to undergo surgery and extended hospitalization, first in Australia and then in the United States, where he was denounced in Congress. General Loan was removed from influence in a purge of Kỳ loyalists, replaced by supporters of President Nguyên Văn Thiêu. On 6 June General Trân Văn Hai, a Thiêu follower, became director of the National Police and Loan soon disappeared from the political arena. On his return to Sài Gòn, he seemed changed, devoting his time to working with orphans.

On the fall of Sài Gòn, American officials ignored Loan's appeal for assistance, but he escaped in a South Vietnamese plane. He then traveled to the United States and settled in northern Virginia where he opened a pizzeria. He operated it until 1991, when publicity about his past led to a sharp decline in business. Loan died of cancer at his home in Burke, Virginia on 14 July 1998.

—Ho Diêu Anh and Spencer Tucker

References: Oberdorfer, Don. *Tet!* Garden City, NY: Doubleday, 1971. Westmoreland, William C. *A Soldier Reports.* New York: Doubleday, 1976. Wirtz, James. *The Tet Offensive: Intelligence Failure in War.* Ithaca, NY: Cornell University Press, 1991.
See also: Media and the War; Nguyên Cao Kỳ; Têt Offensive.

Nguyên Phúc Ánh (Gia Long)

(1761–1820)

Vietnamese emperor, 1802–1820. In 1527 Mac Đăng Dung, a notable at the court of the later Lê dynasty (1428–1788), began a revolt against the ruling emperor and proclaimed himself founding emperor of a new royal family, the Mac. The Macs were never able to establish themselves as the single legitimate rulers possessing heaven's mandate. The Lê family resisted their usurpation, and in 1591, with the help of a powerful clan, the Trịnh lords, captured Hà Nôi (Thăng Long) and the reigning Mac emperor and drove the remainder of the Mac family into exile. This did not mean the return of Lê authority, however, for that family was now dependent on the Trinh lords, who became the primary court faction. Their political manipulations determined the rise and fall of puppet Lê emperors, and only the most pliant remained on the throne. Trinh influence continued at the Lê Court until the dynasty was at last overthrown in 1788.

Even after restoration of Lê power, that weak dynasty was unable to affirm its control over all the land. The Lê dynasty also faced a rival family in the South. These were the Nguyêns, known as Nguyên lords. Although they ruled in the name of the Lê dynasty, in actuality they were independent of its authority, ruling repressively from their seat of power in the city of Phú Xuân (Huê). Unrest and competition among the Lê, Trinh, and Nguyên families weakened government authority throughout Vietnam. Rural dissatisfaction in the South throughout the 1760s brought forth a rebellion in 1771, when three brothers from the village of Tây Sơn began a struggle to depose the Nguyêns. This they accomplished in 1785 with broad-based support from many segments of the population. The Tây Sơn rebels then turned to the North and attacked and defeated the Trinh lords there, seizing Hà Nôi in 1786. When the Lê emperor called on China for help, the Tây Sơn rebels defeated its armies and forced the reigning Lê to flee into exile in Beijing. Thereupon a new dynasty came into being when, in 1788, Nguyên Huê, leader of the Tây Sơns, declared himself Emperor Quang Trung. From the rise of the Mac dynasty in 1527 to the overthrow of the Trinh lords and the Lê family in 1788, Vietnam had been saddled with unstable government and wracked with strife and disorder.

Nguyên Ánh, pretender to the throne, was one of the few surviving members of the Nguyên family that had ruled in the South since the sixteenth century. Born in 1761, he was forced to flee into the marshes and swamps of the Mekong Delta when Gia Đinh (Sài Gòn), the only important territory left under the Nguyên lords, fell to the Tây Sơn in 1778. From the Delta he proclaimed himself emperor but was again defeated by the Tây Sơn in 1783. He then fled to an island in the Gulf of Siam, Phú Quôc, where he continued his struggle.

Nguyên Ánh was totally dedicated to his goal of prevailing over the Tây Sơn dynasty, but the outlook was bleak. Then he met French missionary Pierre Pigneau de Béhaine, later bishop of Adran in India, who strongly supported Nguyên Ánh's cause. He arranged for Nguyên Ánh's son, Nguyên Canh, to visit France in 1787 to seek help from the government. In return for financial support and the use of French naval craft and troops to defeat his rivals, the Nguyêns established the Treaty of Versailles with Louis XVI, granting France commercial and missionary rights, the city of Đà Năng (renamed Tourane by the French), and the island of Côn Sơn (renamed Poulo Condore by the French), a small dot of land in the South China Sea about 50 miles from the southern coast that the French later turned into a prison colony for Vietnamese political activists.

The promised French governmental help failed to materialize; consequently, France did not achieve control of Tourane or Poulo Condore until a new treaty was made with Tư Đức in June 1862. In any case, Pigneau de Béhaine raised the armed forces necessary for Nguyên Ánh to overcome his enemies.

Nguyên Ánh then launched a campaign against those who resisted his rule. After years of struggle, by 1802 the Tây Sơn were either dead or in exile. Nguyên Ánh then founded the Nguyên dynasty (1802–1945), which lasted until the abdication of Bao Đai in 1945. Nguyên Ánh took the dynastic name Gia Long (Gia from the customary name for Sài Gòn, Gia Định; Long from Thăng Long, the ancient name of Hà Nôi) and, after an official investiture by China, declared himself emperor, thus uniting the land for the first time in centuries.

Gia Long changed his capital from Hà Nôi to Huê and the name of his nation from Đai Viêt to Vietnam. Enamored of his giant neighbor to the north, the new emperor promulgated his Gia Long Penal Code, based on the one used by the Chinese Ch'ing dynasty. This new system of law took less note of local and village customs and strengthened the hand of the emperor. He replaced *Chư Nôm*, the written form of Vietnamese then in use, with Chinese as the official written language. He ordered the construction of public granaries, developed an effective postal service, gathered in Cambodia (Kampuchea) as a client state, and spent government funds repairing the Old Mandarin Road. Gia Long allowed a measure of toleration toward French missionary activity but resisted any increase in French commercial growth. He died in 1820 and was succeeded by his son, Chí Đam, who assumed the dynastic name of Minh Mang.

—Cecil B. Currey

References: Buttinger, Joseph. *The Smaller Dragon: A Political History of Vietnam.* New York: Praeger, 1968.
Duiker, William J., ed. *Historical Dictionary of Vietnam.* Metuchen, NJ: Scarecrow Press, 1989.
Olson, James, ed. *Dictionary of the Vietnam War.* New York: Peter Bedrick Books, 1988.
See also: Minh Mang; Nguyên Dynasty; Nguyên Huê (Quang Trung); Pigneau de Béhaine, Pierre; Vietnam: From 938 through the French Conquest.

Nguyên Thái Hoc

(1902–1930)

Leader of the Viêt Nam Quôc Dân Đang (VNQDD). Born in 1902 into a middle-class farmer's family in Thô Tang village, Vĩnh Tường District, Vĩnh Yên Province, Nguyên Thái Hoc in 1921 was admitted into the new Teachers School in Hà Nôi. The attitude of the French instructors and their Vietnamese underlings toward their Vietnamese students made Hoc a nationalist. He was expelled at the end of his third year after quarreling with an instructor over what he considered to be her improper treatment of his classmates. Later he enrolled in the School of Commerce before devoting all his attention to revolution. His close friends described him as a man of simple tastes, calm, intelligent, decisive, and brave.

The mid-1925s saw many events that heightened Vietnamese patriotism. Among these were the failed 18 June 1924 attempt by Pham Hông Thái to assassinate French Indo-China Governor

General Martial Henri Merlin in Hong Kong and the public reaction when Phan Bôi Châu was kidnapped in Shanghai and returned to Vietnam.

Nguyên Thái Hoc made use of the Nam Đông Publishing House, founded by friends in 1925, that published books promoting Vietnamese patriotism. It became so popular that the colonial government closed it down and confiscated its publications. Hoc wrote to French Governor General Alexandre Varenne, proposing political, economic, and social reforms, but received no response. He was already on the colonial government's blacklist.

As his name became known among nationalist activists, several anticolonialist groups urged Hoc to found a revolutionary organization. On 25 December 1927, 36 representatives from 14 provinces in North Vietnam (Tonkin) met secretly in Hà Nôi and established the Viêt Nam Quôc Dân Đang. Its name reflected the influence of Sun Yat-sen and the 1911 Chinese Revolution and the fact that a party of that same name had been organized by respected nationalist activist Phan Bôi Châu in 1923; it had been inactive since Phan Bôi Châu's arrest in Shanghai in 1925.

The VNQDD was the first well-organized Vietnamese revolutionary party to advocate armed revolt to achieve independence. Drawing the bulk of its members from the middle class, it was also the largest such party. Not long after Hoc was elected chairman in late 1927, Phan Bôi Châu became VNQDD honorary chairman.

The French soon launched a large-scale campaign to eradicate the VNQDD. Rather than see the party destroyed, Hoc and his staff resolved to act, even if their attempt was not successful. As Hoc put it, "If we do not succeed, we still do the right thing." The party leadership approved Hoc's call for an uprising, and from 10 to 15 February 1930 the VNQDD struck major French military bases around Hà Nôi, although communication failures prevented these from being simultaneous. Collectively these are known in Vietnamese history as the Yên Báy (or Yên Bái) Uprising.

The French soon put down the uprising. Hundreds of VNQDD members were killed or subsequently executed, and thousands of others ended up in prisons. Hoc refused his comrades' appeals that he flee to China and was arrested on 20 February 1930.

On 23 March 1930 Hoc and 82 party members whom the French thought the most dangerous were tried in a special court (Commission Criminelle). They including a woman, Nguyên Thi Băc, elder sister of Hoc's fiancee Nguyên Thi Giang. The next morning, Hoc and 38 comrades were sentenced to death; the others received prison terms. In early June 1930 the president of France approved 27 death sentences, including that of Hoc.

Before his execution, Hoc's family was allowed to see him for the last time, during which time he begged his mother's forgiveness for not fulfilling his filial obligation. Early on 17 June 1930 Hoc and 18 comrades were moved to Yên Bái and that same morning all were guillotined. Reportedly all met their deaths bravely. One of those executed, Phó Đưc Chính, asked the headsman to let him lie on his back so that he could see the blade fall. Reportedly each shouted "Long live Viêt Nam" before the blade fell. Nguyên Thái Hoc was the last to die.

Nguyên Thái Hoc was romantically linked with Nguyên Thi Giang. She assisted him as a liaison officer, conveying his orders when he frequently changed his whereabouts. One of the first female members of the VNQDD, she opened the way for many hundreds to follow. The women helped distribute weapons, ran propaganda, and collected intelligence.

The day of Hoc's death, Giang was part of the crowd watching the executions. That afternoon, she went to Hoc's home village to visit his mother and pay her regards, and then she committed suicide with a pistol.

Hoc was the eldest child in his family and left a sister and three brothers. One of the brothers joined the VNQDD and was later sentenced to death by the French. Another brother was killed by French soldiers in a raid on his village in November 1947 when he refused to surrender.

Although Hoc and his comrades had not won the decisive victory they sought for their country and people, their revolutionary activity and uprising boosted Vietnamese nationalism.

—Nguyên Công Luân (Lư Tuân)

References: Cao Thê Dung. *Viêt Nam Huyêt Lê Sư.* New Orleans, LA: Đông Hưởng, 1996.
Hoàng Văn Đào. *Viêt Nam Quôc Dân Đang.* Sài Gòn: Published by the author, 1970; reprinted in the United States.
Pham Kim Vinh. *The Vietnamese Culture.* Solana Beach, CA: PM Enterprises, 1995.
See also: Viêt Nam Quôc Dân Đang (Vietnam National Party).

Nguyên Thi Bình
(1927–)

Southern Vietnamese revolutionary who served as a diplomat for the National Front for the Liberation of South Vietnam (NFLSV) and as the Provisional Revolutionary Government's (PRG) foreign minister. Born in Sài Gòn in 1927, Nguyên Thi Bình was the grandniece of one of Vietnam's most famous patriots, Phan Chu Trinh. During the 1950s Madame Bình was one leader of a Sài Gòn rebellion of students and intellectuals known as the Trân Văn Ởn Movement. The French arrested Bình in 1951 and she remained in jail until the signing of the 1954 Geneva Accords. After her release from prison, she joined several resistance groups in Sài Gòn and was elected to the NFLSV's Central Committee in 1962. From 1962 until 1969 Bình served in the Front's diplomatic corps, accepting assignments to Africa and Europe. She led the NFLSV delegation to the Third Congress of the Afro-Asian People's Solidarity Organization in 1963 and in 1965 headed the NFLSV's legation in Algiers. Throughout the mid-1960s Bình toured the world, offering interviews to hundreds of reporters. For many in the West, Madame Bình became the symbol of the NFLSV and its most important spokesperson.

Once the Paris peace talks opened in 1968, Bình assumed the role of chief negotiator for the NFLSV, although official recognition of the Front was one of the major stumbling blocks to successful talks. In 1969 the Provisional Revolutionary Government appointed her as its foreign minister, sending her to Paris as its official representative.

As a negotiator, Bình was steadfast in her determination to exact a settlement that diminished Nguyên Văn Thiêu's monopoly on political power in the South and that coupled the freedom of southern political prisoners with the release of American prisoners of war. During the fall 1972 negotiations, Madame Bình criticized the Tho-Kissinger accord because it did not deal adequately with the prisoner-of-war issue. Eventually, Madame Bình signed the final accord on behalf of the PRG.

After the Vietnam War, Bình served in a variety of governmental positions in Hà Nôi, and in the early 1990s she assumed the vice-presidency of the Socialist Republic of Vietnam.

—Robert K. Brigham

References: *Personalities of the South Vietnam Liberation Movement.* Tran Phu, Vietnam: Foreign Relations Commission of the South Vietnam National Front for Liberation, 1965.
Pike, Douglas. *Viet Cong: The Organization and Techniques of the National Liberation Front of South Vietnam.* Cambridge, MA: MIT Press, 1966.
Porter, Gareth. *A Peace Denied: The United States, Vietnam, and the Paris Agreement.* Bloomington, IN: Indiana University Press, 1975.
Trân Văn Giâu, and Lê Văn Chât. *The South Vietnam Liberation National Front.* Hà Nôi: Foreign Languages Publishing House, 1962.
See also: National Front for the Liberation of South Vietnam (NFLSV); Ngô Đình Diêm; Ngô Đình Nhu; Nguyên Cao Kỳ; Nguyên Hưu Tho; Nguyên Văn Thiêu; Paris Negotiations; Paris Peace Accords; Provisional Revolutionary Government of South Vietnam (PRG); Trân Bưu Kiêm.

Nguyên Thi Đinh
(1920–)

Military leader of the Armed Forces for the Liberation of the South and leader of the National Liberation Front Women's Union during the Vietnam War. Nguyên Thi Đinh was born in 1920 in Bên Tre Province, South Vietnam, into a poor family of ten children. Influenced by her older brother who was involved in revolutionary activities against the French in the early 1930s, Madame Đinh began her participation in the movement as a liaison when she was 16 and also helped with propaganda work. In 1938 she married a member of the Bên Tre Central Committee of the Indo-Chinese Communist Party and gave birth to her first child in 1939. That same year, the French authorities arrested her husband and exiled him; Đinh herself was arrested and exiled in Bà Rá, South Vietnam, in 1940.

Released in 1943 because of heart disease, Đinh joined the Viêt Minh movement in 1944, the same year that her husband died in prison. After participating in the 1945 uprising in Bên Tre, the next year she was elected to the Executive Committee of the Bên Tre Women's Union and was sent to the north in a delegation of southern revolutionaries to visit Hô Chí Minh and request assistance in waging war against the French in the south.

Đinh was in charge of the first shipload of weapons and financial assistance sent to the South in November 1946. She continued Viêt Minh activities, charged with mobilization, and remarried. After the 1954 Geneva Accords, she chose to stay in the South instead of joining her son by her first marriage in moving into the North.

After 1954 Đinh took charge of rebuilding the revolutionary movement and coordinating Viêt Minh cadres remaining in Bên Tre. Later she had charge of disrupting and troubling the Diêm government's Agroville program in Châu Thành and Mo Cày.

In early 1960 Đinh was appointed a member of the Bên Tre Central Committee. She was also a member of the Central Committee for Đông Khởi, a popular uprising in late January 1960 to seize power from Diêm administration officials in villages in Bên Tre. During Đông Khởi, she was the founder of the Long-Haired Army (Đôi Quân Toc Dài), an organization of revolution sympathizers, largely women, established to plan protest demonstrations against the Diêm government and to persuade Army of the Republic of Vietnam (ARVN) soldiers to desert. This was considered the political struggle that went along with military activities.

Đinh became one of the founders of the National Liberation Front (NLF) and helped build its armed forces. She was later appointed general, vice–commander in chief of the Armed Forces for the Liberation of the South, and was also a member of the NLF Central Committee and chair of the Women's Union for the Liberation of the South. When the People's Revolutionary Party, the southern branch of the Lao Đông Party, was formed in 1962, she became a member of its Central Committee. She continued to hold these leadership positions throughout the Vietnam War.

After 1975 Nguyên Thi Đinh continued as a member of the Central Committee of the Vietnamese Communist Party, but she was active only in the women's movement, holding the post of vice-chair of the Women's Union of the Socialist Republic of Vietnam. From May 1982 she was its chair. In 1991 she was elected vice-chair of the Socialist Republic of Vietnam State Council.

—Ho Diêu Anh

References: Eisen, Arlene. Woman and Revolution in Vietnam. London: Zed Books, 1984.
Nguyên Thi Đinh. Trân Hường Nam, ed. Không Còn Con Đường Nào Khác (No Other Way). Hà Nôi: Nhà Xuât Ban Phu Nư, 1968.
See also: Agroville Campaign; Lao Đông Party; National Front for the Liberation of South Vietnam (NFLSV); Vietnam, Socialist Republic of: 1975 to the Present; Vietnamese Communist Party (VCP); Women in the War, Vietnamese.

Nguyên Tường Tam, or Nhât Linh

(1906–1963)

Leader of the Viêt Nam Quôc Dân Đang (VNQDD) and highly respected writer. Born into the family of a poor mandarin in Câm Giàng District, Hai Dường Province in 1906, Nguyên Tường Tam graduated from high school at age 16. In 1930 he traveled to France to attend a university and graduated with a degree in physics and chemistry.

In the mid-1930s Tam founded the Tư Lực Văn Đoàn (Self-Reliance Literary Group) of a dozen modern writers. They advocated cultural reforms, focusing primarily on a literary movement to promote a new style of writing. They also advocated social reforms, including new housing in slum areas.

The Tư Lực Văn Đoàn published journals, such as the *Phong Hóa Weekly* and the *Ngày Nay Weekly,* and a series of novels. Using humorous stories, caricatures, and theme novels, the group radically changed Vietnamese literature. Their novels were best-sellers at the time. Indirectly the group promoted patriotism among Vietnamese youth, although some critics saw this as a kind of romanticism.

In the early 1940s Nhât Linh participated in revolutionary activities, such as organizing the Đai Viêt Dân Chính. He then fled to China, where he was arrested on the orders of Chang Fa Kwei at the same time as Hô Chí Minh. Nhât Linh's party later merged with the Đai Viêt Quôc Dân Đang and the VNQDD into one party.

Returning to Vietnam in 1945, Nhât Linh became minister of foreign affairs in the first coalition government of the Democratic Republic of Vietnam (DRV). He was not present at the meeting that approved the 6 March 1946 preliminary Hô-Sainteny Agreement, but he led the DRV delegation that negotiated with the French at Đà Lat in April 1946. He was to have been chief negotiator in talks with the French in Paris, but he left Vietnam before his scheduled departure for France, reportedly to avoid imminent danger from Viêt Minh groups assigned to assassinate prominent non-Communists.Nhât Linh lived in Hong Kong until 1950, when he returned to Vietnam, settling in the South and steadfastly avoiding politics. In 1958 he tried unsuccessfully to revive his literary movement.

The Diêm government accused Nhât Linh of being involved in the 1960 attempted coup d'état. Nhât Linh committed suicide on 7 July 1963 before his trial in Sài Gòn could begin. Though he was unsuccessful in politics, Nhât Linh is the greatest writer of modern Vietnam.

—Nguyên Công Luân (Lư Tuân)

References: Cao Thê Dung. Viêt Nam Huyêt Lê Sư. New Orleans, LA: Đông Hưởng, 1996.
Hoàng Văn Đào. Viêt Nam Quôc Dân Đang. Sài Gòn: Published by the author, 1970; reprinted in the United States.
Pham Kim Vinh. The Vietnamese Culture. Solana Beach, CA: PM Enterprises, 1995.
See also: Hô-Sainteny Agreement; Viêt Nam Quôc Dân Đang (Vietnam National Party); Vietnamese Culture.

Nguyên Văn Cư

(1934–)

Republic of Vietnam Air Force (VNAF) pilot who bombed the presidential palace on 27 February 1962. Born in 1934, Nguyên Văn Cư was the second son of Nguyên Văn Lôc, a leader of the Viêt Nam Quôc Dân Đang (VNQDD) nationalist party and opponent of Republic of Vietnam (RVN) President Ngô Đình Diêm.

Cư volunteered for the VNAF in 1955, attending several training courses at Bartow Air Force Base, Alabama, and Goodfellow Air Force Base, Texas, from 1955 to 1957. He was an instructor in the VNAF Training Center in Nha Trang and then a fighter pilot of the 514th Fighter Squadron at Biên Hòa Air Force Base.

Cư's father's revolutionary council wanted to assassinate Diêm. They settled on a plan whereby Cư and Pham Phú Quôc, another pilot recruited by Cư from his same squadron, would shoot down Diêm's VNAF C-47 aircraft. Because of problems in carrying this out, the planners decided that the two pilots would attack the Độc Lập (Independence) Palace on the morning of 27 February 1962.

That same day, the two pilots were ordered on a combat mission from Biên Hòa to Gò Công, south of Sài Gòn. When they were over the presidential palace, dense clouds blanketed Sài Gòn. As a result, they had to bring their two AD-6 Skyraider aircraft below the safe altitude to drop bombs. They did strafe the palace with rockets, and one of their 500-lb bombs penetrated a room in which Diêm was located. The bomb failed to detonate because the low altitude did not allow sufficient time for its arming. The only casualty was a Nhu family servant, who was wounded.

Pham Phú Quôc's plane was damaged by ground fire. Forced to land in Nhà Bè near Sài Gòn, he was arrested and imprisoned, but released after Diêm's death the next year. Quôc then returned to duty with the VNAF. In late 1964 while returning from an air raid over North Vietnam, his plane was hit by North Vietnamese anti-aircraft fire and he was killed.

Nguyên Văn Cự's plane was also damaged, but he was able to fly it to Phnom Penh, where he worked as a language teacher until his return to Vietnam after Diêm's overthrow. In 1967 he resigned from the VNAF upon his election to the RVN House of Representatives.

In June 1975 Cự was arrested and sent to a reeducation camp. Released in 1985, he immigrated to the United States in 1991.

—Nguyên Công Luân (Lư Tuân)

Reference: Nguyên Vă Cự and Chu Tư Kỳ (one of the key protagonists behind the attempt), interviews with the author.
See also: Ngô Đình Diêm.

Nguyên Văn Bình
(1910–1991)

Catholic archbishop of Sài Gòn from 24 November 1960 until his death in 1991. Nguyên Văn Bình was born on 1 September 1910. He graduated from Sài Gòn Seminary in 1922 and continued his studies in Rome in 1932. He was ordained a priest in Rome in March 1937 and became a bishop in November 1955. Archbishop Bình was also the president of the Vietnam Episcopal Council.

Despite the aggressive role played by Catholics in the earlier period of the Vietnam War, Nguyên Văn Bình was considered a moderate religious leader. After 1975 his moderate stance helped keep the Catholic Church at relative peace with the new government. He died in Sài Gòn in 1991, at which time the government permitted the Catholic Church in Vietnam to hold memorial services for the archbishop that lasted several days.

—Ho Diêu Anh

Reference: *Who's Who in Vietnam.* Sài Gòn: Vietnam Press Agency, 1974.
See also: Roman Catholicism in Vietnam; Vietnam, Republic of: 1954–1975; Vietnam, Socialist Republic of: 1975 to the Present.

Nguyên Văn Cao
See Văn Cao.

Nguyên Văn Hiêu
(?–1975)

Army of the Republic of Vietnam (ARVN) major general. Brought up in Hong Kong, Nguyên Văn Hiêu was a son of veteran revolutionary Nguyên Văn Hưởng. He graduated from the Đà Lat Military Academy around 1952. Hiêu rose through the ranks and before his death had been chief of staff, II Corps/Tactical Zone 2 (1964); twice commander of the 22d Infantry Division (1964 and 1966); and commander of the 5th Infantry Division (1970).

Hiêu was regarded as one of the most incorruptible ARVN generals. That reputation brought him the post of inspector general of the army under Vice-President Trân Văn Hưởng, who promoted an anticorruption program, which failed despite their enthusiastic efforts. In 1974 Hiêu became deputy commander of III Corps/Military Region III at Biên Hòa.

In early April 1975 Hiêu died by a pistol shot. Official reports held that his death had occurred while he was cleaning his pistol, but there were rumors that he had been murdered.

—Nguyên Công Luân (Lư Tuân)

Reference: Hà Mai Viêt. *Famous Generals of the Republic of Vietnam Armed Forces.* Unpublished manuscript in Vietnamese.
See also: Trân Văn Hưởng.

Nguyên Văn Hinh
(1915–)

General in the State of Vietnam, Republic of Vietnam (RVN), and French Air Force. Born on 20 September 1915 in Vũng Tàu, South Vietnam, the son of Premier Nguyên Văn Tâm, Nguyên Văn Hinh became a naturalized French citizen in 1929. Hinh attended the prestigious Lycée Chasseloup Laubat in Sài Gòn and later Lycée Saint Louis in Paris, France. He graduated from the French Air Force School and in 1938 became an officer in the French Air Force. In July 1948 as a lieutenant he was military aide to Premier Nguyên Văn Xuân. In 1950 Hinh was promoted to major and became a pilot. He was then assigned as chief of staff to Emperor Bao Đai. In 1949, following the Elysée Agreements, Hinh volunteered and became the first air force officer of the State of Vietnam's Armed Forces.

In 1952 Hinh was promoted to major general and that March he became chief of staff of the State of Vietnam's Armed Forces. In 1954 during the confrontation between then Premier Ngô Đình Diêm and the southern religious sects, Hinh at first opposed Diêm; later he asked Emperor Bao Đai to reconcile with Diêm, but Bao Đai refused. On 26 October 1954 Hinh attempted a coup d'état against Premier Diêm. The U.S. government warned Hinh that it would halt military assistance, and the coup collapsed. On 20 November 1954 Hinh left Vietnam for France to be replaced as chief of the general staff by General Nguyên Văn Vy. Hinh's subsequent effort to return to power failed.

After 1954 Hinh rejoined the French Air Force and was made a general, eventually becoming its deputy commander. Hinh retired at the end of 1969 and started a small air cargo company in which Bao Đai also invested.

—Ngô N. Trung

Reference: Biographical Files, Indo-China Archives, University of California at Berkeley.
See also: Bao Đai; Elysée Agreement; Ngô Đình Diêm.

Nguyên Văn Linh (Nguyên Văn Cúc)

(1915–)

Prominent leader in the Indo-Chinese Communist Party (ICP). Born in 1915 at An Phú village, My Văn District, Hưng Yên Province, as a teenager Linh joined a student group associated with the Viêt Nam Quôc Dân Đang (Vietnam National Party) (VNQDD). Later Linh joined the Viêt Nam Thanh Niên Cách Mênh Đông Chí Hôi (Vietnamese Revolutionary Youth Association) in 1929. In 1939 he became a member of the Sài Gòn City Party Standing Committee and in 1946 was named its secretary. In 1947 he became a member of the Southern Region Party Committee. Despite being a northerner, Linh successfully developed broad connections in the South. He grew up in the southwestern region of the South and spent most of his youth in prison, in what were known as "revolution schools." In the early 1950s French intelligence identified Linh, known by the aliases of Nguyên Văn Mưởi and Mưởi Cúc, as secretary of the Special Zone of Sài Gòn.

In September 1960 Linh was secretly elected a member of the Lao Đông (Communist Party) Central Committee. In 1961 he became secretary of the Central Office for South Vietnam (COSVN). Later, during the Vietnam War, he was in charge of mass mobilizations in the Sài Gòn–Gia Đinh Special Zone. Between 1972 and 1973 he was secretary of the Sài Gòn City Party Committee. After the April 1975 takeover of Sài Gòn, Linh again was briefly secretary of the City Party Committee.

In December 1976 Linh was elected to the Politburo of the Vietnamese Communist Party Central Committee and served as secretary of the Secretariat. Six years later, he was dropped from the Politburo and returned to Sài Gòn as secretary of the Party City Committee. In June 1985 he was again elected to the Politburo, and in December 1986 Linh was named general secretary of the Vietnamese Communist Party (VCP).

Linh is credited as the leader who initiated the party-led renovation in Vietnam beginning in 1986. However, as the Communist bloc collapsed, Linh was hesitant to push for more reforms. At the 1991 Seventh Party Congress, Linh retired on grounds of poor health, but remained an advisor to the VCP.

—Ngô N. Trung

Reference: Biographical Files, Indo-China Archives, University of California at Berkeley.
See also: COSVN (Central Office for South Vietnam or Trung Ưởng Cuc Miên Nam); Lao Đông Party; Vietnam, Socialist Republic of: 1975 to the Present.

Nguyên Văn Thiêu

(1923–)

Army of the Republic of Vietnam (ARVN) general and president of the Republic of Vietnam from 1967 to 1975. Born near Phan Rang on 5 April 1923, Nguyên Văn Thiêu joined the Viêt Minh in 1945 but became disillusioned with their ruthless disregard for life. He then fought on the State of Vietnam side with the French, entering the National Military Academy and graduating from there in 1949. He also attended infantry school in France and the staff college in Hà Nôi (1952). As a battalion commander in 1954, he drove the Viêt Minh out of his native village. In 1955 Thiêu commanded the Republic of Vietnam (RVN) Military Academy in Đà Lat.

In 1957 Colonel Thiêu graduated from the Command and General Staff College at Ft. Leavenworth, Kansas. In 1962 he joined the secret Cân Lao Party organized by Ngô Đình Diêm's brother Ngô Đình Nhu. After commanding the ARVN's 1st Infantry Division for two years, Thiêu assumed command of the 5th Infantry Division in 1963, leading one of his regiments against the presidential bodyguard in the coup that brought down Diêm. Promoted brigadier general, he commanded IV Corps.

While serving on the Armed Forces Council in 1964, he cooperated with the coup by Air Vice-Marshal Nguyên Cao Kỳ, who led a faction of the generals referred to as the "Young Turks" against General Nguyên Khánh. Thiêu served as deputy premier in the short-lived government of Dr. Phan Huy Quát until 12 June 1965, when Thiêu became chief of state in Prime Minister Kỳ's new government. Together, in 1966 they made plans to strengthen the armed forces, met with President Lyndon Johnson in Honolulu and Manila, successfully quashed a coup by General Nguyên Chánh Thi, gained Buddhist support, and promised a constitution.

Despite their temporary cooperation, the two leaders were political rivals. Although Thiêu had declined the premier's post in 1965, his determination to challenge Kỳ for the highest office in the 1967 elections led the Armed Forces Council to force Kỳ and Thiêu onto a joint ticket, giving the presidential nomination to Thiêu and the vice-presidential nomination to Kỳ on the basis of seniority. The Thiêu-Kỳ ticket won the election with 34.8 percent of the vote against ten other tickets.

During the 1968 Têt Offensive, Thiêu had gone to his wife's home in the Mekong Delta town of My Tho. Thus, it was Kỳ who handled the counterattack in the capital. As a result, the Ameri-

President Lyndon Johnson and Republic of Vietnam President Nguyên Văn Thiêu at the Honolulu Conference in 1966. In 1945 Thiêu had joined the Viêt Minh but became disillusioned with their ruthless disregard for life.

cans pressed Thiêu to give more responsibility to Kỳ, which led to renewed bickering between them. Thiêu took advantage of the Têt Offensive to push through a general mobilization, which doubled the size of the armed forces. Fighting charges of widespread official corruption, Thiêu launched an anticorruption campaign that led to the replacement of four province chiefs, two corps commanders, and others, but the prospect of negotiations with the Democratic Republic of Vietnam (DRV) in Paris made him more reluctant to broaden the base of his government. His initial refusal to attend the Paris peace talks when they began was an attempt to ensure direct negotiations between the DRV and RVN and also an effort to help Richard Nixon in his race for the presidency against Hubert Humphrey, who had threatened Thiêu with an aid cutoff if he did not affect significant reform.

President Thiêu distributed land to some 50,000 families and by 1968 had gotten laws passed that froze rents and forbade landlords from evicting tenants. He also began the restoration of elected village chiefs so that, by 1969, 95 percent of villages under RVN control had elected chiefs and councils. Chiefs were given a role in national defense and control over Popular Forces (PFs) and police; they also received some government financial support.

After the United States began Vietnamization coupled with the gradual withdrawal of its forces beginning in 1969, Thiêu was faced with the challenge of replacing American units as they left. In 1970 he mobilized large numbers of high school and college students for the war effort, but this resulted in considerable opposition, which in turn led to government arrests and trials. Increased draft calls and payroll taxes produced a surge of support for the National Front for the Liberation of South Vietnam (NFLSV or NLF).

On 26 March 1971 Thiêu presented land to 20,000 people in an impressive ceremony following the passage of the Land-to-Tiller Act, which reduced tenancy to only 7 percent. With the U.S. Congress considering measures to end American involvement in Vietnam, in 1971 Thiêu engineered an election law to disqualify his major opponents, Air Vice-Marshall Kỳ and General Dương Văn Minh. Although the Supreme Court said Kỳ, who had charged Thiêu's government with corruption, could run, he chose not to. Thiêu's election made one-person rule a reality and did serious damage to his government's image.

During Operation LAM SÒN 719, an ARVN attempt at a preemptive strike into Laos to disrupt the People's Army of Vietnam (PAVN) buildup for a major invasion of the South, Thiêu disappointed U.S. Military Assistance Command, Vietnam (MACV) Commander General Creighton Abrams by withdrawing his forces prematurely. However, PAVN units suffered heavy losses to U.S. airpower in Laos and in the 1972 Easter invasion.

As a result of the Paris peace talks, Henry Kissinger brought a draft agreement to President Thiêu, who insisted on 26 changes, accusing the United States of betraying the RVN. His chief objection was that PAVN forces did not have to withdraw from the South but merely promise not to reinforce. Kissinger was furious with Thiêu for torpedoing the agreement, but following LINE-BACKER II, Kissinger secured a new agreement with the DRV—the Paris accords of 23 January 1973—which, however, left ap-

proximately 145,000 PAVN troops in the South. Thiêu, who was the beneficiary of a massive last-minute airlift of military supplies (Operation ENHANCE PLUS), was threatened with a total cutoff of U.S. aid and acquiesced to heavy U.S. pressure to sign.

General Trân Văn Trà, a key PAVN commander in the South, wrote in *Concluding the Thirty Year War* that it was ironic that after the cease-fire there was "not a day on which the guns fell silent" on South Vietnamese battlefields, and yet he conceded that "the puppet administration" had become "stronger politically, militarily and economically." He also pointed out that PAVN and NLF units were in disarray from their 1972 Easter Offensive as well as from fighting in Laos and Cambodia. This permitted Thiêu's forces to recapture some areas, to abolish hamlet and village elections in an effort to keep them in government hands, and to bar neutralist protest activities against the government. The latter was a violation of Article 11 of the Paris accords, but the Communists were violating Article 20 with regard to the neutrality of Laos and Cambodia and had sent 30,000 cadres and 70,000 troops from the DRV to build new base areas from Quang Tri Province south to the Central Highlands. To no one's surprise the "Third Indo-China War" was under way as soon as the dry season came in 1974, and Thiêu's forces drove the PAVN back in Quang Tri Province and other southern positions, even pursuing them into Svay Rieng, the Parrot's Beak region of Cambodia. This proved to be the last ARVN offensive. By the summer, the ARVN was sustaining losses of 500 men per week to reequipped PAVN and NLF forces and had to impose rigid supply controls because of severe shortages.

Thiêu was shocked when the Watergate scandal forced President Nixon to resign in August 1974. This called into question the written and verbal promises that the United States would respond militarily if the RVN were threatened. Nixon had gotten Congress to set a $1 billion ceiling on military aid to the RVN, but the Senate appropriated $700 million, and only about $280 million was actually received because of shipping and other expenses. Ammunition was now rationed, 224 aircraft and 21 riverine units were placed in storage, and only 55 percent of available transport could be fueled.

Sài Gòn was in turmoil, and a People's Anti-Corruption Movement led by a Catholic priest developed into a massive antigovernment crusade. The problem was real, but Thiêu tried to sidestep it and place all blame on the Communists. When the PAVN unleashed their offensive in the Central Highlands, and the Ford administration did not respond in accord with the terms of the Paris accords, Thiêu made the fateful decision to abandon the northern half of the country. To make matters worse, the government made no public announcement and had no plan for its execution. Government supporters in Military Regions I and II felt that they had been abandoned, first by the Americans and then by their own government and army. Although the ARVN put up a good fight at Xuân Lôc, it lost the battle, and four PAVN corps continued toward the capital.

On 21 April 1975 President Thiêu resigned in a tearful address to the nation. Five days later, he left Vietnam, flying to Taiwan and then on to Great Britain. Later he settled in the United States in a suburb of Boston.

—Claude R. Sasso

References: Bùi Diêm, with David Chanoff. *In the Jaws of History.* Boston: Houghton Mifflin, 1987.

Pike, Douglas, ed. *The Bunker Papers: Reports to the President from Vietnam, 1967–1973.* 3 vols. Berkeley, CA: Institute of East Asian Studies, 1990.

Westmoreland, William. *A Soldier Reports.* New York: Doubleday, 1976.

See also: Cân Lao Nhân Vi Cách Mang Đang (Revolutionary Personalist Labor Party); Easter Offensive (Nguyên Huê Campaign); ENHANCE PLUS, Operation; Ford, Gerald R.; Humphrey, Hubert H.; Joint General Staff; Kissinger, Henry Alfred; LAM SƠN 719, Operation; Military Revolutionary Council; Ngô Đình Diêm; Ngô Đình Diêm, Overthrow of; Nguyên Cao Kỳ; Nixon, Richard Milhous; Paris Negotiations; Paris Peace Accords; Vietnam, Republic of: 1954–1975; Vietnam, Republic of: Army (ARVN).

Nguyên Văn Toàn

(1932–)

General in the Army of the Republic of Vietnam (ARVN) and one of its most competent commanders. Born on 6 October 1932 in Lai Thê village, Phú Vang District, Thửa Thiên Province, central Vietnam, Nguyên Văn Toàn graduated from high school at Huê in 1950. He attended the National Military Academy in Đà Lat and then pursued studies in France from 1951 to 1955.

From 1956 to 1957 Toàn was trained at the Joint Armor School at Saumur, France. He also received training at Fort Knox, Kentucky, in 1958 before being assigned to ARVN headquarters. Promoted to major, Toàn then attended the U.S. Army Special Warfare School at Fort Bragg, North Carolina, in 1962.

Toàn returned to Vietnam as a lieutenant colonel and was named commander of the Armor School of the Republic of Vietnam, a post he held until 1964. Toàn participated in the November 1963 military coup that overthrew President Ngô Đình Diêm.

In November 1964 Toàn became commander of the 4th Armor Squadron, a post he held until May 1966. He was then promoted to colonel. In June 1966 he commanded the ARVN 1st Infantry Division. From January 1967 to May 1972 he commanded the 2d Infantry Division. Toàn was promoted to brigadier general in July 1969 and to major general in July 1971.

In May 1972 Toàn became commander of Military Region II. He was forced to give up this post in 1974, because of rumors relating to an inappropriate exploitation of cinnamon in Quang Ngãi Province. In March 1975 Toàn was named commander of Military Region III, but this came too late to save the situation there. In mid-April 1975 he succeeded in stopping the Communist advance in Long Khánh Province, in what was the last significant battle of the Vietnam War. It only gained additional time for evacuation efforts. After the April 1975 Communist victory, Toàn left Vietnam. He now lives in the United States.

—Ngô N. Trung

Reference: Biographical Files, Indo-China Archives, University of California at Berkeley.

See also: Hô Chí Minh Campaign; Ngô Đình Diêm; Ngô Đình Diêm, Overthrow of; Vietnam, Republic of: Army (ARVN).

Nguyên Văn Xuân

(1892–?)

Prominent general and leading figure of the State of Vietnam. Born in 1892 at Trửờng Tho, Gia Đinh Province, the son of Nguyên Văn Cua, owner and publisher of the well-known newspaper *Luc Tinh Tân Văn,* Nguyên Văn Xuân became a naturalized French citizen. A graduate of the Ecole Polytechnique, Xuân married a Frenchwoman and enlisted in the French Army. He fought in World War I, including service in the Battle of Verdun. He remained in the military and from 1939 to 1940 worked as chief of the Troisième Bureau at the Military Affairs Directorate of the Ministry of Colonies. In 1944 he was promoted to lieutenant colonel of artillery. In the spring of 1945 Xuân refused to become minister of war in the Japanese-sponsored Vietnamese government and was imprisoned by the Japanese in Hà Nôi. He also refused after the August 1945 Revolution to join Hô Chí Minh's Provisional Revolutionary Government. He then escaped to the South, perhaps assisted by Japanese officers.

In March 1946 Xuân was promoted to full colonel in the French Army. An advocate of an autonomous, separate republic in the South, on 1 June 1946 Xuân was named vice-premier of the Republic of Cochin China by the French. In December 1946 he left Vietnam for France, but returned to Sài Gòn in September 1947 to announce the establishment of a provisional government for a separate republic in the South and replaced Lê Văn Hoach as premier. In December 1947 Xuân accompanied Chief of State Bao Đai to meet French High Commissioner for Indo-China Emile Bollaert at Ha Long Bay.

On 23 May 1948 Xuân became premier of the Provisional Government of Vietnam. He also kept the post of minister of defense. In those capacities, on 5 June 1948 Xuân signed the Ha Long Bay Agreement with Bollaert that mandated an independent State of Vietnam and the return of Bao Đai. On 20 June 1949 Xuân's government collapsed, but he was promoted to lieutenant general and became vice-premier and minister of defense in the next government until January 1950. On 17 September 1954 Xuân was again named vice-premier, but he resigned a week later. After 1955 Xuân spent most of the rest of his life in France, where he died.

—Ngô N. Trung

Reference: Biographical Files, Indo-China Archives, University of California at Berkeley.

See also: Bao Đai; Bollaert, Emile; France: Army.

Nguyên Viêt Thanh

(?–1971)

Army of the Republic of Vietnam (ARVN) lieutenant general. Nguyên Viêt Thanh graduated from the Đà Lat Military Academy around 1952. Before 1954 Thanh commanded the 16th Battalion and then the 707th Light Infantry Battalion of the Army of the State of Vietnam in the Bùi Chu area of North Vietnam. He then commanded the Long An sector, the 121st Infantry Regiment, an infantry division, and finally the IV Corps/Military Region IV at Cân Thơ.

Thanh was a devout Buddhist and one of the most incorruptible ARVN generals. He was killed in 1971 when the helicopter in which he was supervising a battle accidentally collided with another craft.

Thanh was quite popular with the people in Military Region IV, and in the early 1980s there were reports of his apparition and sanctification. Many people secretly bought small portraits of the general to worship on their family altars.

—Nguyên Công Luân (Lư Tuân)

Reference: Hà Mai Viêt. *Famous Generals of the Republic of Vietnam Armed Forces.* Unpublished manuscript in Vietnamese.

NIAGARA, Operation

(January–March 1968)

Massive U.S. airpower and artillery effort directed at People's Army of Vietnam (PAVN) concentrations in Khe Sanh. By late January 1968 U.S. intelligence detected the presence of 20,000 or more PAVN soldiers in the vicinity of Khe Sanh. American tactics were to allow PAVN units to surround the U.S. Marines there in order to produce the most spectacular targets of the war for American firepower.

U.S. Military Assistance Command, Vietnam (MACV) commander General William Westmoreland chose the name Operation NIAGARA for the coordination of firepower at Khe Sanh; it evoked an appropriate image of cascading shells and bombs. NIAGARA I was an intelligence-gathering effort to pinpoint targets; NIAGARA II was the destruction of these by aircraft and artillery.

Intelligence concerning target selection was generated by a variety of means, including remote sensors, ground and aerial observers, photo reconnaissance, crater analyses, infrared imagery, and analysis of intercepted communications. U.S. Marine and Army Special Forces reconnaissance patrols, Central Intelligence Agency (CIA) personnel, and the MACV Studies and Observation Group (SOG) all provided input.

During the night of 3–4 February 1968 sensor arrays indicated the presence of up to 2,000 PAVN troops in the vicinity of Marine hill outposts near Khe Sanh. This information was used to plot and execute artillery fire against PAVN troop concentrations. PAVN units were devastated, and the intended attack was broken up in what was one of the earliest examples in warfare of a ground attack thwarted on the basis of sensor data.

Khe Sanh had top-priority claim on all U.S. air assets in Southeast Asia. General Westmoreland personally planned B-52 strikes launched from Guam, Thailand, and Okinawa. Meanwhile, the Marines and U.S. Air Force provided fighter-bombers from bases within South Vietnam, and U.S. Navy aviators flew sorties from aircraft carriers in the South China Sea. South Vietnamese and U.S. Army aviation also provided aerial support. Usually there were fighter-bombers overhead at Khe Sanh around the clock. Such aircraft flew 16,769 sorties and delivered 31,238 tons of ordnance in defense of Khe Sanh.

B-52s in ARC LIGHT strikes attacked targets such as troop concentrations, supply areas, and bunker complexes. On average, every 90 minutes one three-plane cell of B-52s conducted bombing runs on locations around Khe Sanh. In some instances, PAVN soldiers were found after an ARC LIGHT strike wandering around in a daze with blood streaming from their noses and mouths. To catch these survivors above ground, artillerymen at Khe Sanh

often placed artillery fire into the ARC LIGHT target area a few minutes after the departure of the heavy bombers. ARC LIGHT attacks delivered a total of 59,542 tons of munitions during the siege. Westmoreland maintained that ordnance delivered by the B-52s is what defeated the PAVN at Khe Sanh.

Nearly 100,000 tons of munitions at a cost of $1 billion were expended by U.S. forces. Photo reconnaissance and direct observation credited NIAGARA with having caused 4,705 secondary explosions, 1,288 PAVN deaths, and the destruction of 1,061 structures and damage to another 158; 891 bunkers were claimed destroyed, with another 99 damaged. Total PAVN casualties were estimated at 10,000.

—Peter W. Brush

Reference: Nalty, Bernard C. *Air Power and the Fight for Khe Sanh.* Washington, DC: Office of Air Force History, 1973.
See also: Air Power, Role in War; ARC LIGHT (B-52 Raids); Artillery Fire Doctrine; Khe Sanh, Battles of; Military Assistance Command, Vietnam (MACV); Studies and Observation Group (SOG); Vietnam, Democratic Republic of: Army (People's Army of Vietnam [PAVN]); Westmoreland, William Childs.

Nitze, Paul Henry

(1907–)

U.S. assistant secretary of defense (1961–1963), secretary of the Navy (1963–1967), and deputy secretary of defense (1967–1969). Born in Amherst, Massachusetts, on 16 June 1907, Paul Nitze graduated from Harvard in 1928. He entered government service in 1941. As a Cold War bureaucrat, Nitze took part in the creation of the North Atlantic Treaty Organization (NATO) and helped formulate the containment policy. In December 1960 he was appointed assistant secretary of defense for international security affairs by President John F. Kennedy, and served as secretary of the Navy from 1963 to 1967.

In April 1967 Nitze and Secretary of Defense Robert McNamara proposed that the United States cease bombing above the 20th parallel in order to begin negotiations, but President Lyndon Johnson rejected this. In June 1967 Nitze was appointed deputy secretary of defense and two months later joined McNamara in formulating the so-called San Antonio formula, a conciliatory proposal modifying the Johnson administration's previous demand for the People's Army of Vietnam (PAVN) de-escalation before peace negotiations could begin, which was rejected by Hà Nôi in October.

Nitze was a member of an ad hoc study group formed to review the request for an additional 200,000 troops following Têt 1968. He warned that any increase in American troops could lead to a direct confrontation with Red China and could jeopardize American commitments worldwide. He recommended instead a strengthening of the Army of the Republic of Vietnam (ARVN) while withdrawing American forces. Although the study group rejected his warning, on 31 March Johnson announced de-escalation.

Nitze resigned from the Defense Department in January 1969. He served until 1974 as a member of the U.S. delegation in the

Lt. Col. F. S. Wood, commanding officer of a battalion in the U.S. 1st Marine Division, escorts Secretary of the Navy Paul Nitze (left) around the base. After the 1968 Tết Communist Offensive, Nitze recommended strengthening of the Army of the Republic of Vietnam while withdrawing American forces.

Strategic Arms Limitation Talks (SALT) negotiations. In 1981 he was head of the delegation negotiating Intermediate Range Nuclear Forces. In 1984 he was named arms control advisor to Secretary of State George Schultz.

—Robert G. Mangrum

References: Davidson, Phillip B. *Vietnam at War: The History 1946–1975.* Novato, CA: Presidio Press, 1988.
Herring, George C. *America's Longest War: The U.S. and Vietnam 1950–1975.* 2d ed. New York: Alfred A. Knopf, 1986.

International Who's Who, 1984–85. London: Europa Publications.
See also: Acheson, Dean G.; Containment Policy; Johnson, Lyndon Baines; Kennedy, John Fitzgerald; McNamara, Robert S.

Nixon, Richard Milhous

(1913–1994)

U.S. congressman (1947–1951); U.S. senator (1951–1953); vice-president (1953–1961); thirty-seventh president of the United States (1969–1974). Born at Yorba Linda, California, on 9 January

1913, Richard M. Nixon attended Whittier College and Duke University Law School. He served in the Pacific during World War II as a Navy lieutenant junior grade and in 1946 won the first of two terms in the House of Representatives. A Republican, Nixon concentrated zealously on the issue of anticommunism and won election to the Senate in 1950. In 1952 Dwight Eisenhower chose Nixon as his vice-presidential running mate. The successful campaign was marred only by Nixon's need to publicly defend himself against charges of profiting from a secret fund of monies raised by his California friends.

In October 1953 Nixon visited French Indo-China as part of his first overseas trip as vice-president. He visited Sài Gòn, Hà Nôi, Vientiane, and Phnom Penh, coming away convinced that the French troubles in the region stemmed from their failure to win the hearts and minds of the Indo-Chinese peoples. Nixon was privately concerned that the Eisenhower administration was not doing enough to prevent the spread of communism in Southeast Asia. He was one of the earliest supporters of a Southeast Asia Treaty Organization (SEATO), with the United States at its head.

When in April 1954 the French found themselves trapped at Điên Biên Phu, Nixon vociferously argued that the United States should intervene militarily. At a National Security Council (NSC) meeting, Nixon spoke in favor of a proposal put forth by Adm. Arthur Radford, then chairman of the Joint Chiefs of Staff, to bomb and destroy Viêt Minh positions with three small tactical atomic bombs. Code-named Operation VULTURE, the plan was rejected by Eisenhower. Continuing to argue the point, Nixon suggested that the United States send more technicians and supplies to Vietnam, and he told an audience of newspaper editors that the executive branch "has to take the politically unpopular position" of stopping the Communists, and "I personally would support such a decision." Despite Nixon's vigor, Eisenhower refused to intervene. The situation only cemented in Nixon's mind the need to halt what he viewed to be Communist aggression in the region, a belief made even more secure in June 1956, when he met with Republic of Vietnam (RVN) President Ngô Đình Diêm and came away with the feeling that, despite Diêm's excesses, the South Vietnamese leader was capable of establishing order in his nation.

After his devastating loss to John F. Kennedy in the 1960 presidential election and a subsequent failure in California's 1962 gubernatorial race, Nixon appeared to be finished politically. But in 1968 he emerged as the unlikely Republican candidate for president. The war in Vietnam held the potential for being the major issue in the 1968 presidential campaign. Nixon had nothing to gain from meeting the issue head-on, and he refused to do so. Concentrating his efforts on denouncing President Lyndon Johnson's record on law and order, Nixon was reported to have a "secret plan" to end the war—a plan that he later admitted to an interviewer never existed. The tactic worked; even Johnson's decision to stop the bombing of the North less than a week before the election could not turn the tide against Nixon.

The entirety of the Nixon presidency must be seen through the prism of Vietnam; that is unquestionably how he saw it. On many occasions, Nixon wrote or stated that ending the Vietnam War was his "first priority"; détente with the People's Republic of China

(PRC) and the Soviet Union (USSR) would follow. Yet he did not seriously entertain an escalation of the conventional war in 1969. Indeed, Nixon was convinced that Hô Chí Minh could achieve his objective of a unified Vietnam under Communist rule if the United States continued to prosecute the war as had been done under Lyndon Johnson. As a result, Nixon drastically changed American military strategy in Vietnam. Refusing for the moment to order the reinstatement of the bombing of the North, Nixon instead looked to withdraw American troops from combat and protect that withdrawal with a widening of the war into Cambodia and Laos. It was this strategy that Nixon hoped would force the North Vietnamese to entertain serious negotiations.

Nixon's plan was immediately put to the test in February 1969 when Hà Nôi launched its spring offensive. General Creighton Abrams asked Nixon, as he had asked Johnson many times before, to bomb North Vietnamese supply lines in Cambodia. Unlike Johnson, Nixon supported the plan from the start. Nixon viewed Southeast Asia as he had visited it as vice-president—not as four separate countries but as one theater of war. He had come to believe that the key to winning the war was in the destruction of the North Vietnamese supply lines that ran through Laos and Cambodia—the Hô Chí Minh Trail.

Nixon gave the approval for Operation MENU, a wide plan for bombing suspected Communist sanctuaries in Cambodia. To skirt what would be certain worldwide condemnation for bombing a technically neutral nation, Nixon ordered that the bombings be kept secret. The MENU bombings succeeded only in driving the North Vietnamese deeper into Cambodia. It also began the chain of abuses of power known collectively as Watergate, as Secretary of State Henry Kissinger ordered the tapping of the phones of several White House aides in an effort to find out who leaked the story about the bombing to the *New York Times*.

Nixon combined the secret bombings with attempts to show the world that American commitment to the war was winding down. In June he ordered an immediate withdrawal of 25,000 troops from Vietnam. The next month he let it be known that, once the American withdrawal was complete, he did not expect to recommit troops to the region anytime soon, as he articulated what would become known as the Nixon Doctrine: Unless directly attacked, the United States should not commit its troops to the defense of a Third World country. Hoping that these moves would show his good faith, Nixon secretly gave the North Vietnamese a 1 November deadline to show some significant steps toward peace. However, Nixon's moves did not satisfy the antiwar movement at home, whose 15 October and 15 November Moratoria against the War were a huge success. As a result, Nixon was forced to let his deadline go by unchallenged. In an effort to regain the initiative, on 2 November Nixon spoke directly to his supporters in the middle class—those whom he dubbed the "great, silent majority of my fellow Americans"— and begged them to help him control dissent in the nation, asking that they recognize that "North Vietnam cannot defeat or humiliate the United States. Only Americans can do that." By the end of the year, Nixon had promised a further withdrawal of 50,000 troops by 15 April 1970.

However, Nixon's response to events threatened to widen the scope of the war just as his withdrawals were becoming significant. Nixon argued that it was the advent of the Democratic Republic of Vietnam (DRV) attack on Cambodia, begun in the wake of the overthrow of the Norodom Sihanouk government on 11 March 1970, that convinced him that he must take further military action there. Other observers note the failure of the MENU bombings as the cause. Either way, the 26 March decision to send American troops into Cambodia to search out and destroy Communist sanctuaries along the border was consistent with Nixon's desire to support his withdrawals by cutting off North Vietnam's western route of supplies. This decision was the most fateful of Nixon's presidency. Nixon had tried to soften the blow by announcing on 20 April the withdrawal of 150,000 more American troops before the end of 1971. However, his 30 April announcement of what had become known as the Cambodian "incursion" led to a firestorm of protest on college campuses, culminating in the deaths of student protesters at Kent State University and Jackson State University.

The Cambodian incursion proved little, except that the Army of the Republic of Vietnam (ARVN) was not yet ready to fight on its own. In an attempt to rectify that situation, as well as take one more step toward cutting the supply lines to the west, in January 1971 Nixon sanctioned an offensive into Laos (LAM SƠN 719) using only ARVN troops. The initiative began on 8 February, but within six weeks ARVN troops were forced to withdraw, leaving the Hồ Chí Minh Trail remaining virtually intact. The Laotian disaster only stiffened Nixon's resolve, and it may have contributed to the harshness of his response to the 13 June 1971 release of the Pentagon Papers in the *New York Times*. Yet despite the criticism that followed in the press, Nixon would not be rushed. Convinced that his February 1972 rapprochement with the People's Republic of China would scare their DRV clients back to the peace table, Nixon continued to withdraw troops and wait.

However, for the fourth straight year, Hà Nội did not bow to Nixon's tactics. The DRV spurned Nixon's request for further talks and, on 30 March 1972 launched what was to that point the largest offensive of the war. Furious, Nixon ordered the resumption of the bombing of the North. On 1 April Nixon authorized Operation LINEBACKER—the bombing within 25 miles of the demilitarized zone; two weeks later, he expanded the bombing zone up to the 20th parallel. On 8 May he ordered the mining of Hai Phòng Harbor, telling the American people that the only way to stop the war was to "keep the weapons of war out of the hands of the international outlaws of North Vietnam." Nixon had become certain that only a massive show of force would convince the North to negotiate. Kissinger and Lê Đức Tho resumed their peace talks within a month of the start of the LINEBACKER bombings; by late fall, the talks were in earnest.

It was soon clear that the only party who could not agree to a truce was RVN President Nguyên Văn Thiêu. In an effort to gain his support, Nixon sent a secret correspondence to Thiêu, promising that, if the North Vietnamese broke the truce, the United States would recommit troops to South Vietnam. But when the North balked at changes in a document already agreed to, Nixon had finally had enough. At Camp David, he told Chairman of the Joint Chiefs of Staff Adm. Thomas Moorer, "I don't want any more of this crap about the fact that we couldn't hit this target or that one. This is your chance to use military power effectively to win the war, and if you don't, I'll consider you responsible." On 17 December Nixon ordered renewed saturation bombing of the North. LINEBACKER II, also known as the "Christmas Bombing," dropped some 36,000 tons of bombs in an 11-day period. On 26 December Hà Nội sent signals about wanting to resume negotiations; on 9 January 1973 in Paris, Secretary of State William Rogers initialed the truce.

Nixon understood that the truce was a particularly weak one, writing later that the only way he had been able to get the North to buy into the deal was to allow them to keep a military presence in the South. As a result, Nixon never believed that the truce meant that the United States was to stop sending monies and supplies to the RVN, which he continued to do until the 30 June 1973 Cooper-Church Amendment precluded him from doing so. Nevertheless, Nixon's memoranda make it clear that he fully expected to uphold his secret pledge to Thiêu and to push the Congress to recommit troops when the DRV violated the peace. However, the 7 November passage of the War Powers Act would have precluded Nixon from making such a move, and his 9 August 1974 resignation in the wake of the Watergate investigation left such a decision to his successor, Gerald R. Ford.

Nixon believed that his policies had won what could have been a lasting peace had the Congress not weakened his hand or that of his successor in terms of enforcing that settlement. In a 1985 defense of his Vietnam policies entitled *No More Vietnams,* Nixon argued that "when we signed the Paris peace agreements in 1973, we had won the war. We then proceeded to lose the peace. . . . In the end, Vietnam was lost on the political front in the United States, not on the battlefront in Southeast Asia." Nixon was also convinced that his numerous escalations of the war, far from being a useless waste of life, shortened that conflict—he would later tell a British audience that his only regret about expanding the war into Cambodia was not having done it sooner.

Most contemporary observers feel that Nixon relegated domestic policies to a secondary role, concentrating instead on the war and his other foreign policy initiatives. This is only partially true. For example, Nixon and his staff developed innovative proposals for welfare reform and for new financial relationships between state and local government. However, these initiatives were defeated by a Congress that, largely because of Nixon's heavy-handed conduct of the war, had become increasingly alienated from his administration.

It was in foreign affairs that Nixon made his mark, again largely because of the war in Vietnam. The success of his overtures to the PRC and the USSR was based largely upon Nixon's success in playing each of these nations against the other, as well as against the North Vietnamese. Nixon called this "linkage diplomacy." As a condition of doing business, Nixon required that both the PRC and USSR lessen their overt commitment to North Vietnam. Although both states continued publicly to support Hồ Chí

President Richard Nixon greets U.S. Army combat troops at Dĩ An. During his 1968 presidential campaign, Nixon was reported to have a "secret plan" to end the war—a plan that, he later admitted, never existed.

Minh, the amount of military and financial aid they gave to North Vietnam decreased dramatically after 1972.

Following his resignation, there were many reports that Nixon would reenter the political arena, but he preferred to play the role of elder statesman, writing eight books between 1978 and 1994. His *No More Vietnams* (1985) was a thoughtful defense of his administration's policies, as well as an acerbic critique of Congress's refusal to fund the requests of the Ford administration for further aid to South Vietnam in 1975. His successors in the White House kept Nixon informed on major foreign policy initiatives; Ronald Reagan and George Bush even solicit his advice on a number of issues. Nixon died on 22 April 1994, following a stroke.

—John Robert Greene

References: Ambrose, Stephen E. *Nixon.* 3 vols. New York: Simon & Schuster, 1987, 1989, 1991.

Greene, John Robert. *The Limits of Power: The Nixon and Ford Administrations.* Bloomington, IN: Indiana University Press, 1992.

Litwak, Robert S. *Détente and the Nixon Doctrine: American Foreign Policy and the Pursuit of Stability, 1969–1976.* Cambridge, MA: Cambridge University Press, 1984.

Nixon, Richard. *No More Vietnams.* New York: Avon Books, 1985.

See also: Abrams, Creighton; Amnesty; Antiwar Movement, United States; Cambodian Incursion; Cooper-Church Amendment; Eisenhower, Dwight David; Federal Bureau of Investigation (FBI); Fishhook; Ford, Gerald R.; Kent State University; Kissinger, Henry Alfred; LAM SƠN 719, Operation; LINEBACKER I, Operation; LINEBACKER II, Operation; Madman Strategy; MENU, Operation; Midway Island Conference; Mitchell, John Newton; Moorer, Thomas H.; Moratorium to End the War in Vietnam; Nguyên Văn Thiêu; Nixon Doctrine; Paris Negotiations; Paris Peace Accords; Parrot's Beak; Pentagon Papers and Trial; Radford, Arthur W.; Rogers, William Pierce; United States: Department of Justice; Vietnamization; VULTURE, Operation; War Powers Act; Washington Special Actions Group (WSAG); Watergate.

Nixon Doctrine

(July 1969)

Foreign policy statement by President Richard M. Nixon. In July 1969 Nixon began his first foreign trip as president with a stop in Guam. Speaking to the press at the island's Naval Air Station, he promised "we will keep our treaty commitments" to Asian nations, but cautioned that "as far as the problems of internal security [and] military defense, except for the threat of a major power involving nuclear weapons, the United States . . . has a right to expect that this problem will be increasingly handled by . . . the Asian nations themselves."

Many interpreted the statement, which the press quickly dubbed the "Nixon Doctrine," as meaning that Nixon planned to abandon Vietnam once American troops had withdrawn. Nixon later argued in his *Memoirs* that such interpretations were false and that the doctrine was meant to be a platform that would allow the United States to "play a responsible role" in helping non-Communist nations win and defend their independence.

—John Robert Greene

References: Greene, John Robert. *The Limits of Power: The Nixon and Ford Administrations.* Bloomington, IN: Indiana University Press, 1992.

Nixon, Richard M. *Memoirs.* New York: Grosset & Dunlap, 1978.

See also: Nguyên Văn Thiêu; Nixon, Richard Milhous; United States: Involvement in Vietnam, 1969–1973; Vietnamization.

Nolting, Frederick, Jr.

(1911–1989)

U.S. ambassador to the Republic of Vietnam (RVN), 1961–1963. Born at Richmond, Virginia, on 24 August 1911, Frederick Nolting received a B.A. from the University of Virginia in 1933, an M.A. from Harvard University in 1941, and a Ph.D. from the University of Virginia in 1942. Nolting was a conservative Democrat and foreign service officer with extensive diplomatic experience in Europe. In 1961 President John F. Kennedy posted the forthright and polite, yet somewhat naive, Virginian, who had no knowledge or firsthand experience with Asia, to the Republic of Vietnam.

The appointment of Nolting to succeed Elbridge Durbrow in Sài Gòn signaled a tactical shift in policy. Dealings with President Ngô Đình Diêm changed from candid exchanges to cordial relations. Backed by General Paul D. Harkins, commander of the Military Assistance Command, Vietnam (MACV), the gracious Nolting, who disliked controversy, supported the regime completely. He applauded the Strategic Hamlet program and upheld the RVN's account of the battle of Ấp Bắc (1963) in a bitter clash with resident correspondents. Calling them green and impractical, he chided reporters for failure to stand behind an ally as he did and for their disinclination to assume that the Communists were suffering reversals in the countryside as the Diêm regime claimed.

Ambassador Nolting identified with the South Vietnamese upper class rather than the society at large. Moreover, he believed that political reforms were less significant than effective operations and, consequently, criticized the country's dissenters for their unwillingness to make common cause with the regime. Opposed to an enlarged U.S. military involvement, he perceived the central issue facing American policymakers as political in nature. Instead of coercion, he advocated placing faith in Diêm's ability to secure the nation against the Viêt Công.

When Buddhists demonstrated in 1963, the State Department ordered Nolting to press President Diêm to reconcile with the dissidents. But he declined and then departed Sài Gòn for a European vacation in the midst of a developing crisis. In his absence, William Truehart, an embassy representative, subverted Nolting's conciliatory approach and cautioned Diêm that he risked forfeiting American assistance if he continued to suppress the Buddhists. A series of heated White House meetings followed in which the recently returned Nolting participated. Kennedy reproved Nolting for his absence and chastised him for faulty intelligence. He then dispatched the ambassador back to his post with instructions to win Diêm's cooperation. Still, Nolting remained hesitant to pressure Diêm and the crisis intensified.

The Kennedy administration, by now dissatisfied with Nolting's performance and reporting, decided to replace him with Henry Cabot Lodge, Jr. Nolting, preoccupied with family concerns and a desire to enter international banking, was ready to resign and return to the United States by the summer of 1963.

Nolting's memoir, *From Trust to Tragedy,* published in 1988, is highly critical of the Kennedy administration while praising Diêm. Nolting died in Charlottesville, Virginia, on 14 December 1989.

—Rodney J. Ross

References: Halberstam, David. *The Best and the Brightest.* Greenwich, CT: Fawcett, 1973.
Hammer, Ellen J. *A Death in November: America in Vietnam, 1963.* New York: E. P. Dutton, 1987.
Karnow, Stanley. *Vietnam: A History.* New York: Viking Press, 1983.
Nolting, Frederick. *From Trust to Tragedy: The Political Memoirs of Frederick Nolting, Kennedy's Ambassador to Diem's Vietnam.* New York: Praeger, 1988.
See also: Âp Băc, Battle of; Durbrow, Elbridge; Harkins, Paul D.; Kennedy, John Fitzgerald; Lodge, Henry Cabot, Jr.; Ngô Đình Diêm; United States: Involvement in Vietnam, 1954–1965.

Nông Đưc Manh

(1940–)
Prominent leader in the Vietnamese Communist Party (VCP) and the Socialist Republic of Vietnam (SRV). Born in 1940 in Băc Thái Province, Nông Đưc Manh is of the Tày ethnic minority. He became a Lao Đông (Communist Party) member in 1963. Starting as a forest worker, he went to the USSR and graduated from the Institute of Forest Technology in Leningrad, and after returning to Vietnam, he graduated from the Lao Đông Nguyên Ái Quôc Advanced School.

Manh was director of the Phu Lường Forestry Farm in Băc Thái Province and vice-chairman and chairman of the People's Committee of Băc Thái Province and secretary of its Party Committee. In 1986 at the Sixth Congress of the Vietnamese Communist Party, he was elected alternate member of the Central Committee. In March 1989 he became a full member. That September he was appointed head of the Commission for Nationalities of the VCP Central Committee. In 1989 he was chosen in a by-election to the Eighth National Assembly and was appointed vice-chairman of the Council of Nationalities of the National Assembly.

In June 1991, during the Seventh Party Congress, Manh was reelected to the VCP Central Committee and appointed to the Political Bureau. In July 1992 he was elected deputy to the Ninth National Assembly, and that September he was elected chairman of the National Assembly. Manh is a protégé of former VCP General Secretary Nguyên Văn Linh; he has never denied rumors that he is a son of Hô Chí Minh.

—Ngô N. Trung

Reference: Biographical Files, Indo-China Archives, University of California at Berkeley.
See also: Hô Chí Minh; Lao Đông Party; Nguyên Văn Linh (Nguyên Văn Cúc); Vietnam, Socialist Republic of: 1975 to the Present.

North Vietnam

See Vietnam, Democratic Republic of: 1945–1954; Vietnam, Democratic Republic of: 1954–1975.

North Vietnamese Army (NVA)

See Vietnam, Democratic Republic of: Army (People's Army of Vietnam [PAVN]).

Nùng

See Montagnards.

Nurses

See United States: Nurses.

O

O'Daniel, John W.

(1894–1975)

U.S. Army general and commander of the Military Assistance and Advisory Group (MAAG), Indo-China, March 1954 to October 1955. Born in Newark, Delaware, on 15 February 1894, John W. "Iron Mike" O'Daniel, while still a student at the University of Delaware, enlisted as a private in the National Guard and saw service on the Mexican border. After graduating from college, he was commissioned as a second lieutenant of infantry. He served in France during World War I and earned the Distinguished Service Cross.

In February 1944 O'Daniel assumed command of the 3d Infantry Division, then on the Anzio beachhead. From 1948 to 1950 he was the U.S. military attaché in Moscow. O'Daniel was never known for his tact, and after that assignment he wrote a magazine article in which he said that Moscow impressed him "as a vast slum." In response, the Soviets accused him of being a spy. During the Korean War, O'Daniel commanded I Corps.

Rising to the rank of lieutenant general, O'Daniel's involvement with Vietnam began when he was commanding general of the U.S. Army in the Pacific. In June 1953 the Joint Chiefs of Staff (JCS) sent him to Vietnam to assess French requirements for military aid. O'Daniel came back with an optimistic report and support for the Navarre Plan.

During his second visit in November 1953, O'Daniel convinced French General Henri Navarre to accept four American officers on his staff and to permit a small increase in the size of the MAAG, then under the command of Maj. Gen. Thomas Trapnell. O'Daniel reported to the JCS what he believed to be "real military progress" and maintained that "prospects for victory are increasingly encouraging." Army Chief of Staff General Matthew B. Ridgeway, however, thought O'Daniel's report overly optimistic.

In February 1954 O'Daniel visited the French position at Điên Biên Phu. Although he generally accepted what he was told in the briefings, several aspects of the French position disturbed him. French bunkers did not appear very strong, and O'Daniel was bothered by the fact that the French had failed to secure the surrounding high ground. In a memo to the JCS he noted, "A force with two or three battalions of medium artillery could make the area untenable."

The French initially objected to O'Daniel being named to replace General Trapnell as MAAG chief. They insisted that O'Daniel be demoted to major general so he would not be equal in rank to Navarre. O'Daniel was willing to accept a temporary reduction, but Ridgeway objected strongly. O'Daniel finally assumed command of the MAAG on 31 March, just weeks before Điên Biên Phu fell.

When O'Daniel assumed command of the MAAG, its primary mission was to provide equipment support. O'Daniel pushed for authority to reorganize and train the Vietnamese Army. He believed that a loose interpretation of the MAAG's responsibility to perform "end use checks of American equipment" could be stretched to cover training. Ridgeway, however, gave strict instructions that he was to "make no commitments whatsoever in regard to training."

In August 1954 the South Vietnamese government requested assistance from the United States in evacuating from the North those Vietnamese who did not wish to remain under Communist control. O'Daniel established the Evacuation Staff Group, headquartered in Sài Gòn. On 16 August U.S. Navy Task Force 90, consisting of 28 ships under command of Rear Adm. Lorenzo S. Sabin, began evacuating French and Vietnamese from Hai Phòng.

In November 1954 the internal political situation in Sài Gòn became very unstable. Rumors were rife that South Vietnamese Chief of Staff General Nguyên Văn Hinh was about to stage a coup against the government of Ngô Đình Diêm. Because of the delicacy of the situation, U.S. Ambassador Donald Heath ordered all U.S. personnel to avoid contact with Hinh. On 12 November, however, O'Daniel became convinced that Hinh was only hours away from launching the coup. Unable to contact Heath, O'Daniel visited Hinh at his home and impressed upon him the negative U.S. reaction such a course of action would trigger. O'Daniel came away from the meeting convinced that he had derailed the coup, but Heath was furious because his orders had been disobeyed.

On 12 February 1955 O'Daniel finally received authority to reorganize and train the South Vietnamese Army. Under the terms of the Collins-Ely Agreement, all American and French advisory training personnel, 68 American and 209 French officers, came under O'Daniel's command by March. When O'Daniel left the MAAG in October 1955, training advisors totaled 142 U.S. and 58 French officers. O'Daniel tried to convince President Diêm to allow a sizable French combat force to remain in South Vietnam, but Diêm believed that the French could not be relied upon and should leave as soon as possible.

O'Daniel's advisory effort focused on preparing the South Vietnamese to resist a conventional attack from North Vietnam. He believed that an army so equipped and organized would also be capable of performing an internal security role. After he retired from the Army in 1955, O'Daniel founded the American Friends of Vietnam, a very effective group that lobbied for American support of the Diêm government. General O'Daniel died in San Diego, California, on 27 March 1975.

—David T. Zabecki

References: *New York Times* (29 March 1975).
Spector, Ronald H. *Advice and Support: The Early Years, 1941–1960.* Washington, DC: U.S. Army Center for Military History, 1983.
The Washington Post (30 March 1975).
See also: American Friends of Vietnam; Điên Biên Phu, Battle of; Navarre, Henri Eugène; Navarre Plan; Ngô Đình Diêm; Nguyên Văn Hinh; Ridgway, Matthew B.

Office of Strategic Services (OSS)

Predecessor to the Central Intelligence Agency (CIA); it assisted the Vietnamese in their fight against the Japanese in World War II. In August 1941 President Franklin D. Roosevelt created the Office of the Coordinator of Information, headed by 58-year-old William Joseph "Wild Bill" Donovan. In May 1942 Donovan's group was renamed the Office of Strategic Services (OSS).

As was their practice worldwide during World War II, OSS operatives in Indo-China sought contact with any group fighting the Axis. Their earliest contact in Vietnam was worldly, Canadian-born, Cal-Texaco executive Lawrence Gordon, who had lived in Hai Phòng until 1940.

In 1941 Cal-Texaco persuaded Gordon to return to Indo-China to oversee its interests. Concurrently, Chief of British Security Sir William Stephenson (later known as "Intrepid") gave him a cover and made him a captain in the British Secret Service. On his way to Vietnam, Gordon met OSS agents in China who arranged to finance his operations. Throughout 1941 and 1942 he traveled across Vietnam pretending to be a freelance oil agent. Gordon set up a vast network of spies, most of them Vietnamese and former Cal-Texaco workers.

In 1942 Gordon was joined by two Americans, somehow living freely in southern Vietnam—former Cal-Texaco employee Harry V. Bernard and Boston-born Chinese American Frank "Frankie" Tan. By 1943 the group, known as the GBT (the initials of the men's last names), had established radio-listening posts all over Indo-China and was providing vital information to, among others, General Claire Chennault's 14th Air Force in China.

Concurrently, the OSS sought to undermine the Japanese by supporting nationalist guerrillas in Indo-China. In Vietnam it soon established ties with Viêt Minh forces led by Hô Chí Minh and Võ Nguyên Giáp. Throughout the war and immediately afterward, OSS agents advocated in their reports to Washington that the United States support Vietnamese independence from France. Even though it is clear that many high administration officials saw these reports and that Donovan leaned in this direction, it is still not clear what President Roosevelt intended. In any case, after Roosevelt's death in April 1945, President Harry S Truman was clearly less sympathetic.

In March 1945 the previously docile French in Vietnam, led by General Marcel Alessandri, planned a revolt against Japanese occupation. The Japanese struck first and arrested most of the French. This Japanese victory greatly harmed GBT/OSS efforts and left the Viêt Minh as the only viable anti-Japanese force in Indo-China. At war's end, Hô, accompanied by OSS agents, entered Hà Nôi on 19 August 1945. When puppet emperor Bao Đai abdicated on 25 August, Hô's "pro-U.S." forces seemed to have won an important victory.

On 2 September 1945 Hà Nôi awoke to a festive day. Nearly a half-million people were present to celebrate "Vietnamese Independence Day." Peter Dewey and Archimedes Patti led the OSS contingent in Hà Nôi.

At the Potsdam Conference, however, Allied leaders thwarted Viêt Minh hopes when it was decided that the Nationalist Chinese would occupy northern Vietnam while the British would occupy the South. During this occupation, the Chinese tolerated Hô's government in the North, but the British soon returned control of the South to the French.

During this period, the cordial OSS–Viêt Minh relationship continued, but the accidental Viêt Minh killing of Lieutenant Colonel Dewey in Sài Gòn on 26 September 1945 foretold the tragic future of U.S.-Vietnamese relations. Hô was "shaken" by the death of an American at Viêt Minh hands while he was seeking U.S. support. In effect, Dewey became the first American serviceman to die at the hands of Hô's soldiers.

On 1 October 1945 President Truman disbanded Donovan's 12,600-member organization, replacing it in early 1946 with the Central Intelligence Group, and in 1947 with the CIA.

—William Head

References: Boettcher, Thomas. *Vietnam: The Valor and the Sorrow.* Boston: Little, Brown, 1985.
Karnow, Stanley. *Vietnam: A History.* New York: Viking Press, 1983.
Smith, Ralph Harris. *OSS: The Secret History of America's First Central Intelligence Agency.* Berkeley, CA: University of California Press, 1972.
See also: Central Intelligence Agency (CIA); Dewey, Albert Peter; Donovan, William Joseph; Hô Chí Minh; Patti, Archimedes L. A.; Roosevelt, Franklin Delano; Truman, Harry S; United States: Involvement in Indo-China through 1954; Viêt Minh (Viêt Nam Đôc Lâp Đông Minh Hôi [Vietnam Independence League]); Võ Nguyên Giáp.

Olds, Robin

(1922–)

U.S. Air Force fighter pilot and commander of the 8th Tactical Fighter Wing (1966–1967). Born on 14 July 1922 in Honolulu, Hawaii, Robin Olds was the son of Army Air Corps Maj. Gen. Robert Olds. Robin Olds graduated from the U.S. Military Academy at West Point in 1943. He became a career Air Force officer and a triple ace, having shot down a total of 17 enemy aircraft during World War II and the Vietnam War. He began his combat career flying a P-38 Lightning and was credited with 107 combat missions, including 24.5 victories, 13 aircraft shot down and 11.5 aircraft destroyed on the ground. During the Vietnam War, he flew a F-4 Phantom II and, using air-to-air missiles, shot down two MiG-17 and two MiG-21 aircraft over North Vietnam.

As commander of the U.S. 8th Tactical Fighter Wing at Ubon Royal Thai Air Force Base, Thailand, from September 1966 until December 1967, Colonel Olds devised and led Operation BOLO, in which U.S. Air Force jets downed seven MiG-21s over North Vietnam on 2 January 1967. Promoted to brigadier general in June 1968, Olds served as commandant of cadets at the U.S. Air Force Academy before retiring from the Air Force in June 1973.

—James H. Willbanks

Col. Robin Olds, commander of the U.S. 8th Tactical Fighter Wing, receives a welcome after his 100th and final combat mission. Olds became a triple ace, having shot down a total of 17 enemy aircraft during World War II and the Vietnam War.

References: Berger, Carl, ed. *The United States Air Force in Southeast Asia, 1961–1973.* Washington, DC: Office of Air Force History, 1977.
Hanak, Walter, ed. *The United States Air Force in Southeast Asia—Aces and Aerial Victories, 1965–1973.* Washington, DC: Office of Air Force History, 1976.
See also: Air Power, Role in War; Airplanes, Allied and Democratic Republic of Vietnam; BOLO, Operation; United States: Air Force.

OMEGA, Project

(August 1966–1 November 1967)

Designation for U.S. Special Forces (SF) operation headquartered at Ban Mê Thuôt to fill a growing need for military intelligence. Established in August 1966, comprised of personnel from the 5th Special Forces Group, and controlled by Detachment B-50 on orders from I Field Force, the OMEGA unit was committed to combat on 11 September and created to supplement Project DELTA. OMEGA supplied corps-level special reconnaissance and long-range patrol capabilities, mainly in the Central Highlands of II Corps Tactical Zone (II CTZ).

OMEGA operated within the framework of the Civilian Irregular Defense Group (CIDG) program. Assuming that well-trained, dependable, ethnic minorities would be most successful in this type of mission, it recruited indigenous troops from the Montagnards and Chinese Nùngs.

Organizationally a smaller version of DELTA, OMEGA consisted of a reconnaissance element and a reaction force (a combined total of about 600 men). A modified B Team served as an advisory command. Reconnaissance responsibilities were divided. Eight reconnaissance teams with six members each (two SF and four indigenous personnel) carried out patrols in specified reconnaissance zones to gather intelligence and conduct terrain analysis. Four roadrunner teams of four scouts each (all indigenous personnel)—dressed in Communist uniforms and equipped with appropriate weapons and documents—operated for extended periods in Communist-controlled territory. The scouts were well paid and the recipients of extra privileges, but they often did not survive their high-risk missions.

The reaction force provided a reinforcing component of a battalion of three Mobile Strike Force Command ("Mike Force") companies, each with 25 SF members and 150 highly trained, airborne-qualified CIDG soldiers. Only later did Republic of Vietnam Special Forces participate. Spending an average of 60 percent of their time in the field, these units gathered information, helped extract compromised teams, and called in air strikes.

During the first nine months of its operation, OMEGA claimed 191 Communist troops killed in action. One of the most important contributions of the SF to the war effort, OMEGA yielded valuable intelligence and negatively affected its enemy's morale. On 1 November 1967 the assets of Detachment B-50 were transferred to Military Assistance Command, Vietnam's Studies and Observation Group (MACV-SOG).

—Paul S. Daum, with assistance from Trevor Curran

References: Kelly, Francis J. *U.S. Army Special Forces, 1961–1971.* Vietnam Studies Series. Washington, DC: Department of the Army, 1973. Simpson, Charles M., III. *Inside the Green Berets: The First Thirty Years, a History of the U.S. Army Special Forces.* Novato, CA: Presidio Press, 1983. Stanton, Shelby L. *Green Berets at War: U.S. Army Special Forces in Southeast Asia, 1956–1975.* Novato, CA: Presidio Press, 1985. _____. *Special Forces at War: An Illustrated History, Southeast Asia 1957–1975.* Charlottesville, VA: Howell Press, 1990.
See also: Civilian Irregular Defense Group (CIDG); DELTA, Project; Mobile Strike Force Commands; Montagnards; SIGMA, Project; United States: Special Forces.

Operation Plan 34A (OPLAN 34A)

U.S.–backed covert harassment and intelligence-gathering efforts conducted along the Democratic Republic of Vietnam (DRV) coastline. Three days before his assassination, President John Kennedy gave his approval to a new covert action program in Vietnam known as Operation Plan 34A, or OPLAN 34A. Activities conducted under this code name included minor raids by mercenaries and South Vietnamese commandos at various locations along the northern coastline of the DRV. The commandos penetrated Communist territory, usually at night, and blew up defensive positions and supply dumps, attacked coastal radar transmitters, and kidnapped individuals marked by intelligence as worthy of interrogation in the South.

Covert U.S. naval operations mounted by the Navy and Marines were not new. Known as DeSoto missions, they consisted of ELINT (electronic intelligence) activities and had been conducted since the 1950s against the Soviet Union, North Korea, and the People's Republic of China. OPLAN 34A were covert intelligence missions. ELINT vessels surveyed northern coastal radar and other electronic installations above the 17th parallel, monitored transmissions, determined radio and radar frequencies used, and pinpointed locations of transmission units.

The first DeSoto mission against the DRV came in 1962. In 1964 the destroyer *Maddox* began conducting electronic surveillance along the northern coast. DeSoto missions had the additional duty to search for ships bringing supplies south to Việt Công units and to counter seaborne resupply efforts by the DRV's Group 759. Another responsibility was to record navigational information for use by OPLAN 34A commando teams landing along the long coastline of the DRV. Those teams regularly traveled to the North from their base at Đà Nẵng using special American-built boats, called "Swifts," sometimes captained by Norwegian skippers. Ironically, these boats were found to be too slow and so were phased out and replaced with Norwegian-built craft called "Nasties," captained by Americans. These craft were armed with twin .50-caliber machine guns on the deckhouse and a combined .50-caliber and 81-mm mortar aft. The crew consisted of an officer and five enlisted men. Occasionally American patrol torpedo (PT) boats, stripped of their torpedo tubes, were also used.

During the night of 30–31 July 1964 an OPLAN 34A group conducted raids against two small islands, Hòn Ngư near Vinh and about three miles offshore, and Hòn Me about eight miles offshore. The strike force was unable to land any commandos, but did fire on island installations before returning to base. The *Maddox,* 120 miles away, monitored resulting radar and radio transmissions.

The *Maddox* later moved no closer than five miles of Hòn Me, on 2 August, when the small North Vietnamese Navy reacted with a PT boat attack against her. On 4 August there was possibly a second strike against the *Maddox* and a sister ship, the destroyer *C. Turner Joy.* In both cases, the destroyers were supported by planes from the carrier *Ticonderoga,* sent to the mouth of the Gulf of Tonkin in spring 1964. These incidents, growing out of OPLAN 34A and DeSoto missions, gave rise to the Tonkin Gulf incidents and the congressional Tonkin Gulf Resolution on 10 August, called by Senator Wayne Morse of Oregon the functional equivalent of a declaration of war.

—Cecil B. Currey

References: Marolda, Edward J., and G. Wesley Pryce III. *A Short History of the United States and the Southeast Asian Conflict, 1950–1975.* Washington, DC: Naval Historical Center, Department of the Navy, 1984.

Preston, Anthony. "The Naval War in Vietnam." In *The Vietnam War: An Almanac,* edited by John S. Bowman. New York: World Almanac Publications, 1985.
See also: DeSoto Missions; ELINT (Electronic Intelligence); Kennedy, John Fitzgerald; Morse, Wayne Lyman; Quach Tom; Tonkin Gulf Incidents; Tonkin Gulf Resolution; Vietnam, Republic of: Commandos.

Order of Battle

The process of determining the identification, disposition, strength, command structure, subordinate units, and equipment of any military force. During military operations, order of battle (OB) is an integral part of the tactical intelligence process, one of the many tools used by military intelligence analysts to determine enemy capabilities and probable courses of action.

All armies go to great lengths to prevent their enemies from obtaining this information. Likewise, all armies engage in deception operations to feed false and misleading information to the opposing forces. For these reasons, OB, like so much else in the realm of military intelligence, is as much an art as it is a science. Intelligence analysts face the daunting task of building a coherent picture of an enemy from partial, often conflicting, and sometimes false information gathered from a wide variety of sources of varying accuracy and reliability.

The OB picture of an enemy force is never complete and never stable. It is a constantly moving picture that changes shape as units loose or build strength, change location, change commanders, and even exchange subordinate units and elements. The OB picture can be considered true and accurate only after the war is over—and perhaps not even then.

The historian uses OB information in much the same manner as the intelligence analyst. Whereas the intelligence analyst is trying to predict the future, the historian is trying to reconstruct the past. Historians use similar research and analytical tools, and they face similar challenges in incomplete, conflicting, and often intentionally misleading information.

Many years after an event, the surviving or available records still might not provide enough information to construct the true picture. The objective of both the intelligence analyst and the military historian is to construct the best picture possible using the best available data.

More than 20 years after the fall of the Republic of Vietnam, OB information on the Vietnam War remains incomplete. In the following tables, the information for U.S. military units is virtually complete and accurate. The information for Republic of Vietnam Armed Forces (RVNAF) is somewhat less complete. The information for Communist troops (People's Army of Vietnam [PAVN] and Viêt Công units) is often incomplete. In many cases, only partial listings of subordinate units are known. In some cases, this information is not available at all. In most cases, it is possible to reconstruct only partial and spotty listings of commanders.

Soldiers of the U.S. 173d Airborne Brigade pass the bodies of their comrades killed during fighting at Đăk Tô in November 1967.

After a firefight, two soldiers of the U.S. 173d Airborne Brigade wait for a helicopter to evacuate them and a dead companion.

I. United States Order of Battle

A. American Joint Commands

The first U.S. military organization arrived in Vietnam in 1950. The mission of the Military Assistance and Advisory Group, Indo-China (MAAG–Indo-China) was to provide assistance and advice to the French forces there. In 1955 MAAG–Indo-China became MAAG-Vietnam, with a mission of providing joint service support to the South Vietnamese. In 1962 the United States also established the Military Assistance Command, Vietnam (MACV) to coordinate the expanding U.S. military activities in Vietnam.

In 1964 MACV was reorganized and absorbed MAAG-Vietnam, which became the Field Advisory Element, MACV. The Field Advisory Element provided the Army of the Republic of Vietnam (ARVN) with advisor teams from corps down to regimental level. In essence, the senior American advisor at any given level functioned as almost a shadow commander. From about mid-1970 the senior U.S. Army officer in each corps tactical zone (CTZ) was considered the senior advisor as well. The one exception was when John Paul Vann became the senior advisor in II CTZ in May 1971. In 1964 the Field Advisory Element had an assigned strength of 4,741 men. It reached its peak in 1968 with 9,430.

MACV was a subordinate unified command of the United States Pacific Command, headquartered in Hawaii. The commander of MACV had control and authority over all U.S. military oper-ations in South Vietnam. This included naval operations in Vietnamese coastal waters and all air missions over South Vietnam. The commander of MACV did not have any control over the air war against North Vietnam, over the high seas operations of the U.S. Seventh Fleet (including air strikes launched from its carriers), nor over any missions carried out by aircraft of the Air Force's Strategic Air Command (SAC).

In theory the commander of MACV reported to the Commander in Chief, Pacific Command (CINCPAC). In practice, however, the commander of MACV often reported directly to the U.S. secretary of defense. In hindsight, it can be seen very clearly that the United States violated the principal of unity of command almost from the start.

U.S. Military Strength in Vietnam

1964	23,310
1965	184,310
1966	385,300
1967	485,600
1968	536,000
1969	484,330
1970	335,790
1971	158,120
1972	24,000

Republic of Vietnam 7th Brigade Marines aboard a CH-21 Shawnee helicopter from the 57th Transportation Company are airlifted to a landing zone ten miles west of the Môc Hóa airstrip.

Military Assistance Advisory Group, Indo-China (MAAG–Indo-China)

Date formed in Vietnam: 17 September 1950
Date reorganized as MAAG-Vietnam: 31 October 1955
Headquarters: Sài Gòn (Chợ Lớn)
Commanding generals:

Brig. Gen. Francis G. Brink	October 1950
Maj. Gen. Thomas J. H. Trapnell	August 1952
Lt. Gen. John W. O'Daniel	April 1954

Military Assistance Advisory Group, Vietnam (MAAG-Vietnam)

Date formed from MAAG–Indo-China: 1 November 1955
Date merged with MACV: 15 May 1964
Headquarters: Sài Gòn
Commanding generals:

Lt. Gen. Samuel T. Williams	November 1955
Lt. Gen. Lionel C. McGarr	September 1960
Maj. Gen. Charles J. Timmes	July 1962

Military Assistance Command, Vietnam (MACV)

Date formed in Vietnam: 8 February 1962
Date inactivated in Vietnam: 29 March 1973
Headquarters: Sài Gòn (Tân Sơn Nhứt Air Base)
Major subordinate commands:

Field Advisory Element, MACV
U.S. Army, Vietnam
I Field Force
II Field Force
XXIV Corps
5th Special Forces Group
III Marine Amphibious Force
Naval Forces, Vietnam
Seventh Air Force
Commanding generals:

Gen. Paul D. Harkins	February 1962
Gen. William C. Westmoreland	June 1964
Gen. Creighton W. Abrams	July 1968
Gen. Frederick C. Weyand	June 1972

Field Advisory Element, MACV

Senior U.S. Army advisors

I Corps Tactical Zone	
Brig. Gen. A. L. Hamblen, Jr.	June 1966
Col. John J. Beeson III	July 1967
Brig. Gen. Salve H. Matheson	January 1968
Col. John J. Beeson III	April 1968
Col. Ronald H. Renwanz	August 1968

Rubble and barbed wire line the streets of Chợ Lớn, a suburb of Sài Gòn.

Brig. Gen. Henry J. Muller, Jr.	September 1969
Brig. Gen. Charles A. Jackson	July 1970
Lt. Gen. James W. Sutherland	October 1970
Lt. Gen. Welborn G. Dolvin	July 1971
Maj. Gen. Frederick J. Kroesen	April 1972
Maj. Gen. Howard H. Cooksey	June 1972

II Corps Tactical Zone

Brig. Gen. James S. Timothy	June 1966
Maj. Gen. Richard M. Lee	August 1966
Col. Charles A. Cannon	November 1966
Maj. Gen. John W. Barnes	November 1967
Col. Robert M. Piper	January 1968
Brig. Gen. Gordon J. Duquemin	December 1969
Brig. Gen. Jack MacFarlane	July 1970
Lt. Gen. Arthur S. Collins, Jr.	October 1970
Maj. Gen. Charles P. Brown	January 1971
Mr. John Paul Vann	May 1971
Maj. Gen. Michael D. Healy	June 1972

III Corps Tactical Zone

Col. Arndt L. Mueller	June 1966
Col. Gus S. Peters	November 1967
Brig. Gen. Donald D. Dunlop	June 1968
Brig. Gen. Carleton Preer, Jr.	May 1969
Brig. Gen. Dennis P. McAuliffe	January 1970
Lt. Gen. Michael S. Davison	October 1970
Maj. Gen. Jack J. Wagstaff	May 1971
Maj. Gen. James F. Hollingsworth	January 1972
Maj. Gen. Marshall B. Garth	September 1972

IV Corps Tactical Zone

Col. George A. Barton	June 1964
Col. Leroy B. Wilson	June 1966
Brig. Gen. William R. Desorby	August 1966
Maj. Gen. George S. Eckhardt	January 1967
Maj. Gen. Roderick Wetheril	June 1969
Maj. Gen. Hal D. McCown	January 1970
Maj. Gen. John H. Cushman	May 1971
Brig. Gen. Frank E. Blazey	February 1972
Maj. Gen. Thomas M. Tarpley	March 1972

B. U.S. Army Major Commands

U.S. Army, Vietnam (USARV) was established in 1965 to coordinate administrative and logistical support to all U.S. Army units operating in Vietnam. Actual command and control of combat units and operations remained with MACV. On paper, the commander of MACV was also the commander of USARV. In practice, the deputy commander of USARV ran the organization on a day-to-day basis.

In November 1965 the Americans established Field Force, Vietnam, as a corps-level headquarters to control ground combat operations. As the number of U.S. ground combat units grew rapidly, II Field Force, Vietnam, was established in March 1966—with Field Force, Vietnam, redesignated I Field Force, Vietnam. Initially the Americans used the designation "field force" rather than corps to avoid confusion with the geographically based corps tactical zones of the Army of the Republic of Vietnam (ARVN). In February 1968, however, the U.S. Army established its third corps-level headquarters, designating it XXIV Corps. Throughout the war, many U.S. divisions and separate brigades came under the operational control of different field forces/corps at different times.

Most U.S. Army combat forces in Vietnam were organized into divisions. Some units operated as separate brigades. In April 1967 three such separate brigades were organized into a provisional division designated Task Force Oregon. That September, Task Force Oregon was formally organized into the 23d Infantry Division, but retaining only one of Task Force Oregon's three brigades and adding two more.

During the war, most U.S. Army units of similar type remained fairly consistent in organization and strength. A typical U.S. division had between 16,570 and 17,730 soldiers. A division's principal combat forces consisted of 10 or 11 maneuver (infantry, armor, or cavalry) battalions and 4 artillery battalions. A typical infantry battalion had 920 officers and soldiers, while a typical artillery battalion had 641.

U.S. Army, Vietnam

Date formed in Vietnam: 20 July 1965
Date inactivated in Vietnam: 15 May 1972
Headquarters: Long Bình
Major subordinate units:
  1st Logistical Command
  1st Aviation Brigade
  18th Military Police Brigade
  34th General Support Group
  525th Military Intelligence Group
  U.S. Army Engineer Command (Provisional)
Deputy commanding generals, MACV:

Maj. Gen. John Norton	July 1965
Lt. Gen. Jean E. Engler	January 1966
Lt. Gen. Bruce Palmer, Jr.	July 1967
Lt. Gen. Frank T. Mildren	June 1968
Lt. Gen. William J. McCaffrey	July 1970
Maj. Gen. Morgan C. Roseborough	September 1972

I Field Force, Vietnam

Date formed in Vietnam: 15 November 1965
Date inactivated in Vietnam: 30 April 1971
Headquarters: Nha Trang
Subordinate combat units:
  1st Cavalry Division
  4th Infantry Division
  3d Brigade, 25th Infantry Division
  1st Brigade, 101st Airborne Division
  173d Airborne Brigade
  41st Artillery Group
  52d Artillery Group
Commanding generals:

Lt. Gen. Stanley R. Larson	November 1965

Lt. Gen. William R. Peers	March 1968
Lt. Gen. Charles A. Cocoran	March 1969
Lt. Gen. Arthur S. Collins, Jr.	March 1970
Maj. Gen. Charles P. Brown	January 1971

II Field Force, Vietnam

Date formed in Vietnam: 15 March 1966
Date inactivated in Vietnam: 2 May 1971
Headquarters: Long Bình
Subordinate units:

    1st Cavalry Division
    1st Infantry Division
    9th Infantry Division
    25th Infantry Division
    101st Airborne Division
    3d Brigade, 4th Infantry Division
    3d Brigade, 82d Airborne Division
    173d Airborne Brigade
    196th Infantry Brigade
    199th Infantry Brigade
    11th Armored Cavalry Regiment
    23d Artillery Group
    54th Artillery Group

Commanding generals:

Lt. Gen. Jonathan O. Seaman	March 1966
Lt. Gen. Bruce Palmer, Jr.	March 1967
Maj. Gen. Frederick C. Weyand	July 1967
Maj. Gen. Walter T. Kerwin, Jr.	August 1968
Lt. Gen. Julian J. Ewell	April 1969
Lt. Gen. Michael S. Davison	April 1970

XXIV Corps

Date formed in Vietnam: 15 August 1968
Date departed Vietnam: 20 June 1972
Headquarters: Phú Bài, August 1968; Đà Nẵng, March 1970
Subordinate units:

    III Marine Amphibious Force (after March 1970)
    1st Cavalry Division
    23d Infantry Division
    101st Airborne Division
    1st Brigade, 5th Infantry Division
    3d Brigade, 82d Airborne Division
    196th Infantry Brigade
    108th Artillery Group

Commanding generals:

Lt. Gen. William B. Rosson	February 1968
Lt. Gen. Richard G. Stilwell	July 1968
Lt. Gen. Melvin Zais	June 1969
Lt. Gen. James W. Sutherland, Jr.	June 1970
Lt. Gen. Welborn G. Dolvin	June 1971

1st Cavalry Division (Airmobile) ("The First Team")

Date formed: 13 September 1921
Date arrived in Vietnam: 11 September 1965 from Ft. Benning
Date departed Vietnam: 29 April 1971 to Ft. Hood

Headquarters: An Khê, September 1965; Biên Hòa, May 1969
Subordinate combat units:

    1st Battalion, 5th Cavalry
    2d Battalion, 5th Cavalry
    1st Battalion, 7th Cavalry
    2d Battalion, 7th Cavalry
    5th Battalion, 7th Cavalry
    1st Battalion, 8th Cavalry
    2d Battalion, 8th Cavalry
    1st Battalion, 12th Cavalry
    2d Battalion, 12th Cavalry
    1st Squadron, 9th Cavalry
    2d Battalion, 17th Artillery
    2d Battalion, 19th Artillery
    2d Battalion, 20th Artillery
    1st Battalion, 21st Artillery
    1st Battalion, 30th Artillery
    1st Battalion, 77th Artillery
    11th Aviation Group

Principal engagements:

    Ia Drang Valley
    Operation MASHER/WHITE WING
    Operation PAUL REVERE II
    Operation BYRD
    Operation IRVING
    Operation PERSHING
    Operation BOLLING
    Têt Offensive
    Khe Sanh
    Operation PEGASUS
    A Shau Valley
    Cambodia 1970

Commanding generals:

Maj. Gen. Harry W. B. Kinnard	July 1965
Maj. Gen. John Norton	May 1966
Maj. Gen. John J. Tolson III	April 1967
Maj. Gen. George I. Forsythe	July 1968
Maj. Gen. Elvy B. Roberts	May 1969
Maj. Gen. George W. Casey	May 1970
Brig. Gen. Jonathan R. Burton	July 1970
Maj. Gen. George W. Putman, Jr.	July 1970

1st Infantry Division ("Big Red One")

Date formed: 22 December 1917
Date arrived in Vietnam: 2 October 1965 from Ft. Riley
Date departed Vietnam: 15 April 1970 to Ft. Riley
Headquarters: Biên Hòa, October 1965; Dĩ An, February 1966; Lai Khê, October 1967; Dĩ An, November 1969
Subordinate combat units:

    1st Battalion, 2d Infantry
    2d Battalion, 2d Infantry
    1st Battalion, 16th Infantry
    2d Battalion, 16th Infantry
    1st Battalion, 18th Infantry
    2d Battalion, 18th Infantry

1st Battalion, 26th Infantry
1st Battalion, 28th Infantry
2d Battalion, 28th Infantry
1st Squadron, 4th Cavalry
1st Battalion, 5th Artillery
8th Battalion, 6th Artillery
1st Battalion, 7th Artillery
6th Battalion, 15th Artillery
2d Battalion, 33d Artillery
1st Aviation Battalion

Principal engagements:
Operation EL PASO II
Operation ATTLEBORO
Operation CEDAR FALLS
Operation JUNCTION CITY
Tết Offensive
Operation QUYET THANG

Commanding generals:

Maj. Gen. Jonathan O. Seaman	October 1965
Maj. Gen. William E. DePuy	March 1966
Maj. Gen. John H. Hay, Jr.	February 1967
Maj. Gen. Keith L. Ware	March 1968
Maj. Gen. Orwin C. Talbott	September 1968
Maj. Gen. Albert E. Milloy	August 1969
Brig. Gen. John Q. Herrion	March 1970

4th Infantry Division ("Ivy Division")

Date formed: December 1917
Date arrived in Vietnam: 25 September 1966 from Ft. Lewis
Date departed Vietnam: 7 December 1970 to Ft. Carson
Headquarters: Pleiku, September 1966; Đăk Tô, March 1968; Pleiku, April 1968; An Khê, April 1970
Subordinate combat units:

1st Battalion, 8th Infantry
2d Battalion, 8th Infantry
3d Battalion, 8th Infantry
1st Battalion, 12th Infantry
2d Battalion, 12th Infantry
3d Battalion, 12th Infantry
1st Battalion, 14th Infantry
1st Battalion, 22d Infantry
2d Battalion, 22d Infantry
3d Battalion, 22d Infantry
1st Battalion, 35th Infantry
2d Battalion, 35th Infantry
2d Battalion, 34th Armor
1st Battalion, 69th Armor
1st Squadron, 10th Cavalry
2d Battalion, 9th Artillery
5th Battalion, 16th Artillery
6th Battalion, 29th Artillery
4th Battalion, 42d Artillery
2d Battalion, 77th Artillery
4th Aviation Battalion

Principal engagements:
Operation ATTLEBORO
Operation JUNCTION CITY
Operation FRANCIS MARION
Đăk Tô
Tết Offensive
Cambodia 1970
Operation WAYNE GREY
Operation PUTNAM TIGER

Commanding generals:

Brig. Gen. David O. Byars	August 1966
Maj. Gen. Arthur S. Collins, Jr.	September 1966
Maj. Gen. William R. Peers	January 1967
Maj. Gen. Charles P. Stone	January 1968
Maj. Gen. Donn R. Pepke	December 1968
Maj. Gen. Glenn D. Walker	November 1969
Maj. Gen. William A. Burke	July 1970
Brig. Gen. Maurice K. Kendall	December 1970

9th Infantry Division ("Old Reliables")

Date formed: 1 August 1940
Date arrived in Vietnam: 16 December 1966 from Ft. Riley
Date departed Vietnam: 27 August 1969 to Ft. Lewis
Headquarters: Bear Cat, December 1966; Đồng Tâm, August 1968
Subordinate combat units:

6th Battalion, 31st Infantry
2d Battalion, 39th Infantry
3d Battalion, 39th Infantry
4th Battalion, 39th Infantry
2d Battalion, 47th Infantry
3d Battalion, 47th Infantry
4th Battalion, 47th Infantry
2d Battalion, 60th Infantry
3d Battalion, 60th Infantry
5th Battalion, 60th Infantry
3d Squadron, 5th Cavalry
2d Battalion, 4th Artillery
1st Battalion, 11th Artillery
3d Battalion, 34th Artillery
1st Battalion, 84th Artillery
9th Aviation Battalion

Principal engagements:
Operation PALM BEACH
Operation ENTERPRISE
Operation JUNCTION CITY II
Tết Offensive
Operation QUYET THANG
Operation DUONG CUA DAN
Operation SPEEDY EXPRESS
Operation RICE FARMER

Commanding generals:

Maj. Gen. George C. Eckhart	December 1966
Maj. Gen. George C. O'Connor	June 1967
Maj. Gen. Julian J. Ewell	February 1968
Maj. Gen. Harris W. Hollis	April 1969

Task Force Oregon
Date formed in Vietnam: 12 April 1967
Date converted to 23d Infantry Division: 22 September 1967
Headquarters: Chu Lai
Subordinate combat units:
    3d Brigade, 25th Infantry Division
    1st Brigade, 101st Airborne Division
    196th Infantry Brigade
Commanding generals:
    Maj. Gen. William B. Rosson   April 1967
    Maj. Gen. Richard T. Knowles   June 1967

23d Infantry Division ("Americal Division")

Date formed in Vietnam: 22 September 1967
Date inactivated in Vietnam: 29 November 1971
Headquarters: Chu Lai
Subordinate combat units:
    11th Infantry Brigade
    196th Infantry Brigade
    198th Infantry Brigade
    2d Battalion, 1st Infantry
    3d Battalion, 1st Infantry
    4th Battalion, 3d Infantry
    1st Battalion, 6th Infantry
    1st Battalion, 20th Infantry
    3d Battalion, 21st Infantry
    4th Battalion, 21st Infantry
    4th Battalion, 31st Infantry
    1st Battalion, 46th Infantry
    5th Battalion, 46th Infantry
    1st Battalion, 52d Infantry
    6th Battalion, 11th Artillery
    1st Battalion, 14th Artillery
    3d Battalion, 16th Artillery
    3d Battalion, 18th Artillery
    1st Battalion, 82d Artillery
    3d Battalion, 82d Artillery
    16th Aviation Group
Principal engagements:
    Operation WHEELER/WALLOWA
    Operation MUSCATINE
    Têt Offensive
    Operation BURLINGTON TRAIL
    Operation LAMAR PLAIN
Commanding generals:
    Maj. Gen. Samuel W. Koster   September 1967
    Maj. Gen. Charles M. Gettys   June 1968
    Maj. Gen. Lloyd B. Ramsey   June 1969
    Maj. Gen. Albert E. Milloy   March 1970
    Maj. Gen. James L. Baldwin   November 1970
    Maj. Gen. Frederick J. Kroesen, Jr.   July 1971

25th Infantry Division ("Tropic Lightning")

Date formed: 10 October 1941
Date arrived in Vietnam: 28 March 1966 from Schofield Barracks
Date departed Vietnam: 8 December 1970 to Schofield Barracks
Headquarters: Cu Chi
Subordinate combat units:
    1st Battalion, 5th Infantry
    4th Battalion, 9th Infantry
    2d Battalion, 12th Infantry
    1st Battalion, 14th Infantry
    2d Battalion, 14th Infantry
    2d Battalion, 22d Infantry
    3d Battalion, 22d Infantry
    4th Battalion, 23d Infantry
    1st Battalion, 27th Infantry
    2d Battalion, 27th Infantry
    1st Battalion, 35th Infantry
    2d Battalion, 35th Infantry
    2d Battalion, 34th Armor
    1st Battalion, 69th Armor
    3d Squadron, 4th Cavalry
    1st Battalion, 8th Artillery
    2d Battalion, 9th Artillery
    7th Battalion, 11th Artillery
    3d Battalion, 13th Artillery
    2d Battalion, 77th Artillery
    6th Battalion, 77th Artillery
    25th Aviation Battalion
Principal engagements:
    Operation PAUL REVERE
    Operation CEDAR FALLS
    Operation JUNCTION CITY
    Operation YELLOWSTONE
    Têt Offensive
    Operation QUYET THANG
    Operation SARATOGA
    Cambodia 1970
Commanding generals:
    Maj. Gen. Frederick C. Weyand   January 1966
    Maj. Gen. John C. F. Tillson III   March 1967
    Maj. Gen. Fillmore K. Mearns   August 1967
    Maj. Gen. Ellis W. Williamson   August 1968
    Maj. Gen. Harris W. Hollis   September 1969
    Maj. Gen. Edward Baultz, Jr.   April 1970

101st Airborne Division (Airmobile) ("Screaming Eagles")

Date formed: 15 August 1942
Date arrived in Vietnam: 19 November 1967 from Ft. Campbell
Date departed Vietnam: 10 March 1972 to Ft. Campbell
Headquarters: Biên Hòa, November 1967; Huê, February 1968; Biên Hòa, June 1968; Huê/Phú Bài, December 1969
Subordinate combat units:
    3d Battalion, 187th Infantry
    1st Battalion, 327th Infantry
    2d Battalion, 327th Infantry
    1st Battalion, 501st Infantry
    2d Battalion, 501st Infantry
    1st Battalion, 502d Infantry

2d Battalion, 502d Infantry
1st Battalion, 506th Infantry
2d Battalion, 506th Infantry
3d Battalion, 506th Infantry
2d Squadron, 17th Cavalry
2d Battalion, 11th Artillery
1st Battalion, 39th Artillery
4th Battalion, 77th Artillery
2d Battalion, 319th Artillery
2d Battalion, 320th Artillery
1st Battalion, 321st Artillery
101st Aviation Group
Principal engagements:
Têt Offensive
Operation CARENTAN II
Operation TEXAS STAR
Operation APACHE SNOW
Operation LAMAR PLAIN
Operation RANDOLPH GLEN
Operation JEFFERSON GLENN
Operation LAM SỜN 719
Commanding generals:

Maj. Gen. Olinto M. Barsanti	November 1967
Maj. Gen. Melvin Zais	July 1968
Maj. Gen. John M. Wright, Jr.	May 1969
Maj. Gen. John J. Hennessey	May 1970
Maj. Gen. Thomas M. Tarpley	January 1971

1st Brigade, 5th Infantry Division (Mechanized)
Date arrived in Vietnam: 25 July 1968 from Ft. Carson
Date departed Vietnam: 27 August 1971 to Ft. Carson
Headquarters: Quang Tri
Subordinate combat units:
1st Battalion, 11th Infantry
1st Battalion, 61st Infantry
1st Battalion, 77th Armor
5th Battalion, 4th Artillery
Principal engagements:
Operation DEWEY CANYON II
Commanding officers:

Col. Richard J. Glikes	July 1968
Col. James M. Gibson	October 1968
Col. John L. Osteen, Jr.	June 1969
Brig. Gen. William A. Burke	April 1970
Brig. Gen. John G. Hill, Jr.	July 1970
Brig. Gen. Harold H. Dunwoody	May 1971

3d Brigade, 82d Airborne Division
Date arrived in Vietnam: 18 February 1968 from Ft. Bragg
Date departed Vietnam: 11 December 1969 to Ft. Bragg
Headquarters: Huê, February 1968; Sài Gòn, September 1968
Subordinate combat units:
1st Battalion, 505th Infantry
2d Battalion, 505th Infantry
1st Battalion, 508th Infantry

2d Battalion, 321st Artillery
Principal engagements:
Operation CARENTAN II
Commanding officers:

Col. Alex R. Bolling, Jr.	February 1968
Brig. Gen. George W. Dickerson	December 1968

11th Infantry Brigade (Light)
Date arrived in Vietnam: 19 December 1967
Date assigned to 23d Infantry Division: 15 February 1969
Date departed Vietnam: 13 November 1971
Headquarters: Đức Phổ, December 1967; Thê Lợi, July 1971
Subordinate combat units:
3d Battalion, 1st Infantry
4th Battalion, 3d Infantry
1st Battalion, 20th Infantry
4th Battalion, 21st Infantry
6th Battalion, 11th Artillery
Principal engagements:
Operation WHEELER/WALLOWA
Operation MUSCATINE
Têt Offensive
Operation BURLINGTON TRAIL
Operation LAMAR PLAIN
Commanding officers:

Brig. Gen. Andy A. Lipscomb	December 1967
Col. Oran K. Henderson	March 1968
Col. John W. Donalson	October 1968
Col. Jack L. Treadwell	April 1969
Col. Hugh F. T. Hoffman	September 1969
Col. Kendrick B. Barlow	March 1970
Col. John L. Insani	September 1970
Col. Warner S. Goodwin	March 1971

173d Airborne Brigade
Date arrived in Vietnam: 7 May 1965 from Okinawa
Date departed Vietnam: 25 August 1971
Headquarters: Biên Hòa, May 1965; An Khê, November 1967; Bồng Sơn, May 1969
Subordinate combat units:
1st Battalion, 503d Infantry
2d Battalion, 503d Infantry
3d Battalion, 503d Infantry
4th Battalion, 503d Infantry
3d Battalion, 319th Artillery
Principal engagements:
Operation ATTLEBORO
Operation CEDAR FALLS
Operation JUNCTION CITY
Đăk Tô
Têt Offensive
Operation McLAIN
Operation COCHISE GREEN
Operation WASHINGTON GREEN

Commanding officers:

Brig. Gen. Ellis W. Williamson	May 1965
Brig. Gen. Paul F. Smith	February 1966
Brig. Gen. John R. Deane, Jr.	December 1966
Brig. Gen. Leo H. Schweiter	August 1967
Brig. Gen. Richard J. Allen	April 1968
Brig. Gen. John W. Barnes	December 1968
Brig. Gen. Hubert S. Cunningham	August 1969
Brig. Gen. Elmer R. Ochs	August 1970
Brig. Gen. Jack MacFarlane	January 1971

196th Infantry Brigade (Light)

Date arrived in Vietnam: 26 August 1966
Date assigned to Task Force Oregon: 22 September 1967
Date relieved from 23d Infantry Division: 29 November 1971
Date departed Vietnam: 29 June 1972
Headquarters: Tây Ninh, August 1966; Chu Lai, June 1967; Tam Kỳ, November 1967; Phong Điền, April 1968; Hôi An, June 1968; Chu Lai, July 1968; Đà Nẵng, April 1971
Subordinate combat units:

2d Battalion, 1st Infantry
1st Battalion, 6th Infantry
3d Battalion, 21st Infantry
4th Battalion, 31st Infantry
1st Battalion, 46th Infantry
3d Battalion, 82d Artillery

Principal engagements:

Operation ATTLEBORO
Operation JUNCTION CITY
Operation WHEELER/WALLOWA
Operation MUSCATINE
Têt Offensive
Operation BURLINGTON TRAIL
Operation LAMAR PLAIN

Commanding officers:

Brig. Gen. Richard T. Knowles	November 1966
Brig. Gen. Frank H. Linnell	May 1967
Col. Louis Gelling	November 1967
Col. Frederick J. Kroesen, Jr.	June 1968
Col. Thomas H. Tackaberry	May 1969
Col. James M. Lee	November 1969
Col. Edwin L. Kennedy	April 1970
Col. William S. Hathaway	November 1970
Col. Rutland D. Beard, Jr.	June 1971
Brig. Gen. Joseph P. McDonough	November 1971

198th Infantry Brigade (Light)

Date arrived in Vietnam: 21 October 1967
Date assigned to Task Force Oregon: 21 October 1967
Date departed Vietnam: 13 November 1971
Headquarters: Dưc Phồ, October 1967; Chu Lai, December 1967
Subordinate combat units:

1st Battalion, 6th Infantry
1st Battalion, 46th Infantry
5th Battalion, 46th Infantry
1st Battalion, 52d Infantry
1st Battalion, 14th Artillery

Principal engagements:

Operation WHEELER/WALLOWA
Operation MUSCATINE
Têt Offensive
Operation BURLINGTON TRAIL
Operation LAMAR PLAIN

Commanding officers:

Col. J. R. Waldie	October 1967
Col. Charles B. Thomas	June 1968
Col. Robert B. Tully	December 1968
Col. Jere D. Whittington	May 1969
Col. Joseph G. Clemons	November 1969
Col. William R. Richardson	July 1970
Col. Charles R. Smith	March 1971

199th Infantry Brigade (Light)

Date arrived in Vietnam: 10 December 1966
Date departed Vietnam: 11 October 1970
Headquarters: Sông Bé, December 1966; Long Bình, March 1967; Biên Hòa, April 1967; Long Bình, July 1967; Gao Ho Nai, March 1968; Long Bình, July 1968
Subordinate combat units:

2d Battalion, 3d Infantry
3d Battalion, 7th Infantry
4th Battalion, 12th Infantry
5th Battalion, 12th Infantry
2d Battalion, 40th Artillery

Principal engagements:

Operation FAIRFAX
Operation UNIONTOWN
Têt Offensive
Phú Tho Racetrack

Commanding officers:

Brig. Gen. Charles W. Ryder, Jr.	December 1966
Brig. Gen. John F. Freund	March 1967
Brig. Gen. Robert C. Forbes	September 1967
Brig. Gen. Franklin M. Davis, Jr.	May 1968
Col. Frederic E. Davison	August 1968
Brig. Gen. Warren K. Bennett	May 1969
Brig. Gen. William R. Bond	December 1969
Col. Joseph E. Collins	July 1970
Lt. Col. George E. Williams	September 1970

11th Armored Cavalry Regiment ("Black Horse")

Date arrived in Vietnam: 8 September 1966
Date departed Vietnam: 5 March 1971
Headquarters: Biên Hòa, September 1966; Long Bình, December 1966; Xuân Lôc, March 1967; Lai Khê, February 1969; Long Gaio, March 1969; Biên Hòa, October 1969; Dĩ An, July 1970
Subordinate combat units:

1st Squadron, 11th Armored Cavalry
2d Squadron, 11th Armored Cavalry
3d Squadron, 11th Armored Cavalry

Principal engagements:
  Operation CEDAR FALLS
  Operation JUNCTION CITY
  Têt Offensive
  Operation TOAN THANG
  Cambodia 1970
Commanding officers:
  Col. William W. Cobb   September 1966
  Col. Roy W. Farley   May 1967
  Col. Jack MacFarlane   December 1967
  Col. Leonard D. Holder   March 1969
  Col. Charles R. Gorder   March 1968
  Col. George S. Patton   July 1969
  Col. James H. Leach   April 1968
  Col. Donn A. Starry   December 1969
  Col. John L. Gerrity   June 1970
  Col. Wallace H. Nutting

U.S. Army Special Forces, Vietnam (Provisional)
Date formed in Vietnam: September 1962
Date inactivated in Vietnam: 30 September 1964
Headquarters: Nha Trang
Subordinate combat units:
  C-3 Operations Detachment
  B-7 Operations Detachment
  B-130 Operations Detachment
  B-320 Operations Detachment
  B-410 Operations Detachment
Commanding officers:
  Col. George C. Morton   September 1962
  Col. Theodore Leonard   November 1963

5th Special Forces Group (Airborne), 1st Special Forces
Date arrived in Vietnam: 1 October 1964 from Ft. Bragg
Date departed Vietnam: 3 March 1971 to Ft. Bragg
Headquarters: Nha Trang
Subordinate combat units:
  Company A (C-3 Operations Detachment)
  Company B (C-2 Operations Detachment)
  Company C (C-1 Operations Detachment)
  Company D (C-4 Operations Detachment)
  Company E (C-5 Operations Detachment)
Commanding officers:
  Col. John H. Spears   August 1964
  Col. William A. McKean   July 1965
  Col. Francis J. Kelly   June 1968
  Col. Jonathan F. Ladd   June 1968
  Col. Harlod R. Aaron   June 1968
  Col. Robert B. Rheault   May 1969
  Col. Alexander Lemberes   July 1969
  Col. Michael D. Healy   August 1969

1st Aviation Brigade
Date formed in Vietnam: 25 May 1966
Date departed Vietnam: 28 March 1973

Headquarters: Tân Sơn Nhứt, May 1966; Long Bình, December 1967; Tân Sơn Nhứt, December 1972
Subordinate operational and combat units:
  11th Aviation Group
  12th Aviation Group
  16th Aviation Group
  17th Aviation Group
  160th Aviation Group
  164th Aviation Group
  165th Aviation Group
  10th Aviation Battalion
  11th Aviation Battalion
  13th Aviation Battalion
  14th Aviation Battalion
  52d Aviation Battalion
  58th Aviation Battalion
  145th Aviation Battalion
  210th Aviation Battalion
  212th Aviation Battalion
  214th Aviation Battalion
  222d Aviation Battalion
  223d Aviation Battalion
  268th Aviation Battalion
  269th Aviation Battalion
  307th Aviation Battalion
  308th Aviation Battalion
  7th Squadron, 1st Cavalry
  1st Squadron, 9th Cavalry
  3d Squadron, 17th Cavalry
  7th Squadron, 17th Cavalry
Commanding officers:
  Brig. Gen. George P. Seneff   May 1966
  Maj. Gen. Robert R. Williams   November 1967
  Brig. Gen. Allen M. Burdett, Jr.   April 1969
  Brig. Gen. George W. Putnam, Jr.   January 1970
  Col. Samuel G. Cockerham   August 1970
  Brig. Gen. Jack W. Hemingway   August 1970
  Brig. Gen. Robert N. Mackinnon   September 1971
  Brig. Gen. Jack V. Mackmull   September 1972

C. U.S. Marine Corps Major Commands
The major Marine Corps headquarters in Vietnam was the III Marine Amphibious Force (III MAF), roughly the equivalent of a U.S. Army corps. Initially, III MAF reported directly to MACV and was responsible for all U.S. combat operations in the north of the country. The Army's XXIV Corps was subordinate to III MAF. The Marines started withdrawing from Vietnam in 1969, and by early 1970 the Army had the preponderance of U.S. forces in northern South Vietnam. In April 1970 the command relationships reversed, with XXIV Corps now the major subordinate command under MACV, and III MAF reporting to it.

A U.S. Marine division was roughly the equivalent of an Army division, although slightly smaller and more lightly equipped. Whereas Army divisions were organized into three or more brigades, Marine divisions were organized into three or more regiments. The key difference between Army brigades and Marine regiments is that the regiments are composed of permanently organic battalions. Army brigades are purely command and control headquarters, with no permanent battalions. An Army division's combat battalions can be grouped and regrouped under the various brigade headquarters as the mission dictates.

The 1st Marine Air Wing (1st MAW) reported directly to III MAF and provided air support independent of the Seventh Air Force. At its peak, the 1st MAW had three helicopter groups and three fighter-bomber groups for a total of approximately 225 rotary and 250 fixed-wing aircraft.

III Marine Amphibious Force

Date formed in Vietnam: 7 May 1967
Date departed Vietnam: 14 April 1971
Headquarters: Đà Nẵng
Major subordinate commands:
    XXIV Corps (until March 1970)
    1st Marine Division
    3d Marine Division
    1st Marine Air Wing
Commanding officers:

Maj. Gen. William R. Collins	May 1965
Maj. Gen. Lewis W. Walt	June 1965
Maj. Gen. Keith B. McCutcheon	February 1966
Lt. Gen. Lewis W. Walt	March 1966
Lt. Gen. Robert E. Cushman	June 1967
Lt. Gen. Herman Nickerson, Jr.	March 1969
Lt. Gen. Keith B. McCutcheon	March 1970
Lt. Gen. Donn J. Robertson	December 1970

1st Marine Division

Date formed: 1942
Date arrived in Vietnam: February 1966
Date departed Vietnam: April 1971
Headquarters: Chu Lai, February 1966; Đà Nẵng, November 1966
Subordinate combat units:
    1st Marine Regiment
    5th Marine Regiment
    7th Marine Regiment
    11th Marine Regiment (Artillery)
    27th Marine Regiment (attached February 1968 from the 5th Marine Division)
Principal engagements:
    Operation UNION
    Operation SWIFT
    Huê
    Operation HOUSTON
    Operation MAMELUKE THRUST
    Operation TAYLOR COMMON
Commanding generals:

Maj. Gen. Lewis J. Fields	February 1966
Maj. Gen. Herman Nickerson, Jr.	October 1966
Maj. Gen. Donn J. Robertson	October 1967
Maj. Gen. Ormond R. Simpson	December 1968
Maj. Gen. Edwin B. Wheeler	December 1969
Maj. Gen. Charles F. Widdecke	April 1970

3d Marine Division

Date formed: 1942
Date arrived in Vietnam: 6 May 1965
Date departed Vietnam: 30 November 1969
Headquarters: Đà Nẵng, May 1965; Huê, October 1966; Quang Tri, March 1968; Đông Hà, June 1968; Đà Nẵng, November 1969
Subordinate combat units:
    3d Marine Regiment
    4th Marine Regiment
    9th Marine Regiment
    12th Marine Regiment (Artillery)
    26th Marine Regiment (attached April 1967 from the 5th Marine Division)
Principal engagements:
    Operation STARLIGHT
    Operation HASTINGS
    Operation PRAIRIE
    Operation PRAIRIE II
    Operation BUFFALO
    Operation KENTUCKY
    Khe Sanh
    Operation LANCASTER II
    Operation DEWEY CANYON
    Operation APACHE SNOW
Commanding generals:

Maj. Gen. William R. Collins	March 1965
Maj. Gen. Lewis W. Walt	June 1965
Maj. Gen. Wood B. Kyle	March 1966
Maj. Gen. Bruno A. Hochmuth	March 1967
Maj. Gen. Rathvon McC. Tompkins	November 1967
Maj. Gen. Raymond G. Davis	May 1968
Maj. Gen. William K. Jones	April 1969

1st Marine Air Wing

Date arrived in Vietnam: May 1965
Date departed Vietnam: 14 April 1971
Headquarters: Đà Nẵng
Commanding generals:

Maj. Gen. Paul J. Fontana	May 1965
Maj. Gen. Keith B. McCutcheon	June 1965
Maj. Gen. Louis B. Robertshaw	May 1966
Maj. Gen. Norman J. Anderson	June 1967
Maj. Gen. Charles J. Quilter	June 1968
Maj. Gen. William G. Thrash	July 1969
Maj. Gen. Alan J. Armstrong	July 1970

D. U.S. Air Force Major Commands

The 2d Air Division controlled air operations in South Vietnam from October 1962 until it was converted to the Seventh Air Force in April 1966. The commander of the Seventh Air Force also served as MACV's deputy commander for air. Not all Seventh Air Force's operations, however, came directly under MACV's control.

When operating against targets in North Vietnam or Laos, the commander of the Seventh Air Force took his orders from the commander of the Pacific Air Force, who reported to CINCPAC. The Seventh Air Force also did not directly control operations of the 1st MAW. Further muddling the air command and control structure, the U.S. Strategic Air Command, based in Omaha, Nebraska, retained direct control over all B-52 bomber missions flown against Southeast Asian targets.

Another organizational anomaly was the Seventh/Thirteenth Air Force, stationed in Udorn, Thailand. The Seventh/Thirteenth was an air division-size organization taking orders from two different higher headquarters. In operational matters, it took its orders from the Seventh Air Force; for logistical matters, it took its orders from the Thirteenth Air Force, based in the Philippines.

When the 2d Air Division was converted to the Seventh Air Force, it had approximately 30,000 personnel and almost 1,000 aircraft. In 1968 the Seventh/Thirteenth had 35,000 personnel and 600 aircraft.

2d Air Division

Date formed in Vietnam: 8 October 1962
Date converted to Seventh Air Force: 1 April 1966
Headquarters: Tân Sơn Nhứt Air Base
Commanding generals:

Brig. Gen. Rollen H. Anthis	October 1962
Brig. Gen. Robert R. Rowland	December 1962
Brig. Gen. Milton B. Adams	December 1963
Lt. Gen. Joseph H. Moore	January 1964

Seventh Air Force

Date formed in Vietnam: 1 April 1966
Date departed Vietnam: March 1973
Headquarters: Tân Sơn Nhứt Air Base
Subordinate combat units:
    834th Air Division
        483d Tactical Airlift Wing
        315th Special Operations Wing
        Airlift Control Center
        3d Tactical Fighter Wing
        12th Tactical Fighter Wing
        31st Tactical Fighter Wing
        35th Tactical Fighter Wing
        366th Tactical Fighter Wing
        Air Force Advisory Group
Commanding generals:

Lt. Gen. Joseph H. Moore	April 1966
Gen. William W. Momyer	June 1966
Gen. George S. Brown	August 1968
Gen. Lucius D. Clay, Jr.	September 1970
Gen. John D. Lavelle	August 1971
Gen. John W. Vogt, Jr.	April 1972

Seventh/Thirteenth Air Force

Date formed in Thailand: 6 January 1966
Date departed Thailand: April 1973
Headquarters: Udorn, Thailand
Subordinate combat units:
    8th Tactical Fighter Wing
    355th Tactical Fighter Wing
    388th Tactical Fighter Wing
    432d Tactical Reconnaissance Wing
    553d Tactical Reconnaissance Wing
    56th Special Operations Wing
Commanding generals:

Maj. Gen. Charles R. Bond	January 1966
Maj. Gen. William C. Lindley	June 1967
Maj. Gen. Louis T. Seith	June 1968
Maj. Gen. Robert L. Petit	June 1969
Maj. Gen. James F. Kirkendall	March 1970
Maj. Gen. Andrew Evans, Jr.	October 1970
Maj. Gen. DeWitt R. Searles	June 1971
Maj. Gen. James D. Hughes	September 1972

E. U.S. Navy Major Commands

The American naval effort in Vietnam was almost as fragmented as the air effort. U.S. Naval Forces, Vietnam, established in April 1966, reported directly to MACV. Naval Forces, Vietnam, controlled operations on inland waterways and coastal operations in the II, III, and IV CTZs. Naval operations in I CTZ were the responsibility of the III MAF. The U.S. Seventh Fleet, which reported to the commander of the Pacific Fleet and then to CINCPAC, controlled all naval operations beyond South Vietnamese coastal waters and all operations directly against North Vietnam.

The main striking force of the Seventh Fleet was Task Force 77 (TF 77). Consisting of two to three attack carriers and supporting escorts, TF 77 first operated from Dixie Station, and then from Yankee Station after mid-1966. Task Group 70.8, a cruiser and destroyer force, conducted antishipping and shore gunfire operations against the North. Task group 70.8's subordinate Task Unit 70.8.9 provided naval gunfire support to MACV's ground forces in the South. TF 73 was the Fleet's logistical support element, including the hospital ships *Sanctuary* and *Repose*. TF 76 was the Fleet's amphibious element. It conducted the initial landings in Đà Nẵng in March 1965, and in 1969 it conducted Operation BOLD MARINER, the largest amphibious operation of the war.

U.S. Naval Forces, Vietnam, consisted of three main task forces. TF 115 was the Coastal Surveillance Force, operating 81 fast patrol boats and 24 Coast Guard cutters. TF 116 operated as the River Patrol Force, and controlled up to three Sea Air Land (SEAL) platoons at any one time. TF 117 was the Riverine Assault Force, the Navy component of the joint Army-Navy Mobile Riverine Force. Naval Forces, Vietnam, also controlled operations of the approximately 50 U.S. Coast Guard vessels that served in Vietnam.

Seventh Fleet
Date began operating in Vietnam waters: 1961
Date ceased major operations in Vietnam waters: mid-1973
Headquarters: Japan
Major subordinate commands:
  Task Force 73
  Task Force 76
  Task Force 77
  Task Group 70.8
Commanding officers:
  Vice-Adm. Roy L. Johnson   June 1964
  Vice-Adm. Paul P. Blackburn, Jr.   March 1965
  Rear-Adm. Joseph W. Williams   October 1965
  Vice-Adm. John J. Hyland   December 1965
  Vice-Adm. William F. Bringle   November 1967
  Vice-Adm. Maurice F. Weisner   March 1970
  Vice-Adm. William P. Mack   June 1971
  Vice-Adm. James L. Holloway III   May 1972

Naval Forces, Vietnam
Date formed in Vietnam: 1 April 1966
Date inactivated in Vietnam: 29 March 1973
Headquarters: Sài Gòn
Subordinate operational units:
  Task Force 115
  Task Force 116
  Task Force 117
  Naval Advisory Group
  3d Naval Construction Brigade
  Military Sea Transportation Service Office, Vietnam
  Coast Guard Command, Vietnam
    Coast Guard Squadron 1
    Coast Guard Squadron 3
Commanding officers:
  Rear Adm. Norvell G. Ward   April 1966
  Rear Adm. Kenneth L. Veth   April 1967
  Vice-Adm. Elmo R. Zumwalt   September 1968
  Vice-Adm. Jerome H. King   May 1970
  Rear Adm. Robert S. Salzer   April 1971
  Rear Adm. Arthur W. Price, Jr.   June 1972
  Rear Adm. James B. Wilson   August 1972

II. Allied Forces Order of Battle

Seven American allies sent military units and personnel to Vietnam. Both Korea and Thailand provided division-sized units. Australia, New Zealand, and the Philippines sent smaller units. Nationalist China and Spain also sent very small groups of advisors and observers to Vietnam. Between 1964 and 1970 Nationalist China had between 20 and 31 soldiers in Vietnam, and from 1966 to 1970 Spain had between 7 and 13. A very small number of British officers also served in Vietnam while seconded to Australian and New Zealand units.

Allied Strength in Vietnam

	Australia	Korea	New Zealand	Philippines	Thailand
1964	200	200	30	20	—
1965	1,560	20,620	120	70	20
1966	4,530	25,570	160	2,060	240
1967	6,820	47,830	530	2,020	2,220
1968	7,660	50,000	520	1,580	6,000
1969	7,670	48,870	550	190	11,570
1970	6,800	48,540	440	70	11,570
1971	2,000	45,700	100	50	6,000
1972	130	36,790	50	50	40

A. Republic of Korea Forces in Vietnam

Of all America's allies, the Republic of Korea sent the largest contingent of combat forces to Vietnam. At their peak in 1968, Korean forces were organized into two divisions, a Marine Corps brigade and associated support elements—a total of 22 maneuver battalions. They were grouped under a corps-sized headquarters, established in August 1966. Highly respected militarily by both allies and foes, the bulk of the Korean forces did not start to withdraw from Vietnam until January 1973.

Republic of Korea Forces, Vietnam Field Command
Date arrived in Vietnam: August 1966
Date departed Vietnam: 17 March 1973
Headquarters: Nha Trang
Major subordinate units:
  Capital Division
  9th Infantry Division
  2d Marine Corps Brigade
  100th Logistical Command

Capital Division ("Tigers")
Date arrived in Vietnam: 29 September 1965
Date departed Vietnam: 10 March 1973
Headquarters: Qui Nhơn
Subordinate combat units:
  The Cavalry Regiment
  1st Infantry Regiment
  26th Infantry Regiment
  10th Field Artillery Battalion
  60th Field Artillery Battalion
  61st Field Artillery Battalion
  628th Field Artillery Battalion

9th Infantry Division ("White Horse")
Date arrived in Vietnam: 27 September 1966
Date departed Vietnam: 16 March 1973
Headquarters: Ninh Hò
Subordinate combat units:
  28th Infantry Regiment
  29th Infantry Regiment
  30th Infantry Regiment
  30th Field Artillery Battalion
  51st Field Artillery Battalion

52d Field Artillery Battalion
966th Field Artillery Battalion

2d Marine Corps Brigade ("Blue Dragons")

Date arrived in Vietnam: 19 October 1965
Date departed Vietnam: February 1972
Headquarters: Hôi An
Subordinate combat units:
    1st Marine Battalion
    2d Marine Battalion
    3d Marine Battalion
    5th Marine Battalion

B. Thailand Forces in Vietnam

The Royal Thai Army Regiment arrived in Vietnam in September 1967 and operated in conjunction with the U.S. 9th Infantry Division. That regiment rotated back to Thailand in August 1968 and was replaced by the Royal Thai Expeditionary Division. At their peak in 1970 Thai forces fielded six maneuver battalions. They began withdrawing shortly thereafter. By September 1971 only one maneuver brigade and its supporting units remained. That force was redesignated the Royal Thai Army Volunteer Force.

Royal Thai Army Regiment ("Queen's Cobras")

Date arrived in Vietnam: 19 September 1967
Date departed Vietnam: 15 August 1968
Headquarters: Bear Cat

Royal Thai Expeditionary Division ("Black Panthers")

Date arrived in Vietnam: 25 February 1969
Date reorganized to brigade strength: 31 August 1971
Headquarters: Bear Cat
Subordinate combat units:
    1st Royal Thai Army Brigade
    2d Royal Thai Army Brigade
    3d Royal Thai Army Brigade
    1st Artillery Battalion (155-mm)
    1st Artillery Battalion (105-mm)
    2d Artillery Battalion
    3d Artillery Battalion
    1st Armored Cavalry Squadron

Royal Thai Army Volunteer Force

Date formed in Vietnam: 1 September 1971
Date departed Vietnam: March 1972
Headquarters: Sài Gòn
Subordinate combat units:
    2d Royal Thai Army Brigade
    1st Artillery Battalion (155-mm)
    1st Artillery Battalion (105-mm)
    2d Artillery Battalion

C. Australian Forces in Vietnam

The Australians were the first American allies to send military forces to Vietnam. The Australian Army Training Team arrived in July 1962. In 1965 the Australian government decided to commit combat forces to Vietnam, establishing the Australian Army Force, Vietnam. In May 1966, this headquarters was converted to the Australian Forces, Vietnam, a joint headquarters controlling both army and air force units. The 1st Australian Task Force was the principal Australian ground combat headquarters.

The Australians rotated entire battalions in and out of Vietnam. At least 12 different maneuver battalions served in Vietnam at one time or another, with three the maximum number of maneuver battalions in Vietnam at any one time between 1968 and 1970.

Australian Army Training Team, Vietnam (AATTV)

Date arrived in Vietnam: 31 July 1962
Date departed Vietnam: 18 December 1972
Headquarters: Sài Gòn

Australian Army Force, Vietnam (HQ, AAFV)

Date arrived in Vietnam: 25 May 1965
Date reorganized as HQ, AFV: 2 May 1966
Headquarters: Sài Gòn

Australian Forces, Vietnam (HQ, AFV)

Date organized from HQ, AAFV: 3 May 1996
Date departed Vietnam: 15 March 1972
Headquarters: Sài Gòn
Subordinate combat units:
    1st Australian Task Force
    1st Australian Logistic Support Group
    Royal Australian Air Force, Vietnam

1st Australian Task Force

Date formed in Vietnam: 1 April 1966
Date departed Vietnam: 12 March 1972
Headquarters: Núi Đât
Subordinate combat units:
    1st Battalion, Royal Australian Regiment
    2d Battalion, Royal Australian Regiment
    3d Battalion, Royal Australian Regiment
    4th Battalion, Royal Australian Regiment
    5th Battalion, Royal Australian Regiment
    6th Battalion, Royal Australian Regiment
    7th Battalion, Royal Australian Regiment
    8th Battalion, Royal Australian Regiment
    9th Battalion, Royal Australian Regiment
    1st Armoured Personnel Carrier Squadron
    3d Cavalry Regiment
    1st Armoured Regiment
    4th Field Artillery Regiment
    12th Field Artillery Regiment
    1st Special Air Service Squadron

2d Special Air Service Squadron

3d Special Air Service Squadron

Australian Army Assistance Group, Vietnam (AAAGV)

Date formed in Vietnam: 6 March 1972

Date departed Vietnam: 31 January 1973

Headquarters: Sài Gòn

D. New Zealand Forces in Vietnam

Throughout most of the Vietnam War, the New Zealand Battalion of the 28th Commonwealth Brigade was serving in Malaysia. The New Zealanders did, however, send the 161st Field Battery, Royal New Zealand Artillery, to provide fire support for Australian forces. Later, they sent one, then another, rifle company.

New Zealand "V" Force

Date arrived in Vietnam: 21 July 1965

Date departed Vietnam: June 1972

Subordinate combat units:

"V" Rifle Company, Royal New Zealand Infantry

"W" Rifle Company, Royal New Zealand Infantry

161st Field Battery, Royal New Zealand Artillery

Number 4 Troop, Royal New Zealand Special Air Service

E. Philippine Forces in Vietnam

In 1965 the Philippine Army had approximately 70 soldiers in Vietnam. In September 1966 the 1st Philippine Civic Action Group (PHILCAG) arrived and concentrated on pacification missions in Tây Ninh Province. Philippine forces reached their peak strength of slightly more than 2,000 in 1966 and 1967. PHILCAG left Vietnam by the end of 1969.

1st Philippine Civic Action Group, Vietnam

Date formed in Vietnam: 14 September 1966

Date departed Vietnam: 13 December 1969

Headquarters: Tây Ninh

Subordinate units:

Philippine Security Infantry Battalion

Philippine Field Artillery Battalion

Philippine Construction Engineer Battalion

Philippine Medical and Dental Battalion

III. Republic of Vietnam Armed Forces

Many units of the Army of the Republic of Vietnam (ARVN) traced their origins to French colonial units that fought against the Việt Minh. Most of those units originally were turned over to the State of Vietnam. After the establishment of the Republic of Vietnam on 26 October 1955, all ARVN units went through a confusing series of reorganizations and mergers.

Between 1957 and 1963 the ARVN established four corps-level commands that divided responsibility for the security of the country into four corps tactical zones (CTZs). Each of the ARVN's 11 infantry divisions were allocated to a corps. Two elite divisions, the Airborne Division and the Marine Division, constituted the country's strategic reserve and were controlled directly by the Joint General Staff.

Within each of the CTZs, the ARVN designated at least one semiautonomous Special Tactical Zone (STZ) for the purpose of focusing military efforts and resources in critical areas. In addition to the regular forces, the commander of each CTZ also controlled the territorial forces, which consisted of the Civil Guard and the Self-Defense Corps. The latter was later designated the Popular Forces (PF) and the former became the Regional Forces (RF).

I Corps

Date formed: 1 June 1957

Headquarters: Đà Nẵng

Area of responsibility: Quang Tri Province, Thừa Thiên Province, Quang Nam Province, Quang Tín Province, Quang Ngãi Province (after November 1963)

Major subordinate units:

1st Infantry Division

2d Infantry Division

3d Infantry Division

1st Ranger Group

1st Armor Brigade

Special Tactical Zones: Quang Đà Special Zone

Commanding generals:

Lt. Gen. Trân Văn Đôn	15 October 1957
Maj. Gen. Lê Văn Nghiêm	7 December 1962
Maj. Gen. Đỗ Cao Trí	21 August 1963
Lt. Gen. Nguyên Khánh	11 December 1963
Maj. Gen. Tôn Thât Xửng	30 January 1964

RVN Military Strength

	Army	Air Force	Navy	Marine Corps	Regional Forces	Popular Forces
1955	170,000	3,500	2,200	1,500	54,000	48,000
1960	136,000	4,600	4,300	2,000	49,000	48,000
1964	220,000	11,000	12,000	7,000	96,000	168,000
1967	303,000	16,000	16,000	8,000	151,000	149,000
1968	380,000	19,000	19,000	9,000	220,000	173,000
1969	416,000	36,000	30,000	11,000	190,000	214,000
1970	416,000	46,000	40,000	13,000	207,000	246,000
1972	410,000	50,000	42,000	14,000	284,000	248,000

Lt. Gen. Nguyên Chánh Thi	14 November 1964
Maj. Gen. Nguyên Văn Chuân	14 March 1966
Lt. Gen. Tôn Thât Đính	9 April 1966
Maj. Gen. Huỳnh Văn Cao	15 May 1966
Gen. Trân Thanh Phong	20 May 1966
Lt. Gen. Hoàng Xuân Lãm	30 May 1966
Lt. Gen. Ngô Quang Trưởng	3 May 1972

II Corps

Date formed: 1 October 1957

Headquarters: Pleiku

Area of responsibility: Kontum Province, Bình Đinh Province, Pleiku Province, Phú Bôn Province, Phú Yên Province, Darlac Province, Khánh Hòa Province, Quang Đưc Province, Tuyên Đưc Province, Ninh Thuân Province, Lâm Đông Province, Bình Thuân Province

Major subordinate units:
    22d Infantry Division
    23d Infantry Division
    2d Ranger Group
    2d Armor Brigade

Special Tactical Zones: 24th Special Tactical Zone

Commanding generals:

Maj. Gen. Trân Ngoc Tám	1 October 1957
Maj. Gen. Tôn Thât Đính	13 August 1958
Lt. Gen. Nguyên Khánh	20 December 1962
Lt. Gen. Đô Cao Trí	12 December 1963
Maj. Gen. Nguyên Hửu Có	15 September 1964
Lt. Gen. Vĩnh Lôc	23 June 1965
Lt. Gen. Lư Lan	28 February 1968
Lt. Gen. Ngô Dzu	28 August 1970
Maj. Gen. Nguyên Văn Toàn	10 May 1972
Maj. Gen. Pham Văn Phú	30 October 1974

III Corps

Date formed: 1 March 1959 (provisional); 20 May 1960 (permanent)

Headquarters: Biên Hòa

Area of responsibility: Phưởc Long Province, Long Khánh Province, Bình Tuy Province, Bình Long Province, Bình Dưởng Province, Biên Hòa Province, Phưởc Tuy Province, Tây Ninh Province, Hâu Nghĩa Province, Long An Province

Major subordinate units:
    5th Infantry Division
    18th Infantry Division
    25th Infantry Division
    81st Ranger Group
    3d Armor Brigade

Special Tactical Zones: Capital Military District, Rưng Sát Special Zone

Commanding generals:

Lt. Gen. Thái Quang Hoàng	1 March 1959
Lt. Gen. Nguyên Ngoc Lê	11 October 1959
Maj. Gen. Lê Văn Nghiêm	5 May 1960
Maj. Gen. Tôn Thât Đính	7 December 1962

Lt. Gen. Trân Thiên Khiêm	5 January 1964
Maj. Gen. Lâm Văn Phát	2 February 1964
Lt. Gen. Trân Ngoc Tám	4 April 1964
Maj. Gen. Cao Văn Viên	12 October 1964
Maj. Gen. Nguyên Bao Tri	11 October 1965
Lt. Gen. Lê Nguyên Khang	9 June 1966
Lt. Gen. Đô Cao Trí	5 August 1968
Lt. Gen. Nguyên Văn Minh	23 February 1971
Lt. Gen. Pham Quôc Thuân	29 October 1973
Lt. Gen. Dư Quôc Đông	30 October 1974
Lt. Gen. Nguyên Văn Toàn	January 1975

IV Corps

Date formed: 1 January 1963

Headquarters: Cân Thơ

Area of responsibility: Gò Công Province, Kiên Tưởng Province, Đinh Tưởng Province, Kiên Hòa Province, Kiên Phong Province, Sa Đéc Province, Vĩnh Long Province, Vĩnh Bình Province, Châu Đôc Province, An Giang Province, Phong Dinh Province, Ba Xuyên Province, Kiên Giang Province, Chưởng Thiên Province, Băc Liêu Province, An Xuyên Province

Major subordinate units:
    7th Infantry Division
    9th Infantry Division
    21st Infantry Division
    4th Ranger Group
    4th Armor Brigade

Special Tactical Zones: 44th Special Tactical Zone

Commanding generals:

Maj. Gen. Huỳnh Văn Cao	1 January 1963
Maj. Gen. Nguyên Hửu Có	4 November 1963
Maj. Gen. Dưởng Văn Đưc	4 March 1964
Maj. Gen. Nguyên Văn Thiêu	15 September 1964
Lt. Col. Đăng Văn Quang	20 January 1965
Maj. Gen. Nguyên Văn Manh	23 November 1966
Lt. Gen. Nguyên Đưc Thăng	29 February 1968
Lt. Gen. Nguyên Viêt Thanh	1 July 1968
Maj. Gen. Ngô Dzu	1 May 1970
Lt. Gen. Ngô Quang Trưởng	21 August 1970
Maj. Gen. Nguyên Vĩnh Nghi	4 May 1972
Maj. Gen. Nguyên Khoa Nam	30 October 1974

1st Infantry Division

Date formed: 1 January 1955

Origins and redesignations:
    21st Mobile Group (French), 1 September 1953
    21st Infantry Division, 1 January 1955
    21st Field Division, 1 August 1955
    1st Field Division, 1 November 1955
    1st Infantry Division, 1 January 1959

Headquarters: Huê

Subordinate combat units:
    1st Infantry Regiment
    3d Infantry Regiment
    51st Infantry Regiment

54th Infantry Regiment
Principal engagements:
    Huê Uprising 1966
    Huê
    Operation LAM SƠN 719
    Spring 1975, Huê
Commanding officers:
    Lt. Col. Lê Văn Nghiêm   1 January 1955
    Col. Tôn Thât Xửng
    Col. Tôn Thât Đính
    Col. Nguyên Văn Thiêu   ca. 1957
    Gen. Đồ Cao Trí   ca. 1963
    Gen. Nguyên Chánh Thi   ca. 1964
    Maj. Gen. Nguyên Văn Chuân   ca. 1965
    Gen. Phan Xuân Nhuân   12 March 1966
    Lt. Gen. Ngô Quang Trưởng   June 1966
    Maj. Gen. Pham Văn Phú   21 August 1970
    Brig. Gen. Lê Văn Thân   ca. 1973
    Maj. Gen. Nguyên Văn Điêm   31 October 1974

2d Infantry Division
Date formed: 1 February 1955
Origins and redesignations:
    32d Mobile Group (French), 3 November 1953
    32d Infantry Division, 1 February 1955
    32d Field Division, 1 August 1955
    2d Field Division, 1 November 1955
    2d Infantry Division, 1 January 1959
Headquarters: Đà Năng, 1955; Quang Ngãi, 1965; Chu Lai, 1972; Hàm Tân, 1975
Subordinate combat units:
    4th Infantry Regiment
    5th Infantry Regiment
    6th Infantry Regiment
Principal engagements:
    Spring 1975, Chu Lai
    Spring 1975, Tam Kỳ
    Spring 1975, Phan Rang
Commanding officers:
    Col. Tôn Thât Đính   1 January 1955
    Lt. Col. Đăng Văn Sơn   22 November 1956
    Lt. Col. Lê Quang Trong   14 June 1957
    Col. Dưởng Ngoc Lăm   23 August 1958
    Col. Lâm Văn Phát   8 June 1961
    Col. Trưởng Văn Chưởng   18 June 1963
    Brig. Gen. Tôn Thât Xửng   6 December 1963
    Brig. Gen. Ngô Dzu   30 January 1964
    Col. Nguyên Thanh Săng   29 July 1964
    Maj. Gen. Hoàng Xuân Lãm   15 October 1964
    Maj. Gen. Nguyên Văn Toàn   10 January 1967
    Brig. Gen. Phan Hòa Hiêp   22 January 1972
    Brig. Gen. Trân Văn Nhưt   27 August 1972

3d Infantry Division
Date formed: 1 October 1971

Origins and redesignations: None
Headquarters: Ái Tư, 1971; Đà Năng, 1972
Subordinate combat units:
    2d Infantry Regiment
    56th Infantry Regiment
    57th Infantry Regiment
Principal engagements:
    Easter Offensive, Quang Tri
    Spring 1975, Đà Năng
Commanding officers:
    Brig. Gen. Vũ Văn Giai   1 October 1971
    Maj. Gen. Nguyên Duy Hinh   9 June 1975

5th Infantry Division
Date formed: 1 February 1955
Origins and redesignations:
    6th Infantry Division, 1 February 1955
    6th Field Division, 1 August 1955
    41st Field Division, 1 September 1955
    3d Field Division, 1 November 1955
    5th Infantry Division, 1 January 1959
Headquarters:
    Sông Mao, 1955; Biên Hòa, 1961; Phú Lởi, 1964; Lai Khê, 1970
Subordinate combat units:
    7th Infantry Regiment
    8th Infantry Regiment
    9th Infantry Regiment
Principal engagements:
    Cambodia 1970
    Easter Offensive, An Lôc
    Phước Long
    Spring 1975, Bên Cát
Commanding officers:
    Col. Vòng A Sáng   1 March 1955
    Col. Pham Văn Đông   25 October 1956
    Lt. Col. Nguyên Quang Thông   18 March 1958
    Col. Tôn Thât Xửng   16 September 1958
    Lt. Col. Đăng Văn Sơn   19 November 1958
    Col. Nguyên Văn Chuân   3 August 1959
    Brig. Gen. Trân Ngoc Tám   20 May 1961
    Col. Nguyên Đửc Thăng   16 October 1961
    Col. Nguyên Văn Thiêu   20 December 1962
    Brig. Gen. Đăng Thanh Liêm   2 February 1964
    Brig. Gen. Cao Hao Hửn   5 June 1964
    Brig. Gen. Trân Thanh Phong   21 October 1964
    Maj. Gen. Pham Quôc Thuân   19 July 1965
    Maj. Gen. Nguyên Văn Hiêu   15 August 1969
    Brig. Gen. Lê Văn Hưng   14 June 1971
    Brig. Gen. Trân Quôc Lich   4 September 1972
    Col. Lê Nguyên Vy   7 November 1973

7th Infantry Division
Date formed: 1 January 1955
Origins and redesignations:
    7th Mobile Group (French)

2d Mobile Group (French)

31st Mobile Group (French), 1 September 1953

31st Infantry Division, 1 January 1955

31st Field Division, 1 August 1955

11th Field Division, August 1955

4th Field Division, 1 November 1955

7th Infantry Division, 1 January 1959

Headquarters: Tam Kỳ, 1955; Biên Hòa, 1955; My Tho, 1961;
Đông Tâm, 1969

Subordinate combat units:

    10th Infantry Regiment

    11th Infantry Regiment

    12th Infantry Regiment

Principal engagements:

    Operations against Hòa Hao Forces 1956

    Cambodia 1970

    Easter Offensive, Cambodian Border

    Spring 1975, Tân An

Commanding officers:

Lt. Col. Nguyên Hữu Có	1 January 1955
Col. Tôn Thât Xửng	15 June 1955
Lt. Col. Ngô Dzu	27 April 1957
Col. Trân Thiên Khiêm	17 March 1958
Col. Huỳnh Văn Cao	30 March 1959
Col. Bùi Đình Đam	22 December 1962
Brig. Gen. Nguyên Hữu Có	1 November 1963
Col. Pham Văn Đông	5 November 1963
Brig. Gen. Lâm Văn Phát	2 December 1963
Col. Bùi Hữu Nhơn	2 February 1964
Col. Huỳnh Văn Tôn	7 March 1964
Brig. Gen. Nguyên Bao Tri	16 September 1964
Brig. Gen. Nguyên Viêt Thanh	9 October 1965
Brig. Gen. Nguyên Thanh Hoàng	3 July 1968
Maj. Gen. Nguyên Khoa Nam	16 January 1970
Gen. Trân Văn Hai	30 October 1974

9th Infantry Division

Date formed: 1 January 1962

Origins and redesignations: None

Headquarters: Phú Thanh, 1962; Sa Đéc, 1963; Vĩnh Long, 1972

Subordinate combat units:

    14th Infantry Regiment

    15th Infantry Regiment

    16th Infantry Regiment

Principal engagements:

    Cambodia 1970

    Easter Offensive, An Lôc

    Spring 1975, Mekong Delta

Commanding officers:

Col. Bùi Dzinh	1 January 1962
Col. Đoàn Văn Quang	7 November 1963
Brig. Gen. Vĩnh Lôc	9 February 1964
Brig. Gen. Lâm Quang Thi	29 May 1965
Maj. Gen. Trân Bá Di	3 July 1968
Brig. Gen. Huỳnh Văn Lac	26 October 1973

18th Infantry Division

Date formed: 16 May 1965 (provisional); 1 August 1965
(permanent)

Origins and redesignations:

    10th Infantry Division, 16 May 1965

    18th Infantry Division, 1 January 1967

Headquarters: Xuân Lôc

Subordinate combat units:

    43d Infantry Regiment

    48th Infantry Regiment

    52d Infantry Regiment

Principal engagements:

    Easter Offensive, An Lôc

    Spring 1975, Xuân Lôc

Commanding officers:

Col. Nguyên Văn Manh	5 June 1965
Brig. Gen. Lử Lan	20 August 1965
Brig. Gen. Đô Kê Giai	16 September 1966
Maj. Gen. Lâm Quang Thơ	20 August 1969
Brig. Gen. Lê Minh Đao	4 April 1972

21st Infantry Division

Date formed: 1 June 1959

Origins and redesignations:

    1st Light Division, 1 August 1955

    11th Light Division, 1 November 1955

    3d Light Division, 1 August 1955

    13th Light Division, 1 November 1955

    Merged as 21st Infantry Division, 1 June 1959

Headquarters: Sa Đéc, 1959; Bắc Liêu, 1960

Subordinate combat units:

    31st Infantry Regiment

    32d Infantry Regiment

    33d Infantry Regiment

Principal engagements:

    Operations against Hòa Hao Forces 1956

    U Minh Forest

    Easter Offensive, An Lôc

    Spring 1975, Mekong Delta

Commanding officers:

Lt. Col. Nguyên Bao Tri	1 June 1959
Lt. Col. Trân Thanh Chiêu	8 September 1959
Col. Trân Thiên Khiêm	2 February 1960
Col. Bùi Hữu Nhơn	December 1962
Col. Cao Hao Hưn	November 1963
Brig. Gen. Đăng Văn Quang	1 June 1964
Col. Nguyên Văn Phước	20 January 1965
Brig. Gen. Nguyên Văn Minh	21 March 1965
Maj. Gen. Nguyên Vĩnh Nghi	13 June 1968
Brig. Gen. Hô Trung Hâu	3 May 1972
Brig. Gen. Chưởng Dzanh Quay	21 August 1972
Brig. Gen. Lê Văn Hưng	9 June 1973

22d Infantry Division:

Date formed: 1 April 1959

Origins and redesignations:

    2d Light Division, 1 August 1955

    12th Light Division, 1 November 1955 (disbanded 31 March 1959; troops incorporated into the 22d Infantry Division)

    4th Light Division, 1 August 1955

    14th Light Division, 1 November 1955

    22d Infantry Division, 1 April 1959

Headquarters: Kontum, 1959; Bà Gi, 1965; Bình Đinh, 1972; Tân An, 1975

Subordinate combat units:

    40th Infantry Regiment

    42d Infantry Regiment

    47th Infantry Regiment

Principal engagements:

    Operations against Hòa Hao Forces 1956

    Easter Offensive, Kontum

    Spring 1975, Bình Đinh

    Spring 1975, Tân An

Commanding officers:

Lt. Col. Trân Thanh Chiêu	1 April 1959
Lt. Col. Nguyên Bao Tri	8 September 1959
Col. Nguyên Thanh Săng	5 November 1963
Brig. Gen. Linh Quang Viên	5 February 1964
Col. Nguyên Văn Hiêu	7 September 1964
Brig. Gen. Nguyên Xuân Thinh	24 October 1964
Brig. Gen. Nguyên Thanh Săng	1 March 1965
Brig. Gen. Nguyên Văn Hiêu	28 June 1966
Brig. Gen. Lê Ngoc Triên	11 August 1969
Col. Lê Đưc Đat	1 March 1972
Brig. Gen. Phan Đình Niêm	28 April 1972

23d Infantry Division

Date formed: 1 April 1959

Origins and redesignations:

    5th Light Division, 1 August 1955

    15th Light Division, 1 November 1955

    23d Infantry Division, 1 April 1959

Headquarters: Nha Trang, 1955; Duc My, 1956; Ban Mê Thuôt, 1961; Long Hai, 1975

Subordinate combat units:

    41st Infantry Regiment

    44th Infantry Regiment

    45th Infantry Regiment

    53d Infantry Regiment

Principal engagements:

    Operations against Hòa Hao Forces 1956

    Cambodia 1970

    Easter Offensive, Kontum

    Spring 1975, Ban Mê Thuôt

Commanding officers:

Lt. Col. Trân Thanh Phong	19 May 1959
Col. Lê Quang Trong	17 May 1963
Brig. Gen. Hoàng Xuân Lãm	14 December 1963
Brig. Gen. Lư Lan	14 October 1964
Brig. Gen. Nguyên Văn Manh	20 August 1965

Brig. Gen. Trưởng Quang Ân	24 November 1966
Brig. Gen. Vo Văn Canh	9 September 1968
Brig. Gen. Lý Tòng Bá	25 January 1972
Brig. Gen. Trân Văn Câm	20 October 1972
Brig. Gen. Lê Trung Tưởng	24 November 1973

25th Infantry Division

Date formed: 1 July 1962

Origins and redesignations: None

Headquarters: Thuân Hòa, 1962; Cây Điêp, 1964; Cu Chi, 1970

Subordinate combat units:

    46th Infantry Regiment

    49th Infantry Regiment

    50th Infantry Regiment

Principal engagements:

    Cambodia 1970

    Easter Offensive, An Lôc

    Spring 1975, Tây Ninh

    Spring 1975, Cu Chi

Commanding officers:

Col. Nguyên Văn Chuân	July 1962
Col. Lư Lan	28 December 1962
Col. Nguyên Viêt Đam	19 March 1964
Brig. Gen. Nguyên Thanh Săng	December 1964
Brig. Gen. Phan Trong Chinh	16 March 1965
Lt. Gen. Nguyên Xuân Thinh	10 January 1968
Brig. Gen. Lư Văn Tư	25 January 1972
Col. Nguyên Hưu Toán	7 November 1973
Brig. Gen. Lý Tòng Bá	April 1975

Airborne Division

Date formed: 1 May 1955

Origins and redesignations:

    1st Airborne Battalion (French), 1 August 1951

    Groupment Aéroporté 3 (French), 1 May 1954

    Airborne Group, 1 May 1955

    Airborne Brigade, 1 December 1959

    Airborne Division, 1 December 1965

Headquarters:

    Tân Sơn Nhưt, 1955

    Quang Tri (Forward HQ), 1972

Subordinate combat units:

    1st Airborne Brigade

    2d Airborne Brigade

    3d Airborne Brigade

    7th Ranger Group

Principal engagements:

    Đăk Tô

    Têt Offensive

    Cambodia 1970

    Operation LAM SỞN 719

    Easter Offensive, Quang Tri

    Spring 1975, Nha Trang

    Spring 1975, Phan Rang

    Spring 1975, Xuân Lôc

Commanding officers:

Lt. Col. Đỗ Cao Trí	1 March 1955
Col. Nguyên Chánh Thi	1 September 1956
Col. Cao Văn Viên	12 November 1960
Lt. Gen. Dư Quốc Đông	19 December 1964
Brig. Gen. Lê Quang Lưởng	11 November 1972

Marine Division:

Date Formed: 1 October 1954

Origins and redesignations:

1st and 2d Battalions de Marche (French)

Marine Infantry Battalion, 1 October 1954

Marine Infantry Group, 16 April 1956

Marine Brigade, 1 January 1962

Marine Division, 1 October 1968

Headquarters:

Sà Gòn, 1954

Vũng Tàu, 1975

Subordinate combat units:

147th Marine Brigade

258th Marine Brigade

369th Marine Brigade

Principal engagements:

Tết Offensive

Cambodia 1970

Operation LAM SƠN 719

Easter Offensive, Quang Tri

Spring 1975, Đà Nẵng

Spring 1975, Vũng Tàu

Commanding officers:

Lt. Col. Lê Quang Trong	1 October 1954
Maj. Pham Văn Liêu	16 January 1956
Capt. Bùi Pho Chi	31 July 1956
Maj. Lê Như Hùng	30 September 1956
Maj. Lê Nguyên Khang	7 May 1960
Lt. Col. Nguyên Bá Liên	16 December 1963
Lt. Gen. Lê Nguyên Khang	26 February 1964
Brig. Gen. Bùi Thê Lân	5 May 1972

IV. People's Army of Vietnam and the National Liberation Front

The People's Army of Vietnam (PAVN) was the lineal successor of the Việt Minh force that defeated the French. Most of the Việt Minh divisions that fought in the Red River Delta and at Điên Biên Phu have continued with the same designations through the 1990s.

As with armies of all Communist nations, the PAVN was organized to give the party tremendous influence over its daily operations. At all echelons political officers had equal authority with commanders, but theoretically different responsibilities.

In October 1945 the Việt Minh organized all of Vietnam into 14 military regions. In 1950 the 14 were reorganized into 9 military regions, with a special military zone in the Central Highlands, another for Hà Nôi, and later another for Sài Gòn–Gia Định. The PAVN retained this system after the 1954 partition and throughout the Vietnam War. Military Regions 5 through 9 comprised South Vietnam. In 1961 Maj. Gen. Trân Lưởng (aka Trân Nam Trung) established the Central Office for South Vietnam (COSVN), representing the Party Central Committee to coordinate all military operations in Military Regions 6, 7, 8, 9, and the Sài Gòn–Gia Định Special Zone. COSVN was primarily located just inside Cambodia, opposite Tây Ninh Province.

The People's Liberation Armed Forces (PLAF) was officially the armed wing of the National Liberation Front (aka Việt Công [VC]). Despite the official fiction that the PAVN and PLAF were separate and distinct, VC military units actually operated under the direct command of COSVN. As the war progressed, PAVN and VC regiments and battalions often were grouped in the same division. VC units suffered huge losses in the 1968 Tết Offensive and many were never again battlefield-effective units. After Tết, PAVN units increasingly carried the weight of the war. The PAVN officially absorbed the PLAF in June 1976.

The PLAF's first corps-level organization was the 559th Transportation Group. Composed of an infantry division, an engineering division, a transportation division, an antiaircraft division, and three sector divisions, the 559th Group ran operations along the Hồ Chí Minh Trail. The PLAF's first corps of main force combat units was LXX Corps, established in October 1970.

The 301st Group, established with three main force divisions in March 1971, was redesignated IV Corps in July 1974. Between October 1973 and March 1975 the PAVN established three other corps, all of which played key command and control roles in the final spring 1975 campaign.

Starting in March 1965 PAVN divisions deploying to the South started the practice of leaving cadre or "frame" units in the North. The frame units raised and trained replacement units and provided the strategic reserve for the defense of the North. Replacement units received the same numerical designation as the frame unit, followed by a letter designation. Thus, the 325th Infantry Division spawned the 325-B, 325-C, and 325-D Infantry Divisions between 1964 and 1966. In 1964 the 325th was redesignated 325-A. The 325-B and 325-C Infantry Divisions were eventually devastated by long combat operations in the South. In 1972 the 325-D Infantry Division was redesignated the 325th Infantry Division. This practice, of course, caused a great deal of confusion among Allied OB analysts.

When the Vietnam War ended in 1975, the North Vietnamese had 685,000 regular troops under arms. The ground forces consisted of 24 divisions and 3 training divisions, 15 surface-to-air missile (SAM) regiments, and 40 antiaircraft artillery gun regiments. The North Vietnamese Navy had 3,000 troops; the Air Force, another 12,000. The Air Force had one light bomber squadron, four MiG-21 interceptor squadrons, two MiG-19 interceptor squadrons, and six MiG-15/17 fighter-bomber squadrons. In addition to the regular forces, the North Vietnamese had some 50,000 troops in the Frontier Force, the Coast Security Force, and the People's Armed Security Force, plus a militia of nearly 1.5 million.

A. PAVN High Command

Commander in Chief and Minister of National Defense:

Sr. Gen. Võ Nguyên Giáp	December 1945–February 1980

Chiefs of Staff:

Maj. Gen. Hoàng Văn Thái	December 1945–1953
Sr. Gen. Văn Tiến Dũng	1953–1980

Commanding Generals, Political General Directorate:

Gen. Nguyên Chí Thanh	June 1950–1961
Lt. Gen. Song Hào	1961–ca. December 1975
Sen. Gen. Chu Huy Mân	ca. April 1977–ca. October 1984

Commanding Generals, Rear Services General Directorate:

Maj. Gen. Đinh Đức Thiên	April 1971–April 1975
Lt. Gen. Bùi Phùng	April 1975–ca. June 1984

First Secretaries, Central Office for South Vietnam (COSVN):

Military Committee/Military Affairs Party Committee

Maj. Gen. Trân Lưởng	May 1961–October 1963
Nguyên Văn Linh	October 1963–1964
Sr. Gen. Nguyên Chí Thanh	1964–June 1967
Pham Hùng	June 1967–May 1975

Commanding Generals, Southern Regional Military Headquarters

Col. Gen. Trân Văn Trà	October 1963–January 1967
Lt. Gen. Hoàng Văn Trà	January 1967–1973
Col. Gen. Trân Văn Trà	1973–May 1975

B. Navy Branch

Date formed: 7 May 1955

Commanding officers:

Maj. Gen. Ta Xuân Thu	January 1959
Sr. Col. Nguyên Bá Phát	March 1967
Sr. Col. Đoàn Bá Khanh	late 1974

Political officers:

Maj. Gen. Ta Xuân Thu	January 1959
Sr. Col. Đoàn Phung	March 1967
Hoàng Trà	April 1970
Sr. Col. Trân Văn Giang	late 1974

C. Air Force Branch

Date formed: 3 March 1955

Commanding officers:

Sr. Col. Đăng Tính	September 1955
Col. Nguyên Văn Tiên	March 1967
Col. Đào Đình Luyên	1970s

Political officers:

Col. Hoàng Thê Thiên	September 1956
Col. Phan Khăc Hy	March 1967
Lt. Col. Đô Long	1970s

D. Air Defense–Air Force Branch

Date formed: 22 October 1963

Subordinate units:

361st Antiaircraft Artillery Division
363d Antiaircraft Artillery Division
365th Antiaircraft Artillery Division
367th Antiaircraft Artillery Division
368th Antiaircraft Artillery Division
369th Antiaircraft Artillery Division
371st Antiaircraft Artillery Division
377th Antiaircraft Artillery Division

Commanding officers:

Sr. Col. Phùng Thê Tài	October 1963
Sr. Col. Lê Văn Trí	April 1973

Political officers:

Sr. Col. Đăng Tính	October 1963
Hoàng Phường	1975

E. Regional Commands

Military Region 1
Area of responsibility: Viêt Băc, Northeast North Vietnam

Military Region 2
Area of responsibility: Tây Băc, Northwest North Vietnam
Commanding officer:

Lt. Gen. Vũ Lâp	ca. April 1979

Military Region 3
Area of responsibility: Southern Red River Delta, North Vietnam
Commanding officer:

Maj. Gen. Hoàng Sâm	ca. 1965

Military Region 4
Area of responsibility: "Panhandle," North Vietnam
Commanding officers:

Maj. Gen. Trân Văn Quang	1965
Lt. Gen. Đàm Quang Trung	ca. December 1975
Lt. Gen. Lê Quang Hòa	ca. December 1975

Military Region 5
Area of responsibility: Quang Tri, Thưa Thiên, Quang Nam, Quang Tín, Quang Ngãi, Bình Đinh, Pleiku, Phú Bôn, and Phú Yên Provinces, South Vietnam
Commanding officers:

Maj. Gen. Nguyên Đôn	1961
Lt. Gen. Hoàng Văn Thái	August 1966
Lt. Gen. Chu Huy Mân	ca. 1970
Lt. Gen. Đoàn Khuê	ca. 1977

Military Region 6
Area of responsibility: Quang Đưc, Tuyên Đưc, Ninh Thuân, Bình Thuân, Lâm Đông, and Bình Tuy Provinces, South Vietnam
Commanding officer:

Sr. Col. Nguyên Trong Xuyên	ca. January 1975

Military Region 7
Area of responsibility: Phước Long, Long Khánh, Phước Tuy, Bình Long, Bình Dưởng, Biên Hòa, Tây Ninh, and Hâu Nghĩa Provinces, South Vietnam

Commanding officers:

Nguyên Văn Xuyên	ca. 1946
Col. Lê Văn Ngoc	ca. 1975
Col. Gen. Trân Văn Trũ	ca. 1976

Military Region 8
Area of responsibility: Long An, Kiên Tường, Kiên Phong, Đinh
Tường, Gò Công, and Kiên Hòa Provinces, South Vietnam
Commanding officer:

Trân Văn Trà	ca. 1946

Military Region 9
Area of responsibility: Châu Đôc, An Giang, Vĩnh Long, Phong
Dinh, Vĩnh Bình, Ba Xuyên, Kiên Giang, Băc Liêu, Chường Thiên,
and An Xuyên Provinces, South Vietnam
Commanding officers:

Lê Đức Anh	ca. December 1965
Phan Ngoc Hùng	ca. 1975

*Sài Gòn–Gia Định Special Zone (merged with Military
Region 7 in October 1967)*
Area of responsibility: Rừng Sát Special Zone, Lòng Tào River,
Tân Sơn Nhưt Air Base, Long Bình

F. Main Force Combat Units
I Military Corps (Quyêt Thăng Corps)
Date formed: 24 October 1973
Subordinate units:

    308th Infantry Division
    312th Infantry Division
    320-B Infantry Division
    367th Antiaircraft Artillery Division
    45th Artillery Brigade
    202d Tank Brigade
    299th Engineer Brigade
    140th Signal Regiment
Principal engagements:
    Spring 1975, Sài Gòn
Commanding officers:

Maj. Gen. Lê Trong Tân	October 1973
Maj. Gen. Nguyên Hoa	ca. March 1975

Political officers:

Maj. Gen. Lê Quang Hòa	October 1973
Maj. Gen. Hông Minh Thi	ca. March 1975

II Military Corps
Date formed: 17 May 1974
Subordinate units:

    304th Infantry Division
    324th Infantry Division
    325th Infantry Division
    367th Antiaircraft Artillery Division
    203d Tank Brigade
    164th Artillery Brigade

    219th Engineer Brigade
    463d Signal Regiment
Principal engagements:
    Spring 1975, Huê
    Spring 1975, Đà Năng
    Spring 1975, Phan Rang
Commanding officers:

Lt. Gen. Hoàng Văn Thái	1974
Maj. Gen. Nguyên Hửu An	1975

Political officer:

Maj. Gen. Lê Linh	1974

III Military Corps (Tây Nguyên Corps)
Date formed: 26 March 1975
Subordinate units:

    10th Infantry Division
    320th Infantry Division
    316th Infantry Division
    40th Artillery Regiment
    675th Artillery Regiment
    234th Antiaircraft Regiment
    593d Antiaircraft Artillery Regiment
    273d Tank Regiment
    7th Engineer Regiment
    29th Signal Regiment
Principal engagement:
    Spring 1975, Sài Gòn
Commanding officer:

Vũ Lăng	March 1975

Political officer:

Đăng Vũ Hiêp	March 1975

IV Military Corps (Cửu Long Corps)
Date formed: 20 July 1974
Subordinate units:

    5th VC Division
    7th Infantry Division
    9th VC Division
    341st Infantry Division
    24th Mobile Artillery Regiment
    71st Antiaircraft Artillery Regiment
    25th Engineer Regiment
    429th Sapper Regiment
    69th Signals Regiment
Principal engagements:
    Spring 1975, Route 14
    Spring 1975, Sài Gòn
Commanding officer:

Maj. Gen. Hoàng Câm	July 1974

Political officer:

Maj. Gen. Hoàng Thê Thiên	March 1975

LXX Military Corps
Date formed: October 1970
Subordinate units:

304th Infantry Division
308th Infantry Division
320th Infantry Division
Principal engagements:
  Route 9
  Laos

232d Group
Date formed: February 1975
Subordinate units:
  3d Infantry Division
  5th Infantry Division
Principal engagements:
  Spring 1975, Sài Gòn
Commanding officers:

Lê Đức Anh	February 1975
Maj. Gen. Nguyên Minh Châu	March 1975

Political officers:

Lê Văn Tưởng	February 1975
Maj. Gen. Trân Văn Phác	March 1975

301st Group
Date formed: 18 March 1971 (reorganized as IV
Corps on 20 July 1974)
Subordinate units:
  5th Division
  7th Division
  9th Division
  28th Artillery Regiment
Principal engagement:
  Cambodia 1971
Commanding officer:

Trân Văn Trà	March 1971

Political officers:

Trân Đô	March 1971

559th Transportation Group
Date formed: 19 May 1959
Subordinate units:
  337th Antiaircraft Artillery Division
  470th Sector Division
  471st Sector Division
  472d Sector Division
  473d Engineering Division
  571st Transportation Division
  968th Infantry Division
Principal engagements:
  Hô Chí Minh Trail
Commanding officers:

Sr. Col. Vo Bam	May 1959
Maj. Gen. Phan Trong Tuê	1965
Sr. Col. Đông Sy Nguyên	1967

Political officer:

Maj. Gen. Hoàng Thê Thiên	1970s

1st Infantry Division
Date formed: 20 December 1965
Subordinate units (1967):
  24th PAVN Infantry Regiment
  32d PAVN Infantry Regiment
  33d PAVN Infantry Regiment
  66th PAVN Infantry Regiment
  88th PAVN Infantry Regiment
  95-B PAVN Infantry Regiment
Subordinate units (1973):
  52d PAVN Infantry Regiment
  101-D PAVN Infantry Regiment
  44th Sapper Regiment
Strength: December 1967, 9,525; December 1972, 3,400
Principal engagements:
  Central Highlands
  Easter Offensive

2d Infantry Division
Date formed: 20 October 1965
Subordinate units (1967):
  1st VC Infantry Regiment
  2d VC Infantry Regiment
  3d PAVN Infantry Regiment
  21st PAVN Infantry Regiment
Subordinate units (1973):
  1st PAVN Infantry Regiment
  52d VC Infantry Regiment
  141st PAVN Infantry Regiment
  368th PAVN Artillery Regiment
Strength: December 1967, 6,450; December 1972, 4,000
Principal engagements:
  Têt Offensive
  Laos
  Easter Offensive, Kontum
  Spring 1975, Đà Năng
  Cambodia 1979
Commanding officers:

Nguyên Năng	October 1965
Lê Hữu Tru	ca. July 1967
Giáp Văn Cường	December 1967
Lê Kích	ca. January 1969
Hô Xuân Anh	August 1969
Nguyên Chơn	ca. February 1971
Dưởng Bá Lời	June 1972
Nguyên Viêt Sơn	September 1972
Nguyên Chơn	June 1973

Political officers:

Nguyên Minh Đức	October 1965
Nguyên Ngoc Sơn	December 1967
Nguyên Huy Chưởng	October 1969
Lê Đình Yên	ca. February 1972
Mai Thuân	ca. February 1975

3d Infantry Division
Date formed: 2 September 1965

Subordinate units (1967):
    18th PAVN Infantry Regiment
    22d PAVN Infantry Regiment
Subordinate Units (1973)
    2d PAVN Infantry Regiment
    12th PAVN Infantry Regiment
    21st PAVN Infantry Regiment
Strength: December 1967, 2,870; December 1972, 3,500
Principal engagements:
    Tết Offensive
    Easter Offensive, Bình Định
    Phước Long
    Spring 1975, Qui Nhơn
    Spring 1975, Vũng Tàu
Commanding officers:
    Sr. Col. Giáp Văn Cường   September 1965
    Lu Giang   ca. April 1968
    Huỳnh Hữu Anh   July 1970
    Trân Trong Sơn   ca. May 1974
    Đô Quang Hưởng   ca. February 1975
    Trân Văn Khuê   ca. March 1975
Political officers:
    Đăng Hòa   September 1965
    Nguyên Nam Khanh   ca. April 1968
    Mai Tân   June 1971

5th VC Division

Date formed: 23 November 1965
Subordinate units (1967):
    27th VC Infantry Regiment
    275th VC Infantry Regiment
Subordinate units (1973):
    6th PAVN Infantry Regiment
    174th PAVN Infantry Regiment
    205th PAVN Infantry Regiment
    275th VC Infantry Regiment
Strength: December 1967, 3,300; December 1972, 3,900
Principal engagements:
    Vũng Tàu
    Cambodia 1971
    Easter Offensive, Lộc Ninh
Commanding officers:
    Bùi Thanh Vân   ca. 1972
    Trân Thanh Vân   ca. 1975
    Vũ Văn Thược   ca. 1975
Political officers:
    Nguyên Văn Cúc   ca. 1972
    Nguyên Xuân Ôn   ca. 1975

6th Infantry Division

Date formed: ca. 1972
Subordinate units (1973):
    24th Infantry Regiment
    207th Infantry Regiment
Strength: December 1972, 2,300

Principal engagement:
    Spring 1975, Xuân Lôc
Commanding officer:
    Đăng Ngoc Si   ca. August 1974

7th Infantry Division

Date formed: 13 June 1966
Subordinate units (1967):
    141st PAVN Infantry Regiment
    165th PAVN Infantry Regiment
    52d PAVN Infantry Regiment
Subordinate units (1973):
    141st PAVN Infantry Regiment
    165th PAVN Infantry Regiment
    209th PAVN Infantry Regiment
Strength: December 1967, 5,250; December 1972, 4,100
Principal engagements:
    JUNCTION CITY, Tây Ninh
    Tết Offensive, Tây Ninh
    Cambodia 1970
    Easter Offensive, Bình Long Province
    Phước Long
    Spring 1975, Xuân Lôc
    Cambodia 1979–1983
Commanding officers:
    Nguyên Hoa   June 1966
    Nguyên Thê Bôn   1967
    Đàn Văn Nguy   ca. 1970
    Lê Nam Phong   September 1973
Political officers:
    Dưởng Thanh   June 1966
    Vưởng Thê Hiêp   1967
    Lê Thanh   ca. 1970
    Tư Vinh   July 1974
    Phan Liêm   March 1975

8th Infantry Division

Date formed: ca. 1975
Principal engagement:
    Spring 1975, My Tho
Commanding officer:
    Sr. Col. Huỳnh Văn Nhiêm   August 1974

9th VC Division

Date formed: 2 September 1965
Subordinate units (1967):
    2d VC Infantry Regiment
    70th VC Infantry Regiment
    101st PAVN Infantry Regiment
    271st VC Infantry Regiment
    272d VC Infantry Regiment
    273d VC Infantry Regiment
    69th VC Artillery Regiment
    84th PAVN Artillery Regiment

Subordinate units (1973):
    95-C Infantry Regiment
    271st VC Infantry Regiment
    272d VC Infantry Regiment
Strength: December 1967, 10,260; December 1972, 4,100
Principal engagements:
    Bình Gia
    Bâu Bàng
    Operation ATTLEBORO
    Operation CEDAR FALLS
    Tết Offensive, Sài Gòn
    Cambodia 1970
    Easter Offensive, Route 13
    Spring 1975, Phước Long
    Cambodia 1978
Commanding officers:

Sr. Col. Hoàng Câm	September 1965
Ta Minh Khâm	1967
Lê Văn Nho	1969
Nguyên Thời Bung	ca. 1969
Vo Văn Dan	ca. 1972

Political officers:

Sr. Col. Lê Văn Tường	September 1965
Nguyên Văn Tong	1967
Nguyên Văn Quang	ca 1969
Pham Xuân Tung	ca 1972
Tam Tung	ca July 1974

10th Infantry Division

Date formed: 20 September 1972
Subordinate units:
    28th PAVN Infantry Regiment
    66th PAVN Infantry Regiment
    95-B PAVN Infantry Regiment
Strength: December 1972, 3,800
Principal engagements:
    Spring 1975, Ban Mê Thuôt
    Spring 1975, Sài Gòn
    Cambodia 1978
Commanding officers:

Nguyên Manh Quân	September 1972
Đô Đức Gia	May 1973
Hô De	mid-1974
Hông Sơn	April 1975
Sr. Col. Phùng Bá Thưởng	September 1976

Political officers:

Sr. Col. Đăng Vũ Hiêp	September 1972
Lã Ngoc Châu	May 1973
Lừu Quý Ngư	1975

303d Infantry Division

Date formed: 19 August 1974
Subordinate units:
    201st VC Infantry Regiment
    205th VC Infantry Regiment

271st VC Infantry Regiment
262d PAVN Artillery Regiment
Principal engagements:
    Spring 1975, Tây Ninh
    Spring 1975, Sài Gòn
    Cambodia 1978
    Chinese Border 1979
Commanding officers:

Đô Quang Hưởng	August 1974
Sr. Col. Trân Hai Phung	1977
Col. Cao Hoài Sai	September 1977

304th Infantry Division

Date formed: 4 January 1950
Subordinate units (1973):
    9th PAVN Infantry Regiment
    24-B PAVN Infantry Regiment
    66th PAVN Infantry Regiment
Strength: December 1972, 5,000
Principal engagements:
    Đáy River
    Điên Biên Phu
    Hòa Bình
    Khe Sanh
    Huê
    Operation LAM SỜN 719
    Easter Offensive, Quang Tri
    Spring 1975, Đà Năng
    Spring 1975, Sài Gòn
Commanding officers:

Hoàng Minh Thao	February 1950
Hoàng Sâm	November 1953
Nam Long	late 1955
Ngô Ngoc Dưởng	ca. 1960s
Mai Hiên	March 1965
Hoàng Kiên	August 1965
Thái Dũng	1967
Hoàng Dan	June 1968
Lê Công Phê	ca. 1973
Nguyên An	ca. 1974

Political officers:

Trân Văn Quang	February 1950
Lê Chưởng	1951
Trưởng Công Cân	late 1955
Trân Huy	ca. 1960s
Trưởng Công Cân	August 1965
Trân Nguyên Do	January 1968
Hoàng Thê Thiên	June 1968

308th Infantry Division

Date formed: August 1949
Subordinate units (1973):
    36th PAVN Infantry Regiment
    88th PAVN Infantry Regiment
    102d PAVN Infantry Regiment

Principal engagements:
    Vĩnh Yên
    Đáy River
    Hòa Bình
    Tu Vũ
    Xóm Phèo
    Black River
    Operation LORRAINE
    Laos 1953
    Điên Biên Phu
    Khe Sanh
    Operation LAM SƠN 719
    Easter Offensive, Quang Tri

Commanding officers:

Vường Thừa Vũ	August 1949
Thái Dũng	June 1968
Nguyên Hửu An	ca. 1972

Political officer:

Song Hào	August 1949

312th Infantry Division

Date formed: 27 October 1950
Subordinate units (1973):
    141st PAVN Infantry Regiment
    165th PAVN Infantry Regiment
    209th PAVN Infantry Regiment
Strength: December 1972, 6,000
Principal engagements:
    Vĩnh Yên
    Hòa Bình
    Black River
    Laos 1953
    Điên Biên Phu
    Têt Offensive
    Laos 1969
    Easter Offensive, DMZ
    Spring 1975

Commanding officers:

Lê Trong Tân	October 1950
Sr. Col. Hoàng Câm	1954
Nguyên Năng	mid-1960s
Lã Thái Hòa	October 1971
Nguyên Chương	early 1975

Political officers:

Trân Đô	ca. 1953
Lê Chiêu	mid-1969
Pham Sinh	October 1971
Nguyên Xuyên	early 1975

316th Infantry Division

Date formed: 1 May 1951
Subordinate units (1973):
    98th PAVN Infantry Regiment
    174th PAVN Infantry Regiment
    176th PAVN Infantry Regiment

Principal engagements:
    Mao Khê
    Black River
    Operation LORRAINE
    Laos 1953
    Điên Biên Phu
    Laos 1969
    Spring 1975, Ban Mê Thuôt
    Chinese Border 1979

Commanding officers:

Lê Quang Ba	1953
Lt. Gen. Vũ Lâp	1958
Sr. Col. Đàn Văn Nguy	early 1975

Political officers:

Chu Huy Mân	May 1951
Col. Hà Quôc Toan	early 1975

320th Infantry Division

Date formed: 16 January 1951
Subordinate units (1973):
    48th PAVN Infantry Regiment
    64th PAVN Infantry Regiment
Strength: December 1972, 3,000
Principal engagements:
    Đáy River
    Khe Sanh
    Operation LAM SƠN 719
    Easter Offensive, Kontum
    Spring 1975, Ban Mê Thuôt
    Spring 1975, Phú Bôn
    Spring 1975, Sài Gòn

Commanding officers:

Văn Tiên Dũng	January 1951
Sùng Lam	ca. 1967
Kim Tuân	ca. 1971
Bùi Đình Hòe	March 1975

Political officers:

Sr. Col. Lường Tuân Khang	ca. 1965
Phi Trieu Mah	ca. 1971
Col. Bùi Huy Bông	March 1975

320-B Infantry Division

Date formed: September 1965 (redesignated 390th Infantry Division on 4 May 1979)
Subordinate units (1973):
    48-B PAVN Infantry Regiment
    64-B PAVN Infantry Regiment
Strength: December 1972, 3,500
Principal engagements:
    Easter Offensive, DMZ
    Chinese Border 1979

Commanding officers:

Pham Thân Sơn	September 1965
Bùi Sinh	early 1966
Hà Vi Tùng	mid-1969

Sr. Col. Lưu Bá Xao	ca. 1973

Political officers:

Nguyên Duy Tưởng	September 1965
Nguyên Huân	early 1966
Trân Ngoc Kiên	mid-1969

324-B Infantry Division

Date formed: ca. 1965
Subordinate units (1967):
    803d PAVN Infantry Regiment
    812th PAVN Infantry Regiment
    90th PAVN Infantry Regiment
Subordinate units (1973):
    29th PAVN Infantry Regiment
    803d PAVN Infantry Regiment
    812th PAVN Infantry Regiment
Strength: December 1967, 7,800; December 1972, 5,000
Principal engagements:
    Huê
    Operation LAM SỞN 719
    Easter Offensive, Huê
    Spring 1975
Commanding officer:

Duy Sơn	ca. 1975

Political officer:

Nguyên Trong Dan	ca. 1975

325th Infantry Division

Date formed: 11 March 1951 (redesignated 325-A Infantry Division in late 1964)
Subordinate units (1964):
    18th Infantry Regiment
    95th Infantry Regiment
    101st Infantry Regiment
Principal engagement:
    Laos 1961
Commanding officers:

Trân Quy Hai	ca. 1953
Maj. Gen. Nguyên Hửu An	1964

Political officers:

Chu Văn Biên	ca. 1951
Hoàng Văn Thái	1955
Quách Sĩ Kha	1961
Nguyên Minh Đưc	1964

325-B Infantry Division

Date formed: November 1964
Subordinate units (1965):
    18-B Infantry Regiment
    24th Infantry Regiment
    33d Infantry Regiment
    95-B Infantry Regiment
    101-B Infantry Regiment
Principal engagement:
    A Shau Valley

Commanding officers:

Vưởng Tuân Kiêt	ca. 1964

Political officers:

Quôc Tuân	ca. 1964

325-C Infantry Division

Date formed: 1965
Subordinate units (1967):
    5th PAVN Infantry Regiment
    6th PAVN Infantry Regiment
    18-C PAVN Infantry Regiment
    95-C PAVN Infantry Regiment
    101-C PAVN Infantry Regiment
Strength: 1967, 7,790
Principal engagements:
    Khe Sanh
    Huê
Commanding officer:

Chu Phưởng Doi	ca. 1965

Political officer:

Nguyên Công Trang	ca. 1965

325-D Infantry Division

Date formed: 1966 (Redesignated the 325th Infantry Division in 1972)
Subordinate units (1972):
    18-D Infantry Regiment
    95-D Infantry Regiment
    101-D Infantry Regiment
Strength: December 1972, 5,000
Principal engagements:
    Easter Offensive, DMZ
    Spring 1975, Huê
    Spring 1975, Đà Năng
    Spring 1975, Sài Gòn
Commanding officers:

Thang Binh	1968
Lê Kích	ca. 1971
Col. Pham Minh Tâm	May 1974

Political officers:

Vũ Đưc Thái	1968
Sr. Col. Nguyên Công Trang	ca. 1971
Col. Lê Văn Dưởng	May 1974

341st Infantry Division

Date formed: February 1962 (disbanded ca. 1963; reconstituted March 1965; disbanded late 1966; reconstituted November 1972)
Principal engagements:
    Spring 1975, Huê
    Spring 1975, Xuân Lôc
    Spring 1975, Sài Gòn
Commanding officer:

Trân Văn Tran	ca. January 1977

Political officer:

Trân Nguyên Do	ca. January 1975

351st Heavy Division
Date formed: 1953
Subordinate units (1954):
    45th Viêt Minh Artillery Regiment
    675th Viêt Minh Artillery Regiment
    367th Viêt Minh Antiaircraft Artillery Regiment
    237th Viêt Minh Heavy Weapons Regiment
    151st Viêt Minh Engineer Regiment
Principal engagement:
    Ðiên Biên Phu
Commanding officer:
    Vũ Hiên   1953

711th Infantry Division
Date formed: 29 June 1971
Subordinate units (1973):
    3d PAVN Infantry Regiment
    35th PAVN Infantry Regiment
    270th PAVN Infantry Regiment
Strength: December 1972, 3,500
Principal engagement:
    Easter Offensive
Commanding officer:
    Nguyên Chơn   June 1972

202d Tank Brigade
Date formed: 5 October 1959
Subordinate unit:
    397th PAVN Tank Battalion
Principal engagements:
    Operation LAM SƠN 719
    Spring 1975, Sài Gòn
Commanding officers:
    Ðào Huy Vũ   October 1959
    Lê Xuân Kiên   June 1965
    Nguyên Văn Lang   November 1971
    Ðô Phưởng Ngư   1972
Political officers:
    Ðăng Quang Long   October 1959
    Vo Ngoc Hai   June 1965
    Hoàng Khoái   1972

V. French Forces in Indo-China

The French military returned to Indo-China immediately following the end of World War II. By the late 1940s all French Union Forces (FUF) in Indo-China came under the control of the French high commissioner, who exercised command through the military commander in chief. In practice, however, French political and military leaders in Paris intervened in local decisions to the point of almost constant interference. That situation improved only slightly between December 1950 and April 1952 when Gen. Jean de Lattre de Tassigny held both offices. French military headquarters was located in Hà Nôi.

A post–World War II amendment to France's Budget Law restricted the use of conscripted French nationals to the defense of "homeland" territory—which included France, Algeria, and French-occupied Germany. Thus, all French regular units sent to Vietnam consisted of volunteers. This, of course, restricted the size of the ethnic French element of the French Expeditionary Force.

French Foreign Legion units in Vietnam consisted largely, but not exclusively, of non-French Europeans. They were organized and equipped the same as regular French units and had French officers.

The North African colonial units were similarly organized, equipped, and led. Because Algeria was considered part of metropolitan France, the Algerian units were allowed to have Algerian officers. Many of the colonial units in Vietnam recruited locally and included varying proportions of Vietnamese in their ranks. The French also raised colonial units in Vietnam, Cambodia, and Laos.

The French Expeditionary Force supposedly was backed by the French-controlled Vietnamese National Army of 100,000 troops. That force, however, never came close to living up to expectations. In 1947 the French had some 115,000 troops in all of Indo-China. In May 1953 the French Expeditionary Force of 189,000 troops consisted of the following:

French Army	54,000
Foreign Legion	20,000
North African	30,000
Vietnamese	70,000
French Air Force	10,000
French Navy	5,000

At any given time, as many as 100,000 troops of the French Expeditionary Force were in static defenses and garrisons. Remaining forces available for offensive operations often were organized into Mobile Groups (groupes mobile, or GM). The GMs were the main French striking units in Indo-China. They were ad hoc regimental combat teams, usually consisting of three infantry battalions, an artillery battalion, and armor support. GMs often worked in conjunction with parachute battalions.

Some GMs were fairly stable, tending to have the same battalions from operation to operation. Others swapped-out battalions on a frequent basis. Typically, GMs numbered some 6,000 men. Variations on the GM concept included several amphibious groups, at least one airborne group, and armored subgroups that operated in conjunction with the GMs.

Much of the fighting in Tonkin between 1951 and 1953 was carried by GMs 1 through 4. Although ethnic French units were heavily represented in the GMs, some were made up of colonial or Vietnamese units. GM 1 consisted of crack North African and Senegalese battalions, while most of GM 3's soldiers were tough Muong mountain troops. GM 9 fought at Ðiên Biên Phu, while GM Nord was part of the Operation CASTOR relief column. GM 100, which was decimated by fighting in the south, was formed around the two battalions of the Korea Regiment—French troops who had fought under the United Nations (UN) command in Korea.

No comprehensive OB sources exist in English for the French forces in Indo-China between 1945 and 1954. The following list was compiled from official French military records. Because the GMs were not regularly constituted units, they do not appear on this list. The one exception to this is GM 1, which also bore the designation Groupe Mobile Nord-Africain. That unit is carried on the French list as a regularly constituted infantry unit between 25 August 1949 and 11 August 1954.

(A note of explanation: Units designated *marche* in the French Army have no equivalent in the U.S. Army; perhaps best translated as "mobile," these units were often assembled for a specific purpose, but, as with an American task force, they tended to become permanent. Also, French artillery groups, commanded by a lieutenant colonel and containing three or more separate batteries, were the equivalent of an American artillery battalion.)

French High Commissioners in Indo-China

Adm. Georges d'Argenlieu	31 August 1945
Emile Bollaert	October 1947
Léon Pignon	5 October 1948
Gen. Jean de Lattre de Tassigny	16 December 1950
Maurice Dejean	3 July 1952
Gen. Paul Ely	9 June 1954
Ambassador Henri Hoppenot	27 July 1955

French Commanders in Chief in Indo-China

Gen. Philippe Leclerc	June 1945
Gen. Jean Valluy	1 October 1946
Gen. Raoul Salan	10 February 1948
Lt. Gen. Roger Blaizot	10 June 1948
Gen. Marcel Carpentier	1 April 1949
Gen. Jean de Lattre de Tassigny	16 December 1950
Gen. Raoul Salan	1 April 1952
Gen. Henri Navarre	29 May 1953
Gen. Paul Ely	9 June 1954
Gen. Pierre Elie Jacquot	1 June 1955

Supreme French Headquarters (HQ) in Indo-China

HQ, French Expeditionary Corps, Far East
    Date formed in Indo-China: 16 September 1945
    Date reorganized in Indo-China: 1 January 1946

HQ, Supreme Command of French Troops, Far East
    Date formed in Indo-China: 1 January 1946
    Date reorganized in Indo-China: 11 June 1948

HQ, Supreme Command of Ground Forces, Far East
    Date formed in Indo-China: 12 June 1948
    Date reorganized in Indo-China: 9 September 1949

HQ, Commander in Chief of Military Forces, Far East
    Date formed in Indo-China: 10 September 1949
    Date reorganized in Indo-China: 31 December 1950

HQ, Joint and Ground Forces, Far East
    Date formed in Indo-China: 1 January 1951
    Date inactivated in Indo-China: 11 August 1954

Major Subordinate French Headquarters
French Forces of the North, China, and Indo-China
    Date formed in Indo-China: end of 1945
    Date reorganized in Indo-China: 1 November 1946

French Troops in Indo-China, North
    Date formed in Indo-China: 2 November 1946
    Date inactivated in Indo-China: 11 August 1954

French Troops in Indo-China, South
    Date formed in Indo-China: 13 September 1946
    Date reorganized in Indo-China: 9 March 1949

Franco-Vietnamese Forces, South
    Date formed in Indo-China: 10 March 1949
    Date reorganized in Indo-China: 5 May 1951

Land Forces, South Vietnam
    Date formed in Indo-China: 6 May 1951
    Date inactivated in Indo-China: 11 August 1954

French Troops, Central Annam
    Date formed in Indo-China: 1 August 1947
    Date reorganized in Indo-China: 9 October 1949

Land Forces, Central Vietnam
    Date formed in Indo-China: 10 October 1949
    Date inactivated in Indo-China: 11 August 1954

Land Forces, Montagnard Plateau
    Date formed in Indo-China: 15 March 1951
    Date reorganized in Indo-China: 31 December 1952

Southern Montagnard Plateau
    Date formed in Indo-China: 1 January 1953
    Date inactivated in Indo-China: 11 August 1954

French Land Forces in Laos and Laotian Land Forces
    Date formed in Indo-China: end of 1945
    Date inactivated in Indo-China: 11 August 1954

Military Command, Cambodia
    Date formed in Indo-China: 1 January 1946
    Date reorganized in Indo-China: 19 January 1949

Forces Command, Cambodia
    Date formed in Indo-China: 20 January 1949
    Date reorganized in Indo-China: 31 March 1951

Land Forces, Cambodia
    Date formed in Indo-China: 1 April 1951
    Date inactivated in Indo-China: 31 October 1953

Divisions

2d Armored Division (elements)
    Date arrived in Vietnam: 14 October 1945
    Date departed Vietnam: 7 October 1946

3d Colonial Infantry Division
    Date arrived in Vietnam: October 1945
    Date departed Vietnam: 12 September 1946

9th Colonial Infantry Division
    Date arrived in Vietnam: end of 1945
    Date departed Vietnam: 1 November 1956

1st Tonkin Marche Division
    Date formed in Vietnam: start of 1951
    Date inactivated in Vietnam: 11 August 1954
    Zone of responsibility: Tonkin, West

2d Tonkin Marche Division
    Date formed in Vietnam: start of 1951
    Date inactivated in Vietnam: 11 August 1954
    Zone of responsibility: Tonkin, North

3d Tonkin Marche Division
    Date formed in Vietnam: 1 November 1951
    Date inactivated in Vietnam: 11 August 1954
    Zone of responsibility: Tonkin, South

4th Tonkin Marche Division
    Date formed in Vietnam: 1 June 1954
    Date Inactivated in Vietnam: 11 August 1954
    Zone of responsibility: Hai Phòng

Foreign Legion Units
Regiments
    1st Foreign Cavalry Regiment
    2d Foreign Infantry Regiment
    3d Foreign Infantry Regiment
    5th Foreign Infantry Regiment
    13th Foreign Legion Demi-Brigade

Separate Battalions
    1st Foreign Parachute Battalion
    2d Foreign Parachute Battalion
    Marche Battalion, 1st Foreign Infantry Regiment
    5th Battalion, 4th Foreign Infantry Regiment
    3d Battalion, 6th Foreign Infantry Regiment

Airborne Units
Regiments
    Colonial Parachute Commando Demi-Brigade (SAS)
    1st Parachute Demi-Brigade (SAS)
    1st Parachute Chasseurs Regiment
    2d Colonial Parachute Commando Demi-Brigade

Separate Battalions
    1st Colonial Parachute Battalion
    2d Colonial Parachute Battalion
    3d Colonial Parachute Battalion
    4th Colonial Parachute Battalion
    5th Colonial Parachute Battalion
    6th Colonial Parachute Battalion
    7th Colonial Parachute Battalion
    8th Colonial Parachute Battalion
    9th Colonial Parachute Battalion
    10th Dismounted Chasseurs Parachute Battalion
    Marche Battalion, 35th Airborne Artillery Regiment

Infantry Units
Regiments
    Korea Regiment
    Mobile Group 1
    6th Colonial Infantry Regiment
    11th Colonial Infantry Regiment
    21st Colonial Infantry Regiment
    22d Colonial Infantry Regiment
    23d Colonial Infantry Regiment
    43d Colonial Infantry Regiment
    1st Algerian Rifle Regiment
    2d Algerian Rifle Regiment
    3d Algerian Rifle Regiment
    7th Algerian Rifle Regiment
    22d Algerian Rifle Regiment
    Moroccan Colonial Infantry Regiment
    1st Moroccan Rifle Regiment
    2d Moroccan Rifle Regiment
    3d Moroccan Rifle Regiment
    4th Moroccan Rifle Regiment
    5th Moroccan Rifle Regiment
    6th Moroccan Rifle Regiment
    24th Senegalese Rifle Marche Regiment
    4th Tunisian Rifle Regiment
    1st Tonkin Rifle Regiment
    Cambodian Composite Regiment

Separate Battalions
    Marche Battalion, 35th Infantry Regiment
    Marche Battalion, 43d Infantry Regiment
    1st Marche Battalion, 49th Infantry Regiment
    Marche Battalion, 110th Infantry Regiment
    Marche Battalion, 151st Infantry Regiment
    1st Marche Battalion, 1st Colonial Infantry Regiment
    1st Marche Battalion, 2d Colonial Infantry Regiment
    Marche Battalion, 5th Colonial Infantry Regiment
    Marche Battalion, 16th Colonial Infantry Regiment
    Marche Battalion, 19th Colonial Infantry Regiment
    1st African Light Infantry Battalion
    1st Marche Battalion, 201st North African Pioneer Infantry Regiment
    1st Marche Battalion, 6th Algerian Rifle Regiment

21st Algerian Rifle Battalion
22d Algerian Rifle Battalion
23d Algerian Rifle Battalion
25th Algerian Rifle Battalion
27th Algerian Rifle Battalion
205th Algerian Rifle Battalion
217th Algerian Rifle Battalion
4th Battalion, Chad Marche Regiment
Marche Battalion, 7th Moroccan Rifle Regiment
1st Marche Battalion, 8th Moroccan Rifle Regiment
1st Moroccan Far East Battalion
2d Moroccan Far East Battalion
3d Moroccan Far East Battalion
5th Moroccan Far East Battalion
8th Moroccan Far East Battalion
9th Moroccan Far East Battalion
10th Moroccan Far East Battalion
11th Moroccan Far East Battalion
17th Moroccan Far East Battalion
207th Moroccan Far East Rifle Marche Battalion
214th Moroccan Far East Rifle Battalion
Marche Battalion, 13th Senegalese Rifle Regiment
26th Senegalese Rifle Marche Battalion
27th Senegalese Rifle Marche Battalion
28th Senegalese Rifle Marche Battalion
29th Senegalese Rifle Marche Battalion
30th Senegalese Rifle Marche Battalion
31st Senegalese Rifle Marche Battalion
32d Senegalese Rifle Marche Battalion
104th Senegalese Battalion
1st French East African Marche Battalion
2d French East African Marche Battalion
3d French East African Marche Battalion
Marche Battalion, 4th Tonkin Rifle Regiment
Annam Battalion
Sài Gòn–Cholon Garrison Battalion
1st Far Eastern Marche Battalion
2d Far Eastern Marche Battalion
3d Far Eastern Marche Battalion
4th Far Eastern Marche Battalion
5th Far Eastern Marche Battalion
6th Far Eastern Marche Battalion
7th Far Eastern Marche Battalion
1st Indo-China Marche Battalion
2d Indo-China Marche Battalion
3d Indo-China Marche Battalion
1st Muong Battalion
2d Muong Battalion
1st Thai Battalion
2d Thai Battalion
3d Thai Battalion
1st Laotian Chasseurs Battalion
2d Laotian Chasseurs Battalion
3d Laotian Chasseurs Battalion
4th Laotian Chasseurs Battalion

5th Laotian Chasseurs Battalion
6th Laotian Chasseurs Battalion
7th Laotian Chasseurs Battalion
8th Laotian Chasseurs Battalion
Phnom Penh Garrison Battalion

Armor and Cavalry Units
Regiments
1st Armored Cavalry Regiment
4th Dragoon Regiment
5th Armored Cavalry Regiment
9th Dragoon Marche Regiment
8th Algerian Spahis Regiment
2d Moroccan Spahis Regiment
5th Moroccan Spahis Regiment
6th Moroccan Spahis Regiment
Far East Spahis Marche Regiment
Far East Colonial Armored Regiment

Separate Squadrons and Battalions
4th Dragoon Battalion
7th Squadron, 1st Moroccan Spahis Marche Regiment
1st Far East Independent Reconnaissance Squadron
2d Far East Independent Reconnaissance Squadron
3d Far East Independent Reconnaissance Squadron
4th Far East Independent Reconnaissance Squadron
5th Far East Independent Reconnaissance Squadron

Artillery Units
Regiments
2d Artillery Regiment
4th Colonial Artillery Regiment
10th Colonial Artillery Regiment
41st Colonial Artillery Regiment
69th African Artillery Regiment
Moroccan Colonial Artillery Regiment

Separate Battalions
Marche Battalion, 64th Artillery Regiment
Marche Battalion, 66th Artillery Regiment
1st Battalion, Far East Colonial Antiaircraft Regiment
21st Aerial Artillery Observation Battalion
22d Aerial Artillery Observation Battalion
23d Aerial Artillery Observation Battalion
24th Aerial Artillery Observation Battalion
261st Antiaircraft Battalion
French East African Colonial Artillery Battalion
Levant Colonial Mountain Artillery Battalion
1st Central Annam Artillery Battalion
2d Central Annam Artillery Battalion

Engineer Units
Battalions
22d Engineer Battalion
26th Engineer Sanitation Battalion

31st Engineer Marche Battalion

61st Engineer Battalion

62d Engineer Battalion

71st Engineer Battalion

72d Engineer Battalion

73d Engineer Battalion

75th Engineer Battalion

61st Colonial Engineer Battalion

71st Colonial Engineer Battalion

72d Colonial Engineer Battalion

73d Colonial Engineer Battalion

—David T. Zabecki

References: Berger, Carl, ed. *The United States Air Force in Southeast Asia, 1961–1973.* Washington, DC: Department of the Air Force, 1977.
Collins, James Lawton, Jr. *The Development and Training of the South Vietnamese Army, 1950–1972.* Washington, DC: Department of the Army, 1975.
Collins, James Lawton, Jr., and Stanley Robert Larsen. *Allied Participation in Vietnam.* Washington, DC: Department of the Army, 1975.
Davidson, Phillip A. *Vietnam at War: The History, 1946–1975.* Novato, CA: Presidio Press, 1988.
Fall, Bernard B. *Street without Joy.* Harrisburg, PA: Stackpole, 1961.
Lanning, Michael Lee, and Dan Crag. *Inside the VC and the NVA: The Real Story of Vietnam's Armed Forces.* New York: Fawcett Columbine, 1992.
Pike, Douglas. *PAVN: People's Army of Vietnam.* Novato, CA: Presidio Press, 1986.
Stanton, Shelby L. *Vietnam Order of Battle.* Washington, DC: U.S. News Books, 1981.
See also: Australia; China, Republic of (ROC; Taiwan); France: Air Force; France: Army; France: Foreign Legion in Indo-China; France: Navy; Korea, Republic of; New Zealand; Philippines; Thailand; United States: Air Force; United States: Army; United States: Marine Corps; United States: Navy; Vann, John Paul; Vietnam, Democratic Republic of: Air Force; Vietnam, Democratic Republic of: Army (People's Army of Vietnam [PAVN]); Vietnam, Republic of: Air Force (VNAF); Vietnam, Republic of: Army (ARVN); Vietnam, Republic of: Navy (VNN).

Order of Battle Dispute

(1967)

In 1965 the United States sent ground troops into Vietnam without having adequate intelligence on the forces U.S. troops were to fight. When Military Assistance Command, Vietnam (MACV) began to issue monthly reports on Communist organization and strength in South Vietnam—order of battle—the figures were at first very incomplete.

As intelligence improved during 1966, the figures for Communist regular combat units came to be reasonably accurate. Order of battle reports, however, contained figures for three other types of Communist personnel:

(1) "Combat support" or "administrative services": those people handling supply, transport, medical care, and other support functions.

(2) "Political cadres" or "political infrastructure": local administrators, tax collectors, police, and other political operatives in the areas of South Vietnam that were partially or wholly under Communist control.

(3) "Irregulars": a variety of guerrilla and militia organizations, of which the two having the least capability for

conventional military combat would eventually become the subject of particular controversy—the "self-defense" militia in Communist-controlled villages and the "secret self-defense" militia in government-controlled villages.

Most Communist personnel in South Vietnam fell in these three categories, but no serious study of their numbers had been made before 1966. Bureaucratic inertia dictated that, for lack of anything better, officers responsible for the order of battle reports repeated each month the unfounded estimate in the previous month's report.

By early 1967 U.S. intelligence officers (mostly in military intelligence in Vietnam, but to some extent also at Central Intelligence Agency (CIA) headquarters in the United States) had compiled enough information to make realistic estimates possible for all categories. This created a major problem. The new estimates, especially for the administrative services and irregulars, were far higher than the old ones. Public support for the war was already shaky in the United States and for the official estimate of total Communist personnel in South Vietnam dramatically to increase, perhaps even double, could have had serious repercussions.

There followed a series of acrimonious conferences at which the CIA argued for comparatively high estimates, and MACV intelligence argued for much lower estimates. In September 1967 an agreement was worked out under which the definitions used in compiling the estimates were drastically changed. U.S. intelligence simply stopped estimating the number of people in the self-defense and secret self-defense militia. Estimates for the "infrastructure" continued to be compiled but were no longer treated as part of the military order of battle. Having dropped these categories, MACV accepted higher estimates of some others (though not as high as CIA estimates) without any increase in the overall total.

The 1968 Têt Offensive came a few months later. Debate continues between those who say the course of combat during Têt proved that MACV estimates had been valid and those who say that Têt proved that MACV had been grossly underestimating Communist strength.

Samuel Adams, a CIA analyst of order of battle issues, was one of the CIA negotiators at the conferences of 1967. He believed that the estimates agreed upon at the September conference had been grossly dishonest—incomplete and inaccurate to an extent that caused dangerous complacency as Têt approached. After retiring from the CIA, Adams made his view public in a May 1975 article in *Harper's* magazine titled, "Vietnam Cover-Up: Playing War with Numbers." The story reached television with a 23 January 1982 CBS documentary, "The Uncounted Enemy: A Vietnam Deception." It argued that the intelligence figures had been deliberately falsified and that General William Westmoreland bore part of the blame.

After the televised special program aired, General Westmoreland filed a libel suit for $120 million against CBS, several CBS employees, and Adams. The trial began in October 1984. Westmoreland at first seemed to be doing well, demonstrating significant misconduct by CBS. But after the defense case began in January 1985, CBS presented considerable evidence for the central thesis of its program: that military intelligence officers under General Westmoreland's command had reported fewer Communist personnel of all types—not just militia but even regular combat troops—than were actually present in South Vietnam. Several such officers testified as witnesses for CBS.

Col. Gains Hawkins, the man immediately responsible for MACV's overall estimates, testified that under pressure from his superiors he had ordered his own subordinates to lower their estimates in mid-1967. He was not aware of any evidence justifying lower estimates; he said that the evidence suggested that the estimates were already too low. On the witness stand, he described the estimates that MACV had presented to other intelligence agencies in August 1967 as "crap."

For the most part, General Westmoreland had not been directly involved; his immediate subordinates had passed down the chain of command what they believed to be his wishes, without necessarily consulting him in detail. General Philip Davidson, chief of intelligence for MACV, had issued a directive in August 1967 that CBS introduced in evidence at the trial:

> In view of General Westmoreland's conversations, all of which you have heard, I am sure that this headquarters will not accept a figure in excess of the current strength figure carried by the press. Let me make it clear that this is my view of General Westmoreland's sentiments. I have not discussed this directly with him but I am 100 percent sure of his reaction.

CBS was able to present two witnesses, however: General Joseph McChristian (Davidson's predecessor as chief of MACV intelligence) and Colonel Hawkins. In May 1967 they had presented directly to Westmoreland more accurate figures that they wanted to substitute for the underestimates in the order of battle.

On 18 February 1985 Westmoreland withdrew his suit in return for a carefully worded statement in which CBS did not retract or apologize for anything in the broadcast, but said that it "never intended to assert, and does not believe, that General Westmoreland was unpatriotic or disloyal in performing his duties as he saw them."

—Edwin E. Moise

References: Adams, Sam. *War of Numbers: An Intelligence Memoir.* South Royalton, VT: Steerforth Press, 1994.
Brewin, Bob, and Sydney Shaw. *Vietnam on Trial: Westmoreland vs. CBS.* New York: Atheneum, 1987.
Moise, Edwin. "Why Westmoreland Gave Up." *Pacific Affairs* 58, no. 4 (Winter 1985–1986): 663–673.

See also: Adams, Samuel A.; Central Intelligence Agency (CIA); Davidson, Phillip Buford, Jr.; Media and the War; Military Assistance Command, Vietnam (MACV); Westmoreland, William Childs.

P

Pacification

Name given to an array of programs that sought to bring security, economic development, and local self-government to rural South Vietnam. Throughout the Vietnam War pacification played an essential role in the conduct of the struggle. Following the 1954 Geneva Accords, leaders of the Republic of Vietnam (RVN) sought to preserve it as a sovereign, non-Communist nation. They relied on various pacification plans to extend rule into the countryside, gain political loyalty, and defeat a Communist insurgency. After 1954 the United States became increasingly involved in supporting the RVN, providing economic and military aid, training its police and local security forces, and supporting the many efforts at pacification. The management and focus of pacification changed during the course of the war, but the underlying philosophy and purpose remained constant.

The prerequisite of pacification was security. To provide local security, the government raised paramilitary forces, the Civil Guard and Self Defense Corps, which in 1964 became the Regional Forces and Popular Forces (RF/PF). In addition, the militia, the People's Self-Defense Force, and police forces had a security role. Revolutionary development (RD) cadre teams lived in the villages, training local citizens and working on self-help projects. The goal was to make secure the villages where people lived, but in some cases, nearby fighting or operational requirements forced peasants from their homes into camps in secure areas. After 1960, to counter the political propaganda and terrorism of the Việt Công Infrastructure (VCI), the Communists' covert command and control organization in South Vietnam, the Sài Gòn government under the Phoenix program used its police forces to identify and arrest members of the VCI. Under the Chiêu Hồi (Open Arms)

Soldiers of the U.S. 101st Airborne Division join children of Ấp Uu Thường hamlet in a baseball game.

Vietnamese refugee children peer through a fence at Phong Điên refugee hamlet.

program, the government used psychological and economic inducements to encourage the Viêt Công (VC) to defect.

The objective of pacification was not just to stem the VC insurgency; it also sought to improve the lives of the people in the countryside. Sài Gòn instituted land reform, provided assistance to refugees and attempted to resettle them, sent out cadres to teach and organize villagers, set up schools and infirmaries, organized local elections, and provided funds for local development projects.

Although pacification programs were conducted by the South Vietnamese government, Americans played an indispensable role as financiers and advisors at all levels of government. The RVN depended on American financial aid and military assistance for its existence as an independent nation. Much of the history of pacification concerns U.S. efforts to push its ally to carry out mutually agreed-upon plans. Despite the disparity between the two nations in size and resources, American attempts to influence the Vietnamese produced frustrating results; frequent disappointments offset the occasional successes.

Measuring meaningful change or progress in the countryside was difficult. The Americans devised a number of nationwide statistical indices, based on standardized questions, to track such things as the expenditure of funds and the distribution of weapons. But in a war for political support and popular loyalty,

tools such as the Hamlet Evaluation System (HES), a monthly report on pacification compiled by U.S. district advisors, proved more useful for managing programs and resources than for assessing change or gauging popular loyalty in a convincing way.

Shortly after taking power, President Ngô Đình Diêm had consolidated his rule by first suppressing his non-Communist political rivals—the Hòa Hao, Cao Đài, and Bình Xuyên sects. He then turned his attention to eliminating Communist political operatives in the South. These efforts bore fruit in the years 1955 to 1959. Although Diêm instituted limited land reform in 1956, his harsh tactics in suppressing his opposition alienated many South Vietnamese, making them amenable to future Viêt Công propaganda. To many, Diêm's policies seemed designed to benefit wealthy landowners, and this gave the Communists an issue to gain popular support.

In 1959 the Politburo in Hà Nôi decided to take active steps to topple Diêm. In 1960 the National Liberation Front (NLF) came into being. It was designed to merge the efforts of Diêm's Communist and non-Communist opponents inside the RVN and to win political support overseas. The NLF recruited and operated within South Vietnam, but direction and leadership largely came from Hà Nôi. The NLF or Viêt Công was a revolutionary organization, combining political indoctrination with military action, tight organization, and coercion to build their movement. Their strategy skillfully blended intimidation and reform and used political and military means to gain control.

Under Mao Zedong's theory of revolutionary warfare, the VC sought to destroy the government's presence in the countryside, isolating the cities from the people. Without a base of popular support, the government would eventually fall. Primary VC targets were local officials, political leaders, and teachers: Sài Gòn's links with the villages. Assassination, kidnapping, or intimidation of these people effectively ended the government's presence in many areas.

Diêm recognized this threat and mounted several projects to counter it. The most ambitious of these was the Strategic Hamlet program of 1962, which sought to put villagers in fortified hamlets and protect them from VC raids and political organizers. The plan was seriously flawed in execution. The government built too many hamlets too quickly, uprooting many villagers from their ancestral homes and herding them into hastily built and inadequate hamlets that offered few amenities and no real protection. Relocating people instead of bringing security to their native villages proved a major defect. The program did not stop the growth of the VC or the erosion of government control in the countryside and was plagued by official corruption.

Dissatisfied with Diêm's leadership and worried about his prosecution of the war, the RVN's armed forces with U.S. acquiescence overthrew him in November 1963. This only worsened matters. Ongoing pacification programs, including the Strategic Hamlets, essentially stopped. Nor did the follow-on efforts that began after Diêm's overthrow, *Chiên Thăng* or *Hợp Tác*, prove effective. The coup also produced political instability in Sài Gòn and turmoil in the provinces, as officials carrying out pacification plans were replaced when the government in Sài Gòn changed, which it frequently did.

In the absence of political stability, and emboldened by signs of Sài Gòn's collapse, Hà Nội began to send conventional army units into South Vietnam in late 1964 to administer the coup de grace. Pacification was on its death bed.

In 1965 President Lyndon Johnson decided to send in U.S. Marine and Army troops. U.S. commander in Vietnam General William Westmoreland and General William DePuy, his operations officer, concluded in February 1965 that pacification was irrelevant at that point. They saw no reason for using fresh troops to prop up a moribund program. In their view, the Viêt Công had won the political war and U.S. forces, with their peerless firepower and mobility, were needed to avert military defeat and to wear down their foe. Attrition became the strategy, and to accomplish it Westmoreland wanted more troops. President Johnson was unwilling to override the judgment of his military leaders. He agreed to send the requested soldiers from the active forces, but decided not to call up the reserves in an effort to limit the political costs of the war.

At the same time, Johnson was conscious that the political war, pacification, could not be long ignored and began in 1965 to ponder how to revive it. Prompted by National Security Advisor McGeorge Bundy and his assistant, Chester Cooper, Johnson first tried to improve American management of pacification by empowering two successive ambassadors, Maxwell Taylor and Henry Cabot Lodge, to act as "proconsuls." As head of the country team, the ambassador was expected to unify and integrate the various programs run by separate American agencies: the Central Intelligence Agency (CIA), the U.S. Agency for International Development (USAID), the State Department, the U.S. Information Agency (USIA), and the U.S. Armed Forces that supported Vietnamese pacification efforts. Throughout 1965 the president resisted suggestions that he appoint a "Vietnam czar" to manage the so-called "other war" (pacification) in Washington. He had no stomach for disrupting normal bureaucratic arrangements in the midst of war.

That reluctance began to soften after Johnson conferred in Honolulu early in February 1966 with South Vietnamese leaders Nguyên Văn Thiêu and Nguyên Cao Kỳ. This conference put the spotlight on pacification. The president sought to energize his own officials in Washington and Sài Gòn, as well as the RVN leadership, and to make clear that the "other war" was equal in importance to the war being fought by American and Army of the Republic of Vietnam (ARVN) forces. Around the time of the Honolulu conference, the pacification program began to show signs of new life under the dynamic but temperamental General Nguyên Đức Thăng, Minister of Revolutionary Development, and the return of political stability in Sài Gòn in 1966 under Thiêu and Kỳ.

After the conference Johnson made two significant appointments. He chose Ambassador William Porter, Lodge's deputy, to pull together the American effort in Sài Gòn to support pacification. To improve military cooperation, Porter was later given a military assistant, Brig. Gen. Willis Crittenberger. To enhance management and improve the support of pacification in Washington, Johnson appointed Robert Komer, who then worked for McGeorge Bundy, as his special presidential assistant for pacification. Johnson granted him authority to deal directly with the secretaries of state and defense, the director of central intelligence, the administrator of USAID, and most significantly the president himself.

Porter and Komer worked closely together, but their efforts were a study in contrasts. Porter became bogged down with administrative chores that Ambassador Lodge insisted he continue to perform. Lodge was reluctant to let Porter take steps that would centralize U.S. management of pacification support or diminish the autonomy of separate U.S. agencies and their programs. Armed with Johnson's mandate, Komer ran roughshod over Washington bureaucrats, cajoling, threatening, and invoking the president's name to improve the management of pacification support, earning the nickname "Blowtorch" for his pains. By the summer of 1966 Komer became convinced that a single manager was needed to run the array of American pacification programs in Vietnam and that the military, with its abundant manpower, effective logistics system, and unique capabilities such as road building, needed to be involved in pacification support, perhaps even in charge. Komer bluntly told Porter, who adamantly opposed military control, that, "The civil side is a mess. Compared to our military operations, it's still farcical."

Johnson was unwilling in the fall of 1966 to strip responsibility for pacification support from the embassy and so he gave Porter and Lodge, as the civilian leaders in Vietnam, one last chance to manage pacification support and show results. The agency that emerged, the Office of Civilian Operations, was hampered by Lodge's continued insistence that Porter devote his time to running the embassy, in spite of the president's admonitions. Convinced that the military would have to be involved, Komer lobbied for the unification of civilian and military support of pacification under General Westmoreland. In May 1967 Johnson finally agreed, appointing Komer as Westmoreland's deputy for pacification, with the rank of ambassador.

Komer established a new organization called Civilian Operations and Revolutionary (later changed to Rural) Development Support, or CORDS, to put under a single manager most American civilian and military programs that supported pacification. CORDS was a unique amalgamation of military and civilian personnel. It also assumed control of some CIA and USAID programs and appointed military advisors to districts and provinces, which gave the new organization access to military support. CORDS was designed to prevent military domination of pacification, a sensitive point for U.S. civilian agencies. Komer regularly met with the U.S. ambassador, RVN leaders and cabinet officials, and Westmoreland and his military staff principals and unit commanders. As a staff principal in Westmoreland's headquarters, Komer could raise issues with the American commander and had access to military logistics, supplies, manpower, and engineering support.

Komer took immediate steps to unify pacification and establish CORDS. He greatly increased the number of American advisors to the RVN Regional Forces and Popular Forces and sought better training and equipment for them, believing the neglected paramilitary forces offered the best opportunity to achieve sustained local security, a key factor absent from earlier pacification efforts. The other critical step was to gain Westmoreland's approval for a new program, named Phoenix, to attack the Việt Công Infrastructure. Over the U.S. military's objections, Westmoreland gave CORDS and not his intelligence chief, the Military Assistance Command, Vietnam (MACV) J-2, responsibility for gathering intelligence on the VCI. Phoenix attempted to mesh the collection efforts of RVN and U.S. civilian and military intelligence agencies. The goal was to obtain timely, accurate information from all sources and make it available to regular and special police so they could arrest members of the infrastructure in a timely manner. Getting the South Vietnamese to agree to this program, enact it into law, and actually set it up took many frustrating months. Westmoreland approved the concept in July 1967; it became operational a year later.

For the first six months of its existence, CORDS worked to unify existing programs, add staff, bring on board additional advisors, and get new efforts such as Phoenix in gear. The 1968 Communist Tết Offensive occurred before CORDS had demonstrated any visible results. At the same time, it proved difficult to get the ministries of newly elected President Thiệu's government to act decisively. Without doubt, Tết set back pacification, but it also had the effect of energizing it. The first comprehensive, integrated pacification plan, the Accelerated Pacification Campaign (APC), from 1 November 1968 to 31 January 1969, materialized from apparent defeat.

The Tết Offensive evoked wildly disparate assessments in Sài Gòn and Washington. In Sài Gòn, American and South Vietnamese officials viewed the Communist military effort as a failure: VC and People's Army of Vietnam (PAVN) losses were high, the anticipated popular uprising failed to occur, and no significant military objectives, except the city of Huê, were held for long. Washington viewed the offensive as a political and psychological defeat, because the Communists had unexpectedly launched an all-out national offensive that hit many cities, and a small raiding party briefly and suicidally entered the U.S. Embassy's grounds. To Komer, the spent offensive offered an opportunity to demonstrate that pacification could indeed make the visible gains that had eluded earlier plans. By March 1968 he was convinced that the failed offensive had left a "vacuum" in the countryside. Severely weakened by losses, the Việt Công, in his view, would be unable to challenge the expansion of the pacification program into contested or Communist-controlled areas. Moreover, increasing the population under RVN control would also help U.S. and South Vietnamese negotiators at the Paris peace talks, scheduled to begin in the fall of 1968.

Komer overcame significant resistance from CORDS and the American command. They were reluctant to embark on the ambitious plan to improve security in 1,000 contested and Communist-controlled hamlets in 90 days. General Creighton Abrams, who had replaced Westmoreland as the American commander, agreed that the Việt Công would be unable to resist, and in September he approved the concept of a special pacification offensive. It took a concerted effort by Ambassador Ellsworth Bunker, Komer, and his deputy, William Colby, to persuade President Thiệu and his generals that they had more than enough Revolutionary Development cadre teams and RF/PF units to carry out the APC offensive. APC set targets for all major pacification programs, ranging from the number of VCI to be arrested to the number of defectors, and committed the RVN's ministries and armed forces to carry it out. Critical to the APC was Abrams's commitment to have U.S. military units support it. During the campaign, nearly half of all U.S. ground operations were launched in support of the APC.

The APC enjoyed mixed success. On the one hand, most statistical goals were reached or exceeded, and the Americans were generally pleased with South Vietnamese performance. The Việt Công offered little overt armed resistance to the expansion, giving credence to the view that they were a depleted military force. Communist cadres seemed to concentrate on solidifying political control of their villages to hold on to what was already theirs. On the other hand, Komer's overriding purpose for the APC was not achieved. The offensive failed to persuade the American press or the government in Washington that the war was being won and that pacification had made real, lasting progress. After the APC, civilian agencies in Washington argued that the recent gains in pacification were fragile and reversible, should the Communists choose to contest them more vigorously.

The APC initiated a period of gains and improvements in pacification that lasted until the 1972 Easter Offensive. The percentage of the population living in government-controlled hamlets rose from 42 percent in 1967 to 80 percent in 1972, according to Hamlet Evaluation Survey (HES) data. Regional Forces and Popular Forces grew from 300,000 in 1967 to 520,000 at the end of 1972 and were better armed and trained; the RVN police went from 74,000 to 121,000 over the same period. The Việt Công lost strength and prominence. The VCI shrank from an estimated 85,000 in August 1967 to 56,000 in February 1972; the ranks of Việt Công guerrilla units dropped from 77,000 in January 1968 to 25,000 in May 1972.

To replenish these losses, Hà Nôi filled many guerrilla units with soldiers from its army, outsiders in South Vietnam's villages. Many key VC leaders and cadre, who were largely native southerners, had been killed or captured or had defected. Their replacements were generally of lower caliber. The APC brought unprecedented success to the pacification program and gave the government the chance, beginning at the end of 1968, to consolidate control over the countryside and build a national political community.

In November 1968 William Colby took over CORDS after Komer was named ambassador to Turkey. He assumed control of an established, functioning organization. Thanks to improvements in the RF/PF under Komer and heavy VC losses during the 1968 Tết Offensive, Colby could afford to be less concerned with local security than his predecessor. Although the RF/PF, police, and Chiêu Hôi and Phoenix programs continued as high-priority items, Colby oriented CORDS toward rural economic development and political programs, taking advantage of improved security. In his view, the RVN needed to develop the political and social resources to sustain itself over the long term, a position that accorded well with President Richard Nixon's Vietnamization policy. The three "selfs" summarized his approach to pacification: "self-defense, self-government, and self-development."

Colby also benefited from extensive military support for pacification under General Abrams. The APC had established a precedent for meshing pacification plans and military operations, and Abrams preached the importance of pacification over attrition to his commanders, trying to change their attitudes toward the "other war." Results were mixed. Some operations, such as WASHINGTON GREEN in Bình Đinh Province in 1968 and 1969, were models of cooperation between U.S. and ARVN units and between American pacification advisors and local governmental officials. WASHINGTON GREEN was designed and carried out specifically to improve security and gain the political loyalty of villagers. Other operations, such as RUSSELL BEACH in Quang Ngãi Province in 1969, proved as inimical to provincial pacification plans as Operation CEDAR FALLS had in 1966, when Westmoreland was in command. Both operations saw the involuntary removal of villagers from their homes into hastily prepared and inadequate refugee camps so that commanders could maximize the use of firepower. Both caused emotional and physical harm to the persons displaced; neither resulted in the long-term improvement of security.

A basic problem for pacification was assessing "progress" in a political war without front lines. It was fought village by village and district by district. The HES attempted to measure the percentage of people living in areas under government control, clearly a different yardstick than persons committed to the government. By its nature, the so-called war for "hearts and minds" had few objective measures, and some that seemed objective, such as the numbers of RF/PF and militia under arms, were not as critical as the subjective evaluations of their combat ability and willingness to fight. American advisors experienced frequent frustration with the performance of both Vietnamese forces in fighting the VC and government officials in carrying out pacification programs honestly and effectively.

As for Communist losses, there were doubts here also. Clearly, the VC and the VCI were weaker in 1972 than in 1967, and programs such as Phoenix and Chiêu Hôi definitely weakened the insurgency. But Phoenix proved so controversial that it is moot whether its overall impact was positive or negative. The Communist leadership's commitment to replace losses and continue the war was unshaken.

Historians and participants disagree over the accomplishments of pacification. The evidence is inconclusive. The war ended with a conventional military offensive, an indication to some that pacification had succeeded and forced the Communists to take up a "big-unit" war in 1972 and 1975. Yet the VC, though weakened, remained formidable in difficult provinces like Hâu Nghĩa and Bình Đinh and were found throughout South Vietnam. They could have continued the insurgency.

Pacification was hard to judge in isolation, because its gains depended to a significant extent on Allied military support and they occurred after the VC suffered heavy losses in Tết 1968. It cannot be determined in retrospect to what degree pacification would have flourished against a stronger foe. In any event, the program did not realize its potential until after the Tết Offensive, too late to affect the growing public and media perception in America that the war was stalemated.

The critical element in pacification was the Vietnamese parties. The Communists were determined to conquer South Vietnam and unify the country, and they adjusted their strategy and tactics several times during the war to attain that end. They would not give up. Some have argued that if a substantial and coordinated civil military pacification program had been launched in 1965, then the war could have been won. That interpretation fails to acknowledge how moribund pacification then was and also underestimates the enormously difficult task of transforming the RVN into a viable nation-state, an outcome that would have taken so long it would probably have exhausted U.S. support.

—Richard A. Hunt

References: Hunt, Richard. *Pacification: The American Struggle for Vietnam's Hearts and Minds.* Boulder, CO: Westview Press, 1995.
Thayer, Thomas. *How to Analyze a War without Fronts.* Boulder, CO: Westview Press, 1985.
See also: Abrams, Creighton; Bundy, McGeorge; Bunker, Ellsworth; Chiêu Hôi (Open Arms) Program; Civilian Operations and Revolutionary Development Support (CORDS); Colby, William Egan; Hamlet Evaluation

System (HES); Honolulu Conference; Johnson, Lyndon Baines; Komer, Robert W.; Lodge, Henry Cabot, Jr.; Mao Zedong (Mao Tse-tung); Ngô Đình Diệm; Nguyên Cao Kỳ; Nguyên Văn Thiêu; Nixon, Richard Milhous; Phoenix Program; Porter, William James; Refugees and Boat People; Strategic Hamlet Program; Taylor, Maxwell Davenport; Territorial Forces; U.S. Agency for International Development (USAID); Vietnamization.

Palme, Olaf J.

(1927–1986)

Swedish premier and internationally known peace and disarmament advocate and critic of U.S. involvement in Vietnam. Born in 1927, Palme attended private schools before receiving an education in politics and economics at Kenyon College in Ohio and a law degree from the University of Stockholm. A Social Democrat, Palme became Europe's youngest elected premier in 1969.

Palme angered Americans in 1968 when he joined the North Vietnamese ambassador to the Soviet Union in a Stockholm demonstration against U.S. Vietnam policy and when he compared Richard Nixon and the Hà Nôi bombings to the actions of Hitler. Palme left office in 1976 but returned to power in 1982 and won reelection in 1985. He was assassinated by an unknown gunman in Stockholm on 28 February 1986.

—Clayton D. Laurie

References: Freeman, Ruth. *Death of a Statesman: The Solution to the Murder of Olaf Palme.* London: R. Hale, 1989.
Mosey, Chris. *Cruel Awakening: Sweden and the Killing of Olaf Palme.* New York: St. Martin's Press, 1991.
See also: Nixon, Richard Milhous.

Palmer, Bruce, Jr.

(1913–)

U.S. Army general and Vietnam War author. Born in Austin, Texas, on 13 April 1913, Bruce Palmer graduated from West Point in 1936, a classmate of William Westmoreland. During World War II, Palmer was the chief of staff of the 6th Infantry Division in the southwest Pacific; from 1946 to 1956 he commanded the 63d Infantry Regiment in Korea. He rose steadily through the ranks to lieutenant general. In May 1965 Palmer commanded Task Force 120 and U.S. Land Forces during the U.S. intervention in the Dominican Republic. From 1965 to 1967 he commanded the XVIII Airborne Corps at Fort Bragg, North Carolina.

From March to July 1967 Palmer commanded II Field Force, the largest U.S. Army combat command in Vietnam. During his tenure as commander, II Field Force executed Operations JUNCTION CITY and MANHATTAN, the two largest operations of the war to that time. From July 1967 to June 1968 Palmer was the deputy commander of U.S. Army, Vietnam (USARV). Although the commander of Military Assistance Command, Vietnam (MACV), General Westmoreland, was also "dual hatted" as USARV commander, the USARV deputy commander actually ran USARV's daily operations.

Promoted to full general, Palmer was vice-chief of staff of the Army from August 1968 to June 1972. When General Creighton Abrams was selected to succeed Westmoreland as chief of staff,

his confirmation was delayed by Senate hearings investigating allegations that U.S. commanders in Vietnam had exceeded their authority by conducting unauthorized air strikes in North Vietnam. During that interim period until October 1972 Palmer served as the acting chief of staff. Palmer retired from the Army in September 1974, his last assignment being commander of the U.S. Army Readiness Command.

Palmer wrote one of the most important books about Vietnam, *The 25-Year War: America's Military Role in Vietnam,* published in 1984. In it Palmer provides a penetrating analysis of the U.S. military decision-making process during the formative years of the war. He also provides a thorough critique of the disjointed operational chain of command for the war: Although the MACV commander controlled military operations within South Vietnam, the commander in chief, U.S. Pacific Command controlled the offensive air war over the North, while B-52 strikes remained under the control of the Strategic Air Command.

Palmer points out that one of the major flaws of the U.S. strategy was in placing too much faith in the air war. Although the air interdiction program was the most effective element of that aspect of the war, it too was weakened by the lack of supporting ground operations. In assessing what military strategy might have worked, Palmer suggests that defeating the insurgent threat in South Vietnam should have been the primary responsibility of the South Vietnamese. According to Palmer, U.S. ground forces should have prevented People's Army of Vietnam (PAVN) regular forces and supplies from moving into South Vietnam by massing in the northern part of the country and cutting lines of communications within Laos. In an August 1995 interview in *The Wall Street Journal,* Bùi Tín, a former colonel on the PAVN general staff, agreed that those very actions would have cost the Communists the war.

In discussing the larger lessons of the war, Palmer emphasizes that the employment of military force is an art, rather than an exact science. He concludes, "It is supremely important that our national leaders, civilian and military, have a fundamental understanding of the capabilities and limitations of military power. Vietnam demonstrated how the lack of such understanding can lead to disastrous failure." Palmer does not imply that all the fault for the failure in Vietnam lay with the nation's political leadership. He also states, "One body of opinion believes that things would have turned out differently had the military not 'had their hands tied.' I have much difficulty with this thesis because I feel that our top-level military leaders must share the onus of failure."

—David T. Zabecki

References: Bell, William G. *Commanding Generals and Chiefs of Staff: 1775–1983.* Washington, DC: U.S. Army Center of Military History, 1983.
Palmer, Bruce, Jr. *The 25-Year War: America's Military Role in Vietnam.* Lexington, KY: University Press of Kentucky, 1984.
Young, Stephen. "How North Vietnam Won the War," *The Wall Street Journal.* (3 August 1995).
See also: Abrams, Creighton; JUNCTION CITY, Operation; Military Assistance Command, Vietnam (MACV); United States: Army; Westmoreland, William Childs.

Paracel and Spratly Islands

Two island groups in the South China Sea; their Vietnamese names are Quân Đao Hoàng Sa (Paracel Islands) and Quân Đao Trường Sa (Spratly Islands). The Paracels, which the Chinese call Xisha, are located about 170 nautical miles from Đà Năng and from the Chinese island of Hai Nan, between 15'45" and 17'05" north latitude and 111'00" and 113'00" east longitude. This archipelago comprises about 15 to 30 islands, depending on the way they are counted.

The Spratlys, which the Chinese call Nansha and the Filipinos call Kalayaan, lie about 250 nautical miles from Cam Ranh Bay, between 6'50" and 12'00" north latitude and 111'30" and 117'20" east longitude. This archipelago is made up of about a hundred large and small islands and covers an area of 160,000 square kilometers; its center is approximately midway between Vietnam and the Philippines.

Several nations of Southeast Asia, China, and Taiwan currently dispute the sovereignty of these islands. After two decades of occupation by the Army of the Republic of Vietnam (ARVN), in 1974 the Paracels were seized by force by People's Republic of China troops. The Spratlys have been claimed not only by Vietnam, the People's Republic of China, and Taiwan but also by the Philippines, Malaysia, and Brunei. Reasons given for the disputes over these islands were, among others, the strategic position of both the Paracels and Spratlys and possible nearby offshore oil deposits. From the Paracels a naval power could control navigation in the northern part of the South China Sea, and from Spratlys it could follow all ship traffic within Southeast Asia between the Pacific and the Indian Oceans. In these disputes, Vietnam and China claim all the islands. China bases its argument on the rights of discovery, while Vietnam emphasizes its continuous occupation since the seventeenth century. The Philippines and Malaysia emphasize the Spratlys' proximity to their territory.

—Pham Cao Dương

References: Chi-kin Lo. *China's Policy toward Territorial Disputes.* New York: Routledge, 1989.
The Hoang Sa and Truong Sa Archipelagoes (Paracels and Spratlys). Hà Nôi: Vietnam Courrier, 1981.
Lafont, Pierre-Bernard. "Les Frontieres en Mer de Chine Meridionale." In *Les Frontieres du Vietnam: Histoire des Frontieres de la Peninsule Indochinoise.* Paris: L'Harmattan, 1989.
Vo Long Te. *Les Archipels de Hoang-Sa et de Truong-Sa Selon Les Anciens ouvrages de l'Histoire et de Geographie.* Sài Gòn: Ministere de la Culture, de l'Education et de la Jeunesse, 1974.
See also: China, People's Republic of (PRC); China, Republic of (ROC; Taiwan); Philippines.

Paris Negotiations

(1968–1973)

Like the war, the Vietnam peace negotiations were long, painful, and frustrating. From the first meeting to the last, the talks lasted four years, eight months, and 17 days, during which more than 20,000 Americans and perhaps three-quarters of a million Vietnamese on both sides were killed.

The stage was set for the talks when President Lyndon Johnson announced on 31 March 1968 that the United States would stop bombing north of the 20th parallel in the Democratic Republic of Vietnam (DRV) and would seek to open negotiations. Four days later Hà Nôi agreed to send a representative to meet with U.S. officials—though only to discuss an "unconditional" halt to the rest of the bombing. After several weeks of haggling about the site, both sides agreed on Paris.

On 10 May in a conference hall on Avenue Kléber, U.S. and DRV negotiators faced each other for the first time. Three days later the talks formally opened. Averell Harriman headed the U.S. delegation and veteran diplomat Xuân Thuy represented the DRV.

During the next five months the DRV continued to insist that nothing else could be negotiated until all air strikes on its territory had stopped. President Johnson hesitated but finally, on the last day of October 1968, announced the halt, although U.S. negotiators refused to call it unconditional, as the DRV demanded.

The next hurdle was widening the talks to include the two South Vietnamese parties. The DRV and its ally, the National Liberation Front (NLF), refused to accept the Sài Gòn government as a legitimate participant. Just as adamantly, the Republic of Vietnam (RVN) refused to recognize the NLF.

To get around the impasse, Harriman and his deputy Cyrus Vance proposed that instead of officially identifying the four parties, negotiators would simply refer to "our side" and "your side." Through this diplomatic fiction, NLF representatives could join the DRV team but without having to be acknowledged by Sài Gòn's delegates; similarly, RVN negotiators could sit with their American allies without having to be acknowledged by the DRV-NLF side. Hà Nôi agreed but South Vietnam's President Nguyên Văn Thiêu balked, delaying the first session until 16 January 1969—four days before Richard Nixon's inauguration as president.

Nixon named Henry Cabot Lodge to replace Harriman as the chief U.S. negotiator; Lodge resigned in November and was replaced the following year by David K. E. Bruce. Meanwhile, in June 1969 the NLF proclaimed the establishment of a new Provisional Revolutionary Government of South Vietnam, giving its delegation the same governmental status as the other three participants.

The start of negotiations brought a flurry of hope that the war might be settled quickly. Instead, the talks fell into a dreary ritual of weekly sessions, during which both sides recited long-standing positions again and again, without ever coming close to agreement.

The Nixon administration, meanwhile, shifted its negotiating effort from the official talks into a new, secret channel. On 4 August 1969 Henry Kissinger, Nixon's national security advisor, held the first secret meeting with Xuân Thuy in Paris. Lê Đức Tho, one of Hà Nôi's senior leaders, took over as the DRV negotiator in subsequent sessions.

For more than three years, while the United States offered various plans for a cease-fire followed by troop withdrawals and negotiations for a political settlement, the DRV insisted in both the official and secret talks that the only way to end the war was for the United States to dissolve the Sài Gòn government, disband its army, and install a new coalition that would then negotiate for a truce. Hà Nội's position began to soften in the summer of 1972, in the aftermath of that year's Easter Offensive. Then, on 8 October 1972 Tho handed Kissinger a draft treaty, agreeing, for the first time, that the Thiệu regime could remain in existence and negotiate with the PRG, after a cease-fire, for a permanent political settlement.

"We have done it!" Kissinger exulted. Over the next ten days he and Tho reached agreement on a final draft. But Thiệu balked, objecting most vehemently to the fact that the draft treaty did not require North Vietnamese troops to leave the South. Thiệu also objected to the proposed National Council of National Reconciliation and Concord, which was to oversee political negotiations and elections for a new South Vietnamese government.

Talks resumed in November, broke off in mid-December, and remained suspended during the 11-day U.S. air assault code-named LINEBACKER II (more widely called the Christmas bombing). Soon after the new year began, Kissinger and Tho returned to Paris, where on 23 January 1973 they initialed a treaty that, except for some minor changes, was essentially the same as their October draft. The formal signing was set for 27 January, bringing the negotiations to a conclusion at last.

—Arnold R. Isaacs

References: Goodman, Allan E. *The Lost Peace: America's Search for a Negotiated Settlement of the Vietnam War.* Stanford, CA: Hoover Institute Press, 1978.
Kissinger, Henry A. *White House Years.* Boston: Little, Brown, 1979.
See also: Bruce, David K. E.; Harriman, W. Averell; Johnson, Lyndon Baines; Kissinger, Henry Alfred; Lê Đức Tho; Nguyễn Văn Thiệu; Nixon, Richard Milhous; Paris Peace Accords; Xuân Thuy.

Paris Peace Accords

(January 1973)

The "Agreement on Ending the War and Restoring Peace in Vietnam," signed in Paris on 27 January 1973, which ended direct U.S. military involvement in the conflict but failed to end the war itself. The signing ceremony itself revealed the hostility that still lay between the warring sides. The foreign ministers of the two South Vietnamese opponents, the Republic of Vietnam (RVN) and the Provisional Revolutionary Government (PRG), would not even put their signatures on the same copy of the document but signed on separate pages, while representatives of the United States and the Democratic Republic of Vietnam (DRV) signed yet a third copy.

The agreement opened by declaring that "the United States and all other countries respect the independence, sovereignty, unity and territorial integrity of Vietnam as recognized by the 1954 Geneva Agreements on Vietnam." This was meaningful because it reflected the position the Communist side had argued for years: that Vietnam was *one* country, not two, and thus their revolution was not "foreign aggression," as Sài Gòn and the United States maintained, but a legitimate struggle to regain national independence and unity.

The agreement's other provisions called for:

- A cease-fire, to take effect 27 January at midnight, Greenwich Mean Time (0800 the next day, Sài Gòn time). Following the cease-fire, Vietnamese forces would remain in place; resupply of weapons, munitions, and war materiel would be permitted but only to replace items destroyed or used up during the truce.
- Withdrawal of all U.S. and other foreign troops within 60 days, with the release of all U.S. war prisoners "carried out simultaneously" with the troop withdrawal. The signers also promised to assist in accounting for missing personnel and to help find, identify, and repatriate the remains of those who had died.
- Negotiations between South Vietnamese parties for a settlement that would "end hatred and enmity" and allow the South Vietnamese people to freely decide their political future. A National Council of National Reconciliation and Concord, with members representing both South Vietnamese sides and a neutral "third force," would oversee the negotiations and organize elections for a new government. Following a settlement in South Vietnam, reunification of the two Vietnams was to be "carried out step by step through peaceful means."

Other clauses covered such matters as establishing an international observer force and respect for the neutrality of Laos and Cambodia.

The withdrawal of U.S. forces was completed as promised. Some 23,000 American troops, the last of a force that had once numbered more than half a million, left during the 60 days following the truce. On the final day, the U.S. command issued its last general order: "Headquarters Military Assistance Command Vietnam is inactivated this date and its mission and functions reassigned." At 1800 the last troops boarded a U.S. Air Force transport and flew out of the country. Only the truce observers, a detachment of Marine embassy guards, a small team of missing in action (MIA) negotiators, and 50 military personnel assigned to the Defense Attaché Office, now remained in the Republic of Vietnam.

The DRV, meanwhile, released 591 American prisoners of war (POWs). Although the POW issue remained contentious for many years afterward, the Hà Nội leadership never wavered from its insistence that it had turned over all the prisoners in its hands at the time of the agreement.

Aside from ending U.S. military involvement, the agreement achieved none of its other objectives. No political settlement was reached, the national reconciliation council was never created, and no election was held. Nor did the fighting stop, or even slow down. Only the United States, among the four signers, observed the cease-fire. For the Vietnamese, the war continued as before.

The failure of the truce was ordained even before it was supposed to take effect. The agreement called for a "cease-fire in place" but made no provision for establishing, even in rough terms, where the forces of each side belonged. Consequently, there was an irresistible temptation for both sides to try to seize as much territory as possible in the final hours. The Communist side—not tied down, as was Sài Gòn's army, by the need to keep

Henry Kissinger (left foreground) and Lê Đức Thọ (background, second from right) initial the cease-fire agreement in Paris. Seated to the left of Lê Đức Thọ is Xuân Thuy, Thọ's chief deputy.

large forces deployed to protect major towns and communications routes—struck more aggressively. In the 36 hours before the cease-fire was to begin, they penetrated more than 400 towns and villages and cut every major highway in the country.

Though not technically violating the agreement, the attacks drastically altered the true battle lines the truce was intended to preserve. Had the RVN actually frozen in place at the cease-fire hour, its enemy would have been left occupying hundreds of positions that were normally under Sài Gòn's control. There was no possibility that President Nguyên Văn Thiêu and his generals would accept that situation, and they did not. Thiêu ordered his forces to keep fighting, even if offensive operations continued after the cease-fire hour.

In about two weeks RVN troops recaptured most of the territory seized in the pre–cease-fire fighting. Had they paused at that point, with more or less "normal" battle lines reestablished, the cease-fire might have taken hold. Instead, they remained on the offensive.

As fighting continued, both sides took the position that military operations, including attacks anywhere in the enemy's zone, were justified by the other side's prior violations of the cease-fire. Because there had never been any agreement on where either side's forces belonged in the first place (in fact, neither ever con-

ceded that its enemy had a right to any territory at all) there was no way to restore the lines that were supposed to have been frozen by the truce. Instead, there was only an endless chain of retaliations in which, over time, even the idea of peace gradually disappeared. Casualties told the story: 51,000 South Vietnamese soldiers were killed in 1973 and 1974, the highest two-year toll of the entire war. Two years after it was signed, the agreement was all but forgotten: "like a dictionary," said one member of the international observer force, "for a language that nobody speaks."

—Arnold R. Isaacs

References: Isaacs, Arnold R. *Without Honor: Defeat in Vietnam and Cambodia.* Baltimore, MD: Johns Hopkins University Press, 1983.
Le Gro, William E. *Vietnam from Ceasefire to Capitulation.* Washington, DC: Center of Military History, 1981.
Porter, D. Gareth. *A Peace Denied: The United States, Vietnam, and the Paris Agreement.* Bloomington, IN: Indiana University Press, 1975.
See also: National Council of National Reconciliation and Concord (NCNRC); Nguyên Văn Thiêu; Paris Negotiations.

Parrot's Beak

Area of Cambodia that projects into South Vietnam above the Mekong Delta, abutting southern Tây Ninh and western Hậu

Nghĩa Provinces, and only 30 miles from Sài Gòn. Highway 1 ran through this densely populated and fertile area from Sài Gòn to the Cambodian capital of Phnom Penh. As in the Fishhook area to the north, Communist forces maintained semipermanent installations in the Parrot's Beak from which they infiltrated into southern III Corps and northern IV Corps. Though Army of the Republic of Vietnam (ARVN) forces had frequently exercised the right of "hot pursuit" into Communist sanctuaries in Cambodia, American forces were not permitted to do so. Beginning in March 1969, however, President Richard Nixon authorized secret B-52 bombing missions, known as Operation MENU, to deter Communist infiltration.

By early 1970 Allied forces had driven main force Communist units across the border into Cambodia, where they regrouped and expanded their support bases. Communist Base Areas 367 and 706 were located in the Parrot's Beak, and these became the primary objectives of the third phase of the so-called Cambodian Incursion, ordered by President Nixon to begin on 1 May 1970. This phase of the Cambodian operation was conducted entirely by ARVN III and IV Corps ground forces; the American 9th Infantry Division provided only artillery and logistical support. Not bound by the 30-mile penetration limit imposed on American forces, ARVN units rapidly moved deep inside Cambodia, uncovering caches of thousands of weapons and millions of rounds of ammunition. ARVN forces successfully engaged both People's Army of Vietnam (PAVN) and Khmer Rouge forces, up to positions north and south of Phnom Penh.

The ARVN penetration into and through the Parrot's Beak was the first real test of Nixon's Vietnamization policy and was termed a great success. But the operation was complicated by the fact that at the same time ARVN forces were engaging PAVN forces they found themselves protecting and evacuating thousands of indigenous Vietnamese, who were being massacred by General Lon Nol's Cambodian forces. On at least two occasions ARVN troops came to the rescue of Cambodian units besieged by retreating PAVN forces.

Although ARVN forces remained inside Cambodia for a time and acquitted themselves well, Lon Nol's army was powerless to impede the reoccupation of the Parrot's Beak by Communist military units. By the end of 1971, despite daily B-52 bombings, Communist bases were again fully operational; they served as the springboard for massive infiltrations during the 1972 Easter Offensive.

—John D. Root

References: Coleman, J. D. *Incursion.* New York: St. Martin's Press, 1991.
Stanton, Shelby L. *The Rise and Fall of an American Army: U.S. Ground Forces in Vietnam: 1965–1973.* San Francisco: Presidio Press, 1985.
See also: Cambodia; Cambodian Incursion; Fishhook; Khmer Rouge; Nixon, Richard Milhous.

PASSAGE TO FREEDOM, Operation
(1954)

Operation transferring Vietnamese refugees south of the 17th parallel after the 1954 Geneva Accords. Fearful of Việt Minh persecution, nearly 1 million Vietnamese took advantage of the Accord's provisions to move south of the 17th parallel. Most were Catholics who, when prompted to flee by U.S. and French propaganda, could solidify a constituency for South Vietnamese Catholic leader Ngô Đình Diêm.

Washington organized a dramatic rescue operation for these refugees in cooperation with French forces and voluntary agencies. The operation was code-named PASSAGE TO FREEDOM by the U.S. Navy and Operation EXODUS by Diêm. According to Louis Wiesner, in *Victims and Survivors: Displaced Persons and Other War Victims in Viet-Nam, 1954–1975,* the operation evacuated 768,672 refugees from the North: 310,848 of these in U.S. ships, 213,635 by French aircraft, 235,000 by French ships, and 9,189 by British and other ships. Washington also provided emergency food, medical care, clothing, and shelter at reception centers in Vũng Tàu and Sài Gòn. In all, the operation cost the U.S. government some $93 million.

The U.S. press promoted American participation in the venture, particularly the activities of U.S. Navy doctor Thomas Dooley, as evidence of U.S. dedication to "freedom-loving people escaping Communist tyranny." By December U.S. government and nongovernment agencies allocated millions of additional dollars to resettle these refugees, deepening America's commitment to nation building in South Vietnam.

—Delia Pergande

References: Hooper, Edwin, Dean Allard, and Oscar Fitzgerald. *The United States Navy and the Vietnam Conflict.* Vol. 1, *The Setting of the Stage to 1959.* Washington, DC: U.S. Government Printing Office, 1976.
Kahin, George McT. *Intervention: How America Became Involved in Vietnam.* New York: Alfred A. Knopf, 1986.
Wiesner, Louis. *Victims and Survivors: Displaced Persons and Other War Victims in Viet-Nam, 1954–1975.* New York: Greenwood Press, 1988.
See also: Geneva Conference and Geneva Accords; Ngô Đình Diêm; United States: Involvement in Vietnam, 1954–1965.

Pathet Lao

Front group for Communist forces in Laos. The name means "Land of the Lao" and was applied for the first time to the clandestine resistance government formed by Prince Souphanouvong in August 1950 to fight against the French. The early history of the Pathet Lao paralleled in almost every respect that of the front group formed by Hồ Chí Minh in 1941, the Việt Minh, which was also controlled by a small core of Communist leaders. Just as the Việt Minh front was formed in a secure base area over the border in China, the Pathet Lao front was formed at a meeting inside the border in the Democratic Republic of Vietnam (DRV). Although the Pathet Lao's program was designed to appeal to non-Communist nationalists with its slogans "Peace, independence, neutrality and prosperity," the Pathet Lao never achieved the same degree of popularity among the Laotians as the Việt Minh did in Vietnam, probably because they were so evidently dependent on the Vietnamese Communists.

—Arthur J. Dommen

Reference: Zasloff, Joseph J., and MacAlister Brown. *Apprentice Revolutionaries: The Communist Movement in Laos, 1930–1985.* Stanford, CA: Hoover Institution Press, 1986.

Refugees board LSM-516 during Operation PASSAGE TO FREEDOM. Fearful of Viêt Minh persecution, nearly 1 million Vietnamese took advantage of the 1954 Geneva Accord's provisions for them to move south of the 17th parallel.

See also: Laos; Souphanouvong; United Front; Viêt Minh (Viêt Nam Ðôc Lâp Ðông Minh Hôi [Vietnam Independence League]).

Patti, Archimedes L. A.

(1913–)

U.S. Army officer serving in the Office of Strategic Services (OSS) who formed a friendship with Hô Chí Minh in 1945 and witnessed the assumption of power by the Viêt Minh in Hà Nôi. Archimedes Patti was born in New York City in 1913, and was educated in the United States and Italy. He entered the U.S. Army in 1936 and worked with the British Intelligence Services during 1942–1944.

Captain Patti's Indo-China experience began on 13 April 1945, when he arrived at the OSS headquarters at Kunming in southern China. The head of the Secret Intelligence (SI) Branch ordered Patti to investigate the establishment in Indo-China of a network using independence-minded Vietnamese to provide intelligence on Japanese troop strengths and movements. This assignment led to Patti's acquaintance with Hô Chí Minh, who offered the services of the Viêt Minh in return for arms and funds from the OSS.

After the Japanese surrender, Patti headed a group of OSS officers who flew into Hà Nôi on 22 August 1945, becoming the first Allied representatives in that city. Ostensibly, their mission was to locate and arrange for the repatriation of Allied prisoners of war. Patti remained in Hà Nôi, seeing Hô and his lieutenant Võ Nguyên Giáp on numerous occasions, until 1 October. In a book he wrote about his experiences, Patti emphasized Hô's aspirations for independence and played down his Communist background. Patti left the U.S. Army in 1957, but continued his work in national security affairs until 1971.

—Arthur J. Dommen

References: Charlton, Michael, and Anthony Moncrieff. *Many Reasons Why: The American Involvement in Vietnam.* New York: Hill & Wang, 1978.
Patti, Archimedes L. A. *Why Vietnam? Prelude to America's Albatross.* Berkeley, CA: University of California Press, 1980.
See also: Dewey, Albert Peter; Hô Chí Minh; Office of Strategic Services (OSS); Viêt Minh (Viêt Nam Ðôc Lâp Ðông Minh Hôi [Vietnam Independence League]); Võ Nguyên Giáp.

PAUL REVERE I–IV, Operations

(1966)

A series of Allied screening operations along the Cambodian border in Pleiku Province from May to December 1966. Throughout 1966 no single Allied force operated primarily in Pleiku Province, but special task forces were formed. Buoyed by the 1st Cavalry's victory in the Ia Drang Valley the previous fall, U.S. Military Assistance Command, Vietnam (MACV) commander General William Westmoreland favored making the western Central Highlands an area of American concentration, hoping for more main force battles with the People's Army of Vietnam (PAVN) to develop. In March and April the 2d Brigade of the 1st Cavalry joined with the newly arrived 3d Brigade of the 25th Infantry Division to conduct

two operations in the Chu Pong area that killed more than 500 PAVN soldiers.

The mission of PAUL REVERE I/THÂN PHONG (10 May–30 July), led by Brig. Gen. Glenn Walker of the 25th Division, was to counter a possible offensive of the PAVN "Yellow Star" Division against the Special Forces border camps. Joining the task force were a battalion of the 2d Brigade and Troop B, 1st Squadron, 9th Cavalry from the 1st Cavalry Division, two Army of the Republic of Vietnam (ARVN) and Republic of Korea (ROK) battalions, and six artillery batteries. For the most part, the relatively small task force sparred with PAVN units over a large area from the Chu Pong Massif to Ðức Cơ, and from the Cambodian border to Plei Me. But U.S. forces did engage in heavy fighting at Chu Pong, killing more than 200 PAVN soldiers while taking only light casualties.

PAUL REVERE II (1–25 August) was a larger operation, again in the Chu Pong War Zone. When patrolling units of the 3d Brigade of the 25th Division began to take casualties, the 2d and 3d Brigades of the 1st Cavalry were airlifted from An Khê in just 12 hours, followed by the insertion of two ARVN and ROK battalions. For nearly three weeks the 1st Cavalry's Maj. Gen. John Norton led 14 battalions against two PAVN regiments in a battle that S. L. A. Marshall called "the whopper of the summer," which resulted in 861 PAVN soldiers killed, 202 captured, and the seizure of more than 300 weapons.

PAUL REVERE III in September was uneventful, but Paul Revere IV (18 October–30 December) was a major search-and-destroy operation along the Cambodian border conducted primarily by the newly arrived 4th Infantry Division, augmented by elements of the 25th Division and by the 2d Brigade of the 1st Cavalry, barely rested after concluding Operation IRVING in Bình Ðịnh Province. The operation centered on the Chu Pong–Ia Drang area, and although U.S. forces suffered heavy casualties in ambushes, a regiment of the PAVN 10th Division left 977 known dead on the battlefields.

—John D. Root

References: Hymoff, Edward. *The First Air Cavalry Division, Vietnam.* New York: M. W. Lads, 1967.
Marshall, S. L. A. *Battles in the Monsoon: Campaigning in the Central Highlands Vietnam, Summer 1966.* New York: William Morrow, 1967.
Westmoreland, General William C. *Report on Operations in SVN, January 1964–June 1968.* Washington, DC: Department of Defense, 1968.
See also: Airmobility; Free World Assistance Program; Ia Drang, Battle of; IRVING, Operation; Military Assistance Command, Vietnam (MACV); Search and Destroy; United States: Army; Westmoreland, William Childs.

Pearson, Lester Bowles

(1897–1972)

Canadian prime minister, 1963–1968. Born on 23 April 1897 in Toronto, Ontario, Lester Bowles Pearson was the son of a Methodist minister. He attended the University of Toronto, from which he received a B.A. degree in 1919, and Oxford University in England, where he earned both B.A. and M.A. degrees. Following the war Pearson returned to the University of Toronto as a lecturer in history.

Pearson's career in the diplomatic service eventually took him to Washington, where he served as Canadian ambassador to the United States from January 1945 to September 1946. He played a pivotal advisory role in the Canadian delegation at the San Francisco Conference in 1945, which established the United Nations. The highlight of Pearson's political career came in 1957, when he became the first Canadian to receive the Nobel Peace Prize for his mediation efforts during the 1956 Suez crisis.

In 1958 Pearson became the leader of the Canadian Liberal Party. He took office as prime minister in 1963, his tenure coinciding with the period of U.S. escalation in Vietnam. Pearson's relationship with President Lyndon Johnson was permanently and negatively altered as a result of an April 1965 convocation address at Temple University in which Pearson suggested that the United States should cease its bombing of North Vietnam. The remark incensed President Johnson and, despite Pearson's subsequent apology, created a rift between the two that never completely disappeared. U.S. Secretary of State Dean Rusk characterized Canadian-American relations in 1967 as "deteriorated."

Pearson was succeeded as prime minister in 1968 by Pierre Trudeau. Pearson's government, although characterized by scandal among members of the Cabinet, succeeded in passing numerous domestic reforms, including a comprehensive Medicare program. In 1969 Pearson accepted one final diplomatic assignment when he agreed to lead a World Bank commission on international development. He died of cancer in Ottawa, Ontario, on 27 December 1972.

—Wes Watters

References: Bothwell, Robert, Ian Drummond, and John English. *Canada since 1945: Power, Politics, and Provincialism.* Toronto: University of Toronto Press, 1981.
English, John. *The Worldly Years: The Life of Lester Pearson.* Toronto: Vintage Books, 1992.
Pearson, Lester B. *Mike: The Memoirs of the Right Honourable Lester B. Pearson.* New York: Quadrangle Books, 1972.
See also: Canada; Johnson, Lyndon Baines; Rusk, Dean.

Peers, William R.

(1914–1984)

U.S. Army general and chairman of the 1969–1970 commission appointed to investigate the cover-up of the My Lai Massacre. Born 16 June 1914 in Stuart, Iowa, William Peers graduated from the University of California, Los Angeles, in 1937 and was commissioned into the U.S. Army through the Reserve Officers' Training Corps. During World War II, he rose to the rank of colonel and commanded Office of Strategic Services (OSS) Detachment 101, a famed guerrilla unit that operated along the India-Burma border.

Cigar smoking and craggy faced, Peers combined intellectual toughness and rock-ribbed integrity with his soldierly skills. In 1967 he took command of the 4th Infantry Division in Vietnam's Central Highlands, where he again demonstrated that he was a tough and determined combat leader. Then, promoted to lieutenant general, he commanded I Field Force, Vietnam.

Subsequently Peers was given the difficult and thankless task of conducting an inquiry into the My Lai cover-up. He set about the task with uncompromising intensity, eventually putting together an exhaustive account that fixed responsibility at several levels.

General Peers served a final tour of duty as deputy commanding general of the Eighth Army in Korea before retiring in 1973. Dissatisfied with the Army's failure to call to account those who had been responsible for My Lai and the cover-up, he then wrote a hard-hitting book entitled *The My Lai Inquiry,* in which he stated those concerns explicitly: "The failure to bring to justice those who participated in the tragedy or were negligent in following it up . . . casts grave doubts upon the efficacy of American justice— military and civilian alike." Peers died in California at the Presidio of San Francisco on 6 April 1984.

—Lewis Sorley

References: Hilsman, Roger. *American Guerrilla.* Washington, DC: Brassey's, 1990.
Peers, William R. *The My Lai Inquiry.* New York: W. W. Norton, 1979.
Peers, William R., and Dean Brelis. *Behind the Burma Road: The Story of America's Most Successful Guerrilla Force.* Boston: Little, Brown, 1963.
U.S. Department of the Army. *The My Lai Massacre and Its Cover-Up: Beyond the Reach of Law? The Peers Commission Report.* New York: Free Press, 1976.
See also: Atrocities during the Vietnam War; My Lai Massacre; Peers Inquiry.

Peers Inquiry

On 16 March 1968 in a hamlet called My Lai, American soldiers from the 23d Infantry ("Americal") Division deliberately murdered as many as several hundred innocent South Vietnamese, including women and children. Members of the division's chain of command thereafter sought to conceal what had taken place.

Not until over a year later did information of the atrocity leak out as the result of a soldier's letter to a number of government officials, prompting appointment of a commission of inquiry. Lt. Gen. William R. Peers headed the investigation. He was given that task by General William Westmoreland, U.S. commander in Vietnam when the My Lai Massacre took place but Army chief of staff when it was revealed. In his book *A Soldier Reports,* Westmoreland notes that he chose Peers because he "had a reputation throughout the Army for objectivity and fairness."

Eventually a number of officers and men were charged with murder and other crimes, and more than a dozen officers were charged with suppression of information relating to the incident. Of those brought to trial by court-martial, only Lt. William L. Calley, Jr. was convicted. He was found guilty of murder and sentenced to life imprisonment, although, because of subsequent actions ordered by President Richard Nixon, he actually served less than five years, much of it in what amounted to house arrest.

Maj. Gen. Samuel W. Koster was demoted one grade and relieved of his assignment as superintendent of the U.S. Military Academy at West Point. All others charged were acquitted or absolved administratively. Lt. Gen. Jonathan O. Seaman made a determination that there was insufficient evidence to bring to trial any of the senior officers except Col. Oran K. Henderson (who was court-martialed and acquitted). Thus, virtually all of those who perpetrated the atrocity and its cover-up escaped serious punishment.

"I found the dismissal of charges, particularly those without benefit of an Article 32 investigation, most difficult to understand," General Peers later wrote in his book *The My Lai Inquiry*. "I was especially disturbed by General Seaman's dismissal of charges against the senior officers, particularly in General Koster's case." His summary judgment on the matter was uncompromising: "Thus the failures of leadership that characterized nearly every aspect of the My Lai incident had their counterpart at the highest level during the attempt to prosecute those responsible."

Richard Nixon's involvement in the aftermath of My Lai was pervasive and malignant. Peers wrote that General Westmoreland had revealed to him that in contemplating an investigation of My Lai "he had encountered considerable resistance from within the Department of Defense, which he strongly suspected had originated in the White House." Westmoreland met with General Alexander Haig, then assigned to the White House staff, and told him that if the obstruction did not cease he would go directly to the president.

The Peers Inquiry, which then proceeded, uncovered devastating and conclusive evidence of what had taken place, going beyond the individuals involved with My Lai and its cover-up to indict the current state of leadership within the Army. "In analyzing the entire episode," wrote General Peers, "we found that the principal breakdown was in leadership. Failures occurred at every level within the chain of command, from individual noncommissioned officer squad leaders to the command group of the division. It was an illegal operation in violation of military regulations and of human rights, starting with the planning, continuing through the brutal, destructive acts of many of the men who were involved, and culminating in aborted efforts to investigate and, finally, the suppression of the truth."

It did not stop there, Peers wrote: "The failure to bring to justice those who participated in the tragedy or were negligent in following it up . . . casts grave doubts upon the efficacy of American justice—military and civilian alike."

In transmitting the report, General Peers added a cover letter that led General Westmoreland to institute a study on military professionalism, conducted at the Army War College, that documented beyond question the validity of General Peers's wider concerns about the health of Army leadership. "A scenario that was repeatedly described in seminar sessions and narrative responses," said the 1970 report, "includes an ambitious, transitory commander—marginally skilled in the complexities of his duties—engulfed in producing statistical results, fearful of personal failure, too busy to talk with or listen to his subordinates, and determined to submit acceptably optimistic reports which reflect faultless completion of a variety of tasks at the expense of the sweat and frustration of his subordinates." There was much rebuilding to be done.

—Lewis Sorley

References: Peers, William R. *The My Lai Inquiry.* New York: W. W. Norton, 1979.

U.S. Department of the Army. *The My Lai Massacre and Its Cover-Up: Beyond the Reach of Law? The Peers Commission Report.* New York: Free Press, 1976.

See also: Atrocities during the Vietnam War; Calley, William Laws, Jr.; My Lai Massacre; Peers, William R.; Westmoreland, William Childs.

PEGASUS–LAM SƠN 207A, Operation

(1–15 April 1968)

Joint military operation conducted from 1 to 15 April 1968 to lift the People's Army of Vietnam (PAVN) siege of Khe Sanh Base. In January 1968 at least two PAVN divisions surrounded the 26th Marine Regiment and an Army of the Republic of Vietnam (ARVN) Ranger battalion at Khe Sanh, just north of Route 9 near the Laotian border. Attention was riveted on Khe Sanh for fear it might become another Điên Biên Phu.

Maj. Gen. John J. Tolson's U.S. 1st Cavalry Division redeployed northward from II to I Corps in January, and Tolson was ordered on 10 March to prepare plans to relieve Khe Sanh. Code-named PEGASUS–LAM SƠN 207A, the operation was to start on 1 April. In addition to the 1st Cavalry, Tolson had two battalions of the 1st Marines, an ARVN airborne task force, an ARVN Ranger battalion at Khe Sanh, and operational control of the 26th Marine Regiment in Khe Sanh. In all, Tolson commanded about 30,000 troops.

The operation required construction of a forward base just north of Cà Lu near Route 9. A joint force of Army and Marine engineers and Navy Seabees completed the base in 11 days. Called landing zone (LZ) Stud, it included a 450-meter landing strip, ammunition bunkers, refueling points, and a communications and operations center.

Lacking intelligence on PAVN forces, Tolson sent Lt. Col. Richard W. Diller's 1st Squadron, 9th Cavalry (1/9th) to find PAVN strong points, destroy antiaircraft guns, and locate landing zones. Under cover of U.S. Air Force and Marine fighters, Diller conducted reconnaissance by fire for six days before the attack. He developed more than 600 tactical air sorties and 12 B-52 missions. The resulting air bombardment of PAVN positions was so effective that not a single aircraft was lost to antiaircraft or artillery fire.

On 31 March the Marines attacked north toward the Demilitarized Zone (DMZ) to confuse PAVN forces. Then on 1 April Col. Stanley S. Hughes's 1st Marines attacked westward afoot on Route 9, with the 11th Marine Engineers improving the road as they advanced. This was the beginning of PEGASUS–LAM SƠN 207A. That afternoon Col. Hubert S. Campbell's 3d Brigade of the 1st Cavalry Division air assaulted to LZs halfway to Khe Sanh. Quickly converting the LZs to firebases, the 3d Brigade cleared parts of Route 9 ahead of the Marines.

On 2 April the 3d Brigade air assaulted a battalion farther west and two 1st Marine companies air assaulted westward to keep up the momentum of attack. The next day Col. Joseph C. McDonough's 2d Brigade of the 1st Cavalry air assaulted into LZs southeast of Khe Sanh, leapfrogging the 3d Brigade. On 4 April Col. David E. Lownds's 26th Marines at Khe Sanh took Hill 471, overlooking the base, while the 2d Brigade attacked an old French fort south of Khe Sanh. Both efforts met heavy PAVN resistance.

On 5 April Col. John E. Stannard's 1st Brigade air assaulted south of Khe Sanh, where it repulsed a sharp PAVN attack. The next day the 3d Brigade met stubborn resistance as it advanced westward along the highway. The ARVN airborne task force assaulted to an LZ north and east of Khe Sanh to block escape routes to Laos; fighting there was sporadic. On 8 April the 1st Cavalry linked up with Khe Sanh and on 11 April the 1st Marines opened Route 9. Tolson planned other attacks in the area, but on April 10 was ordered to disengage to attack into the A Shau Valley.

General Tolson had conducted an aggressive, fast-moving operation that demoralized PAVN troops and relieved Khe Sanh. It was the first full-division air cavalry raid in history.

—John L. Bell

References: Prados, John, and Ray W. Stubble. *Valley of Decision: The Siege of Khe Sanh.* Boston: Houghton Mifflin, 1991.
Stanton, Shelby. *Anatomy of a Division: 1st Cav in Vietnam.* Novato, CA: Presidio Press, 1987.
Tolson, John J. *Airmobility, 1961–1971.* Washington, DC: Department of the Army, 1973.
See also: Airmobility; Khe Sanh, Battles of; United States: Army; United States: Marine Corps; Vietnam, Democratic Republic of: Army (People's Army of Vietnam [PAVN]); Vietnam, Republic of: Army (ARVN).

PENNSYLVANIA, Operation

(June–October 1967)

Diplomatic attempt to end the Vietnam War. In June 1967 Harvard professor Henry Kissinger was in Paris attending a Pugwash meeting, an international conference of scientists and intellectuals. There he met Raymond Aubrac and Herbert Marcovich, two participants who knew of his trips to Vietnam as a consultant to U.S. Ambassador Henry Cabot Lodge. Aubrac was a socialist and an official in the World Health Organization who was personally acquainted with Hô Chí Minh. Hô had stayed at Aubrac's house in Paris in 1946 and was the godfather of Aubrac's daughter. Aubrac wanted to travel with French biologist Herbert Marcovich to the Democratic Republic of Vietnam (DRV) and to appeal personally to Hô Chí Minh for an end to the war and to explore conditions for peace.

Kissinger passed along this information to Secretary of Defense Robert McNamara and Assistant Secretary of State McGeorge Bundy. McNamara discussed the matter with Secretary of State Dean Rusk and President Lyndon Johnson. They were skeptical regarding its possibilities but McNamara persuaded them to let him proceed. He then encouraged Kissinger to set up the unofficial visit, which was given the code name Operation PENNSYLVANIA.

On July 21 1967 Aubrac and Marcovich arrived in Hà Nôi. Kissinger stayed in Paris to serve as an intermediary between them and President Johnson. Aubrac and Marcovich were granted a courtesy visit with an ill Hô Chí Minh and then had substantive discussions with Premier Pham Văn Đông, who insisted on an "unconditional" halt in U.S. bombing of the North (Operation ROLLING THUNDER) as a prelude to official negotiations. He said that the air offensive could end without public announcement because the DRV did not desire to publicly humiliate the

United States. Đông appeared willing to keep this channel open and told the two that in the future they could communicate with him through DRV Consul General Mai Văn Bô in Paris. Aubrac and Marcovich left Hà Nôi on 26 July and met with Kissinger in Paris on their return.

On 8 August McNamara obtained approval from Johnson and Rusk of Đông's terms with the condition that any halt in the bombing lead directly to negotiations and that the DRV not take advantage of the situation to strengthen its forces in the South.

On 17 August Kissinger had a series of meetings with the two intermediaries, who pressed the United States for some means to show that Washington was sincere about a bombing halt. On 19 August Johnson agreed to a halt in the bombing within a ten-mile radius of Hà Nôi from 24 August to 4 September to ensure the safety of the two when they returned to Hà Nôi and to validate Kissinger's role as intermediary. Unfortunately, bad weather beforehand had led to an increased U.S. Navy and Air Force target list, and on 20 August, when the weather cleared, the U.S. flew more than 200 sorties, more than any other previous day of the war.

Aubrac and Marcovich never made it to Hà Nôi. On 21 August Hà Nôi canceled their visa applications, claiming it was unsafe for them to visit the DRV capital. As Robert McNamara noted in his memoirs, "Once again, we had failed miserably to coordinate our diplomatic and military actions." There were subsequent efforts to reestablish the channel, but heavy U.S. bombing continued. Although Johnson publicly endorsed this so-called "no advantage" formula in a 29 September 1967 speech in San Antonio, Texas, on 20 October the DRV broke off the Aubrac and Marcovich channel when Bô announced that there was no reason to talk again. The bombing did not stop for another year.

—Kevin Arceneaux and Spencer C. Tucker

References: Karnow, Stanley. *Vietnam: A History.* New York: Penguin Books, 1984.
Kissinger, Henry. *Diplomacy.* New York: Simon & Schuster, 1994.
McNamara, Robert S., with Brian VanDeMark. *In Retrospect, the Tragedy and Lessons of Vietnam.* New York: Times Books, 1995.
See also: Bundy, McGeorge; Hô Chí Minh; Johnson, Lyndon Baines; Kissinger, Henry Alfred; Lodge, Henry Cabot, Jr.; McNamara, Robert S.; Pham Văn Đông; ROLLING THUNDER, Operation.

Pentagon Papers and Trial

(1971)

U.S. Defense Department study of the course of American Vietnam policy and the trial resulting from publication of the study. By 1967 Secretary of Defense Robert McNamara was questioning the course of the Vietnam War, and he created a task force within the Defense Department to investigate the history of U.S. policy in Vietnam. The task force conducted no interviews; its work was based on written materials, mostly files from the Departments of Defense and State, the Central Intelligence Agency (CIA), and to some extent the White House.

The end product was a history accompanied by the original texts of many of the documents on which it had been based. Formally titled *United States–Vietnam Relations, 1945–1967,* it is commonly referred to as the Pentagon Papers. The narrative and documents totaled well over 7,000 pages arranged in 47 volumes. There were only 15 copies—7 for distribution within the Department of Defense and 8 elsewhere.

Dr. Daniel Ellsberg, a researcher with the RAND Corporation (a "think tank" that had been given 2 of the 15 copies), was one of the study's authors. After the project was completed, he examined the entire manuscript carefully. He had already developed doubts about U.S. Vietnam policy; reading the Pentagon Papers convinced him that the American involvement there had been fundamentally immoral and should be ended immediately.

Ellsberg believed that the evidence that had led to his beliefs about the war should be made available to Congress and the public, and late in 1969 he began photocopying large sections of the Pentagon Papers. After failing to persuade several U.S. senators to make the material public, in March 1971 he delivered it to Neil Sheehan of the *New York Times.*

Sheehan and others at the *Times,* working in extreme secrecy, produced a series of articles intended for publication on ten consecutive days. Each daily installment was made up of a long article plus the original texts of some of the most important supporting documents. The articles were not abridged versions of the corresponding sections of the narrative that had been written by persons within the Department of Defense; they were written by reporters of the *New York Times,* using information from both the narrative and the documents in the Defense Department version. The first installment was published on Sunday, 13 June 1971.

On 14 June Attorney General John Mitchell informed the *New York Times* that "publication of this information is directly prohibited by the provisions of the Espionage Law." He asked that the newspaper cease publication immediately and return the documents to the Department of Defense. The *Times* refused.

On 15 June the Justice Department sought an injunction forbidding the publication of further installments. Judge Murray I. Gurfein of the Southern District of New York issued a restraining order preventing publication for four days to allow time for the case to be argued. This was the first occasion that a U.S. court had restrained a newspaper, in advance, from publishing a specific article.

Ellsberg immediately gave a substantial portion of the Pentagon Papers to *The Washington Post,* which began publishing articles based on this material on 18 June. The Justice Department filed suit against *The Post* the same day.

The Justice Department had obtained the initial restraining order without first proving to Judge Gurfein's satisfaction that such restraint was either necessary or legal. All of the courts that became involved in the case agreed that such an order could not remain in effect for the length of time usually required for the U.S. court system to decide a matter of such importance. The district courts in New York and Washington took only a few days to hand down decisions in favor of the newspapers, citing principles of freedom of the press and a lack of evidence that publication of the Pentagon Papers posed a serious danger to the nation.

The government appealed, and both cases reached the Supreme Court on 24 June. Four justices voted to reject the government's appeal without a hearing and to allow the newspapers to proceed with publication forthwith. The majority, however, voted to combine the two cases and hear them on 26 June.

The two newspapers had refused, as a matter of principle, to reveal what information they intended to publish, or even what portions of the Pentagon Papers Ellsberg had given them. The four volumes of the original study dealing with efforts made through various intermediaries to negotiate an end to the war, the disclosure of which, the government warned, might impede future negotiations, had never been given to either newspaper because Daniel Ellsberg shared the government's view of that risk. Of the material that Ellsberg did furnish, the *Times* exercised some restraint in its disclosure, avoiding the publication of information about which the newspaper felt there might be legitimate national security concerns. *The Post* exercised greater restraint, avoiding the publication of texts from any of the source documents in the Pentagon Papers. Had the newspapers been less secretive, court proceedings might have centered on the articles scheduled for publication, rather than on the whole text of the Pentagon Papers, and the argument that publication would imperil national security might have been strengthened.

On 26 June the Supreme Court heard arguments. By that time, the Justice Department had shifted the legal basis of its case from the Espionage Act to the inherent powers of the presidency. Solicitor General Erwin Griswold argued that the president's responsibility for the conduct of foreign policy and his role as commander in chief of the armed forces required that he have the ability to forbid the publication of military secrets.

On 30 June the court found for the newspapers, 6 to 3. Justices Hugo Black, William J. Brennan, William O. Douglas, Thurgood Marshall, Potter Stewart, and Raymond "Whizzer" White were able to agree on a very short statement, the core of which was that, given the constitutional protection of freedom of the press, a request by the government for prior restraint of publication "carries a heavy burden of showing justification," and the government had not met that burden.

Each of the six, however, wrote a separate concurring opinion; Black and Douglas each joined in the other's opinions, and Stewart and White likewise. No common thread unites all six concurring opinions. Important elements found in various aspects of them included assertions that (1) Congress had passed no law, and indeed had repeatedly rejected proposed laws, under which the government could enjoin publication of government secrets by the press; (2) the government had failed to prove that publication of the Pentagon Papers would cause such dire harm as to justify making an exception to the general principles of the First Amendment; and (3) the government's claims for the inherent powers of the presidency could not be accepted.

Those who dissented—Chief Justice Warren Burger and Justices Harry Blackmun and John Marshall Harlan—were more nearly in agreement with one another. In the realm of foreign affairs, they were willing to grant the executive branch almost unfettered authority to decide which government secrets the press should be forbidden to publish. They did not claim that the government had proved that publication of the Pentagon Papers would cause such dire harm to the nation as would justify an exception to the First Amendment; they did not feel that the government should have been required to provide such proof. They argued that only the executive branch was qualified to decide whether publication threatened the national security and that the courts should enforce the judgment of the executive branch on the press without asking for any detailed explanation of the basis for that judgment.

The Supreme Court had rejected prior restraint of publication in this case. The key to the outcome had rested with Stewart and White, the two justices who had not been willing to find for the newspapers on 25 June without a hearing, but who did find for them on 30 June. They suggested that the government protect its secrets through the deterrent effect of criminal prosecution, rather than prior restraint of publication. The Justice Department did not attempt criminal action against the newspapers, but it did indict Daniel Ellsberg for conspiracy, theft of government property, and violation of the Espionage Act.

The trial of Ellsberg and an alleged coconspirator, Anthony Russo, began 3 January 1973 in Los Angeles. Its verdict might have clarified some of the issues that had been left unresolved by the 1971 decision, but on 11 May the judge dismissed the charges, citing a pattern of government misconduct including the fact that White House "plumbers," a team selected to plug information leaks, in search of evidence against Ellsberg had burglarized the office of Ellsberg's psychiatrist.

Before the end of 1971 two sets of selections from the Pentagon Papers that were much more complete than any newspaper could have published appeared in book form, one published by the U.S. Government Printing Office after formal declassification and the other released by Senator Mike Gravel of Alaska and published by Beacon Press. Between them, these contained essentially all of the narrative history, except for the sections dealing with negotiations to end the war; those sections were published only in 1983. Many of the source documents that had been appendices to the original Pentagon Papers were included in various versions published in 1971, but many others remained unreleased.

—Edwin E. Moise

References: Herring, George C., ed. *The Secret Diplomacy of the Vietnam War: The Negotiating Volumes of the Pentagon Papers.* Austin, TX: University of Texas Press, 1983.
The Pentagon Papers, as Published by the New York Times. New York: Bantam Books, 1971.
The Pentagon Papers: The Defense Department History of United States Decisionmaking on Vietnam. 5 vols. Boston: Beacon Press, 1971–1972.
Schrag, Peter. *Test of Loyalty: Daniel Ellsberg and the Rituals of Secret Government.* New York: Simon & Schuster, 1974.
Ungar, Sanford J. *The Papers & The Papers: An Account of the Legal and Political Battle over the Pentagon Papers.* New York: E. P. Dutton, 1972.
United States–Vietnam Relations, 1945–1967: Study Prepared by the Department of Defense. 12 vols. Washington, DC: U.S. Government Printing Office, 1971.
See also: Ellsberg, Daniel; Gelb, Leslie H.; Gravel, Maurice Robert (Mike); McNamara, Robert S.; Media and the War; Nixon, Richard Milhous; Russo, Anthony J., Jr.; Sheehan, Cornelius Mahoney (Neil); Watergate.

People's Army of Vietnam (PAVN)

See Vietnam, Democratic Republic of: Army (People's Army of Vietnam [PAVN]).

People's Liberation Armed Forces (PLAF)

See National Front for the Liberation of South Vietnam (NFLSV).

People's Republic of China

See China, People's Republic of (PRC).

People's Self-Defense Forces

The Republic of Vietnam (RVN) officially created the People's Self-Defense Forces (PSDF) in the General Mobilization Law of June 1968, the result of the Tết Offensive. The law required all male citizens ages 16 to 17 and 39 to 50 to participate in the PSDF program with the exception of those who volunteered to serve in the military and those in the draft age range (18–38) who were exempted from service for reasons other than poor health. In addition, those over 50, disabled veterans, women, and teenagers under 16 were also encouraged to volunteer for the PSDF in a supporting role. Similar organizations that had existed before 1968 such as Combat Youth, Rural Combatants, and Civil Defense were disbanded and their membership shifted to the PSDF.

The PSDF existed at every level of national undertaking, except the military domain. PSDF committees were chaired, in descending order, by the premier, city mayors or province chiefs, district, village, and hamlet chiefs, or their urban counterparts.

The PSDF force structure had two components: combat and support. The foundation of the combat PSDF was the 11-man team made up of a team leader, a deputy, and three three-man cells. Three such teams formed a section of 35 men under a section leader and a deputy. If an area had more than one section, two or three sections could be joined into a group. This was the largest combat unit, led by a group leader and a deputy. All team, section, and group leaders and deputies were elected by PSDF members on the basis of leadership qualifications. Support elements were all volunteers. They were also organized into teams, sections, and groups but were separated into different categories—elders, women, and teenagers—as dictated by traditional Vietnamese culture.

To ensure that the PSDF could perform its role effectively, a relatively comprehensive training program was devised. A four-week formal training course was conducted at national training centers for team and section leaders.

The PSDF employed guerrilla tactics. It eschewed fixed defense positions but moved to alert positions at night in three-man cells. PSDF members rarely confronted their enemy directly unless that force was small and easy to destroy. When confronted by superior force, PSDF members were to hide their weapons and act as ordinary civilians.

By 1972 the PSDF combat component had more than 1 million members; about half of them were armed with individual weapons and most had received some combat training. The PSDF support component was even larger; it had 2.5 million members. PSDF achievements were not uniform, however; they varied from one locality to another. By and large, where the program was well executed a noticeable improvement in local security followed.

—George J. Gabera

References: Guenter, Lewy. *America in Vietnam.* New York: Oxford University Press, 1978.
Ngô Quang Trưởng. *Territorial Forces.* Washington, DC: U.S. Army Center of Military History, 1981.
See also: Territorial Forces; Vietnam, Republic of: 1954–1975.

Perot, H. Ross

(1930–)

American businessman and politician. Born on 27 June 1930 in Texarkana, Texas, Henry Ross Perot learned the art of business and the importance of relationships from his father, a local cotton broker. At age 19, Perot received an appointment to the U.S. Naval Academy, from which he graduated in 1953. After his four-year period of service, Perot and his wife Margot settled in Dallas, Texas. In 1962 Perot formed Electronic Data Systems Corporation (EDS) to do computing and data processing. By 1968, Perot was a millionaire.

In 1969 National Security Advisor Henry Kissinger sought Perot's assistance in getting the North Vietnamese to improve conditions for U.S. prisoners of war (POWs). In response Perot formed "United We Stand" to collect money and buy newspaper advertisements. The committee sought to use the ads to pressure North Vietnam into improving conditions for the POWs. A week before Christmas 1969 Perot announced that United We Stand would deliver Christmas dinner to the POWs, but DRV authorities refused to cooperate. Perot, however, remained much committed to the POW issue.

In 1978 Perot sent retired Green Beret Colonel Arthur Simons and a team of EDS executives to free two EDS officials from an Iranian prison. In 1992 and 1996 he made unsuccessful runs for the U.S. presidency as a third-party candidate. He remains a controversial business and political leader.

—Michael R. Nichols

References: Mason, Todd. *Perot: An Unauthorized Biography.* Homewood, IL: Business One Irwin, 1990.
Posner, Gerald. *Citizen Perot: His Life and Times.* New York: Random House, 1996.
See also: Kissinger, Henry Alfred; Prisoners of War, Allied; Simons, Arthur D.

PERSHING, Operation

(February 1967–February 1968)

U.S. 1st Cavalry Division operation during 1967 and 1968 in Bình Định Province. It was the largest continuous operation of the 1st Cavalry Division (Airmobile) since arriving in Vietnam. Following inconclusive operations in the longtime Communist stronghold of Bình Định throughout 1966, the 1st Cavalry became the exclusive U.S. presence there.

Under the command of Maj. Gen. John Tolson, PERSHING had as its primary mission to conduct cordon-and-search operations with Army of the Republic of Vietnam (ARVN) forces to rout the entrenched Việt Công (VC) infrastructure and help establish Republic of Vietnam (RVN) government control. Tolson concluded that the more than 900 cordon-and-search operations conducted by the division rendered 50 percent of VC cadre ineffective.

Throughout PERSHING, the 1st Cavalry's three brigades continuously swept the coastal areas and reconnoitered the valleys in pursuit of VC regulars and the 3d People's Army of Vietnam (PAVN) Division, known as the "Yellow Star" division. The 1st Cavalry's complement of 450 helicopters brought a new dimension to airmobility, as armed reconnaissance troops of the 1st Squadron, 9th Cavalry would spot and engage Communist forces, followed by the rapid insertion of infantry battalions. When Communist forces retreated from remote areas like the An Lão Valley, 1st Cavalry units forcibly removed the inhabitants, turning over nearly 100,000 refugees to RVN authorities by August. U.S. Air Force planes then smothered the depopulated areas with crop-destroying Agent Orange, ruining their usefulness as havens for Việt Công labor and recruits. March saw victories over large PAVN forces north of Bông Sơn at Tam Quan, and at Đâm Tra-O Lake to the south.

Until September the entire division operated throughout Bình Định, except for a brief foray in April by the 2d Brigade into southern Quang Ngãi Province, and a June airlift of two battalions of the 3d Brigade to support U.S. forces engaged at Đắk Tô. But on 1 October General William Westmoreland ordered the 3d Brigade to Quang Nam Province in I Corps, where it would remain until January, and on 1 November the 1st Brigade was airlifted to Đắk Tô for a month. By December PERSHING had become a holding operation, with only one full brigade remaining in Bình Định.

When the 22d PAVN Regiment descended from the hills and established entrenched positions near Tam Quan, the last major battle of PERSHING occurred. From 6 to 20 December the 1st Brigade and the 1st Battalion, 50th Infantry (Mechanized) and 22d ARVN units killed 650 PAVN troops. According to Tolson, the battle's significance was that the Bông Sơn Plain "was the least affected of any part of South Vietnam during Tết." In all, PERSHING claimed 5,715 PAVN and 3,367 VC killed, with another 2,323 PAVN and 2,123 VC captured. The 1st Cavalry suffered 852 killed, 22 missing, and 4,119 wounded.

Before rejoining the division in I Corps in late February, the 1st Brigade inflicted 614 more PAVN/VC casualties in Operation PERSHING II. Military Assistance Command, Vietnam (MACV) proclaimed Bình Định province to be "relatively secure," but as Neil Sheehan noted in *A Bright Shining Lie,* the 3d PAVN Division was "the real phoenix of Binh Dinh" and would return in force.

—John D. Root

References: Stanton, Shelby L. *Anatomy of a Division: The First Cav in Vietnam.* Novato, CA: Presidio Press, 1987.
Tolson, Gen. John. *Airmobility, 1961–1971.* Washington, DC: Department of the Army, 1973.

Sgt. George Nemesbathe drinks coconut milk during a break in a search-and-seizure patrol in Operation PERSHING (February 1967–February 1968), the largest continuous operation involving the U.S. 1st Cavalry Division (Airmobile) since arriving in Vietnam.

See also: Airmobility; Đăk Tô, Battle of; IRVING, Operation; MASHER/ WHITE WING, Operation; United States: Army; Westmoreland, William Childs.

Peterson, Douglas "Pete"

(1935–)

First U.S. ambassador to the Socialist Republic of Vietnam (SRV). Born on 26 June 1935 in Omaha, Nebraska, Pete Peterson joined the Air Force in 1954, a year after graduating from high school, and rose to the rank of colonel. A fighter pilot during the Vietnam War, Peterson in 1966 was shot down near Hà Nội and was held prisoner in the Democratic Republic of Vietnam (DRV) for six and a half years. Freed following the war, he obtained a B.S. degree from the University of Arizona in 1976 and retired from the Air Force in 1980.

In 1990 Peterson, a Democrat, was elected to the U.S. Congress from Florida. His only previous political activity was on the Jackson Country Democratic Executive Committee. In 1991 Peterson opposed giving President George Bush authority to use force against Iraq. He said then, "I vowed when I sat in Hanoi that I would never commit troops to battle without the support of the American people."

Peterson served three terms in the House of Representatives, retiring in January 1997. Following normalization of relations between the United States and the SRV, President Bill Clinton nominated Peterson to be the first U.S. ambassador to the SRV. His record of valor and endurance made it difficult for Republicans to block full normalization of relations and an exchange of ambassadors with the SRV. After hearings in February and March 1997, on 10 April the Senate confirmed Peterson, who had announced during the hearings that his top priority as ambassador would be efforts to account for Americans missing in action (MIAs).

Peterson began his ambassadorial duties in May 1997. SRV Premier Võ Văn Kiêt said that Peterson's arrival in Hà Nội affirmed that both countries were interested in closing the past in order to look to the future. Among Peterson's chief tasks was to work toward a trade pact and most-favored nation status for the SRV.

—Spencer C. Tucker

References: Duncan, Philip, and Christine Lawrence. *Congressional Quarterly's Politics in America 1996: The 104th Congress.* Washington, DC: CQ Press, 1997.

The 1995–1996 Official Congressional Directory, 104th Congress. Washington, DC: U.S. Government Printing Office, 1997.
See also: Bush, George Herbert Walker; Clinton, William Jefferson; United States: Involvement in Vietnam, 1975 to the Present.

Pham Công Tắc
(1890–1959)

Leader of the Cao Đài religious sect, Pham Công Tắc was born on 21 June 1890 in Long An. As a 17-year-old student at the Sài Gòn Chasseloup Laubat High School, he took part, along with Phan Bôi Châu and Phan Chu Trinh, in a movement to gain independence for Vietnam. Reportedly, in 1925 during a seance of spiritualism with friends, a spirit revealed himself as God under the name of Cao Đài and instructed Pham Công Tắc and his friends to establish a new religion, Cao Đàism.

In 1941 the French deported Tắc to Madagascar. During his absence, Cao Đài leader Trân Quang Vinh cooperated with the Japanese and formed a Cao Đàist army to resist the French. During the Indo-China War the Cao Đàist forces joined in a loose alliance with the French against the Viêt Minh. In 1946 Tắc returned from exile.

The 1954 French defeat at Điên Biên Phu paved the way for the partition of Vietnam. Tắc was not successful in his efforts to organize a general election to reunify the country. In 1956 he took refuge in Cambodia, where he died in 1959.

—Bùi Đắc Hùm

Reference: Hôi Thánh Cao Đài. *Tiêu Sư Đưc Hô Pháp Pham Công Tắc.* Tây Ninh, Vietnam: Tòa Thánh Tây Ninh, 1992.
See also: Cao Đài; Phan Bôi Châu.

Pham Duy
(1921–)

Well-known musician whose songs are closely associated with the Indo-China and Vietnam Wars. Born in Hà Nôi into the family of Pham Duy Tôn, a renowned writer of the 1920s, his real name was Pham Duy Cân.

Pham Duy attended both the School of Fine Arts and the School of Applied Sciences, but music became his self-taught career. From 1943 to 1945 he traveled with a itinerant theatrical troupe. On the outbreak of the Indo-China War he supported the Viêt Minh against the French as a cultural cadre. Although he had lived in South Vietnam near Sài Gòn in 1945, he soon moved to North Vietnam, where his patriotic songs enjoyed great success. His work and that of other musicians such as Lê Thưởng, Văn Cao, and Lưu Hưu Phươc were important in the fight against the French.

In 1950 the Lao Đông Party instituted a new cultural policy and instructed Pham Duy to publicly renounce his most beloved songs and follow the "socialist" cultural style. That led him in 1951 to leave the Viêt Minh–controlled area and return to Hà Nôi. The same year he moved with his family to Sài Gòn, where he published his songs and hosted several radio musical programs. His wife, Thái Hăng, and her sister Thái Thanh and brother Hoài Băc founded the famous Thăng Long Chorus. Thái Thanh was one of the most important Vietnamese vocalists and helped to popularize Pham Duy's songs.

Between 1954 and 1956 Pham Duy studied at the Institut de Musicologie in Paris. On his return to South Vietnam he continued to compose songs. These included folk and love songs, as well as many of a patriotic and anti-Communist nature. He also traveled in the United States, where he gave performances on American campuses and met with American musicians and singers.

Pham Duy has composed some 500 songs and has written Vietnamese lyrics for some 360 songs from other countries. Because of his anti-Communist stance, the government of the Democratic Republic of Vietnam banned all his music in 1950, a prohibition continued by the Socialist Republic of Vietnam.

—Nguyên Công Luân (Lư Tuân)

References: Pham Duy. *Hôi Ký (Memoirs).* Midway City, CA: PDC Musical Productions, 1991.
Pham Duy. Interview with the author, 24 March 1998.
See also: Vietnamese Culture.

Pham Hùng
(1912–1988)

Prominent official of the Vietnamese Communist Party (VCP), Democratic Republic of Vietnam (DRV), and Socialist Republic of Vietnam (SRV). Born Pham Văn Thiên on 11 June 1912 at Long Hô village, Châu Thành District, Vĩnh Long Province, Pham Hùng in 1928 became involved in activities of the Communist Youth League in the South. In 1930 Hùng joined the Indo-Chinese Communist Party (ICP) and worked in My Tho Province. In 1931 French authorities arrested him and sentenced him to death. The sentence was later remitted to life in prison, and Hùng was exiled to Côn Đao prison. Released after the August 1945 revolution, he was selected as acting secretary of the Southern Region Party Committee.

At the 1951 Second Party Congress Hùng became a member of the party Central Committee. From 1952 he held many important leadership posts in the Central Office for South Vietnam (COSVN) and the Southeastern Region Administrative Resistance Committee. After the 1954 Geneva Accords Hùng became head of the military delegation from the North in the International Commission for Supervision and Control (ICSC) in Sài Gòn. During the Vietnam War Hùng was head of the COSVN and was political commissar for Communist forces in the South. During the 1975 Hô Chí Minh Campaign, Hùng was political commissar of the campaign headquarters.

From 1956 to 1988 Hùng was a member of the VCP Central Committee and the Politburo. He also served continuously as a deputy from the Second through the Seventh National Assemblies. Within the government of the SRV, Hùng held a number of important posts, including minister of interior and vice-chairman of the Council of Ministers. In 1987 he became chairman of the Council of Ministers (premier). Hùng died on 18 March 1988 in Hô Chí Minh City. Hùng was the most powerful leader sent from the North to direct the war in the South, but he helped forge the orthodox policies later blamed for economic ruin.

—Ngô Ngoc Trung

Reference: Biographical Files, Indo-China Archives, University of California at Berkeley.
See also: COSVN (Central Office for South Vietnam or Trung Ưởng Cuc Miên Nam); Hô Chí Minh Campaign; Lao Đông Party; Vietnam, Socialist Republic of: 1975 to the Present.

Pham Ngoc Thao
(1922–ca. 1965)
Viêt Công (VC) mole within the Republic of Vietnam (RVN) military. Pham Ngoc Thao was born in 1922 to Roman Catholic parents. He joined the Viêt Minh after World War II and served as an intelligence agent. Following the 1954 Geneva Accords Thao opted to remain in South Vietnam. He then reported to Bishop Ngô Đình Thuc as a rallier. He was introduced to President Ngô Đình Diêm by the bishop and became an Army of the Republic of Vietnam (ARVN) assimilated captain.

Thao was a VC agent during his time in the ARVN. By 1963 he had been promoted to colonel and was in charge of the Strategic Hamlet program. He duped the Central Intelligence Agency, U.S. military personnel, and even journalists such as Stanley Karnow into believing that he was loyal to the government; his role as a VC agent was not discovered until after the war.

Thao's forces played a key role in seizing strategic installations during the November 1963 coup against Ngô Đình Diêm. In 1964 he succeeded General Nguyên Khánh as press attaché to RVN Ambassador to the United States Trân Thiên Khiêm. He resurfaced in South Vietnam in 1965 when he was involved in another coup attempt that February to force out General Khánh. Although the putschists managed to capture most key points in Sài Gòn, their coup attempt was not successful. Thao escaped in the confusion.

Thao disappeared in mid-1965, and most political observers assumed that General Nguyên Văn Thiêu secured his death. Thao's mission as a VC operative seems to have been to create division within ARVN, thereby weakening the government and crippling RVN military effectiveness.

Another scenario for the Pham Ngoc Thao case has circulated in Vietnam after 1975. This holds that Thao was not a mole. It is based on the assumption that, after rallying to the RVN side, Thao helped its counterintelligence services hunt down dozens of high-ranking cadres and leaders of the Central Office for South Vietnam (COSVN). Moreover, the RVN promoted Thao posthumously to the rank of one-star general and awarded him the title of Liêt Sĩ (heroic war dead). There were other cases where Communist defectors faithfully served the RVN and were killed after the April 1975 Communist victory. As a counterpropaganda measure, the SRV awarded them the same title and paid pensions to their wives.

—Charlotte A. Power and Nguyên Công Luân (Lư Tuân)

References: Fitzgerald, Francis. *Fire in the Lake: The Vietnamese and the Americans in Vietnam.* New York: Random House, 1972.
Karnow, Stanley. *Vietnam: A History.* New York: Penguin Books, 1984.
Post, Ken. *Revolution, Socialism, and Nationalism in Vietnam.* Vol. 4, *The Failure of Counter-Insurgency in the South.* Belmont, CA: Wadsworth, 1990.

See also: Ngô Đình Diêm; Nguyên Khánh; Nguyên Văn Thiêu; Strategic Hamlet Program.

Pham Thê Duyêt
(?–)
Prominent Vietnamese Communist Party (VCP) and Socialist Republic of Vietnam (SRV) government official. Very little information is available about Pham Thê Duyêt's activities during the Indo-China and Vietnam Wars. He was first identified as a prominent national leader in 1982 when he was an alternate member of the VCP Central Committee and vice-chairman of the Vietnam Confederation of Trade Unions. A new member of the VCP Politburo in 1991, Duyêt was seen as a representative for the workers thanks to his extensive activities in the Vietnamese Confederation of Trade Unions.

In 1983 Duyêt was also named a member of the Central Committee of Vietnam's Fatherland Front, an umbrella organization embracing activities to motivate people outside the party. In 1986 Duyêt was elected a full member of the VCP Central Committee and a member of its Secretariat. He was also named acting chairman of the Vietnam Confederation of Trade Unions the same year. In late 1988 Duyêt was promoted to the powerful post of secretary of the VCP Committee of Hà Nôi City and in 1991 to the Politburo. Duyêt is credited with opening up the Hà Nôi administration to more liberal, dynamic, and younger leaders that has led to a surge of development in the capital.

—Ngô Ngoc Trung

Reference: Biographical Files, Indo-China Archives, University of California at Berkeley.
See also: Lao Đông Party; Vietnam, Socialist Republic of: 1975 to the Present.

Pham Văn Đông
(1906–)
One of the three most influential leaders of the Democratic Republic of Vietnam (DRV) and its most public figure. Born in Quang Ngãi Province on 1 March 1906 to an educated, mandarin family, Pham Văn Đông attended the Lycée Nationale in Huê, where his classmates included Võ Nguyên Giáp and Ngô Đình Diêm. During his student years he was actively involved in nationalist organizations. This eventually led to his revolutionary attitude toward the expulsion of the French from Vietnam. In 1930 French authorities arrested him for sedition. He then served eight years on the prison island of Poulo Condore, where he kept up his morale by studying languages, literature, and science.

After the French government outlawed the Communist Party on 26 September 1939, its Central Committee ordered Đông and Giáp to China, there to be trained in guerrilla warfare. In June 1940 in Kuming they met Hô Chí Minh. He instructed them to go to Yenan and learn military techniques and politics. This was soon interrupted by the defeat of the French by Germany, whereupon Hô instructed Đông and Giáp and other Vietnamese Communists in China to return to Vietnam and set up an organization to fight for independence.

Phạm Văn Đông at the Korean War peace talks, Geneva 1954. One of the most influential leaders of the Democratic Republic of Vietnam (DRV), Đông served as the DRV's premier from 1950 to 1975. Throughout the period of U.S. involvement in Vietnam, he maintained a consistent attitude toward the American presence and negotiations.

They soon formed the Viêt Minh and organized camps in the mountains along the Vietnamese-Chinese border. From this base, the Viêt Minh conducted training and propaganda as well as minor ambushes and assassinations. The French and Japanese saw them as only a minor annoyance.

Đông played a leading role in the Viêt Minh during the fight against both the Japanese and the French. He also headed the Viêt Minh delegation to the 1954 Geneva Conference. He initially took a hard line by demanding that the Vietnamese be allowed to settle their own differences. When the French rejected this demand, the conference ground to a halt. From this point on, Zhou Enlai, head of the People's Republic of China delegation; Vyacheslav Molotov, foreign minister of the Soviet Union; and Pierre Mendès-France, French premier, took over the negotiations; Đông's role declined to that of accepting or denying proposals.

Đông sought during the Geneva Conference to maintain the momentum gained by the Viêt Minh on the battlefield, but he was largely unsuccessful. He also wanted the demarcation line drawn at the 13th parallel and a six-months' cease-fire. Đông came away from the conference believing that Zhou had sold out the Viêt Minh as the division was moved to the 17th parallel and the cease-fire was set at two years. As a result, the Viêt Minh ended up with less than they had won on the battlefield.

From 1950 to 1975 Đông served as the DRV's premier. Throughout the period of U.S. involvement in Vietnam, he maintained a consistent attitude toward the American presence and negotiations. He refused any discussions until U.S. bombing of the DRV ended. He also required that any settlement include the creation of a neutral coalition government in Sài Gòn with Viêt Công representatives. Đông's negative attitude toward negotiations with the Americans had everything to do with his experience with the French and the failure of the Geneva Accords.

After the death of Hô on 2 September 1969, Đông became the most public figure in the DRV. He skillfully used the American press to encourage antiwar protestors in the United States by issuing statements that the Vietnamese appreciated their support. In other statements he claimed that the Vietnamese believed that the only viable alternative for President Richard Nixon was the honorable exit they were offering to him. Many of Đông's speeches carried humorous elements, such as when he referred to RVN leaders as puppets. When a reporter asked how he could refer to them as puppets when they acted so consistently against American policy, he replied that they were just "bad puppets."

Đông also played a key role in the secret peace negotiations in Paris between Henry Kissinger and Lê Đức Tho that began in February 1970. His influence was evident in Tho's initial demands for nothing less than a simultaneous armistice and coalition government to include the removal of President Nguyên Văn Thiêu. Negotiations were deadlocked until August 1972 when Đông came to believe that temporary compromise on the matter of Thiêu would allow for a settlement. On 1 August Tho no longer demanded that military and political issues be resolved at one time. He also hinted that the DRV would no longer require Thiêu's withdrawal.

The resolution of final problems in the talks was delayed when, in an 18 October interview with Arnaud de Borchgrave, Đông made reference to the National Council of National Reconciliation and Concord as a "coalition of transition." This again raised the specter of coalition government and temporarily halted the agreement until things could be worked out. The final agreement was signed on 27 January 1973.

Đông continued in office after the capitulation of the Republic of Vietnam on 30 April 1975. He remained as chairman of the Council of Ministers of the Socialist Republic of Vietnam until a series of economic setbacks forced his resignation in December 1986. He then became advisor for the Central Committee of the VCP, although without actual power. Many North Vietnamese regarded Đông as one of their few incorruptible leaders though never, despite his many years as prime minister, a skillful administrator.

—Michael R. Nichols

References: Bain, Chester A. *Vietnam: The Roots of Conflict.* Englewood Cliffs, NJ: Prentice-Hall, 1967.
Davidson, Phillip B. *Vietnam at War, the History: 1946–1975.* Novato, CA: Presidio Press, 1988.
Duncanson, Dennis J. *Government and Revolution in Vietnam.* New York: Oxford University Press, 1968.
Fishel, Wesley R. *Vietnam: Anatomy of a Conflict.* Itasca, IL: F. E. Peacock Publishers, 1968.

Karnow, Stanley. *Vietnam: A History.* Rev. ed. New York: Penguin Books, 1991.

Olson, James S., ed. *Dictionary of the Vietnam War.* New York: Peter Bedrick Books, 1987.

See also: Geneva Conference and Geneva Accords; Hồ Chí Minh; Kissinger, Henry Alfred; Lê Đức Thọ; Mendès-France, Pierre; Molotov (born Scriabin), Vyacheslav Mikhailovich; Ngô Đình Diệm; Nguyên Văn Thiêu; Nixon, Richard Milhous; Paris Negotiations; Paris Peace Accords; Viêt Minh (Viêt Nam Đôc Lâp Đông Minh Hôi [Vietnam Independence League]); Võ Nguyên Giáp; Zhou Enlai (Chou En-lai).

Pham Văn Phú

(1928–1975)

Army of the Republic of Vietnam (ARVN) major general and corps commander. Born in 1928 in Hà Đông, North Vietnam, Pham Văn Phú graduated from the Đà Lat Military Academy. In 1954 Phú was a company officer in the 5th Parachutist Battalion of the Army of the State of Vietnam, fighting alongside the French at Điên Biên Phu.

In the ARVN Phú commanded the Republic of Vietnam (RVN) Special Forces, then the 2d Infantry Division, the Quang Trung Training Center, and then II Corps/Military Region 2 in Pleiku. His troops suffered heavy losses in the withdrawal to the coast ordered by President Nguyên Văn Thiêu in March 1975. General Phú committed suicide on 30 April 1975 in Sài Gòn.

—Nguyên Công Luân (Lư Tuân)

Reference: Hà Mai Viêt. "Famous Generals of the Republic of Viêt Nam Armed Forces" (in Vietnamese). Unpublished manuscript.

Phan Bôi Châu

(1867–1940)

Vietnamese scholar and gentry activist. Born in Nghê An Province on 26 December 1867, Phan resisted the French invaders by supporting King Hàm Nghi and endorsing the Cân Vửơng (Support to the King) Edict. Unsuccessful at first with regional examinations, he studied Vietnamese reformist literature in Huê, came back to Nghê An, and received a degree by 1900. Upon his father's death, he became a devoted activist against the French.

Phan early recognized an Asian need for Western information and political principles as a defense against imperialism. Joining the Duy Tân Hôi (Reformation Society), he perused the writings of Chinese self-strengtheners such as Liang Ch'i-ch'ao yet disapproved of their loathing of force and goal of affecting change from within. Instead Phan favored violent means to oust France, covert links with high Nguyên officials, and assistance from other nations. By 1903 Phan selected Prince Cường Đê as his nominee to assume the throne and wrote *Lửu Câu Huyêt Lê Tân Thư* (Ryukyu's Letter in Bitter Tears), a lament about losing sovereignty to a foreign power.

The Duy Tân Hôi dispatched Phan to Japan to seek foreign aid. He conferred with exiled Chinese and prominent Japanese and believed Japan would play a decisive role in the anticolonial struggle. He penned *Viêt Nam Vong Quôc Sử* (History of the Loss of Vietnam), a complaint of weak Nguyên dynasty leadership and an urgent call for a nationwide resistance. Phan organized the Đông

Du (Exodus to the East), an organization designed to send young Vietnamese to study in Japan.

Phan advocated a reformed Vietnamese monarchy modeled along Meiji lines. His conviction that the Japanese would support Vietnam's national aims was not shared by compatriot Phan Chu Trinh, who also traveled to Japan yet refused to favor Japanese assistance.

Once Japan's government dismantled the Đông Du in 1908, Phan went to Siam and, with other Asian revolutionaries, established the East-Asian League. He hoped the organization would evolve as a firm association of Eastern peoples opposed to European colonialism.

When the Chinese Revolution of 1911 occurred, Phan and Cường Đê hastened to Canton. Subject to the spell of Sun Yat-sen's Guomindang (Kuomintang), Phan discarded the idea of a reformed monarchy for Vietnam. He dissolved the Duy Tân Hôi and created the Viêt Nam Quang Phuc Hôi (Vietnam Restoration Society), with the goal of setting up a Vietnamese democratic republic. Forming an exile regime, he installed Cường Đê as chief executive and himself as vice-president.

Phan's exiled underground inspired resistance in Vietnam between 1907 and 1918. He managed to smuggle in weapons and planned assassinations. In 1925, however, the French captured Phan in Shanghai, tried him, and sentenced him to life in prison. Reports circulated among Vietnamese nationalists that Hồ Chí Minh and his associate Lâm Đức Thu had sold information on Phan's whereabouts to the French secret service. In late 1945 Lâm publicly disclosed this and was subsequently shot to death in front of his home by the Viêt Minh. Prince Cường Đê, however, confirmed the account.

Eventually paroled, Phan lived in restrictive retirement until his death on 29 October 1940 at Huê.

—Rodney J. Ross

References: Buttinger, Joseph. *Vietnam: A Political History.* New York: Praeger, 1968.

Cường Đê. *Cuôc Đời Cách Mang.* Sài Gòn: n.p., 1968.

Duiker, William J. *The Rise of Nationalism in Vietnam, 1900–1941.* Ithaca, NY: Cornell University Press, 1976.

Hoàng Văn Chí. *From Colonialism to Communism.* New York: Praeger, 1964.

Marr, David G. *Vietnamese Anticolonialism, 1885–1925.* Berkeley, CA: University of California Press, 1971.

See also: Cường Đê; French Indo-China; Phan Chu Trinh.

Phan Chu Trinh

(1872–1926)

Vietnamese scholar and gentry reformer. Born in Quang Nam Province on 8 August 1872, Phan defended his home district against the French, decamped to the highlands, and, upon hearing of his father's murder by Cân Vửơng (Support to the King) associates, broke with the resistance. Developing a lasting repugnance to violence, he pondered Chinese studies, passed regional and metropolitan examinations, and in 1903 was appointed to the Board of Rites at Huê.

The next year Phan, critical of the traditional monarchy, resigned and, influenced by Chinese reformers like Liang Ch'i-ch'ao, identified with Western political models. He advocated eliminating the examination system and creating up-to-date schools and businesses. He accompanied Phan Bôi Châu to Japan in 1906, contacted Vietnamese expatriates, and supported the educational efforts of the Duy Tân Hôi (Reformation Society). However, he opposed its endorsement of constitutional monarchy and reliance on Japan to evict France. Instead, Phan favored collaboration with the French, hoping to win reforms through peaceful means.

Back in Vietnam by August 1906, Phan began an open correspondence with Governor General Paul Beau, in which he credited the colonial regime with providing benefits to the populace. Yet he disapproved of its underpinning of a corrupt traditional mandarinate. Willing to postpone independence, he urged Beau to promote economic betterment, individual freedoms, unfettered education, and industrial development. Phan promised Vietnamese cooperation in a joint endeavor toward a modernized Vietnam.

Phan helped to establish the Đông Kinh Nghĩa Thuc (Free School of the Eastern City [Hà Nôi]) to encourage progressive change and prevent bloody revolution. As the school's most admired lecturer, he used the Đông Kinh Nghĩa Thuc to encourage modern ideas in Vietnam. About this time Phan wrote *Tinh Quôc Hôn Ca* (A Ballad to Awaken the National Soul), an original poem publicizing his significant reforms.

In 1908 Phan instigated disorders during the tax uprising in An Nam. Arrested and sentenced to death, he was confined to Côn Sơn island. Once pardoned and freed, he traveled to France and publicly defended tax protestors and reproached the colonial regime. While in Paris during World War I, Phan was jailed in Santé prison but was released by August 1915. He and Hô Chí Minh composed a draft of eight points for Vietnam's liberation that was submitted to the 1919 Paris peace conference. Three years later, Phan penned *Thât Điêu Thư* (Seven Point Letter), a document accusing Emperor Khai Đinh of despicable crimes.

Phan returned to Vietnam in 1925 and published two speeches, one censuring the monarchy and the other considering the possible Vietnamese assimilation of European values. When he died on 26 March 1926 in Sài Gòn, mourners turned out for a seven-day funeral that became a national event.

—Rodney J. Ross

References: Buttinger, Joseph. *Vietnam: A Political History.* New York: Praeger, 1968.
Duiker, William J. *The Rise of Nationalism in Vietnam, 1900–1941.* Ithaca, NY: Cornell University Press, 1976.
Marr, David G. *Vietnamese Anticolonialism, 1885–1925.* Berkeley, CA: University of California Press, 1971.
See also: Beau, Jean-Baptiste-Paul; French Indo-China; Hô Chí Minh; Phan Bôi Châu.

Phan Đình Phùng

(1847–1895)

Most prominent Confucian scholar of the anti–French royalist movement in the late nineteenth century. Born in 1847 in Đông Thái village, La Sơn District, Hà Tĩnh Province, Phan Đình Phùng passed the triennial competitive civil service examination in 1877 with the highest honor and won the title of Đình Nguyên (first

laureate). After serving as head of the district of Yên Khánh in Ninh Bình, he was recalled to the capital and assigned as *ngư sư* (grand censor) in the Đô Sát Viên (Censoriate). When Emperor Tư Đức died (1883) and Emperor Duc Đưc (1883) was dethroned by the then–most-powerful regents, Nguyên Văn Tưởng and Tôn Thât Thuyêt, Phan Đình Phùng protested and was dismissed. In 1884 he was reinstalled as Thâm Biên Sơn Phòng (a mandarin in charge of a mountainous area) in Hà Tĩnh. In 1885 after Huê fell to the French and Emperor Hàm Nghi left the capital to head the Cân Vương (Support to the King) movement, Phan Đình Phùng responded to the emperor's appeal.

With the support of the people from his native village, especially Confucian scholars and former mandarins, Phan Đình Phùng raised an army and chose as his headquarters Mount Vũ Quang, a strategic point that dominates Hà Tĩnh Citadel on the road linking Vietnam with Laos and Thailand. From Vũ Quang his army could operate not only in Hà Tĩnh but also in other provinces, including Quang Bình, Thanh Hóa, and Nghê An. His army was very well trained and organized, and one of his lieutenants, Cao Thăng, was able to produce 300 rifles patterned after the French model of 1874.

During a ten-year period, Phan Đình Phùng caused serious problems for the French. To force him to surrender, the French excavated his ancestors' tombs and arrested his family members. They also launched several attacks against his base in 1895, which were successful. The rebels abandoned Vũ Quang, and Phan Đình Phùng died shortly thereafter of dysentery in December 1895 at age 49.

—Pham Cao Dưởng

References: Đào Trinh Nhât. *Phan Đình Phùng.* Sài Gòn: Tân Viêt, 1950.
Lê Thành Khôi. *Le Viet-Nam: Histoire et Civilisation.* Paris: Editions de Minuit, 1955.
Nguyên Huyên Anh. *Viêt Nam Danh Nhân Tư Điên* (Dictionary of Vietnamese Great Men and Women). Houston: Zieleks, 1990.
Nguyên Thê Anh. *Viêt Nam Dưởi Thơi Pháp Đô Hô* (Viet Nam under French Rule). Sài Gòn: Lửa Thiêng, 1970.
See also: French Indo-China; Tôn Thât Thuyêt; Tư Đức.

Phan Huy Quát

(1909–1979)

Prominent Republic of Vietnam (RVN) politician, foreign minister, and premier. Born on 1 July 1909 in Hà Tĩnh Province, central Vietnam, to Phan Huy Tùng and Trân Thi My Xuân, Phan Huy Quát married the daughter of Đăng Văn Hưởng. His brother-in-law, Dr. Đăng Văn Sung, was a prominent leader of the Đai Viêt Quôc Dân Đang (National Party of Greater Vietnam).

Quát left the Lycée Pellerin in Huê to continue his studies at Lycée du Protectorat in Hà Nôi. He then studied at the Medical School in Hà Nôi, graduating in 1936. He practiced medicine in Hà Nôi, while at the same time engaging in import-export activities.

In 1940 Quát was drafted into the army, where he held the rank of lieutenant in the medical corps. During the early 1940s he founded a new political party, Tân Viêt Nam (New Vietnam). After the August 1945 revolution, Quát was named chairman of the Administrative Committee of Central Vietnam, but he refused to accept that post.

Quát returned to Hà Nôi in 1946 and remained there until his appointment on 1 July 1949 as minister of education in the government of the State of Vietnam. From 1950 to 1954 he was minister of defense in the three consecutive governments of Premiers Nguyên Phan Long, Nguyên Văn Tâm, and Bửu Lôc.

Despite the recommendation of U.S. Ambassador Donald Heath, the next premier, Ngô Đình Diêm, refused in 1954 to give Quát a ministerial post. Quát joined the so-called Caravelle Opposition Group: 18 prominent South Vietnamese politicians who in a news conference of 26 April 1960 at the Caravelle Hotel in Sài Gòn signed a petition calling on Diêm to carry out political reforms.

After the abortive 11 November 1960 coup, Quát was imprisoned. He was released in July 1963 after being acquitted by a military court. Quát returned to the political scene as minister of foreign affairs in the government of Premier General Nguyên Khánh in 1964. In February 1965 the Armed Forces Council named him premier.

A few months after being appointed, Quát had a falling out with Chief of State Phan Khắc Sửu and, under Catholic pressure, Quát resigned the premiership in June 1965. He was the last civilian RVN premier. Quát continued to appear in the international arena and was president of the Asian Section of the World Anti-Communist Alliance until the Communist victory of April 1975. Quát died in the Sài Gòn central prison in 1979.

—Ngô Ngoc Trung

Reference: Biographical Files, Indo-China Archives, University of California at Berkeley.
See also: Ngô Đình Diêm; Nguyên Khánh; Phan Khăc Sửu; Vietnam, Republic of: 1954–1975.

Phan Khăc Sửu
(1905–ca. 1972)
Prominent Republic of Vietnam (RVN) politician and president, 1964–1965. Born on 9 January 1905 in My Thuân village, Cân Thơ, in the heart of the Mekong Delta, Phan Khăc Sửu studied in France for six years. In 1929 he graduated as an agricultural engineer from the Colonial Agriculture Institute at Nogent, Paris. He returned to Vietnam in 1930 and was appointed chief of Economic and Technical Information, a division of the Department of Agriculture in the colonial French administration.

In February 1941 the French authorities arrested Sửu, along with other prominent Vietnamese, for forming a new political party, known as the United National Party for Vietnamese Revolution. According to French police records, this party, founded in October 1940, followed the ideas of Leon Trotsky.

Sentenced to eight years of imprisonment to be followed by eight of banishment, Sửu was kept on Côn Sơn (Poulo Condore) penal island from 1941 to 1945. After his release, Sửu stayed in the guerrilla-controlled Mekong Delta, returning to Sài Gòn in 1948.

On 1 July 1949 Sửu became minister of agriculture, welfare, and labor in the Bao Đai government. He saw this as an opportunity to negotiate with the French for the return of power to the Vietnamese. Disappointed with the French colonial administration, he held the post for only two months. Sửu, who wrote a number of scientific textbooks, then became editor and publisher of the *Dân Quí Daily News.*

On the return of Ngô Đình Diêm to Vietnam in 1954, Sửu became his minister of agriculture, but he soon resigned after Diêm ignored his advice and oppressed the Cao Đài and Hòa Hao religious sects. In 1959 Sửu was elected to the National Assembly but was arrested after the abortive 11 November 1960 coup. In July 1963 a military court condemned him to eight years of solitary confinement. Once again he returned to Côn Sơn penal island but was freed after the 1 November 1963 overthrow of Diêm.

In September 1964 Sửu was named chairman of the High National Council, the consulting and legislative body set up by the new Armed Forces Council headed by General Nguyên Khánh. On 24 October 1964 Sửu was elected by the High National Council as chief of state of the Republic of Vietnam. Sửu named Trân Văn Hưởng as premier, but Hưởng's government was overthrown after only three months. The Armed Forces Council kept Sửu as chief of state and in February 1964 named Phan Huy Quát new premier. Sửu and Quát soon were at political loggerheads over the nomination of several cabinet members, and Quát resigned under Catholic pressure in June 1965.

On 13 June 1965 the Armed Forces Council decided to abolish the High National Council to form a new War Government headed by President Nguyên Văn Thiêu and Premier Nguyên Cao Kỳ, and Sửu was dismissed. In 1966 he was elected to the Constituent Assembly and served as its chairman until the next election in 1967. He ran for the presidency in 1967, but finished third behind General Thiêu and Trưởng Đình Dzu, and retired from politics. He died in Sài Gòn in the early 1970s.

—Ngô Ngoc Trung

Reference: Biographical Files, Indo-China Archives, University of California at Berkeley.
See also: Cao Đài; Hòa Hao; Ngô Đình Diêm; Nguyên Cao Kỳ; Nguyên Khánh; Nguyên Văn Thiêu; Phan Huy Quát; Trưởng Đình Dzu.

Phan Quang Đán
(1918–)
Staunch Vietnamese anti-Communist and anticolonialist. Born at Vinh, Nghê An Province, on 6 November 1918, Phan Quang Đán studied medicine and received his M.D. from Hà Nôi Medical School in 1945, with subsequent studies at the Sorbonne (1949) and Harvard (1954). He formed the League of Food Collectors to save starving people and refused Hồ Chí Minh's offer of a cabinet post in 1945. He then sought refuge in China and served as an advisor to Bao Đai but later broke with him (1949). In 1950 Phan Quang Đán formed his Vietnamese Republican Party and arranged an unsuccessful international forum to engage the Communists in negotiations following the 1954 Geneva Agreement.

Under the Ngô Đình Diêm regime of the Republic of Vietnam (RVN), Phan was arrested and tortured many times, in particular following the 11 November 1960 coup attempt. He was released after the overthrow of Diêm in November 1963.

An elected deputy in the 1966 Constituent Assembly, Phan was unsuccessful, with Phan Khắc Sửu on his ticket, in the presidential election of 3 September 1967. He then joined the RVN government as foreign affairs minister (1969), and later served as a deputy prime minister for social welfare and refugees. Phan's most prominent role in the Vietnam War was his effort to resettle hundreds of thousands of war victims and refugees.

After the defeat of the RVN in May 1975, Phan resettled in the United States. He worked at the East End Family Health Center on St. Thomas Island before retiring to Florida in late 1987 to devote himself to the struggle for freedom and democracy in Vietnam.

—Long Bá Nguyên

References: Fontaine, Ray. *The Dawn of Free Vietnam.* Brownsville, TX: Pan American Business Services, 1992.
Phan, Quang Đán. "From the Homeland to Overseas . . . ," *Viet Marketing and Business Report* 16 (October/November/December 1994): 3–4.
See also: Bao Đai; Ngô Đình Diêm; Phan Khắc Sửu; Vietnam, Republic of: 1954–1975.

Phan Văn Khai

(1933–)

Prominent leader in the Vietnamese Communist Party (VCP) and the Socialist Republic of Vietnam (SRV) and premier of the SRV from September 1997. Born on 25 December 1933 in Sài Gòn, Phan Văn Khai fought against the French in the southern part of Vietnam during the Indo-China War. After the 1954 Geneva Accords, he was regrouped to the North and involved in rural work. From 1960 to 1965 he studied at the National Economics University in the USSR.

From 1965 to 1972 Khai was with the State Planning Commission in Hà Nội and, from 1973 to 1975 with the Reunification Committee of the national government. Over the next several years he served on the Hô Chí Minh City Party Committee and was vice-chairman of the city's Planning Committee. From 1979 he was a Hô Chí Minh City Party Committee standing member, vice-chairman of the People's Committee, and chairman of the city's Planning Committee. In 1985 he became deputy secretary of the Hô Chí Minh City Party Committee and chairman of the city's People's Committee. From 1989 to 1991 he was chairman of the State Planning Commission.

In March 1982 at the Fifth Party Congress Khai became an alternate member of the VCP Central Committee. In 1984 he was elected a full member of the VCP Central Committee, a position that was reconfirmed by the 1986 Sixth Party Congress. In June 1991 at the Seventh Party Congress, he was elected to the Political Bureau of the Central Committee.

In August 1991, at the ninth session of the Eighth National Assembly, Khai became vice-chairman, or vice-premier, of the Council of Ministers of the SRV. At the first session of the Ninth National Assembly he was elected first vice-president of that institution.

Foreign observers credit the Russian-trained Khai with the success of the SRV's economic renovation program. An economist by profession, Khai was considered a technocrat rather than a dynamic leader. Although he was perceived to be lacking a political base and ambition, on 19 September 1997, the VCP Central Committee selected Khai to be chairman of the Councils of Ministers, or premier, replacing Võ Văn Kiêt. The rubber-stamp parliament then elected Khai elected to the post, a mere formality, on 25 September.

—Ngô Ngoc Trung

References: Biographical Files, Indo-China Archives, University of California at Berkeley.
See also: Vietnam, Socialist Republic of: 1975 to the Present.

Philastre, Paul-Louis-Félix

(1837–1902)

French administrator and diplomat, an expert on Vietnamese language and legal procedures considered generally sympathetic to the Vietnamese. Born in Brussels on 7 February 1837, Paul-Louis-Félix Philastre was graduated from the French naval school in 1857 and signed on to the *Avalanche,* bound for China. He arrived in Cochin China in 1861 and in 1863 was named to the post of inspector of indigenous affairs at My Tho in the Mekong Delta. He was appointed chief of native law in 1868. Taken ill, he returned to France and commanded an artillery regiment in the Franco-Prussian War.

In 1873 Philastre returned to Sài Gòn. Under pressure from Paris to resolve the Garnier-Dupuis affair in Tonkin, Admiral Dupré commissioned Philastre his ambassador to the court at Huê. In concert with Emperor Tự Đức, Philastre disavowed Francis Garnier's actions in Tonkin and ordered the evacuation of all French garrisons there. He made the preliminary arrangements for the treaty of protectorate signed at Huê on 15 March 1874, which is sometimes referred to as the Philastre Treaty.

After a year's service in Cambodia, Philastre returned to Huê and served as French chargé d'affaires from 1877 to 1879. He returned to France in 1880 and taught mathematics in Cannes and Nice from 1882 to 1894. He translated into French the Vietnamese legal code and its commentaries; his work was published as *Le Code annamite* ("The Annamite Code") in two volumes in Paris in 1876. Philastre died on 11 September 1902.

—Arthur J. Dommen

References: Buttinger, Joseph. *The Smaller Dragon: A Political History of Vietnam.* New York: Praeger, 1958.
Whitfield, Danny J. *Historical and Cultural Dictionary of Vietnam.* Metuchen, NJ: Scarecrow Press, 1976.
See also: Dupuis, Jean; French Indo-China; Garnier, Francis; Tự Đức.

Philippines

The Philippines assisted the United States in the Vietnam War. After the 1949 Communist victory in China, U.S. strategists feared that the "loss" of Southeast Asia to communism would irretrievably harm America's defense of East Asia, undermining the security of offshore islands from Japan to the Philippines. The Philippine archipelago, located a mere 600 miles across the South China Sea from Indo-China, seemed especially vulnerable if dominoes began to fall.

U.S. officials also perceived the Philippine experience as a prototype for U.S. Vietnam policy. Through 1953 and 1954 American operatives in Manila supported Ramón Magsaysay for secretary of defense and later assisted his successful campaign for the presidency, while aiding his efforts to suppress a strong Communist-directed, peasant-rooted rebellion, the Hukbalahap. Believing comparable outcomes attainable in Indo-China, Washington sent Col. Edward G. Lansdale, who had assisted Magsaysay, to Vietnam in 1954 to implement the psychological warfare techniques he had sharpened in the Philippines. Lansdale promoted Ngô Đình Diệm as the Vietnamese Magsaysay.

Filipino foreign policy followed that of Washington. American military bases in the Philippine Islands had been used to supply the French at Điên Biên Phu and would have been employed to launch the proposed Operation VULTURE, a massive U.S. air strike to aid the French defenders. The U.S. call for united action envisioned Philippine cooperation, and Manila hosted the conference creating the Southeast Asia Treaty Organization (SEATO). The Philippines became a member and by 1955 extended diplomatic recognition to the Republic of Vietnam (RVN).

After the 1954 Geneva Accords, Manila dispatched assistance to the Sài Gòn regime. Operation Brotherhood, made public owing to its benevolent task, assigned Filipino medical personnel to the South Vietnamese countryside and obtained nearly all of its funding from nonpublic Philippine associations. Filipino military veterans employed to execute covert missions in Indo-China staffed the Freedom Company of the Philippines, established in 1955 and controlled by the U.S. Central Intelligence Agency (CIA). It carried out a range of activities, encompassing unconventional military actions north of the Demilitarized Zone (DMZ), authorship of the RVN constitution, and training for President Ngô Đình Diệm's executive guard. Operation Brotherhood was phased out early in the ensuing decade, but the Freedom Company of the Philippines maintained operations to the end of the 1960s. Once the CIA removed its backing at the beginning of that period, the Freedom Company became known as the Eastern Construction Company.

In 1964 the Philippine government joined the Free World Assistance Program or "Many Flags" and, along with South Korea, Australia, New Zealand, Thailand, and Nationalist China (Taiwan), pledged assistance to the Republic of Vietnam. Ostensibly to secure assistance for the Sài Gòn government and to demonstrate regional backing for President Lyndon Johnson's Vietnam commitment, the effort was intended to create the impression that the war was an allied effort. The program began with the goal of seeking noncombat assistance, yet it soon sought the use of Free World soldiers in a military role.

A dispute between the Philippines and the United States soon resulted over the nature of Filipino aid. Manila offered a civic-action detail of nonmilitary engineers and medical units, while Washington preferred military teams conducting unconventional

warfare instruction. In 1965 as the military situation deteriorated, the United States urged President Diosdado Macapagal to win approval for assistance from the Philippine Congress. Despite opposition, the Filipino legislature authorized the Philippine Contingent (PHILCON I), composed of two military surgical groups and a psychological warfare team, but stipulated that the amount of assistance would depend on the extent of Washington's economic support for the Philippines.

After much wrangling over funding, newly elected President Ferdinand Marcos endorsed the deployment of the Philippine Civil Action group (PHILCAG), a 2,300-man engineering group, financed mainly by the U.S. Agency for International Development. Himself opposed to the employment of combat troops, Marcos won the Philippine Congress's sanction to fund PHILCAG for 12 months, and by September 1966 the unit began debarking in Vietnam. Secret economic concessions by President Johnson smoothed the procurement of PHILCAG. Yet, by 1967 antipathy to PHILCAG in the Philippines caused the unit's reduction in size. Before its return home in 1969, nine Filipinos in PHILCAG had died in action.

—Rodney J. Ross

References: Blackburn, Robert M. *Mercenaries and Lyndon Johnson's "More Flags": The Hiring of Korean, Filipino and Thai Soldiers in the Vietnam War.* Jefferson, NC: McFarland, 1994.
Kahin, George McT. *Intervention: How America Became Involved in Vietnam.* New York: Alfred A. Knopf, 1986.
Karnow, Stanley. *In Our Image: America's Empire in the Philippines.* New York: Random House, 1989.
See also: Free World Assistance Program; Lansdale, Edward Geary; Order of Battle; Southeast Asia Treaty Organization (SEATO); U.S. Agency for International Development (USAID); VULTURE, Operation.

Phoenix Program

Program to identify and eliminate the Việt Công Infrastructure (VCI) in South Vietnam. The VCI represented the political and administrative arm of the insurgency in South Vietnam and logistically supported Việt Công (VC) operations, recruited new members, and directed terrorist activities against Allied forces.

Initially, the South Vietnamese intelligence apparatus and elimination forces proved inadequate at gathering intelligence. Hence, in May 1967 Robert Komer, whom President Lyndon Johnson chose to oversee pacification efforts in South Vietnam, arrived in Vietnam to head U.S. Civilian Operations and Revolutionary Development Support (CORDS). This organization combined U.S. and Vietnamese civilian and military intelligence and pacification programs and was placed within the Military Assistance Command, Vietnam (MACV) chain of command.

Supervised by CORDS, financially supported by and directed by the Central Intelligence Agency (CIA), a new program, ICEX or Intelligence Coordination and Exploitation, began building district intelligence and operations coordinating centers (DIOCCs) to collect, disseminate, and forward information to field units. Additional centers were also built at the province level.

In early 1968 questions were raised regarding whether the CIA in Vietnam had violated the sovereignty of the Republic of Vietnam (RVN). To justify the legality of ICEX, William Colby, chief of the CIA's Far East Division, sought and obtained a decree signed by President Nguyên Văn Thiêu formally establishing an organization named Phụng Hoàng to assume ICEX operations. The name Phụng Hoàng (Phoenix) was chosen because of its symbolic meaning. It became the deadliest weapon against the VCI. With renewed fervor, American and RVN personnel began collecting and analyzing data while concurrently arresting and neutralizing targeted individuals.

The DIOCCs circulated, to every district and province in South Vietnam, blacklists of known VCI operatives so that Phoenix forces could arrest and interrogate these individuals. The blacklists consisted of four rankings from A to D, with A being the most wanted. District and province intelligence centers distributed these lists to Phoenix field forces who would then apprehend or neutralize the individuals. These forces included Vietnamese units such as the National Police (NP), the National Police Field Force (NPFF), Provincial Reconnaissance Units (PRUs), and U.S. Navy Sea Air Land teams (SEALs). If not neutralized (killed) by these units, the targeted individual was transported to a provincial interrogation center (PIC). After PIC personnel, namely CIA advisors and their Vietnamese counterparts, gathered sufficient intelligence they sent the information up the chain of command for analysis by DIOCC and CORDS officials.

With the advent of Vietnamization and the withdrawal of American personnel, the Phoenix program suffered. Also, public pressure generated by news reports led to congressional interest in the program. Reporters described Phoenix as nothing more than an assassination program. This culminated in Phoenix being one of the programs to come under congressional investigation, and in 1971 William Colby, then deputy to the MACV commander for CORDS (and future director of the CIA), appeared before a House Committee to explain it.

Another factor in the program's demise was the 1972 Easter Offensive. This People's Army of Vietnam (PAVN) invasion of South Vietnam forced the RVN to focus its military strength against conventional rather than unconventional forces. Hence, in spring 1972 the National Police assumed responsibility for Phoenix and by December 1972 the United States ended its role in the program.

Despite the media's negative reports, top-ranking CIA officials as well as VC and Democratic Republic of Vietnam (DRV) leaders agree that the Phoenix program was a success. According to available sources, from 1968 to 1972 captured VCI numbered around 34,000; of these 22,000 rallied to the RVN government, while those killed numbered some 26,000.

Proof of Phụng Hoàng's success could be seen in Quang Tri Province during the 1972 Easter Offensive. For the first time there were front lines, behind which civilians and troops could move freely at night. Most bridges in rear areas did not have to be guarded as in the past. And when Communist forces took northern Quang Tri Province, they were unable to find trustworthy sympathizers at the village level.

—R. Blake Dunnavent

References: Andrade, Dale. *Ashes to Ashes: The Phoenix Program and the Vietnam War.* Lexington, MA: Lexington Books, 1990.
Colby, William. *Lost Victory: A Firsthand Account of America's Sixteen-Year Involvement in Vietnam.* Chicago: Contemporary Books, 1989.
DeForest, Orrin, and David Chanoff. *Slow Burn: The Rise and Fall of American Intelligence in Vietnam.* New York: Simon & Schuster, 1990.
Herrington, Stuart A. *Silence Was a Weapon: The Vietnam War in the Villages.* Novato, CA: Presidio Press, 1982.
See also: Central Intelligence Agency (CIA); Civilian Operations and Revolutionary Development Support (CORDS); Colby, William Egan; Counterinsurgency Warfare; Komer, Robert W.; Pacification; Psychological Warfare Operations (PSYOP); Territorial Forces; Vietnam, Republic of: Special Forces (Lực Lượng Đặc Biệt [LLDB]).

Phoumi Nosavan
(1920–1985)

Laotian general and political leader. Phoumi Nosavan was born on 27 January 1920 in Savannakhet. His mother was from Mukdaharn—across the Mekong River in Thailand—and he was a cousin once removed of Marshal Sarit Thanarat. Phoumi Nosavan took part in the nationalist movement as one of the leaders of the Lao Pen Lao and played a role in liberating Savannakhet from the Japanese. He joined the Lao Issara independent government and accompanied its leaders in exile (1946–1949). After a short-lived flirtation with the Viêt Minh during the Indo-China War, he joined the Royal Lao Army as a lieutenant in 1950. He rose rapidly through staff appointments, becoming chief of staff in 1955. He was commander of the Fifth Military Region in 1956 and went to France to study at the Ecole de Guerre in 1957.

Returning to Laos, he caught the eye of the U.S. Central Intelligence Agency (CIA) and was one of the prime movers behind the Committee for the Defense of National Interests (CDNI). As a colonel he joined the government of Phoui Sananikone in January 1959 as vice-minister of defense. He was involved in the unsuccessful effort to remove Phoui from power in December 1959, when he was promoted to brigadier general. In the succeeding government he was made defense minister and organized his own political party, the Paxa Sangkhom. After the fraudulent elections of 25 April 1960, he was once again defense minister in the government of Tiao Somsanith.

When Captain Kong Le overthrew the government in a coup d'état on 9 August 1960 and seized control of Vientiane, Phoumi flew from Luang Prabang to Ubon, and thence to Bangkok, where his appeal to Marshal Sarit to help him restore the pro-Western Somsanith government won him promises of aid. Phoumi was also backed by the CIA and the U.S. Defense Department, which ordered that aid be furnished to him at his base at Savannakhet.

After an unsuccessful attempt to patch things up with the new prime minister, Prince Souvanna Phouma, Phoumi formed a Counter–Coup d'Etat Committee (later renamed Revolutionary Committee) under the nominal leadership of Prince Boun Oum. With backing from Thailand and the United States (clandestine, because the United States still recognized the legal government in Vientiane), Phoumi attacked and captured Vientiane in December, forcing Prince Souvanna to flee to Cambodia.

The initial hopes that the United States had placed in Phoumi to defeat the Communists in Laos were soon dashed, as it became apparent that his troops controlled little of Laos outside the major towns. Eventually, Phoumi and Prince Boun Oum became the leaders of the rightist faction in a tripartite agreement brokered with international help for a coalition government with the Neutralists and Pathet Lao. Phoumi became deputy premier in this government, which took office in June 1962.

Phoumi continued his support to Prince Souvanna Phouma until February 1965, when he was caught in a rightist coup plot, apparently of others' making, and fled to Thailand. He was convicted in absentia by a commission of the National Assembly of numerous crimes, including corruption.

In spite of several attempts to restore his reputation in Laos and personal appeals to Prince Souvanna Phouma, Phoumi never returned to Laos and died in a comfortable exile in Thailand on 3 November 1985.

—Arthur J. Dommen

Reference: Dommen, Arthur J. *Conflict in Laos: The Politics of Neutralization.* Rev. ed. New York: Praeger, 1971.
See also: Kong Le; Laos; Souvanna Phouma.

PIERCE ARROW, Operation

(August 1964)
Air strikes launched against the Democratic Republic of Vietnam (DRV) as a result of the Tonkin Gulf incidents. When it was reported that DRV torpedo boats had attacked two U.S. destroyers in the Gulf of Tonkin on the night of 4 August 1964, President Lyndon Johnson quickly ordered retaliatory air strikes, code-named PIERCE ARROW. The targets were DRV naval vessels at a number of locations along the North Vietnamese coast and a petroleum storage facility at Vinh. Sixty-four sorties were flown from the aircraft carriers *Ticonderoga* and *Constellation.*

U.S. military planners would have preferred a dawn attack and President Johnson was determined that it be made early enough so that he could announce it before too much of the American public had gone to bed for the night, but there were long delays. The *Ticonderoga* was short of strike aircraft and more were flying in from the Philippines; the *Constellation,* coming west from Hong Kong at top speed, was not yet in position. When President Johnson went on radio and television to announce the air strikes it was 1037 in North Vietnam and 2337 in Washington. At this point, only four of the *Ticonderoga*'s aircraft, and none from the *Constellation,* were in the air. No bombs fell for another 90 minutes.

The petroleum storage facility at Vinh, important to the supply systems supporting Communist forces both in Laos and in South Vietnam, was the priority target and was destroyed. Of the naval vessels attacked, most were coastal patrol vessels known as "Swatow boats." The Americans sank at least one of these but probably not more than three. A few torpedo boats and one submarine chaser were also attacked; none of these seem to have been sunk, although they suffered damage and personnel casualties.

Two U.S. aircraft were shot down, both from *Constellation.* Lt. (jg) Everett Alvarez, attacking vessels in the harbor at Hòn Gai, was forced to bail out of his A-4C Skyhawk. Captured, he re-

mained a prisoner until 1973. Lt. (jg) Richard Sather, attacking Swatow boats off the mouth of the Ma River, was killed when his A-1H Skyraider crashed into the sea.

Each side claimed victory, exaggerating its success in the action; the United States claimed eight vessels sunk while the DRV claimed eight aircraft shot down. The American public approved of the air strikes overwhelmingly, so much so that public opinion polls showed a dramatic improvement in ratings of the president's overall handling of the situation in Southeast Asia.

—Edwin E. Moise

Reference: Moise, Edwin E. *Tonkin Gulf and the Escalation of the Vietnam War.* Chapel Hill, NC: University of North Carolina Press, 1996.
See also: Aircraft Carriers; Alvarez, Everett, Jr.; DeSoto Missions; Johnson, Lyndon Baines; Operation Plan 34A (OPLAN 34A); Tonkin Gulf Incidents.

Pigneau de Béhaine, Pierre

(1741–1799)
French Catholic bishop who became advisor to Emperor Gia Long and probably did as much as any single Frenchman to involve France in Vietnam. Pierre Pigneau de Béhaine, the Bishop of Adran, was born on 2 November 1741 at Origny-Sainte-Benoîte (Aisne). In 1765 Pigneau left for Pondichéry and from there was sent in 1767 to the province of Hà Tiên in southern Vietnam to head a Catholic seminary. During the wars between the Tây Sơn brothers and the Nguyên forces in southern Vietnam, Pigneau befriended and spirited to safety on an island in the Gulf of Siam the 16-year-old nephew of the Nguyên lords, Nguyên Phúc Ánh, the future Emperor Gia Long.

From this incident on, Pigneau devoted his life to the restoration of the Nguyêns to power. Partly through Pigneau's tireless lobbying on behalf of Nguyên Phúc Ánh and his raising of troops from among French navy deserters, this aim was finally accomplished in 1802. Pigneau was not to live to see it; he died of dysentery on 9 October 1799. Pigneau de Béhaine was buried on 16 December 1799 in Gia Định in the presence of the crown prince, all court mandarins, the king's bodyguard of 12,000 men, and 40,000 mourners. Nguyên Phúc Ánh composed a funeral oration, which was read aloud.

—Arthur J. Dommen

References: Buttinger, Joseph. *The Smaller Dragon: A Political History of Vietnam.* New York: Praeger, 1958.
Whitfield, Danny J. *Historical and Cultural Dictionary of Vietnam.* Metuchen, NJ: Scarecrow Press, 1976.
See also: Nguyên Phúc Ánh (Gia Long); Vietnam: From 938 through the French Conquest.

Pignon, Léon

(1908–1976)
French high commissioner in Indo-China, 1948–1950. Born 19 April 1908 in Angoulême, France, Léon Pignon studied at the Ecole Coloniale before joining the French Ministry for the Colonies in 1932. His many assignments included a stint in

Tonkin prior to the outbreak of the Second World War. Returning to France in 1938, he was imprisoned by the Germans and held until 1942. Following the war he returned to foreign service, performing in numerous capacities, including commissioner for foreign affairs, commissioner of the republic in Cambodia, and assistant to High Commissioner for Indo-China Georges Thierry d'Argenlieu.

A strong proponent of the French Empire, Pignon succeeded d'Argenlieu as high commissioner in 1948. He refused to negotiate with the Viêt Minh but did work with Bao Đai to enhance the facade of Vietnamese independence. The Elysée Agreement, containing an outline for a unified Vietnam but one in which France maintained control of its defense, diplomacy, and finance, was completed in March 1949. Pignon's short tenure as high commissioner ended the following year.

Pignon continued to serve France, first as a delegate to the United Nations Trusteeship Council and then as director of political affairs for the Ministry of French Overseas Territories. He died in Paris on 4 April 1976.

—David Coffey

References: Karnow, Stanley. *Vietnam: A History.* New York: Viking Press, 1983.
International Who's Who 1976–1977. London: Europa Publications, 1977.

See also: Bao Đai; Bollaert, Emile; d'Argenlieu, Georges Thierry; Elysée Agreement.

PIRANHA, Operation
(September 1965)

Allied military operation that began on 7 September 1965 and ran for three weeks on the Batangan Peninsula along the coast of southern Quang Ngãi Province, about 15 miles south of Chu Lai. PIRANHA followed on the conclusion of Operation STARLITE, a weeklong battle in August notable for being the first major U.S. ground operation in the Vietnam War. During STARLITE, battalions from the III Marine Amphibious Force engaged the 1st Viêt Công Regiment on the Batangan Peninsula in the first regimental-size U.S. ground operation since the Korean War. STARLITE involved both amphibious landings and helicopterborne assaults, and in just one week the Marines claimed 964 Viêt Công (VC) killed and possibly diverted an attack on the new U.S. base at Chu Lai.

Operation PIRANHA targeted another VC buildup, possibly by remnants of their battered 1st Regiment, a few miles farther south on the Batangan Peninsula. The coast there also was reported to be a place of entry for the seaborne infiltration of enemy supplies. PIRANHA differed significantly from STAR-

Infantrymen of the U.S. 26th Marines, 3d Division prepare to form an assault line during a search for Viêt Công in the Batangan Peninsula.

LITE in that a relatively small number of Marines coordinated with several battalions of the Army of the Republic of Vietnam (ARVN) 2d Division and a battalion of Vietnamese Marines. Though lasting two weeks longer, the results of PIRANHA were less spectacular than STARLITE, but U.S. Marine forces still counted 183 VC killed in action—66 of them in a single cave blown up by Marine engineers when the VC refused to surrender. South Vietnamese forces claimed an additional 66 VC killed. Marine casualties in PIRANHA were extremely light. Both STARLITE and PIRANHA may have disabused the VC of any illusion that they could defeat U.S. Marines in a stand-up battle, but Quang Ngãi Province remained a Communist sanctuary well into 1968.

—John D. Root

References: Simmons, Brig. Gen. Edwin H. "Marine Corps Operations in Vietnam, 1965–1966." In *The Marines in Vietnam, 1954–1973: An Anthology and Annotated Bibliography,* 2d ed. Washington, DC: History and Museums Division, Headquarters, U.S. Marine Corps, 1985.
Stanton, Shelby L. *The Rise and Fall of an American Army: U.S. Ground Forces in Vietnam, 1965–1973.* Novato, CA: Presidio Press, 1985.
See also: STARLITE, Operation; United States: Marine Corps.

PIRAZ Warships

(1965–1973)

U.S. destroyers, frigates, and cruisers operating in the Gulf of Tonkin to provide support for Allied war planes. To give early warning of air attack, U.S. Navy surface combatants first took up station in April 1965 between the Democratic Republic of Vietnam (DRV) and aircraft carriers on Yankee Station. The surface warships soon assumed other duties, such as vectoring U.S. aircraft against DRV MiGs. In the first successful performance of that mission, the destroyer *Joseph Strauss* in June 1965 controlled two F-4 Phantoms to an interception of two MiG-17s, thus contributing to the initial American aerial victories of the conflict.

Formalized in July 1966, the patrols were dubbed PIRAZ for "Positive Identification Radar Advisory Zone." In addition to early warning and fighter control duties, PIRAZ ships were to provide a precise navigational reference point for U.S. aircraft, to track all planes flying over the Gulf of Tonkin and eastern areas of North Vietnam, to keep U.S. aircraft from crossing into People's Republic of China airspace, and to direct search-and-rescue helicopters to downed aircrews.

Because these multiple missions frequently involved tracking literally hundreds of aircraft simultaneously, the vessels assigned to PIRAZ were inevitably the most modern surface warships, especially those equipped with the new computerized Naval Tactical Data System and with antiaircraft missile batteries for self-defense. As an index of the complex tasks involved, the nuclear-powered cruiser *Long Beach* kept track of about 30,000 U.S. aircraft sorties during a four-month tour in 1967 and followed over 400 DRV flights in the spring of 1968.

Several times PIRAZ warships fired missiles at North Vietnamese fighters. On 23 May 1968 the *Long Beach* downed a MiG with a Talos missile at a range of 65 miles, the first instance in

which a ship had hit a hostile plane with a guided missile. In September the nuclear cruiser destroyed a second MiG at a similar distance.

On at least one occasion, North Vietnamese aircraft directly challenged a PIRAZ warship, when in July 1972 five MiGs attacked the frigate *Biddle;* she shot down two of the attackers, while suffering no damage herself.

PIRAZ warships enjoyed even greater successes by controlling U.S. interception of DRV planes. For instance, in just one week during October 1972, the nuclear frigate *Truxtun* directed U.S. fighters to six air-to-air victories. The top-scoring ship in this field was the cruiser *Chicago,* whose radarman Master Chief Larry Nowell won the Navy's Distinguished Service Medal in August 1972 for vectoring Navy and Air Force fighters to 12 successful interceptions.

But it was in the performance of more mundane duties that the PIRAZ warships made their greatest contribution; they also validated the Navy's newest electronic and missile systems. In so doing, they helped demonstrate the capabilities of the surface warship in a navy dominated by carrier aviation.

—Malcolm Muir, Jr.

References: Marolda, Edward J. *By Sea, Air, and Land: An Illustrated History of the U.S. Navy and the War in Southeast Asia.* Washington, DC: Naval Historical Center, 1994.
Muir, Malcolm, Jr. *Black Shoes and Blue Water: Surface Warfare in the United States Navy, 1945–1975.* Washington, DC: Naval Historical Center, 1996.
See also: Airplanes, Allied and Democratic Republic of Vietnam; United States: Navy; Warships, Allied and Democratic Republic of Vietnam.

Pistols

During the Indo-China War French forces used quantities of both domestic and foreign pistols. Based primarily on a Browning design, the French M1935A and M1935S pistols are chambered for the 7.65-mm "long" cartridge. Both pistols are recoil-operated, semiautomatic weapons attaining a muzzle velocity of 1,132 feet per second and are fed by eight-round detachable box magazines. The M1935A is 7.6 inches long and weighs 1.62 pounds. The M1935S is 7.4 inches long and weighs 1.75 pounds.

French forces also used large numbers of German 9-mm P38s and P08 Lugers as well as American .45-caliber 1911 and 1911A1 Colts. Experience with these weapons spurred designers at the Saint Etienne Arsenal to develop a new French service pistol.

The resulting 9-mm M1950 is essentially a modification of the U.S. .45-caliber Colt 1911A1 chambered for the German 9-mm parabellum cartridge. It is 7.6 inches long and weighs 1.8 pounds. The M1950 utilizes a nine-round detachable box magazine and produces a muzzle velocity of 1,156 feet per second.

During the Vietnam War the standard sidearm issued to U.S. forces was the .45-caliber Model 1911A1. Designed by John Browning and originally designated the Model 1911 after its year of adoption, the pistol was first manufactured by Colt's Patent Firearms Company of Hartford, Connecticut.

In 1926 the Model 1911 was slightly modified and redesignated the Model 1911A1. Over 2.4 million .45-caliber 1911 and

1911A1s were produced for the U.S. government by various manufacturers.

The .45-caliber Model 1911A1 is a recoil-operated semiautomatic utilizing a .45-caliber rimless cartridge. It is 8.62 inches long, weighs 2.43 pounds, features a seven-round, detachable box magazine, and achieves a muzzle velocity of 830 feet per second.

The government also purchased a variety of commercial pistols for special-purpose use, and individual personnel at times carried privately purchased or captured sidearms. Secondary military-issued pistols included the .32- and .380-caliber Colt semiautomatic pistol and the .38-caliber Colt Detective Special Revolver, Colt Police Positive Revolver, Colt Special Official Police, Colt Combat Masterpiece, Smith & Wesson Model 10, and the Smith & Wesson Military and Police Revolvers.

During the Indo-China and Vietnam Wars, Việt Minh, People's Army of Vietnam (PAVN), and Việt Công (VC) forces utilized a wide variety of sidearms. The quality of these weapons ranged from primitive, homemade "zip-guns" to captured World War II Japanese and well-made French and American pistols. Large numbers of weapons were also imported from other Communist countries. Produced by both the Soviet Union and the People's Republic of China, the most commonly used sidearm was the Soviet-designed Tokarev TT Model 1933 semiautomatic pistol, designated the Type 51 in Chinese nomenclature.

Modified at the Tula arsenal by Fedor V. Tokarev from a Colt-Browning design, the TT Model 1933/Type 51 is chambered for a bottlenecked 7.62-mm cartridge. Fed by an eight-round, in-line detachable box magazine, the TT Model 1933/Type 51 is 7.68 inches long, weighs 1.88 pounds, and achieves a muzzle velocity of 1,378 feet per second.

—Jeff Kinard

References: Chant, Christopher, ed. *How Weapons Work.* London: Marshall Cavendish, 1976.
Flayderman, Norm. *Flayderman's Guide to Antique American Firearms . . . and their Values.* 5th ed. Fort Lauderdale, FL: 1994.
Rosa, Joseph G., and Robin May. *An Illustrated History of Guns and Small Arms.* London: Peerage Books, 1984.
Smith, W. H. B., revised by Joseph E. Smith. *Small Arms of the World.* 9th ed. Harrisburg, PA: Stackpole, 1969.
See also: Grenades, Hand: Allied and Democratic Republic of Vietnam; Grenades, Launched: Allied and Democratic Republic of Vietnam; Machine Guns, Allied and People's Army of Vietnam; Rifles; Rockets.

Plain of Jars

Rolling plain in Xieng Khouang Province of northern Laos near the border of Vietnam famed for a large number of stone urns or jars, the origin of which remains a mystery. The plain is crossed from east to west by Route 7, the road coming from northern Vietnam to join the south-north road from Vientiane to Luang Prabang, Route 13, at the Sala Phou Khoun road junction. There is an airfield, originally built by the French, at Phone Savan. Other major towns are Khang Khay on the east, Xieng Khouang on the south, and Muong Soui on the west. These towns were largely destroyed between 1963 and 1973 during the Vietnam War. The plain was very heavily bombed by U.S. planes, and unexploded

ordnance continues to kill people in the area. An ordnance defusing team has worked to correct the situation, supported by international aid from foreign governments, including the United States, and nongovernmental organizations.

—Arthur J. Dommen

See also: Air Power, Role in War; Geography of Indo-China and Vietnam; Laos.

Plain of Reeds

Location, primarily in Kiên Phong and Kiên Tường Provinces about 40 miles west of Sài Gòn, that was a stronghold for Communist guerrilla operations throughout the war. Formed by a depression in the Mekong River Delta, the plain consists largely of harsh, sparsely populated marshland. Its principal crop is rice, harvested annually; often the area is below water. Because few of the peasants owned their own land, they lived in oppressive economic conditions, and the Việt Minh manipulated the local population against the French, who called the area *Plaine des Joncs.*

Similarly, the Việt Công controlled the population against American and South Vietnamese forces. Although no large American units were deployed against the small-scale guerrilla maneuvers, two significant battles took place there, one from 1 to 8 January 1966, another on 29 July 1969. Also in 1969 the U.S. Navy conducted Operation BARRIER REEF, successfully inhibiting the Communists' ability to traverse the plain en route to heavily populated areas farther south. Additionally, the plain was a staging area for the 1970 incursions into Cambodia against guerrilla sanctuaries and resupply routes. The final battles in the area occurred in 1972 during the Easter Offensive.

—Charles J. Gaspar

References: Andrade, Dale. *Trial by Fire: The 1972 Easter Offensive.* New York: Hippocrene Books, 1995.
Coleman, J. D. *Incursion.* New York: St. Martin's Press, 1991.
Schreadley, R. L. *From the Rivers to the Sea.* Annapolis, MD: Naval Institute Press, 1992.
See also: Cambodian Incursion; Easter Offensive (Nguyên Huê Campaign); Mekong Delta.

Poetry and the Vietnam Experience

Poetry that documents the attitudes toward the Vietnam War—as well as the origins, development, and conduct of the war—is both pervasive and significant. Although only a few poems by French writers reflect that country's involvement, the Vietnamese tradition of poetic expression produced a large body of work, both personal and political, written by soldiers and civilians of the Democratic Republic of Vietnam (DRV) and the Republic of Vietnam (RVN). Unfortunately, except for the efforts of American poets John Balaban, Yusef Komunyakka, Kevin Bowen, and Bruce Weigl, most of these poems are not available in translation. Only the Vietnamese expatriate Thích Nhât Hanh published a significant collection in English. His *The Cry of Vietnam* (1968) contains 15 poems about the devastation of war and the horrors inflicted by all sides. Also a number of poems by Vietnamese, Cambodian, and Lao refugee poets appeared in the numerous volumes of the Viêt Nam Forum Series and the Lac-Viêt Series published after 1983 by the Council on Southeast Asia Studies at Yale University. In Viêt Nam Forum 14 (1994), for instance, Viêt Thanh Nguyên, then a Ph.D. candidate at the University of California, Berkeley, wrote in a moving poem about a burning ash heap that he was "yearning to find a clue/ in the ash to my people,/ severed from me with the finality of a butcher's cleaver."

More than any other group, however, American poets, both veterans and nonveterans, in thousands of poems written during and after the war best chronicled the changing, often conflicting attitudes and experiences of men and women fighting in Southeast Asia.

Their poetry ranges from often bawdy ballads sung by American fighter pilots, collected in Joseph F. Tuso's *Singing the Vietnam Blues* (1990), and the short, sometimes humorous verses published in publications such as the satiric *Grunt* magazine or the *Pacific Stars and Stripes,* to immensely ambitious and moving works that rank with the best poetry of the age. Poetry about Vietnam falls into three general categories: political protest poems, usually written by established poets who had not been to Vietnam; verse novels, in which chronologically linked poems depict one person's experiences at war; and the hundreds of usually short, personal lyrics that present individual scenes, character sketches, or events.

The first significant protest volume was *A Poetry Reading against the Vietnam War* (1966), edited by Robert Bly and David Ray. The next year, Walter Lowenfels edited the anthology *Where Is Vietnam?,* in which the 87 contributing poets include James Dickey, Lawrence Ferlinghetti, and Denise Levertov. Two more collections followed: *Out of the Shadow of War* (1968) and *Poetry against the War* (1972). Although a few poems are set in Southeast Asia, most of the works presented in these anthologies reflect the writers' attitudes to U.S. involvement in Vietnam by references to the political scene, the war as seen on TV or reported in the newspapers, and to antiwar themes in general. These anthologies and the numerous individual poems that were published served to define and sustain the general intellectual opposition to the war.

Of the verse novels, three stand out: *Vietnam Simply* (1967) by Dick Shea, *How Audie Murphy Died in Vietnam* (1972) by McAvoy Layne, and *Interrogations* (1990) by Leroy Quintana. In discursive, often sardonic selections, Shea presents the observations of a Navy lieutenant about the entrance of U.S. Marines into the war and other scenes and events in 1965 Vietnam. By means of short, staccato verses, Layne's book traces a Marine recruit (who bears the name of the legendary American war hero) through basic training and combat, then becomes allegorically fanciful as "Audie" is captured by the Viêt Công and holds telephone conversations from Hà Nôi with the president of the United States, yet still hums "The Theme from Marlboro Country." Quintana, the only Hispanic veteran to publish a major collection of poetry, shows how a young army draftee experiences training, combat, and the aftermath of the war, where even "on city streets, in restaurants, bars" he "still walk[s] the jungle in camouflage," his "M-16 mind still on recon patrol." Each of these verse novels pre-

sents young men whose innocent acceptance changes to experienced disillusion about the American presence in Vietnam.

This subject—the movement from innocence to experience—was perhaps the most universal theme explored by American poets, most of whom served in Vietnam, either in the military or as conscientious objectors. Many of them interrupted their college educations to go to war, then returned to earn graduate degrees in various writing programs and teach in universities. Before the 1975 fall of Sài Gòn, many poet-veterans joined protest organizations such as the Vietnam Veterans Against the War, using their poems to substantiate their opposition not only to war in general but to the Vietnam War in particular.

What characterizes the majority of the individual poems is their specificity. Presenting much more shattering detail than did World War I poets such as Rupert Brooke, Siegfried Sassoon, and Wilfred Owen, these poets wrote about immediate wartime experiences: firefights, the death of a friend, smells of the jungle, rocket attacks, being wounded, seeing Vietnamese women and children killed, corpses in body bags, rape, arrival into and departure from Vietnam, street scenes, the beauty of the countryside, memories of the war after ending their tours, bombing missions, and letters from home. Brutally frank, much of the language of these poems represents the actuality of the discourse that prevailed, filled with the soldiers' jargon and profanity, often requiring the use of a glossary because of the many references to historical events as well as specific people and place-names.

The themes of the poems are both universal and particularly modern. Many show the horrors of war, the deaths of innocent civilians, the tragic ending of youthful lives, and the general sundering of moral and ethical values. Reflecting the consciousness of the 1960s and 1970s, however, a large number of poems mirror the feelings of all participants as America's longest war began to seem more and more unwinnable: the sense of loss of individuality, the feeling of guilt at having participated, the impossibility of anyone's understanding the totality of the experience, the realization of having been betrayed by higher authority, and most often, the anger and bitterness at feeling like what fiction writer Larry Heinemann called not a cog in a mighty machine but merely "a slab of meat on the table." There are also many poems that contain racial and ethnic themes, using both black versus white and white versus Asian conflicts.

Of the hundreds of war veteran poets, a few achieved literary prominence. In 1994 Army veteran Yusef Komunyaka won the Pulitzer Prize for his *Neon Vernacular: New and Selected Poems* (1993). All of the selections in one of his earlier books, *Dien Cai Dau* (1988), are about the war and present not only richly metaphoric poems about Hà Nôi Hannah, Bob Hope, and night patrols but also offer the acute vision of a black soldier. Another major prizewinning poet is former Marine W. D. Ehrhart, whose numerous collections of poetry, four nonfiction books, and many edited anthologies made him one of the most prolific and widely known Vietnam War writers. In *A Generation of Peace* (1977), his poem "A Relative Thing," which details the feelings of many returned veterans, reminds America that "We are your sons," and that "When you awake,/we will still be here."

The oldest of the major poets was Walter McDonald, who was a career officer teaching at the Air Force Academy when he was assigned to Vietnam in 1969. An editor as well as a fiction writer, McDonald was best known for his many volumes of poems such as *After the Noise of Saigon* (1988), in which the subject of war is balanced by poems about flying and scenes set in west Texas. Another professor was Bruce Weigl, whose 1967–1968 Army service in Vietnam sparked a number of collections such as *Song of Napalm* (1988), in which most of his war poems appear. The title poem is a haunting testament to his wife as he confesses his inability to forget aspects of the war. Also a college teacher, John Balaban spent three years in Vietnam, the first two as a conscientious objector. He published fiction and numerous translations of Vietnamese poetry, and his collections *After Our War* (1974), nominated for a National Book Award, and *Blue Mountain* (1982) contain memorable poems such as "The Guard at the Binh Thuy Bridge" and "April 30, 1975," a poem written about the last day of the war.

Among the other poets and their major books are Michael Casey, *Obscenities* (1972); David Huddle, *Stopping by Home* (1988); Kevin Bowen, *Playing Basketball with the Viet Cong* (1994); D. F. Brown, *Returning Fire* (1984); Horace Coleman, *Between a Rock and a Hard Place,* in *Four Black Poets* (1977); Gerald McCarthy, *War Story* (1977); Bill Shields, *Nam Poems* (1987); Steve Mason, *Warrior for Peace,* with an introduction by Oliver Stone (1988); Bryan Alec Floyd, *The Long War Dead* (1976); Perry Oldham, *Vinh Long* (1976); and D. C. Berry, *Saigon Cemetery* (1972).

Individual works by most of these and other poets can be found in the following anthologies: *Winning Hearts and Minds,* edited by Larry Rottman, Jan Barry, and Basil T. Paquet (1972); *Listen: The War,* edited by Fred Kiley and Tony Dater (1973); *Demilitarized Zones,* edited by Jan Barry and W. D. Ehrhart (1976); *Carrying the Darkness,* edited by W. D. Ehrhart (1985, 1989); *Shallow Graves: Two Women in Vietnam,* by Wendy Wilder Larsen and Trân Thi Nga (1986); and *Unaccustomed Mercy,* edited by W. D. Ehrhart, with an introduction and bibliography by John Clark Pratt (1989).

Coincident with the dedication of "The Wall," the Vietnam Veterans Memorial in Washington, D.C., the first major gathering of and public readings by Vietnam War creative writers was held in New York City on 23 March 1984. There, W. D. Ehrhart defined what became apparent in most of the poetry that had been and was to be published. Although most veteran-poets did write about many other subjects, it was the war that consumed them in their art and inspired their best poems because, according to Ehrhart, that experience was "the single most important experience of [one's] life." Accordingly, the poetry of the Vietnam War provides a historical, intellectual, and emotional chronology of men and women at war that is indeed unique.

—John Clark Pratt

References: Beidler, Philip D. *American Literature and the Experience of Vietnam.* Athens, GA: University of Georgia Press, 1982.
_____. *Re-Writing America: Vietnam Authors in Their Generation.* Athens, GA: University of Georgia Press, 1991.
Gotera, Vince. *Radical Visions: Poetry by Vietnam Veterans.* Athens, GA: University of Georgia Press, 1994.
Lomperis, Timothy J., and John Clark Pratt. *Reading the Wind: The Literature of the Vietnam War.* Durham, NC: Duke University Press, 1987.
Newman, John. *Vietnam War Literature.* 3d ed. Metuchen, NJ: Scarecrow Press, 1996.
See also: Art and the Vietnam War; Drama and the Vietnam Experience; Fiction, U.S., and the Vietnam Experience; Film and the Vietnam Experience; Prose Narrative and the Vietnam Experience; Vietnam Veterans Against the War (VVAW).

Pol Pot

(1928–1998)

Cambodian Communist revolutionary leader who gained international infamy as the architect of a genocidal policy. Born Saloth Sar of ethnic Khmer parents in the village of Prek Sbau near the provincial capital of Kompong Thom on 25 May 1928, Pol Pot adopted his present revolutionary name in 1976. His reclusive nature, as well as his concealment and falsification of details of his life, has created confusion surrounding his birth and early years. Although it has been widely reported that Pol Pot was born into a peasant family in the depths of poverty, his biographer David Chandler has pointed out that his father was a prosperous farmer who owned land, cattle, and a house. His family also had connections with the royal palace in Phnom Penh. His cousin Meak and

Pol Pot, leader of the Khmer Rouge. In July 1997 Pol Pot became the centerpiece in a show trial in western Cambodia by the Khmer Rouge leadership and was sentenced to life under house arrest.

his sister Saroeun, both members of the royal ballet, became consorts of Prince Sisowath Monivong. Meak bore Monivong a son shortly before he became king in 1927, and during his reign she held a desirable position in charge of the women of the palace and, after his death, served until the early 1970s as a senior teacher with the ballet. Saroeun returned to Kompong Thom after Monivong's death. In addition, Sar's older brother Loth Suong worked as a clerk at the palace from the late 1920s until 1975.

In the mid-1930s Sar and an older brother went to live with Meak and Suong in Phnom Penh. Never known to have mentioned his palace connections or these years, Sar instead stressed his rural origins, more in keeping with the picture he wished to project.

After arriving in Phnom Penh, Sar spent several months at a Buddhist monastery, where he studied Buddhism and became literate in the Khmer language. After five years at the College Norodom Sihanouk (1942–1947), he studied carpentry at the Ecole Technique. In 1949 he continued his education at the Ecole Française de Radio-Electricité in Paris, where he joined the French Communist Party, probably in 1952.

In 1953, upon his return to Cambodia, Pol Pot joined the anti-French, Vietnamese-dominated underground movement and the Communist Party. He taught history and geography in a private school for the next decade, and emerged as a well-known left-wing journalist. In 1960 Cambodia's secret Communist Party elected him to its Central Committee and named him secretary-general in 1963, a post to which he was reelected in 1971 and 1976. Distrusting Prince Norodom Sihanouk's 1963 invitation to join in forming a new government, Sar—now a full-time militant known as Brother Secretary or Brother Number One—fled into the jungles and organized the Khmer Rouge, a Communist guerrilla army.

In March 1970 General Lon Nol seized power in Cambodia. After visiting the Democratic Republic of Vietnam (DRV) and the People's Republic of China in 1969 and 1970, Pol Pot became military commander of the Cambodian Communist component of the National Front, the Sihanouk-led government in exile that sought to overthrow Lon Nol's pro-U.S. regime. The ensuing five-year civil war gave Pol Pot not only an opportunity to increase his military power but the chance to devote attention to political matters and organizational development. These contributed greatly to the Khmer Rouge seizure of Phnom Penh on 16 April 1975.

From 1976 to 1978 Pol Pot was prime minister of Democratic Kampuchea. He envisioned an agricultural utopia populated by the new Cambodian collectivist man. Declaring the "Year Zero," he emptied Phnom Penh and turned the country into one vast concentration camp, with the population as rural forced labor. Khmer Rouge actions obliterated the middle class with its intellectuals and professionals. In all, up to 2 million Cambodians died, some 25 percent of the population.

One source quotes Pol Pot in 1977 saying, "Although a million lives have been wasted, our party does not feel sorry." In December 1978 the Socialist Republic of Vietnam (SRV) invaded Cambodia and created the People's Republic of Kampuchea. In 1979 Pol Pot received sanctuary in Thailand and the Khmer Rouge used that country as the base for its insurgency, first against the Vietnamese-installed government in Phnom Penh and later to attempt to sabotage a UN–brokered peace plan and election.

Pol Pot's power stemmed in part from the mystery surrounding him. He gave his last public interview in 1980, and the last available photograph dates from the same year. In September 1985 the Khmer Rouge faction of the Kampuchean coalition government announced that Pol Pot was relinquishing command of the rebel army that had battled the Vietnamese since 1978. This had long been sought by Western nations supporting the rebel alliance and by the SRV as a first step toward ending the six-year civil war, but it left unclear Pol Pot's real status.

In the years to follow, Pol Pot's travels, exact role in the Khmer Rouge, and even whether he remained alive were the stuff of much speculation in the West. Then in late July 1997 Pol Pot at last surfaced, the centerpiece in a show trial in western Cambodia by the Khmer Rouge leadership. Found guilty, he was sentenced to life under house arrest. His trial was probably the result of the killing the month before of Khmer Rouge leader Son Sen and his family on Pol Pot's orders. Fearing for their own lives, the remaining leaders arrested Pol Pot and held him. He spent his last months in a three-room wooden shack near the Thai border in the Dangrek Mountains region. Pol Pot died in his sleep on 15 April 1998, reportedly of a heart attack. But no autopsy was conducted, and there were suspicions he might have been murdered by some of his lieutenants who feared increasing pressure on the part of Washington for his trial and their possible implication in his misdeeds. Among the Khmer Rouge, not everything is as it seems.

—Paul S. Daum, with assistance from Joseph Ratner

References: Becker, Elizabeth. *When the War Was Over: Cambodia's Revolution and the Voices of Its People.* New York: Simon & Schuster, 1986.
Chandler, David P. *Brother Number One: A Political Biography of Pol Pot.* Boulder, CO: Westview Press, 1992.
Moritz, Charles, ed. *Current Biography 1980.* New York: H. W. Wilson, 1980.
Shawcross, William. *Sideshow: Kissinger, Nixon, and the Destruction of Cambodia.* New York: Simon & Schuster, 1979.
See also: Cambodia; Heng Samrin; Hun Sen; Khmer Rouge; Lon Nol; Sihanouk, Norodom; Vietnamese Invasion and Occupation of Cambodia.

Poland

Polish People's Republic; member, with Canada and India, of the International Commission for Supervision and Control (ICSC) established in the 1954 Geneva Accords. A socialist state, Poland joined other Warsaw Pact members in support of the Democratic Republic of Vietnam (DRV) during the Vietnam conflict. Polish diplomat Janusz Lewandowski secured an opening for negotiations between the United States and the DRV (Operation MARIGOLD) in June 1966, which was torpedoed by U.S. bombings near Hà Nôi. A second attempt to host negotiations in November 1966 also failed due to U.S. refusal to halt its bombings of the North.

The International Commission of Control and Supervision (ICCS), established by the Paris peace accords of 1973, consisted of representatives from Hungary, Poland, Indonesia, and Canada. Not long afterward Canada withdrew and was replaced by Iran. The ICCS disbanded on 30 April 1975.

—Robert G. Mangrum

References: Davidson, Phillip B. *Vietnam at War.* Novato, CA: Presidio Press, 1988.
Karnow, Stanley. *Vietnam: A History.* New York: Penguin Books, 1984.
Summers, Harry G. *Vietnam War Almanac.* New York: Facts on File, 1985.
See also: International Commission for Supervision and Control (ICSC); MARIGOLD, Operation.

Popular Forces

See Territorial Forces.

Porter, William James

(1914–1988)

American diplomat and chief negotiator for the U.S. delegation to the Paris peace talks, 1971–1973. Born in Great Britain on 1 September 1914, Porter entered the U.S. Foreign Service in 1936 as private secretary to the U.S. legation in Budapest, Hungary. An expert on the Middle East, Porter held a variety of posts as a political officer, advisor, and ambassador in such locations as Lebanon, Cyprus, Algeria, Baghdad, Jerusalem, and Morocco.

In 1965, at the request of Ambassador Henry Cabot Lodge, Porter became deputy ambassador to the Republic of Vietnam (RVN). Lodge relieved Porter of routine duties and gave him "full charge" of "community building," the so-called pacification program designed to win the loyalty of the South Vietnamese people. Porter had charge of all nonmilitary aspects of the U.S. effort in the RVN, and although he had reservations about his role and felt that Lodge did not give full support to his ideas, Porter pulled together a number of agencies that previously overlapped and duplicated functions. His Office of Civilian Operations (OCO) trained and installed agricultural and educational workers and community organizers. Such efforts at pacification and rural development won the praise of Henry Kissinger and convinced President Lyndon Johnson that the government was on the right course. However, after 18 months under Porter's control the program fell short of Washington's expectations, and it was reassigned to military control.

Porter's next major assignment and most significant role in the Vietnam War period came with his September 1971 appointment by President Richard Nixon to replace David K. E. Burns as chief U.S. delegate at the Paris peace talks, which had begun in May 1968. His dynamic, unconventional style bolstered the 19-member U.S. delegation and moved the talks forward. Porter took the offensive, unnerving the other side by adopting their own tactics. He postponed meetings, lectured opposing delegates, and was unwilling to let the other side use the negotiations as a stage for propaganda. Complementing Kissinger's efforts with Democratic Republic of Vietnam delegate Lê Đức Tho, Porter is credited with breaking the deadlocked negotiations, opening the way to the withdrawal of U.S. troops, an agreed-upon cease-fire, and the return of U.S. prisoners of war.

Following his Vietnam service, Porter was reassigned as ambassador to the Republic of Korea and then, in 1973, under secretary of state for political affairs. He continued to play an influential role in U.S. Southeast Asia policy, including the restructuring and streamlining of the Foreign Service officer corps. In 1974 President Nixon named him ambassador to Canada. Porter's last post was as ambassador to Saudi Arabia from 1975 to 1977. Porter died of cancer on 15 March 1988 in Fall River, Massachusetts.

—Gary Kerley

References: *Current Biography Yearbook 1974.* New York: H. W. Wilson, 1975.
Herring, George C. *LBJ and Vietnam: A Different Kind of War.* Austin, TX: University of Texas Press, 1994.
Olson, James S., ed. *Dictionary of the Vietnam War.* Westport, CT: Greenwood Press, 1988.
The Pentagon Papers: The Defense Department History of United States Decisionmaking on Vietnam, vol. 2. Boston: Beacon Press, 1971.
See also: Johnson, Lyndon Baines; Kissinger, Henry Alfred; Lodge, Henry Cabot, Jr.; Nixon, Richard Milhous; Pacification; Paris Negotiations.

Post-Traumatic Stress Disorder (PTSD)

Term developed to describe and treat stress reactions in Vietnam War veterans. It has since been used for diagnosis and treatment of sufferers of other traumas such as natural disaster, hostage and prisoner-of-war (POW) experiences, and violent crime. As defined in the most recent edition of the American Psychiatric Association's *Diagnostic and Statistical Manual,* 4th edition (DSM-IV), five conditions are necessary for the diagnosis of post-traumatic stress disorder (PTSD):

1. The existence of a traumatic experience "outside the normal range of human experience." This experience may have come in undergoing or witnessing the imminent threat of death, violent physical injury, or systematic physical abuse, and must have resulted at the time in intense fear, helplessness, or horror.

2. Persistent reexperiencing of the stressor event. The individual is subject to vivid and uncontrollable memories and/or recurrent dreams of the event and may lose track of his or her current surroundings entirely, in what has come to be called a "flashback." There may be intense psychological or physiological reactions to external or internal cues that remind the individual of the event.

3. Persistent avoidance of thoughts, people, places, and other aspects associated with the traumatic event, along with a numbing of emotional responses and/or feelings of detachment from other people. There may also be partial amnesia about the past event and/or an inability to project a normal life for the future. Three indicators in this category are required.

4. Increased arousal, including at least two of the following: sleep problems, outbursts of anger, difficulty in concentrating, hypervigilance, and an exaggerated startle response.

5. A duration of the condition for at least one month.

On a rainy Veterans Day, a veteran breaks down as he and others pay their respects to those who died in the Vietnam War.

The condition may occur immediately after the traumatic event, or, in the case of "delayed stress," may not manifest itself for months or even years after the event.

According to the National Vietnam Veterans Readjustment Study (NVVRS), commissioned by Congress in 1983 and published in 1990, approximately 15.2 percent of Vietnam-theater veterans suffer from PTSD. These figures, on the whole, agree with previous studies conducted by the Department of Veterans Affairs and the Centers for Disease Control, and are surprisingly low when compared with statistics gathered for other wars; estimates for World War II, for example, exceed 30 percent. However, it is difficult to make accurate comparisons, since the definition of the disorder has changed since previous wars, and since most previous statistics were gathered from reported cases during and shortly after the war, whereas statistics for Vietnam veterans are for the most part based on surveys of veterans after combat—sometimes years later—and extrapolated for the remainder of the veteran population.

In previous wars, stress reactions to combat had variously been known as "shell shock," "combat fatigue," and other names, and in the first edition of the DSM had been described under the categories of stress disorders. But in the second edition of the DSM, published in 1968, all references to stress disorders were removed, and there remained no official diagnosis or treatment for the reactions observed in combat troops or returned veterans. Instead, after 1968 individuals exhibiting psychological problems were diagnosed as having "inability to adjust to adult life," schizophrenia, alcoholism, or borderline personality disorder. Of the Vietnam veterans reporting or exhibiting stress problems during and after the war, between 62 percent and 77 percent were diagnosed in the last three categories. Stress disorders were not returned to the DSM until the third edition in 1980, although some psychologists and psychiatrists had begun using the term "Vietnam War Syndrome" as early as 1969.

In December 1970 psychiatrist Robert Jay Lifton, who had been active in the antiwar movement, began a series of experimental "rap groups" with members of the New York chapter of Vietnam Veterans Against the War (VVAW). These rap groups were a form of group therapy in which veterans talked through their experiences during and after the war. In 1973 Lifton described both the rap groups and his conclusions drawn from them in what was to become one of the most influential books about Vietnam veterans: *Home from the War*. It is important to note, however, that in this book, which was to become the basis for diagnosis and treatment of PTSD throughout the helping professions, Lifton acknowledged that he had used a nonrepresentative sample of veterans (that is, disaffected veterans in an activist organization) and that his goal was primarily to train a group of vocal advocates against the war.

By the end of the war the original rap group participants had in fact begun giving public talks about the causes and symptomatology of stress reactions in veterans, and hundreds of rap groups modeled on the ones in New York had been established around the country. They had also joined the lobbying efforts by veterans' groups for better systems of counseling for veterans.

In 1972 Lifton and his colleague Chaim Shatan, with the help of the National Council of Churches, sponsored the "First National Conference on the Emotional Needs of Vietnam-Era Veterans" in St. Louis, Missouri. The conference was attended by Veterans Administration (VA) officials, who were there introduced to Lifton's work and his conclusions and recommendations for the counseling systems that would later be put into place within the VA. In fact, when Congress approved funding for such counseling systems in 1979, the models used were the assumptions and methods established by the original rap groups.

The most important part of the new counseling system was the establishment of Veteran Outreach Centers, or what have now come to be called Vet Centers, places outside normal VA facilities, where veterans could talk to other veterans in an atmosphere less official than that of a major medical facility, and where other services could be provided along with psychological counseling, such as job training and benefits counseling. As early as 1977 VA Director Max Cleland called in Shad Meshad, who had instituted just such a system of storefront counseling centers already in use by the Brentwood VA center in Los Angeles, to help establish these new centers. The Vet Centers, although still under the general jurisdiction of the VA, were given a separate administrative identity under a new reporting chain to the Readjustment Counseling Services (RCS) division.

As counseling began in these new facilities, and within the already existing VA medical centers, there was still no officially recognized definition of the disorders being treated. However, in 1976 Lifton and his colleagues, as part of a task force for the American Psychiatric Association, had begun work on such a definition, and in 1980 their definition was published in the third edition of the *Diagnostic and Statistical Manual* (DSM-III). Although slightly modified and clarified in the two subsequent versions of the DSM (an interim edition, DSM-III-R, was published in 1987), the definition today remains essentially the same as the one first established not only in the 1980 official publication but also in Lifton's original work in the early 1970s.

In 1996 there were over 200 Vet Centers throughout the United States, as well as counseling and other psychiatric services available in VA medical centers around the country. Services in the Vet Centers have been extended to veterans of later wars and may soon be made available to World War II and Korean War veterans.

Development of the definitions and treatment of PTSD, however, has gone far beyond the original intent of dealing with Vietnam veterans' problems. The treatment of trauma-related stress symptoms in general has developed into a major field of psychological research, with its own research institutes, journals, and on-line databases, both inside and outside the VA, and has even entered the realm of popular self-help books, one such book (Judith Herman's *Trauma and Recovery*) having appeared on the *New York Times* best-seller list in 1992. Lifton's original book itself has been reissued several times, and the subject of PTSD became a staple of Vietnam War fiction, film, memoir, and even literary criticism. PTSD became almost synonymous with the Vietnam War experience.

However, as previously noted, only 15.2 percent of Vietnam-theater veterans were estimated to suffer from PTSD; as stated above, this is an estimate based on a survey sample, not a tabulation of reported cases. Furthermore, a disturbing number of reported cases were found to be based on erroneous reporting of the supposed traumatic event or reported symptoms. And in the development of diagnostic instruments and treatment methods, it was found that assumptions originally made about Vietnam veterans have had to be modified, not only for other types of trauma such as rape, natural disaster, and childhood abuse, but also for treatment of women—even women veterans.

It is possible that the developmental history of PTSD definitions and treatment has led to these discrepancies. The diagnostic and treatment research, as noted, was originally done with a nonrepresentative sample of veterans and a presupposed outcome; further, statistical data on recovery rates and numbers of cases were not collected until the definitions had been established, five years after the end of the war. Meanwhile, cases that might have been reported have been diagnosed under other categories of disorder and treated accordingly.

PTSD is a serious condition affecting a statistically small but numerically important segment of the veteran population. Work now in progress through the National Center for PTSD, as well as other organizations and private research efforts, will no doubt clarify and update original work done in the field so as to be of use not only to veterans but also to other sufferers from stress reactions in the future.

—Phoebe S. Spinrad

References: American Psychiatric Association. *Diagnostic and Statistical Manual of Mental Disorders*. 4th ed. Washington, DC: American Psychiatric Association, 1994.

Brende, Joel Osler, and Erwin Randolph Parson. *Vietnam Veterans: The Road to Recovery*. New York: Plenum Press, 1985.

Camp, Norman M., Robert H. Stretch, and William C. Marshall. *Stress, Strain, and Vietnam: An Annotated Bibliography of Psychiatric and Social Sciences Literature*. New York: Greenwood Press, 1988.

Figley, Charles R., and Seymour Leventman, eds. *Strangers at Home: Vietnam Veterans since the War*. New York: Praeger, 1980.

Hendin, Herbert, and Ann Pollinger Haas. *Wounds of War: The Psychological Aftermath of Combat in Vietnam*. New York: Basic Books, 1984.

Herman, Judith Lewis, M.D. *Trauma and Recovery*. New York: Basic Books, 1992.

Kulka, Richard A., et al., eds. *National Vietnam Veterans Readjustment Study: Tables of Findings and Technical Appendices*. New York: Brunner/ Mazel, 1990.

_____. *Trauma and the Vietnam War Generation: Report of Findings of the National Vietnam Veterans Readjustment Study*. New York: Brunner/ Mazel, 1990.

Lifton, Robert Jay. *Home from the War: Vietnam Veterans, Neither Victims nor Executioners*. New York: Simon & Schuster, 1973.

Scott, Wilbur J. *The Politics of Readjustment: Vietnam Veterans since the War*. New York: Aldine de Gruyter, 1993.

Solomon, Zahava. *Combat Stress Reaction: The Enduring Toll of War*. New York: Plenum Press, 1993.

Sonnenberg, Stephen M., Arthur S. Blank, Jr., and John A. Talbott, eds. *The Trauma of War: Stress and Recovery in Vietnam Veterans*. Washington, DC: American Psychiatric Press, 1985.

See also: Fiction, U.S., and the Vietnam Experience; Film and the Vietnam Experience; Lifton, Robert Jay; Vietnam Veterans Against the War (VVAW).

Potsdam Conference

(16 July–1 August 1945)

The final meeting of Allied leaders in World War II. The "Big Three"—Winston Churchill, Joseph Stalin, and Harry S Truman—met at the Potsdam Conference between 16 July and 1 August 1945. Gathering in the Cecilienhof Palace in a suburb of Berlin, the Allied leaders were poised to address many of the same issues confronted previously at Teheran in 1943 and at Yalta in February 1945. Questions over Germany; conflicts over Eastern Europe, especially Poland; and disputes over other territorial claims all remained to be resolved. As the war neared its end, suspicions came to the fore.

Several aspects of the conference affected French Indo-China. First, the United States denied the French representation at Potsdam, despite Charles de Gaulle's petitions. Second, a minor item of the agenda involved procedures for the Japanese surrender in Vietnam. The British were to receive the surrender south of the 16th parallel, while the Chinese Nationalists would take the Japanese surrender in the North. This scheme proved to be a disaster, primarily through miscasting.

In the South British commander General Douglas Gracey, a highly paternalistic colonial officer, violated Lord Mountbatten's orders to avoid Vietnam's internal problems by affirming that "civil and military control by the French is only a question of weeks." In the North, while Chinese forces plundered and pillaged, Hô Chí Minh was nonetheless able to proclaim the independence of the Democratic Republic of Vietnam (DRV).

—Brenda J. Taylor

Reference: Gormly, James L. *From Potsdam to the Cold War*. Wilmington, DE: Scholarly Resources, 1990.

See also: French Indo-China; Gracey, Douglas D.; Jiang Jieshi (Chiang Kai-shek); Truman, Harry S; Vietnam, Democratic Republic of: 1945–1954.

Poulo Condore (Côn Sơn)

One of 14 islands in the Côn Sơn Island group located in the South China Sea approximately 75 miles southeast of Vietnam's Cà Mâu Peninsula and 156 miles south of Vũng Tàu. The island is integral to the history of Vietnam's relations with the West. In the early eighteenth century, first the British and then the French explored the possibility of using it as the headquarters for their trade in East Asia. In 1787 its cession to France was part of the price the French hoped to extract from Nguyên Phúc Ánh (later Nguyên Emperor Gia Long) for the assistance they proposed to offer him in defeating the Tây Sơn Rebellion. It was eventually ceded to France by Nguyên Emperor Tư Đức in 1862 as part of the spoils of a war that marked the beginning of the French conquest of Vietnam.

The French soon converted the island into a prison where they incarcerated Vietnamese who opposed French colonial administration. A principal feature of the prison complex was its "tiger cages." These were cells approximately five feet square and nine feet high, roofed with metal bars that served as overhead walkways for guards. Three or more prisoners were forced to spend their days and nights shackled to the cell floor, fed on little more, and often less, than unsalted rice and water. Thus immobilized, prisoners often experienced permanent paralysis or disfigurement, while malnutrition frequently led to tuberculosis and death. This means of confinement often served to harden the spirit of defiance among the prisoners who survived it, among whom were some of the leading lights of the Vietnamese revolution: Phan Chu Trinh, Lê Duân, Lê Đưc Tho, and Pham Văn Đông.

After the expulsion of the French, the Republic of Vietnam (RVN) employed the renamed Côn Sơn Correctional Facility to house Communists who were not members of the Viêt Công Armed Forces, and thus not protected by the Geneva Convention. Also sent there were non-Communist opponents of the RVN government. Except for some prisoners of war (POWs) guilty of murder in POW camps, no PAVN POWs were held at Côn Sơn. Conditions of incarceration on the island were harsh, and the Red Cross ultimately documented ill treatment there and judged it to be in violation of the Geneva Convention.

Vietnamese and U.S. leaders, however, continually denied the existence of any "relics" of French penal administration and maintained that nothing was being done on Côn Sơn Island that deprived prisoners of "physical necessities and human dignity." A U.S. advisor went so far as to insist that the facility, which had grown into the largest prison in the Free World, was as salubrious as "a Boy Scout recreational camp." These officials thereby constructed a public relations time bomb that exploded with devastating effect in the wake of the joint Vietnamese and American incursion into Cambodia in the spring of 1970.

Then eager to demonstrate that the Republic of Vietnam was worthy of such continued U.S. support and sacrifice, President Richard M. Nixon encouraged the dispatch of a ten-member congressional investigatory team that he hoped would return with a glowing report of progress toward political stability and democracy. This delegation sought to measure that progress by visiting Vietnamese prisons and by speaking with the students who were at the forefront of opposition to the administration of President Nguyên Văn Thiêu. Upon hearing from Câu Loi Nguyên, a student recently released from detention on Côn Sơn, that many student leaders were in the island's tiger cages, congressional aide (later California Senator) Tom Harkin, Don Luce of the World Council of Churches, and Congressmen Augustus Hawkins and William Anderson visited the island and returned with evidence of political repression so embarrassing to the credibility of the Vietnamese and U.S. governments that it ultimately helped convince Congress to begin to curtail further assistance to the Republic of Vietnam.

Thus, Côn Sơn Island, which figured in the introduction of direct Western political influence in Vietnam, also played a role in its eclipse. The site of the prison complex has been preserved as a monument to the Vietnamese independence movement. A full-scale replica of a tiger cage is on display at the War Crimes Museum in Hô Chí Minh City.

—Marc Jason Gilbert

References: Buttinger, Joseph. *The Smaller Dragon: A Political History of Vietnam.* New York: Praeger, 1958.

Brown, Holmes, and Don Luce. *Hostages of War: Saigon's Political Prisoners.* Washington, DC: Indochina Mobile Education Project, 1973.

Ciabatari, Jane. "Senator Harkin Returns to the Tiger Cages of Con Son." *Parade* (8 October 1995): 19.

Leslie, Jacques. *The Mark: A War Correspondent's Memoir of Vietnam and Cambodia.* New York: Four Walls Eight Windows, 1995.
See also: Hayden, Thomas E.; Lê Duân; Lê Đưc Tho; Missing in Action and Prisoners of War; Viêt Công and People's Army of Vietnam; Nguyên Phúc Ánh (Gia Long); Pham Văn Đông; Phan Chu Trinh.

Powell, Colin L.

(1937–)

U.S. Army general and first African American to serve as chairman of the Joint Chiefs of Staff. Born on 5 April 1937 to an immigrant Jamaican family in the Harlem section of New York City, Colin Powell in 1958 graduated from City College of New York with a degree in Geology and received a Reserve Officers' Training Corps (ROTC) commission as an infantry second lieutenant.

Powell was profoundly influenced in his military thinking by his experiences in Vietnam. His first tour of duty in Vietnam came in 1962 and 1963, when he was assigned as an advisor to an Army of the Republic of Vietnam (ARVN) infantry battalion near the Laotian border. During that tour he was wounded when he stepped into a punji pit in a rice paddy, impaling his foot on one of the sharpened stakes. In 1968 Powell returned to Vietnam. During this second tour he again was injured, this time in a helicopter crash; later he was decorated for helping to rescue other troops from the burning wreck.

During Powell's second tour he served as an assistant operations officer in the 23d ("Americal") Division, widely known as the "hard luck division" of the war. In that position Powell became involved with the My Lai Massacre investigation. Although the massacre occurred several months before Powell returned to Vietnam, he was assigned the responsibility of drafting the 23d Division's first official response to rumors circulating through military units in the country. Powell reported that the rumors were unfounded. Later, investigators came to consider Powell's report as part of the cover-up, but he staunchly maintained he knew nothing about the massacre until much later, when word of it became public in November 1969.

In 1973 Powell was selected as a White House Fellow. From there he went on to a string of high-profile jobs, including senior military assistant to Secretary of Defense Caspar Weinberger, commanding general of V Corps in Germany, assistant to National Security Advisor Frank Carlucci, and national security advisor to President Ronald Reagan. In October 1989 Powell became chairman of the Joint Chiefs of Staff.

In this position Powell was responsible for overseeing the Persian Gulf War and the beginnings of the post–Cold War military drawdown. He also was responsible for crafting America's military strategy. As with many of the officers of his generation, he had seen firsthand the failure of the gradual "squeezed" application of military power and of using military forces to attempt to send political signals. As a result, Powell championed the concept of decisive military force.

What has become known as the "Powell Doctrine" was clearly stated in the January 1992 edition of the *National Military Strategy of the United States,* issued under his signature. Reflecting almost exactly what was not done in Vietnam, it states:

Once a decision for military action has been made, half-measures and confused objectives extract a severe price in the form of a protracted conflict which can cause needless waste of human lives and material resources, a divided nation at home, and defeat. Therefore, one of the essential elements of our national military strategy is . . . the concept of applying decisive force to overwhelm our adversaries and thereby terminate conflicts swiftly with a minimum loss of life.

Powell retired from the Army in September 1993. During his tenure as chairman of the Joint Chiefs, he was awarded the Presidential Medal of Freedom by President Bush and again by President Clinton. In 1995 Colin Powell considered but declined a run for the presidency on the Republican ticket.

—David T. Zabecki

References: Adler, Bill. *The Generals: The New American Heroes.* New York: Avon Books, 1991.

Barry, John. "The Very Model of a Political General: On Duty with Powell, from Vietnam to the Gulf." *Newsweek* (11 September 1995): 25–26.

Powell, Colin. *My American Journey: An Autobiography.* New York: Random House, 1995.

Roth, David. *Sacred Honor: A Biography of Colin Powell.* San Francisco: Harper, 1993.

See also: My Lai Massacre; Schwarzkopf, H. Norman, Jr.

PRACTICE NINE, Project

See McNamara Line.

PRAIRIE, Operation

(August 1966–January 1967)

Code name for the combat operations of the U.S. 3d Marine Division in the Côn Thiên and Gio Linh regions of I Corps in 1966 and early 1967. The Marine assignment was to stop the People's Army of Vietnam (PAVN) 324B Division from crossing the Demilitarized Zone (DMZ) and invading Quang Tri Province. Operation PRAIRIE, following Operation HASTINGS, was launched on 3 August 1966 and continued until 31 January 1967. A second stage of Operation PRAIRIE commenced on 1 February 1967 and concluded on 18 March 1967. During the conduct of both stages of the operation, the 3d Marine Division claimed more than 2,000 PAVN soldiers killed. In driving the North Vietnamese back across the Bên Hai River, the Marines also succeeded in preventing the PAVN from establishing a major operating base in northern Quang Tri Province. However, the Marines sustained casualties of 200 dead and well over 1,000 wounded, and PAVN units were able to regroup and later in 1967 recrossed back into South Vietnam.

—James H. Willbanks

References: Pearson, Willard. *The War in the Northern Provinces, 1966–1968.* Washington, DC: Department of the Army, 1975.

Shulimson, Jack. *U.S. Marines in Vietnam: An Expanding War 1966.* Washington, DC: History and Museums Division, Headquarters, U.S. Marine Corps, 1982.

Stanton, Shelby L. *Vietnam Order of Battle.* New York: Galahad Books, 1986.

Telfer, Gary L., Lane Rogers, and Keith Fleming. *U.S. Marines in Vietnam: Fighting the North Vietnamese, 1967.* Washington, DC: History and Museums Division, Headquarters, U.S. Marine Corps, 1984.

See also: HASTINGS, Operation; United States: Marine Corps; Vietnam, Democratic Republic of: Army (People's Army of Vietnam [PAVN]).

Prisoners of War, Allied

(1964–1973)

In accordance with the Paris peace accords, a total of 565 American military and 26 civilian prisoners of war (POWs) were released by the Democratic Republic of Vietnam (DRV) in February and March 1973, and two military persons and two civilians held in the People's Republic of China were released at the same time. The civilians included contract pilots; Central Intelligence Agency (CIA), State Department, and Voice of America personnel; and agricultural specialists, missionaries, and other nonmilitary personnel. Six foreign nationals—two Canadians, two South Koreans, and two Filipinos—also departed. At various points during the war, Hà Nôi had turned over a total of 12 POWs to visiting "peace delegations," and early in the war the Viêt Công released a few prisoners. A small number of Americans escaped from the Viêt Công or from Communist forces in Laos. Although many pilots shot down over hostile territory evaded capture until being rescued, no one actually brought into the prison system successfully escaped from North Vietnam. A few civilians and the accused defector Bobby Garwood came home after the 1973 release.

Estimates of POWs who died in captivity vary. The North Vietnamese listed 55 deaths. One American source cited 54 military and at least 13 American and foreign civilians; another source gives the number as 72 Americans. For prisoners so injured and mistreated, the casualty rate was amazingly low in the North Vietnamese camps. The returned POWs cited 8 known deaths of military personnel in the Hà Nôi system—2 considered outright murder, 3 from a combination of brutality and neglect, and 3 from appallingly substandard medical care. The large number of deaths of military personnel and civilians occurred in the jungle camps in the South.

Justifiably proud of their communication network, command structure, and memory bank, which attempted to register every individual in the system, the POWs recorded at least 766 verified captives at one point or another. But accountability for those outside the North Vietnamese prison system was less certain. Of the hundreds who disappeared in Laos, only ten came home in 1973, and no one knows the fate of the many captives of local Viêt Công units. At the time of release, more than 2,500 men were still listed as missing in action (MIA). Many of those most likely died when shot down, but their deaths were not confirmed. Others known to be alive on the ground and even in the prison system mysteriously disappeared.

All but 71 of the military personnel who returned in early 1973 were officers, primarily Air Force or Navy aviators shot down during combat missions. With the exception of a handful of Air Force personnel, the enlisted men consisted of Army and Marine personnel captured in the South. The fliers had received survival and captivity training; for the most part those captured in the South had not. The first pilot captured by the North Vietnamese was Navy Lt. (jg) Everett Alvarez, shot down on 5 August 1964 in the first bombing raid on the DRV following the Gulf of Tonkin incidents. But the longest-held POW was Army Special Forces Capt. Floyd James Thompson, whose light reconnaissance plane was shot down by small-arms fire on 26 March 1964. He spent five years in solitary confinement, three with the Việt Công in the South and two more after being moved to North Vietnam. Thompson suffered a broken back in the crash, numerous illnesses, and a heart attack during his almost nine years of captivity, becoming the longest-held American POW in history.

Most of the POWs were aviators shot down during the ROLLING THUNDER bombing campaign of North Vietnam, February 1965 through November 1968; 1967 produced the most captives. The Têt Offensive in the first half of 1968 generated the most captives on the ground; almost half the Army and Marine POWs came in that year. Eighteen of the 26 civilian POWs released in 1973 were captured during a one-week period, the first week of February 1968. With the end of ROLLING THUNDER, the number of captives dropped off dramatically from late 1968 through early 1972, virtually all of them taken in the South or in Laos. The LINEBACKER bombings lead to an upsurge of captives in the spring of 1972, and during LINEBACKER II 44 aviators were shot down in December 1972 alone. Only one pilot was added in 1973, captured on January 27, the day that the Paris peace accords were signed. The 131 POWs captured in 1972 and 1973 experienced a short and very different captivity from those held in the earlier years.

Among the military POWs, one commentator surveying the 356 aviators held in 1970 recorded that the average flier was approximately 32 years old, an Air Force captain or Navy lieutenant, and married with two children. They were for the most part career-minded officers, skilled pilots of high-performance aircraft, highly disciplined, intensely competitive, and college graduates with a minimum of 135 IQ, and the senior officers were even more of an elite group.

American POWs were held in 11 different prisons in North Vietnam, 4 in Hà Nội, 6 others within 50 miles of the city (more or less up and down the Red River), and 1 on the Chinese border. The most famous of these was North Vietnam's main penitentiary, Hoa Lò Prison in downtown Hà Nội, which the POWs dubbed the "Hanoi Hilton." They gave the other prisons names as well—Briarpatch, Faith, Hope (Sơn Tây), Skidrow, D-1, Rockpile, Plantation, the Zoo, Alcatraz, and Dogpatch.

From the first captive on, a test of wills existed between the Hà Nội Camp Authority and the American military personnel over the Code of Conduct, which had been promulgated in 1955 in response to the allegedly disgraceful performance of American POWs during the Korean conflict. The Vietnam POWs were determined to maintain a record of honor that would reflect well upon themselves personally, the U.S. military, and the nation. The Camp

Authority employed every means at its disposal, including isolation, torture, and psychological abuse, to break POW discipline. Senior commanders such as Air Force Lt. Col. Robinson Risner, Navy Comdr. James Stockdale, Navy Lt. Comdr. Jeremiah Denton, and many others emerged as the leaders in the POW resistance campaign. And tough younger resisters such as Bud Day, George Coker, John Dramesi, George McKnight, and Lance Sijan, to name but a few, played significant roles in the effort. Stockdale, Day, and Sijan (posthumously) received the Medal of Honor for their performance as POWs.

The POW experience broke down roughly into several periods. From 1965 through 1969 prisoners were isolated, kept in stocks, bounced from one camp to another, malnourished, and brutally tortured to break their morale, discipline, and commitment to the Code of Conduct. After the death of Hồ Chí Minh in September 1969, the torture ended and conditions improved in the camps. Following the Sơn Tây Raid in November 1970, the North Vietnamese closed the outlying camps and consolidated all the POWs in Hà Nội. Compound living began in what the prisoners called Camp Unity. In February 1971 Air Force Col. John Flynn, the highest-ranking POW, who had spent most of his captivity isolated from the others, assumed command and organized the military community into the 4th Allied POW Wing. A few Thais and South Vietnamese POWs, who had distinguished themselves in working with the Americans, were included in the Wing. From this point on, the greatest attention was given to how the POWs would return home. Amnesty was tendered to those who had cooperated with the enemy if they would now adhere to the Code of Conduct. All but a few accepted the offer. During the final two years, the collective POW story was collected, shaped, and honed.

With the end of the war, the POWs returned home in Operation HOMECOMING to great fanfare as the only heroes of a frustrating war. Much to the dismay of senior POW officers, the Defense Department decided that POWs who had collaborated would not be prosecuted. Only Robert Garwood, when he returned to the United States in 1979, faced court-martial. Although many divorces resulted from their captivity, the Vietnam POWs adjusted relatively well. Ten years later, only about 30 had been treated for psychological or mental problems, although 2 had committed suicide and 3 died of other causes. Almost half were still in the military.

The POW story is recorded in the more than 50 individual and collective participant narratives.

—Joe P. Dunn

References: Doyle, Robert C. *Voices from Captivity: Interpreting the American POW Narrative.* Lawrence, KS: University Press of Kansas, 1994.
Dunn, Joe P. "The Vietnam War and the POWs/MIAs." In *Teaching the Vietnam War: Resources and Assessments.* Los Angeles: Center for the Study of Armament and Disarmament, California State University–LA, 1990.
Howes, Craig. *Voices of the Vietnam POWs: Witnesses to Their Fight.* New York: Oxford University Press, 1993.
Hubbell, John G., et al. *P.O.W.: A Definitive History of the American Prisoner of War Experience in Vietnam, 1964–1973.* New York: Reader's Digest Press, 1976.
Rowan, Stephan A. *They Wouldn't Let Us Die: The Prisoners of War Tell Their Story.* Middle Village, NY: Jonathan David Publishers, 1973.

See also: Alvarez, Everett, Jr.; Denton, Jeremiah A. Jr.; Garwood, Robert "Bobby" Russell; Hà Nội Hilton (Hoa Lò Prison); HOMECOMING, Operation; LINEBACKER I, Operation; LINEBACKER II, Operation; McCain, John S., III; ROLLING THUNDER, Operation; Stockdale, James B.

Prisoners of War, Việt Công and People's Army of Vietnam

See Missing in Action and Prisoners of War, Việt Công and People's Army of Vietnam.

Project 100,000

Great Society program designed to extend the social and economic benefits of military service to disadvantaged or underqualified Americans. Johnson administration officials, in an effort to attack poverty and its detrimental effect on the American family, hoped that by easing military admission standards underprivileged young men could gain valuable skills, discipline, and useful benefits that would enhance employment opportunities and help stabilize families.

In 1964 the Presidential Task Force on Manpower Conservation headed by Assistant Secretary of Labor Daniel Patrick Moynihan of New York issued a report titled "One Third of a Nation: A Report on Young Men Found Unqualified for Military Service," which indicated that approximately 600,000 men failed the Armed Forces Qualification Test (AFQT) each year. In response to this finding the Johnson administration directed the Selective Service System to channel disqualified men into government-backed training and referral programs. This effort failed, as fewer than 4 percent of the 134,000 participants referred, only 2,200 secured jobs, and of these only 189 received any viable training.

In March 1965 a second Moynihan report, "The Negro Family: The Case for National Action," found that a major factor in the deterioration of the African American family was the absence or weakness of father figures stemming from a legacy of subjugation and present-day discrimination. The report sparked a particularly intense debate between the White House, leaders of the civil rights movement, and social scientists. President Lyndon Johnson's June 1965 speech at Howard University reflected a shift in the federal approach to civil rights from action on segregation and legal protection to an attack on social and economic ills, such as housing, employment, and education.

Blacks represented 11 percent of the population but only 8.5 percent of the military in 1964. The government rationale was that blacks should be proportionately represented in the U.S. military. Furthermore, military experience would benefit the black family insofar as it could inculcate responsible behavior among young black males. In short, military experience would produce stronger father figures who would return as veterans, use their benefits, and be more productive in their respective communities. Special attention would now be turned to blacks and other underprivileged Americans who failed the initial military entrance test and would normally not be eligible to join the Armed Forces.

Announced in August 1966, Project 100,000 sought to, as Defense Secretary Robert McNamara termed it, "rehabilitate" the nation's "subterranean poor" by extending the benefits of military service to those previously excluded due to mental or physical inaptitude. The goal was to bring 100,000 of these previously ineligible men into the Army and Marines each year by relaxing entrance requirements.

Between 1966 and 1972 (when the program was terminated) the U.S. military accepted some 350,000 Project 100,000 men. The majority of these reflected the administration's focus: A high percentage came from broken homes or low-income families; most were high school dropouts; many had low IQs or read at a grade-school level; 41 percent were black; and the majority, black and white, were from the South.

Despite its altruistic facade, Project 100,000 had practical as well as political implications for the U.S. effort in Vietnam by adding badly needed bodies to America's manpower pool. More than half of the Project 100,000 men went to Vietnam and most of these received combat-related assignments (one report indicates that Project 100,000 men died at almost twice the rate of nonproject combat troops, although this is disputed). Many black leaders, such as Dr. Martin Luther King, saw this as evidence of institutional racism, citing disproportionately high casualties among black soldiers. Also, the expanded manpower pool helped Johnson to avoid calling up the Reserves—something he repeatedly refused to consider—as the demand for more troops intensified. Critics of the program cited increased disciplinary problems and poor military performance among the Project 100,000 and other relaxed-standards inductees; they were, for example, more likely to be absent without leave (AWOL), and because they received no special training many failed to meet the demands of the job. These soldiers were also more likely to receive courts-martial or less-than-honorable discharges. But many special-standards inductees performed well, and some combat commanders preferred them to more educated troops in the field.

As a social engineering program, Project 100,000 largely failed. Few of the men received training or developed skills that would benefit them in civilian life as the project's advocates had envisioned. Many, especially those with less-than-honorable discharges, came away from the experience worse off than before.

With decreased force demands after 1969, Project 100,000 quotas dropped accordingly. The project was terminated in 1972 with the advent of an all-volunteer military. Although the military maintained some special-standards recruitment for several years, the number inducted represented only a tiny percentage of the total force.

—Paul R. Camacho and David Coffey

References: Baskir, Lawrence M., and William A. Strauss. *Chance and Circumstance: The Draft, the War, and the Vietnam Generation.* New York: Alfred A. Knopf, 1978.
Dougan, Clark, Samuel Lipsman, et al. *A Nation Divided. The Vietnam Experience,* edited by Robert Manning. Boston: Boston Publishing, 1984.
Hsiao, Lisa. "Project 100,000: The Great Society's Answer to Military Manpower Needs in Vietnam." *Vietnam Generation—A White Man's War: Race Issues and Vietnam* 1, no. 2 (Spring 1989): 14–37.
Moynihan, Daniel P. *Maximum Feasible Misunderstanding: Community Action in the War on Poverty.* New York: Free Press, 1970.

Rainwater, Lee, and W. L. Yancey. *The Moynihan Report and the Politics of Controversy.* Cambridge, MA: MIT Press, 1967.

Starr, Paul. *The Discarded Army: Veterans after Vietnam.* New York: Charterhouse, 1973.

See also: African American Personnel in U.S. Forces in Vietnam; Conscientious Objectors (COs); Draft; Johnson, Lyndon Baines; King, Martin Luther, Jr.; McNamara, Robert S.

Prose Narrative and the Vietnam Experience

Nonfiction prose narrative dealing with the American involvement in Vietnam takes a number of different forms: biography, memoir, combat narrative, oral history collections, and journalistic reporting. Sometimes the categories blur, not only among themselves but between fiction and nonfiction, memoir and formal history. Of the thousands of titles that have been published, this overview concentrates on the most often referenced books within the various subgenres.

The most prevalent type of prose narrative is, of course, the combat narrative, usually written by a former combatant and often indistinguishable from memoir. Most of these narratives take the following pattern: A new recruit arrives in-country, usually with high ideals of what the war was about and what service entails. He is immediately faced with the severe physical hardships and danger of combat conditions, and may either become disillusioned or grow to admire the fortitude of the other troops. In any case, the pattern is essentially the traditional one of a "coming of age." The focus is normally on the narrator's own development, and other individuals presented in the narrative tend to be "types." However, even where serious attempts are made to create accurate portraits of people with whom the narrator has served, we generally do not see any development in them; they remain background for the narrator's own development and very often sounding boards for his opinions. Vietnamese—both South and North—are also normally portrayed as background figures.

As might be expected, the chief events in these combat narratives are military engagements: usually two or more minor engagements and finally one major battle in which the narrator's views are solidified. But in some narratives, the culminating event is not a battle but rather an "atrocity" event: a rape, the killing of a civilian, the desecration of an enemy's body, and so on. This is particularly true of Philip Caputo's *A Rumor of War* (1977), perhaps one of the most famous books of its kind.

Caputo, a Marine who was in fact charged with ordering the killing of two Vietnamese civilians (the charges were subsequently dropped), shapes his narrative around the attitudes and events leading up to the event in question, in an attempt to explain how such things happen—and, of course, implying that they happened with great frequency. The narrator of such books emerges from the experience with an understanding of the destructive influence of war, and especially of the Vietnam conflict, on combatant and noncombatant alike.

Interestingly enough, even the nondisillusioned narratives of this type may include an "atrocity" event. In David Christian's *Victor Six* (1991), for example, actually a celebration of a particular unit's prowess in combat, members of the unit at one point dese-crate the body of a dead enemy just for the experience of doing so. This event is held up as an evil omen for the unit, and surely enough, shortly afterward the unit meets its first defeat, and most of its members are killed or wounded. The heroes have ceased to be heroic, and so must be defeated; they have betrayed the cause and must be punished.

In Craig Roberts and Charles W. Sass's *The Walking Dead* (1989), also a fairly positive memoir of the war, there is another variation on this theme: One member of a unit who has killed a suspected Viêt Công collaborator in anger later talks another man out of doing the same thing, telling him that the momentary anger is not trustworthy, and the deed will haunt him afterward.

Other motifs in these narratives are the loss of a best friend in combat and the first encounter with the gruesome carnage of war. In the "disillusioned" narrative, such scenes often become almost inverted conversion experiences, causing a loss rather than a gaining of faith. *A Rumor of War* contains a typical scene of this sort, as does Lynda Van Devanter's *Home before Morning* (1983), one of the few such narratives by a woman. Van Devanter's repeated question "Why, why, why?" about the maimed and dying soldiers she has seen as a combat nurse remains unanswered, implying that the war itself has no purpose.

Among other "disillusioned" memoirs and combat narratives are W. D. Ehrhart's *Vietnam-Perkasie* (1983), Tim O'Brien's *If I Die in a Combat Zone* (1973), and Ron Kovic's *Born on the Fourth of July* (1976). Later made into a film, Kovic's book follows a paralyzed veteran home and through the peace movement, and has sometimes been said to overlap into the fiction category. Combat narratives focusing on the positive development of the individual and the unit mission, and assuming a more positive view of military service and often of the war itself, include Michael Lee Lanning's *The Only War We Had: A Platoon Leader's Journal of Vietnam* (1987) and its sequel, *Vietnam, 1969–1970: A Company Commander's Journal* (1988); Larry Chambers's *Recondo: LRRPs in the 101st Airborne* (1992); Lynn Hampton's *The Fighting Strength: Memoirs of a Combat Nurse in Vietnam* (1990), an interesting counterview to Van Devanter's more jaundiced one; Eric Bergerud's *Red Thunder, Tropic Lightning* (1993); and Otto J. Lehrack's *No Shining Armor: The Marines at War in Vietnam* (1992).

Oral histories are particularly pervasive forms of narrative emerging from the Vietnam conflict, perhaps more so than in any other American overseas engagement. The most widely read of these are Mark Baker's *Nam* (1981), which is unfortunately marred by its failure to document the speakers' identities and units of service, so that the accuracy of the accounts cannot be verified, and Al Santoli's *Everything We Had* (1981), which is more extensively documented but includes at least one questionable narrative. Women's experiences have been assembled in such collections as Catherine Marshall's *In the Combat Zone* (1987) and Keith Walker's *A Piece of My Heart* (1985), and the African American experience has been documented in Wallace Terry's *Bloods* (1982). Al Santoli's *To Bear Any Burden* (1985) adds more oral histories to his earlier collection, and in addition presents numerous accounts of Southeast Asian experiences both during and after the war. The fall of Sài Gòn and the flight of the refugees from South Vietnam is further presented in the oral histories collected by Larry Engelmann in *Tears before the Rain: An Oral History of the Fall of South Vietnam* (1990). And Bob Greene's *Homecoming* (1989) addresses the experiences of troops returning from the war, in a collection that is not specifically "oral" history but rather letters written by veterans in response to questions he posed in one of his newspaper columns.

One narrative that is difficult to categorize is Michael Herr's *Dispatches* (1977), an account of his experience as a journalist in the field and in his bureau's Sài Gòn headquarters. Originally written as a series of travel pieces for *Esquire* and revised for the purposes of book publication, this narrative perhaps inadvertently describes the journalists' milieu as strongly as it does that of the soldier in the field. Some of the episodes have been questioned as to their accuracy, particularly where the book versions differ from the magazine versions, but on the whole, Herr presents a view of the American involvement that has become pervasive in all the literature: Vietnam as metaphor as much as event, the shaping influence of post-1965 American society, and at the same time a reflection of what it shaped. His closing statement is one of the most often quoted in all of Vietnam literature: "Vietnam, Vietnam, Vietnam, we've all been there."

—Phoebe S. Spinrad

References: Beidler, Philip. *American Literature and the Experience of Vietnam.* Athens, GA: University of Georgia Press, 1982.

Butler, Deborah A. *American Women Writers on Vietnam: Unheard Voices, a Selected Annotated Bibliography.* New York: Garland, 1990.

Jason, Philip K., ed. *Fourteen Landing Zones: Approaches to Vietnam War Literature.* Iowa City, IA: University of Iowa Press, 1991.

Lewis, Lloyd B. *The Tainted War: Culture and Identity in Vietnam War Narratives.* Westport, CT: Greenwood Press, 1985.

Pratt, John Clark. *Vietnam Voices.* New York: Viking Press, 1984.

Searle, William, ed. *Search and Clear: Critical Responses to Selected Literature and Films of the Vietnam War.* Bowling Green, OH: Popular Press 1988.

Wilson, James C. *Vietnam in Prose and Film.* Jefferson, NC: McFarland, 1982.

Wittman, Sandra M. *Writing about Vietnam: A Bibliography of the Vietnam Conflict.* Boston: G. H. Hall, 1989.

See also: Art and the Vietnam War; Drama and the Vietnam Experience; Fiction, U.S., and the Vietnam Experience; Film and the Vietnam Experience; Media and the War; Poetry and the Vietnam Experience.

Protective Reaction Strikes

Designation for 1970 air strikes conducted to suppress North Vietnamese air defenses that targeted U.S. reconnaissance flights. Although all American "offensive" bombing operations against North Vietnam were informally suspended by 31 October 1968, there was an "understanding" between the United States and the Democratic Republic of Vietnam (DRV) that U.S. reconnaissance flights would continue. When these were fired on, Washington authorized U.S. Seventh Air Force commander General John D. Lavelle to retaliate against DRV air defense installations south of the 19th parallel.

The rules of engagement stipulated that, as soon as DRV radar guidance systems locked on American aircraft, escorts would at-

tack the sites. In April 1970 Protective Reaction Strikes expanded to target surface-to-air missile (SAM) and antiaircraft installations protecting the Hồ Chí Minh Trail south of the 20th parallel as well as Communist infiltration across the Demilitarized Zone (DMZ). Over 1,100 Protective Reaction Strike sorties were flown in 1970.

In the fall of 1972 General Lavelle was called before the House and Senate Armed Forces Committee to answer charges that, between November 1971 and March 1972, he had launched 28 Protective Reaction Strike missions involving 147 sorties in violation of existing guidelines. Although Lavelle defended his actions by intimating that he had been "encouraged" by higher authorities to do so, he was relieved of his command, reduced in rank, and retired.

—Edward C. Page

References: Lewy, Guenter. *America in Vietnam.* New York: Oxford University Press, 1978.

Morrocco, John. *Rain of Fire: Air War, 1969–1973. The Vietnam Experience,* edited by Robert Manning. Boston: Boston Publishing, 1984.

See also: Air Defense, Democratic Republic of Vietnam; Lavelle, John D.

Provincial Reconnaissance Units (PRUs) (Đơn Vi Thám Sát Tinh)

In April 1969 the government of the Republic of Vietnam (RVN) created a special paramilitary force as an addition to its National Police forces. Provincial Reconnaissance Units (PRUs) were detached in platoon-sized units and assigned to provincial headquarters to carry out "special missions." They were part of the Phượng Hoàng or Phoenix program, specifically targeted against the Việt Công (VC) infrastructure in the South. The "special missions" translated to killing or capturing VC political cadre, tax collectors, intelligence agents, administrators, and propagandists. Additionally they were to destabilize VC influence among the peasant population and encourage support for the RVN government.

The PRUs were under the authority of the RVN National Police but in reality were directed, armed, and trained by the U.S. Central Intelligence Agency (CIA). Since they were part of the police forces, they were not subject to the control and discipline of the RVN armed forces. However, the U.S. Military Assistance Command, Vietnam (MACV) provided approximately 100 U.S. advisors to these units, and the PRUs were commanded by Army of the Republic of Vietnam (ARVN) officers. General Creighton Abrams recognized the political nature of this unit and reluctantly bowed to CIA pressure to commit military resources to the program. Abrams's chief frustration was that MACV had no operational control over the PRUs.

PRU members were physically hard men; in many cases they were criminals or were VC or People's Army of Vietnam (PAVN) defectors who had personal grudges to settle because of real or imagined offenses committed against them by the Communists. Some of them at times tortured captives and behaved in such a manner as to further alienate the peasant population against the central government. Since they knew what their fate would be if captured, PRU personnel were not terribly concerned with the treatment of those that fell into their hands. Critics of U.S. involvement often accused the U.S. advisory personnel of participating in PRU actions or of training PRUs in torture techniques; however, in reality U.S. advisors had little control over the PRUs. Any policy conflicts that arose between U.S. military officers and PRUs were often resolved at the highest levels of the RVN government. National Police routinely practiced torture and cruel interrogation techniques on their own people as part of routine criminal arrest procedures and, as an organ of state, were very influential in the internal politics of the RVN. Further hampering MACV's attempts to either control the PRUs or protest their actions, the CIA often sided with the National Police and the Sài Gòn government, praising the results the PRUs were achieving. As part of the Phoenix program they freely operated against the VC infrastructure as well as political enemies of the government of the RVN.

Since they engaged in clandestine operations they were armed with a variety of weapons. Most of their small arms were a mixture of obsolete American types: M1 carbines, submachine guns, and Browning Automatic Rifles (BARs). They received some M16 rifles as government forces began to be reequipped by the United States. The CIA is reported to have liberally supplied the PRUs with Russian and Chinese weapons, primarily the AK47 rifle and SKS carbine. For assassination missions they utilized silenced weapons such as the British 9-mm Sten submachine gun and Smith & Wesson Model 39 .22-caliber and 9-mm pistols, also known as "hush puppies." They wore a polyglot mixture of uniforms, the most common being the "black pajamas"—common peasant garb throughout Vietnam—or "tiger stripe" camouflage uniforms. They rarely if ever wore the "leopard" pattern camouflage uniform, which was authorized only for National Police field forces engaged in military operations.

In 1970 General Abrams directed MACV to withdraw its support from these forces. He ordered advisors with the PRUs not to participate in field operations or sanction torture. Abrams was quite satisfied to leave the problems caused by the PRUs to the CIA. It was during this period that MACV began to streamline and consolidate the entire RVN military establishment, attempting to end the numerous private armies that existed within the system. The PRUs, like other RVN territorial forces, did not undergo this reorganization, as they were not part of the military establishment. The PRUs continued to operate under the auspices of the government of the RVN until the end of hostilities in 1975.

—J. A. Menzoff

References: Clarke, Jeffery J. *Advice and Support: The Final Years 1965–1973.* Washington, DC: US Army Center of Military History, 1988.
Spector, Ronald H. *After Tet: The Bloodiest Year in Vietnam.* New York: Vintage Books, 1993.
See also: Abrams, Creighton; Central Intelligence Agency (CIA); Phoenix Program; Vietnam, Republic of: National Police.

Provisional Revolutionary Government of South Vietnam (PRG)

Communist alternative or rival to the government of the Republic of Vietnam. Meeting between 6 and 8 June 1969, representatives of the Alliance of National, Democratic and Peace Forces (ANDPF) and the National Liberation Front (NLF) met and established the Provisional Revolutionary Government of South Vietnam (PRG). Huỳnh Tân Phát was its first president; he and other PRG leaders had earlier been active in the National Front for the Liberation of South Vietnam (NFLSV). The PRG's first minister of justice was Trương Như Tang, who in his memoir provides a list of the PRG leadership. Tang states that most PRG cabinet ministries were located within the Iron Triangle of South Vietnam. The PRG's proposed capital site was An Lôc.

The PRG's major responsibilities included foreign policy. Its best-known spokesperson was Madame Nguyên Thi Bình, foreign minister and earlier head of the NLF delegation at the Paris peace talks. In 1969 the PRG received diplomatic recognition from Communist states in eastern and central Europe, Cambodia, China, Cuba, Mongolia, North Korea, North Vietnam, Syria, and the Soviet Union.

General Trân Văn Trà headed the PRG delegation on the Four-Power Joint Military Commission responsible for supervision of the 1973 cease-fire and for implementation of prisoner exchanges. He was also the major PRG representative present at Độc Lập Palace when Sài Gòn fell on 30 April 1975. In that role, Trân Văn Trà served on the Military Management Committee immediately in charge of the city. Despite its aspirations of playing a significant role in a reunited Vietnam, the PRG was quickly integrated into the Socialist Republic of Vietnam. Madame Nguyên Thi Bình became minister of education for the Socialist Republic, one of only a few PRG leaders to receive an important position in the SRV.

—Ernest C. Bolt, Jr.

References: Nguyên Khăc Viên. *Vietnam, A Long History.* Hà Nôi: Gioi Publishers, 1993.
Trân Văn Trà. *Vietnam: History of the Bulwark B2 Theatre.* Vol. 5, *Concluding the 30-Years War* (in Vietnamese). Hô Chí Minh City: Văn Nghê, 1982. Translated in *Southeast Asia Report* 1247, no. 82783 (2 February 1983).
Truong Nhu Tang, with David Chanoff and Doan Van Toai. *A Vietcong Memoir: An Inside Account of the Vietnam War and Its Aftermath.* New York: Vintage Books, 1986.
See also: Huỳnh Tân Phát; National Front for the Liberation of South Vietnam (NFLSV); Nguyên Thi Bình; Trân Văn Trà; Trương Như Tang.

Proxmire, William

(1915–)

U.S. senator, 1957–1988. Born on 11 November 1915 at Lake Forest, Wisconsin, William Proxmire graduated from Yale in 1938 and, two years later, received an M.B.A. from Harvard. He enlisted as a private in the Army at the outbreak of World War II and rose through the noncommissioned ranks to master sergeant. Serving in counterintelligence, in 1946 he was commissioned a lieutenant. In 1948 he earned a master's degree in Public Administration from Harvard. In 1950 he won election to the Wisconsin State Assembly and served one term. Thereafter he ran unsuccessfully for governor in 1952, 1954, and 1956. Surprisingly, following the death of Joseph McCarthy in 1957, Proxmire, a liberal Democrat, won election to fill the controversial and conservative senator's vacant seat.

Proxmire made an instant impression in the Senate, most of which was negative. A maverick, he butted heads with top Washington power brokers such as Senators Lyndon Johnson and John Kennedy. He opposed excessive military spending and the growing military-industrial complex that, he maintained, threatened social, educational, and civil rights programs. Still, he supported U.S. intervention in Southeast Asia and remained hawkish well into the Johnson administration. After the 1968 Têt Offensive he joined increasingly persistent legislative efforts to end the Vietnam War and signed the Hatfield-McGovern Amendment. Later he opposed the B-1 bomber and the C-5A jumbo cargo plane.

A social liberal, Proxmire became increasingly conservative on fiscal issues. Although he favored space exploration, he opposed the costly space shuttle program. He also spoke out against privilege, perks, frivolous government spending, and the federal bailouts of Lockheed Corporation and New York City. He sponsored the Consumer Credit Protection Act and, in 1976, rose to the chairmanship of the Senate Banking, Housing, and Urban Affairs Committee.

Senator Proxmire retired in 1989 but resides and maintains an office in Washington. He is the author of several books and articles, including *Report from Wasteland: America's Military-Industrial Complex* and *Uncle Sam: The Last of the Big Time Spenders.*

—David Coffey

References: *Current Biography Yearbook, 1978.* New York: H. W. Wilson, 1978.
Who's Who in American Politics, 1996. New Providence, NJ: R. R. Bowker, 1995.
See also: Church, Frank Forrester; Hatfield, Mark Odum; Hatfield-McGovern Amendment; Humphrey, Hubert H.; Johnson, Lyndon Baines; Kennedy, John Fitzgerald; Mansfield, Michael Joseph; McCarthy, Joseph Raymond; McGee, Gale William; McGovern, George S.

Psychological Warfare Operations (PSYOP)

Quite early in this most "ideological" of wars, the U.S. Military Assistance Command, Vietnam (MACV) was well aware of the importance of psychological operations (PSYOP) in Vietnam. Throughout the war the Joint U.S. Public Affairs Organization (JUSPAO), a joint services and combined Allied organization, was responsible for supervising, coordinating, and evaluating all U.S. PSYOP in North and South Vietnam, Laos, and Cambodia, and for providing PSYOP support to Republic of Vietnam (RVN) programs. MACV commander General William Westmoreland and his successor General Creighton Abrams remained strong supporters of PSYOP, as were many of their staff. It is simply another myth of the Vietnam War that the United States, stubbornly fixated on a World War II–style conventional conflict, was unaware of the "other war."

JUSPAO's mixture of military and civilian personnel was well suited to the dual nature of this war and at least testified to the American military's early awareness that "winning the hearts and minds of the people" was fully as important a PSYOP target as the armed conflict. In fact, JUSPAO's stated first mission priority was to bolster the image of the government of the RVN. The second priority was the Chiêu Hôi—"Open Arms"—defector program,

established by the RVN government in 1963. The program was directed toward, and was most successful with, the indigenous Viêt Công (VC). Allied surrender appeals in Vietnam were usually closely tied to Chiêu Hôi. The North Vietnamese, of course, could hardly be expected to rally in significant numbers to the RVN government and remain separated from their families.

In addition to its combat PSYOP, the U.S. effort enlightened civilians about RVN government programs and provided information services that would normally come under the heading of "nation building," and was, in turn, supported by JUSPAO and other military and civilian agencies in-country. In dealing with the VC in areas they dominated, JUSPAO PSYOP often became something closer to civil affairs (CA) than in any previous U.S. conflict.

In this war there were basically four military PSYOP targets: the Viêt Công guerrillas in the South, People's Army of Vietnam (PAVN) regulars, the civilian population of South Vietnam, and civilians of North Vietnam. Psychological operations directed toward each target had to be quite distinct.

On 1 December 1967 the 4th Psychological Operations Group (POG) was activated, with its headquarters in Sài Gòn but with its four battalions (the 6th, 7th, 8th, and 10th) operating in direct support of U.S. and Allied forces in each of the four Corps Tactical Zones (CTZs). In the field PSYOP was initially conducted by four psychological operations companies, again one in each of the major CTZs. Finally, 13 HA (command and control), 13 HB (loudspeaker) and 33 HE (audiovisual) three-man teams were deployed by the 4th POG's battalions to units and areas in the field. The HA teams provided command and control to the HB and HE teams and supported pacification and stability operations as well. The HE teams were ideal for "one-on-one" PSYOP, as they gave medical civilian assistance (MEDCAP), distributed leaflets and posters, showed movies (revolutionary development, public safety, RVN image, and Disney films), carried out public opinion polls, reported local attitudes and opinions, and gathered information on Communist weapons and food caches as well as intelligence on the local VC infrastructure. Usually each Allied division had one attached HE team. The 4th POG's battalions also provided direct PSYOP support to U.S. Army combat divisions, brigades, and regiments, as well as training the Army of the Republic of Vietnam (ARVN) to assume its duties when "Vietnamization" of the struggle had been completed.

Each battalion was under the operational control of the senior U.S. commander in each CTZ. The 4th POG was under the control of MACV, although JUSPAO continued to provide support to military PSYOP activities in the field. By the time the 4th POG was activated, the U.S. military advisor team in each RVN province included a PSYOP officer, usually a lieutenant or captain. At the regional/corps level the advisory staff included military and civilian PSYOP officers, although at the district level the U.S. military advisor rarely had any PSYOP assets. In addition, in February 1968 the 4th POG established mobile advisory teams, each consisting of a PSYOP-trained officer and noncommissioned officer (NCO), to establish unit PSYOP programs or to evaluate existing programs. Team personnel acted as PSYOP advisors to units that lacked their own PSYOP capability. Adding to their labors in the field, leaflet distributors and loudspeaker teams often worked with civic action groups and the defector Kit Carson Scouts.

As might be expected, this insurgency conflict saw considerable overlapping of missions, but also an intelligent sharing of resources. For example, JUSPAO would receive prisoners of war who had defected as a result of MACV operations and use them for their own PSYOP.

A useful means of improving PSYOP coordination between the U.S. Army and the ARVN was the Combined PSYOP Center (CPOC), established at each CTZ in 1969. The CPOCs pooled, collated, evaluated, and distributed PSYOP intelligence and planned combined operations. Each CPOC differed to some degree in its functions and team composition, but each was headed by a Vietnamese with an American as his deputy.

Civilian PSYOP operations could often be mounted on a quick, ad hoc basis: When a local defense guard was injured by a booby trap while working in a rice field outside Phường Tho village in December 1970, the PSYOP liaison team attached to the 1st Armored Cavalry Division quickly exploited the incident. A tape was made informing the local people of the man's injuries and pointing out that the victim could just as easily have been an innocent villager or a child and that through the villagers' payment of taxes the VC was able to purchase such weapons of indiscriminate warfare.

The most intensive civilian PSYOP of the war was that conducted by U.S. Army Special Forces among the indigenous Montagnard tribes of the Central Highlands. Special Forces worked through the Civilian Irregular Defense Group (CIDG), originally established by the Central Intelligence Agency, and welded them into an effective field force that both protected the villages and engaged in offensive operations.

Army PSYOP in Vietnam utilized practically all of the themes of previous U.S. psywars, including the surrender pass, "Happy POW," "Allied Might," nostalgia, good soldier–bad leaders, and other reliable methods. The "nostalgia" theme seemed to enjoy great success. The 1st Infantry Division's G-5 broadcast a "family appeal" designed to make insurgents think of home and family. Another typical leaflet, addressed to the VC, depicted a lissome Vietnamese beauty amid a traditional rural landscape, and carried this plaintive message from her husband: "Take a husband, my love. . . . Don't delay for the fires here in the South burn fiercely. My arms are torn from my body and with my life's blood I write this last plea. . . ."

A new theme was the offer of money for defectors or for weapons. One such leaflet promised as much as the equivalent of $20,000 U.S. for any Communist infantry company that defected with its commander, political officer, platoon leader, and at least 80 percent of its men. Another listed a price scale for weapons turned in by defectors. As in other U.S. wars, the surrender pass gained such credibility that the defector needed reassurance that he was not required to carry such a leaflet to receive good treatment. Another typical leaflet warned:

Members of the NVA [North Vietnamese Army], gunships and artillery will hit your positions. . . . The darkness of the

jungle will no longer hide you. Our electronic devices will detect and locate your positions at any time, day or night. . . . Gunships, artillery, and air strikes will continuously hit your positions if you choose to remain in this area.

Some leaflets simply showed, in full color, a plentifully stocked marketplace in an RVN city. JUSPAO also brought back the bomber leaflet of World War II in the Pacific. This time the bomber was the B-52 and the target was troops in the field. The message: This weapon is deadly, and there is nothing you can do about it except give up.

JUSPAO personnel undoubtedly enjoyed composing the "disillusioning" leaflet carrying photos of Communist China's Mao Zedong and Zhou Enlai (Chou En-lai) at their historic meetings with President Richard Nixon. The reaction, particularly among the selfless, indoctrinated cadres, to the widely disseminated spectacle of this "Imperialist," this "Mad Bomber" cordially conferring with the "Elder Brothers" of the anti-imperialist forces must have indeed been sobering ("Who are you fighting now?" "THIS IS WHAT YOU DIDN'T KNOW, BUT IT IS GOOD FOR YOU TO KNOW"). To rub in the point, JUSPAO several months later disseminated another leaflet, this time showing Leonid Brezhnev amiably proposing a toast to the same accursed Richard Nixon.

Many of these themes, of course, could overlap. A surrender pass might emphasize nostalgia, or a nostalgia leaflet could point out the terrible killing power of the Allies, or a "gory" leaflet might paint a contrast with the good life in the South. In fact, most leaflets used one or more themes. All but a few specialized U.S. PSYOP leaflets in Vietnam were written by Vietnamese nationals, although JUSPAO or other U.S. authorities often suggested the themes.

U.S. loudspeaker operators had to adopt new approaches to deal with a situation in which civilians and insurgents were seemingly inextricably intertwined. The new messages often concentrated upon the burdens heaped by the VC on the people:

You had to work very hard to get rice and money. If you report to the ARVN and Allied forces when the VC come to collect taxes, the RVN troops and Allied forces will come to chase the VC cadre from your area.

Loudspeaker teams brought their messages close-in, but they also suffered the only PSYOP battlefield fatalities of the war, with 11 killed in action.

The 4th POG disseminated a number of apparently effective news journals for both civilians and Communist troops. Among these were a daily two-page news summary *Tin Chiến Trường* ("News from the Front"), and *Canh Hoa*, a single-page news update distributed during field operations.

The dissemination of U.S. and Allied PSYOP showed considerable technical improvement. With new lightweight presses, photocopiers, and the Polaroid camera, PSYOP troopers could produce, in many cases, almost complete PSYOP in the field. Creative psywarriors could copy captured VC self-criticism diaries, with their depressing sentiments in the subject's verifiable handwriting, perhaps attach a photo of the author, and run off thousands of copies for dropping over the diarist's comrades, within a matter of hours.

The U.S. Air Force developed improved, side-mounted speakers on its own psywar-converted venerable C-47 transport aircraft, and the helicopter finally made accurate leaflet dissemination possible. By all accounts, most of the contested areas of South Vietnam had been well "papered" long before the end of hostilities.

Tactical radio also finally came into its own in this war. The 4th POG operated a 50,000-watt radio station at Pleiku in II Corps area, targeting Communist troops within a 200-mile radius. Audiovisual teams informed and entertained civilian audiences with propaganda and Hollywood efforts.

Allied PSYOP also employed television for the first time in the field, beginning in 1966. The novel medium attracted large crowds, sometimes including the VC, who occasionally shot up the sets, a tactic that definitely could backfire.

U.S. PSYOP in Vietnam had its deficiencies, of course. Soldiers served their one-year tour of duty in Vietnam and then rotated back to the States at the time when they were beginning to understand how things worked "in-country." Many PSYOP personnel remained deficient in language qualifications, and fewer than 40 percent were PSYOP or Army school trained. Conventional tactical unit commanders often remained unaware of the mission or value of PSYOP. Some commanders even pressed PSYOP tactical units into showing movies to their troops. Combat officers seconded to PSYOP units often expressed reservations about their assignments and believed, with considerable justification, that this was anything but a "career enhancing" move.

The very nature of psychological operations complicates any evaluation of its success. A study circa late 1968 of 337 *hôi chánhs* throughout CTZ I claimed that no less than 90 percent were "influenced by what [they] read." A full 96 percent said that they had seen PSYOP leaflets, and 91 percent said that they had heard aerial broadcasts. Yet such reports may on occasion be exercises in self-promotion. It is much more difficult to dismiss convincingly the no less than 200,000 defectors who came over to the Allied side, or the numerous captured documents inveighing against the "deceits" and "tricks" of Allied PSYOP.

The U.S. PSYOP effort in Vietnam can be termed a substantial, albeit temporary, success.

—Stanley Sandler

References: Chandler, Robert W. *War of Ideas: U.S. Propaganda Campaign in Vietnam.* Boulder, CO: Westview Press, 1981.
Sandler, Stanley. *"Cease Resistance: It's Good for You," A History of U.S. Army Combat Psychological Operations.* Fort Bragg, NC: U.S. Army Special Operations Command, n.d.
U.S. Army. Special Operations Command, Directorate of History and Archives, Fort Bragg, NC.
See also: Abrams, Creighton; Chiêu Hôi (Open Arms) Program; Civic Action; Civilian Irregular Defense Group (CIDG); Civilian Operations and Revolutionary Development Support (CORDS); Kit Carson Scouts; Montagnards; Pacification; Westmoreland, William Childs.

Pueblo Incident

(1968)

Incident involving a U.S. Navy vessel captured by the Democratic People's Republic of Korea (North Korea) on 23 January 1968.

Originally a light cargo vessel, in 1967 the 970-ton, 176-foot *Pueblo* was refitted and recommissioned as an Auxiliary General Environmental Research vessel (AGER). The *Pueblo* was, in fact, a "spy ship," equipped with electronic and cryptographic gear and manned—in addition to its regular crew—by communications technicians specially trained in electronic intelligence operations. Although to fulfill its mission the ship had to operate near hostile waters, the *Pueblo* was lightly armed, carrying only two .50-caliber machine guns.

On 23 January 1968 the *Pueblo*, captained by Comdr. Lloyd Bucher, was attacked by North Korean forces approximately 15 miles off Wonsan, North Korea. One seaman was killed and several crew members wounded. The crew were then held prisoner in North Korea until 22 December 1968, when they were released at Panmunjon Bridge. During their captivity they were tortured and forced to sign confessions.

After their release the Navy convened a court of inquiry to investigate the seizure of the *Pueblo* and the conduct of the crew during their captivity. The court recommended the court-martial of Bucher and the officer in charge of intelligence operations on the *Pueblo*. Navy Secretary John Chafee overruled the recommendation, stating that the men had "suffered enough." The episode, occurring while the United States was involved in the Vietnam War, was a blow to American prestige and a severe indictment of the Navy command structure, which had sent an inadequately armed vessel on a dangerous mission without adequate support.

—Kenneth R. Stevens

References: Brandt, Ed. *The Last Voyage of USS Pueblo.* New York: W. W. Norton, 1969.
Bucher, Lloyd M., with Mark Rascovich. *Bucher: My Story.* Garden City, NY: Doubleday, 1970.
Schumacher, F. Carl, Jr., and George C. Wilson. *Bridge of No Return: The Ordeal of the U.S.S. Pueblo.* New York: Harcourt Brace Jovanovich, 1971.
See also: ELINT (Electronic Intelligence); Korea, Democratic People's Republic of; United States: Navy.

Puller, Lewis B., Jr.

(ca. 1945–1994)

Vietnam War hero and prizewinning biographer. Lewis Puller was born at Camp Lejeune, North Carolina, circa 1945, son of Marine Corps General Lewis B. ("Chesty") Puller, the most decorated Marine. In 1967 he graduated from the College of William and Mary.

In 1968 Marine 2d Lieutenant Puller had been in Vietnam only three months when he was horribly wounded. His body was nearly cut in half when he triggered a booby-trapped howitzer shell. Puller was heavily disfigured and lost both of his legs just below his hips and most of both hands. He later wrote, "I had no idea that the pink mist that engulfed me had been caused by the vaporization of most of my right and left legs." Puller was awarded the Silver Star and two Purple Hearts.

Somehow Puller willed himself to live, although he said "the psychological and emotional wounds never healed." He returned to William and Mary to earn a law degree. In 1971 he had turned against the war, although he could not bring himself to return his medals: "They had cost me too dearly," he wrote, "and although I now saw clearly that the war in which they had been earned was a wasted cause, the medals still represented the dignity and caliber of my service and of those with whom I had served." In 1978 in Virginia he ran unsuccessfully for Congress as a Democrat and, beginning in 1979, worked as a senior lawyer at the Defense Department. At the time of his death in 1994 he was on leave of absence as writer-in-residence at George Mason University.

In 1991 Puller published *Fortunate Son.* Written in tribute to his father—the most decorated soldier in the history of the Marine Corps—the book chronicles his own fight against depression and alcoholism. William Styron, in a review for the *New York Times,* called it "a dark and corrosive autobiography." It won the 1992 Pulitzer Prize for biography.

Although Puller called his book "an affirmation of life—there are second chances," he never quite healed. He and his wife had only recently separated when, on 11 May 1994, he died at his home in Mount Vernon, Virginia, of a self-inflicted gunshot wound. His wife said of him, "To the list of names of victims of the Vietnam War, add the name of Lewis Puller."

—Spencer C. Tucker

References: *New York Times* (12 and 14 May 1994).
Newsweek (23 May 1994).
Puller, Lewis B. *Fortunate Son: The Autobiography of Lewis B. Puller, Jr.* New York: Bantam Books, 1991.
See also: Prose Narrative and the Vietnam Experience.

Q

Quach Tom

(1932–1997)

Vietnamese commando who parachuted into North Vietnam in a Central Intelligence Agency (CIA)-sponsored operation. An ethnic Hmong born in Hòa Bình Province in 1932, Quach Tom served with the French during the Indo-China War. In 1965 he was recruited into a South Vietnamese commando unit; the following year, as a sergeant, he was deputy commander of a team that parachuted into North Vietnam under CIA auspices to disrupt infiltration into the South.

Democratic Republic of Vietnam (DRV) authorities had been informed in advance of the parachute drop, and Quach was the only member of his unit not immediately captured. In fact, he managed to avoid capture for nearly three months, longer than any other commando sent into the North by U.S. authorities.

In 1996 declassified documents revealed that the U.S. government had lied to the "widows" of commandos sent into the North by declaring all of them dead. Quach's wife was so notified and was paid a $50 gratuity. Sedgwick Tourison, a former Defense Intelligence Agency analyst, has identified some 360 surviving commandos.

Quach survived almost 19 years of harsh imprisonment, including torture and near starvation. Released following the end of the Vietnam War, he lived in Vietnam in poverty. Quach arrived in the United States in 1996. His lawyer, John C. Mattes, sued in federal court on behalf of the commandos and has lobbied both Congress and President Bill Clinton for compensatory legislation. Such legislation was introduced by Senators John Kerry (D-Massachusetts) and Bob Kerrey (D-Nebraska) to provide $20 million to the commandos, about $40,000 each. It came too late for Quach Tom; he died in Chamblee, Georgia, on 26 August 1997.

—Spencer C. Tucker

References: *New York Times* (27 August 1997).
Tourison, Sedgwick D. *Project Alpha: Washington's Secret Military Operations in North Vietnam.* New York: St. Martin's Press, 1997.
See also: Central Intelligence Agency (CIA); Hmong; Kerry, John Forbes; Operation Plan 34A (OPLAN 34A); Vietnam, Republic of: Commandos.

Quadrillage/Ratissage

Key elements in the "oil slick" *(tache d'huile)* pacification method pursued by the French in Vietnam during the Indo-China War. The technique involved splitting up the territory to be pacified into grids or squares. Once this gridding *(quadrillage)* had been accomplished, each square was then "raked" *(ratissage)* by pacification forces familiar with the area. If carried out on a regular basis by a sufficient number of troops, it could be successful, but French forces in Indo-China never had the numbers of men necessary.

—Spencer C. Tucker

Reference: Fall, Bernard. *The Two Viet Nams.* Rev. ed. New York: Praeger, 1964.
See also: *Tache d'huile.*

Quang Tri, Battle of

(1972)

One of the opening battles of the three-pronged 1972 People's Army of Vietnam (PAVN) Easter Offensive. In preparation for the battle, Hà Nôi had moved long-range 130-mm field guns and 152-mm howitzers to positions just north of the Demilitarized Zone (DMZ). On 30 March 1972, under supporting fire from heavy artillery, the PAVN launched a coordinated ground attack spearheaded by T-54 and PT-76 tanks south across the DMZ and from the west through Khe Sanh. Four PAVN divisions moved into Quang Tri Province in Military Region I. The newly formed Army of the Republic of Vietnam (ARVN) 3d Division, charged with defending Quang Tri, was overwhelmed by the PAVN onslaught, and many units fled in panic. The situation for the ARVN was exacerbated by friction between its troops and Republic of Vietnam (RVN) Marines also operating in the area. Thus, the continuity of the RVN defensive effort in Quang Tri Province was fatally weakened from the beginning.

In addition to these problems, cloud cover during the first two weeks of April inhibited U.S. close air support; when the weather cleared in mid-April, however, B-52 strikes were heavy. Undaunted, PAVN forces crossed the Cam Lô–Cửa Viêt River barrier and attacked Quang Tri City from three directions, while heavy artillery struck hard at ARVN forces south of the city. On 27 April cloud cover returned and the PAVN 304th Division increased the intensity of its attack. Thousands of South Vietnamese refugees flooded Highway 1, streaming south toward Huê; the PAVN targeted the road, indiscriminately shelling the capital city and the road south. So many civilians were killed by PAVN direct and indirect fire on a 0.3-mile stretch of Highway 1 at Trường Phước Bridge, 10 miles south of Quang Tri, that the place was known to most Vietnamese as "*Đoan Đường Kinh Hoàng*" (the Road of Horrors). Đông Hà fell on 28 April, and on 1 May PAVN forces took Quang Tri City, with the rest of the province falling under its control two days later.

The offensive then stalled and degenerated into a stalemate. Toward the end of the summer RVN forces, buoyed by massive B-52 air support and somewhat rejuvenated by new senior leadership, launched a counteroffensive. After weeks of intense house-to-house fighting, on 15 September ARVN forces recaptured Quang Tri City. The fighting and bombing had almost completely obliterated the city, and RVN forces had suffered more than 5,000 casualties, but the North Vietnamese attackers had been stopped and pushed back. This action and the ARVN victories at Kontum and An Lôc effectively foiled the North Vietnamese Easter Offensive of 1972.

—James H. Willbanks

References: Clarke, Jeffrey J. *Advice and Support: The Final Years.* Washington, DC: U.S. Army Center of Military History, 1988.
Ngo Quang Truong. *The Easter Offensive of 1972.* Washington, DC: U.S. Government Printing Office, 1980.
Turley, G. H. *The Easter Offensive.* Novato, CA: Presidio Press, 1985.
See also: An Lôc, Battle of; Easter Offensive (Nguyên Hué Campaign); Vietnam, Democratic Republic of: Army (People's Army of Vietnam [PAVN]); Vietnam, Republic of: Army (ARVN); Vietnamization; Võ Nguyên Giáp.

Quôc Ngư

Literally translated as "national language," a writing system for Vietnamese based on the Roman alphabet. *Quôc ngư* was created in the seventeenth century by Catholic missionaries from Portugal, Spain, Italy, and France to translate prayer books and catechisms. The most important role in this process has been attributed to Alexandre de Rhodes, a French Jesuit priest, who published his *Dictionarium Annamiticum Lusitanum et Latinum* in Rome in 1651.

Until the middle of the nineteenth century, *quôc ngư* was used only by Catholic missionaries and their followers. It began to be taught in schools in Cochin China (South Vietnam) when this part of the country became a French colony. The colonial administration used it as a means to eliminate the political and cultural influence of Vietnamese Confucian scholars. The first newspaper published in *quôc ngư* was the *Gia Đinh Bá,* and its first writers were Trưởng Vĩnh Ký and Huỳnh Tinh Cua. Later, at the beginning of the twentieth century, Confucian scholars in the Đông Kinh Nghĩa Thuc school used *quôc ngư* as an instrument to spread new ideas and knowledge of Western science among the population. However, only when the traditional triennial examinations were abolished between 1915 and 1918 did *quôc ngư* become established as the national writing system for the Vietnamese language, replacing Chinese characters.

—Pham Cao Dưởng

References: Nguyên Đình Hòa. *Language in Vietnamese Society: Some Articles by Nguyen Dinh Hoa.* Carbondale, IL: Asia Books, 1980.
Nguyên Khăc Kham. "Vietnamese National Language and Modern Vietnamese Literature," *East Asian Cultural Studies* (Tokyo) 15, no. 1–4 (1976): 177–194.
Nguyên Thê Anh. "Introduction à la connaissance de la peninsule indochinoise: Le Viet Nam." In *Tuyên Tâp Ngôn Ngư Văn Tư* (Viet Nam—Essays on Vietnamese Language and Writing). Campbell, CA: Dòng Viêt, 1993.
See also: de Rhodes, Alexandre; French Indo-China.

R

Radford, Arthur W.
(1896–1973)

Chairman of the U.S. Joint Chiefs of Staff, 1953–1957. Born in Chicago, Illinois, on 27 February 1896, Arthur Radford graduated from the U.S. Naval Academy in 1916. He was on transatlantic convoy duty during World War I and thereafter encouraged the development of naval airpower. Rising through the ranks to rear admiral, he was in the Pacific theater during World War I, where he commanded aircraft carriers against Japanese forces in various island campaigns. After the war he promoted naval aviation and led the U.S. Pacific Fleet in the Korean War. In 1953 President Dwight D. Eisenhower appointed him chairman of the Joint Chiefs of Staff.

To Radford, Indo-China was extremely significant. Predicting ominous results if France was defeated there, he urged the Joint Chiefs to employ American air strikes in support of the French at Điên Biên Phu in 1954. Confident of victory, Radford thought France had gained the upper hand against the Viêt Minh. When in March French Chief of Staff General Paul Ely asked for U.S. military intervention to boost France's bargaining position at the Geneva Conference, Radford favored implementing Operation VULTURE—a proposed U.S. bombing mission.

Despite Admiral Radford's enthusiasm for air raids, President Eisenhower refused to contemplate bombing in the absence of endorsements from Congress and the Allies, particularly Britain. Supported by Secretary of State John Foster Dulles and Vice-President Richard Nixon, Radford tried to garner congressional sanction for the chief executive's discretionary use of air strikes. But a number of prominent legislators turned down the plea, since the United Kingdom declined participation in an effort to save the French.

During discussions about possible American involvement in Indo-China, Radford advanced some unique notions. Besides his recommendation for the employment of tactical nuclear arms at Điên Biên Phu, he suggested that the United States assist in forming an "International Volunteer Air Corps." For political reasons, General Ely rejected Radford's idea to increase the number of U.S. advisors available to train Vietnamese forces and showed only slight concern when Radford urged the use of psychological and unconventional methods.

Two years later, Radford offered the National Security Council a modified strategy to defeat an aggressor in Southeast Asia. He argued that the United States should contain the Democratic Republic of Vietnam with airpower. The U.S. Army would play only a restricted role; South Vietnamese ground forces would bear primary responsibility for stopping the invader. Army strategists expressed dissatisfaction with Radford's concepts.

Radford retired from the Navy in 1957 and died on 17 August 1973 at Bethesda Naval Hospital near Washington, D.C.

—Rodney J. Ross

References: Arnold, James R. *The First Domino: Eisenhower, the Military, and America's Intervention in Vietnam.* New York: William Morrow, 1991. Short, Anthony. *The Origins of the Vietnam War.* London: Longman, 1989. Spector, Ronald H. *Advice and Support: The Early Years, 1941–1960.* Washington, DC: U.S. Army Center of Military History, 1983.
See also: Điên Biên Phu, Battle of; Eisenhower, Dwight David; Ely, Paul Henri Romuald; Twining, Nathan Farragut; VULTURE, Operation.

Radio Direction Finding

The study of radio signal origins, targets, frequency of communications, and extent of command nets. Radio direction finding (RDF) and associated signals intelligence activities were utilized by the major antagonists in Indo-China, at least as early as the beginning of World War II.

RDF provides essential information about command structure and unit deployment. Two of the most important signals intelligence activities are to locate enemy headquarters and track troop movements. During the Indo-China War, Viêt Minh communications, including RDF data gathered by an American facility in Manila, were exchanged for signals intelligence from French intercept stations in Vietnam and Laos. Subsequently, during the Vietnam War, the Army Security Agency, the Air Force Security Service, and the Naval Security Group were deployed in the Indo-China region under the operational control of the National Security Agency (NSA), which had responsibility for the centralized coordination, direction, and performance of American signals intelligence.

Ground installations included Phú Bài, Đà Nẵng, Pleiku, Tân Sơn Nhứt, Côn Sơn Island, and Cam Ranh Bay in South Vietnam; Nakhon Phanom and Udorn in Thailand; bases in the Philippines; and the cooperating British facility at Little Sai Wan in Hong Kong. Phú Bài, equipped and technically assisted by Taiwan, had previously been the only similar installation within the Republic of Vietnam. Mobile capabilities included U.S. Navy ships and aircraft; U.S. Army aircraft, as well as teams at division and separate brigade level; U.S. Marine Corps elements; and U.S. Air Force aircraft such as the EC-47, EC-121, and EC-130.

Allied RDF depended on obtaining two or more readings, from different locations, of the direction of a Communist transmitter. A line of position (LOP) would be plotted for each reading. After obtaining several LOPs on a transmitter, the lines would converge on a common point, or fix—the physical location of the transmitter. Techniques used by the Communists in attempts to thwart RDF included using mobile transmitters carried by vehicles, transmitting in extremely short bursts, repeatedly changing frequency and power output, and ceasing transmission upon the approach of Allied aircraft.

The limitations of RDF were demonstrated when U.S. intelligence analysts were misled into thinking that a Communist division was deployed along the Cambodian border, when in fact it had approached Biên Hòa to participate in the Tết Offensive. To deceive Allied intelligence, the division's transmitters had been left at a border site.

Throughout the Vietnam War there were numerous incidents of swift reaction to RDF information, enabling ground forces, artillery, tactical aircraft, and B-52 bombers to attack Communist forces, often precluding or disrupting operations. Eventually, airborne RDF, by which a single aircraft could rapidly obtain a fix on a transmitter, became the most important single source of intelligence for Allied ground commanders in Indo-China.

Notable instances of RDF successes include the 1967 Battle of Đăk Tô, as well as the 1968 Battle of Khe Sanh. With the assistance of RDF, every company and battalion of the two North Vietnamese divisions besieging Khe Sanh were located. During the Tết Offensive, RDF was particularly useful at Ban Mê Thuôt and Nha Trang. In the Mekong Delta, as other sources of information dried up during Tết, the Mobile Riverine Force became almost completely dependent on RDF for intelligence.

—Glenn E. Helm

References: Bergen, John D. *Military Communications: A Test for Technology.* Washington, DC: U.S. Army Center of Military History, 1986.

Fulghum, David, Terrence Maitland, and the editors of Boston Publishing. *South Vietnam on Trial: Mid-1970 to 1972. The Vietnam Experience,* edited by Robert Manning. Boston: Boston Publishing, 1984.

LeGro, William E. "The Enemy's Jungle Cover Was No Match for the Finding Capabilities of the Army's Radio Research Units." *Vietnam* 3 (June 1990): 12–20.

"U.S. Electronic Espionage: A Memoir." *Ramparts* (August 1972): 35–50.

See also: Đak Tô, Battle of; Khe Sanh, Battles of; Tết Offensive: Overall Strategy; Tết Offensive: The Sài Gòn Circle.

RANCH HAND, Operation

(1961–1971)

Code name for missions involving the aerial spraying of herbicides. RANCH HAND operations evolved from two primary objectives: to deny Communist forces the use of thick jungle cover through defoliation and to deny them access to food crops in South Vietnam.

In 1961, in the face of increasing pressure from the Viêt Công, Republic of Vietnam (RVN) President Ngô Đình Diêm intensified his requests for U.S. assistance. On 30 November 1961 President John F. Kennedy approved the use of herbicides in Vietnam.

Political and other events leading to that decision signaled its importance. While the agricultural use of herbicides in the United States was climbing, with annual spraying occurring on over 53 million acres, the use by the military had steadily declined for a decade, despite the fact that the small Special Aerial Spray Flight (SASF) was upgrading its aircraft from the C-47 to the C-123

Provider. After an extremely effective defoliation experiment at Camp Drum, New York, in 1959, and following a visit to Vietnam by Vice-President Lyndon Johnson in May 1961, a joint U.S.-RVN counterinsurgency center was established. Its principal task was to evaluate the use of herbicides against guerrilla food sources and the thick jungle foliage that shielded Viêt Công activities. Dr. James Brown, deputy chief of the Army's Chemical Warfare Center, supervised the tests.

Difficulties abounded. Little was known about the multitude of vegetation found in South Vietnam, and the only airplane available for testing was the old C-47, although some tests included other delivery systems, such as the H-34 helicopter and a ground-based turbine sprayer. However, the success of these tests led Brown to recommend, through General Maxwell Taylor and Walt W. Rostow, that the SASF from Langley Air Force Base, Virginia, be deployed to Vietnam. Expecting President Kennedy's approval, on 28 November 1961 six C-123s, under the FARM GATE Program—with newly installed MC-1 spray tanks capable of holding 1,000 gallons of herbicide—departed their home station on the first leg of a deployment to South Vietnam.

After a month's delay in the Philippines, on 7 January 1962 three C-123s arrived at Tân Sơn Nhứt Airport outside Sài Gòn; their crews expected to remain there on temporary duty (TDY) for less than 90 days. They began operational missions on 12 January. Initially their assignment was to clear foliage along a major roadway north of Sài Gòn; later, mangrove forests near the coast and rice-growing areas in the Mekong Delta were added as approved targets.

Although the aircrews were using Agents Purple and Blue (military code names for specific herbicides), the results were somewhat less successful than expected. As a result of further testing in Florida, the number of nozzles on each wing boom was decreased from 42 to 35. This was done to increase the droplet size of the herbicide to between 300 and 350 micrometers, which was expected to minimize drift.

Another concern was the extremely dangerous mission profile. To ensure accurate delivery of the herbicide, the aircrews needed to fly very low, about 150 feet above the ground, in a straight and level flight path and at a relatively slow airspeed of about 130 miles per hour. In this environment the aircraft were vulnerable to everything from small-arms fire to antiaircraft artillery, especially after 1963. Although tactics changed somewhat throughout the war, the basic herbicide delivery parameters kept the crews constantly at risk.

In the early years of the war, the small detachment, still composed primarily of TDY aircrews, gradually expanded its operations. Defoliation missions for the three aircraft increased from 60 in 1962 to 107 in 1963 to 273 in 1964. Significantly, the difficulty of the aerial tactics increased as operations were expanded from the relatively flat areas surrounding lines of communication in the South to the rugged topography of the mountain passes in the more northern provinces.

In October 1964 following the Tonkin Gulf incidents, tactics were further complicated. Previously, crop destruction missions were flown by South Vietnamese helicopter pilots; on 3 October

RANCH HAND aircrews, initially with South Vietnamese observers, flew against crop targets in War Zone D north of Sài Gòn. Because crops were planted in tightly defined areas, such as in valleys or small openings in the jungle, delivery tactics in these controlled target areas necessitated the use of more dangerous maneuvering and even dive-bombing approaches to the target box. With this range of tactics and the addition of a fourth aircraft in December 1964, the unit had established its value in the war effort.

As a prologue to future growth, 1965 was an important year. To meet the need for more experienced aircrews, TDY personnel were replaced with aircrews assigned for a full year's rotation. In November three additional aircraft (by then known as the UC-123B) were added to the inventory. Furthermore, while Agent Blue continued to be used against crops, the less costly and more effective Agent Orange was added for jungle defoliation missions. Finally, 1965 saw a detachment of aircraft deployed to Đà Nẵng Air Base for operations against the Hồ Chí Minh Trail.

This pattern of exponential growth continued. In 1966 the unit had 14 authorized aircraft; in 1968 the number was 25; in 1969, 33 of the improved C-123K model aircraft were authorized. With this growth came, in October 1966, a change in name from the 309th Spray Flight to the 12th Air Commando Squadron; nearly concurrently, the unit moved to Biên Hòa Air Base to increase the logistical efficiency of the operations.

With the expansion to squadron status, RANCH HAND aircrews assumed a number of collateral duties, including flying airlift missions during the 1968 Tết Offensive and flying classified missions in Laos and Thailand. Still, the squadron's primary workload increased: In 1965 RANCH HAND aircrews flew only 897 missions covering 253 square miles of jungle; in 1968, the squadron's busiest year, 5,745 herbicide sorties were flown in addition to 4,000 collateral sorties.

The contraction of RANCH HAND operations occurred quickly. In 1969 the results of a five-year study at the National Cancer Institute reached the Department of Defense, culminating a series of earlier, preliminary studies that indicated serious health problems might occur with exposure to herbicides. Public disapproval also erupted when the Cambodian government made an unsubstantiated claim that 170,000 acres of its land had been intentionally sprayed with herbicides. These concerns, along with a drastic decrease in funding from a requested $27 million to $3 million under Vietnamization, caused a rapid decline in the number of operational sorties flown.

In mid-1970 the unit was reduced to eight aircraft, reassigned to Phan Rang Air Base as a flight, and restricted from using Agent Orange, replacing that herbicide with the less effective Agent White. On 7 January 1971, after nine years of operations, RANCH HAND aircrews flew the last three herbicide missions of the war.

—Charles J. Gaspar

References: Buckingham, William. "Operation Ranch Hand." *Air University Review* 34 (1983): 42–53.
Cecil, Paul. *Herbicidal Warfare: The Ranch Hand Project in Vietnam.* New York: Praeger, 1986.
Wolfe, William. "Health Status of Air Force Veterans Occupationally Exposed to Herbicides in Vietnam." *JAMA* 264 (10 October 1990): 1824–1832.
See also: Airplanes, Allied and Democratic Republic of Vietnam; Defoliation; FARM GATE, Operation; Herbicides.

RAND Corporation

U.S. government–funded "think tank" that contemplated various war scenarios for nuclear war but also for the limited war in Vietnam. RAND began as an outgrowth of both British and American operational research groups in World War II. These groups had been composed of scientists from all fields who examined data, theorized about the facts, and predicted future operations. Fearing that these organizations would fade with the end of the war, General Henry "Hap" Arnold sought support for the creation of a permanent U.S. government agency. Finally, in March 1946 Theodore Von Karman, head of the Army Air Force Scientific Advisory Board, officially started Air Force Project RAND (Research and Development). General Curtis LeMay, deputy chief of air staff for research and development, had charge of oversight and guidance for the program.

A nonprofit organization, the RAND Corporation was made up of a body of thinkers: physicists, political strategists, economists, and mathematicians. The charter read: "Project RAND is a continuing program of scientific study and research on the broad subject of air warfare with the object of recommending to the Air Force preferred methods, techniques, and instrumentalities for this purpose." Initially, analysts attempted solely to impose a rational order on the concept of nuclear war. In areas of tactics, RAND officials broke the military sides down into mathematical odds based on the reasonable options available to both sides. RAND analysts wrote essays on where to attack, why armies attacked, and the best weapons to use in a given situation. Their essays and pamphlets influenced an entire generation of military and political leaders. In the 1960s RAND devotees moved into positions of considerable influence with the inauguration of President John F. Kennedy and the appointment of Secretary of State Robert S. McNamara.

Many RAND ideas became national policy during the Vietnam War. McNamara's approach to American involvement in Vietnam in early 1965 stemmed from RAND strategist William Kaufmann's concepts of "limited war." Kaufmann advocated not victory but stalemate, in which no larger power would be drawn into the war and the United States could convince the Democratic Republic of Vietnam (DRV) that the costs of fighting were higher for the Vietnamese than for the Americans. He called for "discreet" methods of destruction rather than the use of nuclear weapons. Assistant Secretary of Defense John McNaughton was a student of RAND policymaker Thomas Schilling. McNaughton advocated the gradual increase of troop strengths and adherence to the limited war concept.

The Vietnam conflict disillusioned many intellectuals within RAND, especially Bernard Brodie, one of its founders. Brodie came to the realization that Communist leaders were not irrational barbarians but shared many of the same concerns over nuclear weapons expressed by U.S. leaders. Brodie moved away from the idea of providing options for the use of nuclear weapons. He believed that no options existed and that the best option for the United States and the world was a policy of not using or threatening to use weapons of mass destruction.

The war also disillusioned Dr. Daniel Ellsberg, a researcher with RAND and one of the authors of a lengthy (47-volume) study of how the United States came to be involved in Vietnam: *United States–Vietnam Relations, 1945–1967,* commonly referred to as "The Pentagon Papers." Ellsberg made copies of portions of the study available to the press.

Still, throughout the 1970s and 1980s RAND continued to author strategies for nuclear war, and RAND alumni such as James Schlesinger remained key figures in the government.

—Michael R. Nichols

References: FitzGerald, Frances. *Fire in the Lake: The Vietnamese and the Americans in Vietnam.* Boston: Little, Brown, 1972.

Kaplan, Fred. "Scientists at War: The Birth of the RAND Corporation." *American Heritage* (June/July 1983): 49–64.

————. *The Wizards of Armageddon.* New York: Simon & Schuster, 1983.

See also: Ellsberg, Daniel; Kennedy, John Fitzgerald; LeMay, Curtis Emerson; McNamara, Robert S.; McNaughton, John T.; Pentagon Papers and Trial; ROLLING THUNDER, Operation; Schlesinger, James R.; Vietnam, Democratic Republic of: 1954–1975.

Raven Forward Air Controllers (FACs)

Individuals controlling air strikes in Laos. The Raven Forward Air Controller program began during the winter of 1965–1966 with the assignment of U.S. Air Force enlisted personnel who had been trained as forward air guides by the Air Commandos. Using the radio call sign of "Butterfly," these men directed attacks by the Royal Lao Air Force and the U.S. Air Force in northern Laos while riding aboard aircraft from Air America and Continental Air Services.

In October 1966, with growing numbers of U.S. Air Force fighter-bombers employed in Laos, General William E. Momyer, commander of the Seventh Air Force, inaugurated what was known as the Steve Canyon program to replace the enlisted forward air guides. Under this program, officers who had spent six months in South Vietnam as forward air controllers were eligible to volunteer for a six-month tour in Laos. Assigned to the U.S. Embassy in Vientiane and wearing civilian clothes, they would use the radio call sign "Raven" to direct air strikes in support of Central Intelligence Agency (CIA)-led guerrilla forces in northern Laos, or Military Region II. (Later, they would perform the same task in southern Laos as the war expanded into that part of the country in the late 1960s.)

The Ravens, free from usual military restraints, sometimes irritated their more traditional superiors. Although frequently accused of immature personal behavior, no one doubted their skill or courage. Flying at low levels over the battlefields of Laos, these volunteer airmen played a vital role in bringing airpower to bear against the Communist Pathet Lao and their North Vietnamese allies. The cost proved high: Between 1966 and 1973 more than 30 Ravens lost their lives in the little-noticed but frequently vicious sideshow to the main conflict in Vietnam.

—William M. Leary

Reference: Robbins, Christopher. *The Ravens.* New York: Crown, 1987.

See also: Air America; Central Intelligence Agency (CIA); Continental Air Services; Laos; Momyer, William W.; Pathet Lao.

Read, Benjamin Huger
(1925–1993)

U.S. State Department official, 1963–1965. Born on 14 September 1925 in Philadelphia, Benjamin Huger Read was reared in Conshohocken, Pennsylvania, and educated at Williams College, receiving a B.A. degree in 1949. He graduated from the University of Pennsylvania Law School in 1952 and was admitted to the Pennsylvania bar the same year. He then worked in various legal capacities, including that of public defender in Philadelphia until 1958, at which time he departed for Washington as a legislative aide to Senator Joseph Clark of Pennsylvania, for whom he worked for five years.

In 1963 Read became executive secretary to U.S. Secretary of State Dean Rusk. Rusk, along with Secretary of Defense Robert McNamara and National Security Advisor McGeorge Bundy, belonged to a group known around Washington as the "awesome foursome" because of their "Tuesday lunches" with President Lyndon Johnson at the White House. As a result of his association with Rusk, Read had access to the top foreign policy group around President Johnson. Read worked diligently to keep Secretary Rusk, who had virtually no personal staff, apprised of continuing developments in the State Department regarding Vietnam. To ensure secrecy, Read at one point reduced access to the file codenamed MARIGOLD to only six people.

Read worked with Vice-President Hubert Humphrey in the 1968 presidential campaign and left the State Department in 1969 to become director of the Woodrow Wilson International Center for Scholars at the Smithsonian Institution. In 1973 he became the founding president of the German Marshall Fund, which the Federal Republic of Germany established in appreciation for the Marshall Plan. Read later served as undersecretary of state for management in the Carter administration and aided in efforts to secure the release of the U.S. hostages in Iran. At the time of his death in Washington, D.C., on 18 March 1993, Reed was president of Ecofund '92, a group associated with the 1992 Earth Summit meeting in Rio de Janeiro.

—Wes Watters

References: Cooper, Chester L. *The Lost Crusade: America in Vietnam.* New York: Dodd, Mead, 1970.

Herring, George C. *LBJ and Vietnam: A Different Kind of War.* Austin, TX: University of Texas Press, 1994.

————, ed. *The Secret Diplomacy of the Vietnam War: The Negotiating Volumes of the Pentagon Papers.* Austin, TX: University of Texas Press, 1983.

New York Times (19 March 1993).

Schoenbaum, Thomas J. *Waging Peace and War.* New York: Simon & Schuster, 1988.

See also: Bundy, McGeorge; Humphrey, Hubert H.; Johnson, Lyndon Baines; MARIGOLD, Operation; McNamara, Robert S.; Rusk, Dean.

Reagan, Ronald

(1911–)

Actor; governor of California, 1967–1975; president of the United States, 1981–1989. Ronald Reagan was born on 11 February 1911 in Tampico, Illinois. This popular movie star and spokesman for General Electric was never involved in the Vietnam War or even visited Vietnam. Even so, Vietnam was central to his career and to his agenda as politician and president. A staunch anti-Communist, Reagan strongly supported U.S. intervention in Vietnam. During his 1966 California gubernatorial campaign, he propelled himself into office by strongly assailing student antiwar protestors on the campuses of the University of California, particularly those at Berkeley.

In his gubernatorial and presidential campaigns between 1966 and 1980, Reagan, a conservative Republican, reaffirmed his continuing suspicion of the Soviet Union and his belief that U.S. intervention in Vietnam was justified both morally and strategically. As president, he saw it as part of his mission of national regeneration to eradicate the effects of the Vietnam trauma upon the United States and restore his country's pride and self-confidence. He also continued the policy of nonrecognition of the Socialist Republic of Vietnam. Ironically, in practice Reagan was extremely cautious in committing U.S. military forces in action abroad, and his concern to avoid long and politically damaging foreign military entanglements was symptomatic of the continuing legacy of Vietnam for American politicians. However, throughout the 1980s his administration actively opposed left-wing movements in Central America with an ideological determination similar to that directed toward Vietnam in the 1950s and 1960s.

Reagan retired from public life following his second term as president. Suffering from Alzheimer's disease, he has remained in virtual seclusion on his California ranch.

—Priscilla Roberts

References: Cannon, Lou. *President Reagan: The Role of a Lifetime.* New York: Simon & Schuster, 1991.

Dallek, Robert. *Ronald Reagan: The Politics of Symbolism.* Cambridge, MA: Harvard University Press, 1984.

Johnson, Haynes. *Sleepwalking through History: America in the Reagan Years.* New York: W. W. Norton, 1991.

Reagan, Ronald. *My Early Life; or, Where's The Rest of Me.* New York: Sidgwick and Jackson, 1981.

_____. *Ronald Reagan: An American Life.* New York: Simon & Schuster, 1990.
See also: Antiwar Movement, United States; Bush, George Herbert Walker; Carter, Jimmy; Vietnam, Socialist Republic of: 1975 to the Present.

Red Cross Recreation Workers

See United States: Red Cross Recreation Workers.

Red River Delta

The geographical heartland of Vietnam. The Red River Delta, an alluvial accumulation at the mouth of the Red River in northern Vietnam, extends from 50 miles north of Hà Nôi southeastward to the Gulf of Tonkin. More shallow and narrow than the Mekong River Delta 800 miles to the extreme south, the flat and fertile Red River Delta is encircled by bordering highlands and plateaus and houses a concentrated population of rice farmers.

The Red River Delta is of late geological origin, formed by silt carried along by the Black and Clear Rivers that empty their deposits into the Red River 30 miles north of Hà Nôi. Consequently, the Delta is developing toward the open sea to the extent of 200 feet yearly. The Black and Clear Rivers likewise channel into the Red, as a rule, about 141,000 cubic feet of surging water each second, which saturates the Delta region from Viêt Trì to the shoreline. However, in arid years the rate could drop under 24,600 cubic feet, meaning the Red River's moisture fails to touch the parched rich lands in its path.

When rains exceed normal, the Red River ascends to perilous levels. Since China's reign over Tonkin, hydraulic controls have been used to check, route, and garner the overflow by construction of dikes, canals, and dams. By 1968 two large overhead dikes had been erected that funneled the Red River down the Delta and regulated its raging waters.

Spreading over 15,000 miles, the entire system aids transportation with a line of roadways atop the dikes. Despite their vulnerability to air attack, the U.S. Joint Chiefs of Staff, except for the destruction of levees around Nam Đinh in 1972, did not officially recommend their targeting.

Tonkin's Red River Delta has experienced continuous food scarcity, which has been partially offset by imports, mainly from the People's Republic of China (PRC) and the USSR. Rice surpluses shipped north from the Mekong Delta, as well as the use by Tonkinese farmers of intensive agricultural techniques like night soil, irrigation, and planting a second crop, have contributed to meeting the food needs of a growing population.

The Red River Delta offers Indo-China the best opportunity for industrialization. With proximate mineral abundance in the Annamite Cordillera and northern Mountains as well as climatic variety encouraging industrial staples such as cotton and sugar cane, the Hà Nôi regime's goal of economic well-being by way of industrial development could be fostered, added by Hai Phòng's entry to the Gulf of Tonkin and its road and rail connections. The Delta area already has established secondary industries such as cement, paper, textiles, and chemicals.

—Rodney J. Ross

References: Buttinger, Joseph. *Vietnam: A Political History.* New York: Praeger, 1968.

Dutt, Ashok K., ed. *Southeast Asia: Realm of Contrasts.* Boulder, CO: Westview Press, 1985.

Fisher, Charles A. *Southeast Asia: A Social, Economic and Political Geography.* New York: E. P. Dutton, 1966.
See also: Dikes; Geography of Indo-China and Vietnam; Mekong Delta; Tonkin.

Reeducation Camps

Camps established in Vietnam, Cambodia, and Laos following the victories of Communist forces there. They were based on the dozen "Production Camps" established in North Vietnam after 1947. Many more were added after 1954, and all were renamed "Reeducation Camps." The most notorious of these were Lý Bá Sư, named for its camp chief, and Công Trời (Gate to Heaven).

After the Communist victory in April 1975, many more such camps were built in South Vietnam, a number of them located at former U.S./Republic of Vietnam (RVN) military bases. These camps held officials of the defeated RVN government, former Army of the Republic of Vietnam (ARVN) soldiers, former schoolteachers, and employees of the U.S. military. Figures on the numbers of prisoners held vary, but Ginette Sagan and Stephen Denney estimated that over 1 million Vietnamese were kept in more than 150 camps, subcamps, and prisons. They claimed that some 500,000 prisoners were released within the first three months; 200,000 remained in the camps between two and four years; some 240,000 spent at least five years; and that in 1983 some 60,000 people remained. This coincides closely with figures released in 1980 by the government of the Socialist Republic of Vietnam (SRV) when it informed Amnesty International that 1 million Vietnamese were held for "short reeducation courses," and about 40,000 were detained for longer purposes.

In addition to political prisoners detained after 30 April 1975, reeducation camps also kept common lawbreakers. These individuals had been sentenced by courts or incarcerated without trial by decision of district Public Security chiefs under authority of Resolution 49 to three-year terms, which could be renewed without limit.

Conditions in the camps varied widely. Although the systematic brutality of such camps in the early Soviet Union was not the pattern in Vietnam, there were occasional beatings, torture, and even executions. Medical care also varied widely, and hard physical labor was interposed with political study sessions. Each camp had an incommunicado ward of dark cells. Here inmates violating camp regulations were put in stocks, for periods ranging from one week to—the longest time known—14 months.

One of the instructions for the camp guards, who freely shared it with the prisoners, was the following: "We [Public Security personnel] must exploit prisoner labor to the fullest extent for the benefit of our socialist society . . . as the Soviet Union has done." Beatings and torture were freely meted out to prisoners incarcerated for criminal offenses, even for stealing a bit of food. Political prisoners were treated somewhat better, although any escape attempt would bring torture and even death, apparently under orders from higher authorities.

The SRV freed many of the inmates in the 1970s and 1980s. Beginning in 1982 the SRV on several occasions publicly offered to permit camp inmates to depart from the country. Such an offer was made by Premier Pham Văn Đông in May 1984. In arguing for a favorable U.S. response, that September Secretary of State George Shultz estimated there were about 10,000 inmates of Hà Nội's reeducation camps who would leave the country if permitted to do so.

In September 1987 Hà Nội announced that it was releasing 6,685 prisoners, among them several hundred military and civilian personnel of the former RVN government, including 2 ministers, 18 administrative officials, 9 ARVN generals, 248 officers of field rank, and 117 junior officers. In June 1989 Foreign Minister Nguyên Cò Thach claimed that only about 120 people remained interned.

In 1990 the U.S. State Department handled arrangements to bring some 2,000 Vietnamese who had been in the camps to the United States. Early that year a U.S. government spokesman said that about 100,000 former camp inmates were among the 600,000 Vietnamese who had applied to emigrate to the United States.

The situation in Laos was far worse. Tens of thousands may have perished there. Among those executed in "seminar camps," as the Laotian reeducation camps were known, were government officials, army officers, and members of the Lao royal family, including King Savang Vatthana, the queen, and their eldest son. General Vang Pao put the toll there at more than 46,000 people.

—Spencer C. Tucker and Nguyên Công Luân

References: Đoàn Văn Toai. *The Vietnam Gulag.* New York: Simon & Schuster, 1986.
Nguyên Long. *After Saigon Fell.* Berkeley, CA: University of California Press, 1981.
Sagan, Ginette, and Stephen Denney. *Violations of Human Rights in the Socialist Republic of Vietnam.* Palo Alto, CA: Aurora Foundation, 1983.
Vang Pao, Maj. Gen. Speech delivered at the Vietnam Seminar, Texas Tech University, Lubbock, Texas, 18 April 1996.
See also: Laos; Refugees and Boat People; Vietnam, Socialist Republic of: 1975 to the Present.

Refugees and Boat People

Fleeing their homeland on crowded fishing boats, makeshift vessels, and unseaworthy craft, Vietnamese refugees by the hundreds and thousands, known as "boat people," became an ever-visible reminder of the Vietnam War and its bitter legacy. In the spring of 1975 more than 60,000 people took to the South China Sea during the death throes of the Republic of Vietnam in desperate efforts to reach ships of the U.S. Seventh Fleet. This first wave of boat people, rescued under U.S. Operation FREQUENT WIND, consisted of prominent political and military figures and those whose U.S. or Sài Gòn connections marked them for Communist retribution. The group also included professionals such as doctors, lawyers, professors, and journalists.

After the great exodus of April 1975, only 377 boat people made their way during the next eight months to first-asylum countries such as Malaysia, Indonesia, Singapore, the Philippines, and Hong Kong. These were intended as only temporary sanctuaries but in some cases became permanent homes. The number of refugees jumped dramatically the following year, when an estimated 5,619 people departed Vietnam. In 1977 the total number of boat people rose to 21,276, despite official estimates that one-third of refugees died at sea from bad weather and starvation and despite rape, pillage, and murder at the hands of pirates. Many who escaped were former RVN soldiers, fishermen, farmers, and businessmen, including northerners who had fled the DRV in 1954 and were now again fleeing communism.

Though changes in the reunited Vietnam came gradually at first with the post–April 1975 nationalization of major industries,

Fleeing their homeland on crowded fishing boats, makeshift vessels, and unseaworthy craft, Vietnamese refugees, also known as "boat people," became an ever-visible reminder of the Vietnam War and its bitter legacy.

in June 1977 the Vietnamese Communist Party Central Committee, during the Fourth Party Congress, announced the complete transformation of the South to socialism. Confiscation of private businesses and properties, freezing of assets, currency changes, collectivization of farmland, and forced removals to New Economic Zones (NEZ) all took a heavy toll on many ethnic Chinese, or Hoa, as the Vietnamese called them.

Another change after the reunification of Vietnam—perhaps less tangible than the others but possibly causing the greatest distress—was the process of indoctrination and reeducation in labor camps. The loss of personal freedom and fear for one's life served as powerful incentives to leave the country.

To avoid what they saw as a bleak future in Vietnam, many Hoa, who for generations prospered in commerce and dominated the private business sector in banking and trading in the South, now opted to leave. Victims of a class war and viewed with suspicion by the government for suspected loyalty to China, many ethnic Chinese were encouraged to leave by the Public Security Bureau—the political police—after paying bribes and a departure fee of five taels ($1,500) per adult. Trafficking in refugees became, from 1977 to 1979, a thriving enterprise for the Hà Nội government.

Vietnam's war with China in 1979 also sparked a major migration of ethnic Chinese in northern Vietnam to China and a mass exodus of Hoa from Sài Gòn. Of 1.7 million ethnic Chinese in Vietnam, the majority of the 1.4 million who lived in the South left. This created a huge vacuum in Vietnam's already weakened economy. Encouragement of the Hoa to leave did not extend to those who were not ethnic Chinese. Ethnic Vietnamese who were caught or suspected of trying to escape were severely punished.

It was not until 1979, when the exodus of boat people reached alarming proportions, that the world community became interested in their plight. An international crisis was precipitated when Thailand, Malaysia, Singapore, Indonesia, and the Philippines (the so-called ASEAN countries) as well as Hong Kong announced that they were no longer capable of absorbing additional refugees into the already overcrowded camps, where most waited for the resettlement process. The estimate of boat people in 1979 stood roughly at 100,000 with some 10,000 to 15,000 arriving each month.

In July 1979 ASEAN nations issued statements that they would no longer accept refugees unless the West guaranteed resettlement there. In response, United Nations (UN) Secretary General Kurt Waldheim convened a conference in Geneva to address the problem. This meeting, attended by representatives of 65 countries, resulted in both monetary aid to the United Nations High Commissioner for Refugees (UNHCR) and pledges for the resettlement of 260,000 refugees (including a U.S. pledge to double its admission rate from 7,000 to 14,000 Indo-Chinese per month). The UNHCR also exacted a promise from Hà Nội to stem the flow of illegal departures and to establish a program of orderly departure. By 1980 and 1981 the flow of refugees leaving Vietnam fell drastically, temporarily alleviating the crisis.

In 1979 another refugee problem took on urgency. Border disputes between Vietnam and Cambodia that year led 150,000 Cambodian Khmer to cross the Thai border into UNHCR camps. By early 1980 there were an additional 500,000 to 700,000 refugees on the border.

Even in 1995, after the resettlement of nearly 480,000 Vietnamese to the United States and 210,000 to other countries around the world since 1975, the boat people still constituted the bulk of refugees in Southeast Asia: some 46,000 as of 31 January 1995. Southeast Asian governments, with UNHCR cooperation, announced their intentions to close the camps, which safeguarded over 840,000 Vietnamese who fled their homeland after 1975. A lucky few would receive offers to resettle in the West; most would be compelled to return to Vietnam. The possibility of violence over forced repatriation of the remaining refugees was a source of concern for UNHCR. In many of the camps, stranded boat people said they would rather die than return to Vietnam.

In January 1996 the UNHCR said there were 39,000 Vietnamese remaining in the camps. The United Nations also announced that it would stop paying for the refugee camps and would close them all by July, a sign of its determination to end a lingering problem.

—Thomas T. Phu

References: Dalglish, Carol. *Refugees from Vietnam.* London: Macmillan, 1989.

Dougan, Clark, and David Fulghum. *The Fall of the South. The Vietnam Experience,* edited by Robert Manning. Boston: Boston Publishing, 1984.

Shenon, Philip. "Boat People Prefer Death to Homeland." *New York Times* (16 March 1995).

United Nations High Commissioner for Refugees. *Resettlement Section: Statistics Concerning Indochinese in East and South East Asia.* Geneva: United Nations, 1995.

U.S. Department of State, Bureau of Public Affairs. *Indochinese Refugees.* Washington, DC: U.S. Government Printing Office, 1981.

See also: Chinese in Vietnam; FREQUENT WIND, Operation; International Rescue Committee; Sino-Vietnamese War; United Nations and the Vietnam War; Vietnamese Invasion and Occupation of Cambodia.

Regional Forces

See Territorial Forces.

Reinhardt, George Frederick

(1911–1971)

U.S. diplomat; ambassador to the Republic of Vietnam (1955–1957). Born on 21 October 1911 in Berkeley, California, G. Frederick Reinhardt received a B.A. from the University of California in 1933 and a master's degree from Cornell University in 1935. He attended the Cesare Alfien Institute of Diplomacy in Florence, Italy, before becoming a U.S. Foreign Service officer in 1937. After holding minor posts in Austria, Latvia, Estonia, and the Soviet Union, Reinhardt served with the U.S. military during the Second World War, most notably as a staff advisor to General Dwight D. Eisenhower. In 1945 Reinhardt became first secretary and consul general in Moscow, gaining valuable, early exposure to Cold War dynamics. Returning to the United States in 1948, he spent the next seven years in various capacities within the State Department.

In 1955 President Eisenhower named Reinhardt ambassador to the fledgling Republic of Vietnam (RVN). Reinhardt's chief objective, despite strong misgivings voiced by his predecessor, J. Lawton Collins, was to solidify the relationship between the United States and Prime Minister Ngô Đình Diêm. Although he was the top U.S. official in Vietnam, Reinhardt exercised little personal control over the U.S. mission. Still, by the end of his tenure in 1957, Reinhardt had fulfilled his government's wishes—the United States was firmly committed to the RVN.

Reinhardt served briefly as ambassador to the United Arab Republic and minister to Yemen before becoming ambassador to Italy in 1961. He retired in 1968 to join the Stanford Research Institute in Geneva, Switzerland. Ambassador Reinhardt died in Geneva on 22 February 1971.

—David Coffey

References: Findling, John E. *Dictionary of American Diplomatic History.* New York: Greenwood Press, 1989.

Spector, Ronald H. *Advice and Support: The Early Years of the U.S. Army in Vietnam, 1941–1960.* Washington, DC: U.S. Army Center of Military History, 1983.

See also: Collins, Joseph Lawton; Eisenhower, Dwight David; Geneva Conference and Geneva Accords.

Republic of Vietnam

See Vietnam, Democratic Republic of: 1945–1954; Vietnam, Republic of: 1954–1975.

Research and Development (R&D) Field Units

U.S.-sponsored research and development initiatives in Southeast Asia. In 1961 the U.S. Defense Department Advanced Research Projects Agency established two research and development (R&D) field units in Southeast Asia: the Combat Operations Research Center (CORC) in Sài Gòn and the Combat Development and Test Center (CDTC) in Bangkok, Thailand. Both were joint and combined operations. They included personnel from all U.S. forces, as well as all forces from the host country, and British and Australian military personnel.

CORC was located at Military Assistance Command, Vietnam (MACV) headquarters. CDTC was housed at the Thai Ministry of Defense. Both units had several missions, but the primary mission of each was to conduct counterinsurgency-related R&D for U.S. forces. In addition, each unit was to conduct R&D to enhance the capabilities of the host nation's forces, the results of which did not have to be suitable for U.S. use. Although the bulk of the work of both units consisted of testing equipment developed in R&D laboratories in the United States, both also initiated projects of their own.

The CORC was intended primarily to conduct testing that required a combat environment. Early projects included the first in-country tests of the Colt AR-15 rifle, an evaluation of personnel-detection radar, and tests of the Canadian-built Caribou cargo aircraft, which had excellent short-field capabilities and was thought to be useful for delivering supplies to remote outposts.

The primary purpose of the CDTC was to conduct testing that required the Southeast Asia environment but that did not require, or could not be conducted in, a combat environment. Early projects included measurement of radio propagation characteristics

at the geomagnetic latitude of Thailand and Vietnam; tests of personnel detection devices, such as the AN/GSS-9 break-wire detector and a seismic intrusion detector; tests of a portable loudspeaker unit for propaganda purposes; and tests of U.S. military vehicles in paddy fields and rain forests. Not all CDTC activities involved hardware testing. One project involved an anthropological study of northeast Thailand near Laos to evaluate the potential for growth of an insurgency in that area.

Locally initiated projects at the CDTC included one for the Thai Army to develop a water buffalo–drawn sled to provide troops with mobility in mud flats, a magnetic detector device for rapidly inspecting sampans for concealed weapons as they floated along a canal, and an "electronic ear" to aid sentries in listening for movement of infiltrators.

Since the initial focus of the R&D field units was counterinsurgency, they became less and less relevant to U.S. forces as the war escalated to conventional levels; they continued to operate until 1971, however. The CDTC in particular added to the military capabilities of the host nation.

—Joseph P. Martino

See also: Counterinsurgency Warfare; Thailand.

Reserve Forces

President Lyndon Johnson's July 1965 decision not to call up reserve forces for service during the Vietnam War was one of the most important, fateful, and unfortunate decisions of the entire war. Johnson's decision forced the U.S. armed services, and particularly the Army, to support rapid and massive expansion without recourse to the assets in manpower, knowledge, experience, and leadership represented by the National Guard and the Army Reserve. It rendered those elements havens for draft evaders, resulting in humiliation and frustration among dedicated longtime professionals within the reserve forces. In addition, reserve force units were stripped of essential equipment to support new formations being organized to go to Vietnam in their place, so that when—much later and in small numbers—some reserve force units were called up, they were less ready and represented themselves less well than they could have done at the outset.

The military establishment had expected Johnson to approve the employment of the reserves. Secretary of Defense Robert McNamara had recommended it. Among senior military leaders only General William Westmoreland was opposed. All contingency plans for operations as extensive as the deployments then being ordered for Vietnam were based on the availability of reserve forces.

Then, at the very last moment, President Johnson drew back. Large formations were being sent to Vietnam, he told the American people; more would be required later, and they would also be sent. But reserve forces would take no part in this. Instead, draft calls would be increased to provide the needed additional manpower. For the Army, this meant growing from about 965,000 in early 1965 to more than 1,527,000 by mid-1968. The increases, as General Creighton Abrams later ruefully observed, consisted "entirely of privates and second lieutenants."

As the war went on, year after year, and the Army grew ever larger to meet insatiable demands, levels of experience and maturity in the force continued to drop, particularly among junior officers and noncommissioned officers. Further dilution resulted from the prospect of repetitive tours in Vietnam for those in the regular Army. Many, again especially among the junior leadership, came under heavy family pressure and resigned rather than go through yet another separation at risk. There was a parallel development in terms of increasing problems of poor discipline, racial strife, and drug abuse in the armed forces. The conclusion seems inescapable that there was a causal relationship between the two trend lines.

The Joint Chiefs of Staff made repeated appeals to the president and Secretary McNamara on the need to call up reserve forces. Each time they were rebuffed. It was not until early 1968, when the North Koreans seized the U.S. electronic surveillance ship *Pueblo,* and the sense of crisis caused by this action was then strongly reinforced by the Têt Offensive in Vietnam, that a small number of units from the reserve forces were brought to active duty.

In May 1968 a small number of additional units were called up, and a few were eventually dispatched to Vietnam, usually after extended periods of postmobilization training. Deployments were in some cases delayed by individual and class-action lawsuits challenging the legality of the call-ups. Eventually the Supreme Court ruled that the mobilization was legal, ending these suits. All those mobilized had been returned to inactive status by December 1969.

A subsequent assessment by the Army War College's Strategic Studies Institute concluded that, insofar as the Army was concerned, "mobilization for the Vietnam War occurred far too late to be of any political significance, and was far too small to be of any military significance."

—Lewis Sorley

References: National Guard Association of the United States. *The Abrams Doctrine: Then, Now and in the Future: A National Guard Association Symposium: Report and Transcript.* Washington, DC: National Guard Association, 1994.
Sorley, Lewis. "Creighton Abrams and Active-Reserve Integration in Wartime." *Parameters* (Summer 1991): 35–50.
Stuckey, Col. John D., and Col. Joseph H. Pistorius. *Mobilization of the Army National Guard and Army Reserve: Historical Perspective and the Vietnam War.* Carlisle Barracks, PA: Strategic Studies Institute, U.S. Army War College, 15 November 1984.
See also: Johnson, Lyndon Baines; McNamara, Robert S.; *Pueblo* Incident; Têt Offensive: Overall Strategy; Têt Offensive: The Sài Gòn Circle; United States: Army.

Revers Report
(1949)

Secret French report on policy and military strategy in Indo-China that became famous when its contents were leaked. The report was the work of French Chief of Staff General Georges Revers, picked by Premier Henri Queuille to head a fact-finding mission to Indo-China in May 1949.

The Revers Report recommended consolidating French military resources, including the evacuation of Cao Băng, in order to concentrate on defense of the vital Red River Delta area. Revers also sharply criticized the Bao Đai government for its corruption and other deficiencies and blamed French policy for leaving Bao Đai so few of the attributes of independence that he could only set up "a government composed of twenty representatives of phantom parties, the best organized of which would have difficulty in rallying twenty-five adherents."

Revers recommended strictly respecting the agreements with Bao Đai that created a Vietnamese national army, and doing away with a large number of civil servants, who seemed determined to hold on to their prerogatives regardless of the cost. These criticisms were seen as an attack on Léon Pignon in Sài Gòn.

Viêt Minh radio began broadcasting extracts of the report in August. This fact, however, was hushed up in Paris until 18 September, when police officers called to end a fight on a bus between a military man recently returned from Indo-China and two Vietnamese found several sections of the Revers Report in a briefcase in the possession of one of the latter. Investigation revealed that Revers had imprudently and unofficially given a copy of his report to a fellow officer, General Mast, whom some suspected of being Revers's candidate to replace Pignon in Sài Gòn as high commissioner. Mast had, for his part, passed along sections of the report to various Vietnamese, whence it had been conveyed to the Viêt Minh. The story was first reported in December by *Time* magazine and became known as the "affair of the generals." The scandal and its political ramifications rocked French politics for months afterward.

—Arthur J. Dommen

References: Dalloz, Jacques. *The War in Indo-China, 1945–54.* Translated by Josephine Bacon. Savage, MD: Barnes and Noble, 1990.
Gras, Général Yves. *Histoire de la Guerre d'Indochine.* Paris: Editions Denoël, 1992.
Hammer, Ellen J. *The Struggle for Indochina.* Stanford, CA: Stanford University Press, 1954.
See also: Blaizot, Roger; Indo-China War; Pignon, Léon.

Rheault, Robert B.
(1925–)

U.S. Army officer and commander of 5th Special Forces Group, 1969. Rheault was born on 31 October 1925 in Massachusetts. Graduating from West Point in 1946, he was commissioned in the infantry, eventually making his way into the Special Forces.

In the summer of 1969 Rheault was assigned to Vietnam to command the 5th Group. Soon thereafter, Thái Khắc Chuyên, a Vietnamese employed to gather cross-border intelligence, came under suspicion as being a double agent. With Colonel Rheault's knowledge and approval, members of his command murdered Chuyên. When a sergeant who was involved talked about the matter with the Central Intelligence Agency (CIA), things started to come unraveled. General Creighton Abrams, then American commander in Vietnam, summoned Rheault to Sài Gòn. Rheault maintained there was no truth to rumors that Chuyên had been killed, insisting that he was instead on a special mission. When officers of Rheault's command confessed the murder to Army criminal investigators, Rheault was exposed as a liar. Abrams relieved him of command, and soon thereafter court-martial charges were brought against Rheault and others.

The defendants were able to generate enough political pressure to cause President Richard Nixon to have the charges against them dismissed. Colonel Rheault was then offered another assignment but elected to retire instead. "I approved it," he later said of the murder in an oral history interview. "I take responsibility for it." But he continued to argue that what he had done was proper and appropriate.

—Lewis Sorley

References: Rheault, Col. Robert B. Oral History Interviews. Carlisle Barracks, PA: U.S. Army Military History Institute, 1987, 1988.
Simpson, Col. Charles M., III. *Inside the Green Berets.* New York: Berkeley Books, 1984.
Sorley, Lewis. *Thunderbolt: General Creighton Abrams and the Army of His Times.* New York: Simon & Schuster, 1992.
See also: Abrams, Creighton; Atrocities during the Vietnam War; Nixon, Richard Milhous; United States: Special Forces.

Richardson, John H.
(1913–)

U.S. Central Intelligence Agency (CIA) station chief in Sài Gòn, 1962–1963.

Hammond Richardson had served in Greece and the Philippines prior to his 1963 posting to Sài Gòn. He developed a close relationship with Republic of Vietnam (RVN) President Ngô Đình Diêm and his brother Ngô Đình Nhu. Nevertheless, Richardson and William Colby laid the groundwork for the coup against Diêm during the summer of 1963. In his reports to Washington, Richardson expressed doubt that the RVN could survive under Diêm and argued for covert U.S. assistance in carrying out the coup.

As a result of his close ties to Nhu, he was mistrusted by the RVN generals conspiring against Diêm, so Lucien Conein acted as the go-between. Reporting the situation in August, Richardson noted that the Ngô family was determined to hold out but that the conspiracy would succeed. But experiencing second thoughts about the coup, Richardson changed his instructions to Conein. When Ambassador Henry Cabot Lodge discovered this, he ordered Conein to report directly to him about discussions with the conspirators. Richardson's changing position, coupled with his still-close ties with the Diêm regime, led Lodge to request Richardson's recall. Richardson left Sài Gòn on 5 October 1963.

—Robert G. Mangrum

References: Hammer, Ellen J. *A Death in November: America in Vietnam 1963.* New York: Oxford University Press, 1987.
Karnow, Stanley. *Vietnam: A History.* New York: Viking Press, 1983.
Rust, William J. *Kennedy in Vietnam.* New York: Charles Scribner's Sons, 1985.
See also: Conein, Lucien Emile; Lodge, Henry Cabot, Jr.; Ngô Đình Diêm; Ngô Đình Nhu.

Ridgway, Matthew B.
(1895–1993)

U.S. Army general and chief of staff, 1953–1955. Born at Fort Monroe, Virginia, on 3 March 1895, Matthew B. Ridgway graduated from West Point in 1917 and spent all of World War I at a border post. After the war he returned to West Point as an instructor. In 1925 he graduated from the Infantry School; he then served in various posts in the United States and overseas. In 1935 he graduated from the Command and General Staff School; two years later he graduated from the Army War College. In July 1939 he was promoted to lieutenant colonel. In December 1941 Ridgway was a temporary colonel and in January 1942 a temporary brigadier general. He then took over command of the 82d Infantry Division and oversaw its conversion to the 82d Airborne Division. In early 1943 he led the division to the Mediterranean and dropped with it into Sicily (July 1943), led elements of the 82d at Salerno (September 1943), and parachuted with his troops into France as part of the D-day invasion (6 June 1944). Ridgway led the XVII Airborne Corps in the unsuccessful MARKET-GARDEN Offensive to take Arnheim, The Netherlands. Participating in the Rhineland and Ruhr campaigns, he was promoted to lieutenant general in June 1945. After holding other commands, in August 1949 Ridgway became Army deputy chief of staff. During the Korean War he took over command of Eighth Army (December 1950), reorganizing United Nations (UN) forces in the midst of a Chinese offensive. In April 1951 President Harry Truman appointed Ridgway to take the place of fired UN commander General Douglas MacArthur. Truman selected Ridgway to take the place of retiring General Dwight Eisenhower as North Atlantic Treaty Organization (NATO) supreme Allied commander, Europe, and he was promoted to general (May 1952). In October 1953 Ridgway returned to the United States as chief of staff of the Army.

Ridgway opposed U.S. involvement in France's colonial war in Indo-China. When Secretary of State John Foster Dulles and Chairman of the Joint Chiefs of Staff Admiral Arthur Radford urged intervention during the Điên Biên Phu crisis, Ridgway advised against rashness. Remembering the protracted Korean conflict, Ridgway criticized Operation VULTURE's proposed U.S. air strikes against Viêt Minh positions, since he believed ground operations would inevitably follow. He argued that between five and ten combat divisions with supporting engineering units would be required to root out the foe. Moreover, he pointed out necessities like huge construction expenses, home front mobilization, and increased conscription of draftees. The political nature of the war, Ridgway said, would mean an extended commitment. His arguments influenced President Dwight D. Eisenhower's decision against intervention in 1954.

Ridgway recognized the problems inherent in the defense doctrine of "massive retaliation" and was a chief spokesman for the concept of "flexible response." He remained skeptical of U.S. Vietnam policy and served as one of President Lyndon Johnson's senior advisors known as the "Wise Men." He died on 26 July 1993 in Fox Chapel, Pennsylvania.

—Rodney J. Ross and Spencer C. Tucker

References: Dupuy, Trevor N., Curt Johnson, and David L. Bongard. *The Harper Encyclopedia of Military Biography.* New York: HarperCollins, 1992.

Halberstam, David. *The Best and the Brightest.* Greenwich, CT: Fawcett, 1973.

Ridgway, Matthew. *Soldier: The Memoirs of Matthew B. Ridgway.* New York: Harper and Brothers, 1956.

Spector, Ronald H. *Advice and Support: The Early Years, 1941–1960.* Washington, DC: U.S. Army Center of Military History, 1983.

See also: Eisenhower, Dwight David; Johnson, Lyndon Baines; Mac-Arthur, Douglas; Radford, Arthur W.; Truman, Harry S; VULTURE, Operation; "Wise Men."

Rifles

During the Indo-China War, French forces used a variety of rifles. These included the German 8-mm 98K as well as U.S.-made .30-caliber M1 Garands, and M1 and M2 carbines. During the latter part of France's involvement in Indo-China, the standard rifle was the 7.5-mm rifle M1949 (MAS) (designation for St. Etienne Arsenal).

Well made and reliable, the M1949 is an excellently designed combination of previously proven ideas and new innovations. The M1949 is a gas-operated semiautomatic weapon chambered for the French 7.5-mm M1929 cartridge. It is fed by a ten-round detachable box magazine, is 43.3 inches in length, and weighs 10.4 pounds. Its muzzle velocity is 2,705 feet per second. Although not issued with a bayonet, the M1949 features an integral grenade launcher as well as mounting grooves for detachable telescopic sights.

Combat experiences in Vietnam spurred a rapid evolution in U.S. infantry rifles. Early military advisors in Southeast Asia were issued a variety of World War II and Korean War vintage weapons, including the .30-caliber M1 and M2 carbines and the .45-caliber M1A1 Thompson and M3A1 submachine guns.

As U.S. involvement in Vietnam escalated, the American military adopted the 7.62-mm M14 rifle as its standard rifle. Based on the .30-caliber M1 Garand action, the M14 features a number of improvements. Chambered for the 7.62-mm North Atlantic Treaty Organization (NATO) cartridge, the M14 is capable of both semiautomatic and automatic fire. Although retaining the Garand's basic action, the M14 features an improved gas system and a detachable 20-round magazine, increasing both rate of fire and accuracy.

A total of 1,381,581 M14s were produced by Harrington and Richardson Arms Company, Thompson Products, Winchester-Western Arms Division of Olin Mathieson Corporation, and the Springfield Armory. The M14 is 44.14 inches long, weighs 8.7 pounds, and achieves a muzzle velocity of 2,800 feet per second. Replaced in the Air Force and Army with the M16 and M16A1, the M14 continued service with a number of Marine Corps units.

In the late 1950s Eugene Stoner and the Armalite Corporation developed a new weapon, the AR-15 rifle. After obtaining manufacturing rights from Armalite, Colt's Patent Fire Arms Manufacturing Company began producing it for the U.S. government in the early 1960s. Adopted as the 5.56-mm rifle M16, the new weapon exhibited a number of advanced innovations, including an improved gas system and reduced weight and caliber.

The M16 and M16A1 select-fire weapons introduced the smaller 5.56-mm (.223-caliber) cartridge. The M16A1 is 39 inches long, weighs 6.3 pounds without its 20-round detachable box magazines, and produces a muzzle velocity of 3,250 feet per second.

The M16 had originally been developed for air base security and not as an infantry weapon. Consequently, when first introduced into field service in Vietnam it evidenced a number of shortcomings. Its susceptibility to jamming under adverse conditions earned the M16 the mistrust of troops in the field. Modifications to the cartridge and to the weapon itself, as well as improved training, resulted in a greatly improved rifle, which was then re-designated the M16A1. Advantages of the M16A1 include its light weight—reducing fatigue among troops carrying it—and the reduced cartridge size, permitting larger quantities of ammunition to be carried in the field.

The Viêt Minh used a variety of rifles of varying origin. These included World War II and older weapons. At the end of 1945, the Viêt Minh acquired more than 30,000 Japanese 6.5-mm and 7.7-mm small arms. They also purchased American-manufactured small arms from the Chinese Nationalists.

During the Vietnam War Viêt Công and People's Army of Vietnam (PAVN) arms ranged from modern Soviet and Chinese assault rifles to crudely fashioned single-shot weapons. As during the war with France, Communist forces in Vietnam utilized any weapons available. These included French Model 49 and Chinese Type 50 submachine guns, World War II vintage German 98Ks, Soviet Model 44s, and captured U.S. weapons.

Two weapons most associated with Communist forces in Vietnam are the Simonov SKS carbine and the Kalashnikov AK47 assault rifle. Both are of Soviet design and were produced by both Soviet bloc countries and the People's Republic of China. Simple and robust, they are ideal for issue to poorly trained troops in adverse conditions.

The semiautomatic Simonov SKS carbine is equipped with a folding bayonet and like the AK47 is chambered for the intermediate-sized 7.62-mm M1943 cartridge. It is fed by a ten-round nondetachable box magazine, is 40.16 inches long, and weighs 8.8 pounds. The muzzle velocity is 2,410 feet per second.

The selective-fire 7.62-mm Automat Kalashnikov assault rifle was issued in a number of variations. The original AK design, commonly known as the AK47, is composed predominantly of milled steel components and was issued with either wooden or folding metal stocks. The later AKM is a modification of the AK47, differing mainly in the extensive use of stamped metal in its construction. Both weapons utilize a 30-round detachable box magazine, are 34.25 inches long, and produce a muzzle velocity of 2,410 feet per second. The construction changes, however, reduced the AK47's 10.58-pound weight to the AKM's 8.87 pounds, which was a significant improvement.

—Jeff Kinard

References: Chant, Christopher, ed. *How Weapons Work.* London: Marshall Cavendish, 1976.

A member of the U.S. 1st Battalion, 5th Infantry Regiment, 25th Infantry Division readies his rifle as he peers cautiously into a tunnel during an ambush patrol against the Việt Công on the outskirts of Cu Chi. Combat experiences in Vietnam spurred a rapid evolution of U.S. infantry rifles. As U.S. involvement in Vietnam escalated, the American military adopted the M16 (pictured here) as its standard infantry firearm.

Sgt. David Weiner, a still photographer with the U.S. Marine photography laboratory at Phú Bài, prepares to go into the field with a company in the 3d Division. Weiner is carrying an M14, an earlier rifle that many considered superior to the Vietnam-era M16.

Flayderman, Norm. *Flayderman's Guide to Antique American Firearms . . . and their Values.* 5th ed. Fort Lauderdale, FL: n.p., 1994.

Rosa, Joseph G., and Robin May. *An Illustrated History of Guns and Small Arms.* London: Peerage Books, 1984.

Smith, W. H. B., revised by Joseph E. Smith. *Small Arms of the World.* 9th ed. Harrisburg, PA: Stackpole, 1969.

See also: Grenades, Hand: Allied and Democratic Republic of Vietnam; Grenades, Launched: Allied and Democratic Republic of Vietnam; Machine Guns, Allied and People's Army of Vietnam; Pistols.

Rigault de Genouilly, Charles
(1807–1873)

French admiral who in 1857 carried out the first major European military incursion into Vietnam. Charles Rigault de Genouilly was born on 12 April 1807. He rose through naval ranks, and in the spring of 1847 he commanded one of two French ships that Admiral Cécille sent to Tourane (now Đà Nẵng) to rescue Catholic missionary Dominique Lefèbvre. On

15 April 1847 these French ships sank three Vietnamese vessels at Tourane.

Rigault de Genouilly came to command French units at Sebastopol during the Crimean War. Sent to China in 1856 to command French naval forces there, the next year he participated in a joint operation with British forces against the Chinese port of Canton. After bombarding that port, Rigault de Genouilly personally led a landing party in taking the town (December 1857). The combined forces then attacked Tien-Tsin, at which point the Chinese government agreed to open six ports to international trade under European control (Treaty of Tientsin, 27 June 1858).

The success of the China operations freed the French China Squadron for employment elsewhere. Both Spain and France sought redress from Vietnam for the execution of missionaries, and Emperor Napoleon III hoped to secure a port there in the fashion of Hong Kong. It was no accident that the French chose to penetrate southern Vietnam first; it was the newest part of the country and its inhabitants were not as wedded to Vietnamese institutions. Indeed, the French conquest proved more difficult the farther it moved north.

In January 1858 Rigault de Genouilly received instructions issued in Paris the previous November. Operations in Indo-China were to be only an appendix, and entirely subordinate, to those in China, but Paris instructed him to halt persecution and ensure toleration of Catholics in Indo-China. Paris thought this could best be achieved by occupying Tourane, mistakenly considered the key to the entire kingdom. Future Indo-China operations would be entirely at Rigault's discretion.

On 31 August 1858 Rigault de Genouilly's squadron of 14 vessels and 3,000 men anchored off Tourane. He believed that decisive military action would bring fruitful negotiations with the Vietnamese. On 1 September he landed his troops, including 300 Filipino troops sent by Spain. These stormed the Tourane forts after only perfunctory resistance, taking them and the port and inaugurating the first phase of the French conquest of Indo-China.

Within a few months, heat, disease, and a lack of supplies forced the French from Tourane. Admiral Rigault de Genouilly then shifted his attack southward to the fishing village of Sài Gòn, selected because of its proximity and the importance of the rice trade. It fell to the French after a brief fight on 17 February 1859. This attack was subsequently criticized in Paris, and in November 1859 Rigault de Genouilly was replaced by Admiral Page, who was instructed by Paris not to seek territorial concessions but to sign a treaty with the Vietnamese that would guarantee religious liberties and French consuls in the major Vietnamese ports. In 1867 and again in 1870 Admiral Rigault de Genouilly served as France's minister of marine. He died on 4 April 1873.

—Spencer C. Tucker

References: Jenkins, E. H. *A History of the French Navy.* Annapolis, MD: Naval Institute Press, 1973.

Lê Thành Khôi. *Histoire de Viêt Nam des origines à 1858.* Paris: Sudestasie, 1981.

Taboulet, Georges. "Les origines immédiates de l'intervention de la France en Indochine (1857–1858)." *Revue d'histoire des colonies françaises* 344 (1954–1955): 281–302.

Thompson, Virginia. *French Indo-China.* New York: Octagon Books, 1968.

See also: French Indo-China; Lefèbvre, Dominique; Napoleon III.

Riverine Craft

Throughout the Indo-China and Vietnam Wars navies played vital roles in seaborne and coastal operations. During the Vietnam War perhaps the most important role played by the Republic of Vietnam (RVN) and U.S. navies was in the use of naval craft to conduct riverine ("brown-water") operations along the inland waterways of Vietnam. All riverine craft involved had one common prerequisite: shallow draft. Without this no boat could navigate rivers and especially canals during the dry season.

To implement Operation GAME WARDEN and SEALORDS (Southeast Asia Lake Ocean River Delta Strategy) the U.S. Navy's riverine force, the Mobile Riverine Force (MRF), required small, heavily armed shallow-draft boats. The river patrol boat (PBR) fit these requirements and became the workhorse of the River Patrol Force. The PBR was adapted from a 1965 design by the founder of the Hatteras Yacht Company, Willis Slane. It appeared in two versions: the MK-I and the MK-II. Built by United Boatbuilders, the MK-I consisted of a 31-foot fiberglass hull with two diesel-powered water jets instead of propellers. The MK-I had a beam of 10 feet 10 inches and displaced 14,500 pounds with a draft of 2 feet 2 inches; however, when operating at high speeds up to 30 knots or on "the step" (when planing), the PBR had only a 9-inch draft. About 160 MK-Is were built in 1966. The MK-IIs, built in 1967, had only three design modifications from the MK-I. The length was increased to 31 feet 11 inches and the beam to 11 feet 2 inches. Displacement also increased to 16,000 pounds; however, this had minimal effect on the boat's speed and draft. Both versions of the PBR contained the same weaponry. The main armament consisted of twin .50-caliber machine guns mounted in a turret forward and a single .50-caliber machine gun aft. In addition, several starboard and port mounts existed for M60 machine guns; a 40-mm automatic grenade launcher was also on board. Although naval designers placed small amounts of ceramic armor at weapons stations and the coxswain's "flat," firepower and speed were this small boat's advantages.

The fast patrol craft (PCF), although not initially selected for riverine operations, proved valuable along the larger rivers during SEALORDS, which enabled the shallower-draft PBRs to move onto smaller waterways. The Navy adapted the PCF, or Swift boat, from the Sewart Seacraft Company vessel used by oil companies to transport crews to and from offshore rigs in the Gulf of Mexico. From 1965 to 1967 the Navy had two versions constructed, which included the MK-I and MK-II. The MK-I was about 50 feet in length, had a beam of 13 feet 1 inch, and displaced 19 tons, yet had a draft of only 3 feet 6 inches. This diesel-powered, dual-propeller–driven boat could make 25 knots. About 104 MK-Is were built between 1965 and 1966. The MK-II, of which only eight were constructed, had only three modifications: The length was increased to 51 feet 4 inches, the beam to 13 feet 7 inches, and the displacement to 19.5 tons. The armament consisted of a .50-caliber machine gun mounted atop an 81-mm mortar aft and twin .50-caliber machine guns mounted in a turret on top of the pilot house.

The only craft designed keel-up for use in Vietnam was the assault patrol boat (ASPB). The ASPB, the MRF's destroyer and minesweeper, was about 50 feet long, had a beam of 15 feet 3 inches, and displaced 28 tons. Equipped with diesel engines, the ASPB could make 15 knots. The Navy had over 30 of these boats built and shipped to Vietnam by late 1967. The boat's armament included a 20-mm cannon mounted in a turret forward, an 81-mm mortar aft, one .50-caliber machine gun amidships, and one aft.

The bulk of the MRF's brown-water fleet were conversions of the World War II LCM-6, or mechanized landing craft. The three predominant versions of the LCM-6 included the monitor, the ATC (armored troop carrier), and the CCB (command-and-communications boat). All of the conversions had two propellers powered by diesel engines that gave them a top speed of 6 knots. Additionally, although each conversion displaced different tonnage, they all drew 3 to 3 feet 5 inches of water. The monitor was 60 feet long, had a beam of 17 feet 6 inches, and displaced 75 tons. This craft had an 81-mm mortar in a pit amidships, and aft two .50-caliber and M60 machine guns along with one 20-mm cannon. A turret forward housed a 40-mm cannon and a .50-caliber machine gun. A modified monitor, dubbed a "Zippo," mounted two flamethrowers forward. The ATCs were 56 feet long and had a beam of 17 feet 6 inches. Each ATC displaced 66 tons and could carry 40 troops. The ATC's armament included one 20-mm cannon, two .50-caliber machine guns, and either four .30-caliber or four M60 machine guns. The CCBs maintained the same specifications of the monitor except for the mortar pit amidships. Instead the CCBs had radar and radio equipment. Other LCM-6 conversions included helipad craft and tankers for the brown-water fleet. All of the conversions had standoff armor to predetonate incoming rockets.

The patrol air cushion vehicle (PACV) was an experimental craft adopted for naval purposes. This strange contraption for Vietnam resembled hover ferries used to cross the English Channel. It had a length of 39 feet and a beam of 22 feet 9 inches. The PACV displaced 15,680 pounds and, when airborne, had a hull-borne clearance of 4 feet. Installed with a gas turbine engine that operated both the air screw and lift fan, the PACV could easily reach 70 knots. For armament the PACV had two .50-caliber machine guns above the pilot house.

Until Vietnamization, the most common boats in the Vietnamese Navy's (VNN's) river fleet or River Assault Groups (RAGs) included STCAN/FOMs (Services Techniques des Construction et Armes Navales/France Outre Mere), LCVPs (personnel landing craft vehicles), LCM-6s or LCM-8 conversions such as monitors, and RPCs (river patrol craft). The FOMs remained from French involvement in Vietnam and, following French withdrawal, became part of the VNN. The FOM was 36 feet long and could make 10 knots. Its armament included one .50-caliber machine gun forward and three .30-caliber machine guns dispersed amidships and aft. The converted LCVP was 35 feet 9 inches in length and had a beam of 10 feet 6 inches. Displacing 26,600 pounds, the LCVP could make 9 knots and drew only 3 feet 5 inches of water. Each LCVP would have a variety of weapons such as .30-caliber and .50-caliber machine guns. In an attempt to replace the FOMs, 34 RPCs were built in 1965. They had a length of 35 feet 10 inches and beam of 10 feet 10 inches. The RPC's two diesel-driven propellers enabled the boat to navigate at 14 knots with a displacement of 26,000 pounds, drawing only 3 feet 6 inches of water. Each RPC had either one set of twin .30-caliber and a set of .50-caliber machine guns or two sets of twin .30-caliber machine guns.

Although both navies used and experimented with other craft, these represent the primary craft used by the American and Vietnamese navies.

—R. Blake Dunnavent

References: Cutler, Thomas J. *Brown Water, Black Berets: Coastal and Riverine Warfare in Vietnam.* Annapolis, MD: Naval Institute Press, 1988.
Marolda, Edward J. *By Sea, Air, and Land: An Illustrated History of the U.S. Navy and the War in Southeast Asia.* Washington, DC: Naval Historical Center, 1994.
Schreadley, R. L. *From the Rivers to the Sea: The United States Navy in Vietnam.* Annapolis, MD: Naval Institute Press, 1992.
U.S. Naval History Division. *Riverine Warfare: Vietnam.* Washington, DC: U.S. Government Printing Office, 1972.
See also: GAME WARDEN, Operation; MARKET TIME, Operation; Mekong Delta; Mobile Riverine Force; Riverine Warfare; SEALORDS (Southeast Asia Lake Ocean River Delta Strategy); United States: Navy; Vietnam, Republic of: Navy (VNN).

Riverine Warfare

The contest for control of the waterways of South Vietnam. The Mekong Delta was the geostrategic center of the Republic of Vietnam (RVN). With an area of 40,000 square kilometers and nearly 8 million inhabitants, it constituted almost one-fourth of the country's territory and held about half of its population. Even more importantly, the Delta was the agricultural production center of the entire region—the rice bowl of Southeast Asia.

The Delta is a flat alluvial plain created by the Mekong River and its many tributaries. Only one hard-surfaced road, Highway 4, traversed the Delta south of Sài Gòn. On the other hand, the region had some 2,400 kilometers of navigable natural waterways, interconnected by another 4,000 kilometers of human-made canals of varying width, depth, and condition. It was a perfect area for river-borne operations.

Although virtually no People's Army of Vietnam (PAVN) units operated in the Mekong Delta, it was a major Viêt Công (VC) stronghold. Home of the VC 9th Division, in mid-1966 the area held an estimated 28 VC battalions and 69 separate companies, totaling some 82,500 troops. Almost one-third of all VC actions against the RVN took place in the Delta, and the VC controlled an estimated 24.6 percent of the region's population. As part of their overall strategy, the VC attempted to cut off the flow of rice from the Delta.

The Delta constituted the Army of the Republic of Vietnam's (ARVN's) IV Corps Tactical Zone. Three ARVN divisions—the 7th, 9th, and 21st—were stationed there. The RVN Navy (VNN) also operated six river assault groups and 11 coastal groups in the waters in and adjacent to the Delta. The RVN river assault groups were patterned directly after the Dinassauts, operated by the French in the Indo-China War.

The American military first entered the Delta in 1957 when U.S. Navy advisors replaced their French counterparts. By 1966 no American ground units were yet in the Delta, but the U.S. Army's 13th Combat Aviation Brigade provided support to the ARVN. The U.S. Navy had two task forces operating in Delta waters. Task Force (TF) 115, under Operation MARKET TIME, patrolled the coastal areas to prevent VC infiltration and resupply from the sea. In Operation GAME WARDEN, TF 116, also known as the River Patrol Force, worked the rivers. Operating with a Navy helicopter attack squadron, SEAL teams, and a minesweeping division, the River Patrol Force conducted reconnaissance patrols, salvage operations, day and night ambushes, and hit-and-run raids.

The concept of a joint Army-Navy riverine force for the Delta emerged from a March 1966 study by the Military Assistance Command, Vietnam (MACV), entitled *Delta Mobile Afloat Force Concept and Requirements*. Its missions were to secure U.S. base areas and lines of communication, conduct offensive operations against VC forces in the area, isolate the most heavily populated and key food-producing areas from the VC, interdict VC supply routes, and provide reserve and reaction forces for ARVN units operating in the IV Corps Tactical Zone.

One of the principal reasons behind the concept of the Mobile Riverine Force (as it came to be designated) was the lack of a suitable land base area for a large U.S. ground force in the densely populated Delta. The MACV plan called for the establishment of a relatively small land base, created by dredging. It would house units of the force's support structure and equipment the force would not need while afloat. In June 1966 General William Westmoreland personally selected a site near My Tho for the new base, which was christened Đồng Tâm.

The planners felt that at least a brigade-sized unit was needed in the Delta. The original concept called for a force consisting of two river assault groups (later called river assault squadrons), supported by five self-propelled barracks ships. The plan was approved by the Department of Defense on 5 July 1966, but at the same time, Secretary of Defense Robert McNamara decided to cut the number of barracks ships from five to two.

As a result of McNamara's decision, the authorized force had afloat berthing space for only one of a brigade's three maneuver battalions. The Navy created berthing space for another battalion by providing a towed barracks barge. The force, however, could still maintain only two battalions afloat. As a result, the brigade habitually operated with only two battalions, while the third secured the land base at Đồng Tâm.

The Army element of the Mobile Riverine Force (MRF) was the 2d Brigade of the 9th Infantry Division. Under its first commander, Col. William B. Fulton, the 2d Brigade consisted of the 3d and 4th Battalions, 47th Infantry Regiment; the 3d Battalion, 60th Infantry; and the 3d Battalion, 39th Artillery—a towed 105-mm unit. The 9th Infantry Division was activated specifically for the

Vietnam War at Fort Riley, Kansas, on 1 February 1966. Its lead elements arrived in Vietnam on 16 December 1966.

Initially the division's 1st and 3d Brigades operated from Bearcat, just south of Sài Gòn and north of the Mekong Delta, in the III Corps Tactical Zone. The 2d Brigade operated from Đồng Tâm.

The Navy component of the Mobile Riverine Force was River Assault Flotilla 1, also known as the Riverine Assault Force and Task Force 117. Under the initial command of Capt. Wade C. Wells, TF 117 consisted of the 9th and 11th River Assault Squadrons, which were further organized into river assault divisions. A river assault squadron could carry a battalion, and a river assault division could carry a company. By the time the Mobile Riverine Force was disbanded, TF 117 had grown to four river assault squadrons, with the addition of the 13th and the 15th.

A 400-man river assault squadron was a powerful flotilla. It consisted of up to three command-and-communications boats (CCBs), five monitors, 26 armored troop carriers (ATCs), 16 assault support patrol boats (ASPBs), and one refueler, plus a supporting underwater demolition team (UDT), an explosive ordnance detachment (EOD), and a riverine survey team.

During the life of the Mobile Riverine Force, many local innovations improved the equipment and operating procedures. Perhaps the most important was the mounting of artillery on barges, which greatly increased the mobility—and therefore the operational range—of the brigade's artillery battalion. Each barge carried two 105-mm howitzers, their crews, and basic loads of ammunition. Field artillery requires stationary firing platforms and fixed aiming points, which meant that the barges had to be beached along a river or canal bank in order to fire effectively. This did, however, allow for direct support fire to ground units once they were landed. Other important innovations included the building of helicopter landing platforms on the ATCs and the use of helicopter landing barges.

The Mobile Riverine Force was not a true joint task force with a single commander. According to *MACV Planning Directive 12-66* of 10 December 1966, Army units of the force came under the commanding general of II Field Force, who exercised operational control through the designated subordinated headquarters, in this case the 9th Infantry Division. Navy units of the force came directly under the operational control of the commander, U.S. Naval Forces in Vietnam. The document further stipulated that the relationship between Army and Navy units would be one of coordination, with the Navy providing close support to the Army. Although in U.S. practice the doctrinal concept of close support implies that the supported force directs operations, the determination of mission and area of operation of the Mobile Riverine Force was a constant source of friction between the Army and Navy component commanders.

In practice, the target and area of operations usually was selected by the commander of the 2d Brigade or a higher-echelon Army commander. The 2d Brigade and TF 117 commanders then agreed on the general timing and task organization of the mission. At that point a joint planning staff developed the scheme of maneuver in the target area. From there they worked backwards to work out the details of the assault or landing, the water movement, and the loading phases. Then the final operations plan was briefed to the two commanders, usually aboard the MRF's flagship, the landing ship *Benewah.*

The operations of the MRF consisted of coordinated airmobile, ground, and waterborne attacks, supported by air and naval forces. Once the force made contact with the VC, commanders quickly moved to cut off possible escape routes by moving units into blocking positions on the VC flanks and rear. After directing artillery fire, helicopter gunship fire, and tactical air strikes into the VC positions, ground troops then swept the area. During the MRF's first year of operations, these tactics proved very effective. The VC often were disoriented and caught by surprise. Prior to the arrival of the MRF in the Delta, the VC had anticipated attacks primarily coming from the land and air. Their defenses, therefore, almost always faced away from the water.

Over time the VC learned to deal with the new situation. While under way, the principal security threats to the MRF came from command-detonated mines in the waterway and ambushes along the shore, with heavy fire from recoilless rifles and B-40 rockets. While anchored, the most critical threats were from floating mines, swimmer saboteurs, and suicide attack boats. The MRF developed security measures to deal with all of these.

During operations all troop movements were controlled and coordinated from the joint tactical operations center on the flagship. The Army element of the staff normally was supervised by the brigade executive officer. The brigade commander operated with his forward command group from a firebase. During daylight hours, they were usually aloft in a command-and-control helicopter. Battalion command posts were divided into forward and rear tactical operations centers. The battalion commander operated from the forward command post aboard the command ship of the river assault squadron. The battalion rear command posts were controlled by the executive officers and located aboard ship at the mobile riverine floating base.

Operating in a riverine environment presented special challenges. Salt water in the lower reaches of the Delta caused maintenance problems, often corroding weapons, especially the steel links of belted machine gun ammunition. Operations had to be planned around such constraints as tides, water depth, water obstructions, bridge clearances, and the suitability of river and canal banks for landing sites.

Wet and marshy terrain also caused immersion foot, dermatophytosis, and other foot problems. These diseases increased at high rates whenever the troops operated on land for more than two continuous days. Soldiers in the Delta almost never wore socks. Once a soldier got into the water—which was unavoidable—wet socks inside his boots would keep his feet wet that much longer after he got out of the water. It was simply impossible to carry enough dry socks and impractical to stop to change socks every time feet got wet.

The main body of the 2d Brigade arrived in Vietnam on 31 January 1967. On 15 February the VC attacked an oceangoing freighter on the Lòng Tào, the main shipping channel between Vũng Tàu on the coast and Sài Gòn. In reaction to this attack, the 3d Battalion, 47th Infantry was ordered to conduct operations in the Rừng Sát Special Zone, a tangled area of mangrove swamp at the northeastern corner of the Delta. The resulting operation, RIVER RAIDER I, was the first joint operation between U.S. Army and Navy units that would later form the MRF. The operation lasted from 16 February to 20 March, with Army units supported by River Assault Division 91 of River Assault Squadron 9.

The 2d Brigade's headquarters became operational at Đồng Tâm on 10 March. A month later, the first of the river assault divisions moved to Đồng Tâm and began operations with the 3d Battalion, 47th Infantry. The Mobile Riverine Force became fully operational on 1 June 1967. Between then and March 1968 the MRF conducted a series of wide-ranging riverine and combined airmobile and riverine operations designated CORONADO I through XI.

The Navy component of the Mobile Riverine Force continued to grow. By the fall of 1968 it reached its full strength of four river assault squadrons, including 184 river assault craft, four barracks ships, two barracks barges, three repair ships, two support ships, and two resupply ships, as well as various other craft. About the same time, the MRF was reorganized into two Mobile Riverine Groups. Group Alpha had five river assault divisions and Group Bravo had three.

In mid-1968 the 9th Infantry Division underwent a major change in its mission. On 25 July the division headquarters relocated from Bearcat to Đồng Tâm and the other two brigades also moved into the Delta. For the first time, an entire U.S. infantry division was in the Mekong Delta. As part of this shift, the 2d Brigade's mission changed to an almost exclusive focus on the pacification of Kiên Hòa Province. The 2d Brigade finally received its third maneuver battalion afloat, but the newly restricted area of operations greatly reduced the mobility advantages demonstrated during the wider-ranging operations of the MRF's first year. Mobile Riverine Group Alpha continued to support the 2d Brigade in Kiên Hòa Province, while Mobile Riverine Group Bravo carried out operations in the southern Delta with units of the 2d, 3d, and 4th Battalions of the Republic of Vietnam Marine Corps.

In November 1968 Mobile Riverine Group Bravo initiated the first of the SEALORDS (Southeast Asia Lake Ocean River Delta Strategy) operations, designed to keep Communist forces away from the rivers and canals in western Long An and Kiên Tường Provinces. On 1 February 1969 the 25 river assault craft of River Assault Division 91 were turned over to the RVN Navy. The 9th Infantry Division, meanwhile, was informed that it was to be the first division withdrawn from Vietnam, with the 2d Brigade to be the first unit deactivated. As part of the Vietnamization process, TF 117 started turning over the rest of its boats to the RVN Navy. On 25 August 1969 the Mobile Riverine Force, and with it River Flotilla 1 and the 2d Brigade, 9th Division, were deactivated.

On both tactical and operational levels the Mobile Riverine Force was one of the success stories of the Vietnam War. While it operated, the MRF effectively wrested control of the northern Delta from the VC and opened Highway 4 for the first time since 1965, which in turn freed the flow of agricultural products from the Delta for both export and domestic use.

One intriguing question remains about the composition of the Mobile Riverine Force. By doctrine, the U.S. Marine Corps is organized and trained for amphibious warfare missions. It seems odd then that U.S. Marine units in Vietnam were deployed in the mountainous north of the country and that a brigade of a newly raised Army division was assigned the amphibious mission that is supposed to be the Marine Corps' raison d'être.

—David T. Zabecki

References: Croizat, Victor. *The Brown Water Navy: The River and Coastal War in Indochina and Vietnam, 1940–1972.* Dorset, UK: Blandford Press, 1984.
Cutler, Thomas J. *Brown Water, Black Berets: Coastal and Riverine Operations in Vietnam.* Annapolis, MD: Naval Institute Press, 1988.
Fulton, William B. *Riverine Operations, 1966–1969.* Washington, DC: Vietnam Studies, Office of the Chief of Military History, 1985.
Sheppard, Don. *"Riverine": A Brown Water Sailor in the Delta, 1967.* Novato, CA: Presidio Press, 1992.
See also: Dinassauts; GAME WARDEN, Operation; MARKET TIME, Operation; McNamara, Robert S.; Mobile Riverine Force; Riverine Craft; SEAL (Sea, Air, Land) Teams; SEALORDS (Southeast Asia Lake Ocean River Delta Strategy).

Rivers, L. Mendel
(1905–1970)

U.S. congressman, 1941–1970, and staunch supporter of American involvement in Vietnam. Born in Gumville, North Carolina, on 28 September 1905, L. Mendel Rivers later moved to South Carolina and in 1940 was elected to the U.S. House of Representatives as a Democrat. He was reelected to the House 15 consecutive times.

Over the years Rivers became one of the staunchest advocates of the U.S. military establishment and of escalating military procurements. As chairman of the House Armed Services Committee, he had significant influence on military legislation and appropriations. In return for his unswerving support, various administrations rewarded him with an enormous number of military installations for his district.

Rivers's views on the Vietnam War were hawkish and remained so. His only serious criticism of the war was that it had not been fought vigorously enough. After the 1968 Tết Offensive, he went so far as to recommend the use of nuclear weapons against the Democratic Republic of Vietnam (DRV). Rivers also supported the military in opposing civilian systems analysts often favored by the Department of Defense. He conducted hearings in support of an ultimately unsuccessful proposal to abolish the Office of Systems Analysis, a creation of Secretary of Defense Robert McNamara. Rivers died in Birmingham, Alabama, on 28 December 1970.

—Eric Jarvis

References: Baritz, Loren. *Backfire.* New York: Ballantine Books, 1985.
Gibbons, William Conrad. *The U.S. Government and the Vietnam War, Parts 1–3.* Princeton, NJ: Princeton University Press, 1986.
Hopkins, George W. "From Naval Pauper to Naval Power: The Development of Charleston's Metropolitan-Military Complex." In *The Martial Metropolis: U.S. Cities in War and Peace,* edited by Roger W. Lotchin. New York: Praeger, 1984.

New York Times (29 December 1970).
The Washington Post (29 December 1970).
See also: Goldwater, Barry Morris; McGee, Gale William; McNamara, Robert S.; Stennis, John Cornelius; Tết Offensive: Overall Strategy; Tết Offensive: The Sài Gòn Circle.

Road Watch Teams (RWTs)

U.S. Central Intelligence Agency (CIA)-sponsored teams monitoring North Vietnamese traffic down the Hồ Chí Minh Trail in Laos. Road Watch Teams (RWTs) originated in mid-1966 and were eventually controlled jointly by the CIA in Laos and the Military Assistance Command, Vietnam (MACV), Studies and Observations Group (SOG) in Sài Gòn.

Because of the prohibition against U.S. military personnel conducting "ground combat operations" in central and northern Laos, participants in the RWT program were indigenous Laotians. Teams were composed of 6 to 12 men each. Individual teams were sometimes inserted overland, but the usual procedure was by helicopter. Each team was assigned a Royal Laotian officer or sergeant to identify team members. The teams were not to engage in combat and had as their primary mission surveillance of the Hồ Chí Minh Trail. Their operational area ran from the southern boundary of the People's Republic of China to the northern Cambodian border.

U.S.-led reconnaissance (recon) teams from SOG's Operation 35 (Ground Studies Group) were the exception to the ban on American combat forces in Laos. By presidential order they were authorized to reconnoiter in Laos up to 20 kilometers from the Republic of Vietnam (RVN) border. Operation 35's zone of operations (code-named PRAIRIE FIRE) ran from the Demilitarized Zone (DMZ) south to the northern Cambodian border. RWTs and Operation 35 teams were purposely kept separated. RWTs operated deeper, beyond limitations set for Operation 35 in Laos. RWT members reported enemy activity via short-burst, coded radio transmissions to U.S. aircraft flying around-the-clock designated orbits over Laos. The U.S. Air Force utilized this information to conduct bombing missions against enemy truck convoys. RWTs also assessed damage from these strikes, and they aided propaganda leaflet drops over Laos. The RWT project was a model of cooperation between the U.S. Air Force, U.S. Special Forces, and the CIA.

—Harve Saal and Spencer C. Tucker

References: Saal, Harve. *MACV-Studies and Observation Group (SOG).* 4 vols. Milwaukee, WI: Jones Techno-Comm, 1990.
Secord, Richard, with Jay Wurts. *Honored and Betrayed. Irangate, Covert Affairs, and the Secret War in Laos.* New York: John Wiley & Sons, 1992.
See also: Central Intelligence Agency (CIA); Laos; STEEL TIGER, Operation; TIGER HOUND, Operation; United States: Special Forces.

Rockefeller, Nelson A.
(1908–1979)

Governor of New York, 1959–1973; vice-president of the United States, 1974–1977. Nelson Rockefeller was born on 8 July 1908 at Bar Harbor, Maine. He majored in economics at Dartmouth

College and graduated from there in 1930. One of the heirs to the vast Standard Oil fortune of John D. Rockefeller, he was determined to win distinction in the political arena, where his ultimate ambition, never attained, was to become president of the United States. A liberal Republican, he was successively coordinator of the Office of Inter-American Affairs (1940–1944); assistant secretary of state for American republics' affairs (1944–1945); chairman of the International Development Advisory Board (Point Four Program) (1950–1951); undersecretary of health, education, and welfare (1953–1954); and special assistant to the president (1954–1955). In 1958 he was elected to the first of four successive terms as governor of New York. Throughout the 1960s he was a leading candidate for the Republican presidential nomination.

A firm anti-Communist and leader of the internationalist wing of the Republican Party, believing implicitly in the prevailing Cold War orthodoxy, Rockefeller was originally a strong supporter of the U.S. commitment to Vietnam. In the 1964 election campaign he attacked President Lyndon Johnson's Vietnam policies as insufficiently firm and assertive. Rockefeller was fully supportive of the military escalation from 1965 to 1967. During the 1968 presidential campaign, Rockefeller announced that he would not attack Johnson's prosecution of the war, with which he sympathized. He did advance a program for peace, a rather impractical proposal that envisaged the supervision of Vietnam by a neutral international peacekeeping force, and free elections to decide whether or not North and South Vietnam should be reunited.

At the 1968 Republican convention both he and Richard Nixon supported and won a platform plank favoring peace negotiations. This was over the opposition of Ronald Reagan's followers, who urged a more aggressive prosecution of the war. After Nixon's election, Rockefeller loyally supported his policies toward Vietnam. In the turmoil that followed Nixon's resignation, President Gerald Ford selected Rockefeller as his vice-president, a move that angered the conservative wing of the Republican Party. Nelson Rockefeller died on 27 January 1979 of a heart attack in New York City.

—Priscilla Roberts

References: Dietz, Terry. *Republicans and Vietnam, 1961–1968*. Westport, CT: Greenwood Press, 1986.

Persico, Joseph. *The Imperial Rockefeller*. New York: Simon & Schuster, 1982.

See also: Elections, U.S.: 1968; Ford, Gerald R.; Goldwater, Barry Morris; Johnson, Lyndon Baines; Nixon, Richard Milhous; Reagan, Ronald.

Rockets

Rockets were used extensively in the Vietnam War by both Allied and Communist military forces. They were used principally in antiarmor/antibunker, artillery, and aerial ground support roles. Antiarmor rockets were employed by both sides. The United States employed M20 and M72 antiarmor weapons that fired high-explosive antitank (HEAT) rockets. The M20 was a 3.5-inch rocket launcher. It was known as the "super bazooka" because it replaced the earlier M9A1 2.36-inch bazooka of World War II fame. The M20 was in turn replaced by the M72 light antitank weapon (LAW), which was a one-man, single-shot 66-mm rocket launcher. The rockets these launchers fired were used primarily in an antibunker role.

Communist forces used the Chinese Type 51 rocket launcher modeled on the American M20 super bazooka. The 90-mm HEAT rocket this launcher fired was used in its traditional role against tanks and armored personnel carriers. Việt Công (VC) and People's Army of Vietnam (PAVN) units used artillery rockets principally because of their deficiency in field artillery early in the war. This deficiency was alleviated by the extensive employment of mortars and mines in coordination with these rockets. Rockets had the advantages of mobility and relative undetectability. Their components were of man-portable weight, and, because of their low trajectory, they were often able to escape detection by U.S. AN/MPQ-4 (Q-4) countermortar radar.

The Communists relied on three principal types of artillery rockets. The first two, the BM 14-16 and BM 21, came from the USSR and the third, the Type 63, came from China. The BM 14-16 represented an early 1950s 16-round 140-mm multiple-rocket system. The BM 21 was a 40-round 122-mm multiple-rocket system. Both systems were initially truck mounted. The Type 63 was a 12-round 107-mm multiple-rocket system. It could be either truck or towed-carriage mounted.

In guerrilla warfare, single rocket tubes, wooden stakes, and sandbags were frequently used to fire these rockets. The DKZ-B antibuilding and antipersonnel launcher, for instance, was a tripod-mounted tube from a BM 21. The Type 63 was also often fired from a single-round launcher. It was greatly favored because three could be transported as easily as one 122-mm rocket.

Such rockets were primarily area-fire weapons that were launched against towns, firebases, and airfields. Often overcaliber rockets were created by attaching larger warheads to the original assemblies. However, if properly employed, the circular error probability (CEP) of the Soviet rockets allowed them to function almost as point-attack weapons.

Aerial rockets were used exclusively by Free World forces. Between 1965 and 1973 U.S. procurement of 2.75-inch rockets reached almost 16 million units. Warhead variants included fragmentation, phosphorus, flechette, and armor piercing. Aerial Rocket Artillery (ARA) battalions were created by the U.S. Army to provide firepower support for ground operations. These battalions were originally composed of UH-1B/C helicopters, each equipped with 48 2.75-inch rockets. In 1968 the AH-1G Huey Cobra was introduced; it carried 76 rockets. These rockets contained either high-explosive or flechette (beehive) antipersonnel warheads. The early WDU-4/A warhead carried 6,000 flechettes and was later superseded by the WDU-4A/A model, which carried 2,200 heavier flechettes with better penetrative power. In 1970 these battalions were given the new designation Aerial Field Artillery (AFA).

The U.S. Navy also deployed artillery rockets aboard LSMRs (landing ships medium, rocket) and IFSs (in-shore fire support ships) in support of amphibious operations.

—Robert J. Bunker

References: Doleman, Edgar D. *Tools of War. The Vietnam Experience,* edited by Robert Manning. Boston: Boston Publishing, 1984.
Ott, David Ewing. *Field Artillery, 1954–1973.* Vietnam Studies. Washington, DC: U.S. Government Printing Office, 1975.
Robinson, Anthony, Anthony Preston, and Ian V. Hogg. *Weapons of the Vietnam War.* New York: Gallery Books, 1983.
Rosser-Owen, David. *Vietnam Weapons Handbook.* Wellingborough, Northants, UK: Patrick Stephens, 1986.
Stockholm International Peace Research Institute. *Anti-Personnel Weapons.* London: Taylor & Francis, 1978.
See also: Armor Warfare; Artillery, Allied and People's Army of Vietnam; Bombs, Dumb; Bombs, Smart (PGMs); Grenades, Hand: Allied and Democratic Republic of Vietnam; Grenades, Launched: Allied and Democratic Republic of Vietnam; Helicopters, Employment of, in Vietnam; Mortars, Allied and Democratic Republic of Vietnam.

Rogers, William Pierce

(1913–)

U.S. secretary of state, 1969–1973. William P. Rogers was born in Norfolk, New York, on 23 June 1913. In 1934 he graduated from Colgate University and in 1937 he earned a law degree at Cornell. A New York lawyer of impeccable establishment credentials, he had a long record of public service, beginning with stints as assistant district attorney in New York County (1938–1942 and 1946–1947), where he served under Thomas E. Dewey; counsel to the U.S. Senate War Investigating Committee (1947); and chief counsel to the U.S. Senate Investigations Sub-Committee of the Executive Expenditures Committee (1947–1948). At this time he first met the young Congressman Richard Nixon, with whom he worked on the Alger Hiss case. During the Eisenhower administration, he was appointed assistant attorney general (1953–1958), eventually winning promotion to attorney general (1958–1961).

Unlike most prominent New York lawyers, Rogers was a personal friend of Nixon, whom he assisted when the latter set up a legal practice in New York after his defeat in the 1962 California gubernatorial election. In 1968 newly elected President Nixon rewarded Rogers by appointing him secretary of state. Rogers had no background in foreign policy, and his appointment reflected Nixon's desire to keep control of foreign policy in his own hands. Rogers was no match for the dominating, driven, and intellectually brilliant National Security Advisor Henry Kissinger, under whose direction the National Security Council within a few weeks wrested from the State Department the crucial power to set the agenda for U.S. foreign policy discussions.

Throughout his term as secretary of state, Rogers remained a marginal figure, entirely overshadowed by the able, flamboyant, and publicity-hungry Kissinger. Nixon said of his two subordinates: "Henry thinks Bill isn't very deep, and Bill thinks Henry is power-crazy." Nixon and Kissinger often kept Rogers in ignorance of major foreign policy initiatives, including arms control, secret negotiations to end the Vietnam War, and the opening of China (of which he first learned through newspaper accounts of Kissinger's 1971 trip to Beijing).

On Vietnam and Indo-China, Rogers normally favored caution, conciliation, and negotiation over the generally more militant instincts of Nixon and Kissinger. In February 1969 he and Secretary of Defense Melvin Laird persuaded Nixon to temporar-

ily defer resumption of U.S. bombing of North Vietnam, although in March, over Rogers's objections, the president finally authorized this course. In November when Nixon delivered a major speech on Vietnam, Rogers unsuccessfully urged him to stress negotiations rather than the military threat to Vietnam. In April 1970 he opposed the U.S. invasion of Cambodia, preferring to continue the existing policy of minor cross-border raids by Army of the Republic of Vietnam (ARVN) forces. He also spoke against the February 1971 ARVN attack on the Hồ Chí Minh Trail in southern Laos, an operation that ended in an inglorious military rout. In the spring of 1972 Rogers was dubious as to the utility of the U.S. mining of Hai Phòng Harbor and the bombing of Hà Nôi, measures that were, as so often occurred, implemented against his advice.

In an unusual twist, Kissinger briefed Rogers in full on the final version of the Paris Peace Accords, which were signed in January 1973, and of which Rogers became a strong supporter. Equally unusual was that Kissinger stayed at home out of the limelight while Rogers went to Paris to sign the Accords. In September 1973 Nixon asked for Rogers's resignation and replaced him with his great rival and bureaucratic nemesis, Kissinger. Rogers returned to the practice of law in New York City, taking little further interest in foreign affairs.

—Priscilla Roberts

References: Ambrose, Stephen E. *Nixon: Ruin and Recovery 1973–1990.* New York: Simon & Schuster, 1991.
_____. *Nixon: The Triumph of a Politician 1961–1972.* New York: Simon & Schuster, 1989.
Isaacson, Walter. *Kissinger: A Biography.* New York: Simon & Schuster, 1992.
See also: Kissinger, Henry Alfred; Laird, Melvin R.; Nixon, Richard Milhous; Paris Peace Accords.

ROLLING THUNDER, Operation

(2 March 1965–31 October 1968)

Prolonged U.S. bombing campaign against North Vietnam. ROLLING THUNDER became the longest bombing campaign ever conducted by the U.S. Air Force. The bombing cost the Democratic Republic of Vietnam (DRV) more than half its bridges, virtually all of its large petroleum storage facilities, and nearly two-thirds of its power-generating plants. It also killed an estimated 52,000 of its citizens. DRV air defenses cost the United States nearly 1,000 aircraft, hundreds of prisoners of war, and hundreds of airmen killed or missing in action. Although the Air Force, Navy, and Marines flew almost a million sorties (one plane, one mission) to drop nearly three-quarters of a million tons of bombs, ROLLING THUNDER failed to achieve its major political and military objectives. In the overwhelming judgment of history, ROLLING THUNDER stands as the classic example of airpower failure.

Preparations for an extended bombing campaign against North Vietnam began in early 1964. Over the course of the year competing plans emerged. The U.S. Air Force (USAF), led by chief of staff General Curtis E. LeMay, advocated an "all-out" assault wrapped around 94 targets. The USAF's air campaign was designed to bomb the DRV "back to the Stone Age" by destroying its industrial base and war-making capability. The State Department advocated an escalating campaign that would increase in intensity with the number of targets, expanding over time until the Hà Nội regime stopped supporting the Việt Công (VC) and agreed to allow the Republic of Vietnam (RVN) to develop as an independent, non-Communist state. The Navy, because its planes did not have the range to strike targets deep inside North Vietnam, proposed an interdiction campaign south of 20 degrees north latitude, concentrating on roads, bridges, and railroads in the southern panhandle.

President Lyndon Johnson and his advisors turned to airpower in 1965 out of frustration. The war was going poorly in South Vietnam. The RVN political situation remained unstable and Việt Công guerrillas, with growing support from the DRV, seemed very close to achieving victory. Based on their perceptions of the accomplishments of airpower in World War II and in Korea, Air Force and Navy airpower advocates promised what airpower enthusiasts have always promised: quick victory at an acceptable cost by striking at an enemy's vital centers. They argued that by "holding hostage" the small industrial base of North Vietnam, Hà Nội would be faced with the choice of either abandoning its efforts inside South Vietnam or risking economic ruin.

In the early nineteenth century, Prussian military theorist Carl von Clausewitz wrote, "The first, supreme, the most far-reaching act of judgment that the statesman and commander have to make is to establish . . . the kind of war on which they are embarking; neither mistaking it for, nor trying to turn it into, something that is alien to its nature." The war in Vietnam was not World War II nor Korea, a fact that seemingly escaped airpower leaders. Furthermore, President Johnson's objectives were both limited and negative. The limited objective was to secure the right of the RVN to exist as a free and independent state. The DRV did not have to be destroyed to achieve this objective. It had only to be persuaded to desist from supporting the insurgents. The negative objective was to avoid military action that might risk Chinese or Soviet intervention. Such limited and negative objectives were not readily amenable to what airpower—at least theoretically—can deliver: decisive victory through vigorous offensive action. Although airpower had never been decisive in warfare, the U.S. Air Force was structured and equipped to deliver that kind of victory in total, nuclear war with the Soviets. The Air Force, and to a lesser extent the Navy, were not structured, equipped, nor doctrinally inclined to engage in limited warfare. Unfortunately, their leaders probably did not realize that they did not know how to fight this kind of war.

On 2 March 1965 the first ROLLING THUNDER mission took place when 100 U.S. Air Force and Republic of Vietnam Air Force (VNAF) sorties struck the Xóm Bang ammunition depot 35 miles north of the Demilitarized Zone (DMZ). Twelve days passed before the second ROLLING THUNDER missions were flown when USAF and Navy planes struck an ammunition dump 100 miles southeast of Hà Nội. ROLLING THUNDER was under way, and before it ended three years and nine months later, nearly 900 American planes would be shot down trying to accomplish its three objectives.

The first objective was strategic persuasion. Emanating from deterrence theory, the concept behind strategic persuasion was to employ airpower in ever-intensifying degrees in an effort to persuade the DRV to stop supporting the Việt Công and enter negotiations to end the war. When ROLLING THUNDER began, strategic persuasion was its primary objective. Military planners and civilian officials alike seemed convinced that when faced with vigorous demonstrations of American power, Hà Nội would demur.

By July no one in Hà Nội had blinked. But in Sài Gòn General William C. Westmoreland, commander of Military Assistance Command, Vietnam (MACV), had asked Secretary of Defense Robert McNamara to pass along his request for 44 combat maneuver battalions to take the war to the Việt Công. This was the beginning of a massive buildup of ground forces, and ROLLING THUNDER switched from strategic persuasion to interdiction. For the next three years and five months ROLLING THUNDER was primarily an effort at reducing the flow of troops and supplies moving from North Vietnam to the battlefields of the south.

The third objective was to boost the morale of RVN political and military elites by demonstrating U.S. resolve. After the assassination of President Ngô Đình Diêm in the military coup of early November 1963, the political situation in Sài Gòn had been unsettled. A large portion of the Army of the Republic of Vietnam spent a disproportionate amount of time on "coup alert," either protecting a given regime or preparing to overthrow it. Meanwhile, the VC was growing stronger in the countryside. The air war against the North was meant as a demonstration of U.S. resolve to stay the course.

Targets in ROLLING THUNDER included ammunition depots and storage areas; highways and railroads; bridges and marshaling yards; warehouses; petroleum, oil, and lubricant storage facilities (the DRV had no refineries); airfields; army barracks; and power-generating plants. North Vietnam possessed three factories worthy of the name: the Thái Nguyên Steel Works, an ammunition plant, and a cement factory. They were all eventually destroyed. The target list grew from the original 94 devised by the Joint Chiefs of Staff (JCS) in 1964 to nearly 400 targets by late 1967.

ROLLING THUNDER went through five phases. In phase one, from March through June 1965, a variety of targets, including ammunition depots, radar sites, and barracks, were struck as Washington tried to convince the DRV of the seriousness of its intentions. Hà Nội responded by increasing its support for the VC, who had started attacking American air bases in the south. When U.S. troops began arriving in substantial numbers to protect those bases, the focus of ROLLING THUNDER switched from strategic persuasion to interdiction. Although the bombing retained the objective of persuading the DRV to withdraw its support from the VC and negotiate an end to the conflict, after July 1965 ROLLING THUNDER remained basically an interdiction campaign.

During phase two, from July 1965 to the end of June 1966, despite several bombing halts to accommodate bad weather and to allow for unsuccessful diplomatic efforts aimed at starting negotiations, the bombing focused on roads, bridges, and railroads. There were two kinds of targets: numbered and unnumbered. The former included such targets as the Hàm Rồng (Dragon Jaw)

Bridge in Thanh Hóa Province and the Thái Nguyên Steel Works, which had designated target numbers. Those targets were difficult to strike, not only because they were well defended but also because the targeting process for attacking a numbered target was cumbersome and time consuming. Clearance procedures that extended from Sài Gòn through Honolulu to the Pentagon, the State Department, and into the White House were not unusual. More than 75 percent of the interdiction effort in 1965 and 1966 concentrated on trucks, railroad rolling stock, locomotives, and boats moving along the rivers and down the coast of North Vietnam. In 1965 and 1966, according to Pentagon estimates, attacks on these "fleeting" targets accounted for 4,600 trucks destroyed and another 4,600 damaged. Some 4,700 boats were reportedly sunk and 8,700 damaged, while 800 railroad cars and 16 locomotives were destroyed and another 800 railroad cars were damaged.

The attacks were costly. In the first 20 months of ROLLING THUNDER, over 300 planes were shot down, and the General Accounting Office estimated that it cost the United States $6.60 to inflict $1.00 worth of damage in North Vietnam. The price for bombing the DRV was going to go up. Meanwhile, between 150,000 and 200,000 North Vietnamese were pressed into various forms of active and passive antiaircraft defenses, ranging from managing air-raid shelters to manning antiaircraft guns or firing away at planes with rifles and submachine guns. Another 500,000 Vietnamese worked at repairing roads, railroad beds, and bridges. Accordingly, the flow of troops and supplies moving from north to south doubled during the first year of ROLLING THUNDER.

In January 1966 U.S. Commander in Chief, Pacific, Admiral Ulysses S. Grant Sharp, told the JCS that the destruction of North Vietnam's petroleum, oil, and lubricant (POL) storage facilities would make it difficult for them to support the war in the South. The Việt Cộng and People's Army of Vietnam (PAVN) units in the South were likely to "wither on the vine." At the end of June 1966 phase three of ROLLING THUNDER got under way.

The concerted attack on the DRV's POL facilities lasted through the summer and into early autumn. In that time, estimates were that 70 percent of North Vietnam's POL storage capacity had been destroyed. The remaining 30 percent had been dispersed; that is, put into caches of a hundred or more 55-gallon drums and placed in the middle of villages, near pagodas, churches, schools, or dikes—areas that U.S. bombers were not likely to strike. Despite the bombing of petroleum storage facilities, the movement of troops and supplies continued and the ground war inside South Vietnam intensified.

Phase four began in October 1966 with a shift to industrial targets and electric power-generating capabilities. Targets in and around Hà Nội, previously kept off-limits for fear of inflicting collateral damage on nonmilitary structures and causing civilian casualties, were struck. The Thái Nguyên Steel Works, North Vietnam's only cement plant, power-generating plants, and transformers were bombed. After May 1967 sporadic attacks on what remained of the industrial infrastructure, the transportation system, and the "fleeting" targets continued. But one thing was becoming increasingly evident: The bombing was not having the desired effect. Meanwhile, by mid-1967 over 600 aircraft had been shot down, and, at home,

the antiwar movement increasingly focused on the bombing as a cruel and unusual technology unleashed on a "peaceful and peace-loving people."

The 1968 Têt Offensive, which began in late January and lasted through February and into March, ushered in the final phase of ROLLING THUNDER. On 31 March President Johnson, in an effort to get peace negotiations started, limited the bombing of North Vietnam to areas in the southern panhandle below 19 degrees north latitude. Seven months later, on 31 October 1968, to boost the prospects for the Democratic Party's nominee for the presidency in the November elections, Johnson ended ROLLING THUNDER.

For the most part, ROLLING THUNDER was over. Escorted reconnaissance flights were flown, and, from time to time, attacks on North Vietnam were undertaken. Officially these were called ROLLING THUNDER missions, but they were rare, sometimes covert, and always militarily inconsequential.

During ROLLING THUNDER over 643,000 tons of bombs fell on North Vietnam. The bombing destroyed 65 percent of North Vietnam's POL storage capacity and an estimated 60 percent of its power-generating capability. At one time or another, half of its major bridges were down. Nearly 10,000 trucks, 2,000 railroad cars, and a score of locomotives were destroyed. Of the 990 Air Force, Navy, and Marine aircraft lost over North Vietnam during the war, most were shot down flying ROLLING THUNDER missions. By 1967 it was costing the United States $9.60 to inflict $1.00 worth of damage on its enemy. Air Force pilots flying the F-105 Thunderchiefs, the primary fighter-bombers involved in ROLLING THUNDER, stood a 50 percent chance of surviving a one-year tour. In some squadrons, attrition rates reached 75 percent.

Although the bombing intensified in 1967, its effect was not apparent on the battlefields of South Vietnam. According to MACV's own estimates, the flow of troops and supplies moving from North Vietnam into South Vietnam doubled each year of ROLLING THUNDER. The North responded to the bombing of its roads, bridges, and railroads by building redundancy into its transportation system so that by 1968 it was capable of handling three times as much traffic through the panhandle as it could in 1965.

Other than perhaps boosting the morale of a few ARVN generals and RVN politicians, ROLLING THUNDER failed to achieve its objectives. Its primary failure was one of strategy. Conventional airpower used on North Vietnam had very little impact on the unconventional war in South Vietnam. Although after 1965 increasing numbers of PAVN troops were entering the war in the South, until 1968 the conflict was basically an unconventional and guerrilla war. Airpower leaders, especially Air Force generals, blinded by their perceptions of airpower gained in World War II and Korea, were unable to devise a strategy appropriate to the war at hand. At best, their concept of guerrilla war was the kind of partisan warfare carried out by Tito in Yugoslavia during World War II. They had little or no understanding of people's war as articulated by Mao Zedong or Hô Chí Minh.

There are three more specific reasons for the failure of ROLLING THUNDER. First, the DRV was a preindustrial, agricultural country.

It was not vulnerable to the kind of bombing that played a role in defeating industrial powers such as Nazi Germany and Imperial Japan. North Vietnam had no war-making industries. Its primitive economy could not be held hostage to an emerging industrial base. Besides, its leadership held that reunification was more important than industrialization.

Second, for all its sound and fury, the potential effectiveness of the bombing was hampered by politically conceived constraints. Although airpower enthusiasts in the Air Force and Navy make too much of this point, there is something to it. President Johnson exercised far more control than was prudent or necessary, partly out of fear of prompting Chinese or Soviet intervention and partly out of his inherent distrust of generals.

Third, the North Vietnamese were a very determined foe. Hà Nội remained constant in its war aims, which were both total and limited. Against South Vietnam, Hà Nội had the total war aim of overthrowing the RVN government and reunifying the country under a single, Communist system. As an expedient, Hà Nội might be willing to delay realization of that objective, but, despite setbacks on the battlefield in 1965, 1968, and again in 1972, the DRV leadership remained true to that total objective until final victory in 1975. The destruction of three factories, half their bridges, and 60 percent of their power-generating capability failed to dissuade them. Against the United States, war aims of the DRV were limited. Hà Nội had only to compel the United States to withdraw both its troops from South Vietnam and its support for the RVN. To accomplish this, they had to make the war more costly for the Americans than it was worth. The defeat inflicted on the air forces of the United States during ROLLING THUNDER helped realize that objective. In July 1969, under the rubric of Vietnamization, the withdrawal of American forces began. By 1972 the return of American prisoners of war (POWs) was a primary American war objective. Most of those POWs were airmen shot down during ROLLING THUNDER.

In retrospect, ROLLING THUNDER has become the classic example of an airpower failure. The Air Force generals and Navy admirals who planned and executed ROLLING THUNDER were victims of their own historical experiences. Most were former bomber pilots who believed too much in the efficacy of strategic bombing. They had neither the training, the experience, nor the inclination for fighting an unconventional war against a preindustrial, agrarian foe. In the minds of airpower leaders, the very concept of limited war was an oxymoron. Furthermore, Air Force doctrine and most of its equipment were not suited to the kind of war that developed in Vietnam. But most of all, the failure of ROLLING THUNDER was a result of the inability of airpower leaders, especially those in the USAF, to devise a strategy appropriate to the war at hand.

—Earl H. Tilford, Jr.

References: Cable, Larry. *Unholy Grail: The U.S. and the Wars in Vietnam, 1965–68.* London: Routledge, 1991.

Clausewitz, Carl von. *On War.* Edited and translated by Michael Howard and Per Paret. Princeton, NJ: Princeton University Press, 1976.

Clodfelter, Mark. *The Limits of Air Power: The American Bombing of North Vietnam.* New York: Free Press, 1989.

Littauer, Raphael, and Norman Uphoff, eds. Air War Study Group, Cornell University. *The Air War in Indochina.* Boston: Beacon Press, 1971.

Thompson, James Clay. *Rolling Thunder: Understanding Policy and Program Failure.* Chapel Hill, NC: University of North Carolina Press, 1979.

Tilford, Earl H., Jr. *Crosswinds: The Air Force's Setup in Vietnam.* College Station, TX: Texas A&M University Press, 1993.

See also: Air Defense, Democratic Republic of Vietnam; Air Power, Role in War; Antiaircraft Artillery, Allied and Democratic Republic of Vietnam; Bombs, Dumb; Bombs, Smart (PGMs); Johnson, Lyndon Baines; LeMay, Curtis Emerson; LINEBACKER I, Operation; LINEBACKER II, Operation; McCone, John Alex; McNamara, Robert S.; Momyer, William W.; Ngô Đình Diêm, Overthrow of; RAND Corporation; Sharp, Ulysses Simpson Grant, Jr.; Vietnam, Republic of: Air Force (VNAF); Yankee Station.

Roman Catholicism in Vietnam

The Roman Catholic Church left a significant mark on Vietnam, more so than in any other part of Asia except the Philippines. The first Catholic missionaries arrived in Vietnam in the fifteenth century, but Catholic proselytizing made its greatest inroads two centuries later. In 1622 French Jesuit Alexandre de Rhodes arrived in Vietnam. He transcribed the Vietnamese language into the Roman alphabet and converted thousands of Vietnamese to Catholicism. He also successfully petitioned the Vatican to train indigenous priests and promoted a partnership of French religious and commercial interests to sponsor future Vietnam projects. This union of missionaries and merchants laid the groundwork for French colonization of Indo-China.

By 1700 hundreds of thousands of Vietnamese had embraced Catholicism. Some merchants converted to ingratiate themselves with Western traders, while others saw Catholicism as an escape from the traditions of Confucian society and oppressive mandarins. Often whole districts and villages converted and turned to priests as community leaders.

Vietnamese government attitudes toward Catholics vacillated. The missionaries' technical information and connections to European arms suppliers encouraged toleration, yet some government officials feared that Christianity's emphasis on individual salvation would undermine the Confucianist society's reverence for state authority. Vietnamese Catholics' divided loyalties and adherence to Vatican decrees made them a potentially subversive force. The emperors also correctly assumed that most Catholic missionaries were allied with European advocates of imperial conquest. Consequently, Vietnamese governments, to varying degrees, limited Catholic activities, jailed priests, deported missionaries, and persecuted converts.

By the nineteenth century France used Vietnam's increasing hostility toward Catholicism as a pretext for military intervention and colonial domination, as in the case of the arrest of Catholic missionary Dominique Lefèbvre. Although Vietnamese Catholics often refused to support French forces, the dying mandarinal regime executed an estimated 20,000 of them for allegedly cooperating with France.

Once France established imperial control, the Catholic Church enjoyed a privileged position and became one of the largest landholders in Indo-China. The French hoped Catholicism would dis-

U.S. Marines in a 60-mm mortar section of the 1st Regiment, 3d Division, choose a bivouac site near a Catholic church, a symbol of an older Western presence in Vietnam. An estimated 2.9 million Catholics remained in Vietnam after April 1975.

seminate Western culture and eventually shift the religious balance from Buddhism.

Vietnamese Catholics both supported and resisted the return of French colonial forces after World War II. Still, the Việt Minh accused all Catholics of collaboration, attacked their villages, and, after the 1954 Geneva Accords, confiscated church property and arrested priests. With help from the U.S. and South Vietnamese governments, the church launched a propaganda campaign, proclaiming "The Virgin has gone South" to entice an estimated 800,000 Catholics among nearly a million North Vietnamese refugees to flee the Communist-controlled North.

Life for the approximately 600,000 Catholics who stayed in the Democratic Republic of Vietnam (DRV) was not easy. The Liaison Committee of Patriotic and Peace Loving Catholics encouraged them to "reintegrate" into society. Although the church supposedly retained links to the Vatican, most of its foreign priests had fled to the South or had been expelled. The church also lost control of its property, including its schools, hospitals, and orphanages. Officially, Catholics were free to worship, but they were forbidden to question collective socialism.

Republic of Vietnam (RVN) President Ngô Đình Diêm welcomed the Catholics who moved South after 1954. Diêm was a devout Catholic, and he and U.S. officials viewed these refugees as a critical part of his regime's anti-Communist constituency and allocated millions of dollars to resettle them. Prominent Catholics worldwide urged support for Diêm's nationalist struggle against communism and contributed to the misconception that the RVN was a predominantly Catholic nation. Under Diêm, Catholics enjoyed special advantages in commerce, education, and the professions. They occupied positions of power at all government levels and helped polarize South Vietnamese society and politics. They strongly rejected accommodation with the Communists, the democratic left, or southern insurgents, many of whom merely sought land reform and social justice. In fact, Diêm's brother, Ngô Đình Thuc, served as archbishop of Huê and exercised great influence within the government and among Vietnamese Catholics. Such patronage and intransigence precipitated a political crisis that eventually toppled Diêm and led to increased military control.

As the insurgency of the National Liberation Front (NLF) strengthened, Catholics were among its first targets. NLF leaders pushed rural anti-Communists, especially Catholics, out of land development centers and villages, increasing the RVN's refugee burden. Southern Catholics became a wandering underclass, dependent on the uncertain aid of the government and private agencies. Thousands lost faith in the RVN government and fled the country in anticipation of the 1975 Communist takeover.

An estimated 2.9 million Catholics remained in Vietnam after April 1975. The new regime promised to rebuild churches, but the government still viewed Catholicism as a reactionary force and urged church members to join a Communist Party–controlled "renovation and reconciliation" movement. When Catholics continued to oppose Communist authority, the state created various organizations to recruit recalcitrant elements of the Catholic community and unite them behind socialism. Despite efforts to create the impression of cooperation, Hà Nội officials continue to view the church as a subversive force. An estimated 4 to 6 million Catholics continue to practice in Vietnam under three archdioceses and 22 dioceses, but surveillance of Catholic activities by the Religious Affairs Committee persists.

—Delia Pergande

References: Buttinger, Joseph. *Vietnam: A Political History.* New York: Praeger, 1968.
Cima, Ronald, ed. *Vietnam: A Country Study.* Washington, DC: U.S. Government Printing Office, 1989.
Karnow, Stanley. *Vietnam: A History.* Rev. ed. New York: Penguin Books, 1991.
Wiesner, Louis. *Victims and Survivors: Displaced Persons and Other War Victims in Viet-Nam, 1954–1975.* New York: Greenwood Press, 1988.
See also: Buddhists; Confucianism; de Rhodes, Alexandre; Lefèbvre, Dominique; Ngô Đình Diêm; Ngô Đình Thuc.

Romney, George W.

(1907–1995)

Presidential candidate for the Republican nomination in 1967 and cabinet member under President Richard Nixon. Born on 8 July 1907 to Mormon missionaries in Chihuahua, Mexico, George Wilcken Romney was raised in both Utah and Idaho. He attended several colleges, but never graduated. He also served as a Mormon missionary to Scotland and England for two years in the late 1920s. Romney went to Washington as a speechwriter for Massachusetts Democratic Senator David T. Walsh. In 1954, having joined the Nash-Kelvinator Corporation six years earlier, he became president of American Motors, the product of a merger between Nash-Kelvinator and the Hudson Motor Company.

In 1962 Romney ran for governor of Michigan against Democratic incumbent John B. Swainson. Winning by 78,000 votes, he became the first Republican governor of Michigan in 14 years. He was reelected in both 1964 and 1966. A liberal Republican, Romney supported civil rights initiatives as well as government social programs. He opposed the war in Vietnam. Romney was immensely popular in Michigan but seemed stiff in national politics. In 1967 he was the first to announce his candidacy for the Republican presidential nomination. Initially the front-runner in early campaigning in New Hampshire, Romney in the following weeks was ridiculed for a statement in which he said that he had originally supported the Vietnam War because he had been "brainwashed" by generals and diplomats during a 1965 visit there.

Appointed housing secretary by President Richard Nixon, Romney found himself increasingly frustrated because he remained outside the president's inner circle, which prevented him from beginning any meaningful domestic reforms. He resigned in 1972 after Nixon's reelection and retired from public life.

In 1979 Romney began service as chairman of the National Center for Citizen Involvement. He emerged politically in 1994 to campaign for his son, Mitt, who ran unsuccessfully against Edward Kennedy for a Senate seat in Massachusetts. Romney died at his home in Bloomfield Hills, Michigan, on 26 July 1995, at the age of 88.

—Michael R. Nichols

Reference: *New York Times* (27 July 1995).
See also: Nixon, Richard Milhous.

Roosevelt, Franklin Delano

(1882–1945)

President of the United States, 1933–1945. Born on 30 January 1882 in Hyde Park, New York, Franklin Delano Roosevelt was educated at Groton and Harvard. He served as assistant secretary of the Navy in President Woodrow Wilson's administration (1913–1920) and was a two-term governor of New York (1928–1932). Elected president during the Great Depression, Roosevelt put the full weight of the government behind the recovery effort.

As early as November 1941 Roosevelt had made public pronouncements concerning the territorial integrity of Indo-China and had proposed a multilateral nonaggression pact with Japan concerning the Pacific region. The Japanese attack on the United States at Pearl Harbor on 7 December nullified Roosevelt's overtures.

In the early years of the Second World War, President Roosevelt and other government officials regularly supported the self-determination of all peoples, prodding European leadership to establish timetables for colonial independence. As the war progressed, questions concerning the resolution of French Indo-China persisted. In a January 1944 memo to Secretary of State Cordell Hull, the president reiterated his stance, proposing the establishment of a trusteeship whereby developed nations would prepare native elites for eventual self-government. Although it was a compromise to Roosevelt's goal of colonial independence, the trusteeship seemed to offer the best hope for the stability of indigenous societies while they moved toward independence. Roosevelt especially condemned the French administration of Indo-China, stating that "the people are worse off than they were at the beginning. . . . France has milked it for one hundred years. The people of Indo-China are entitled to something better than that."

The president coupled his humanitarian concern for the Indo-Chinese with his genuine belief that the colonial system would jeopardize postwar peace by interfering with trade and sowing discord between the great powers. In February 1945 he declared at a press conference that China's Jiang Jieshi (Chiang Kai-shek) and the Soviet Union's Joseph Stalin supported his plans for an Indo-Chinese trusteeship. Within a few months, however, Roosevelt reversed his stance, promising to not interfere with colonial rule. Several factors contributed to this policy shift. America's most important ally, British Prime Minister Winston Churchill, had clearly stated his opposition to tampering with European colonial possessions, and Free French leader Charles de Gaulle no less resolutely contested U.S. interference.

The Roosevelt administration recognized that insistence on colonial self-rule could create excessive strains between the Allies and imperil cooperation in Western Europe, the most vital arena of U.S. foreign policy. Additionally, defense planners argued that postwar national security would require the United States to maintain control over several former Japanese-controlled islands. Imposition of trusteeships could easily be applied to the United States as well as to the European colonial powers. Roosevelt, therefore, although still favoring independence, reluctantly acceded to the return of Indo-China to France.

Roosevelt died in office on 12 April 1945 while convalescing in Warm Springs, Georgia, depriving the postwar world of his calm confidence and those who favored Indo-Chinese self-determination of an influential proponent.

—Brenda J. Taylor

References: Anderson, David L., ed. *Shadow on the White House: Presidents and the Vietnam War, 1945–1975.* Lawrence, KS: University Press of Kansas, 1993.
Dallek, Robert. *F.D.R. and American Diplomacy.* New York: Oxford University Press, 1979.
Williams, William Appleman, ed. *America in Vietnam: A Documentary History.* Garden City, NY: Anchor Press, 1985.
See also: de Gaulle, Charles André Marie Joseph; Jiang Jieshi (Chiang Kai-shek); Potsdam Conference; Truman, Harry S; United States: Involvement in Indo-China through 1954.

Rostow, Eugene Victor

(1913–)

U.S. undersecretary of state for political affairs, 1966–1969. The son of Russian Jewish immigrants, Eugene V. Rostow was born on 25 August 1913 in Brooklyn, New York. He attended Yale University, earning an A.B. in 1933 and an LL.D. in 1937. In 1938 he became an instructor at Yale. Throughout his career Rostow combined teaching with government service and extensive writing.

Rostow believed that the United States was the only nation with the capability and the resolve to maintain geopolitical stability in the chaotic years following the Second World War. He became convinced that the United States, having accepted the role of peacekeeper, could expect that the Soviet Union and China would periodically test American resolve and that the Korean War justified that conclusion. Rostow saw the United States as maintaining a policy of containing communism while simultaneously avoiding armed confrontation. This, he believed, was the primary U.S. role in Vietnam.

Rostow worked extensively within the Johnson administration. Following the assassination of President John F. Kennedy, he urged President Lyndon Johnson to appoint a panel to determine responsibility for Kennedy's death; his suggestion led to the establishment of the Warren Commission. He also served as an advisor during arms control talks between the United States and the Soviet Union. Later he became undersecretary of state in charge of political affairs.

Rostow believed that the Vietnam War was a morass Johnson had inherited. Two presidents—Dwight D. Eisenhower and John F. Kennedy—had made a commitment to protect South Vietnam, and in 1961 Kennedy had expanded the obligation by increasing political, economic, and military aid to the region. Rostow believed that Johnson was obligated to fulfill U.S. responsibilities in Vietnam, as established by the Southeast Asia Treaty Organization (SEATO) treaty, the United Nations charter, and the policies of former presidents backed by several Congresses. He strongly supported Johnson's Vietnam policies and believed that Johnson's position of restraint in the use of force, coupled with maximum diplomatic effort, represented the best approach in dealing with the Vietnam situation. Rostow maintained that the Gulf of Tonkin Resolution was a constitutional mandate similar to a declaration of war. With its passage, there was little doubt in his mind that Johnson had the "full weight of the nation" behind his policies. Critics would have vilified the administration had it not acted following the resolution's passage.

Rostow admitted that the United States made mistakes in Vietnam that negatively affected foreign policy decisions for many years after the war. Errors notwithstanding, he remains convinced that the United States helped establish a strong economic infrastructure in Southeast Asia. Rostow left government service in 1969, returning to Yale University to teach.

—Dean Brumley

References: Goulden, Steven L. *Political Profiles: The Johnson Years.* New York: Facts on File, 1976.
Halberstam, David. *The Best and the Brightest.* New York: Penguin Books, 1983.
Johnson, Lyndon Baines. *The Vantage Point: Perspectives of the Presidency, 1963–1969.* New York: Holt, Rinehart and Winston, 1971.
Rostow, Eugene V. *Law, Power, and the Pursuit of Peace.* Lincoln, NE: University of Nebraska Press, 1968.
_____. *Toward Managed Peace: The National Security Interests of the United States, 1759 to the Present.* New Haven, CT: Yale University Press, 1993.
See also: Johnson, Lyndon Baines; Tonkin Gulf Resolution.

Rostow, Walt Whitman

(1916–)

Chairman, State Department Policy Planning Council, 1961–1966; special assistant to the president for national security affairs, 1966–1969. Walt W. Rostow was born in New York City on 7 October 1916. An economist, he studied at Yale University and was a Rhodes Scholar at Oxford University. During World War II, Rostow served in the Office of Strategic Services (OSS), where he was one of the analysts on the Strategic Bombing Survey.

After the war Rostow worked briefly in the State Department and then became an assistant to the assistant secretary of the Economic Commission for Europe before returning to the academic world in 1950. For the next ten years he taught economics at the Massachusetts Institute of Technology and was also an associate of the Institute's Central Intelligence Agency–supported Center for International Studies. Rostow's academic work centered on the possibility of providing an alternative to Marxist models and historical theories of economic development.

During the election campaign of 1960, Rostow was an informal advisor to Democratic presidential candidate Senator John F. Kennedy, with whom he had been close since 1958. Initially he was appointed deputy to the Special Assistant to the President for National Security Affairs McGeorge Bundy. In early February 1961 he passed on to Kennedy and enthusiastically endorsed a report by Brig. Gen. Edward G. Lansdale, which suggested that a serious crisis was impending in South Vietnam and recommended a major expansion of U.S. programs in that country. Rostow argued

that the options of bombing North Vietnam or occupying its southern regions be considered, an outlook that made him one of the strongest hawks in the administration, a stance he would retain throughout the Vietnam War era.

In October 1961 Rostow and General Maxwell D. Taylor undertook a mission to Vietnam to assess the situation there and the merits of potential U.S. courses of action. Their report recommended that the United States change its existing advisory role to one of "limited partnership" with the Republic of Vietnam (RVN). The report also advocated increased American economic aid and military advisory support to the country. A secret annex suggested that 8,000 American combat troops be deployed there. All except the last of these recommendations were implemented.

In late 1961 Rostow was appointed a State Department counselor and chairman of the department's Policy Planning Council. He continued to be one of the administration's strongest advocates of an assertive U.S. policy in Vietnam, constantly urging increased military pressure against the Democratic Republic of Vietnam (DRV). By late 1964 he believed that escalating U.S. military measures, including the commitment of American ground forces, a naval blockade, and bombing of North Vietnam, would convince Hà Nội that victory over the RVN was impossible.

When these measures were implemented in 1965, Rostow urged their expansion, as he continued to do after his March 1966 appointment as special assistant to the president for national security affairs. In the Johnson administration's final years Rostow's confidence in an eventual favorable outcome of the war remained unshaken, even in light of mounting public protests and the inconclusive progress of the war. In 1967 he called for the extension of the U.S. bombing program and opposed an unconditional bombing halt, although in late 1967 he did endorse proposals by Secretary of Defense Robert McNamara to try to reduce U.S. casualties and shift more of the burden of fighting to the South Vietnamese. In an increasingly divided and demoralized administration, he remained a committed hawk, opposed to the post–Tết Offensive decision of March 1968 to open negotiations with the DRV.

After his resignation in January 1969, Rostow joined the University of Texas at Austin as a professor of economics and history. In his voluminous writings since then, he has always defended U.S. policy in Vietnam, arguing that U.S. involvement in the war gave other Southeast Asian nations the breathing space they required to develop strong economies and become staunch regional anti-Communist bastions.

—Priscilla Roberts

References: Berman, Larry. *Planning a Tragedy: The Americanization of the War in Vietnam.* New York: W. W. Norton, 1982.
Gibbons, William Conrad. *The U.S. Government and the Vietnam War.* Parts 2 and 3. Princeton, NJ: Princeton University Press, 1986, 1989.
Halberstam, David. *The Best and the Brightest.* New York: Random House, 1972.
Rostow, Walt W. *The Diffusion of Power, 1957–1972: An Essay in Recent History.* New York: Macmillan, 1972.
See also: Bundy, McGeorge; Bundy, William P.; Clifford, Clark M.; Johnson, Lyndon Baines; Kennedy, John Fitzgerald; McNamara, Robert S.; Rusk, Dean; Taylor, Maxwell Davenport.

Route Coloniale (RC) 4, Battles for

See LÊ HỒNG PHONG II, Operation.

Rowe, James N.

(1938–1989)

U.S. Army officer and five-year captive of the Việt Cộng. Born in McAllen, Texas, on 8 February 1938, James N. "Nick" Rowe was six years old when his older brother died just three months short of graduating from the U.S. Military Academy. Sixteen years later Rowe himself graduated from West Point and was commissioned in the field artillery. In July 1963 he went to Vietnam as a member of Special Forces A-Detachment A-23. Less than four months later, on 29 October, he was captured by the Việt Cộng while on patrol with South Vietnamese irregular forces near Tân Phú in the Mekong Delta.

Knowing that Communist forces had a standing policy of summarily executing all captured Special Forces soldiers, Rowe hid his identity. He attempted to escape at least three times, and earned the nickname "Mr. Trouble" from his captors. He was a prisoner of war (POW) in the Delta for more than five years, spending most of his time in a cramped bamboo cage. During that time, two of his fellow captives died.

The Việt Cộng eventually learned Rowe's true identity. On 31 December 1968 as he was being led to his execution, Rowe struck his guard and made a break for a clearing. Waving a mosquito net over his head, Rowe managed to attract the attention of a U.S. helicopter crew. The aircraft almost fired on the black pajama–clad figure, when the crew spotted Rowe's red beard. They landed and picked him up.

Rowe had been a first lieutenant when he was captured, but over the five-year period he was routinely promoted to captain and then to major. He also received the Silver Star for his actions while a POW. After returning from Vietnam, he wrote a book about his experiences. In 1974 Rowe left the active Army and went into the Reserves. In 1981 he returned to active duty and established the Army's Survival, Evasion, Resistance, and Escape (SERE) training program, designed to teach soldiers how to avoid and deal with capture.

In 1985 Rowe assumed command of the 1st Special Warfare Training Battalion at Fort Bragg, North Carolina. After that assignment he was promoted to colonel and sent to the Philippines as a military advisor to the Corazon Aquino government. His background, however, made him a high-profile figure and a lucrative target. On 21 April 1989 Rowe's car was ambushed as he was being driven to work at the Joint U.S. Military Advisory Group headquarters. Two hooded gunmen poured more than 20 bullets into his car, hitting Rowe once in the head. He died on the way to the hospital. Several days later, the New People's Army, the military wing of the Philippines' Communist Party, claimed responsibility for the deed.

—David T. Zabecki

References: Miles, Donna. "A Real Hero: Col. Nick Rowe Assassinated in the Philippines." *Soldiers* (June 1989): 24–25.
New York Times (22 April 1989).

Rowe, James N. *Five Years to Freedom.* Boston: Little, Brown, 1971.
See also: Prisoners of War, Allied; United States: Special Forces.

Rubin, Jerry

(1938–1994)

Leading antiwar activist. Born on 14 July 1938 in Cincinnati, Ohio, Jerry Rubin received a B.A. from the University of Cincinnati in 1961 and was active in the Free Speech Movement at the University of California, Berkeley, in 1964. In 1965 Rubin helped organize a teach-in at Berkeley involving 12,000 students. As a leader of the Vietnam Day Committee, he was recognized as a skilled organizer with a flair for gaining media attention. In August 1965 the committee staged well-publicized attempts to stop troop trains in the San Francisco area.

Rubin believed that the antiwar movement was a generational conflict between young and old and advised followers "not to trust anyone over thirty." In 1967 he moved to New York City, where he met Abbie Hoffman and organized a march on the Pentagon that October. In January 1968 Rubin, Hoffman, and Paul Krassner formed the Youth International Party, or Yippies, which staged demonstrations in Chicago to coincide with the August 1968 Democratic National Convention. Rubin was one of the "Chicago Eight" tried in 1969 on charges of conspiracy and intent to riot.

In the late 1970s Rubin turned to spiritualism and self-help and self-improvement programs before becoming a Wall Street securities analyst. By 1991 he was an independent marketer of health-food drinks in Los Angeles. He died on 28 November 1994 after being struck by a car two weeks earlier while jaywalking.

—Clayton D. Laurie

References: *New York Times* (30 November 1994).
Rubin, Jerry. *Do It! Scenarios of the Revolution.* New York: Simon & Schuster, 1970.
_____. *Growing (Up) at 37.* New York: Evans, 1976.
The Washington Post (30 November 1994).
See also: Antiwar Movement, United States; Chicago Eight; Democratic Party National Convention, 1968; Hayden, Thomas E.; Hoffman, Abbie; March on the Pentagon; Youth International Party ("Yippies").

Rules of Engagement (ROE)

According to the Department of Defense Dictionary, Joint Publication 1–02, "directives issued by competent military authority which delineate the circumstances and limitations under which United States forces will initiate and/or continue combat engagement with other forces encountered." Rules of engagement (ROE) often have two primary purposes. The first is to limit the destruction of property and the injury and death of noncombatants. The second—particularly important in a conflict like the Vietnam War without front lines or often a clearly identifiable enemy—is to prevent casualties from friendly fire.

For the ground and air war in South Vietnam, the competent military authority was the Commander, Military Assistance Command, Vietnam (COMUSMACV), with supplementation by the U.S. Joint Chiefs of Staff (JCS). But for the air war in North

Vietnam it was ultimately the president of the United States and his secretary of defense through the JCS.

In a conventional conflict, in which lines of contact between enemy and friendly forces are generally well defined, destruction of property is considered a necessary evil of war, and injury inflicted on noncombatants is difficult to control or prevent. In a conflict like the war in Vietnam involving insurgency and counterinsurgency, with no clearly defined front lines and the resulting prosecution of the war among the civilian population—whose support is actively sought by the insurgents—rules of engagement were necessary to prevent losses and retain the support of the populace.

The rules of engagement imposed by the JCS in South Vietnam were primarily designed to keep the war limited and to prevent international incidents in border areas and in the Demilitarized Zone. The JCS also prescribed rules for B-52 strikes in the South, for example requiring that targets for such strikes must be at least one kilometer from any area inhabited by noncombatants. The problem, of course, was the difficulty in identifying who were truly noncombatants and who were guerrillas.

The air war over North Vietnam was executed in stages and was completely controlled from Washington by the White House and the Pentagon. President Lyndon Johnson and Secretary of Defense Robert McNamara spent long hours poring over maps of the North, planning raids, and searching for just the right pressure points to bring the North Vietnamese to the negotiating table. Washington not only dictated the strategy of the air war but the tactics as well, including types and numbers of bombs to be dropped, flight patterns, formation size, attack approaches, and times of attack. Most missions were directed at lines of communication: roads, bridges, and railroads. Nonmilitary facilities were generally not targeted, except for power plants and other installations that indirectly affected North Vietnam's ability to support the war. However, the extended bombing campaign caused considerable damage to civilian structures and the deaths of many noncombatants, both because of proximity to military targets and because pilots flying through intense antiaircraft fire could not always drop their bombs with precision.

In South Vietnam there were three types of operations employed in the conduct of the war: search and destroy, clearing, and securing. Search and destroy was the primary tactic of U.S. forces. It meant taking the war to the Communists by searching them out and then bringing massive firepower to bear. The objective of clearing operations, usually done by regular forces of the Army of the Republic of Vietnam (ARVN), was to drive large enemy forces out of populated areas so that pacification could take place. Securing operations were conducted primarily by ARVN Regional and Popular Forces or police to protect pacification teams and eliminate local guerrilla units.

In an effort to protect the South Vietnamese civilian population and their property, the COMUSMACV issued more than 40 directives on ROE (an example of which is included below). These contained explicit guidance on the proper treatment of civilians and their property as well as on the discriminating use of firepower. ARVN forces, however, were not specifically bound to comply with these ROE directives, although efforts were made at every level by American advisors to gain their compliance.

Search-and-destroy tactics meant the substitution of firepower for maneuver to minimize friendly casualties. Although the Military Assistance Command, Vietnam (MACV) maintained that its forces closely followed very restrictive ROE, massive firepower employed on a relatively random basis often alienated the civilian population and provided the Communists with an excellent source of propaganda. With emphasis on achieving "body counts" associated with the strategy of attrition, there was strong incentive for commanders to circumvent the ROE. In addition, the fact that ROE were often misunderstood or received "creative application" while sanctions against violators were virtually nonexistent created an environment in which allegations of war crimes may have been well founded, as in the case of the 1968 My Lai Massacre.

Two uses of firepower to prosecute the war that have received considerable criticism in relation to ROE were harassment and interdiction (H&I) fires and free fire zones. H&I fires were unobserved fires placed on likely Communist positions or routes of movement, usually selected by map or aerial reconnaissance. Although proponents and critics were equally vocal in their support or denigration of this practice, there is little statistical information to support one stand or the other. What is certain is that a large quantity of firepower was expended on these types of missions, and the likelihood of injuring or killing unsuspecting noncombatants was just as high as for Communist forces.

The term "free fire zone" connotes the indiscriminate use of firepower and often provoked an emotional reaction from Americans. However, free fire zones were established only in uninhabited areas or areas totally under Communist control, and permission had to be obtained from Vietnamese province and district chiefs before an area could be designated a free fire zone. Although these areas were generally free of noncombatants and their property, thereby avoiding property destruction, there was no guarantee that noncombatants would not inadvertently wander into designated free fire zones and become subject to attack. Likewise, this so-called unrestrictive fire control measure may have on occasion increased the likelihood of two uncoordinated friendly elements placing one another under fire, believing that the other was an enemy force.

—Arthur T. Frame

MACV [Military Assistance Command, Vietnam] Rules of Engagement

1. UNINHABITED AREAS.

a. Fire may be directed against VC [Việt Công]/NVA [North Vietnamese Army] forces in contact in accordance with normal artillery procedures.

b. Unobserved fire may be directed at targets and target areas, other than VC/NVA forces in contact, only after approval by Province Chief, District Chief, Sector Commander, or Subsector Commander and U.S./FWMAF [Free

World Military Assistance Forces] Military Commander, as appropriate, has been granted.

c. Observed fire may be directed against targets of opportunity which are clearly identified as hostile without obtaining Province Chief, District Chief, Sector Commander, or Subsector Commander and U.S./FWMAF Military Commander's approval.

d. Approval by Province Chief, District Chief, Sector Commander, or Subsector Commander and U.S./FWMAF Military Commander, as appropriate, is required, before directing fire on targets of opportunity not clearly identified as hostile.

2. VILLAGES AND HAMLETS.

a. Fire missions directed against known or suspected VC/NVA targets in villages and hamlets occupied by noncombatants will be conducted as follows:

(1) All such fire missions will be controlled by an observer and will be executed only after approval is obtained from the Province Chief or District Chief, as appropriate. The decision to conduct such fire missions will also be approved by the attacking force battalion or task force commander, or higher.

(2) Villages and hamlets not associated with maneuver of ground forces will not be fired upon without warning by leaflets and/or speaker system or by other appropriate means, even though fire is received from them.

(3) Villages and hamlets may be attacked without prior warning if the attack is in conjunction with a ground operation involving maneuver of ground forces through the area, and if in the judgement of the ground commander, his mission would be jeopardized by such warning.

b. The use of incendiary type ammunition will be avoided unless absolutely necessary in the accomplishment of the commander's mission or for preservation of the force.

3. URBAN AREAS.

a. Fire missions directed against known or suspected VC/NVA targets in urban areas must preclude unnecessary destruction of civilian property and must by nature require greater restrictions than the rules of engagement for less populated areas.

b. When time is of the essence and supporting weapons must be employed to accomplish the mission or to reduce friendly casualties, fire missions will be conducted as follows:

(1) All fire missions will be controlled by an observer and will be executed only after GVN [Government of Vietnam]/RVNAF [Republic of Vietnam Armed Forces]/U.S. approval. The decision to conduct the fire mission in urban areas will be retained at corps/field force or NAVFORV [Naval Forces, Vietnam] level. Approval must be obtained from both the corps commander and the U.S. field force level commander. This approval is required for the employment of any U.S. supporting weapons in urban areas to include U.S. weapons in support of RVNAF.

(2) Prior to firing in urban areas, leaflets and loudspeakers and other appropriate means will be utilized to warn and to secure the cooperation and support of the civilian populace even though fire is received from these areas.

(3) Supporting weapons will be used only on positively located enemy targets. When time permits, damage to buildings will be minimized.

(4) The use of incendiary type munitions will be avoided unless destruction of the area is unavoidable and then only when friendly survival is at stake.

(5) Riot control agents will be employed to the maximum extent possible. CS [riot control] agents can be effectively employed in urban area operations to flush enemy personnel from buildings and fortified positions, thus increasing the enemy's vulnerability to allied firepower while reducing the likelihood of destroying civilian property. Commanders must plan ahead and be prepared to use CS agents whenever the opportunity presents itself.

4. THE ABOVE STATED PROCEDURES WILL NOT BE VIOLATED OR DEVIATED FROM EXCEPT, WHEN IN THE OPINION OF THE RESPONSIBLE COMMANDER, THE SITUATION DEMANDS SUCH IMMEDIATE ACTION THAT THESE PROCEDURES CANNOT BE FOLLOWED. SUCH SITUATIONS INCLUDE PRESERVATION OF THE FORCE OR THE RIGHT OF SELF-DEFENSE.

5. RVN [Republic of Vietnam]/CAMBODIAN BORDER AREAS.

a. Fire missions within 2000 meters of the RVN/Cambodian border will be observed, except under circumstances where fires are in defense of friendly forces and observation of such fires is not possible. These requirements are in addition to applicable control procedures stated elsewhere in this directive.

b. Fire missions with intended target areas more than 2000 meters from the RVN/Cambodian border may be unobserved, subject to applicable control procedures stated elsewhere in this directive.

c. Fire missions will not be conducted when dispersion could result in fire being placed on or over the RVN/Cambodian border.

d. Commanders will review and comply with the provisions of MACV Rules of Engagement—Cambodian when planning for operations near the Cambodian/RVN border.

(Cited in Ott, David E. *Field Artillery, 1954–1973*. Vietnam Studies Series. Washington, DC: Department of the Army, 1975, pp. 173–175.)

References: Kinnard, Douglas. *The War Managers*. Wayne, NJ: Avery Publishing Group, 1985.
Krepinevich, Andrew F., Jr. *The Army and Vietnam*. Baltimore: Johns Hopkins University Press, 1986.
Ott, David E. *Field Artillery, 1954–1973*. Vietnam Studies Series. Washington, DC: Department of the Army, 1975.
Palmer, Gen. Bruce, Jr. *The 25-Year War: America's Military Role in Vietnam*. New York: Simon & Schuster, 1984.

Westmoreland, General William C. *A Soldier Reports.* New York: Da Capo Publications, 1989.
See also: Air Power, Role in War; Artillery, Allied and People's Army of Vietnam; Artillery Fire Doctrine; Atrocities during the Vietnam War; Attrition; Body Count; Free Fire Zones; Friendly Fire; Harassment and Interdiction (H&I) Fires; My Lai Massacre.

Rusk, Dean

(1909–1994)

U.S. secretary of state, 1961–1969. David Dean Rusk was born in rural Cherokee County, Georgia, on 9 February 1909. He worked his way through Davidson College in North Carolina, graduating in 1931. That year he entered Oxford University on a Rhodes Scholarship and earned a B.S. in 1934 and an M.A. the following year. Returning to the United States, he taught at Mills College in Oakland, California, and attended the University of California Law School. In 1940 he entered the Army Reserve as a captain. On active duty in Washington, D.C., he worked in military intelligence. In 1943 he was transferred to the Far East, serving in China and Burma, where he became deputy chief of staff to General Joseph Stilwell. Discharged in 1946 with the rank of colonel, Rusk joined the State Department.

In the State Department he held a variety of important posts and worked with such issues as the establishment of the State of Israel and the United Nations. In 1950 he became assistant secretary of state for Far Eastern affairs, and as such was involved in the formulation of Korean War policy. He supported the policy of containment and encouraged the decision to remove General Douglas MacArthur. But in 1952 Rusk left the State Department to assume the presidency of the Rockefeller Foundation. In 1960 President-elect John F. Kennedy chose Rusk as his secretary of state over such notables as Chester Bowles and Adlai Stevenson, who became Rusk's subordinates.

Upon assuming office, Rusk immediately confronted myriad international problems, the most serious being Communist threats in Cuba, Southeast Asia, and Berlin. A staunch anti-Communist, he largely worked behind the scenes in the Kennedy administration, offering advice only when it was solicited. But he believed that Communist aggression had to be met with determination and feared that China would intervene in Vietnam. He had little faith in Ngô Đình Diệm, and urged a stronger American commitment in South Vietnam. Along with Secretary of Defense Robert McNamara, Rusk usually deferred to the Pentagon position on Southeast Asia.

When Lyndon Johnson assumed the presidency after Kennedy's assassination, Rusk continued as secretary of state. Under Johnson, he took a much more active role. He quickly became one of Johnson's most trusted advisors. As antiwar sentiment intensified, many of Johnson's advisors, such as Secretaries of Defense Robert McNamara and Clark Clifford, began to mirror the public's exasperation. Rusk steadfastly supported Johnson's position. He backed Pentagon calls for larger troop commitments to Southeast Asia and the bombing of North Vietnam. He urged Johnson to stay the course, despite mounting pressure to end U.S. involvement in the war. Rusk did not, as is often suggested, oppose

negotiations with Hà Nội. He constantly warned against the appearance of weakness in the face of Communist aggression, but in 1967 suggested that Johnson pursue negotiations. Rusk left office in 1969 when the Republican administration of Richard Nixon took office.

Throughout his career Rusk displayed marked ability and an intense loyalty to his superiors. Though admirable, his loyalty proved damaging as, with the exception of Johnson, no other political figure became more closely associated with America's failure in Vietnam than Rusk. He was also an outsider. A southerner among Ivy League easterners, he never fell in with the "Wise Men." Rusk also found himself an outcast. Shunned by more prestigious academic institutions, he eventually accepted a position at the University of Georgia, where he taught international law until his retirement in 1984. His memoir, *As I Saw It,* was published in 1990 to much less hoopla than Robert McNamara's subsequent effort. Rusk died at his home in Athens, Georgia, on 20 December 1994.

—David Coffey

References: *Current Biography Yearbook, 1961.* New York: H. W. Wilson, 1961. *Current Biography Yearbook, 1995.* New York: H. W. Wilson, 1995. Halberstam, David. *The Best and the Brightest.* New York: Random House, 1972.
Isaacson, Walter, and Evan Thomas. *The Wise Men: Six Friends and the World They Made.* New York: Simon & Schuster, 1986.
Karnow, Stanley. *Vietnam: A History.* New York: Viking Press, 1983.
See also: Bowles, Chester B.; Bundy, McGeorge; Bundy, William P.; Clifford, Clark M.; Containment Policy; Halberstam, David; Johnson, Lyndon Baines; Kennedy, John Fitzgerald; MacArthur, Douglas; McNamara, Robert S.; Ngô Đình Diệm; Pearson, Lester Bowles; Read, Benjamin Huger; Stevenson, Adlai E.; Truman, Harry S; "Wise Men."

Russell, Richard B., Jr.

(1897–1971)

One of the most powerful members of the U.S. Senate during the years of the Vietnam War. Born in Winder, Georgia, on 12 November 1897, Richard Russell received a law degree from the University of Georgia in 1918. He practiced law and then was elected as a Democrat to the state legislature. In 1931, at age 39, Russell became the youngest governor in Georgia history. Two years later he was elected as a Democrat to the U.S. Senate from that state, a seat he held for the next 38 years. As chairman of the Senate Armed Services Committee from 1951 to 1969, he was highly influential during the Vietnam War era.

Russell was confronted with a difficult problem concerning the Vietnam War. On the one hand, he believed that American involvement in the war had been a mistake from the beginning and that Southeast Asia offered no security threat to the United States. On the other hand, mindful of the need to be loyally supportive of the president as well as the soldiers in the field, Russell never joined the growing antiwar faction in the Senate. Indeed, he was openly critical of the peace movement and its public protests.

This paradoxical stance caused him much frustration, exacerbated by White House failure to heed his opinions about the war. In spite of grave misgivings Russell supported the government's war policies to the end of his life. He died in office in Washington, D.C., on 21 January 1971.

—Eric Jarvis

References: Fite, Gilbert C. *Richard B. Russell Jr., Senator from Georgia.* Chapel Hill, NC: University of North Carolina Press, 1991.
Gibbons, William Conrad. *The U.S. Government and the Vietnam War, parts 1–3.* Princeton, NJ: Princeton University Press, 1986.
Halberstam, David. *The Best and the Brightest.* Greenwich, CT: Fawcett Publications, 1969.
New York Times (22 January 1971).
The Washington Post (22 January 1971).
See also: Fulbright, J. William; Humphrey, Hubert H.; Johnson, Lyndon Baines; McGee, Gale William; Proxmire, William; Stennis, John Cornelius.

Russo, Anthony J., Jr.

(1936–)

Indicted codefendant in the Pentagon Papers trial (1972–1973). Born on 14 October 1936 in Suffolk, Virginia, Anthony J. Russo, Jr. received a B.S. from the Virginia Polytechnic Institute in 1960 and an M.S. from Princeton in 1963. He also attended Princeton's Woodrow Wilson School of Public and International Affairs, from which he received a masters degree in 1964. That year he joined the RAND Corporation. Russo worked in Vietnam for two years (from February 1966 to January 1968), analyzing crop destruction programs and interviewing Viêt Công prisoners in the RAND-conducted study "Viêt Công Morale and Motivation." During this period he became highly disillusioned with U.S. policy in Southeast Asia. Terminated by RAND in July 1968, Russo was allowed a six-month grace period to complete his work. He was, by this time, a devoted antiwar crusader and a fledgling member of the counterculture. After leaving RAND, he engaged in social and civil rights work in the Los Angeles area.

Russo had met Daniel Ellsberg in Vietnam, but the two did not become close friends until 1968, when they worked together at RAND's Santa Monica, California, headquarters. When Ellsberg decided to copy the volumes of sensitive documents that came to be known as the Pentagon Papers, he called Russo for help. Russo secured the use of a Xerox machine belonging to an advertising agency owned by his friend Linda Sinay. Russo then assisted in the photocopying of some 7,000 pages of Vietnam-related material.

Only days after the first installments of the Pentagon Papers appeared in the *New York Times* in June 1971, the FBI questioned Russo. He refused to cooperate. On 23 June he was subpoenaed by a federal grand jury in Los Angeles, but he declined to testify on the grounds that he might incriminate himself. Granted full immunity, he again refused to cooperate in the case against Ellsberg by offering secret testimony; he preferred to go public. Cited for contempt, Russo was jailed on 16 August. He later claimed that during his 47-day imprisonment he had been chained, tortured, and held in solitary confinement.

On 1 October a federal judge ordered Russo's release and further ruled that he be given a transcript of any grand jury testimony he provided. Pending appeal, Assistant U.S. Attorney David Nissen would not supply a copy of confidential testimony, and Russo again refused to testify. On 29 December 1971 the grand jury returned a new 15-count criminal indictment, charging Ellsberg and Russo with conspiracy, theft and misuse of government property, and espionage. The Pentagon Papers trial began in Los Angeles on 10 July 1972.

The trial that began as a test of First Amendment rights quickly became a lesson in the abuse of governmental power. The unfolding Watergate drama brought new revelations into play. On 11 May 1973, citing governmental misconduct, Federal Judge William Matthew Byrne declared a mistrial and dismissed all charges against Ellsberg and Russo. Russo remained a staunch antiwar campaigner and worked zealously for the impeachment of President Richard Nixon. He eventually resumed his career in social work.

—David Coffey

References: Schrag, Peter. *Test of Loyalty: Daniel Ellsberg and the Rituals of Secret Government.* New York: Simon & Schuster, 1974.
Ungar, Sanford J. *The Papers and the Papers: An Account of the Legal and Political Battle over the Pentagon Papers.* New York: E. P. Dutton, 1972.
See also: Ellsberg, Daniel; Pentagon Papers and Trial; Watergate.

S

Sabattier, Gabriel

(1892–1966)

French Army lieutenant general, commander of French forces in Tonkin in 1945, and delegate-general of Indo-China. Born in Paris on 2 August 1892, Gabriel Sabattier entered Saint-Cyr in 1913. He was promoted to lieutenant in 1915 and to captain in 1916. Sabattier was sent to Morocco in 1928; six years later he became French military attaché to China with the rank of lieutenant colonel. In November 1940 he went to Indo-China with the rank of colonel, and in 1941 he commanded French troops in the short war with Thailand. The next year he was commander of French troops in southern Vietnam as a brigadier general.

In 1944 Sabattier became commander of the Tonkin Division. He sought permission from the French Army commander in Indo-China, Lt. Gen. Eugène Mordant, to begin preparations to wage guerrilla warfare in the event of a Japanese attack, including the establishment of mountain supply caches. Mordant refused, fearful of provoking the Japanese.

Sabattier became alarmed by reports that the Japanese might be intending something, and on the morning of 8 March 1945 he ordered his troops placed on "armed exercise" status. Anxious not to alarm the Japanese, Mordant canceled Sabattier's alert the next morning, but some units either did not get the word or disobeyed the order. Later that day the Japanese carried out their well-planned coup.

The Japanese failed on the 9th to attack Sabattier's two forces positioned just to the west and northwest of Hà Nôi. This enabled some 6,000 men to evacuate their camps. In their retreat westward the French hoped for assistance from the U.S. Air Force; commander of the Fourth Air Force General Claire Chennault was in favor of such action, but a pessimistic President Franklin Roosevelt opposed it, despite pleas from Paris.

Maj. Gen. Marcel Alessandri commanded the Second Tonkin Brigade. On 11 March 1945 he decided to disarm his Indo-Chinese riflemen and leave them behind to fend for themselves. Most were staunchly loyal to the French and the action wounded them deeply; later the Viêt Minh used this as an example of French perfidy.

Sabattier and Alessandri hoped the Japanese would be content to control the populous Delta regions, allowing French forces that escaped the initial coup to remain in the Tonkin highlands until the end of the war.

In late March Paris granted Sabattier full civil and military powers as part of his title as delegate-general. Sabattier installed himself in the Điên Biên Phu area and busied himself with political activities, turning over military matters to Alessandri.

But the Japanese were determined to get rid of the French altogether. Their military actions against the French made retreat to Yunnan the only viable course of action. The French had to destroy their artillery and vehicles at river crossings because of lack of adequate ferries and rafts, and the Japanese blocked the two most important border exits at Lào Cai and Hà Giang.

In all, some 5,000 French troops made the 600-mile-long anabasis to southern China, where they were accorded a chilly reception. Sabattier continued as the senior French military representative there for some three months. But on 15 August 1945, in a fateful decision, Provisional President of the French Republic Charles de Gaulle replaced Sabattier, naming Admiral Georges Thierry d'Argenlieu as high commissioner for Indo-China and instructing him "to restore French sovereignty in the Indo-China Union." Sabattier returned to France at the end of 1945. He died in Paris on 22 May 1966.

—Spencer C. Tucker

References: Dalloz, Jacques. *The War in Indo-China, 1945–1954.* Translated by Josephine Bacon. Savage, MD: Barnes and Noble, 1990.
Marr, David G. *Vietnam 1945: The Quest for Power.* Berkeley, CA: University of California Press, 1996.
Patti, Archimedes L. A. *Why Viet Nam? Prelude to America's Albatross.* Berkeley, CA: University of California Press, 1980.
Sabattier, Gabriel. *Le Destin de l'Indochine: Souvenirs et documents, 1941–1951.* Paris: Plon, 1952.
See also: Alessandri, Marcel; d'Argenlieu, Georges Thierry; Franco-Thai War; Mordant, Eugène; Roosevelt, Franklin Delano.

Sài Gòn Military Mission

Effort by Allen Dulles of the Central Intelligence Agency (CIA) and Secretary of State John Foster Dulles to accomplish two tasks simultaneously: to weaken the government of the Democratic Republic of Vietnam (DRV) and to support and strengthen former emperor Bao Đai's State of Vietnam non-Communist government south of the 17th parallel. Organized in the summer of 1954, shortly after the Geneva Conference, the Sài Gòn Military Mission (SMM) was headed by Air Force Col. (later Maj. Gen.) Edward Lansdale, who for some time had been on loan to the CIA. His orders called for him to serve in Sài Gòn as assistant air attaché on embassy duty, but his real mission was to assist in the birth of a southern government capable of successfully competing with and opposing Hô Chí Minh's DRV. Lansdale had an unlimited budget and complete operational freedom. He was authorized to put together a small team to help him. Those he selected included many CIA operatives, some on loan from active or reserve military units and some career agents.

Lansdale was in place, although without his team members, before Ngô Đình Diêm, Bao Đai's newly appointed prime minister, arrived in Sài Gòn on 26 June 1954. The two met at Independence

(Độc Lập) Palace and within three weeks were fast friends, largely due to Lansdale's sympathetic and receptive manner, behind which he couched his advice. He urged Diệm to become more a "man of the people" to create a loyal bureaucracy and to implement a number of social, economic, and political reforms, including building schools, repairing roads, and teaching personal and public hygiene, all suggesting to rural inhabitants benefits that might be theirs if they supported the Sài Gòn government. Lansdale also counseled Diệm to establish service clubs after the model of Rotary International, and helped Filipinos set up Operation BROTHERHOOD and the Freedom Company in Vietnam. He also persuaded Diệm to take advantage of the provision of the Geneva Accords that, during the first 300 days, allowed civilians living in either zone to remove to the other. Aided by the Seventh Fleet and American air transport (Civil Air Transport, a CIA front organization), some 1.5 million people ultimately came south (the Great Migration), while perhaps 90,000 resettled in the North. It was a coup for Diệm and for Lansdale.

Using the Great Migration as a cover, Lansdale sent part of his team, under the leadership of Lucien Conein, into the North to carry out acts of sabotage. Conein and the northern team recruited and trained two groups of Vietnamese who would serve as "stay-behind" agents: the Hòa and Bình teams. Conein and the others buried caches of weapons and attempted unsuccessfully to close the port of Hai Phòng, to contaminate northern petroleum supplies, and to sabotage rail and bus transportation before they were called back south at the end of the population exchange. Most of their efforts were ultimately futile. Northern officials quickly rolled up the Hòa and Bình teams and located the caches.

The SMM had better luck in the south. It foiled an attempted assassination of Diệm by his army chief of staff, set up a Palace Guard under the leadership of Filipino Napoleon Valeriano, and contacted various leaders of the Hòa Hao and Cao Đài sect armies, bribing many of them to give up their independence for commissions in the Army of the Republic of Vietnam (ARVN). SMM members recall going to meetings with such men, carrying suitcases crammed with CIA-supplied bribe money. Many sect generals and their men became part of the ARVN, strengthening the hand of Diệm. Cao Đài General Nguyên Thành Phường demanded and received $3.6 million for his loyalty, in addition to monthly payments for his troops. General Trân Văn Soái, a Hòa Hao warlord, cost $3 million.

This additional manpower gave Diệm the courage to stand up to the Bình Xuyên sect in fighting that began 26 April 1955. By 9 May Bình Xuyên troops had been driven from Sài Gòn into southern swamps. Yet perhaps the most successful action of the SMM was its support of Diệm when he called for a nationwide election in 1955 to determine whether the country should remain under the leadership of Bao Đai or become an independent republic with him as its president. Lansdale counseled restraint; he told Diệm there should be no stuffing of ballot boxes and that voting should be fair; Diệm ignored the advice. The polls opened on 23 October 1955. Diệm won the election, receiving 98 percent of the overall vote and in Sài Gòn 605,025 votes, one-third more than the

total number of 450,000 registered voters. Diệm garnered 5.7 million votes; Bao Đai received only 63,000. Lansdale left Vietnam soon afterward. The work of the SMM had ended.

—Cecil B. Currey

References: Currey, Cecil B. *Edward Lansdale: The Unquiet American.* Boston: Houghton Mifflin, 1988.
Interviews with most of the principals.
See also: Bao Đai; Bình Xuyên; Cao Đài; Conein, Lucien Emile; Dulles, Allen Welsh; Dulles, John Foster; Hòa Hao; Lansdale, Edward Geary; Ngô Đình Diệm; United States: Involvement in Vietnam, 1954–1965; Vietnam, Republic of: 1954–1975.

Sainteny, Jean
(1907–1978)

Key French diplomat in negotiations with Hô Chí Minh and the Viêt Minh at the end of World War II. Jean Sainteny was born in Vésinet (Seine-et-Oise) on 29 May 1907. From 1929 to 1940 he pursued a banking career, first in Indo-China (1929–1931) and then in Paris. A Resistance hero during the Second World War, he was a key figure in Marie-Madeleine Fourcade's Alliance network. In March 1944 he carried to Britain plans of German coastal defenses that were vital in Allied planning for the June 1944 Normandy invasion.

After the liberation, Sainteny held a series of key diplomatic posts in Southeast Asia. In 1945 General Charles de Gaulle named him head of the French military mission to China. On 3 October that same year he was appointed commissioner for Tonkin and North An Nam, a post he held until 1 December 1947.

Sainteny and Hô Chí Minh negotiated what became known as the Hô-Sainteny Agreements of 3 March 1946. These provided for French recognition of the independence of the Democratic Republic of Vietnam (DRV) within the Indo-China federation and the French Union, the return of 15,000 French troops into northern Vietnam (but with a phased five-year withdrawal), and a plebiscite for southern Vietnam to determine if it wished to join the DRV. Had these agreements been fully implemented there would have been no Indo-China War.

In June 1946 Sainteny returned to France with Hô Chí Minh to take part in negotiations at the Fontainebleau Conference, which were torpedoed while he was away by the actions of the French proconsul in Indo-China, Admiral Thierry d'Argenlieu. From 1954 to 1958 Sainteny was the senior French representative ("delegate") to the Democratic Republic of Vietnam. He left the DRV in 1957 "on temporary leave," his mission of protecting French property a failure. After Charles de Gaulle's return to power in 1958, Sainteny was elected to the National Assembly on the Gaullist ticket. From 1959 to 1962 he was commissioner general for tourism, and from 1962 to 1966 he was minister for war veterans and war victims under Premier Georges Pompidou. He was a director of Air France from 1967 to 1972 and an officer in many other organizations. Sainteny made several trips to the DRV during the Vietnam War, providing useful information on DRV policies. Jean Sainteny died in Paris on 25 February 1978. His memoir *Histoire d'une Paix Manquée: Indochine 1945–1947* (1953) leaves no doubt that a policy of open negotiation with the Viêt Minh would have prevented all the unhappy events that followed.

—Spencer C. Tucker

References: Fall, Bernard. *The Two Viet Nams.* Rev. ed. New York: Praeger, 1964.

Fourcade, Marie-Madeleine. *Noah's Ark: A Memoir of Struggle and Resistance.* New York: E. P. Dutton, 1974.

Sainteny, Jean. *Histoire d'une Paix Manquée: Indochine, 1945–1947.* Paris: Amiot-Dumont, 1953.

See also: d'Argenlieu, Georges Thierry; de Gaulle, Charles André Marie Joseph; Fontainebleau Conference; Hô Chí Minh; Hô-Sainteny Agreement; Indo-China War.

Salan, Raoul Albin Louis

(1899–1984)

French Army general, commander of French forces in Indo-China (1952–1953), and once France's most decorated soldier. Raoul Salan was born in Roquecourbe near Toulouse on 10 June 1899, the son of a physician. He went to war at age 18 in 1917, and he won the Croix de Guerre and in subsequent years 85 other decorations. Salan later graduated from the military academy at Saint-Cyr and served in the colonial infantry in Algeria, Morocco, and the Middle East.

In 1924 Salan had his first tour in Indo-China. At the beginning of the Second World War, he commanded a battalion of Senegalese troops in Africa. At first loyal to Vichy, in 1943 he changed sides and campaigned with General Jean de Lattre de Tassigny's forces in southern France.

At the end of the war Salan took part in peace negotiations that secured the Chinese withdrawal from northern Vietnam, and, as commander of French troops in Tonkin, in April 1946 he signed the accords establishing the size and location of French and Vietnamese garrisons within the Democratic Republic of Vietnam (DRV). In 1948 Salan commanded all French troops in the Far East.

In 1952 de Lattre, then French high commissioner for Indo-China, appointed Salan field commander of French military forces. Salan succeeded de Lattre as commander in chief on the latter's death in January 1952. As military commander, Salan followed largely defensive tactics against the Viêt Minh. The inability of French forces to halt a Viêt Minh invasion of Laos in April 1953—a seemingly easy task—led to Salan's replacement by General Henri Navarre. Following the Battle of Điên Biên Phu, Salan returned to Indo-China with General Paul Ely on a fact-finding mission that recommended an evacuation of all French troops from North Vietnam and French concentration on the area south of the 16th parallel.

Salan was politicized by the French defeat in Indo-China. In November 1954 a rebellion against French rule broke out in Algeria, and in December 1956 Salan was named commander of French forces there. Nicknamed the "Mandarin" or the "Chinaman" for his cunning, Oriental impassivity, and Asian experiences, Salan was distrusted by many of his fellow officers and was an unpopular command choice. In 1957 he was the target of a right-wing assassination attempt. Salan supported General

Charles de Gaulle's return to power following the May 1958 right-wing settler uprising in Algiers and the end of the Fourth French Republic. In December 1958 de Gaulle, who shared in the general distrust of Salan, removed him from command.

Salan retired in Algeria in 1959 and eventually joined other generals, colonial troops, and European settlers in plotting to keep Algeria French. Exiled to Spain in 1960, he was active in forming the Secret Army Organization (OAS), which employed terrorism in metropolitan France. In April 1961 Salan and three other generals led a coup in Algiers and held power there for four days. De Gaulle managed to hold the loyalty of the bulk of the army; however, Algiers fell to loyalist forces, and Salan went into hiding. In July he was sentenced in absentia to death for treason. Captured in Algiers in April 1962, he was sentenced to life in prison and stripped of military honors. President de Gaulle pardoned him in June 1968 and in 1982 President François Mitterand restored him to the rank of full general and reinstated his pension. Salan spent his last years writing about his experiences in Indo-China and Algeria. He died in Paris on 3 July 1984.

—Spencer C. Tucker

References: *The International Who's Who, 1983–1984.* 47th ed. London: Europa Publications, 1983.

Salan, General Raoul. *Indochine Rouge: Le Message d'Ho Chi Minh.* Paris: Presses de la Cité, 1975.

_____. *Mémoires: Fin d'un Empire, "Le Viet-Minh Mon Adversaire" October 1946–October 1954.* Paris: Presses de la Cité, 1954.

_____. *Le Sens d'un Engagement, 1899–1946.* Paris: Presses de la Cité, 1970.

See also: de Lattre de Tassigny, Jean Joseph Marie Gabriel; France: Army; LORRAINE, Operation; Na San, Battle of; Navarre, Henri Eugène.

Salisbury, Harrison E.

(1908–1993)

New York Times editor and correspondent, 1949–1973. Harrison Salisbury was born in Minneapolis, Minnesota, on 14 November 1908. He graduated from the University of Minnesota with a B.A. in 1930 and then joined the United Press as a correspondent, a position he held until 1948. In 1949 he became the Moscow correspondent for the *New York Times.* Salisbury developed an interest and expertise in Soviet and Far East affairs that would place him among America's most distinguished journalists. In 1955 he won the Pulitzer Prize for international reporting. He produced a number of books inspired by or related to his Soviet experience, including *American in Russia, Moscow Journal,* and *The Nine Hundred Days: The Siege of Leningrad.*

Salisbury played a controversial role in the reporting of the Vietnam War. In December 1966 he was the first American newsman to be admitted to the Democratic Republic of Vietnam (DRV). For several weeks he sent back controversial dispatches that asserted the heavy U.S. bombing campaign was not having the anticipated incapacitating effects upon the DRV's economy, but that it was killing thousands of innocent civilians. He also emphasized that, despite the bombing, North Vietnamese morale remained high. President Lyndon Johnson and Pentagon officials, together with some journalists, strongly criticized Salisbury as a

Communist mouthpiece, and, among other things, for "lending aid and comfort to the enemy." But others applauded his reporting as an exercise in honesty and courage, presenting unpalatable but necessary facts to the American public. This episode initiated a greater willingness on the part of well-established newspapers to challenge official administration accounts of the progress of the Vietnam War. Salisbury's articles failed, however, to win Pulitzer recognition. Despite substantial support from editors and correspondents, the decision to award Salisbury the coveted prize was overruled.

Until his death, Salisbury continued to travel and write extensively. In his later years he developed considerable expertise on China and produced several books, including *To Peking and Beyond, China: 100 Years of Revolution,* and *The Long March: The Untold Story.* He died of a heart attack on 15 July 1993 in Providence, Rhode Island.

—Priscilla Roberts

References: Karnow, Stanley. *Vietnam: A History.* New York: Viking Press, 1983.
Salisbury, Harrison. *Behind the Lines: Hanoi, December 23, 1966–January 7, 1967.* New York: Harper & Row, 1967.
_____. *A Journey for Our Times: A Memoir.* New York: Harper & Row, 1983.
_____. *A Time of Change: A Reporter's Tale of Our Time.* New York: Harper & Row, 1988.
_____. *Without Fear or Favor: The New York Times and Its Times.* New York: Harper & Row, 1980.
See also: Burchett, Wilfred; Fall, Bernard B.; Johnson, Lyndon Baines; Media and the War.

San Antonio Formula

(29 September 1967)
President Lyndon Johnson's proposed formula for peace talks between the Democratic Republic of Vietnam (DRV) and the United States. On 29 September 1967 President Johnson delivered a speech in San Antonio, Texas, in which he publicly offered to stop "all aerial and naval bombardment" of North Vietnam if DRV leader Hô Chí Minh would agree immediately to enter productive peace negotiations. Johnson also demanded that while discussions proceeded that the DRV not take advantage of a bombing cessation or limitation to infiltrate men or supplies into the South.

Johnson's offer stemmed from the so-called "Pennsylvania Channel," the private diplomatic initiative of two French intermediaries, Herbert Marcovich and Raymond Aubrac. Henry Kissinger, at the time a private citizen, traveled to Hà Nôi to present Johnson's proposal, which later became known as the San Antonio Formula. The DRV leadership rejected the offer, labeling it "insulting" and noted that it was conditional—dependent on "prompt productive discussions."

Secretary of Defense Robert S. McNamara recommended the deletion of the offensive language, but debate over this continued within the administration. President Johnson renewed the offer again on 31 March 1968, following the January Têt Offensive and his own decision not to seek reelection. Although Hà Nôi never responded positively to it, the San Antonio Formula did serve as the basis for future negotiations.

—Mary L. Kelley

References: Clifford, Clark. *Counsel to the President: A Memoir.* New York: Random House, 1991.
Cooper, Chester L. *The Lost Crusade.* New York: Dodd, Mead, 1970.
McNamara, Robert S. *In Retrospect: The Tragedy and Lessons of Vietnam.* New York: Random House, 1995.
See also: Hô Chí Minh; Johnson, Lyndon Baines; Kissinger, Henry Alfred; McNamara, Robert S.

Sanctuaries

Places of refuge or protection. In the Vietnam War context they were places where the Viêt Công (VC) and People's Army of Vietnam (PAVN) soldiers could retreat and be safe from attack. Although places like the U Minh Forest and the Iron Triangle were sometimes referred to as sanctuaries, Communist forces there were not safe from attack, and thus they were not true sanctuaries. In theory, Cambodia and Laos became sanctuaries during the war because their so-called neutrality was used by VC and PAVN forces to gain protection from attack throughout the war.

Cambodia and Laos, both former protectorates under the French Indo-China Union, had declared their neutrality soon after gaining independence. Laos had become a constitutional monarchy in 1949, and in 1962 a conference at Geneva officially proclaimed that country's neutrality. On the other hand, Cambodia's Prince Norodom Sihanouk declared his country neutral soon after the French withdrew in 1954 and tried to preserve that neutrality throughout the war. Presidents John Kennedy and Lyndon Johnson publicly declared that the United States would honor both countries' proclaimed neutrality.

According to the 1907 Hague Convention, the definition of neutrality includes the statement, "A neutral country has the obligation not to allow its territory to be used by a belligerent. If the neutral country is unwilling or unable to prevent this, the other belligerent has the right to take appropriate counteraction."

As early as May 1959 the DRV formed a military unit in Laos to funnel arms and supplies to Communist guerrillas there and began construction of an infiltration route through the Laotian panhandle and eastern Cambodia to transport soldiers and supplies into South Vietnam. Known as the Hô Chí Minh Trail, this avenue was used and even expanded throughout the war. Also, by the mid-1960s rest, resupply, and training bases had been established across the Republic of Vietnam (RVN) border in Cambodia for VC and PAVN troops, and war supplies were being landed at the port of Sihanoukville and brought overland to these sanctuaries.

In response, in 1963 the United States began the first of several bombing campaigns against the Hô Chí Minh Trail that would continue until 1974. In addition, limited U.S. artillery and air attacks were directed across the border into Cambodia beginning in 1966 in response to Communist fire from those sanctuaries. In March 1969, with tacit approval from Prince Sihanouk, secret B-52 bombing raids hit PAVN base areas inside Cambodia, and in April 1970 U.S. and Army of the Republic of Vietnam (ARVN) forces, with the approval of President Richard Nixon, conducted an "incursion" into Cambodia to destroy Communist bases. Likewise, a U.S.-supported (without U.S. ground troops) ARVN raid against the Hô Chí Minh Trail in Laos, Operation LAM SỞN 719, was conducted in February 1971. What had begun as sanctuaries, because of violations of neutrality, became extensions of the battlefield.

—Arthur T. Frame

References: Clarke, Jeffrey J. *Advice and Support: The Final Years, 1965–1973.* Washington, DC: U.S. Army Center of Military History, 1988.
Herring, George C. *America's Longest War: The United States and Vietnam, 1950–1975.* 2d ed. New York: Alfred A. Knopf, 1986.
Karnow, Stanley. *Vietnam: A History.* New York: Penguin Books, 1984.
Lewy, Gunther. *America in Vietnam.* New York: Oxford University Press, 1978.
Stanton, Shelby L. *The Rise and Fall of an American Army: U.S. Ground Forces in Vietnam, 1965–1973.* New York: Dell, 1985.
See also: BARREL ROLL, Operation; Cambodia; Hô Chí Minh Trail; Iron Triangle; LAM SỞN 719, Operation; Laos; MENU, Operation; Sihanouk, Norodom; STEEL TIGER, Operation; TIGER HOUND, Operation; White Star.

Sarraut, Albert

(1872–1962)

French politician, premier, and governor-general of Indo-China (1911–1914 and 1917–1919). Albert Sarraut was born in Bordeaux on 28 July 1872. Trained in the law, he was a deputy from the Aude to the National Assembly from 1902 to 1924 and senator from 1926 to 1940. Sarraut fought in World War I as a lieutenant and won the Médaille Militaire at Verdun in 1916.

Sarraut's greatest contribution to France was in colonial affairs. He was governor-general of Indo-China from November 1911 to January 1914, when severe illness forced his return to France, and from January 1917 to May 1919. As governor-general he represented the best in French liberal republican ideals and helped shift French policy from assimilation to association.

Sarraut worked to improve administration by a policy of fewer but better-trained civil servants, restoring examinations for appointment, and opening more posts to natives, but his efforts to stiffen language requirements met considerable resistance and had little success. Sarraut also carried out judicial reform. He insisted on uniformity throughout the Union and worked to revise legal codes to ensure justice for the natives and to end torture and corporal punishment. He worked to improve medicine and promoted the building of hospitals and clinics. Sarraut also worked to raise the standard of living through attention to public works and by improving education. He opened more secondary schools to natives and discouraged sending Vietnamese to study in France. Virginia Thompson, in *French Indo-China,* called him the first governor-general "to win native devotion" and "the most popular man France ever sent to the colony."

From 1920 to 1940 Sarraut was almost continuously a minister of state. From 1920 to 1924 and from 1932 to 1933 he was minister of colonies. As leader of the Radical Party, Sarraut was briefly premier in 1933 and again in 1936 (during the German remilitarization of the Rhineland, when he sought but failed to secure punitive action against Germany).

From 1947 to 1958 Sarraut was on the High Council of the French Union. He died in Paris on 26 November 1962.

—Spencer C. Tucker

References: Bernstein, S. *Histoire du parti radical.* 2 vols. Paris: Presses de la Foundation Nationale des Sciences Politiques, 1980–1982.
Hammer, Ellen J. *The Struggle for Indochina.* Stanford, CA: Stanford University Press, 1954.
Hutton, Patrick H., ed. *Historical Dictionary of the Third French Republic, 1870–1940.* Vol. 2. New York: Greenwood Press, 1986.
Sarraut, Albert. *Grandeur et servitude coloniales.* Paris: Editions du Sagittaire, 1931.
_____. *La Mise en valeur des colonies françaises.* Paris: Payot, 1923.
Thompson, Virginia. *French Indo-China.* New York: Octagon Books, 1968.
See also: French Indo-China.

Schlesinger, Arthur M., Jr.

(1917–)

Prominent American scholar; special assistant to the president (1961–1964). Born 15 October 1917 in Columbus, Ohio, Arthur M. Schlesinger, Jr. earned a degree in history from Harvard University in 1938. His book, *The Age of Jackson,* won the Pulitzer Prize for History in 1946, and Schlesinger, who did not have an advanced degree, became a tenured associate professor of history at Harvard; he was made a full professor in 1954. Schlesinger sought to downplay class conflict in American history and instead focused on the great programs that improved life in America; he also emphasized the examination of heroism.

In 1961 Schlesinger joined President John F. Kennedy's circle of advisors as a special assistant. After the president's death, he published *A Thousand Days: John F. Kennedy in the White House,* which became a best-seller and won a National Book Award and a Pulitzer Prize.

In 1966 he joined the faculty of the City University of New York and began to examine the Vietnam conflict. At first Schlesinger opposed an American withdrawal from Vietnam for fear of Chinese encroachment, but, gradually dismayed by the increasing American involvement, he pushed for de-escalation and negotiation. Yet, Schlesinger refused to blame the problems in Vietnam on any specific U.S. policy or individual. He lambasted revisionist policy analysts who blamed a deliberately aggressive American foreign policy. He believed that in foreign policy moral considerations should not exceed national interests.

Alarmed by the growing power of the presidency, Schlesinger wrote *The Imperial Presidency,* which studied the gradual assumption of power by the executive branch, mainly through the conduct of an independent foreign policy and war making. In 1978 he published *Robert Kennedy and His Times.*

—Laura Matysek Wood

References: Anderson, Patrick. *The President's Men.* Garden City, NY: Anchor Books, 1968.
Depoe, Stephen. *Arthur M. Schlesinger, Jr. and the Ideological History of American Liberalism.* Tuscaloosa, AL: University of Alabama Press, 1994.
See also: Fall, Bernard B.; Kennedy, John Fitzgerald; Salisbury, Harrison E.

Schlesinger, James R.

(1929–)

Director, Central Intelligence Agency, January to June 1973; secretary of defense, June 1973 to November 1975. Born on 15 February 1929 in New York City, James Schlesinger earned a B.A. (1950), an M.A., and then a Ph.D. (1956) at Harvard University. He began his career as a college teacher and then became the director of Strategic Studies at the RAND Corporation. Schlesinger served in several positions during the Nixon administration, including brief stints as director of central intelligence and as Nixon's last secretary of defense, although he was largely ignored in Vietnam-related policy making.

A measured opponent of détente with the Soviet Union, Schlesinger clashed with Congress when he argued against proposed cuts in allocations to the North Atlantic Treaty Organization (NATO). President Gerald Ford disliked the often imperious Schlesinger but retained him in his cabinet to appease conservative Republicans. Schlesinger continued his criticism of détente, often grumbling against Ford's attempts to continue arms talks with the Soviets.

In terms of Vietnam, Schlesinger was one of the more moderate voices among Ford's national security advisors. He argued in favor of Ford's plan to grant limited amnesty to Vietnam-era draft offenders, and he was one of the first cabinet members, as early as September 1974, to push for a swift withdrawal of all U.S. Embassy personnel from Sài Gòn. Ford ultimately ignored Schlesinger's counsel on Vietnam, widening the rift between the two men. Ford even suspected that Schlesinger defied a presidential order during the *Mayaguez* crisis and that he had refused to order a fourth air strike on the Cambodian mainland. On 2 November 1975 Ford replaced Schlesinger with former White House Chief of Staff Donald Rumsfeld. Schlesinger went on to serve as President Jimmy Carter's secretary of energy and then reentered academic life. Schlesinger later became a senior advisor for Lehman Brothers in Washington, D.C.

—John Robert Greene

Reference: Greene, John Robert. *The Presidency of Gerald R. Ford.* Lawrence, KS: University Press of Kansas, 1995.
See also: Central Intelligence Agency (CIA); Ford, Gerald R.; *Mayaguez* Incident; Nixon, Richard Milhous; RAND Corporation.

Schwarzkopf, H. Norman, Jr.

(1934–)

U.S. Army general. Schwarzkopf was born on 22 August 1934 in Trenton, New Jersey. He attended Bordentown Military Institute and Valley Forge Military Academy before going on to the U.S. Military Academy at West Point, from which he graduated in 1956. His father, also an army general, had a checkered career, having left the service in the late 1920s to head the New Jersey State Police. As such, he headed the investigation of the Lindbergh kidnapping. At the outbreak of World War II, the elder Schwarzkopf rejoined the Army. From 1942 to 1948 he led the U.S. mission to Iran. At the age of 12, Norman, Jr. accompanied his father to Iran. After one year he was sent to Europe, where he received some schooling in Switzerland.

Following graduation from West Point, Schwarzkopf held normal career assignments before serving two tours in Vietnam. His first tour was as an advisor to Army of the Republic of Vietnam (ARVN) airborne troops. During his second tour, as an infantry battalion commander, he received his third Silver Star and a second Purple Heart.

During the 1983 Grenada invasion, Schwarzkopf served as Army chief advisor to the admiral commanding the invasion. Later, as commander of Central Command, he was charged with ousting Iraqi forces from Kuwait during Operation DESERT STORM in 1991. Remembering Vietnam and the gradual escalation strategy, he insisted on a maximum buildup of forces before any military action was taken against the Iraqis. Following DESERT STORM he retired from the Army as a full general in 1991. Schwarzkopf believed that the Gulf War may have finally brought the American people to terms with Vietnam.

—Robert G. Mangrum

References: Birnbaum, Jesse. "Stormin' Norman on Top." *Time* (4 February 1991).
Dallas Morning News (21 April 1991; 10 August 1991; 20 September 1992).
Schwarzkopf, H. Norman. *It Doesn't Take a Hero.* New York: Bantam Books, 1992.
See also: Powell, Colin L.

SCOTLAND, Operation

(November 1967—March 1968)

U.S. Marine Corps operation in Quang Tri Province. Succeeding Operation ARDMORE, Operation SCOTLAND began on 1 November 1967 in western Quang Tri Province. Initially, the 3d Battalion, 26th Marines (3/26th) encamped at the Khe Sanh Combat Base, with the 1st Battalion, 26th Marines (1/26th) positioned on strategic hills west and north. In January 1968 the 2d Battalion, 26th Marines (2/26th) reinforced Khe Sanh, as it appeared that three People's Army of Vietnam (PAVN) divisions were massing in the area. After several quiet weeks, on 20 January a company of the 1/26th, joined by a reaction force from the 3/26th, engaged a PAVN battalion entrenched between Hills 881 South and 881 North, killing 103, while losing 7 dead and 35 wounded. The second Battle of Khe Sanh had begun.

On 21 January PAVN forces failed to take Hill 861, losing 47 killed, but overran the village of Khe Sanh and showered artillery shells and rockets on the area, blowing up a large ammunition dump. The previous day's action had deterred a simultaneous attack on Hill 881S. The Marines had thwarted a PAVN plan to use both hills as firebases. The Army of the Republic of Vietnam (ARVN) 37th Ranger Battalion then joined the five Marine battalions in and around Khe Sanh, now supported by 46 artillery pieces, five 90-mm tank guns, and 92 106-mm recoilless rifles. Despite the widely reported dangers and miseries experienced by its defenders, Khe Sanh Combat Base itself never was seriously threatened by ground forces. Less well known, but perhaps more significant militarily, is the valor displayed by the Marines on the outlying hills and listening posts. Two companies occupied Hill 881S, perhaps the most isolated Marine firebase in Vietnam, while three companies and a reinforced platoon occupied Hills 861, 861A, 558, and 950. From these outposts overlooking the Khe Sanh plateau, the Marines directed artillery and air strikes on moving PAVN units. PAVN forces held Hill 881N, from which they launched 5,000 122-mm rockets at Khe Sanh. From 881S, Marines could observe these launches and alert the base; thus, they became a target themselves and were shelled heavily, losing 40 killed and 150 wounded, proportionally greater casualties than at Khe Sanh proper.

The night of 5 February a battalion of the PAVN 325C Division assaulted a Marine company on the west slope of Hill 861A, breaching the perimeter but leaving 109 dead after hand-to-hand fighting. Marine casualties were 7 killed and 35 wounded. The next day a regiment of the PAVN 304th Division overran Làng Vei Special Forces camp southwest of Khe Sanh. But the worst day for the 26th Marines was 25 February, when a PAVN company ambushed the 3d Platoon, Company B, 1/26th, patrolling south of the base, and also decimated a relief platoon. Company B lost almost two-thirds of its men, including every soldier in the so-called "Doomed Patrol," whose bodies were not recovered until two weeks later. By mid-March, PAVN units began their exit from the Khe Sanh area, although the shelling continued. On 24 March a patrol from Company A, 1st Battalion, 9th Marines (1/9th), killed 31 PAVN soldiers in fighting northwest of the base. In the last encounter, on 30 March, Company B, 1/26th Marines, attacked an entrenched PAVN battalion south of the base, killing 34 while losing 5.

Operation SCOTLAND officially ended on that day, with the 26th Marines counting more than 1,600 PAVN dead (excluding thousands killed by bombing). Their own casualties officially numbered 205 killed and 1,668 wounded. John Prados and Ray Stubbe, however, have identified by name 353 Marines killed between 20 January and 31 March alone. Operation PEGASUS (1–15 April), a combined Army, Marine, and ARVN force, effected the relief of Khe Sanh as the PAVN withdrawal continued. It accounted for 1,304 PAVN dead, while U.S. forces sustained 92 killed (51 Marines) and 667 wounded; the ARVN lost 33 men and 206 wounded. Meanwhile, Marines from the 3/26th moved from Hill 881S to attack PAVN forces still entrenched around Hill 881N, killing more than 200, while losing 6 men.

The day PEGASUS ended, the Marines launched Operation SCOTLAND II, which lasted until 28 February 1969. Initially, the 3/26th Marines swept the valley floor west from Khe Sanh toward Hill 881S and found themselves stepping over hundreds of skeletal remains. The 1/9th Marines endured intense fighting against PAVN bunker complexes near Hill 689, losing 9 dead, 53 wounded, and 32 missing in action. Ironically, the 3/26th Marines took more casualties leaving Khe Sanh than during the siege itself, with 301 killed and more than 1,500 wounded by 11 July. The Khe Sanh base was abandoned by 27 June, even though at least ten PAVN battalions remained in western Quang Tri. Now employing mobile tactics, by the end of SCOTLAND II Marines had killed more than 3,000 and captured 64 PAVN soldiers while suffering 435 dead and 2,395 wounded.

—John D. Root

References: Prados, John, and Ray W. Stubbe. *Valley of Decision: The Siege of Khe Sanh.* Boston: Houghton Mifflin, 1991.
Shore, Moyers S., II. *The Battle for Khe Sanh (1969).* Washington, DC: U.S. Marine Corps, 1977.
See also: Khe Sanh, Battles of; PEGASUS–LAM SƠN 207A, Operation; United States: Marine Corps; Vietnam, Democratic Republic of: Army (People's Army of Vietnam [PAVN]).

SEA DRAGON, Operation

(25 October 1966–31 October 1968)

Two-year-long U.S. Navy campaign designed to cut the southward flow of munitions and to bombard positions of military significance in the Democratic Republic of Vietnam (DRV). Designated Operation SEA DRAGON, the first U.S. surface ship foray into waters north of the Demilitarized Zone (DMZ) occurred on 25 October 1966 when the destroyers *Mansfield* and *Hanson* commenced patrols to counter Communist waterborne logistics movements from North Vietnam into Quang Tri Province. Although this initial sweep was unproductive, by February 1967 SEA DRAGON ships had extended their raids 230 miles above the DMZ to the 20th parallel.

The vessels involved were usually the older gunships of the Seventh Fleet. At the height of the campaign in May 1967 two cruisers and 12 destroyers were assigned to SEA DRAGON missions. Normal tactics called for surface action groups to make high-speed dashes from 20 miles offshore to logistics choke points such as the mouths of the Song Giang and Kiên Giang Rivers. Targeted were radar stations, coastal guns, and supply craft, although truck columns, boat repair facilities, bridges, and surface-to-air missile (SAM) sites were occasional victims. The U.S. ships also detected and analyzed Communist radar transmissions.

Results of these strikes were frequently gratifying. For instance, in May 1967 SEA DRAGON raiders damaged or destroyed 160 of the 420 waterborne logistics craft (WBLC) that had been detected. After one year of this effort, Seventh Fleet headquarters calculated that SEA DRAGON warships had sunk or damaged 2,000 logistics craft and had drastically stemmed the flow of supplies from the DRV to the South.

The U.S. effort did not go unchallenged, and the North Vietnamese increased their shore batteries in both numbers and caliber. Mobile and difficult to locate, these guns often subjected SEA DRAGON ships to heavy fire. During the summer of 1967 DRV batteries engaged U.S. warships between 10 and 15 times monthly. For example, on 2 August 1967 the heavy cruiser *St. Paul* was bracketed by nearly 100 shell bursts, which inflicted minor structural damage on the vessel. Two months later on 18 October, as many as 12 shore batteries fired over 200 rounds at the heavy cruiser *Newport News* and the Australian destroyer *Perth,* both of which were steaming near Sâm Sơn. The *Perth* took a direct hit, which disabled her Tartar missile system. Overall, 29 SEA DRAGON ships were damaged, 5 sailors were killed, and 26 wounded.

With President Lyndon Johnson's bombing halt of April 1968, U.S. forces were restricted to waters from the DMZ 150 miles north to the 19th parallel, a one-third reduction in the operating area. The SEA DRAGON campaign ended altogether on 31 October 1968, when U.S. units withdrew south of the DMZ, but Seventh Fleet cruisers, frigates, and destroyers ranged north one last time from April to September 1972 to fire over 110,000 rounds in retaliation for the Easter Offensive.

—Malcolm Muir, Jr.

References: Marolda, Edward J. *By Sea, Air, and Land: An Illustrated History of the U.S. Navy and the War in Southeast Asia.* Washington, DC: Naval Historical Center, 1994.

Muir, Malcolm, Jr. *Black Shoes and Blue Water: Surface Warfare in the United States Navy, 1945–1975.* Washington, DC: Naval Historical Center, 1996.

Uhlig, Frank, Jr., ed. *Vietnam: The Naval Story.* Annapolis, MD: Naval Institute Press, 1986.

See also: Artillery, Allied and People's Army of Vietnam; Australia; Naval Bombardment; Sea Power in the Vietnam War; United States: Navy; Warships, Allied and Democratic Republic of Vietnam.

Sea Power in the Vietnam War

Sea power is useful only in how it ultimately affects events on land, but historically this influence has often been powerful, sometimes even decisive. One noted analyst, Bernard Brodie, writing in the 1960s, dissected the many advantages to be derived by a state from naval dominance: (1) sea power protects the movement over water of one's own military forces and their supplies; (2) it guards friendly shipping from enemy attacks; (3) it prevents an enemy from using the sea to transport their own forces; (4) it exerts military and economic pressure on an enemy by preventing them from maintaining trade; and (5) it bombards land targets. During the conflict in Southeast Asia, the United States exercised every one of these advantages and yet could not achieve its desired results.

Unlike the great struggles for the sea in the two world wars, the United States and its allies enjoyed from the beginning of the Vietnam War unquestioned—and essentially unchallenged—supremacy on the broad oceans. Thus, there was no clash approaching the scope of the Battles of Jutland or Leyte Gulf fought in the South China Sea. Nevertheless, this supremacy did not garner the expected fruits, an anomaly due partly to the nature of the struggle, but also partly to the unreadiness of the United States to exploit its advantages at sea.

American sea power, configured during the 1950s for nuclear war, was unready to rapidly move U.S. military forces and supplies 7,000 miles to the theater of action. Lacking adequate sea lift in 1965, the United States was forced to use the time-consuming practice of chartering foreign merchantmen to transport the equipment and supplies badly needed in South Vietnam. The buildup of American forces took years. Given the nature of the war, time was a luxury that American leaders could not afford to waste.

Better executed was the American task of protecting shipping from enemy attacks. Whereas the Democratic Republic of Vietnam (DRV) had only a small navy composed of coastal craft, U.S. Navy vessels were at hazard only in port or in rivers, where individual ships might be struck by Communist saboteurs or mines. Following certain widely publicized Viêt Công successes early in the war, the U.S. Navy instituted Operation STABLE DOOR, an effective long-term venture to secure South Vietnamese ports.

The Navy was also largely able to prevent the North Vietnamese from transporting their military forces and supplies southward by sea. Beginning in March 1965 the Navy's MARKET TIME patrols of airplanes, destroyers, and small craft augmented by Coast Guard cutters was so effective at reducing the flow of Communist supplies down the coast that the North Vietnamese were forced to rely much more heavily on the Hồ Chí Minh Trail and to open the Sihanouk Trail to the Mekong Delta.

The United States was less successful in using sea power to prevent North Vietnam from maintaining trade with its Communist-bloc supporters. The Johnson administration, wary of intervention by the People's Republic of China (PRC) or the USSR, made no effort to close the principal North Vietnamese port, Hai Phòng. When the Nixon administration finally ordered the mining of Hai Phòng Harbor in retaliation for the DRV's 1972 Easter Offensive, the move proved one of the most effective ploys of the war. No vessels entered the port for over 300 days. Thus, North Vietnam's imports, especially of critical munitions, were slashed by 85 percent.

As for the last of Brodie's advantages conferred by sea power, the U.S. Navy made ample use of its ability to bombard shore targets. With a 1,500-mile coastline and averaging only 80 miles in width, Vietnam was especially suited for such operations. Operating off South Vietnam, Allied warships lent direct fire support to friendly troops. From 1966 to 1968, and again in 1972, U.S. gunships in Operation SEA DRAGON shelled targets above the DMZ. Of course, naval aircraft flying from carriers on station in the Gulf of Tonkin also delivered a great weight of explosives against North Vietnamese targets. Political limitations hobbled these air and surface strikes, making them far less militarily effective than they might have been.

Sea power exerted pressure in another time-honored fashion: force projection through amphibious assaults and riverine operations, although here too the potential advantages were neglected or exploited halfheartedly. Landings by U.S. and South Korean Marines failed, usually because of security leaks, to achieve important results. For instance, Operation BOLD MARINER in January 1969, the largest amphibious action of the war, resulted in the capture of only one Viêt Công sapper company.

In the Mekong Delta, the U.S. Navy conducted riverine ("brown-water") patrols, code-named Operation GAME WARDEN, beginning in March 1966. However, the hastily improvised river patrol boats (PBRs) were too few in number, and their Jacuzzi waterjet pumps were prone to fouling, while their truck engines made such noise as to render surprise almost impossible. Moreover, the top officers in the Navy, such as the aviator chiefs of naval operations (CNOs), were most interested in the carrier war. Not until after the 1968 Têt Offensive did the patrol craft reach the minimum number (250 boats) deemed necessary for successful large-scale operations. By that point the tide of the war had turned. In somewhat similar fashion, the Mobile Riverine Force, designed to carry specially trained soldiers to attack Việt Công bastions in the Mekong Delta, was handicapped by a lack of speedy troop carriers and the substitution of the Army's 9th Division for Marines (assigned to I Corps in the North).

With the collapse of South Vietnam in 1975, Allied sea power was harnessed one last time, in this case to rescue friendly military personnel and civilians fleeing the final Communist offensive. In Operation FREQUENT WIND, in April U.S. Marines and soldiers evacuated thousands of Americans and Allied civilian and military personnel from Sài Gòn. Over the next several months Seventh Fleet warships plucked from the South China Sea tens of thousands of refugees ("boat people").

If the war in Southeast Asia demonstrated some of the capabilities of sea power, the struggle also showed some of its inherent limitations in such a conflict. But if sea power in the end could not bring decisive weight to bear, it nonetheless helped for a decade to stymie the DRV effort to conquer South Vietnam.

—Malcolm Muir, Jr.

References: Cutler, Thomas J. *Brown Water, Black Berets: Coastal and Riverine Warfare in Vietnam.* Annapolis, MD: Naval Institute Press, 1988.
Hagan, Kenneth J. *This People's Navy: The Making of American Sea Power.* New York: Free Press, 1991.
Hooper, Edwin B. *United States Naval Power in a Changing World.* New York: Praeger, 1988.
Uhlig, Frank, Jr. *Vietnam: The Naval Story.* Annapolis, MD: Naval Institute Press, 1986.
See also: BOLD MARINER, Operation; FREQUENT WIND, Operation; GAME WARDEN, Operation; MARKET TIME, Operation; Riverine Craft; Riverine Warfare; SEA DRAGON, Operation; United States: Navy; Warships, Allied and Democratic Republic of Vietnam.

Seabees

See United States: Seabees

SEAL (Sea, Air, Land) Teams

U.S. Navy special operations force. In 1961 President John F. Kennedy believed that the United States needed unconventional warfare capability to combat Communist-inspired "Wars of National Liberation." He personally encouraged the U.S. Army to expand its Special Forces and authorized them to wear the distinctive green beret. The other two services quickly followed suit; the U.S. Air Force formed Air Commando squadrons and the U.S. Navy established the SEALs. The naval unconventional warfare specialists evolved from the underwater demolition teams (UDTs) or "frogmen" employed in World War II and the Korean War. They were trained to operate underwater and on land and were parachute qualified, hence the acronym SEAL (sea, air, land). Their missions consisted of intelligence gathering, raids, ambushes, prisoner captures, and disruption of enemy rear-area operations. In addition, they projected U.S. military power by training forces friendly to the United States in a fashion similar to that of the Army's Special Forces. Each of the two SEAL teams consisted of approximately 200 officers and men; one team was permanently stationed on the East Coast and the other on the West Coast of the United States.

The training program was grueling; once selected, a candidate had to complete the 25-week Basic Underwater Demolition/SEAL (BUD/S) course and the Army's 3-week Airborne School. After finishing the formal school courses, a candidate was posted to an operational UDT or SEAL team for six months' probation. If an individual failed to meet unit standards he would be returned to the fleet. SEAL personnel continually enhanced their combat skills by attending such courses as advanced diving or Army Ranger School. Individuals were also selected to attend foreign special warfare schools, such as Britain's Royal Marine Commando Course or Special Air Service Selection and Training. All SEALs received training in the use of a variety of small arms, hand-to-hand combat, patrolling, land and water navigation, and other specialized skills.

The major doctrinal difference between the UDTs and SEALs was that UDT missions primarily stopped at the water's edge, whereas SEALs conducted missions inland up to a distance of 20 miles. SEALs could infiltrate hostile shores using a variety of methods: disembarking from submerged submarines and swimming to the beach or using different types of small boats to gain access to land. These included river patrol boats (PBRs), fast patrol craft (PCF), mechanized landing craft (LCM), light SEAL support craft (LSSC), SEAL team assault boats (STABs), and medium SEAL support craft (MSSC). These vessels ranged in size from 20 to 36 feet in length and carried different types of armaments, providing a wide variety of mobility and fire support for assault and reconnaissance missions.

In addition, three submarines—*Grayback, Perch,* and *Tunny*—were reconfigured to carry UDT/SEAL teams on covert missions and remained dedicated to support naval unconventional warfare operations. In the Vietnam War, SEALs were allotted two air squadrons: one squadron of UH-1 Iroquois helicopter gunships ("Seawolves") and one squadron of OV-10 Broncos ("Black Ponies"). The OV-10 was a dual-propeller–driven light aircraft that carried a wide array of ordnance. It could respond quickly to calls for assistance and had the capability of loitering over target areas for extended periods. These two squadrons operated primarily in the Mekong River Delta.

From 1962 until 1964 SEALs trained Republic of Vietnam (RVN) Biệt Hai naval commandos (the RVN's unconventional force that conducted patrol and other operations using armed and upgraded civilian junks) and the regular naval UDTs, the Liên Đôi Người Nhái (LDNN). American UDT personnel also conducted hydrographic surveys along the RVN coast and made covert incursions into the Democratic Republic of Vietnam (DRV) to collect intelligence and carry out coastal mapping. In 1963 SEALs supported numerous raids into the DRV by LDNN forces. The object of these raids was to destroy coastal rail lines, power plants, and harbor facilities. Personnel assigned to either SEAL Team 1 or SEAL Team 2 regularly saw service in the RVN as part of fleet deployment rotations. Neither team was permanently stationed in the RVN but regularly assigned personnel for tours of duty there. Twenty separate SEAL detachments of varying strengths were established in the RVN under the Commander of Naval Forces, Vietnam (COMNAVFORV).

In early 1964 several SEAL detachments were assigned to the U.S. Military Assistance Command, Vietnam's Studies and Observations Group (MACV-SOG). MACV-SOG was responsible for all covert operations conducted in the RVN and included all branches of the U.S. military, the Central Intelligence Agency (CIA), and the RVN's special warfare forces. Operations into the DRV continued as well as numerous missions throughout the Mekong Delta to capture Việt Cộng and People's Army of Vietnam (PAVN) personnel, weapons, and documents.

In 1965 MACV, acting jointly with COMNAVFORV, ordered the SEALs into a specific area of operations, the Rửng Sát Special Zone (RSSZ). Located seven miles south of Sài Gòn, the Rửng Sát was a thick mangrove swamp crisscrossed by rivers, all emptying into the South China Sea. It was one of the most difficult areas in Vietnam in which to conduct military operations. Further hampering Allied efforts to patrol the area, the Rửng Sát was habitat to numerous varieties of poisonous snakes, crocodiles, and venomous insects. South China Sea predators such as sharks and poisonous sea snakes inhabited the area's saltwater inlets. This area was a Việt Cộng (VC) stronghold and presented a direct threat to Sài Gòn.

SEAL operations in the RSSZ consisted of hunter-killer teams of three to seven men each that targeted VC land concentrations and small boat traffic on the waterways and canals. SEALs patrolled specific areas using small boats or swam and waded through thick mud to establish ambushes. SEALs assaulted VC-controlled villages and other substantial targets using small craft that carried machine guns and mortars and provided increased firepower. SEALs also targeted the Communist infrastructure by killing or capturing VC leaders whenever possible. Throughout the course of the war SEAL patrols and VC units engaged in a constant deadly game of ambush and counterambush in the Rửng Sát. By mid-1966 SEAL operations were so effective that the RSSZ was no longer a VC safe haven.

In 1967 MACV-SOG ordered an increase in SEAL operations throughout the Mekong Delta. SEALs also provided intelligence to, and scouted for, the combined U.S. Army-Navy Mobile Riverine Force. The Mobile Riverine Force consisted of the U.S. Army's 9th Division backed by U.S. Navy small boats. These consisted of armored fire support ships (dubbed "monitors" because of their resemblance to Civil War ironclads), landing craft, supply, and fire support barges. This force was tasked with conducting conventional operations in the Mekong Delta.

From 1968 to 1970 SEAL and UDT personnel continued to engage in covert operations along the entire RVN coast as well as conventional operations within their designated operational areas. UDT personnel kept the shipping channels clear of mines and explosives and helped facilitate navigation by removing wrecked ships or deepening the waterways by clearing natural obstacles. SEALs in advisory duty, working with Army Special Forces, assisted and trained the ARVN's Provincial Reconnaissance Units (PRUs). The PRUs recruited personnel from Vietnamese Chiêu Hồi centers, and some from prisons and jails, to perform counterterrorist missions within the RVN. The American advisors tried to exert great control and discipline over these rather unsavory characters to ensure they functioned as soldiers and not bandits. Despite the 1970 Washington announcement of "Vietnamization," the pace of SEAL/UDT operations continued unabated.

SEALs played a key role in Operation BRIGHTLIGHT (1970–1972), the attempted rescue of prisoners of war (POWs) held by the VC in the Mekong Delta. In this operation, SEALs acted in conjunction with raids mounted by the ARVN and U.S. Army Special Forces against suspected VC POW camps. Despite success, including the recovery of numerous ARVN POWs, not one American POW was found during BRIGHTLIGHT. In many instances the Allied raiders found empty camps—termed "empty holes"—or large caches of weapons and equipment, but the failure to rescue American POWs in RVN locations continually frustrated MACV planners. Raid after raid demonstrated the Allied command's failure to use intelligence in a timely manner, despite possessing special operations forces capable of rapid response.

The waning years of the Vietnam War (1970–1972) saw SEAL and UDTs continuously involved in advising and training the LDNN and accompanying them on forays into the DRV. Covert coastal mapping and hydrographic surveys also continued. The last SEAL platoons were withdrawn from the RVN in 1972.

From their inception and deployment to the RVN, U.S. Navy SEALs established an enviable combat record. Their unique personnel selection and unsparing training program produced successful combat results with very low casualties. During the Vietnam War, 49 naval special warfare personnel died in action and none were captured. In 1973 the UDTs were disbanded and their missions absorbed by SEAL teams. SEAL units continue to give the U.S. Navy an unconventional warfare option.

—J. A. Menzoff

References: Bosiljevac, T. L. *SEALs: UDT/SEAL Operations in Vietnam.* Boulder, CO: Paladin Press, 1990.
Marolda, Edward J., and Oscar P. Fitzgerald. *The United States Navy in the Vietnam Conflict: From Military Assistance to Combat.* Vol. 2. Washington, DC: Naval Historical Center, Department of the Navy, 1986.
Thompson, Leroy. *U.S. Elite Forces–Vietnam.* Carrollton, TX: Squadron/ Signal Publications, 1985.
See also: Mobile Riverine Force; Riverine Craft; Riverine Warfare; United States: Navy; United States: Special Forces; Vietnam, Republic of: Navy (VNN); Vietnam, Republic of: Special Forces (Lực Lượng Đặc Biệt [LLDB]).

Seale, Bobby

(1936–)

Political activist and cofounder of the Black Panther Party for Self-Defense (BPP), which advocated black power and black opposition to the Vietnam War. Born in Dallas, Texas, on 22 October 1936, Bobby Seale served three years with the U.S. Air Force before enrolling in Merritt College in Oakland, California. While attending college, Seale met Huey P. Newton and in 1966 the two formed the Black Panther Party for Self-Defense after reading the Student Non-Violent Coordinating Committee pamphlet "How the People in Lowndes County Had Armed Themselves." Seale served as the chairman and minister of information, and Newton became defense minister. The party had grown out of their anger about living conditions and police mistreatment of African Americans in Oakland.

Seale wrote a ten-point party platform demanding political freedom, exemption from military service, black control of black communities, full employment, better housing, education, community health, and an end to police brutality; this program reflected much of the rhetoric of the late Malcolm X, who declared that African Americans formed a "colony within the mother country" and called for armed self-defense. Seale also wrote for and edited the *Black Panther* newspaper and authored a history of the BPP, *Seize the Time: The Story of the Black Panther Party and Huey P. Newton* (1970).

Clad in black leather jackets and berets and carrying weapons, the BPP became the most visible of the black radical groups. This visibility also attracted the attention of the Federal Bureau of Investigation (FBI), which launched a large-scale counterinsurgency effort, a domestic counterintelligence program (COINTELPRO), to create dissension and undermine the BPP. Seale, one of the FBI's key targets, was arrested and put on trial as one of the Chicago Eight for his part in protest activities at the 1968 Democratic Party National Convention. His case attracted nationwide attention when Judge Julius Hoffman ordered Seale bound and gagged in the courtroom when he attempted to act in his own defense. His case was separated from the other defendants, and Seale was sentenced to 48 months in prison for 16 acts of contempt. Seale was then charged with killing a BPP informant in New Haven, Connecticut; the contempt charges were dismissed, and the murder trial ended with a hung jury.

Internal dissension caused by COINTELPRO, power struggles, and violent clashes with police and other black nationalist groups led to the demise of the BPP by the early 1970s. Seale, however, remained active and ran for mayor of Oakland in 1973, narrowly losing a close election to the incumbent. In 1968 he published his autobiography, *A Lonely Rage*. Seale, a gifted orator, continued to lecture on black issues across the country. He also served as a minority recruiter and consultant for Temple University in Philadelphia, where he resides. In the 1980s Seale attracted attention with the publication of his *Barbeque with Bobby* celebrity cookbook.

—Laura Matysek Wood

References: O'Reilly, Kenneth. *"Racial Matters." The FBI's Secret File on Black America 1960–1972.* New York: Free Press, 1989.

Seale, Bobby. *A Lonely Rage: The Autobiography of Bobby Seale.* New York: Times Books, 1968.

————. *Seize the Time: The Story of the Black Panther Party and Huey P. Newton.* New York: Random House, 1970.

Williams, Michael W., ed. *The African American Encyclopedia.* Vol. 1. New York: Marshall Cavendish, 1993.

See also: Antiwar Movement, United States.

SEALORDS (Southeast Asia Lake Ocean River Delta Strategy)

(1968–1971)

U.S. combined-force interdiction, harassment, and pacification effort in the Mekong Delta of South Vietnam. In October 1968 newly appointed Commander Naval Forces, Vietnam Vice-Adm. Elmo R. Zumwalt, Jr., established SEALORDS or Task Force 194 to operate along the canals and less-traveled rivers and waterways of the Mekong Delta to interdict Viêt Công infiltration routes from Cambodia; to harass Communist forces; and, with the assistance of ground and air forces, to pacify the Delta. This idea emerged when Zumwalt realized that water barriers or blockades could be placed in and around the Delta and along the Cambodian border. To create this program, Zumwalt combined all Naval Forces, Vietnam (NAVFORV) assets: Task Force 115, the Coastal Surveillance Force; Task Force 116, the River Patrol Force; and Task Force 117, the Mobile Riverine Force. Zumwalt believed that these forces together could project an offensive deep into the Mekong Delta and along less frequently traveled but still vital waterways of IV Corps Tactical Zone (CTZ).

In early October, prior to the inception of SEALORDS, the Coastal Surveillance Force expanded its mission to include river incursions into the III and IV CTZs. These initial forays into territory previously dominated by the Viêt Công destroyed numerous structures, sampans, and tax collection stations. Such operations proved the practicality of transiting the waterways and caught the insurgents off guard. Thus, on 18 October 1968 when SEALORDS became official, the tempo of these transits increased.

Since river incursions had already proved valuable, Zumwalt wanted to establish a patrol barrier on the Vĩnh Té Canal bordering Cambodia. But first he had to test the validity of his barrier concept. The admiral suggested that the new riverine commander, or First Sea Lord, Capt. Robert S. Salzer, establish a blockade along the canal in the center of the western part of the Delta. If this worked, then it would be feasible to move the barrier up to the Vĩnh Té Canal. Salzer immediately drew up the plan for the operation, subsequently code-named SEARCH TURN.

After approval by Military Assistance Command, Vietnam (MACV) head General Creighton W. Abrams, the initial assault began on 1 November 1968. Four days later NAVFORV established an interdiction barrier that consisted of a 24-hour riverboat patrol. SEARCH TURN's area of operations (AO) encompassed the Rach Giá–Long Xuyên Canal from the Bassac River to the Rach Soi Canal and then southwest on the latter canal to the Gulf of Thailand. The success of Operation SEARCH TURN, combined with transits of the Rach Gang Thân River and the Vĩnh Té Canal, contributed to the establishment of Operation TRÂN HƯNG ĐẠO along the Cambodian border on 21 November 1968.

On 6 December SEALORDS expanded with a new barrier, GIANT SLINGSHOT. This operation, so named because the AO encompassed the east and west branches of the Vàm Co River (Vàm Co Tây [west] and Vàm Co Đông [east]) that flowed along converging routes on either side of the Parrot's Beak and joined near the town of Bên Lức, forming what looked like a giant slingshot. The Parrot's Beak, a beak-shaped extension of Cambodian territory, extended southeastward to within a few miles of Sài Gòn. From their base camps in nearby Cambodia, the Communists had but a short trip to the Republic of Vietnam capital; hence, the largest amounts of infiltration had occurred here. Before the inception of GIANT SLINGSHOT, friendly movement on these rivers did not exist, thus Admiral Zumwalt sought to stop infiltration and make these rivers accessible to the local inhabitants. The AO extended from the confluence of the Vàm Co River northeastward along the Vàm Co Đông to an area five miles southwest of Tây Ninh, the capital of Tây Ninh Province. It also extended from the Nhà Bè River west along the Vàm Co Tây to Mộc Hóa, the capital of Kiên Tường Province.

In the final months of 1968 an idea emerged for a fourth barrier. The concept was to connect Trần Hưng Đạo in the West to GIANT SLINGSHOT in the East. This new operation, BARRIER REEF, or the Border Interdiction Campaign, began on 2 January 1969. The AO was located in the Plain of Reeds, a vast open area that during the rainy months became a huge shallow lake. The AO extended from the GIANT SLINGSHOT on the Vàm Co Tây along the Lagrange Canal from Tuyên Nhơn to Ấp Bắc and westward along the Ông Lớn Canal to the upper Mekong River at An Long. The Lagrange–Ông Lớn Canal bisected many secondary canals leading from the Cambodian border toward the populous portion of the Delta east-southeast of the Plain of Reeds, including the city of My Tho.

In addition to these operations, Zumwalt established on 27 June 1969 Sea Float, a mobile advance tactical support base (MATSB), composed of 11 Ammi pontoons heavily laden with mortars, rockets, and machine guns and capable of operating a wide range of river craft and providing living quarters for boat crews while floating in midstream on the Cửa Lớn River in An Xuyên Province on the Cà Mâu Peninsula. Then in September 1969 Zumwalt activated Breezy Cove, an advance tactical support base (ATSB) containing similar defensive measures as the MATSB, also located in An Xuyên on the riverbank of the Ông Đốc.

Despite the offensive nature of SEALORDS, Zumwalt had created the barrier plans with one overarching goal: to enable the Republic of Vietnam Navy to take over as American forces withdrew. Known as ACTOV (Accelerated Turnover to Vietnamese), the Navy's Vietnamization program began in the fall of 1968, and by April 1971 all SEALORDS operations had been turned over to the RVN Navy.

—R. Blake Dunnavent

References: Cutler, Thomas J. *Brown Water, Black Berets: Coastal and Riverine Warfare in Vietnam.* Annapolis, MD: Naval Institute Press, 1988.
Dunnavent, R. Blake. "SEALORDS: The Riverine Interdiction Campaign in Vietnam." Master's thesis, Texas Tech University, 1992.
Marolda, Edward J. *By Sea, Air, and Land: An Illustrated History of the U.S. Navy and the War in Southeast Asia.* Washington, DC: Naval Historical Center, 1994.
Schreadley, R. L. *From the Rivers to the Sea: The United States Navy in Vietnam.* Annapolis, MD: Naval Institute Press, 1992.
See also: GAME WARDEN, Operation; Geography of Indo-China and Vietnam; MARKET TIME, Operation; Mekong Delta; Mobile Riverine Force; Riverine Craft; Riverine Warfare; United States: Navy; Vietnam, Republic of: Navy (VNN); Zumwalt, Elmo R., Jr.

Search and Destroy

U.S. military tactic of attrition used in Vietnam between 1965 and 1968. Developed by General William Westmoreland and his deputy, Brig. Gen. William DePuy, search and destroy emerged not from the conclusions of study committees, think-tank reports, or tactical doctrine developed at the U.S. Army Command and General Staff College. As with many U.S. tactics, its development depended on military capabilities at the given time. It was an ad hoc approach that grew out of discussions between Westmoreland and DePuy. Charles MacDonald, spokesman at the U.S. Army Center of Military History, revealed that Westmoreland turned to his trusted associate and said, "Bill, what should we call this?" DePuy responded, "How about search-and-destroy?"

Although Westmoreland would later deny that search and destroy was even a specific tactic, it was certainly the dominant approach followed by American fighting units of all sizes in Vietnam. Search and destroy relied on the assumption that American firepower and technology were so superior and could cause such severe casualties that neither the Việt Công (VC) nor the People's Army of Vietnam (PAVN) would be able to withstand the punishment the United States could visit upon them. Search and destroy was to be an aggressive military tool. Ground forces, transported by Army aviation helicopter units and supported by artillery, would locate enemy forces and destroy both them and occasionally their base areas. It emphasized attacking the Communist forces rather than acquiring territory. Troopers struck into areas of supposed Communist strength to "find, fix, and finish" their enemy. Mission accomplished, they withdrew to their home base until ordered out on the next such operation. Westmoreland believed that the Communists, unable to stand against such forays, would seek peace.

Not everyone agreed with this approach. Air Force Chief of Staff General John P. McConnell and Marine Corps Commandant General David M. Greene opposed it. Army General James Gavin called for U.S. military aid to Vietnam to be restricted to sending forces to certain enclaves, providing those locations with protection, and freeing troops of the Army of the Republic of Vietnam (ARVN) to carry the brunt of the fight. General Edward Lansdale argued that the main American commitment should be directed toward countrywide pacification and counterinsurgency rather than employing combat maneuver battalions.

Westmoreland wanted no static defensive posture, was unwilling to confine his command to a defensive role, and repudiated the enclave strategy. An early indication of his desire to expand in-country operations came in the summer of 1965 when he ordered the 173d Airborne deployed to the Central Highlands; it had only arrived in Vietnam on 7 May. On 26 June the Pentagon gave Westmoreland authority to assign U.S. troops to field action. Two days later (28 June), 3,000 soldiers of the 173d moved into War Zone D, 20 miles northwest of Sài Gòn. Perhaps Westmoreland felt he had no choice. Previous military preparation had equipped and prepared the Army only to fight in Europe: to contain a Soviet strike through the Hof Corridor or Fulda Gap in Germany on its way to the Rhine. Suddenly faced with Vietnam, planners sent military forces intact to Southeast Asia. Surely they could easily handle a fight with irregular guerrilla forces.

Westmoreland has been soundly criticized for adopting this tactic of attrition. It grew from his erroneous assumption that American soldiers and firepower could inflict devastating losses

U.S. Army Pfc. Jerome Alexander and Sp4c. George Lightfoot, Company B, 2d Battalion, 1st Infantry, 196th Light Brigade, fire at a suspected Viêt Công position during a search-and-destroy mission 10 kilometers west of Tây Ninh. The dominant approach followed by American fighting units of all sizes in Vietnam, search and destroy emphasized attacking Communist forces rather than acquiring territory.

on Communist forces in Vietnam while keeping U.S. casualties to an acceptable level.

Westmoreland's hopes were doomed by wartime reality. The level of attrition he was able to bring to bear on the Communists was neutralized by the fact that over 200,000 North Vietnamese males, replacements for PAVN losses in battle, reached draft age every year. Westmoreland's army never came close to inflicting that many casualties in any 12-month period. A bigger problem with Westmoreland's tactics was the fact that the Communists rather than U.S. forces generally initiated hostilities—they chose locations for battle that were favorable to them and often ended combat when they saw fit, leaving the site of an attack along safe avenues of retreat.

Dave Richard Palmer roundly criticized Westmoreland's war of attrition as an indication of his failure to conceive of an alternative, as irrefutable proof of the absence of any strategy, and as an approach demonstrating that the U.S. Army was strategically bankrupt in Vietnam. Others also criticized the strategy, but Westmoreland stubbornly relied on search and destroy throughout his tenure as commander of U.S. Military Assistance Command, Vietnam (MACV). Following the 1968 Tết Offensive, however, MACV public affairs officers did not often use the term search and destroy, replacing it with the phrase "reconnaissance in force." An observer would have been hard-pressed, however, to note any actual change in American approaches to locating Communist forces.

—Cecil B. Currey

References: MacDonald, Charles, interview with the author.
Palmer, Dave Richard. *Readings in Current Military History.* West Point, NY: Department of Military Art and Engineering, U.S. Military Academy, 1969.
Shaplen, Robert. *The Road from War: Vietnam, 1965–1970.* New York: Harper & Row, 1970.
See also: Attrition; Bến Súc; Casualties; Clear and Hold; DePuy, William E.; Gavin, James M.; Military Assistance Command, Vietnam (MACV); United States: Army; Westmoreland, William Childs.

Search-and-Rescue (SAR) Operations

The location and rescue of downed aircrewmen. From April 1962 until April 1975 a total of 2,254 U.S. Air Force aircraft were destroyed in combat or other operations in Southeast Asia. In all, 8,588 U.S. Air Force, Army, Navy, and Marine fixed-wing and rotary-wing aircraft were lost in the Vietnam War. Thousands of aircrewmen were killed, were reported missing in action, or were taken prisoner. The U.S. Air Force's Aerospace Rescue and Recovery Service (ARRS) played a key role in minimizing these losses.

On 1 April 1962 Detachment 3, Pacific Air Rescue Center (Det 3, PARC) was established at Tân Sơn Nhứt Air Base in Sài Gòn. This detachment possessed no rescue aircraft and was only able to coordinate operations that relied on Army, Marine, and Vietnamese Air Force helicopters and search aircraft.

The first Air Force search-and-rescue (SAR) helicopters, Kaman HH-43Bs, arrived at Nakhon Phanom Royal Thai Air Force Base (RTAFB), Thailand, in June 1964. With a combat radius of less than 100 miles, these choppers were virtually useless for aircrew recovery. A real rescue capability did not exist until a year later when the first modified Sikorsky CH-3C/Es arrived at Udorn RTAFB, Thailand. These were soon replaced with air-refuelable HH-3Es that could reach any point in North Vietnam. The even larger Sikorsky HH-53s, introduced in late 1967, gave rescue forces a formidable aircrew recovery capability.

Additionally, the introduction of helicopters with more powerful engines and better hovering characteristics, armor, and the jungle penetrator survivor extraction system made it possible for rescue forces to use the inhospitable jungle, karst formations, and mountains to their advantage. When a fighter-bomber received battle damage over North Vietnam, the pilot tried to keep his crippled aircraft aloft until it reached either the Gulf of Tonkin or, if traveling west, one of several designated jungle regions called SAFE (Selected Area for Evasion) areas.

Although technological advances helped the ARRS overcome some of the problems of geography and terrain, Democratic Republic of Vietnam (DRV) air defenses remained troublesome throughout the war. With help from the Soviet Union and the People's Republic of China, the DRV built what was believed to be the world's third best air defense system (after that of the Soviet Union and, perhaps, Israel). It included SA-2 surface-to-air missiles (SAMs), MiG interceptors, and at least 2,000 antiaircraft guns ranging in caliber from 14.5-mm heavy machine guns to 23-mm, 37-mm, 57-mm, and 85-mm guns, many with radar control. From 1965 to 1972 these weapons claimed 35 rescue aircraft. An additional 10 rescue aircraft suffered noncombat operational losses, and 71 rescue men perished.

Tactics and improved equipment helped to overcome expanding DRV defenses. The greatest innovation was the search-and-rescue task force (SARTAF) that included a control aircraft, two to four fighter-bomber escorts, and at least two rescue helicopters. The types of aircraft in the SARTAF changed as better airframes became available. Tactics evolved, with flexibility as the primary principle.

The airborne mission control airplane was the nerve center of the SARTAF. Originally Grumman HU-16 amphibians performed this role. In 1965 these were replaced by four-engine Douglas HC-54s, which, the following year, were replaced by Lockheed HC-130P Hercules four-engine turboprops with the call sign "Crown" and later "King." Douglas A-1 Skyraiders, hefty, propeller-driven attack aircraft designed in World War II for the Navy and produced in the 1940s and early 1950s, excelled in the rescue escort (RESCORT) mission. In 1972, when all Air Force and Navy A-1s were turned over to the South Vietnamese Air Force, Vought A-7 single-engine jets proved to be a poor replacement.

The helicopters evolved from HH-43s to the HH-3s to the HH-53s, some of which, by 1971, had a limited nighttime recovery capability. The HH-43s were designed to suppress aircraft fires and pick up crews in the vicinity of bases, but the HH-43Fs were modified to perform limited long-range aircrew recovery. But the HH-3 and HH-53 "Jolly Green Giants" could, with refueling from Crown/King HC-130Ps, remain aloft up to 18 hours. These choppers almost always flew in pairs, with the "low bird" making the actual pickup, while the "high bird" was available as a backup should the low bird be shot down.

Aircrew recovery was a bright spot in the long air war. Some 3,883 lives were credited to the ARRS. Of these, 2,807 were U.S. military: 926 Army, 680 Navy, and 1,201 Air Force. Rescue forces also saved 555 Allied military men, 476 civilians, and 45 other people, including a Việt Công who had his leg blown off in a minefield and an East German sailor who was flown from a freighter off the coast of South Vietnam to Đà Nẵng, where an emergency appendectomy was performed.

—Earl H. Tilford, Jr.

References: Berger, Carl, ed. *The United States Air Force in Southeast Asia: An Illustrated Account.* Washington, DC: Office of Air Force History, 1984. Tilford, Earl H., Jr. *A History of U.S. Search and Rescue Operations in Southeast Asia, 1961–75.* Washington, DC: Office of Air Force History, 1980.
See also: Airborne Operations; Airplanes, Allied and Democratic Republic of Vietnam; EAGLE PULL, Operation; Helicopters, Allied and Democratic Republic of Vietnam; Helicopters, Employment of, in Vietnam; Medevac; Sơn Tây Raid.

Sharp, Ulysses Simpson Grant, Jr.

(1906–)

U.S. Navy admiral and commander in chief, U.S. Pacific Command, 1964–1968. Born in Chinook, Montana, on 2 April 1906, Ulysses S. Grant Sharp's grandmother was the sister-in-law of Civil War general and U.S. President Ulysses S. Grant. In 1927 he graduated from the U.S. Naval Academy and was commissioned an ensign. Between 1927 and 1942 he served on a number of ships at sea and in Washington, D.C. In 1942 he assumed command of a destroyer-minesweeper in the Atlantic and the next year commanded a destroyer in the Pacific. In late 1944 he was in the United States in staff and command posts. After a year at the Naval War College, in 1950 he assumed command of a destroyer squadron operating near the Korean coast. Just prior to the Inchon landing, he was attached to the invasion planning staff.

In 1951 he became an operations officer on the Second Fleet (Atlantic) commander's staff and soon became chief of staff, a post he held until late 1953. He then commanded a destroyer, followed by two years as deputy chief of staff for plans and operations for the Pacific Fleet and one year as commander of Cruiser Division Three.

Between 1957 and 1959 Sharp was assistant director, and later director, of the Strategic Plans Division of the Office of the Chief of Naval Operations. He next served as commander of the Cruiser-Destroyer Force in the U.S. Pacific Fleet and briefly as First Fleet commander. From 1960 to 1963 Sharp served as deputy chief of naval operations (plans and policy) and was deeply involved in the planning of naval operations during the 1962 Cuban missile crisis.

In September 1963 Sharp became commander of the U.S. Pacific Fleet and in June 1964 commander in chief of the Pacific Command (CINCPAC), the largest U.S. unified command. It contained more than 940,000 Army, Navy, Marine, and Air Force personnel, 7,500 aircraft, and 560 ships. As CINCPAC, Sharp was responsible for the defense of an area of 85 million square miles, extending across the Pacific to the Indian Ocean, and from the Aleutian Islands to the Antarctic. Sharp also held such associated posts as U.S. military advisor to the Southeast Asia Treaty Organization (SEATO) and U.S. military representative to the Philippine–U.S. Mutual Defense Board and the Australia–New Zealand–United States Council (ANZUS).

Sharp oversaw air strikes against North Vietnamese torpedo boat bases following the August 1964 Gulf of Tonkin incident. Subsequently, the Joint Chiefs of Staff (JCS) placed him in overall supervision of military actions in Vietnam. As CINCPAC, Admiral Sharp had overall military responsibility for the air operations of ROLLING THUNDER, the bombing of North Vietnam that began in early 1965, even though ultimate authority lay with President Lyndon Johnson. His view of operational objectives often differed sharply with those of Secretary of Defense Robert McNamara and the JCS, especially Chief of Naval Operations Admiral Thomas H. Moorer.

McNamara and President Johnson believed that limited bombing could be used to force a diplomatic solution. Sharp, Moorer, and most service leaders balked at such an idea. Admiral Sharp was as convinced as Air Force generals that strategic bombing against the Democratic Republic of Vietnam would have been successful. He chafed under what he saw as "absurd" restrictions on strategic airpower.

In August 1968 Sharp retired as CINCPAC and from active duty. He then served as a consultant to the president of Teledyne Ryan Aeronautical Company and as a director of the San Diego Gas & Electric Company. He also wrote an article, "We Could Have Won in Vietnam Long Ago" (*Reader's Digest,* May 1969), and a book, *Strategic Direction of the Armed Forces* (1977).

In 1978 Sharp wrote *Strategy for Defeat: Vietnam in Retrospect.* In this book Sharp declared that if, beginning in 1965, the United States had undertaken massive and constant B-52 LINEBACKER-style raids against North Vietnam that America could have won the war without fear of Soviet or Chinese intervention.

Sharp received numerous U.S. Navy medals and awards from many foreign governments. In 1971 Montana State University awarded him an honorary doctorate. He resides in San Diego, California.

—William Head

References: Momyer, William. *Air Power in Three Wars.* Washington, DC: U.S. Government Printing Office, 1978.
Sharp, U. S. G. *Strategy for Defeat: Vietnam in Retrospect.* San Rafael, CA: Presidio Press, 1978.
Tilford, Earl H., Jr. *Crosswinds: The Air Force Setup in Vietnam.* College Station, TX: Texas A&M University Press, 1993.
Westmoreland, Gen. William C., and Adm. U. S. G. Sharp. *Report on the War in Vietnam.* Washington, DC: U.S. Government Printing Office, 1968.
See also: Johnson, Lyndon Baines; McNamara, Robert S.; Moorer, Thomas H.; ROLLING THUNDER, Operation.

Sheehan, Cornelius Mahoney (Neil)

(1936–)

Among the first and finest correspondents of the Vietnam War. Born on 27 October 1936 in Holyoke, Massachusetts, Cornelius

Mahoney (Neil) Sheehan graduated from Harvard in 1958 and served three years with the Army in Korea and Japan. He joined United Press International (UPI) in Tokyo and was sent to Sài Gòn in April 1962. Sheehan did not question the righteousness of the Vietnam conflict or U.S. involvement but soon learned to suspect the false optimism of senior military officials, such as U.S. General Paul Harkins, and to listen to field advisors, such as Lt. Col. John Paul Vann, who admitted mistakes.

Sheehan first angered U.S. officials with his reporting of the January 1963 Battle of Ấp Bắc, in which an Army of the Republic of Vietnam (ARVN) division experienced a stunning defeat by allowing a surrounded Việt Cộng (VC) battalion to escape practically unscathed. Vann called Ấp Bắc "a miserable damn performance," but Harkins proclaimed it a victory, announcing 101 VC killed (only 3 bodies were found), while significantly understating ARVN casualties and material losses. Washington accepted Harkins's characterization of the battle and assailed the press, especially Sheehan, for misrepresenting it.

The Republic of Vietnam (RVN) government began to harass American correspondents after they reported that the May 1963 Buddhist crisis might bring down the government. When Ngô Đình Nhu's security troops raided Buddhist pagodas in August, Sheehan had to smuggle the true story out while the U.S. Embassy endorsed Nhu's version of events. That September both he and David Halberstam revealed that the CIA was backing dissident generals in a planned coup against Ngô Đình Diêm, but Sheehan's editors killed his story and recalled him to Tokyo, causing him to miss the story of the coup and assassinations of Diêm and his brother Nhu. But in January 1964 Sheehan rebutted Ambassador Henry Cabot Lodge's report of significant progress in the Mekong Delta, concluding that the war there was "a long way toward being lost." Sheehan then left Vietnam to join the staff of the *New York Times*.

Returning in 1965 to what was becoming an American war, Sheehan was among the first to dispatch firsthand accounts of the bloody fighting in the Ia Drang Valley. When he left again in 1966, still neither dove nor hawk, Sheehan had concluded that not only would General William Westmoreland's strategy of attrition not destroy the enemy's will to fight, but that it was certain to cost thousands of civilian and American lives.

Sheehan continued to cover the war from Washington but would not return to Vietnam until 1972. Following the 1968 Tết Offensive, that March he and fellow journalist Hedrick Smith revealed Westmoreland's request for 206,000 more troops. Sheehan's notoriety increased with a lengthy March 1971 article in the *New York Times Book Review* that questioned whether American leaders had committed war crimes in Vietnam. But his biggest story came soon thereafter when Daniel Ellsberg gave him a copy of a secret 46-volume "history" of America's involvement in Vietnam commissioned by Secretary of Defense Robert McNamara in 1967. Sheehan led a team in editing the documents as *The Pentagon Papers*, excerpts of which appeared in June 1968 issues of the *New York Times* and *The Washington Post*.

In 1972 Sheehan began an extended leave from the *New York Times* to write one of the most ambitious books about the war, *A*

Bright Shining Lie: John Paul Vann and America in Vietnam (1988). Vann had left the U.S. Army in 1963 but returned to Vietnam to serve as a high-ranking civilian advisor until his 1972 death in a helicopter crash. At Vann's funeral Sheehan recognized that "We were burying the whole era of . . . boundless self-confidence that led us to Vietnam," and that Vann's career could serve as a metaphor for America's involvement. Even Vann had lost the sense of reality because he could not admit defeat. More than biography, Sheehan's book is a virtual history of the American phase of the Vietnam War, a penetrating analysis of how intelligent men had behaved stupidly and brought upon the United States and the people of Southeast Asia an enormous tragedy. The book earned Sheehan a Pulitzer Prize and a National Book Award.

A Bright Shining Lie was not Sheehan's last word on the war. His three post-1975 visits to Vietnam are recounted in *After the War Was Over* (1995). Sheehan currently resides in Washington, D.C.

—John D. Root

References: Prochnau, William. *Once Upon a Distant War: David Halberstam, Neil Sheehan, Peter Arnett—Young War Correspondents and Their Early Vietnam Battles.* New York: Vintage Books, 1995.
Sheehan, Neil. *A Bright Shining Lie: John Paul Vann and America in Vietnam.* New York: Random House, 1988.
Wyatt, Clarence R. *Paper Soldiers: The American Press and the Vietnam War.* Chicago: University of Chicago Press, 1993.
See also: Ấp Bắc, Battle of; Ellsberg, Daniel; Halberstam, David; Harkins, Paul D.; Lodge, Henry Cabot, Jr.; McNamara, Robert S.; Ngô Đình Nhu; Pentagon Papers and Trial; Vann, John Paul; Westmoreland, William Childs.

SHINING BRASS, Operation

(October 1965)

U.S. Special Forces cross-border operations into Laos to locate and disrupt North Vietnamese infiltration along the Hồ Chí Minh Trail into South Vietnam. Operation SHINING BRASS began in September 1965 and was carried out by 12-man teams that normally included 3 Americans and 9 Montagnard civilians under the control of the Military Assistance Command, Vietnam Studies and Observation Group (MACV-SOG). The command and control center was in Đà Nẵng at Marble Mountain; forward operating bases were usually located in Special Forces Civilian Irregular Defense Group (CIDG) camps along the border with Laos. The primary mission during the early days of SHINING BRASS was the location of targets for aerial bombing, but at times, when they had no other choice, the teams had to fight. Later their operations were expanded to include emplacing antipersonnel devices, engaging People's Army of Vietnam (PAVN) or Pathet Lao personnel in open combat, assessing B-52 bomb damage, and controlling air strikes. Eventually, there were three battalions of American-led Vietnamese used as a reaction force to carry out larger missions in Laos. The authorized areas for operations were specified strips of Laos along the border that stretched 20 kilometers into the country.

Initially SOG commanders were not allowed to lift reconnaissance teams in by helicopter, although they were authorized to extricate them by air if necessary. As the Laotian border consisted of some of the most rugged terrain in Southeast Asia, daily movements of reconnaissance teams were severely limited. Because of the difficulty of movement, helicopter infiltration was ultimately authorized and soon became the norm. Reconnaissance teams were able to direct air strikes on known targets through a rather elaborate procedure that included securing permission on a target-by-target basis from the U.S. ambassador to Laos. SHINING BRASS became one of the largest and most important Special Forces strategic reconnaissance and interdiction campaigns in Southeast Asia. SHINING BRASS was renamed PRAIRIE FIRE in 1968, and finally PHU DUNG in April 1971.

—James H. Willbanks

References: Kelly, Francis J. *U.S. Army Special Forces, 1961–1971.* Washington, DC: Department of the Army, 1973.

Simpson, Charles M. *Inside the Green Berets.* Novato, CA: Presidio Press, 1983.

Stanton, Shelby L. *The Green Berets at War.* Novato, CA: Presidio Press, 1985.

See also: Civilian Irregular Defense Group (CIDG); Hồ Chí Minh Trail; Laos; Montagnards; Studies and Observation Group (SOG); United States: Special Forces.

Shoup, David M.

(1904–1983)

Commandant, U.S. Marine Corps, 1960–1963. Born on 30 December 1904 in Battle Ground, Indiana, David Shoup graduated from DePauw University in 1926. As a colonel in World War II, he earned the Medal of Honor for actions in November 1943 while commanding a Marine regiment on Betio, a bitterly contested island of Tarawa Atoll. Shoup was promoted to brigadier general in April 1953; in November 1959 he became a lieutenant general and chief of staff of the Marine Corps. In August 1959 President Dwight Eisenhower nominated Shoup as the commandant of the Marine Corps. Upon assuming this post in January 1960, Shoup was promoted to full (four-star) general.

General Shoup believed strongly that the military should serve the national interest as defined by its civilian leaders. He refused to participate in what he referred to as the "hate-the-Communists" movement. Shoup would fight the Communists if required by circumstances, but he said that he did not find it necessary to hate them. He was opposed to the massive military buildup in Southeast Asia, and, after his retirement, he continued his crusade against the Vietnam War. In the April 1969 edition of *Atlantic Monthly,* Shoup collaborated with Col. James Donovan, USMC (Ret.), in a widely reviewed article that held that anticommunism provided the perfect climate and foundation to nurture a "new American militarism" in the defense establishment. General Shoup died on 13 January 1983 in Alexandria, Virginia.

—W. E. Fahey, Jr.

References: Shoup, Gen. David M. "The New American Militarism." *Atlantic Monthly* (April 1969).

Washington, DC: History and Museums Division, Marine Corps Historical Center, U.S. Marine Corps Headquarters.

See also: United States: Involvement in Vietnam, 1954–1965; United States: Marine Corps.

SIGMA, Project

U.S. military long-range reconnaissance initiative, 1966–1967. General William Westmoreland launched Project DELTA (Special Forces Detachment B-52) in October 1964 to conduct secret, long-range reconnaissance into Việt Công (VC) sanctuaries. Encouraged by the success of DELTA, in August 1966 Westmoreland organized Projects OMEGA (Detachment B-50) and SIGMA (Detachment B-56). Whereas Project DELTA operated country-wide under the direction of the Military Assistance Command, Vietnam (MACV) commander, OMEGA and SIGMA were created to give the commanders of I and II Field Forces, Vietnam, a long-range reconnaissance capability to use in remote areas of their corps tactical zones (CTZs).

OMEGA and SIGMA were similarly organized. Each consisted of approximately 900 Civilian Irregular Defense Group (CIDG) troops and 125 U.S. Special Forces (SF) personnel. Each included a reconnaissance element, a reaction force, and an advisory command element, organized as a modified B detachment.

The reconnaissance element was composed of eight "Roadrunner" teams and eight reconnaissance teams. The "Roadrunner" teams, made up of four indigenous personnel each, conducted long-distance reconnaissance over trail networks by infiltrating Việt Công–held territory, using members dressed in regional People's Army of Vietnam (PAVN)/VC uniforms and armed with appropriate weapons and carrying proper paperwork.

The reconnaissance teams, composed of two U.S. Special Forces personnel and four indigenous members, conducted saturation patrols throughout specified reconnaissance zones, gathering detailed intelligence on PAVN/VC movements, routes, and installations, and generated detailed terrain analysis.

Backing up the reconnaissance elements were three Mobile Strike Force Command ("Mike Force") reaction companies, each consisting of 150 highly trained, airborne-qualified CIDG personnel, led by 25 SF officers and men. Mike Force companies were employed to exploit small contacts, to aid in the extraction of compromised teams, and to perform reconnaissance-in-force missions.

Project SIGMA forces also participated in raids on prisoner-of-war camps in conjunction with mobile strike forces, but none of these missions was successful in recovering any American or Allied prisoners of war.

Project SIGMA was located at Camp Hô Ngoc Tao near Thu Đức, along Highway 1 between Sài Gòn and Long Bình. SIGMA forces were first sent into combat during Operation GOLF on 11 September 1966. Project SIGMA performed 15 operations in War Zones C and D before its assets were transferred to MACV's Studies and Observation Group (SOG) on 1 November 1967.

—James H. Willbanks

References: Kelly, Francis J. *U.S. Army Special Forces, 1961–1971.* Washington, DC: Department of the Army, 1985.

Simpson, Charles M. *Inside the Green Berets: The First Thirty Years.* Novato, CA: Presidio Press, 1983.

Stanton, Shelby L. *Green Berets at War.* Novato, CA: Presidio Press, 1985.
_____. *Vietnam Order of Battle.* New York: Galahad Books, 1986.
See also: Civilian Irregular Defense Group (CIDG); DELTA, Project; Mobile Guerrilla Forces (MGF); Mobile Strike Force Commands; OMEGA, Project; Studies and Observation Group (SOG); United States: Special Forces.

SIGMA I and II

U.S. military assessment operations, "war games." In 1963, as the political and military situation in South Vietnam deteriorated, the U.S. Joint Chiefs of Staff staged a "war game" code-named SIGMA I. The outcome confirmed some of the worst fears that a military victory over the Viêt Công in South Vietnam would require more than 500,000 American combat troops. In September 1964 the Joint Chiefs of Staff conducted another war game of the situation in South Vietnam. Code-named SIGMA II, this simulation was conducted to assess the potential impact of a major air offensive against North Vietnam. The players, who included National Security Advisor McGeorge Bundy, Defense Department aide John Mc-Naughton, General Earle Wheeler, and General Curtis LeMay, formed two teams, one representing the United States and the other the Democratic Republic of Vietnam. The results of this game were no more encouraging than those of SIGMA I; the war game report concluded that "industrial and military bombing" of North Vietnam "would not quickly cause cessation of the insurgency in South Vietnam." Indeed, it seemed, from the results of SIGMA II, at least, that the United States had little chance of stopping a Viêt Công victory. Despite these findings, political and diplomatic events during the next eight months pushed the United States closer to military intervention on a large scale.

—James H. Willbanks

References: Karnow, Stanley. *Vietnam: A History.* New York: Viking Press, 1983.
McNamara, Robert S. *In Retrospect: The Tragedy and Lessons of Vietnam.* New York: Times Books, 1995.
See also: Bundy, McGeorge; LeMay, Curtis Emerson; McNaughton, John T.; United States: Involvement in Vietnam, 1954–1965; Wheeler, Earl, G.

Sihanouk, Norodom

(1922–)
The leading figure of modern Cambodia—at various times prince, king (1941–1955; 1993–1997), prime minister (1955–1960), head of state (1960–1993), palace prisoner, and guerrilla figurehead—who tried in vain to keep his country out of the Vietnam War. Born in Phnom Penh on 31 October 1922, the son of Prince Norodom Suramarit and Princess Sisowath Kossamak of a line going back to the emperors of Angkor, Norodom Sihanouk was educated at the Ecole François Baudoin in Phnom Penh and the Lycée Chasseloup Laubat in Sài Gòn, where he excelled at music, literature, and drama. When King Monivong, his maternal grandfather, died on 23 April 1941, the French, who exercised a protectorate over Cambodia, picked Sihanouk to succeed him in preference to Monivong's son, Prince Sisowath Monireth.

In the first of many gestures designed to show his independent will, Sihanouk expressed his support for the Japanese when they temporarily interned the French administration in Indo-China on 9 March 1945 and proclaimed the end of the French protectorate. Sihanouk assumed the additional position of prime minister, but his power was overshadowed by an ambitious politician, Sơn Ngoc Thanh, whom the Japanese imposed as foreign minister. Sihanouk was obliged to accept the return of the French following Japan's surrender, but distanced himself from a *modus vivendi* signed in January 1946 by his uncle, Prince Monireth. Elections held under a French-inspired constitution in 1946 and 1947 resulted in big wins for the Democratic Party, the only one with a grassroots organization. Sihanouk viewed this as a challenge by rivals, and within five years, motivated by an unshakable belief that he knew what was best for Cambodia, he managed to eliminate the Democrats and secure a firm grip on Cambodia's political evolution that he was not to give up until 1970.

In 1953 Sihanouk embarked upon what he called a "royal crusade for independence" involving exchanges with Paris, travels abroad (including to the United States, where he was unimpressed by his reception by the Eisenhower administration), and even a well-publicized period of "exile" that ended finally in an agreement that consecrated Cambodia's juridical independence on 9 November 1953. He also formed a liaison at this time with a *métisse* beauty contestant, Monique Izzi, who later became his wife and queen.

The instrument of Sihanouk's political power in a Cambodia whose independence and sovereignty had been reinforced by the favorable armistice terms negotiated by the Cambodian delegation at the 1954 Geneva Conference on Indo-China was the Sangkum Reastr Niyum (People's Socialist Community). His founding of the Sangkum followed by a month his dramatic announcement on 2 March 1955 that he was abdicating the throne. Persuading his father to succeed him, Sihanouk took the title *Samdech Upayuvareach* (the Prince who has been King). Also in April he attended the Afro-Asian Conference in Bandung, which increased his feeling of self-importance and convinced him that Cambodia's foreign policy should henceforth be nonaligned. For his own diversion, he played the saxophone, produced films with pseudohistorical themes, and fathered countless children.

But Sihanouk's efforts to keep Cambodia at peace proved only temporarily successful. First, he experienced increasing difficulties with his two powerful neighbors, Thailand and the Republic of Vietnam. Their pro-Western regimes gave sanctuary to armed dissidents, which under the name of Khmer Serei broadcast anti-Sihanouk propaganda to Cambodia. A more serious threat to Sihanouk's control, however, was the growing use of Cambodia's eastern border provinces by Viêt Công and North Vietnamese forces fighting the Sài Gòn government. Such use of Cambodian territory was carefully camouflaged by Hà Nôi and the South Vietnamese National Liberation Front, which went to great lengths to maintain correct relations with Sihanouk's government, supporting its stands on foreign affairs, for example, in their radio broadcasts.

When his father died in 1960, Sihanouk chose to leave the throne vacant and took the title head of state as a way of letting people know who was in charge. By the mid-1960s he was again having difficulties controlling Cambodia's destiny. The situation on the border was now marked by repeated bombings of Cambodian villages by South Vietnamese and U.S. planes. In late 1963 Sihanouk ended the small U.S. economic and military aid programs in Cambodia and in April 1965 he severed diplomatic relations entirely. Trying to counterbalance the influence of Hà Nôi, whose demands on Cambodia now included the furnishing of rice and other goods for its soldiers, Sihanouk steered ever closer to China. But here too there was no salvation in sight, as the Cultural Revolution absorbed China's attention and his old friend Zhou Enlai had little influence left. Moreover, Sihanouk suspected China of being involved in the only insurgency within Cambodia's borders, an agrarian-based movement that instigated a popular uprising against the army in the western region of Samlaut in 1967 and whose leaders Sihanouk habitually derided as "Khmer Rouge."

In 1969 Sihanouk renewed diplomatic relations with the United States and named a "national salvation government" headed by General Lon Nol to try to deal with the mounting insecurity in the countryside and to reverse his previous socialist economic policies, which were unpopular with the emerging middle class. The situation continued to deteriorate, and at the beginning of March 1970 demonstrations took place in Phnom Penh against the Viêt Công and North Vietnamese presence in Cambodia. On 18 March, taking advantage of Sihanouk's absence abroad, the National Assembly unanimously voted to depose him as head of state.

Sihanouk arrived in Beijing hours later and issued a call for armed resistance to the leaders in Phnom Penh. It was the decisive moment in his career. Assured of China's and North Vietnam's backing, he refused to accept the Phnom Penh decision and proceeded to establish a broad political front and a military command, even though this meant accepting the preponderant influence of the Khmer Rouge, the only Cambodian group with the organization and the means to wage a guerrilla war against the Phnom Penh government and its U.S. backers. Sihanouk continued to reside in Beijing, with the exception of one hurried visit to guerrilla bases in Cambodia in 1973, until after the Khmer Rouge capture of Phnom Penh in April 1975.

Sihanouk was returned to the royal palace in Phnom Penh by the Khmer Rouge as their virtual prisoner. In the egalitarian society they were trying to create by radical policies, they had no use for someone who represented in their eyes both the feudalism and the nexus of connections to Western democracies of the past. They used him only as a tool to preserve their seat at the United Nations (UN). Sihanouk has written movingly of his detestation for the Khmer Rouge. The leader of the Khmer Rouge was Pol Pot, who was responsible for the execution of several of Sihanouk's children. Khmer Rouge xenophobia extended to the newly reunified Vietnam, and Sihanouk's cozy relations with Hà Nôi also became a thing of the past.

A Chinese plane spirited Sihanouk to safety just before invading Vietnamese troops entered Phnom Penh in 1978. But he was once more an exile, far from his beloved Kampuchea, as it was now known. He divided his time between China and North Korea, where his "great friend" Kim Il-sung ruled unopposed. Once again he assumed the role of figurehead leader of a resistance move-

ment, this time a coalition of two small non-Communist groups and the Khmer Rouge, who were still supported by China, in a drawn-out struggle against the Vietnamese-installed people's republic of president Heng Samrin and prime minister Hun Sen. Once again he ensured that Cambodia's UN seat was preserved for his side.

This situation was to last for a decade, until the withdrawal of Vietnamese troops from Cambodia and an internationally brokered peace agreement under UN peacekeeping safeguards allowed Sihanouk to return in triumph to the refurbished royal palace in Phnom Penh in November 1991. Expressing annoyance at UN interference in Cambodia's affairs, Sihanouk immediately declared that the policies of Hun Sen's government had been correct and likened them to those of the Sangkum instead of presiding impartially over a four-sided Supreme National Council as called for in the peace plan. In an astute move, he adopted the title *Samdech Euv* (Father Prince) and embraced Hun Sen as his adopted son. Elections to the National Assembly in May 1993 gave his followers, who had capitalized on his popularity in the countryside, a majority; however, they were forced to share power with the former Phnom Penh government in a two-sided arrangement in which his son, Prince Norodom Ranariddh, became first prime minister.

Sihanouk, never forgiving those who had deposed him, declared himself to have been retroactively head of state since 18 March 1970. No one in Phnom Penh dared contest his right to be head of state. A new constitution tailored to the requirements of the situation made him king once more, although Sihanouk himself modestly proclaimed he would reign but not rule in a parliamentary democracy in which he would remain above politics.

Sihanouk was once again at center stage. The only factors that detracted from his triumph were his health and the Khmer Rouge. Cancer of the bone marrow forced him to spend months at a time in Beijing undergoing radiation treatment by Chinese doctors. Meanwhile the Khmer Rouge, having boycotted the elections, renewed insurgency while avoiding criticizing Sihanouk. With the future thus mortgaged, and with a successor to the throne still undecided, Sihanouk could still feel some uncertainty about whether he would go down in history as his country's benefactor or as a publicity-hungry manipulator willing to deal with anyone and everyone as circumstances dictated.

On 5 July 1997 Second Premier Hun Sen seized power in Cambodia and ousted First Premier Ranariddh, Sihanouk's son, who then fled abroad. In the coup a number of prominent Ranariddh supporters were slain. After trying without success to mediate a solution, in October 1997 Sihanouk left Cambodia, saying that he did not know when and if he would ever return.

—Arthur J. Dommen

References: Chandler, David P. *The Tragedy of Cambodian History: Politics, War and Revolution since 1945.* New Haven, CT: Yale University Press, 1991.
Hamel, Bernard. *Sihanouk et le Drame Cambodgien.* Paris: Editions L'Harmattan, 1993.
Osborne, Milton. *Sihanouk: Prince of Light, Prince of Darkness.* Honolulu, HI: University of Hawaii Press, 1994.

See also: Cambodia; China, People's Republic of (PRC); Heng Samrin; Hun Sen; Khieu Samphan; Khmer Rouge; Lon Nol; Pol Pot; Vietnamese Invasion and Occupation of Cambodia; Zhou Enlai (Chou En-lai).

Simons, Arthur D.

(1918–1979)

U.S. Army officer and strike force commander of 1970 Sơn Tây raid. Born in Missouri on 28 June 1918, Arthur D. "Bull" Simons graduated from the University of Missouri in 1941 with a degree in Journalism and a Reserve Officers' Training Corps (ROTC) commission. He originally was assigned to the field artillery, commanding a 75-mm pack howitzer battery in New Guinea during World War II. Later in the war he commanded a Ranger company in the invasion of the Philippines.

Simons also served in Korea and in the 1950s joined the Special Forces. In 1960 he led a 107-man team, code-named WHITE STAR, that organized a clandestine army in Laos. His team eventually recruited and organized 12 battalions of volunteer Meo tribesmen. Simons went to Southeast Asia four times, always in unconventional operations.

On the night of 20 November 1970 Colonel Simons, at the age of 52, led a 56-man strike team into Sơn Tây Prison, 23 miles from Hà Nội. When they got there they discovered that the American prisoners of war (POWs) had been moved weeks earlier and the prison was empty. Simons's team, nonetheless, got in and out without sustaining a single casualty and inflicted many enemy casualties in the process.

At the time some people considered the Sơn Tây raid a dismal failure. For the American POWs, however, it was a much needed psychological boost—proof that they had not been abandoned by their country. After the raid the North Vietnamese reacted by consolidating the widely scattered POWs, many of whom had been held in virtual solitary confinement for more than five years. Subsequently, they were together and could give each other support.

Simons received the Distinguished Service Cross from President Richard Nixon. In 1971 he retired from the Army after being passed over for promotion to brigadier general. Secretary of the Army Melvin R. Laird personally intervened with General William C. Westmoreland, then Army chief of staff. Westmoreland explained to Laird that it was impossible for him to overrule the promotion board. Simons had been a fine colonel and an outstanding combat commander but he was not, after all, a graduate of the War College. Laird tried three times, and even President Nixon sought to get Simons promoted, but the Army bureaucracy would not yield.

Although Simons retired from the Army, his combat days were not over. In early 1979 he led a commando raid to free two American engineers held captive for ransom by the Iranian government. The raid was organized and financed by the employer of the two engineers, H. Ross Perot, chairman of Electronic Data Systems. Simons's team accomplished its mission by inciting a mob attack on the prison where the Americans were held. Some 11,000 Iranian citizens, also held in the prison, were freed in the process.

Simons never accepted any payment for leading the Iran raid. A month after he returned from Iran, Simons suffered a heart attack. He died in Dallas, Texas, on 21 May 1979.

Within the Army, Simons was considered a soldier's soldier—a warrior rather than a uniformed bureaucrat. Despite his hardcore image, he was a careful and methodical planner of operations who prided himself on his ability to bring his troops out alive. Simons was fond of saying: "Soldiers are entitled to leadership from men who can 'smart their way out of it.' I don't want people to get their ass shot off for nothing. That's what leaders are for, to not let that happen."

—David T. Zabecki

References: Schemmer, Benjamin F. The Raid. New York: Harper & Row, 1976.
———. "Requiem for a Warrior: Col. Arthur D. "Bull" Simons." Armed Forces Journal International (November 1979): 44–46.
The Washington Post (23 May 1979).
See also: Laird, Melvin R.; Nixon, Richard Milhous; Prisoners of War, Allied; Sơn Tây Raid; United States: Special Forces; Westmoreland, William Childs.

Sino-Vietnamese War

(17 February–5 March 1979)

Sometimes referred to as the Third Vietnam War, this 18-day war fought between two former allies, the People's Republic of China (PRC) and Socialist Republic of Vietnam (SRV), seemed to many a strange event indeed. To critics of American involvement in Vietnam it was proof of the historical animosity between the two powers and the fact that self-interest is more important in relations between states than ideology. The causes of the war were border disputes between the two states, the SRV's treatment of its Chinese minority, the PRC's determination to punish Vietnam for its invasion of Cambodia, and China's desire to weaken ties between Vietnam and the Soviet Union.

There had been border disputes between the two states for some time, as the common frontier between the PRC and SRV had been demarcated in colonial times by the French. Although the actual territory in dispute was quite small, beginning in 1974 border incidents had multiplied. According to the SRV there were 21,175 such incidents in 1978, and negotiations over the disputed territory, begun in 1977, had broken off in 1978. More important economically were quarrels between the two states over the Paracel and Spratly Islands in the South China Sea and territorial waters in the Gulf of Tonkin, both of which were spurred on by the possibility of oil deposits.

The second major cause of the war was Vietnam's treatment of its Chinese minority, known as the Hoa. In the late 1970s some 1.5 million Hoa lived in Vietnam, many of whom had been there for generations. The largest concentration of Hoa, some 1.2 million, lived in Chợ Lớn, the Chinese section of Sài Gòn, a former market grown into a bustling commercial center. Many Hoa, who were an important economic element of the country, refused to become Vietnamese citizens. In March 1978 the government abolished private trading, although it allowed many of the Chinese merchants to continue their enterprises after that date because they were essential to the economy of the country. Once the government established its own state-run shops, however, those in private enterprises were ordered to register for productive work. This would have meant the removal of the Chinese into the countryside for agricultural work, which was part of the government plan to reduce population in Sài Gòn.

Faced with this prospect, some 170,000 Chinese fled overland into China. Many more attempted to escape by sea to Hong Kong and other points. This latter exodus was prompted in part by provocateurs—either persons working for the government in an effort to rid the country of a minority population or Chinese gangsters prompted by greed. They informed the Chinese community that war with China was inevitable. These "agents" extracted money from the Chinese in return for providing escape by sea. Although there had been a steady flow of refugees from Vietnam after 1975, by 1978 it had become a flood and had reached crisis proportions from the opposition of Southeast Asian countries to take in the large numbers arriving on their shores; many, of course, perished on the seas in their flimsy craft or were set upon by pirates. The loss of these individuals was certainly a serious blow to the Vietnamese economy. The PRC protested, canceled aid to Vietnam, and withdrew some 5,000 to 8,000 technical advisors. Beijing accused Hà Nôi of deliberately expelling its Chinese minority. The exodus slackened off after July 1979 when Hà Nôi announced it would take major steps to prevent illegal departures, but it was nonetheless a serious cause of friction between the PRC and the SRV.

The third major cause of the war was disagreement between the two states over the 1978 Vietnamese invasion of Cambodia. Beijing regarded Kampuchea as being within its sphere of influence, and in early February 1979 PRC Vice-Premier and Chief of Staff of the People's Liberation Army Teng Hsiao-ping said, "Vietnam must be punished severely, and China is considering taking appropriate counteraction." Chinese leaders also hoped that military action by the PRC against the SRV would relieve pressure on the Khmer Rouge, which it was supporting militarily.

A fourth cause of the conflict has been suggested by historian Bruce Elleman. He believes that the Chinese leadership used the brief war as a means to expose as a fraud Soviet assurances of military support for Vietnam.

Whatever the reasons for the war, the PRC appeared to enjoy tremendous advantages over its opponent. It had a population of nearly a billion people and regular army of 3.6 million. But the 1979 war with Vietnam revealed Chinese weakness rather than military prowess. With the exception of a month-long clash with India in 1962, the People's Liberation Army (PLA) had not fought a major war since the Korean conflict. It was basically an infantry army, sadly deficient in many respects, and commanded by old men.

For its war with Vietnam the PRC massed 18 divisions totaling 180,000 men; 8 divisions made up the initial invading force. Eventually the Chinese had 600,000 men available for deployment. Vietnam seemed at a serious military disadvantage. Its entire military establishment was only approximately 615,000 men, centered on 25 infantry divisions, plus a number of independent regiments and specialized units. It was a modern army, relatively well equipped, well disciplined, and hardened in war. Unfortunately, it was also widely dispersed. Six of its divisions were stationed in

Laos and 14 in Kampuchea. That left in Vietnam itself only 5 divisions, 4 of which protected Hà Nôi. Guarding the border with China were some 70,000 well-armed members of the Border Security Force; lightly armed militia units were also available. The Vietnamese had emplaced obstacles and minefields along the border and had covered possible invasion approaches by artillery and mortars.

On 17 February 1979 Chinese forces led by General Hsu Shih-yu attacked simultaneously at some 43 points along the border. This was both to spread the Vietnamese defenders and to probe for weak spots. The main attacks were along the half-dozen traditional invasion routes to Hà Nôi. The Chinese offensive consisted of heavy artillery barrages followed by human-wave infantry attacks. The Chinese hoped to secure the key mountain passes as quickly as possible. Meeting intense Vietnamese opposition, the Chinese nonetheless accomplished this within several days, the railheads of Đăng Đa and Lào Cai falling on 17 and 19 February, respectively. After penetrating to an average depth of only about five miles, the Chinese then halted their advance for two days to replenish ammunition and bring in additional troops; soon there were some 200,000 Chinese troops inside Vietnam.

Cao Băng and Hà Giang both fell on 22 February; by that date the Chinese controlled all the frontier passes. The Chinese resumed their advance a day later; also on the 23d the Vietnamese made two small counterattacks into Chinese territory, both of which had only limited success.

The Chinese hoped to force SRV Defense Minister Võ Nguyên Giáp into redeploying units from Kampuchea and Laos, but Giáp refused to panic, choosing instead to wait and see where the major Chinese thrust would develop. As Vietnamese frontier towns continued to fall, Giáp was forced to act. On 3 March he committed the 308th Division to the battle for the key railhead city of Lang Sơn. He also moved a second division north from Đà Năng to support Vietnamese forces fighting around Móng Cái on the coast, and he ordered one division from Kampuchea, although it did not arrive in Tonkin before the end of the war. Had the war lasted longer, Giáp would have been forced to shift other divisions from Kampuchea. It was not until 5 March, however, that Giáp ordered a general mobilization.

By the beginning of March the Chinese advance had bogged down. On the average the Chinese had advanced about 20 miles into Vietnam. Then on 5 March Beijing abruptly announced that it had accomplished its ends and was withdrawing its forces. The Chinese carried out scorched-earth policies, destroying what they could not carry away with them. The Vietnamese simply watched the Chinese depart. By 15 March the Chinese had withdrawn from Vietnam. Total casualties on both sides were some 45,000; after the war the Chinese exchanged 1,636 Vietnamese prisoners for 238 Chinese.

The war exposed many Chinese weaknesses, especially in communications (for which they had relied largely on bugles and whistles), transport, and weaponry. One remarkable aspect of the war was that neither side committed its air forces. China had about 1,000 planes in southern China that it could have used, but none were sent over Vietnam. The Vietnamese had in all approximately 485 combat aircraft, but for unknown reasons used none of them in defense of their territory.

Beginning on 22 February the Soviet Union initiated an airlift of supplies to Vietnam and over the next year doubled its military advisors (there were about 3,000 serving in Vietnam at the start of the war) and increased naval units in Vietnamese waters (in May 1979 the first Soviet submarines arrived at Cam Ranh Bay, where the Russians had been given naval facilities). Despite these Soviet moves, one long-term effect of the war was that it exposed the weakness of the Soviet-Vietnam ties, effectively ending the SRV-USSR military pact.

—Spencer C. Tucker

References: Elleman, Bruce. "Sino-Soviet Relations and the February 1979 Sino-Vietnamese Conflict." Paper presented at "After the Cold War: Reassessing Vietnam," symposium at the Center for the Study of the Vietnam Conflict, Texas Tech University, Lubbock, Texas, April 1996.
O'Ballance, Edgar. *The Wars in Vietnam, 1954–1980.* Rev. ed. New York: Hippocrene Books, 1981.
Young, Marilyn B. *The Vietnam Wars, 1945–1990.* New York: Harper-Collins, 1991.
See also: Cambodia; China, People's Republic of (PRC); Paracel and Spratly Islands; Refugees and Boat People; Union of Soviet Socialist Republics (USSR) (Soviet Union); Vietnam, Socialist Republic of: 1975 to the Present; Vietnamese Invasion and Occupation of Cambodia.

SLAM

Military acronym for Seek, Locate, Annihilate, and Monitor. In September 1967, stung by the media's negative portrayal of the siege of Côn Thiên as another Điện Biên Phu, U.S. Military Assistance Command, Vietnam (MACV) commander General William Westmoreland introduced the SLAM concept to Operation NEUTRALIZE. Devised by General William M. Momyer, commander of the U.S. Seventh Air Force, it involved close coordination of the entire spectrum of Allied fire support to break the siege. Naval gunfire, tactical air support, B-52 bomber strikes, artillery, and other ground weapons were combined in a devastating concentration of firepower.

Beginning on 11 September SLAM elements pounded known and suspected Communist positions in an area roughly the size of Manhattan for 49 days. Momyer personally coordinated the strikes from a combined intelligence center in Sài Gòn. Of 820 B-52 sorties in September, 790 were SLAM missions. Altogether, over 3,100 Air Force, Navy, and Marine air sorties resulted in the delivery of almost 40,000 tons of bombs on targets around Côn Thiên, turning the surrounding area into a moonscape of water-filled craters. By early October the siege of Côn Thiên was lifted.

The success of SLAM convinced Westmoreland that massed firepower alone could thwart future sieges of isolated posts. It was, he later wrote in his memoir, *A Soldier Reports,* "a demonstration that was destined to contribute to my confidence" during the 1968 siege of Khe Sanh four months later. After Côn Thiên, Westmoreland criticized the media for its pessimism as well as his counterpart Võ Nguyên Giáp for foolishly providing such a target-rich environment for SLAM attacks. "If comparable in any

way to Dien Bien Phu," Westmoreland concluded, "it was a Dien Bien Phu in reverse."

—Edward C. Page

References: Maitland, Terrence, and Peter McInerney. *A Contagion of War. The Vietnam Experience,* edited by Robert Manning. Boston: Boston Publishing, 1984.
Morrocco, John, et al., eds. *Thunder From Above: Air War 1941–1968. The Vietnam Experience,* edited by Robert Manning. Boston: Boston Publishing, 1984.
Westmoreland, William C. *A Soldier Reports.* Garden City, NY: Doubleday, 1976.
See also: Côn Thiên; Khe Sanh, Battles of; Momyer, William W.; Westmoreland, William Childs.

Smith, Walter Bedell

(1895–1961)

U.S. Army officer and diplomat. Walter Bedell Smith was born in Indianapolis, Indiana, on 5 October 1895. Smith joined the Indiana National Guard in 1911, was commissioned in 1917, and saw action in France during World War I. He rose steadily through the ranks of the peacetime Army. A gifted staff officer, he quickly won the respect of George C. Marshall, future Army chief of staff, and by 1942 General Dwight D. Eisenhower requested Smith as his chief of staff. Thus began an association that would last until the end of the war.

Although he preferred a command assignment after the cessation of hostilities, Smith accepted the U.S. ambassadorship to the Soviet Union. He remained in that post until 1949, when he briefly commanded the First Army. In 1950 President Harry Truman appointed Smith director of central intelligence. During his tenure at the Central Intelligence Agency (CIA), he reorganized and reformed the agency, vastly improving the type and quality of intelligence it provided.

In February 1952 President Dwight Eisenhower appointed Smith undersecretary of state. Much of his efforts while at the State Department were devoted to resolving problems in Indo-China. At a National Security Council meeting in January 1954 Smith argued for American intervention to relieve the French garrison at Điện Biên Phu. He did not advocate the deployment of ground troops at this time but fully supported the use of air assets. In May Smith attempted to convince the British to join the United States in an intervention for the same purpose. The British refused, and Smith remained in Europe to lead the U.S. delegation to the 1954 Geneva Conference, where he played an important role in the ending of the first Indo-China War. He presented a plan to Soviet Foreign Minister Vyacheslav Molotov for an immediate armistice followed by a plebiscite. Smith articulated U.S. resolve to support any anti-Communist government in South Vietnam. At the end of the negotiations Secretary of State John Foster Dulles instructed Smith not to sign the Geneva Accords. Ironically, Smith's ideas served as a framework for the final settlement. In addition, Smith declared U.S. support for the security of the government of South Vietnam.

Smith resigned his State Department post in late 1954. He died in Washington on 9 August 1961.

—Richard D. Starnes

References: Billings-Yun, Melanie. *Decision against War: Eisenhower and Dien Bien Phu, 1954.* New York: Columbia University Press, 1988.
Cable, James. *The Geneva Conference of 1954 on Indochina.* New York: St. Martin's Press, 1986.
Crosswell, D. K. R. *The Chief of Staff: The Military Career of General Walter Bedell Smith.* New York: Greenwood Press, 1991.
See also: Dulles, John Foster; Eden, Anthony; Eisenhower, Dwight David; Geneva Conference and Geneva Accords; Knowland, William F.; Molotov (born Scriabin), Vyacheslav Mikhailovich; Truman, Harry S.

SOMERSET PLAIN/LAM SƠN 246, Operation

(August 1968)

Joint U.S./Army of the Republic of Vietnam (ARVN) military operation in the A Shau Valley. SOMERSET PLAIN/LAM SƠN 246 occurred after the successful April–May 1968 joint U.S. 1st Cavalry Division/ARVN Operation DELAWARE, in which U.S. and South Vietnamese forces captured large amounts of war material and supplies in the A Shau Valley. The U.S. Military Assistance Command, Vietnam (MACV) then decided to launch a follow-on operation to destroy the Communist forces and gain control of the valley, which had long been a Communist stronghold. While the 1st Cavalry continued its operations, the 101st Airborne Division (Airmobile) would move into the A Shau and block retreating People's Army of Vietnam (PAVN) forces. Combined U.S. and ARVN forces would then force the North Vietnamese into a decisive engagement.

SOMERSET PLAIN began in early August 1968 as the 1st Cavalry's 1st Squadron, 9th Cavalry guided in the initial assault elements from the 101st. The Allied airmobile forces faced intense antiaircraft fire: Seventeen helicopters were lost or damaged. The North Vietnamese also brought down one U.S. Air Force F-4 fighter-bomber.

Once the 101st had secured their landing zones, they proceeded to link up with ARVN and 1st Cavalry units. PAVN forces broke contact and refused to be committed to a major action against the Allies. The operation became a series of patrols with minimal fighting. The major combat units of the 101st withdrew from the A Shau while their reconnaissance teams emplaced mines and booby traps and set out sensors.

On 19 August helicopters lifted out the remaining 101st personnel as SOMERSET PLAIN terminated. For insignificant PAVN losses, the 101st had sustained significant losses in aviation assets.

—J. A. Menzoff

References: Olson, James S., ed. *Dictionary of the Vietnam War.* New York: Greenwood Press, 1988.
Stanton, Shelby. *The Rise and Fall of an American Army: U.S. Ground Troops in Vietnam, 1965–1973.* Novato, CA: Presidio Press, 1985.
See also: Airmobility; DELAWARE–LAM SƠN 216, Operation; Helicopters, Employment of, in Vietnam; United States: Army; Vietnam, Democratic Republic of: Army (People's Army of Vietnam [PAVN]); Vietnam, Republic of: Army (ARVN).

Sơn Tây Raid

(20–21 November 1970)

Raid against a Democratic Republic of Vietnam (DRV) prison camp believed to hold U.S. prisoners of war (POWs). Planning for the Sơn Tây raid began on 5 June 1970 when U.S. Air Force (USAF) Brig. Gen. Donald D. Blackburn, a special operations expert, undertook a study to determine the feasibility of rescuing up to 50 POWs from Sơn Tây Prison, located about 25 miles north of Hà Nội. Meanwhile, a heavy rainy season forced the Sơn Tây River from its banks and fouled the well at the prison. On 14 July the Sơn Tây POWs were moved to another compound. Some guards and other DRV military personnel remained at the prison, however.

On 8 August Blackburn formed a task group to plan and carry out the raid. Brig. Gen. Leroy J. Manor, commander of the USAF's Special Operations Force (SOF) at Eglin Air Force Base, Florida, and Army Col. Arthur "Bull" Simons had charge of the raid. Over the next three weeks they assembled a planning team to work out the details of "Operation IVORY COAST," a code name chosen to confuse anyone who might hear it. Training for the raid began on 20 August at Eglin's range, an area of swamps, brush, and rivers the size of Rhode Island.

The plan called for Army Rangers to be flown to Sơn Tây by one HH-3 and four HH-53 Aerospace Rescue and Recovery Service (ARRS) "Jolly Green Giant" helicopters. The choppers would be supported by five Special Operations Force A-1E Skyraiders and two SOF "Combat Talon" C-130Es. According to the plan, the HH-3 was to crash-land inside the compound. Rangers would pour out of that helicopter to "neutralize" any opposition while other Rangers, landed outside the walls, would break in to complete the rescue operation.

Training was completed by mid-November and the force assembled at Takhli Royal Thai Air Force Base (RTAFB), Thailand. With a typhoon developing over the Gulf of Tonkin, General Manor decided to launch at the first possible opportunity—the first dark night with little or no moonlight. This was 20 November 1970. At 1600 that day the raiders learned of their destination. By 2330 the task force was airborne and headed for the DRV.

Meanwhile, an Air Force and Navy air armada descended on North Vietnam. Navy A-6 Intruders flew toward Hai Phòng at low altitude to simulate a B-52 attack. Other Navy jets dashed inland to confuse North Vietnamese radar operators. Air Force RF-4 reconnaissance jets flew low over Hà Nội, setting off flares, while Air Force and Navy F-4 Phantoms circled on MiG Combat Air Patrol (MIGCAP). North Vietnamese defenses were completely befuddled. Some radar operators reported B-52 attacks. One even announced that an atomic bomb had been dropped on Hà Nội.

Over Sơn Tây the two C-130s dropped pallets of napalm as reference points. In a moment of confusion, three rescue helicopters attacked a North Vietnamese sapper school, located a quarter of a mile from the Sơn Tây Prison. After blasting the watch towers with their Gatling-like miniguns, two of the helicopters pulled away, but one landed about 50 Rangers led by Colonel Simons. They burst into the school, where a huge firefight erupted. It took about two minutes to realize a mistake had been made and another three minutes to get the helicopter back and the Rangers out. The Rangers, who took no casualties, left scores of People's Army of Vietnam (PAVN) troops dead or bewildered and so confused they could not interfere with operations going on nearby.

Within six minutes of hitting the ground at the wrong compound, the Rangers were back on the ground and battering their way into Sơn Tây Prison.

Meanwhile, the HH-3E had crash-landed inside the walls at Sơn Tây, and Army Rangers were already killing the guards and searching for prisoners. To their great disappointment, no prisoners were found. Twenty-seven minutes after the raid began the helicopters were airborne and headed back to Thailand. The only American casualty was an Air Force flight mechanic who broke his ankle when the HH-53 in which he was riding performed a sharp downward turn to avoid an air-to-air missile fired by a pursing MiG. One USAF F-105F Wild Weasel was shot down, but its two-man crew was rescued by a pair of Jolly Green Giant helicopters.

The raid succeeded tactically; had American POWs been present they would have been rescued. On another level Hà Nôi was sent the message that the United States was far from beaten. A substantial force, inserted only a few miles from their capital, had wreaked considerable havoc before successfully withdrawing. Finally, to make any further such efforts more difficult, Hà Nôi ordered all POWs moved to several central prison complexes. This afforded the prisoners more contact with each other, which boosted morale.

—Earl H. Tilford, Jr.

References: David, Heather. *Operation Rescue.* New York: Pinnacle Books, 1970.
Schemmer, Benjamin F. *The Raid.* New York: Harper & Row, 1976.
Tilford, Earl H., Jr. *A History of United States Air Force Search and Rescue Operations in Southeast Asia, 1961–1975.* Washington, DC: Office of Air Force History, 1980.
See also: Helicopters, Allied and Democratic Republic of Vietnam; Helicopters, Employment of, in Vietnam; Prisoners of War, Allied; Search-and-Rescue (SAR) Operations; Simons, Arthur D.

Sông Bé, Battle of
(27 October 1967)

People's Army of Vietnam (PAVN) attack on the Army of the Republic of Vietnam (ARVN) base at Sông Bé. During the Vietnam War the area around the village of Sông Bé was one of five Allied-controlled enclaves in Communist-dominated Phước Long Province, located near the Cambodian border less than 75 miles north of Sài Gòn. The jungle-covered province was a major route of passage for Communist troops and supplies moving from Cambodian sanctuaries to War Zone D, a Communist base area centered to the southeast of the province. During fall 1967, in order to draw Allied forces to the peripheries of South Vietnam and practice mass assaults prior to the 1968 Tết Offensive, PAVN and Việt Công (VC) forces initiated a series of battles. The first was at Côn Thiên, the second at Sông Bé, and there were subsequent attacks on Lộc Ninh and Đăk Tô.

Just after midnight on the morning of 27 October the 88th PAVN Regiment attacked the headquarters of the 3d Battalion, 9th ARVN Infantry Regiment, located two and a half miles south of Sông Bé. The assault opened with nearly 200 rounds of mortar and recoilless rifle fire striking the small ARVN installation, de-

fended by 200 men. PAVN troops from at least two of the three battalions of the 88th Regiment then attacked with four-to-one superiority in three waves, each of which reached the outpost perimeter before being driven off. As the PAVN attacks finally ceased at dawn, 50 ARVN soldiers aggressively pursued the withdrawing Communist troops until they disappeared into the jungle. The ARVN lost 13 killed while PAVN forces suffered 134 dead and lost 37 individual and 20 crew-served weapons.

—Glenn E. Helm

References: Davidson, Philip B. *Vietnam at War.* Novato, CA: Presidio Press, 1988.
Westmoreland, William C. *A Soldier Reports.* Garden City, NY: Doubleday, 1976.
Wirtz, James J. *The Tet Offensive: Intelligence Failure in War.* Ithaca, NY: Cornell University Press, 1991.
See also: Côn Thiên; Đăk Tô, Battle of; Lộc Ninh, Military Operations near; Tết Offensive: Overall Strategy; Tết Offensive: The Sài Gòn Circle; Vietnam, Democratic Republic of: Army (People's Army of Vietnam [PAVN]); Vietnam, Republic of: Army (ARVN); War Zone C and War Zone D.

Souphanouvong
(1909–1995)

Laotian prince and Communist leader, the first president of the Lao People's Democratic Republic (1975–1991). Prince Souphanouvong was born in Luang Prabang on 13 July 1909, the son of viceroy Prince Bounkhong and Mom Khamouane. He studied in Hà Nôi and Paris, becoming an *ingénieur des ponts et chaussées* (civil engineer). He returned to Indo-China in 1936 and was assigned by the Indo-China civil service to Vietnam.

At the time of the Japanese surrender in 1945, Souphanouvong was at Vinh. From there, he traveled to Hà Nôi, where he met Hô Chí Minh, who had just proclaimed the Democratic Republic of Vietnam. Hô sent Souphanouvong to Savannakhet with a Vietnamese escort to rally anti-French forces there, both Lao and Vietnamese. He arrived in Vientiane on 30 October 1945 and was made foreign minister of the Laotian independent government and commander in chief of its fledgling armed forces.

During the French reoccupation of Thakhek in central Laos in March 1946, Souphanouvong was badly wounded when French aircraft strafed his sampan. He remained in Thailand with the other members of the government in exile, but split with this government in 1949 and made his way to North Vietnam, where he joined Hô. In August 1950 he presided over the formation of a resistance government, the Pathet Lao, that was allied with the Việt Minh. But the 1954 Geneva Conference did not recognize this rival government.

Souphanouvong joined short-lived coalition governments led by his half brother Prince Souvanna Phouma in 1957 and 1962. A popular figure, Souphanouvong was elected to the National Assembly by a wide margin in the 1958 elections. He was imprisoned with other Pathet Lao leaders by a rightist government in Vientiane in 1959 but escaped in May 1960. Although a member of the Politburo of the (Communist) Lao People's Revolutionary Party, Souphanouvong was mainly a figurehead leader of the Pathet Lao and its legalized political party, the Neo Lao Hak Sat. During the war years he remained in hiding at the Pathet Lao base area of Sam Neua Province or in North Vietnam. He returned to Vientiane in 1974 to assume the chairmanship of the National Political Consultative Council, a quasi-legislative body set up by the Vientiane Agreement of 1973.

When the Communists dissolved the third coalition government and seized power in December 1975, Souphanouvong was elected by a people's congress to be the president of the Lao People's Democratic Republic. In 1986, after suffering a stroke, he was forced to hand over effective power to an acting president and retired to his home, where he received visiting delegations from other socialist nations but played no other role in the conduct of state affairs. He was replaced as president in 1991 by Kaysone Phomvihan and died in Vientiane on 9 January 1995.

—Arthur J. Dommen

Reference: Zasloff, Joseph J., and MacAlister Brown. *Apprentice Revolutionaries: The Communist Movement in Laos, 1930–1985.* Stanford, CA: Hoover Institution Press, 1986.
See also: Geneva Conference and Geneva Accords; Laos; Pathet Lao; Souvanna Phouma; Vientiane Agreement.

Southeast Asia Treaty Organization (SEATO)

U.S.-sponsored collective security arrangement for Southeast Asia. Instigated by President Dwight D. Eisenhower and forged by Secretary of State John Foster Dulles, the Southeast Asia Treaty Organization (SEATO) was created by the Pact of Manila of 8 September 1954. As a consequence of the failure earlier that year to create a united front during the Điên Biên Phu crisis and the Chinese Communist threat after the Geneva Conference, Eisenhower and the National Security Council agreed an alliance was essential to bind the imperiled countries of Southeast Asia. With French assent and the domino theory in mind, Eisenhower directed Dulles to negotiate an accord in order to contain any Communist aggression against the free territories of Vietnam, Laos, and Cambodia, or Southeast Asia in general.

Meeting in September at Manila, representatives of the United States, the United Kingdom, France, Australia, and New Zealand conferred with delegates from the Philippines, Thailand, and Pakistan. President Eisenhower desired Asian cooperation to dodge accusations of forming an exclusively Occidental alliance, yet major neutrals like Indonesia and India declined participation. The signatories established a slack defensive arrangement for the mutual protection of the Southeast Asian region.

SEATO contained a protocol that thwarted the Geneva Accord's provisions designed to neutralize the new Indo-China states by naming Laos, Cambodia, and southern Vietnam as lands that, if endangered, could menace the tranquility and safety of the treaty's signers. Dulles insisted that the attached clause was necessary, despite its questionable legality, so that a blanket of security could be thrown around the region. Although France opposed full membership by its former colonies, Paris and Sài Gòn approved of the protocol's safeguard for a limited time over the military re-

groupment zone below the 17th parallel. But Cambodia's Norodom Sihanouk rejected the provision, and international accords affecting Laos in 1962 excluded it.

Ratified by the U.S. Senate in 1955, SEATO differed from the North Atlantic Treaty Organization (NATO) in that it failed to establish an effective multilateral defense system. Without permanent armed forces, members were to confer in case of aggression against a signatory or protocol state. No combined military reply to an attack was required. In fact, no treaty obligation compelled the United States to quell internal disorder nor oppose an invasion. SEATO fell short of gaining general support throughout the area because so few regional nations became members. The Eisenhower administration relied on SEATO, regardless of its shortcomings, to discourage potential Communist aggressors and to provide a diplomatic facade behind which the Republic of Vietnam emerged with a recognizable political boundary south of the 17th parallel.

SEATO proved its usefulness in the next decade. The protocol cover for Indo-Chinese countries provided legitimacy for U.S. involvement in South Vietnam in order to restrain the North Vietnamese. Yet shortly after the fall of Sài Gòn, SEATO expired, self-dissolved in a terse observance on 30 June 1977 at Bangkok, Thailand.

—Rodney J. Ross

References: Arnold, James R. *The First Domino: Eisenhower, the Military and America's Intervention in Vietnam.* New York: William Morrow, 1991.
Hess, Gary R. *Vietnam and the United States.* Boston: Twayne, 1990.
Moss, George Donelson. *Vietnam: An American Ordeal.* Englewood Cliffs, NJ: Prentice-Hall, 1994.
See also: Dulles, John Foster; Eisenhower, Dwight David; Geneva Conference and Geneva Accords; United States: Involvement in Vietnam, 1954–1965.

Souvanna Phouma

(1901–1984)

Laotian prince, parliamentarian, and statesman, who played a major role in his country's independence movement and became the leader of the Neutralist faction in three successive coalition governments. Born in Luang Prabang on 7 October 1901, the son of Prince Bounkhong, viceroy of the Kingdom of Luang Prabang, and Princess Thongsi, Souvanna Phouma was educated at the Lycée Albert Sarraut in Hà Nôi and received degrees in architectural engineering from the University of Paris and in electrical engineering from the University of Grenoble.

Souvanna Phouma entered the Public Works Service in 1931 at Vientiane. In 1940 he was chief of the Architectural Office at Luang Prabang. In 1945 he became chief of the Public Works subdivision at Vientiane and was made director of Public Works for Laos when the Japanese took over from the French in Indo-China on 9 March 1945.

When Souvanna Phouma's half brother, the viceroy Prince Phetsarath, formed an independent government after the Japanese surrender, Souvanna Phouma was a minister, as was another half brother, Prince Souphanouvong. After the French reoccupied Laos in 1946, the three brothers and other ministers fled across the Mekong to Thailand and spent the next three years in exile in Bangkok, returning only when the French gave greater independence to Laos.

Souvanna Phouma became prime minister for the first time on 21 November 1951, his Progressive Party having won 16 out of 35 seats in the elections to the National Assembly that year. His government, having presided over Laos's participation in the 1954 Geneva Conference that ended the Indo-China War, lasted until 20 October 1954.

Souvanna Phouma became prime minister again on 21 March 1956, on a platform of reintegrating the pro-Communist Pathet Lao rebel faction, which his foreign minister at Geneva had promised to do by means of internal negotiations. Although the Pathet Lao were under the titular leadership of Prince Souphanouvong, the negotiations between the government and the Pathet Lao proved to be a long, drawn-out process that brought Souvanna Phouma into conflict with U.S. policy, which opposed a prospective coalition with the Pathet Lao. But Souvanna Phouma persisted in his efforts, claiming that Souphanouvong was not a Communist and that a neutral Laos had the support of neighboring China, with which he was on good terms—although China was not represented in Vientiane. His relations with the Democratic Republic of Vietnam (DRV), on the other hand, remained tense because of the Hà Nội government's continued armed support of the Pathet Lao.

Finally, in November 1957 negotiations resulted in signed agreements under which the Pathet Lao restored to the authority of the royal government the provinces of Sam Neua and Phong Saly and promised to integrate its soldiers into the royal army and to participate in elections as a legalized political party. A coalition government with Souvanna Phouma as prime minister was constituted. But after the Pathet Lao's political party, the Neo Lao Hak Sat, won a stunning electoral victory in partial elections to the National Assembly in May 1958, Souvanna Phouma faced a cabinet crisis and was compelled to resign on 23 July 1958. He then went to France as ambassador.

Returning to Laos, Souvanna Phouma was reelected to the National Assembly in 1960, and was subsequently elected its chairman. Kong Le, the royal army captain who staged a coup in August of that year, turned to Souvanna Phouma to form a government in the wake of the previous cabinet's resignation, and the prince became prime minister once more on 16 August. Following charges of pressure on the National Assembly, Souvanna Phouma resigned at the end of August and was then called upon by the king to form a new cabinet to include certain rightist ministers. However, the deal fell through and the rightists went into rebellion against him, with covert U.S. support, from their base at Savannakhet in southern Laos.

In December 1960 the rightists attacked Kong Le's troops that defended Vientiane, and Souvanna Phouma fled to safety in Phnom Penh, where he continued to maintain he was the legal prime minister. His government was no longer recognized by the United States and its allies, notably Thailand, and he set up his headquarters at Khang Khay on the Plain of Jars. After sporadic heavy fighting between the rightist army, supported by U.S. advi-

sors, and Kong Le's neutralist army, now allied with the Pathet Lao and the Democratic Republic of Vietnam (DRV) and supplied by a Soviet airlift, a cease-fire was negotiated at Ban Namone on 3 May 1961. A 14-nation conference convened in Geneva the following month to deal with the Laos crisis, and, after lengthy deliberations, it gave support to a coalition government with Souvanna Phouma as prime minister.

The second coalition soon fell apart under the pressure of renewed hostilities in the kingdom involving People's Army of Vietnam (PAVN) troops and U.S.-supported Hmong irregulars, but Souvanna Phouma remained in office throughout the war years, recognized by all foreign powers (including North Vietnam, which maintained an embassy in Vientiane) and eventually reconciled with the United States.

A fresh round of negotiations beginning in October 1972 resulted in a new agreement, signed on 21 February 1973, and a bilateral coalition, the third. The Pathet Lao and North Vietnamese maintained pressure, and on 2 December 1975 proclaimed the dissolution of the coalition and the advent of a people's republic in which the hitherto clandestine Laotian Communist party, the Lao People's Revolutionary Party, held exclusive power. Souvanna Phouma, who had suffered a heart attack in July 1974, resigned and was named advisor to the government of the Lao People's Democratic Republic, an honorary post he held until his death in Vientiane on 11 January 1984 at the age of 82.

—Arthur J. Dommen

References: Dommen, Arthur J. *Conflict in Laos: The Politics of Neutralization.* New York: Praeger, 1971.
Stuart-Fox, Martin, and Mary Kooyman. *Historical Dictionary of Laos.* Asian Historical Dictionaries No. 6. Metuchen, NJ: Scarecrow Press, 1992.
See also: Geneva Conference and Geneva Accords; Kong Le; Laos; Pathet Lao; Phoumi Nosavan; Plain of Jars; Souphanouvong.

Special Forces

See United States: Special Forces; Vietnam, Republic of: Special Forces (Lực Lượng Đặc Biệt [LLDB]).

Special Services

See United States: Special Services.

Spellman, Francis Joseph
(1889–1967)

American Roman Catholic cardinal and strong supporter of U.S. involvement in Vietnam. Francis Spellman was born in Whitman, Massachusetts, on 4 May 1889. He graduated from Fordham University in 1911 and then attended the North American College in Rome. Ordained in 1916, Spellman had already forged friendships with influential Italian ecclesiastics who would help his career and lay the groundwork for his appointment as New York's archbishop in 1939. Spellman was elevated to cardinal on 21 February 1946. He was one of the most politically influential religious leaders outside the Vatican after World War II and obdurately supported American intervention in Vietnam. Government officials at all levels sought his favor and viewed his ardent nationalist and anti-Communist convictions as representing those of his church and 26 million American Catholics.

A domino theory advocate, Spellman urged more U.S. support for French troops fighting Communist insurgents in Indo-China. After France's defeat in 1954, he rallied American support for Ngô Đình Diêm, a Vietnamese nationalist and Catholic he first met in 1950, as leader of South Vietnam. The Cardinal helped organize a pro-Diêm lobby in Washington and encouraged Catholic relief groups to supplement U.S. and Sài Gòn aid programs. Although distancing himself from Diêm before the 1963 coup, Spellman hawkishly supported military escalation and served as vicar of the U.S. Armed Forces. Some antiwar protesters called the conflict "Spellman's war." As Pope Paul VI promoted a negotiated peace, Spellman argued that the Vietnam conflict was a "holy war" against communism that required total American victory. This break with the Vatican, and the American public's increasing polarization over Vietnam, diminished the cardinal's influence by the time of his death in New York City on 2 December 1967.

—Delia Pergande

References: Buttinger, Joseph. *Vietnam: A Dragon Embattled.* New York: Praeger, 1967.
Cooney, John. *The American Pope: The Life and Times of Francis Cardinal Spellman.* New York: Times Books, 1984.
See also: American Friends of Vietnam; Antiwar Movement, United States; Ngô Đình Diêm; Roman Catholicism in Vietnam.

Spock, Benjamin M.
(1903–1998)

Noted writer and antiwar activist. Born in New Haven, Connecticut, on 2 May 1903, Benjamin Spock received his B.A. from Yale and an M.D. from Columbia. He cast his first presidential vote for Calvin Coolidge but by the 1930s was a staunch supporter of Franklin Roosevelt's New Deal. Between 1944 and 1946 Lt. Comdr. Spock practiced psychiatry in the U.S. Naval Reserve and wrote *The Common Sense Book of Baby and Child Care,* which would become the world's second best-selling book after the Bible. Immersed in his practice immediately after the war, Spock uncritically accepted American policies. In 1960 he campaigned for John F. Kennedy, appearing on television with Jacqueline Kennedy to garner the "mother's vote." Spock then supported Lyndon Johnson's candidacy in 1964, accepting his campaign promises for peace.

Frustrated by President Johnson's failure to act, Spock began to speak against the war and to urge draft resistance. On 5 January 1968 he was indicted with four others for conspiring to counsel, aid, and abet violations of the Selective Service law and hinder administration of the draft. All but one of the "Boston Five" were found guilty, fined, and sentenced to two years' imprisonment. The U.S. First Circuit Court of Appeals reversed the convictions of Spock and one other defendant, declaring that "vigorous criticism of the draft and of the Vietnam war is free speech protected by the First Amendment, even though its effect is to interfere with the war effort." The remaining two were ordered retried based on an error in the judge's charge to the jury.

In 1972 Spock ran for the presidency as the candidate of the Pacifist People's Party. He also wrote two books about that time: *Decent and Undecent: Our Personal and Political Behavior* (1970) and *Raising Children in a Difficult Time* (1974). Spock died at his home in San Diego, California, on 16 March 1998.

—Brenda J. Taylor

Reference: Mitford, Jessica. *The Trial of Dr. Spock.* New York: Alfred A. Knopf, 1969.
See also: Antiwar Movement, United States; Draft; Spring Mobilization to End the War in Vietnam; United States: Department of Justice.

Spratly Islands
See Paracel and Spratly Islands.

Spring Mobilization to End the War in Vietnam
(15 April 1967)

First of the mass demonstrations in the United States against the war sponsored by national coalitions. A conference of liberal and leftist antiwar activists held in Cleveland, Ohio, on 26 November 1966 formed the Spring Mobilization Committee to End the War in Vietnam and set 15 April 1967 as the date to hold major demonstrations in New York and San Francisco. Previous antiwar actions had been locally organized and dispersed around the country or smaller rallies sponsored by individual groups. Organizers hoped that by focusing on only two sites they could draw impressive crowds that would effectively pressure the Johnson administration to alter its policy. The leadership of the "Spring Mobe," which included veteran activists A. J. Muste (until his death in mid-February), Dave Dellinger, and Robert Greenblatt, brought in James Bevel of the Southern Christian Leadership Conference to direct the planning. The coalition also continued the precedent of a nonexclusion policy that invited cooperation regardless of political ideology, a stance that led some of the more conservative groups to withhold their formal endorsements. Still, the events received broad support. The spring mobilization revealed the breadth of antiwar public opinion.

On 15 April the New York crowd reached perhaps 200,000 people who marched from Central Park to the UN building. Martin Luther King, Jr., joining an antiwar coalition event for the first time, served as keynote speaker. The rally also featured Benjamin Spock, Pete Seeger, and Stokely Carmichael, among others. The demonstration attracted people from a wide variety of political views, professions, racial and ethnic groups, ages, religions, and lifestyles, many of whom were protesting for the first time. Participants faced taunts and thrown objects from unsympathetic onlookers. Preceding the New York march, nearly 150 people held a collective draft card burning in Central Park's Sheep Meadow, organized by Cornell University's We Won't Go group. In San Francisco, 50,000 people rallied in Kezar Stadium to hear such speakers as Coretta Scott King, Julian Bond, and Robert Scheer. The turnout was the city's most impressive to date.

The Spring Mobilization was the largest demonstration in the nation's history to that point, and it clearly revealed the degree of political opposition to the government's Vietnam policy. Far more than a radical fringe, the antiwar movement was representative of the American mainstream. This impressive challenge drew more attacks from the White House and Congress, whose members inaccurately criticized antiwar forces as Communist dominated and accused the protesters of providing encouragement to the enemy in continuing the war. Frustrated but undaunted, the movement continued to grow and demonstrate its disapproval.

—Mitchell K. Hall

References: DeBenedetti, Charles, and Charles Chatfield. *An American Ordeal: The Antiwar Movement of the Vietnam Era.* Syracuse, NY: Syracuse University Press, 1990.
Halstead, Fred. *Out Now! A Participant's Account of the American Movement against the Vietnam War.* New York: Monad Press, 1978.
Wells, Tom. *The War Within: America's Battle over Vietnam.* Berkeley, CA: University of California Press, 1994.
See also: Antiwar Movement, United States; Dellinger, David; King, Martin Luther, Jr.; Muste, Abraham J.; Spock, Benjamin M.

Staley, Eugene

(1906–1989)

International economist who led a fact-finding mission to South Vietnam in 1961. Born in Friend, Nebraska, on 3 July 1906, Eugene Staley received a B.A. from Hastings College in 1925 and a Ph.D. from the University of Chicago in 1928. He began his academic career as an assistant professor at the University of Chicago in 1931 and held a variety of posts, including professor of international economic relations at Johns Hopkins School of Advanced International Studies, before joining the Stanford Research Institute as senior international economist in 1950.

In 1961 President John F. Kennedy called upon Staley to visit South Vietnam and make recommendations for bolstering Ngô Đình Diệm's regime and the U.S. role in accomplishing it. Staley's team spent most of June and July evaluating the situation. Findings ranged beyond economics to social and political reform, troop strengths, and the structured isolation of rural peasants from the Việt Công.

Reporting to Kennedy in August, Staley stressed the need for a self-sustaining Vietnamese economy. He insisted that without meaningful and continued social and political reform, military action could not render desirable results. But the most lasting of Staley's unexpectedly military-oriented recommendations centered on the protection of the civilian population. To this end he advocated substantial major increases in Army of the Republic of Vietnam (ARVN) forces, the Civil Guard, and local militias. He also advised the issue of better arms and equipment at the local level. Finally, he called for the construction of a network of strategic hamlets.

The strategic hamlet idea was not original. In 1959 the Diệm regime launched the Agroville program, a proposed network of protected communities designed to isolate the rural population from the Việt Công. The program proved a disaster. Only a small fraction of the 80 proposed communities were ever completed.

Two years later Sir Robert Thompson, a counterinsurgency expert with the British Advisory Mission in Sài Gòn, advanced the strategic hamlet idea, providing as a positive example his experience against Communist insurgents in Malaya. Diệm balked at Thompson's advice until Staley's advocation (meaning U.S. funding and assistance) induced speedy acceptance. The plan appeared conceptually sound but was, in reality, poorly suited for South Vietnam. Begun with high expectations in 1962, the strategic hamlet program was fraught with corruption from the start. The United States abandoned the effort within a year.

Staley remained a prominent international economist. His writings and research activities largely focused on weighty economic issues, namely the betterment of underdeveloped nations. Staley died in Palo Alto, California, on 31 January 1989.

—David Coffey

References: Asprey, Robert B. *War in the Shadows: The Guerrilla in History.* New York: William Morrow, 1994.
Fall, Bernard B. *The Two Viet-Nams: A Political and Military Analysis.* New York: Praeger, 1963.
See also: Agroville Campaign; Ngô Đình Diệm; Strategic Hamlet Program; Thompson, Robert Grainger Ker.

STARLITE, Operation

(18–24 August 1965)

U.S. Marine Corps operation aimed at eliminating the 1st Việt Công (VC) Regiment. Operation STARLITE began on 18 August 1965 near the Van Tường Peninsula in Quang Tri Province. Marine planners designed a three-pronged attack. It called for elements of the 7th Marines at Chu Lai to move south and block any VC escape north while units of the 4th Marines were helicoptered to three landing zones (LZs), named Red, White, and Blue, west and southwest of the hamlets Nam Yên and An Cường. These Marines would then drive the VC northeastward toward the sea. Finally, elements of the 3d Marines would land on the beach due east of these hamlets, with amphibian and armored support, and drive west and north.

Despite stiff resistance from VC forces, STARLITE succeeded in pushing the insurgents to the coast. Close air support, tanks, and naval gunfire were critical to the operation's outcome. STARLITE terminated on 24 August. The VC sustained 614 dead; the Marines lost 45 killed.

—R. Blake Dunnavent

References: Shulimson, Jack, and Charles M. Johnson. *U.S. Marines in Vietnam: The Landing and the Buildup, 1965.* Washington, DC: History and Museums Division, U.S. Marine Corps Headquarters, 1978.
Stanton, Shelby L. *The Rise and Fall of an American Army: U.S. Ground Forces in Vietnam, 1965–1973.* Novato, CA: Presidio Press, 1985.
See also: Airmobility; Amphibious Warfare; Armor Warfare; Naval Bombardment; PIRANHA, Operation; Tanks, Allied and Democratic Republic of Vietnam; United States: Marine Corps.

STEEL TIGER, Operation

(April 1965–December 1968)

U.S. air interdiction campaign over the Hồ Chí Minh Trail, particularly in the northern panhandle of Laos. Operation STEEL

TIGER represented yet another unsuccessful use of limited air-power in the Vietnam War. Although air planners hoped STEEL TIGER would complement the larger ROLLING THUNDER campaign, the political dangers of bombing Laos haunted the Johnson administration. Concern over possible Chinese or Soviet intervention, coupled with the potential wrath of the world community that had guaranteed Laotian neutrality in 1962, drove Washington to restrict Navy and Air Force target lists. In fact, civilians in Washington selected the targets. This information was then sent on to air planners in Sài Gòn for implementation. The Air Force subsequently used F-105 Thunderchiefs, Lockheed AC-130 Spectre gunships, and numerous other aircraft stationed in South Vietnam and Thailand, while the Navy flew strike missions from aircraft carriers stationed in the South China Sea.

As with most limited uses of airpower, STEEL TIGER did not stop the flow of North Vietnamese men and materials to the South. The Hồ Chí Minh Trail was an elaborate network of intertwined truck tracks and footpaths through deep jungle terrain. Visibility from the air was poor and damage assessments were largely inaccurate. If U.S. airmen bombed a critical choke point, the North Vietnamese either repaired it quickly or transferred the movement of supplies to bicycles. During the monsoon season most of the traffic on the Trail was by foot, which complicated air operations even further.

The development of target lists in Washington led to an additional problem: The command and control of air operations over the Laotian panhandle became hopelessly muddled. Although the Navy played a large role in STEEL TIGER, both Navy and Air Force planners were loath to compromise their autonomy by fully cooperating with each other. Navy pilots, in turn, less than affectionately referred to STEEL TIGER missions as "truck busting." Although many trucks were destroyed along the Trail, a simple cost-benefit analysis showed that the insurgents in the South, while receiving fewer supplies than before, were still getting enough to prosecute the war. In contrast, hitting one North Vietnamese truck on the Hồ Chí Minh Trail cost the United States thousands of dollars.

In 1968 STEEL TIGER merged with Operation TIGER HOUND, which had focused on interdicting Communist supply routes in the southern Laotian panhandle. The newly christened Operation COMMANDO HUNT was to interdict supplies from the Democratic Republic of Vietnam all along the Hồ Chí Minh Trail.

—Lincoln Hill

References: Berent, Mark. *Steel Tiger.* New York: Putnam, 1990.
Berger, Carl, ed. *The United States Air Force in South East Asia 1961–1973.* Washington, DC: U.S. Government Printing Office, 1984.
Gurney, Gene. *Vietnam: The War in the Air.* New York: Crown, 1985.
See also: Air Power, Role in War; BARREL ROLL, Operation; COMMANDO HUNT, Operation; ROLLING THUNDER, Operation; TIGER HOUND, Operation.

Stennis, John Cornelius

(1901–1995)

U.S. senator, 1947–1989. John C. Stennis was born in Kemper County, Mississippi, on 3 August 1901. He graduated from Missis-sippi State University in 1923 and the University of Virginia Law School in 1928. First elected to the U.S. Senate from Mississippi in 1947, he was a conservative Democrat who opposed social welfare programs and supported military appropriations. Although wary of American entanglements overseas and skeptical about South Vietnam, he supported President Lyndon Johnson's policies, believing that once committed the United States could not retreat. A member of the powerful Senate Armed Services Committee, he became the chair in 1969. He favored a maximum use of American airpower against both the Democratic Republic of Vietnam and Việt Công positions in the South. Increasingly concerned that the war was draining the armed forces stockpile of weapons and supplies, he began to express a fear that the war might establish a precedent for American entry into future wars without congressional approval. Although he supported President Richard Nixon's Southeast Asia policies, Stennis worked to limit presidential war-making power. In 1971 he and Senator Jacob Javits cosponsored the War Powers Act. He was defeated for reelection in 1988.

On his retirement from the Senate, Stennis returned to Mississippi, where he died on 23 April 1995. His long service on the Senate Armed Services Committee led the Navy in December 1995 to name a new carrier, the *John C. Stennis* (CVN 74), after him.

—Robert G. Mangrum

References: Congressional Quarterly. *Congress and the Nation.* Vol. 7, *1985–1988.* Washington, DC: Congressional Quarterly, 1990.
Davidson, Phillip B. *Vietnam at War: The History, 1946–1975.* Novato, CA: Presidio Press, 1988.
Karnow, Stanley. *Vietnam: A History.* New York: Penguin Books, 1984.
Olson, James S., ed. *Dictionary of the Vietnam War.* New York: Greenwood Press, 1988.
Summers, Harry G. *Vietnam War Almanac.* New York: Facts on File, 1985.
Who's Who in America, 1984–1985. New Providence, NJ: Marquis Who's Who, 1984.
See also: Fulbright, J. William; Humphrey, Hubert H.; Javits, Jacob Koppel; Johnson, Lyndon Baines; McGee, Gale William; Proxmire, William.

Stevenson, Adlai E.

(1900–1965)

U.S. presidential candidate; U.S. ambassador to the United Nations, 1961–1965. Born on 5 February 1900 in Los Angeles, California, Adlai Ewing Stevenson II attended the Choate School in Wallingham, Connecticut, in 1916 and 1917. He entered Princeton University the next year and graduated in 1922. Despite less than impressive grades he managed to gain admission to Harvard Law School but flunked out after his second year. After moving to Chicago and trying to develop a career in journalism, Stevenson finished law school at Northwestern University in 1926 and subsequently was admitted to the Illinois bar.

Stevenson then practiced law in Chicago, and from 1933 to 1935 he severed as special U.S. government counsel. During the Second World War he was special assistant to the secretary of the Navy. After the war Stevenson held a variety of posts within the State and War Departments, acquiring a reputation for expertise in foreign affairs for his work as a member of the U.S. delegation to the 1945 United Nations Conference in San Francisco.

In 1948 Stevenson was elected governor of Illinois on the Democratic ticket. He instituted economic reforms, reorganized the state administration, attacked corruption, and vetoed a loyalty oath bill. He was twice the Democratic nominee for president (1952 and 1956) but was defeated both times by Dwight D. Eisenhower.

A Cold War liberal, Stevenson favored anticommunism, internationalism, and containment. Stevenson hoped to become President John F. Kennedy's secretary of state, but Dean Rusk got the job instead. In December 1960 Kennedy announced his intention to appoint Stevenson ambassador to the United Nations (UN). He served in that post under Presidents Kennedy and Lyndon Johnson from 1961 until his death in 1965. Regarded with suspicion and mistrust by Kennedy loyalists, who thought him weak and indecisive, Stevenson never enjoyed close rapport with the president.

Stevenson visited Vietnam in April 1953 during the Indo-China War. He observed strong support among the people for insurgent leader Hô Chí Minh but never grasped the reasons why. To counter Hô, Stevenson advocated land reform, national independence, and free elections. He also believed in the domino theory and worried that if Vietnam fell to the Communists, the rest of Southeast Asia would soon follow. Such views shaped his later responses.

Stevenson may have had private misgivings about military escalation but, if so, kept them to himself. In 1964 he supported President Lyndon Johnson's campaign against Republican "hawk" Senator Barry Goldwater. Later Stevenson went on record in favor of applying containment in Southeast Asia. Specifically, he wanted to restrict Chinese Communist expansion there primarily by political and economic means and hoped to enlist Japanese and Indian assistance in the endeavor. In the fall of 1964, when UN Secretary General U Thant pressed for face-to-face negotiations between North Vietnam and the United States, Stevenson supported the idea but elicited no enthusiasm from Rusk or Johnson.

A controversy developed over his real views soon after his death. In November 1965 CBS newsman Eric Severeid reported his impression that Stevenson was ready to resign in a protest over Vietnam. During a previous encounter in June 1965 with the writer Paul Goodman, an antiwar advocate, Stevenson denied any intention of leaving the Johnson administration, stating "That's not the way the game is played." Later he composed but never sent a letter to Goodman, couched in standard Cold War rhetoric, in which he endorsed the Johnson policy of containing Chinese Communist aggression by standing strong in South Vietnam. Subsequently he remained outwardly a Cold War warrior. Whatever his private doubts, he publicly supported the defense of South Vietnam against "Communist aggression." Stevenson died suddenly on 14 July 1965 of a heart attack in London.

—Mark T. Gilderhus

References: Broadwater, Jeff. *Adlai Stevenson and American Politics: The Odyssey of a Cold War Liberal.* New York: Twayne, 1994.
Martin, John Bartlow. *Adlai Stevenson and the World.* Garden City, NY: Doubleday, 1978.
_____. *Adlai Stevenson of Illinois.* Garden City, NY: Doubleday, 1977.
Walton, Richard J. *The Remnants of Power: The Last Tragic Years of Adlai Stevenson.* New York: Coward-McCann, 1968.
See also: Containment Policy; Domino Theory; Goldwater, Barry Morris; Johnson, Lyndon Baines; Kennedy, John Fitzgerald; Rusk, Dean; U Thant.

Stilwell, Richard G.

(1917–1991)

U.S. Army general; chief of staff, Military Assistance Command, Vietnam (1963–1965). Born in Buffalo, New York, on 24 February 1917, Richard Stilwell graduated from the U.S. Military Academy in 1938 and entered the Army as a second lieutenant. He spent much of his 38-year career in administrative positions, serving capably during the Second World War, the Korean War, and in Vietnam. He progressed steadily through the ranks while establishing himself as a leading military thinker. In the first of two tours in Vietnam, Stilwell served as chief of operations (1961–1963) and later chief of staff (1963–1965), Military Assistance Command, Vietnam (MACV). In 1965 he became chief of the Joint U.S. Military Advisory Group, Thailand, but in 1967 he returned to the United States to command the 1st Cavalry Division at Fort Hood, Texas.

In 1968 Stilwell began a second tour of duty in Southeast Asia as commander of XXIV Corps. In 1972 he assumed command of the Sixth Army at San Francisco, California. The following year he was promoted to full (four-star) general and was given overall command of UN forces in South Korea. He retired from the Army in 1976, but in 1981 he joined the Reagan administration as deputy undersecretary of defense for policy formulation, a post he held until 1985. Thereafter he operated a consulting firm in Arlington, Virginia. General Stilwell died in Arlington on 25 December 1991.

—David Coffey

References: *New York Times* (26 December 1991).
Who Was Who in America with World Notables, 1989–1993. Chicago: Marquis Who's Who, 1993.
See also: Military Assistance Command, Vietnam (MACV); United States: Army.

Stockdale, James B.

(1923–)

Highest-ranking U.S. Navy prisoner of war (POW) in Vietnam. Born on 23 December 1923 in Galesburg, Illinois, James B. Stockdale graduated from the U.S. Naval Academy in 1946. After three years of sea duty, he was selected for flight training, earning his wings in 1950.

Commander Stockdale commanded the squadron that flew cover for U.S. ships during the Tonkin Gulf incidents of August 1964, and he was carrier air-group (CAG) commander on the USS *Oriskany* when he was shot down over North Vietnam on 9 September 1965. Stockdale kept secret during his long captivity and repeated torture sessions that he believed no North Vietnamese attack had occurred on 4 August 1964.

Stockdale was the leader of the Alcatraz Gang, the POW's Hall of Fame for hard-line resisters, and he authored the standard orders on adhering to the Code of Conduct. While Stockdale acted as the intellectual and political leader of the POWs, his wife Sybil founded the National League of Families of American Prisoners and Missing in Southeast Asia.

Following his return from Vietnam in 1973, Stockdale was named president of the Naval War College. He was awarded the Medal of Honor in 1976. After retirement from the Navy as a vice-admiral in 1978, he served as president of The Citadel. He was then a Hoover Institution Fellow, and ran unsuccessfully as H. Ross Perot's running mate in the 1992 presidential election.

—Joe P. Dunn

References: Howes, Craig. *Voices of the Vietnam POWs: Witnesses to Their Fight.* New York: Oxford University Press, 1993.
Hubbell, John G., et al. *P.O.W.: A Definitive History of the American Prisoner of War Experience in Vietnam, 1964–1973.* New York: Reader's Digest Press, 1976.
Stockdale, James B. *A Vietnam Experience: Ten Years of Reflection.* Stanford, CA: Hoover Institution Press, 1984.
Stockdale, Jim, and Sybil Stockdale. *In Love and War: The Story of a Family's Ordeal and Sacrifice during the Vietnam Years.* New York: Harper & Row, 1984.
See also: Hà Nôi Hilton (Hoa Lò Prison); McCain, John S., III; Prisoners of War, Allied; Tonkin Gulf Incidents.

Strategic Hamlet Program

The most ambitious and well-known effort by President Ngô Đình Diêm to pacify the countryside and neutralize the Viêt Công insurgents. The Strategic Hamlet program sought to provide security and a better life for the rural populace by settling them in protected hamlets, where government cadres could carry out economic and political programs. Following in the wake of a similar effort, the Agroville campaign, the Strategic Hamlet program was inaugurated in 1961 and officially ended early in 1964, but it began to wane even before Diêm was overthrown in November 1963.

The concept of the Strategic Hamlet program derived from British counterinsurgency expert Sir Robert Thompson's experiences in quashing the Malayan emergency in the 1950s. Between 1961 and 1965 Thompson served as head of the British Advisory Mission and advised the Diêm government on counterinsurgency or pacification programs. His notion was to organize villagers to provide for their own defense. In Malaya, the failure of the Chinese insurgents, who were ethnically different from the villagers, to penetrate the population meant that little more was required than to organize a home guard, a local security force supported by local police. The government could then relocate the Chinese squatters. The situation in Vietnam was more complex. The Viêt Công were well established in all areas of the country and were of the same ethnicity as the villagers. Therefore, the insurgents were not easily identified and segregated from the rest of the people.

Thompson's notion was to bring security to where the people already lived. Relocation was to be minimal. Thompson estimated at the start of the program that only 5 percent of the hamlets, those in Viêt Công–controlled areas, would have to be moved to new sites. The strategic hamlets were intended to isolate the insurgents physically and politically from the people, their recruiting base.

American civilians—notably Roger Hilsman and Walt Rostow in the State Department, as well as embassy personnel in Sài Gòn—favored the program, but American military leaders criticized the concept of strategic hamlets, believing that it tied military forces into a defensive posture. Lt. Gen. Lionel McGarr, head of the U.S. Military Assistance and Advisory Group (MAAG), thought this role more appropriate for police than regular forces. He urged military clearing operations instead of tying down forces in static positions.

Diêm undertook the Strategic Hamlet program on his own without first informing the Americans, merely presenting them with a fait accompli. But Diêm had his own reasons for embarking on the program. He saw it as a way to get assistance from the United States while managing the program himself. Aware of the danger of being perceived by the Vietnamese as an American puppet, he wanted to control the program in order to fend off critics, retain independence, and resist Washington's pressure for political reforms.

Diêm and his brother, Ngô Đình Nhu, who carried out the program, significantly changed Thompson's original concept. Thompson proposed surrounding existing hamlets with security forces, but Diêm and Nhu decided that security should begin within the hamlets and embarked on an ambitious plan to build fortified hamlets, which in practice involved relocating villagers. Nhu established three goals. First, the government would link the people in fortified hamlets in a communications network, allowing them to summon local defense and reaction forces in case of emergency. Second, the program would unite the people and bind them to the government. Third, the government would work to improve living standards.

Nhu wanted half of South Vietnam's 14,000 hamlets to be completed by early 1963 and another 5,000 by early 1964. The remainder would be swept along by example. To meet these ambitious quotas Nhu exerted severe pressure on province chiefs, despite their lack of authority over local officials. Nhu's plans led to overexpansion, creating far more hamlets than Sài Gòn's forces could protect or its cadres could administer. Under pressure from Sài Gòn to show results, province officials often appeased Nhu with meaningless data. In 1962 the government designated 2,600 settlements in I, II, and III Corps as "completed," but American officials ruefully concluded that the definition of "completed" varied greatly from hamlet to hamlet in terms of quality of defenses and percentage of the population under government control. Pressure to meet unrealistic goals encouraged a focus on the superficial aspects of the program, such as erecting fences, which often sufficed to officially reclassify an existing settlement as a strategic hamlet. The program imposed onerous burdens on the people, such as controls on their movement and demands for guard duty. According to the U.S. Embassy, most villagers viewed the program as a security measure, not as an element of revolution.

In May 1963 General Paul Harkins, head of U.S. Military Assistance Command, Vietnam (MACV), criticized the program's execution as superficial, because it left Communist-controlled hamlets and salients in government areas. He urged Diêm to expand the program more logically to consolidate his hold on the countryside.

Women and children of the strategic hamlet of Đá Bàn, Republic of Vietnam, 1963. The purpose of the Strategic Hamlet program was to provide security and a better life for the rural populace by settling them in protected hamlets, where government cadres could carry out economic and political programs.

The Communists initially limited their opposition to disseminating propaganda that compared the strategic hamlets to prisons and inserting agents to collect taxes, recruit, and stir up resentment toward the government. By the summer of 1963 they shifted tactics, directly attacking hamlets and severing links between them and nearby reaction forces. The hamlets were vulnerable because there were too many that were poorly built and weakly defended. The Communists' new approach bore results, and the number of government-run strategic hamlets drastically fell. By July 1964, for example, only 30 of the 219 strategic hamlets in Long An Province remained under government control.

After the Strategic Hamlet program had ended, Thompson criticized its implementation on three grounds. First, using the Cần Lao Party, Nhu attempted to control the program from the top down instead of winning political and popular support at the bottom. Second, by emphasizing the Republican Youth, he created divisions between the youth and the village elders, the traditional leaders. Third, Nhu failed to understand the extent of Viêt Công penetration and was unprepared to take the harsh measures necessary to eliminate it within the hamlets.

Faulty execution compromised a promising pacification program. Not only did the Strategic Hamlet program fail to halt the insurgency, but it manifested the arbitrary and repressive aspect of Diêm's rule. It was also plagued by corruption. The inadequacy

of the Strategic Hamlet program served as a metaphor for the regime's failure to stem the insurgency, to gain and hold the support of the people, and to win the confidence of the Kennedy administration, which acquiesced in Diêm's overthrow.

The failure of the Strategic Hamlet program had a larger significance: Pacification would be supplanted as a strategy for fighting the war. Two successor pacification efforts in 1964, *Chiên Thăng* and *Hợp Tác*, were also poorly executed and failed to reverse Sài Gòn's declining fortunes in the countryside. In late 1964 the emboldened Communists began to infiltrate conventional People's Army of Vietnam (PAVN) units into South Vietnam to administer the coup de grace. It was a situation beyond the scope of pacification to remedy, forcing Washington to intervene with a bombing campaign and ground troops.

—Richard A. Hunt

References: Colby, William E. *Lost Victory: A Firsthand Account of America's Sixteen-Year Involvement in Vietnam.* Chicago: Contemporary Books, 1989.

Hunt, Richard. *Pacification: The American Struggle for Vietnam's Hearts and Minds.* Boulder, CO: Westview Press, 1995.

Osborne, Milton. *Strategic Hamlets in Vietnam.* Data Paper 55. Ithaca, NY: Cornell University Southeast Asia Program, April 1965.

Thompson, Sir Robert. *Defeating Communist Insurgency.* New York: Praeger, 1966.

See also: Agroville Campaign; Harkins, Paul D.; Hilsman, Roger; Malaysia; Military Assistance and Advisory Group (MAAG), Vietnam; Ngô Đình Diêm; Ngô Đình Nhu; Pacification; Rostow, Walt Whitman; Staley, Eugene; Thompson, Robert Grainger Ker.

Students for a Democratic Society (SDS)

A leading organization in the campus-based antiwar movement of the 1960s. When it first appeared in January 1960 the goals of the Students for a Democratic Society (SDS) were to support the civil rights movement and politically organize the urban poor. Tom Hayden, a University of Michigan student, served as the organization's first secretary and worked hard to popularize its ideas. The SDS grew in size and notoriety in mid-1962 when it issued the Port Huron Statement, which called for "true democracy" in the United States and an end to the arms race. It also energized student activists to increase their involvement with the liberal wing of the Democratic Party.

The involvement of the SDS with traditional politics was short-lived, however. The limited progress of the civil rights movement and America's increasing involvement in Vietnam radicalized Hayden and his colleagues. By 1964, and especially after the Gulf of Tonkin incidents, the SDS began to organize more and more campus demonstrations, including "teach-ins," to protest the Vietnam War. SDS members circulated "we won't go" petitions among young men of draft age and developed a militant (and sophisticated) draft resistance program to serve their needs. As a result of these activities, membership in the SDS grew rapidly. In 1965–1966 the number of SDS chapters at U.S. colleges and universities doubled from 124 to 250, with an actual overall membership of some 31,000 people.

Toward the end of the 1960s dissension began to overtake the organization. Those who saw America's involvement in Vietnam beginning to wind down wanted to shift focus to domestic and cultural issues. Others continued to advocate the importance of politics but in a more violent, revolutionary vein. Antiwar demonstrations soon became more unruly. During the "Stop the Draft" week of October 1967, for example, SDS leader Carl Davidson demanded that protesters burn down government draft centers. Still worse was the 1968 Democratic National Convention in Chicago, where SDS members and their sympathizers fought with, and were battered by, riot police in the streets.

At its peak SDS had approximately 400 chapters, but Vietnamization, a growing revulsion with student violence, and the fragmentation of the New Left into different political arenas, such as women's liberation, led to its demise. The organization's impact was significant, however. Although it did not change U.S. foreign policy, it did help block or scale back the number of military options Presidents Lyndon Johnson and Richard Nixon were initially prepared to use. As a result, Vietnamization became the only viable option the Nixon administration had left to extricate itself from a political and military dead end.

—Tracy R. Szczepaniak

References: Gitlin, Todd. *The Sixties: Years of Hope, Days of Rage.* New York: Bantam Books, 1987.

Miller, James. *Democracy Is in the Streets: From Port Huron to the Siege of Chicago.* New York: Simon & Schuster, 1987.

O'Neill, William L. *Coming Apart: An Informal History of America in the 1960s.* New York: Times Books, 1971.

Viorst, Milton. *Fire in the Streets: America in the 1960s.* New York: Simon & Schuster, 1979.

See also: Antiwar Movement, United States; Democratic Party National Convention, 1968; Hayden, Thomas E.; Johnson, Lyndon Baines; May Day Tribe; Nixon, Richard Milhous; Teach-Ins, Sit-Ins; Weathermen.

Studies and Observation Group (SOG)

U.S. Military Assistance Command, Vietnam, subordinate command primarily concerned with covert operations and intelligence gathering. In 1964 the U.S. Military Assistance Command, Vietnam (MACV) organized the Studies and Observation Group (commonly known as MACV-SOG). Supposedly created to evaluate the success of the military advisor program, this mission was actually a cover for highly classified clandestine operations conducted throughout Southeast Asia. MACV-SOG was activated in January 1964 as a MACV subordinate command (and not a Special Forces unit) under the direction of the special assistant for counterinsurgency and special activities (SACSA) in the Joint Chiefs of Staff at the Pentagon. SOG was a joint-service (Army, Air Force, Navy, and Marines) command that by 1966 included more than 2,000 U.S. personnel, most of whom were Army Special Forces, and 8,000 indigenous personnel, including South Vietnamese and Montagnard troops. U.S. forces assigned to MACV-SOG also included personnel from the Air Force 90th Special Operations Wing, Navy SEALs, and Marine Force Recon. MACV-SOG's area of responsibility included Burma, Cambodia, Laos, the Democratic Republic of Vietnam (DRV), and the Republic of Vietnam (RVN), as well as the Chinese provinces of Yunnan, Kwangsi, Kwangtung, and Hainan Island.

SOG was divided into a number of different groups: (1) the Psychological Studies Group, operating out of Huê and Tây Ninh, made false radio broadcasts from powerful transmitters; (2) the Air Studies Group, complete with UH-1F "Green Hornet" and H-34 helicopters, a C-130 squadron, and a C-123 squadron, specialized in dropping and recovering special intelligence groups into Laos, Cambodia, and North Vietnam; (3) the Maritime Studies Group concentrated its efforts on commando raids along the DRV coast and the Mekong Delta; and (4) the Ground Studies Group carried out the greatest number of missions, including ambushes and raids, monitoring the location of American prisoners of war, assassinations, kidnapping, rescue of airmen downed in Communist-controlled territory, long-range reconnaissance patrols, training and dispatching agents into North Vietnam to run resistant movement operations, and harassment and booby-trapping of infiltration routes and ammunition supply facilities.

In 1967 SOG reorganized its ground strike elements into three field commands: Command and Control Central (CCC) located in Kontum, Command and Control North (CCN) in Đà Nẵng, and Command and Control South (CCS) in Ban Mê Thuôt. CCC was responsible for classified unconventional warfare operations throughout the triborder region of Laos, Cambodia, and Vietnam. CCN was responsible for special unconventional warfare missions into Laos and North Vietnam. CCS was responsible for clandestine unconventional warfare operations inside Việt Công–dominated areas of South Vietnam and throughout Cambodia. These organizations included Spike Recon Teams (each composed of three U.S. Special Forces and 8 indigenous personnel), Hatchet Forces (composed of five U.S. Special Forces and 30 indigenous personnel) and SLAM (seek, locate, annihalate, monitor) companies.

In March 1971 MACV-SOG's CCN, CCC, and CCS were redesignated as Task Force Advisory Elements 1, 2, and 3, respectively, and were charged with advising the RVN Strategic Technical Directorate Liaison Service, but this change had little impact on the actual activities of the former SOG commands. Over the years, MACV-SOG personnel earned a total of six Medals of Honor. MACV-SOG was deactivated on 30 April 1972.

—James H. Willbanks

References: Simpson, Charles M. *Inside the Green Berets: The First Thirty Years.* Novato, CA: Presidio Press, 1983.
Stanton, Shelby L. *Green Berets at War.* Novato, CA: Presidio Press, 1985.
_____. *Vietnam Order of Battle.* New York: Galahad Books, 1986.
See also: Civilian Irregular Defense Group (CIDG); DELTA, Project; Montagnards; OMEGA, Project; SEAL (Sea, Air, Land) Teams; SIGMA I and II; United States: Special Forces.

Sullivan, William Healy

(1922–)
American diplomat; ambassador to Laos, 1964–1969. Born on 12 October 1922 in Cranston, Rhode Island, William H. Sullivan graduated from Brown University in 1943 and spent over two years in the Navy as an officer on minesweepers and destroyers in the Atlantic and Pacific during World War II. After the war he entered the Fletcher School of Law and Diplomacy at Tufts University, earning a master's degree in Latin American Studies. Sullivan joined the Foreign Service in 1947. He went on to serve in a variety of positions in Washington and abroad, including postings to Bangkok, Calcutta, Tokyo, and The Hague.

In 1961 Sullivan came to the attention of W. Averell Harriman, who had been charged by President John F. Kennedy with negotiating an end to the Laos crisis. Over the objections of more senior foreign service officers, Harriman designated the junior Sullivan as deputy U.S. representative to the Geneva Conference. Working closely together, Harriman and Sullivan successfully concluded the Declaration on the Neutrality of Laos signed on 23 July 1962. The relationship between the two men continued after the Geneva Conference, with Sullivan serving as special assistant to Undersecretary of State Harriman, working on Southeast Asian affairs.

In December 1964 Sullivan arrived in Laos as U.S. ambassador. Over the next four years, he was responsible for the conduct of military operations against an increasingly aggressive Communist threat. "The secret war in Laos," author Charles Stevenson has emphasized, "was William Sullivan's war." The ambassador insisted on an efficient, closely controlled country team. He imposed two conditions on his subordinates. First, the thin fiction of the Geneva Accords had to be maintained to avoid possible embarrassment to the Lao and Soviet governments; military operations,

therefore, had to be carried out in relative secrecy, largely by Central Intelligence Agency (CIA)-led Hmong tribesmen. Second, no regular U.S. ground troops were to become involved, although American airpower would be necessary. In general, Sullivan successfully carried out this policy.

Sullivan enjoyed a role that Senator Stuart Symington once described as "a military proconsul." He ran the war with a firm hand, occasionally clashing with U.S. military authorities in South Vietnam. Sullivan usually won these bureaucratic battles, as he had the confidence of President Lyndon B. Johnson. Sullivan's informative and often witty cables were appreciated by Johnson and his national security advisor, Walt Rostow.

Sullivan left Laos in March 1969, just as the North Vietnamese introduced major new forces into the country and expanded the war. As deputy assistant secretary of state for East Asian and Pacific affairs, he helped to formulate the proposals that the United States would put forward at the Paris peace talks on Vietnam. Sullivan then acted as chief deputy to National Security Adviser Henry Kissinger in Paris and played an important role in negotiating the agreement that was signed on 27 January 1973.

Sullivan served as ambassador to the Philippines from 1973 to 1977. His last assignment was as ambassador to Iran from 1977 to 1979. When the administration of President Jimmy Carter rejected Sullivan's advice that the United States accept the fundamentalist revolution in Iran and try to steer it in a more moderate direction, he resigned from the Foreign Service.

—William M. Leary

References: Castle, Timothy N. *At War in the Shadow of Vietnam: U.S. Military Aid to the Royal Lao Government, 1955–1975.* New York: Columbia University Press, 1993.
Stevenson, Charles A. *The End of Nowhere: American Policy towards Laos since 1954.* Boston: Beacon Press, 1972.
Sullivan, William H. *Obbligato, 1939–1979: Notes on a Foreign Service Career.* New York: W. W. Norton, 1984.
See also: Carter, Jimmy; Harriman, W. Averell; Johnson, Lyndon Baines; Kennedy, John Fitzgerald; Kissinger, Henry Alfred; Laos; Paris Negotiations; Paris Peace Accords; Rostow, Walt Whitman; Taylor-McNamara Report.

Summers, Harry G., Jr.

(1932–)
U.S. Army officer and analyst of U.S. Vietnam policy. Born in Covington, Kentucky, on 6 May 1932, Harry G. Summers lied about his age and enlisted in the Army when he was only 15. During the Korean War he served as an infantry squad leader, earning the Silver Star. While still an enlisted man, he earned a college degree, and in 1957 he received a direct commission as a second lieutenant of infantry.

Summers served in Vietnam from February 1966 to June 1967. He was an assistant operations officer for II Field Force; then operations officer of the 1st Infantry Division's 1st Battalion, 2d Infantry; then again an assistant operations officer at II Field Force. He was wounded twice. After his Vietnam tour, Summers attended the U.S. Army Command and General Staff College, where Colin Powell was one of his classmates.

Summers returned to Vietnam in July 1974 as chief of the Negotiations Division of the Four Party Joint Military Commission. In that capacity, he flew to Hà Nội to negotiate with members of the North Vietnamese General Staff. When People's Army of Vietnam (PAVN) forces overran Sài Gòn, Summers was in the last helicopter to leave the American Embassy on 30 April 1975.

In 1979 Summers joined the faculty of the U.S. Army War College Strategic Studies Institute. While there he wrote *On Strategy*, a brilliant and scholarly book that was the first and perhaps most influential analysis of America's failure in Vietnam. After retiring from the Army as a colonel, Summers became a widely noted military commentator and writer and the editor of *Vietnam* magazine.

Summers's writing, and *On Strategy* in particular, have had a profound impact on American military thinking. In the continuing debate over the U.S. performance on Southeast Asian battlefields, Summers is a leading voice on the side that maintains that U.S. forces never lost a battle. Retired Col. David Hackworth, a leading voice in the opposite camp, maintains that American tactics failed dismally. Tactical performance, however, is only a peripheral piece of Summers's broader, more significant argument.

On Strategy focuses primarily on the strategic level of war. It analyzes U.S. conduct of the war within the framework of classic Clausewitzian theory and the time-tested principles of war first articulated by British Maj. Gen. J. F. C. Fuller in the 1920s. Summers points out that America had no clearly defined goal and no strategic objective in Vietnam. He also shows that the lack of internal political support for the war violated Clausewitz's concept of the "Remarkable Trinity," which requires a unity of purpose among the government, the military, and the people before any nation's war effort can succeed.

According to Christopher Bassford, Summers's arguments were tremendously influential both inside and outside the military. They underlie many important statements of American national policy, most significantly the 1984 "Weinburger Doctrine." Many of the ideas in the U.S. Army's 1993 capstone manual of war-fighting doctrine, *FM 100–5 Operations,* are paraphrased directly from *On Strategy*. Summers also influenced the trend among U.S. Senior Service Colleges (War Colleges) to add to their curriculum the systematic study of Clausewitz's writings.

—David T. Zabecki

References: Bassford, Christopher. *Clausewitz in English: The Reception of Clausewitz in Britain and America 1815–1945.* New York: Oxford University Press, 1994.
Summers, Harry G. *On Strategy: A Critical Analysis of the Vietnam War.* Novato, CA: Presidio Press, 1984.
See also: Four-Party Joint Military Commission (FPJMC); Hackworth, David H.; Powell, Colin L.

SUNFLOWER, Operation

(5 January–15 February 1967)
Peace initiative following the failure of Operation MARIGOLD. Operation SUNFLOWER consisted of a direct U.S. approach to Hà Nội through the Democratic Republic of Vietnam (DRV) Embassy in Moscow and a parallel attempt in London by British Prime Minister Harold Wilson, working with Soviet Premier Aleksei Kosygin.

Lingering questions about MARIGOLD probably motivated both the United States and the DRV. These included whether the North Vietnamese had been serious about negotiating and whether the United States had been willing to use Janusz Lewandowski's Ten Points (his draft of the U.S. bargaining position) as the basis for a settlement.

In Moscow, the U.S. and DRV representatives essentially restated previous positions: Washington insisted on mutual de-escalation according to Phase A and Phase B (in Phase A, the United States stops the bombing; in Phase B, both sides de-escalate after an adequate time) and Hà Nội demanded an unconditional halt to U.S. acts of war on the North as a precondition for talks. This impasse killed the Moscow channel; on 15 February the DRV terminated contact.

While Wilson pursued his peace overture with Kosygin, the U.S. position on the sequence of de-escalatory moves hardened. This was complicated by a letter from President Lyndon Johnson to Hồ Chí Minh. Although Wilson's "impropriety" in presenting a U.S. offer without permission contributed to the problems, U.S. "bungling" doomed this channel, strained American-British relations, and confused the Soviet Union and the DRV.

SUNFLOWER, during which both the DRV and United States perceived the other becoming more rigid in its negotiating stance, stands as a diplomatic debacle. Certainly MARIGOLD and SUNFLOWER together add up to a tragedy of errors, but even perfect diplomacy could not have surmounted the fact that the two sides held irreconcilable positions. Diplomatic success would have to await changes in the military situation that forced the parties from their intransigent positions.

—Paul S. Daum, with assistance from B. J. Rogers

References: Cooper, Chester L. *The Lost Crusade: America in Vietnam.* New York: Dodd, Mead, 1970.
Herring, George C. *LBJ and Vietnam: A Different Kind of War.* An Administrative History of the Johnson Presidency Series. Austin, TX: University of Texas Press, 1994.
———, ed. *The Secret Diplomacy of the Vietnam War: The Negotiating Volumes of the Pentagon Papers.* Austin, TX: University of Texas Press, 1983.
Kraslow, David, and Stuart H. Loory. *The Secret Search for Peace in Vietnam.* New York: Random House, 1968.
Radvanyi, Janos. *Delusion and Reality: Gambits, Hoaxes, and Diplomatic One-Upmanship in Vietnam.* South Bend, IN: Gateway Editions, 1978.
See also: Kosygin, Aleksei Nikolayevich; MARIGOLD, Operation.

SUNRISE, Operation

(March 1962–August 1963)
Early pacification effort. Operation SUNRISE was a pilot project in the Strategic Hamlet program. The plan called for Army of the Republic of Vietnam (ARVN) troops to establish hamlets in one of the least secure areas in South Vietnam: an inhospitable area of scrub, jungle, and rubber plantations located north of Sài Gòn in Bên Cát District, Bình Dương Province, in War Zone D. It was the

brainchild of Ngô Đình Diệm and his brother Nhu and was paid for by the U.S. government.

In November 1962 correspondent Peter Arnett reported that only 4 of the planned 14 hamlets called for in the operation had been constructed and that Bên Tưởng, the main hamlet, "was falling apart" and that the "experimental hamlets had in fact become expensive internment camps." General William Westmoreland noted in August 1963 that "the showplace strategic hamlet of Ben Tuong—the first-built of all strategic hamlets in Operation Sunrise—was overrun by the Viet Cong." It was, nonetheless, "a mecca for visiting congressmen and journalists, proof that American money was being spent wisely and well." Stanley Karnow wrote that John Donnell and Gerald Hickey, two Vietnamese-speaking RAND researchers whom he knew in Vietnam, concluded that the Bên Cát test was being bungled. Operation SUNRISE failed in its attempt at forced relocation of the peasants into strategic hamlets, and the National Liberation Front (NLF) once again took control of the area. The operation ended in August 1963.

—Paul S. Daum, with assistance from B. J. Rogers

References: Arnett, Peter. *Live from the Battle Field: From Vietnam to Baghdad: 35 Years in the World's War Zones.* New York: Simon & Schuster, 1994.
Karnow, Stanley. *Vietnam: A History.* New York: Viking Press, 1983.
Westmoreland, Gen. W. C. "Report on Operations in South Vietnam, January 1964–June 1968." In *Report on the War in Vietnam (As of 30 June 1968).* Washington, DC: U.S. Government Printing Office, 1968.
See also: Hickey, Gerald Cannon; Ngô Đình Diệm; Ngô Đình Nhu; Strategic Hamlet Program; Westmoreland, William Childs.

Surface-to-Air Missiles (SAMs)

A chief component in the Democratic Republic of Vietnam (DRV) air defense system. On 24 July 1965 a Soviet-built radar-guided surface-to-air missile (SAM) exploded northwest of Hà Nôi amid a flight of four U.S. Air Force F-4C aircraft. Code-named the SA-2 "Guideline" by the North Atlantic Treaty Organization (NATO) and known to the Soviets as the S-75, this missile ushered in a new era in air combat. SA-2 missiles carried a high-explosive warhead of approximately 300 pounds. The missile could reach speeds up to Mach 3.5, but not until it was well over 25,000 feet in altitude. Unlike predicted antiaircraft artillery (AAA) fire, the SA-2 could compensate for aircraft maneuvers by using an electronic guidance system. Its introduction also denied U.S. aircraft the ability to operate at medium or high altitudes in the vicinity of SA-2 batteries. The Americans would have to introduce new technologies and tactics before they could regain these preferred operating altitudes.

Of all the SAMs in the DRV inventory, the SA-2 and SA-7 were the most potent. The SA-2 was a significant weapon, although it shot down relatively few aircraft. Of the approximately 9,000 missiles fired between 1965 and 1972, fewer than 2 percent reached their targets, including 15 B-52 bombers shot down during Operation LINEBACKER II (1972). Nevertheless, the SA-2 triggered the creation of a permanent electronic combat doctrine in American military aviation. This took time, however, and until late 1966

American formations in the vicinity of active SA-2 battalions would have to perform evasive maneuvers and sometimes jettison their bombs in order to escape missile launches. Even if aircraft pressed on with their bomb runs, bombing accuracy was often hindered by SA-2 activity. Without appropriate radar detection equipment, American aviators were rarely aware that an SA-2 had targeted them until a missile was on the way. Then they would evade the missile by diving to low altitudes (where the SA-2 was less effective), but this maneuver brought the aircraft into the range of lethal (AAA).

DRV missile sites were usually carved out of the countryside and designed to allow for the quick setup of an SA-2's radar vans, service vehicles, and missile launchers. A typical site was set up in a "Star of David" pattern. The lines of the six-pointed star were roads and pathways for vehicles and there was a missile launcher at each of the star's points. Electric and communications cables were laid out ahead of time to allow for fast connections. Most important, the sites were quickly and expertly hidden. Until the advent of aircraft such as the U.S. Air Force "Wild Weasel," it was virtually impossible to pinpoint the location of an active SA-2 site until its missiles roared off the launch rails.

The SA-2 was also "soldier-proof" in that it was durable and had large knobs and switches. It required little training to operate, especially when compared to similar Western systems. Each operator in the fire control battery had a highly specialized function, and only the battery commander could make decisions for the crew based on orders from higher authorities. Initially, Soviet technicians manned the sites with their North Vietnamese trainees (the latter assumed more and more responsibilities as the conflict progressed).

The SA-2 required a high degree of operator skill to engage fighters, for there was an appreciable delay before the missile would respond to a command to change direction. Nevertheless, the North Vietnamese quickly proved themselves masters of hit-and-run missile attacks from camouflaged sites. The shuttling of missile battalions between these prepared sites amounted to a deadly shell game, especially during Operation ROLLING THUNDER (1965–1968). What made the shell game deadly was that SA-2 battalions often remained in a dispersed status, hidden in the countryside, until ready to resume firing. The battalions required about three hours to "shut down and pack" and four to six hours to "unpack" and begin operations.

After the bombing halt of 1968, SA-2 battalions, heretofore seen only in the DRV, began deploying along the Hô Chí Minh Trail. SA-2s were also deployed with ground units in the South during the 1972 Easter Offensive, which also saw the first appearance of the small, handheld SA-7 "Grail" infrared-guided missile. It was a "tail chase" weapon. Like the SA-2, the "Grail" could be outmaneuvered by jet fighter aircraft if the latter had enough warning, but this missile proved to be the bane of low-flying aircraft such as Army helicopters and Air Force O-2s, OV-10s, A-1s, and even A-37s. When possible, slow-maneuvering aircraft operated above 10,000 feet to fly above the range of this missile, or they resorted to using decoy flares.

Thus, by 1972 the DRV's SAM system was one of the most sophisticated and formidable in the world. Through 1968 alone, it was partially responsible for the downing of 922 fixed-wing aircraft over the DRV. The system also forced the United States to respond by developing an equally sophisticated method of aerial attack. This method, which included new aircraft, early precision guided munitions, and substantial improvements in electronic warfare, did slow the rate of U.S. losses, but it never completely overcame the threat posed by DRV SAMs.

—Patrick K. Barker

References: Momyer, William W. *Airpower in Three Wars.* Washington, DC: U.S. Government Printing Office, 1978.
Morocco, John. *Thunder from Above: Air War 1941–1968. The Vietnam Experience,* edited by Robert Manning. Boston: Boston Publishing, 1984.
Nordeen, Lon O., Jr. *Air Warfare in the Missile Age.* Washington, DC: Smithsonian Institution Press, 1985.
See also: Air Defense, Democratic Republic of Vietnam; Antiaircraft Artillery, Allied and Democratic Republic of Vietnam; BARREL ROLL, Operation; LINEBACKER I, Operation; LINEBACKER II, Operation; Rockets; ROLLING THUNDER, Operation.

T

Tache d'huile

"Oil slick"; French term for the pacification technique of first securing key population centers and then expanding outward from them, much as an oil slick spreads on water. This process, pioneered by Marshal Louis Hubert Gonzalve Lyautey (1854–1934) in Morocco, worked well in flat, open areas where there were only a few watering holes, but it was not well suited to Vietnam. Nonetheless, the French attempted to utilize the oil slick method throughout the Indo-China War, first securing the population centers and then attempting to expand their control into the countryside. In Vietnam it never had a chance of success because French forces were insufficient for the task.

—Spencer C. Tucker

Reference: Maurois, André. *Lyautey.* New York: D. Appleton, 1931.
See also: *Quadrillage/Ratissage.*

Taiwan

See China, Republic of (ROC; Taiwan).

Tân Sơn Nhứt

Major Republic of Vietnam Air Force (VNAF) and U.S. Air Force (USAF) base; headquarters, U.S. Military Assistance Command, Vietnam (MACV). Tân Sơn Nhứt was a major air operations command center and logistics base near Sài Gòn. In October 1961 the first U.S. air control unit was established there, and later in October the first USAF tactical reconnaissance missions were flown out of Tân Sơn Nhứt. MACV's Army air operations section was colocated at Tân Sơn Nhứt with the joint USAF-VNAF air operations center in August 1964. In 1967 the base became headquarters to MACV. Handling 70,000 sorties per month by 1969, Tân Sơn Nhứt became the busiest airfield in the world. Because of its operational and logistical importance, Tân Sơn Nhứt was the target of Communist military assaults. The most serious of these occurred during the 1968 Tết Offensive. During the early morning hours of 31 January, four infantry battalions supported by a sapper battalion assaulted the base. The attacking force penetrated 650 yards into the base and wreaked considerable havoc until it was repulsed in the early afternoon. Tân Sơn Nhứt fell to People's Army of Vietnam (PAVN) forces during the 1975 Communist offensive. After the war it was rebuilt and currently serves as a major air terminus for the Socialist Republic of Vietnam (SRV).

—Timothy G. Grammer

References: Berger, Carl, ed. *The United States Air Force in Southeast Asia, 1961–1973: An Illustrated Account.* Rev. ed. Washington, DC: U.S. Government Printing Office, 1989.

Cinna, Ronald J., ed. *Vietnam: A Country Study.* Washington, DC: U.S. Government Printing Office, 1989.
Heiser, Joseph M. *Vietnam Studies: Logistic Support.* Washington, DC: Department of the Army, 1974.
See also: Air Power, Role in War; Hồ Chí Minh Campaign; Tết Offensive: Overall Strategy; Tết Offensive: The Sài Gòn Circle; United States: Air Force; Vietnam, Republic of: Air Force (VNAF).

Tanks, Allied and Democratic Republic of Vietnam

Allied forces in Vietnam deployed an assortment of armored fighting vehicles: light tanks, tank-destroyers, and medium tanks. The vast majority of these were of U.S. manufacture. Allied light tanks were represented by the M24, the M41, and the M551.

The lightly armored M24 Chaffee tank with its 75-mm gun was a mainstay of French and Army of the Republic of Vietnam (ARVN) armor forces. Although it served with distinction in the Battle of Điên Biên Phu, the M24 had no cross-country ability. Replaced in ARVN units by the M41A3 in 1965, it was for the most part relegated to static pillbox duty at South Vietnamese installations.

The M41A3 Walker Bulldog mounted a 76-mm gun, weighed 25.9 tons, and used a crew of four men. The M42 Duster variant had twin 40-mm antiaircraft guns mounted on an M41 chassis and was used by U.S. Army forces.

The M551 Sheridan was designated an armored reconnaissance airborne assault vehicle and was deployed in Army armored cavalry squadrons beginning in January 1969. Because of its light aluminum hull, it weighed only 15.7 tons. This vehicle had a crew of four and mounted an unusual 152-mm gun capable of firing both antitank guided missiles and high-explosive antitank (HEAT) rounds that could be used against both vehicular and personnel targets. The Sheridan was unpopular with its crews because of its vulnerability to mines and rocket-propelled grenades, lack of "jungle-busting ability," and the problem surrounding its special combustible cartridge cases that were apt to cause a catastrophic secondary explosion if the tank hit a mine.

The M50A1 Ontos was a lightly armored tank-destroyer fielded by U.S. Marine Corps antitank battalions. Its name meant "the thing" in Greek and aptly described its appearance, which featured six 106-mm recoilless rifles jutting from its turret. Problems with this vehicle centered on its touchy fire-by-wire system, which resulted in more than one tragedy to friendly forces, and its great vulnerability to mines. As a result, it ended up being relegated to static perimeter defense.

The LVTP5A1 (land vehicle tracked, personnel) amphibian tractor (commonly referred to as an "amtrac") was employed by the Marine Corps in its amphibious tractor battalions. The

A flame-throwing tank of the U.S. 1st Tank Battalion, 1st Marine Division. This type of tank was able to spray napalm 100 to 150 yards.

Marines, lacking armored personnel carriers, initially used the LVTP5A1 in their stead, but its vulnerability to mines led to their abandoning the practice.

The M48A3 Patton was the mainstay of Army and Marine tank battalions in Vietnam. Originally introduced in 1953, it mounted a 90-mm gun, weighed 47 tons, and had a crew of four. Its xenon searchlight provided it with infrared capability for nighttime engagements. This tank was initially deployed in Vietnam with the first wave of Marines in 1965. Some 370 of the tanks were serving in 1969 at the peak of U.S. involvement. A flamethrower variant of this tank was able to spray napalm 100 to 150 yards. Other variants included a vehicle with an attached 20-ton expendable mine roller and a command tank with a 2-ton dozer kit. ARVN forces were supplied with Pattons beginning in September 1971 as part of the Vietnamization process.

Some confusion exists over the employment of the M60 main battle tank in Vietnam. It did not see service there; however, two vehicles based on its chassis were present. The first was the M728 combat engineer vehicle (CEV), which carried a 165-mm demolition gun, and the other was the armored vehicle launched bridge (AVLB).

The only non-U.S. tanks used by Allied forces in the Vietnam War were 26 British Centurion 5 tanks deployed there by Australian forces in 1968. The Centurion 5s had 84-mm guns and saw service near Vũng Tàu.

Communist forces in Vietnam deployed Soviet and Chinese-variant self-propelled guns, amphibious tanks, and main battle tanks. Elements of the People's Army of Vietnam (PAVN) armored force, officially created in October 1959, appeared in South Vietnam on less than half a dozen occasions prior to the end of 1973. After that period, as American forces were withdrawn, the use of PAVN armor in the South became more common. It played a dominant role in the final 1975 offensive.

Unlike American self-propelled guns that functioned as indirect artillery, World War II–vintage Soviet vehicles such as the SU76 and SU122 were principally used as assault guns by PAVN forces. The SU76 weighed 11 tons and had a crew of four. It was based on the obsolete T70 chassis, mounted a 76-mm gun, and was lightly armored. The more common SU122 was based on the T34 chassis, mounted a 122-mm gun, and was more heavily armored. It had a crew of five and weighed almost 31 tons.

The PT76 amphibious tank, initially built in 1952, was very popular with the PAVN because of its versatility. It mounted a 76-mm gun and weighed 13.8 tons. The Chinese Type 62 variant of this vehicle mounted an 85-mm gun and weighed 17.7 tons. About 400 of these vehicles were supplied to the PAVN, but they suffered from extremely thin armor that made them highly vulnerable to tank guns.

The Soviet T34, a renowned World War II main battle tank, was also supplied to the PAVN. It weighed 26.3 tons, carried a 76-mm gun, and had a crew of four. The T34 and its T34/85 variant that carried an 85-mm gun, while decently armored, were no match for the newer American M48. For this reason, they were rarely seen in South Vietnam and were used primarily for training purposes. They were superseded by the Soviet T54 (Chinese T59) and its slightly improved T55 variant. This tank mounted a 100-mm gun, weighed 35.7 tons, and had a crew of four. About 600 of these tanks were in use by the PAVN armored force and saw considerable service in South Vietnam later in the war.

—Robert J. Bunker

References: Arnold, James R. *Armor. The Illustrated History of the Vietnam War.* New York: Bantam Books, 1987.
Dunstan, Simon. *Vietnam Tracks: Armor in Battle, 1945–1975.* Novato, CA: Presidio Press, 1982.
Pimlott, J. C. "Armour in Vietnam." In *Armoured Warfare*, edited by J. P. Harris and F. H. Toase. New York: St. Martin's Press, 1990.
Rosser-Owen, David. *Vietnam Weapons Handbook.* Wellingborough, Northants, UK: Patrick Stephens, 1986.
Starry, Donn A. *Armored Combat in Vietnam.* New York: Bobbs-Merrill, 1980.
See also: Armor Warfare; Armored Personnel Carriers (APCs); Grenades, Launched: Allied and Democratic Republic of Vietnam; Mines, Antipersonnel and Antitank; Rockets.

Tây Sơn Uprising
(1771–1789)

General uprising led by three brothers from Tây Sơn (Bình Định Province) that ended in the capture of Gia Định (including present Hồ Chí Minh City) and Thăng Long (now Hà Nội) and the weakening of the Nguyên lords in the south and the Trinh lords and the Lê dynasty in the north. The rebellion began as a peasant protest against the corrupt rule of the Nguyên lords.

In 1771 the oldest of the three brothers, Nguyên Nhạc (Hồ Nhạc by birth) began to attack the Nguyên lords and eventually, with the help of his brothers Nguyên Lữ and Nguyên Huê (or Hồ Lữ and Hồ Huê) captured all of the south. The Tây Sơn, as the rebels were known, then attacked the Trinh, rulers in Thăng Long. The Tây Sơn then returned south, where Nguyên Nhạc declared himself King of the Center, headquartered in Quy Nhơn. Nguyên Huê became King of the North, stationed in Thuân Hòa, and Nguyên Lữ was made King of the South, operating out of Gia Định.

After successfully defeating the Nguyên and Trinh Lords, the Tây Sơn brothers entered into an uneasy alliance with the Lê emperors. Emperor Lê Chiêu Thông, realizing he was too weak to withstand the Tây Sơn movement, called upon the Chinese to res-

cue his dynasty. The Chinese sent 200,000 troops to Vietnam and encountered immediate resistance from Nguyên Huê. On the fifth day of the Tết holiday, 1789, the Tây Sơn rebels attacked the Chinese near Thăng Long in what became known as the Battle of Đông Đa. The outcome was an overwhelming victory for the Tây Sơn and repulsion of the Chinese invaders.

The victory over the Chinese propelled the three brothers to national power and they then set out on an ambitious course to redistribute land and wealth to the peasants. Unfortunately, all three brothers died in the early 1790s before their program could be completed. Within a decade the surviving Nguyên lord, Nguyên Ánh, came to power and reestablished the dominance of the Nguyên Dynasty under the name Gia Long.

The Tây Sơn rebellion is important for several reasons, among them the introduction of *nôm* as the official Vietnamese language and the mass mobilization of the peasant class. The Battle of Đông Đa is still celebrated in Vietnam as one of the country's greatest military achievements.

—Robert K. Brigham

References: Lê Thành Khôi. *Histoire du Viet Nam: Des origines à 1858.* Paris: Sudestasie, 1981.
Trường Bửu Lâm. *Resistance, Rebellion, and Revolution: Popular Movements in Vietnamese History.* Singapore: Institute of Southeast Asian Studies, 1984.
Viet Chung. "Recent Findings on the Tay Son Insurgency." *Vietnamese Studies* 81 (1985): 30–62.
Whitfield, Danny. *Historical and Cultural Dictionary of Vietnam.* Metuchen, NJ: Scarecrow Press, 1976.
See also: Hà Nội (Đông Đa), Battle of; Lê Dynasty; Nguyên Dynasty; Nguyên Phúc Ánh (Gia Long); Trinh Lords; Vietnam: From 938 through the French Conquest.

Taylor, Maxwell Davenport
(1901–1987)

U.S. Army general; military representative of the president, 1961–1962; chairman of the Joint Chiefs of Staff, 1962–1964; ambassador to Vietnam, 1964–1965; presidential consultant on Vietnam, 1965–1968. Born in Keytesville, Missouri, on 26 August 1901, Maxwell D. Taylor graduated from West Point in 1922 and during World War II participated in campaigns with the 82d Airborne Division in Sicily and Italy, where he made a dramatic trip to Rome while the city was still behind enemy lines. On D day he parachuted into German-held France at the head of the 101st Airborne Division. Taylor later commanded the 101st in Operation MARKET GARDEN and was wounded. In the defense of Bastogne, Belgium, during the Battle of the Bulge, the entire division earned a presidential citation, the first time this had happened.

After the war, Taylor served as superintendent of the U.S. Military Academy from 1945 to 1949, commander of the American Military Government in Berlin in 1949, commander of Eighth Army and United Nations forces in Korea in 1953, commander of the U.S. Army Far East and UN Command in 1955, and Army chief of staff from 1955 to 1959.

Taking issue with the doctrine of massive nuclear retaliation supported by Chairman of the Joint Chiefs of Staff Admiral Arthur

W. Radford, Taylor favored a larger military capable of flexible response. When Radford's view prevailed, and the 1960 budget called for 55,000 fewer men than he had advocated, Taylor resigned in July 1959.

Taylor then wrote *The Uncertain Trumpet* (1960), urging a reappraisal of military policy. He advocated a buildup of conventional forces and the doctrine of flexible response. Taylor had been warning for years that brush-fire wars, not nuclear conflicts, presented the greatest military challenge to the United States. In April 1961 President John F. Kennedy called on Taylor to study the role of the Central Intelligence Agency (CIA) in the Bay of Pigs fiasco. In July he took on the newly established post of military representative of the president. Serving as Kennedy's chief military advisor, he also had the responsibility of apprising the president on the adequacy of U.S. intelligence operations. The position made him the president's senior military representative at home and abroad.

In October 1961 Kennedy sent Taylor and Walt Rostow on a fact-finding mission to Vietnam. Taylor recognized a "double crisis of confidence" there: doubts about American determination to hold Southeast Asia and doubts that Republic of Vietnam (RVN) President Ngô Đình Diêm's methods could defeat the Communists. He advocated sending additional military aid and advisors while at the same time urging RVN reforms. Taylor highly recommended the dispatch of 8,000 ground combat troops under the cover of a "flood control team" to overcome Diêm's sensitivity on the issue of foreign combat troops. He also wanted intensive training of local self-defense forces and a large increase in helicopters, fighter-bombers, reconnaissance aircraft, and support personnel. Kennedy approved the recommendations, with the exception of sending ground combat troops. This report, flawed by its de-emphasis of political problems and underestimation of the Communists, marked the zenith of Taylor's influence.

In October 1962, in an unprecedented move, Kennedy recalled Taylor from retirement to serve in the nation's highest military position: chairman of the Joint Chiefs of Staff (JCS). Taylor and Secretary of Defense Robert McNamara were in general agreement on strategy and shared similar management styles that favored clear-cut decisions and emphasis on detail. The two made three trips to Vietnam together; perhaps the most important came in September 1963, when they noted great military progress and expressed confidence that it would continue. Two of their conclusions remain disturbing. The first, that "the security of South Vietnam remains vital to United States security," inhibited discussion of disengagement. The second, advocacy of a training program for the Vietnamese that would allow the United States to withdraw the bulk of its personnel by the end of 1965, showed stunning naiveté about Vietnamese political and military potential.

Taylor was critical of the 1963 coup against Diêm, faulting the State Department and the CIA. In January 1964 he informed McNamara that the JCS favored the elimination of many military restrictions and sought "bolder actions." Taylor advocated both an intensified counterinsurgency program and selected air and naval strikes against North Vietnam. He saw bombing as a deterrent to Hà Nôi's "aggression," a morale-booster in the South, and a means to bring the North to the negotiating table. He continued to stress this two-part program in years to come.

Taylor undertook his most controversial role in July 1964, when he succeeded Henry Cabot Lodge as U.S. ambassador to the RVN. When he arrived in Sài Gòn, Taylor was seemingly in a powerful position, in control of American military forces. He and Military Assistance Command, Vietnam (MACV) commander General William Westmoreland began to "Americanize" the war. Taylor had little patience for the political complexities of the RVN, nor could he understand its leaders. By December relations between the ambassador and Prime Minister Nguyên Khánh became so strained that Taylor demanded he resign, while Khánh threatened to ask Washington for Taylor's recall.

In early 1965 Taylor foresaw the probability of a U.S. troop commitment, which, according to journalist Stanley Karnow, "rattled him." He now embraced the notion that the United States should avoid Asian land wars and told President Lyndon Johnson that the Vietnamese lacked motivation rather than manpower. In February Westmoreland requested two Marine battalions to protect the air base at Đà Nẵng. Taylor differed with Westmoreland over the introduction of U.S. combat troops, and in March he returned to Washington to voice his objections to what he saw as a first installment in an inevitably increasing American commitment. He believed that a major U.S. commitment would take too much of the burden from the Army of the Republic of Vietnam (ARVN) and encourage it to let the United States fight the war.

Taylor did not oppose the introduction of U.S. troops per se but he did advocate their restrained use. He supported an enclave strategy that would secure major cities, towns, and U.S. military bases, mainly along the coast, by aggressive patrolling, rather than Westmoreland's search-and-destroy strategy. Taylor also opposed the immediate dispatch of additional U.S. troops.

During the April 1965 Honolulu Conference Taylor had a brief argument on the troop issue with McNamara and Westmoreland. This conference saw a major shift in U.S. policy from counterinsurgency to large-scale ground war. It also represented a first step from Taylor's enclave strategy to Westmoreland's big-unit search-and-destroy strategy. Taylor's defeat on this issue ended the fiction of an all-powerful ambassador and was, according to journalist David Halberstam, the "last time that Max Taylor was a major player, his farewell in fact."

Returning to Washington in July 1965, Taylor was haunted by a sense of failure. Johnson thought that his intransigence had created unnecessary friction with RVN leaders, some of whom saw Taylor as too outspoken—more soldier than statesman—to function as a diplomat. He nonetheless retained an important advisory role and joined the group of Johnson's senior policy consultants known as the "Wise Men." His memoir, *Swords and Ploughshares* (1972), received mixed reviews. As late as 1973 Taylor still hoped for an acceptable outcome to the war.

One of the major American military figures of the twentieth century, Maxwell Taylor died in Washington on 19 April 1987.

—Paul S. Daum, with assistance from Elizabeth W. Daum

References: Cooper, Chester L. *The Lost Crusade: America in Vietnam.* New York: Dodd, Mead, 1970.

Halberstam, David. *The Best and the Brightest.* New York: Random House, 1972.

Isaacson, Walter, and Evan Thomas. *The Wise Men: Six Friends and the World That They Made. Acheson, Bohlen, Harriman, Kennan, Lovett, McCloy.* New York: Simon & Schuster, 1986.

Karnow, Stanley. *Vietnam: A History.* New York: Viking Press, 1983.

Kinnard, Douglas. *The Certain Trumpet: Maxwell Taylor & The American Experience in Vietnam.* Washington, DC: Brassey's, 1991.

Taylor, Gen. Maxwell D. *Responsibility and Response.* New York: Harper & Row, 1967.

_____. *Swords and Plowshares.* New York: W. W. Norton, 1972.

_____. *The Uncertain Trumpet.* New York: Harper & Row, 1960.

Taylor, John M. *General Maxwell Taylor: The Sword and the Pen.* New York: Doubleday, 1989.

Trân Văn Đôn. *Our Endless War: Inside Vietnam.* Novato, CA: Presidio Press, 1978.

Young, Marilyn B. *The Vietnam Wars, 1945–1990.* New York: HarperCollins, 1991.

Zaffiri, Samuel. *Westmoreland: A Biography of General William C. Westmoreland.* New York: William Morrow, 1994.

See also: Central Intelligence Agency (CIA); Eisenhower, Dwight David; Enclave Strategy; Flexible Response; Honolulu Conference; Johnson, Lyndon Baines; Joint Chiefs of Staff; Kennedy, John Fitzgerald; Lodge, Henry Cabot, Jr.; McNamara, Robert S.; Ngô Đình Diêm; Nguyên Khánh; Radford, Arthur W.; Rostow, Walt Whitman; Rusk, Dean; Search and Destroy; Taylor-McNamara Report; Westmoreland, William Childs; "Wise Men."

Taylor-McNamara Report

(2 October 1963)

Report on U.S. government fact-finding mission to South Vietnam in September 1963. The Kennedy administration was eager to see immediate results after its 1961 commitment of U.S. military advisors and increased financial support to the Republic of Vietnam (RVN). Despite this, Viêt Công (VC) forces still controlled much of the South Vietnamese countryside and enjoyed widespread popular support.

On 2 January 1963 inferior VC forces defeated a well-equipped, American-advised Army of the Republic of Vietnam (ARVN) force in the Battle of Âp Băc. This prompted President Kennedy to send Roger Hilsman and Michael Forrestal to Sài Gòn in February 1963 to study the situation. Their report was relatively optimistic but noted that progress was slower than had been hoped and that increased U.S. air attacks against Communist bases might alienate the population in the countryside.

Less promising was the deteriorating relationship between RVN President Ngô Đình Diêm and the Kennedy administration. Diêm refused increased American military and political participation in the war but simultaneously welcomed material and financial assistance. Washington was deeply concerned about the growing opposition to Diêm's regime among the South Vietnamese people. Beginning in May 1963 a series of Buddhist demonstrations and self-immolations showed the widespread opposition to Diêm, his brother Ngô Đình Nhu, and Nhu's wife.

Therefore, Kennedy sent a new fact-finding mission to South Vietnam on 10 September 1963 led by Marine Corps General Victor Krulak and State Department official Joseph Mendenhall. Their conflicting report caused even greater confusion in Washington.

Another mission to South Vietnam was dispatched in late September 1963, led by Chairman of the Joint Chiefs of Staff General Maxwell Taylor and Defense Secretary Robert S. McNamara. The group included William Bundy of the Defense Department, the CIA's William Colby, White House advisor Michael Forrestal, and diplomat William Sullivan. Their major goals were to evaluate the progress of the war, recommend courses of action, and assess the prospects of a coup d'état (plans for an attempt to overthrow Diêm had been in progress since May).

The eight-day visit (24 September–1 October) resulted in different opinions. Taylor was convinced by U.S. Military Assistance Command, Vietnam (MACV) commander General Paul Harkins's optimistic evaluation of the war and thought that some 1,000 U.S. advisors might be withdrawn by the end of the year if the war continued to go well. Most of the civilian members of the mission were not as optimistic and agreed with Ambassador Henry Cabot Lodge's warning about Diêm's political fragility. They were even more convinced of this after a meeting with Diêm in Sài Gòn, when he rejected McNamara's concerns over South Vietnamese political unrest.

The mission returned to Washington on 2 October. Their subsequent report, called the Taylor-McNamara Report, reflected their own mixed opinions. They expressed optimism about the war's progress yet warned that the Ngô brothers' policies could endanger this: "The political situation in South Viet-Nam remains deeply serious. The United States has made clear its continuing opposition to any repressive actions in South Viet-Nam. Although such actions have not yet significantly affected the military effort, they could do so in the future." The mission believed that there was only a slight chance of a military coup and did not recommend that the United States support such a coup "at this time."

They also recommended selective economic and psychological measures that would convince Diêm to change his course of policy but would not endanger the progress of the war. These measures included a major reduction in U.S. economic and military aid to the RVN and the recall of John Richardson, pro-Diêm chief of the CIA station in Sài Gòn.

In spite of the intentions of the Kennedy administration, these measures did not change President Diêm's domestic policy. They did, however, signal U.S. dissatisfaction with Diêm's regime and helped encourage the 1 November 1963 coup against him.

—Zsolt J. Varga

References: Moss, George Donelson. *Vietnam: An American Ordeal.* Englewood Cliffs, NJ: Prentice-Hall, 1990.

Ruskin, Marcus G., and Bernard B. Fall. *The Vietnam Reader: Articles and Documents on American Foreign Policy and the Viet-Nam Crisis.* New York: Vintage Books, 1965.

Rust, William J. *Kennedy in Vietnam.* New York: Charles Scribner's Sons, 1985.

Young, Marilyn B. *The Vietnam Wars: 1945–1990.* New York: HarperCollins, 1991.

See also: Âp Băc, Battle of; Bundy, William P.; Colby, William Egan; Forrestal, Michael V.; Harkins, Paul D.; Hilsman, Roger; Kennedy, John Fitzgerald; Krulak, Victor H.; Lodge, Henry Cabot, Jr.; McNamara, Robert S.;

Mendenhall, Joseph A.; Ngô Đình Diêm; Ngô Đình Diêm, Overthrow of; Ngô Đình Nhu; Sullivan, William Healy; Taylor, Maxwell Davenport.

Taylor-Rostow Mission

(18–25 October 1961)

U.S. fact-finding mission to the Republic of Vietnam. In response to a letter from Republic of Vietnam (RVN) President Ngô Đình Diêm, President John F. Kennedy on 13 October 1961 asked his special military advisor General Maxwell D. Taylor to make a fact-finding trip to Sài Gòn. The mission was headed by Taylor but also included Deputy Special Assistant to the President for National Security Affairs Walt Rostow. The mission was in Vietnam between 18 and 25 October 1961.

In his memoirs, *Swords and Plowshares,* General Taylor recalled that he arrived in Sài Gòn on the very day that President Diêm had declared a state of emergency following a National Liberation Front (NLF) attack on a provincial capital near Sài Gòn. A serious flood in the Mekong Delta region and increasing NLF violence had also upset the nation.

Taylor was bothered by what he felt was the poor quality of U.S. political reporting. He was dismayed by the unpopularity of President Diêm, yet he remained convinced that there was no one better qualified to run the country than this man of "stubborn courage and basic integrity." Walt Rostow apparently agreed.

Accordingly, the official Taylor-Rostow report to President Kennedy on 3 November 1961 supported the domino theory claim that the troubles in Vietnam were part of a Communist plan to take over all of Southeast Asia. The situation was considered serious, but the report concluded that the threat of bombing could help keep the Communists at bay. The report recommended that the United States express its willingness to help defend the RVN by upgrading the U.S. Military Assistance and Advisory Group (MAAG) to the U.S. Military Assistance Command, Vietnam (MACV), and by improving various intelligence and aid projects. Its most controversial suggestion was that U.S. military forces be sent to the Mekong Delta region to assist in flood control. These units were to fight only if fired upon, but their main purpose was clearly to improve the low morale of South Vietnam's military.

In subsequent meetings, President Kennedy did not accept the troop proposal, but he did agree to change MAAG to MACV and to increase both economic aid and the number of U.S. military advisors. These measures were largely implemented in December 1961, after a reluctant Diêm signed a letter promising to try and broaden the base of his support.

The Taylor-Rostow Mission marked a significant escalation of U.S. support for South Vietnam. Following closely upon similar recommendations from Vice-President Lyndon Johnson, the mission both reinforced the domino theory and argued for a far stronger U.S. commitment. After this point, it would be very hard for the United States to withdraw aid without a serious loss of prestige.

—Peter K. Frost

References: Herring, George. *America's Longest War.* 2d ed. New York: Alfred A. Knopf, 1986.

Hilsman, Roger. *To Move a Nation.* New York: Doubleday, 1967.

Taylor, Maxwell D. *Swords and Plowshares.* New York: W. W. Norton, 1972.

See also: Domino Theory; Johnson, Lyndon Baines; Kennedy, John Fitzgerald; Military Assistance and Advisory Group (MAAG), Vietnam; Military Assistance Command, Vietnam (MACV); National Front for the Liberation of South Vietnam (NFLSV); Ngô Đình Diêm; Rostow, Walt Whitman; Taylor, Maxwell Davenport.

Teach-Ins, Sit-Ins

Antiwar protest activities. Both the civil rights movement and the Vietnam War ushered in new ways to protest U.S. government policies during the 1960s. In particular, teach-ins and sit-ins afforded Americans the opportunity to express their discontent peacefully. Although teach-ins provided a forum to denounce the Vietnam War, sit-ins were associated both with the civil rights movement and antiwar protests.

Teach-ins were first used in response to America's growing involvement in Vietnam. In February 1965 the United States began what would become a three-year bombing campaign (Operation ROLLING THUNDER) against North Vietnam. A number of University of Michigan faculty members wrote President Lyndon Johnson to protest this escalation of what had heretofore been a limited, "brush-fire" war. When Johnson subsequently sent 3,000 Marines to Đà Nẵng in the Republic of Vietnam, on 10 March 1965 the Michigan group organized a teach-in. On 24 March more than 3,000 students and faculty members participated in the first teach-in. They used the forum to question the Vietnam War and argued against it until dawn. Within six weeks of the Michigan forum, virtually all major universities (and several smaller ones) held their own teach-ins. The movement culminated on 15 May 1965 with a National Teach-In, in which more than 100 schools held antiwar forums on their own campuses.

In the case of sit-ins, civil rights advocates initially used them in the 1950s to protest segregation. As a peaceful form of protest, the sit-in did not gain notoriety until the 1960s, when college administration buildings and Reserve Officers' Training Corps (ROTC) detachments throughout the United States became targets of antiwar sit-ins. The most notorious sit-in occurred during the week of 23–30 April 1968, when between 700 and 1,000 students took over five buildings at Columbia University. A key goal of the sit-in was to pressure the individual school administration to break its ties with the Institute for Defense Analysis, a group of universities (sponsored by the Pentagon) that advised the Johnson administration on military matters.

Overall, teach-ins and sit-ins raised questions and public awareness about the Johnson administration and its policies. They fueled the antiwar movement, put the administration on the defensive, and provided people with a nonviolent (and respectable) way to express their opposition to the war. Neither teach-ins nor sit-ins, however, stopped the Vietnam War. Still, their effects were far from negligible, but things deteriorated. As the United States continued to escalate the war, its opponents abandoned teach-ins and sit-ins for more violent forms of protest.

—Tracy R. Szczepaniak

References: Gitlin, Todd. *The Sixties: Years of Hope, Days of Rage.* New York: Bantam Books, 1987.
Miller, James. *Democracy Is in the Streets: From Port Huron to the Siege of Chicago.* New York: Simon & Schuster, 1987.
O'Neill, William L. *Coming Apart: An Informal History of America in the 1960s.* New York: Times Books, 1971.
Viorst, Milton. *Fire in the Streets: America in the 1960s.* New York: Simon & Schuster, 1979.
See also: Antiwar Movement, United States; Democratic Party National Convention, 1968; Hayden, Thomas E.; King, Martin Luther, Jr.; ROLLING THUNDER, Operation; Students for a Democratic Society (SDS).

Television and the Vietnam Experience

The Vietnam War was known as America's first "television war" because it was the first war for which television was a primary means of providing information to the American public. For much of the war, at least from 1964 through 1973, reports were broadcast in two- or three-minute segments on nightly news telecasts of the three major U.S. television networks. Even the final storming of Sài Gòn and the evacuation of the last Americans from the embassy roof in 1975 was watched by millions of Americans sitting in their living rooms. Television viewers were eyewitnesses to the war, and this helped to shape their opinions of it.

Television coverage of the war has both its critics and its defenders. Critics claim that television producers attempted to make their coverage visually dramatic, using short "sound bites" aimed at viewers' emotions rather than their intellect, which resulted in distorted views of events. More severe critics charged that reporters with a decidedly liberal bias provided coverage that was not only distorted but intentionally inaccurate and bordered on propaganda. Extremes of this view suggest that television helped decide the war's outcome.

One problem with television coverage of the war was that it was limited to available video footage. The U.S. military permitted almost all coverage (press accreditation cards directed "full cooperation and assistance" without censorship from U.S. units), and U.S. and Army of the Republic of Vietnam (ARVN) successes and mistakes were equally available and were aired based on the reporter's or producer's judgment. The Communists, however, controlled access to information and events and limited coverage to footage provided by the state or foreign correspondents deemed acceptable to the state. This produced propaganda footage that only showed the People's Army of Vietnam (PAVN) and Việt Công (VC) in a favorable light.

Defenders of Vietnam War television coverage present it as essentially accurate and evenhanded. They agree that it was not perfect; mistakes were made and some inaccuracies were reported, but they argue that the print media was equally prone to make mistakes. Supporters claim that sources of inaccuracies were often military or White House representatives—military and embassy public affairs officers who conducted daily press briefings, unceremoniously nicknamed the "five o'clock follies." Optimistic, often glowing reports of progress presented at these briefings often did not coincide with information reported from the field.

Two related events that came to signify the controversy surrounding the media in general and television reporting in particular were the 1968 siege at Khe Sanh and the Tết Offensive, both of which were Allied tactical and operational victories. Television and print media reporting of the battle at Khe Sanh emphasized the parallels with the French defeat at Điên Biên Phu that brought about the French withdrawal from Indo-China. Although there were some similarities, the comparison was inaccurate and obscured the actual events and outcome. In fairness, however, whether influenced by media coverage or reaching their own conclusions, several government officials also were guilty of the inaccurate comparison—not the least of these was President Lyndon Johnson, who required the Joint Chiefs of Staff to attest in writing that Khe Sanh would not go the way of Điên Biên Phu.

Television reporting of the 1968 Tết Offensive has borne the brunt of criticism. Critics claim that coverage focused on the sensational to the point of being inaccurate. General William Westmoreland believed this played a large role in turning the American public against the war, transforming the failed Communist offensive into a "psychological victory." In his book *Big Story,* journalist Peter Braestrup supported the charge. However, in the face of continually optimistic forecasts of victory expressed by the military and the Johnson administration, there is little wonder that televised reporting of the Tết attacks, which fell hard upon American and South Vietnamese strongholds, caused journalists such as Walter Cronkite, and those who trusted his interpretation, to view the war as a no-win situation.

Discounting the debate that still sometimes flares over the media's role in the Vietnam War, one positive result of television reporting is the extensive video archives amassed primarily by the major networks. These have been helpful in producing numerous documentaries about the war, many of which are available on videotape, enabling individuals to study the war at home.

—Arthur T. Frame

References: Arlen, Michael. *Living Room War.* New York: Viking Books, 1969.
Braestrup, Peter. *Big Story.* New Haven, CT: Yale University Press, 1983.
Herr, Michael. *Dispatches.* New York: Alfred A. Knopf, 1977.
Lewinski, Jorge. *The Camera at War.* New York: Simon & Schuster, 1978.
Vietnam: A Television History. Videotape produced by WGBH-TV, Boston. New York: Sony, 1983.
Vietnam: The Ten Thousand Day War. Videotape produced by Michael Mclear. Los Angeles: Embassy Home Entertainment, 1987.
See also: Cronkite, Walter Leland; "Five O'Clock Follies"; Johnson, Lyndon Baines; Joint U.S. Public Affairs Office (JUSPAO); Khe Sanh, Battles of; Media and the War; Tết Offensive: Overall Strategy; Tết Offensive: The Sài Gòn Circle; Westmoreland, William Childs.

Territorial Forces

Republic of Vietnam (RVN) military units similar in status to the U.S. National Guard or traditional militia. The Territorial Forces comprised the Regional Forces and the Popular Forces (RF/PF), popularly known as "Ruff-Puffs." Territorial Forces constituted about one-half of the RVN's military strength during the 1960s and 1970s, and even though they were always poorly supplied and

A U.S. Marine lance corporal and a South Vietnamese soldier raise an American flag at an outpost where 14 Marines trained home guards.

supported, they were the closest thing to a grassroots rural security system ever developed in the RVN.

The Regional Forces traced their roots to the 68,000-man Civil Guard created in April 1955 from the remnants of the Vietnamese National Army, French Union Forces, and other auxiliary units. In 1964 the Civil Guard was renamed the Regional Forces and was integrated into the RVN Armed Forces under control of the Joint General Staff.

Regional Forces had as their original mission the manning of 9,000 fixed outposts scattered throughout South Vietnam, half of which were in the Mekong Delta. After 1955 their duties expanded to include fighting the Việt Cộng, providing support to the militia as a provincial quick reaction force, and guarding the nation's infrastructure by protecting communications and transportation systems and government installations.

The basic Regional Forces unit was the rifle company that could be augmented as required by river boat companies, mechanized platoons, heavy-weapons platoons, reconnaissance units, and administration and logistical support companies. Typically, Regional Forces operated in company-sized units, but they were capable of multicompany operations. In 1967 there were 888 Regional Force companies, but the number increased to 1,119 in 1968 and to 1,810 by 1973.

The Regional Forces went through several configurations during their history, evolving from separate companies to company groups, battalions, and finally mobile groups. In 1969, for example, the first mobile units were created. These grew in number to 31 mobile battalions and 232 mobile companies by the end of 1970. By late 1974 plans were made to establish 27 Regional Forces mobile groups, similar in makeup to the French *Groupement Mobiles* of the Indo-China War. Only 7 such mobile groups were operational by the time of the fall of South Vietnam in April 1975. At the latest stage of its development, the Regional Forces consisted of 312,000 personnel.

The Popular Forces traced their origins to the 48,000-man Self-Defense Corps created by the Ministry of the Interior in 1956. They were part-time, volunteer, village militia, whose basic unit of organization was the team. This varied in strength depending on the size and population of the province or district but generally consisted of from four to ten men per 1,000 inhabitants. Popular Force teams were later increased in size to 30-man platoons. These teams were essentially infantry units, and their equipment and mode of subsistence were more austere than those of the Regional Forces.

Popular Forces teams, whose members held regular jobs in the community, performed security duties and protected their home villages, hamlets, and districts from Việt Cộng attack. Inherently close to the population, they manned local outposts and watch towers, conducted night patrols and reconnaissance missions, laid ambushes, and searched houses for arms caches.

The Popular Forces were integrated into the South Vietnamese Armed Forces in 1964 and were placed under the control of the Joint General Staff. Below this level, they were administered by the Central Self-Defense Corps Directorate in Sài Gòn, which controlled offices at the province and district level, and commission-

ers in the villages. Unlike the Regional Forces, Popular Forces did not have a formal rank structure beyond team and squad leader designations, but all members received a monthly salary. Popular Forces totaled 220,800 members in 8,100 platoons in 1973.

Between 1961 and 1965 the Territorial Forces were under the authority of Army of the Republic of Vietnam (ARVN) corps and division commanders, who often used them as auxiliaries on search-and-destroy operations, for which they were ill suited because of their inadequate training and often meager and outdated arms and equipment. This resulted in large losses, depressed morale, and numerous desertions. Although the Territorial Forces could theoretically call on the ARVN in times of crisis, the regular military routinely failed to provide the Territorial Forces the level of tactical or logistical support they needed.

The ARVN always viewed such groups as second-rate units, and most officers and noncommissioned officers (NCOs) sought to avoid service with them. To many South Vietnamese, however, the Territorial Forces were an alternative to the ARVN and they often served as a haven for deserters and draft evaders. Yet, in 1965 when Regional Forces troops began to receive similar pay and reenlistment bonuses as ARVN soldiers, and after June 1968 when a General Mobilization Law made every male citizen age 18 to 38 liable for service in either ARVN or the Territorial Forces, recruitment levels in the latter were boosted to record levels.

From 1965 to 1969, when the United States dominated the ground war, the ARVN filled most local security needs with only limited assistance from the Territorial Forces. Thus, the Territorial Forces received scant support from either the ARVN or its allies. Yet, when U.S. forces began to withdraw and the ARVN began to take on more of the fighting, and greater emphasis was placed on rural security, pacification, and Vietnamization, Regional and Popular Forces took on a new importance. For the first time they were deployed outside their home areas to serve with ARVN formations. As a result, U.S. Military Assistance Command, Vietnam (MACV) sought changes in the Territorial Forces to improve their capabilities. MACV now recognized that the war could not be won without providing security in the hamlets, a role that Regional and Popular Forces could perform if adequately supported. Territorial Forces were to provide real and lasting security for the countryside by keeping Communist insurgents away from the people, while the police eliminated the Việt Cộng infrastructure. In the meantime, the ARVN would combat Communist main force units even as U.S. forces departed.

MACV had started the push to create more Regional and Popular Forces units in 1967 as being a cheaper and ultimately more efficient and successful alternative to ARVN divisions. RVN leaders resisted this move. Anticipating the ultimate withdrawal of American forces, they believed that the better-equipped and heavier ARVN divisions would be far more successful against the Việt Cộng and the People's Army of Vietnam (PAVN) than the lightly equipped and poorly trained Territorial Forces. Yet, with the start of the Civilian Operations and Revolutionary Development Support (CORDS) program in 1967, the number of men in Territorial Forces units increased from 300,000 in 1967 to over 530,000 by 1971.

Major improvements were also made in training. Starting in 1967 MACV created over 350 mobile advisory teams (MATs), consisting of U.S. Army personnel, who trained and advised the Territorial Forces on small-unit tactics and pacification techniques while actually living among them for months at a time. The Americans also built and helped staff 12 provincial training centers throughout South Vietnam that operated until 1972.

Equipping the Territorial Forces was a major undertaking, as most units carried a wide variety of weapons, most of World War II vintage. After 1969, however, Territorial Forces received larger quantities of M16 rifles, M60 machine guns, light anti-tank weapons, M79 grenade launchers, and modern radio sets. But the Territorial Forces remained dependent on the ARVN for their ground and air transport, heavy firepower, and artillery support.

The improved Territorial Forces took on an increased combat role at a much higher cost between 1968 and 1972 as U.S. units withdrew and the ARVN assumed the primary responsibility for the war. During this period the ARVN lost almost 37,000 soldiers killed in action compared to Regional and Popular Force losses of over 69,300 personnel. Because of their size, exposure in the countryside, and lighter equipment, the Territorial Forces were often subject to a higher rate of attack by Communist units than regular ARVN formations, and except for 1968 it was always more dangerous to serve in a Regional or Popular Forces unit than in the ARVN.

Still charged primarily with local defense tasks after the American withdrawal and still too lightly armed and equipped to withstand massive and sustained attacks from regular PAVN units supported by tanks and artillery, the Territorial Forces were overwhelmed and largely destroyed during the final Communist offensive in 1975.

Overall, Regional and Popular Forces performed well while surmounting many obstacles and handicaps. In most areas in which they operated they markedly improved rural security efforts. Even though they received less than 20 percent of the total South Vietnamese defense budget and lacked organic firepower, they accounted for roughly 30 percent of the Communist combat deaths inflicted by South Vietnamese Armed Forces, depending on the year, and consumed only 2 to 4 percent of the total cost of the war.

—Clayton D. Laurie

References: Donovan, David. *Once a Warrior King*. New York: Ballantine, 1985.

Krepinevich, Andrew F., Jr. *The Army and Vietnam*. Baltimore: Johns Hopkins University Press, 1986.

Lewy, Guenther. *America in Vietnam*. New York: Oxford University Press, 1978.

Ngô Quang Trưởng. *Territorial Forces*. Washington, DC: U.S. Army Center of Military History, 1981.

Summers, Harry G., Jr. *Vietnam War Almanac*. New York: Facts on File, 1985.

Trần Đình Tho. *Pacification*. Washington, DC: U.S. Army Center of Military History, 1980.

See also: Civilian Operations and Revolutionary Development Support (CORDS); Hồ Chí Minh Campaign; Military Assistance Command, Vietnam (MACV); Strategic Hamlet Program; Vietnam, Republic of: Army (ARVN).

Tết Offensive: Overall Strategy
(1968)

Decisive turning point of the Vietnam War. On 6 July 1967 the top leadership of the Democratic Republic of Vietnam (DRV) gathered in Hà Nội for the state funeral of Senior General Nguyễn Chí Thanh, who had been the military commander in the South and a member of the Vietnamese Communist Party's Politburo. After the funeral members of the Politburo met to consider plans to bring the Vietnam War to a speedy and successful conclusion.

Militarily, the war had not been going well for the Việt Cộng (VC) and People's Army of Vietnam (PAVN), who were unable to compete with U.S. military firepower and mobility. Thanh had been in favor of scaling back operations in South Vietnam and conducting an even more protracted war to wear the Americans down. DRV Defense Minister General Võ Nguyên Giáp, however, favored trying to end the war in one master stroke. In essence, he wanted to repeat his triumph over the French at Điện Biên Phu. With Thanh now dead, there was no other major opponent on the Politburo to Giáp's plan. (However, according to Colonel Bùi Tín, a former member of the PAVN general staff, the plan for the master stroke actually was proposed by Thanh in January 1967.)

Giáp's plan borrowed from Chinese Communist doctrine and was based on the concept of the "General Offensive." Following the General Offensive—in something of a one-two punch—would come the "General Uprising," during which the people of South Vietnam would rally to the Communist cause and overthrow the Sài Gòn government. The General Uprising was a distinctly Vietnamese element of revolutionary dogma.

The success of Giáp's plan depended on three key assumptions: The Army of the Republic of Vietnam (ARVN) would not fight and would in fact collapse under the impact of the General Offensive, the people of South Vietnam would follow through with the General Uprising, and American will to continue would crack in the face of the overwhelming shock.

The General Offensive was set for Tết 1968, the beginning of the Lunar New Year and the most important holiday in the Vietnamese year. The plans, however, were a tightly held secret, and the exact timing and objectives of the attack were withheld from field commanders until the last possible moment. Giáp's buildup and staging for the Tết Offensive was a masterpiece of deception. Starting in the fall of 1967, VC and PAVN forces staged a series of bloody but seemingly pointless battles in the border regions and the northern part of South Vietnam near the Demilitarized Zone (DMZ).

The battles at Lộc Ninh and Đắk Tô were part of Giáp's "peripheral campaign" designed to draw U.S. combat units out of the urban areas and toward the borders. The operations also were designed to give Communist forces experience in larger-scale conventional attack formations. In January 1968 several PAVN divisions began to converge on the isolated U.S. Marine outpost at Khe Sanh in northern I Corps, near the DMZ.

The Têt Offensive began in Huê at 0340 on 31 January 1968. Pictured here is the destruction in the city from the subsequent fighting, seen from the Huê Citadel.

Khe Sanh was a classic deception, and Giáp depended on the Americans misreading history and seeing another Điên Biên Phu in the making. It worked. From 21 January 1968 until the point when the countrywide attacks erupted at Têt, the attention of most of the U.S. military and the national command structure was riveted on Khe Sanh. The battle became an obsession for President Lyndon Johnson, who had a scale terrain model of the Marine base built for the White House situation room.

Meanwhile, the Communists used the Christmas 1967 ceasefire to move their forces into position, while senior commanders gathered reconnaissance on their assigned objectives. In November 1967 troops of the 101st Airborne Division had captured a Communist document calling for the General Offensive/General Uprising, but U.S. intelligence analysts dismissed it as mere propaganda. Such a bold stroke seemed too fantastic, because U.S. intelligence did not believe the Communists had the capability to attempt it.

One senior U.S. commander was not thrown off by the peripheral campaign. Lt. Gen. Frederick C. Weyand, commander of U.S. II Field Forces headquartered in Long Bình some 15 miles east of Sài Gòn, did not like the pattern of increased Communist radio traffic around the capital, combined with a strangely low number of contacts made by his units in the border regions. On 10 January 1968 Weyand convinced General William Westmoreland to let him pull more U.S. combat battalions back in around Sài Gòn. As

a result, there were 27 battalions (instead of the planned 14) in the Sài Gòn area when the attack came. Weyand's foresight would be critical for the Allies.

The countrywide Communist attacks were set to commence on 31 January, but the secrecy of Giáp's buildup cost him in terms of coordination. At 0015 on the morning of 30 January Đà Nẵng, Pleiku, Nha Trang, and nine other cities in the center of South Vietnam came under attack. Commanders in Việt Công Region 5 had started 24 hours too early. This was apparently because they were following the lunar calendar in effect in South Vietnam rather than a new lunar calendar proclaimed by the DRV leadership for all of Vietnam.

As a result of this premature attack, the Têt holiday cease-fire was canceled, ARVN troops were called back to their units, and U.S. forces went on alert and moved to blocking positions in key areas. Giáp had lost the element of surprise.

At 0130 in the morning on 31 January the Presidential Palace in Sài Gòn was attacked. By 0340 the city of Huê was under attack and the Têt Offensive was in full swing. Before the day was over, five of six autonomous cities, 36 of 44 provincial capitals, and 64 of 245 district capitals were under attack.

With the exception of Khe Sanh, the ancient capital of Huê, and the area around Sài Gòn, the fighting was over in a few days. Huê was retaken on 25 February, and the Chợ Lớn area of Sài Gòn was finally cleared on 7 March. By 20 March PAVN units around

U.S. Marines riding on an M48 tank as the 90-mm gun fires into the jungle during a road sweep. Despite heavy losses in the Tết Offensive, North Vietnamese Army and Viêt Công soldiers remained active in the countryside, and Allied forces spent months clearing areas near cities and bases.

Khe Sanh began to melt away in the face of overwhelming American firepower.

Militarily, the Tết Offensive was a tactical disaster for the Communists. By the end of March 1968 they had not achieved a single one of their objectives. More than 58,000 VC and PAVN troops died in the offensive, with the Americans suffering 3,895 dead and the ARVN losing 4,954. Non-U.S. Allies lost 214. More than 14,300 South Vietnamese civilians also died.

Giáp had achieved great surprise, but he was unable to exploit it; he had violated the principle of mass. By attacking everywhere he had superior strength nowhere. Across the country the attack had been launched piecemeal, and it was repulsed piecemeal. Giáp also had been wrong in two of his three key assumptions. The people of South Vietnam did not rally to the Communist cause, and the General Uprising never took place—even in Huê, where Communist forces held the city for the longest time. Nor did the ARVN fold. It required significant stiffening in certain areas, but on the whole it fought and fought well.

The biggest loser in the Tết Offensive was the Viêt Công. Although a large portion of the PAVN conducted the feint at Khe Sanh, VC guerrilla forces had led the major attacks in the South, and they suffered the heaviest casualties. The guerrilla infrastructure developed over so many years was wiped out. After Tết 1968 the war was run entirely by the North. The VC were never again a significant force on the battlefield. When Sài Gòn fell in 1975, it was to four PAVN corps.

Giáp, however, had been absolutely correct on his third major assumption. His primary enemy did not have the will. With one hand the United States delivered the Communists a crushing tactical defeat—and then proceeded to give them a strategic victory with the other. Thus, the Tết Offensive is one of the most paradoxical of history's decisive battles.

The Americans and the South Vietnamese government and military had been caught by surprise by both the timing and the intensity of the Communist offensive but had still won overwhelmingly. Communist forces, and especially the VC, were badly hurt. As a follow-up, U.S. military planners immediately began to formulate plans to finish off the Communist forces in the South. Westmoreland and Joint Chiefs of Staff chairman General Earle Wheeler were preparing to request an additional 206,000 troops to finish the job, when a disgruntled staff member in the Johnson White House leaked the plan to the press. The story broke in the *New York Times* on 10 March 1968. With the fresh images of the besieged U.S. Embassy in Sài Gòn still in their minds, the press and the public immediately concluded that the extra troops were needed to recover from a massive defeat.

The Tết Offensive was the psychological turning point of the war. U.S. military historian Brig. Gen. S. L. A. Marshall probably summed up the Tết Offensive best: "a potential major victory turned into a disastrous defeat through mistaken estimates, loss of nerve, and a tidal wave of defeatism."

—David T. Zabecki

References: Braestrup, Peter. *Big Story.* Boulder, CO: Westview Press, 1977.

Oberdorfer, Don. *Tet!* New York: Doubleday, 1971.

Palmer, Bruce, Jr. *The 25-Year War: America's Military Role in Vietnam.* Lexington, KY: University Press of Kentucky, 1984.

Palmer, Dave. *Summons of the Trumpet.* Novato, CA: Presidio Press, 1978.

Summers, Harry G. *On Strategy: The Vietnam War in Context.* Carlisle Barracks, PA: U.S. Army War College, Strategic Studies Institute, 1981.

Young, Stephen. "How North Vietnam Won the War" (interview with former Colonel Bui Tin). *Wall Street Journal* (3 August 1995).

Zabecki, David T. "Battle for Saigon." *Vietnam* (Summer 1989): 19–25.

See also: Bùi Tín; Đăk Tô, Battle of; Huê, Battle of; Khe Sanh, Battles of; Lôc Ninh, Military Operations near; Nguyên Chí Thanh; Têt Offensive: The Sài Gòn Circle; Võ Nguyên Giáp; Westmoreland, William Childs; Weyand, Frederick C.; Wheeler, Earle G.

Têt Offensive: The Sài Gòn Circle
(1968)

The primary Communist objectives during the 1968 Têt Offensive were the South Vietnamese capital of Sài Gòn and the major U.S. and Army of the Republic of Vietnam (ARVN) bases in nearby Long Bình and Biên Hòa. The vital strategic area, which roughly formed a 29-mile zone around the capital, was called the "Sài Gòn Circle."

As a gesture of confidence in the ARVN, the U.S. Command on 15 December 1967 turned over sole responsibility for the defense of Sài Gòn to the South Vietnamese military. The main task of securing the capital fell to the ARVN 5th Ranger Group, supported by the 2d Battalion, U.S. 13th Artillery, the only U.S. combat unit remaining inside the city.

Thirty-nine maneuver battalions of the U.S. II Field Forces (an organization basically equivalent to a corps), meanwhile, were earmarked for operations against Viêt Công (VC) and People's Army of Vietnam (PAVN) base camps near the Cambodian border. These operations were a direct response to the "peripheral campaign" of PAVN General Võ Nguyên Giáp, who was attempting to draw U.S. forces away from the major cities prior to launching the Têt Offensive.

Giáp's deception plan almost worked. If the American border campaign had continued on schedule, there would have been only 14 U.S. and Free World combat battalions inside the Sài Gòn Circle when the Têt attacks were launched on 31 January 1968. But the commander of II Field Force, Lt. Gen. Frederick C.

Refugees flee Têt Offensive attacks. By the end of the Têt Offensive, the Viêt Công and People's Army of Vietnam forces had failed to achieve any of their principal objectives, and they had suffered huge numbers of casualties in the process.

Weyand, did not like the operational patterns that were emerging. His units on the Cambodian border were making too few contacts, while at the same time, Communist radio traffic around Sài Gòn was increasing.

On 10 January 1968 Weyand took his concerns to General William C. Westmoreland. As a result of that meeting, Westmoreland allowed Weyand to pull more of his battalions in toward the capital. When the Communist attacks were finally launched, there were 27 combat battalions back inside the Sài Gòn Circle. Weyand's keen analysis of the situation and subsequent action turned the battle before it even started.

One of the primary indicators of the importance the Communists placed on the Sài Gòn Circle objective was reflected in the command structure for the attacks. The entire operation was under the command of Lt. Gen. Trân Văn Trà, the second highest-ranking PAVN general. Just prior to Christmas 1967, Trà shifted his headquarters from the "Fishhook" area of Cambodia to the outskirts of Sài Gòn. This, in part, accounted for the increased communications traffic noted by Weyand. Trà's new headquarters was colocated with that of Col. Trân Văn Đắc, chief VC political officer for the area. They were joined by Maj. Gen. Trân Đô, VC commander for the operation. In all, the Communists had a force equivalent of 35 battalions, organized into one PAVN and two VC divisions.

The combined Communist command had eight major objectives for the Sài Gòn Circle, which they believed would cripple the Sài Gòn government and trigger the anticipated "General Uprising." In Sài Gòn itself, VC and PAVN forces were to seize and neutralize all the key government command, control, and communications centers; take the artillery and tank depots at Gò Vâp; neutralize Tân Sơn Nhưt Air Base and the U.S. Military Assistance Command, Vietnam (MACV) command center there; seize Chợ Lớn, the ethnic Chinese district of Sài Gòn; and destroy the Newport Bridge linking Sài Gòn to Long Bình and Biên Hòa on Highway 1. In Long Bình the primary objective was the massive U.S. logistics depot and U.S. II Field Force headquarters. In Biên Hòa the targets were the U.S. Air Base and ARVN III Corps headquarters. In addition, supporting forces on the outer edges of the Circle were to block any attempts by the U.S. 25th Infantry Division to reinforce Sài Gòn from Cu Chi along Highway 1 and prevent the U.S. 1st Infantry Division from reinforcing from Lai Khê along Highway 13.

Because of secrecy in the planning and buildup for the attacks, Communist forces suffered coordination problems. On 30 January, one day before the countrywide attacks were scheduled to start, Viêt Công Region 5 commanders launched attacks against Đà Nẵng and 11 other cities in the north of the country. As a result, the Tết holiday cease-fire was canceled and U.S. and ARVN units were moved into alert positions.

The official start of the Tết Offensive came at 0130 on the morning of 31 January, when a 14-man platoon from the Viêt Công's C-10 sapper battalion attacked the Sài Gòn Presidential Palace. Forty-five minutes later, a 19-man platoon from the same battalion attacked the U.S. Embassy. Two American military police (MPs), Sp4c. Charles L. Daniel and Pfc. William Selbast, were killed in the initial assault, but not before they managed to sound the alarm and kill the VC platoon leader and his assistant.

Although the attacks spread throughout the city, General Weyand coordinated the American response from his command post at Long Bình. As the morning wore on, his most pressing headache was, ironically, the most militarily insignificant—the U.S. Embassy. VC sappers never did enter the embassy building, but it took until well into the morning to clear them out of the courtyard. The American media, meanwhile, flashed images around the world of the seat of U.S. power in Vietnam under siege. The result was a psychological impact far out of proportion to its actual importance. As the fighting progressed, Weyand sent his deputy commander, Maj. Gen. Keith Ware, into the city to form "Task Force Ware" and assume command of all U.S. forces inside the city proper.

A few blocks north of the city, another platoon of the ubiquitous C-10 sapper battalion attacked the National Radio Station. They were accompanied by a PAVN specialist who carried prerecorded tapes announcing the General Offensive and General Uprising. The Communist troops seized the radio station with little difficulty, but they were prevented from making their broadcast when the link to the remote transmission tower was severed at the last minute on a prearranged signal from the station's technicians.

The ARVN depot complex at Gò Vâp on the northern edge of the city was the objective of the VC 101st Regiment. The plan called for the Communist troops to overrun the depot, capture the artillery and tanks stored there, and use those weapons for the continued assault on Tân Sơn Nhưt Air Base, about a mile to the west. The VC were accompanied by PAVN specialist troops to help them in the use of the weapons. The Communists succeeded in capturing the depot, only to discover that the tanks had been moved elsewhere the week before. They did manage to capture 12 105-mm artillery pieces, but the withdrawing ARVN troops had the presence of mind to take the guns' firing locks with them. The VC had the big guns, but they were useless. Thus, a key element of the attack on Tân Sơn Nhưt faltered.

During the evening of 30 January a large VC force had infiltrated into the Vinatexco textile factory across Highway 1 on the west side of Tân Sơn Nhưt. At about 0320 the next day three VC battalions stormed across the road and attacked the western end of the air base. In less than an hour, Communist forces were on the runway and the fighting became hand-to-hand.

With its main headquarters under threat, MACV sent a call for help to the 25th Infantry division at Cu Chi, about 20 miles to the northwest of Sài Gòn. The 3d Squadron, 5th Cavalry was already on alert for a possible relief mission to Tân Sơn Nhưt. Squadron Commander Lt. Col. Glenn K. Otis immediately sent his Troop C down the road. Suspecting VC ambushes, however, Otis flew ahead of the troop in his command and control helicopter, spotting the ambush sites, attacking them from the air, and leading his troops around them. Troop C, vastly outnumbered, crashed into the rear of the Communist attack about 0600. It was mauled in the process, but the momentum of the VC attack was halted temporarily.

Otis flew back to Cu Chi and then led his Troop B back down the same road. When they arrived at Tân Sơn Nhưt Otis deployed them at a 90-degree angle to Troop C, fixing the VC in an "L." Otis then brought in his air cavalry troop and attack helicopters to finish off the VC. Otis and three of his soldiers were later awarded the Distinguished Service Cross. The 3d Squadron, 4th Cavalry also won a Presidential Unit Citation. Years later, Otis finished his military career as a four-star general and commander of U.S. Army forces in Europe.

Thirteen miles to the east of Sài Gòn, the VC 5th Division simultaneously attacked the Long Bình–Biên Hòa complex. They were opposed primarily by the U.S. 9th Infantry Division's 2d Battalion, 47th Infantry, a mechanized unit commanded by Lt. Col. John B. Tower. Company A was sent to relieve the attack on the large prisoner-of-war compound between the two cities, and Company B was sent to reinforce the besieged garrison at Long Bình. Just as Company B arrived at 0630, VC sappers managed to blow up part of the huge Long Bình ammunition storage dump. The massive explosion could be heard and seen for miles around, but miraculously few Allied casualties resulted.

Company C, meanwhile, was sent into Biên Hòa City to relieve the attack on the ARVN III Corps headquarters compound. Company C had to fight its way through the middle of the VC 275th Regiment astride Highway 1 and through the flank of the VC 274th Regiment that was attacking the U.S. air base at Biên Hòa. At 0545 it plowed into the rear of the VC 238th Battalion inside the city. Dismounting from their armored personnel carriers (APCs), the soldiers engaged in city fighting more typical of World War II than of Vietnam. By that evening the city was secure.

While Company C was fighting to clear the city, Troop A of the 3d Squadron, 5th Cavalry was sent to relieve the attack on Biên Hòa Air Base. It had to fight its way down Highway 1 and through Company C's fight inside the city. Once it reached the air base, Troop A linked up with the 101st Airborne Division's 2d Battalion, 506th Infantry, which had been brought in at dawn by helicopter. Together they fought all day to eject Communist forces from the air base. At the end of the day, Troop A's lone tank had taken 19 hits and lost two crews, but it was still in action. Both Troop A and the 2/47th Infantry won Valorous Unit Citations for their actions on 31 January.

Most of the fighting inside the Sài Gòn Circle was over in a matter of days, except in Chợ Lớn, the teeming ethnic Chinese district of Sài Gòn. Initially, the area was attacked by the VC 5th and 6th Local Force (LF) Battalions, but as the fighting elsewhere petered out, most Communist survivors filtered into Chợ Lớn. The key to Chợ Lớn was the Phú Thọ Racetrack, the hub of most of the key streets. By holding it the VC could deny its use to the Americans as a helicopter landing zone.

The VC 6th LF Battalion had little trouble taking the racetrack, and from there it fanned out to consolidate control of the district. Communist political officers worked the streets to drum up support for the General Uprising, while others served arrest and execution warrants for the district's leaders. A monthlong reign of terror in Chợ Lớn had begun.

Early on 31 January General Weyand ordered units of the 199th Light Infantry Brigade into Chợ Lớn to reinforce the ARVN

Rangers there. Company A, 3d Battalion, 7th Infantry reached Chợ Lớn about 0800. Six blocks from the racetrack they were ambushed and had to continue fighting their way house-to-house. By 1300 they were within two blocks of the racetrack. Their initial attack on the track was repulsed by a well-dug-in VC defense. The Americans tried again at 1630, this time with helicopter gunship support. Once the racetrack fell, the Americans consolidated the position and brought in reinforcements that night by air.

The next day U.S. troops fanned out from the racetrack and started the long and torturous process of retaking Chợ Lớn. By 3 February the South Vietnamese had five ranger, five marine, and five airborne battalions inside Sài Gòn. The Americans had committed seven infantry, one MP, and six artillery battalions. On 5 February the ARVN 5th Ranger Group started a "final push" to clear Chợ Lớn. For political and prestige reasons the South Vietnamese asked the Americans to pull back and let the ARVN finish the job. Five days later, the South Vietnamese asked the Americans to come back in.

Most of Chợ Lớn was finally cleared by 7 March, but sporadic fighting continued to erupt in Sài Gòn for the remainder of the month. In one of those final aftershocks, on 31 March Sài Gòn Police Chief Maj. Gen. Nguyên Ngọc Loan was caught on film summarily executing a suspected VC prisoner. The image became one of the most famous of the Vietnam War and produced reactions of horror and outrage throughout the world. It was, unfortunately, only one of many such incidents on both sides during the two months of fighting.

A few weeks later, Colonel Đắc, VC chief political officer for Sài Gòn, defected. The Tết Offensive was over. The VC and PAVN forces had failed to achieve any of their eight principal objectives, and they had suffered huge numbers of casualties in the process.

—David T. Zabecki

References: Braestrup, Peter. *Big Story.* Boulder, CO: Westview Press, 1977.
Hoàng Ngọc Lung. *General Offensives of 1968–69.* Washington, DC: U.S. Army Center of Military History, 1981.
Oberdorfer, Don. *Tet!* New York: Doubleday, 1971.
Palmer, Dave. *Summons of the Trumpet.* Novato, CA: Presidio Press, 1978.
Zabecki, David T. "Battle for Saigon." *Vietnam* (Summer 1989): 19–25.
See also: Huê, Battle of; Nguyên Ngọc Loan; Tết Offensive: Overall Strategy; Trân Đô; Trân Văn Trà; Võ Nguyên Giáp; Ware, Keith L.; Westmoreland, William Childs; Weyand, Frederick C.

TEXAS, Operation

(20–24 March 1966)
Combined U.S. Marine/Army of the Republic of Vietnam (ARVN) reaction force to relieve a besieged Republic of Vietnam (RVN) Regional Forces camp at An Hòa, approximately 15 miles south of Chu Lai in Quang Ngãi Province. Operation TEXAS, known to the ARVN as LIÊN KÊT-28, resulted from a 19 March 1966 attack by the 1st Viêt Công (VC) Regiment on the An Hòa base, which was garrisoned by a single Regional Forces company. U.S. Marine helicopters flew in ARVN reinforcements and evacuated the wounded, but it appeared that An Hòa could not be held. At dawn on 20 March the 3d Battalion, 7th Marines and the 5th

ARVN Airborne Battalion were flown to within a mile of the fort and immediately went into battle, forcing the Việt Công to withdraw. The 2d Battalion, 4th Marines were then helicoptered from Chu Lai to a position 4 miles to the south of An Hòa to intercept the retreating VC regiment. The tactic worked, and the Allied forces successfully trapped the VC force and annihilated them during two more days of fierce fighting. In just four days the Marines accounted for 405 known VC dead, and the ARVN claimed an additional 218 for a total of 623. U.S. Marine and ARVN casualties in Operation TEXAS/LIÊN KÊT-28 were termed "light."

—John D. Root

References: Simmons, Brig. Gen. Edwin H. "Marine Corps Operations in Vietnam, 1965–1966." In *The Marines in Vietnam, 1954–1973: An Anthology and Annotated Bibliography,* 2d ed. Washington, DC: History and Museums Division, Headquarters, U.S. Marine Corps, 1985.
Stanton, Shelby L. *The Rise and Fall of an American Army: U.S. Ground Forces in Vietnam, 1965–1973.* Novato, CA: Presidio Press, 1985.
See also: Territorial Forces; United States: Marine Corps; Vietnam, Republic of: Army (ARVN).

TEXAS STAR, Operation

(1 April–5 September 1970)
Military operation in I Corps conducted by the U.S. 101st Airborne Division (Airmobile) in cooperation with the Army of the Republic of Vietnam (ARVN) 1st Infantry Division. One brigade of the 101st assumed responsibility for pacification support and development programs. The other two carried out offensive sweeps through the western part of the Republic of Vietnam's two northern provinces of Quang Tri and Thừa Thiên. Operation TEXAS STAR clearly reflected U.S. military priorities for 1970: Vietnamization of the war, reduction of U.S. casualties, meeting the timetable of withdrawal of U.S. forces, and U.S. combat operations only if intended to "stimulate a negotiated settlement."

TEXAS STAR utilized lessons learned in Operation RANDOLPH GLEN (7 December 1969–31 March 1970), developed in coordination with the ARVN 1st Infantry Division and Vietnamese provincial officials to meet the objectives both of an integrated pacification/development plan and an autonomous Vietnamese military capable of self-defense. Emphasis on these two goals had led, however, to a reduction in Allied offensive capability that enabled People's Army of Vietnam (PAVN) forces time to upgrade their own capabilities and return to areas abandoned in 1969. PAVN proximity to population centers threatened the pacification effort along the coastal plains, and by April 1970 PAVN forces in Thừa Thiên Province outnumbered those during the 1968 Tết Offensive. Operation TEXAS STAR represented an effort to regain the initiative of the 1969 A Shau Valley campaigns lost during RANDOLPH GLEN's pacification efforts.

Using a network of fire support bases, active patrolling, and aerial reconnaissance, TEXAS STAR attempted to halt PAVN infiltration. The five-month operation included action at Fire Support Bases (FSBs) Arsenal, Bastogne, Gladiator, Granite, Henderson, Kathryn, Los Banos, Maureen, Mink, O'Reilly, Ripcord, Sarge, and Tomahawk. At FSB Maureen on the night of 7 May, Pfc. Kenneth

M. Kays, a medic with Company D, 1st Battalion, 506th Infantry earned the Medal of Honor. In the fighting the division's Ranger reconnaissance teams suffered heavy losses, including, on 11 May, an entire six-man team from Lima Company, 75th Infantry (Rangers). The 2d Squadron, 17th Cavalry, within the 101st's tactical area of responsibility, played a major role in supplying aerial reconnaissance and surveillance, but paid a high price in casualties and lost aircraft.

On 8 July the largest action of the year saw troopers of the 2/17th engage PAVN forces on the move near Khe Sanh. An intense daylong battle resulted in 139 PAVN killed and 4 captured.

The battle of FSB Ripcord was the costliest of the year. After an exploratory insertion on 12 March and a failed attempt to make the hill into a firebase, on 1 April the 101st "Screaming Eagles" moved off the hill to a more secure area. After ten days of firefights, on 10 April the 2d Battalion, 506th Infantry, commanded by Lt. Col. Andre C. Lucas (posthumously awarded the Medal of Honor), secured the hill without opposition. After a relatively quiet seven weeks, during which a PAVN division code-named F-4 moved into the area, on 1 July the siege of FSB Ripcord began. From 1 to 23 July the firebase came under assault from rockets and 120-mm mortars. Two factors influenced Acting Division Commander Brig. Gen. Sidney Berry to disengage. On 18 July a U.S. Chinook helicopter was shot down and crashed into the main U.S. artillery ammunition dump; this destroyed the heart of Ripcord's defenses. And two days later Capt. Charles Hawkins, commanding Company A, 2/506th, reported that the opposing PAVN forces were between 9,000 and 11,000 men. On the morning of 23 July, having suffered heavy losses, the 300 remaining defenders of Ripcord executed a fighting withdrawal. American losses at Ripcord totaled 112 killed, 698 wounded, and 1 missing in action (of these casualties, 61 killed, 345 wounded, and 1 missing in action were during the July siege). U.S. Military Assistance Command, Vietnam, claimed for Operation TEXAS STAR 1,782 PAVN casualties. Other sources believe the toll was actually higher.

—Paul S. Daum, with assistance from Francis Ryan

References: Hawkins, Capt. Charles. Interviews with the author, 24–25 January 1996.
Kamps, Charles T., Jr. *The History of the Vietnam War.* New York: Exeter Books, 1987.
Linderer, Gary. "The 101st Airborne Division: The Vietnam Experience." In *101st Airborne Division: Screaming Eagles,* edited by Robert J. Martin. Paducah, KY: Turner, 1995.
Sigler, David Burns. *Vietnam Battle Chronology: U.S. Army and Marine Corps Combat Operations, 1965–1973.* Jefferson, NC: McFarland, 1992.
Stanton, Shelby L. *The Rise and Fall of an American Army: U.S. Ground Forces in Vietnam, 1965–1973.* Novato, CA: Presidio Press, 1985.
_____. *Vietnam Order of Battle.* New York: Galahad Books, 1986.
See also: Airmobility; Khe Sanh, Battles of; Pacification; Tết Offensive: Overall Strategy; United States: Army; Vietnam, Democratic Republic of: Army (People's Army of Vietnam [PAVN]); Vietnamization.

Thailand

Southeast Asian nation and close ally of the United States during the Vietnam War. Thailand provided both military bases and combat forces to assist the Republic of Vietnam (RVN). Although

Thai partisans help prepare a joint Thai-Vietnamese-French operation against the invading Communist-led Viêt Minh in 1954. During the Vietnam War, Thailand was a close U.S. ally, providing both military bases and combat forces to assist the Republic of Vietnam.

the Thais had traditionally maintained a policy of nonintervention in Southeast Asia and had gotten along with the Vietnamese, they became suspicious of Communist intentions. Fearing the fall of Cambodia and Laos to guerrillas, the Thais wanted above all to preserve their own independence while taking a more active role in regional defense matters. Accordingly, the Thai government responded to President Lyndon Johnson's call for "Free World Military Forces" and joined 40 other nations in sending forces or other support to the RVN. Thai support to Johnson's "Many Flags" campaign took the form of combat troops, which by 1969 totaled nearly 12,000 men in South Vietnam.

The first Thai contribution to the Vietnam War effort came in September 1964, when a 16-man Royal Thai Air Force contingent arrived in South Vietnam to assist in flying and maintaining some of the cargo aircraft operated by the RVN Air Force. The Royal Thai Military Assistance Group was established in Sài Gòn in February 1966.

Later in 1966 the Thai government announced that it was considering sending combat troops to aid the South Vietnamese against the Communists. Public support for this idea was overwhelmingly positive; 5,000 men volunteered almost immediately, including some 20 Buddhist monks and the prime minister's son. In January 1967 the Thai government officially announced that it would send a reinforced combat battalion to South Vietnam.

In September 1967 the first elements of the Royal Thai Volunteer Regiment, the "Queen's Cobras," arrived in Vietnam and moved to Bear Cat (near Biên Hòa), where it was colocated with the U.S. 9th Infantry Division. The Queen's Cobras began combat operations almost immediately, launching Operation NARASUAN in October 1967. The Thai soldiers quickly proved themselves to be a well-trained and resourceful force. In addition to participating in combat operations, Thai units were also active in civic action projects in their area of operations, building schools and roads and treating the civilian population with their medical units.

Even as the Queen's Cobras were conducting combat operations, the Thai government began to consider increasing its commitment to South Vietnam. Discussions between the Thai government and the U.S. Military Assistance Command, Vietnam (MACV), led Thailand to increase its troop strength in South Vietnam to an entire division. In July 1968 the Queen's Cobras were replaced by the Royal Thai Army Expeditionary Division, the "Black Panthers," which arrived incrementally and eventually included two brigades of infantry, three battalions of 105-mm field artillery, and an armored cavalry unit. The Black Panthers were joined by 48 U.S. Army advisors to assist in their operations. The area of operations (AO) assigned to the Thai force in the III Corps Tactical Zone was characterized by a low level of action because the land was used by the Communist forces as a source of food and clothing; thus, offensive actions were not as significant in the Thai AO as in other areas. Nevertheless, Thai forces fought very effectively, primarily conducting search-and-clear operations supported by their own artillery firing from two Thai firebases. They also conducted extensive psychological warfare operations and continued their civic action projects. In August 1970 the Black

Panthers Division was redesignated the Royal Thai Army Volunteer Force, a title it retained throughout the rest of its time in South Vietnam.

In addition to the ground forces, the Royal Thai Air Force contributed C-47 and C-123 cargo aircraft to what they called their Victory Flight. In 1971 as part of the general drawdown of forces in Vietnam, Royal Thai forces were gradually withdrawn; the last Thai troops left Vietnam in April 1972. During the course of its commitment to the RVN, Thailand provided more military support than any other country except the United States and South Korea.

Thailand also contributed bases to the American war effort in Southeast Asia. The U.S. Air Force operated from Thailand with the 8th, 355th, 366th, and 388th Tactical Fighter Wings and the 307th Strategic Wing. Strategic bombing operations over both North and South Vietnam often originated in Thailand. In addition to the Air Force, the United States also stationed the 46th Special Forces Company in Thailand. This unit was tasked with assisting Thai forces in resisting Communist terrorist (CT) guerrilla activity along Thailand's northeastern Laotian border and in the south on the Malay Peninsula. Several U.S. servicemen were killed during the period 1967–1973 in the anti-CT campaign. CT forces also conducted a number of raids on U.S. Air Force bases, notably at Udorn and U-Tapao, causing U.S. casualties. The bodies of these CT sappers almost invariably turned out to be North Vietnamese. Other U.S. forces in Thailand included the U.S. Army 9th Logistical Command, 44th Engineer Group and 40th Military Police (Battle) at Korat, the 29th Signal Group at Bangkok, and the U.S. Marine Corps Marine Air Group 15 at Nam Phong in 1972.

—James H. Willbanks

References: Larsen, Stanley Robert, and James Lawton Collins, Jr. *Allied Participation in Vietnam.* Washington, DC: U.S. Government Printing Office, 1975.
Stanton, Shelby L. *Vietnam Order of Battle.* New York: Galahad Books, 1986.
See also: Civic Action; Free World Assistance Program; Johnson, Lyndon Baines; Korea, Republic of; Military Assistance Command, Vietnam (MACV); Order of Battle.

Thành Thái

(?–1954)

Tenth emperor of the Nguyên dynasty (1889–1907). Thành Thái was the son of Emperor Duc Đưc (1883). The French placed him on the throne after the death of Emperor Đông Khánh (1885–1889). Thành Thái was intelligent, open minded, and deeply influenced by the reform movement. However, it was during his reign that the French forced the Huê Court to eliminate the position of Kinh Lược Băc Kỳ (Viceroy of Tonkin) and let its functions be taken over by the French Resident Superior. The French also eliminated the Cơ Mât Viên (Secret Council), the highest council of the imperial court, and replaced it with the Council of Ministers headed by the French Resident in Huê.

These events profoundly affected Thành Thái and made him openly anti-French. He secretly contacted members of the Đông Du movement and, for a time, planned to flee the country. On 3

September 1907 the French forced him to abdicate. They replaced him with his son, Vĩnh San, who became Emperor Duy Tân. From 1907 to 1915 Thành Thái was kept in Vũng Tàu (Cap Saint-Jacques); he was then sent into exile on Réunion Island. He returned to Vietnam in 1947 and died seven years later in Sài Gòn.

—Pham Cao Dưỡng

References: Hoàng Trong Thước. *Hô Sơ Vua Duy Tân (Thân Thê và Sư Nghiêp).* San Francisco: Nhà Xuât Ban Mo Lang, 1993.

Lê Thành Khôi. *Le Viet-Nam: Histoire et Civilisation.* Paris: Editions de Minuit, 1955.

Nguyên Huyên Anh. *Viêt Nam Danh Nhân Tư Điên (Dictionary of Vietnamese Great Men and Women).* Houston: Zieleks, 1990.

Nguyên Thê Anh. *Viêt Nam Dưởi Thơi Pháp Đô Hô (Vietnam under French Domination).* Sài Gòn: Lửa Thiêng, 1970.

See also: Duy Tân; French Indo-China; Nguyên Dynasty.

Thích Quang Đức
(1897–1963)

Buddhist monk whose act of self-immolation in front of invited media was the subject of Malcolm Browne's photograph, a "graven image" of the Vietnam experience. Thích ("Venerable") Quang Đức, born in 1897 in Hôi Khánh, Khánh Hòa Province, became a Buddhist at age 7, a monk at 15, and later the most venerable bonze at Thiên Mu, Vietnam's most famous pagoda, located near Huê. There, after May 1963 anti-Buddhist actions carried out by President Ngô Đình Diêm's minority Catholic government, the Buddhists decided to respond.

On 11 June 1963 Thích Quang Đức arrived by automobile at Sài Gòn's intersection of Phan Đình Phùng and Lê Văn Duyêt Streets. Approximately 700 monks and nuns surrounded him, chanted, burned incense, prayed, and blocked traffic. Doused with gasoline by one of his disciples and then ignited, Thích Quang Đức died without crying out or moving. Thích Quang Đức's death as a martyr protesting the actions of President Diêm's government produced worldwide indignation, widespread antigovernment protests within Vietnam, and a growing realization within the Kennedy administration that Diêm was himself part of the Vietnam problem.

Buddhists, who claimed that the venerable's heart did not burn, removed it to Sài Gòn's Xá Lơi Pagoda, where there is a special altar at which to pray, honor the man, and commemorate the event. Although eventually some 30 monks and nuns burned

Thích Quang Đức's death as a martyr protesting the actions of President Ngô Đình Diêm's government produced worldwide indignation, widespread antigovernment protests in Vietnam, and a growing realization within the Kennedy administration that Diêm was himself part of the Vietnam problem.

themselves, Thích Quang Đức's act—as the first—remained the most shocking and served as the catalyst for the impending demise of Diêm and his regime.

—Paul S. Daum, with assistance from Trevor Curran

References: Curran, Trevor, and Elizabeth Daum. Interview with Buddhist monks, Thiên Mu Pagoda, Huê, Socialist Republic of Vietnam (8 August 1995).
Esper, George, and the Associated Press. *The Eyewitness History of the Vietnam War, 1961–1975.* New York: Ballantine Books, 1983.
Halberstam, David. "Diem Asks Peace in Religious Crisis." *New York Times* (12 June 1963).
Prados, John. "We Are Spiritual in the Material World: The Rise of Buddhist Activism in South Vietnam." *VVA Veteran* 15, no. 2 (February 1995): 1, 23–24, 40–41.
See also: Buddhists; Media and the War; Ngô Đình Diêm; Ngô Đình Nhu.

Thích Trí Quang

(1922–)

Buddhist monk and opponent of the Diêm regime. Trí Quang was born in Quang Bình Province in November 1922 to a family of well-to-do peasants. The French believed him a Viêt Minh sympathizer and kept him under surveillance until 1953, although they did allow him to teach and edit a journal. At the time of the 1954 Geneva Accords Trí Quang was in Huê.

Thích Trí Quang was a patriot but was not sympathetic to the Communists. In 1955 his parents and brother were arrested as landlords during land reform movements in the northern province of Quang Bình. This prompted Thích Trí Quang to become the president of the Buddhist Association for Central Vietnam. Buddhist monks such as Thích Trí Quang believed that if the United States left Vietnam and Ngô Đình Diêm's regime was ended, peace talks could be held and the country reunited.

The core of conflict in 1963 was that while the Republic of Vietnam (RVN) officially professed religious freedom, incidents of local discrimination and repression created doubts. By 1963 the Buddhists in the RVN organized and discussed political action in response to Diêm's repression.

On 8 May 1963 a confrontation occurred between Buddhists, who had gathered in Huê to celebrate the 2,527th birthday of Buddha, and Catholics. Thích Trí Quang was scheduled to give a speech but Maj. Đăng Sĩ, a Catholic, refused to allow it to be broadcast. Sĩ ordered his officers to throw a concussion grenade at the crowd to disperse them, and a woman and eight children died.

In the weeks that followed, Buddhist protests escalated and the government often resorted to brutal means to quell the unrest. Thích Trí Quang and the monks kept up the pressure until Diêm was overthrown.

In 1964 Thích Trí Quang again mobilized Buddhists during the tenuous rule of General Nguyên Khánh. After 1964 the Buddhists were relatively quiet until 1966 when Nguyên Cao Kỳ fired I Corps commander General Nguyên Chánh Thi, a close friend of Thích Trí Quang. This time the United States was determined to stand behind Kỳ, and General Thi was exiled to the United States. Thích Trí Quang went on a hunger strike, but the power of the

Buddhists was broken. Thích Trí Quang was arrested and transferred to a Sài Gòn hospital.

In 1975 when the People's Army of Vietnam took control of the RVN, Thích Trí Quang was placed under house arrest. Eventually released, he has since lived in self-imposed obscurity.

—Charlotte A. Power

References: FitzGerald, Francis. *Fire in the Lake: The Vietnamese and the Americans in Vietnam.* New York: Random House, 1972.
Post, Ken. *Revolution, Socialism, and Nationalism in Vietnam.* Vol. 4, *The Failure of Counter-Insurgency in the South.* Belmont, CA: Wadsworth, 1990.
See also: Buddhists; Ngô Đình Diêm; Nguyên Cao Kỳ; Nguyên Chánh Thi; Roman Catholicism in Vietnam.

Thiêu Tri

(?–1847)

Third emperor of the Nguyên dynasty (1841–1847). His real name was Miên Tông; Thiêu Tri was his ruling name. Thiêu Tri ascended the throne in 1841. This gentle poet and emperor maintained all the works and policies of his father, Emperor Minh Mang (1820–1841), although he was less severe toward the Catholics. His short reign was marked by the French bombardment of Đà Năng in 1847 and the Vietnamese abandonment of Trân Tây Thành (Cambodia). He was the author of three collections of poems in Chinese characters.

Thiêu Tri died in 1847. Western pressure on Vietnam increased under his successor, Tư Đức, last emperor of an independent Vietnam.

—Pham Cao Dưỡng

References: Nguyên Huyên Anh. *Viêt Nam Danh Nhân Tư Điên (Dictionary of Vietnamese Great Men and Women).* Houston: Zieleks, 1990.
Quôc Sư Quán. *Quôc Triêu Chánh Biên Toát Yêu (A Summary of the History of Our Current Dynasty).* Sài Gòn: Nhóm Nghiên Cưu Sư Đia, 1971.
Trân Trong Kim. *Viêt Nam Sư Lược (Outline of Vietnamese History).* Sài Gòn: Bô Giáo Duc, Trung Tâm Hoc Liêu, 1971.
See also: Minh Mang; Tư Đức; Vietnam: From 938 through the French Conquest.

Thomas, Allison Kent

(1914–)

U.S. Office of Strategic Services (OSS) officer sent to work with the Viêt Minh at the end of World War II. Born on 21 September 1914, Allison Kent Thomas grew up in Lansing, Michigan, and attended Michigan State University before receiving his LL.B. from the University of Michigan Law School in 1939. His newly established legal practice ended when he was drafted in June 1941. He graduated from Officers Candidate School (OCS) at Benning, Georgia, and was commissioned a second lieutenant in 1942.

Sent to Alabama to train raw recruits, he became involved in intelligence work and was assigned to look for trainees of foreign backgrounds who might be subversive risks. Then a message came from War Department headquarters announcing an initiative to recruit French-speaking members of the military. Thomas volunteered, having studied the language for two years in school.

At his interview in Washington, D.C., he was asked only one question: "*Quel age avez vous?*" In this way he was recruited by the Office of Strategic Services (OSS).

While awaiting overseas assignment, Thomas took a Berlitz course in French. Later in London he lived with a French-speaking family. Then he was sent to France, assigned to the small OSS detachment at General George Patton's Third Army headquarters, where he worked with the French Resistance, interviewing and debriefing various agents. Thomas may have been the first to learn, while talking with the agent code-named "Gallois," of Hitler's plans to burn Paris before it could be liberated.

When OSS work in Europe was largely completed, Thomas was sent to China. He arrived in Kunming 1 April 1945. By then a major, Thomas headed a small unit, the "Deer Team," sent into northern Tonkin to train Việt Minh soldiers. On 16 July 1945 Thomas and his men parachuted from a Dakota cargo plane, landing near the village of Kim Lũng (now Tân Trào). In the weeks that followed Thomas worked with Hồ Chí Minh, Võ Nguyên Giáp, and other Việt Minh leaders to carry out his assignment. Thomas and his men arrived in Hà Nội on 9 September and spent the next week wandering the city, buying souvenirs, and saying good-bye to friends. The evening before his departure for Kunming, he attended a private dinner with Hồ and Giáp and asked Hồ if he was a Communist. "Yes," Hồ replied, "but we can still be friends, can't we?"

Thomas arrived back in Michigan before the end of September and returned to the practice of law, ultimately becoming a partner in the firm of Hubbard, Fox, Thomas, White, and Bengston. He is now retired.

—Cecil B. Currey

Reference: Thomas, Allison Kent, interviews with the author.
See also: Conein, Lucien Emile; Deer Mission; Dewey, Albert Peter; Hồ Chí Minh; Office of Strategic Services (OSS); Patti, Archimedes L. A.; Võ Nguyên Giáp.

Thompson, Robert Grainger Ker

(1916–1992)

British counterinsurgency expert. Born in England on 12 April 1916, Robert Grainger Ker Thompson served the British government for many years in Asia before being assigned to Vietnam. In the 1930s he was stationed in Malaya in a variety of posts and during World War II spent six years in the Royal Air Force. After the war he returned to Malaya. Between 1957 and 1961 he served first as deputy, then as secretary of defense of the Federation of Malaya. A noted expert in counterinsurgency, Thompson was instrumental in suppressing the Malayan Emergency, a Communist-mounted insurgency. In the 1960s he advised the United States in counterinsurgency operations, urging the Americans to apply the lessons of Malaya to Vietnam.

At the request of the United States he went to Vietnam as head of the British Advisory Mission (1961–1965). In this capacity he urged President Ngô Đình Diệm to embark on the Strategic Hamlet program. In 1969 he toured South Vietnam on behalf of President Richard Nixon. An opponent of large conventional military operations that often alienated the population and did not deal with the root causes of insurgency, he advocated police and military programs that bolstered the Sài Gòn government's political support in the countryside.

Thompson derived the concept of the Strategic Hamlet program from his experiences in the Malayan Emergency. His idea was to organize South Vietnamese villagers to provide their own defense. A network of strategic hamlets would, according to Thompson, serve to isolate the insurgents physically and politically from the people and cut them off from their recruiting base.

In Malaya the failure of the largely Chinese insurgents, who were ethnically different than the Malay villagers, to penetrate the population meant that little more was required to end the insurgency than to organize a home guard—a local security force supported by local police. The government could devote its efforts to relocating Chinese squatters. The situation in South Vietnam was more complex, because the Việt Công (VC) movement had established itself in all areas of the country. With its tightly knit political and military organization, the VC was embedded in the structure of many villages and was harder to displace. Because the insurgents were of the same ethnicity as the villagers, it was not easily to identify and segregate the VC.

The premise of Thompson's Strategic Hamlet programs was to bring security to where the people lived. At the start of the program in 1962 Thompson estimated that only 5 percent of the hamlets, those in Việt Công–controlled areas, would have to be moved to new sites. But that was not how the Republic of Vietnam government carried out the program. Far too many people were relocated into hastily built fortified settlements, which failed to segregate the people from the insurgents or to improve their lives. Most peasants regarded the program as onerous because it forced them from their homes. Others viewed it as a means to control the rural population. The program, which faltered after a promising start, ended in failure after the overthrow of Diệm in 1963.

Thompson criticized the program as implemented by Diệm's brother Ngô Đình Nhu on three grounds. First, using the Cần Lao Party, Nhu attempted to control the program from the top down instead of winning political and popular support at the bottom. Second, by emphasizing the Republican Youth, he created divisions between the youth and village elders, the traditional local leaders. Third, he failed to understand the extent of penetration of the VC and was unprepared to take the harsh measures necessary to eliminate it within the hamlets.

Although he exercised less influence after the failure of the Strategic Hamlet program, Thompson remained involved in Vietnam, writing influential books *(Peace Is Not at Hand* and *Defeating Communist Insurgency)* and advising the Americans on how to deal with the VC. After the 1968 Tết Offensive, when counterinsurgency or pacification again became a prominent part of the war effort, Thompson's views enjoyed a new appeal. In 1969 he advised President Richard Nixon, who wanted to strengthen the ability of the Republic of Vietnam to cope with the Communists, to enlarge the police and give them a greater role in order to end the insurgency. Thompson died on 16 May 1992.

—Richard A. Hunt

References: Hunt, Richard A. *Pacification: The American Struggle for Vietnam's Hearts and Minds.* Boulder, CO: Westview Press, 1995.
Thompson, Robert. *Defeating Communist Insurgency: The Lessons of Malaya and Vietnam.* New York: Praeger, 1966.
See also: Counterinsurgency Warfare; Malaysia; Ngô Đình Diêm; Ngô Đình Nhu; Nixon, Richard Milhous; Pacification; Strategic Hamlet Program.

THUNDERHEAD, Operation

(29 May–19 June 1972)

Secret search-and-rescue mission conducted in North Vietnam. U.S. Navy intelligence had received information of a possible escape attempt by two to five prisoners from a prisoner-of-war (POW) camp near Hà Nôi. As a result, from 29 May to 19 June 1972 numerous sorties were flown under Lt. Comdr. Edwin Towers's direction to search for the escaped prisoners in enemy territory. Primary surveillance was performed by Navy SEAL teams and HH-3A helicopters at a cost of one man killed. Upon its termination, the mission was labeled a failure because the prisoners had not been extracted.

The fate of the prisoners remained unknown for a year. When released in 1973, they stated that they had spent several months planning an escape attempt. However, increased prison security, stemming from the breakdown in negotiations between Washington and Hà Nôi, led to the attempt being called off. This increased security also prevented notifying American authorities that the escape attempt had been called off.

—Rajesh H. Chauhan

References: Gropman, Alan L. *Air Power and the Airlift Evacuation of Kham Duc.* U.S. Air Force Southeast Asia Monograph Series, Vol. 5, Monograph 7. Washington, DC: Office of Air Force History, 1985.
Lavalle, A. J. C. *Air Power and the 1972 Spring Invasion.* U.S. Air Force Southeast Asia Monograph Series, Vol. 2, Monograph 3. Washington, DC: Office of Air Force History, 1985.
Towers, Edwin L. *Hope for Freedom: Operation Thunderhead.* La Jolla, CA: Lane & Associates, 1981.
See also: Prisoners of War, Allied; SEAL (Sea, Air, Land) Teams.

Tiger Cages

Confinement cells at the Republic of Vietnam (RVN) prison on Côn Sơn Island that held prisoners of war and political opponents. Built by the French, the so-called tiger cages have been described as subsurface cement cells approximately six feet by ten feet in size, topped by bars, with ceilings so low that inmates could barely stand. But according to descriptions by visiting U.S. officials, the cells were entirely above ground, located in two covered, windowless buildings with bars forming the ceiling, and a catwalk on top, measuring six feet three inches by ten feet six inches by ten feet. Such facilities were pictured in a 1970 *Life* magazine article.

In any case, Sài Gòn claimed that all Côn Sơn prisoners were humanely treated and confined only temporarily in the tiger cages. But in July 1970 U.S. Congressmen William Anderson (D-Tennessee) and Augustus Hawkins (D-California), staff aide Thomas Harkin, and Don Luce of the World Council of Churches inspected the prison and reported "paralyzed" tiger cage victims

who were denied adequate food, water, and exercise. Subsequently, the International Red Cross cited the RVN government for violations of the Geneva Convention.

In 1974 antiwar protesters maintained a "Tiger Cage vigil" at the U.S. Capitol, demanding that the RVN government release its prisoners.

—Mary L. Kelley

References: Guenter, Lewy. *America in Vietnam.* New York: Oxford University Press, 1978.
Nguyên Tiên Hưng, and Jerrold L. Schecter. *The Palace File.* New York: Harper & Row, 1986.
See also: Missing in Action and Prisoners of War, Viêt Công and People's Army of Vietnam.

TIGER HOUND, Operation

(1965–1973)

Allied air operation in the panhandle region of Laos designed to reduce Communist infiltration along the Hô Chí Minh Trail. In 1965 Allied leaders estimated that the Communists used the Hô Chí Minh Trail to bring 4,500 troops and 300 tons of supplies per month into South Vietnam. Planned by U.S. Air Force Col. John F. Groom, Operation TIGER HOUND began in December 1965 and focused on infiltration routes in Military Regions (MRs) I and II in the area from Tchépone near the 17th parallel south to Cambodia. It augmented air operations in the northern panhandle designated STEEL TIGER (Mu Già Pass to the 17th parallel), which began in April.

Unlike Operation BARREL ROLL in northern Laos, these operations were not constrained by strict rules of engagement (the need to have U.S. Embassy or Laotian government permission to attack potential targets). The panhandle was seen as an extension of the South Vietnamese battlefield and was thus under the control of U.S. General William Westmoreland.

In TIGER HOUND the Allies employed C-47s and later C-130s as airborne battlefield command and control centers (ABC&CCs); Air Force O-1s and A-1Es as well as Laotian T-28s and Army OV-1 Mohawks with side-looking and infrared radar for forward air control (FAC); RF-101s and RF-4Cs for target detection; UC-123s to defoliate the jungle; and B-57s, F-100s, F-105s, AC-47 gunships, C-130 flare ships, Marine and Navy jets, and Army gunship helicopters as the primary strike aircraft for day and night attacks.

The primary targets in TIGER HOUND were trucks, storage and bivouac areas, bridges, buildings, and antiaircraft artillery (AAA) sites. The secondary mission was to cut roads and create traffic choke areas. TIGER HOUND pilots were also to supply frequent detailed photos of infiltration targets to General Westmoreland's headquarters. Unlike BARREL ROLL, which was to support Royal Laotian Government forces and Hmong irregulars under General Vang Pao, TIGER HOUND and STEEL TIGER focused on interdiction of Communist ground forces and support for Army of the Republic of Vietnam (ARVN) and American long-range armed reconnaissance units.

By 31 December 1965 U.S. pilots had flown 425 sorties, 51 of them at night. In the first half of 1966 TIGER HOUND gained momentum, and by May B-52s had flown over 400 saturation bombing sorties against bridges, roads, and encampments, destroying an additional 3,000 structures, 1,400 trucks, dozens of bridges, and 200 antiaircraft positions.

Despite these impressive numbers, infiltration continued and U.S. Air Force commanders decided they needed a long-loitering aircraft. In June they deployed eight modified World War II A-26s. They also used AC-47s, AC-119 "truck killers," and AC-130 gunships with flare capability for night raids. The Americans also set up in Nakhon Phanom an MSQ-77 Skyport radar with a 200-mile range to improve bombing results. Despite this effort, the Communists increased the number of AAA sites, later including surface-to-air missiles (SAMs), and by the summer of 1966, 22 TIGER HOUND and STEEL TIGER planes had been shot down.

By this time, TIGER HOUND and STEEL TIGER operations had been blended into Seventh Air Force duties and placed under the TIGER HOUND task force. Overall operational responsibility was delegated to the Seventh Air Force commander.

After a summer monsoon lull, full operations resumed between October 1966 and April 1967. U.S. pilots flew over 2,000 sorties per month. By the end of 1967 B-52 operations had also increased, totaling 1,718 (compared to 617 sorties in 1966). By late 1967 most TIGER HOUND strike aircraft had been equipped with Starlight scopes to increase target detection at night. In 1967 a large number of TIGER HOUND raids were carried out at night, often by B-57 "Canberra" bombers in night camouflage. In November and December 1967 the Allies placed a line of seismic and acoustic sensors along infiltration roads and trails. The sensors transmitted troop and truck movements to high-flying EC-121s. In turn, they sent the raw data to the Air Force Infiltration Surveillance Center in Nakhon Phanom, built and run by Task Force Alpha commanded by Brig. Gen. William P. McBride.

After President Lyndon Johnson halted the air war in North Vietnam on 31 March 1968, Operation TIGER HOUND was reduced to a less intense routine until it, along with all Allied air operations in Laos, ended in April 1973. From 1965 to 1972 Allied planes dropped over 1.1 million tons of bombs on the Hô Chí Minh Trail in the southern Laotian panhandle. Despite its impressive numbers, TIGER HOUND failed to stop Communist infiltration.

—William Head

References: Berger, Carl, ed. *The United States Air Force in Southeast Asia, 1961–1973: An Illustrated Account.* Washington, DC: Office of Air Force History, 1984.
Momyer, Gen. William H. *Airpower in Three Wars.* Washington, DC: Office of Air Force History, 1978.
Morrocco, John. *Rain of Fire: Air War, 1969–1973. The Vietnam Experience,* edited by Robert Manning. Boston: Boston Publishing, 1984.
————. *Thunder From Above: Air War, 1941–1968. The Vietnam Experience,* edited by Robert Manning. Boston: Boston Publishing, 1984.
Schlight, John. *The Air War in South Vietnam: The Years of the Offensive, 1965–1968.* Washington, DC: Office of Air Force History, 1988.
Tilford, Earl H., Jr. *Crosswinds: The Air Force's Setup in Vietnam.* College Station, TX: Texas A&M University Press, 1994.
See also: Air Power, Role in War; Airplanes, Allied and Democratic Republic of Vietnam; BARREL ROLL, Operation; Hô Chí Minh Trail; Laos;

Logistics, Allied and People's Army of Vietnam/Viêt Công; STEEL TIGER, Operation.

Tinker v. Des Moines

U.S. court case relating to the Vietnam War. On Thursday and Friday, 16 and 17 December 1965 several public school students in Des Moines, Iowa, including John Tinker, Mary Beth Tinker, and Chris Eckhardt, wore black arm bands to school to mourn the dead in Vietnam and to demonstrate support for the Christmas truce there. They were suspended and sent home for violating a ban on the wearing of arm bands that had been passed earlier in the week by the Des Moines School Board.

The board upheld the ban at its 3 January 1966 meeting, by which time the suspended students had returned to school. The Tinker and Eckhardt families, aided by the Iowa Civil Liberties Union, decided to pursue the matter in federal court. On 1 September 1966 District Judge Roy Stephenson ruled in favor of the school district, acknowledging that the arm bands were indeed a form of speech. He did not, however, feel that the ban deprived the students of their First Amendment rights.

The U.S. Court of Appeals for the Eighth Circuit upheld the lower court ruling by virtue of a split vote in November 1967. The U.S. Supreme Court accepted the case and overturned the lower decisions on 24 February 1969. The Court's seven-to-two ruling noted that the wearing of arm bands was a protected act of symbolic speech and espoused the idea that students have rights that are not left "at the schoolhouse gate."

The arm band incident, borne out of a sincere objection to U.S. policy in Vietnam, resulted in the addition of a landmark symbolic speech and students' rights case to American constitutional law.

—Wes Watters

Reference: Rappaport, Doreen. *Tinker vs. Des Moines: Student Rights on Trial.* New York: HarperCollins, 1993.
See also: Antiwar Movement, United States.

Tô Hữu

(1920–)
Prominent Vietnamese Communist Party (VCP) and Socialist Republic of Vietnam (SRV) official; well-known poet. Born Nguyên Kim Thành in 1920 in Phu Lai, Thừa Thiên Province, Tô Hữu joined the Đoàn Thanh Niên Dân Chu (Democratic Youth League) in 1936. In 1938 he joined the Indo-Chinese Communist Party (ICP). Arrested by French authorities in 1939, Hữu served time in Thừa Thiên, Lao Bao, and Qui Nhơn prisons. In 1942 Hữu escaped and in 1945 led the uprising against the French at Huê. In 1951 he joined the party Central Committee. Hữu built his career in the party's propaganda apparatus, and, although widely unappreciated as a poet, his works appeared in textbooks in the Vietnamese educational system. Hữu was notorious for paeans dedicated to the USSR.

In December 1976 Hữu became an alternate member of the VCP Politburo in charge of cultural affairs and ideology. He was also vice-chairman of the Council of Ministers in charge of economics. In September 1985 Hửu instigated a currency reform that he had modified on his own initiative and which was a great failure. In June 1986 after the economic collapse of the SRV, Hửu was dropped from the post of vice-premier, and at the December 1986 party congress he was ousted from the Politburo and disappeared from the Vietnamese political scene.

—Ngô N. Trung

Reference: Biographical Files, Indo-China Archives, University of California at Berkeley.
See also: Vietnam, Socialist Republic of: 1975 to the Present; Vietnamese Communist Party (VCP).

TOÀN THẮNG (Complete Victory), Operation

(8 April–25 May 1968)
First of many Allied military operations with the same code name that took place in the vicinity of Sài Gòn. On 8 April 1968 Allied military forces commenced 11 separate operations in the Republic of Vietnam (RVN) Capital Military District. U.S. Military Assistance Command, Vietnam (MACV) combined these actions into Operation TOÀN THẮNG, which became the central focus of Allied attentions from 1968 until U.S. armed forces withdrew from South Vietnam. The operation was motivated by the 1968 Têt Offensive and was designed to stop Viêt Công (VC) and People's Army of Vietnam (PAVN) attacks on Sài Gòn. TOÀN THẮNG initially included almost 80 U.S. and Army of the Republic of Vietnam (ARVN) combat battalions, but later included over 100 Allied battalions. U.S. units committed to the operation included the 3d Brigade, 9th Infantry Division; 1st Infantry Division; 25th Infantry Division; and 199th Infantry Brigade (Separate). Allied units included all ARVN forces assigned to the Capital Military District as well as the 1st Australian Task Force.

On 3 May 1968 Washington and Hà Nôi announced that peace talks would soon begin in Paris, and MACV and ARVN commanders sought to strengthen the defenses around the South Vietnamese capital in anticipation of renewed VC/PAVN attacks. Such precautions were indeed warranted because on 4 May the VC launched another major operation against Sài Gòn. Known as "Mini-Têt," this lasted until the end of the month. Attacks were concentrated on the Sài Gòn–Biên Hòa highway bridge that linked these two vital South Vietnamese cities. RVN Marines, however, repulsed the attacks and held the bridge. On 6 May the U.S. 25th Infantry Division (Tropic Lightning) counterattacked and decisively defeated VC units near Tân Sơn Nhứt Airport.

Despite Allied precautions, the well-equipped VC 267th Local Force Battalion infiltrated Sài Gòn and occupied several key locations. The 38th ARVN Ranger Battalion engaged the intruders and eventually triumphed despite heavy losses. The Rangers were then dispatched to the VC-occupied Bình Tiên Bridge, and, after two days of grueling combat, they secured the span.

The most serious threat came as two VC battalions captured the Y-Bridge linking downtown Sài Gòn with the Nhà Bè District. Additionally, the VC further fortified several built-up areas around the bridge. The U.S. 2d Battalion, 47th Infantry (Mechanized) and the 5th Battalion, 60th Infantry (Mechanized), 9th Infantry Division were sent to secure this vital artery. It took six days of hard fighting for the Americans, employing all available weapons, to destroy the VC units and retake the bridge and surrounding area in what was the most costly action fought by American troops during this offensive.

TOÀN THẮNG's initial phase ended on 25 May 1968. Mini-Têt, however, continued into June as the 5th ARVN Ranger Group worked to clear VC incursions into the Chợ Lớn section of Sài Gòn.

—J. A. Menzoff

Reference: Stanton, Shelby. The Rise and Fall of an American Army: U.S. Ground Forces in Vietnam, 1965–1973. Novato, CA: Presidio Press, 1985.
See also: Khe Sanh, Battles of; National Front for the Liberation of South Vietnam (NFLSV); Têt Offensive: Overall Strategy; Têt Offensive: The Sài Gòn Circle; United States: Army; Vietnam, Republic of: Army (ARVN).

Tôn Đức Thăng

(1888–1980)
Prominent Vietnamese Communist Party (VCP), Democratic Republic of Vietnam (DRV), and Socialist Republic of Vietnam (SRV) official. Born on 20 August 1888 in My Hòa Hưng village, Đinh Thành canton, Long Xuyên Province, Tôn Đức Thăng in 1906 went to Sài Gòn and received vocational training at the Technique School. He later worked at Ba Son shipyard. In 1913 Thăng went to France by ship and worked at Toulon. At the end of 1919 the French government deported him because of his support for the 1917 Russian Bolshevik Revolution. Thăng returned to Vietnam and worked in Sài Gòn. From 1920 to 1925 he was a member of a secret labor union at Ba Son shipyard.

In 1927 Thăng joined the Viêt Nam Thanh Niên Cách Mênh Đông Chí Hôi (Vietnamese Revolutionary Youth Association), predecessor of the Vietnamese Communist Party, and was named a member of the Executive Committee of the Southern Region Party Committee. At the end of 1928 he was arrested on a murder charge, tried and sentenced to 20 years of hard labor, and exiled to Côn Đao Island. He was freed on 23 September 1945.

In October 1945 Thăng took part in activities of the Southern Region Party Committee and was elected deputy to the National Assembly of the Democratic Republic of Vietnam. In April 1946 he was a member of the DRV delegation to France. At the 1951 Second Party Congress Thăng was elected to the party Central Committee. He also became chairman of Mặt Trân Liên Viêt (Liên Viêt Front) and head of the Standing Committee of the National Assembly. In July 1960 Thăng became vice-president of the DRV. He became president after the 2 September 1969 death of Hô Chí Minh and served in that capacity until his own death on 30 March 1980. Thăng is remembered as a veteran of the early days of the VCP and a lifelong friend of Hô Chí Minh.

—Ngô N. Trung

Reference: Biographical Files, Indo-China Archives, University of California at Berkeley.
See also: Hô Chí Minh; Lao Đông Party; Vietnam, Democratic Republic of: 1945–1954; Vietnam, Socialist Republic of: 1975 to the Present; Vietnamese Communist Party (VCP).

Tôn Thât Đình

(1926–)

Army of the Republic of Vietnam (ARVN) general; key figure in the coup against President Ngô Đình Diêm. Born on 20 November 1926 in Huê, Tôn Thât Đình attended the French Armor School at Samur and later became the protégé of Ngô Đình Cân, warlord of central Vietnam and brother of Diêm. Đình's courage had impressed Cân, but more important for Đình was his ambition and vanity. His closeness to the Ngô family and the trust that Diêm placed in him led to his appointment in 1961 as the youngest ARVN general. Đình converted to Roman Catholicism in the early 1960s and became an active member of the Personalist Labor Party under Diêm's brother Ngô Đình Nhu.

As one of the architects of the 1 November 1963 coup against Diêm, General Trân Van Đôn established early in the planning that General Đình's adherence would secure the coup's success. Đình's support was vital because he controlled ARVN forces surrounding Sài Gòn. Using Đình's vanity to advantage, Đôn treated Đình to women and food for several nights and then paid a fortune-teller to predict that he would be elevated to prominence.

This prompted Đình to ask Diêm to name him as minister of the interior. Diêm refused and scolded the young general for proposing it. Taking advantage of this disappointment, Đôn convinced Đình to join the coup plotters. Still, the conspirators did not entirely trust Đình and assigned men to kill him if he changed his mind.

Knowing that a coup was in the works, Nhu confronted Đình about a suspicious assignment given to Col. Nguyên Hữu Có. Đình's angry response was that he would kill "the little traitor." This convinced Nhu of his sincerity. Nhu then proceeded to let Đình know that he knew about the conspiracy and revealed his own plans for a preemptive coup, Operations BRAVO I and BRAVO II. General Đình was assigned a pivotal role—to march into Sài Gòn against a staged uprising. Đình immediately revealed the plans to Đôn and the other generals.

On 29 October Đình ordered Col. Lê Quang Tung and his special forces out of Sài Gòn in accordance with Nhu's plans. In a key maneuver, Đình also convinced the regime that he could conduct BRAVO II more effectively if he had control over all of the forces in the region, including troops under the command of Diêm loyalist General Huỳnh Văn Cao. Still believing Đình to be on their side, Diêm and Nhu allowed the general to deploy troops throughout Sài Gòn near key government installations such as the radio station, presidential palace, and police headquarters.

When the coup began on the morning of 1 November, Diêm repeatedly attempted to call Đình but could not get an answer. In a final test of loyalty for Đình by the conspiring generals, Đình was allowed to speak with Diêm while many of the plotters listened to his words. Đình won their confidence when he proceeded to shout obscenities at Diêm, telling him that he was finished.

Following the coup on 4 November Prime Minister Nguyên Ngoc Thơ appointed Đình minister of interior. A few months later, on 29 January 1964 during a coup led by General Nguyên Khánh, Đình was placed under arrest with several other figures for allegedly plotting to negotiate a peace settlement with Hà Nôi.

With the rise of General Nguyên Cao Kỳ, Đình again took command of an ARVN corps. On 10 April 1966 during the Buddhist uprising, Kỳ appointed Đình as I Corps commander to replace the rebellious general Nguyên Chánh Thi. Đình, however, lost favor when he expressed his resentment at Kỳ's tactics in crushing the Buddhist movement. In the summer of 1966 he lost command of his corps. Đình was elected to the RVN Senate in 1967 and served there until April 1975, when he left Vietnam. He now lives in Virginia and is engaged in writing his memoirs.

—Michael R. Nichols

References: Duncanson, Dennis J. *Government and Revolution in Vietnam.* New York: Oxford University Press, 1968.
Karnow, Stanley. *Vietnam: A History.* Rev. ed. New York: Penguin Books, 1991.
Olson, James, ed. *Dictionary of the Vietnam War.* New York: Peter Bedrick Books, 1987.
Smith, R. B. *An International History of the Vietnam War.* 3 vols. New York: St. Martin's Press, 1988.
See also: BRAVO I and BRAVO II, Operations; Huỳnh Văn Cao; Lê Quang Tung; Ngô Đình Cân; Ngô Đình Diêm; Ngô Đình Diêm, Overthrow of; Ngô Đình Nhu; Nguyên Cao Kỳ; Nguyên Chánh Thi; Nguyên Hữu Có; Nguyên Khánh; Trân Văn Đôn.

Tôn Thât Thuyêt

(1835–1913)

Influential mandarin, member of the Board of Regents, and leader of the Cân Vương (Support to the King) movement of the mid-1880s. He was responsible for the *binh biên* (military event) of the thirteenth day of the fifth month of the Ât Dâu Year (1885) at Huê against the French. Born in 1835 in Huê, Tôn Thât Thuyêt began his career as a military officer. After several years of service in the royal army throughout the country, he was called back to Huê to become minister of the armed forces, then member of the Board of Regents in 1883 on the death of Tư Đưc. Strongly patriotic and anti-French, Tôn Thât Thuyêt removed pacifists who accepted French domination, retrained the army, consolidated fortifications around the capital, and established a military base at Tân Sơ, Quang Tri Province, in anticipation of a war against the French. He also sent emissaries to neighboring countries seeking support.

Confronted by the arrogant and incompetent General Roussel de Courcy, commander in chief of French forces in North Vietnam, when he arrived at Huê, Tôn Thât Thuyêt ordered the Vietnamese army to attack the French at Mang Cá fort near the capital in the evening of the twenty-second day of the fifth month of the Ât Dâu Year (5 July 1885). This attack failed, and Tôn Thât Thuyêt fled to Tân Sơ, bringing with him young Emperor Hàm Nghi.

From Tân Sơ and on behalf of Hàm Nghi, Tôn Thât Thuyêt issued an appeal to mandarins, scholars, and the people asking them to support the monarch in his fight against the French. There was a wide response to this, beginning an anti-French movement known as the Phong Trào Cân Vương (Supporting the King Movement). In 1886 Tôn Thât Thuyêt went to China to seek assistance from the Ch'ing dynasty. He died there in 1913.

—Pham Cao Dưỡng

References: Lê Thành Khôi. *Le Viet-Nam: Histoire et Civilisation.* Paris: Editions de Minuit, 1955.

Nguyên Huyên Anh. *Viêt Nam Danh Nhân Tư Điên* (Dictionary of Viet-namese Great Men and Women). Houston: Zieleks, 1990.

Nguyên Thê Anh. *Viet Nam Dưới Thơi Pháp Đô Hô* (Viet Nam under French Domination). Sài Gòn: Lửa Thiêng, 1970.

See also: French Indo-China; Hàm Nghi; Tư Đức.

Tonkin

Northernmost of the three former French colonies that make up present-day Vietnam. Tonkin, the region surrounding the Red River and bordering on China, received its name during the reign of Vietnamese emperor Lê Lơi, who defeated and expelled the Chinese in 1427 after a 20-year occupation and established the longest-lasting dynasty in Vietnamese history. Lê Lơi established his imperial capital at the present site of Hà Nôi, which he called "Đông Kinh," from which Tonkin was derived.

After August 1883 Tonkin and An Nam were ruled by titular Vietnamese emperors under a French-imposed "protectorate." In Huê, the emperor and his mandarins continued to "rule," observed by the French "resident superior," who answered to the French governor-general in Hà Nôi.

—Arthur T. Frame

References: Buttinger, Joseph. *Vietnam: A Political History.* New York: Praeger, 1968.

Karnow, Stanley *Vietnam: A History.* New York: Penguin Books, 1984.

See also: An Nam; Cochin China; French Indo-China; Lê Dynasty; Lê Lơi (Lê Thái Tô); Minh Mang; Nguyên Phúc Ánh (Gia Long); Vietnam: Prehistory to 938; Vietnam: From 938 through the French Conquest.

Tonkin Gulf Incidents

(1964)

Major event in the history of U.S. involvement in Vietnam that prompted the Tonkin Gulf Resolution. On 31 July 1964 the U.S. Navy destroyer *Maddox* started a reconnaissance cruise off the coast of North Vietnam. The destroyer carried extra radio gear and personnel to monitor Democratic Republic of Vietnam (DRV) radio communications, but not enough of either to give the ship the capabilities of a true electronic espionage vessel.

Around the time of the cruise, the United States also scheduled an unusually intense string of covert operations (DeSoto Missions) against the North Vietnamese coast. These were carried out by relatively small vessels (mostly Norwegian-built "Nasty" boats), having Vietnamese crews but operating under American orders, based in the vicinity of Đà Năng, and were part of a program called Operation Plan 34A (OPLAN 34A). Two islands off the North Vietnamese coast were to be attacked on the night of 30–31 July; two points on the North Vietnamese mainland were to be shelled on the night of 3–4 August; one island was to be shelled, and the crew of one fishing boat was to be seized and taken south for interrogation, on 5 August. One of the *Maddox*'s main missions was to learn about North Vietnamese coastal defenses, and it was apparently believed that more would be learned if those defenses were in an aroused state during the patrol.

On the evening of 1 August the *Maddox* approached within gun range of the island of Hòn Me (one of the two islands shelled by OPLAN 34A vessels on the night of 30–31 July) and the coastal defense forces became more aroused than the Americans had planned. On the afternoon of 2 August three DRV torpedo boats came out from the island and attacked the destroyer. The attack was unsuccessful, and the torpedo boats suffered varying degrees of damage and crew casualties from the *Maddox*'s guns and from strafing by four U.S. Navy aircraft from the carrier *Ticonderoga,* which reached the scene as the torpedo boats were retreating from the attack. The American belief that they actually sank one of the torpedo boats was mistaken, as was the Vietnamese belief that they had shot down one of the planes. President Lyndon Johnson was annoyed that the torpedo boats had not all been sunk but he decided not to order any further retaliation, partly because he had reason to believe that the attack had been a result of confusion in the North Vietnamese chain of command rather than a deliberate decision by the government in Hà Nôi.

On 3 August the *Maddox* and another destroyer, the *C. Turner Joy,* went back into the Gulf of Tonkin to resume the patrol, operating under orders more cautious than those with which *Maddox* had gone into the Gulf on 31 July. The new orders kept the destroyers farther from the North Vietnamese coast and completely out of the extreme northern section of the Gulf. These limitations seriously reduced the ability of the destroyers to collect useful information.

Many sailors on the destroyers, including the patrol commander, Capt. John Herrick, thought that another attack by North Vietnamese torpedo boats was likely. For about two hours on the night of 4 August, such an attack seemed to be in progress, but the situation was very confused; the *C. Turner Joy* was firing at objects on the radar screens that were invisible to the *Maddox*'s radar, while the *Maddox*'s sonar equipment was picking up sounds interpreted as the motors of DRV torpedoes, which could not be heard by the sonar equipment on the *C. Turner Joy.* Those who were aboard the destroyers that night are still divided on the issue; some think that they were attacked by torpedo boats, while others think that what appeared on their radar screens was nothing but weather-generated anomalies, seagulls, foam on the crests of waves, or other natural disturbances. The overall weight of the evidence is with those who deny that an attack occurred.

In Washington, after some initial uncertainty, it was decided that there had been a genuine attack. Intercepted North Vietnamese radio messages seemed to provide the clinching evidence. The texts of the messages have never been released; it seems likely that they were in fact descriptions of the combat between *Maddox* and the three torpedo boats on 2 August, being misinterpreted by the Americans as references to a more recent event.

President Johnson, believing that an attack had occurred, ordered retaliatory air strikes (Operation PIERCE ARROW), which were carried out on the afternoon of 5 August. He also asked for and quickly obtained a congressional resolution (the Tonkin Gulf Resolution), passed almost unanimously, authorizing him to do whatever was necessary to deal with Communist aggression in Vietnam. The Tonkin Gulf incidents were politically very profitable for President Johnson in the short run; public opinion polls showed not just overwhelming approval of the way he had handled the crisis but a dramatic improvement in the public's rating of his handling of the Vietnam War as a whole. In the long run, however, the cost to the president's credibility was considerable. It became plain that Congress and the public had been misled about the administration's intentions and about the relationship between the OPLAN 34A raids and the Tonkin Gulf incidents. Eventually, many people came to doubt that there had been any attack on the night of 4 August but suspected that the report of such an attack had been a deliberate lie rather than the honest mistake it had been.

—Edwin E. Moise

Reference: Moise, Edwin E. *Tonkin Gulf and the Escalation of the Vietnam War.* Chapel Hill, NC: University of North Carolina Press, 1996.
See also: DeSoto Missions; ELINT (Electronic Intelligence); Johnson, Lyndon Baines; Operation Plan 34A (OPLAN 34A); PIERCE ARROW, Operation; Stockdale, James B.; Tonkin Gulf Resolution.

Tonkin Gulf Resolution

(1964)

Congressional resolution passed in response to the Tonkin Gulf incidents. During 1964 senior Johnson administration officials became increasingly convinced that an acceptable conclusion of the war in South Vietnam would require some form of armed attack on North Vietnam and began to consider obtaining a congressional resolution that endorsed U.S. military action. President Lyndon Johnson, wary of the prospect of a major war in Vietnam, was especially determined not to get into such a war without a prior commitment of congressional support. As he put it, "I'm gonna getem on the takeoff so they'll be with me on the landing."

In May and June 1964 senior administration officials produced drafts of a possible resolution. They decided not to present these to Congress, however; there seemed too little chance of such a resolution being passed without a politically damaging debate.

In early August it was reported that North Vietnamese torpedo boats had twice attacked U.S. Navy destroyers on the high seas (the Tonkin Gulf incidents): on the afternoon of the 2d and on the evening of the 4th. A revised draft of the resolution was quickly presented to the Congress. The crucial passages read:

Whereas naval units of the Communist regime in Vietnam, in violation of the principles of the Charter of the United Nations and of international law, have deliberately and repeatedly attacked United States naval vessels lawfully present in international waters, and have thereby created a serious threat to international peace; and

Whereas these attacks are part of a deliberate and systematic campaign of aggression that the Communist regime in Vietnam has been waging against its neighbors and the nations joined with them in the collective defense of their freedom. . . .

Congress approves and supports the determination of the President, as Commander in Chief, to take all necessary

measures to repel any armed attack against the forces of the United States and to prevent further aggression.

. . . the United States is, therefore, prepared, as the President determines, to take all necessary steps, including the use of armed force, to assist any member or protocol state of the Southeast Asia Collective Defense Treaty requesting assistance in defense of its freedom.

The members of Congress were given the impression that the heart of the resolution, the aspect they should consider voting for or against, was the passage about supporting the president in repelling armed attacks on U.S. forces. They were told that they should not worry about the implications of the next paragraph that authorized the president to do whatever he felt necessary to assist South Vietnam, since the administration had no intention of escalating American involvement in the war. Most accepted these assurances and the resolution passed on 7 August, unanimously in the House of Representatives and with only two dissenting votes, by Ernest Gruening (D-Alaska) and Wayne Morse (D-Oregon), in the Senate.

After Johnson had sent U.S. combat forces to Vietnam and cited the Tonkin Gulf Resolution as his authority, many who had voted for the resolution regretted their action, and some began to investigate the circumstances. They found that the first attack (on 2 August 1964) had not been so clearly unprovoked as they had been told; that there was reason to doubt that the second attack (on 4 August) had ever happened; and that the administration had been working on preliminary drafts of such a resolution, which it wanted precisely because it was considering an escalation of the war long before the incidents had arisen. By 1968 the resulting disillusionment had become a serious liability for the administration.

When Senator Morse first proposed in 1966 that Congress repeal the Tonkin Gulf Resolution, there was hardly any support. Sentiment gradually shifted, however, and the Resolution was finally repealed by a vote in both houses of Congress at the end of 1970.

—Edwin E. Moise

Reference: Moise, Edwin E. *Tonkin Gulf and the Escalation of the Vietnam War.* Chapel Hill, NC: University of North Carolina Press, 1996.
See also: Gruening, Ernest Henry; Johnson, Lyndon Baines; Morse, Wayne Lyman; Tonkin Gulf Incidents.

Trần Bửu Kiêm

(1921–)

Southern Vietnamese revolutionary; foreign relations specialist for the National Front for the Liberation of South Vietnam (NFLSV). Born in 1921 in Cân Thơ, Trần Bửu Kiêm attended the school of law at Hà Nôi University and was active in the August Revolution (1945). From 1946 to 1949 he served as the secretary general of the Administrative and Resistance Committee for the Nam Bô region (southern Vietnam) and as the president of the South Vietnam Students' Union for Liberation. In 1962 he joined the NFLSV and was elected to its Central Committee. From 1963 until late in 1964 Kiêm served as the Front's secretary general. In 1964 he replaced Nguyên Văn Hiêu as the NFLSV's chairman of the Commission for Foreign Relations and resigned his position as secretary general.

As the NFLSV's chief diplomat, Kiêm promoted the Front's neutralization plan to nonaligned nations and Western Europe. He called for the creation of a coalition government in South Vietnam with a neutral foreign policy. Kiêm and the NFLSV's international strategists understood that the United States would reject such a plan but realized its propaganda value. True to predictions, policy-makers in Washington quickly condemned such a scheme, claiming that it was tantamount to surrender to the Communists. Other world leaders, such as President Charles de Gaulle of France and Prince Norodom Sihanouk of Cambodia, disagreed and urged the Johnson administration to consider neutralization as a possible solution to the Southeast Asian crisis. It now seems clear that Kiêm's success hampered the ability of the United States to build a coalition of supportive or at least sympathetic allies.

When the peace talks opened in Paris in 1968, Kiêm joined Madame Nguyên Thi Bình as the NFLSV's representatives. According to some Vietnamese sources, while in Paris Kiêm had a confrontation with a senior-level official and was called home to undergo self-criticism. Kiêm later returned to Paris under the aegis of the Provisional Revolutionary Government of South Vietnam (PRG), but it was clear that he had lost considerable power and prestige. In 1974 he accepted the position of PRG minister to the president's office, and later he was a member of the new National Assembly of the Socialist Republic of Vietnam. By 1977 Kiêm's political activity was confined to membership in the Fatherland Front.

—Robert K. Brigham

References: Herring, George C., ed. *The Secret Diplomacy of the Vietnam War: The Negotiating Volumes of the Pentagon Papers.* Austin, TX: University of Texas Press, 1983.
Personalities of the South Vietnam Liberation Movement. Tran Phu, Vietnam: Foreign Relations Commission of the South Vietnam National Front for Liberation, 1965.
Pike, Douglas. *Viet Cong: The Organization and Techniques of the National Liberation Front of South Vietnam.* Cambridge, MA: Massachusetts Institute of Technology Press, 1966.
Trường Như Tang. *A Viet Cong Memoir: An Inside Account of the Vietnam War and Its Aftermath.* New York: Vintage Books, 1985.
See also: National Front for the Liberation of South Vietnam (NFLSV); Nguyên Thi Bình; Nguyên Văn Thiêu; Paris Negotiations; Paris Peace Accords; Provisional Revolutionary Government of South Vietnam (PRG).

Trân Đô
(1923–)

Commander of Viêt Công (VC) forces in South Vietnam and prominent Vietnamese Communist Party (VCP) official. Born in 1923 in Thái Bình Province in the Red River Delta, Trân Đô's real name is Ta Ngoc Phách. Đô joined the Revolutionary Youth Movement at age 18 and later joined the Vietnamese Communist Party. Soon he was arrested by the French and held in Hoa Lò prison, later known as the "Hà Nôi Hilton." He was then sent to the notorious Sơn La Prison, in a remote mountainous area northeast of Hà

Nôi near the Laos border. There Đô met, and was trained by, Nguyên Lương Bằng, a Communist leader who later became vice-president of the Democratic Republic of Vietnam (DRV) and the reunited Socialist Republic of Vietnam (SRV). Đô escaped from Sơn La Prison in 1944.

Once out of prison, Đô rejoined the party and worked in a special task force to protect party leaders in 1945. In 1946 Đô joined the army and in 1952 became the political commissar of Division 312, commanded by General Lê Trong Tân, who later was chief of staff of the People's Army of Vietnam (PAVN). Đô also reportedly served as political commissar of the Right Bank Military Region (Nam Đinh Province) in the North. From 1945 to 1955 Đô held high party and military posts in the Viêt Minh. He also played an important part in the Battle of Điên Biên Phu. In 1958 Đô was a major general of the PAVN. He was one of the high-ranking officers to be elected an alternate member of the VCP Central Committee in September 1960.

Đô was sent south at the beginning of the Vietnam War. In 1963 he was identified as a member of the Military Committee, and head of the Political Department of the Central Office for South Vietnam (COSVN), the office through which Hà Nôi controlled and directed all military and political activities under the name of the National Front for the Liberation of South Vietnam (NFLSV) and its military arm, the People's Liberation Armed Forces (PLAF). Đô was one of five deputy commanders of the PLAF during the war.

Đô was believed to be one of the DRV's principal field commanders in the South in charge of political affairs in a triumvirate with Generals Nguyên Chí Thanh and Trân Văn Trà. Đô wrote a number of important articles and drafted COSVN directives under the pseudonym of Chín Vinh. During his years in the South, he lived with his fellow soldiers in jungle camps and underground bunkers, constantly confusing and evading American forces. Although many South Vietnamese resented the leadership of northerners in the South, Đô was a capable leader who prevented factionalism from disrupting the VC war effort.

Đô also helped plan and execute the Têt Offensive in January 1968. Although the attacks resulted in tens of thousands of casualties for the VC and North Vietnamese, he admitted later that the results worked in their favor. He stated that "In all honesty, we didn't achieve our main objective. . . . As for making an impact in the United States, it had not been our intention—but it turned out to be a fortunate result." During the Offensive there were rumors about Đô's death, but intelligence sources confirmed that Đô had been only slightly wounded in a February 1968 B-52 strike.

In December 1976 Đô was elected a member of the VCP Central Committee and a National Assembly deputy. In the 1980s he was named chairman of the National Assembly's Committee of Cultural and Educational Affairs. Đô was also once identified as vice-minister of Culture and Information. In 1987 he was elected vice-chairman of the National Assembly and vice-chairman of the State Council (equivalent to vice-president) of the SRV.

Reportedly, Đô's demands for reform in the midst of the collapse of the USSR and the end of communism in Eastern Europe led in 1991 to his removal from all party and government posts.

He is now under close surveillance, especially as he had written several petitions for political reforms and democracy in Vietnam.

—Michael R. Nichols and Ngô N. Trung

References: Biographical Files, Indo-China Archives, University of California at Berkeley.

Davidson, Phillip B. *Vietnam at War, the History: 1946–1975.* Novato, CA: Presidio Press, 1988.

Karnow, Stanley. *Vietnam: A History.* Rev. ed. New York: Penguin Books, 1991.

Olson, James S., ed. *Dictionary of the Vietnam War.* New York: Peter Bedrick Books, 1987.

Smith, R. B. *An International History of the Vietnam War.* London: Macmillan, 1983.

See also: COSVN (Central Office for South Vietnam or Trung Ửơng Cuc Miên Nam); Hà Nôi Hilton (Hoa Lò Prison); National Front for the Liberation of South Vietnam (NFLSV); Nguyên Chí Thanh; Nguyên Lửơng Băng; Têt Offensive: Overall Strategy; Têt Offensive: The Sài Gòn Circle; Trân Văn Trà; Vietnam, Socialist Republic of: 1975 to the Present; Vietnamese Communist Party (VCP).

Trân Hửng Đạo

(1228–1300)

Trân dynasty (1225–1400) prince and general. Also known as Hửng Đạo Vửơng, Trân Quôc Tuân, or Đửc Thánh Trân, Trân Hửng Đạo was born in 1228. He is credited with having twice defeated a Mongol army in the second half of the thirteenth century. His first victory took place in 1285, two years after a huge army of 500,000 Mongols led by Thoát Hoan (Toghan), a son of Hôt Tât Liêt (Kublai Khan), invaded and occupied a major part of the country, including Thăng Long, the capital. Two years later, in 1287, Thoát Hoan returned with 200,000 men. At first, the Mongols were successful in regaining control of the northern part of the country and the Trân army had to withdraw to Thanh Hóa in the South. After a series of victories at Hàm Tử (Hửng Yên Province) and Chửơng Dửơng, the Trân recaptured the capital and then crushed the Mongols in a battle at the Bach Đăng River. Thoát Hoan escaped to China by hiding himself in a bronze tube.

Trân Hửng Đạo has been considered the most important hero in Vietnamese history. In addition to his great military achievement, his famous answer to King Trân Nhân Tông is familiar to every Vietnamese. When the king asked whether it would be a good idea to surrender to prevent the people's suffering, Trân Hửng Đạo replied, "Your Majesty, if you want to surrender, please have my head cut off first." His *Hich Tửơng Sĩ* (Proclamation to Generals and Officers) is regarded as a classic work in Vietnamese thirteenth-century literature, as is his *Binh Thử Yêu Lửơc* (Essentials of Military Art). Following his death in 1300, temples were built in his honor at Kiêp Bac and in many other places throughout the country, where he has been honored and even worshipped as a Thánh (saint) and respectfully referred to as Đửc Thánh Trân. Before 1975 the Republic of Vietnam Navy selected him as its patron saint.

—Pham Cao Dửơng

References: Hà Văn Tân and Pham Thi Tâm. *Cuôc Kháng Chiên Chông Xâm Lửơc Nguyên Mông Thê Ky XIII.* Hà Nôi: Nhà Xuât Ban Khoa Hoc Xã Hôi, 1972.

Lê Thành Khôi. *Histoire du Viet-Nam des Origines à 1858.* Paris: Sud-estasie, 1981.

Nguyên Huyên Anh. *Viêt Nam Danh Nhân Tử Điên* (Dictionary of Vietnamese Great Men and Women). Houston: Zieleks, 1990.

Tran Trong Kim. *Viêt Nam Sử Lửơc* (A Short History of Viet Nam). Sài Gòn: Bô Giáo Duc, Trung Tâm Hoc Liêu, 1971.

See also: Vietnam: From 938 through the French Conquest.

TRÂN HửNG ĐAO I and II, Operations

See SEALORDS (South East Asia Lake Ocean River Delta Strategy).

Trân Kim Tuyên

(?–1995)

Head of the Republic of Vietnam (RVN) Office of Political and Social Studies and one of many officers to plot against President Ngô Đình Diêm. Born in the late 1910s, Trân Kim Tuyên attended medical school and practiced medicine in Hà Nôi. A staunch Catholic, he helped Ngô Đình Nhu find refuge when he was hunted by the Communists. In 1954 Tuyên fled to the South as part of the relocation provided for in the Geneva Accords. Ngô Đình Nhu then appointed him to direct the secret police. Tuyên also headed the Office of Political and Social Studies, a Central Intelligence Agency (CIA)-assisted organization that kept track of dissenters. He also organized an infiltration network into the North. Although physically unimposing, he was one of the most feared figures in the RVN.

In the late 1950s Tuyên came to believe that the Diêm government was too weak and corrupt and invited a future Communist takeover. In early 1963 after Lt. Col. Vửơng Văn Đông's coup attempt failed, Tuyên decided to plan his own coup. Tuyên quietly consulted with leading military and civilian officials, as well as several senior Army of the Republic of Vietnam (ARVN) officers. Among those he consulted were young air force pilot Nguyên Cao Kỳ and Col. Pham Ngoc Thao, a clandestine Communist agent. He also filled his faction with disgruntled junior officers and many dissidents that he had blacklisted.

Hoping to begin their coup before other conspirators could act, Tuyên and Thao planned a quick movement against Diêm. CIA officer Lucien Conein learned of their plans and informed General Trân Thiên Khiêm, ARVN chief of staff. Khiêm prevented the coup and Nhu exiled Tuyên to Egypt as consul general. Tuyên traveled no farther than Hong Kong, where he continued to work against Diêm. He returned to the RVN following Diêm's 1963 assassination but played no important political role. He fled South Vietnam just before the fall of Sài Gòn in April 1975. Tuyên ran a hostel in Cambridge, England, until his death in 1995.

—Michael R. Nichols

References: Fishel, Wesley R., ed. *Vietnam: Anatomy of a Conflict.* Itasca, IL: F. E. Peacock, 1968.

FitzGerald, Frances. *Fire in the Lake: The Vietnamese and the Americans in Vietnam.* Boston: Little, Brown, 1972.

Karnow, Stanley. *Vietnam: A History.* Rev. ed. New York: Penguin Books, 1991.

Olson, James S., ed. *Dictionary of the Vietnam War.* New York: Peter Bedrick Books, 1987.

Smith, R. B. *An International History of the Vietnam War.* Vol. 2, *The Struggle for South-East Asia, 1961–65.* New York: St. Martin's Press, 1985.
See also: Conein, Lucien Emile; Ngô Đình Diêm; Ngô Đình Diêm, Overthrow of; Ngô Đình Nhu; Nguyên Cao Kỳ; Pham Ngoc Thao; Trân Thiên Khiêm.

Trân Thiên Khiêm
(1925–)
Leading Republic of Vietnam (RVN) military and political figure and one of the leaders of the coup against President Ngô Đình Diêm. Born on 15 December 1925 in Sài Gòn, Trân Thiên Khiêm graduated from Đà Lat Military Academy in 1947, joined the Vietnamese army as a young man, and quickly advanced in rank. In November 1960 he directed loyal troops who saved Diêm from an attempted revolt, during which Army of the Republic of Vietnam (ARVN) paratroopers surrounded the presidential palace. This led to his appointment as Army chief of staff and his rise to one of the most powerful figures in South Vietnamese politics. In early 1963 he halted another coup attempt, this one headed by Dr. Trân Kim Tuyên and Col. Pham Ngoc Thao.

Later in 1963 Khiêm became involved in the coup plot led by Generals Trân Văn Đôn, Lê Văn Kim, and Dương Văn Minh that resulted in the assassination of Diêm. Afterward Khiêm became military commander of the Sài Gòn region, but did not feel properly recompensed. He joined with other disgruntled officers and General Nguyên Khánh in their conspiracy against the military junta. After this coup of 30 January 1964 Khiêm became minister of defense.

After Khánh's August 1964 resignation, Khiêm sought to head the government. Unable to decide on any one figure, the Armed Forces Council compromised by creating a triumvirate of Khiêm, Khánh, and Minh to rule until a permanent government could be formed. But in October Khánh exiled both Minh and Khiêm. In October 1964 Khiêm became ambassador to the United States, and from November 1965 to May 1968 he was ambassador to the Republic of China (Taiwan).

Khiêm returned to Sài Gòn in May 1968 to become minister of the interior; he served as deputy prime minister for five months in 1969. Later that same year he became prime minister, a post he held until 1975. While acting in this political capacity, Khiêm became involved in a significant narcotics trade. The money he received from the sale of heroin was used to fund his political machines. In April 1975 as Communist forces moved into Sài Gòn he escaped South Vietnam and eventually settled in the United States.

—Michael R. Nichols

References: Bain, Chester A. *Vietnam: The Roots of Conflict.* Englewood Cliffs, NJ: Prentice-Hall, 1967.
Duncanson, Dennis J. *Government and Revolution in Vietnam.* New York: Oxford University Press, 1968.
Fishel, Wesley R., ed. *Vietnam: Anatomy of a Conflict.* Itasca, IL: F. E. Peacock, 1968.
FitzGerald, Frances. *Fire in the Lake: The Vietnamese and the Americans in Vietnam.* Boston: Little, Brown, 1972.
Karnow, Stanley. *Vietnam: A History.* Rev. ed. New York: Penguin Books, 1991.
Nguyên Khắc Viên. *Vietnam: A Long History.* Hà Nôi: The Gioi Publishers, 1993.
Olson, James S., ed. *Dictionary of the Vietnam War.* New York: Peter Bedrick Books, 1987.
Smith, R. B. *An International History of the Vietnam War.* Vol. 2, *The Struggle for South-East Asia, 1961–65.* New York: St. Martin's Press, 1985.
See also: Dương Văn Minh; Lê Văn Kim; Military Revolutionary Council; Ngô Đình Diêm; Ngô Đình Diêm, Overthrow of; Nguyên Khánh; Pham Ngoc Thao; Trân Kim Tuyên; Trân Văn Đôn.

Trân Văn Chương
(1898–1986)
Republic of Vietnam (RVN) official; ambassador to the United States, 1954–1963. Born on 2 June 1898 in Phu Lý, North Vietnam, Trân Văn Chương was from a prominent Vietnamese family. His father was Trân Văn Thông, governor of Hai Dương, and his mother was Bùi Thi Lan, sister of Bùi Quang Chiêu, who in 1923 founded the Constitutional Party. Chương was the older brother of Trân Văn Đô, once foreign minister of the Republic of Vietnam. In 1912 he married into another prominent Vietnamese family. His wife, Thân Thi Nam Trân, was the daughter of Thân Trong Huê, a high official of the royal court and by marriage a relative of the royal family.

In 1913 Chương went abroad to study in Algeria and France. He obtained his doctorate of law in France in 1922 and returned to Vietnam following graduation, although he became a naturalized French citizen in 1924. From 1925 to 1933 he practiced law in the South. He continued to practice law in northern and central Vietnam from 1933 to 1945.

Beginning in the 1930s Chương became involved in politics. In 1938 he became vice-chairman of the High Council of Economic and Financial Affairs of Indo-China. From 1941 to 1943 he was a member of the High Council of Indo-China.

Chương remained in close contact with Japanese officials during the Japanese occupation. After the 9 March 1945 coup d'état, he became minister of foreign affairs and then vice-premier in Trân Trong Kim's Japanese-installed government. The Communists arrested Chương on 21 December 1946 but later released him. He then fled to Phát Diêm, a Catholic stronghold in the North, and remained there until his return to Hà Nôi in July 1947. French authorities put Chương under house arrest at Hòn Gai City in Quang Ninh Province before allowing him to live in Đà Lat in the Central Highlands. In 1949 they allowed Chương to go to France, where he lived until becoming a cabinet minister in the first government of Ngô Đình Diêm in July 1954. Chương was then ambassador to the United States until he resigned in August 1963 to protest RVN government oppression of the Buddhist movement.

Chương died in July 1986 in Washington D.C., killed by his only son, Trân Văn Khiêm. Chương was the father of two daughters, one of whom was Trân Thi Lê Xuân, who became Madame Ngô Đình Nhu, wife of the younger brother of Ngô Đình Diêm.

—Ngô N. Trung

Reference: Biographical Files, Indo-China Archives, University of California at Berkeley.

See also: Ngô Đình Diêm; Ngô Đình Nhu; Ngô Đình Nhu, Madame (Trân Lê Xuân).

Trân Văn Đô
(1904–)

Prominent Republic of Vietnam (RVN) political leader; first foreign minister in the Ngô Đình Diêm government. Born on 15 November 1904 in Phu Lý in northern Vietnam into a prominent family, Trân Văn Đô was the younger brother of Trân Văn Chưởng, father of Madame Ngô Đình Nhu. Đô later married a daughter of Lưu Văn Lang, a prominent southerner. He studied at Lycée Albert Sarraut in Hà Nôi, then at the University of Hà Nôi School of Medicine.

From 1928 Đô studied in France, where he graduated as a doctor of medicine in 1931. He then returned to Vietnam and practiced medicine, first in Sài Gòn and then in Gò Công Province. He also wrote for the newspaper *Đông Nai*. During the Japanese occupation he was for a brief time in 1945 director of the Health Department of the Southern Region. Đô also participated in social relief activities after August 1945.

In 1949 Đô founded a newspaper, *Tinh Thân,* to support Ngô Đình Diêm. In 1951 he refused to become minister of health in Trân Văn Hửu's administration, despite the advice of U.S. Ambassador Donald Heath. In July 1951 Đô enlisted in the Army of the State of Vietnam with the rank of major and was appointed deputy commander of Military Medical Corps. Promoted to lieutenant colonel the next year, he commanded the Military Medical Corps.

In 1953 Đô joined the Công Nông Chánh Đang (Political Party of Workers and Peasants), predecessor of Cân Lao Nhân Vi Cách Mang Đang (Revolutionary Personalist Labor Party), which included core members of the Esprit Group formed by Ngô Đình Nhu to support his brother, Ngô Đình Diêm. Promoted to full colonel, Đô continued to serve as a military medical doctor until July 1954, when he became minister of foreign affairs in the first government of Ngô Đình Diêm. In this capacity he was the representative of the State of Vietnam at the 1954 Geneva Conference.

In 1955 Đô was ousted from the Cân Lao Nhân Vi Cách Mang Đang ruling party, accused of supporting the Bình Xuyên. He was one of 18 prominent leaders who held a news conference at the Caravelle Hotel in Sài Gòn on 26 April 1960, calling on President Diêm to carry out political reforms. Đô served as a vice-premier in the 1965 Phan Huy Quát government and as minister of foreign affairs in the cabinet of Premier Nguyên Văn Lôc from 1967 to 1968. After the collapse of the RVN in April 1975 Đô took refuge in Paris.

—Ngô N. Trung

Reference: Biographical Files, Indo-China Archives, University of California at Berkeley.
See also: BRAVO I and BRAVO II, Operations; Heath, Donald R.; Ngô Đình Diêm; Ngô Đình Diêm, Overthrow of; Ngô Đình Nhu; Ngô Đình Nhu, Madame (Trân Lê Xuân); Phan Huy Quát.

Trân Văn Đôn
(1917–)

Army of the Republic of Vietnam (ARVN) general; one of the key participants in the 1963 overthrow of President Ngô Đình Diêm. Trân Văn Đôn was born in Bordeaux, France, in 1917 while his father was attending medical school. Đôn became a French army officer during World War II, after which he returned to Vietnam and rose through the ranks of the French-sponsored Vietnamese forces. He initially supported Diêm, but corruption and other shortcomings within the Diêm government turned him against the regime. In July 1963 Đôn began discussing with other disillusioned army leaders the possibility of a coup.

Đôn, the ARVN chief of staff, and his deputy, General Lê Văn Kim, met with Central Intelligence Agency (CIA) representatives on 23 August 1963. Đôn and Kim made it clear that the Kennedy administration must realize that Diêm, his brother Nhu, and Nhu's wife should be removed, an act they were prepared to undertake if supported by Washington. This message was passed on to Ambassador Henry Cabot Lodge, who forwarded the information to Washington. Đôn and other generals proposed to Diêm that he declare martial law to strengthen the military in its fight against the Viêt Công. Their real purpose was to strengthen their own position for a coup. Self-immolations by Buddhist monks beginning in June of 1963 were a problem for Diêm and he agreed to declare martial law in the hopes that he could use it to crack down on the Buddhists with the army taking the blame. This action, however, forced the Kennedy administration to take a stand against Diêm.

After the 1 November 1963 coup, Đôn continued to serve in the army until he was forced to retire in 1965. Two years later he was elected to the Senate and remained an influential figure in South Vietnam. The day before the fall of Sài Gòn in April 1975, he arranged to leave the country for the United States.

—Charlotte A. Power

References: Olson, James S., ed. *Dictionary of the Vietnam War.* New York: Peter Bedrick Books, 1987.
Post, Ken. *Revolution, Socialism, and Nationalism in Vietnam.* Vol. 4, *The Failure of Counter-Insurgency in the South.* Belmont, CA: Wadsworth, 1990.
See also: Conein, Lucien Emile; Lê Văn Kim; Lodge, Henry Cabot, Jr.; Ngô Đình Diêm; Ngô Đình Diêm, Overthrow of; Ngô Đình Nhu; Ngô Đình Nhu, Madame (Trân Lê Xuân).

Trân Văn Giàu
(1911–)

Vietnamese Communist intellectual. Considered by many the leading Stalinist within the Vietnamese revolutionary movement, Giàu was born in 1911 at Ta Nam in South Vietnam. Giàu founded several southern front organizations for the party and oversaw the successful merger between the National United Front and the Viêt Minh in 1945. In 1946 Giàu and several other Stalinists were made to go through *kiêm thao* (self-criticism) for their excesses after the August Revolution. Giàu lost much of his political power but became a very influential historian of the modern revolution, publishing several important books. He often wrote under the pseudonym Tâm Vu, as he did in his most important essay, "People's War against Special War," in which he outlined the village and district-level struggles that undermined the will to fight within the Army of the Republic of Vietnam (ARVN). In 1996 he was living in Hô Chí Minh City.

—Robert K. Brigham

References: Huỳnh Kim Khánh. *Vietnamese Communism, 1925–1945.* Ithaca, NY: Cornell University Press, 1982.
Marr, David G. *Vietnam: World Bibliographical Series.* Oxford, UK: Clio Press, 1992.
_____. *Vietnamese Tradition on Trial, 1920–1945.* Berkeley, CA: University of California Press, 1981.
Pike, Douglas. *Viet Cong: The Organization and Techniques of the National Liberation Front of South Vietnam.* Cambridge, MA: Massachusetts Institute of Technology Press, 1966.
Tâm Vu (Trân Văn Giàu). "People's War against Special War." *Vietnamese Studies,* no. 11 (1967).
See also: National Front for the Liberation of South Vietnam (NFLSV); Viêt Minh (Viêt Nam Đôc Lâp Đông Minh Hôi [Vietnam Independence League]); Vietnam, Republic of: Army (ARVN).

Trân Văn Hai

(1925–1975)

Army of the Republic of Vietnam (ARVN) brigadier general. Born in Phong Dinh province (Cân Thơ) in 1925, Trân Văn Hai graduated from the Đà Lat Military Academy in 1951. He was widely known as incorruptible, outspoken, and a brave officer. During the 1968 Têt Offensive Hai commanded the Ranger Branch Command and supervised the raid to clear the Communist force that had infiltrated into the Chơ Lơn business district. He was then assigned to the post of national police chief. In 1970 Hai commanded Special Tactical Area 44. He then took command of the 7th Infantry Division at Đông Tâm, near My Tho.

At midnight on 30 April 1975 Hai committed suicide at division headquarters at Đông Tâm.

—Nguyên Công Luân (Lư Tuân)

Reference: Hà Mai Viêt. "Famous Generals of the Republic of Viêt Nam Armed Forces" (in Vietnamese). Unpublished manuscript.

Trân Văn Hương

(1903–mid 1980s)

Born on 1 December 1903, Trân Văn Hương was educated at Harvard University. He was a schoolteacher before he joined the Viêt Minh resistance movement against the French. Hương served as mayor of Sài Gòn in 1954 and again in 1964. He became Republic of Vietnam (RVN) prime minister in a civilian government orchestrated by General Nguyên Khánh. Hương, whose reputation was based on his opposition to Ngô Đình Diêm, was in his early sixties when Khánh appointed him prime minister. Khánh seems to have chosen him because he was part of the "old guard."

During Hương's first three months as prime minister, Buddhists and other political factions staged protest demonstrations. Hương did not rely on either the Buddhists or the Catholics when making political appointments but drove both into opposition and delivered himself to the military council, the strongest faction that did not want a civilian government.

The younger officers in Army of the Republic of Vietnam (ARVN) (commonly referred to as "Young Turks") wanted the old guard forcibly retired. Although Hương was part of this group he was left alone when on 20 December 1964 the other leaders were rounded up and held at Kontum. He managed to retain his post until 27 January 1965, when the military deposed him and returned Khánh to power.

After the 1968 Têt Offensive, President Nguyên Văn Thiêu appointed Hương prime minister again, a post he held until 1969. In 1971 Hương became vice-president of South Vietnam; he remained in that position until 21 April 1975 when Thiêu resigned. By this time Hương was 72 and feeble. He attempted to negotiate a settlement of war, and on April 28 he transferred authority to General Dưởng Văn Minh, on the eve of the North Vietnamese victory. He chose to stay in Vietnam when people were fleeing the country before the collapse of the RVN. Hương was widely respected by Vietnamese because he was both outspoken and incorruptible. Partly for that reason the Communist leadership left him alone, even though he adamantly refused to meet with them to the time of his death in the mid-1980s.

—Charlotte A. Power

References: Karnow, Stanley. *Vietnam: A History.* New York: Viking Press, 1983.
Moss, George Donelson. *Vietnam: An American Ordeal.* Englewood Cliffs, NJ: Prentice-Hall, 1990.
Post, Ken. *Revolution, Socialism, and Nationalism in Vietnam.* Vol. 4, *The Failure of Counter-Insurgency in the South.* Belmont, CA: Wadsworth, 1990.
See also: Dưởng Văn Minh; Ngô Đình Diêm; Nguyên Khánh; Nguyên Văn Thiêu; Viêt Minh (Viêt Nam Đôc Lâp Đông Minh Hôi [Vietnam Independence League]).

Trân Văn Lăm

(1913–)

Prominent Republic of Vietnam (RVN) political figure and foreign minister, 1969–1973. Born on 30 July 1913 in Sài Gòn, Trân Văn Lăm studied at Petrus Ký High School in Sài Gòn from 1927 to 1934. In 1935 he went to Hà Nôi to pursue higher education at the School of Medicine and Pharmacy, from which he received a degree in pharmacy in 1939.

A prominent Catholic, in 1952 Lăm became a member of the Sài Gòn City Supervisory Council. A year later he was appointed president of the Third District Administrative Council. In 1954 he became southern commissioner of the State of Vietnam government. In 1956 he was elected a deputy to, and served as the president of, the National Constituent Assembly.

Lăm continued as president of the first RVN National Assembly from 1957 to 1958 and was the leader of the majority block in the Assembly from 1959 to 1961, when he was chosen a judge of the Supreme Court and of the Constitutional Court. From 1961 to 1963 he was RVN ambassador to Australia. In 1967 he was elected to the RVN Senate, one of two houses in the National Assembly.

In September 1969 Lăm became minister of foreign affairs. He was one of the four signatories of the 1973 Paris peace accords that ended U.S. involvement in the Vietnam War. Reelected to the Senate in 1973, Lăm was elected its president until the Communist takeover in April 1975, when he emigrated to Australia. He remains a prominent commentator on Vietnamese affairs.

—Ngô N. Trung

Reference: Biographical Files, Indo-China Archives, University of California at Berkeley.
See also: Paris Peace Accords; Vietnam, Republic of: 1954–1975.

Trân Văn Trà
(1918–1996)

People's Army of Vietnam (PAVN) general; chairman, Military Affairs Committee of the Central Office of South Vietnam (COSVN) (1964–1976); minister of defense, Provisional Revolutionary Government of South Vietnam (PRG) (1969–1976). Trân Văn Trà was born to middle-class parents in 1918 in Quang Ngãi, a coastal province in south-central Vietnam. He received an elementary education and later became a railroad worker, but he quit his job to join the Viêt Minh resistance during World War II. He quickly became a senior officer in the South and led a 200-man guerrilla band near the Laotian border.

In 1954 Trà became deputy chief of staff to Defense Minister Võ Nguyên Giáp. He spent the next nine years in the North and studying in the Soviet Union and China. He also became an alternate member of the Central Committee of the Lao Đông (Communist) Party. In 1963, under the alias Anh Thư, he took command of a Viêt Công (VC) cadre group in the Mekong Delta. He also used the aliases Tư Chi and Trân Nam Trung (loyal to the South).

In 1964 General Trà became chair of the Military Affairs Committee, Central Office of South Vietnam, a position he held until 1976. He commanded the VC attack on Sài Gòn during the Têt Offensive in 1968. From 1969 to 1976 he was Minister of Defense for the Provisional Revolutionary Government of South Vietnam.

In March 1973 Trà returned to Hà Nôi to plan the final attack on South Vietnam. Between 1973 and 1975 Trà's task was facilitated by growing economic woes in the South, increasing morale problems among the Army of the Republic of Vietnam (ARVN), and waning U.S. support exacerbated by the April 1974 resignation of President Nixon.

Despite disagreement with other Communist leaders such as Lê Đức Tho, Lê Duẩn, and Giáp, in October 1974 Trà began the final campaign. Supported by fresh supplies of Soviet weapons, the offensive moved forward with success throughout the remainder of the year. Trà planned the final assault on Sài Gòn led by General Văn Tiên Dũng and four crack PAVN divisions.

In spite of last-minute efforts by President Thiêu to enlist U.S. aid, ARVN forces crumbled in March and were in full retreat by early April. On 7 April 1975 Lê Đức Tho and Trà arrived at the battlefront to oversee the final phase of the taking of Sài Gòn. On the 21st Thiêu resigned. On 30 April General Dưởng Văn Minh surrendered and Tho and Trà arrived that afternoon to end the war.

From May 1975 to January 1976 Trà served as head of the Military Occupation Force, Sài Gòn (later Hô Chí Minh City). From 1976 to 1981 he served on the Politburo of the Vietnamese Communist Party (VCP) and in the new Socialist Republic of Vietnam as chair, Inspectorate Council of Ministers.

In 1982 Trà published his controversial five-volume work, *History of the Bulwark B2 Theatre*. In it he criticized wartime policies of the Democratic Republic of Vietnam (DRV), especially the 1968 Têt Offensive and the willingness (or, as Trà says, desire) to sacrifice Viêt Công manpower in what he believed was an ill-conceived and needless campaign. Such candor led to his ouster from the Politburo and the banning of the book in Vietnam. Even though the Vietnamese government rescinded the ban in the late 1980s and allowed Trà to participate in various conferences reappraising the Communist role in the Vietnam War, he lived under something of a "house arrest" situation. Trà, one of the "grand old men" of the revolution, was allowed to meet visiting dignitaries and veterans groups from the United States in controlled settings. After a long illness, Trà died in Sài Gòn on 20 April 1996.

—William Head

Reference: Trân Văn Trà. *History of the Bulwark B2 Theatre. Vol. 5, Concluding the 30-Year War.* Hô Chí Minh City, Vietnam: Văn Nghê Publishing House, 1982.
See also: COSVN (Central Office for South Vietnam or Trung Ưởng Cuc Miên Nam); Hô Chí Minh Campaign; Lê Duẩn; Lê Đức Tho; Têt Offensive: Overall Strategy; Têt Offensive: The Sài Gòn Circle; Vietnamese Communist Party (VCP); Võ Nguyên Giáp.

Transportation Group 559

Organization responsible for opening the supply network through Laos to South Vietnam. In May 1959 General Võ Nguyên Giáp, a reluctant convert to aggressive action in the South, ordered General Vo Bam to begin work on a secret project to move war supplies into South Vietnam through eastern Laos. Bam formed the 559th Transportation Group (work began in the fifth month of 1959). Group 759, organized that July, was to arrange resupply by sea.

Land resupply was by far the most important means of support for the insurgency in the South, however. Bam's Group 559 did its work well and soon opened a "modest track" to the South. Vastly expanded and made more sophisticated over the years, this communications network, which became known as the Hô Chí Minh Trail, was vital to Hà Nôi's military victory. Group 559 also supplied the Pathet Lao, the Communist army in Laos.

—Spencer C. Tucker

Reference: Currey, Cecil B. *Victory at Any Cost. The Genius of Viet Nam's Gen. Vo Nguyen Giap.* Washington, DC: Brassey's, 1997.
See also: Hô Chí Minh Trail; Logistics, Allied and People's Army of Vietnam/Viêt Công; Order of Battle; Võ Nguyên Giáp.

Triêu Âu
(225–248)

Also known as Bà Triêu (Lady Triêu) or Triêu Thi Trinh; leader of the revolt against Chinese rule in 248 in Cửu Chân, present Thanh Hóa Province. Bà Triêu has been considered one of the most

701

important heroines in Vietnamese history, second only to Hai Bà Trưng (Trưng Trắc and Trưng Nhi). She is also famous for her statement, "I want to ride a strong wind, push away the fierce wave with the sole of my foot, kill the whale in the East Sea, sweep up the country to save our people from hell, instead of following the step of common people to bend my back to serve men as their concubines." Together with her brother, Triêu Quốc Đat, she led a revolt in 248 against the Wu.

In battle Bà Triêu wore golden armor, sat on the head of an elephant, and fought bravely. After six months of fighting, her small army was defeated and Bà Triêu killed herself at age 23. To show respect to the heroine, King Lý Nam Đê (544–548) ordered the erection of a temple in her honor.

—Pham Cao Dương

References: Nguyên Huyên Anh. *Viêt Nam Danh Nhân Tư Điên* (Dictionary of Vietnamese Great Men and Women). Houston: Zieleks, 1990.
Pham Cao Dương. *Lich Sư Dân Tôc Viêt Nam. Quyên I: Thơi Kỳ Lâp Quôc* (History of the Vietnamese People. Vol. 1, The Making of the Nation). Fountain Valley, CA: Truyên Thông Viêt, 1987.
Taylor, Keith W. *The Birth of Vietnam.* Berkeley, CA: University of California Press, 1983.
See also: Trưng Trắc and Trưng Nhi; Vietnam: Prehistory to 938.

Triêu Đà

(258–137 B.C.)

Chao T'o, in Chinese, also known as Triêu Vũ Vương, founder of the Triêu dynasty (207–111 B.C.) and the Nam Viêt (Nan Yueh, in Chinese) Kingdom that covered the Chinese provinces of Kwang-tung and Kwang-si and the northern part of present Vietnam. Born in northern China in 258 B.C., Triêu Đà began his career as an officer in the army of Ch'in Shih Huang Ti. When the Chinese failed to pacify South China because of the resistance of the local Viêt (Yueh), he was sent to the south in 214 B.C. as a lieutenant to the governor of the district of Nan Hai in present Canton. This assignment provided opportunities for him to build up his own power. In 207 B.C. he attacked the Kingdom of Âu Lac of An Dương Vương Thuc Phán in the Red River Delta of North Vietnam and incorporated it into his Nan Hai district in 207 B.C. When Shi Huang-ti died and the Ch'in Empire disintegrated, Đà proclaimed himself king of Nam Viêt and chose for a capital Phiên Ngung (currently Canton). He died in 137 B.C. at the age of 121.

To most Vietnamese, Triêu Đà is a Viêt king because he was the founder of a southern kingdom carved within the former territory of the Viêt (Yueh) with the Viêt as the main population, completely separated from the Ch'in in the north. Later, he replaced the Thuc of the Vietnamese Kingdom of Âu Lac and continued to defend the interests of the Viêt against Empress Lư's policy of not selling iron tools and female animals to Nam Viêt in 196 B.C. This was also Emperor Gia Long's view when he initially chose Nam Viêt as the name for his new kingdom instead of Vietnam. Many others consider the two Kwang provinces as Vietnamese territory.

—Pham Cao Dương

References: Lê Thành Khôi. *Histoire du Viet-Nam des Origines à 1858.* Paris: Sudestasie, 1981.

Pham Cao Dương. *Lich Sư Dân Tôc Viêt Nam. Quyên I: Thơi Kỳ Lâp Quôc* (History of the Vietnamese People. Vol. 1, The Making of the Nation). Fountain Valley, CA: Truyên Thông Viêt, 1987.
Taylor, Keith W. *The Birth of Vietnam.* Berkeley, CA: University of California Press, 1983.
See also: Nguyên Phúc Ánh (Gia Long); Vietnam: Prehistory to 938.

Trinh Lords

Rulers of northern Vietnam (Tonkin) from 1592 to 1786. By the beginning of the sixteenth century, the later Lê dynasty (1428–1788) had fallen victim to the perpetual struggle for land and status among the families of Vietnam's imperial bureaucrats and feudal landlords. Two of these families, the closely related Nguyên and Trinh, overthrew a third, the Mac, which managed to supplant the Lê dynasty with its own imperial mandate from 1527 to 1592. After the defeat of the Mac, the Trinh restored the Lê dynasty, but only as puppet rulers, and strove to consolidate and expand their northern lands and influence at the expense of their onetime allies, the Nguyên lords. During the struggle with the Mac, the Nguyên family had developed its own power base in the South and by that war's end were masters of all of Vietnam below the 17th parallel. For the next 184 years, the Trinh intermittently fought to bring the Nguyên-held lands under their authority, but Nguyên fortifications built astride the narrow coastal plain and the resources provided by the Nguyên conquest of the Mekong Delta enabled them to withstand Trinh assaults. The Trinh succeeded in introducing some administrative and military reforms and in 1711 issued an edict intended to check the greed of provincial mandarins and landlords. The Trinh were, however, unable to halt the continuing efforts of landowners, court notables, and mandarins to seek landed wealth at the expense of the peasantry. As a result, the regime was repeatedly menaced by peasant insurgencies and eventually fell prey to the populist Tây Sơn Rebellion. Between 1786 and 1789 Tây Sơn armies defeated the Trinh, their nominal Lê overlords, and even a Chinese army, but their leaders did not govern long enough to eradicate the lust for power and economic self-interest that plagued Vietnam's traditional ruling elites. These traits persisted with fateful results for Vietnam's stability during the dynasty subsequently established by the Trinh's old rivals, the Nguyên, who had managed to survive, if only barely, the challenge of the Tây Sơn Rebellion.

—Marc Jason Gilbert

References: Buttinger, Joseph. *The Smaller Dragon: A Political History of Vietnam.* New York: Praeger, 1958.
Nguyên Khăc Viên. *Vietnam: A Long History.* Hà Nôi: Foreign Language Publishing House, 1987.
Whitfield, Danny J. *Historical and Cultural Dictionary of Vietnam.* Metuchen, NJ: Scarecrow Press, 1976.
See also: Lê Dynasty; Nguyên Dynasty; Tây Sơn Uprising.

Truman, Harry S

(1884–1972)

President of the United States (1945–1952); responsible for initiating U.S. involvement in Vietnam. Born in Lamar, Missouri, on 8 May 1884, Harry Truman served in the U.S. Army in World War I as an artillery captain. In 1923 he entered politics under the tutelage of the Kansas City Pendergast machine and served as a county judge until 1935. Truman was elected to the U.S. Senate in 1934 and served until elected vice-president in 1944. He became president upon the 12 April 1945 death of Franklin Delano Roosevelt.

In July 1945 Truman met at Potsdam with Winston Churchill (replaced during the conference by Clement Atlee) and Joseph Stalin to negotiate the map of Europe and discuss the end of the war in the Pacific. Truman and Churchill made a far-reaching determination concerning Southeast Asia. The Allied chiefs of staff divided French Indo-China along the 16th parallel for "operational purposes," allowing the Japanese to surrender to the Chinese north of that line and to the British to the south. Although Roosevelt had favored independence, postwar leaders made no provisions for Indo-Chinese self-determination and Truman ignored the question as the threat of communism in Europe began to eclipse all other concerns.

In 1946, reacting to the Communist threat in Greece and Turkey, Truman enjoined Congress to aid in preserving democracy: "The free peoples of the world look to us for support in maintaining their freedoms." Truman and U.S. policymakers articulated through the Truman and Marshall Plans George F. Kennan's "containment" doctrine. This "policy of firm containment [of Russia] . . . with unalterable counterforce at every point where the Russians show signs of encroaching," which Kennan publicly introduced in the journal *Foreign Affairs,* dominated foreign relations throughout the Cold War and was extended to Southeast Asia. Believing French collaboration to be crucial in Europe, Undersecretary of State Dean Acheson convinced Truman in March 1950 to allocate $15 million of a pending military aid bill for Western Europe to assist the French in defeating the Việt Minh. On 28 June 1946, three days after hostilities broke out in Korea and four weeks before Truman signed the aid bill, eight C-47 cargo aircraft transported to Vietnam the first of this aid, which by 1954 grew to a total of $3 billion.

Truman's decision to assist the French in Indo-China was motivated by several events: the 1949 Russian detonation of an atomic bomb, the Communist victory in China that same year, and Joseph McCarthy's ensuing attack on the administration for supposed "softness" on communism. Subsequent administrations escalated U.S. participation in Vietnam. President Lyndon Johnson, believing he had inherited from Truman, Eisenhower, and Kennedy a pledge to protect Southeast Asia from communism, later uttered these words within hours of his presidential oath following Kennedy's assassination: "I am not going to lose Vietnam. I am not going to be the President who saw Southeast Asia go the way China went."

During the war Johnson visited Truman several times seeking a public endorsement of his policies, but Truman refused to make a public statement; privately, he was disenchanted with Johnson's leadership. Truman died in Kansas City, Missouri, on 26 December 1972.

—Brenda J. Taylor

References: Anderson, David L., ed. *Shadow on the White House: Presidents and the Vietnam War, 1945–1975.* Lawrence, KS: University Press of Kansas, 1993.

McCullough, David. *Truman.* New York: Simon & Schuster, 1992.
Williams, William Appleman, ed. *America in Vietnam: A Documentary History.* Garden City, NY: Anchor Press, 1985.
See also: Acheson, Dean G.; Containment Policy; Eisenhower, Dwight David; Johnson, Lyndon Baines; Kennan, George Frost; United States: Involvement in Indo-China through 1954.

Trưng Trắc and Trưng Nhi

(?–43)

Also known as Hai Bà Trưng (The Two Ladies Trưng) or Trưng Vương or Trưng Nữ Vương (Queens Trưng); sisters and Vietnamese heroines, who led the first uprising of Vietnamese against Chinese rule in A.D. 40. Trưng Trắc and Trưng Nhi were daughters of the Lạc Tướng (Lạc Lord) of Mê Linh, in present Vĩnh Phú Province. They led a revolt after Tô Định, the greedy and inept prefect of Giao Chi, killed Trưng Trắc's husband, Thi Sách, lord of Chu Diên. This triggered a general revolt against the unpopular Hán regime. Angered by the Hán's assimilation policy and the seizing of land and power from the local nobility in favor of Hán immigrants who had just moved to Vietnam following Wang Mang's usurpation of the Hán throne (A.D. 9–23), the uprising quickly spread throughout the Chinese colonies, from Cửu Chân (now Thanh Hóa) to Hợp Phô (in present Kwang Tung Province, China). Chinese governors and colonial forces retreated to China proper. Trưng Trắc and Trưng Nhi proclaimed themselves queens, choosing Mê Linh as the capital.

After two years of intensive preparation, the Chinese counterattacked with an army commanded by Ma Viên (Ma Yuan), its most famous general at the time. Hai Bà Trưng were defeated at the Battle of Lãng Bạc and committed suicide in 43 by leaping into the Hát River.

Hai Bà Trưng are considered by many Vietnamese to be the most important and most revered heroines in Vietnam's history. Temples were erected in their honor, and the anniversary of their deaths has become Vietnamese Women's Day. Ceremonies are organized annually in their honor on the sixth day of the second month of the lunar calendar.

—Pham Cao Dương

References: Bùi Quang Tung. "Cuộc Khởi Nghĩa Hai Bà Trưng Dưới Mắt Sử Gia." (The Two Trung Ladies' Uprising in Historians' Eyes). In *Đại Học,* publication of Huế University, no. 10 (July 1959): 1–16.
Nguyên Huyên Anh. *Việt Nam Danh Nhân Tự Điên* (Dictionary of Vietnamese Great Men and Women). Houston: Zieleks, 1990.
Pham Cao Dương. *Lịch Sử Dân Tộc Việt Nam. Quyên I: Thời Kỳ Lập Quốc* (History of the Vietnamese People. Vol. 1, The Making of the Nation). Fountain Valley, CA: Truyên Thông Việt, 1987.
Taylor, Keith W. *The Birth of Vietnam.* Berkeley, CA: University of California Press, 1983.
See also: Triêu Âu; Vietnam: Prehistory through 938; Women in the War, Vietnamese.

Trường Chinh (Đăng Xuân Khu)

(1907–1988)

General secretary, Indo-Chinese Communist Party (1941–1956); Democratic Republic of Vietnam (DRV) official; general secretary,

Vietnamese Communist Party (1986). Born in Tonkin's Nam Định Province in 1907, Đặng Xuân Khu was the son of an activist teacher who soon recruited his son to the anti-French nationalist movement. Expelled from his provincial school for political agitation, Khu went to Hà Nội in 1928 to finish his secondary education at Lycée Albert Sarraut, later studying at the Hà Nội College of Commerce. After an effort at teaching, he joined Hồ Chí Minh's Việt Nam Thanh Niên Cách Mệnh Đồng Chí Hội, or Thanh Niên (Vietnam Revolutionary Youth Association), and wrote articles for several underground Communist publications. He was one of the founders, in 1930, of the Indo-Chinese Communist Party (Đặng Công San Dương) and was quickly valued for his propagandistic skills.

Seized by French authorities in 1931, he was convicted of subversion and consigned to Sơn La Prison. Upon his release in 1936 he worked enthusiastically on Communist Party activities. As a cover in late 1936 Khu began work for a Hà Nội newspaper, *Le Travail* (Work), living under the pseudonym of "Qua Ninh." Greatly impressed with Mao Zedong's activities in China, Khu had already adopted the alias Trưởng Chinh, or "Long March." In 1938 Trưởng Chinh, as Qua Ninh, in collaboration with Võ Nguyên Giáp, who wrote under the name Vân Đình, published *The Peasant Problem, 1937–1938,* arguing that a Communist revolution could be both peasant- and proletarian-based. Leftist journalist Wilfred Burchett described the book as a masterly analysis and a profound study that formed the basis for the Communist Party and later Việt Minh policies toward the peasantry.

When French authorities banned the Communist Party in 1939, Trưởng Chinh fled to safety in China. In 1940 he became head of the Indo-Chinese Communist Party's propaganda department and in May 1941 began work as the Indo-Chinese Communist Party's secretary-general.

When Hồ Chí Minh in 1941 organized the Việt Nam Độc Lập Đồng Minh Hội, or Việt Minh (Vietnam Independence League), a consortium of several different nationalist parties under Communist leadership, Trưởng Chinh became a leading member, successfully helping to portray it as nothing more than an anti-French and anti-Japanese resistance movement dedicated to the overthrow of foreign dominance in Vietnam. In 1945 he played a leading part in the August Revolution and helped draft the constitution of the Democratic Republic of Vietnam (DRV). The next year he became a member of the DRV's first National Assembly.

Trưởng Chinh served as director of Việt Minh propaganda and oversaw intelligence and counterintelligence activities during the first Indo-China War (1946–1954). In 1946 he published *The August Revolution* and, the next year, *The Resistance Will Win.* He was largely responsible for the new name adopted by northern Communists in 1951, the Lao Đông, or "Workers" Party. Within a short time Trưởng Chinh was named secretary-general of the new party and by 1953 was second only to Hồ Chí Minh in the northern hierarchy.

In his writings and speeches in the early 1950s, Trưởng Chinh dictated a strict new party cultural line that imposed severe restrictions on writing, music, and poetry. All had to promote party policies.

A longtime friend and comrade of Võ Nguyên Giáp, Trưởng Chinh became suspicious of his meteoric rise in the party hierarchy and his control of military forces. After a bitter struggle, Trưởng Chinh succeeded in having the army placed under the control of political commissars. In 1950 he ordered the execution of Trần Chí Châu, Giáp's chief of logistical services, and accused Giáp of "lack of judgment in his selection of responsible personnel" and of stumbling into "useless massacres [of soldiers in combat], which had no other purpose than to promote personal interests." Although they would vote together on later issues, the two were never again close.

About this time Trưởng Chinh fell onto hard times. Hồ Chí Minh named him vice-chairman of the Land Reform Committee in 1954 and he implemented a draconian program of agrarian reform that included large-scale dispossession and innumerable executions of "landlords," often no more than landless peasants guilty only of being disliked by their neighbors and consequently charged by them in ad hoc Land Tribunal Courts as counterrevolutionaries. Trưởng Chinh demonstrated his zeal for land reform by denouncing his own father. His attempts to impose total collectivization of agriculture based on the Communist pattern greatly diminished production and threatened famine.

Although Giáp voiced the actual charges, it was Hồ Chí Minh who dismissed Trưởng Chinh from his positions as land reform vice-chairman and as secretary-general of the Lao Đông Party. He was forced to make an official statement admitting "serious mistakes" and "left-wing deviationism" (being more orthodox than the party line required). Despite this he retained his number three position within the Politburo and remained influential within the party leadership.

His eclipse did not last long. By 1958 he was one of four vice-premiers of the DRV and the same year became chairman of the National Scientific Research Commission. He left those offices two years later to become chairman of the Standing Committee of the National Assembly, a job he held for some time. In April 1961 he became a member of the Presidium of the Fatherland Front and in August 1964 served as a member of the National Assembly delegation to Indonesia.

His influence waned by 1968, as he urged a "socialist construction" of the North, while some others (notably Lê Duân, who served as first secretary) wanted the DRV to concentrate on winning the war in the South. Trưởng Chinh insisted that "military action can only succeed when politics are correct," adding that "politics cannot be fulfilled without the success of military action." Lê Duân and his faction won the argument, thus paving the way for the 1968 Tết Offensive. Absent from view in Hà Nội from March to April 1969, Trưởng Chinh was probably in East Germany seeking medical treatment. After the 1975 fall of South Vietnam, he again rose in influence. In 1986, following the death of Lê Duân, he was again secretary-general of the Vietnamese Communist Party, a position he held from July until December, probably resigning at that point because severe economic problems in the Socialist Republic of Vietnam had eroded his political base. However, he continued to serve as an advisor to the Politburo until his accidental death in October 1988.

A dour and private man most comfortable working behind the scenes, Trương Chinh was primarily devoted to theory and party doctrine and, of all his comrades, was probably the most knowledgeable about Communist ideology.

—Cecil B. Currey

References: Pham Binh, Châu Phong, Lê Mai, Bùi Tín, Trân Công Mân, and Cao Pha, interviews with the author.
The Washington Post (18 December 1986).
"Who's Who in North Vietnam." Washington, DC: Office of External Research, U.S. Department of State, 1972.
Who's Who in the Socialist Countries. New York: Saur, 1978.
See also: Burchett, Wilfred; Hô Chí Minh; Lao Động Party; Lê Duân; Mao Zedong (Mao Tse-tung); Vietnam, Democratic Republic of: 1954–1975; Vietnam, Socialist Republic of: 1975 to the Present; Vietnamese Communist Party (VCP); Võ Nguyên Giáp.

Trương Đình Dzu

(1917–mid-1980s)

Prominent South Vietnamese politician and unsuccessful candidate for the presidency of the Republic of Vietnam (RVN). Born on 10 November 1917 into a poor family from Qui Nhơn, central Vietnam, Trương Đình Dzu became a prominent lawyer. In 1961 he declared his intention to run for the RVN presidency against incumbent President Ngô Đình Diêm, but he was pressured to withdraw when accused of illegal fund transfers out of the country.

In 1967 Dzu again ran for the presidency. His slogan of "Negotiation Now" called for negotiations to end the war. He won 17.2 percent of the vote, finishing behind the winning ticket of Nguyên Văn Thiêu and Nguyên Cao Kỳ, who garnered 35 percent. Four days after the election, Dzu and two other candidates, Phan Khắc Sửu and Hoàng Cơ Bình, held a news conference in front of the National Assembly building, charging fraud on the part of the military ticket to rig the elections. Military leaders accused Dzu of being a "pseudo-pacifist" and of illegally opening a San Francisco bank account.

In February 1967 Dzu and other leftists such as Âu Trường Thanh, Trân Thúc Linh, and Hô Thông Minh were put under police surveillance. Dzu was brought before a Special Military Court and on 26 July 1968 sentenced to five years of hard labor.

Thanks to public pressure in the RVN and from abroad, Dzu was released that December. After the April 1975 Communist victory, Dzu was sentenced to reeducation and reportedly died in the mid-1980s.

—Ngô N. Trung

Reference: Biographical Files, Indo-China Archives, University of California at Berkeley.
See also: Elections (National), Republic of Vietnam: 1955, 1967, 1971; Ngô Đình Diêm; Nguyên Cao Kỳ; Nguyên Văn Thiêu.

Trương Như Tang

(1923–)

Southern Vietnamese revolutionary and founding member of the National Front for the Liberation of South Vietnam (NFLSV);

minister of justice in the Provisional Revolutionary Government (PRG) (1969–1975). Born in Sài Gòn in 1923, Trương Như Tang received his education in pharmaceutical studies at the Grall Hospital and the University of Hà Nôi. In 1945 he earned his master's degree in political science in Paris. During the last days of the Indo-China War he served in the national navy. After the war he accepted the position of chief comptroller for the Industry and Commerce Bank of Vietnam. From this vantage point Tang was an unlikely revolutionary. However, in 1956 he joined several other prominent individuals in Sài Gòn to oppose the rule of Republic of Vietnam (RVN) President Ngô Đình Diêm. These contacts led him to the group of revolutionaries who founded the National Front for the Liberation of South Vietnam on 20 December 1960.

Despite his clandestine revolutionary activities, Tang continued to hold important positions in Sài Gòn, including director general of the National Sugar Company. During the early 1960s his secret activities were disclosed, and he spent a significant amount of time in a Sài Gòn prison. He then traded in his professional life for one of a full-time revolutionary in the jungles of Tây Ninh Province. Throughout the Vietnam War, Tang was a dedicated revolutionary, but he became disillusioned after the war as he saw the Southern revolutionaries pushed aside by their northern compatriots. He was especially bitter about the composition of the postwar national government in Hà Nôi, believing that too many important southern revolutionaries had been discarded.

Although Tang maintained that he never was a Communist, the Lao Động Party did reward him with a ministry post after the fall of Sài Gòn. By 1976, however, he was already making plans for his escape from Vietnam. He now lives in self-imposed exile in Paris.

Tang is perhaps best known in the West for his 1985 book, *A Viet Cong Memoir.* This highly controversial book retraces his life from his birth to his role in the modern Vietnamese revolution. There is considerable debate among scholars as to whether Tang, an avowed non-Communist, is representative of the NFLSV's membership and leadership.

—Robert K. Brigham

References: Dellinger, David. *Vietnam Revisited: Covert Action to Invasion to Reconstruction.* Boston: South End Press, 1986.
Pike, Douglas. *Viet Cong: The Organization and Techniques of the National Liberation Front of South Vietnam.* Cambridge, MA: Massachusetts Institute of Technology Press, 1966.
Thayer, Carlyle A. *War by Other Means: National Liberation and Revolution in Viet-Nam, 1956–1960.* Sydney: Allen & Unwin, 1989.
Trương Như Tang. *A Viet Cong Memoir: An Inside Account of the Vietnam War and Its Aftermath.* New York: Vintage Books, 1985.
See also: National Front for the Liberation of South Vietnam (NFLSV); Nguyên Hữu Tho; Nguyên Thi Bình; Provisional Revolutionary Government of South Vietnam (PRG).

Tsuchihashi Yūitsu

(ca. 1895–?)

Japanese Army lieutenant general and commander of Japanese forces in Indo-China during the critical period between December

1944 and the end of the Second World War. Born in 1895 (?), Tsuchihashi Yūitsu graduated from the Japanese Military Staff College in 1920. Fluent in French, he served concurrently as military attaché to France and Belgium between 1937 and 1940. In early 1939 Tsuchihashi went to Hà Nôi to meet with French Governor-General Jules Brevié concerning the interdiction of American supplies for the Guomindang (Nationalist) government of Jiang Jieshi (Chiang Kai-shek) in China that were routed through Indo-China. The French refused, and the next year the Japanese sent occupation troops into Indo-China.

Tsuchihashi assumed command of Japanese forces in Indo-China in December 1944. Tokyo worried that the United States would soon mount an amphibious assault on Vietnam from the Philippines and thought it best to neutralize the French first before having to deal with an American invasion. In March 1945 Tsuchihashi carried out a coup against the French administration and military forces in Indo-China. Tsuchihashi surrendered his forces north of the 16th parallel to the Chinese at Hà Nôi on 28 September 1945.

—Spencer C. Tucker

References: Marr, David G. *Vietnam 1945: The Quest for Power.* Berkeley, CA: University of California Press, 1996.

Patti, Archimedes L. A. *Why Viet Nam? Prelude to America's Albatross.* Berkeley, CA: University of California Press, 1980.

See also: French Indo-China; Japan; Mordant, Eugène; Sabattier, Gabriel.

Tư Đức

(1829–1883)

Fourth ruler of the Nguyên dynasty (1847–1883), second son of Emperor Thiêu Tri (1840–1847) and Empress Tư Dũ, and the last emperor of an independent Vietnam. His real name was Hông Nhâm; Tư Đức was his ruling name. He was born in 1829 and became emperor in 1847. He is also known as Đức Tông Anh Hoàng Đê or Vua Đức Tông. Intelligent, dedicated, and very hardworking despite poor health, this gentle scholar, poet, and monarch could have been a great emperor in Vietnamese history but for the French invasion of the country. In the year of his ascension to the throne, French warships shelled Đà Năng. Eleven years later, in 1858, using as an excuse the persecution of Catholics, the French and their Spanish allies attacked, seized this citadel, and began their invasion of Vietnam. Biên Hòa, Gia Đinh, and Đinh Tường, the three eastern provinces of South Vietnam, were lost to the French in the Treaty of 1862; then came the loss of Vĩnh Long, An Giang, and Hà Tiên, the three Western provinces, in 1867. The rest of the country became a French protectorate in 1884. At the same time Tư Đức had to face several uprisings in the North, some of which were led by Catholic followers.

Tư Đức is well known in Vietnamese history for his many efforts in culture and education. Under him, the Nha Sĩ Khoa and the Cát Sĩ Khoa were added to the traditional and regular civil service examinations. He also created two cultural institutions, the Tập Hiên Viên and the Khai Kinh Điên, to bring mandarins and scholars together to discuss with him literature, poetry, and state business. He was receptive to new ideas brought up to him by the great reformer Nguyên Trường Tô, who was sent to France in the late 1860s and early 1870s to study means of modernizing Vietnam. Unfortunately, this was too late and the plan was not supported by the conservative mandarins, who dominated the court at this time.

Tư Đức promoted the use of *Chư Nôm* (a writing system for Vietnamese that used Chinese characters with alterations) and was the author of nine collections of poetry and other writings in both Chinese characters and *Nôm*. Under his order the most comprehensive work on Vietnamese history was written by several scholars at the Quôc Sư Quán, the National Historical Institute. Tư Đức died on 19 July 1883, just before the Huê Court was to sign the Treaty of Quý Mùi (25 August 1883), accepting a French protectorate over the rest of Vietnam.

—Pham Cao Dưởng

References: Lê Hữu Muc. *Huân Dich Thâp Điêu: Thánh Du Cua Vua Thánh Tô, Diên Nghia Cua Vua Dức Tông* (Ten Moral Maxims: Imperial Teachings by Emperor Thanh To and Translated into Nom by Emperor Duc Tong). Sài Gòn: Phu Quôc Vu Khanh Đăc Trách Văn Hoa, 1971.

Lê Thành Khôi. *Le Viet-Nam: Histoire et Civilisation.* Paris: Editions de Minuit, 1955.

Nguyên Huyên Anh. *Viêt Nam Danh Nhân Tư Điên* (Dictionary of Vietnamese Great Men and Women). Houston: Zieleks, 1990.

Quôc Sư Quán. *Quôc Triêu Chánh Biên Toát Yêu* (Summary of the History of Our Current Dynasty). Sài Gòn: Nhom Nghiên Cửu Sư Đia, 1971.

Trân Trong Kim. *Viêt Nam Sư Lược* (Outline of Vietnamese History). Sài Gòn: Bô Giáo Duc, Trung Tâm Hoc Liêu, 1971.

See also: Hàm Nghi; Minh Mang; Thiêu Tri; Vietnam: From 938 through the French Conquest.

Tư Vê

Self-defense (militia) force made up of young citizens in cities to fight against the French at the beginning of the first Indo-China War (1946–1954). It was also called Tư Vê Thành (city self-defense force) or Tư Vê Chiên Đâu (self-defense combat force). The Tư Vê were neither Communists nor members of the Vietnam Independence League (Viêt Nam Đôc Lâp Dông Minh Hôi, or Viêt Minh).

During the fighting in Hà Nôi between 19 December 1946 and 17 February 1947, the Tư Vê fought very bravely, despite being poorly armed and trained. The 60 days they were able to contain the French in the capital bought the time necessary for the Vê Quôc Đoàn, the regular military force, to withdraw safely to mountainous areas and follow the Democratic Republic of Vietnam (DRV) strategy for the "preservation of its main force" *(bao toàn chu lưc)*. Part of the Hà Nôi Tư Vê force later formed two regiments: the Trung Đoàn Thu Đô (Regiment of the Capital) and the Trung Đoàn Thăng Long (Thăng Long Regiment), both of which became famous in the history of Vietnamese resistance against the French.

—Pham Cao Dưởng

References: Ban Nghiên Cửu Lich Sư Quân Đôi. *Lich Sư Quân Đôi Nhân Dân Viêt Nam, tâp I.* Hà Nôi: Nhà Xuât Ban Quân Đôi Nhân Dân, 1977.

Gras, Général Yves. *Histoire de la Guerre d'Indochine.* Paris: Plon, 1979.

Nguyên Khăc Viên. *The Long Resistance, 1858–1975.* Hà Nôi: Foreign Language Publishing House, 1975.

See also: Indo-China War; Viêt Minh (Viêt Nam Đôc Lâp Đông Minh Hôi [Vietnam Independence League]).

Tunnel Rats

Soldiers who fought the Viêt Công (VC) and People's Army of Vietnam (PAVN) in their underground tunnels and bunkers. Only the U.S. Army 1st and 25th Infantry Divisions maintained formal units of these troops, and the 1st Infantry devoted the most effort to their development and training. Even so, the units were small. The 1st Division only had two squads, each led by a lieutenant, and the numbers never exceeded 13 men at any one time. Lt. Randolph Ellis and Lt. Jerry Sinn, two long-serving team commanders, formalized the teams and gave them the discipline and procedural guidelines commonly found in elite units like the British Special Air Service (SAS) and the American Special Forces. Robert Woods, the first team sergeant, served for three years and contributed as much as anyone to the specific skills and tactics used by the teams. Each of the 1st Division teams also had a radio telephone operator (RTO) and a medic, as well as two former Viêt Công, Hiêp and Tiên, who acted as advisors and translators.

A tunnel rat's basic equipment was a .38-caliber revolver, a flashlight, and a knife. Standard procedure required three men in the tunnels at a time. The biggest success for tunnel rats during the Vietnam War came between 9 and 11 August 1968, in support of the 11th Armored Cavalry and the 5th Army of the Republic of Vietnam (ARVN) Division. The team led by Sergeant Woods killed 3 VC soldiers in an underground firefight and forced 153 more backward out of a tunnel into captivity.

Outside of the 1st Infantry Division, most tunnel rats were usually ill-trained volunteers. Still, they occasionally scored notable successes. In II Corps in the Central Highlands Mike Neil found a hospital 60 feet inside a hill. Paul Boehn located a classroom and a mess hall. This author found an armory and a hospital with an electrocardiogram in Cambodia. Moreover, many of the reports of weapons captured during the war in all of the military regions were the result of explorations by tunnel rats.

Lt. Col. George Eyster, who served with the 1st Division's 3d Brigade, was among the first Americans to die in tunnel warfare, but, surprisingly, most of the tunnel rats survived. Some, such as Sergeant Woods and Capt. Herbert Thornton of the 1st Division or Sgt. Pete Rejo in the 25th Division, survived because of their aggressiveness and skill. Woods and Thornton had the dubious distinction of being on a Viêt Công bounty list, and prisoners knew their names and reputations. All 1st Division tunnel rats were wounded at least once. Wounds or the approach of the end of their tours in Vietnam forced the retirement of all the tunnel rats, both inside and outside the 1st Division.

—James T. Gillam

Tunnel rats, such as the soldier shown here, fought the Viêt Công and People's Army of Vietnam in their underground tunnels and bunkers. A tunnel rat's basic equipment was a .38-caliber revolver, a flashlight, and a knife.

References: Browne, Malcolm. *The New Face of War.* New York: Bobbs-Merrill, 1965.

Burchett, Wilfred G. *Vietnam: The Inside Story of the Guerrilla War.* New York: International Publishers, 1965.

Ebert, James R. *A Life in a Year: The American Infantryman in Vietnam 1965–1972.* Novato, CA: Presidio Press, 1993.

Mangold, Thomas, and John Pennycate. *The Tunnels of Cuchi.* East Rutherford, NJ: Berkeley Publishing, 1987.

See also: CEDAR FALLS, Operation; Cu Chi, Tunnels of; Iron Triangle; United States: Army.

Twining, Nathan Farragut

(1897–1982)

U.S. Air Force general; chairman of the Joint Chiefs of Staff (JCS), 1957–1960. Born 11 October 1897 in Monroe, Wisconsin, Nathan F. Twining joined the Oregon National Guard and served on the U.S.-Mexican border before entering West Point in 1917. He completed the shortened wartime course there in November 1918 and was commissioned an infantry lieutenant. After attending flying school, in 1926 he formally transferred to aviation. In 1937 Twining graduated from the Command and General Staff School. During the Second World War he rose steadily in rank and responsibilities, commanding in succession the Thirteenth Air Force, the Fifteenth Air Force, and the Twentieth Air Force.

Later Twining commanded the Air Material Command and then the Alaskan Command. In 1950 after serving as head of Air Force personnel, Twining was appointed Air Force vice-chief of staff. In June 1953 he became Air Force chief of staff.

Twining supported President Dwight Eisenhower's contention that the threat of "massive retaliation" would eliminate "brush-fire" wars. In 1954 during the Indo-China War he advocated the use of atomic weapons at Điên Biên Phu, believing this would lift the siege and strengthen deterrence, but he opposed the use of covert U.S. military advisors. Twining believed that the Viêt Minh's lack of sophisticated air defense capability would make U.S. airpower virtually invulnerable over Indo-China. During the 1954–1955 Quemoy and Matsu crisis, when the People's Republic of China shelled and threatened to invade the islands, Twining urged an American commitment to defend them. As chief of staff, Twining was an advocate of Air Force expansion, including the B-52 bomber and the ballistic missile program.

Twining's hawkish stance led President Eisenhower to appoint him chairman of the JCS after the expiration of Admiral Arthur Radford's term in 1957. Twining retired from the military in 1960. In 1966 he wrote *Neither Liberty nor Safety,* in which he discussed the change in the world's strategic balance since the Second World War. He opposed the Strategic Arms Limitations and the Anti-Ballistic Missile treaties as dangerous to deterrence. Twining died on 29 March 1982 at Lackland Air Force Base in Texas.

—Stephen R. Maynard

References: Dupuy, Trevor N., Curt Johnson, and David L. Bongard. *The Harper Encyclopedia of Military Biography.* New York: HarperCollins, 1992.

Mrozek, Donald J. "Nathan F. Twining: New Dimensions, a New Look." In *Makers of the Modern Air Force,* edited by John L. Frisbee. Washington, DC: Pergamon-Brassey's, 1989.

See also: Eisenhower, Dwight David; Radford, Arthur W.; VULTURE, Operation.

U

U Thant
(1909–1974)

United Nations (UN) secretary-general (1962–1972). Born in Panataw, Burma, in 1909, Thant was trained as an educator. After World War II, he became Burma's press director and director of broadcasting. In 1952 he went to the United Nations as an alternate in Burma's delegation to the UN General Assembly, and in 1957 he became that country's permanent UN ambassador. After the death of Dag Hammarskjøld in September 1961, Thant was unanimously elected as acting secretary-general by the General Assembly, and on 30 November 1962 secretary-general.

Immediately following the August 1964 Tonkin Gulf incidents, Thant spoke directly with President Lyndon Johnson and offered to arrange a meeting of low-level diplomats from all warring sides. Democratic Republic of Vietnam leader Hô Chí Minh was interested, but Johnson, preoccupied with that fall's presidential election, was not. The idea, however, intrigued Adlai Stevenson, U.S. ambassador to the United Nations. In January 1965 he suggested to Thant that together they make preliminary plans for talks that would take place in Burma. Thant quickly agreed, and over several weeks the two diplomats tried to sell the Johnson administration on their plan, which became known as the "Rangoon initiative." But on 30 January the Johnson administration officially rejected the plan.

Thant tried another tack, suggesting another Geneva peace conference, despite Johnson's July 1964 statement that he would never agree to a second meeting. When Johnson again refused, a furious Thant called a news conference and made public Washington's obstruction of his peace efforts. Caught off guard, the administration denied that such initiatives had ever been undertaken.

That summer Stevenson and Thant approached Britain and France, hoping those governments would take the lead in the search for a negotiated peace. It was not to be. Stevenson died in London in July while on a trip designed to advance these initiatives, and the plan perished with him. Thant retired as secretary-general on 1 January 1972. He died at New York City on 25 November 1974. His memoirs were published posthumously.

—John Robert Greene

References: Kraslow, David, and Stuart H. Loory. *The Secret Search for Peace in Vietnam.* New York: Random House, 1968.
U Thant. *View from the UN: The Memoirs of U Thant.* Garden City, NY: Doubleday, 1978.
See also: Hô Chí Minh; Johnson, Lyndon Baines; Stevenson, Adlai E.; Tonkin Gulf Incidents; United Nations and the Vietnam War.

Uniforms

French Expeditionary Forces Uniforms and equipment used by the French Army represented a mix of French, British, and American items. French uniforms of the period were a combination of standard issue service dress and field uniforms that reflected the climate of Southeast Asia. The service dress was a khaki uniform with the standard insignia of the French armed forces. This uniform was modified for the heat and humidity of Indo-China by adding a shorts and knee sock ensemble. Headgear consisted of either the peaked cap, side cap, kepi, or beret. A "safari" or "bush" jacket and trousers were also issued as a service or "walking out" uniform.

Field uniforms of the French forces were initially British or American World War II dress. The items most utilized during the period were American green herringbone twill trousers and heavy canvas twill camouflage shirts. Later, uniforms of French design and manufacture consisted of loose-fitting, multipocketed shirts and trousers in either green or camouflage pattern. Camouflage uniforms gained in popularity among airborne and commando units. By the end of the conflict, multipatterned uniforms became a distinctive designator for all special forces–type units and the Foreign Legion. The American M1 steel helmet was universally issued to the Expeditionary Force, as were canvas webbing and belts for field service. The French also distributed a broad-brimmed floppy "bush" hat that was preferred by the troops in the field to the helmet or any other type of soft cap. French forces also used a canvas and rubber boot designed for service in the humid tropical climate of Indo-China.

Viêt Minh, People's Army of Vietnam, and Viêt Công The Viêt Minh and later the Viêt Công were essentially peasant armies, and this was reflected in their uniforms. The Viêt Minh wore various military-styled clothing. Shirts had shoulder loops. Headgear usually consisted of a pith hat marked with a simple yellow star on red. Footgear worn by most Vietnamese Communist soldiers from 1947 to 1975 was the well-known rubber-tire sandal, named Bình Tri Thiên for the area where they were first made: Quang Bình, Quang Tri, and Thưa Thiên Provinces. When meeting the public, Hô Chí Minh often wore this kind of footgear, which Americans referred to as Hô Chí Minh sandals or simply "Ho-Chis."

After the 1949 Communist victory in China, the People's Republic of China (PRC) began to send weapons and supplies to Hô Chí Minh's forces, and the Viêt Minh began to be uniformed similarly to China's People's Liberation Army. The uniform consisted of a four-pocket jacket and loose-fitting trousers in a mustard brown color. In the later stages of the Franco-Vietnamese conflict, uniforms were gray-green.

The Viêt Minh adopted the Chinese-style "Mao" soft cap or used captured French bush hats. As uniforms became more standard to the Viêt Minh, a fiber and cloth sun or pith helmet became

Sp4c. Richard Campion's hat, beads, and medallions, which would have been forbidden in 1965, were common in the fragmented U.S. Army of 1971.

the official headgear. This was not a helmet in the true sense, as it offered no ballistic protection. In rare instances, specialized units such as antiaircraft units wore Russian-style steel helmets. Footgear consisted of copies of standard Chinese boots or sandals.

The dress uniform of the Democratic Republic of Vietnam's People's Army of Vietnam (PAVN) remained essentially Chinese style with a system of collar tabs and epaulets for rank and unit identification. The PAVN added a peaked or service cap for officers and the sun helmet with national identification markings for other ranks. The ensemble was completed by a leather belt with metal belt buckle denoting the insignia of the PAVN and either boots or shoes of a "sneaker"-like appearance. For field service, PAVN soldiers wore a loose-fitting, green, cotton, two-pocket button shirt and pants of the same color. Soldiers used a system of webbing to carry personal equipment and ammunition. To hide their involvement during the early stages of the Vietnam War, many North Vietnamese units were dressed similarly to the Việt Công.

The People's Liberation Forces (PLF) or Việt Công (VC) wore mostly civilian clothing during the war. By the early 1960s the VC standardized uniform consisted of a black loose-fitting shirt and pants. This was common peasant garb in Vietnam, referred to by Americans as "black pajamas." In jungle workshops, the VC man-

ufactured soft khaki-brimmed bush hats and web gear to supply their regular or "main force" units. These were similar to those of the PAVN and other Communist-bloc nations. They also depended heavily on the capture of Army of the Republic of Vietnam (ARVN) clothing and equipment. Shoes were usually locally made sandals, often constructed from truck tires and referred to by Americans as Ho-Chis.

In some U.S. training centers, typical VC were depicted as wearing black pajamas and conic hats. The VC did not wear the latter, which would hinder movement and combat activities, but this mistaken notion probably led to the deaths of many peasants.

Republic of Vietnam Armed Forces (RVNAF) RVNAF forces were uniformed similarly to those of the United States, as the Americans supplied and trained those forces. In the initial stages of the war, the Army of the Republic of Vietnam (ARVN) dress and service uniform was a modified American khaki dress uniform with service cap (or beret, if part of a special unit) and black oxford shoes. For field service, the ARVN used the standard U.S.-style green utility or "fatigue" uniform, consisting of a two-button pocket shirt and trousers with national rank and insignia. American helmets, webbing, and black leather boots completed the field uniform. The ARVN also used either the U.S. Army or Marine soft caps (known as the "baseball" or "engineer" hat, respectively). RVNAF special units (army rangers, airborne, special forces, and Marines) often wore locally fabricated camouflage field uniforms to denote their elite status. Montagnards, who were auxiliaries to the ARVN as members of the Civilian Irregular Defense Group (CIDG), generally wore black pajamas or camouflage uniforms provided by U.S. Army Special Forces.

After 1973 most ARVN soldiers wore field dress similar to that of the U.S. Army at the time: loose coats with four pockets and loose trousers with six pockets.

United States Army and Marines American forces in Southeast Asia arrived in an advisory role that expanded as regular U.S. combat forces were committed to the war. The U.S. Army service dress (Class B) consisted of a khaki short-sleeved shirt, trousers, and either service or overseas cap with appropriate rank and insignia. Black shoes or "low-quarters" and a black web belt with metal buckle completed the uniform; however, airborne-qualified personnel were authorized to wear their black "jump boots" with the service uniform. The service uniform was worn as a duty uniform by those assigned to headquarters and support offices or for arriving and departing Vietnam. U.S. Army Special Forces wore the distinctive green beret with either the Class B or field uniform.

The American fatigue or field uniform consisted of green shirt and trousers (OG-107) with boots, helmet, and web gear. The official issue soft cap was the baseball-style hat, which was universally despised by American soldiers. Rank and insignia were worn on the shirt and hat.

The climate of Vietnam quickly proved the complete unsuitability of field uniforms designed for temperate or cold weather. In 1966 the United States began to issue a field uniform designed for operations in tropical climates. "Jungle fatigues" consisted of a coat with four large slanted pockets with six-pocketed loose-fitting trousers. This uniform became standard throughout the balance of the Vietnam War and was issued universally to all branches of the service, including naval personnel engaged in ground operations. The coat design initially had epaulets, but these were removed and the buttons were covered in later versions of the jacket. American special units required camouflaged uniforms for jungle operations. U.S. research and development produced several camouflage patterns considered consistent with operations in Southeast Asia. The two most suitable were the green and black "tiger stripes," preferred by Army Special Forces and Navy SEAL (Sea, Air, Land) teams, and the "leaf" pattern, used by long-range reconnaissance patrol (LRRP) personnel and Rangers, which continued as the battle dress uniform (BDU) of U.S. armed forces. In 1967 the U.S. Marine Corps began to issue leaf-patterned jungle fatigues to all Marines in Vietnam, but the complete change did not take place until after the U.S. withdrawal.

One of the items most popular with the soldiers but hated by the command structure for its "unmilitary" appearance was the "hat, hot weather," or "boonie," a narrow-brimmed soft hat designed to offer protection from the sun, humidity, and rain. This was issued between 1967 and 1968 for field service only in Vietnam and was universally loved by most Americans in field units. In 1970 General Creighton Abrams restricted the boonie to recon-naissance units and required that the baseball cap again be standard issue for all Army personnel in Southeast Asia. However, soldiers continued to wear the boonie until the end of American involvement, despite the official prohibition. The Marines continued to issue their own distinctive soft cap throughout the conflict.

American technology developed another innovation for Southeast Asia, the "jungle boot." It likewise came to signify U.S. presence in Vietnam. The black leather combat or jump boot proved unsuitable in Vietnam, and in 1966 the soldiers were issued a canvas web and rubber field boot with a steel plate to offer a modicum of protection against mines and booby traps. Later versions of the boot did not have the steel plate. This popular jungle boot was worn by Allied forces during the conflict. The boonie hat, jungle boot, and M16 rifle identified the U.S. ground soldier during the Vietnam War.

—J. A. Menzoff

References: Bonds, Ray, ed. *The Vietnam War: The Illustrated History of the Conflict in Southeast Asia.* New York: Crown, 1983.
Katcher, Philip. *Armies of the Vietnam War, 1962–1975.* London: Osprey, 1980.
Russell, Lee. E. *Armies of the Vietnam War.* 2d ed. London: Osprey, 1983.
See also: Civilian Irregular Defense Group (CIDG); Military Decorations; Montagnards; National Front for the Liberation of South Vietnam (NFLSV); United States: Army; United States: Marine Corps; United States: Navy; United States: Special Forces; Vietnam, Democratic Republic of: Army (People's Army of Vietnam [PAVN]); Vietnam, Republic of: Army (ARVN); Vietnam, Republic of: Marine Corps (VNMC); Vietnam, Republic of: Special Forces (Lực Lượng Đặc Biệt [LLDB]).

UNION I and II, Operations

(21 April–5 June 1967)

Successive U.S. Marine Corps operations in Quang Nam and Quang Tín Provinces in southern I Corps, areas long Việt Cộng (VC) and People's Army of Vietnam (PAVN) strongholds, in which Army of the Republic of Vietnam (ARVN) forces were unable to establish outposts beyond the district capitals. Until 1967 the U.S. Marines lacked assets to control the Phước Ha/Quê Sơn Valley.

On 20 April, while moving along a ridgeline outside of Thăng Bình, a company of the 2d Battalion, 1st Marines was hit by concentrated automatic weapons and grenade fire from the 3d PAVN Regiment. Operation UNION I began the next morning with the insertion of the 3d Battalion, 5th Marines and the 1st Battalion, 1st Marines. The 1st ARVN Ranger Group also participated. Heavy fighting ensued in the Phước Ha/Quê Sơn Valley and lasted until 25 April, when PAVN forces began to withdraw. As contact diminished, only units of the 5th Marines remained in the area.

On 10 May these Marines successfully assaulted PAVN mortar emplacements on Hill 110, but Communist forces mauled several Marine companies coming to assist. For the next five days, the 5th Marines continuously assaulted entrenched PAVN positions on the valley floor. Supported by air strikes and artillery fire, they finally overran the PAVN defenses, and the operation officially ended on 17 May. Over the 27 days of the operation, the Marines counted 865 PAVN dead and claimed another 777 "probable" battle deaths. They also took 173 prisoners. Marine casualties were 110 killed and 473 wounded.

Launched nine days later, Operation UNION II was designed to entrap the 3d and 21st PAVN Regiments, spotted in a valley in northern Quang Tín Province. On 26 May two battalions of the 5th Marines and the 6th ARVN Regiment were inserted. For two days, the 3d Battalion, 5th Marines battled units of the 3d PAVN Regiment 20 miles northwest of Tam Kỳ, killing 171. Marine casualties were 37 killed and 66 wounded. On 2 June, the 1st Battalion, 5th Marines, supported by artillery fire and 138 air strikes, overran entrenched hillside positions of the 21st PAVN Regiment north of Thiên Phước. In bunker-to-bunker fighting, the Marines killed 540 PAVN soldiers, while suffering 73 killed and 139 wounded. The operation ended on 5 June.

Operations UNION I and II, brief as they were, were the bloodiest Marine engagements to date. The two operations produced a total of 1,566 PAVN dead, 196 captured, and 184 weapons seized. Marine losses for both operations totaled 220 killed and 714 wounded. For action in UNION I and II, the 5th Marine Regiment won the Presidential Unit Citation.

—John D. Root

References: Simmons, Brig. Gen. Edwin H. "Marine Corps Operations in Vietnam, 1967." In *The Marines in Vietnam, 1954–1973: An Anthology and Annotated Bibliography,* 2d ed. Washington, DC: History and Museums Division, Marine Corps Historical Center, U.S. Marine Corps Headquarters, 1985.
Stanton, Shelby L. *The Rise and Fall of an American Army: U.S. Ground Forces in Vietnam, 1965–1973.* Novato, CA: Presidio Press, 1985.
See also: United States: Marine Corps; Vietnam, Democratic Republic of: Army (People's Army of Vietnam [PAVN]); Vietnam, Republic of: Army (ARVN).

Union of Soviet Socialist Republics (USSR) (Soviet Union)

The history of relations between the Soviet Union and the Democratic Republic of Vietnam (DRV) until well into the decisive 1960s has been characterized by Douglas Pike in *Vietnam and the Soviet Union* as "nominal and cursory, having neither much intercourse and emotional attachment for either party." Then during the Vietnam War and for a decade afterward until the mid-1980s, relations were very close. The Soviet Union fully supported the DRV's war effort militarily, economically, and diplomatically. While Mikhail Gorbachev was in power, from 1985 to the mid-1990s, however, relations between the USSR/Russia and the DRV/Socialist Republic of Vietnam (SRV) steadily deteriorated until there was little intercourse between the two on any front.

The Bolshevik Revolution was profoundly meaningful for Vietnamese revolutionaries, although early Bolshevik leaders had little knowledge of Southeast Asia. Hồ Chí Minh attended the fifth Comintern Congress in Moscow in 1924, which denounced Western imperialism and colonialism, including French control of Indo-China. And he visited Moscow frequently between 1924 and 1941. Although there existed extensive sentimental and psychological ties, there were few specific political and diplomatic connections. Hồ considered the Comintern of limited usefulness.

The Stalin years (1929–1953) were ones of complete indifference on the part of the USSR. Joseph Stalin regarded anticolonial activity as sometimes useful but always undependable, believing that something would invariably go wrong. Furthermore, throughout the whole period, Stalin and his government were preoccupied with internal Soviet and European problems, namely the survival of Stalin, his system, and the Soviet Union. Vietnam was hardly a concern. During World War II, Hồ received no Soviet assistance in his struggle against the Japanese, and Soviet reaction to Hồ's declaration of independence in August 1945 was guarded. In fact, the Soviet Union did not recognize the Democratic Republic of Vietnam until January 1950, 13 days after the People's Republic of China (PRC) had done so.

Because the Soviet Union sought good relations with France, political support for the Việt Minh throughout the Indo-China War remained restrained. In addition, Stalin never trusted Hồ, regarding him as too independent. Yet behind the scenes, the Soviet Union funneled large and increasing amounts of military aid to the Việt Minh through the PRC, amounting to some $1 billion. That aid was an important factor in the Việt Minh's victory against the French. Vietnam's leaders hoped this benign neglect by the Soviet Union would change after Stalin's death in 1953.

After Stalin's death, the new Soviet leaders wanted to relax tensions with the West. As part of this new foreign policy, Moscow supported the holding of an international peace conference in Geneva in 1954 to settle the Indo-China War. During the conference, the Soviet delegation, led by Foreign Minister V. M. Molotov, forced the Việt Minh to compromise by accepting terms less favorable than its military achievements might otherwise have dictated, which may have had something to do with French rejection of the European Defense Community (EDC). Consequently, after the Geneva Conference, relations were cool between the DRV and the Soviet Union.

When Nikita Khrushchev achieved complete power by 1956, DRV leaders held great hopes. Khrushchev shifted Soviet interests from European to a global scope that included Asia. He saw potential advantages in Vietnam and in its renewed war and stepped up military and economic aid, thus deepening relations. Soviet economic aid propelled rapid economic development in the DRV. Yet as the war intensified, Khrushchev became more cautious. Originally his goal was to oust the West from Asia, but the increasing Sino-Soviet dispute complicated efforts. Khrushchev feared that a quick and total victory by the Communists in Vietnam would only help China and cause an unnecessary confrontation with the United States. By the end of his rule in 1964 Khrushchev had completely soured on Vietnam, regarding the war as too risky and the DRV leaders as crafty and manipulative. All that prevented a total Soviet disengagement was the coup that ousted Khrushchev in October 1964.

The war was the central event in Vietnamese-Soviet relations. It dictated day-to-day events and locked the two in an association. Soviet Premier Aleksei Kosygin's visit to Hà Nội in February 1965 initiated full and close relations. Soviet and Vietnamese leaders signed economic and military treaties, in which the Soviet Union pledged full support for the DRV's war effort. The Soviets and the

DRV leadership planned military strategy and entered into discussions to determine the DRV's needs to implement such a strategy. The USSR would supply the DRV with all the necessary war materiel, including air defenses for the North and offensive weapons to be employed in the South.

The Soviet Union also conducted a propaganda war against the United States in world forums, such as the United Nations, and at times threatened to send Soviet and Eastern European "volunteers" to Vietnam. The Soviet Union hoped to use the war to seek an ideological advantage over China, as the dispute between the two Communist powers became increasingly bitter. Yet it became clear that the Soviet Union would not directly intervene in the war, and its policies remained ambiguous and cautious. But as the war intensified, so did Soviet aid—until it amounted to some 80 percent of all supplies reaching the DRV.

After the 1968 Têt Offensive, the Soviets believed for the first time that a total victory was possible. Yet, as the war continued, the Soviet spirit waned; its leaders and people increasingly wearied of the war. They believed that little more was to be gained from a war that was proving very expensive for the Soviet Union. Therefore, the Soviets fully endorsed the peace talks that began in Paris in 1968. When the talks deadlocked in 1972, the Soviet Union pressured the DRV to accept a compromise settlement with the Republic of Vietnam (RVN) and the United States in January 1973. The success of the 1975 military offensive came as a great surprise to both the DRV and the Soviet leadership, however.

The Vietnam War proved a great victory for the Soviet Union, which supported the North fully and yet avoided a confrontation with the United States. It served Soviet interests well by keeping the United States fully occupied in an area not of crucial importance to the USSR. Historians are in disagreement, however, regarding Soviet influence over DRV decision making during the war.

Economic relations between the two countries were largely a one-way street. The Soviet Union poured billions of rubles into Vietnam but few rubles returned to the USSR. A formal economic treaty was first signed in 1955 and was then renewed yearly. Economic aid consisted of food, oil, and other basic necessities; the expansion and modernization of industries and farming; services, such as sending Soviet economic and military advisors to Vietnam and the sending of Vietnamese to the USSR for education and training; and, of course, military aid. During the war years (1965–1975), military aid—weapons, aircraft, rockets, air defenses, munitions, food, and fuel—was central. Economic aid was entirely geared to the war effort. By the 1970s Soviet aid was huge and diverse, amounting to some $1 billion or more each year. It would have been impossible for the DRV to have continued the war without it. After the DRV's 1975 victory, governmental ineptness led to the near collapse of the economies of both the North and the South. The Soviet Union had to send the Socialist Republic of Vietnam basic food and oil supplies.

Immediately after the war, a more intimate relationship than ever before developed. This was in part the result of a precipitous decline in relations between China and Vietnam. Wars with China and Cambodia proved costly between 1978 and 1979 and drove

Vietnam into near total dependency on the Soviet Union. In November 1979 the Soviet Union signed a friendship pact with the SRV, in return for which it obtained naval and air bases. Ironically, many of these were former U.S. bases in South Vietnam. The Soviet presence was everywhere. By the mid-1980s the relationship had become very close, to the point that Vietnam was considered a Soviet client state.

After Mikhail Gorbachev came to power in 1985, Soviet relations steadily declined. Gorbachev enacted major changes in Soviet foreign policy, moving away from militarily and ideologically oriented policies to those based on economics. Furthermore, Gorbachev achieved a rapprochement with China. Those changes greatly reduced the value of Vietnam to the Soviet Union. In Soviet eyes, Vietnam became just another poor country that drained crucial economic resources. Vietnam, in turn, criticized Gorbachev's wide-ranging political and economic reforms. The collapse of communism in Eastern Europe in 1989, and then in the Soviet Union itself two years later, profoundly shocked Vietnamese leaders. Vietnam faded from the attention of Russia's new leaders, who felt absolutely no ideological affinity toward the country. Economic and military aid completely stopped. Because of Russia's huge and growing economic crisis, trade itself greatly declined and would be conducted only on a basis of full equality and in hard currency. A few Russian entrepreneurs found Vietnam an attractive place to buy cheap consumer goods to sell in Russia, but criminal behavior of some Vietnamese workers and students in Russia caused problems. Relations between the two countries reached a low ebb with no sign of improvement.

—Michael Share

References: Edmonds, Robin. *Soviet Foreign Policy: The Brezhnev Years.* Oxford, UK: Oxford University Press, 1983.
Gaiduk, Ilya V. *The Soviet Union and the Vietnam War.* Chicago: Ivan R. Dee, 1996.
Longmire, R. A. *Soviet Relations with South-East Asia.* London: Kegan Paul, 1989.
Pike, Douglas. *Vietnam and the Soviet Union: Anatomy of an Alliance.* Boulder, CO: Westview Press, 1987.
See also: Gorbachev, Mikhail Sergeyevich; Khrushchev, Nikita Sergeyevich; Kosygin, Aleksei Nikolayevich; Paris Negotiations; Paris Peace Accords; Vietnam, Democratic Republic of: 1945–1954; Vietnam, Democratic Republic of: 1954–1975; Vietnam, Socialist Republic of: 1975 to the Present.

UNIONTOWN, Operation

(December 1967-March 1968)

U.S. Army 199th Infantry Brigade (Light) operation in War Zone D. In 1966 the U.S. Army was hurriedly raising units to meet the demands created by the conflict in Southeast Asia. The 199th Infantry Brigade (Light) was formed by combining the 3d Battalion, 7th Infantry and 4th Battalion, 12th Infantry; both units were based at Fort Benning, Georgia, the U.S. Army's Infantry Center. The light infantry brigade concept called for a rapidly deployable force with minimal heavy equipment and fire support assets. The brigade was to be mixed in task forces with aviation, transportation, logistical, and artillery support from existing forces in

Vietnam. U.S. Military Assistance Command, Vietnam (MACV) and, later, U.S. Army, Vietnam (USARV) were designated as the controlling headquarters for the 199th.

The brigade remained under severe pressure to meet the army's deployment schedule, which required it to be in theater by November 1967. Despite late-November shortages in personnel and equipment, the brigade moved by air and sea to arrive at the port of Vũng Tàu in early December. It then moved to its permanent base camp at Long Bình, which would remain "home" to the 199th for the duration of its Vietnam service.

In December 1967 Operation UNIONTOWN commenced as the 199th, supported by the 11th Armored Cavalry Regiment ("Black Horse"), moved into War Zone C and engaged Việt Công (VC) and People's Army of Vietnam (PAVN) forces. Operation UNIONTOWN continued until March 1968. On 17 December 1967 the brigade's 4th Battalion, 12th Infantry regiment conducted its first airmobile combat assault. The 199th continued to be used as a "quick reaction force" in the Sài Gòn area during the conflict.

MACV assigned the 199th to cooperate with Army of the Republic of Vietnam (ARVN) forces to provide security for the greater Sài Gòn area. During the 1968 Tết Offensive, the 199th fought insurgents in the capital before being relieved by the 5th ARVN Ranger Group. Other elements of the brigade conducted the defense at Long Bình. As the Tết Offensive continued, the brigade moved to positions near Biên Hòa. Meanwhile, the 1st Infantry Division had split War Zones C and D and opened Route 13 between Sài Gòn and Quan Lợi, and the "Redcatchers" of the 199th supported 1st Infantry operations in that area.

The 199th was later combined with the 196th Light Infantry Brigade (Separate) to form the 23d Infantry Division (Americal). It served through the remainder of the war in Quang Ngãi Province.

—J. A. Menzoff

Reference: Stanton, Shelby. *The Rise and Fall of an American Army: U.S. Ground Forces in Vietnam, 1965–1973.* Novato, CA: Presidio Press, 1985.
See also: Airmobility; Military Assistance Command, Vietnam (MACV); Tết Offensive: Overall Strategy; Tết Offensive: The Sài Gòn Circle; United States: Army; Vietnam, Republic of: Army (ARVN).

United Front

Groups, factions, or organizations united to achieve a political objective. The principal organizational strategy used by the Vietnamese Communists to win power, the united front is a powerful weapon in the hands of a small but highly dedicated and disciplined party that relies on mobilizing sentiment to achieve political aims, sometimes through the use of revolutionary violence.

Patterned on Lenin's use of the Soviets by the Bolsheviks in 1917, the first notable example of the united front in Indo-China was the Việt Minh, organized by Hồ Chí Minh while he was still in China in 1941. The Việt Minh served to mobilize Vietnamese nationalists in the war against the French, although its Communist domination became increasingly more apparent as the war continued. Similarly, the Communist-dominated National Front for

the Liberation of South Vietnam or National Liberation Front (NLF), established in December 1960, and the Pathet Lao in Laos included among their membership many non-Communist nationalist groups.

As Lê Duẩn, who is generally credited with being the driving force of the united front strategy following Hồ's death in 1969, explained in a 1970 newspaper article: "The Front is an organization in which contradictions could be reconciled. The Front includes many different classes that united on the basis of a common and fixed program of action. . . . Being the leader of the revolution and possessing a political line that adequately represents the nation's common interests, our Party [the Communist Party of Vietnam] is naturally recognized as the leader of the Front. Revolutionary and national interests require that we permanently strengthen and consolidate the Party's leading role in the Front, firmly maintain the Party's political line and its independent organs, and oppose every tendency to minimize the Party's role and to dissolve the Party in the Front."

—Arthur J. Dommen

Reference: Lê Duẩn. "Under the Glorious Party Banner, for Independence, Freedom, and Socialism, Let Us Advance and Achieve New Victories." *Nhân Dân* (Hà Nội) (14 February 1970); translated in JUSPAO (Sài Gòn), Viet Nam Documents and Research Notes No. 77 (April 1970), p. 14.
See also: Hồ Chí Minh; Lê Duẩn; National Front for the Liberation of South Vietnam (NFLSV); Pathet Lao; Việt Minh (Việt Nam Độc Lập Đồng Minh Hội [Vietnam Independence League]).

United Nations and the Vietnam War

The role of the United Nations in the Vietnam War was negligible for a number of reasons. One resulted from the structure of the organization. Each member of the United Nations (UN) Security Council has the power to veto resolutions. Both the United States, which supported the Republic of Vietnam (RVN), and the Soviet Union, which openly supported the Democratic Republic of Vietnam (DRV), used the veto to block resolutions that they perceived to be critical of their Southeast Asian policies.

Another obstacle blocking a meaningful UN role was that neither the DRV nor the RVN were member states of the United Nations. The Soviet Union had proposed admitting the two nations in 1957, but the United States rejected the idea. American diplomats were unwilling to recognize the partition of Vietnam with a Communist regime in the North.

Secretary-General of the United Nations U Thant of Burma believed that solution of the Vietnam problem lay outside the UN mandate. Many representatives of the United Nations agreed with his interpretation, including France, which championed the principle of nonintervention.

The 1954 Geneva Accords that ended the Indo-China War also weakened the ability of the United Nations to intervene in Vietnam. These agreements called for national elections in Vietnam in 1956, but made no provision for UN participation. This rendered unlikely any debate concerning Vietnam in the UN General Assembly.

Despite these obstacles, U Thant attempted in 1964, 1968, and 1970 to negotiate a settlement of the Vietnam War. U Thant used his outstanding credentials as a neutralist and the power of his position to try to broker a peace agreement. His 1964 initiative came closest to success. With the tacit approval of President Lyndon B. Johnson, U Thant made arrangements for talks to take place in Rangoon, Burma. The Soviet Union acted as intermediary to transmit the offer to Hà Nôi. The timing seemed fortuitous because it coincided with an attempt by Soviet Premier Nikita Khrushchev to get the North Vietnamese to negotiate. The DRV leadership listened to Khrushchev's suggestion because the Soviet Union was its major supplier of armaments, especially surface-to-air missiles. However, hopes for a negotiated settlement were soon dashed. Khrushchev's fall from power in October 1964 brought a hardened policy against negotiations and in favor of increased assistance to Hà Nôi. But the change in Soviet leadership was not the only problem. Washington had already rejected his suggestions that September concerning a basis for a peace settlement. U Thant's two other attempts at negotiation made no headway because of a hardening of positions on both sides resulting from the escalation of the war.

Although the United Nations failed to play an active role in the Vietnam War, it enjoyed success in other issues that stemmed from the conflict. U Thant made some progress in limiting the use of defoliants such as Agent Orange. The United Nations also brokered a ban on biological weapons in April 1972, in part the result of a storm of international criticism over their use during the war. The United Nations accomplished much in easing the suffering of many Vietnamese displaced by the war. This included protection of thousands of Vietnamese refugees (the "boat people") who fled following the 1975 collapse of the Republic of Vietnam. The United Nations also supervised the emigration of Amerasian children from Vietnam to the United States.

—Eric W. Osborne

References: Boyd, Andrew. *Fifteen Men on a Powder Keg: A History of the U.N. Security Council.* New York: Stein & Day, 1971.
Karnow, Stanley. *Vietnam: A History.* Rev. ed. New York: Penguin Books, 1991.
Lewin, Isaac. *War on War.* New York: Shengold, 1969.
Olson, James S., and Randy Roberts. *Where the Domino Fell: America and Vietnam, 1945–1990.* New York: St. Martin's Press, 1991.
See also: Amerasians; Khrushchev, Nikita Sergeyevich; Johnson, Lyndon Baines; Refugees and Boat People; U Thant.

United States: Air Force

When the United States entered the Vietnam War, the U.S. Air Force (USAF) dominated the defense establishment. The Air Force won its separate service status in 1947 based on the theory that strategic bombing—the destruction of an enemy's industrial war-making capabilities—was a potentially decisive element in warfare. In 1961 the Strategic Air Command dominated the Air Force, and its budget was greater than that for the entire U.S. Army.

In November 1961 President John F. Kennedy ordered the 4400th Combat Crew Training Squadron to the Republic of Vietnam (RVN) under the code name Operation FARM GATE. The air commandos of Operation FARM GATE had three missions. Their overt mission was to train pilots for the Republic of Vietnam Air Force (RVNAF). Their covert mission was to fly close air support missions in response to the needs of the Army of the Republic of Vietnam (ARVN). Their hidden agenda was to keep the U.S. Army from taking over the close air support function with newly developed helicopter gunships.

The air commandos managed to train several squadrons of RVNAF pilots and performed well in close air support of ARVN and U.S. Army Special Forces units scattered about the countryside. But the Viêt Công and increasing numbers of People's Army of Vietnam (PAVN) troops were still gaining the upper hand against the ARVN. By 1964 the situation was grim. Beginning in March 1964 Air Force leaders called for bombing campaigns against North Vietnam. After a series of retaliation raids against North Vietnam, beginning with the Gulf of Tonkin incidents in August 1964, President Lyndon Johnson ordered Operation ROLLING THUNDER, a bombing campaign directed against the Democratic Republic of Vietnam (DRV), which began on 2 March 1964.

ROLLING THUNDER had three objectives. The first was strategic persuasion—airpower used in ever-intensifying degrees to persuade the DRV to stop supporting the Viêt Công and negotiate an end to the war. Although strategic persuasion remained an objective throughout ROLLING THUNDER, after the massive deployment of U.S. ground forces to South Vietnam began in July 1965, the focus of ROLLING THUNDER switched to interdiction of roads and railroads, primarily in the panhandle of North Vietnam. A continuous but relatively minor objective was to boost the morale of South Vietnamese military and political elites.

ROLLING THUNDER became the longest bombing campaign ever conducted by the U.S. Air Force; it lasted three years and nine months—from 2 March 1965 to 31 October 1968. During that time, the Air Force, Navy, and Marine Corps flew more than 700,000 sorties over North Vietnam, with the Air Force flying nearly 500,000 of those sorties. DRV air defenses claimed over 700 aircraft. In some Air Force F-105 units in 1966 and 1967, attrition rates ran between 50 and 75 percent for a one-year tour. During ROLLING THUNDER, 600,000 tons of bombs fell on North Vietnam.

ROLLING THUNDER's ultimate failure came as a result of an inappropriate strategy that dictated a conventional air war on the DRV to affect what was basically an unconventional war in the RVN. The bombing failed to accomplish its two primary objectives: strategic persuasion and interdiction. The DRV was a preindustrial, largely agricultural country with virtually no military industries. Destroying its three small factories (a cement plant, a gunpowder factory, and a steel mill) had no impact on the war in South Vietnam or on Hà Nôi's ability to prosecute that war. Furthermore, according to U.S. Military Assistance Command, Vietnam's (MACV) own figures, infiltration actually increased, as the flow of troops and supplies moving into South Vietnam doubled each year of ROLLING THUNDER. Amid growing public dissatisfaction with the war, in March 1968 President Johnson limited ROLLING THUNDER strikes to the southern panhandle of North

Sgt. Richard L. Moser, Detachment I, 460th Tactical Reconnaissance Wing, signals the pilot to start the engine of a U.S. Air Force RB-57. These planes flew above the Hô Chí Minh Trail searching for truck convoys.

Vietnam. He ended the campaign one week before the 1968 presidential elections, many believed in an attempt to bolster the prospects of Democratic Party presidential candidate Vice-President Hubert H. Humphrey.

Throughout the Vietnam War, most USAF air action focused on South Vietnam, where from 1962 until 23 January 1972 some 4 million tons of bombs fell, making it the most bombed country in the history of aerial warfare. Much of this bomb tonnage fell as a result of B-52 ARC LIGHT missions directed against suspected Viêt Công and PAVN encampments and troop concentrations. Airpower played a key role in keeping four PAVN divisions at bay during the siege of Khe Sanh in 1967 and 1968. During the Easter Offensive of 1972, B-52s and tactical aircraft pounded PAVN units when they were halted by concerted ARVN ground action throughout South Vietnam, especially at Kontum, a key to the Sài Gòn defenses.

Undoubtedly hundreds, perhaps thousands, of American and Allied soldiers owe their lives to the USAF's quick response to calls for close air support. Critics, however, ask why airpower was not more effective despite the scope of the effort. Did the tremendous capability the USAF had for moving troops and supplies around the RVN actually prolong the war by enabling the Army to continue to fight a war that it really did not know how to fight? Was airpower counterproductive in that images of napalm exploding over South Vietnamese villages seemed to support the more extravagant claims of the antiwar movement that a cruel technology was being unleashed on peaceful peasants?

Meanwhile, when ROLLING THUNDER ended on Halloween night 1968, the bombing did not stop. It only shifted across the Annamite Mountains to focus on the Hô Chí Minh Trail in Laos. Operation COMMANDO HUNT, a pure interdiction campaign, officially began on 15 November 1968. Before it ended in late April 1972 nearly 3 million tons of bombs fell on Laos, most of that on infiltration corridors, mountain passes, and supply caches along the Trail.

Propeller-driven, side-firing gunships, of which the AC-130 was premier, became the key to the truck war portion of COMMANDO HUNT. At night, gunships roamed up and down the Hô Chí Minh Trail, blasting trucks with their computer-aimed 40-mm cannon and, later in the war, 105-mm howitzers. During what has become the classic example of industrial-age aerial warfare, a managerial ethos took control of COMMANDO HUNT operations, with success determined by statistical compilations that included estimates of how many trucks had been destroyed or damaged. The total number of trucks *estimated destroyed* rose from 9,012 in 1969 to a high of 12,368 in 1970. Since Central Intelligence Agency figures indicate that there were only 6,000 trucks in all of North Vietnam and Laos combined, these figures remain highly suspect.

Undoubtedly COMMANDO HUNT efforts did result in some constriction along the supply arteries into South Vietnam, but the extent of damage inflicted is difficult to estimate. During this period, the nature of the war changed from a guerrilla insurgency to a conventional war with some unconventional aspects, meaning that by 1971 it took far more resources to supply PAVN forces

fighting in the South than it did to support Viêt Công guerrilla units five years earlier.

The changed nature of the war became evident when the DRV launched its massive Easter Offensive on 30 March 1972. Some 14 PAVN divisions poured out of South Vietnam's Central Highlands and Cambodia (after traveling down the Hô Chí Minh Trail during COMMANDO HUNT operations), while others crossed the Demilitarized Zone (DMZ) that separated the two Vietnams. The United States responded with Operation LINEBACKER, later dubbed LINEBACKER I, a massive air campaign in which the Air Force played a key role.

LINEBACKER I began on 9 May 1972, with the aerial mining of Hai Phòng Harbor. Meanwhile, Air Force, Navy, and Marine squadrons began pounding infiltration routes not only in the southern panhandle but also on the highways and railroads leading from Hà Nôi to the Chinese border. LINEBACKER I was the first air campaign in which precision-guided munitions, laser and electro-optically guided bombs, were used as part of a coherent strategy. By the time LINEBACKER I ended on 23 October 1972, 155,548 tons of bombs had been dropped on North Vietnam, and the PAVN offensive had been halted.

LINEBACKER I was the most effective employment of airpower during the Vietnam War, and it succeeded because the nature of the war had changed. This was conventional airpower used on North Vietnam to stop a conventional invasion. LINEBACKER I is a classic aerial interdiction campaign but one with a "strategic" dimension in that it finally compelled Hà Nôi's leaders to negotiate seriously. As a result, the United States and the DRV reached an agreement on terms for a cease-fire in late October.

At this point, the RVN's leadership, who had been excluded from meaningful roles in the peace negotiations, objected. President Nguyên Văn Thiêu saw this agreement as a sellout of his country and demanded substantive changes before he would sign it. The chief U.S. negotiator, National Security Advisor Henry A. Kissinger, and Hà Nôi's top negotiator, Lê Đức Tho, resumed talks in November, but they quickly stalemated.

To break this stalemate, President Richard M. Nixon ordered LINEBACKER II. Initially intended as a 3-day bombing campaign aimed at forcing the DRV to return to the negotiation table, LINEBACKER II began on 18 December 1972. It continued for 11 days and featured 739 B-52 sorties against targets in and around Hà Nôi, Hai Phòng, and other major North Vietnamese cities. The USAF, Navy, and Marines added 2,000 fighter-bomber sorties. In total, B-52s dropped 15,000 tons of bombs while the fighter-bombers added another 5,000 tons. DRV defenses brought down 15 B-52s, nine fighter-bombers, a Navy reconnaissance jet, and an Air Force HH-53 "Jolly Green Giant" rescue helicopter. On 26 December Air Force F-4 Phantoms used radar bombing techniques to destroy the surface-to-air (SAM) missile assembly area in downtown Hà Nôi. That night, after specially equipped IRON HAND flights blasted 30 SAM sites around the country, 120 B-52s struck ten targets within a 15-minute period. The DRV was virtually helpless, and its leadership asked if peace talks could resume. President Nixon agreed, but the bombing continued until Hà Nôi and

Washington established an agenda for the talks. On 29 December LINEBACKER II came to an end.

The Air Force's role in the Vietnam War is historically controversial. Airpower enthusiasts point to LINEBACKER II as vindication of strategic bombing doctrine. Critics answer that the nature of the war had changed so that in 1972 the DRV was susceptible to that kind of attack, but that would not have been the case had similar attacks been undertaken earlier, as claimed by Air Force leaders such as General Curtis E. LeMay.

From 1962 though August 1973 when the U.S. Congress mandated an end to the bombing of Cambodia, nearly 8 million tons of bombs fell on Southeast Asia. About half, 4 million tons, fell on South Vietnam, much of it in B-52 ARC LIGHT missions directed against suspected Viêt Công and PAVN camps in the countryside. That made South Vietnam the most bombed country in the history of aerial warfare, a dubious distinction for an ally. For its part, the Air Force lost 2,257 aircraft to hostile action or accidents during the Vietnam War. The majority of aircraft were shot down by light antiaircraft fire, mostly over South Vietnam. Losses over North Vietnam came to 990 aircraft, about 700 of which were USAF planes, and 2,800 airmen perished.

—Earl H. Tilford, Jr.

References: Berger, Carl, ed. *The United States Air Force in Southeast Asia, 1961–1973: An Illustrated Account.* Washington, DC: Office of Air Force History, 1984.

Clodfelter, Mark. *The Limits of Air Power: The American Bombing of North Vietnam.* New York: Free Press, 1989.

Littauer, Raphael, and Norman Uphoff, ed. *The Air War in Indochina.* Rev. ed. Boston: Beacon Press, 1971.

Schlight, John. *The Years of the Offensive: 1965–1968.* Washington, DC: Office of Air Force History, 1988.

Tilford, Earl H., Jr. *Crosswinds: The Air Force's Setup in Vietnam.* College Station, TX: Texas A&M University Press, 1993.

See also: Air Defense, Democratic Republic of Vietnam; Air Power, Role in the War; ARC LIGHT (B-52 Raids); COMMANDO HUNT, Operation; Johnson, Lyndon Baines; LeMay, Curtis Emerson; LINEBACKER I, Operation; LINEBACKER II, Operation; Nixon, Richard Milhous; Order of Battle; ROLLING THUNDER, Operation.

United States: Air National Guard (ANG)

In January 1968 President Lyndon B. Johnson ordered 14,000 Air Force and Navy Reservists mobilized in response to the North Korean seizure of the U.S.S. *Pueblo*. The ANG subsequently mobilized 9,343 personnel on 25 January 1968. A second mobilization, announced on 11 April 1968 in response to the Têt Offensive, involved 1,333 Air Guardsmen; they entered federal service on 13 May.

While the Johnson administration debated what to do with the Guardsmen mobilized in January, those called up in May were quickly integrated into active force operations. Cannon Air Force Base (AFB), New Mexico, hosted two ANG fighter units that trained Air Force pilots as forward air controllers and combat crewmen. An ANG medical evacuation unit transported military patients within the continental United States and the Caribbean. Those units called up in May returned to the United States the following December.

On 3 May 1968 the first of four ANG fighter squadrons equipped with F-100s began to arrive in Vietnam and were soon flying combat missions. In addition, some 85 percent of one active duty fighter squadron were ANG volunteers. The four ANG fighter units were quickly and effectively integrated into combat operations. In Vietnam they flew 24,124 sorties and amassed 38,614 combat hours. Those numbers would rise to approximately 30,000 sorties and 50,000 combat hours if the predominantly ANG 355th tactical Fighter Squadron, a regular USAF unit, is included. The ANG squadrons returned to the United States between April and June 1969.

To help stabilize the situation following the North Korean seizure of the *Pueblo*, two ANG fighter squadrons were dispatched to the Republic of Korea during the summer of 1968 to replace Air Force units. They left federal service in May and June 1969.

An ANG tactical reconnaissance wing (TRW) also was activated in January 1968. It served as the primary Air Force tactical reconnaissance unit in the continental United States. Elements of its squadrons rotated temporary duty assignments in Asia from July 1968 until April 1969, providing photo reconnaissance support. Its demobilization began in December 1968 and lasted until the following June.

ANG volunteers also supported Air Force operations in Southeast Asia. ANG airlifters had become involved there on a significant scale beginning in 1965 and flew regular missions until 1972. In July 1970 two EC-121s from the ANG left the United States for Thailand. During the next six months about 60 Guardsmen were rotated through the theater on 30- to 60-day tours during Operation COMMANDO BUZZ. Their aircraft served as flying radar stations and airborne control platforms for U.S. tactical air operations over North Vietnam and the Gulf of Tonkin until January 1971.

Despite problems encountered, the 1968 mobilizations demonstrated that the Air Guard had emerged as a combat reserve force with units capable of rapid global deployment. The ANG's performance helped to pave the way for the total force policy in the 1970s. Air Guardsmen had demonstrated that well-trained units supplied with modern equipment that were integrated into the Air Force's peacetime operations were capable of performing up to the professional standards of their active force counterparts.

—Charles J. Gross

References: Gross, Charles J. "A Different Breed of Cats: The Air National Guard and the 1968 Reserve Mobilizations." *Air University Review* (January–February 1983): 94–95.

_____. *Militiaman, Volunteer, and Professional: The Air National Guard and the American Military Tradition.* Washington, DC: National Guard Bureau, 1996.

_____. *Prelude to the Total Force: The Air National Guard, 1943–1969.* Washington, DC: Office of Air Force History, 1985.

National Guard Bureau (NGB). *A NGB Activity Input to Project Corona Harvest on Air National Guard Support of U.S. Air Force Operations in Southeast Asia, 1954 to March 31, 1968.* Vol. I. Washington, DC: National Guard Bureau, 1970.

See also: Airplanes, Allied and Democratic Air Power, Role in War; Republic of Vietnam; United States: Air Force; United States: Army.

United States: Army

As in all of America's wars, the vast majority of the troops who fought in Vietnam were U.S. Army soldiers. U.S. Army involvement in Vietnam started with the formation of the Military Assistance Advisory Group, Indo-China (MAAG, Indo-China) on 17 September 1950. In 1955 MAAG, Indo-China was redesignated MAAG, Vietnam. The primary MAAG mission was to provide service support, combat arms training, and field advisors to the Republic of Vietnam Armed Forces (RVNAF). Although the MAAG was a joint command, the majority of its personnel as well as its commander came from the Army.

With the expansion of the American role in Vietnam, the U.S. Military Assistance Command, Vietnam (MACV) was formed on 8 February 1962. MAAG, Vietnam continued in existence for two more years, but MACV eventually took over all advisory functions. As with MAAG, Vietnam, MACV was a joint command, but the vast majority of its personnel and its commander were from the Army. MACV became the principal U.S. command in Vietnam. Under it came the U.S. Army Vietnam (USARV), the U.S. Seventh Air Force, the III Marine Amphibious Force, and U.S. Navy units inside Vietnam. Advisors to the Army of the Republic of Vietnam (ARVN) came from the Field Advisory Element of MACV, which at its height in 1968 provided 9,430 advisors.

USARV was established in Vietnam on 20 July 1965. Its primary mission was to control all Army logistical and administrative units

U.S. soldiers check their position on a map during a search-and-destroy mission in 1966.

Table 1. U.S. Army Manpower in Vietnam

Year	Strength
1960	800
1961	2,100
1962	7,900
1963	10,100
1964	14,700
1965	116,800
1966	239,400
1967	319,500
1968	359,800
1969	338,300
1970	254,800
1971	141,200
1972	16,100

in Vietnam. The commanding general of MACV was also the commander of USARV. In day-to-day operations, however, the deputy commander of USARV actually ran things.

Operations of U.S. Army combat units were controlled by corps-level headquarters, commanded by a lieutenant general. Corps are flexible organizations, to which divisions and other units can be assigned as needed for specific operations. Throughout the course of the war, many divisions were assigned to more than one corps at different times. Since the ARVN was

organized into four corps on a regional basis, the American corps were called "field forces" to avoid confusion. I Field Force controlled operations in the north of the country, while II Field Force controlled operations in the south. In 1968 a third corps was formed and actually called a corps. XXIV Corps, which initially came under the operational control of the III Marine Amphibious Force (MAF), controlled Army units near the Demilitarized Zone (DMZ) and in the extreme north of the country. In March 1970 the command relationship reversed, with III MAF subordinate to XXIV Corps.

The division, commanded by a major general, is normally the largest tactical unit in the U.S. Army. At the height of the war, 7 of the Army's 19 divisions were in Vietnam, 6 were in the United States, 4 were in Germany, and 2 were in Korea. A Vietnam-era division was a fixed unit, normally consisting of 10 or 11 infantry battalions, 4 artillery battalions, an armored cavalry squadron, an aviation battalion, and various support battalions.

Between the division headquarters and the battalions, each division had three brigades, intermediate-level headquarters commanded by a colonel. A brigade controlled three to five maneuver battalions. Brigades were not fixed organizations, and battalions were attached and detached from them as needed for specific operations.

Table 2. U.S. Army Units in Vietnam

Unit type	1965	1966	1967	1968	1969	1970	1971	1972
Divisions	0	3	5	7	7	5	2	0
Infantry Battalions	2	32	57	79	81	61	28	2
Tank Battalions/ Cavalry Squadrons	0	3	9	11	12	10	5	0
Direct Support Artillery Battalions	1	15	28	34	33	20	9	0
General Support Artillery Battalions	0	8	18	23	26	25	16	0
Combat Engineer Battalions	0	10	16	19	20	14	7	0
Construction Engineer Battalions	2	6	14	15	14	14	13	0
Signal Battalions	1	9	26	26	28	23	16	2
Aviation Companies/ Air Cavalry Troops	16	62	90	127	142	135	100	40
Special Forces Detachments	76	93	98	88	79	60	7	1

Notes: Under divisions, figures for battalions and companies are totals, including divisional and nondivisional units. Direct Support Artillery Battalions were almost always divisional units, armed with 105-mm howitzers. General Support Artillery Battalions included divisional and nondivisional units armed with 155-mm howitzers, and nondivisional units armed with 175-mm guns and 8-inch howitzers. Figures for Special Forces include A, B, and C detachments.

Table 3. Organization of a Typical Infantry Division

Divisional Headquarters Company	1
Brigade Headquarters Company	3
Divisional Artillery Headquarters Company	1
Infantry Battalions	10
Armored Cavalry Squadrons	1
105mm Artillery Battalions (DS)	3
155mm Artillery Battalions (GS)	1
Aviation Battalion	1
Medical Battalion	1
Signal Battalion	1
Engineer Battalion	1
Maintenance Battalion	1
Supply & Transport Battalion	1
Military Police Company	1
Officers	1,330
Warrant Officers	260
Enlisted	20,700

Notes: A brigade HQ normally controlled three to five battalions. The Divisional Artillery HQ controlled the division's three Direct Support battalions and one General Support battalion, plus any other nondivisional battalions designated to reinforce the division for a specific operation. Some divisions had more than 10 infantry battalions. The infantry battalions of the 1st Cavalry Division were called "cavalry" battalions but were airmobile infantry units. Some divisions also had tank battalions. The 1st Cavalry Division, 23rd Infantry Division, and 101st Airborne Divisions had much larger Aviation Groups, each consisting of three battalions.

The battalion, commanded by a lieutenant colonel, is the basic tactical unit in the U.S. Army. The structure of the infantry battalions underwent several changes during the war, and the battalions in Vietnam eventually were organized much differently than similar units in Germany or in the United States. By 1968 the standard light infantry battalion in Vietnam had four rifle companies, a combat support company, and a headquarters and headquarters company. The combat support company provided the battalion reconnaissance section and the heavy (4.2-inch) mortar platoon. The headquarters company provided battalion administration, maintenance, and supply functions. Typical infantry battalion strength was 43 officers, 2 warrant officers, and 875 enlisted soldiers.

More than any other twentieth-century American war, Vietnam was a company commander's war—a war of small unit actions. The infantry rifle company, commanded by a captain, consisted of a company headquarters, three rifle platoons, and a mortar platoon. The rifle platoon, led by a lieutenant, had three rifle squads and a weapons squad. The rifle squad was led by a staff sergeant and divided into two fire teams, each led by a sergeant. The weapons squad had two M60 machine guns and one 90-mm recoilless rifle. The mortar platoon had three 81-mm mortars. A rifle squad had 10 soldiers; a rifle platoon had one officer and 41 soldiers; and a rifle company had 6 officers and 158 enlisted soldiers.

The Army also had several separate brigades and regiments that operated independent from the divisions. In some special cases, divisional brigades were detached to operate separately. Separate brigades were augmented with support elements to make them semiself-sufficient. Rather than being commanded by a colonel, these separate brigades often were commanded by a brigadier general. The 11th Armored Cavalry Regiment also was a brigade-sized separate unit that operated directly under the control of a field forces headquarters.

There has been much criticism of the U.S. Army's field performance and poor morale and the lack of professionalism among its officer corps. Much of that criticism is accurate and justified, but some of it is overstated. The mentality of careerism and "ticket-punching" among the officer corps has been well documented in *Crisis in Command* by Richard A. Gabriel and Paul L. Savage. Although the typical infantry, artillery, or armor enlisted man spent his entire 12-month tour of duty assigned to a combat unit, the average officer spent only six months with such a unit. The original purpose of this policy was to give as many officers as possible the opportunity for combat experience. The effect, however, was that the enlisted men came to believe that their officers were not being subjected to the same risks as they were, and this led to a loss in confidence in the officer corps.

Armies—all armies at all times—can never be anything more than reflections of the societies from which they are drawn. The careerism and ticket-punching mentality of the Vietnam-era officer corps was adopted from American business and government. Secretary of Defense Robert McNamara himself was a driving force in pushing the military to be more similar to big business. But the "bottom line" in business is measured clearly in terms of dollars and cents. It is impossible to measure military operations in those terms. Hence the business-like fixation with quantification of results led during the Vietnam War to ghoulish practices such as "body counts."

The Army's replacement system was another source of severe problems. Unlike previous wars, where American soldiers went into combat with their units "for the duration," soldiers in Vietnam served only 12 months. This meant that there was constant turnover within units, which made it impossible for leaders to develop the cohesion, teamwork, and personal bonding so necessary for a unit to survive and succeed in combat. The individual replacement system was made possible by America's tremendous transportation capabilities and it was far easier to manage than rotating entire units in and out of the combat zone. Therefore, at the managerial level, the U.S. Army chose administrative expedience over combat effectiveness. The individual soldiers, however, paid the price.

Among all the wars in America's history, Vietnam was unique in that the Army Reserve and National Guard were not mobilized. In all previous wars, a large portion (often the majority) of the force was comprised of National Guardsmen and Reservists. In World War II, for example, Reservists and Guardsmen accounted for 29 percent of all Army officers, 62 percent of the battalion commanders, and 84 percent of the company commanders. After the 1968 Têt Offensive, there was a small-scale call-up, and eventually 7,040 Guardsmen and 3,500 Reservists did serve in Vietnam—some 3 percent of the force there.

The reason for the lack of large-scale reserve involvement was the Johnson administration's reluctance to send too strong a signal to both the American people and to the world at large. This lack of a strong signal, however, served to convince the American people that the involvement in Vietnam was not something that affected the country's vital interests. General Creighton Abrams recognized this only too well. When he became chief of staff of the Army in 1972, he purposely reconfigured the Army's force structure in such a way that any future large-scale deployments of the Army would be impossible without mobilizing its reserve components. This, in fact, is exactly what happened during the 1991 Persian Gulf War and the Bosnia peacekeeping mission beginning in 1996.

Although the typical soldier on the ground often had no idea why he was in Vietnam, morale was generally good during the early part of the war. This changed when more of the American public began to oppose the war in the aftermath of the 1968 Têt Offensive. Opposing the war was one thing, but many Americans, most particularly many in the antiwar movement, committed the terrible error of focusing their anger and frustration on the soldiers fighting the war. As word of the disgraceful treatment of returning soldiers filtered back to the battlefield, the soldiers in the jungles and rice paddies came to believe that they had been betrayed by the very people who had sent them to Vietnam in the first place. From that point on, morale fell apart, and with it, discipline and combat effectiveness.

Between 1961 and 1975 a total of 30,868 U.S. Army soldiers died in Vietnam as the result of hostile action; 7,193 died from other causes. A total of 201,536 U.S. Army soldiers were wounded in action.

—David T. Zabecki

References: Gabriel, Richard A., and Paul L. Savage. *Crisis in Command: Mismanagement in the Army.* New York: Hill & Wang, 1978.

Hackworth, David. *About Face.* New York: Simon & Schuster, 1989.

Krepinevich, Andrew, Jr. *The Army and Vietnam.* Baltimore: Johns Hopkins University Press, 1986.

Palmer, Bruce. *The 25-Year War: America's Military Role in Vietnam.* New York: Simon & Schuster, 1984.

Palmer, Dave. *Summons of the Trumpet: U.S.-Vietnam in Perspective.* Novato, CA: Presidio Press, 1978.

Stanton, Shelby. *The Rise and Fall of an American Army: U.S. Ground Forces in Vietnam 1965–1973.* Novato, CA: Presidio Press, 1985.

_____. *Vietnam Order of Battle.* Washington, DC: U.S. News Books, 1981.

See also: Abrams, Creighton; African American Personnel in U.S. Forces in Vietnam; Antiwar Movement, United States; Casualties; Draft; Herbert, Anthony; Johnson, Lyndon Baines; McNamara, Robert S.; Military Assistance and Advisory Group (MAAG), Vietnam; Military Assistance Command, Vietnam (MACV); Order of Battle; United States: Air Force; United States: Navy; United States: Special Forces; Westmoreland, William Childs.

United States: Coast Guard

On 29 April 1965 President Lyndon Johnson authorized deployment of U.S. Coast Guard cutters to Vietnam to assist the Navy in preventing arms and supplies from being smuggled to Viêt Công guerrillas. Coast Guard Squadron One, with 17 82-foot patrol boats (WPBs) and 250 men, was established on 27 May 1965. The cutters were operated by two officers and nine enlisted men. Each ship was armed with five .50-caliber machine guns and a trigger-fired, flat-trajectory, 81-mm mortar. The twin-screwed cutter, powered by diesel engines, had a speed of 17 knots. WPBs were radar equipped, displaced 70 tons, and were shallow-draft—6.5 feet—for working close to shore.

The squadron, divided into two divisions, arrived in Vietnam in July 1965. Division 11, based at Phú Quôc Island in the Gulf of Thailand, patrolled the Cambodian border and Gulf coast of Vietnam. Division 12 was based at Đà Nẵng and patrolled the 17th parallel and the coastline south of the Demilitarized Zone (DMZ). A third division of nine cutters was sent to Vietnam on 22 February 1966. Division 13, stationed at Cát Lở, patrolled the rivers and coastal area of the Mekong Delta region south of Sài Gòn.

Cutter crewmen boarded and searched hundreds of thousands of junks and sampans, deterring coastal smuggling of arms and ammunition. WPBs were under way on patrol 70 percent of the time—in all weather. Cutters are credited with engaging and destroying most of the Democratic Republic of Vietnam (DRV) steel-hulled supply trawlers interdicted. Patrol boats supported Special Forces and Marine amphibious operations and routinely provided close-in fire support and illumination with their mortars for outposts under attack and troop operations ashore.

As the Vietnam conflict escalated, Navy Secretary Paul Nitze requested that the Coast Guard "assist the Department of the Navy by assigning five high endurance cutters to augment Market Time forces." Coast Guard Squadron Three, consisting of five 311-foot Coast Guard high-endurance cutters (HECs), was commissioned at Pearl Harbor on 24 April 1967. Headquartered at Subic Bay in the Philippines, the squadron kept three cutters on patrol continuously during Operation MARKET TIME.

Cutters interdicted and destroyed DRV supply trawlers, provided naval gunfire support (NGFS), engaged in medical and civil action programs (MEDCAPs), and supported patrol boat operations. When Navy destroyers were withdrawn from MARKET TIME on 30 June 1969, Coast Guard HECs continued to maintain the outer barrier. During Squadron Three's deployments, high-endurance cutters spent 75 percent of their time under way, 20 percent in upkeep, and 5 percent on port visits. From April 1967 to January 1972, 4,500 officers and men and 30 ships participated in deployments with Squadron Three. Cutters retained their white paint schemes during deployments.

On 20 February 1966 U.S. Military Assistance Command, Vietnam (MACV) made an urgent request for the assistance of Coast Guard Explosive Loading Detachments (ELDs). The increasing volume of ammunition arriving in Vietnam was handled by inexperienced Vietnamese stevedores who lacked equipment and skills to safely unload explosives. Two eight-man detachments arrived on 5 June 1966 and were assigned to the Army's 1st Logistical Command (1st Log). The detachments supervised Vietnamese stevedores unloading ammunition at Nhà Bè and U.S. Army operations at Cam Ranh Bay. By teaching the Vietnamese more efficient procedures and introducing better equipment, operations were made safer and unloading times were cut in half. In August 1968 the Navy requested a Coast Guard ELD for Đà Nẵng. After a near disastrous ammunition accident, in March 1968 an ELD was assigned to the Army at Qui Nhơn. During the entire Vietnam conflict, there was never a major explosive incident due to accident or hostile action at any port where Coast Guard ELDs were assigned.

On 20 July 1966 General William Westmoreland requested the assistance of a Coast Guard Port Security and Waterways Detail (PS&WD). The PS&WD inspected Army port facilities, trained Army boat crews, and advised 1st Log's commanding general on port security. On 3 December 1966 a Coast Guard marine inspector was assigned to Sài Gòn to assist the Navy's Military Sea Transportation Service (MSTS) in resolving problems aboard the 300 merchant ships supporting U.S. forces. On 1 July 1968 the position was expanded to a Merchant Marine Detail and attached to the U.S. Embassy in Sài Gòn. A Coast Guard Aids to Navigation Detail, working out of Sài Gòn, deployed buoy tenders, positioned and maintained buoys, and fixed aids at ports and along the coast to support U.S. military operations.

On 3 April 1968 Coast Guard helicopter pilots began flying rescue missions with the HH-3E and HH-53C helicopters of the Air Force's 37th Aerospace Rescue and Recovery Squadron stationed at Đà Nẵng. Flying those "Jolly Green Giants," the pilots' mission was to rescue U.S. pilots downed behind enemy lines in North and South Vietnam. The exchange pilot program continued until 1973, and Coast Guard aviators were highly decorated for their daring rescues under fire.

On 14 December 1965 the Defense Department requested that the Coast Guard build an electronic navigation system that would provide precision guidance for Air Force aircraft operating in North and South Vietnam; it had to be in operation in eight months. On 8 August 1966 Operation TIGHT REIGN's LORAN-C chain went on-air as scheduled. Electronic signals that were beamed from 625-foot-high transmitting towers at two stations in Thailand and one station in Vietnam were monitored by another station in Thailand. To provide better coverage of the Hồ Chí Minh Trail, the Coast Guard built a second transmitting station in Vietnam at Tân My in 1969. Just 42 miles below the DMZ, Tân My LORAN Station became the northernmost U.S. installation in Vietnam during the withdrawal.

After U.S. forces withdrew in 1973, the LORAN chain continued to operate, but with Coast Guardsmen replaced by civilian technicians at the two stations in Vietnam. The crew of LORAN station, Côn Sơn Island, destroyed electronic equipment before being evacuated by helicopter on 29 April 1975, the day before Sài Gòn fell.

Eight thousand Coast Guardsmen served in Vietnam from 1964 to 1973, 3,500 with units in-country. Seven Coast Guardsmen were killed in action.

—Alex Larzelere

References: Kaplan, Hyman R. *Coast Guard in Vietnam.* Washington, DC: U.S. Coast Guard, Public Information Division, 1971.
Larzelere, Alex. *The Coast Guard at War. Vietnam, 1965–1975.* Annapolis, MD: Naval Institute Press, 1997.
Schreadley, R. L. *From the Rivers to the Sea.* Annapolis, MD: Naval Institute Press, 1993.
Tulich, Eugene N. *The United States Coast Guard in Southeast Asia during the Vietnam Conflict.* Washington, DC: U.S. Coast Guard, Public Affairs Division, 1986.
See also: MARKET TIME, Operation; Military Assistance Command, Vietnam (MACV); Sea Power in the Vietnam War; Search-and-Rescue (SAR) Operations; United States: Navy; Warships, Allied and Democratic Republic of Vietnam.

United States: Department of Justice

U.S. government executive department founded in 1870 to enforce federal law, represent the government in federal cases, determine jurisdiction, and ensure governmental compliance under federal law; branches include the Civil Rights Division and the Federal Bureau of Investigation (FBI); headed by the attorney general of the United States. Between 1965 and 1973 the Johnson and Nixon administrations encountered growing domestic opposition to the war in Vietnam. Presidents Lyndon B. Johnson and Richard M. Nixon believed that Communists were responsible for the antiwar movement, that protests threatened domestic order and stability, and that demonstrators were a source of support for the Vietnamese Communists. Both administrations used the Department of Justice and its investigatory branch, the FBI, to infiltrate, subvert, and monitor protest groups.

The Johnson administration gathered intelligence and sought possible legal actions against domestic critics of the war. In 1965 Attorney General Nicholas Katzenbach pledged to initiate a nationwide investigation of antiwar organizations and suggested federal indictments for draft resistance and sedition. FBI Director J. Edgar Hoover ordered his agency to link antiwar leaders to Communists, and soon FBI agents secretly infiltrated organizations. The FBI also reinitiated counterintelligence programs (COINTELPROs), covert programs directed against dissident domestic groups. Katzenbach's successor Ramsey Clark refused, however, to support legislation outlawing draft resistance, nor did he cancel large protest marches on Washington. Yet Johnson and the Justice Department increased legal pressure on the antiwar movement. The FBI interrogated protest leaders and recruited university officials to report on student protesters, and the Justice Department briefly ended draft deferments for college students who protested the war in Vietnam. The Johnson administration also prepared a list of federal statutes violated by protesters; it included aiding deserters, advocating insurrection by mail, damaging government property, impeding the protection of the president, and sabotaging U.S. military facilities. On 5 January 1968 the Justice Department indicted several prominent antiwar leaders, including the pediatrician Dr. Benjamin Spock, for conspiracy to counsel, aid, and abet young men to violate draft laws. A hesitant Clark prosecuted Spock and four others, but all were eventually acquitted or the charges against them were dropped.

Nixon's attorney general John Mitchell took a more confrontational approach to the antiwar movement to appease right-wing politicians who believed that Johnson was reluctant to prosecute protesters for treason. Mitchell's actions also reflected Nixon's belief that demonstrators were allied with Communists. In 1969 Mitchell ordered the Justice Department to increase electronic surveillance operations by relaxing restrictions on federal wiretapping. Nixon also urged Hoover to wiretap the phones of journalists who questioned Vietnam policy. Mitchell tried to justify the questionable wiretapping before the Supreme Court by arguing that the president needed wide latitude in conducting national security. In 1972 the Supreme Court rejected his arguments in *U.S. v. U.S. District Court for the Eastern District of Michigan.* Nixon also enlisted the help of presidential aide Tom Huston to study new investigation techniques. The subsequent but aborted Huston Plan of 1970 proposed far-reaching (and often illegal) activities including wiretaps, burglaries, opening mail, and infiltration. The Huston Plan called for the creation of an interagency domestic intelligence apparatus under White House control, combining elements of the FBI, the Central Intelligence Agency (CIA), and other agencies, which too was illegal. Although Nixon approved the plan, Hoover refused to go along. This willingness on the part of the White House to circumvent or break existing laws foreshadowed the events that contributed to the Watergate scandal.

—Mark A. Esposito

References: Elliff, John T. *Crime, Dissent, and the Attorney General: The Justice Department in the 1960s.* Beverly Hills, CA: Sage Publications, 1971.
Kutler, Stanley. *The Wars of Watergate: The Last Crisis of Richard Nixon.* New York: Alfred A. Knopf, 1990.
Wells, Tom. *The War Within: America's Battle over Vietnam.* Berkeley, CA: University of California Press, 1994.
See also: Antiwar Movement, United States; Federal Bureau of Investigation (FBI); Huston Plan; Johnson, Lyndon Baines; Katzenbach, Nicholas; Mitchell, John Newton; Nixon, Richard Milhous; Spock, Benjamin M.; Watergate.

United States: Involvement in Indo-China through 1954

Nineteenth- and twentieth-century American missionaries and entrepreneurs saw Asia as fertile ground for trade and for Christianizing and Westernizing the inhabitants of that continent, with each goal complementing the others. The center of that Asian activity was mainland China, and the United States was concerned by gains there registered first by Russia and then Japan.

When the French moved into Indo-China in the mid–nineteenth century, the U.S. government began to take special notice of that area. Initial U.S. interest in the region was based on concern that the French posed a threat to American interests in China. It is ironic that the United States first chose to confront Japan over Vietnam; in July 1941 Japan established bases in South Indo-China. This threat to Siam, Malaya, and the Netherlands East Indies brought a joint U.S., United Kingdom, and Netherlands economic embargo, and it was this that brought the Japanese to the decision to attack Pearl Harbor.

During the Second World War, the United States provided assistance to the Viêt Minh through the Office of Strategic Services (OSS). The Viêt Minh helped rescue downed American pilots and provided intelligence information on the Japanese. OSS agents, including Capt. Archimedes Patti, did not conceal their admiration for the Viêt Minh and assured it that the United States would stand on its side against French colonialism. Furthermore, the Atlantic Charter provided encouragement to Hô Chí Minh and Vietnamese nationalists by its support for the right of national self-determination. By 1945, however, growing fear of Russian activity worldwide prompted the United States to support French colonialism in Southeast Asia.

In the Second World War's last months, President Franklin Roosevelt suggested U.S. support for a trusteeship over the region. He believed that France had performed poorly as a colonial power and should not be allowed to reclaim Indo-China. His successor Harry Truman, more concerned about communism than colonialism, made the initial commitment to the French presence in Vietnam almost immediately at the war's end.

In August 1945 the Truman administration ordered 12 U.S. merchant ships, originally assigned to carry U.S. servicemen home from war, to transport French combat troops to Sài Gòn. The French government intended to reestablish itself in Indo-China, and the U.S. government did not seek to prevent it. U.S. diplomats in Indo-China, however, notified Washington on several occasions of growing nationalism in the area. Any attempt by the French to reclaim its colony, many feared, would spark a long, bloody conflict. Such warnings were indeed prophetic. A little more than a year after the conclusion of World War II, war erupted in Indo-China. At the center of the conflict was the Communist leader Hô Chí Minh and his nationalist organization, the Viêt Minh. During the course of World War II, the Viêt Minh made significant contributions to the Allied cause, especially in locating downed airmen. This did not go unnoticed by members of the U.S. intelligence community, who often praised Hô, but usually noted that he was, after all, a Communist. The anti-Communist ethos that had pervaded the United States since 1917 made it virtually impossible for that generation's leaders to ally themselves too closely with any Communist, Marshal Tito of Yugoslavia notwithstanding.

Whatever the suspicions, Hô Chí Minh employed the words of Thomas Jefferson in proclaiming Vietnam's independence on 2 September 1945. He hoped for eventual support from the United States and Great Britain. At that moment, the British were arming French prisoners of war, and just over one month later, U.S. Secretary of State Dean Acheson publicly noted that the United States would not oppose the reestablishment of French control in Vietnam. Hô made several direct appeals to Washington, always praising the United States as champion of the rights of small nations and noting that it was the Viêt Minh, not the French, who contributed to the Allied war effort, but such appeals went unanswered. In spite of the coolness in Washington, U.S. officials on the scene continued to support Hô's goal of an independent Vietnam.

Without support from either the United States or Britain, Hô was forced to seek a temporary arrangement with France. Though criticized by many of his own supporters, on 6 March 1946 he concluded an agreement with Jean Sainteny, in which the French promised to withdraw all troops by 1952 and recognize the Democratic Republic of Vietnam. The situation was complicated when French High Commissioner for Indo-China Georges Thierry d'Argenlieu arbitrarily created the Republic of Cochin China.

Despite such impediments, Hô traveled to France in the hope that he could finalize what was at best an ambiguous arrangement. The discussions at Fontainebleau accomplished little. By August Hô concluded that the French never intended to allow complete independence. The talks were subsequently canceled, and Hô returned home. Pressure for war was building on both sides, and fighting began in December 1946.

For policymakers in the U.S. State Department in the winter of 1946, Vietnam presented yet another in a long list of problems requiring attention. In December of that year Albert Low Moffat, head of the State Department's division on Southeast Asia, traveled to Hà Nôi to assess the situation. After careful observation, he concluded that Hồ Chí Minh was first and foremost a Vietnamese nationalist, determined to win independence for his people. He added that Hồ might be viewed less as a tool of international communism and more as an Asian Tito. Other officials in Vietnam agreed with Moffat's assessment of the Việt Minh leader. The people of Vietnam would, they argued, reject any other proposed head of state.

Disregarding positive reports from officials in Vietnam, most Washington policymakers believed that the United States must continue to support the French effort in order to gain their crucial backing for America's strategy in Europe. This revealed that, from the outset, the U.S. position on Vietnam was hostage to its European policy. With Germany disarmed, France was the major power in Europe to contain a possible Soviet invasion. Before the end of 1946 the United States had sent $160 million to aid the French effort in Vietnam.

Debate continued through 1949 on how the United States should view Hồ Chí Minh, especially in comparison to the French puppet Bao Đai. In a May 1949 memorandum (included in Williams et al.'s *America in Vietnam: A Documentary History*), Secretary of State Acheson noted: "Question whether Ho as much nationalist as Commie is irrelevant. All Stalinists in colonial areas are nationalists. With achievement national aims . . . their objective necessarily becomes subordination . . . to Commie purposes. . . ."

The fall of Nationalist China, combined with Soviet recognition of Hồ's regime, solidified Washington's belief that Vietnam was permanently assimilated into the worldwide Communist movement. After 1949 U.S. commitment to France was never in serious doubt. The Korean War that began in 1950 strengthened this.

In 1950 the U.S. government established a Military Assistance and Advisory Group (MAAG) in Vietnam to help train a viable army, to screen French requests for aid, and to make helpful suggestions regarding strategy. The French generally ignored MAAG and seemed insulted that Americans presumed to give them advice. Despite such French recalcitrance, Washington continued to pour in aid. No one seriously questioned what might happen should France fail in Indo-China.

After President Truman left office in 1953, the Vietnam situation grew more complex by the day. President Dwight D. Eisenhower, though unhappy with the French refusal to heed U.S. advice, adopted the previous administration's position totally and with no serious review or reevaluation.

The French military effort, in fact, was going badly, and opposition to the war was growing among the population in France. For that reason, Paris began to talk about a negotiated settlement after the Korean armistice in July 1953. The United States, while still involved in fighting in Korea, had actively opposed negotiations with the Việt Minh and assured Paris of material aid, short of combat troops or nuclear weapons.

In the spring of 1954, as the situation at Điên Biên Phu deteriorated, Washington seriously considered military intervention.

Among those arguing for such a course was Vice-President Richard Nixon. A plan for U.S. military intervention, code-named Operation VULTURE, was never implemented, in large part because of British opposition. London, believing the battle was too far gone and placing hopes in the conference at Geneva, refused to participate. Congressional leaders informed President Eisenhower that they would not support such an operation if the British refused participation.

The May 1954 fall of Điên Biên Phu and the subsequent Geneva Accords marked the beginning of the end of French influence in Vietnamese affairs. It was not long before the United States replaced the French.

—Francis H. Thompson

References: Herring, George C. *America's Longest War: The United States in Vietnam, 1950–1975.* 2d ed. New York: Alfred A. Knopf, 1986.
Kahin, George M. *Intervention: How America Became Involved in Vietnam.* Garden City, NY: Anchor Books, 1987.
Williams, William A., John McCormick, et al., eds. *America in Vietnam: A Documentary History.* New York: W. W. Norton, 1985.
Young, Marilyn. *The Vietnam Wars, 1945–1990.* New York: Harper Perennial, 1991.
See also: Acheson, Dean G.; Central Intelligence Agency (CIA); Containment Policy; d'Argenlieu, Georges Thierry; Điên Biên Phu, Battle of; Eisenhower, Dwight David; Geneva Conference and Geneva Accords; Hồ Chí Minh; Hồ-Sainteny Agreement; Military Assistance and Advisory Group (MAAG), Vietnam; Nixon, Richard Milhous; Office of Strategic Services (OSS); Patti, Archimedes L. A.; Roosevelt, Franklin Delano; Sainteny, Jean; Truman, Harry S; Việt Minh (Viêt Nam Độc Lâp Đông Minh Hôi [Vietnam Independence League]); VULTURE, Operation.

United States: Involvement in Vietnam, 1954–1965

With the French capitulation at Geneva in 1954, the United States, by its own decision, assumed responsibility for South Vietnam. Long frustrated with the French, both for their political handling of Indo-China and for what was perceived as their weak military performance against the Việt Minh, the United States sought to play the decisive hand in the future of the area. At first, President Dwight Eisenhower attempted to work with the French and other Western allies to contain communism in Southeast Asia. He and Secretary of State John Foster Dulles engineered the Southeast Asia Treaty Organization (SEATO) in September 1954, which under a separate protocol gave Laos, Cambodia, and South Vietnam a special protected status. Eisenhower sent General J. Lawton Collins to attempt to continue a U.S.-French joint effort in the region.

In the spring of 1955 Eisenhower abandoned the allied approach and moved in a unilateral direction as the United States dedicated itself to building a strong Vietnamese nation in the South under the leadership of the enigmatic Ngô Đình Diêm. Eisenhower tried to persuade the French to support the Diêm option, but they hated the aristocratic nationalist almost as much as Diêm distrusted them.

The French attempted to maintain a military presence in South Vietnam by continuing to train its military establishment, but the United States assumed this role in early 1956, and France was squeezed out within a few months. The United States began to structure the South Vietnamese armed forces into a carbon copy of its own military and prepared the country to fight a mid-intensity conventional war against an invasion from the North. Only the slightest attention was given to counterinsurgency.

Diêm faced an almost impossible task in a war-ravaged country, "a political jungle of warlords, sects, bandits, partisan troops and secret societies," as one commentator described it. First, he had to deal with the influx of about 900,000 refugees, mostly Catholics, into the predominantly Buddhist South. The Viêt Minh left cadres behind in the South; later they were the vanguard of insurrection. In the spring of 1955 various contenders for power, including the religious sects (the Cao Đài and the Hòa Hao), the Sài Gòn gangsters (Bình Xuyên), and several coup factions in the military, challenged Diêm's regime. In the midst of Diêm's multiple crises, Washington was ready to cut its ties, but amazingly Diêm overcame the challenges and solidified his position in the country, consequently retaining the relationship with his U.S. benefactors.

Seizing on the momentum of his victories, Diêm announced that the Geneva-mandated reunification elections in 1956 would not be held, and with the assistance of Central Intelligence Agency (CIA) operative Col. Edward Lansdale, Diêm successfully ousted Emperor Bao Đai, converted the State of Vietnam into the Republic of Vietnam (RVN), and claimed its presidency. Although the RVN was not the citadel of democracy that the United States proclaimed and Diêm not the model leader, the United States had cast its lot with him.

Full-scale insurrection against Diêm resurfaced in 1957. The origins were primarily indigenous, with little direction from the North. However, the U.S. military mission continued to concentrate on building the Republic of Vietnam Armed Forces (RVNAF) along conventional lines to repel an external aggressor. Diêm, though, focused on the internal threat and employed counterinsurgency military measures. These forces were poorly trained and equipped, and the social programs component was halfhearted.

U.S. economic assistance was generous, in excess of $250 million per year through the Eisenhower years—80 percent of which went to the military. The result was an economically dependent South Vietnamese client-state. As U.S. involvement increased, the first American military casualties occurred in July 1959, when two U.S. advisors were killed in a terrorist attack at Biên Hòa Air Base.

The nature of the U.S. advisory role changed in the early 1960s. In December 1960 Hà Nôi announced the birth of the National Liberation Front (NLF) in South Vietnam, although the organization had already existed for at least a couple of years. President John F. Kennedy feared that Indo-China was a prime theater for Soviet-sponsored "wars of national liberation," and he prepared to meet this global challenge. Influenced by his reading of *The Uncertain Trumpet* (1960) by former Army Chief of Staff General Maxwell Taylor, Kennedy extended Taylor's proposal for a more "flexible military response" to include low-intensity warfare and assigned this counterinsurgency role to the U.S. Army Special Forces. The regular military was not enthusiastic about counterinsurgency and did little more than pay it lip service.

Although the primary area of concern in Indo-China during the first months of the Kennedy administration was Laos, by spring 1961 the focus began to shift to Vietnam. Kennedy authorized the expansion of the RVNAF from 150,000 to 200,000 men and sent more U.S. advisors—civilian specialists in government, economic affairs, and technical areas as well as military personnel, including Green Berets. With the National Security Council and the Joint Chiefs of Staff considering combat troops, Kennedy dispatched advisors Maxwell Taylor and Walt Rostow to South Vietnam in October 1961 to report on the situation. Their pessimistic report called for more assistance of all kinds, including a task force that would include combat troops. Vice-President Lyndon Johnson on an earlier trip had broached the subject with Diêm, who did not want U.S. troops. Diêm believed that the presence of American forces would provide the Viêt Công with a significant propaganda issue, and he was concerned about the impact of greater American involvement on his non-Communist opposition in the South. But most importantly, he feared that American combat troops would lead to the United States assuming control of the war and ultimately the country. Diêm wanted unlimited American aid with no interference in internal politics or the conduct of the war.

Kennedy stepped up assistance but rejected the idea of combat troops. He remarked that the first group of troops would engender requests for more. "It's like taking a drink. The effect wears off, and you have to take another." At the same time that he refused to authorize combat troops, Kennedy also rejected a negotiated settlement in Vietnam similar to one he was seeking in Laos. Thus, Kennedy opted for a midposition between fighting and negotiating—a commitment of aid and advisors, which he recognized from the beginning might prove unsuccessful. But for the most part, Kennedy was optimistic. Like his Secretary of Defense Robert McNamara and others of his "best and brightest" advisors (to employ journalist David Halberstam's characterization), Kennedy viewed Vietnam predominantly as a military problem to be "managed" successfully. This sanguine approach characterized American policy in 1962.

The upgrading of the Military Advisory and Assistance Group (MAAG) to Military Assistance Command, Vietnam (MACV) in February 1962 was symbolic and substantive. The number of advisors rose from 3,200 in December 1961 to 9,000 by the end of 1962. The increased American presence with helicopters, new weapons, civic action programs, and expanded training had a short-term positive impact on the war, but this advantage largely eroded by the end of the year. American optimism and cultural hubris did not. As one foreign journalist noted, "probably the only people who have the historical sense of inevitable victory are the Americans."

Despite talk about winning hearts and minds, U.S. leaders never persuaded RVN President Diêm to undertake the reforms needed to win support for his government nor to address seriously the corruption that engulfed the country. The high-profile Strategic Hamlet program ultimately failed as Diêm misused it, primarily to bring the rural countryside under his personal control. Diêm resented American "interference" and increasingly came to fear the escalating American presence as much as his internal enemies. His concerns were not totally unwarranted.

As American journalists began to attack Diêm and American Vietnam policy, the buoyancy of 1962 quickly waned. Increasingly, Kennedy became frustrated by Diêm and his pernicious brother Ngô Đình Nhu. Diêm's heavy-handed and inept handling of the Buddhist uprising in the spring and summer of 1963 weakened American support for his regime. Despite the official rhetoric, disenchantment with the ARVN's capacity and willingness to fight grew. With his advisors greatly divided over what to do about Diêm, Kennedy was wavering and evasive through the fall, finally tacitly acquiescing to a coup effort by South Vietnamese generals against Diêm in November 1963. However, Kennedy personally was devastated by Diêm's murder during the coup. When Kennedy was assassinated three weeks later, Lyndon Johnson inherited a growing political and military quagmire.

Johnson retained the Kennedy team to run the war, and he continued the same basic policies. After an extensive policy review in March 1964, the president concluded that "the only reasonable alternative" was "to do more of the same and do it more efficiently." Johnson expanded the number of advisors (from 16,300 when he took office to 23,300 by the end of 1964), and he increased assistance by $50 million. He hoped to keep Vietnam on the back burner at least through the 1964 presidential election, and he proceeded cautiously. However, at the same time, he authorized secret plans for possible military action against North Vietnam. Through intermediaries, the Johnson administration warned Hà Nôi that the United States was prepared to inflict a heavy punishment on the Democratic Republic of Vietnam (DRV) if it continued to support the insurgency in the South. But North Vietnam responded by mobilizing its own forces for war, expanding the Hô Chí Minh Trail, and preparing to infiltrate regular People's Army of Vietnam (PAVN) units into the South.

Meanwhile, political intrigue and instability dominated the South Vietnamese government and the ARVN. The war against the guerrillas was being lost. The Viêt Công controlled more than 40 percent of the territory and more than 50 percent of the population. In many areas, the Viêt Công was so entrenched that only massive military force would dislodge them.

On 2 August 1964 the budding crises between the United States and North Vietnam intensified with a DRV attack on the USS *Maddox,* which was engaged in electronic espionage in the Gulf of Tonkin off the coast of the DRV. The United States prepared for a possible military retaliation. Two nights later, another attack may have occurred, although Võ Nguyên Giáp told McNamara in November 1995 that it never happened. In any case, the Johnson administration opted for the opportunity to send a message. The United States launched air strikes against the DRV, and Johnson seized the moment to extort from the frenzied Congress the Southeast Asian Resolution, better known as the Gulf of Tonkin Resolution, which authorized the president to employ military power against the DRV. Senator Ernest Gruening of Alaska, one of only two senators to vote against the resolution, correctly labeled it a "predated declaration of war."

After the Gulf of Tonkin incident, Johnson reverted to a cautious strategy. During the fall presidential campaign against Vietnam hawk Barry Goldwater, Johnson emphasized that he did not wish to widen the war or "send American boys to do what Asian boys should do." He did not respond to terrorist attacks that took American lives in South Vietnam in November and December, but the administration was preparing a retaliatory bombing program against the North to be unleashed at the proper moment.

In early 1965 all the pieces began to fall in place. In response to another provocation, Johnson ordered a retaliatory bombing in early February. Individual reprisal attacks soon transformed into Operation ROLLING THUNDER, a sustained bombing campaign, and in reaction to the desperate military situation in the South, American ground troops followed in March. In July Johnson authorized independent American combat operations and began the massive American troop buildup. The advisory days were over. This was now America's war in Vietnam.

—Joe P. Dunn

References: Anderson, David L. *Trapped by Success: The Eisenhower Administration and Vietnam, 1953–61.* New York: Columbia University Press, 1991.
Duiker, William J. *U.S. Containment Policy and the Conflict in Indochina.* Stanford, CA: Stanford University Press, 1994.
Herring, George C. *America's Longest War: The United States and Vietnam, 1950–1975.* 2d ed. New York: Alfred A. Knopf, 1986.
Kahin, George M. *Intervention: How America Became Involved in Vietnam.* New York: Alfred A. Knopf, 1986.
Krepinevich, Andrew F., Jr. *The Army and Vietnam.* Baltimore: Johns Hopkins University Press, 1986.
See also: Central Intelligence Agency (CIA); Collins, Joseph Lawton; Fishel, Wesley Robert; Gruening, Ernest Henry; Halberstam, David; Johnson, Lyndon Baines; Kennedy, John Fitzgerald; Lansdale, Edward Geary; McNamara, Robert S.; Ngô Đình Diêm; Ngô Đình Diêm, Overthrow of; ROLLING THUNDER, Operation; Rostow, Walt Whitman; Southeast Asia Treaty Organization (SEATO); Taylor, Maxwell Davenport; Tonkin Gulf Incidents; Tonkin Gulf Resolution.

United States: Involvement in Vietnam, 1965–1968

In 1965 the United States made the fateful decision to commit major ground combat forces to the war in Vietnam, thus deepening an involvement, which to that point had consisted primarily of logistical, financial, and advisory support to the South Vietnamese. At the end of 1964 about 23,500 Americans had been serving in Vietnam. By the close of 1968 that number had grown to 525,000. Commencement of this buildup was precipitated by February 1965 Viêt Công attacks on American installations near Pleiku in the Central Highlands. Retaliatory air strikes by the United States, deployment into Vietnam of additional air assets, and a consequent need to protect the growing complement of aircraft and their airfields added to the necessity for an increased U.S. troop presence. To that end, in early March 1965 President Lyndon Johnson authorized the deployment of some 3,500 U.S. Marines to the area around Đà Nẵng, followed in April by the assignment of the Army's 173d Airborne Brigade to Biên Hòa and Vũng Tàu.

Also in early March 1965 President Johnson sent U.S. Army Chief of Staff General Harold K. Johnson on a mission to Vietnam. Returning to Washington at midmonth, General Johnson submitted

Soldiers from two companies of the U.S. 101st Airborne Division rest during a jungle march south of Đà Nẵng.

to the president a report containing 21 recommendations, including an intensified air war against North Vietnam and the deployment of many more ground forces to Vietnam. Most of these proposals were approved, and in mid-June Secretary of Defense Robert McNamara announced additional deployments to a level of 75,000 men.

In closing his report, General Johnson had raised the question of how much more the United States would have to contribute. In the margin, Secretary McNamara wrote a blank check: "Policy is: Anything that will strengthen the position of the GVN [government of Vietnam] will be sent." Meanwhile General Johnson set in motion within the Army staff a study of how the war was being conducted that would have an enormous, but much delayed, impact on American involvement.

Reports through the late spring of 1965 indicated that the Army of the Republic of Vietnam (ARVN) could not survive without extensive additional assistance. On 28 July President Johnson announced to Americans that he was sending 50,000 more troops and that draft calls would be increased. "Additional forces will be needed later," he added, "and they will be sent as requested." Significantly, the president did not approve calling up reserve forces. The U.S. command in Vietnam quickly submitted requests for even more forces, and the buildup of American troops moved into high gear.

Shortly after the series of retaliatory air strikes against targets in North Vietnam were conducted in early February 1965, President Johnson authorized a continuing air campaign against the North that became known as Operation ROLLING THUNDER. Commencing in early March 1965 this bombing continued unabated, except for certain suspensions and restrictions, until 31 October 1968. It was in the conduct of the air war, however, that the greatest controversy arose over the administration's "graduated response" approach. The Joint Chiefs of Staff, as well as the field command, sought to apply massive force in the shortest possible time. Instead, frustrating impediments to this strategy were imposed by the civilian hierarchy. Even though the scope and magnitude of the air war continued to increase, albeit punctuated by numerous pauses of varying duration, the incremental approach permitted the Communists to make adjustments at successive levels and to put in place a continuously improving air defense system. After leaving office, Johnson reportedly told President Richard Nixon that all the pauses had been useless and that he regretted having ordered them. That notwithstanding, in March 1968 Johnson scaled back the bombing of North Vietnam to below the 20th parallel only, and in November of that year terminated it altogether.

In June 1964 General William Westmoreland had taken command of Military Assistance Command, Vietnam (MACV). This was an ominous appointment, for it was he who devised the strategy of attrition and search-and-destroy tactics that characterized the ground war through the end of his tenure. The measure of merit under this approach became the body count; the defining objective and the so-called crossover point became the point at which enemy soldiers were being killed at a greater rate than they could be replaced by infiltration from North Vietnam or by in-country recruitment in South Vietnam. "Accompanying the strategy," stated the Pentagon Papers, "was a subtle change of emphasis—instead of simply denying the enemy victory and convincing him that he could not win, the thrust became defeating the enemy in the South." But that was not all: "Written all over the search and destroy strategy was total loss of confidence in the RVNAF [Republic of Vietnam Armed Forces] and a concomitant willingness on the part of the U.S. to take over the war effort."

Seeking to achieve this elusive goal, General Westmoreland made repeated requests for additional troops. In February 1966, only months after the first major increases, he came in with requirements that would raise the troop ceiling to 429,000. In 1967 he was back with further requests for major troop augmentation, beyond the 470,000 that by that point had been authorized. This time he presented two alternatives, one described as a "minimum essential" add-on of 80,500 troops, the other an "optimum" of some 200,000 additional, which would have brought the total authorized to 670,000. Washington approved neither of these packages; only a scaled down addition to a new total of 525,000 was authorized. Tolerance for additional commitments was running out.

With these forces, Westmoreland mounted large multibattalion operations aimed at bringing Communist main force units to battle. The first of these engagements took place in the Ia Drang Valley in November 1965, when elements of the newly deployed 1st Cavalry Division (Airmobile) took on some 2,000 People's Army of Vietnam (PAVN) troops from three different regiments. In *We Were Soldiers Once . . . and Young*, Lt. Gen. Harold Moore, whose battalion had been in the thick of it, called the battle "one month of maneuver, attack, retreat, bait, trap, ambush, and bloody butchery." When it was over, the Americans had inflicted an estimated 3,561 deaths on the Communists, losing 305 of their own in the process. "What that said to two officers who had learned their trade in the meat-grinder campaigns in World War II," wrote Moore of Westmoreland and his operations officer, Maj. Gen. William DePuy, "was that they could bleed the enemy to death over the long haul with a strategy of attrition."

The American military establishment in the Republic of Vietnam (RVN) grew larger and more pervasive with each passing year. An elaborate system of base camps was developed, ports and airfields built or improved, and massive logistical support provided. Naval and Air Force elements grew proportionately, with naval gunfire as well as air elements contributing to the massive firepower at MACV disposal.

Meanwhile the essence of Communist control over the populace, the Viêt Công infrastructure in the hamlets and villages, continued essentially undisturbed as pacification in the countryside and improvement of South Vietnamese forces were largely ignored. One positive development was that in May 1967 American support for pacification was pulled together under MACV control.

During 1967 General Westmoreland made three trips to the United States. Addressing various audiences, including the National Press Club, he said, "we have reached an important point when the end begins to come into view. I have never been more encouraged," he said in November, only weeks before the Communist 1968 Têt Offensive changed everything.

After the Têt Offensive, General Earle G. Wheeler made a trip to Vietnam and brought back a request for the deployment of some 206,000 additional American troops. This was yet another bombshell. General Westmoreland had been describing the Têt Offensive as a battlefield victory for Allied forces, one that had cost the Communists severe losses. Now this request for hundreds of thousands more troops seemed to undermine the credibility of that claim, just as the fact of the Têt Offensive itself had undermined Westmoreland's optimistic forecasts of the preceding year.

The request precipitated a comprehensive review of American policy on Vietnam. The result was a series of dramatic changes. The troop request was denied, the high-water mark of American commitment to the war was reached and passed, and Westmoreland was replaced as U.S. commander in Vietnam.

General Westmoreland was not happy with the outcome of his tenure in command. Recalling bitterly "the prideful creatures in the bureaucratic jungles of Washington and Saigon," in his memoirs he summed up the experience in these terms: "As American commander in Vietnam, I underwent many frustrations, endured much interference, lived with countless irritations, swallowed many disappointments, bore considerable criticism."

Meanwhile the Pentagon Papers offered their own summation of the situation: "At this writing, the U.S. has reached the end of the time frame estimated by General Westmoreland in 1965 to be required to defeat the enemy. It has committed 107 battalions of its own forces and a grand total of 525,000 men. The strategy remains search and destroy, but victory is not yet in sight."

On 3 July 1968 General Creighton Abrams formally assumed command of MACV, replacing General Westmoreland. Abrams had, however, been de facto commander since shortly after the Têt Offensive. The successive increments of troop increases requested by Westmoreland, even though many of them had been scaled back, had brought the troop ceiling to 549,500 by the time Abrams took command. Actual deployments never exceeded 543,400, however, and on Abrams's watch there were no requests for more troops. Abrams understood the war and the dominant influence of the domestic support base, and he understood the need to work within the limits of that fragile and waning support. For a number of years, public, congressional, and, to some extent, even media backing had been strong, but that had been squandered as year after year went by with no discernible progress in bringing the war to a successful conclusion.

After the 1968 Têt Offensive, the Johnson administration changed its policy for the war from seeking military victory brought about largely by American forces to capping U.S. involvement and shifting the main burden to larger and more capable South Vietnamese forces. In that context, Abrams changed the tactics from search and destroy to clear and hold, the measure of merit from body count to population security, and the philosophy to conducting "one war" in which pacification, improvement, and modernization of the RVN armed forces and the conduct of military operations were integrated and of equal importance.

"The tactics changed instantly when General Abrams took over," recalled General Donn Starry. "We need to be more flexible tactically inside South Vietnam," Abrams had told President Johnson earlier in the year, and during the remainder of 1968 he set about arranging just that. Two early priorities were closing down the static defense of Khe Sanh, getting those forces into a more mobile role, and doing something about protecting Sài Gòn from the frequent rocket and mortar attacks that had plagued it for years.

Soon Abrams had a planning element working on the combined campaign plan for the coming year, one that incorporated the essentials of the study that General Harold K. Johnson had commissioned in the spring of 1965. Known as Program for the Pacification and Long-Term Development of South Vietnam (PROVN), the study maintained that the way the war was being prosecuted under Westmoreland was not working, indeed could not work, and that a radical redirection of effort was required to achieve success. When the study was first introduced in March 1966, it had, not surprisingly, been rejected by Westmoreland and the MACV staff. Nor had it found many advocates elsewhere. Now it had one very important sponsor, Abrams himself. "The critical actions are those that occur at the village, district, and provincial levels," the study maintained. "This is where the war must be fought; this is where the war and the object which lies beyond it must be won." That object was the security and loyalty of the South Vietnamese people, the single-minded pursuit of which was to be the focus of the final years of American involvement in Vietnam.

—Lewis Sorley

References: Herring, George C. *America's Longest War: The United States and Vietnam, 1950–1975.* New York: John Wiley & Sons, 1979.
Johnson, Lyndon Baines. *The Vantage Point: Perspectives of the Presidency, 1963–1969.* New York: Holt, Rinehart and Winston, 1971.
Karnow, Stanley. *Vietnam: A History.* New York: Viking Press, 1983.
Kinnard, Douglas. *The War Managers.* Hanover, NH: University Press of New England, 1977.
Lewy, Guenter. *America in Vietnam.* New York: Oxford University Press, 1978.
McNamara, Robert S., with Brian VanDeMark. *In Retrospect: The Tragedy and Lessons of Vietnam.* New York: Times Books, 1995.
Palmer, Gen. Bruce, Jr. *The 25-Year War: America's Military Role in Vietnam.* Lexington, KY: University Press of Kentucky, 1984.
Westmoreland, Gen. William C. *A Soldier Reports.* New York: Doubleday, 1976.
See also: Attrition; Body Count; Johnson, Lyndon Baines; McNamara, Robert S.; Military Assistance Command, Vietnam (MACV); Reserve Forces; Search and Destroy; Taylor, Maxwell Davenport; Têt Offensive: Overall Strategy; Têt Offensive: The Sài Gòn Circle; Westmoreland, William Childs; Wheeler, Earle G.

United States: Involvement in Vietnam, 1969–1973

With the advent of a new administration in Washington came formalization of the drastically changed approach to the war in Vietnam initiated by the predecessor government following the 1968

Têt Offensive. Vietnamization, the process of progressively turning the primary burden of fighting the war back over to the South Vietnamese as American forces disengaged, became the dominant theme.

Withdrawal of successive increments of U.S. ground forces, euphemistically termed redeployments, began in August 1969, when 25,000 were brought home. Three key criteria had been established to guide the pace and magnitude of these withdrawals: improvement of South Vietnam's armed forces, enemy activity, and progress in the Paris peace negotiations. As Henry Kissinger observed in *White House Years,* however, the withdrawals took on a life of their own and continued at a steady rate regardless of other developments. "The last elements of flexibility were lost," Kissinger wrote, "when the Defense Department began to plan its budget on the basis of anticipated troop reductions; henceforth to interrupt withdrawals would produce a financial shortfall affecting the procurement of new weapons."

In April 1970 President Richard Nixon announced that 150,000 U.S. troops would be brought out in three increments over the coming year, and in April 1971 that an additional 100,000 would come out by the end of November of that year. By the time the Communists launched the 1972 Easter Offensive, U.S. forces were down to only 69,000 men, including just one combat brigade. Military Assistance Command, Vietnam (MACV) Commander General Creighton Abrams, an Army officer by then bereft of Army forces, fought his last battle with air and naval elements.

During these years, a superb team of top leaders was directing American affairs in Vietnam. Ambassador Ellsworth Bunker headed the country team, Abrams led the military establishment, and William Colby (who held ambassadorial rank) directed the American aspects of pacification. Stressing "one war," the harmonization of all elements of the program, these leaders were in a race to make the South Vietnamese self-sufficient before the withdrawal of U.S. forces was completed. If that eventuality had not been clear enough when the first withdrawal increment of 25,000 was announced at Midway in June 1969, it certainly became so the following month at Guam when the president enunciated what came to be known as the Nixon Doctrine. Its essence was, as its architect recalled in *RN: The Memoirs of Richard Nixon,* that henceforth the United States "would furnish only the materiel and the military and economic assistance to those nations willing to accept the responsibility of supplying the manpower to defend themselves."

The revised tactics specified by Abrams involved American combat units in thousands of small patrols by day and ambushes by night. Early in his tenure, Abrams also issued an order specifying that there would be no bombing or use of heavy artillery against inhabited areas without his personal approval. The Program for the Pacification and Long-Term Development of South Vietnam (PROVN) study had pointed out that it made no difference to the peasant whether destruction was caused by enemy or friendly combat actions; it was just as devastating no matter the source. "My problem is colored blue," observed Abrams, referring to how friendly forces are usually depicted on military maps, as he set about trying to curb the indiscriminate use of the massive American firepower. Abrams told his commanders, "We've got to go beyond smashing up the enemy's main-force units. We have to do that selectively, but the way to get off the treadmill is to get after his infrastructure and guerrillas."

Much of that infrastructure was in the villages, where Việt Công functionaries collected taxes, organized carrying parties, distributed propaganda, provided guides for military units, procured food and medicine, and often imposed their will on the populace through terrorism and intimidation. Under Ambassador Colby, MACV support for pacification, including the Phoenix program that targeted the Việt Công infrastructure, sought not only to root out this influence but simultaneously to strengthen the mechanisms of the RVN government at every level as remaining American units fought to buy time for Vietnamization and pacification to develop and prosper.

Abrams had perceived that the Communists, rather than being served by a logistical "tail" as was common in warfare, were forced to push out in front of planned operations a logistical "nose" of caches, prepared positions, and the like that were essential to their battlefield success. Finding and seizing these caches and positions became a primary objective, one that preempted many planned Communist attacks.

But the really big caches were in base areas across the border in Laos and Cambodia. In the spring of 1970 President Nixon authorized U.S. forces to do something about those sanctuaries. Launching attacks coordinated with simultaneous South Vietnamese thrusts, at the end of April American forces drove into Cambodia on a 60-day rampage that captured thousands of tons of weapons and ammunition, supplies of every description, and piles of documents. The latter included bills of lading and other proof that the Communists had indeed, as MACV had been maintaining for years but the Central Intelligence Agency (CIA) had consistently denied, been using the Cambodian port of Sihanoukville as a major route for bringing in supplies, arms, and munitions. A major benefit of the Cambodian incursion was choking off that lifeline. The operation was also assessed as having bought up to a year's additional time for Vietnamization to progress, as well as providing increased security for the dwindling American forces still in the theater. In his book *No More Vietnams*, Richard Nixon called it "the most successful military operation of the entire Vietnam War."

In late January 1971 there followed another attempt to sweep enemy sanctuaries and interfere with logistical operations along the Hồ Chí Minh Trail. Known as Operation LAM SƠN 719, this consisted of a large-scale raid by South Vietnamese forces into southern Laos. U.S. forces had by this time been prohibited by statute from engaging in ground operations in Laos or Cambodia, so they played a supporting, albeit critically important, role in the operation. American engineers upgraded Route 9 to the Laotian border near Khe Sanh, American artillery fired into Laos from positions near the border, massive American logistical support was provided to the South Vietnamese, and U.S. aviation of every description supported a multidivision thrust toward Communist base areas around Tchépone.

Again much materiel was captured or destroyed, and the Communists took horrifying casualties in resisting the incursion, but the results were mixed. Because of congressional restrictions, South Vietnamese units had been operating for the first time without their American advisors. This proved particularly disadvantageous when it came to calling for the various kinds of assistance, from artillery to medevac to close air support. Meanwhile the Communists, relieved of any necessity to leave forces to defend the North by the perception that U.S. policy foreclosed ground intervention there, were able to concentrate virtually their entire military establishment in the path of the invading forces. An unprecedented density of antiaircraft weaponry proved particularly effective.

The Republic of Vietnam Armed Forces (RVNAF), still inexperienced in the conduct of multidivision operations, struggled with significant problems of command and control, and when token elements reached Tchépone, the operation was terminated earlier than had been planned. Nevertheless, severe losses had been imposed on the Communists, and additional time was gained for Vietnamization to proceed. As the American pullout continued, it also became clear that LAM SƠN 719 was the last major action in which U.S. ground elements would take part.

One measure of the effectiveness of the cross-border operations into Cambodia and Laos was that it took the Communists until the spring of 1972 to gear up for another major offensive. When it came, however, it provided a severe test of the expanded and improved South Vietnamese armed forces, now left with only air, naval, and logistical support from the Americans. In what came to be known as the Easter Offensive, at the end of March People's Army of Vietnam (PAVN) forces struck in force at three key locations—along the Demilitarized Zone (DMZ), north of Sài Gòn around An Lộc, and in the Central Highlands at Kontum.

These attacks triggered major retaliatory strikes by U.S. air and naval forces, including renewed bombing of Hà Nội and Hai Phòng in North Vietnam for the first time since the halt ordered by President Lyndon Johnson in November 1968. Large numbers of additional ships and aircraft were dispatched to the theater of war, and Hai Phòng and North Vietnam's other major ports were mined, an action often urged by military leaders but never before authorized by civilian authorities.

The South Vietnamese fought well, and Abrams noted in a report to Secretary of Defense Melvin Laird that they had made great progress over the past year in "integrating their various elements of air, armor, artillery and infantry. This has been outstanding." American support had been important, crucially important, especially at An Lộc, where B-52s literally saved the day. But Abrams made sure everybody understood that no amount of American support would have mattered had the South Vietnamese not been up to the challenge.

In late June 1972 Abrams departed Vietnam after five years of service there and headed home to be Army chief of staff. He was succeeded as Commander, U.S. Military Assistance Command, Vietnam (COMUSMACV) by General Fred Weyand, his deputy for the past two years and a man with vast experience in the war. Weyand had commanded the 25th Infantry Division in combat in

Vietnam and then II Field Force at the time of the 1968 Têt Offensive. After duty as a principal on the Army Staff in the Pentagon, he went to Paris as Joint Chiefs of Staff representative on the U.S. negotiating team, and then finally returned to Vietnam. Now he had inherited the difficult and thankless task of closing down the American expeditionary force.

Apparent progress in the Paris peace talks had hit a snag in late autumn of 1972, and although Secretary of State Kissinger had reported virtually on the eve of the U.S. presidential election that "peace is at hand," that prospect faded away. Ever-narrowing U.S. expectations and aspirations for the war now focused on getting back American prisoners of war. On 18 December President Nixon unleashed the most concentrated bombing campaign of the war on North Vietnam. The onslaught continued until 31 December, when the North Vietnamese agreed to resumption of the peace talks. Agreement was then swiftly reached, and on 23 January 1973 the document was initialed by Henry Kissinger and Lê Đức Tho.

At that point, the United States was virtually out of the war. Left behind in South Vietnam were a small Defense Attaché Office and the U.S. Embassy. Also left behind were the North Vietnamese forces with whom the South Vietnamese had been struggling for these many years. The peace agreement, fatally flawed, provided for a cease-fire. The Americans went home, but Communist forces remained largely where they were—in position to fight on.

When American troop withdrawals began, commanders on the ground had expected that a substantial residual force would remain in Vietnam, one that would continue to work with the South Vietnamese much as had American forces in Korea following an earlier war. Eventually it became clear that this was not going to be the case.

The reality was that there were set for the South Vietnamese a series of increasingly difficult hurdles: first to become capable of defeating the Viêt Công insurgency; then to defeat both the Viêt Công and the PAVN; then to do this without help from U.S. ground forces; then to do it without help from U.S. air or naval forces, either; and finally to do it without even American financial or logistical assistance. They accomplished all but the last, when Congress slashed financial aid to a former ally while North Vietnam's backers stayed the course.

—Lewis Sorley

References: Clarke, Jeffrey J. *Advice and Support: The Final Years, 1965–1973.* Washington, DC: U.S. Army Center of Military History, 1988. Kissinger, Henry A. *White House Years.* Boston: Little, Brown, 1979. Nixon, Richard M. *RN: The Memoirs of Richard Nixon.* New York: Grosset & Dunlap, 1978. Palmer, Dave R. *Summons of the Trumpet: U.S.-Vietnam in Perspective.* Novato, CA: Presidio Press, 1978. Sorley, Lewis. *Thunderbolt: General Creighton Abrams and the Army of His Times.* New York: Simon & Schuster, 1992.
See also: Abrams, Creighton; ARC LIGHT (B-52 Raids); BÌNH TÂY I-IV, Operations; Bunker, Ellsworth; Civilian Operations and Revolutionary Development Support (CORDS); Clear and Hold; Colby, William Egan; Easter Offensive (Nguyên Huê Campaign); Hamburger Hill (Battle of Âp Bia Mountain); Kissinger, Henry Alfred; Laird, Melvin R.; LAM SƠN 719, Operation; Military Assistance Command, Vietnam (MACV); Nixon, Richard Milhous; Pacification; Paris Peace Accords; Vietnamization; Weyand, Frederick C.

United States: Involvement in Vietnam, 1973–1975

U.S. involvement in Vietnam steadily diminished between the signing of the Paris peace accords in 1973 and the collapse of the Sài Gòn government in 1975. This period is often cynically referred to as the "decent interval," but the greatest significance of American policy during this period may well be the surprisingly little amount of controversy that it generated.

The Paris peace accords, signed on 27 January 1973 by representatives of the United States, the Democratic Republic of Vietnam (DRV), the Republic of Vietnam (RVN), and the Provisional Revolutionary Government (PRG), called for a cease-fire, the withdrawal of all U.S. military forces within 60 days, the return of all captured personnel, efforts to locate missing persons on both sides, and the beginning of talks aimed at achieving "national conciliation and concord."

After some delays and threats by the United States not to withdraw after all, issues surrounding the return of American prisoners of war (POWs) were resolved, and 591 captured U.S. personnel were returned under Operation HOMECOMING in March 1973. After stating firmly on 29 March that "All our American POWs are on their way home," President Richard Nixon announced that the last American forces were also returning.

U.S. military involvement in Southeast Asia did not cease, however. Immediately after the Paris agreement, a number of U.S. bases were signed over to the RVN, enough planes and helicopters were brought in to give the Republic of Vietnam Armed Forces (RVNAF) the fourth largest air force in the world, and at least 9,000 U.S. servicemen hastily resigned their commissions so that they could be legally retained by the Vietnamese as civilians. President Nixon also ordered occasional reconnaissance flights over North Vietnam so that he could match his previous promises to supply $4.75 billion in reconstruction aid with threats to drop the aid and resume bombing if the cease-fire failed to hold. The U.S. Air Force dropped 250,000 tons of bombs on Cambodia in the first six months of 1973; this was more tonnage than had been dropped on Japan in World War II. Heavy bombing also took place in Laos.

Meanwhile President Nixon began to experience political trouble at home on a number of issues, including the emerging Watergate scandal. The decline in his political power combined with an increasing war weariness among Americans to undercut his military efforts in Southeast Asia. Despite intense Nixon administration lobbying, Congress cut the amount of aid authorized for Vietnam from $2.3 billion in fiscal year 1973 (1 July 1972 to 30 June 1973) to $1 billion in 1974. The dramatic increase in the price of oil following the Arab oil embargo and resulting inflation further eroded the buying power of this appropriation. By 1974 the United States was no longer able to replace RVNAF equipment at the level permitted by the Paris peace accords, and operations by the Republic of Vietnam Air Force had to be cut by as much as 50 percent.

The Nixon administration faced even more difficulties in its own air war. Deeply upset by the disclosure of illegal bombings in Cambodia, on 10 May 1973 a rebellious, heavily Democratic Congress cut off all funding for further U.S. air operations in the the-

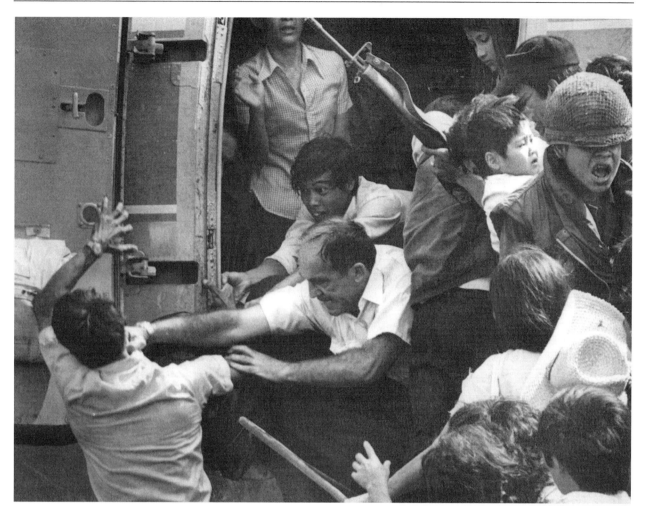

An American official punches a man to try to break him from the doorway of an airplane already loaded with refugees seeking to flee Nha Trang, 1 April 1975.

ater. By late June Congress went beyond that to pass a law forbidding further military operations of any sort in Southeast Asia. President Nixon's angry veto was overridden after negotiations extended the final deadline to 15 August 1973. By 6 November 1973 Congress overrode another Nixon veto and the War Powers Act became law. This required the president to inform Congress within 48 hours of the dispatch of U.S. troops to another country and said that the troops must be withdrawn within 60 days unless Congress explicitly authorized their presence.

In August 1974 after the Watergate scandals forced President Nixon to resign from office and Gerald Ford assumed the presidency, American interest in Vietnam declined even further. Secretary of State Henry Kissinger still talked of preserving American credibility in the region and lobbied hard for continued aid, but a generally hostile Congress cut appropriations to only $700 million for fiscal year 1975. Even charges that Americans might still be held against their will in Vietnam were largely discounted by a war-weary public. Ambassador Graham Martin and other embassy officials in Sài Gòn were thus faced with the difficult task of trying to counter the demoralizing effects of U.S. aid cuts on a government that the Americans themselves had once played a crucial role in maintaining, but now regarded as too feeble and corrupt to be worth trying to save.

The decline in American interest in Vietnam became clear to the North Vietnamese and Provisional Revolutionary Government forces when the United States did not respond to the 7 January 1975 capture of the provincial capital of Phước Bình, and hence the province of Phước Long. DRV military leaders now felt that they could push into the Central Highlands. When a disastrous retreat destroyed key elements in the ARVN, DRV forces continued on toward the main southern cities. The final phase of the war had begun. During this period, the U.S. Congress voted an additional $300 million in humanitarian aid but refused to discuss having U.S. troops reenter the war. As Henry Kissinger sadly stated on 17 April 1975, "The Vietnam debate has run its course."

The Sài Gòn government surrendered on 30 April 1975, a mere 55 days after the final Communist offensive began. The speed of that offensive, combined with Ambassador Graham Martin's determination to keep up morale, meant that many Vietnamese who should have been evacuated by the Americans were left behind. As television screens in America displayed dramatic images of Americans being evacuated by helicopter from the roof of the U.S.

Embassy in Sài Gòn, Communist forces quickly solidified their power in Cambodia and Laos as well.

Fortunately for the United States, Kissinger's remark about the finality of debate over the U.S. involvement in Vietnam signaled not only the cessation of all military efforts but also a lack of scapegoating over who was to blame for the tragedy. Unlike the earlier angry charges that the Democrats had "lost" China and, to a lesser extent, Korea, Americans this time around did not engage in a great debate over responsibility for the defeat. The sacrifices of the U.S. military, the clear incompetence and corruption of the Sài Gòn forces, and the scope of the effort—not just by the relatively liberal Democratic President Lyndon Johnson but also by the deeply conservative Republican President Richard Nixon—combined to give Americans a more realistic sense of their power to implement policy.

—Peter K. Frost

Reference: Isaacs, Arnold R. *Without Honor: Defeat in Vietnam and Cambodia.* New York: Vintage Books, 1984.
See also: Ford, Gerald R.; FREQUENT WIND, Operation; Hô Chí Minh Campaign; HOMECOMING, Operation; Nixon, Richard Milhous; Kissinger, Henry Alfred; Martin, Graham A.; Missing in Action, Allied; Paris Peace Accords; Prisoners of War, Allied; Television and the Vietnam Experience; War Powers Act; Watergate.

United States: Involvement in Vietnam, 1975 to the Present

After the fall of the Republic of Vietnam (RVN) in April 1975, the United States conducted a punitive policy toward Vietnam. Not only did Washington refuse to normalize relations with the newly reunited state, but it actively sought to isolate Vietnam politically, economically, and diplomatically.

Socialist Republic of Vietnam (SRV) leaders fully believed that the United States would fulfill its part of the 1973 Paris peace accords, in which the United States agreed to supply some $3.3 billion dollars over a five-year period in reconstruction aid. Foreign aid was vital to rebuild and develop a nation devastated by war. Instead, the trade embargo that had applied to the Democratic Republic of Vietnam (DRV) under the Trading with the Enemy Act was extended to all of Vietnam. The United States also pressured other nations, most importantly Japan, to adhere to the embargo. Furthermore, the United States blocked credits and loans from the World Bank, the International Monetary Fund, and the Asian Development Bank, and some $150 million in Vietnamese assets in the United States were frozen. The United States vetoed all of Vietnam's requests to join the United Nations, which would have given it international legitimacy. The Ford administration adopted this policy to punish the SRV for a war that America lost.

In 1977 the Carter administration cautiously sought to move away from this punitive policy. Washington appeared receptive to establishing diplomatic relations with Vietnam, provided it give a "proper accounting" of the fate of some 2,500 Americans missing in action (MIAs). Between spring 1977 and fall 1978 a series of preliminary talks between the two countries came close to a tentative agreement. Washington even dropped its veto of Viet-

namese membership in the United Nations. However, the talks fell apart over Vietnamese demands for billions of dollars in war reparations. Washington flatly rejected this, contending that Vietnam itself completely violated the Paris accords by invading the RVN in 1975. Carter declared that aid would follow the normalization of relations but could not be linked to either normalization or to the MIA issue. Negotiations temporarily broke down.

In 1978 Vietnam dropped its demands for war reparations as a precondition for recognition. However, by then Washington was far less enthusiastic about normalizing relations with Vietnam. Congress and the American public were decidedly not interested. The Carter administration became concerned over Vietnamese troop buildups along their Cambodian border, a heightened Soviet influence in the region, and a growing exodus of Vietnamese refugees. Most importantly, the Carter administration was moving toward establishing full relations with China. Because of worsening relations between Vietnam and China that would culminate in a full-scale border war in 1979, the administration believed that normalizing relations with Vietnam could jeopardize good relations with China. Once the United States established full relations with China in 1978, Vietnam was ignored. Then in November 1978 Vietnam signed a treaty of alliance with the Soviet Union, putting it solidly in the Soviet camp when the Cold War heated up again in the late 1970s.

Vietnam's invasion and subsequent occupation of Cambodia, the unresolved issue of MIAs, and other problems led to little progress between the SRV and United States in normalizing diplomatic relations or in ending the crippling trade embargo that was costing Vietnam billions of dollars in potential loans and credits.

The MIA issue was the most stubborn and sensitive question dividing the two states. American television and cinema exploited the issue by conveying the impression that Americans were still imprisoned in Vietnam, which was bolstered by polls and by congressional sentiment. Some 1,750 Americans were listed as missing in Vietnam, nearly 2,400 in all of Southeast Asia. Nevertheless, the U.S. Department of Defense considered virtually all MIAs legally dead, their bodies simply impossible to find in the inaccessible jungles, mountains, and seas.

MIAs were not unique to the Vietnam War. World War II and Korea, for example, had 80,000 and 8,000 MIAs, respectively, still unaccounted for, a far higher percentage than in Vietnam. Despite numerous reports of sightings by refugees and international aid organization representatives, none have ever been confirmed. American veterans even conducted forays into Laos searching for MIAs, again without any success.

When Ronald Reagan assumed the presidency in 1981, he promised to deal forthrightly with the MIA question. His tough position, that Vietnam be held accountable for all MIAs, was strongly supported by several nongovernmental groups, most significantly the National League of POW/MIA Families. In a speech before the group's national meeting in 1988, Reagan declared that Americans still felt "great pain" over the issue, and the lack of progress poisoned any prospects for normalization.

Seeking to break the stalemate in the mid-1980s, Vietnam made concessions. In July 1985 for the first time Vietnam permitted an American inspection team to visit a potential MIA burial site. Additional searches were made during 1985, and remains of more than 30 airmen who had been shot down were returned to the United States. In 1987 and again in 1989 former Chairman of the Joint Chiefs of Staff General John Vessey visited Vietnam on behalf of the Reagan and Bush administrations to discuss the issue. Vietnam pledged full cooperation. Between 1985 and 1990 remains of nearly 200 American servicemen were returned. Possible leads, no matter how small, were thoroughly investigated. Vietnam provided Americans access to war records, archives, and even Vietnamese cemeteries. In 1991 the United States opened an office in Hà Nôi to coordinate efforts in its search for MIAs. By 1995, 35 different searches had been conducted.

Besides the MIA question, misunderstandings on other issues also divided the two states. First, the United States declared that any negotiations for normalization could not occur until after all Vietnamese troops withdrew from Cambodia. Washington considered Vietnam's occupation as part of a growing Soviet assertiveness in the world. Under strong pressure from Soviet leader Mikhail Gorbachev, who was seeking rapprochement with China and an end to a very costly stalemate, Vietnam agreed to withdraw all its forces by September 1989. In return, China and the Association of South East Asian Nations (ASEAN) bloc agreed to cut its support for the Khmer Rouge guerrilla fighters and end Vietnam's international isolation.

Second, the Orderly Departure Program, carried out under the auspices of the United Nations, was designed to promote an orderly resettlement in the West, mainly the United States, of Vietnamese political refugees who might otherwise try to flee by sea. After years of stalling by Vietnam, the program started functioning properly at the end of the decade. Furthermore, virtually all of the estimated 35,000 Amerasians (children of American fathers and Vietnamese mothers) and their families were resettled in the United States. In 1990 an agreement was also signed that allowed tens of thousands of officials and officers of the former RVN government and army to emigrate to the United States. Thus, one by one, once-serious problems were resolved to mutual satisfaction.

Significant progress occurred after 1990. The Clinton administration moved cautiously, though steadily, toward a full normalization of economic and political ties. Most significantly, the American trade embargo was finally lifted in February 1994. That action allowed American trade and investment. The United States dropped its veto on credits and loans to Vietnam from international lending associations. Yet some trade restrictions still impeded American companies from taking a greater role in developing what many consider to be Southeast Asia's "next dragon." Humanitarian aid, as well as cultural and educational exchanges, both governmental and private, increased. American tourism also skyrocketed as veterans and Vietnamese Americans returned to visit friends and relatives. In January 1995 American and

An Air America helicopter crewman helps evacuees up a ladder on top of a Sài Gòn building in April 1975.

Vietnamese officials signed an agreement exchanging liaison offices in their respective capitals. Finally, despite opposition from the MIA lobby and Republican conservatives, in July 1995 President Bill Clinton extended full diplomatic ties to the Socialist Republic of Vietnam. On 6 August 1995 Secretary of State Warren Christopher looked on as the American flag was raised over the U.S. Embassy in Hà Nôi.

In the final step in establishing full diplomatic relations between the United States and the SRV, President Clinton nominated Representative Douglas "Pete" Peterson (D-Florida), a former POW in Vietnam, as the first U.S. envoy to the SRV. The Senate confirmed Peterson in April 1997, and he took up his duties in Hà Nôi in May. In June Secretary of State Madeleine K. Albright visited Hà Nôi and met with SRV leaders. She also traveled to Hô Chí Minh City, the first U.S. secretary of state to do so since the war, and laid the cornerstone for a new American consulate there.

—Michael Share

References: Sar Desai, D. R. *Vietnam: The Struggle for National Identity.* Boulder, CO: Westview Press, 1992.
Williams, Michael. *Vietnam at the Crossroads.* London: Pinter, 1992.
Young, Marilyn. *The Vietnam Wars, 1945–1990.* New York: HarperCollins, 1991.
See also: Bush, George Herbert Walker; Carter, Jimmy; Clinton, William Jefferson; Ford, Gerald R.; Khmer Rouge; Missing in Action, Allied; Peterson, Douglas "Pete"; Prisoners of War, Allied; Reagan, Ronald; Vietnam, Socialist Republic of: 1975 to the Present; Vietnamese Invasion and Occupation of Cambodia.

United States: Marine Corps

U.S. Marine Corps involvement in the Vietnam War began in April 1962 when Marine helicopter units deployed to the Mekong Delta to lift Army of the Republic of Vietnam (ARVN) units into battle. On 8 March 1965 two battalions of the 9th Marine Expeditionary Brigade (MEB), the first U.S. ground troops in Vietnam, arrived by sea and air at Đà Nẵng. As a steady stream of Marine ground and aviation units poured into Vietnam, the 9th MEB became the III Marine Amphibious Force (MAF), and the Marines' mission expanded from the defense of the Đà Nẵng air base to meeting the Communist threat throughout the five northernmost provinces of South Vietnam. In May another Marine base with a jet-capable airstrip was established 55 miles south of Đà Nẵng at Chu Lai.

Unlike the U.S. Army, whose leaders believed that the primary threat to the Republic of Vietnam was the presence of large units of Communist forces, the Marines preferred to place their emphasis on pacification. Effective pacification required eradication of the National Liberation Front (NLF) political and military infrastructure in the thousands of hamlets and villages in Vietnam. The Marines devised a program of civic action platoons. Each merged a squad of Marines with one of Vietnamese militia to provide defense at the hamlet level. Civic action proved successful on a limited scale, but pacification was never given as much emphasis by Military Assistance Command, Vietnam (MACV) as large-unit search-and-destroy operations.

In August 1965 the Marines launched Operation STARLITE, a regimental-sized attack against a large Viêt Công (VC) force lo-cated south of Chu Lai. STARLITE proved to be a large battle. Further Marine operations between 1965 and 1966 were predominantly against small Viêt Công units in the southern I Corps.

In July MACV obtained evidence that a People's Army of Vietnam (PAVN) division had crossed the Demilitarized Zone (DMZ) and taken up positions in Quang Tri Province. This threat forced the Marines to downplay their pacification program, deploy northward, and construct a series of combat bases parallel to and south of the DMZ. During the second half of 1966 and into 1967 the Marines fought a series of bloody battles with well-equipped North Vietnamese regulars in such places as the Rockpile, Côn Thiên, Gio Linh, Khe Sanh, and Cam Lô. The Marines constructed large bases at Phú Bài and Đông Hà to support these operations.

By 1967 the Marines found themselves fighting two wars: In southern I Corps, the 1st Marine Division fought a counterinsurgency war against the VC, while to the north the 3d Marine Division waged a more conventional war against the PAVN. By mid-summer 1967 total Marine casualties in Vietnam exceeded those for the Korean War. Despite the best efforts of the Marines, the

A U.S. Marine wears a gas mask as he enters a tear gas–filled village, previously a Viêt Công stronghold in the An Lão Valley. Unlike General Westmoreland, who emphasized firepower, search and destroy operations, and attrition, the Marines preferred to emphasize pacification.

Serving as a forward point for his unit, a Marine moves slowly, cautious of enemy pitfalls. Walking point on patrol was one of the most dangerous things an American soldier could do in Vietnam.

large bases of Đông Hà, Đà Nẵng, Chu Lai, and Phú Bài continued to be regular targets for Communist rocket attacks.

In late 1967 General William Westmoreland ordered U.S. Army units into southern I Corps, allowing the deployment of more Marine units further north. January 1968 saw major PAVN attacks against Marines at Khe Sanh and, at the end of the month, the Tết Offensive throughout South Vietnam. In the latter, ground attacks were launched against all five provincial capitals in I Corps, and the important city of Huế was temporarily captured by a combined PAVN/VC force. Heavy fighting continued into the spring. To meet this threat, General Westmoreland increased the number of U.S. Army units in what had initially been a Marine area.

Fighting in northern areas tapered off in late 1968. In the area around Đà Nẵng, the Marines launched an Accelerated Pacification Plan designed to take back what had been lost in the Tết Offensive. As 1969 began, the 3d Marine Division adopted Army-style high mobility operations that de-emphasized reliance on fixed positions. Pacification yielded successes.

By mid-1969 the withdrawal of ground and aviation units from Vietnam had begun. Marine positions in northern South Vietnam became the responsibility of the U.S. Army and the Army of the Republic of Vietnam (ARVN). The 1st Marine Division continued operations around Đà Nẵng, where earlier fighting had occurred: Arizona Territory (20 miles southwest of Đà Nẵng), Dodge City (6 to 12 miles south of Đà Nẵng), Gò Nôi Island, and the Quế Sơn Valley. By October 1969 as a part of President Richard Nixon's Vietnamization policy, the 3d Marine Division had left Vietnam.

In March 1970 the Army XXIV Corps replaced III MAF as the dominant U.S. headquarters in I Corps. The Marine area of responsibility shrank to what it had been in the beginning, essentially Quang Nam Province with its capital at Đà Nẵng. Marine combat bases were either razed or turned over to U.S. Army or ARVN forces. During the 1971 invasion of Laos, U.S. Marine participation was limited to transportation and engineering support. In April 1971 the III MAF headquarters transferred to Okinawa.

At the time of the 1972 PAVN Easter Offensive, only a few hundred Marines remained in Vietnam. Marine F-4 Phantom jets provided tactical air support for South Vietnamese armed forces. Other Marines performed duties as air and naval gunfire spotters and advisors to the Vietnamese Marine Corps. No Marine ground combat troops went ashore.

The Vietnam War was the longest and, in many ways, the largest war in Marine Corps history. By 1972 a total of 12,926 Marines had been killed in Vietnam and another 88,542 wounded. This was a larger number of casualties than the Marine Corps had suffered in World War II (74,913). Approximately 800,000 Marines served in the Corps during the period 1965–1972, the years of major Marine involvement in Vietnam.

—Peter Brush

References: Moskin, Robert J. *The U.S. Marine Corps Story.* New York: McGraw-Hill, 1977.

Simmons, Edwin H., ed. *The Marines in Vietnam, 1954–1973. An Anthology and Annotated Bibliography.* Washington, DC: Headquarters, U.S. Marine Corps, 1985.

_____. *The United States Marines.* New York: Viking Press, 1976.

See also: Amphibious Warfare; Civic Action; Clear and Hold; Đà Nẵng; Huế, Battle of; Marine Combined Action Platoons (CAPs); Order of Battle; Pacification; STARLITE, Operation; Vietnam, Republic of: Marine Corps (VNMC); Westmoreland, William Childs.

United States: Navy

The U.S. Navy played an important role during the entire course of the Southeast Asian struggle. From supplying the French with ships and aircraft to evacuating the last refugees in 1975, the U.S. Navy undertook, usually with success, a multitude of missions, many of them novel or unanticipated.

This record is all the more impressive in that the Navy of the early 1960s was not especially well prepared for a conflict like that in Vietnam. For over a decade the service had been largely oriented in doctrine and force structure to nuclear war: time-honored techniques such as shore bombardment and amphibious assault were neglected and conventional pieces of ordnance such as shipboard guns and iron bombs were in short supply. Some of the Navy's newest surface warships had been commissioned with

U.S. Navy attack planes are launched from the 7th Fleet carrier Constellation *off the North Vietnamese coast. President Nixon's decision to cut land and sea supply lines into North Vietnam demanded increased activity by planes on the several aircraft carriers in the Gulf of Tonkin area.*

only missiles aboard. The Navy's most modern fighter, the F-4 Phantom II, was armed only with long-range missiles designed to shoot down Soviet bombers attacking American carriers. Naval intelligence was focused largely on the support of nuclear operations. Fleet support ships were mostly World War II veterans with outdated equipment and slow transit speeds.

Following the August 1964 Tonkin Gulf incidents and the commitment of the Seventh Fleet to a widening war, the Navy scrambled to redress these deficiencies. Cruisers and destroyers updated their gunnery skills with frequent exercises. Several gun cruisers and the battleship *New Jersey* won stays from the mothball fleet or were returned to service. Existing attack aircraft were modified to carry conventional munitions, and 250- and 500-pound bombs were produced on an emergency basis. The F-4 Phantom received a pod-mounted 20-mm cannon to give it a dogfighting capability, and a hurried program of base expansion at Subic Bay provided essential repair and replenishment support to a much larger fighting force.

Aside from renewing prior capabilities, the Navy added to its arsenal. New planes just entering service, such as the RA-5C and the A-6 Intruder, endowed the fleet with enhanced reconnaissance and strike capabilities. Strike aircraft acquired Shrike missiles to enable them to hit back at North Vietnamese antiaircraft radars. The service life of shipboard artillery pieces was significantly extended by the addition of "Swedish additive" or titanium dioxide to ammunition charges.

Over the next decade of conflict, the Navy performed a host of missions. Most in the public eye were the Seventh Fleet carrier operations directed against Communist forces in both North and South Vietnam, but also on occasion in Laos and Cambodia. Less dramatically, surface warships gave fire support to friendly troops ashore and, in Operation SEA DRAGON, mounted harassment and interdiction raids along the North Vietnamese coastline. Another principal mission of the Navy was to stop maritime infiltration from the north. Navy MARKET TIME patrols, begun in 1965, established a three-tiered shield of long-range aircraft, medium-sized surface ships, and fast patrol craft (or "Swift boats").

Ashore, the Navy's small Sài Gòn advisory group expanded prominently in May 1965 with the establishment of Naval Forces, Vietnam command. To carry the war to enemy forces operating in the Mekong Delta, the Navy improvised a brown-water fleet of fiberglass patrol boats, shallow-draft landing craft, and fire support monitors. This effort hampered Communist forces all the way to the Cambodian border. SEAL (Sea Air Land) teams and Navy helicopter units searched out opposing troops far from the sea; river convoys resupplied Army and Marine soldiers. On several occasions, the Navy put Marines ashore in amphibious assaults.

Additionally, U.S. naval personnel served throughout the war as advisors to their South Vietnamese counterparts, engaged in civic action, and implemented naval aspects of the Vietnamization policy. From 1964 to 1973, 2,636,000 sailors and Marines served in the Southeast Asian operational theater. Fourteen Navy men won the Medal of Honor; 2,551 U.S. naval personnel lost their lives (excluding Marines).

In the last stages of the war, naval forces provided aerial support and naval bombardment to counter the 1972 Democratic Republic of Vietnam (DRV) Easter Offensive and to prosecute the subsequent LINEBACKER campaign. Aerial mining of North Vietnamese harbors proved especially effective in forcing the Communists to resume negotiations. With the collapse of South Vietnam in 1975, the U.S. Navy extricated American and friendly personnel from South Vietnam.

These successes aside, the Navy was, in the end, hurt severely by the Vietnam War. Apart from the decline in popular support and the racial unrest that it shared with the other U.S. military services, the Navy found it difficult to pay for costly operations in Southeast Asia during a ten-year period in which defense appropriations declined markedly. As the Soviet Navy grew in size and capability during the same decade, the U.S. Navy faced the wholesale obsolescence of its many World War II–era ships. To keep its principal sea control arm—its aviation component—at strength, the Navy cut back on its forces tailored for other missions; even so, aircraft in the Navy inventory dropped from 10,598 in 1964 to 7,681 in 1973. Especially hurt were the Navy's antisubmarine elements as the specialized antisubmarine carriers went to the scrap yards. New construction was deferred with funding going into other operations. For the 1967 and 1968 fiscal years, the nuclear-powered frigates *California* and *South Carolina* were the only two major surface combatants authorized by Congress.

But overall, the Navy's record was creditable. Certainly the Vietnam War proved the need for a navy with multiple capabilities. Guns, denounced as antediluvian in a missile navy, demonstrated their virtues in reliability, economy, and continuous availability in all types of weather. The aircraft carrier, under severe criticism as outdated or irrelevant with the loss of its nuclear strike mission to submarines, showed its versatility once again.

—Malcolm Muir, Jr.

References: Hooper, Edwin B., Dean C. Allard, and Oscar P. Fitzgerald. *The Setting of the Stage to 1959.* Vol. 1, *The United States Navy and the Vietnam Conflict.* Washington, DC: U.S. Navy, Naval History Division, 1976.

Love, Robert W., Jr. *History of the U.S. Navy.* Vol. 2, *1942–1991.* Harrisburg, PA: Stackpole, 1992.

Marolda, Edward J. *By Sea, Air, and Land: An Illustrated History of the U.S. Navy and the War in Southeast Asia.* Washington, DC: Naval Historical Center, 1994.

Marolda, Edward J., and Oscar P. Fitzgerald. *From Military Assistance to Combat.* Vol. 2, *The United States Navy and the Vietnam Conflict.* Washington, DC: Naval Historical Center, 1986.

Muir, Malcolm, Jr. *Black Shoes and Blue Water: Surface Warfare in the United States Navy, 1945–1975.* Washington, DC: Naval Historical Center, 1996.

See also: DeSoto Missions; FREQUENT WIND, Operation; GAME WARDEN, Operation; Gayler, Noel Arthur Meredyth; LINEBACKER I, Operation; LINEBACKER II, Operation; MARKET TIME, Operation; Mobile Riverine Force; *New Jersey* (BB-62); Operation Plan 34A (OPLAN 34A); Order of Battle; Riverine Craft; Riverine Warfare; SEA DRAGON, Operation; Sea Power in the Vietnam War; SEAL (Sea, Air, Land) Teams; Tonkin Gulf Incidents; United States: Coast Guard; United States: Marine Corps; United States: Seabees; Warships, Allied and Democratic Republic of Vietnam; Yankee Station.

United States: Nongovernmental Organizations, 1954 to the Present

American nongovernmental organizations (NGOs) played a significant role in U.S. involvement in Vietnam, providing emergency relief and economic development assistance during years of attempted nation building and escalated military conflict. Even after the U.S. government severed ties with Vietnam in 1975, some NGOs orchestrated refugee evacuations, organized reconciliation movements, and channeled the only American aid available to the Vietnamese people.

Although some NGOs provided assistance to refugees during the Indo-China War, more followed with substantial aid programs after the 1954 Geneva Accords. Groups such as CARE, Catholic Relief Services, International Rescue Committee, Mennonite Central Committee, and Church World Service entered South Vietnam with the humanitarian goal of helping people escape political and military upheaval. They also hoped to save South Vietnam from Communist revolution and stabilize a new "nation" with democratic and capitalist institutions. Encouraged by the State Department's Advisory Committee for Voluntary Foreign Aid, these agencies assisted U.S., French, and South Vietnamese government efforts to evacuate nearly a million refugees, mostly Catholic, fleeing the Communist-controlled North.

Between 1954 and 1964 American NGOs provided millions of dollars to resettle refugees and helped develop economic projects in villages and cities and build houses, hospitals, schools, cultural centers, and orphanages in South Vietnam. Private agencies worked closely with U.S. and Sài Gòn officials, who encouraged their projects by granting funds, authorizing programs, advising personnel, and providing transportation and security. The majority of food distributed by NGOs was made available by the U.S. government through Public Law 480, or the Food for Peace program. As the Communist insurgency intensified, NGOs' connections and dependence on the U.S. and Republic of Vietnam (RVN) governments politicized and compromised their humanitarian aims.

Still, NGO activity increased dramatically after 1964 as American military intervention heightened the need for humanitarian assistance. By 1970, 33 American NGOs operated in South Vietnam with 374 expatriate staff and programs in excess of $27 million. The war divided NGOs into conflicting camps. Some agencies supported U.S. policy and continued to depend on government funding and security. A few even distributed Food for Peace food aid to Army of the Republic of Vietnam (ARVN) troops and assisted minority populations to provide intelligence information. Other NGOs refused government funds and tried to distance themselves from U.S. actions. The Mennonite Central Committee and American Friends Service Committee offered aid to people on both sides of the conflict and openly criticized U.S. policy. In 1971 International Voluntary Services, a major recipient of government resources, was expelled from the RVN for its condemnation of American military actions.

Once the United States pulled out of Vietnam and ended diplomatic relations in 1975, most NGOs followed and concentrated their efforts on relocating thousands of refugees (the "boat people") fleeing the Communist regime. Private agencies that pushed for reconstruction aid and reconciliation found it difficult to circumvent the U.S. government policy of isolating Vietnam by withholding economic aid and humanitarian assistance. Once the political climate improved with the Cambodian peace agreement in 1991, Washington altered its stance and allowed some funds to be channeled through private agencies for disaster relief, agricultural needs, and health programs. NGOs continue to play a pivotal role in promoting improved relations with Vietnam and in encouraging the U.S. government to allow more aid programs to reconstruct and develop the region.

—Delia Pergande

References: Meinertz, Midge Austin, ed. *Witness in Anguish.* New York: Vietnam Christian Service, 1975.

Minear, Larry. "Private Aid and Public Policy: A Case Study." *IndoChina Issues* (June 1988): 1–8.

Rawlings, Stuart. *The IVS Experience from Algeria to Vietnam.* Washington, DC: International Voluntary Services, 1992.

Spencer, Dao, ed. *Directory of U.S. NGOs Vietnam Programs.* New York: U.S. NGO Forum on Viet Nam, Cambodia and Laos, 1992.

See also: American Friends of Vietnam; Refugees and Boat People.

United States: Nurses

U.S. military nurses arrived in Vietnam early in the conflict. In March 1962, 13 U.S. Army nurses arrived at the Eighth Field Hospital, Nha Trang. The first members of the Navy Nurse Corps were stationed in Sài Gòn at the same time. Air Force nurses soon followed, and the number of military nurses serving in Vietnam rose steadily after 1966 to a peak of 900 in January 1969. This coincided with the number of troops deployed, which was at its highest number of 543,400 in April 1969. Nurses served as flight nurses, in hospitals throughout Vietnam, and on board the hospital ships USS *Repose* and *Sanctuary.*

The work of nurses closely paralleled that of physicians and medical corpsmen. Most patients were either wounded in battle or sick with infectious diseases. Care of those infected with tropical diseases was primarily supportive, providing liquids, medications for relief of symptoms, nourishment, and rest. Nurses were often infected themselves, and most days lost from work were related to tropical diseases.

Nurses received wounded personnel in the field in hospitals of varied sizes and equipped with varied resources. The wounded men had been stabilized by a medic or corpsman and transported, most often by helicopter, to one of 19 medical facilities. Although physicians were responsible for the triage of wounded men, nurses often shared this task and were sometimes delegated triage decisions because physicians were needed to begin treatment or surgery.

For those whose wounds were so severe that treatment was futile, nurses focused on pain relief and psychological support. Some nurses reported that comforting the dying soldier was an essential task, so that the soldier and his family would know that he had not died alone.

Most wounded had suffered either small-arms injuries or explosive injuries from mines or booby traps. Small-arms fire typically caused severe tissue damage, interfered with blood supply to the wound, and often resulted in multiple wounds. Explosive devices caused large and contaminated wounds. After surgery had been performed on the wounded, nurses were primarily concerned with prevention of infection, relief of pain, tissue regeneration, and psychological support.

The role of nurses was significantly challenged by the soldiers in Vietnam and conflicts in American culture during the 1960s and 1970s. Not only was the war unpopular, but the country was also struggling with civil rights issues and the women's movement. Alcohol and drug abuse complicated an already complex social milieu, and the traditional role of nurses in providing neutral, unconditional support was made much more difficult. Additionally, many nurses encountered the same psychological trauma as the soldiers for whom they cared.

Nurses served aboard fixed-wing evacuation flights, transporting patients, most often to Okinawa or Japan, for further treatment or rehabilitation. These nurses were trained in trauma and critical care and worked with significantly more independence than did nurses prior to the war.

The Vietnam War brought at least three changes in the nursing profession. First, nurses developed practice specialties, much like physicians had already begun to do. They were particularly successful in the specialties of trauma and critical care and anesthesia. Second, the war afforded many opportunities for nurses to practice more independently and with greater professional autonomy. Nurses, physicians, and patients were able to observe the benefit of increased flexibility and effectiveness in nurses' activities. Third, in 1966 men were authorized by Congress to join the three nurses' corps. Men ultimately made up about one-fourth of the nurse corps and were most commonly found in anesthesia and surgical specialties. Men were a valuable addition to the nurse corps; however, many soldiers found female nurses an important factor in morale. This same phenomena has been reported in other American wars and is probably related to the socialization of women as comforters.

Several studies and biographies of nurses who served in Vietnam reveal experiences of a more personal nature. First, women there were socially isolated, restricted to the hospital, the barracks, and occasionally the officers' club. Second, many nurses were frustrated by their inability to see a patient through his recovery. The excellent transport and treatment systems were key factors in the low mortality rate, but these denied the nurses and physicians the ability to see progress and recovery. Third, nurses, like soldiers, experienced difficulty in readjusting to life at home after their Vietnam experience.

One nurse was killed in the Vietnam War: 1st Lt. Sharon Lane was killed by hostile action while on duty at the 312th Evacuation Hospital, Chu Lai, on 8 June 1969. The contribution of nurses to the American military effort during the war was recognized in 1993 with the dedication of a statue, sculpted by Glenna Goodacre, that was placed near the Vietnam Veterans Memorial; it depicts three women assisting a fallen soldier.

—Rhonda Keen-Payne

References: Donahue, M. Patricia. *Nursing: The Finest Art.* St. Louis, MO: C. V. Mosby, 1985.
Kalisch, Phillip A., and Beatrice Kalisch. *The Advance of American Nursing.* 3d ed. Boston: Little, Brown, 1994.
_____. "Nurses under Fire: The World War II Experience of Nurses on Bataan and Corregidor," *Nursing Research* (November/December 1966).
Kirkpatrick, Sandra. "Battle Casualty." *American Journal of Nursing* (July 1968).
Norman, Elizabeth M. "A Study of Female Military Nurses in Vietnam during the War Years 1965–1973." *Journal of Nursing History* (November 1986).
Smith, Winnie. *American Daughter Gone to War.* New York: William Morrow, 1992.
See also: Casualties; Medevac; Medicine, Military; Vietnam Veterans Memorial; Women in the War, U.S.

United States: Red Cross Recreation Workers

The Supplemental Recreation Activities Overseas (SRAO) program, one of five services offered by the American Red Cross in Vietnam, provided a variety of recreational activities for American troops. The first SRAO center opened in Đà Nẵng in October 1965. Subsequently another 27 centers were established throughout South Vietnam, including Biên Hòa, Nha Trang, Cam Ranh Bay, Quang Tri, Phú Bài, Qui Nhởn, Xuân Lôc, Long Bình, Pleiku, Sài Gòn, Chu Lai, An Khê, and Cu Chi. Between 1965 and 1972, 627 female SRAO workers, commonly called "doughnut dollies," served in Vietnam.

All of the women were college graduates who volunteered to serve in the SRAO. After only a two-week training program in Washington, D.C., they were immediately sent to Vietnam. Once there, they were required to wear the standard blue uniforms, despite being in a war zone. These young women provided refreshments and recreational activities, visited hospitals, wrote letters for patients, and listened to the men talk about their experiences and feelings. Often the only American civilian females with whom the soldiers came in contact, they frequently took on the surrogate roles of mother, sister, and girlfriend.

Although nonveterans rarely recognize or appreciate their invaluable work, in fact SRAO women immeasurably boosted the morale of approximately 300,000 American troops each month. Like all Americans serving in Vietnam, military and civilian, the SRAO women were subjected daily to the horrors of war and confronted fear, violence, and death. Three SRAO women were killed in Vietnam: Hanna E. Crews, Virginia E. Kirsch, and Lucinda J. Richter. Considering that 8 of the more than 7,500 military women who served in Vietnam were killed, the deaths of three SRAO workers is significant. Although the American Red Cross continued to work in Vietnam in other capacities, the SRAO program officially ended in May 1972 as the last American combat troops were withdrawn.

—Lori M. Geist

References: Dickerson, Sharon Lewis. "American Red Cross Women in Vietnam." In *Celebration of Patriotism and Courage: Dedication of the Vietnam Women's Memorial.* Washington, DC: Vietnam Women's Memorial Project, 1993.
Marshall, Kathryn. *In the Combat Zone.* New York: Penguin Books, 1987.

Walker, Keith. *A Piece of My Heart.* New York: Random House, 1985.
See also: Women in the War, U.S.

United States: Seabees

U.S. Navy construction engineers, their name being derived from the pronunciation of the initial letters of "construction battalion." Seabee involvement in Vietnam began on 25 January 1963, when two 13-man Seabee Technical Assistance Teams entered the country in support of U.S. Army Special Forces. The Seabees built Special Forces camps, performed civic action tasks, and completed projects in support of the Civilian Irregular Defense Group (CIDG). Seabee teams remained active in Vietnam to the end of U.S. involvement, their numbers growing to 17 teams there by 1969.

The first full Naval Mobile Construction Battalion landed in Vietnam on 7 May 1965 to build an airfield for the Marines at Chu Lai. In June 1965 Construction Mechanic Third Class Marvin G. Shields, USN, became the first Seabee to win the Medal of Honor. His team, STAT 1104, had been performing construction at a camp at Đông Xoài when a battalion-sized Việt Công force attacked. Shields gave his life defending the camp and helping wounded comrades.

From 1965 to 1969 the Seabee commitment in South Vietnam rapidly increased, necessitating first the transfer of Atlantic Fleet battalions to the Pacific through a change of home port, then deployment of Atlantic Fleet battalions directly to Vietnam and the reestablishment of nine additional battalions. Finally, in May 1968 2 reserve battalions were called to active duty, bringing to 21 the number of battalions rotating to Vietnam at one time or another. In addition, two Amphibious Construction Battalions lent support to the Vietnam effort and two Construction Battalion Maintenance Units were active.

Seabee battalions in Vietnam were under the immediate control of two Naval Construction Regiments. Together they formed the Third Naval Construction Brigade, which provided overall control of Seabee units operating in Vietnam. Seabees were also assigned to such non-Seabee units as the Naval Support Activities at Đà Năng and Sài Gòn. During the war, the total Seabee community grew from 9,400 men in mid-1965 to more than 26,000 in 1969.

Seabee accomplishments in Vietnam were impressive. Seabees built critically needed roads, airfields, cantonments, warehouses, hospitals, bunkers, and other facilities. The mobile search-and-destroy strategy adopted by the U.S. military during the first years of the war shaped their mission. In addition to the many Seabee teams active at remote locations, construction battalions built large coastal strongholds in I Corps area. Seabees were especially active at Đà Năng, Phú Bài, Chu Lai, and Đông Hà. In 1966 Seabees entered Quang Tri Province and built a hilltop fort of concrete bunkers at Làng Vei, which overlooked a feeder line of the Hồ Chí Minh Trail. In 1967 Seabees built the 2,040-foot-long "Liberty Bridge" across the Thu Bồn River, 80 miles southwest of Đà Năng.

During the bitter struggle of the 1968 Tết Offensive, Seabees built and fought in direct support of the Marine Corps and Army.

At Huê, Seabees repaired badly needed bridges. When sniper fire drove them under cover, they organized their own combat teams and silenced the snipers. In addition to supporting combat forces, Seabees completed innumerable civic action projects while in Vietnam, including the construction of schools, hospitals, housing, and wells.

By the end of 1968 most major base construction was complete and the Seabees began to pull out. The last battalion left Vietnam in November 1971. The three Seabee teams still there finished their tasks and were gone by the end of 1972.

—Vincent A. Transano

References: Naval Facilities Engineering Command Archives, NAVFAC Historical Program Office, Naval Construction Battalion Center, Port Hueneme, CA.
"Naval Facilities Engineering Command History, 1965–1974." Vol. 2. Report Symbol OPNAV 5750–1. Washington, DC: NAVFAC Historian's Office, 1975, unpublished.
Tregaskis, Richard. *Southeast Asia: Building the Bases.* Washington, DC: U.S. Government Printing Office, 1975.
See also: Civic Action; Civilian Irregular Defense Group (CIDG); Huê, Battle of; Search and Destroy; United States: Army; United States: Marine Corps; United States: Navy.

United States: Special Forces

Elite U.S. Army troops who played a key role in counterinsurgency operations during the Vietnam War. Realizing the need for specialized units that were expert in conducting unconventional warfare (UW) operations behind enemy lines, Office of Psychological Warfare (OPW) chief Brig. Gen. Robert A. McClure suggested their formation. On 20 June 1952 the first permanent UW unit since the Second World War was formed at Fort Bragg, North Carolina. It used U.S. Army personnel and became a fixture of the U.S. military. Known as the U.S. Special Forces (USSF), it carried on the traditions of Roger's Rangers, Francis Marion, Darby's Rangers, Merrill's Marauders, the 1st Special Service Force, and the Office of Strategic Services (OSS).

Under Public Law 597 of 30 June 1952, the "Lodge Bill," recruiting of Special Forces volunteers began. The guidelines specifying requirements for voluntary service were drafted as U.S. Army Special Regulation 600-160-10 for implementation on 25 April 1952. The basic oath required verbally of each volunteer stated in part: "I volunteer for Special Forces training and duty. I further volunteer to perform frequent aircraft flights, glider flights, parachute jumps, and to participate in realistic combat training. . . ."

Training stressed infiltration and land navigation techniques and the use of parachutes and small boats. Individually suited, specialized training followed and included sabotage, intelligence gathering, communications, medicine, and weaponry. Army volunteers who successfully completed the secret training were assigned directly to Special Forces. Many in the Army's hierarchy were displeased, but by the 1960s both President John F. Kennedy and his senior military advisor General Maxwell D. Taylor were strong advocates for an enhanced Special Forces capability.

SF were the chief instrument of U.S. counterinsurgency policy in Vietnam. The goal was not so much to destroy enemy armed

U.S. Special Forces soldiers operating a recoilless rifle use field telephones to maintain contact with their command post. U.S. Special Forces were elite U.S. Army troops that played a key role in counterinsurgency operations during the Vietnam War.

forces as to win the allegiance of the people by inspiring them to defend themselves.

Personnel from the 1st Special Forces Group on Okinawa first entered Vietnam in the summer of 1957. During the following few months, they trained 58 Vietnamese soldiers in special forces techniques at a training center in Nha Trang, later designated the Military Assistance Command, Vietnam (MACV) Recondo School. These Vietnamese formed the nucleus of the Vietnamese Special Forces (Lực Lượng Đặc Biệt [LLDB]).

In 1960 the USSF mission expanded to include training 60 Army of the Republic of Vietnam (ARVN) Ranger companies. To do this, 30 instructors from the 7th Special Forces Group deployed to Vietnam. In early 1961 this arrangement was changed when four men from the 1st Special Forces Group and five other soldiers replaced the 7th SF instructors as a Mobile Training Team (MTT). Such teams rotated from Okinawa for the next two years to train the Rangers. These teams operated under the control of the Central Intelligence Agency's (CIA's) Combined Studies Group (CSG).

The impetus for increased USSF operations in Vietnam was addressed in the 11 May 1961 National Security Action Memorandum No. 52 in which President Kennedy directed Secretary of Defense Robert S. McNamara to examine "increasing the counter-guerrilla resources" of the United States. In both his 1961 message to Congress on the defense budget and in his State of the Union address, Kennedy announced his intention to expand the mili-

tary's capability to conduct unconventional warfare. On 21 September 1961 the 5th Special Forces Group (Airborne), 1st Special Forces was activated at Fort Bragg. Its mission was to train personnel in counterinsurgency methods to be used in Vietnam.

Also in 1961 USSF began training ethnic minorities in Vietnam, and this became the basis of the Civilian Irregular Defense Group (CIDG). The purpose was to reestablish government control over remote areas and to provide forces capable of combating the Communist insurgents. By August about 10,000 Rhadé had been organized into village defense and mobile strike forces. The program relied on fortified camps, and by 1965 over 80 CIDG camps had been established. During 1961 the CIA used one SF team to train Vietnamese Special Forces to conduct reconnaissance and harassment operations in North Vietnam. On 1 May 1962 the CSG was attached to MACV headquarters.

In addition to training local inhabitants to defend themselves, to gather intelligence, and to conduct small offensive operations, USSF was deeply involved in civic action programs to encourage civilians to identify more closely with the South Vietnamese government and to improve the living conditions of the people. This was done through such efforts as digging wells, building schools, and providing medical care.

In July 1962 Secretary McNamara directed that the CIA's paramilitary operations be transferred to MACV. This was to place SF units under Army control and to emphasize offensive operations rather than pacification. Code-named Operation PARASOL-SWITCHBACK, the transfer was complete by 1 July 1963.

As a result of the increased number of camps being opened, the 5th Special Forces Group at Fort Bragg, North Carolina, sent 76 command and support personnel to Vietnam in September 1962. By November 24 SF detachments operated in Vietnam on temporary duty (TDY), six-month tours. In September MACV established Headquarters, U.S. Army Special Forces Vietnam, Provisional (USASFV[P]). In February 1963 the headquarters occupied semipermanent facilities at Nha Trang Air Base. Operation SWITCHBACK was completed as scheduled. By that time, the SF had trained 52,636 villagers, 10,904 reaction force soldiers, 515 medical personnel, 3,803 scouts, and 946 trail watchers; also 879 villages had been secured. Total USSF personnel in Vietnam had risen to 646.

USSF were frustrated in their efforts to improve the quality of the LLDB primarily because of incompetent Vietnamese leadership and mistrust of the Sài Gòn government. Part of the concept of the CIDG and border camps was that, once an area was deemed secure, the camps would be turned over to ARVN or LLDB control, and the defenders would become part of the South Vietnamese Army. Traditional Vietnamese disregard of ethnic minorities, who often composed CIDG forces, and the incompetency of ARVN officers many times led to the abandonment of camps or to the unwillingness of the CIDG to fight for the government. The CIDG often showed themselves more loyal to their USSF advisors than to the Sài Gòn regime.

On 1 November 1963 along with the CIDG program, the CIA relinquished their surveillance responsibilities along the Laotian and Cambodian borders to the USASFV(P) headquarters. By June 1964, 18 border camps had been established. As the SF mission shifted from training indigenous forces to watching infiltration routes into South Vietnam, these camps became increasingly tempting targets for the North Vietnamese. In July 1964 a Việt Cộng (VC) force attacked the camp at Nam Đồng. For this battle, USSF camp commander Capt. Roger Donlon received the first Medal of Honor issued since the Korean War.

Programs to increase the number of indigenous minorities participating in the CIDG effort and to expand CIDG operations, along with greater emphasis on observation along the borders, soon outstripped USSF resources available in Vietnam.

On 1 October 1964 the 5th Special Forces Group officially arrived in Vietnam. Many SF teams, however, were understaffed. Replacements often had little to no SF experience, and shortages of personnel with communications and medical skills became critical. Duty tours for USSF teams in Vietnam increased from six months to one year. This resulted in troop replacements on an individual rather than team basis, which had a detrimental effect on team operations. USSF reached its highest strength in Vietnam on 30 September 1968 with 3,542 assigned personnel.

Other activities in which USSF were involved included acting as guides for U.S. units to orient them to a particular area. From 1964 to 1966 USSF trained and fielded three long-range reconnaissance projects: DELTA, SIGMA, and OMEGA. All had USSF

leadership with indigenous battalions as reaction forces. In September 1966 General William C. Westmoreland, MACV commander, directed the 5th SF Group to establish the MACV Recondo School to train U.S. and Allied personnel from major combat units in long-range reconnaissance techniques. Despite having a permanent headquarters in Vietnam, the USSF was unable to prevent MACV from employing SF and CIDG as regular infantry in offensive operations against the People's Army of Vietnam (PAVN) or VC. Although results of such operations were often disastrous, the CIDG was usually successful in defending camps against Communist attacks. By 1967 increased use of night operations, extensive training, and missions based on effective intelligence resulted in more effective operations being conducted by SF detachments, such as B-36 Mobile Guerrilla Force (MGF), identified as Project RAPID FIRE. In November 1967 following the 3 September transfer of Projects SIGMA and OMEGA to MACV Studies and Observations Group (MACV-SOG), Detachment B-36 assumed the added responsibility of developing tactical and strategic reconnaissance in III Corps.

Although USSF composed most of the personnel in MACV-SOG operations, SOG was not subordinate to the 5th Special Forces Group and not answerable to MACV, but uniquely supervised by the president of the United States. Under MACV-SOG direction, combined USSF indigenous mercenary teams conducted operations into North Vietnam, Laos, and Cambodia to gather intelligence about PAVN activities along the Hồ Chí Minh Trail. The Provincial Reconnaissance Unit was the armed wing of the PHOENIX program, and MACV-SOG continued to draw off experienced USSF personnel. This only added to the overall shortage of qualified USSF personnel for 5th Special Forces Group missions.

On 27 August 1969 General Creighton Abrams, who succeeded Westmoreland as MACV commander, ordered the phaseout of the CIDG program, with the camps and CIDG soldiers to be transferred to ARVN control. A total of 38 light infantry battalions, comprised primarily of ethnic minorities, joined the ARVN under this program.

On 1 March 1971 the 5th Special Forces Group ceased all operations in South Vietnam and departed for the United States. Some USSF personnel remained in Vietnam, however, as instructors with the Special Mission Advisory Group (SMAG). These instructors readied Vietnamese soldiers to assume MACV-SOG's unconventional warfare role as the Special Mission Service (SMS). As SMAG was deactivated on 1 April 1972, USSF instructors became advisors to the SMS and the graduated SMAG students. Teams from the 1st Special Forces Group (SFG) continued to train ARVN and Cambodian soldiers until 22 February 1973 when the 1st SFG ceased operations in South Vietnam. The combined USSF-Vietnamese organization, Strategic Technical Directorate (STD), operated under the auspices of the closed MACV-SOG until 12 May 1973, when it was disbanded.

—Richard L. Kiper, Harve Saal, and Spencer C. Tucker

References: Donahue, James C. *Mobile Guerrilla Forces with the Special Forces in War Zone D.* Annapolis, MD: Naval Institute Press, 1996.

Kelly, Francis J. *U.S. Army Special Forces, 1961–1972.* Washington, DC: Department of the Army, 1973.

Saal, Harve. *MACV, Studies and Observations Group (SOG). Behind Enemy Lines, A History of the Men and Missions.* 4 vols. Milwaukee, WI: Jones Techno-Comm, 1991.

Simpson, Charles M., III. *Inside the Green Berets (The Story of the Special Forces).* New York: Berkley Publishing, 1984.

Stonton, Shelby L. *Green Berets at War. U.S. Army Special Forces in Southeast Asia, 1956–1975.* Novato, CA: Presidio Press, 1985.

Sutherland, Ian D. W. *1952/1982: Special Forces of the United States Army.* San Jose, CA: R. James Bender, 1990.

See also: Abrams, Creighton; Civilian Irregular Defense Group (CIDG); Counterinsurgency Warfare; DELTA, Project; Kennedy, John Fitzgerald; McNamara, Robert S.; Military Assistance Command, Vietnam (MACV); Montagnards; OMEGA, Project; Phoenix Program; Road Watch Teams (RWTs); SEAL (Sea, Air, Land) Teams; SIGMA, Project; Studies and Observation Group (SOG); Taylor, Maxwell Davenport; Vietnam, Republic of: Special Forces (Lực Lưởng Đặc Biệt [LLDB]); Westmoreland, William Childs.

United States: Special Services

Organization providing recreational activities for military personnel. The U.S. Army Special Services program in Vietnam began on 1 July 1966, when responsibility for providing diversified, comprehensive recreational activities for U.S. and Allied military forces was transferred from the U.S. Navy to the U.S. Army, Vietnam (USARV) with operational responsibility assigned to the 1st Logistical Command. General William Westmoreland considered recreational facilities critical both for maintaining troop morale and for providing on-base diversions so that American soldiers would not overwhelm the Vietnamese economy. Special Services facilities helped to fulfill this need.

The Special Services program consisted of arts and crafts, entertainment, library, rest and recuperation (R&R), recreation (sports and motion pictures), and service facilities. Military personnel assumed responsibility for R&R and recreation, but civilian volunteers, both women and men, supervised and staffed the remaining branches. Initially USARV supplied only the organizational structure and technical and supervisory administrative personnel. Individual units provided all other administrative and logistical support, including the assignment of full-time military personnel and local national employees to each facility. In March 1970, however, Special Services was reorganized and centralized as the USARV Special Services Agency (Provisional). At that time, 31 craft shops and photography laboratories, six entertainment offices, 23 service clubs, and 39 libraries, most housed in permanent structures, were in operation.

Civilian librarians also administered 250 field library units, arranging the distribution of 190,000 magazine subscriptions and 350,000 paperbacks. Recreation specialists directed a variety of leisure activities, coordinated United Service Organizations (USO) tours of commercial entertainers and celebrities, and produced and acted in small theater productions. They created Command Military Touring Shows, sending military personnel to entertain soldiers in areas that commercial shows could not visit for security reasons.

The majority of Special Services programs and services were located in base camps and command areas, inaccessible to fighting units but well placed to provide diversionary activities for support personnel and field units rotating into the base camps that General Westmoreland wanted isolated from the local economy. However, the Command Military Touring Shows and the field distribution of expendable reading materials did provide recreational support to the soldier in the field, as did the R&R program.

Although the exact number is unknown, between 200 and 300 civilians, about 75 percent of them women, served with Special Services in Vietnam between 1966 and 1972. Two recreation specialists assigned to service clubs died of nonhostile causes—Dorothy Phillips in a 1967 plane crash near Qui Nhơn and Rosalyn Muskat in a 1968 jeep accident at Biên Hòa.

—Ann L. Kelsey

References: "General Historical Records." National Archives Branch Depository, Records of the United States Army, Vietnam (USARV), RG 472. Headquarters, U.S. Army, Vietnam, Special Services Agency (Provisional), Entertainment Branch, College Park, MD.

"General Records." National Archives Branch Depository, Records of the United States Army, Vietnam (USARV), RG 472. Headquarters, U.S. Army, Vietnam, Office of the Civilian Personnel Director, Office of the Director, College Park, MD.

Westmoreland, William C. *A Soldier Reports.* Garden City, NY: Doubleday, 1976.

See also: United States: Red Cross Recreation Workers; Women in the War, U.S.

University of Wisconsin Bombing

(August 1970)

24 August 1970 bombing on the campus of the University of Wisconsin. As New Left protest groups, led by Students for a Democratic Society (SDS), began to disintegrate in 1969, a few radicals sought to attract attention. The most radical of these groups was the Weathermen.

In October 1969 most of the New Left antiwar groups had agreed to a moratorium on further action. After the May 1970 violence at Kent State University left four people dead, many students and the SDS ceased their protests. A few protesters, however, turned to violence. Led by Mark Rudd, a small, radical group of students—the Weathermen—turned to bombings and guerrilla warfare.

After a bizarre open convention at Flint, Michigan, on Christmas Day 1969, at which they openly advocated violence, the Weathermen went underground and operated in small "affinity groups" and revolutionary cells. Soon bombs set by the Weathermen began going off around the country. On 21 February 1970 Weathermen firebombed the home of Judge John Murtagh, who was presiding over a trial of a group of Black Panthers. On 6 March 1970 a townhouse in Greenwich Village exploded, killing three Weathermen, who had been assembling a bomb when it detonated prematurely. Other Weathermen cells bombed the New York City police headquarters in June 1970. Weathermen bombs also exploded in Chicago, California, and Long Island, but none resulted in deaths.

That changed on 24 August 1970, when a Weathermen bomb exploded in Sterling Hall on the main University of Wisconsin campus at Madison. Known as Army Math, the building was the home of the Army Mathematics Research Center (AMRC). The purpose of the bombers was to strike a blow at the "government war machine." The bomb destroyed the work of five professors and the doctoral work of 24 graduate students. It also caused $6 million in damage, injured three people, and killed Robert Fussnach, a 33-year-old graduate student. His death shocked and angered many radicals.

The bombing was carried out by Madison residents Karl and Dwight Armstrong and University of Wisconsin students David Fine and Leo Burt. The Federal Bureau of Investigation immediately launched an extensive manhunt and between 1972 and 1976 all the bombers except Burt were caught. In 1973 Karl Armstrong was sentenced to 23 years in prison (later reduced to 10 years); Dwight Armstrong and Fine received 7-year sentences. Burt remains at large. Although terrorist bombings continued for the next several years, the number of Weathermen attacks dropped dramatically after the University of Wisconsin bombing.

—Laura Matysek Wood

References: Dougan, Clark, Samuel Lipsman, and the editors of Boston Publishing. *A Nation Divided. The Vietnam Experience,* edited by Robert Manning. Boston: Boston Publishing, 1984.
Jacobs, Harold, ed. *Weathermen.* Berkeley, CA: Ramparts Press, 1970.
Kutler, Stanley I., ed. *Encyclopedia of the Vietnam War.* New York: Charles Scribner's Sons, 1996.
Unger, Irwin. *The Movement: A History of the American New Left, 1959–1972.* New York: Dodd, Mead, 1974.
See also: Antiwar Movement, United States; Federal Bureau of Investigation (FBI); Weathermen.

U.S. Agency for International Development (USAID)

Also known as the Agency for International Development (AID); it was the agency responsible for administration of the economic aid program of the United States to the Republic of Vietnam (RVN). With the 1954 Geneva Accords and the temporary establishment of two separate Vietnams, the economic assistance program of the U.S. government to the South Vietnamese came under the administration of the Agency for International Development, which evolved out of the International Cooperation Administration (ICA).

USAID administered the economic assistance program through its field agency in the RVN, the United States Operation Mission (USOM). USAID provided not only American economic support to the government of Ngô Đình Diêm, but the economic foundation for the survival of the new South Vietnamese government.

Between 1955 and 1960 U.S. economic aid averaged from $220 to $270 million a year, or over 20 percent of the gross national product of the RVN. During this period, USAID provided economic assistance through a variety of programs that addressed education, agriculture, public health, public safety, local government, public works, industrial development, land reform, and refugee resettlement. USAID monies were used for the construction of schoolhouses and universities, the establishment of health centers and hospitals, the purchase of agricultural technology,

and for the construction of highways, hydroelectric facilities, and industrial centers. Public safety projects included support for the development of a national police force and local security forces. USAID monies were also funneled into local government, assisting in the 1956 election of a Constituent Assembly to draft a national constitution and in the election of local representatives to the RVN National Assembly.

USAID assistance also provided the support necessary to cope with the immediate crisis involving the resettlement of refugees from North Vietnam. Following the 1954 agreement that established a temporary partition of the country, perhaps 1 million refugees fled the North for the South. Many of these were Catholics who provided the principal political base for RVN Prime Minister Ngô Đình Diêm in his anti-Communist crusade. USAID provided the economic assistance to resettle these refugees and, in the process, promoted a land reform campaign to gain their loyalty to the Diêm government. USAID assistance also provided support for the construction of houses, mechanical equipment to farm the land, and daily subsistence needs.

The largest resettlement project involved land reclamation at Cái Săn in Kiên Giang Province along the Gulf of Thailand extending back into An Giang Province. Some 100,000 refugees cleared and drained nearly 200,000 acres of swampland and dug 20 kilometers of irrigation canals for rice cultivation over a five-year period. This became the showpiece for Diêm's refugee resettlement program. Instead of outright ownership of the land they had reclaimed, the refugees were asked to sign tenancy contracts for lands to be purchased in installments from the government. This, however, led to peasant resentment rather than allegiance to the government. The mismanagement of the Cái Săn land reform project showed that projects supported by USAID economic assistance and implemented by the South Vietnamese government were often inconsistent with U.S. political objectives.

The land development program was a USOM idea to resettle refugees in Land Development Centers (LDCs) on supposedly abandoned lands in the Mekong Delta and in undeveloped lands in the Central Highlands, with the same purpose of gaining peasant allegiance to the government. USAID monies provided assistance for the program. The highlander resettlement program, begun in 1955 as part of the land development program, resettled Montagnards into defensible areas and made Montagnard lands available to Vietnamese refugees. This in turn alienated many Montagnards and promoted the development of the ethnonationalist Montagnard movement.

During the early years of American involvement, USAID worked primarily through Vietnamese government channels in Sài Gòn to advance economic and political objectives. Although USAID personnel made inspection trips to rural areas outside Sài Gòn, they relied primarily on Vietnamese government officials to implement the projects supported through USAID economic assistance. Because USAID officials primarily worked and lived in Sài Gòn, they often failed to properly supervise USAID projects in the field. American monies and assistance were thus often wasted or used for purposes other than those originally intended. In this regard, the economic and political objectives that directed those projects were often subverted by the Vietnamese government bureaucracy and Vietnamese political officials.

By the early 1960s USAID had formed the internal Office of Rural Affairs and began to expand its efforts outside of Sài Gòn by sending civilian advisors to more rural areas. USAID advisors began to move into rural provinces and to take a more active and independent role in economic assistance programs. USAID continued to fund engineering projects, such as road and bridge construction; industrial and agricultural production; public health projects, including the drilling of wells and the establishment of health centers; and education projects such as the construction of schools. USAID monies provided equipment for development and construction, supplies such as cement and tin for roofs, and seeds for agricultural production. The intent was to improve the standard of living for the civilian population and thereby attract their support for the Sài Gòn government.

One of the more notable programs funded by USAID was the International Volunteer Service (IVS). Founded as a private, non-profit organization in 1953, IVS served as a model for the Peace Corps and first came to the RVN in 1957. In Vietnam, IVS was funded primarily by USAID, but monies also came from the RVN government during the early years and from private agencies as well. In contrast to most USAID officials, IVS workers were required to study Vietnamese and received instruction in Vietnamese culture. They signed up for a two-year tour in Vietnam, with assignments at the village level ranging from developing agriculture to teaching English. IVS saw its function as humanitarian and divorced from USAID political objectives. Don Luce served as IVS director from 1961 to 1967 but resigned to protest U.S. political and military policies that affected IVS work at the village level. IVS resisted USAID pressure to become more politically involved, and the Sài Gòn government stopped approving its projects in 1971.

By mid-1965 USAID economic support for pacification programs reached approximately $500 million per year to build support for the Sài Gòn government. At the same time, however, the war escalated and long-term development programs often took a backseat to more immediate security concerns and pacification efforts. After 1967 USAID economic assistance was channeled through Civilian Operations and Revolutionary Development Support (CORDS), established under the Military Assistance Command, Vietnam (MACV) to organize all civilian aid programs involved in the pacification effort under the military chain of command.

—David M. Berman

References: Hunt, Richard A. *Pacification: The American Struggle for Vietnam's Hearts and Minds.* Boulder, CO: Westview Press, 1995.
Luce, Don, and John Sommer. *Viet Nam: The Unheard Voices.* Ithaca, NY: Cornell University Press, 1969.
Sheehan, Neil. *A Bright Shining Lie: John Paul Vann and America in Vietnam.* New York: Random House, 1988.
Wiesner, Louis A. *Victims and Survivors: Displaced Persons and Other War Victims in Viet-Nam, 1954–1975.* New York: Greenwood Press, 1988.
See also: Civic Action; Civilian Operations and Revolutionary Development Support (CORDS); Land Reform; Marine Combined Action Platoons (CAPs); Michigan State University (MSU) Advisory Group; Military Assistance Command, Vietnam (MACV); Montagnards; Pacification; Strategic Hamlet Program.

U.S. Army, Vietnam, Installation Stockade (USARVIS)

Infamous U.S. military correctional facility in Vietnam. Rarely called it by its official name, the U.S. Army, Vietnam, Installation Stockade (USARVIS) was located in a headquarters and logistical complex on the outskirts of Long Bình in Biên Hòa Province. Most soldiers knew it as Long Bình Jail, or LBJ. Early in its involvement in Vietnam, the United States established a military prison at a former tennis court at Pershing Field near Sài Gòn. Soldiers called it "the stockade." It was moved to Long Bình in the summer of 1966, a change necessitated by the huge American troop buildup and the consequent need to house the increasing number of military offenders.

Long Bình was a good location. Newly arrived GIs were processed at Long Bình, where they saw firsthand what would happen to them if they broke the rules, and many did. Offenders were sent to LBJ from all four Army Corps Tactical Zones (CTZs). Few officers or senior noncommissioned officers (NCOs) were confined within its perimeter of cyclone fence and concertina wire, but there were exceptions. One was Lt. William Calley, who stayed there for some weeks prior to his transshipment back to the United States. Another was Col. Robert Rheault, commander of the U.S. Fifth Special Forces Group, and six of his officers, charged with the premeditated murder of a suspected double agent.

LBJ soaked up those who went absent without official leave (AWOL) and those who refused orders. It housed those convicted of drug abuse, combat refusal, and "fragging." Men convicted of war crimes passed through its gates, and incorrigible discipline busters inevitably ended up at LBJ after their courts-martial. Rapists, thieves, black marketeers, and murderers all came to know LBJ well.

Periods of incarceration at LBJ were "lost time" and did not count toward the fulfillment of one's 365-day tour. The memory of time spent in the stockade became an indelible part of some men's lives, and even hardened noncommissioned officers spoke of LBJ in the early days in hushed tones. The simple threat of being sent there was sufficient to keep many GIs obedient to orders; they would rather face the enemy than serve time at LBJ.

Initially, the Military Police Corps assigned to LBJ as guards and other personnel those who had little or no professional training as confinement facility specialists. Size, weight, and toughness seemed to be primary qualifications for a job there. Guards demanded unthinking obedience at all times and imposed their own rigid and exacting disciplinary standards. Infractions of rules brought about special confinement in "the box," a metal conex container that stood in the open absorbing the blazing rays of the tropical sun, or other punishments such as filling endless sandbags, guard-administered baths at midnight in the shower facility during which some inmates nearly drowned, or surreptitious beatings.

For the first two years of LBJ's existence at Long Bình, official treatment of prisoners regularly exceeded normally allowable limits. That was the era in which the legend of Long Bình Jail was formed. Then on 29 August 1968 prisoners seized the stockade compound and set out on a rampage of destruction. They fired the buildings, tore down what would not burn, and beat any guard within reach. The commander of LBJ, Lt. Col. Vern Johnson, never recovered from the beating he received and was invalided out of the service.

Commanders thereafter oversaw the reconstruction of LBJ into a gleaming, modern correctional institute. Guards took appropriate training in a new military occupational specialty (MOS) and became "correctional facility specialists." Social services were upgraded. Punishments became less arbitrary and more rational. The kitchen at LBJ became famous for the quality of its food, attracting many officers who came there for meals from units all over Long Bình.

As the U.S. Army's pullout began, LBJ's population dwindled. In 1972 the Army closed the facility, transferring the few remaining prisoners and guards to the original stockade area at Pershing Field in Sài Gòn. USARVIS's existence terminated on 29 March 1973, as the last combat troops departed from Vietnam.

—Cecil B. Currey

References: Author interviews with more than 200 personnel associated with the USARVIS.
See also: Atrocities during the Vietnam War; Calley, William Laws, Jr.; Desertion, Allied and Communist; Long Bình.

UTAH, Operation

(4–7 March 1966)

Code name (LIÊN KÊT-26) for a combined U.S. Marine Corps and Army of the Republic of Vietnam (ARVN) assault northwest of Quang Ngãi City in I Corps against People's Army of Vietnam (PAVN) and Việt Công (VC) main force units. Planning for the operation began on the evening of 3 March 1966, when Brig. Gen. Jonas Platt, commanding Task Force Delta, learned that the 36th (also called the 21st) PAVN Regiment had taken up a position seven miles northwest of the city. He sent Col. Oscar Peatross, who commanded the 7th Marines, to meet with Brig. Gen. Hoàng Xuân Lãm, commanding general of the 2d ARVN Division at Quang Ngãi City. They agreed on a combined operation using one ARVN and one Marine battalion.

On the morning of 4 March Marine Air Group (MAG) 36, commanded by Col. William Johnson, airlifted the 1st Airborne Battalion of the 2d ARVN Division, followed by Companies F, G, and H of the 2d Battalion, 7th Regiment, U.S. Marines, commanded by Col. Leon Utter, from Chu Lai to southwest of the hamlet of Châu Nhai, 15 kilometers northwest of Quang Ngãi City. Despite meeting heavy PAVN resistance at the landing zones, the landing was completed.

Paddies, hamlets, Hills 97 and 85 to the southwest, and Hill 50 to the northeast stood out as major features. Hill 50 presented the strongest opposition and extensive fighting occurred at Châu Nhai, southwest of that hill. Artillery saturation of PAVN strongholds produced the largest fire mission to date in the Chu Lai area (1,900 rounds in two hours).

To encircle the PAVN forces, Generals Platt and Lãm expanded the operation with additional U.S. Marine units (by order of insertion: 3/1st, commanded by Lt. Col. James Young; 2/4th, commanded by Col. Paul "P.X." Kelley; 1/7th, commanded by Col. James Kelley; and a company from 2/7th) and ARVN reinforcements (the 37th Ranger Battalion, 2d Division Strike Company, and an armored personnel carrier troop, and from Sài Gòn, the 5th Airborne Battalion). By midday on 5 March Company L, 3/1st, with support from the 1st ARVN Airborne Battalion, took Hill 50 after three and one-half hours of combat.

Most of the action had ended by early morning of 6 March. Near An Tuyêt, however, Company B, 1/7th (commanded by Capt. Robert Prewitt) came under attack. A dangerous helicopter mission resupplied them with ammunition, and Company B successfully repelled an attack by two PAVN companies. Ordered to relieve the beleaguered command, Company B, 2/4th discovered that the main PAVN force had withdrawn.

Fighting in the northern area of Operation UTAH was unexpectedly light. On 6 March three Marine battalions (2/7th, 3/1st, 1/7th) discovered abandoned defensive complexes, including caves and tunnels with weapons, supplies, and documents. On 7 March the operation came to an end when the Marines destroyed the PAVN fortifications on Hill 50.

In this short, hard fight the Marines sustained casualties of 98 dead and 278 wounded; ARVN forces lost 30 killed and 120 wounded. Edward Simmons lists PAVN killed at 586 (Marines claimed 358; ARVN, 228), while Shelby Stanton states there were 632 known enemy casualties.

—Paul S. Daum, with assistance from Trevor Curran

References: Shulimson, Jack. *U.S. Marines in Vietnam, 1966: An Expanding War.* Marine Corps Vietnam Series. Washington, DC: History and Museums Division, Marine Corps Historical Center, U.S. Marine Corps Headquarters, 1982.
Simmons, Edward H. "Marine Corps Operations in Vietnam, 1965–1966." In *The Marines in Vietnam, 1954–1973: An Anthology and Annotated Bibliography,* 2d ed. Marine Corps Vietnam Series. Washington, DC: History and Museums Division, U.S. Marine Corps Headquarters, 1985.
Stanton, Shelby L. *The Rise and Fall of an American Army: U.S. Ground Forces in Vietnam, 1965–1973.* Novato, CA: Presidio Press, 1985.
See also: United States: Marine Corps; Vietnam, Democratic Republic of: Army (People's Army of Vietnam [PAVN]); Vietnam, Republic of: Army (ARVN).

V

Valluy, Jean-Etienne

(1899–1970)

French Army general and commander in chief in Indo-China from the end of 1946 to February 1948. Born on 15 May 1899 at Rive-de-Gier (Loire), Jean-Etienne Valluy entered the French military academy of Saint-Cyr in 1917. Upon graduation, he chose service with colonial troops and served in the Middle East and Morocco; he was promoted to captain in 1929. Valluy was posted in China from 1937 to 1939. Between 1940 and 1941 he was a prisoner of war in Germany. In 1941 he was promoted to lieutenant colonel, and from 1941 to 1943 he served in French West Africa. Promoted to brigadier general in September 1944, he served as chief of staff of the French First Army and fought with it in France and Germany and commanded the 9th Division d'Infanterie Coloniale (DIC). In November 1945 he left for Indo-China with his division as part of General Jacques-Philippe Leclerc's expeditionary corps. He soon found himself at the cutting edge of French efforts first to conciliate the Viêt Minh and then to confront them with a show of force. It was on his orders that Col. Pierre-Louis Dèbes gave the ultimatum to the Viêt Minh to evacuate Hai Phòng and then bombarded the town.

On succeeding Leclerc as commander in chief, Valluy demonstrated a high degree of military ability with the forces placed at his disposal. By the end of 1947 the French military position in Tonkin was as favorable as it was ever to be during the First Indo-China War (1946–1954). Regarded as one of the most intelligent generals to serve in Indo-China, with a good grasp of the political nature of the war, Valluy was nevertheless opposed to what he considered Emile Bollaert's premature offer of negotiations with the Viêt Minh.

Following his return to France in February 1948, Valluy was called upon to participate in several high-level missions to Indo-China. He died in Paris on 4 January 1970.

—Arthur J. Dommen

Reference: Gras, Général Yves. *Histoire de la Guerre d'Indochine.* Paris: Editions Denoël, 1992.
See also: Bollaert, Emile; Dèbes, Pierre-Louis; France: Army; Leclerc, Jacques-Philippe; Viêt Minh (Viêt Nam Dôc Lâp Dông Minh Hôi [Vietnam Independence League]).

Văn Cao

(1923–1995)

Acclaimed Vietnamese musician and composer of the national anthem of the Democratic Republic of Vietnam (DRV) and Socialist Republic of Vietnam (SRV). Born on 11 November 1923 in Hai Phòng to a poor working family, Nguyên Văn Cao was a gifted artist, well known as Văn Cao. Famous in Vietnam in many fields and best known as a composer, he was also a poet, painter, and stage decorator. He wrote his first song, "Buôn Tàn Thu" ("Feeling Blue in Late Fall") at age 16; it is still a favorite among Vietnamese. Other romantic favorites are "Thiên Thai" ("Paradise"), "Làng Tôi" ("My Village"), and "Trường Chi" (the name of a male character in a well-known Vietnamese folktale).

Văn Cao joined the Viêt Minh as a commando and composed a number of songs. He wrote "Tiên Quân Ca" ("Marching Forward") in November 1944; it soon became the song of the Viêt Minh and was sung in front of the Hà Nôi Opera House on 17 August 1945, when the red flag with yellow star that became Vietnam's national flag was introduced. Hô Chí Minh himself chose "Marching Forward" as the national anthem. The song's lyrics read in part, "Our flag, red with the blood of victory, bears the spirit of our country. . . . The path to glory passes over the bodies of our foes." In the 1970s there was some discussion about changing the national anthem, but popular support led to its retention. This was reconfirmed in 1993.

Although Văn Cao continued as a member of the Communist Party, in the 1960s he fell into disgrace after he joined Nhân Văn Giai Phâm, an opposition group that included many famous writers and poets. It had emerged in 1957 when Hô Chí Minh followed China's "Let a Hundred Flowers Bloom" and allowed limited freedom of expression. Văn Cao stopped composing until late 1975 when he produced "Mùa Xuaân Đâu Tiên" ("The First Spring"). Supposedly praising the Communist April 1975 victory, it was more of a lamentation and was not welcomed by the authorities. It was his last musical work.

In the early 1980s the Vietnamese Communist Party (VCP) held a competition for a new national anthem, solely because the party leadership disliked Văn Cao. The idea of a new national anthem was dropped after almost all party favorites among composers convinced the party leaders that none of the entries was comparable to Văn Cao's anthem.

Văn Cao's talents were again recognized during *đôi mơi* in the 1990s, and at age 70 he was awarded the coveted Medal of Independence. After a long illness, Nguyên Văn Cao died on 10 July 1995. Loved and admired by generations of Vietnamese, he was accorded a large funeral.

—Spencer C. Tucker

References: *New York Times* (14 July 1995).
Sài Gòn Giai Phong (Sài Gòn) (16 July 1995).
See also: Hô Chí Minh; Viêt Minh (Viêt Nam Dôc Lâp Dông Minh Hôi [Vietnam Independence League]); Vietnam, Democratic Republic of: 1945–1954; Vietnam, Democratic Republic of: 1954–1975; Vietnam, Socialist Republic of: 1975 to the Present.

Văn Tiên Dũng
(1917–)

People's Army of Vietnam (PAVN) general; Army commander in chief (1974–1980); defense minister, Socialist Republic of Vietnam (1980–1986). Văn Tiên Dũng was born on 1 May 1917 in Hà Đông Province near Hà Nôi. Dũng was of peasant ancestry and as a boy worked in a French textile factory. In the 1930s he joined the Indo-Chinese Communist Party and fought against the French occupation of Vietnam; after 1940 he fought the Japanese. Dũng became a protégé of General Võ Nguyên Giáp, who moved him up through the ranks of the military. In 1953 Giáp appointed Dũng his chief of staff, a position he held during the victory over French forces at Điên Biên Phu.

In the 1950s and early 1960s Dũng served as an alternate member of the Politburo, and throughout the 1960s he remained second in command of the Army to Giáp, who used Dũng as an example of true Communist ideals at work: a peasant who had worked hard and risen through the ranks.

In March 1964 Dũng wrote a series of articles in the Communist Party newspaper *Nhân Dân* defending party domination of the Army. Colonel General Dũng argued that "the absolute and total leadership of the Party is the decisive factor for our army to maintain its proletarian class character and to fulfill successfully all revolutionary tasks." Dũng completely embraced the party line and ideals.

In the early 1970s Dũng became a member of the Democratic Republic of Vietnam (DRV) Politburo. In March 1973 he oversaw the infiltration of large numbers of PAVN troops into the Republic of Vietnam (RVN). PAVN and Viêt Công (VC) units set up a headquarters in Lôc Ninh, 75 miles north of Sài Gòn, moved battalions of labor troops through the jungles, positioned armored vehicles, began construction on an oil pipeline, and laid out a radio grid to communicate with Hà Nôi. Dũng described these efforts as "strong ropes inching gradually, day by day, around the neck, arms, and legs of a demon, awaiting the order to jerk tight and bring the creature's life to an end." The fact that the Communists could amass such a force so short a distance from Sài Gòn testified to the failure of the Army of the Republic of Vietnam (ARVN) in the early 1970s.

General Dũng waited for the right moment to strike, seeking to avoid a prolonged street fight for Sài Gòn. It would not serve his government's purposes if that city were reduced to rubble. Dũng was content to wait while continuing the military buildup and conducting small-scale attacks. Another consideration was concern about the willingness of China and the Soviet Union to replenish military stocks.

An elderly Vietnamese couple in a refugee center near Đà Năng.

The right moment came on 1 March 1975 when Dũng unleashed his forces in the Central Highlands. By late March thousands of refugees were fleeing into Đà Nẵng from Huê. Đà Nẵng, the RVN's second largest city, fell to Dũng's forces on 30 March. Dũng then shifted his offensive to the South to take Sài Gòn before the May rains. The last major military engagement, at Xuân Lôc, 35 miles northeast of Sài Gòn, lasted two weeks. Once the PAVN captured the road to Biên Hòa Airport they headed straight for Sài Gòn, finally rolling into the RVN capital on 29 April.

Dũng had completed his task of liberating Sài Gòn before 1 May. His book, *Our Great Spring Victory,* describes the final military campaign and collapse of the RVN government. He went on to lead the invasion of Cambodia in 1979 and also directed the Sino-Vietnamese clash in 1979. Dũng replaced Giáp as minister of national defense in February 1980. He was dismissed from this position and expelled from the Politburo in 1986. Thereafter he faded into obscurity.

—Charlotte A. Power

References: Karnow, Stanley. *Vietnam: A History.* New York: Penguin Books, 1984.
Post, Ken. *Socialism in Half a Country.* Vol. III, *Revolution, Socialism, and Nationalism in Vietnam.* Belmont, CA: Wadsworth, 1989.
See also: Hô Chí Minh Campaign; Lao Đông Party; Sino-Vietnamese War; Vietnam, Democratic Republic of: Army (People's Army of Vietnam [PAVN]); Vietnamese Invasion and Occupation of Cambodia; Võ Nguyên Giáp.

Vance, Cyrus Roberts

(1917–)

Department of Defense official, secretary of the Army (1962–1963); deputy secretary of defense (1964–1967); negotiator at the Paris peace talks (1968). Born at Clarksburg, West Virginia, on 27 March 1917, Cyrus Vance moved to New York City at an early age and was educated at Kent School and Yale University. He was admitted to the bar in 1942 and after World War II served as a civil case lawyer. During the war, he was a destroyer gunnery officer in the Pacific. As assistant counsel to Lyndon Johnson's Senate Preparedness Investigative Subcommittee in the 1950s, Vance contributed to the creation of the National Aeronautics and Space Administration (NASA).

Vance supported the John F. Kennedy–Johnson ticket in 1960 and joined the Kennedy administration as general counsel to the secretary of defense. As counsel, Vance handled two difficult assignments: obtaining the release of the Bay of Pigs prisoners in Cuba and supervising a reorganization of the Department of Defense. This reorganization strengthened the authority of the secretary and improved strategic planning and logistics.

In 1962 Vance was appointed secretary of the Army. Supporting new uses of aviation to improve the Army's mobility, Vance helped create the 11th Air Assault Division (Test) that proved the air assault concept. Renamed the 1st Cavalry Division (Airmobile), this unit went to Vietnam in 1965. Vance also organized the Army Concept Team in Vietnam (ACTIV) to experiment with ways to improve counterinsurgency warfare capabilities.

Appointed deputy secretary of defense in 1964, Vance concurred with the decision to bomb North Vietnam after the Gulf of Tonkin incidents and with Operation ROLLING THUNDER in 1965. One of Vance's responsibilities after August 1964 was approving covert raids against the Democratic Republic of Vietnam (DRV). By 1966 Vance doubted the effectiveness of the expanded air war, and in 1967 he became disenchanted with the whole war. A back ailment prompted his resignation in 1967.

President Johnson recalled Vance as an informal advisor in March 1968. He was one of the "Wise Men" who recommended that the president halt the bombing of the DRV and seek a negotiated settlement to the war.

Vance's most trying assignment was serving with Averell Harriman as deputy negotiator at the Paris Peace Conference in 1968. Harriman and Vance were unable to get substantive talks started while bombing continued. President Johnson would not stop the bombing unless the DRV guaranteed that it would not seek military advantage. Hà Nôi would give no guarantees nor talk about substantive issues until the bombing stopped. Without success, Vance explored different formulas for a bombing halt. Finally, in November 1968 President Johnson declared a bombing halt after the DRV tacitly agreed not to use it to advantage or to block South Vietnamese participation in the conference. At this point, the Republic of Vietnam (RVN) balked at having representatives of the National Liberation Front (NLF) present, and the United States had to pressure South Vietnam not to disrupt the conference. When Vance resigned in early 1969, the conference was on the verge of substantive discussions. He served as secretary of state under President Jimmy Carter (1977–1981) and continued thereafter as a respected negotiator and advisor on international affairs.

—John L. Bell

References: Johnson, Lyndon B. *The Vantage Point: Perspectives of the President, 1963–1969.* New York: Holt, Rinehart and Winston, 1971.
McLellan, David S. *Cyrus Vance.* Vol. 20, *The American Secretaries of State and Their Diplomacy,* edited by Robert H. Ferrell. Totawa, NJ: Rowman & Allanheld, 1985.
See also: ACTIV (Army Concept Team in Vietnam); Carter, Jimmy; Harriman, W. Averell; Johnson, Lyndon Baines; Paris Negotiations; Paris Peace Accords; ROLLING THUNDER, Operation; Tonkin Gulf Incidents; "Wise Men."

Vang Pao

(1931–)

Best-known military leader of the anti-Communist Hmong, he rose through the ranks from simple soldier to general and confounded some of Hà Nôi's best strategists in the war in Laos.

Vang Pao was born at Nong Het, Laos, in 1931. As a teenager, he was a guide and a courier for the French against the Japanese, and in 1947 he was recruited by the French as a soldier in their irregular forces in Laos. In March 1948 he was promoted to corporal and sent to noncommissioned officers school at Luang Prabang, where he graduated first in his class. In January 1949 Vang Pao was promoted to chief corporal and sent to the National Gendarmerie school, where he again graduated first in his class and was promoted to sergeant major. He received two further promotions, attaining the rank of adjutant in October 1950.

Vang Pao distinguished himself in the war of ambushes and small, sharp engagements against the Viêt Minh that centered on the Plain of Jars. He also understood the vital importance of having the civilian population on his side. He applied for officers' candidate school and graduated as the only Hmong, and seventh in his class of 56, in March 1952. Three months after his graduation, Vang Pao was a second lieutenant in the 14th infantry company of the Royal Laotian Army stationed at Muong Hiem near the border of Luang Prabang and Sam Neua Provinces. By the time of the 1954 Viêt Minh siege of Điên Biên Phu, Vang Pao had risen to first lieutenant and had command of his own irregular unit. In December 1954 he was made captain.

When the Vietnam War escalated in January 1961, Vang Pao was a lieutenant colonel. As the senior officer in the region, he made appeals to American and Thai officers for weapons to arm 7,000 of his Hmong followers. An arrangement was worked out to the mutual satisfaction of the two sides. Thereafter, Vang Pao led his well-armed Hmong irregulars, sometimes called the *Armée Clandestine* (Secret Army), in fighting against the Pathet Lao and North Vietnamese.

Vang Pao respected the North Vietnamese as soldiers but thought that they lacked his troops' ability to improvise. He observed that North Vietnamese commanders always followed the same routine when they were planning an attack, and he found that he could throw off their plans by moving his mobile units around immediately beforehand, sometimes inducing his adversaries to call off the attack.

Vang Pao rose to the command of Military Region II and was a major general when the 1973 cease-fire intervened. After the Communist takeover in 1975, Vang Pao was evacuated to Thailand in a small U.S. plane and eventually settled in the United States, where he became a citizen and remained active in the affairs of the Hmong exile community.

—Arthur J. Dommen

References: Hamilton-Merritt, Jane. *Tragic Mountains: The Hmong, the Americans, and the Secret Wars for Laos, 1942–1992.* Bloomington, IN: Indiana University Press, 1993.
Quincy, Keith. *Hmong: History of a People.* Cheney, WA: Eastern Washington University Press, 1988.
See also: Hmong; Laos; Long Chieng; Pathet Lao; Plain of Jars.

Vann, John Paul

(1924–1972)

U.S. Army officer; critic of military strategy; U.S. Agency for International Development (USAID) official. John Paul Vann was born on 2 July 1924 in Norfolk, Virginia. He was drafted in 1943 and trained as a navigator. When the Air Corps moved to separate from the Army in 1947, Vann transferred to the infantry and received a commission. After fighting in Korea, he received a degree from Rutgers University in 1955, graduated from the Command and General Staff College in 1958, and earned an M.B.A. from Syracuse University in 1959. He was promoted to lieutenant colonel in 1961.

Vann served his first tour of duty in Vietnam from March 1962 to April 1963. Part of his duties included advising a South Vietnamese infantry division in the Mekong Delta. What he saw in Vietnam dismayed him, particularly at the Battle of Ấp Bắc; despite what the president was being told by his military advisors, Vann believed that the war was being lost and that it could be won if the right tactics and military might were applied. When his reports were ignored, he leaked information to journalists covering the fighting in Vietnam. He was then reassigned to the Pentagon where his words still fell on deaf ears. After 20 years in the Army, Vann retired on 31 July 1963 and began to speak out publicly on the war.

Vann returned to Vietnam in March of 1965 as pacification representative of the Agency for International Development. He was so successful that in 1966 he was made chief of the civilian pacification program for the provinces surrounding Sài Gòn. In 1967 he denounced General William Westmoreland's strategy and warned that the Communists were still a threat; the Tết Offensive of 1968 seemed to support his point of view. Because Vann's critique was aimed at trying to improve the war effort, he was promoted in May 1971 to senior advisor for the Central Highlands and given command over U.S. military forces and the civilians in the pacification program. Vann also indirectly commanded the South Vietnamese troops in the area. His position was equivalent to that of a U.S. Army major general, but he was still a civilian. In effect, he was the third most powerful American in Vietnam. After directing the defense against a People's Army of Vietnam (PAVN) offensive, Vann was killed in a helicopter crash in the Central Highlands on 9 July 1972.

Vann was a complex and compelling figure. Dedicated to winning the war, he nonetheless openly criticized the American strategy. He condemned indiscriminate bombing of the countryside as cruel and morally wrong. Vann believed America to be the greatest power on earth, a position it was destined to hold forever, and which it should use to bring peace and prosperity to the world. There was much wrong about the war in Vietnam, but not the war itself, and he could not accept an American defeat. He seemed to embody the American dilemma in Vietnam.

—Laura Matysek Wood

Reference: Sheehan, Neil. *A Bright Shining Lie: John Paul Vann and America in Vietnam.* New York: Random House, 1988.
See also: Ấp Bắc, Battle of; Order of Battle; Pacification; Sheehan, Cornelius Mahoney (Neil); U.S. Agency for International Development (USAID).

Vessey, John W.

(1922–)

Chairman of the U.S. Joint Chiefs of Staff, who served as a field artillery battalion commander in Vietnam. Born in Minneapolis, Minnesota, on 29 June 1922, John Vessey in 1939 enlisted in the National Guard. As a battery first sergeant during the Second World War, he earned a Bronze Star and a battlefield commission at Anzio. After the war, Vessey stayed in the Army as an officer but did not complete his college degree until he was 41 years old. In Vietnam he commanded the 25th Infantry Division's 2d Battalion, 77th Field Artillery. On 21 March 1967—during Operation JUNCTION CITY—all three of Vessey's batteries occupied Fire Support Base GOLD when it came under attack from elements of five battalions under the control of the 272d Viêt Công Regiment. Vessey's gunners fired over 1,000 rounds of direct fire in defense of the base, including 30 "beehive" rounds. It was the first large-scale combat use of fléchette-firing antipersonnel rounds. Vessey received the Distinguished Service Cross for the action.

In 1970 at age 48, Vessey qualified as an Army helicopter pilot. In August 1974 he assumed command of the 4th Infantry Division. From 1982 to 1985 he was chairman of the Joint Chiefs of Staff. Following his retirement at the rank of full general, Vessey played a prominent role in normalizing relations between the Socialist Republic of Vietnam and the United States when he served as the Bush administration's negotiator with Hà Nôi on prisoner of war and missing in action issues.

—David T. Zabecki

Reference: Webb, Willard J., and Ronald Cole. *The Chairmen of the Joint Chiefs of Staff.* Washington, DC: Historical Division, Joint Chiefs of Staff, 1989.
See also: Artillery, Allied and People's Army of Vietnam; Artillery Fire Doctrine; Bush, George Herbert Walker; JUNCTION CITY, Operation; Missing in Action, Allied; Vietnam, Socialist Republic of: 1975 to the Present.

Vientiane Agreement

(21 February 1973)

Cease-fire agreement to end the war in Laos, signed at Vientiane, Laos, on 21 February 1973 by Pheng Phongsavan, representing the Royal Lao government, and Phoumi Vongvichit, representing the Lao Patriotic Forces (usually called the Pathet Lao). The agreement resulted from negotiations between the two sides that began on 17 October 1972 and consisted of 14 articles in five chapters.

The principal provisions were:

- Implementation of a cease-fire throughout Laos beginning at noon on 22 February (Article 2);
- Withdrawal of all foreign military personnel and regular and irregular forces from Laos, the dissolution of all foreign military and paramilitary organizations in Laos, the disbanding of all special forces and the dismantling of their bases within 60 days from the establishment of the Provisional Government of National Union (PGNU) and the National Political Consultative Council (NPCC) (Article 4);
- Reciprocal repatriation of all persons, regardless of nationality, who were captured or detained during the war, within 60 days from the establishment of the NPCC (Article 5);
- Responsibility to provide information about those reported missing during the war upon completion of repatriation of captured personnel (Article 5);
- Establishment by the two sides of the PGNU and the NPCC within 30 days of the signing of the present agreement (Article 6);
- Holding of free and democratic general elections for a national assembly and a permanent coalition government under procedures to be agreed upon by the two sides (Article 6);
- The PGNU to be composed of an equal number of representatives of the two sides, plus two agreed intellectuals (Article 7);
- The NPCC to be composed of an equal number of representatives of the two sides, plus a number of intellectuals to be determined (Article 8);
- Neutralization of Vientiane and Luang Prabang (Article 9);
- Temporary maintenance of the zones controlled by each side pending establishment of the national assembly and the permanent coalition government (Article 10A);
- Promotion of normal relations between the zones of temporary control (Article 10B);
- Holding of discussions with the United States regarding the latter's contributing to healing the wounds of war and postwar reconstruction (Article 10C);
- Formation of a joint commission to oversee implementation of the agreement (Article 11);
- Continuation of the work of the International Commission for Supervision and Control (Article 12);
- Continuation of negotiations between the two sides on protocol to implement the agreement (Article 13).

The "special forces" mentioned in Article 4 referred to the Hmong irregulars in the North and the Kha irregulars in the South, both of whom had been supported during the war by the U.S. Central Intelligence Agency (CIA).

Insofar as Article 5 related to U.S. prisoners of war (POWs) and missing in action (MIAs), the Pathet Lao released no prisoners captured before the cease-fire (although they did release one captured afterward) and provided no information about MIAs. Resolution of these matters between the United States and Laos had to wait for more than ten years, when cooperative efforts were begun to search for remains and to collect information on the missing. At the time of the cease-fire, there were more than 300 Americans unaccounted for in Laos.

The protocol mentioned in Article 13 was signed on 14 September 1973.

The PGNU and NPCC were finally established on 5 April 1974. Prince Souvanna Phouma was prime minister of the PGNU in Vientiane, and Prince Souphanouvong was chairman of the NPCC, which was based in Luang Prabang.

—Arthur J. Dommen

References: Dommen, Arthur J. *Laos: Keystone of Indochina.* Boulder, CO: Westview Press, 1985.
New York Times (22 February 1973). (This contains the complete text of the Vientiane Agreement.)
See also: International Commission for Supervision and Control (ICSC); Laos; Missing in Action, Allied; Pathet Lao; Prisoners of War, Allied; Souphanouvong; Souvanna Phouma; Vientiane Protocol.

Vientiane Protocol

(14 September 1973)

Protocol giving effect to the Vientiane Agreement of 21 February 1973. The 14 September 1973 Vientiane Protocol resulted from negotiations between the Royal Lao Government and the Lao Patriotic Forces (Pathet Lao) and consisted of 21 articles, of which the most important follow:

- Article 1 provided for establishment of the Provisional Government of National Union (PGNU), which was to be headed by a prime minister and two deputy prime ministers and consist of 25 ministers and secretaries of state (deputy ministers).
- Article 2 allocated the ministerial portfolios in the PGNU.
- Article 3 committed the PGNU to follow policies of peace, national unity, neutrality, independence, democracy, and prosperity in accordance with the recommendations of the future National Political Consultative Council (NPCC).
- Article 4 enshrined the principle of unanimity of decision in all important matters, while maintaining the responsibility of each side for its own ministries.
- Article 5 stipulated the structure of the NPCC to consist of 42 members and various commissions.
- Article 6 provided for decisions in the NPCC by consensus.
- Article 9 gave the NPCC a major role in organizing general elections.
- Article 10 provided for mixed police forces in Vientiane and Luang Prabang to maintain security.
- Article 12 provided for demarcating the cease-fire lines in places where tension existed between the forces of the two sides.
- Articles 14–16 dealt with the joint commission's control of troop movements and withdrawal of foreign troops and war materials.
- Article 17 stipulated the disbanding of the special forces.
- Article 18 provided for notifying the joint commission of the numbers and nationalities of captured foreign personnel and the names of those reported to be missing.

The joint commission held meetings to work out procedures for release of prisoners and exchange of information on the missing. But because implementation of such actions had been tied under the Vientiane Agreement into the timetable for formation of the PGNU and NPCC, which was seriously delayed, there was little or no compliance with these provisions before political and military tensions rose once again over such issues as violations of the cease-fire and the king's role in opening the National Assembly that had been carried over from the previous Royal Lao Government.

—Arthur J. Dommen

References: Dommen, Arthur J. *Laos: Keystone of Indochina*. Boulder, CO: Westview Press, 1985.
New York Times (15 September 1973). (This contains the text of the Vientiane Protocol.)
See also: Laos; Pathet Lao; Vientiane Agreement.

Viêt Minh (Viêt Nam Ðôc Lâp Ðông Minh Hôi [Vietnam Independence League])

Communist front organization created to help the Indo-Chinese Communist Party achieve its overall objectives. The Viêt Nam Ðôc Lâp Ðông Minh Hôi, commonly known as the Viêt Minh (Vietnam Independence League), was founded at the Eighth Plenum of the Indo-Chinese Communist Party in May 1941. The Viêt Minh served as the organizational nexus for the development of a broad, national program. According to Hô Chí Minh, the front was needed to organize the masses in resistance to French colonial rule and occupying Japanese forces. The purpose of the Viêt Minh was tactical, never strategic. Its flexibility allowed the party to alter its course quickly for current conditions. Perhaps the most important aspect of the front was its attention to the "national question." By downplaying class revolution in favor of national liberation, the party attempted to involve all elements of society in the national struggle. Anticolonialism, patriotism, and nationalism were the only prerequisites for joining the national united front. The Viêt Minh purposefully made temporary alliances with its "enemies" in order to achieve its more immediate objectives.

The Viêt Minh–led August Revolution is one of the defining moments of the modern Vietnamese revolution. Shortly after the Japanese invasion of 1940, the Viêt Minh planned for that inevitable moment of contradiction when the Japanese would turn their guns on the French colonialists. This moment came on 9 March 1945 when Japanese soldiers carried out a relatively bloodless coup against French colonial forces. When the Japanese surrendered five months later, this left a political void in Indo-China. Through their revolutionary training, the Viêt Minh were prepared to exploit this situation to its fullest potential, and as a result, marched into Hà Nôi to proclaim Vietnamese independence. The Viêt Minh front also fielded an army headed by Võ Nguyên Giáp. It seized power during the (1945) August Revolution.

On 2 September 1945 the political leader and founder of the Viêt Minh, Hô Chí Minh, read aloud in Ba Ðình Square an official pronouncement declaring an end to French colonialism, Japanese occupation, and the Nguyên dynasty. Shortly after Hô's declaration of independence, the Indo-Chinese Communist Party announced that it was dissolving, leaving the Viêt Minh front as the only official party apparatus. In 1951 the party resurfaced officially with the formation of the Vietnamese Workers' Party (Ðang Lao Ðông Viêt Nam). At this time, the Viêt Minh was itself dissolved. According to revolutionary theory, the broad-based front was to be revised whenever historical circumstances changed drastically. The Communists therefore reconstituted the Viêt Minh as the Liên Viêt front during the Indo-China War, and shortly after the Geneva Accords, the Fatherland Front was born.

There is some question as to the actual date of the reconstitution of the Viêt Minh front as the Liên Viêt front (Liên Hiêp Quôc Dân Viêt Nam). Some scholars have suggested that the Viêt Minh lasted only until the war with France (1941–1946) began. Hoàng Văn Ðào, in *Viêt Nam Quôc Dân Ðang*, gives April 1946 as the date for the reconstitution of the Liên Viêt front. Others suggest, however, that it was the Viêt Minh that battled the French from 1946 to 1954. In any case, the Viêt Minh has popularly been associated with the army that handed the French their humiliating defeat at the Battle of Điên Biên Phu and that served the Democratic Republic of Vietnam (DRV) so faithfully since its 1945 inception.

—Robert K. Brigham

References: Duiker, William J. *The Rise of Nationalism in Vietnam, 1900–1941.* Ithaca, NY: Cornell University Press, 1976.
History of the August Revolution. Hà Nôi: Foreign Languages Publishing House, 1972.
Hoàng Văn Đào. *Việt Nam Quốc Dân Đang.* Sài Gòn: Published by the author, 1970.
Huynh Kim Khanh. "The Vietnamese August Revolution Reinterpreted." *Journal of Asian Studies* 30, no. 4 (August 1971): 761–782.
Marr, David G. *Vietnamese Tradition on Trial, 1920–1945.* Berkeley, CA: University of California Press, 1981.
Woodside, Alexander B. *Community and Revolution in Modern Vietnam.* Boston: Houghton Mifflin, 1976.

See also: August Revolution; Điên Biên Phu, Battle of; French Indo-China; Geneva Conference and Geneva Accords; Hô Chí Minh; Indo-China War; Japan; Lao Đông Party; Nguyên Dynasty; United Front; Vietnamese Communist Party (VCP); Võ Nguyên Giáp.

Việt Nam Quốc Dân Đang (Vietnam National Party)

Vietnamese nationalist political party before the Second World War. The Việt Nam Quốc Dân Đang, or Vietnam National Party (in Chinese, Viet Nam Guomindang), was established on 27 December 1927 in Hà Nôi by a group of young men led by Nguyên Thái Hoc. This moderate socialist party, known to most adults in Vietnam as the Việt Quốc and usually referred to as the VNQDD, was the first revolutionary party in Vietnam, preceding by three years the establishment of the Indo-Chinese Communist Party (ICP).

Although the VNQDD bears the same name as the Nationalist Chinese Party, it was not created by the Chinese. Sun Yat-sen's program may have inspired VNQDD founders to adapt the party name, but it had no direct relation to or get any support from the Chinese Guomindang until after the failed uprising in February 1930. Some assert that, had it received even modest military support from the Chinese Nationalists, Vietnamese history might have developed quite differently after the 1930 Yên Bái uprising.

The VNQDD was organized along clandestine lines and held together with strict discipline. The party's strength grew quickly. Most adherents were teachers, colonial government employees, and army noncommissioned officers (NCOs). Beginning in 1928 the VNQDD attracted considerable Vietnamese support but also the attention of French colonial authorities after a VNQDD death squad killed several French and Vietnamese officials notorious for their cruelty toward the Vietnamese population.

With French authorities about to carry out a large-scale crackdown against the VNQDD, its leadership believed it had no choice but to carry out uprisings where possible. After this decision, Nguyên Thái Hoc made his well-known remark: "If we fail to succeed we will still build a good cause."

At midnight 10–11 February 1930 VNQDD company-sized forces launched surprise attacks against French colonial army bases northeast of Hà Nôi at Yên Bái, Hưng Hoa, Lâm Thao, and Sơn Tây, as well as grenade attacks in the heart of the capital. On 12 February VNQDD forces attacked French military camps at Đáp Câu, Pha Lai, east of Hà Nôi. The next day they conducted other attacks at Kiên An and Vĩnh Bao. Việt Quôc forces numbered from 50 to 300 fighters at each location.

The greatest VNQDD success came at Yên Bái, where the rebels killed a dozen French officers and noncommissioned officers and controlled the town for a day before being expelled by French counterattacks. Although they met fierce resistance, the French soon reoccupied all of their positions.

The VNQDD relied mostly on homemade cement and black powder grenades, captured rifles, and a few pistols. Although they fought bravely, without effective weapons the VNQDD squads were doomed to defeat. Ineffective communications also meant that word of the attacks did not reach many regional commanders and surprise was lost.

French reprisal raids all over North Vietnam crushed the VNQDD. Many hundreds of its members were executed. Among them, Nguyên Thái Hoc and 12 others were guillotined in Yên Bái on 17 June 1930. Their dauntless behavior and the calmness and dignity with which they faced the guillotine made them nationalist heroes in Vietnam.

The following months saw several thousand VNQDD members sentenced to prison terms of from five years to life. Those who escaped arrest fled mainly to China, where they reorganized the party. Along with the VNQDD, many other movements, including the Communists, got limited support from the Chinese government.

In August 1945 the Việt Minh seized power and set up a provisional government. This violated an agreement between member parties of the Việt Nam Cách Mênh Đông Minh Hôi, which included Hô Chí Minh's Việt Minh (Việt Nam Đôc Lâp Đông Minh Hôi), and the VNQDD.

After August 1945 hundreds of VNQDD members in exile returned to Vietnam, but many of them were killed by the Việt Minh when they crossed the border from China. When the main non-Communist parties moved from China back to Vietnam and their local cells revived, the Nationalists joined together in the opposition to the Việt Minh. Armed clashes between the Việt Minh and the Nationalists occurred regularly in major cities of North Vietnam. After the 6 March 1946 Hô-Sainteny Agreement that allowed French army units to deploy in key cities, the Nationalists found themselves under attack from the French as well as the Việt Minh. At the end of 1946 when the Indo-China War erupted, several thousand VNQDD and other opposition party members were massacred by the Việt Minh in a bloody purge. The survivors fled to China. Others, to escape sure death, fled to French-controlled areas.

After the 1954 Geneva Accords, many VNQDD members from North Vietnam, including those from Việt Minh–controlled areas, gathered in South Vietnam. They were deeply divided after years of Communist oppression and lack of strong leadership. Although they were fervent anti-Communists, virtually all of the factions found themselves in opposition to the government of the Republic of Vietnam (RVN). Those VNQDD members who survived the Vietnam War years were again persecuted by the Communist regime after 30 April 1975. Although many former VNQDD members found refuge in the West and have continued to campaign for democracy and human rights in Vietnam, they remain divided politically. The VNQDD still enjoys respect in overseas Vietnamese political communities; many Vietnamese regard it as the foremost anti-Communist spiritual force.

—Nguyên Công Luân (Lư Tuân)

References: Hoàng Văn Đào. *Việt Nam Quốc Dân Đang.* Sài Gòn: Published by the author, 1970.

Karnow, Stanley. *Vietnam: A History.* New York: Penguin Books, 1984.

See also: French Indo-China; Hô-Sainteny Agreement; Viêt Minh (Viêt Nam Đôc Lâp Đông Minh Hôi [Vietnam Independence League]).

Viêt Nam Thanh Niên Cách Mang Đông Chí Hôi (Vietnam Revolutionary Youth Association)

Vietnamese anticolonial organization. Known commonly as Thanh Niên (Youth), the Viêt Nam Thanh Niên Cách Mang Đông Chí Hôi was founded by Hô Chí Minh in 1925 as a new anticolonial organization that attempted to unite political and social issues. The Thanh Niên advocated a new Vietnamese society dependent upon national liberation and land reform. To accomplish these goals, the Thanh Niên relied almost exclusively on new revolutionary theory and the blending of Marxist-Leninist teachings with Vietnamese patriotism. The specific revolutionary strategy of the Thanh Niên consisted of three distinct phases: organization, agitation, and insurrection. This reliance on the theoretical perspective distanced the Thanh Niên from other anticolonial organizations and ensured its success during the brutal French purges. In short, Hô Chí Minh's revolutionary organization represented the beginnings of Vietnamese communism.

Two of the Thanh Niên's most significant contributions to the resistance movement were its use of the term *cách mang* (revolution) and its acknowledgment of a more stratified anticolonial society. For the Communist leaders, *cách mang* meant the basic transformation of the political structure and the process of rule, not merely the removal of the right to rule. In this way, the revolutionary process was an ongoing dialectic between the people and the party. For years, the party considered all Vietnamese to be anticolonials and it was only with the development of revolutionary thought within the Thanh Niên that the term "intermediary elements" began to be applied to friends of the most oppressed classes. This thinking helped the Thanh Niên develop the front concept where the party could make temporary alliances with non-Communists to achieve the revolution's overall goals.

From 1925 to 1927 the Thanh Niên headquarters was located in Canton. Here, over 300 Vietnamese revolutionaries received training. The center published several periodicals on various political subjects. Among the most important of these publications were *Đường Cách Mang* (The Road to Revolution) and the weekly newspaper *Thanh Niên* (Youth). By 1927, however, the Thanh Niên had been caught up in the revolutionary activities in China and fell victim to Guomindang Communist sweeps. The Thanh Niên activities came to an abrupt halt in 1927, but Vietnamese revolutionaries continued their activities within Vietnam's own borders until mid-1929.

The Thanh Niên movement was an important first step in Vietnam's modern revolution. Before its organization, Vietnamese revolutionaries were still searching for ideas and techniques to liberate Vietnam. After the Thanh Niên, Vietnam's anticolonialists, led by Hô Chí Minh, embraced a revolutionary movement with a clear ideological base.

—Robert K. Brigham

References: Duiker, William J. *The Communist Road to Power in Vietnam, 1900–1941.* Boulder, CO: Westview Press, 1981.

Huynh Kim Khanh. *Vietnamese Communism, 1925–1945.* Ithaca, NY: Cornell University Press, 1982.

Marr, David G. *Vietnamese Tradition on Trial, 1925–1945.* Berkeley, CA: University of California Press, 1981.

Woodside, Alexander B. *Community and Revolution in Modern Vietnam.* Boston: Houghton Mifflin, 1976.

See also: Hô Chí Minh; Jiang Jieshi (Chiang Kai-shek); Lao Đông Party; Trân Văn Giàu; Viêt Minh (Viêt Nam Đôc Lâp Đông Minh Hôi [Vietnam Independence League]); Vietnamese Communist Party (VCP); Võ Nguyên Giáp.

Vietnam: Prehistory to 938

Legends and Prehistory Vietnamese consider the founder of their nation to be Hùng Vương, or King Hùng, of the Hông Bàng dynasty (2879–258 B.C.). The country was then called Văn Lang, and the capital was located at Phong Châu in present Vĩnh Phú Province, where a temple dedicated to Hùng Vương was later erected. According to legend, this kingdom was very large. It occupied a great part of southern China, North Vietnam, and part of central Vietnam. Approximately, it covered those areas occupied by the Bách Viêt (One Hundred Yuehs), non-Chinese people living in South China south of the Yangtze River.

Hùng Vương and his 18 successors, who bore the same title of Hùng Vương, divided their kingdom into 15 *bô* (districts) and administered them through the *lac hâu* (civil chieftains), *lac tướng* (military chieftains), and the *bô chính* (subaltern officials). The throne was hereditary and so probably were the titles of *lac hâu* and *lac tướng*. Rice fields were called *lac điên* (lac fields), and people who lived on them were called *lac dân* (lac people).

Whether Hùng Vương, the Hông Bàng dynasty, and the Văn Lang kingdom really existed or are simply legendary is still a controversy of Vietnamese history. Based on indications found in Chinese sources and facts from recent archaeological discoveries, many scholars have tried to prove that the Hùng Vương did in fact exist. Nonetheless, every year, Vietnamese in Vietnam and throughout the world, on the tenth day of the third month of the lunar calendar, celebrate the anniversary of King Hùng.

Beginning with discoveries by the French in the 1920s and 1930s of stone age sites in Hòa Bình and Băc Sơn in North Vietnam and that of a bronze age site in Đông Sơn, Thanh Hóa Province, archaeological research has made important progress. In the 1960s and 1980s Vietnamese archaeologists excavated several new sites, such as Tân Van in Lang Sơn Province, Núi (Mount) Do in Thanh Hóa, Quỳnh Vân in Nghê An, and Phung

Nguyên in Phú Tho. These discoveries prove that Vietnam has been continuously inhabited by humankind since a very early time in its history.

In Vietnam an original civilization different from that of China widely developed. The most important features of this civilization were a wet rice cultivation using tidewater movement; a matrilineal organization of society; the worship of ancestors and of the god of the soil; the building of shrines in high places; and a cosmological dualism in which are opposed the mountain and the sea, the winged race and the aquatic race, the men of the heights and those of the coasts. This Austro-Asiatic civilization, as it is known to archaeologists, corresponds to the Dongsonian civilization. To many scholars, it is the Hùng Vương era.

The Thuc (258–207 B.C.) and the Triêu (207–111 B.C.) In 258 B.C., Văn Lang was invaded by a neighbor king, Thuc Phán, and annexed to his territory. A new kingdom, Âu Lac, was formed, and Thuc Phán became An Dương Vương. Cô Loa, not far from Hà Nôi, was chosen as the new capital. Here a citadel in spiral form was built that later became the most ancient and important historical vestige of ancient Vietnam.

In 207 B.C. An Dương Vương was defeated by Triêu Đà (Chaoto), a former general of the Ch'in. Âu Lac was combined with Triêu Đà's territory to make a new kingdom, Nam Viêt (Nan Yueh). Phiên Ngung (Canton) became its capital. Triêu Đà and his successors ruled ancient Vietnam until 111 B.C., when Nam Viêt was invaded by the Han to become a Chinese colony. During this time, the country was divided into two *quân* (districts): Giao Chi and Cửu Chân. Each was headed by a legate and enjoyed an indirect and loose control from Canton.

Chinese Domination (111 B.C.–A.D. 938) During the first 100 years of their domination, the Chinese brought almost no change to their southern colony. The two Triêu legates in Giao Chi and Cửu Chân submitted without resistance and were confirmed in office. The *lac hâu* and the *lac tưởng* were allowed to keep their territories and lead their own people. No rebellion was recorded. At the beginning of the first century A.D., however, the Chinese governors changed their policies. Through the effort of two governors, Tích Quang (Si Kuang) and Nhâm Diên (Jen Yen), Vietnamese culture was Sinicized and lands were seized to give to new Chinese immigrants at the expense of local nobles. This new policy reached its climax under Tô Đinh (Su Ting) and led to the important uprising of Trưng Trắc and her sister Trưng Nhi, in 39 A.D. Hai Bà Trưng (the Two Ladies Trưng) spread their rebellion over 65 fiefs, covering all the territories from Cửu Chân to Hợp Phô (Kwang Tung). Tô Đinh fled to Canton.

The reaction of the Han Court was slow. But after two years of careful preparation, in the year 42, a large Chinese army, raised from several provinces in southern China and commanded by the old and famous general Mã Viên (Ma Yuan), moved south to counterattack. The Ladies Trưng were defeated at a bloody battle at Lãng Bac in the spring of 43. They chose suicide by leaping into the Hát River.

After the failure of Hai Bà Trưng, the Han tightened their control over both Giao Chi and Cửu Chân. Ancient Vietnam was no longer administered as a protectorate; it became a Chinese province and was strictly controlled. Rebellions also occurred more often and provided Vietnam with a longer list of national heroes, among them Bà Triêu (248), Lý Bôn (or Lý Nam Đê) (544–548), Triêu Quang Phuc (or Triêu Viêt Vương) (549–571), Lý Tự Tiên and Đinh Kiên (687), Mai Thúc Loan (or Mai Hac Đê) (722), Phùng Hưng (766–791), and Dương Thanh (819).

These rebellions finally ended with the great victory of Ngô Quyên over the Chinese on the Bach Đăng River in 938. This important battle opened a new era in Vietnamese history. The country was again independent after more than a thousand years of Chinese rule.

The ten centuries of Chinese domination nonetheless greatly affected Vietnam and its people. Under Chinese influence, the country slowly separated from other nations of Southeast Asia to become a part of East Asia. Its territory was smaller than that of the legendary Văn Lang; however, its boundaries were much better defined, and both lowlands and highlands were more systematically administered. A Vietnamese people emerged of ancient local elements and new localized immigrants from the North. In writing, Chinese characters were officially used, and Chinese traditions and customs were widespread. Confucianism, Taoism, and Mahayana Buddhism were introduced and served as the base for Vietnamese intellectual and spiritual life in the following centuries, even to the present.

The Vietnamese and their culture were not completely Sinicized, however. The combination of local and northern elements was slowly realized throughout the whole ten centuries. What was first foreign took root and became local. Ancient Vietnam was the southern nation (Nước Nam, or Nam Quôc) facing China as the northern nation (Băc Quôc) in the coming millennium.

—Pham Cao Dưởng

References: Coedes, Georges. *The Making of South East Asia.* Translated by H. M. Wright. Berkeley, CA: University of California Press, 1966.
Higham, Charles. *The Archaeology of Mainland Southeast Asia.* New York: Cambridge University Press, 1989.
Lê Thành Khôi. *Histoire du Viet Nam des Origines à 1858.* Paris: Sudestasie, 1981.
Pham Cao Dưởng. *Lich Sử Dân Tôc Viêt Nam, Tâp I: Thời Kỳ Lâp Quôc* (History of the Vietnamese People, Vol. I: The Formation of the Nation). Fountain Valley, CA: Truyên Thông Viêt, 1987.
Taylor, Keith W. *The Birth of Vietnam.* Berkeley, CA: University of California Press, 1983.
Trân Trong Kim. *Viêt Nam Sử Lược* (Outline of Vietnamese History). Sài Gòn: Bô Giáo Duc, Trung Tâm Hoc Liêu, 1971.
Uy Ban Khoa Hoc Xã Hôi Viêt Nam. *Lich Sử Viêt Nam, Tâp I* (History of Vietnam, Vol. I). Hà Nôi: Nhà Xuât Ban Khoa Hoc Xã Hôi, 1971.
Văn Tân, Nguyên Linh, Lê Văn Lân, Nguyên Đông Chi, and Hoàng Hưng. *Thời Đai Hùng Vương: Lich Sử, Kinh Tê, Chính Tri, Văn Hóa, Xã Hôi* (The Hùng Vương Era: History, Economy, Politics, Society). Hà Nôi: Nhà Xuât Ban Khoa Hoc Xã Hôi, 1976.
Viên Khao Cô Hoc, Uy Ban Khoa Hoc Xã Hôi Viêt Nam. *Nhửng Phát Hiên Mởi Vê Khao Cô Hoc Năm 1984* (New Archaeological Discoveries in 1984). Thành Phô Hô Chí Minh, 1985.
See also: Lý Bôn; Ngô Quyên; Trưng Trắc and Trưng Nhi.

Vietnam: 938 through the French Conquest

The victory of Ngô Quyên over the Southern Han on the Bach Đăng River in 938 opened a new era in Vietnamese history. It marked an end to 1,000 years of Chinese domination (111 B.C.–A.D. 938) and inaugurated the grand period of national independence. During the next nine centuries (938–1884), the Vietnamese successfully built a new country—to use their own term, a southern nation (Nam Quôc, or Nước Nam) facing China as a northern nation (Bắc Quôc). Several tentative Chinese efforts to regain the control of their former colony failed except for a 20-year period under the Mings (1407–1427). However, the imprint of Chinese civilization on Vietnam persisted and proved to be of a permanent nature.

At the same time, in their Nam Tiên (March to the South), the Vietnamese expanded their territory from south of Đèo Ngang (Ngang Pass) to the point of Cà Mâu at the expense of the Chams and the Khmers. "Resisting the North" (*Bắc cư*) and "conquering the South" (*Nam chinh*) became major themes of Vietnamese history as was the development of an original Vietnamese culture and civilization.

Vietnamese Dynasties   In 939 Ngô Quyên declared himself king. He chose Cô Loa, the ancient capital of the Thuc before the invasion of Triêu Đà, for the new capital. Many Vietnamese historians view this decision as the most significant action by this national hero. It showed his determination to put the Chinese domination behind and opened a new period of independence for his country. Ngô Quyên's dynasty did not last long, however. He died in 944, and his children were unable to maintain order. Ancient Vietnam soon fell into serious troubles, especially in 965. Vietnamese historians refer to these years as the Period of the Twelve Lords (Mười Hai Sứ Quân). It lasted until 968 when Đinh Bô Lênh reunified the kingdom.

The Đinh dynasty was able to gain recognition by the Chinese. Đinh Tiên Hoàng, who called himself Đê (Đinh Tiên Hoàng Đê—First Emperor of the Đinh), named the country Đai Cô Viêt and systematically organized his court and the administration of the country. The dynasty he founded lasted only 12 years; he was assassinated in 980. His commanding general, Lê Hoàn, managed to replace him and founded the Tiên Lê (Early Lê, 980–1009) dynasty. Lê Hoàn, or Lê Đai Hành, defeated the Sung invasion, preserving national independence. He also launched a victorious expedition against Champa in the South in 982.

With the liberation of the country from the Chinese by Ngô Quyên, the preservation of national unity by Đinh Bô Linh, and the consolidation of national independence and security from foreign invasion or infiltration under Lê Hoàn, the Ngô, the Đinh, and the Tiên Lê laid a solid foundation for an independent Vietnam that future dynasties would develop to create a great southern nation before it was conquered by the French in the second half of the nineteenth century.

The following Vietnamese dynasties succeeded the Tiên Lê:

The Lý (1010–1225)
The Trân (1225–1400)
The Hô (1400–1407)
The Hâu (Posterior) Trân (1407–1413)
    and the Ming Domination (1407–1428)
The Hâu (Posterior) Lê (1428–1788)

The Mac (1527–1592)
The Nguyên Tây Sơn (1788–1802)
The Nguyên (1802–1945)

The Preservation of Independence and Cultural Development

The Sung invasion of Đai Cô Viêt in 980 was not the only Chinese effort to regain control of their former southern colony. The Chinese tried several times to reconquer Đai Viêt (the name given to the country by the Lý), and each time they were defeated. Vietnamese efforts to preserve their independence from China added more names to their list of heroes, among them Lý Thường Kiêt and Tôn Đan of the eleventh century; Trân Hưng Đao, Trân Quang Khai, Trân Khánh Dư, and Pham Ngū Lao of the thirteenth century; Lê Lơi (or Lê Thái Tô), Nguyên Trãi, and many others of the fifteenth century; and closer to the present, Quang Trung (Nguyên Huê) of the late eighteenth century.

In fighting Chinese domination and invasion, the Vietnamese used the rich experience they learned from their enemy. Despite its independent spirit, the Vietnamese monarchy under the Lý, Trân, Lê, and Nguyên never thought of giving up the methods of government inherited from the Chinese empire. Instead it modeled its institutions after the examples in China, particularly in the use of Confucianism, as the major influence in the education of the country's elite, and the organization of competitive examinations to recruit mandarins for the state government and administration. The Văn Miêu, or Temple of Literature, was built in 1070 in the capital of Thăng Long, and the first examination was organized in 1075. Chinese characters were always used as the country's official writing system at the expense of Nôm (the written form of the Vietnamese language, using derivatives of Chinese characters) until the early twentieth century. Buddhism and Taoism had a role equal to Confucianism under the Lý and at the beginning of the Trân, but gradually these lost their primary importance in state life. This evolution is reflected in Vietnamese poetry and literature.

Nam Tiên, or March to the South   At the time Vietnam became independent from China in the tenth century, its southern border did not pass the Đèo Ngang. Nam Tiên, or the effort to expand the national territory further to the south, was another constant trait of Vietnamese history before the coming of the French. This was accomplished at the expense first of the Chams and later the Khmers. In 1069 after a successful military campaign, Lý Thánh Tông seized the Cham capital and imprisoned the Cham king, whose liberation was exchanged for the cession of three Cham districts, Đia Ly, Ma Ling, and Bô Chính, which later became Quang Bình and Quang Tri Provinces. In the early fourteenth century two more Cham districts, the Ô and the Rí, were given to Đai Viêt in exchange for Princess Huyên Trân in marriage. Those districts became Thừa Thiên Province. In the fifteenth century the Chams had to give up all their territory north of the present province of Quang Nam; in 1471 the Vietnamese took their capital of Vijaya. This loss was vital, because, once the Vietnamese had secured a permanent foothold south of Hai Vân Pass, the remaining Cham country was quickly subdued. In the seventeenth century the remnants of this old and Indianized kingdom were definitively absorbed, although a petty Cham king still retained nominal independence in the region of Phan Rang until 1822.

But the Nam Tiên of the Vietnamese did not end there. The elimination of Champa brought them into direct contact and conflict with the Khmers in the Mekong River Delta. This part of the lower plain of future Cochin China came under virtual Vietnamese control in the last decades of the eighteenth century.

French Conquest The main reason often cited for the French intervention and conquest of Vietnam was to protect the persecuted Catholic missionaries and their Vietnamese followers. The French action, however, was also to gain a "balcony" over the Pacific Ocean and was carried out at the same time as the Anglo-French intervention in China to open up trading ports.

The French conquest of Vietnam began with an attack on Đà Nẵng in 1858 and later the South. Gia Định Province fell in 1859, Đinh Tường in 1861, and Biên Hòa in 1862. These three oriental provinces of the South became a French colony following the Treaty of 1862. Then the three western provinces, Vĩnh Long, An Giang, and Hà Tiên, were colonized from 1867 to 1875. The rest of the country became a French protectorate in 1884, following two French attacks on North Vietnam in the early 1870s and 1880s and the signing of treaties in 1883 and 1884.

—Pham Cao Dương

References: Chesneaux, Jean. *Contribution à L'Histoire de la Nation Vietnamienne.* Paris: Editions Sociales, 1955.

Lê Thành Khôi. *Le Viet-Nam: Histoire et Civilisation.* Paris: Editions de Minuit, 1955.

Nguyên Thê Anh. *Viêt Nam Dưởi Thơi Pháp Đô Hô* (Vietnam under French Domination). Sài Gòn: Lửa Thiêng, 1970.

Phan Khoang. *Viêt Nam Pháp Thuôc Sử: 1862–1945* (The History of Vietnam under French Rule, 1862–1945). Sài Gòn: Phu Quôc Vu Khanh Đăc Trách Văn Hoa, 1971.

Trân Trong Kim. *Viêt Nam Sư Lược* (Outline of Vietnamese History). Sài Gòn: Bô Giáo Duc, Trung Tâm Hoc Liêu, 1971.

See also: Confucianism; French Indo-China; Lê Dynasty; Lê Lơi (Lê Thái Tô); Ngô Quyên; Nguyên Huê (Quang Trung); Trinh Lords.

Vietnam, Climate of

Vietnam is entirely located in the tropical belt lying between the equator and the Tropic of Cancer. Although there are variations in temperature, depending on the season and altitude, the primary seasonal changes are marked variations in rainfall. The rainy season extends from early May to November in the lowlands below Cape Dinh at 11 degrees 20 minutes north and the Central Highlands, with annual rainfall averaging approximately 79 inches (200 centimeters) in lowland regions. It rains in the coastal area in central Vietnam above Cape Dinh from November to April. The typhoon season lasts from July through November, with the most severe storms occurring along the central coast. In the North, the rainy season extends from mid-April to mid-October; the city of Hà Nôi has a mean annual rainfall of 69 inches (172 centimeters); and in the mountains, annual precipitation sometimes exceeds 160 inches (40 centimeters). During the Vietnam War, heavy rains and impenetrable fog frequently forced sharp curtailments of airborne missions during the long monsoon season. Inclement weather was also responsible for bombing inaccuracies, and many targets had to be bombed repeatedly before they were finally hit.

Daily temperatures in the North fluctuate considerably in the Red River Delta region. In the dry season, temperatures may vary 45 degrees Fahrenheit (25 degrees Celsius) during one day. The South is more tropical. Temperatures in Sài Gòn (Hô Chí Minh City) vary only between 64 and 91 degrees Fahrenheit (between 18 degrees and 33 degrees Celsius) throughout the year. Temperatures in the Central Highlands are somewhat cooler, running from a mean of about 63 degrees Fahrenheit (17 degrees Celsius) in winter to 68 degrees Fahrenheit (20 degrees Celsius) in summer.

—Louise Mongelluzzo

Reference: Marshall, S. L. A. *Battles in the Monsoon.* New York: William Morrow, 1967.

See also: Geography of Indo-China and Vietnam.

An American GI in Vietnam carried as much as 100 pounds of gear—an enormous burden in a country where daytime temperatures could soar to 90 degrees, rains could be heavy, and the terrain is generally flat and swampy or steep and heavily forested.

Vietnam, Democratic Republic of: 1945–1954

By May 1945 the Việt Nam Độc Lập Đông Minh Hội, or Việt Minh (Vietnam Independence League), controlled a free zone in the mountainous region of the North. Under the control of Hồ Chí Minh and the Indo-Chinese Communist Party (ICP), it was ready to grab power when Japan surrendered at the end of World War II. Việt Minh troops then marched into Hà Nội, occupying key locations, an event that later came to be known as the August Revolution. On 2 September 1945 in Ba Đình Square, Hồ Chí Minh read his Vietnamese declaration of independence and proclaimed the establishment of the Democratic Republic of Vietnam (DRV), a new government meant to embrace all three regions of the country: Tonkin, An Nam, and Cochin China.

Hồ's hopes were dashed from the beginning. According to the terms of the Potsdam Agreement, British troops under Maj. Gen. Douglas Gracey arrived south of the 16th parallel while Chinese soldiers, loosely commanded by General Lư Hán, moved into the North. Both were charged with disarming and repatriating Japanese forces. Gracey did his best to disrupt Việt Minh attempts to govern in his domain, while the Chinese soldiery looted the North. Simultaneously, Paris sent agents into the region to restore French rule. The Việt Minh even faced natural disasters. A prolonged drought was followed that August by flooding in the Red River Delta region. Then there was a cholera epidemic. In the midst of this chaos, Hồ tried to establish his government.

Hồ Chí Minh had little with which to work: no rice stocks, a bankrupt treasury with only a few disintegrating banknotes and coins, no bureaucracy, no foreign recognition of his nation, and no one experienced in running a nation. Nor was support for the Việt Minh solid even among Vietnamese. Rival parties struggled for their share of power. To quiet them, on 11 November 1945 Hồ dissolved the Indo-Chinese Communist Party and on 6 January 1946 held elections for a new National Assembly in which opposition parties were allowed to serve, although without real power. A few months later, with Hồ gone to France, acting president Võ Nguyên Giáp ordered armed units into action. From 11 to 13 July his units seized property, arrested opponents, and shut down newspapers, while his thugs murdered hundreds who opposed the Communist government.

Then a new problem arose. France and China signed an accord whereby China agreed to remove its troops from Indo-China by 31 March 1946. In return, France surrendered all its claims to former concessions in China and received Chinese approval to return French troops to Tonkin. Despite opposition from many of his followers, Hồ acquiesced in this development; at least the Chinese would be gone.

In negotiations with the French, Hồ proposed the formation of an independent Vietnam within the French Union. Paris disagreed, insisting that it must retain Cochin China as a colony, but it would recognize Tonkin and Annam as an autonomous state. Hồ now offered to accept recognition of Vietnam as a "free" state and to drop insistence on the word "independent." He also argued that no more than 15,000 French soldiers should return to the North. The French delegation led by Jean Sainteny accepted these stipulations, and the two sides signed an accord on 6 March 1946. They opened a conference at Đà Lạt on 18 April 1946 to work out details. Little was accomplished. Newly promoted to the rank of full general, Võ Nguyên Giáp, as minister of the interior, ordered his armed forces to be ready to fight if necessary and began to plan ways to procure weapons.

Hồ left Hà Nội on 31 May 1946 for a four-month-long conference at Fontainebleau that began on 6 July and continued into August. During this absence, French High Commissioner for Indo-China Adm. Thierry d'Argenlieu announced recognition of a Republic of Cochin China, further sundering the third of Vietnam's three zones from Hồ's influence. Also during Hồ's absence, a series of incidents between Giáp and the French military heightened tensions. French aircraft bombed Việt Minh positions and French infantry attacked Việt Minh roadblocks. D'Argenlieu gave orders to the French army to occupy certain northern provinces and to establish puppet governments in the mountains (the Thái-Ky and Nùng-Thái Republics) to diminish Việt Minh authority. On 25 June French soldiers seized the governor-general's mansion in Hà Nội used by the Việt Minh. General Giáp warned top French commander, Lt. Gen. Jean-Etienne Valluy, to stop these incidents, but they continued. During those troubled times, the DRV celebrated its first birthday on 2 September 1946.

In October 1946 Hồ Chí Minh returned home. His months in France had been futile; its government had refused meaningful concessions. Eager to consolidate power now that Giáp had eliminated so many rivals, Hồ directed his National Assembly to approve a new constitution, effective 8 November 1946, that formalized the DRV's status. The assembly then dissolved, not to meet again until 1953, with most Nationalist members eliminated.

In the summer of 1946 the French insisted on usurping control of the port of Hai Phòng from the Việt Minh. The Việt Minh refused. On 29 August French troops with tanks and armored vehicles occupied the post office, police station, and customs house and expelled Việt Minh personnel. Both sides exchanged gunfire. The French did not withdraw for nearly two weeks. On 20 November the French seized a Chinese junk suspected of carrying arms for the Việt Minh. In retaliation, the Việt Minh captured three French soldiers and barricaded themselves with the captives deep within Hai Phòng. Another firefight ensued as the French tried to free their comrades. On 23 November the French in Hai Phòng issued an ultimatum that the Việt Minh evacuate Hai Phòng and gave two hours for a response. When the Việt Minh refused, the French used tanks, airplanes, artillery, and naval gunfire to shell the city, causing extensive civilian casualties. They also insisted that the Việt Minh surrender control of the Hà Nội/Hai Phòng road. The Việt Minh resisted, and General Giáp began to prepare for war.

Hồ made a fruitless appeal to Paris as Giáp continued military preparations. On 19 December 1946 Giáp issued a national call to arms, and the next morning Hồ broadcast a message asking his people to fight to the end. Giáp needed time to move troops, materiel, and factories back into the northern wilderness, the Việt Bắc, or "Greenhouse" as Giáp called it, where he felt that the Việt Minh would be safe from French attack. His soldiers bought him the time. The last of them did not retreat from the fighting in Hà Nôi until 17 February 1947.

The Viêt Minh government had been reduced to one in exile, controlling an area only some 50 miles in radius and lying 80 miles north of Hà Nôi. However, it was largely secure from the French, whose wheelbound military could get close to, but not into, the Viêt Băc. General Valluy tried, launching Operation LEA—a combined riverine and air assault—on 7 October 1947. His men closed on Hô's headquarters so rapidly that Hô and Giáp saved themselves only by hiding for some hours in a hole in the ground. With the help of a peasant, Hô escaped safely across French lines. French soldiers failed to identify him, but did kill the scholar Nguyên Văn Tô, whom they mistook for Hô.

Valluy's forces made later assaults as well, ultimately claiming to have killed 9,500 Viêt Minh during actions in late 1947. Dissatisfied with these results, Paris recalled Valluy, replacing him with Lt. Gen. Roger C. Blaizot, who accomplished no more than his predecessor. Giáp knew that he did not have to win many battles to achieve victory in the war. He only had to make the French quit.

A combat lull fell over both sides between 1948 and 1950, but the DRV improved its situation, when in 1949 Mao Zedong, Communist ruler of the People's Republic of China, gave the DRV legal recognition. During that hiatus, the DRV's army grew to about 300,000. Blaizot was followed by Lt. Gen. Marcel Carpentier, who was replaced by General Jean de Lattre de Tassigny, who was followed by General Raoul Salan and, finally, General Henri Navarre. None were able to stop the Viêt Minh.

In 1950, with Hô's approval, Giáp committed his divisions to battle at Đông Khê and Cao Băng, grinding down the French. In 1951 he continued his attacks, at Vĩnh Yên, Mao Khê, and the Đáy River, suffering savage setbacks. Trying again in 1952 he lost another 9,000 men, and so Giáp backed away from frontal confrontations for a time and again relied on guerrilla warfare. In late 1952 the French unsuccessfully counterattacked in Operation LORRAINE and other assaults. Despite French efforts, by 1953 the Viêt Minh controlled most of rural Vietnam and some of the villages and towns and had extended operations into Laos. General Navarre commanded 84 battalions, yet was unable to smash his enemies. Then he concocted a plan to force a set-piece battle with the Viêt Minh at Điên Biên Phu. After fighting bravely for 55 days against General Giáp's besieging soldiers, the French surrendered on 8 May 1954. The DRV had finally defeated the French in the North. The future of Hô's nation would now depend on the great powers, their representatives already gathering for a meeting at Geneva.

—Cecil B. Currey

References: Davidson, Phillip B. *Vietnam at War: The History, 1946–1975.* New York: Oxford University Press, 1988.
Harrison, James Pinckney. *The Endless War: Vietnam's Struggle for Independence.* New York: McGraw-Hill, 1982.
Võ Nguyen Giáp. *Unforgettable Months and Years.* Translated by Mai Elliott. Ithaca, NY: Cornell University Press, 1975.
————. Interviews with the author, December 1988 and July 1991.
See also: August Revolution; d'Argenlieu, Georges Thierry; Fontainebleau Conference; Gracey, Douglas D.; Hai Phòng, Shelling of; Hô Chí Minh; Hô-Sainteny Agreement; Lao Dông Party; LEA, Operation; LOR-RAINE, Operation; Lư Hán; Navarre, Henri Eugène; Sainteny, Jean; Viêt Minh (Viêt Nam Đôc Lâp Đông Minh Hôi [Vietnam Independence League]); Võ Nguyên Giáp.

Vietnam, Democratic Republic of: 1954–1975

The leaders of the Democratic Republic of Vietnam (DRV) never deviated from their goal of unifying the whole of Vietnam under Communist rule. The 1954 Geneva Accords provided that Vietnam was one state temporarily divided at the 17th parallel pending national elections. The final declaration, however, was unsigned, and neither the United States nor South Vietnam accepted its operative terms. The Geneva compromise was a great disappointment to DRV leaders, who were induced to accept less, for the time being, by their Soviet and Communist Chinese allies in order to prevent the possibility of U.S. entry into the conflict.

In the mid-1950s DRV leaders retained two goals: the Marxist consolidation of strength (political and economic) in the North and the "struggle for national reunification." In a step toward attaining the first goal and eliminating the dissension and factionalism that characterized Vietnamese culture, DRV leaders sought to obtain the loyalty of the masses by carrying out "land reform," this in spite of the fact that the North, unlike the South, consisted almost entirely of small landholders. In December 1953 the National Assembly of the DRV called for the confiscation of land and property of the entire "landlord" class. Although there were landholders who had abused the poor, the party was not interested in justice as much as it was interested in class warfare.

Following the example of other Communist nations, especially the People's Republic of China, the peasantry was encouraged to denounce and try landholders, with the aim of temporarily redistributing their holdings among landless peasantry. This resulted in execution or death by starvation of up to 100,000 "landlords." This so-called land reform work was temporarily halted during the 300-day period of free movement provided by the Geneva Accords across the 17th parallel in an effort to limit emigration south. The Viêt Minh blocked the emigration of approximately 400,000 people, but more than 928,000 civilians made it to South Vietnam.

When the 300 days ended, people's courts resumed their ideologically driven work, accusing landholders of being American lackeys or imperialists and denouncing those who committed suicide as "saboteurs." Those who opposed this policy, including party members who refused to participate, were consigned to forced labor camps to study Marxist-Leninist teachings. Many of the condemned landholders had only marginal holdings, and unrest led Hô Chí Minh to admit publicly that cadres had committed errors and excesses. This was followed, as in China, by a campaign to "rectify errors," which ended the terror and led to the release of thousands of survivors. Some victims were also allowed to take revenge on land reform cadres. However, this did not prevent a number of peasant revolts, the most serious of which occurred in Hô's native province of Nghê An on 2 November 1956. Apparently religious oppression and the party's plans to collectivize land recently awarded to individual peasant farmers sparked the

By 1953 the Việt Minh controlled most of rural Vietnam and some of the villages and towns and had extended operations into Laos. Here trucks of the Việt Minh 308th Division parade down the crowd-lined streets of Hà Nội in October 1954. By then, French forces had pulled out, and Việt Minh forces officially took possession of the town.

uprising of Catholics in Cêm Trưởng village, Quỳnh Lưu District. It was crushed by the 325th People's Army of Vietnam (PAVN) Division, resulting in the death or deportation of thousands of peasants. Several hundred peasants made it on foot to South Vietnam with the intervention of the International Commission for Supervision and Control. Although land reform succeeded in increasing the number of those dependent on the party's power, it adversely affected crop production, and famine was averted only through Soviet assistance.

Economic reconstruction of the DRV was essential to continuing the Vietnamese revolution. Politburo member Lê Duân

noted: "The basic problem is the conversion of small individual production into large-scale socialist production. We must construct almost from scratch the entire material and technical base, economic foundation and superstructure for a socialist nation. . . ."

Soviet-bloc aid to the DRV was, according to Bernard Fall, comparable to U.S. aid levels for the Republic of Vietnam (RVN). From 1955 to 1961 grants and loans for economic aid exceeded $1 billion. Despite impressive advances in industrial development, agriculture continued to lag behind that of the RVN, which had a smaller population, yet produced more rice. Although many peasants resisted collectivization of the land, the process of forming lower-stage agricultural cooperatives was completed by 1962.

The other preoccupation of the DRV leadership was reunification. In accordance with the 1954 Geneva Conference agreement, Việt Minh soldiers were regrouped into the North, but political cadres remained in the South to prepare for the 1956 elections. But the RVN government of Ngô Đình Diêm, whose brother had been killed by the Communists and whose regime became repressive, rebuffed all demands of DRV Premier Pham Văn Đông for national elections.

By the summer of 1956 Diêm's "denunciation of Communists" campaign had allegedly eliminated 90 percent of the party's cells in the South. After the Geneva Accords, the DRV left approximately 3,500 armed guerrillas in South Vietnam, in remote locations such as the U Minh Forest of the Mekong Delta, where they received direction from Politburo member Lê Duân. But the DRV was constrained by the global strategy of the Communist Party of the Soviet Union (CPSU), which at their January 1956 Moscow meeting proclaimed a policy of peaceful coexistence with the West. Resistance to this policy was voiced by Trưởng Chinh, who had attended the CPSU Congress with Lê Đưc Tho, at the Ninth Plenum of the Central Committee in April 1956. As head of the Regional Committee of the South, Lê Duân proposed before the Plenum the organization of 20 main force battalions and guerrilla units in friendly villages. His work, *The Path of Revolution in the South,* encouraged a more activist approach, with the party leading the masses. This, along with Diêm's campaign in the South, undermined the primacy of political struggle and led the Eleventh Plenum in December 1957 to launch a program of assassination of Diêm government supporters, ranging from "wicked landlords" to village officials and teachers. This campaign was officially labeled "extermination of traitors."

Thirty-seven armed companies were organized in the South by October 1957 on orders from Hà Nôi. With the insurgency under way, President Diêm rebuffed DRV efforts to arrange trade normalization. Lê Duân was recalled to Hà Nôi as acting first secretary of the party and traveled with Hô Chí Minh to Moscow to seek support for the new approach.

In February 1951 Hô had changed the name of the Communist Party to the Đang Lao Đông Viêt Nam (Vietnamese Workers' Party), popularly known as the Lao Đông (or Workers' Party), the intention being to mask communism and widen nationalist support throughout Vietnam. In January 1959 the Lao Đông Party's Fifteenth Plenum decided to use armed force to topple the Diêm government. In May 1959 the DRV government authorized the formation of Group 559, which began work on enlarging the Hô Chí Minh Trail; meanwhile Group 779 began seaborne infiltration.

In September 1960 the Third Congress of the Lao Đông Party named Lê Duân as secretary-general. The Congress also made it clear that the Vietnamese revolution retained "two strategic tasks," namely to "carry out the socialist revolution in the North" and to "achieve national reunification." In regard to the first, it is worth noting that in 1960 the DRV obtained a long-term loan from the Soviets, which provided for the construction of 43 indus-

trial plants, including eight thermal power stations. The People's Republic of China (PRC) provided a similar loan to enlarge 29 existing plants, including the Thái Nguyên steel mill complex and a large fertilizer factory in Băc Giang, which also produced explosives for the PAVN. A First Five Year Plan was initiated in 1961 on the Soviet model, with central planning and priority given to heavy industry. Steel and coal production, electric power generation, rolling stock, and other basic industries became the focus. The Soviets also constructed a machine tool plant and a superphosphate factory. The Chinese built roads and plants, Mongolia provided 100,000 breed cattle, and East Germany sent an ocean fishing fleet and supplies to build a hospital. Only about 10 percent of the DRV's trade was with non-Communist nations. Industrial production as a percentage of the gross national product increased from 31.4 percent in 1957 to 53.4 percent by 1964.

To facilitate the second task of the revolution and recognizing that its operatives in the South were on the verge of open guerrilla war, on 20 December 1960 the party created the National Liberation Front (NLF) and its military branch. This apparently liberal, nationalist front to overthrow the Diêm regime was in fact tightly controlled by the DRV through the newly revived Central Office for South Vietnam (COSVN), but the party's success in concealing this linkage gave the NLF insurgency worldwide sympathy. Military units in the Western Highlands and the Mekong Delta were consolidated into the People's Liberation Armed Forces (PLAF), better known to their enemies as the Việt Công (VC). The creation of the People's Revolutionary Party in 1962 (in effect, a branch of the Lao Đông Party) was another step toward the takeover of the South.

The DRV accepted the Kennedy administration–initiated Geneva Accords of 1962 on Laos, but failed to live up to its provisions to reduce its advisors with the Pathet Lao and remove its personnel on way stations along the Hô Chí Minh Trail. When the Ninth Plenum of the Central Committee in December 1963 decided to escalate the war effort in South Vietnam, the Communists received crucial support from the PRC, which provided 90,000 rifles and machine guns to the Việt Công in 1962 alone.

After the August 1964 Tonkin Gulf incidents and the ouster of Premier Nikita Khrushchev that October, DRV leaders appealed to the Soviets for more aid, while at the same time working to preserve their ties with the Chinese. This was reflected in the February 1965 visit of Soviet Premier Aleksei Kosygin to Hà Nôi, which was followed by aid agreements in April and June and a Soviet-bloc conference in Moscow (October 1966) that promised $1 billion in military and financial aid. The Chinese had agreed in July 1965 to provide the DRV with $200 million in "national defense and economic supplies." The DRV decision to move to big unit (conventional) war could not have been made without these pacts.

In an effort to exploit Việt Công successes, the leadership also decided in 1964 to send regular PAVN troops down the Hô Chí Minh Trail to the South. Up to this point, most of those sent to the South were native Việt Minh southern veterans who had been regrouped in the North in accordance with the 1954 Geneva Agreements. By 1964 the Trail had been prepared to accommodate greater infiltration and, as a result of Soviet and Chinese assistance, it could now handle trucks and other vehicles. However, the attempt of the PAVN and VC to cut South Vietnam in two from the Central Highlands to the coast was frustrated by the 1965 entry of U.S. ground troops into the conflict. The U.S. 1st Cavalry Division (Airmobile) defeated three PAVN regiments in the Ia Drang Valley late that year.

The commitment of 200,000 U.S. troops to the Republic of Vietnam led the Twelfth Plenum of the Central Committee in December 1965 to decide upon protracted war. Big-unit war proved costly in the face of a continuing U.S. troop buildup. By 1967 declining volunteers and heavy casualties forced more PAVN and VC units to seek refuge in sanctuaries in "neutral" Laos and Cambodia. When the Fourteenth Plenum of the Central Committee met in late 1967, it finalized plans for a "general offensive, general uprising" (the Tết Offensive), despite the presence of 500,000 U.S. troops. Reportedly, Defense Minister General Võ Nguyên Giáp opposed risking so much, but he accepted the decision when the party shifted the brunt of the fighting to VC units. Although the party's hopes for a general uprising of the South Vietnamese populace proved illusory, the shock of a countrywide offensive was sufficient to persuade the Johnson administration to seek a negotiated end to the conflict, including a halt to bombing above the 20th parallel.

The 1968 Tết Offensive would not have been possible without massive Soviet and Chinese aid. Moscow had begun operating some North Vietnamese air defense missile batteries in July 1965, and until March 1968 the Chinese had up to 170,000 troops in the DRV, staffing air defenses (three antiaircraft divisions), building the logistic system, and repairing roads and bridges. Chinese reports indicate that they suffered 20,000 casualties in U.S. bombing. The DRV Air Force was forced by the destruction of its airfields to operate out of bases in southern China that were off limits to U.S. aircraft.

Nonetheless, according to British Consul General in Hà Nội John Colvin, the United States had won the air war by the end of 1967 because DRV ports and rails were out of action. As Philip B. Davidson notes in *Vietnam at War: The History, 1946–1975*, Colvin claimed that by that date the DRV "was no longer capable of maintaining itself as an economic unit, nor of mounting aggressive war against its neighbor." Factories, schools, and hospitals, along with most of the civilians in Hà Nội, Hai Phòng, Nam Định, Việt Trì, and Thanh Hóa, were moved outside city limits, leaving the former bustling inner cities nearly empty. This slowed and changed the focus of industrial production as well. The Tết Offensive had also failed to such an extent that the Việt Cộng never recovered its former strength, and North Vietnamization of its forces became necessary.

Seeking an end to all bombing of the North, the DRV agreed to talks in Paris, but adopted the tactic of "fighting and talking," which was designed to exacerbate differences between the United States and the RVN and to intensify antiwar pressures in the United States. Not surprisingly, these talks achieved little. There was an understanding, however, that, in return for a complete bombing halt over the North, the Communists would refrain from attacks on the cities. When the latter was violated by an offensive in February 1969, the Nixon administration initiated the secret bombing of Communist sanctuaries in Cambodia and announced its Vietnamization policy. The DRV leadership could not protest because it denied having troops in Cambodia, but the bombing of Cambodia prompted them to agree to secret talks in Paris.

Hồ Chí Minh's death in September 1969 temporarily resolved the debate in Hà Nội in favor of those who wanted a guerrilla war. U.S. and Army of the Republic of Vietnam (ARVN) pacification efforts achieved successes between 1970 and 1971, but intensive efforts to rebuild Communist forces were under way. The U.S. incursion into Cambodia to support the forces of Lon Nol in 1970 and the U.S. encouragement of the ARVN effort to destroy Communist bases and cut the Hồ Chí Minh Trail in southern Laos (Operation LAM SƠN 719) probably forced the North Vietnamese to postpone by one year the great offensive approved by the Nineteenth Plenum. By 1971 the USSR had provided the DRV some $3 billion in economic and military assistance, while the PRC had provided an additional $1 billion. Both governments gave additional aid increases for the upcoming offensive.

The Nixon administration had arranged summits with both Beijing and Moscow in 1972 to obtain PRC and USSR cooperation in bringing about a negotiated settlement in Vietnam. Nonetheless, the DRV launched an all-out offensive with 14 PAVN divisions in a conventional attack that employed Soviet-supplied tanks and artillery. The Nguyên Huế (or Easter Offensive) was timed to impact the U.S. presidential election and was launched when there were only 6,000 U.S. combat troops in Vietnam. But President Richard Nixon's decision to escalate dramatically the air war, resume the bombing of the North, target PAVN forces in the South, and mine Hai Phòng Harbor resulted in a crushing PAVN defeat, with losses estimated at 100,000 troops.

Receiving pressure from both the Soviets and the Chinese, Hà Nội sought a settlement through the secret Henry Kissinger–Lê Đức Tho talks in Paris. The breakthrough came on 8 October 1972, with agreement to an immediate cease-fire in place, followed by a completion of the U.S. troop withdrawal and an exchange of prisoners. But key to the agreement was the concession that North Vietnamese troops did not have to leave territory they occupied inside South Vietnam. This and other substantive problems caused RVN President Nguyên Văn Thiêu to balk, delaying the final agreement. Hà Nội agreed to reopen the negotiations but stalled, hoping the Nixon administration would be compelled to make further concessions based on congressional deadlines or antiwar pressures. When the DRV discontinued the talks on 13 December, President Nixon ordered the intense LINEBACKER II bombing, which convinced the DRV to settle, since its air defenses were devastated and its economy was in ruins. DRV leaders claimed that the bombing had produced suffering akin to a holocaust. DRV claims to the contrary, U.S. newsman Michael W. Browne of the *New York Times* on visiting Hà Nội observed that "the damage caused by American bombing was grossly overstated by North Vietnamese propaganda."

In return for an end to the bombing, DRV leaders agreed to return to the Kissinger–Lê Đức Tho talks and ultimately agreed to the cease-fire agreement, privately assuring the United States that they would arrange a cease-fire in Laos as well, but claiming that they could not do the same in Cambodia. The DRV was left in control of about 20 percent of the South and redeployed troops in Cambodia to their former jungle sanctuaries on the RVN border.

With the removal of U.S. combat troops and advisors, the DRV concentrated on rebuilding its own forces. Soviet heavy artillery, air defense missiles, and armored vehicles were moved south during the next two years. A captured COSVN directive describing the post cease-fire period stated, "This period will be a great opportunity for revolutionary violence, for gaining power in South Vietnam. . . ."

The third Indo-China War began almost immediately. The Canadians, representatives on the International Commission of Supervision and Control, withdrew in frustration since they were being arrested and treated as prisoners by the PLAF. They reported that the most serious violations were North Vietnamese disregard for Lao and Cambodian neutrality and continuing infiltration into the RVN.

Secretary of State Kissinger visited Hà Nôi in February 1973 to confront the Communists with a report of more than 200 cease-fire violations, but DRV leaders wanted only to discuss the money promised them for reconstruction. As Kissinger noted in *White House Years,* he assured them that they could not "have their aid and eat Indochina too." Sài Gòn's effort to regain lost territory and the passage of the Case-Church Amendment that ended funding for U.S. forces in Southeast Asia prompted the Twenty-First Plenum of the Central Committee in October 1973 to approve "strategic raids" on isolated ARVN bases in order to clear their "logistics corridor," cut key communication with Sài Gòn, regain lost territory, and begin preparation for a culminating offensive to win the war. Critical to PAVN's success was the movement of troops and materiel down the Hô Chí Minh Trail, the construction of an oil pipeline, and a paved highway from Quang Tri in the north through the Central Highlands to Lôc Ninh in the South. Also important was the aggressive initiative of theater commander General Trân Văn Trà, who persuaded Lê Duân to back his plan for attacking Phước Long Province, despite concerns over the level of war materiels and the U.S. reaction.

When the United States did not react to the seizing of Phước Long Province in December 1974, the DRV, confident that the Ford administration would not send in airpower, pushed ahead with an all-out invasion of the South (the Hô Chí Minh Campaign), which they anticipated would take two years to complete. But RVN President Nguyên Văn Thiêu's precipitous abandonment of the Central Highlands was the beginning of a rout as PAVN forces, led by General Văn Tiên Dũng and reequipped with modern Soviet tanks and weapons, completed the conquest of the RVN well ahead of schedule. Sài Gòn fell on 30 April 1975. The DRV also celebrated the victories of its allies in Cambodia and in Laos, where PAVN divisions were instrumental in the Pathet Lao victory.

Chief of the Soviet Armed Forces General Viktor Kulikov had hurried to Hà Nôi after the capture of Phước Long Province to offer an estimated 400 percent increase in military aid to complete the destruction of the RVN. The Communist Chinese, who had assumed the aid burden for the Khmer Rouge in Cambodia, also provided critical military aid. During the war years, they provided about 500,000 tons of grain per year to help feed the urban population of the North.

During the second and third Indo-China Wars, the combined losses of the DRV and the RVN were at least 1 million troops. The DRV suffered heavy bomb damage in six industrial cities, and 32 towns required major rebuilding. Another challenge facing Vietnam was trying to feed the 49 million people of the reunified country, especially considering that the Socialist transformation of the South was made a high priority.

—Claude R. Sasso

References: Doyle, Edward, et al., and the editors of Boston Publishing. *The North. The Vietnam Experience,* edited by Robert Manning. Boston: Boston Publishing, 1984.
Duiker, William, J. *The Communist Road to Power in Vietnam.* Boulder, CO: Westview Press, 1981.
Fall, Bernard. *The Two Viet Nams.* Rev. ed. New York: Praeger, 1964.
Kissinger, Henry A. *White House Years.* Boston: Little, Brown, 1979.
See also: Agricultural Reform Tribunals; Cambodia; China, People's Republic of (PRC); Easter Offensive (Nguyên Huê Campaign); Hô Chí Minh; Hô Chí Minh Campaign; Hô Chí Minh Trail; International Commission for Supervision and Control (ICSC); Kissinger, Henry Alfred; Lao Đông Party; Laos; Lê Duân; Lê Đức Tho; LINEBACKER II, Operation; National Front for the Liberation of South Vietnam (NFLSV); Paris Negotiations; Paris Peace Accords; Union of Soviet Socialist Republics (USSR) (Soviet Union); Viêt Minh (Viêt Nam Đôc Lâp Đông Minh Hôi [Vietnam Independence League]); Vietnam, Democratic Republic of: 1945–1954; Vietnamese Communist Party (VCP).

Vietnam, Democratic Republic of: Air Force

During Operation ROLLING THUNDER (1965–1968), 90 percent of U.S. air attacks against the Democratic Republic of Vietnam (DRV) were against its southern panhandle. The other 10 percent, as one participant noted, were against "the center of hell, with Hà Nôi as its hub." The area above the 20th parallel proved hellish for attackers because it was protected by the most sophisticated integrated air defense network yet seen in war. A significant component of this network was the DRV Air Force, which sporadically worked in concert with antiaircraft artilleries (AAA) and surface-to-air missiles (SAMs) to exact a high price of U.S. aircraft striking North Vietnamese targets.

Prior to the August 1964 Gulf of Tonkin incident, the DRV's Air Force was obsolete and insignificant. It had only 30 trainer aircraft, 50 transports, and four light helicopters. Only two modern airfields—Gia Lâm in Hà Nôi and Cát Bi near Hai Phòng—could sustain prolonged jet operations, and only 20 radar sets protected these meager resources from possible attack. However, almost immediately after the confrontation in the Gulf of Tonkin, the People's Republic of China provided a limited number of MiG-15 and MiG-17 jet aircraft, which were based at Phúc Yên airfield near Hà Nôi. China provided these as a precaution against future U.S. air strikes and in the expectation that the DRV was about to embark on a period of prolonged war. This prodded

After a Việt Công attack that leveled a two-block area, three Vietnamese women move back into the Chợ Lớn area in a district in Sài Gòn in hopes of salvaging their meager belongings.

the Soviet Union to replace the Chinese as the DRV Air Force's main sponsor and supplier.

Between 1965 and 1966 the North Vietnamese and their Soviet sponsors began to build what would become a fearsome air defense system. By the end of 1965 the DRV had some 75 MiG fighters and eight IL-28 light bombers. North Vietnamese pilots spent most of the year training for what would become their sole mission throughout the war—air defense. There were only ten fighter engagements between U.S. and DRV pilots during that year, resulting in the loss of six North Vietnamese aircraft while the Americans lost two.

The agile MiG-21, which became the primary DRV Air Force interceptor during the war, first arrived in December 1965. Also by the end of the year, the DRV established the rudiments of a centralized intercept network that could detect approaching American aircraft from multiple directions. Both developments allowed the DRV Air Force to increase its level of activity in 1966.

Things began slowly during the first half of 1966 when the North Vietnamese pilots averaged 1 interception a month, but during the last half of the year there were an average of 12 engagements a month. By year's end, despite the loss of 29 aircraft in air-to-air combat (American losses were 11 aircraft), 70 MiG fighters

remained, including 15 MiG-21s. Clearly, the DRV Air Force was on the brink of a new level of aggressiveness, proficiency, and tactical maturity that would allow it to make U.S. attacks costly.

In 1967 the F-105 "Thunderchief" and the F-4 "Phantom" continued to perform the overwhelming number of bombing missions against the DRV. What they now encountered was indeed "the center of hell": 200 SAM sites, 7,000 AAA guns, and approximately 110 MiGs (including 18 MiG-21s), all working together under a sophisticated ground-control intercept system. The role of the SAMs and MiGs was to destroy enemy aircraft, force them to jettison their bombs prematurely, or compel them to dive into the lethal range of AAA fire. The role of ground fire was to force the attacker back up into the SAM/MiG belt to suffer the same fate. Not surprisingly, the dense air defense system worked, although MiG operations were not as important as SAM defenses and AAA fire. U.S. losses grew from 171 aircraft in 1965 to 326 in 1967; the cost of causing $1 worth of damage grew from $6.60 to $9.60; and the U.S. success rate in air combat, based on an average of 20 encounters per month in 1967, was a mere three to one (75 DRV versus 25 U.S. aircraft lost). However, the three-to-one ratio did include 15 MiGs destroyed on the ground in attacks against three of the DRV's five principal airfields. The attacks disrupted DRV activities to the point that by the end of 1967 there were only 10 to 30 MiG aircraft working in the DRV, and they operated at irregular intervals. The North Vietnamese moved the rest of their MiGs, for retraining and regrouping, to air facilities in southern China. There some 100 aircraft stayed even after ROLLING THUNDER ended in March 1968. The remaining 50 or so MiGs in the DRV then individually challenged U.S. aircraft, still operating below the 20th parallel, until the complete American bombing halt of 31 October 1968.

After the bombing halt, the DRV Air Force operated at a reduced tempo until 1972. At that point, it had an estimated 206 MiGs, including 93 MiG-21s. With the reintroduction of U.S. air strikes above the 20th parallel in Linebacker I and II, the North Vietnamese Air Force once again served as a necessary component of the DRV's still-lethal air defense system. U.S. aircraft reached their objectives without significant interference by North Vietnamese fighters, but 23 U.S. airplanes went down between February and October 1972. Thus, the DRV Air Force remained to the end what it was in the beginning—a limited (but effective) air defense tool designed to harass and disrupt U.S. air attacks against the DRV.

—Peter R. Faber

References: Clodfelter, Mark. *The Limits of Air Power.* New York: Free Press, 1989.

Sharp, U. S. G. "Report on Air and Naval Campaigns against North Vietnam and Pacific Command-Wide Support of the War, June 1964–July 1968." In *Report on the War in Vietnam.* Washington, DC: U.S. Government Printing Office, 1969.

See also: Air Defense, Democratic Republic of Vietnam; Air Power, Role in War; Antiaircraft Artillery, Allied and Democratic Republic of Vietnam; Order of Battle; ROLLING THUNDER, Operation; Surface-to-Air Missiles (SAMs).

Vietnam, Democratic Republic of: Army (People's Army of Vietnam [PAVN])

Military establishment of the Democratic Republic of Vietnam (DRV), comprising regular and reserve ground forces and small naval and air components. Over a 30-year span, the People's Army of Vietnam (PAVN) evolved from a small insurgent group into one of the world's largest armed forces. The PAVN's roots can be traced to the various nationalist military units that battled the French and Japanese during the 1930s and 1940s. The impetus to build an army came with the Viêt Minh resistance during the Second World War. Originally an umbrella organization that included non-Communist elements, by 1944 the Viêt Minh was dominated by Hô Chí Minh's Communist Party. On 22 December of that year the party laid the foundation for what would become the PAVN with the establishment of the first Armed Propaganda Team. Comprised of 31 men and 3 women and commanded by Võ Nguyên Giáp, this unit became the party's first full-time formation and served a political as well as military role. Supplied with only a few old weapons, including muzzle-loading flintlocks, the Armed Propaganda Team provided the model for future units.

Under Giáp's leadership, the task of army building went forward. Armed Propaganda Teams, various guerrilla bands, and other independent resistance groups were combined in May 1945 to form the Vietnam Liberation Army with Giáp in overall command. Later that year, this small force of only a few thousand people spearheaded the August Revolution, after which Hô proclaimed Vietnamese independence and the founding of the Democratic Republic of Vietnam (DRV).

Renamed the Vietnam National Defense Army, the force remained largely a guerrilla army, capable of only small-unit operations as practiced during the struggle against the Japanese. But with the DRV's formation came an aggressive drive to expand the army. This coincided with the French decision to reassert primacy in Vietnam and the resultant Indo-China War (1946–1954). The fledgling DRV military force was soon designated the People's Army of Vietnam.

Although the army grew steadily during the war, initially it lacked organization, training, and weapons. Forced to rely on captured French and Japanese equipment, the PAVN fought a largely defensive guerrilla war. Victories along the northern border with China allowed the establishment of staging areas and training bases in that country. It also opened the door to increased assistance from the People's Republic of China (PRC). The Viêt Minh prosecuted the war in various phases, building to large-scale conventional warfare. The first PAVN infantry division, formed in 1949, went into action in 1951 and was followed by five more, but throughout the war most of the fighting was done by regional or local forces while the regulars were used sparingly and withheld for major actions such as the Battle of Điên Biên Phu. Local units supplied reconnaissance and logistical support and often bolstered combat formations; regional forces carried out much of the everyday fighting. The acquisition of field artillery (captured French and recently supplied Chinese guns) to augment heavily employed mortars led to the advent of heavy divisions and helped facilitate the shift to conventional warfare and the 1954 victory at Điên Biên Phu that prompted the French withdrawal from Vietnam. Throughout the Indo-China War, a lack of transport vehicles forced the Viêt Minh to rely almost exclusively on thousands of porters to supply forces in the field. At war's end, the PAVN numbered some 380,000 soldiers, of whom approximately 120,000 were considered regulars. The Viêt Minh had been nominally a united front organization, and the PAVN reflected this on a small scale.

With victory over the French came a rapid consolidation by the Communists of both political and military organizations. The Communist Party held sway in the DRV as the PAVN's composition boldly illustrated; an overwhelming majority of PAVN officers were party members, and most of the soldiers had received political indoctrination.

The 1954 Geneva Accords that mandated a partition of Vietnam allowed a 300-day regroupment period during which almost 1 million people fled the North for the South. Some 80,000 Viêt Minh soldiers, mostly regional and local troops who had carried the bulk of the fighting in the South, returned to the North. Some 10,000 veterans remained in the South and would form the core of the future People's Liberation Armed Forces (PLAF).

The unification of Vietnam became the Communist Party's overriding goal. In 1956 Lê Duân, an influential member of the

A People's Army of Vietnam detachment swings down a road in North Vietnam as civilians stand by watching, 14 August 1965.

party's Central Military Committee, went to the South to assess the situation and prepare for the job of unification. The following year, PAVN guerrillas attacked Minh Thanh in Thu Dâu Môt Province, signaling the beginning of the Vietnam War.

DRV leaders now focused on the modernization and professionalization of their army. The government mandated compulsory military service and intensified training for all officers and noncommissioned officers (NCOs). It also instituted uniform regulations and formalized the command structure. It established formal ranks and insignia for a force that had operated without these mainstays of Western armies. The influx of war materiel from the PRC and the USSR—namely artillery, T-34 medium tanks, and airplanes—led to the formation of artillery and armor units and a small air force. The army still lacked adequate transport and remained heavily infantry oriented.

Unification drove military planning in the late 1950s. The Fifteenth Party Plenum in May 1959 determined that the time was ripe to press the initiative. Acting on Lê Duân's recommendations, the party moved to build an army in the South based upon the Armed Propaganda Team that could evolve into a conventional

force. The 1954 Geneva Accords restricted the PAVN to areas north of the 17th parallel; therefore, the chief instrument of insurrection in the South became the National Front for the Liberation of South Vietnam or National Liberation Front (NLF), a nominally indigenous united-front organization that opposed the U.S.-supported Republic of Vietnam (RVN) and its President Ngô Đình Diêm.

Although the DRV denied any involvement in the southern insurrection, it was clearly involved. The NLF's military branch—the People's Liberation Armed Forces (known to the United States as the Viêt Công)—was comprised largely of southern volunteers and carried out most of the fighting against RVN and U.S. forces prior to 1968. It contained main force and guerrilla components and reached a total strength of almost 400,000 before the 1968 Têt Offensive.

Although Hà Nôi insisted that the southern guerrilla war be self-sufficient, it provided vital assistance in the form of experienced leadership, technical support, and supplies. The DRV directed the southern effort through its command apparatus, later known as the Central Office for South Vietnam (COSVN). Additionally, PAVN soldiers who had gone north during the regroupment were infiltrated to the South, forming the bulk of PLAF main force units. Still, throughout the Vietnam War, the PAVN and the PLAF viewed themselves as separate entities. After the war, Hà Nôi claimed sponsorship of the PLAF—much to the disgust of many PLAF veterans.

The most important aspect of the DRV's early involvement was logistical support. The 1959 commitment to escalate its involvement in the South led to the creation of Group 559 to infiltrate troops and supplies southward on the Hồ Chí Minh Trail, which was constantly expanded and improved by PAVN engineers and defended by PAVN infantry and antiaircraft units. Group 759 was charged with supplying southern forces by water, while Group 959 was developed to support the Pathet Lao in Laos. These efforts, especially that of Group 559, contributed hugely to the Communist victory.

Until 1965 the PLAF conducted a usually low-level "people's war," employing its guerrilla forces against the Army of the Republic of Vietnam (ARVN) and its Regional and Popular Forces. Political action was equally important to the southern effort, and NLF and Communist Party cadres worked to exploit local dissatisfaction with the Sài Gòn government. But with the commitment of U.S. combat troops, the DRV found it increasingly necessary to augment PLAF formations and finally to commit regular units. The PAVN initially operated in the Central Highlands south of the Demilitarized Zone (DMZ) to keep U.S. and ARVN forces from concentrating PLAF activities further south. This was especially the case prior to the 1968 Tết Offensive, as entire PAVN divisions moved below the DMZ in a diversionary effort to draw U.S. and ARVN attentions from the targeted areas in the South.

Tết became a military disaster that destroyed the fighting effectiveness of the PLAF, who bore the brunt of the fighting and took devastating losses. Thereafter PAVN regulars assumed the leading combat role and took on an increasingly conventional profile with a large influx of tanks, artillery, and surface-to-air missiles (SAMs). The regular PAVN divisions, which mainly conducted the 1972 Spring Offensive in the wake of the withdrawal of U.S. ground troops, were beaten back by the ARVN with the aid of substantial U.S. air support. After almost three years of preparation that included massive troop and equipment buildups, the PAVN unleashed its final offensive—the 1975 Hồ Chí Minh Campaign directed by Senior General Văn Tiên Dũng—that overpowered ARVN defenders and culminated in the fall of Sài Gòn.

The PAVN was also responsible for the DRV's defense. PAVN regional and local forces augmented by as many as 2 million civilian militia stood guard against ground attack and staffed coastal defenses. The PAVN, with substantial technical assistance from the PRC and the USSR, operated what became one of the worlds heaviest air defense systems, including tightly arrayed radar-guided SAM and antiaircraft gun sites. A small PAVN naval contingent operated a few dozen small craft—mostly patrol and torpedo boats—and devoted itself to coastal defense. Its most notable Vietnam War participation came during the 1964 Tonkin Gulf incidents. The PAVN's air branch grew steadily during the conflict—thanks to the influx of Soviet warplanes—but never assumed more than a limited defensive posture against the U.S. Air Force.

PAVN tactics were dictated by its various stages of engagement and ranged from guerrilla to big-unit conventional warfare. "Death Volunteer" units attracted much attention. These pressed the close-in battle against French strong points, especially at Điên Biên Phu, but against the Americans, all troops pressed in close. Such "hugging tactics" were intended to place PAVN troops too close for U.S. forces to risk using artillery for fear of killing their own personnel. These tactics achieved mixed success against U.S. forces but proved eminently effective against all but the most elite ARVN troops.

Training and combat cohesion were critical elements of PAVN success. Its conscripts were highly motivated and received nearly four months of basic training before reporting to their units for specific training requirements. More importantly, in contrast to their counterparts in the South, PAVN NCOs and technical personnel received extensive military and political motivational training as well as technical instruction. The result was an army of conscripts led by a technically competent and highly motivated noncommissioned officer corps. The officers corps received even more intensive training. All activities, social and military, were centered around the unit. The result was a tightly knit, intensely cohesive force. Additionally, all PAVN units contained both military and political leaders of equal stature. Military and political objectives were inseparable.

Logistics were key to PAVN success. Its units were weapons-intensive formations with few logistics and support personnel. Thus, supplies were husbanded carefully and dispersed in hidden caches around likely operating areas and stockpiled near the objective well in advance of an offensive. When necessary, local labor was recruited or conscripted to haul supplies to new locations or units in the field. For example, tens of thousands of porters were recruited to transport supplies and heavy weapons used at Điên Biên Phu. Likewise, the deployment of regular forces to South Vietnam was preceded by logistics preparations along the deployment route. The construction of barracks and rest facilities along the Hồ Chí Minh Trail began in 1965, each base being about one day's march apart. The PAVN ultimately constructed two fuel pipelines along the trail before it dispatched tanks to the South. Storage areas were built underground in staging areas within PAVN sanctuaries inside Cambodia and South Vietnam's A Shau Valley, from which supplies were then transported to caches deeper in South Vietnam. Sea and river transport was used whenever possible. Communist flag merchant ships also carried supplies to Cambodia's Sihanoukville (Kompong Som) for transport into South Vietnam. In fact, this was the most common delivery means for heavier materials prior to 1970. Cambodia's entry into the war in 1972 cut this supply route. Supplies were also smuggled through Vietnam's coastal waters until 1975, although U.S. and RVN interdiction efforts proved increasingly successful. By 1973 the bulk of PAVN supplies entered South Vietnam via the Hồ Chí Minh Trail.

Equipment was initially a PAVN weakness. Regular divisions were equipped with a homogenous array of weapons after 1951. Originally the small arms were of Japanese origin, but French small arms predominated in the regular infantry until 1960.

Artillery and mortars initially came from surrendered French and Japanese stocks, but beginning in the early 1960s they were gradually replaced by Soviet and Communist Chinese weapons. By 1965 PAVN divisions contained artillery regiments equipped with Soviet 122-mm guns and howitzers, in addition to a wide range of mortars (60- to 160-mm) and rocket launcher systems (120- to 130-mm).

Small arms were standardized around Communist-bloc models as numbers became available. The 7.62-mm SKS carbine and AK47 assault rifle were the standard infantry weapons, while the Soviet RPD light machine gun or its Chinese version provided the squad's automatic fire support element. Every platoon had Soviet-produced rocket-propelled grenade launchers (RPG-7s) after 1965. These supplemented the battalion's 57-mm and 75-mm recoilless rifles. Soviet and American heavy machine guns (12.7-mm and .50-caliber, respectively) could also be found in the battalion's heavy weapons company, but mortars were the primary heavy support weapon below division level.

Tanks were introduced in the 1950s. Captured French and Japanese models were discarded after 1954 and were replaced in limited quantities by Chinese and Soviet light and medium tanks. The PT76 was the first tank the PAVN deployed southward. It was relatively easy to infiltrate into South Vietnam because its light weight and amphibious capabilities enabled it to cross rivers and use all but the most primitive roads. The heavier and more powerful T54 medium tank was not deployed until after the Hồ Chí Minh Trail was improved in 1968. Organized into independent battalions, tanks were deployed against key objectives and astride critical lines of communications. The movement of its armored units signified PAVN intentions after 1970. Since the DRV did not produce its own tanks, these almost irreplaceable weapons were husbanded even more carefully than were supplies, and they were held in reserve for decisive battles. During the 1972 Spring (Easter) Offensive, the PAVN used T54s for the first time (at Đông Hà). But PAVN commanders seemed not to grasp the importance of combined armor-infantry tactics. Several tanks moved forward to attack without any infantry support and were destroyed easily by ARVN M72s. Heavy losses in the failed 1972 Spring Offensive put a temporary halt to offensive operations until more tanks could be acquired. The PAVN employed nearly 400 medium tanks in the vanguard of the final offensive that conquered Sài Gòn in 1975. That drive marked the PAVN's successful transition to a highly trained mechanized infantry force equal to all but the world's very best conventional armies.

The PAVN was General Giáp's creation. Its tactics, strategy, and organizational structure all emanated from his genius. His protégés and assistants served him well, if not perfectly. General Nguyên Chí Thanh ably commanded the PLAF and the war effort in the South from 1965 until his death in 1967. But he and General Giáp grossly overestimated the South Vietnamese people's desire for "revolution" and his forces suffered accordingly. The 1968 Tết Offensive was a major military disaster, but it paid unexpected political dividends.

Giáp and his generals learned from their mistakes. They modified their tactics to minimize their exposure to U.S. firepower.

Few can fault Senior General Văn Tiến Dũng's 1975 drive on Sài Gòn. More significantly, PAVN military strategy was integrated with that of their political leaders and diplomats. Thus, the DRV's military and diplomatic activities were mutually supporting, something that their opponents never achieved during either the Indo-China or Vietnam War. The PAVN could also rely on the excellent Communist support system that provided food, labor, and military intelligence.

At war's end in 1975, the PAVN numbered nearly 1 million troops, despite loses announced in April 1995 at 1.1 million Communist fighters killed between 1954 and 1975—a figure that includes both Viêt Công guerrillas in South Vietnam and PAVN personnel. PLAF formations were either disbanded or absorbed by the PAVN. But the fighting was far from over. In 1978 the PAVN invaded Cambodia and occupied the country until 1989. In response to this, PRC forces attacked into northern Vietnam in early 1979 but withdrew after intense resistance from PAVN regular and regional forces. By the mid-1980s the PAVN represented the world's third largest standing army, trailing only the PRC and the USSR. Severe economic conditions and the loss of Soviet aid prompted dramatic force reductions, but the PAVN remains a formidable armed force.

—Carl O. Schuster and David Coffey

References: Lanning, Michael L., and Dan Cragg. *Inside the VC and the NVA*. New York: Ballantine Books, 1992.
Miller, David. "Giap's Army." *War Monthly* 28 (July 1976): 26–33.
Pike, Douglas. *The People's Army of Vietnam*. Novato, CA: Presidio Press, 1986.
Terzani, Tiziano. *Giai Phong: The Fall and Liberation of Saigon*. New York: St. Martin's Press, 1976.
Võ Nguyên Giáp. *Big Victory, Great Task*. New York: Praeger, 1968.
See also: COSVN (Central Office for South Vietnam or Trung Ưởng Cuc Miên Nam); *Đâu Tranh;* Điên Biên Phu, Battle of; Easter Offensive (Nguyên Huê Campaign); Hồ Chí Minh Campaign; Hồ Chí Minh Trail; Indo-China War; Khe Sanh, Battles of; Lê Duân; Nguyên Chí Thanh; Order of Battle; Sino-Vietnamese War; Tết Offensive: Overall Strategy; Tết Offensive: The Sài Gòn Circle; Tonkin Gulf Incidents; Văn Tiến Dũng; Vietnamese Invasion and Occupation of Cambodia; Võ Nguyên Giáp.

Vietnam, Republic of: 1954–1975

The 1954 Geneva Conference ending the Indo-China War temporarily divided Vietnam at the 17th parallel. The Viêt Minh regrouped into the North where Hồ Chí Minh's Democratic Republic of Vietnam (DRV) held sway. The State of Vietnam, headed by Emperor Bao Dai, dominated the South. A Demilitarized Zone (DMZ) separated the two, and national elections to reunify the country were to be held within two years of the Geneva Agreement—in 1956.

Bao Dai, then living in France, called on nationalist and Catholic leader Ngô Đình Diêm to head a government. Bao Dai needed Diêm's support and that of his brother Ngô Đình Nhu, who had set up the influential Front for National Salvation in Sài Gòn as an alternative to the Viêt Minh. Another factor influencing Bao Dai was his belief that Washington backed Diêm. On 18 June 1954 Bao Dai appointed Diêm as prime minister. Diêm returned to Sài Gòn on 26 June, and on 7 July officially formed his new government, which technically embraced all Vietnam.

The United States did back Diêm and supplied increasing amounts of aid to his government, the power base of which was quite narrow: Catholics, the landed gentry, and fervent anti-Communist nationalists. Many of the rich and powerful and Francophiles opposed him. This soon included most of the nationalist parties and religious sects. Many observers believed that Diêm would not last long in power, but he proved to be an adroit political manipulator. Certainly a key in this was that Washington channeled all aid directly to his government. This U.S. decision, effective in October 1954, undercut remaining French authority in the South.

At the same time, Washington pressured Paris to withdraw its remaining forces, and the last left the country in April 1956. American officers, meanwhile, arrived to train the South Vietnamese armed forces. This angered Army commander General Nguyên Văn Hinh, a naturalized Frenchman, and led to a test of wills between him and Diêm. When Diêm ordered Hinh to leave the country, Hinh refused to go and for a time there was talk of a coup. This ended when President Dwight D. Eisenhower sent General J. Lawton Collins to South Vietnam as special ambassador. He informed Sài Gòn officials that Washington would deal only with Diêm. Hinh then went into exile in France.

Internationally the United States supported Diêm by taking the lead in the September 1954 creation of the Southeast Asia Treaty Organization (SEATO), which extended protection to South Vietnam. President Eisenhower sent high-ranking U.S. officials to Vietnam, including both Secretary of State John Foster Dulles and Vice-President Richard Nixon. In May 1957 Diêm traveled to the United States and spoke to a joint session of Congress.

Meanwhile Diêm moved quickly to consolidate power in South Vietnam. By this time, a number of opposition groups were carrying out armed resistance to the government, including the Cao Đài and the Hòa Hao religious sects and the Đai Viêt Party. In 1955, using Army units loyal to him and money bribes from Washington, Diêm defeated the Bình Xuyên—Sài Gòn–based gangsters who had their own well-organized militia. He also moved against the Cao Đài and the Hòa Hao, which also had armed support.

In 1955 Diêm defied an effort by Bao Đai to remove him from office. He turned the tables by calling for a referendum in which the people would choose between them. Diêm would easily have won any honest contest, but he ignored appeals of U.S. officials and falsified the results so that the announced vote was 98.2 percent in his favor.

On 26 October 1955, using the results of the referendum as justification, Diêm proclaimed the Republic of Vietnam (RVN) with himself as president. Washington recognized him in this position, and its aid was vital in his growing strength. U.S. assistance jumped from $100,000 in 1954 to $325,800,000 in 1955; from 1955 to 1966 Washington provided economic assistance totaling almost $2 billion, not including military equipment. Such aid enabled Diêm to reject talks with Hà Nôi over the elections called for by the Geneva Accords, which the Viêt Minh, confident of electoral victory, so ardently sought.

Diêm spent the vast bulk of Washington's aid on the military. Perhaps three-quarters of U.S. assistance went into the military budget and the remainder into the bureaucracy and transportation. Only modest amounts were set aside for education, health, housing, and community development. Also, most nonmilitary aid stayed in the cities, which held only a minority of the population. U.S. financial assistance freed Diêm from the necessity of carrying out economic reforms or income taxes that would have brought real reform and benefits to the impoverished classes in the cities or in the countryside.

Diêm was out of touch with the peasants in the countryside, and little was done to carry out much-needed land reform. In 1961, 75 percent of the land was owned by 15 percent of the population; by 1962, although slightly more than a million acres of land had been transferred to the peasants, this was less than a quarter of the acreage eligible for expropriation and purchase. Between 1955 and 1960 less than 2 percent of Washington's aid to Sài Gòn went for agrarian reform.

In 1956 Diêm launched his Tô Công (denunciation of Communists) campaign to locate arms caches in the South as well as to arrest hundreds of those in Viêt Minh political cadres who had remained in the South to prepare for the planned national elections, a violation of the Geneva Agreements. But in part, this campaign was retaliation to DRV policies regarding landowners and opposition leaders. Diêm also imprisoned many non-Communist patriots, and he estranged South Vietnam's ethnic minorities. His effort to impose Vietnamese culture on the Montagnards reversed long-standing French policy. The Montagnards also suffered heavily in Diêm's efforts to relocate rural populations into government-controlled areas in the Strategic Hamlet program. This led dissident Montagnards to form the ethnonationalistic movement of FULRO (Le Front Unifié de Lutte des Races Opprimées, or United Struggle Front for Oppressed Races).

Diêm refused to enter into economic talks with the DRV or to hold the elections called for in the Geneva Accords. He announced that his government was not a party to the agreements and thus not bound by them, and the U.S. government supported Diêm in that stand. Both Washington and Sài Gòn claimed that no elections could be held until there was a democratic government in Hà Nôi, although this was not a part of the 1954 agreements.

On 4 March 1956 the South Vietnamese elected a 123-member national legislative assembly; a new constitution, heavily weighted toward control by the executive, came into effect on 26 October 1956. The country was divided into 41 provinces, which were subdivided into districts and villages.

These apparent reforms were largely a sham, as Diêm increasingly subjected the South to authoritarian rule. Diêm completely dominated the National Assembly. The government was also highly centralized. The central administration appointed officials, even those at the local level. Diêm oversaw administrative appointees, and most province chiefs were military officers loyal to him. The Catholic Diêm installed Catholics in key positions; many of them were Catholics from central Vietnam and northerners who had recently come south. Other posts went to his supporters and his friends. Political loyalty rather than ability was the test for positions of leadership in both the government and the military.

The aloof and arrogant Diêm proved an adroit practitioner of the divide-and-rule concept. Rarely did he reach out for advice beyond his immediate family circle (perhaps his closest advisor was his older brother, Bishop Ngô Đình Thuc). Diêm also delegated authority to his brother Ngô Đình Nhu, who controlled the secret police and was the organizer of the Personalist Labor Party (Cân Lao Party).

By 1960 opposition within South Vietnam against Diêm was growing, even in the cities that had benefited most under his regime. In April 1960, 18 prominent South Vietnamese issued a manifesto protesting governmental abuses. They were promptly arrested. On 11–12 November 1960 there was a near-coup when paratroop units surrounded the presidential palace and demanded that Diêm purge his administration of certain individuals, including his brother Nhu. Although Diêm outmaneuvered the protesters, clearly time was running out for his regime. On 27 February 1962 there was another coup attempt when two Vietnamese Air Force pilots tried to kill Diêm and his brother Nhu by bombing and strafing the presidential palace.

Dozens of Diêm's political opponents disappeared and thousands more languished in prison camps. Then, in December 1960 the National Liberation Front for South Vietnam was officially established with Hà Nôi's blessing. It came to be completely dominated by the Lao Đông Party (the renamed Communist Party) Central Committee of the Democratic Republic of Vietnam.

Washington was now having second thoughts about Diêm. When President John F. Kennedy took office, he demanded that Diêm institute domestic reforms. But there seemed to be no alternative to Diêm's rule, and Kennedy expanded the U.S. Special Forces presence in that country. In May 1961 Kennedy sent Vice-President Lyndon Johnson to the RVN on a fact-finding mission. Although Johnson had private reservations concerning Diêm, he publicly hailed him as the "Winston Churchill of Southeast Asia." Less than a week after Johnson's return to Washington, Kennedy agreed to increase the size of the Army of the Republic of Vietnam (ARVN) from 170,000 to 270,000 men. These troops tended to be poorly trained in guerrilla warfare, indifferently led, and inadequately provided for.

With ARVN generally performing poorly in the field, in 1962 Washington dramatically increased the U.S. military presence in the RVN. Only belatedly did U.S. officials seek to address problems through a counterinsurgency program. In 1961, with strong U.S. backing, Diêm began the Strategic Hamlet program. Run by Nhu, it forcibly resettled peasants into new fenced and armed compounds, supposedly to provide health and education advantages as well as protection from the Viêt Công. Riddled with corruption, the program was a vast and expensive failure and soon alienated much of the peasantry from the regime.

Madame Ngô Đình Nhu, who acted as the first lady of the state (Diêm was celibate), embarked on her own bizarre puritanical campaign that outlawed divorce, dancing, beauty contests, boxing, gambling, fortune-telling, prostitution, adultery, and even certain music. The harsh punishments for violations of these new rules further antagonized elements of the population.

In January 1963 ARVN suffered a stinging military defeat in the Battle of Âp Bắc. That summer, Buddhist protests and rallies became more frequent and intense. On 8 May, Buddha's 2,527th birthday, in Huê thousands demonstrated against a ban imposed on flying their multicolored flag; riot police killed nine demonstrators, and this led to Buddhist demonstrations throughout the country. In June elderly Buddhist monk Thích Quang Đức publicly burned himself alive in protest. By November six more monks had emulated Thích Quang Đức. Madame Nhu exacerbated the crisis by referring to these self-immolations as "barbecues."

Many Americans now came to believe that Diêm should be ousted. Nhu was particularly embarrassing to Washington. He was responsible for the August 1963 raids on Buddhist pagodas that damaged many of them and led to the arrest of over 1,400 Buddhists.

In August Henry Cabot Lodge replaced Frederick Nolting as U.S. ambassador to Sài Gòn. The U.S. Central Intelligence Agency (CIA) had already reported that an influential faction of South Vietnamese generals wanted to overthrow Diêm. Lodge gave this new credence. Washington was initially opposed to a coup, preferring that Diêm purge his entourage, especially the Nhus. But it was clear that to insist on this would alert Nhu and probably result in a bloodbath, since Nhu had troops loyal to him in the capital. At the end of August Washington assured the generals of its support and President Kennedy, in the course of a television interview, publicly criticized Diêm.

Following some of the worst government outrages against the Buddhists, on 2 October Washington suspended economic subsidies for RVN commercial imports, froze loans for developmental projects, and cut off financial support of Nhu's 2,000-man Vietnamese Special Forces. This action was a clear signal to the dissidents.

Shortly after midnight on 1 November 1963 Major Generals Dương Văn Minh, Tôn Thât Đính, and Trân Văn Đôn began a takeover of power. In the coup, both Diêm and Nhu, whom Washington assumed would be given safe passage out of the country, were murdered.

Diêm's death began a period of political instability in the RVN government. Washington never could find a worthy successor to him. No subsequent leader of the RVN had his air of legitimacy or as much respect from the general public, and economically and socially, except for the confusion at the beginning of his rule, life had never been better for the South Vietnamese than under Diêm. He was a fervent patriot who strongly defended morality and social order. He was also greatly interested in improving the economy and did succeed in reforming the bureaucracy.

U.S. leaders, who had seen in Diêm a nationalist alternative to Hô Chí Minh and means to stop Communist expansion, soon found themselves taking direct control of the war in Vietnam. The United States, which could not win the war with Diêm, also could not win the war without him.

Diêm was followed by a military junta led by General Dương Văn Minh as chief of state. The new regime was no more responsive to the people of South Vietnam and indeed brought political instability. Members of the new 12-member Military Revolutionary Council fell to quarreling among themselves. Minh had boasted that the collective leadership would ensure that no one else would have Diêm's power. But Minh, the nominal leader, showed no inclination to govern, preferring to play tennis, tend to his orchids, and pursue an interest in exotic birds.

On 30 January 1964 there was another coup, this time against Minh, led by 37-year-old Maj. Gen. Nguyên Khánh. U.S. officials, caught by surprise, promptly hailed Khánh as the new leader because he promised to rule with a strong hand. However, although shrewd and energetic, Khánh showed no more aptitude for governing than had Minh. Khánh's own history of changing sides hardly engendered trust.

Khánh purged some generals, although he allowed Minh to remain on as titular head of state. Khánh's aides also arranged the execution of Maj. Nguyên Văn Nhung, who had worked for Minh and was one of those responsible for the murder of Diêm. Militant Buddhists, alarmed that Khánh's victory might lead to a return to power of Catholics and those faithful to Diêm, were again active. To increase their influence, the heads of various Buddhist sects agreed to form a political alliance. Many ARVN officers also turned against Khánh for his attempt to try rival Generals Trân Văn Đôn and Lê Văn Kim on fabricated charges.

Khánh sought to resurrect the Đai Viêt Quôc Gia Liên Minh nationalist party and manipulate it to his advantage. He persuaded Đai Viêt leader and Catholic physician Dr. Nguyên Tôn Hoàn to return from exile in Paris to serve as premier. Khánh hoped to play the Đai Viêt against other parties. When it was clear that the Đai Viêt was hopelessly splintered, Khánh named himself as premier with Hoàn as his deputy. Hoàn then began to conspire with the Buddhists and other opposition groups against Khánh. Political instability in the RVN was now rampant, and that year there were seven changes of government. As RVN governments rose and fell, nothing alarmed the Americans as much as the possibility that one of them might enter into accommodation with the Communists.

Hà Nôi, meanwhile, followed the political instability in the South with keen interest. At the end of 1963 the DRV leadership decided that the time was ripe to escalate sharply its support for the war in the South. In a major shift in policy requiring considerable economic sacrifices, the DRV decided to send native northerners south to fight, to introduce the latest models of Communist small arms, and to authorize direct attacks against Americans in the South.

The war was escalating. In March 1964 Secretary of Defense Robert McNamara visited the RVN and vowed U.S. support for Khánh. McNamara barnstormed the country, describing Khánh in memorized Vietnamese as the country's "best possible leader." On his return to the United States, McNamara publicly pronounced improvement in the RVN, but privately he told President Johnson that conditions had deteriorated since his last visit there and that 40 percent of the countryside was now under Viêt Công control or influence. Washington agreed to furnish Khánh with additional aid. But although more than $2 million a day was arriving in the country, little of it went to public works projects or

reached the peasants. Khánh, despite promises to McNamara to put the country on "a war footing," steadfastly refused to do so, fearful of antagonizing wealthy and middle-class city dwellers, whose sons would be inducted into the army. In August 1964 came the Tonkin Gulf incidents with the U.S. Congress giving President Johnson special powers to wage war in Southeast Asia.

By summer 1964 Khánh was in serious difficulty and pleading for major action against the DRV as a distraction from his domestic political difficulties. U.S. air strikes following the Tonkin Gulf incidents seem to have energized him. He announced a state of emergency and imposed censorship and other controls. He also hastily put together a new constitution for the RVN, promoting himself to the presidency and dismissing former figurehead chief of state Dương Văn Minh.

Sài Gòn responded with protests. In August students took to the streets and were soon joined by Buddhists, who complained that too many Diêm supporters were in key positions. Khánh met with Buddhist leaders, but revealed his real strength by telling them that he would discuss their complaints with U.S. Ambassador Maxwell Taylor. Taylor in turn urged Khánh not to yield to minority pressure. On 25 August when thousands of demonstrators gathered outside his office to demand his resignation, Khánh bravely appeared before them and announced he did not plan to establish a dictatorship. That afternoon, however, he quit and the Military Revolutionary Council met to choose a new head of state.

After lengthy political maneuvering, a triumvirate emerged of Generals Khánh, Minh, and Trân Thiên Khiêm. Khánh retained the premiership, but flew off to Đà Lat as chaos took over in the capital. Order was restored only after two days of rioting. Khánh, meanwhile, named Harvard-educated economist Nguyên Xuân Oánh to be prime minister in his absence. Turbulence continued as the government was threatened by dissident army units in the Mekong Delta and militant Buddhists from Huê. Buddhist demands had grown to include a veto over government decisions.

In November there were new riots in Sài Gòn protesting Khánh's rule, and Ambassador Taylor urged him to leave the country. By this time, a faction of younger military officers had come to the fore. Known as the "Young Turks," they were headed by Nguyên Cao Kỳ, one of the younger officers in the coup against Diêm, who had been promoted to major general and given charge of the Republic of Vietnam Air Force (VNAF). The faction also included army Maj. Gen. Nguyên Văn Thiêu. Disillusioned by the ineffective national government, in mid-December 1964 the Young Turks overthrew the Military Revolutionary Council of older officers.

In late January 1965 a new Armed Forces Council decided that Premier Trân Văn Hương should be ousted. Khánh replaced him as premier, but in February General Lâm Văn Phát ousted Khánh. On 17 February Dr. Phan Huy Quát became premier with Phan Khăc Sửu as chief of state. Quát, a physician with considerable governmental experience, appointed a broadly representative cabinet. The Armed Forces Council also announced the formation of a 20-member National Legislative Council.

That same month, after Communist attacks that specifically targeted U.S. military personnel, President Johnson authorized retaliatory bombings of the DRV. Operation ROLLING THUNDER, the sustained bombing of North Vietnam, began on 24 February.

On 11 June 1965 the RVN government collapsed and the Armed Forces Council chose a military government with Kỳ as premier and Nguyên Văn Thiêu in the relatively powerless position of chief of state. It was the ninth government in less than two years. Kỳ took steps to strengthen the armed forces. He also instituted needed land reforms, programs for the construction of schools and hospitals, and price controls. His government also launched a much-touted campaign to remove corrupt officials. At the same time, however, Kỳ instituted a number of unpopular repressive actions, including a ban on newspapers.

In March 1965 U.S. Marine battalions—the first U.S. combat troops—had arrived in South Vietnam to defend the Đà Nẵng airfield. U.S. Army divisions soon followed. By the end of 1965 there were nearly 200,000 U.S. military personnel in South Vietnam.

The new government was soon embroiled in controversy with the Buddhists and powerful ARVN I Corps commander General Nguyên Chánh Thi, one of the members of the ten-member National Leadership Committee; the other nine members sought to remove him from his post. In March 1966 workers in Đà Nẵng began a general strike, and Buddhist students in Huê also began protests. Soon Thi's removal was no longer the central issue as Buddhist leaders pushed for a complete change of government. With it evident that there was growing sympathy for the movement among the civil service and many ARVN units, in early April Kỳ announced that the Communists had "taken over" in Đà Nẵng. In fact, it is unclear what role, if any, they played.

On 10 April Kỳ appointed General Tôn Thất Đính as the new commander of I Corps, but Đính could not assert his authority with Thi still in Huê. After a significant military operation to suppress the Buddhists and rebel ARVN units, Thi accepted his dismissal on 24 May and went into exile in the United States. Tensions also eased with Buddhist leaders when Kỳ agreed to dissolve the junta and hold elections for an assembly with constituent powers. In June, supported by U.S. forces, Kỳ's troops ended opposition in Huê.

Kỳ's popularity and political clout had also been enhanced by a February 1966 meeting with President Lyndon Johnson in Hawaii. The two delegations agreed on the need for social and economic reforms in the RVN and national elections. In May a government decree set up a committee to draft election laws and procedures. In September 1966 a 117-member constituent assembly was elected. It met in Sài Gòn the next month to begin drafting a constitution, which was completed in March 1967. The new constitution provided for a president who had wide powers and a premier and cabinet responsible to a bicameral legislature (the new upper house was commonly referred to as the Senate) with strengthened authority. The judiciary was also to be coequal to the executive and legislative branches. The president would serve a four-year term and could stand for reelection once. The president still had wide powers, including command of the armed forces and the ability to promulgate laws and initiate legislation. The two-house legislature was to be chosen by universal suffrage and secret ballot.

Local elections were held in May 1967 with elections for the Lower House in October. The constitution allowed for political parties, but it specifically forbade those promoting communism "in any form." Unfortunately, the complex electoral law involved the use of ten-member lists, and voters in 1967 had to choose from 48 such slates, a process that favored well-organized voting blocks.

Tensions were high between Kỳ and Thiêu. At first the two men got along fairly well, but then both openly vied for control of the government. Kỳ was later sharply critical of Thiêu, who he said "wanted power and glory but not to have to do the dirty work." Although the more senior Thiêu had stepped aside in 1965 to allow Kỳ to take the premier's post, his determination to challenge Kỳ for the highest office in the 3 September 1967 elections led the Armed Forces Council to force the two men onto a joint ticket, giving the presidential nomination to Thiêu and the vice-presidential nomination to Kỳ simply on the basis of military seniority. The Thiêu-Kỳ ticket won the election with only 34.8 percent of the vote; the remaining vote was split among ten other slates.

Thiêu gradually consolidated power. As with his predecessors, he ruled in authoritarian fashion. He was, however, more responsive to the Buddhists, Montagnards, and peasants. He arranged for distribution of land to some 50,000 families, and by 1968 he had secured passage of laws that froze rents and forbade landowners from evicting tenants. Thiêu also restored local elections. By 1969, 95 percent of villages under RVN control had elected chiefs and councils. Village chiefs also received control over the local Popular Forces (PFs) and some central government financial support.

After the United States began the withdrawal of its forces in 1969, Thiêu was faced with the challenge of replacing U.S. military units. In 1970 he mobilized many high school and college students for the war effort. This brought considerable opposition, which in turn led to arrests and trials. Increases in the numbers of draftees and in taxes produced a surge of support for the Communists.

On 26 March 1971 Thiêu presented land to 20,000 people in an impressive ceremony in accordance with passage of the Land-to-Tiller Act, which turned over land to those who worked it. This reduced tenancy to only 7 percent. The government took responsibility to compensate former landowners for the confiscated land.

In 1971 Thiêu pushed through a new election law that had the practical effect of disqualifying his major opponents, Kỳ and Dương Văn Minh. It required that candidates obtain the support of at least 40 national assembly members or 100 provincial/municipal councilors. Opposition groups argued that the purpose of the new law was to exclude them from political power. The Senate rejected the law, but it was reinstated by the Lower House, the result of bribery and intimidation.

Although the Supreme Court ruled that Kỳ, who had charged Thiêu's government with corruption, might run, he chose not to do so. Dương Văn Minh, the other chief candidate, also dropped out. Thiêu's reelection in October 1971 made one-man rule a reality and did serious injury to the RVN government's image abroad.

In October 1972 Thiêu announced his opposition to the agreement negotiated in Paris by the DRV and the United States and torpedoed it. Following massive bombing of the North, in January 1973 Hà Nôi and Washington then concluded a new agreement, which was this time imposed on Sài Gòn. The last American combat troops left South Vietnam at the end of March. Vietnamization imposed severe hardships on the RVN. Although the United States turned over massive amounts of equipment to the RVN, Congress curtailed funding. This severely reduced the ability of South Vietnamese forces to fight the high-technology war for which they had been trained.

In January 1974 Thiêu announced the renewal of the war. In August under increasing pressure over Watergate and his handling of the war, Richard Nixon resigned the presidency and the RVN lost its most ardent supporter. In January 1975 the Communists began a major offensive in the Central Highlands. Years of warfare and corruption and the loss of U.S. support all sapped the will of the South Vietnamese to resist. Thiêu's response to this was at best poor, and his precipitous abandonment of the Central Highlands was a disaster. Kỳ later charged that Thiêu turned a tactical withdrawal into a rout that led to the eventual disintegration of the entire RVN military. ARVN resistance now collapsed, and, with Communist forces closing in the capital, on 25 April Thiêu departed the country for Taiwan. Three days later, Vice-President Trân Văn Hưởng transferred authority as chief of state to General Dưởng Văn Minh. On 30 April Communist forces captured Sài Gòn. Minh formally surrendered to Col. Bùi Tín, the highest officer of the Communist forces. The Communists now occupied Đôc Lâp Palace, and the Republic of Vietnam came to an end.

—Spencer C. Tucker

References: Herring, George C. *America's Longest War: The United States and Vietnam, 1950–1975.* 2d ed. New York: Alfred A. Knopf, 1986.
Karnow, Stanley. *Vietnam: A History.* New York: Viking Press, 1983.
Nguyên Cao Kỳ. *Twenty Years and Twenty Days.* New York: Stein & Day, 1976.
Spector, Ronald H. *Advice and Support: The Early Years, 1941–1960. The U.S. Army in Vietnam.* Washington, DC: U.S. Army Center of Military History, 1983.
See also: Bao Đai; Bình Xuyên; Cao Đài; Caravelle Group; Đai Viêt Quôc Dân Đang (National Party of Greater Vietnam); Dulles, John Foster; Dưởng Văn Minh; Eisenhower, Dwight David; Elections (National), Republic of Vietnam: 1955, 1967, 1971; FULRO (Le Front Unifié de Lutte des Races Opprimées); Hòa Hao; Honolulu Conference; Johnson, Lyndon Baines; Kennedy, John Fitzgerald; Lodge, Henry Cabot, Jr.; McNamara, Robert S.; Military Revolutionary Council; National Assembly Law 10/59; Ngô Đình Diêm; Ngô Đình Diêm, Overthrow of; Ngô Đình Nhu; Nguyên Chánh Thi; Nguyên Khánh; Nguyên Văn Hinh; Nguyên Văn Thiêu; Nixon, Richard Milhous; Nolting, Frederick, Jr.; Phan Khăc Sửu; ROLLING THUNDER, Operation; Strategic Hamlet Program; Taylor, Maxwell Davenport; Territorial Forces; Thích Quang Đức; Tôn Thât Đình; Tonkin Gulf Incidents; Trân Thiên Khiêm; Trân Văn Đôn; Trân Văn Hưởng; United States: Special Forces.

Vietnam, Republic of: Air Force (VNAF)

Despite its own efforts and the support of its sponsors, the Republic of Vietnam Air Force (VNAF) (1955–1975) failed to develop into an independent, war-winning organization.

Prior to 1964 the VNAF was a small and neglected organization. It received its first consignment of American-built aircraft from France in the summer of 1955. The released items included 28 F-8F fighter-bombers, 35 C-47 transport aircraft, and 60 L-19 reconnaissance aircraft. Three years later, the United States replaced the already obsolescent F-8F with a combat version of the propeller-driven T-28 trainer. The American AD-6 fighter-bomber subsequently complemented the T-28, and by the end of 1962 the VNAF had one squadron each of AD-6s and T-28A/Bs, three L-19 liaison squadrons of 15 aircraft each, and a number of C-47s. These aircraft performed tactical infantry support missions that included airlift operations, artillery spotting, close air support (CAS), interdiction, medical evacuation, and reconnaissance.

There were multiple reasons why the VNAF performed badly prior to 1964. First, there were less than a dozen fully qualified flight leaders in the Air Force, and even they were unmotivated and unreliable. They showed, for example, an obvious distaste for night combat, all-weather operations, and deployments away from the comforts of home. Second, the Vietnamese had an unresponsive command and control system. Before a pilot could attack a ground target, he had to get permission from the province chief, regional commander, Joint General Staff, and perhaps even President Ngô Đình Diêm himself. As a result, the government's fear of civilian casualties made real-time tactical air support against fast-moving guerrilla units almost impossible. Third, ground commanders did not appreciate the value of airpower, even in unconventional warfare. They seldom asked the VNAF to protect ground convoys, escort helicopter assault operations, or fly more CAS and interdiction missions on their behalf. Lastly, logistics and maintenance support remained a chronic problem. In mid-1962 available aircraft averaged, for example, seven AD-6s, 11 T-28s, and 11 L-19s. There were, therefore, too many missions for the number of aircraft available, and it remained an open question whether the relatively untrained Vietnamese pilots, flying only in daylight (and with broken instruments), had any idea of how to combat their foe.

With the upsurge of Viêt Công activity in 1963 and 1964 and the introduction of North Vietnamese regulars into combat in 1965, the VNAF expanded in size and responsibilities. In 1964 it had 8,400 men and 190 aircraft. It also had 248 helicopters and 140 aircraft on loan from the United States, although there were restrictions on their use. During the same year, the durable A-1 "Skyhawk" replaced the increasingly ineffectual T-28. By 1965 the South Vietnamese had 150 A-1s, which quickly became the backbone of the VNAF. The air arm continued to grow. By 1968 it had 16,000 men, 398 aircraft (including the A-37 "Dragonfly" and C-130 "Hercules"), and its first squadron of compact F-5 "Freedom Fighter" jets.

With increased size also came more responsibilities. Although the United States and Republic of Vietnam first conducted joint air operations in December 1961, they became a formal requirement in Operation ROLLING THUNDER between 1965 and 1968. In February 1965 Washington and Sài Gòn agreed to conduct a limited bombing campaign against the Democratic Republic of Vietnam (DRV), starting with inconsequential targets below the 19th parallel. The motive was simple—President Lyndon Johnson's administration hoped that a limited air campaign would convince the DRV to stop aiding and abetting the guerrilla campaigns in Laos and the Republic of Vietnam. The campaign began on 2 March 1965 when 104 American aircraft attacked DRV targets while 19 South Vietnamese fighter-bombers struck the naval facilities at Quân Khê. This initial strike began a limited (but significant) contribution by the VNAF to Operation ROLLING THUNDER. The VNAF provided a minimum of three strike/reconnaissance missions for each of the on-again, off-again periods of the campaign. The contribution would have been larger if not for the growing number of missions required in the South. By mid-1968 the VNAF was responsible for 25 percent of all combat sorties flown within its borders.

Thus from 1964 to 1968 the role of the VNAF did grow, but the organization still had problems. Although the VNAF had 550 pilots by 1967, finding qualified, English-speaking recruits remained a problem. Second, high accident rates only aggravated existing repair and maintenance problems, particularly because the VNAF relied on the army for most of its supplies. Third, the command and control system had simplified, but now Air Force units responded only to orders from VNAF Headquarters in Sài Gòn. Lastly, and because U.S. units had their own equipment to replenish, the Vietnamese remained woefully short of new and improved helicopters and aircraft. In 1968, for example, the VNAF received only eight new UH-1H "Huey" helicopters from the United States. As a result of all these problems, the performance of VNAF units was irregular during the climactic 1968 Têt Offensive.

Vietnamization dominated the last phase of the Vietnam War and with it came Project ENHANCE, a crash program by the United States to provide the VNAF enough resources to fight by itself. From a numerical standpoint, the results were impressive. By the time of the American withdrawal in 1972, the VNAF had a $542.8 million budget, 49,454 personnel, 39 operational squadrons (including 16 fighter/fighter-bomber units), and 27 squadrons either in training or scheduled for activation.

Nevertheless, in 1975 when the final DRV offensive came against the South, much of the VNAF simply melted away. The reasons for its failure were fourfold. First, even after 20 years, the Air Force's supply system remained chaotic and unreliable. Second, in 1974 and 1975 the U.S. Congress tightened its purse strings. The VNAF now had to scramble for critical spare parts and fuels, supplies of which had only filled the gaps left after the DRV's 1972 Easter Offensive. Third, North Vietnamese units introduced handheld SA-7 surface-to-air missiles in the South. As a result, CAS, airmobile, and interdiction missions became more hazardous and significantly less effective. Lastly, the United States did build up the VNAF, but only with low-performance, short-range aircraft that had no electronic warfare equipment or sophisticated fire-control systems. These aircraft were ideal for low-intensity warfare, but not for the largely conventional war that they then faced.

—Peter R. Faber

References: Clarke, Jeffrey J. *Advice and Support: The Final Years, 1965–1973.* Washington, DC: U.S. Government Printing Office, 1988.
Futrell, Robert F. *The United States Air Force in Southeast Asia: The Advisory Years to 1965.* Washington, DC: U.S. Government Printing Office, 1981.

See also: Air Power, Role in War; Airplanes, Allied and Democratic Republic of Vietnam; Hô Chí Minh Campaign; Ngô Đình Diêm; Order of Battle; ROLLING THUNDER, Operation; Vietnamization.

Vietnam, Republic of: Army (ARVN)

Successor to the French-led Vietnamese National Army (VNA) of the Indo-China War, the Army of the Republic of Vietnam (ARVN) grew from an initial VNA strength of 150,000 in 1950 to nearly 1 million troops at the time of its collapse in 1975. Suffering from corruption, poor leadership, and low morale throughout its existence, the ARVN never achieved the mobility and combat cohesion required to counter its better-motivated Viêt Công (VC) and People's Army of Vietnam (PAVN) opponents. As a result, it suffered defeats in most of its engagements against the VC and could defeat PAVN units only when supported by massive U.S. firepower. Still, many of its best units were outstanding, proving the military maxim that well-led and well-trained troops will nearly always perform effectively in combat. Unfortunately for the Republic of Vietnam (RVN), its army as a whole enjoyed neither effective leadership nor thorough training.

ARVN traced its roots to November 1949, when the French government and Vietnamese Emperor Bao Đai signed a formal agreement to establish a Vietnamese National Army to resist the Communist-dominated Viêt Minh, who were fighting to drive the French from Indo-China. Four divisions were to be formed by the end of 1952, but recruitment was slow. Very few Vietnamese recognized Bao Đai's authority, and most were ambivalent about his government, which they believed was controlled by the French. Another inhibiting factor for the Vietnamese was the degree of French control over the VNA; most of its early combat formations were led by French officers and noncommissioned officers (NCOs). The French were also reluctant to provide the VNA with modern equipment, instead turning over weapons procured for their own pre–World War II army. Weapons and transportation assets given to the VNA were obsolete and in very poor condition, not a policy upon which to build an effective army.

The fourth VNA division was not raised until just before the French defeat in 1954. The French had established a training school system in the interim, so the initial development of a professional NCO corps and technical services had begun. However, the French took the instructors and most of the technicians with them when they left Indo-China. Their departure left the State of Vietnam with an army of four indifferently trained divisions and an inexperienced NCO corps led by a very small and generally corrupt cadre of Vietnamese officers. Worse, the training system was poorly staffed, inadequately funded, and oriented toward the training of officers. Plans to raise three more divisions by 1958 were scrapped.

The Americans took over on the French departure. Their combat tactics, doctrine, and philosophy were radically different from that of the French. Whereas the French had preferred to await developments and then maneuver to force their enemy to attack, the Americans preached a more aggressive, firepower-based approach to war. Material superiority and logistics were the key. The Americans did not alter the French-based training school system,

A member of the Republic of Vietnam Army's (ARVN's) 7th Division leads a blinded comrade. Suffering from poor leadership, low morale, and corruption throughout its existence, the ARVN never achieved the mobility and combat cohesion required to counter its better-motivated Việt Công and People's Army of Vietnam opponents.

but did work hard to model the ARVN after the U.S. Army and in the process generously provided both weapons and advisors. The initial training of the troops and NCOs was left as before and the provision of unit transport was considered a Vietnamese government responsibility. The result was an army the units of which had good firepower and were well advised, but lacked the mobility and command and control to employ their equipment effectively.

The ARVN's most debilitating deficiency, however, was the pervasive corruption—much of it due to the promotion system used by President Ngô Đình Diêm's government—that infected the ARVN leadership and handicapped its logistics structure. The Diêm government, which replaced the Bao Đai regime in 1955, ruled Vietnam by a combination of oppression and patronage. This extended to the Army, where senior leadership positions were awarded on the basis of social position and loyalty to the regime rather than integrity and ability. This resulted in a force comprised of more than 60 percent Buddhists (as were most Vietnamese) led by a senior officer corps that was almost entirely Catholic (as was Diêm).

This had its most serious impact on the logistics and technical services, where senior officers operated their units to their own personal financial benefit. These officers achieved and retained

their positions, not by providing efficient support to units in the field but rather by sharing their "bounty" with their superiors and sponsors. Combat leaders also practiced a form of corruption based on overreporting the strength of their units and pocketing the surplus pay. Many units, especially in the Popular Forces, were therefore much smaller than their establishment. Finally, ARVN soldiers were very poorly paid and had to buy their own rations. Given that a private's pay in 1964 barely paid for a month's rice, it is no wonder that small-scale pilferage and looting was endemic to the Army. The United States started correcting these problems in 1964, but despite much progress under the Vietnamization program, corruption was never eliminated.

The ARVN's last ten years were marked by an intensive U.S. training program concentrated on junior officers and NCOs. Units that performed well in operations received newer equipment and training. Helicopters were provided to decrease dependence on roads. Logistics and technical service units also received greater training and emphasis. Unfortunately, this had two negative effects. The first was that it exacerbated divisions within the officer ranks. The junior officers were trained in American tactics and procedures, while senior officers remained welded to French traditions. This resulted in the senior officers not understanding staff plans or intentions. Nor did they comprehend their subordinate units' requirements or activities. Worse, these senior officers tried to run their units from deep in the rear, feeling no need to observe the situation at the front. Junior commanders believed that their seniors were out of touch with the actual situations on the ground. This distrust and division over operations would have fatal consequences in 1975.

The second negative effect was that the ARVN became dependent upon U.S. support. Where the French had taught units to repair their equipment and parts themselves, the Americans taught them to identify the defective part and replace it with one acquired from the logistics system. Although faster than before, it also relied totally upon American largesse. As U.S. support ebbed, the ARVN had growing inventories of unserviceable equipment that the logistics services could do little to reduce. Many units entered combat with only a portion of their assigned equipment in operating order. This had disastrous effects during the 1975 PAVN offensive.

At its peak, ARVN numbered nearly 1 million troops organized into three echelons. The first and best were the 450,000 troops of the regular army. They were organized in formations of 13 divisions, seven Ranger groups, and various independent elite battalions and regiments. Nearly 200,000 regulars were also assigned to support units. ARVN's second echelon was its Regional Forces. These were assigned to the Military Region Commanders, of which there were four. The third and final echelon was made up of the Popular Forces, which were the ARVN's least trained and equipped units. In rural areas they came under the control of village councils and provided security for particular villages. They also provided security for cities, installations, and key provincial facilities. Regional and Popular Forces (known to American GIs as the "Ruff-Puffs") totaled nearly 525,000 troops. The Civilian Irregular Defense Group (CIDG) rounded out the Vietnamese armed forces but were not part of the ARVN. Rather they were part-time soldiers who defended their villages and towns or augmented the Popular and Regional Forces in doing so.

In 1975 most Vietnamese and senior American leadership took an optimistic view of the ARVN. It had seemingly stood up well against the PAVN 1972 Easter Offensive. The ARVN's almost desperate reliance on American airpower in that offensive was overlooked. As PAVN pressure built in the spring of 1975, President Nguyên Văn Thiêu's intended strategic realignment of his

South Vietnamese soldiers make a parachute assault from U.S. Air Force C-123 transports.

An Army of the Republic of Vietnam patrol discovers a Communist outpost with an improvised bulletin board in Tân Phước. The patrol ripped the posters and signs from the board before continuing their search for Viêt Công rebels.

forces seemed a simple expedient to halt what appeared to be a limited PAVN offensive in the Central Highlands. However, following the French tradition in which they had been trained, neither Thiêu nor his staff, corps, and division commanders involved had studied the ground or roads over which the units would move. Thus, as refugees and overloaded military vehicles crammed onto the overloaded road system, units became bunched up. Many officers simply left their units. PAVN forces had only to press their attack and unit cohesion broke down. Only elite Ranger and Airborne units stood their ground, paying a heavy price in the process. Seven regular ARVN divisions melted away. Despite much desperate rallying and troop movements, the situation could not be saved.

ARVN never had the consistent leadership and direction required in an effective combat force. Its best junior NCO and officer leadership was siphoned off into elite units that were used as "fire brigades" to shore up battered positions or hold key locations and terrain. Thus, regular ARVN units suffered from uneven leadership at the junior officer and NCO level. This was exacerbated by failings in the senior leadership. Generally troops were squandered in wasteful tactics or ineffective deployments. Although the ARVN had an abysmal reputation with its opponents and allies, it would be unfair to characterize it as a uniformly poor army. Its units stood alone for two years against a better-equipped, better-trained, and more highly motivated force. Its better performances and sacrifices are often overlooked in its overall defeat.

—Carl O. Schuster

References: Davidson, Phillip B. *Vietnam at War: The History, 1946–1975.* Oxford, UK: Oxford University Press, 1988.
Momeyer, William W. *Airpower in Three Wars.* Washington, DC: U.S. Government Printing Office, 1978.
Ngo Quang Truong. *The Easter Offensive of 1972.* Indochina Monographs. Washington, DC: U.S. Army Center of Military History, 1980.
Pike, Douglas. *PAVN: People's Army of Vietnam.* Novato, CA: Presidio Press, 1986.
See also: Civilian Irregular Defense Group (CIDG); Ngô Đình Diêm; Nguyên Văn Thiêu; Order of Battle; Territorial Forces; Vietnam, Republic of: Marine Corps (VNMC); Vietnam, Republic of: Special Forces (Lực Lường Đặc Biêt [LLDB]); Vietnamization.

Vietnam, Republic of: Commandos

South Vietnamese military formations that entered North Vietnam (1961–1968) to gather intelligence, conduct sabotage, and disrupt infiltration into the South. The commando program was run by the U.S. government and Central Intelligence Agency (CIA). From 1961 to 1968 more than 50 commando teams were sent into North Vietnam by sea and by air. Democratic Republic of Vietnam (DRV) authorities were routinely notified of these activities and were able to capture most of the commandos immediately. Reportedly every member of these teams was either captured or killed, or disappeared. The longest evasion was by Quach Tom, who managed to avoid capture for nearly three months. By the end of the Vietnam War in 1975 more than 300 commandos still languished in DRV prisons.

To compound the tragedy for the program's participants, documents declassified in 1996 revealed that the U.S. government had lied to the families of the commandos by declaring all of them dead and paying their "widows" $50 gratuities. Sedgwick Tourison, a former Defense Intelligence Agency analyst who has written about the commandos, has identified some 360 survivors.

John C. Mattes, Quach Tom's lawyer, sued in federal court on behalf of the commandos and lobbied Congress and President Bill Clinton for legislation to provide compensation. Congressional hearings were held in 1996 and Senators John Kerry (D-Massachusetts) and Bob Kerrey (D-Nebraska) introduced legislation to provide some $20 million to the former commandos, about $40,000 each.

—Spencer C. Tucker

Reference: Tourison, Sedgwick D. *Project Alpha: Washington's Secret Military Operations in North Vietnam.* New York: St. Martin's Press, 1997.
See also: Central Intelligence Agency (CIA); Clinton, William Jefferson; Kerry, John Forbes; Operation Plan 34A (OPLAN 34A); Quach Tom.

Vietnam, Republic of: Đà Lat Military Academy

Republic of Vietnam (RVN) military academy, first established in December 1948 as the Officers School of Vietnam at Đâp Đá in Huê after the proclamation of the State of Vietnam. After two classes, in 1950 the school moved to Đà Lat with the name of Combined-Arms Military School.

Under the State of Vietnam, the school graduated 11 classes. After the declaration of the Republic of Vietnam by President Ngô Đình Diêm in 1955, the school was reformed with new curriculum, beginning with Class 12 in late 1955. The concept of "combined arms" was to train cadets as platoon leaders but with a general knowledge of all combat arms (artillery, armor, and engineer, including vehicle repair).

In 1960 the school was renamed the Military Academy of Vietnam (VNMA), and a new facility was built near the old installation. Its curriculum and military ceremonies combined those of West Point, St. Cyr, and the traditions of Vietnam.

During the war, the VNMA provided ARVN units with excellent officers. Up to 30 April 1975 the VNMA graduated 29 classes, totaling more than 6,500 officers. Classes 30 and 31 were still in training when the RVN collapsed.

—Nguyên Công Luân (Lư Tuân)

See also: Vietnam, Republic of: Army (ARVN).

Vietnam, Republic of: Marine Corps (VNMC)

The Vietnamese Marine Corps began in the latter period of French control in Indo-China. On 13 October 1954 President Ngô Đình Diêm signed a government decree creating within the naval establishment a corps of infantry to be designated the Marine Corps (VNMC). In 1955 the Vietnamese Naval Forces passed from French to Vietnamese command. Although French in origin, all further evolution of the VNMC was in cooperation with the U.S. Marine Corps (USMC).

In 1954 U.S. Marine Lt. Col. Victor Croizat became the first senior U.S. advisor to the VNMC. The first Vietnamese Marines were formed from colonial-era commandos who came south when Vietnam was partitioned by the 1954 Geneva Accords. USMC advisory efforts permeated every aspect of VNMC training—force expansion, logistics, and field operations. Under U.S. tutelage the VNMC increased its size from 1,150 marines when Croizat arrived to a corps of nine infantry battalions, three artillery battalions, and supporting units.

During the Vietnam War, the VNMC earned a solid reputation as a fighting force, particularly compared to the regular Army of the Republic of Vietnam (ARVN). The VNMC, along with Ranger and Airborne units, constituted Sài Gòn's elite national reserve, deployed to exploit battlefield successes and redress emergency situations.

The VNMC fought throughout the national area of South Vietnam, from anti-infiltration duties in the Mekong Delta to waging conventional war against North Vietnamese forces along the Demilitarized Zone (DMZ). The VNMC participated in the recapture of Huê during the 1968 Têt Offensive and in the 1970 invasion of Cambodia. During the 1972 invasion of Laos, VNMC units took on the difficult task of blunting the People's Army of Vietnam (PAVN) counterattack that had forced regular ARVN units to abandon their firebases on the drive to Tchépone.

During the 1972 Easter Offensive, it was the severely outnumbered Vietnamese Marines who fought most effectively against 45,000 invading PAVN troops reinforced with Soviet tanks, surface-to-air missiles (SAMs), antiaircraft weapons, and long-range artillery. Fighting with their USMC advisors after almost all U.S. forces had left Vietnam, VNMC units were instrumental in defeating this major PAVN drive to break the vital Quang Tri defensive line and capture the important city of Huê. Reflecting their USMC training, the VNMC staged counterattacks against superior forces, including their first ever amphibious assault, launched from U.S. naval vessels. During this fighting, the VNMC units suffered 20 percent combat casualties.

USMC advisors finally left South Vietnam in 1973. In 1975 with the collapse of the Republic of Vietnam government, the VNMC split into two forces. In the final hours, Vietnamese Marines fought PAVN forces near Đà Năng and near the presidential palace in Sài Gòn. Fewer than 250 VNMC ultimately escaped to the United States after the fall of Sài Gòn.

—Peter W. Brush

References: Croizat, Victor J. "Vietnamese Naval Forces: Origin of the Species." *U.S. Naval Institute Proceedings* (February 1973): 48–58.

Melson, Charles D., and Curtis G. Arnold. *U.S. Marines in Vietnam, 1954–1973. An Anthology and Annotated Bibliography.* Washington, DC: Headquarters, U.S. Marine Corps, 1985.

Turley, G. H. *The Easter Offensive: Vietnam, 1972.* New York: Warner Books, 1985.

See also: Easter Offensive (Nguyên Huế Campaign); Hồ Chì Minh Campaign; Order of Battle; Tết Offensive: Overall Strategy; Tết Offensive: The Sài Gòn Circle; United States: Marine Corps; Vietnam, Republic of: Air Force (VNAF); Vietnam, Republic of: Army (ARVN).

Vietnam, Republic of: National Police

An outgrowth of the colonial police established when Indo-China was a French colony. The Republic of Vietnam (RVN) National Police were organized much like the French Metropolitan Police forces—with responsibility for the preservation of social order and apprehension of criminals. When Vietnam achieved independence followed by partition, the government in the South created its own police forces and used the French model. It was a national police under the Interior Ministry with the director general of police subordinate to the minister of the interior. It consisted of a well-trained general police or gendarmerie exclusively responsible for the maintenance of order in the major cities and provincial towns. In the urban environment, the police were responsible to the mayors or province chiefs and performed general police duties. In addition to the gendarmerie, police forces consisted of criminal police who carried out criminal investigations and, like the French Compagnies Républicaines de Sécurité (CRS, a paramilitary force of approximately 15,000 police officers responsible for riot control and maintenance of public order and security during periods of social unrest), provided an immediate reserve of trained men to supplement the Army of the Republic of Vietnam (ARVN) if required. Unlike under the French, the National Police did not have a dual control between the Ministry of the Interior and the Ministry of Defense. In another difference, the RVN gendarmerie was part of the Ministry of Defense. Because of the complex nature of Vietnamese politics, control of the police was often given to the ruler's most trusted advisor.

In 1954 Emperor Bao Đai appointed Ngô Đình Diêm as prime minister. At the time, the National Police was totally controlled by the Bình Xuyên gang, headed by Lê Văn Viên. He organized several Public Security battalions, efficiently controlling the national highway from Sài Gòn to Vũng Tàu. But Diêm routed the Bình Xuyên and other warlords in 1955.

Refusing to honor the Geneva Accords provision for national elections in 1955, Diêm defeated Bao Đai in southern elections and, supported by the United States, proclaimed the Republic of Vietnam (RVN) in October 1955 with himself as president. Diêm gave control of the National Police to his brother Ngô Đình Nhu.

Under Nhu, the character of the police changed. He added a secret police to watch dissidents and ordered the secret police to infiltrate labor unions and social organizations and to build a network of informants to report any potential enemies directly to him. His wife, the flamboyant Madame Nhu, in addition to being the de facto "first lady" of Vietnam, shared with her husband the control of the police forces. The secret police was authorized to arrest and interrogate anyone without warrant. Nhu also increased the size of the police from approximately 20,000 men in 1960 to almost 32,000 in 1963. The Ngô brothers and other wealthy families engaged in graft and other forms of corruption while the police protected many criminal enterprises such as prostitution, narcotics, weapons trading, and smuggling. The police basically ensured social order and practiced selected suppression of criminal activity within the RVN.

With the renewal of the insurgency in the South, the National Police soon took on more military roles. As the insurgency grew, the Diêm regime used the police and military to combat not only Communists but Buddhists and other dissidents. On 1 November 1963 a coup led by General Dưởng Văn "Big" Minh toppled the Diêm regime. Both Diêm and Nhu were killed. Increasingly the RVN used the National Police as a paramilitary force. The National Police was still segregated from the military but performed military roles almost exclusively.

In 1965 the National Police force was expanded to approximately 41,000 personnel. Police officers were exempt from military draft or service. The National Police, as part of civilian government, was not under the control of the RVN military establishment. It conducted special intelligence gathering and counterintelligence, often duplicating the military efforts. In addition, it was responsible for protecting RVN officials and government buildings, again duplicating efforts of the ARVN military police and special forces units.

The National Police Field Force (NPFF) consisted of company-sized units stationed throughout the RVN and was organized and trained as light infantry by the U.S. Military Assistance Command, Vietnam (MACV). These police officers seldom engaged in any law enforcement, but most often engaged in counterinsurgency operations. They were separate from the Regional Forces/Popular Forces (RF/PF), which fell loosely under the control of the ARVN or MACV. After 1964 the gendarmerie became part of the criminal investigation section of the Military Police Command.

In 1969 as part of a campaign to root out and destroy the Communist infrastructure, Provincial Reconnaissance Units (PRUs) were added to the National Police. The National Police, in conjunction with the U.S. Central Intelligence Agency (CIA), were the controlling forces in the Phoenix program. Police intelligence detachments coordinated with CIA operatives to gather data on known Viêt Cong (VC) and were also tasked to assist in crime control with U.S. authorities.

The National Police wore a tan service uniform and peaked cap marked with their insignia. From 1956 until 1965 the police also wore a white dress uniform for formal occasions. For routine police duties, they were armed with a .38-caliber revolver, but, as the war progressed, M1 carbines and later M16 rifles were added. The NPFF companies were authorized to wear distinctive brown-spotted camouflage uniform dubbed the "leopard" pattern. They were armed as light infantry with M1 rifles, submachine guns, light machine guns, and mortars. The PRUs wore little in the way of standard uniforms, but were equipped with a wide variety of small arms.

The National Police performed an important role for the RVN during the Vietnam conflict. Their duties ranged from political suppression to direct combat with Communist forces. During the 1968 Tết Offensive, they fought with great distinction in Sài Gòn, yet their efforts seemed nullified when Director of National Police General Nguyên Ngoc Loan executed a VC prisoner before American television cameras. The conduct of the PRUs is more suspect, and the National Police, as a whole, must share blame for excesses committed by the PRUs.

—J. A. Menzoff

References: Becker, Harold K. *Police Systems of Europe: A Survey of Selected Police Organizations.* Springfield, IL: Charles C. Thomas, 1973.
Clarke, Jeffery J. *Advise and Support: The Final Years, 1965-1973.* Washington, DC: U.S. Army Center for Military History, 1988.
Karnow, Stanley. *Vietnam: A History.* Rev. ed. New York: Penguin Books, 1991.
See also: Ngô Đình Diêm; Ngô Đình Nhu; Provincial Reconnaissance Units (PRUs) (Đơn Vi Thám Sát Tinh).

Vietnam, Republic of: Navy (VNN)

The Vietnam Navy (VNN) came into existence, fought its battles, and faded into history in a short span of 20 years (1955–1975), but during that time the VNN, with the assistance of American advisors, became one of the world's largest navies with 42,000 men and women, 672 amphibious ships and craft, 20 mine warfare vessels, 450 patrol craft, 56 service craft, and 242 junks.

The organizational changes to the Vietnam Navy during those two decades reflected the evolution in the service's mission and responsibilities. Initially, the chief of the general staff of the Vietnamese armed forces, an Army officer, controlled the Navy staff and its chief. With the encouragement of U.S. Navy advisors, the general staff established the billet of chief of naval operations, which handled the administration, if not the operational control, of the naval service.

In the early years, the Navy's combat forces consisted of the Sea Force (renamed Fleet Command in January 1966), River Force, and Marine Corps (made a separate military service in April 1965). Recognizing that the sea was a likely avenue of approach for Communists infiltrating from the Democratic Republic of Vietnam (DRV) or moving along the South Vietnamese littoral, the Navy in April 1960 established the paramilitary Coastal Force and in July 1965 formally integrated it into the Navy.

The different missions of the Navy's combat forces determined how they were operationally controlled. The units involved in open sea and coastal patrol missions operated first in five Sea Zones, then in four Naval Zones (after October 1963), and finally in four Coastal Zones (after April 1965). The Coastal Zones, from the 1st in the North to the 4th in the Gulf of Siam, corresponded to the Army's I, II, III, and IV Corps areas. Coastal Force junks patrolled the offshore waters from 28 bases along the coast. The regional operations of the Coastal Force were directed from coastal surveillance centers set up in Đà Nẵng, Cam Ranh, Vũng Tàu, and An Thới.

The River Force, organized into river assault groups on the French model of the Dinassaut (naval assault divisions), initially served the Army divisions closest to its Mekong Delta naval bases at Sài Gòn, My Tho, Vĩnh Long, Cân Thơ, and Long Xuyên. In the early 1960s the Navy also formed the River Transport Escort Group to protect the vital foodstuffs being convoyed to Sài Gòn and the River Transport Group to move Army forces throughout the Delta. In April 1965 the Joint General Staff established the III and IV Riverine Areas to manage River Force operations. The Navy was given sole responsibility for handling operations in the Rừng Sát "Special Zone," a maze of rivers and swamps south of Sài Gòn.

During the 1950s and 1960s the United States supplemented the modest force of ships and craft turned over to the VNN by the French with hundreds of naval vessels, including escorts (PCE), patrol rescue escorts (PCER), motor gunboats (PGM), large support landing ships (LSSL), large infantry landing ships (LSIL), tank landing ships (LST), medium landing ships (LSM), and minesweeping launches (MLMS). These vessels improved the ability of the oceangoing force to patrol the 1,200-mile coastline, provided gunfire support for troops ashore, and assisted in carrying out amphibious landings and open-sea operations.

The River Force received a fleet of smaller vessels, including specially converted mechanized landing craft (LCM), that served as monitors, command boats, troop transports, minesweeping boats, patrol vessels, and fuel barges. The United States also provided the river sailors with 27 American-built river patrol craft (RPC). Unfortunately, these vessels proved to be too noisy, underarmed, and easily slowed by river vegetation.

Armed with these combatants, the Vietnam Navy played an increasing role in the fight for South Vietnam. Along with American naval forces, the Fleet Command and the Coastal Force seized or destroyed thousands of junks, sampans, and other craft ferrying munitions and personnel along the coast. The Coastal Force also carried out many amphibious raids, patrols of shallow inlets and river mouths, and troop lifts. These operations played an important part in the Allied campaign to deny the Communists easy access to the coastal regions. For instance, during Operation IRVING in October 1966, ground forces and junk units in II Coastal Zone cooperated to kill 681 Viêt Công guerrillas. Even though Communist forces sometimes overran the triangular-shaped fortifications of the Coastal Force, they more often failed to overcome the defenders.

In addition to offshore patrol, Fleet Command ships also patrolled the larger Mekong Delta rivers and protected merchant ships moving between the sea and the Cambodian capital of Phnom Penh. The VNN paid a price for its success on the rivers, however. In one period during 1966, river mines sank an LSSL and damaged an LSIL and a utility landing craft (LCU). Mines also sank several of the command's minesweeping launches in the Rừng Sát during 1966 and 1967.

Although the VNN sometimes crowned its operations with victory and its sailors often fought bravely, serious deficiencies plagued the service throughout its existence, but especially during the 1960s. Careerism and political activity on the part of many naval officers weakened the war effort. The coup d'état against President Ngô Đình Diêm in November 1963 and the political troubles of 1965 and 1966, in which the Navy figured prominently, damaged the morale of officers and sailors alike and distracted them from their military mission.

The training of sailors, many educationally unprepared in the technical skills essential for the operation of complex vessels, weapons, and equipment, was generally inadequate. Low pay and austere living conditions prompted many sailors to desert the colors over the years and frustrated recruitment.

The material condition of the Navy raised even more serious concerns. Hull and equipment deterioration in the World War II–era ships and craft was a serious problem, as was the lack of sufficient spare parts, supplies, and fuel. Compounding the problem was the inability of the ship and boat repair facilities in South Vietnam to handle the workload generated by the high-intensity operations undertaken from 1967 to 1969. Because of these personnel and material problems, the Vietnam Navy rarely had 50 percent of its ships and craft in operation for ocean, coastal, or river missions.

The VNN's fortunes rose, albeit temporarily, with Washington's decision to turn the war effort over to the Vietnamese and withdraw U.S. military forces from Southeast Asia. In early 1969 President Richard Nixon formally adopted as U.S. policy the so-called Vietnamization program. The naval part of that process, termed Accelerated Turnover to the Vietnamese (ACTOV), involved the phased transfer to Vietnam of the U.S. Navy's river and coastal combatant fleet. As entire units came under Vietnam Navy command, control of the various combat operations passed to that naval service as well. Hence, the VNN took on sole responsibility for river assault operations when the joint U.S. Army-Navy Mobile Riverine Force lowered its colors and transferred 64 riverine assault craft to the VNN in the summer of 1969.

The Vietnam Navy performed well during the Allied push into Cambodia in the spring of 1970. On 9 May a combined Vietnamese-American naval task force, under Vietnamese command, steamed up the Mekong River and secured control of that key waterway from Communist forces. The combined flotilla stormed Neak Luong, a strategic ferry crossing point on the river. Then, the Vietnamese contingent of river combatants pushed on to Phnom Penh. In July 1970 the U.S. Navy ceased its offensive missions on I Corps's Cửa Việt and Perfume Rivers and by the end of the year closed its other major operations throughout South Vietnam. During that time, U.S. Naval Forces, Vietnam transferred to the VNN 293 river patrol boats and 224 riverine assault craft. The Vietnam Navy grouped these fighting vessels into riverine assault interdiction divisions (RAIDs), river interdiction divisions (RIDs), and river patrol groups (RPGs).

The same process worked with the offshore patrol operation in 1970 and 1971. As part of the U.S. Navy's ACTOV program and the U.S. Coast Guard's Small Craft Assets, Training, and Turnover of Resources (SCATTOR) program, the United States transferred to the VNN complete control of the coastal and high seas surface patrol operations. The American naval command transferred four

A coastal patrol fleet of sailing junks. Operated by civilians, these boats were meant to blend in with river traffic and watch for Viêt Công supply shipments.

Coast Guard cutters, each equipped with five-inch guns; radar escort picket ship *Camp* (DER 251); *Garrett County* (LST 786); and various harbor control craft, mine craft, and logistic support vessels. In the midst of this activity, U.S. and Vietnamese naval forces managed to sink or turn back all but 1 of the 11 ships from the DRV that attempted to infiltrate contraband into South Vietnam during 1971. By August 1972 the VNN took on responsibility for the entire coastal patrol effort when it took possession of the last of 16 American coastal radar installations.

In addition to ships and craft, the U.S. Navy, under the Accelerated Turnover to the Vietnamese, Logistics (ACTOVLOG) program, transferred its many combat and logistic support bases to the Vietnam Navy. The first change of command occurred in November 1969 at My Tho; the last, in April 1972 at the former centers of American naval power in South Vietnam, the bases at Nhà Bè, Bình Thuy, Cam Ranh Bay, and Đà Năng. By 1973 the Vietnam Navy possessed the material resources to carry on the fight alone. The 42,000-sailor naval service marshaled a force of over 1,400 ships and craft to meet the Communists on the rivers and canals of South Vietnam and in the South China Sea. The relatively young, dramatically expanded, and still developing Vietnam Navy had great potential, but it needed time to mature.

The Vietnam Navy never got that time. Disenchanted with the American venture in Southeast Asia, Congress drastically cut financial support for the Vietnamese armed forces during 1973 and 1974. The Vietnam Navy was compelled to reduce its overall operations by 50 percent and its river combat and patrol activities by 70 percent. To conserve scarce ammunition and fuel, Sài Gòn laid up over 600 river and harbor craft and 22 ships. The Communists did not target the waterways during this period, but the respite was short-lived.

In little more than a month, during the spring of 1975, Communist ground forces seized all of northern and central South Vietnam, bypassing any VNN concentrations. The Vietnam Navy's ships and sailors soon joined the hurried exodus of troops and civilians from the I and II Corps areas. With the 30 April fall of Sài Gòn, many of the VNN's ships and craft put to sea and gathered off Côn Sơn Island southwest of Vũng Tàu. The flotilla of 26 Vietnam Navy and other vessels, with 30,000 sailors, their families, and other civilians on board, joined the U.S. Seventh Fleet when it embarked the last of the refugees fleeing South Vietnam and headed for the Philippines.

—Edward J. Marolda

References: Marolda, Edward J. *By Sea, Air, and Land: An Illustrated History of the U.S. Navy and the War in Southeast Asia.* Washington, DC: Naval Historical Center, 1994.
Marolda, Edward J., and Oscar P. Fitzgerald. *From Military Assistance to Combat, 1959–1965.* Vol II, *The United States Navy and the Vietnam Conflict.* Washington, DC: Naval Historical Center, 1986.
Schreadley, R. L. *From the Rivers to the Sea: The United States Navy in Vietnam.* Annapolis, MD: Naval Institute Press, 1992.
See also: Dinassauts; MARKET TIME, Operation; Mobile Riverine Force; Order of Battle; Riverine Craft; Riverine Warfare; Sea Power in the Vietnam War; United States: Coast Guard; United States: Navy; Warships, Allied and Democratic Republic of Vietnam.

Vietnam, Republic of: Rural Development Cadre Training Center

Republic of Vietnam (RVN) training facility founded in 1966 under the Rural Development Ministry. As most U.S. aid to the RVN went for military assistance, rural development (RD) took second place. RD operations at the hamlet level were conducted by RD teams, each with more than 50 members clad in black pajamas and armed with light weapons. They took charge of their own security and had charge of renovating hamlet and village administrative and security infrastructure, training militia, running political indoctrination, and setting up dispensaries and primary schools.

To train these cadres, the RVN established a large facility near Vũng Tàu. Supported by direct U.S. assistance and commanded by Col. Nguyên Bé, the center was highly successful. Usually 6,000 to 7,000 students, many of them women, were in training at any one time. Discipline and morale were excellent. In 1970 the facility was renamed the National Cadres Training Center.

—Nguyên Công Luân (Lư Tuân)

See also: Pacification.

Vietnam, Republic of: Special Forces (Lực Lương Đăc Biêt [LLDB])

Republic of Vietnam (RVN) elite military units. The Army of the Republic of Vietnam Special Forces (LLDB, or Lực Lương Đăc Biêt) came into being at Nha Trang in February 1956 under the designation of First Observation Battalion/Group (FOG).

By 1960 most LLDB were involved in counterinsurgency operations within South Vietnam. Their training was conducted in Sài Gòn. A smaller number of LLDB personnel were involved in the FOG program. At Long Thanh, they received training in intelligence gathering, sabotage, and psychological operations (PSYOP).

The primary duties of the LLDB included recruitment and training of one- to four-member teams sent into North Vietnam on intelligence, sabotage, and psychological warfare missions. Although these teams did create some problems for the Hà Nôi government by minor sabotage, intelligence gathering, and fomenting unrest, Hà Nôi declared, apparently with justification, that all such agents were captured, interrogated, and executed.

In 1961 the LLDB and Army of the Republic of Vietnam (ARVN) 1st Infantry Division conducted a joint operation against Communist infiltrators in northern Quang Tri Province. That fall, LLDB units began Operation EAGLE at Bình Hưng with a night parachute assault.

In September 1962 the U.S. Army Special Forces arrived in Vietnam. Special Forces personnel took over the Central Intelligence Agency's border surveillance and Civilian Irregular Defense Group (CIDG) programs and began working with the LLDB. In 1963 the LLDB established its headquarters at Nha Trang, where it had its own support structures and where the Vietnamese Special Forces Command was established. LLDB organizational structure underwent considerable change in the 1960s, but it continued to expand and that same year was given the additional duty of operating with the CIDG.

In 1964 the U.S. Army's 5th Special Forces Group was officially assigned to Vietnam. The LLDB worked very closely with this command and, although the United States funded the CIDG camps, the LLDB assumed ultimate responsibility for them. These camps were commanded by Vietnamese Special Forces, assisted by U.S. Special Forces advisors.

From 24 June to 1 July 1964 under Project DELTA, LLDB teams made five parachute insertions into Laos to gather intelligence. By 1965 LLDB personnel were working closely with the ARVN in recruiting and training as well as sending teams into Communist sanctuaries to gather information.

In March 1970 with the anticipated gradual withdrawal of U.S. Special Forces personnel from Vietnam and the acknowledged failure of the CIDG program, in part through fraud and corruption, both the ARVN and U.S. Military Assistance Command, Vietnam (MACV) agreed to convert CIDG camps into ARVN Ranger camps. With the elimination of the CIDG, the LLDB were no longer needed and were disbanded. Some former LLDB personnel were formed into a new clandestine unit known as the Vietnamese Special Mission Service (SMS).

Approximately 5,000 personnel served in the RVN Special Forces during the war. After the April 1975 fall of South Vietnam, some former LLDB personnel escaped to the United States, but others served long years in reeducation camps.

—Harve Saal, Spencer C. Tucker, and Vu Đ Hiêu

References: Kelly, Francis J. *The Green Berets in Vietnam 1961–71.* Washington, DC: Brassey's, 1991.
Saal, Harve. *MACV–Studies and Observations Group (SOG).* Vol. I, *Historical Evolution;* Vol. IV, *Appendixes.* Milwaukee, WI: Jones Techno-Comm, 1990.
See also: Central Intelligence Agency (CIA); Civilian Irregular Defense Group (CIDG); Psychological Warfare Operations (PSYOP); United States: Special Forces; Vietnam, Republic of: Army (ARVN).

Vietnam, Socialist Republic of: 1975 to the Present

On 30 April 1975 Communist forces captured Sài Gòn, capital of the Republic of Vietnam (RVN), officially bringing the Vietnam War to a close. A military administration now took charge of the south. In April 1976 general elections were held for a single National Assembly, which convened in June and the next month declared that the reunified country would be known as the Socialist Republic of Vietnam (SRV) with its capital at Hà Nôi. Sài Gòn was renamed Hô Chí Minh City. Tôn Đức Thăng was elected president and Pham Văn Đông the premier.

In December 1976 the Lao Đông Party renamed itself the Đang Công San Viêt Nam (Vietnamese Communist Party, VCP). This occurred during the Fourth Party Congress (the fourth since the 1930 founding of the party and first since 1960). These meetings, supposed to be held every five years, were rubber-stamp sessions for policies developed by the party Politburo. These policies were then explained by cadres to local units to obtain feedback

and create solidarity, and perhaps even slight modification, before the Congresses met.

The Fourth Congress decreed the need to develop socialism throughout the SRV. It stressed the need to speed industrialism, which was seen as the chief means to socialism. Heavy industry received priority in a second five-year plan (1976–1980). In September 1977, sponsored by a record number of nations, the SRV was admitted to the United Nations.

The SRV faced staggering problems, including rebuilding the war-ravaged country, knitting the two halves of the country together after decades of division and war, reconciling very different patterns of economic development, and providing for the needs of a burgeoning population that would double in the next 20 years.

The Communist Party retained its monopoly on power; indeed, the constitution guaranteed it as "the only force leading the state and society." Immediately after the war the government conducted a political purge in the South. There were some deaths, but nothing like the bloodbath feared and so often predicted by Washington. Thousands of former RVN officials and military officers were sent to reeducation camps for varying terms, there to be politically indoctrinated and to undergo varying degrees of physical and mental discomfort, even torture.

Efforts were also made to force people out of the cities, especially Hô Chí Minh City, by far the nation's largest metropolitan area. Its population had swelled in the last years of the war, and the concentration of population in urban areas of the South meant that perhaps a third of the arable land lay idle. So-called new economic areas were created to develop new land and to get other areas back into cultivation.

Economically Vietnam had, even in the best of times, been a poor, developing nation. In the immediate aftermath of the war, the Vietnamese set about quite literally picking up the pieces of war. In addition to the ravages of the war, Vietnam had inherited vast amounts of scrap metal and over $1 billion in unused U.S. military equipment. The broken machines of war fueled the scrap-metal furnaces of the country for years afterward, and the country exported American military hardware. In another move to gain badly needed foreign currency, the government sent some 200,000 Vietnamese abroad to work in the USSR and Eastern Europe. These workers had to pay the Vietnamese government 40 percent of their salaries and sent home an estimated $150 million a year.

The government introduced farm collectivization in South Vietnam. This effort, led by Đô Mười, met silent but determined peasant resistance. New regulations governing business practices led to the collapse of light and medium industry in the South. As a consequence, the policy was soon abandoned. Economic unrest, however, helped fuel an exodus of refugees from the SRV.

Floods in North and central Vietnam in the summer of 1978 helped hasten the collapse of agricultural cooperatives. In 1981 the government introduced the new "*khoán san phâm*" system, a contractual arrangement with incentives. Local authorities granted each peasant family land to farm. The peasants paid a fixed rent for the use of the land and were able to sell surplus produce on the private market.

During the April 1982 Fifth Congress of the Communist Party, there was much criticism of previous policy "errors." That September the government issued a new currency at the rate of one new note for ten of the old. By the end of that year, there was rising criticism of government policy, even within the controlled National Assembly.

Vietnam had no official ties with the United States in these years, although both countries would have benefited economically from these if they had been established early on. Such an opportunity came in 1977, when President Jimmy Carter was prepared to normalize relations. In March Assistant Secretary of State Richard Holbrooke began talks with Vietnamese officials to explore U.S. recognition, but with Hà Nôi insisting on reparations said to have been promised by the Nixon administration, Washington halted negotiations until the summer of 1978 when the SRV dropped this demand. Talks did not proceed then, however, because of what Washington saw as Hà Nôi's callous disregard for the plight of the refugees (the boat people), SRV preparations for an invasion of Cambodia, the SRV's conclusion of a treaty of friendship and cooperation with the USSR that November, and a decision by the Carter administration to make normalization of relations with China a priority over Vietnam.

Meanwhile relations deteriorated between the SRV and Cambodia (Kampuchea). The December 1978 Vietnamese invasion of Cambodia and subsequent occupation of that country until September 1989 made normalization of relations between the United States and the SRV impossible. Also troubling from Washington's point of view was Hà Nôi's refusal to cooperate on prisoner of war/missing in action (POW/MIA) matters, which remained a volatile political issue in the United States. It is worth noting, however, that Hà Nôi never made an issue of resolution of its own MIAs, announced in 1995 to total some 330,000 Viêt Công and People's Army of Vietnam (PAVN) personnel.

The invasion of Cambodia led the United States to strengthen its 1975 trade embargo of Vietnam. This included blocking vital loans from multilateral agencies such as the International Monetary Fund, the World Bank, and the Asian Development Bank; forestalling significant international aid; and stifling the SRV's domestic economic development. President Carter also committed the United States to aiding Cambodian guerrilla groups that opposed the Vietnamese presence there. The Cambodian incursion made the SRV something of an international pariah.

Throughout the second half of the decade of the 1970s, SRV relations with China continued to deteriorate for a variety of reasons, including territorial disputes, the forced exit of many Chinese from the SRV, the invasion of Cambodia, and Sino-Soviet tensions in which Vietnam took the side of the USSR. The Soviet Union provided important support for the SRV economy, amounting to perhaps $2.25 billion a year (more than half of this in military assistance). Sino-SRV tensions exploded into war when Chinese troops crossed the northern Vietnamese frontier briefly in February 1979. Vietnam decreed a general mobilization. Although Chinese troops soon withdrew from Vietnam and the SRV was not forced to remove its troops from Cambodia, the cost was high for Vietnam; many of its villages in the border area were destroyed.

The SRV continued to maintain a large military establishment. In the mid-1980s with 1.2 million people armed, it possessed the world's fourth largest armed forces. This figure did not include Public Security personnel, estimated to number over 1 million people. The military consumed up to a third of the national budget, and a bloated government bureaucracy also consumed revenues. As a result, the economy remained vastly undermechanized. In the mid-1980s there was not a single rice threshing machine in the country. It appeared to many foreign observers that Vietnam worked more effectively at war than at peace, perhaps because the Vietnamese had had little experience with the latter. Vietnam was very much an insular and xenophobic society.

In 1985 famine spread in the SRV, the result of failed farm collectivization and botched currency reform. Inflation was rampant, running between 400 and 600 percent per year by 1985. Economic growth of 2 percent per year was being outstripped by the birthrate, which at 3 percent was one of the highest in the world. Agricultural production, which had risen after the 1981 reforms, fell again. All of this led to striking changes both in policy and leadership announced at the December 1986 Sixth National Communist Party Congress.

At the Congress, the leadership announced changes based on material incentives, decentralized decision making, and limited free enterprise. Party secretary and hard-liner Lê Duân had died in July 1986, and Premier Pham Văn Đông, Lê Đưc Tho, and Trưởng Chinh all retired. In all, 6 of 13 Politburo members were dropped. Nguyên Văn Linh and Võ Văn Kiêt, two leading proponents of change, came to the fore. Linh replaced Trưởng Chinh as party secretary and the most powerful figure in the state. He was credited with overseeing the tentative steps toward a free market economy that had helped the South remain more prosperous than the North. Võ Văn Kiêt was vice-premier and chairman of the state planning commission.

Linh's reform program, known as *đôi mơi* (renovation), produced progress. It introduced the profit incentive for farmers, allowing them to market produce privately. Individuals could also set up private businesses. Companies producing for export were granted tax concessions, and foreign-owned firms could operate in the country and repatriate their profits (with a guarantee against being nationalized). But Linh said there was no need for Vietnam to emulate the example of East European states and allow opposition political parties and free elections. There was, however, some easing of restrictions on the media. Attempts were also made to open Vietnam to the West (including talks in August 1987 on the MIA issue with a U.S. delegation headed by retired U.S. Army general and former chairman of the Joint Chiefs of Staff John Vessey, Jr.). The regime also sought reconciliation with former South Vietnamese officials and groups once considered enemies of the SRV. In September 1987 the SRV announced that it was releasing 6,685 military and political prisoners, including generals and senior officials of the former RVN government. In 1988 to promote foreign investment, the constitution was amended to remove derogatory references to a number of Western countries.

Đôi mơi registered successes. Inflation was cut dramatically from 300 percent in 1987 to 8.5 percent in 1994. Food production and consumerism increased. But the reform was uneven as party bureaucrats and conservatives inhibited its spread.

In March 1988 Pham Hùng, chairman of the Council of Ministers (premier) since the previous July, died at age 75; Võ Văn Kiêt followed him as acting premier, but in June 1988 Đô Mười, a candidate introduced by the Communist Party Central Committee, was elected premier by the National Assembly. At that time, Mười was seen as a transitional figure.

Economic reforms continued, although they produced uneven results. Most advances came in the cities rather than in the countryside, where 80 percent of the population lived. Vietnam remained a poor country with per capita income of less than $200 a year. In 1989 some 75,000 people fled the country, largely to escape economic poverty.

The leadership came to realize that the SRV had to join the Southeast Asia development race or forever be left behind. Cambodia was the main problem for both the West and in Hà Nôi's relations with China. Leaving Cambodia would end SRV diplomatic isolation and lead to Western investment. Driven largely by economic reasons, in July 1988 Vietnam began withdrawing its troops from Cambodia, an operation completed in September 1989. The Vietnamese also reduced their troop strength in Laos. And Foreign Minister Nguyên Cơ Thach traveled to Washington for talks, becoming the highest-ranking Hà Nôi official to do so.

Not unrelated to this, in 1989 Soviet leader Mikhail Gorbachev embarked on reform programs that resulted in reduced aid to Vietnam. The Soviets also sharply cut back on their military presence, especially at Cam Ranh Bay, which had become the largest Soviet military base outside the USSR. Soviet aid ended altogether in 1991, and the USSR announced that henceforward all trade between the two countries would be in dollars at world market prices. The cutback in Soviet aid was another reason for Vietnam to try to mend its fences with Beijing, and in September 1990 Deputy Prime Minister Võ Nguyên Giáp traveled to China for talks.

At the same time there were signs of political struggle in Vietnam. General Secretary Linh announced his plan to retire at the next party Congress, and the battle between conservatives and reformers intensified. The conservatives, led by Lê Đức Tho (who died in October 1990) and his brother, Interior Minister Mai Chí Tho, used the collapse of communism in Eastern Europe to try to halt any movement toward political pluralism. In 1990, prompted by fears that the upheaval seen in Eastern Europe might infect Vietnam, the government ordered the arrests of hundreds of people, most of them in the South—some of them for what the government referred to as too much contact with westerners. There was also a public campaign against reported efforts of "reactionary forces overseas" to sabotage the state and socialism.

The leadership of the SRV was deeply divided. In June 1991 the party held its Seventh Congress, and the leaders announced that they would continue economic reforms but stand firm against political changes in the fashion of Eastern Europe. Linh stated that pluralism would create political instability and "difficulties and obstacles for the entire renovation process."

In August 1991 there was a major cabinet shake-up. The VCP Seventh National Congress elected Đô Mười as general secretary of the VCP to succeed Linh, and Võ Văn Kiêt became premier, replacing Đô Mười. Võ Nguyên Giáp, who had been removed as minister of defense in 1986 and had been retained only as vice-premier in charge of family planning, now lost that post as well. Nguyên Cơ Thach was removed from the foreign ministry; Mai Chí Tho, from the interior ministry. Nguyên Manh Câm, the SRV's former ambassador to the Soviet Union and member of the 146-person Central Committee, replaced Thach; General Bùi Thiên Ngô became minister of the interior; and General Đoàn Khuê, army chief of staff, became the new defense minister. At the same time, Vietnam announced its intention to patch up relations with China.

Relations with the United States also improved. In February 1991 talks between the Bush administration and Vietnam led Hà Nôi to allow Washington to set up a "temporary" office in the Vietnamese capital to coordinate efforts to locate Americans missing in action during the Vietnam War. Relations between the two states continued to improve as Hà Nôi took steps to account for American MIAs. U.S. businesses that saw themselves losing out as many other nations invested in Vietnam also applied pressure, and in September 1993 President Bill Clinton allowed American firms to compete for development projects in the SRV that were to be funded by international lending institutions. Then on 3 February 1994 Clinton normalized relations with the SRV. In 1997 the two countries exchanged ambassadors. The SRV also agreed to assume debts, now worth about $140 million, incurred by the Sài Gòn government for roads, power stations, and grain shipments before its fall in 1975. Hà Nôi took this step to help pave the way for most-favored nation trading status.

The much-delayed Vietnamese Eighth Communist Party Congress took place at the end of June 1996 in Hà Nôi in a meeting hall that featured giant portraits of Marx and Lenin. The delay reflected concerns in the party about threats from corruption and what it referred to as "peaceful evolution," a perceived Western plot to undermine remaining Communist one-party states. In the weeks leading up to the Congress, the 170-person Central Committee of the 2.2 million-member Communist Party met repeatedly in an effort to resolve some of these issues.

At the Congress the country's ruling septuagenarian leaders—party General Secretary Đô Mười (age 79), Premier Võ Văn Kiêt (73), and President Lê Đức Anh (75)—were reelected to five-year terms, although many expected that this would be probably only for another year or two. Apparently there was some discussion that the top leaders might retire, but the leadership believed that this was not the time to change. Rising stars in the new Politburo were the young and liberal former mayor of Hô Chí Minh City (now secretary of the Hô Chí Minh City Party Committee), Trương Tân Sang (47), and Nông Đức Manh (56), chairman of the National Assembly. Other possibilities were two deputy prime ministers in their fifties, Trân Đức Lương and Phan Văn Khai, and the head of the army's political department, General Lê Kha Phiêu (64).

In September 1997 the National Assembly elected Phan Văn Khai as premier, replacing Võ Văn Kiêt. The Russian-trained Khai, an economist and technocrat from the South, was perceived as one of the architects of the economic reforms.

PAVN influence remained strong. The party Congress increased representation of military and internal security forces on the 19-member Politburo from four to six and gave the military three of five positions on a new standing committee charged with conducting day-to-day affairs. This was seen as an effort by the party leadership to protect the country's political and social structure. From the mid-1980s to 1996 the PAVN shrank by 50 percent to an army of about 550,000 soldiers, navy of 40,000, air force of 15,000, and paramilitary force of 15,000. These figures do not include the Public Security force. The military budget remains high, however, having risen every year since 1992.

The most contentious issue for the party leadership was the pace of liberalization. The leadership wanted continued rapid economic growth, but this had begun to transform Vietnam in ways that made some party leaders uneasy. Still, the leadership decided to continue the delicate balancing act of attracting increased foreign investment and aiming for an annual growth rate of 10 percent per year while continuing to accord primacy to less productive state-run economic enterprises. Foreign investors were made nervous, however, when the Congress called for expansion of party cells within business enterprises, including joint ventures with foreign companies. Even the PAVN was involved in these activities, managing hotels and a travel agency, mining coal, and entering into 49 joint ventures with foreign companies worth up to $.5 billion. Foreign observers believed that SRV insistence on maintaining centralized control and pouring money into inefficient state-owned enterprises would make it difficult to meet growth targets. The Congress did ease restrictions on "social evils," including foreign advertising.

From 1990, when outside investment in Vietnam was negligible, to 1996 foreign companies committed $20 billion in investments, and thousands of foreign enterprises were registered to do business there. U.S. investment in the SRV rose from just $3.3 million in 1993 to $1.2 billion in 1995, although the United States was only the sixth largest investor, trailing Taiwan, Japan, Hong Kong, Singapore, and the Republic of Korea.

Inflation was substantially reduced by 1992, and since then economic growth has averaged 8 percent per year. With the official currency, the đông, shrinking in value (by 1985 $1 bought 10,000 đông), however, U.S. dollars were the preferred currency. Corruption, red tape, poor infrastructure, and lack of regulations inhibited investment. The main attractions for foreign investment were low wages, untapped natural resources, and the country's great need to modernize.

Although Vietnam with its population of 75 million (ranked thirteenth in the world and with half the people born after the Vietnam War) aspires to be one of the Asian "tigers," chronic problems remain. Per capita spending is low. In 1993 the average Vietnamese spent just $1,040 compared with $24,750 for each American. SRV per capita income of $250 per year is also among the world's lowest. There is also a growing disparity between rich and poor, many of the "new rich" being Communist officials and their associates.

The central issue for an aging SRV leadership remains whether Vietnam can modernize using the Chinese model, successful thus far, without the party relaxing political control. Ironically the party is itself the chief obstacle to reform, as shown by its refusal to privatize state-run industries.

The party sees its chief enemies as the multiparty system, the dollar's pervasive influence (in 1995 Western economists calculated that between $600 million and $2 billion were circulating in the country), the residue of war (would the South rise again?), corruption, poor management, regional autonomy, Buddhist agitation, growing crime and disrespect for authority, and the menace of China.

Making Vietnam a single entity economically has also yet to be accomplished. Even in 1996 the North, its soil depleted and forests fast disappearing, trails the South economically. One of the ironies of the Vietnam War may indeed be that the South won after all, at least in the adoption of modified capitalism and in its standard of living; Hồ Chí Minh City is the economic engine driving the rest of the country. Northern leaders, however, oppose yielding political power.

—Spencer C. Tucker

References: Nguyên Khắc Viên. *Vietnam, A Long History.* Hà Nôi: Foreign Languages Publishing House, 1987.
See also: Carter, Jimmy; Clinton, William Jefferson; Đô Mười; Embargo; Lao Đông Party; Lê Đức Anh; Lê Đức Tho; Nguyên Văn Linh (Nguyên Văn Cúc); Nông Đức Manh; Pham Văn Đông; Phan Văn Khai; Reeducation Camps; Sino-Vietnamese War; Trường Chinh (Đăng Xuân Khu); Vietnamese Invasion and Occupation of Cambodia; Võ Vân Kiêt.

Vietnam Information Group (VIG)

Johnson administration public relations vehicle. Harassed and criticized by the news media and "doves" in Congress over his Vietnam policies, President Lyndon B. Johnson established the Public Affairs Policy Committee for Vietnam in August 1965. Early in the U.S. involvement in the war, Johnson noted that "the greatest chink in our armor is public opinion." This organization, redesignated the Vietnam Information Group (VIG) in 1967, prepared Vietnam-related material from the Johnson administration for public consumption.

The VIG released the most optimistic information available concerning U.S. involvement in the Republic of Vietnam. Its principal task was to discredit Johnson administration opponents and win both U.S. and foreign favor. Director Harold Kaplan and his staff monitored public reactions to the war and attempted to deal with problems as soon as they appeared.

In an aggressive campaign to mobilize the "silent center" in American politics, Johnson ordered the U.S. Embassy and military command in Vietnam to "search urgently for occasions to present sound evidence of progress in Vietnam." The VIG offered the resulting reams of favorable statistics as proof of U.S. progress in Vietnam.

A loose organization similar to the VIG continued to prepare position papers and press releases during President Richard Nixon's administration. Nixon used the term "silent majority" for a slightly more successful appeal in seeking support for his Vietnam policies.

—Stanley S. McGowen

References: Herring, George C. *America's Longest War: The United States and Vietnam, 1950–1975.* 2d ed. Philadelphia, PA: Temple University Press, 1986.

_____. *LBJ and Vietnam: A Different Kind of War.* Austin, TX: University of Texas Press, 1994.

Johnson, Lyndon B. *The Vantage Point: Perspectives of the Presidency, 1963–1969.* New York: Holt, Rinehart and Winston, 1971.

Small, Melvin. *Johnson, Nixon, and the Doves.* New Brunswick, NJ: Rutgers University Press, 1988.

See also: Johnson, Lyndon Baines; Media and the War.

Vietnam Veterans Against the War (VVAW)

U.S. antiwar organization. Vietnam Veterans Against the War (VVAW) was founded in April 1967 by 6 of 20 American veterans who had marched under a banner with that legend in an antiwar demonstration in New York City. By November of that year VVAW had increased their membership to 40; by the end of 1968 to 300. Their main headquarters remained in New York City, but advertising in national magazines allowed them to broaden their membership, and affiliated chapters were formed in cities across the country. By the time of the organization's dissolution in 1973, VVAW leaders claimed a membership of several thousand, although it was not clear then, and grew even less clear as time passed, how many of these reported members really held active membership, how many were government infiltrators, and how many of the participating members had really seen service in Vietnam.

The initial goal of VVAW was to add credence to the antiwar movement by giving it the visible presence of veterans themselves, those who had seen firsthand the events and conditions being protested by those who opposed the war. Members participated in many of the major demonstrations throughout 1968, including the protests surrounding the Democratic National Convention in Chicago, but, in addition, they found a new and specialized area of concern in 1969 with the publicizing of the My Lai Massacre in the American press. After this, their primary focus was on atrocities committed by U.S. troops in the war and on the psychologically damaging effect that the war itself had on troops.

In September 1970 VVAW staged a lengthy demonstration called Operation RAW (Rapid American Withdrawal), in which 100 participants, not all of them Vietnam veterans, marched from Morristown, New Jersey, to Valley Forge, Pennsylvania. The veterans (and perhaps nonveterans as well) were dressed in fatigues and carried combat weapons. Along the way, they staged "guerrilla theater" to represent war atrocities. Although the marchers encountered some hostility along their route, they were greeted enthusiastically by a group of 1,500 people at their termination point at Valley Forge, where speeches were delivered by such figures as entertainers Jane Fonda and Donald Sutherland and attorney Mark Lane.

During 1970 VVAW leaders had been in touch with Robert Jay Lifton, a New York psychiatrist and antiwar activist who had begun speaking publicly in 1969 about the damaging effect of the war on combatants' psyches and on the inevitability of atrocities

in what was, as he put it, the "atrocity-producing" environment of war. In November 1970 VVAW member Jan Crumb of the New York City office approached Lifton about methods of both dealing with veterans' psychological problems and effectively creating public opposition to the war that had caused these problems.

In December 1970 Lifton and fellow psychiatrist Chaim Shatan of New York University began, with members of the New York VVAW chapter, a series of "rap groups," a form of group therapy in which participants explored their "guilt" and then determined to "animate" it by actively exposing the evil of war. These rap groups were later to become the staple form of Veterans Administration (VA) treatment for war-related stress, particularly in the Veterans Outreach Centers (Vet Centers) established in 1979. (An account of the original rap group sessions and their outcome is given in Lifton's 1973 book, *Home from the War.*)

In February 1971 VVAW members, especially those participating in the rap groups, staged a media event in Detroit, the "Winter Soldier Investigation." Some 115 VVAW members and associates, including Lifton himself, gave testimony about "war crimes" they had participated in and/or witnessed. The main funding sources for this event were Jane Fonda and Mark Lane. Selected speeches of the testifying participants were published in a 1972 report, *The Winter Soldier Investigation.* Later, in his 1978 book, *America in Vietnam,* Guenter Lewy cited evidence that he had found in military records to indicate that many of the participants in the event had not been present at the scenes they claimed to be describing, and that some of them had not seen service in Vietnam at all. This remains a hotly debated issue.

Continuing their public antiwar activities in 1971, VVAW members and supporters, again led primarily by rap group participants, staged "Dewey Canyon III," held in Washington, D.C., in April 1971. (The name was an allusion to DEWEY CANYON I and II, wartime operations in Laos.) The main feature of this event, which included a memorial service at the Tomb of the Unknown Soldier at Arlington Nation Cemetery, was the discarding of medals by an estimated 1,000 veterans on the Capitol steps.

As always, a debate arose as to whether all the participating members of the demonstration were genuine veterans and whether all the medals thrown at the Capitol had been officially awarded to the men discarding them. Some men in uniform, upon being interviewed, acknowledged that they were not veterans, and the count of the most prestigious medals discarded, when correlated with those known to be still in their owners' possession, did not tally with the number issued. Ironically, however, some genuine veterans may have been deliberately excluded from the demonstration. Lynda Van Devanter, a former Army nurse who served at Pleiku during the war, reported in her memoir, *Home before Morning* (1984), that, when she attempted to join the demonstration, she was told not to march with the veterans because she "didn't look like a vet." She took this to mean that, as a female, she might give the impression, as the march representative phrased it, that "we were swelling the ranks with nonvets."

VVAW demonstrations continued throughout 1971 and 1972, but public demonstrations were not the only means that the VVAW found to oppose the war publicly. Throughout the 1970s, even after the dissolution of the organization itself, members and former members campaigned relentlessly for treatment of veterans' psychological disabilities and were instrumental in defining post-traumatic stress disorder as a recognized psychological condition, in establishing VA counseling centers, and in staffing the centers as they were developed.

In a 1984 interview with Myra MacPherson, former director of the VA Readjustment Counseling Services, Dr. Arthur S. Blank, Jr. estimated that 10 percent of current Vet Center team leaders were former VVAW members. Furthermore, among the most prominent writers and editors of popular and professional works on post-traumatic stress disorder were former members or associates of the VVAW, including participants in the Winter Soldier Investigation and Dewey Canyon III: Lifton, Shatan, Charles Figley, Arthur Egendorf, Jack Smith, John Kerry, and Shad Meshad, to name just a few. Their reports and interpretations of their experiences in the war and with veterans became the standard view of veterans and the war throughout the helping professions.

Nor did VVAW influence end with demonstrations and counseling services; it proved to be a powerful voice in public perceptions of the veteran and the war, even as far afield as literary studies. The organization's poetry anthology, *Winning Hearts and Minds* (1972), edited by founding members Jan Barry, Larry Rottman, and Basil Paquet, was one of the first collections of poetry written primarily by veterans and became a model of its kind for future writing; and *The New Soldier* (1971), edited by John Kerry, did the same for oral histories of the war. Furthermore, former members of the VVAW went on to found other organizations, both antiwar organizations during the war and veterans' organizations afterward. The most famous of these veterans' organizations is Vietnam Veterans of America, founded by former VVAW member Robert O. Muller.

Regardless of how many veterans belonged to the VVAW during its six-year existence or how much press coverage it received for any of its given events, it cannot be denied that the organization was and continues to be one of the most influential of its kind in all subsequent reference to the war and to those who served.

—Phoebe S. Spinrad

References: Lewy, Guenter. *America in Vietnam.* New York: Oxford University Press, 1978.

Lifton, Robert J. *Home from the War: Vietnam Veterans, Neither Victims nor Executioners.* New York: Simon & Schuster, 1973.

MacPherson, Myra. *Long Time Passing.* New York: Doubleday, 1984.

Scott, Wilbur J. *The Politics of Readjustment: Vietnam Veterans since the War.* New York: Aldine De Gruyter, 1993.

Van Devanter, Lynda. *Home before Morning.* New York: Warner Books, 1984.

See also: Antiwar Movement, United States; Fonda, Jane Seymour; Kerry, John Forbes; Lifton, Robert Jay; Post-Traumatic Stress Disorder (PTSD); Prose Narrative and the Vietnam Experience.

Vietnam Veterans Memorial

In the late 1970s sensitivity developed surrounding how to remember those who had perished in the Vietnam War. First, without ceremony, a small, nondescript plaque was added to the Tomb of the Unknown Soldier. Next, Congress became interested in a politically neutral option known as "Vietnam Veterans Week." From outside the bureaucracy came the more successful idea—the establishment of a memorial in Washington, D.C.

Jan Scruggs, disturbed by Michael Cimino's powerful film, *The Deer Hunter* (1978), became obsessed with constructing "a memorial to all the guys who served in Vietnam." From this humble dream, the Vietnam Veterans Memorial emerged. However, the early history of the Memorial was embroiled in controversy.

Scruggs, an enlisted man wounded in 1969; Bob Doubek, a former Air Force officer; and Jack Wheeler, a West Point graduate who had attended Yale Law School, became the team that navigated the challenges of the next several years. Incorporated as a nonprofit organization on 27 April 1979, the Vietnam Veterans Memorial Fund fought its first battles in the political arena. With the assistance of Senators Charles Mathias (R-Maryland), who had earlier opposed the war, and John Warner (R-Virginia), the bill approving the Memorial passed the Senate on 30 April 1980. Importantly, the site designated for the Memorial, Senator Mathias's idea originally, was on the Washington Mall, near the Lincoln Memorial. In signing the bill (PL 96-297) authorizing the Memorial into law on 1 July 1980, President Jimmy Carter recognized that "We are ready at last to acknowledge . . . the debt which we can never fully repay to those who served."

Although Scruggs had expected spontaneous contributions, when President Carter signed the authorization bill the Fund had collected only about $250,000. Then, in November 1980 Fund leaders learned that the original target of $2.5 million was naive; they would need $6 to $10 million to complete the project.

A major factor in the turnaround of the fund-raising effort came when the American hostages held in Iran were returned: The heroes' welcome activated many citizens to demand that more tangible recognition be given to those who had served their country in Vietnam. Surprisingly, by the end of 1981 the Fund had over $8 million dollars. An astounding number of Americans—over 650,000—contributed less than $10 each to make possible this enormous success. Later, possibly as a result of disagreements over the design of the Memorial, some controversy about the expenditures of these monies surfaced, but a General Accounting Office audit found that all $9.3 million received as of May 1984 had been properly budgeted.

The design competition ran smoothly, partly because billionaire H. Ross Perot donated $160,000 to underwrite it. Scruggs's idea that the Memorial contain the names of all who perished was central; Wheeler suggested that a landscaped, horizontal design be used; Doubek drafted a proposal that the Memorial be apolitical, not addressing the war's causes or conduct. To further the democratic process of the competition, and thus to enhance the healing process, the Fund agreed to an open selection process with eight judges from the disciplines of architecture and landscape art. By the March 1981 deadline 1,421 entries were submitted. After a week of deliberations, the judges announced their unanimous decision: Maya Ying Lin's design of a polished, black, V-shaped wall that would contain the names of all who died in Vietnam.

The Vietnam Veterans Memorial in Washington, D.C. The Veterans Day dedication of the memorial in November 1982 marked a historic turning point in America's search for a healing closure to the divisive war. More than 150,000 people attended the dedication.

The design was both praised and attacked. Lin, then an undergraduate at Yale University, had seen geometric forms used at the war memorial at Thiepval, France, where the memorial remembered those fallen in the Somme Offensive of World War I, and she had attended the memorial ceremony at Yale, when the names of those graduates killed in Vietnam were added to walls listing those who had died in other wars. Despite these impressive models and praise for her design as "reverential" and a "fitting mark of respect," critics saw the wall, which was carved into a gentle embankment, as a "degrading ditch" and a "wailing wall for antiwar demonstrators." Lin, responding to these critics, added short eulogistic words explaining that the list of names memorialized those who made the ultimate sacrifice in Vietnam, but she did not negotiate about keeping the list of names in chronological order, a crucial aspect of the Memorial's powerful effect.

Although this accommodation satisfied most critics, some still wanted a more traditional design. James Watt, then secretary of the interior, delayed construction until a compromise could be reached. After much controversy, the Memorial's critics accepted Lin's design if a representational statue and flag could be added later. In March 1982 just before the deadline if the dedication were to occur on Veterans Day, Watt signed the construction permit.

From the start, the most demanding work involved polishing the black granite and inscribing the names. Arriving from Bangalore, India, the stone was separated into 140 differently sized panels in Vermont and then shipped to Memphis, Tennessee. There the process of cutting the names into the panels took place. Because the angles and depth (.015 inch) of the letters had been designed to assure that the sun would cast no shadows that might obscure or change the appearance of a name, the stonecutters needed to proceed with great care. Despite the enormity of these tasks, construction proceeded on schedule.

The Veterans Day dedication in November 1982 marked a historic turning point in America's search for a healing closure to the divisive war. More than 150,000 people attended. At the National Cathedral, the salute began on Wednesday, 10 November, with a candlelight vigil, a 56-hour nonstop service at which all 58,000 names were read. Emotional reactions outside, when soldiers first encountered the Wall, ran high. One medic felt joy as he found that a buddy he had worked on was not listed; others experienced survivor guilt on seeing the names of dead comrades. The National Salute ended on Saturday with a parade, and, after the dedication on Sunday, the crowd dispersed, beginning a practice of leaving flowers, notes, and other memorabilia as tokens of love and loss.

Even after the dedication, controversy raged over the items yet to be added. Frederick Hart, a sculptor who placed third in the overall design competition, was chosen to create the statue; earlier he had said that Lin's design was "[nihilistic] contemporary art done in a vacuum." For her part, Lin called the addition of Hart's realistic sculpture like "drawing moustaches on other people's portraits." However, as issues of placement and size were resolved, Lin came to accept both the flag and the statue well before the 1984 rededication of the double memorial.

Experiencing the memorials together one recognizes the powerful artistic qualities supporting the purposes of reflection and healing. At the flag, the standard patriotic feeling is quietly muted by the inscription's reference to the war's trying conditions. The nearby statue of three soldiers emphasizes the melting-pot quality of the war, while its details create a sense of the reality. Importantly, these soldiers are tired heroes, weary but stoic survivors of a difficult war.

As one moves to the Wall itself, the viewer experiences what Robin Wagner-Pacifici and Barry Schwartz called "a kind of *coincidentia oppositorum*—an agency that brings . . . opposed meanings together without resolving them." Forming a wide "V," the arms of the Wall, each 246 feet long, embrace the visitor. At the apex, 10 feet below the highest panels, one feels an almost pastoral quiet. The names, listed in chronological order by the soldier's date of death, emphasize both the individual soldier's story and the significance of time, a crucial aspect for soldiers who spent a clearly delimited period of time in the war zone. Facing the Wall, the viewer sees not only the names but also the reflections of trees and clouds and himself or herself and feels drawn in, a part of a war that affected so many Americans.

From this position of quiet reflection, one notices that the arms open, signifying the soldier's return to an environment that was still warlike, for the nation was still divided even when the war itself ended. However, looking toward the horizon, the visitor sees along one arm the Washington Monument and along the other the Lincoln Memorial and begins to sense a placement of this war and suffering in the nation's history.

The strength of that experience has caused countless visitors to make one or more pilgrimages to what has become an almost sacred shrine. Often, visitors will take a rubbing of an individual soldier's name, much as one might of a headstone in a cemetery. In return, many visitors leave memorabilia, and this exchange becomes another example of the interactive nature of the Memorial. More than 30,000 items have been collected as of 1995. Ranging from American flags to medals to notes, letters, and poems, these items continue to be cataloged and stored at the Museum and Archeological Regional Storage Facility in Glenn Dale, Maryland. With an estimated 2.5 million visitors annually, this fast-growing collection has created its own cultural history and is a powerful testimonial to the effects of the war on the nation's people.

Likewise, from the troubled drama of its beginnings, the Vietnam Veterans Memorial has inspired a number of other artifacts to augment the originally intended therapeutic process. Scruggs's coauthored book, *To Heal a Nation* (1985) became, in 1987, a television movie. Laura Palmer's book *Shrapnel in the Heart* (1987) reproduced several letters left at the Memorial, while Duncan Spencer and Lloyd Wolf's *Facing the Wall* (1986) evocatively chronicles in text and color photographs one day's events at the Memorial. Further, a half-size replica of the Wall, known as the Moving Wall, has been shown throughout the United States.

On Veterans Day 1993 near the Wall, the Vietnam Women's Memorial Project dedicated its own statue. Created by sculptor Glenna Goodacre, the seven-foot statue of three women was designed to balance Hart's statue. Because 90 percent of the women who served in Vietnam were nurses, the statue emphasizes the nurse's role by showing three women assisting a fallen soldier. As with the Wall, however, the statue is meant to be inclusive, and it thus memorializes all of the approximately 11,500 American women who served in Vietnam as well as the 8 who died there.

Further complementing the Vietnam Veterans Memorial is the Korean War Veterans Memorial, which was dedicated on 27 July 1995. On the opposite side of the Reflecting Pool from the Vietnam Veterans Memorial, this monument also asks that the viewer prioritize the experiences of the individual soldier while simultaneously considering the historical contexts of the war.

Despite its contentious and troubled beginnings, the Vietnam Veterans Memorial has become a powerful cultural memorial for those touched, either directly or indirectly, by America's most divisive twentieth-century war. Still the subject of much critical discussion, the most profound effects are felt by those who experience the therapeutic value of its quiet healing touch. Today the Memorial commemorates the over 58,000 men and women who gave their lives in Vietnam, and, by implication, it remembers all Americans whose lives were touched by the war.

—Charles J. Gaspar

References: Allen, Leslie. "The Wall." *American Heritage* (February/March 1995): 92–103.
Gaspar, Charles J. "The Search for Closure: Vietnam War Literature and the Vietnam Veterans Memorial." *War, Literature, and the Arts* (Spring 1989): 19–34.
Scruggs, Jan C., and Swerdlow, Joel. *To Heal a Nation.* New York: Harper & Row, 1985.
Sturken, Marita. "The Wall, the Screen, and the Image: The Vietnam Veterans Memorial." *Representations* 35 (1991): 118–142.
Wagner-Pacifici, Robin, and Barry Schwartz. "The Vietnam Veterans Memorial: Commemorating a Difficult Past." *American Journal of Sociology* (September 1991): 376–420.
See also: Art and the Vietnam War; Casualties; Film and the Vietnam Experience; Lao Đông Party; Prose Narrative and the Vietnam Experience; Women in the War, U.S.

Vietnamese Communist Party (VCP)

The Vietnamese Communist Party was an outgrowth of Hô Chí Minh's Viêt Nam Thanh Niên Cách Mang Đông Chí Hôi (Vietnam Revolutionary Youth Association) in the late 1920s. Radical youths within the Thanh Niên rejected the reformist policies of other Vietnamese patriotic and nationalistic groups in favor of the new political ideology of communism. In 1928 and 1929 the Thanh Niên was radicalized by these young Vietnamese, and by 1930 a unified Communist Party emerged in Vietnam.

Hô's party separated itself from other anticolonial groups in Vietnam during the 1930s by relying on revolutionary theory. The Communist Party developed a plan for the seizure of power based on a three-phased strategy: organization, agitation, and insurrection. During the first two phases in the 1930s, many members of the party, including Pham Văn Đông and Lê Đực Tho, were arrested and sent to French prisons. These, however, proved to be the breeding ground for young Vietnamese revolutionaries, as many of the party's cadres were politicized there.

Even in the dark days of the 1930s Hô's party recruited thousands of new cadres from the lower middle class and peasants. Lacking an industrial proletariat, the Communist Party modified traditional Marxist-Leninist teachings to meet Vietnam's particular needs. The party also emphasized the radical nature of its revolution, that is, replacing one existing social system with another. Communist leaders were careful, however, not to deter potential allies. In May 1941 at the Communist Party's Eighth Plenum, its leaders founded the Viêt Nam Đôc Lâp Đông Minh Hôi, or Viêt Minh, a national front organization that served as the organizational nexus of the revolution.

The creation of the Viêt Minh allowed the party to mobilize all anticolonial forces in Vietnam under one banner. To accomplish this task, the Communists emphasized national liberation as the primary goal of the party and claimed that social revolution was an expected outcome in the decades to come. This allowed the party to expand its base of support and make temporary alliances with non-Communist Vietnamese to defeat the French. In February 1951, Hô changed the name of the Indo-Chinese Communist Party (ICP) to the Đang Lao Đông Viêt Nam (Vietnamese Workers' Party), popularly known as the Lao Đông (or Workers' Party). His intention was to play down communism and widen nationalist support throughout Vietnam. It remained the party name until 1986.

After the 1954 military victory over the French at Điên Biên Phu, the party turned its attention to reuniting the country under the socialist banner. According to the 1954 Geneva Accords, the party would control Vietnam north of the 17th parallel, and elections in two years were to reunify the country. The Geneva Accords, however, were not observed on both Vietnamese sides, and in 1955 non-Communists and the United States established a counterrevolutionary alternative south of the 17th parallel. From 1954 until 1960 the party tried to unify all of Vietnam through political means.

In 1960 the party's leadership accepted the recommendations of Secretary-General Lê Duân and adopted armed violence in opposition to the American-backed Sài Gòn regime. The party then created the National Front for the Liberation of South Vietnam (NFLSV), another united front, to mobilize all disaffected southerners in opposition to the government of Ngô Đình Diêm. The character and nature of the southern revolution have been the subject of heated debate. The Communist Party denied any relationship with the NFLSV during the war, but later, Võ Nguyên Giáp and others admitted the total subordination of the NFLSV.

From 1960 to 1975 the party battled the United States and its allies. In April 1975 the party presided over the reunification of the country in the name of socialism, victorious in its efforts begun earlier in the century.

—Robert K. Brigham

References: Duiker, William J. *The Rise of Nationalism in Vietnam, 1900–1941.* Ithaca, NY: Cornell University Press, 1976.
Herring, George C. *America's Longest War: The United States and Vietnam, 1950–1975.* 2d ed. New York: Alfred A. Knopf, 1986.
Huynh Kim Khanh. *Vietnamese Communism, 1925–1945.* Ithaca, NY: Cornell University Press, 1982.

Marr, David G. *Vietnamese Tradition on Trial, 1925–1945.* Berkeley, CA: University of California Press, 1981.

Thayer, Carlyle A. *War by Other Means: National Liberation and Revolution in Viet-Nam, 1954–1960.* Sydney: Allen & Unwin, 1989.

Woodside, Alexander B. *Community and Revolution in Modern Vietnam.* Boston: Houghton Mifflin, 1976.

See also: Điên Biên Phu, Battle of; Geneva Conference and Geneva Accords; Hồ Chí Minh; Lao Đông Party; Lê Duân; Lê Đức Thọ; National Front for the Liberation of South Vietnam (NFLSV); Ngô Đình Diêm; Pham Văn Đồng; Viêt Minh (Viêt Nam Đôc Lâp Đồng Minh Hôi [Vietnam Independence League]); Viêt Nam Thanh Niên Cách Mang Chí Hôi (Vietnam Revolutionary Youth Association).

Vietnamese Culture

Although there is no consensus about the origins of the Vietnamese people, artifacts from a number of ancient sites in Vietnam indicate that the early ancestors of today's Vietnamese had both a written language and developed culture. Vietnamese archaeologists date the beginning of their civilization to the Phung-Nguyên culture of the late third millennium B.C. They regard this as advanced Neolithic or early Bronze Age culture. Phung-Nguyên sites covered tens of thousands of square yards and thousands of inhabitants. This gave way over the next thousands of years to a more hierarchical society centered on small village or family groups, culminating in what Vietnamese archaeologists called the Dong-son civilization from the seventh century B.C. to the first century A.D. Burial sites of this period of the legendary Hung kings have yielded considerable bronze artifacts. Bronze drums, rectangular stone axes, and bronze axes believed patterned after those of stone, all dating from this period, have been recovered from numerous sites in North Vietnam.

Most anthropologists believe that the Viet people lived first in what is today southern China. Pushed out of that area by the Chinese, they moved south and settled in the Red River Delta, mixing there with other Austro-Asian groups including Malaysians and Indonesians pushing northward.

Early Vietnamese had a self-contained sea-oriented culture. They fished and farmed and lived in a hierarchical society based on a system of hereditary privilege, mutual obligation, and personal loyalty, the people living in villages or small communities under the rule of the Lac lords. Many of the people tattooed their bodies in the belief that this would ward off peril from the sea. Women have traditionally enjoyed relatively high status in Vietnamese history, and this was true at this time as well. Indeed, when the Vietnamese rose up against Chinese rule, they were led by women.

In addition, there were the original aboriginal inhabitants, who the Vietnamese pushed out of the deltas and into the highlands. The French referred to these people collectively as the Montagnards ("mountain dwellers"). Today there are in Vietnam some 60 different minority ethnic groups with their own languages and cultures.

Vietnamese geography—the country extends over 1,200 miles from north to south—has meant that the climate of the country varies widely according to region. Distance and differing climates and living conditions affected dietary habits and outlook, much as Americans of New England and the Deep South differ in their culture. Despite this diversity, the population of the country is overwhelmingly Vietnamese, and Vietnam is largely a unified country in terms of language, customs, and traditions.

The Vietnamese language is in the Mon-Khmer group and reflects contributions from many ethnic groups. It is semimonosyllable with many disyllabic words and even some trisyllables—or to be more accurate, two-word and three-word compounds. Rich in its six tones, Vietnamese is a singing and musical language.

During the thousand years of Chinese rule, the Vietnamese adopted many Chinese words, modifying and employing them in Vietnamese patterns. To the end of the nineteenth century, Vietnamese still used Chinese characters for writing, but they pronounced them their own way. They also employed *Chữ Nôm*, a transcription of spoken Vietnamese that used Chinese characters with alterations.

In the seventeenth century, Catholic missionaries introduced *quốc ngữ* (national language), a romanized transcription of the spoken Vietnamese language. It has been mandatory in Vietnam since the beginning of the twentieth century. The colonial administration used *quốc ngữ* to eliminate the political and cultural influence of Vietnamese Confucian scholars. But it also greatly facilitated popular education and the training of skilled workers. This was a two-edged sword for the French, for it also brought the cultural and education concepts that were to help undermine their position in Vietnam.

Although China occupied Vietnam for a thousand years and the Vietnamese are unique among the peoples of Southeast Asia in adopting Chinese cultural patterns, the Vietnamese retained a sense of nationalism and cultural identity. While they assimilated Chinese culture and philosophy, the Vietnamese also slightly modified them to their own use, and despite the long Chinese occupation, the Vietnamese preserved their identity, language, and traditions. Thus, Vietnamese women have traditionally enjoyed higher social status than women in many Asian countries, and, while Vietnamese celebrate the Chinese Lunar New Year, known in Vietnam as Têt, there are significant differences in it.

The Vietnamese effort to maintain a distinct cultural identity, especially regarding China, has been a constant element in their history. Vietnamese military victories over Chinese invaders helped to fuel this sense of Vietnamese nationalism.

The Vietnamese adopted Confucianism and Taoism, but in moderate and more tolerant forms. Buddhism reached full development in Vietnam during the Lý dynasty (1010–1225). French and Portuguese priests brought Catholicism in the sixteenth century, and Protestantism arrived in the early twentieth century.

The Communists opposed both Catholicism, mainly because of its Western orientation and value systems, and Buddhism, because of its spirit of nonviolence and philosophy of "cause and effect."

Most Vietnamese practice veneration of their ancestors and believe that, when a person dies, his or her soul lives on. Dead and living coexist in the world and remain in communication with each other. Many believe that, because the souls of the dead can affect the living, descendants must provide for them and remember them on the anniversaries of their birthdays and marriages as well as holy days. Such days also serve to cement family ties. Ancestral tombs must be properly maintained, and houses contain altars honoring the ancestors.

Failure to venerate the departed, it is believed, will cause their souls to wander aimlessly and carry out destructive acts. Thus, the failure to practice ancestor worship could be destructive not only to an individual but to society as well. Vietnamese consider it their personal duty to provide for the aged. Older people are held in high esteem, and even verbal criticism of them or the departed is not tolerated.

Vietnamese families are patriarchal, and Vietnamese highly regard filial loyalty. Such strong family ties have often led to nepotism, however. For men, the societal ideal is *quân tử* ("kiun tseu" in Chinese): a preference for honesty and honor over material possessions.

Polygamy was legal in Vietnam during the French period, but marriage to concubine(s) had to be approved by the first wife. A new Family Law, introduced by Madame Ngô Đình Nhu and passed by the Republic of Vietnam Congress in 1959, ended the practice. However, polygamy still exists, particularly in northern Vietnam and in part because of the impact of warfare in decimating so many males.

Vietnam has a rich literature, especially poetry, both in Chinese characters and in *Chữ Nôm*. In the twentieth century all forms of literature prospered, including novels and poetry in *quốc ngữ*. In the late 1930s a new literary movement, known as the Tự Lực Văn Đoàn (Self-Reliance Literary Group), sought to revolutionize literature and promote positive change in Vietnamese society. The leader of this movement, Nguyên Tường Tam (pen name Nhất Linh), later became a leader of the Quốc Dân Đang and, in 1946, foreign minister of the Democratic Republic of Vietnam (DRV). He is still regarded as Vietnam's greatest modern writer.

Music, mostly songs, is by far the principal form of entertainment in Vietnam. Traditional Vietnamese music on a pentatonic scale is rich in folk songs and musical dramas such as *chè cô* (old musical plays), traditional in North Vietnam for thousands of years. *Cai lường* (modern musical drama) dates from the early twentieth century and is very popular throughout Vietnam, particularly in the South. Some of its instruments come from China, and some are those invented and played by Vietnamese only, such as the *đàn bâu,* or mono-string.

Western-scale diatonic music arrived in Vietnam with the French. At first, Western music drew the interest of only those who were close to the French or had attained a Western education. Songs composed by Vietnamese began appearing in the 1930s. This "new music," as it was called, developed quickly and came to be regarded as weapon in the fight for national independence as these songs changed from romantic songs and those praising nature to heroic and patriotic themes. After the proclamation of the Democratic Republic of Vietnam (DRV) and with the war against the French, the DRV government aggressively promoted nationalist and anti-French music. "Field cultural shows" with songs, poems, and plays helped instill high morale in Viêt Minh troops before they went into battle against the French. Some of the most influential musicians in this period were Văn Cao, Pham Duy, and Lưu Hưu Phước.

During the Vietnam War, the DRV government promoted anti-American songs, although in the North there was always a clandestine interest in South Vietnamese and Western music, carried by radio broadcasts from South Vietnam, Australia, the Voice of America (VOA), and British Broadcasting Corporation (BBC). The VOA, BBC, and Radio France International still broadcast South Vietnamese pre-1975 music.

There was little interest during the period of the State of Vietnam in promoting anti-Communist songs. This came in South Vietnam only after 1955. However, South Vietnamese were not interested in music composed on government order, and the only songs that were popular were those by freelance composers, which included those praising Army of the Republic of Vietnam (ARVN) soldiers, and in any case tended to be of higher artistic value. Most music in the South consisted of love songs. Although the Republic of Vietnam (RVN) government employed entertainment groups to serve its combat troops, these groups presented love songs more than heroic and patriotic songs.

After the 1975 Communist victory, books and music from South Vietnam flooded North Vietnam. Hà Nội then permitted songs from the pre-1975 South Vietnam, except for those critical of communism and all songs by Pham Duy.

Other fine arts are not as popular. Painting, wood-block printing, carving, and sculpture draw on both ancient China and the modern West. Although some Vietnamese kings left behind famous architectural constructions, these are not as imposing as those of China. Vietnamese have chosen to regard this as a sign that their rulers were not as tyrannical as those in other countries. Some dozen temples, relics of the Cham kingdom, built many hundreds of years before the Vietnamese invasions, do remain and today draw many foreign tourists. The film industry, still in its infancy, has yet to attract a foreign audience.

Nearly all Western sports are played in Vietnam, but the national favorite is soccer. Before 1975 the Republic of Vietnam won several Asian Games gold medals in soccer, tennis, and table tennis.

Education is highly prized in Vietnam. As in China, education was the chief path to positions of influence. Many renowned mandarins were born into poor peasant families but rose to positions of influence by reason of their success in the mandarinate examinations. A noble's or mandarin's child could claim no special privilege other than that gained through education and examination.

Rice is the staple diet in Vietnam. As with many Asian peoples, Vietnamese also consume a lot of pork fat. Almost all Vietnamese season their food with fish sauce, or *nước mắm,* which has a 16 to 18 percent protein content. Probably the two greatest Vietnamese delicacies for Americans are *phở* (noodle soup) and *cha giç* (meat roll).

Traditionally, peasants dressed in a pajamalike garment, black in the South and deep brown in the North. City dwellers dress in Western-style clothing. Vietnamese women alone wear the *áo dài* (literally, long dress).

Wars have greatly affected Vietnamese culture, especially after the division of the country following the 1954 Geneva Accords. South Vietnam adopted the worldwide standard 12-grade general education system. The curriculum somewhat overworked students of average ability and below, but it did produce a large number of professionals such as doctors, engineers, and professors. Artists, poets, and composers had complete creative license, providing they did not propagandize for the Communists. Leftist opinions and antiwar music were not banned. Freedom of press was limited, but much less strictly than in many countries at war. Many South Vietnamese easily assimilated Western ways, especially during the Vietnam War.

In North Vietnam, education and culture were tightly controlled and subordinated to Communist Party goals. Romantic poetry and music not conforming to Communist teachings were strictly forbidden. In this period and indeed until the break with Beijing in 1975, most official Vietnamese songs of the DRV, and later the Socialist Republic of Vietnam (SRV), conformed closely to those of the People's Republic of China.

Education in the North was in a ten-grade system in which students had to attend political indoctrination lessons four hours per week, and children of Communist cadres received preferential treatment. Many customs and traditions were banned, including saying "thank you," labeled as against the "new way of life." Many believed that the Vietnamese language in the North deteriorated from improper usage and the influence of Chinese Communist political literature.

The land reform campaign in the North had as one of its principal aims the eradication of traditional social and cultural structures in the countryside. Landholders and village notables were considered enemies of the Socialist Revolution because they were the political and cultural leaders. Between 1956 and 1957 the Nhân Văn Giai Phâm (Humanist Masterpieces) movement arose in opposition to this and included a large number of well-known writers, artists, composers, and poets who had been members of the Việt Minh. It and other dissident movements were crushed on Hồ Chí Minh's order.

Since the 1980s the SRV government has restored many institutions and regulations of the former RVN. The South was defeated militarily and politically, but it triumphed culturally in that the SRV has surrendered unconditionally to South Vietnamese culture, especially in music and mores.

Most Vietnamese living in the West are proud of their culture and have made great efforts to preserve and promote it.

—Nguyên Công Luân (Lư Tuân)

References: Pham Duy. *Hôi Ký*. Midway City, CA: P.D.C. Musical Productions & Pham Duy, 1991.
Pham Kim Vinh. *The Vietnamese Culture*. Solana Beach, CA: PM Enterprises, 1994.
Pham Văn Sơn. *Việt Sử Toàn Thư*. Sài Gòn: Thư Lâm Ấn Thư Quán, 1960; reprinted at Glendale, CA: Dainamco, n.d.
Vũ Ký. *Luận Cương Về Văn Hóa Việt Nam*. Brussels: Trung Tâm Văn Hóa Xã Hội Việt Nam, 1995.
See also: Buddhists; *Quốc Ngữ*.

Vietnamese Invasion and Occupation of Cambodia

(25 December 1978–26 September 1989)

The Vietnamese invasion and occupation of Cambodia from December 1978 to September 1989 isolated the Socialist Republic of Vietnam (SRV) from much of the international community, exacerbated troubled relations with the People's Republic of China (PRC), led to a brief war in 1979 between the PRC and the SRV, proved a serious drain on the Vietnamese economy, and delayed normalization of relations between Vietnam and the United States. It also drove the Khmer Rouge from power.

The background of the conflict lay not in ideology but in traditional animosity between Vietnam and Cambodia. Khmer Rouge leaders were also bitter that in the 1960s the Vietnamese Communists, anxious to keep their own useful accommodation with Prince Norodom Sihanouk's government intact, had given the Khmer Rouge no support. This permanently embittered Khmer Rouge leaders, who were, in any case, instinctively anti-Vietnamese. After entering into an uneasy alliance with the Vietnamese Communists after Sihanouk's fall, Khmer Rouge leaders believed that they had been betrayed a second time after the Vietnamese Communists signed the 1973 Paris peace accords. Khmer Rouge leaders ordered the Vietnamese to leave Cambodian territory and even launched a purge to eliminate pro-Vietnamese elements within the Khmer Rouge. These purges killed nearly all the "Khmer Việt Minh," those Cambodians who had fought against the French and had gone on to live in the Democratic Republic of Vietnam (DRV) until 1970, when the government there had ordered them south to help lead the Cambodian resistance.

From the spring of 1973 the Vietnamese Communists no longer played any role in the Khmer Rouge fight against the Lon Nol government. They remained in their Cambodian sanctuaries, however; and from time to time there were armed clashes between them and the Khmer Rouge.

In April 1975 the Khmer Rouge defeated the Lon Nol government. After they came to power, the Khmer Rouge ordered the people out of the capital of Phnom Penh and larger towns and put them to work in agricultural labor camps in the countryside. All private property was abolished, and paper money disappeared, replaced by ration tickets earned by productive labor. Schools were closed and Buddhist temples destroyed. Thousands of people died, including many ethnic Vietnamese; some 200,000 Vietnamese were expelled from the country.

In January 1976 the Khmer Rouge promulgated a new constitution and changed the name of the country to the Democratic Republic of Kampuchea. In April Prince Sihanouk resigned as head of state. Khieu Samphan took his place, but Pol Pot, another Khmer Rouge leader, was the dominant figure in the cabinet. Meanwhile the government announced that 800,000 people, or roughly 10 percent of the population, had died in the war that brought the Khmer Rouge to power.

There had long been border disputes between Vietnam and Cambodia, and by 1977 these led to serious fighting. In September Vietnam claimed that four Kampuchean divisions had invaded its Tây Ninh Province. In September and December Vietnam retaliated. The December incursion saw 60,000 troops, supported by tanks and artillery, striking as far as the outskirts of Svay Rieng and Kompong Cham. It led to the first public disclosure of the conflict, and on 31 December 1977 an angry radio broadcast from Phnom Penh denounced the Vietnamese. A week later the Vietnamese withdrew, most probably on their own accord, but the Khmer Rouge declared that it had won a "historic victory" and rejected calls for negotiations. The Khmer Rouge also proceeded to carry out a violent purge centered on its armed forces in the eastern part of the country that were supposed to defend the regime from the Vietnamese. Up to 100,000 Cambodians were executed. Many Khmer Rouge fled into Vietnam to avoid being arrested and killed. Later they formed the backbone of the Vietnamese-sponsored anti–Khmer Rouge resistance.

Kampuchea also laid claim to much of Cochin China (southernmost Vietnam), which had a large Khmer minority, and to small islands in the Gulf of Thailand. In 1960 Sài Gòn had claimed seven of these, including the largest island of Phú Quôc, and landed troops. There was a major clash between the two states in May 1975 over these islands, almost certainly prompted by the belief that there was oil in the area.

As the border conflicts escalated, Hà Nôi supported an anti–Khmer Rouge resistance. Eastern Cambodia had been an important part of the People's Army of Vietnam (PAVN) and Viêt Công logistics system during the Vietnam War, and ties between the people there and Vietnam were strong. This was strengthened by the fact that many of those opposed to the Khmer Rouge fled to the border area. Hà Nôi now organized those who had fled to Vietnam, including many ex–Khmer Rouge fighters, into anti–Khmer Rouge units to fight alongside the Vietnamese Army against Kampuchean forces. Much of this fighting occurred in the Parrot's Beak area.

Fighting along the border escalated, and from June 1978 both sides used aircraft, with Chinese pilots flying on the Kampuchean side. Although Hà Nôi made several offers to negotiate, all these were rebuffed by the Khmer Rouge.

Although Kampuchea remained largely cut off from the outside world, stories of mass killings there began to circulate. In October 1978 Hà Nôi claimed that the Khmer Rouge had killed 2 million Kampucheans. At the time, this was thought to be propaganda, but clearly something was happening. Kampuchea, regarded as a rice bowl in Southeast Asia, was close to starvation.

Tensions between Vietnam and Kampuchea were abetted by the fact that the two states became proxies in the developing Sino-Soviet rivalry. Kampuchea was a client state of China; Vietnam, of the Soviet Union. Loyalties of the Communist world divided accordingly; most of the Warsaw Pact nations and Cuba, then relying heavily on financial assistance from the Soviet Union, supported Vietnam; North Korea supported Kampuchea.

At the beginning of December 1978 several anti–Khmer Rouge factions came together to form the Kampuchean National Front led by Khmer Rouge defector Heng Samrin, former deputy commander in eastern Cambodia. Hà Nôi gave the Front full support, including military assistance, and it soon fielded an army of 20,000.

Finally, on 25 December 1978 the Vietnamese Army invaded Cambodia on a broad front. Initially the SRV committed 12 divisions, or half of its army, to the operation. Ultimately there were 200,000 Vietnamese troops in Cambodia, along with Heng Samrin's army. Pol Pot's army numbered only approximately 60,000 in

four divisions and three independent regiments, and it was armed with a mix of weapons. Heavily outnumbered and outgunned, the Khmer Rouge retreated into the countryside and waged guerrilla warfare. Heng Samrin and his forces took Phnom Penh unopposed and soon had all principal Kampuchean cities under their control. Heng Samrin became president of the country, but only the presence of several Vietnamese divisions enabled him to remain in power. The Soviet Union, Laos, the SRV, and most other Communist states recognized the new government. In January 1979 the USSR used its veto in the UN Security Council to kill a resolution demanding the withdrawal of all foreign troops from Kampuchea. Heng Samrin, meanwhile, entered into treaties with the SRV and Laos.

With his forces down to only about 25,000 troops, Pol Pot continued to conduct guerrilla warfare, concentrating what remained of his army in the thick jungles of northeastern Kampuchea near the Thai border. China, meanwhile, aided the Khmer Rouge, funneling this assistance through Thailand. Thai generals profited handsomely from the misery, allowing the transit of military assistance to the Khmer Rouge and securing gems and timber from their area of control.

In yet another ironic legacy of the Vietnam War, the United States also aided the Khmer Rouge. Supposedly, Washington sent military assistance only to the non–Khmer Rouge resistance groups, but it was an open secret that much of this aid was in fact used by the Khmer Rouge. Only the Vietnamese occupation prevented the Khmer Rouge from returning to power and continuing their genocidal policies. Indeed, it was only because of the Vietnamese invasion that the mass killings of Cambodians by the Khmer Rouge were confirmed.

China, meanwhile, threatened the SRV with force to punish Hà Nôi for the invasion of Kampuchea, and divisions of the PRC's People's Liberation Army actually invaded Vietnam in a brief war in February and March 1979. The Chinese invasion did not drive the Vietnamese from Cambodia. That came about from the sheer expense of the operation and resultant drain on the Vietnamese economy, and the SRV's attendant isolation in the international community at a time when the leadership recognized the need to revitalize the national economy and secure foreign investment.

Finally, in May 1988 Hà Nôi announced that it would withdraw 50,000 troops, about half of its forces, from Cambodia by the end of the year. In July the Phnom Penh government and rebel coalition met for the first time face-to-face in inconclusive peace talks in Indonesia. On 5 April 1989 Hà Nôi and Phnom Penh announced jointly that all Vietnamese troops would leave Cambodia by the end of September, even if no settlement was found. On 26 September 1989 Vietnam announced that all its troops had withdrawn from Cambodia. Some 25,000 Vietnamese troops had died there.

In late 1990, after prolonged negotiations, rival Cambodian factions, including the Vietnamese-installed regime—then headed by Hun Sen—and the Khmer Rouge, agreed to a supreme national council headed by Prince Sihanouk. The United Nations also mounted a vast peacekeeping operation and supervised elections. The Khmer Rouge—into 1996 at least—had not returned to power.

—Spencer C. Tucker

References: Becker, Elizabeth. *When the War Was Over.* New York: Simon & Schuster, 1986.
Chanda, Nayan. *Brother Enemy.* New York: Harcourt Brace Jovanovich, 1986.
Chen, King C. *China's War with Vietnam, 1979: Issues, Decisions, and Implications.* Stanford, CA: Hoover Institute Press, 1987.
Etcheson, Craig. *The Rise and Fall of Democratic Kampuchea.* Boulder, CO: Westview Press, 1984.
Hardy, Gordon, Arnold R. Isaacs, and MacAlister Brown. *Pawns of War.* Boston: Boston Publishing, 1987.
Isaacs, Arnold R. *Without Honor: Defeat in Vietnam and Cambodia.* Baltimore: Johns Hopkins University Press, 1983.
O'Ballance, Edgar. *The Wars in Vietnam, 1954–1980.* Rev. ed. New York: Hippocrine Books, 1981.
See also: Cambodia; China, People's Republic of (PRC); Heng Samrin; Kampuchean National Front; Khmer Rouge; Lon Nol; Pol Pot; Sihanouk, Norodom; Union of Soviet Socialist Republics (USSR) (Soviet Union); Vietnam, Socialist Republic of: 1975 to the Present.

Vietnamese National Army (VNA)

French-created indigenous Vietnamese force established to fight the Viêt Minh. In the 8 March 1949 Elysée Agreement, France recognized the Associated State of Vietnam within the French Union, complete with its own military, the Vietnamese National Army (VNA), to operate in conjunction with French forces against the Viêt Minh. Although Chief of State Bao Ðai was the nominal supreme commander of the VNA from 1949 to 1955, in effect it remained under control of the French High Command.

The VNA met with a mixed reception from French commanders, who for the most part persisted in the practice of recruiting Vietnamese for their own forces. This angered the Bao Ðai government and made VNA recruitment more difficult. Typical was the attitude of French military commander in Indo-China (1949–1950) Marcel Carpentier. He welcomed the expanded military support promised by the VNA, but wanted it firmly in French hands. U.S. Maj. Gen. Graves B. Erskine reported that Carpentier told him that Vietnamese troops were unreliable, would not make good soldiers, and were not to be trusted on their own. Erskine said that he replied, "General Carpentier, who in hell are you fighting but Vietnamese?" Carpentier steadfastly refused to allow U.S. military aid to be channeled directly to the Vietnamese.

Jean de Lattre de Tassigny (commanding general and French high commissioner in Indo-China, 1950–1951) felt differently. One of his chief policies was *le jaunissement* (yellowing): the building up and training of wholly Vietnamese units. At the time of his arrival in Indo-China, the VNA numbered only 11 battalions and nine gendarmerie units. De Lattre launched a program to increase this to 25 battalions, four armored squadrons, and eight artillery batteries, along with support units. De Lattre also saw to it that some of his best officers and men volunteered to serve as cadres. But this effort came too late, and de Lattre left Indo-China in December 1951.

The goal was a VNA force of 115,000 troops, but in May 1951 it had less than 40,000. In July 1951 the Trân Văn Hửu government decreed a "general mobilization" to conscript 60,000 men for two months' training, something that de Lattre applauded. The small number of officer candidates (1,000) and specialists (600) attracted under this plan were less than a quarter the number actually needed. Even this modest plan soon encountered difficulties, as fewer than half the number of officer candidates reported for duty at training schools in Thu Ðưc and Nam Ðinh. The government called up only half of the planned number of conscripts, and these did not receive their full training. Less than 10 percent of them were induced to join the VNA.

Recruiting for the VNA continued to lag, and in January 1952 the Bao Ðai government cut the quota for enlisted specialists from 800 to 500 and the training period for officer candidates from 12 months to only 8. Of 1,000 officer candidates projected as required in the mobilization plan, only 690 were in training. The VNA also suffered from a severe lack of trained senior officers, and it had no general staff, chief of staff, or minister of defense.

The VNA suffered chiefly from conflict between the French and the Bao Ðai government and a lack of financial support. Bao Ðai wanted the new units under his personal control, but the French refused; they accused the Vietnamese of delaying the recruitment of new units. Yet until the VNA was genuinely independent of French control, it was unlikely to attract many recruits. In May 1953 the Viêt Minh showed the VNA's true situation when, for the second time in less than two years, three companies attacked the training school, Centre d'Instruction Technique No. 3 at Nam Ðinh and captured much of its 600-member student body and all school weapons without incurring any casualties.

In 1953 the VNA had two types of battalions: the Bataillon Vietnamien (BVN), armed with French weapons and having a base camp and administrative support elements, and the Tiêu Ðoàn Khinh Quân (TDKQ, or Light Infantry Battalion), armed with the U.S. M1 Garand and M1 Carbine rifles, but without significant base and support elements.

General Henri Navarre also wanted to increase the size of the VNA, form progressively larger units (first mobile groups and then divisions), and give it operational autonomy and more responsibility. He planned to bring it to 54 battalions before the end of the year and to double that in 1954. In fact, he succeeded in creating 107 new battalions of 95,000 troops, although the VNA was never well trained and led.

In 1955 the Ngô Ðình Diêm government took over the VNA, and it became the nucleus of the Army of the Republic of Vietnam (ARVN).

—Gary Kerley and Spencer C. Tucker

References: Clayton, Anthony. *Three Marshals of France: Leadership after Trauma.* London: Brassey's, 1992.
Ðồng Văn Khuyên. *The RVNAF.* Washington, DC: U.S. Army Center of Military History, 1980.
Duicker, William J. *Historical Dictionary of Vietnam.* Metuchen, NJ: Scarecrow Press, 1989.
Fall, Bernard B. *The Two Viet-Nams: A Political and Military Analysis.* Rev. ed. New York: Praeger, 1967.

Herring, George C. *America's Longest War: The United States and Vietnam, 1950–1975.* Rev. ed. Philadelphia, PA: Temple University Press, 1986.

Spector, Ronald H. *Advice and Support: The Early Years, 1941–1960. The U.S. Army in Vietnam.* Washington, DC: U.S. Army Center of Military History, 1983.

See also: Bao Đai; Carpentier, Marcel; de Lattre de Tassigny, Jean Joseph Marie Gabriel; Ngô Đình Diêm; Viêt Minh (Viêt Nam Đôc Lâp Đông Minh Hôi [Vietnam Independence League]); Vietnam, Republic of: Army (ARVN).

Vietnamization

Vietnamization is an American term used to describe the process of progressively turning primary responsibility for conduct of the Vietnam War back over to the South Vietnamese. In his book *Lost Victory,* Ambassador William Colby, who led American support for pacification during the critical period, defined Vietnamization broadly as the "practical consequences of the Nixon Doctrine, that is, withdrawal of American troops and reinforcement of South Vietnamese forces to withstand the North Vietnamese." Secretary of Defense Melvin Laird is often credited with coining the term "Vietnamization" in the spring of 1969, although General Creighton Abrams had almost a year earlier told a White House meeting that he was training the South Vietnamese army for the purpose of "Vietnamizing" the war.

Whatever the program's origins, Colby's definition is comprehensive enough to include the many elements essential if Vietnamization were to succeed: improving and modernizing the armed forces, providing pacification of the rural areas, strengthening the political apparatus, delivering essential services to the populace, nurturing a viable economy, and, most important of all, ensuring security for the people. From these goals derived a host of subsidiary tasks: from expanding and improving the police and territorial forces to land reform, from control of inflation to hamlet and village elections, and from rooting out the Viêt Công infrastructure to increasing the rice harvest. Ambassador Ellsworth Bunker noted in a reporting cable that South Vietnam's plan for community defense and local development had "three overall objectives: self-defense, self-government, and self-development, which explains why the Vietnamese refer to 'Vietnamization' as 'the three selfs.'"

George Jacobson, a longtime American official serving in the U.S. Embassy, used to tell visitors that opinions varied as to whether security for the people was 10 percent of the pacification process or 90 percent, but everyone agreed that it was the *first* 10 percent or the *first* 90 percent. In other words, without security, nothing else could proceed. Perhaps even more important than the regular armed forces, therefore, were the territorial forces and the People's Self-Defense Force. The latter, sponsored by President Nguyên Văn Thiêu when all his advisors were cautioning against it, resulted in half a million weapons being issued to ordinary citizens.

Neutralizing the Viêt Công infrastructure was another crucially important task. The enemy needed guerrilla forces and the cadre in the South Vietnamese hamlets and villages, General Abrams stressed. "If anything," he said, "they're more important to him than the caches, or more important to him than the actual strength of his rifle battalions."

Dealing with the enemy infrastructure was, in Abrams's view, the way to get off the treadmill that U.S. forces had been on in Vietnam. Ambassador Bunker agreed. "It seemed to me we started late in training the Vietnamese and that we had a lot to make up," he said in an oral history interview. "In the beginning, I think we had misjudged the war and thought it would be a short-term proposition, that we could finish it ourselves." In due course, the remarkable combination of Bunker, Abrams, and Colby was in place, and the "making up" began in earnest.

In *No More Vietnams,* Richard Nixon recalled of Vietnamization that "our whole strategy depended on whether this program succeeded." Thus, "our principal objectives shifted to protecting the South Vietnamese at the village level, reestablishing the local political process, and winning the loyalty of the peasants by involving them in the government and providing them with economic opportunity. General Creighton Abrams had initiated this shift in strategy when he took command of our forces in Vietnam in 1968," Nixon acknowledged.

Of course, the Americans could only help and, as Abrams once observed, they could only help so much. The rest was up to the Vietnamese. Ambassador Bunker admired what they were able to achieve in the midst of so much conflict. "I think his posture was remarkably enlightened," he said of President Thiêu. "Considering that the country was at war, I think it was quite remarkable how well the government functioned."

That aspect of Vietnamization was at least equal in importance to progress in building up military forces that could maintain security as American forces progressively withdrew. Among the many indicators of effective government functioning was skillful handling of refugees. Land reform was another. "The record will show that the GVN did quite a remarkable job on land distribution, one of their major achievements," said Bunker. Resurgence of the agricultural sector was yet another. In 1969, for example, South Vietnam had its best rice crop since 1964, an achievement made all the more impressive by the impediments of an ongoing war and labor shortages induced by simultaneous expansion of the armed forces, territorial forces, and police. "It certainly brought prosperity in the Delta and the South," said Bunker. "I can recall going down there later in my tour and seeing farmers and people riding motorcycles where they used to ride bicycles, and seeing antennae over the houses in the villages, seeing people using tractors where they had used oxen before to plow."

In one of his reporting cables, Ambassador Bunker remarked that "pacification is tough to measure—it's something that one judges by feel, like politics." By the time the Paris peace agreement was signed, he later recalled, that feeling was unmistakable. "The country was quiet," he said. "One could travel anywhere in Vietnam."

Soon the last American forces had been withdrawn, and the South Vietnamese were left to cope with the continued war as best they might, eventually without major financial or material assistance from their former American allies, much less the swift retribution that had been promised in the event the DRV violated the

Members of the 1st Army of the Republic of Vietnam (ARVN) Division move along a trail near Fire Support Base O'Reilly in Thừa Thiên Province. As part of Nixon's Vietnamization program, ARVN troops had taken over the firebase earlier in 1970, but abandoned it in September after a two-month siege.

agreement. Thus, the accomplishments of Vietnamization were squandered.

—Lewis Sorley

References: Bunker, Ellsworth. *The Bunker Papers: Reports to the President from Vietnam, 1967–1973.* Edited by Douglas Pike. 3 vols. Berkeley, CA: Institute for East Asian Studies, 1990.

Clarke, Jeffrey J. *Advice and Support: The Final Years, 1965–1973.* Washington, DC: U.S. Army Center of Military History, 1988.

Colby, William, with James McCargar. *Lost Victory.* Chicago: Contemporary Books, 1989.

Nguyên Duy Hinh. *Vietnamization and the Cease-Fire.* Washington, DC: U.S. Army Center of Military History, 1980.

Thompson, Robert. *No Exit from Vietnam.* New York: D. McKay, 1969.

See also: Abrams, Creighton; Bunker, Ellsworth; Civil Operations and Revolutionary Development Support (CORDS); Colby, William Egan; ENHANCE PLUS, Operation; Jacobson, George D.; Nixon, Richard Milhous; Pacification.

Võ Nguyên Giáp

(1911–)

Vietnamese leader of the military struggle from 1944 to 1980 against Japan, France, the United States, Cambodia, and China. Widely recognized as a master logistician, Võ Nguyên Giáp also became adept at tactics and strategy. He drew his understanding of military science from many sources, including patriotic inspiration from his own country's past heroes, such as Trưng Trắc and Trưng Nhi, Lý Bôn and Ngô Quyên, Trân Hưng Đạo and Nguyên Huê. He learned from the writings of Sun Tzu and Mao Zedong, from Hô Chí Minh and Lenin. He knew of Napoleon's campaigns, and he assiduously studied the writings of T. E. Lawrence. From all these, as well as his own field experiences, he welded together an approach to combat that confounded his enemies.

Võ Nguyên Giáp was born on 25 August 1911 to a townswoman, Nguyên Thi Kiên, and her husband, Võ Quang Nghiêm, in the tiny village of An Xá, along the banks of the Kiên Giang River, subdistrict of Quang Ninh, district of Lê Thuy, in the province of Quang Bình in central An Nam, just north of the 17th parallel. He was the sixth of eight children, the first three having died in infancy.

Giáp completed his primary education in local schools and in 1925 moved to Huê to study at the Quôc Hoc, or Lycée Nationale. Regarded by school authorities as an agitator, he was expelled in 1927 and worked for a time as a journalist. He also joined the Tân Viêt Cách Mênh Đang (Revolutionary Party for a New Vietnam), which soon split into two factions. Giáp allied himself with the Communist wing and thereafter lived a double life as journalist and secret revolutionary.

Giáp was caught in a police dragnet at the end of 1930 and sentenced to serve two years at hard labor at Lao Bao, a French prison in the mountains near Laos. There he met his future wife, 15-year-old Nguyên Thi Quang Thái, daughter of a railroad employee in Vinh. Given an early release, Giáp moved to Vinh, into the home of Professor Đăng Thái Mai, a former teacher of literature at the Quôc Hoc. There he met Mai's daughter, Đăng Bích Hà, a toddler, born in 1919, who called him Chú (Uncle) and who one day would became his second wife.

After moving to Hà Nôi, Giáp studied at the Lycée Albert Sarraut, graduating in 1934. Thereupon he accepted a job as teacher of history and French at Lycée Thăng Long (Rising Dragon). He simultaneously published a newspaper, *Hôn Tre Tâp Mơi* (Soul of Youth, new edition), which was shut down by authorities after its fifth issue. Thereupon Giáp published *Le Travail* (Work) and initiated at least 11 other short-lived journals. He also began studies at the School of Law of the University of Hà Nôi, and in 1938 he received his *license en droit* with a concentration in political economy.

Giáp joined the Communist Party in 1937, and sometime before April 1939 married Quang Thái. In early 1940 they had a daughter, Hông Anh (Red Queen of Flowers). In April 1940 the party ordered him to flee into southern China. He left behind his wife and daughter, never again to see Quang Thái, who was arrested by the French in May 1941 and tortured to death in Hoa Lò (The Oven) prison in Hà Nôi.

Traveling with Pham Văn Đông, Giáp reached southern China and there met Nguyên Âi Quôc, now calling himself Hô Chí Minh. Under Hô's orders, Giáp returned to the mountains of northern Tonkin between 1941 and 1945 and, with his cadre, worked among the hill tribes (Nùng, Thô, Mán Trăng, Mán Tiên, Tày

Võ Nguyên Giáp (left) with Hô Chí Minh. Now viewed as a "national treasure," Giáp makes appearances on ceremonial occasions, but is otherwise closely watched by his government.

[Tai], Dao, Hmong, and others), converting them to the anti-French cause. One of his followers, Chu Văn Tân, became a leader in the first armed resistance organization, the Army for National Salvation. Meanwhile Hồ organized a new group, the Việt Nam Độc Lập Đông Minh Hôi (Vietnam Independence League), or Việt Minh. Its rivals for power included the Đang Đai Việt, a nationalist middle-class urban group; the Việt Nam Quốc Dân Đang, an older group founded in 1927 by radical intellectuals; and the Việt Nam Cách Mênh Đông Minh Hôi, founded in 1942 under Chinese sponsorship.

Giáp's Việt Minh cadres were most successful in enlisting support among both lowland Vietnamese and hill people. He insisted on such a rigid code of conduct for his agents that tribal women began calling them "men without cocks." French efforts between 1942 and 1944 to destroy this fledgling movement came to be called the time of the "white terror."

On 22 December 1944 Giáp formed 34 men into the Việt Nam Tuyên Truyền Giai Phóng Quân (Vietnam Armed Propaganda and Liberation Brigade). First attacks against the French came on 24 December when Giáp's unit struck outposts at Phai Khát and Nà Ngân. During a later attack on the town of Thai Nguyên on 20 August 1945, Giáp learned that the Japanese had surrendered, and he marched his men into Hà Nôi. Between 19 and 30 August, Hồ's Việt Minh grabbed power from the Red River to the Mekong Delta. Giáp became minister of the interior of the new Democratic Republic of Vietnam (DRV) and was later named to the rank of full general and commander of all Việt Minh military forces.

Military incidents with the French in Tonkin, particularly at Hai Phòng, caused Giáp to issue a national call to arms on 19 December 1946. Retreating in the face of French strength, by early 1947 the Việt Minh government and Giáp's army were once again hiding in the remote fastnesses of northern Vietnam. In the next years Giáp put together an army of nearly 300,000 troops and militia and made a series of attacks against French troops and positions, sometimes sustaining savage casualties. In 1953 he launched a drive into Laos, having already gained control of most of central and northern Vietnam outside the coastal lowlands. French military commander General Henri Navarre, seeking a "set-piece" battle with Giáp's forces, chose to commit 10,000 troops to an isolated valley in northwest Vietnam astride Giáp's line of communication to Laos at Điên Biên Phu.

Giáp secretly brought recently obtained artillery into the surrounding mountains, a development the French considered impossible. He also massed 50,000 troops and laid siege for 55 days to French strong points in the valley. The French surrendered on 8 May 1954 and, at Geneva, gave up further efforts to control Vietnam north of the 17th parallel.

Giáp also led the military campaign against the southern Republic of Vietnam (RVN) and the United States during the 1960s and 1970s. Giáp, like Mao, believed that revolutionary warfare against a government passed through three stages: guerrilla warfare, strategic defense, and counteroffensive. Giáp was long concerned that the United States might invade the North and, when he believed his forces strong enough, frequently orchestrated frontal attacks on U.S. positions, as in the Ia Drang Valley (Novem-

ber 1965), at Khe Sanh (January 1968), and in the Tết Offensive (January 1968). Militarily opposed to the latter, he bowed before the greater political influence of Lê Duân, "the Flame of the South," General Nguyên Chí Thanh, and their allies in the Politburo. These individuals, all dedicated to the overthrow of the RVN, faulted Giáp for his reticence to use his units boldly below the 17th parallel and consistently called for increased military action in the South.

The Tết Offensive destroyed the Viêt Công and forced the People's Army of Vietnam (PAVN) troops to carry the burden of the war. Still, Tết was a strategic victory for the Communists, even if a tactical defeat. Following Hồ's death (2 September 1969), Giáp shared power with Lê Duân, who controlled domestic affairs, and Pham Văn Đồng, who presided over the Foreign Ministry. Giáp's goals were to prolong the war, to inflict setbacks to U.S. President Richard Nixon's policy of Vietnamization, and to impose continuing casualties on U.S. troops. Not until 1970 did Giáp order new offensives, concentrating on the conquest of southern Laos and destabilization of Cambodia's border region.

In 1972, with some dismay because he felt the time was not yet ripe, Giáp planned his Nguyên Hué, or Easter Offensive. The Politburo had called for the offensive, assuming that, with U.S. forces all but withdrawn, the Republic of Vietnam was ripe for attack. Once again Giáp's misgivings were proven correct. Throughout most of the RVN, after initial withdrawals, the Army of the Republic of Vietnam (ARVN) held its positions when buttressed with massive American air strikes. Nixon also ordered extensive bombings of the DRV and mining of Hai Phòng Harbor. The PAVN suffered more than 100,000 casualties. Still, when it was over, Giáp's divisions occupied territory never before controlled, and the terms of the 1973 peace agreement did not require their removal.

Ironically, although he retained his post of minister of defense, the Politburo then stripped Giáp—who had opposed the entire offensive—of his command of the PAVN and gave it to his chief of staff and longtime disciple, General Văn Tiên Dũng. It was Dũng who led the Hồ Chí Minh offensive, the final assault on the South in 1975. Thereafter Giáp's life consisted of a round of visits to countries, most of which were Communist: Cuba, Algeria, the USSR, East Germany, Hungary, Poland, China, Yemen, Madagascar, Mozambique, Ethiopia, Guinea, Benin, Congo, and Angola. Appointed to head the Ministry of Science and Technology, Giáp opposed the 1978 Vietnamese invasion of Cambodia and played only a supervisory role in it and in the conflict with China that began in 1979. In 1986 Giáp retired as minister of defense, and in August 1991 he was forced to give up his remaining post as vice-premier in charge of family planning. Now viewed as a "national treasure," Giáp lives quietly with his wife at their villa, appearing on ceremonial occasions, but closely watched by his government, which fears he might lead a military coup against it.

—Cecil B. Currey

References: Currey, Cecil B. *Victory at Any Cost: The Genius of Viet Nam's Gen. Vo Nguyen Giap.* Washington, DC: Brassey's, 1997.

Davidson, Phillip B. *Vietnam at War: The History, 1946–1975.* Novato, CA: Presidio Press, 1988.

Turley, Gerald H. *The Easter Offensive: The Last American Advisors, Vietnam, 1972.* Novato, CA: Presidio Press, 1985.

Văn Tiên Dũng. *Our Great Spring Victory.* New York: Monthly Review Press, 1977.

Võ Nguyên Giáp. *Dien Bien Phu.* Hà Nôi: Foreign Languages Publishing House, 1962.

———. *Unforgettable Days.* Hà Nôi: Foreign Languages Publishing House, 1978.

Võ Nguyên Giáp, interviews with the author, December 1988 and July 1991.

Who's Who in the Socialist Countries. New York: Saur, 1978.

See also: *Đâu Tranh;* Điên Biên Phu, Battle of; Easter Offensive (Nguyên Huê Campaign); Hô Chí Minh; Ia Drang, Battle of; Khe Sanh, Battles of; Lê Duân; Navarre, Henri Eugène; Nguyên Chí Thanh; Nixon, Richard Milhous; Pham Văn Đông; Têt Offensive: Overall Strategy; Têt Offensive: the Sài Gòn Circle; Transportation Group 559; Văn Tiên Dũng; Viêt Minh (Viêt Nam Đôc Lâp Đông Minh Hôi [Vietnam Independence League]); Vietnam, Democratic Republic of: Army (People's Army of Vietnam [PAVN]).

Võ Trân Chí

(?–)

Prominent figure in the Vietnamese Communist Party (VCP). Little is known about Võ Trân Chí's activities during the Vietnam War except that he was a guerrilla leader in the Sài Gòn area.

In 1977 Chí was elected secretary of the VCP Committee of the 5th District of Hô Chí Minh City, the main commercial section of the former Sài Gòn. In 1986 he became secretary of the VCP Committee of Hô Chí Minh City, a position he retained through 1996. Chí was promoted to the Politburo in June 1991. A protégé of SRV Premier Võ Văn Kiêt, Chí was regarded as a staunch conservative. Approximately 70 years old in June 1996, he was dropped from the Politburo at the Eighth Communist Party Congress.

—Ngô Ngoc Trung

Reference: Biographical Files, Indo-China Archives, University of California at Berkeley.

See also: Vietnam, Socialist Republic of: 1975 to the Present; Vietnamese Communist Party (VCP); Võ Văn Kiêt.

Võ Văn Kiêt

(1922–)

Prominent leader in the Vietnamese Communist Party (VCP) and the Socialist Republic of Vietnam (SRV). Born on 23 November 1922 into a peasant family in Trung Hiêp village, Vũng Liêm District, Vĩnh Long Province, Võ Văn Kiêt became a revolutionary in 1938 and joined the Indo-Chinese Communist Party the next year. He was active as a leader in the anti-French youth movement, and from 1941 to 1945, while in Rach Giá, he joined the provincial party committee and participated in an attempt to seize power in the August 1945 armed uprising at Vũng Liêm.

After the uprising, Kiêt was deputy secretary of the party committee of Rach Giá Province. During the early period of the Indo-China War, he was a political commissar with the People's Army of Vietnam (PAVN) guerrilla units in the South. In 1950 he was transferred to Bắc Liêu Province, where he became provincial party secretary. In 1955 Kiêt was on the Southern Region Party Committee and deputy secretary of Hâu Giang Inter-Zone. He then became party secretary of the Sài Gòn–Gia Đinh Zone.

At the 1960 Third Party Congress, Kiêt became an alternate member of the Central Committee's Executive Committee. He was also on the Central Committee for the Southern Region and continued as party secretary for the Sài Gòn–Gia Đinh Zone. Kiêt then became party secretary for the Southwestern Zone. In 1972 he was again elected to the Executive Committee of the Central Committee. From 1972 to 1975 he worked at the central committee level on the Southern Region's Standing Committee.

At the time of the 1975 PAVN/Viêt Công victory, Kiêt was secretary of the Special Party Committee of the Military Management Committee and vice-chairman of the Military Management Committee of Sài Gòn. Later he became deputy party secretary and chairman of the Hô Chí Minh City People's Committee. He was elected as a deputy to the Sixth National Assembly of the SRV.

At the 1976 Fourth Party Congress, Kiêt joined the Central Committee's Executive Committee and was chosen an alternate member of the Politburo, assigned to the position of party secretary of Hô Chí Minh City. At the 1982 Fifth Party Congress, Kiêt was elected to the Politburo. At the same time, the National Assembly appointed him a vice-chairman of the Council of Ministers and chairman of the State Planning Committee.

At the 1986 Sixth Party Congress, Kiêt was elected to the Central Committee's Executive Committee and the Politburo. In 1987 he was elected to the Eighth National Assembly and appointed as first vice-chairman of the Council of Ministers. On the March 1988 death of Premier Pham Hùng, Kiêt became acting premier. In June Đô Mười, a candidate introduced by the Communist Party Central Committee, was elected premier by the National Assembly, replacing Kiêt. At the 1991 Seventh Party Congress, Kiêt joined the Central Committee's Executive Committee and rejoined the Politburo. In June 1991 Kiêt became chairman of the SRV Council of Ministers, replacing Đô Mười.

Considered easygoing and charming, Kiêt was regarded as a moderate within the VCP and an advocate of changes based on material incentives, decentralized decision making, and limited free enterprise. He also favored normalization of relations with the United States.

—Ngô Ngoc Trung

Reference: Biographical Files, Indo-China Archives, University of California at Berkeley.

See also: Pham Hùng; Vietnam, Socialist Republic of: 1975 to the Present; Vietnamese Communist Party (VCP).

Vogt, John W., Jr.

(1920–)

U.S. Air Force general. Born in Elizabeth, New York, on 19 March 1920, John W. Vogt, Jr. enlisted in the Army Air Corps in 1941; he was commissioned and received his pilot's wings in 1942. During World War II, he was a fighter pilot in the 63d and 360th Fighter Squadrons in Europe. Vogt rose through the ranks, and from 1965 to 1968 he served as deputy for plans and operations, Pacific Air

Forces in Honolulu, Hawaii. In this capacity he participated in the planning and direction of the air campaign against North Vietnam. In 1972 he was named commander of the Seventh U.S. Air Force in Vietnam, while serving concurrently as deputy commander of Military Assistance Command, Vietnam (MACV). The 1972 Easter bombardment of the North was carried out under his direction. Vogt presided over the pullout of U.S. forces from Vietnam through the remainder of 1972 to March 1973, after which his headquarters was moved to Nakhom Phanom Royal Thai Air Force Base. In the fall of 1973 he departed Thailand to assume command of Pacific Air Forces in Hawaii and then a tour as commander of the U.S. Air Force in Europe. He retired from active duty in August 1975.

—Robert G. Mangrum

References: Olson, James S. *Dictionary of the Vietnam War.* New York: Greenwood Press, 1988.
Sumners, Harry G. *Vietnam War Almanac.* New York: Facts on File, 1985.
See also: Air Power, Role in War; LINEBACKER I, Operation; LINEBACKER II, Operation; Military Assistance Command, Vietnam (MACV); ROLLING THUNDER, Operation; United States: Air Force.

Vũ Hông Khanh

(1898–1993)

Prominent leader of the Viêt Nam Quôc Dân Đang (Vietnam National Party, or VNQDD). Born in 1898 in Thô Tang village (as was Nguyên Thái Hoc), Vĩnh Tương District, Vĩnh Yên Province, Vũ Hông Khanh's real name was Vũ Văn Giang. A graduate of the Hà Nôi Teachers School, he was assigned a teaching post in Kiên An Province. He was one of the first to join the VNQDD.

In the 1930 uprising, Khanh commanded the VNQDD force attacking French colonial bases in Hai Phòng City and Kiên An Province. His force failed to take its objectives and caused only light damage. After the uprising, Khanh fled to south China, where, along with Nguyên Hai Thân, Nghiêm Kê Tô, and others, he helped reorganize the VNQDD. In the process, he encountered difficulties because, despite Jiang Jieshi's (Chiang Kai-shek's) support, local Chinese authorities did not always favor the nationalist Vietnamese.

In August 1945 right after Hô Chí Minh took over Hà Nôi, Khanh directed VNQDD militia units in attacks against Japanese troops in Hà Giang Province and other border areas. That September he returned to Hà Nôi to work with Nguyên Hai Thân, chairman of the Viêt Nam Cách Mang Đông Minh Hôi (VNCMDMH), a coalition of several nationalist parties.

In early 1946 Khanh became vice-chairman of the Central Military Commission of the Democratic Republic of Vietnam (DRV), of which Võ Nguyên Giáp was the chairman. Khanh was a cosignatory of the 6 March 1946 preliminary agreement between Hô Chí Minh and French representative Jean Sainteny. Many of his nationalist colleagues were critical of Khanh for this agreement, which they saw as a sellout to the French.

When the Viêt Minh launched their offensive to eliminate the nationalist opposition, Khanh led VNQDD militia units in the northern border areas against both them and the French. In 1948

he went to southern China where, a year later, he convened a congress and founded the Măt Trân Cách Mang Liên Minh (Allied Revolution Front). Jiang Jieshi's government recognized it as the Vietnamese government in exile.

After the Chinese Communists defeated the nationalists, in November 1949 Vũ Hông Khanh led three infantry divisions of Vietnamese and Chinese across the border into Vietnam. His troops promptly came under attack by both the Viêt Minh and French Army. Fierce fighting and supply shortages, coupled with an appeal from Bao Đai, chief of state of the newly established State of Vietnam, led Khanh to side with the State of Vietnam. In 1952 he became minister of youth in the cabinet of Premier Nguyên Văn Tâm. Khanh did not hold any government post after 1954, but he remained a VNQDD leader in South Vietnam. In June 1975 the Communists sentenced him to prison. Released in 1979, he was kept under house arrest in his home village of Thô Tang until his death on 14 November 1993.

—Nguyên Công Luân (Lư Tuân)

References: Cao Thê Dung. *Viêt Nam Huyêt Lê Sư.* New Orleans, LA: Đông Hưởng, 1996.
Hoàng Văn Đào. *Viêt Nam Quôc Dân Đang.* Sài Gòn: Published by the author, 1970; reprinted in the United States.
Pham Kim Vinh. *The Vietnamese Culture.* Solana Beach, CA: PM Enterprises, 1995.
See also: Bao Dai; Hô Chí Minh; Hô-Sainteny Agreement; Nguyên Hai Thân; Pham Duy; Sainteny, Jean; Văn Cao; Võ Nguyên Giáp.

Vu Oanh

(?–)

Prominent Vietnamese Communist Party (VCP) and Socialist Republic of Vietnam (SRV) official. During the Vietnam War, Oanh was political commissar of a division commanded by General Văn Tiên Dũng, who led the victorious 1975 Hô Chí Minh Campaign. In 1972 Oanh was deputy chief of the VCP Central Committee Organization Department, one of the most important bodies in charge of personnel matters.

In December 1976 at the Fourth VCP Congress he was elected as an alternate member, and in 1979 he was named chief of the VCP Central Committee's Agriculture Department. Three years later, he became a full member of the Fifth VCP Central Committee, and in 1985 he was named chairman of the Vietnamese Collective Farmers Federation. In 1986 Oanh was elected as a member of the VCP Central Committee's Secretariat. In June 1991 during the Seventh Party Congress, he was promoted to the Politburo in charge of mass mobilization.

Oanh was apparently the architect of the SRV's new policy of opening up to the outside world in the wake of political upheaval in the USSR and Eastern Europe. Oanh was a deputy to the National Assembly from Hòa Bình Province, as well as chairman of its Economic Committee. Approximately 67 years old, Oanh retired from the Politburo at the Eighth Communist Party Congress in June 1996.

—Ngô Ngoc Trung

Reference: Biographical Files, Indo-China Archives, University of California at Berkeley.

See also: Vietnam, Socialist Republic of: 1975 to the Present; Vietnamese Communist Party (VCP).

Vũ Quôc Thúc
(1920–)

Prominent Vietnamese intellectual who participated in Republic of Vietnam (RVN) politics throughout the Vietnam War era. Born in Nam Đinh Province, North Vietnam, on 5 August 1920, Vũ Quôc Thúc attended the University of Hà Nôi and then the University of Paris, where he received his doctorate in law (1950) and agrégé in economics (1952). Following World War II, he joined the Viêt Minh to fight against the French, but then left Vietnam for France to pursue graduate study. Returning to Vietnam, he became minister of education and youth in Prince Bửu Lôc's cabinet (1953–1954). After the 1954 Geneva Agreements, Vũ Quôc Thúc and several colleagues founded the first national university in Sài Gòn. He continued teaching at its school of law until the April 1975 defeat of the RVN. He held various important positions such as governor of the central RVN bank, advisor to President Ngô Đình Diêm, head of the RVN Post-War Planning Group, and minister of state in charge of reconstruction and development. His most important contributions during the Vietnam War were his coauthored joint reports with Eugene Staley (1961) and D. E. Lilienthal (1968) on Vietnam postwar reconstruction and development programs, which were submitted to the presidents of the United States and the Republic of Vietnam.

Vũ Quôc Thúc left Vietnam for France in July 1978 and became a full professor at the University of Paris, where he taught until his retirement in 1988.

—Nguyên Bá Long

References: Lilienthal, D. E., and Vũ Quôc Thúc. *The Postwar Development of the Republic of Vietnam: Policies and Programs.* New York: Praeger, 1970.
Vũ Quôc Thúc. *L'Economie communaliste du Vietnam.* Hà Nôi: Press Universitaire du Vietnam, 1952.
_____. "Le Vietnam vainquer et vaincu." *L'Appel de la Nation* 40 (June/July 1995): 12–15.
See also: Ngô Đình Diêm; Staley, Eugene.

VULTURE, Operation
(March–April 1954)

Proposed air strike to relieve French military forces trapped at Điên Biên Phu during March and April 1954. With an international conference on Asian matters scheduled to begin at Geneva on 26 April 1954, the French government hoped to improve its negotiating position by winning a major battle against the Viêt Minh. Confident that his forces could defeat the Viêt Minh in a set-piece battle, General Henri Navarre introduced a force in November 1953 that grew to more than 13,000 men, including 7,000 frontline troops, at Điên Biên Phu in northwest Vietnam. Viêt Minh General Võ Nguyên Giáp's forces occupied the hills surrounding Điên Biên Phu and on 13 March 1964 began an assault that soon made the French position untenable.

On 20 March French chief of staff General Paul Ely arrived in Washington, D.C., to brief U.S. officials, including President Dwight D. Eisenhower, members of the National Security Council, and the Joint Chiefs of Staff, on the situation in Vietnam. He informed them that French forces needed American support in order to hold Điên Biên Phu. Adm. Arthur W. Radford, chairman of the Joint Chiefs, recommended to Eisenhower that the United States be prepared to respond if the French made an emergency request for assistance. This would include direct aerial intervention if necessary. Despite opposition within the Joint Chiefs from Army Chief of Staff Matthew B. Ridgway, Radford encouraged Ely to believe that the United States would intervene if the French government requested it. This was the origin of Operation VULTURE.

Throughout the crisis, U.S. and French military officers developed plans for intervention at Điên Biên Phu—code-named VULTURE by Navarre's staff. These plans shifted in scope and intensity according to the condition of the French garrison. The general outline called for an air attack by between 60 and 100 U.S. B-29 bombers from the Philippines, supported by several hundred jet fighters from American aircraft carriers. A plan to strike Viêt Minh forces in the mountains surrounding Điên Biên Phu itself was dropped because French radar was inadequate to support close fire. Another strategy called for bombing raids on Viêt Minh bases and supply lines near the Chinese border. And, on at least one occasion, Admiral Radford suggested the use of nuclear bombs.

French expectations were further raised on 29 March when Secretary of State John Foster Dulles, in a speech to the Overseas Press Club in New York City, said that, since China supported the Viêt Minh with the purpose of dominating Southeast Asia, other nations should meet the threat with "united action." President Eisenhower seconded Dulles's call for united action in a press conference two days later, but he pointedly neither promised nor ruled out direct U.S. assistance.

On 3 April Dulles and Radford met with congressional leaders, including Republican Senate Majority Leader William F. Knowland and Democratic Senate Minority Leader Lyndon B. Johnson, to seek their support for intervention if the president decided it was necessary. The legislators insisted on three conditions to make congressional approval likely: (1) intervention had to be a multinational effort—a united action including Britain and the British Commonwealth nations; (2) France had to promise to accelerate independence for its Indo-China colonies; and (3) France had to agree not to withdraw from the war once the United States became involved.

Meanwhile in Paris, Ely received a desperate cable from Navarre on 4 April, asking for a U.S. bombing attack on Viêt Minh positions at Điên Biên Phu. The French War Committee that night formally requested immediate intervention through U.S. ambassador C. Douglas Dillon.

In a 7 April press conference, Eisenhower said that the possible loss of Indo-China to communism illustrated the "falling domino principle." The idea was not new, but this marked the first occasion that the "domino theory" had been applied in public.

Eisenhower, however, refused comment when asked if the United States would act unilaterally in Indo-China.

Dulles flew to London and Paris in April in an effort to set up a program of united action. Following a meeting with British Foreign Secretary Anthony Eden, the two issued a communiqué on 13 April, supporting the principle of "collective defense." But as Dulles traveled to Paris, Eden stated in the House of Commons that the statement meant only willingness to examine "possibilities" rather than any specific obligation. Given the restrictions earlier expressed by congressional leaders, there was now no likelihood of U.S. military intervention over Điên Biên Phu.

The French government still hoped that Điên Biên Phu could be rescued, and French Premier Joseph Laniel held out the prospect of French agreement on the European Defense Community (EDC), which the United States desired, in return for it. When Dulles attended a foreign ministers conference in Paris on 22 April, he informed French officials that without French approval of the EDC there was no chance that the United States would intervene. Foreign Minister Georges Bidault retorted that, if Điên Biên Phu fell, France would have no interest in the EDC and would pull out of Southeast Asia completely.

The following day, Bidault received a message from officials in Indo-China that the final battle for Điên Biên Phu had begun. The only alternatives, he informed Dulles, were Operation VULTURE or a cease-fire. That evening, Laniel asked Britain to participate in the united action that was a condition for intervention. Eden returned to London, where Prime Minister Winston Churchill held an emergency meeting of the cabinet, which decided against military involvement in Vietnam. A few hours later, Eden so informed Bidault. This marked the end of serious discussion about Operation VULTURE. In a press conference on 29 April, Eisenhower called for a solution somewhere between the "unattainable," by which he meant a complete victory against Vietnamese Communists, and the "unacceptable," the defeat of all anti-Communist defenses in Southeast Asia.

On 7 May 1954 Viêt Minh forces overran French defenses at Điên Biên Phu and forced the garrison to surrender. The Indo-China phase of the Geneva Conference began the next day, and on 21 July 1954 the conferees arranged a cease-fire agreement that partitioned Vietnam at the 17th parallel.

In the aftermath of Điên Biên Phu, the United States established, in 1955, the Southeast Asia Treaty Organization (SEATO), linking the United States, France, Britain, Australia, New Zealand, Thailand, Pakistan, and the Philippines in a defense coalition. A separate protocol extended the pact to Cambodia, Laos, and Vietnam.

In January 1956 the United States assumed from France the role of training and supporting the South Vietnamese military. Between 1955 and 1961 the Eisenhower administration sent more than $1 billion in aid to the Republic of Vietnam.

—Kenneth R. Stevens

References: Billings-Yun, Melanie. *Decision against War: Eisenhower and Dien Bien Phu, 1954.* New York: Columbia University Press, 1988.
Eden, Anthony. *Full Circle.* Boston: Houghton Mifflin, 1960.
Eisenhower, Dwight D. *Mandate for Change, 1953–1956: The White House Years.* Garden City, NY: Doubleday, 1963.
Ely, Paul. *L'Indochine dans la Tourmente.* Paris: Librairie Plon, 1964.
Radford, Arthur W. *From Pearl Harbor to Vietnam: The Memoirs of Admiral Arthur W. Radford.* Edited by Stephen Jurika, Jr. Stanford, CA: Hoover Institute Press, 1980.
See also: Bidault, Georges; Điên Biên Phu, Battle of; Dulles, John Foster; Eden, Anthony; Eisenhower, Dwight David; Ely, Paul Henri Romuald; Geneva Conference and Geneva Accords; Johnson, Lyndon Baines; Laniel, Joseph; Navarre, Henri Eugène; Radford, Arthur W.; Southeast Asia Treaty Organization (SEATO); Taylor, Maxwell Davenport; Twining, Nathan Farragut; Võ Nguyên Giáp.

W

Wallace, George Corley, Jr.

(1919–)

U.S. presidential candidate; governor of Alabama. Born 25 August 1919 to a poor family in Barbour County, Alabama, George C. Wallace, Jr. worked his way through college and law school at the University of Alabama. In 1943 he married Lurleen Burns of Tuscaloosa, who succeeded him as governor of Alabama in 1968. During World War II Wallace served as a flight engineer on B-29s and flew 14 combat missions over Japan.

After the war and a series of minor political appointments, Wallace was elected circuit judge for a three-county area around Clayton, Alabama. In 1962, capitalizing on his stand to preserve "segregation now, segregation tomorrow, segregation forever," he was elected governor of Alabama by the largest popular vote margin in the state's history. After gaining national attention with his June 1963 "stand in the school house door," a symbolic effort to stall the integration of the University of Alabama, Wallace catapulted to the national political scene.

His populist image, combined with warnings about the intrusive power of the federal government over states and individuals alike, struck a chord among millions of Americans during the turbulent Vietnam War era. In February 1967 Wallace was quoted as saying, "The Vietnam War is the most important matter facing the American people."

Wallace called for a more vigorous pursuit of military victory by bombing the roads and highways leading from Hà Nôi to China and mining Hai Phòng Harbor. Wallace ran for the presidency in 1968 on the American Independent Party ticket; retired Air Force Gen. Curtis E. LeMay was his running mate. After LeMay refused to rule out the use of nuclear weapons in Vietnam, Wallace sent him on a tour of Vietnam to keep him out of the country until after the election.

At home, Wallace excoriated the antiwar movement and warned that any student at any college or university in Alabama who advocated a victory by the Viêt Công would be expelled. At a July 1967 press conference he stated, "Some of these professors in some of these colleges . . . who are advocating a victory of the Vietcong [sic] . . . should be dragged by their beards before a federal judge and put in the penitentiary."

Both in his political career and in his advocacy of a more vigorous war, Wallace was prescient. Every successful presidential candidate since 1968 has incorporated elements of Wallace's calls for welfare reform, law and order, and trimming of the federal bureaucracy. In 1972, President Richard M. Nixon stepped up the air war against North Vietnam to include attacks on the railroad and highway links to China and the mining of Hai Phòng Harbor.

During his run for the Democratic Party presidential nomination in 1972, Wallace was seriously wounded by a would-be assassin. He won several state primaries but ultimately withdrew from the campaign. He was not, however, finished politically. Over the next 15 years he was twice more elected governor of Alabama and made a vigorous final run for the Democratic Party nomination in 1976 before withdrawing and endorsing Governor Jimmy Carter of Georgia. Wallace retired from politics in 1987 at the end of his fourth term as governor of Alabama. He lives quietly in retirement in Montgomery, Alabama.

—Earl H. Tilford, Jr.

References: Frady, Marshall. *Wallace.* New York: New American Library, 1972.
Lesher, Stephan. *George Wallace: American Populist.* Reading, MA: Addison-Wesley, 1994.
Wallace, George, C., Jr. *Hear Me Out: This Is Where I Stand.* Anderson, SC: Droke House, 1968.
See also: Elections, U.S.: 1968; LeMay, Curtis Emerson.

Walt, Lewis W.

(1913–1989)

U.S. Marine Corps general. Born on 16 February 1913 in Harveyville, Kansas, Lewis Walt graduated in 1936 from the Colorado School of Mines and was commissioned a lieutenant in the Marines. Seeing service in China in 1937 and 1938, he was an original member of the 1st Marine Raider Battalion in the Solomons in 1942, and he also saw action on Guadalcanal, Cape Glouster, and Peleliu; in Korea he commanded the 5th Marine Regiment (1952–1953). Promoted to brigadier general in 1962, in June 1965 he assumed command of the 3d Marine Division in Vietnam as a major general, while serving concurrently as commander of III Marine Amphibious Force (MAF). When III MAF was elevated to the first corps-level headquarters in Marine Corps history, Walt was given command and promoted to lieutenant general in 1966; he had under his control U.S. Naval Forces, Vietnam. He also served as senior advisor and coordinator of the Army of the Republic of Vietnam's I Corps, supervising the corps buildup between 1965 and 1967.

Walt insisted on a balance of small-unit patrols, large-unit operations, and a program of pacification that consisted of Marine Combined Action Platoons (CAPs) operating with Vietnamese in the countryside. Walt and the Marines placed much more emphasis on small-unit operations and pacification than did General William Westmoreland in his strategy of large-unit actions.

After returning to the United States, Walt served as assistant commandant of the Marine Corps; he was promoted to full general in June 1969. He retired from the Marine Corps in February 1971. In 1972 Walt served as director of the Senate's investigation on international narcotics traffic. Later he was executive director of the USMC Youth Foundation. In 1976 he published *Strange War, Strange Strategy: A General's Report on Vietnam.* Lewis Walt died in Gulfport, Mississippi, on 26 March 1989.

—Robert G. Mangrum

References: Karnow, Stanley. *Vietnam: A History.* New York: Penguin Books, 1984.

Millet, Allan R. *Semper Fidelis: The History of the United States Marine Corps.* New York: Macmillan, 1980.

Moskin, J. Robert. *The U.S. Marine Corps Story.* Rev. ed. New York: McGraw-Hill, 1982.

Olson, James S., ed. *Dictionary of the Vietnam War.* New York: Greenwood Press, 1988.

Walt, Lewis W. *Strange War, Strange Strategy: A General's Report on Vietnam.* New York: Funk & Wagnalls, 1976.

See also: Marine Combined Action Platoons (CAPs); United States: Marine Corps; Vietnam, Republic of: Army (ARVN); Westmoreland, William Childs.

War Powers Act

(1973)

U.S. congressional effort to limit the president's war-making powers and to ensure more legislative control of the nation's military. The War Powers Resolution of 1973 (Public Law 93-148, 93rd Congress, H.J. Resolution S42, 7 November 1973), simply known as the War Powers Act, requires that the president consult with Congress before military forces are sent into combat abroad, or to areas where hostilities are likely, and to report in writing within 48 hours after troops are deployed. The president must then terminate the use of military force within 60 to 90 days. The deployment can continue for another 60 days, and for another 30 days beyond that if the president certifies to Congress in writing that the safety of the force so requires. Unless Congress authorizes a continuation through a declaration of war, a concurrent resolution, or other appropriate legislation, the deployment cannot be continued beyond 90 days.

The War Powers Act was introduced by Senator Jacob K. Javits of New York after the 1970 U.S. invasion of Cambodia. At the time many believed it was a direct result of the American experience in Vietnam. Javits outlined his rationale in his 1973 book, *Who Makes War: The President versus Congress,* and stated that the act was an effort to learn from the lessons of Vietnam that had cost the United States so heavily in blood, treasure, and morale. Although the act was passed only months after the final American withdrawal, many scholars claim that it was not just a reaction to that conflict but the product of a slow, evolutionary debate on the respective war powers of Congress and the president that had been going on for decades. The act was an attempt by the legislative branch to reassert some of the authority over the military that it had lost to the president after 1941. The law, passed by Congress (House, 284–135; Senate, 75–18) on 7 November 1973 over the veto of President Richard Nixon, gave more authority to Congress to limit the war-making powers of the chief executive.

President Nixon vetoed the bill in the belief that it could imperil the nation in times of crisis. He also argued that it granted Congress authority over troop deployments in violation of Article II of the Constitution that granted such powers to the president. Other critics maintained that the act placed inflexible restrictions on the president's ability to conduct foreign policy.

Supporters held that the act served as a necessary restraint on the president's power and inherently compelled communication between the executive and legislative branches in times of emergency. Although many flaws have been found in the act, it has not been amended since passage.

In April 1975 President Gerald Ford submitted four reports under the act that announced the use of the armed forces to evacuate refugees and U.S. nationals from Cambodia and Vietnam. On 15 May 1975 President Ford again reported to Congress that he had ordered U.S. forces to rescue the crew and retake the ship *Mayaguez,* which had been seized by Cambodian navy patrol boats on 12 May.

—Clayton D. Laurie

References: Fisher, Louis. *Presidential War Power.* Lawrence, KS: University of Kansas, 1995.

Javits, Jacob K. *Who Makes War: The President versus Congress.* New York: William Morrow, 1973.

Stern, Gary M., and Morton Halperin, eds. *The U.S. Constitution and the Power to Go to War: Historical and Current Perspectives.* Westport, CT: Greenwood Press, 1994.

See also: Cooper-Church Amendment; Ford, Gerald R.; FREQUENT WIND, Operation; Hatfield-McGovern Amendment; Javits, Jacob Koppel; *Mayaguez* Incident; Nixon, Richard Milhous; Stennis, John Cornelius.

War Resisters League (WRL)

Pacifist organization advocating nonviolence; support group for conscientious objectors. The War Resisters League (WRL) played an important role in the antidraft and anti–Vietnam War protests of the 1960s and 1970s. The WRL was founded in 1932 by Jessie Wallace Hughan as the American branch of the Fellowship of Reconciliation (FOR), which was founded in England in 1914.

Hughan wanted the WRL to unite political, humanitarian, and philosophical objectors to war. By February 1937 over 12,000 Americans had signed the WRL pledge: "War is a crime against humanity. I therefore am determined not to support any kind of war, international or civil, and to strive for the removal of all causes of war."

In 1945 the WRL had 2,300 active members. Following World War II it served as a radical action organization, although it refrained from advocating illegal actions such as not registering for the draft. In the late 1940s the WRL became a support group for those advocating civil disobedience and revolution. Although its membership declined in the 1950s and early 1960s, with the unpopularity of the Vietnam War and growing opposition to it, by 1972 the WRL had 15,000 members. Headquartered in New York City, the WRL's office also later housed Daniel Berrigan's office of the Catholic Peace Fellowship; the Committee for Nonviolent Action; *Liberation,* a radical magazine edited by David Dellinger and A. J. Muste; and other New York–based radical pacifist groups.

By 1963 under the leadership of Dellinger and David McReynolds, who had come to New York in 1956 as a WRL staff member and national council member of FOR, the WRL focused its protests on the escalating Vietnam War and Selective Service inductions. On 16 May 1964 the WRL cosponsored a demonstration in New York City at which 12 men burned their draft cards.

Between 1964 and 1973 membership in the WRL grew from 3,000 to 15,000 people. From 1965 through 1983 the WRL's Workshop in Nonviolence produced *WIN,* a widely read "movement" magazine, and published *WRL News.* In late 1967 the WRL organized "Stop the Draft Week" and endorsed a number of "teach-ins" and demonstrations, including the 1971 May Day demonstrations. Because of its growing visibility and antiwar activities, the WRL was the target of Central Intelligence Agency (CIA) infiltration and periodic seizures by the Internal Revenue Service (IRS).

Beginning in 1965 David McReynolds became the WRL's primary spokesperson and the liaison between the WRL and other mass mobilization protest movements. He traveled to Vietnam twice during the war and was instrumental in organizing and encouraging antiwar activities. The first major WRL peace demonstration on the Vietnam War issue came on 9 October 1963. In 1964 McReynolds drafted a "Memo on Vietnam," calling for the unconditional withdrawal of U.S. troops. That December the WRL cosponsored the first nationwide demonstration against the Vietnam War. As a pacifist, McReynolds stated that the United States "had no right to dictate the history of Vietnam."

In 1965 the U.S. Congress passed a law making the burning of draft cards illegal, but on 5 November of that year McReynolds and four others burned their draft cards at a rally in Union Square. McReynolds, however, was classified 4-F and not 1-A and was not arrested.

After the Vietnam War, WRL membership again declined, and it turned its attention to issues such as U.S. policy in the Middle East and Central America, amnesty for draft resisters, and nuclear disarmament. The WRL denounced the 1979 Soviet invasion of Afghanistan and protested the 1982 Israeli invasion of Lebanon. David McReynolds continued to be the spokesperson and principal figure in the WRL. The organization's records are housed in the depository at the Swarthmore College Peace Collection in Pennsylvania.

—Gary Kerley

References: DeBenedetti, Charles. *An American Ordeal: The Antiwar Movement of the Vietnam Era.* Syracuse, NY: Syracuse University Press, 1990.
McReynolds, David. "Pacifists and the Vietnam Antiwar Movement." In *Give Peace a Chance: Explaining the Vietnam Antiwar Movement,* edited by Melvin Small and William D. Hoover. Syracuse, NY: Syracuse University Press, 1992, pp. 53–70.
Olson, James S., ed. *Dictionary of the Vietnam War.* Westport, CT: Greenwood Press, 1988.
Wittner, Laurence S. *Rebels against War: The American Peace Movement, 1941–1960.* New York: Columbia University Press, 1969.
Zaroulis, Nancy, and Gerald Sullivan. *Who Spoke Up? American Protest against the War in Vietnam, 1963–1975.* New York: Doubleday, 1984.

See also: Antiwar Movement, United States; Berrigan, Daniel; Conscientious Objectors (COs); Dellinger, David; Draft; Fellowship of Reconciliation (FOR); Muste, Abraham J.

War Zone C and War Zone D

Geographical areas important because of their proximity to Sài Gòn—capital of the Republic of Vietnam, home to about 40 percent of its population and most of its industry, and psychological heart of the South. The terms War Zone C and War Zone D have disputed origins. General William Westmoreland attributes them to the HOP TAC plan of 1964, which defined four zones: A and B just north of Sài Gòn and including its suburbs, then C and D farther north and radiating fanlike from northwest to northeast, all within III Corps Tactical Zone (III CTZ). Several experts mention the earlier existence of these zones as 1950s French designations, People's Army of Vietnam (PAVN) classifications prior to U.S. involvement, or American references prior to 1964. General Bruce Palmer, Jr. writes that older bases inside South Vietnam, usually close to major population centers, were often called "war zones."

Located northwest of Sài Gòn, War Zone C served as the main PAVN approach from Cambodia to Sài Gòn, and included routes of the Hồ Chí Minh Trail and elaborate, concealed, and even deep underground facilities with command posts, ammunition and supply dumps, and hospitals. Some of these installations were connected by tunnel complexes. Under Communist control since before the 1954 partition of Vietnam, War Zone C later served as the headquarters of the Central Office for South Vietnam (COSVN) and therefore was a National Liberation Front (NLF) stronghold and sanctuary.

The borders of War Zone C ran from Bên Cát, the northeastern point of the Iron Triangle, due north on the western side of Route 13 to the Cambodian border, then followed the border southwest to Tapang Raboa, from which a west-east arc ran through Tây Ninh City back to Bên Cát. Portions of three provinces fell within War Zone C: the northern half of Tây Ninh, the western half of Bình Long, and northwestern Bình Dương. The distance from east to west measured about 50 miles; the north-south distance varied from about 30 miles in the west to about 50 miles in the east along Route 13. (It should be pointed out, however, that some references include only parts of Tây Ninh Province in a much smaller War Zone C.)

The varied terrain included land that was flat and potentially marshy (dry in summer, muddy in winter); rolling hills as one progressed toward Cambodia; dense tropical rain forest with massive teak and mahogany trees; and the landmark Núi Bà Đen, or Black Woman Mountain (3,235 feet above sea level).

War Zone D was located northwest of Sài Gòn. With its terrain of heavy—often triple canopy—jungle, rain forest, and elephant grasses, War Zone D provided the main access from the central part of the country to Sài Gòn. Like Zone C, it also included branches of the Hồ Chí Minh Trail and tunnel complexes. Part of a PAVN guerrilla force, Unit 250, appeared in Zone D in October 1957 and within a year had grown to battalion size. In January 1961 the Politburo decision to escalate the war in the South led to a 15 February meeting in War Zone D to unify all armed units into an integrated command known as the People's Liberation Armed Forces (PLAF), more widely known as the Việt Công. In time the PLAF would name War Zone D "the forbidden zone." The borders of War Zone D ran due north from Bến Cát on the eastern side of Route 13 parallel to the border of War Zone C, to Chơn Thành at the split of Routes 13 and 14, then northeast and east on Route 14 through Chí Linh and Đồng Xoài to Bu Nard; it then ran due east for 10 miles, then due south for 25 miles to Thanh Sơn, then due west for 10 miles; after following the Đồng Nai River and Route 20 south for a few miles, it went southwest for about 10 miles, crossing Route 20 before heading 20 miles due west along 11 degrees east latitude parallel to Route 1 via Biên Hòa (headquarters of III Corps); northwest about 10 miles to Phú Cường to rejoin Route 13 north, parallel to the Iron Triangle, and then north 12 miles back to Bến Cát. (Again, boundaries differ depending on the source; some place the eastern border of Zone D as far as the III CTZ–II CTZ line; others shrink the area to include only an inexact reference to the jungle area north of Biên Hòa.) War Zone D included northeast Bình Dương, northern Biên Hòa, southern Phước Long, and northern and western Long Khánh Provinces. Distance from east to west measured about 40 miles; north-south distance about 30 miles.

Forces operating within War Zones C and/or D included the U.S. 1st, 4th, and 25th Infantry Divisions, 11th Armored Cavalry Regiment, 1st Cavalry Division, 196th Infantry Brigade, and 173d Airborne Brigade; the ARVN 5th Division; and the PLAF 9th Division.

The 1st Infantry Division's 1st and 3d Brigades, located at Phước Vinh and Lai Khê, respectively, occupied areas vital to PLAF lines of communication. In both Zones C and D, from its first significant battle near Bầu Bàng on 12 November 1965 through its last at Phú Hòa Đông between 15 and 28 September 1969, the 1st Infantry Division participated in operations or battles each year. The 11th Armored Cavalry carried out joint military operations with the 1st Infantry Division from 8 May 1967 to 12 April 1969. A year later the 11th Armored Cavalry joined the 1st Cavalry Division to conduct Operation MONTANA RAIDER in Zone C. On 9 May 1970 the 11th Armored Cavalry, under the 1st Cavalry Division, moved from its support position in War Zone C into the Fishhook area of Cambodia. The 1st Cavalry Division, in III Corps (III CTZ) in 1969, engaged Communist forces north of the Đồng Nai River in War Zone D and took part in a half-dozen major battles in War Zone C, including those of Landing Zones (LZs) Grant, Carolyn, Jamie, and Ike and Fire Support Bases (FSBs) Becky and Ike.

Major U.S. operations in War Zone C, including EL PASO II, ATTLEBORO, JUNCTION CITY, and YELLOWSTONE, saw the long and costly involvement of the 196th Infantry Brigade; the 173d Airborne Brigade; the 1st, 4th, and 25th Infantry Divisions; and various ARVN units.

Herbicide warfare targeted War Zones C and D heavily: along Route 13, the initial Operation RANCH HAND test site selected by Republic of Vietnam (RVN) President Ngô Đình Diệm in 1961; Routes 13 and 14 in 1962; BIG PATCH, for chemical crop destruction, in 1964 in Zone D; SHERWOOD FOREST in Bời Lời Woods in Zone C in 1965; and PINK ROSE in 1966–1967, with two target areas in Zone C and one in Zone D, the third and last effort combining defoliation with incendiaries to produce forest fires.

U.S. Army Special Forces had about a dozen active A camps in War Zone C and a half-dozen in Zone D. In War Zone D, BLACKJACK 31 and HARVEST MOON, which included the first mass Special Forces–led Civilian Irregular Defense Group (CIDG) combat parachute drop of the Vietnam War, stand out as successful 1967 offensive operations utilizing the concepts of the Mobile Guerrilla Force and Mobile Strike Force, respectively.

Westmoreland stated that operations in War Zones C and D had "shortcomings but probably saved Saigon from enemy control." The constant struggle in these zones between PLAF/PAVN forces and those of the United States and the RVN centered on the control of Sài Gòn, which was crucial to the outcome of the war.

—Paul S. Daum, with assistance from Francis Ryan

References: Buckingham, William A., Jr. *Operation Ranch Hand: The Air Force and Herbicides in Southeast Asia, 1961–1971.* Washington, DC: Office of Air Force History, 1982.
Cambria, Frank (Captain, 11th Armored Cavalry Regiment, RVN, 1970–1971). Interviews with the author, August–December 1995.
Haldane, Robert, ed. *The First Infantry Division in Vietnam, 1965–1970.* Paducah, KY: Turner, 1993.
Hatch, Gardner, ed. *11th U.S. Cavalry: Blackhorse.* Paducah, KY: Turner, 1990.
Martin, Robert, ed. *1st Air Cavalry Division: Memoirs of the First Team, Vietnam, August 1965–December 1969.* Paducah, KY: Turner, 1995.
Palmer, Bruce, Jr. *The 25-Year War: America's Military Role in Vietnam.* Lexington, KY: University Press of Kentucky, 1984.
Rogers, Bernard William. *Cedar Falls–Junction City: A Turning Point.* Vietnam Studies Series. Washington, DC: Department of the Army, 1974.
Stanton, Shelby L. *The Rise and Fall of an American Army: U.S. Ground Forces in Vietnam, 1965–1973.* Novato, CA: Presidio Press, 1985.
Turley, William S. *The Second Indochina War: A Short Political and Military History, 1954–1975.* Boulder, CO: Westview Press, 1986.
Westmoreland, William C. *Report on the War in Vietnam (as of 30 June 1968). Part II. Report on Operations in South Vietnam, January 1964–June 1968.* Washington, DC: U.S. Government Printing Office, 1968.
See also: ATTLEBORO, Operation; Cambodian Incursion; Civilian Irregular Defense Group (CIDG); COSVN (Central Office for South Vietnam or Trung Ương Cuc Miên Nam); Defoliation; HARVEST MOON, Operation; Hô Chí Minh Trail; Iron Triangle; JUNCTION CITY, Operation; Mobile Guerrilla Forces (MGF); Mobile Strike Force Commands; National Front for the Liberation of South Vietnam (NFLSV); RANCH HAND, Operation; United States: Army; United States: Special Forces; Vietnam, Democratic Republic of: Army (People's Army of Vietnam [PAVN]); Vietnam, Republic of: Army (ARVN); YELLOWSTONE, Operation.

Ware, Keith L.

(1915–1968)

U.S. Army general and commander of the 1st Infantry Division (March–September 1968). Born in Denver, Colorado, on 23 November 1915, Keith Ware was inducted into the Army in July 1941. He completed Officer Candidate School (OCS) at Fort Benning, Georgia, and was commissioned a second lieutenant of infantry in 1942. He participated in the Allied invasion of North Africa, the campaigns in Sicily and Italy, and the invasion of southern France. In December 1944 near Sigolsheim, France, Lieutenant Colonel

Ware led a patrol against four machine gun positions, killing many defenders. Half of his patrol members, including himself, were wounded but Ware refused medical attention until the enemy positions had been captured. For this action he received the Medal of Honor.

After World War II Ware attended Army professional schools, served on the Army staff in Washington, and was an instructor at West Point. Promoted to colonel in 1953, he commanded an infantry regiment in Korea (1955–1956), then attended the National War College. Other assignments included service at Supreme Headquarters Allied Powers Europe (SHAPE). He was promoted to brigadier general in 1963 while serving with the 2d Armored Division at Fort Hood, Texas. In September 1964 Ware was appointed deputy chief of information for the Army and then chief in February 1966. In July 1966 he was promoted to major general.

Ware reported to Vietnam for assignment as deputy commanding general, I Field Force, Vietnam (IFFV) in December 1967. He then served as deputy commanding general of IIFFV prior to assuming command of the 1st Infantry Division ("Big Red One"). Ware was an inspirational leader whose dream had been to command the division in combat.

On 13 September 1968 General Ware was killed in action when his command helicopter was hit by hostile ground fire and crashed in the jungle southeast of Lôc Ninh. His command sergeant major, Joseph A. Venable, six other members of the general staff, and the general's canine companion, King, died with him. Ware was the fourth general officer killed in Vietnam. His name now honors a scholarship program for the 1st Infantry Division.

—John F. Votaw

References: *First Infantry Division in Vietnam*. Vol. 2, 1 May 1967–31 Dec. 1968. Published in Vietnam by the 1st Infantry Division, n.d.
Official Biography of Major General Keith L. Ware. Department of the Army, n.d.
See also: Casualties; United States: Army.

Warnke, Paul C.

(1920–)

General counsel for the U.S. Department of Defense, 1966–1967; assistant secretary of defense for international security affairs, 1967–1969. Born in Webster, Massachusetts, on 31 January 1920, Paul Warnke graduated from Yale in 1941. He served as an officer in the U.S. Coast Guard during the Second World War. In 1948 he received a law degree from Columbia University. From then until 1966 he practiced law in Washington, D.C. That year he joined the Defense Department as general counsel, and in 1967 he was named assistant secretary of defense for international security affairs.

A staunch opponent of the Vietnam War, Warnke helped convince Secretary of Defense Robert McNamara of its hopelessness and later exerted considerable influence over McNamara's successor Clark Clifford. General William Westmoreland derisively credited Warnke with moving the once-hawkish Clifford to an antiwar position. With the election of Richard Nixon, Warnke left the De-

fense Department and returned to the practice of law as a partner in Clifford's firm.

Called back to government service by President Jimmy Carter in 1977, Warnke headed the Arms Control and Disarmament Agency for two years and was the chief U.S. negotiator to the second Strategic Arms Limitation Talks (SALT II). From 1978 to 1981 he served as special consultant to the secretary of state on arms control. Returning to the private sector, Warnke formed with Clifford a new high-profile law firm in Washington, D.C.

—David Coffey

References: Karnow, Stanley. *Vietnam: A History*. New York: Viking Press, 1983.
Who's Who in American Politics, 1996. New Providence, NJ: R. R. Bowker, 1995.
See also: Clifford, Clark M.; McNamara, Robert S.; Westmoreland, William Childs.

Wars of National Liberation

Loosely described as revolutionary wars, internal wars, or insurrections. Theoretically, wars of national liberation are organized violence from within a state aimed at overthrowing the government and restructuring the state's political—and often its economic and social—order. To some the Vietnam War fit this pattern. The U.S. government, however, took the position that the organized violence did not come primarily from within but from external Communist-sponsored aggression and was therefore an invasion by an outside power.

It could be argued that Premier Nikita Khrushchev's 1961 pronouncement of Soviet sponsorship of wars of national liberation fed the U.S. slide to full involvement in combating the Vietnam insurgency. The growth of the Soviet nuclear arsenal during the 1950s and 1960s seemed to negate U.S. strategic superiority. With both the USSR and the People's Republic of China (PRC) avowing support to limited wars of this type—which the United States interpreted as Communist-supported insurgency—Washington policymakers developed the strategy of "flexible response." This called for nuclear deterrence and the maintenance of conventional forces to deter a conventional attack or fight limited wars.

From one point of view many aspects of the Vietnam insurgency match the characteristics of a revolutionary war. The National Liberation Front (NLF), or Viêt Công, and Central Office for South Vietnam (COSVN) provided an organized, disciplined leadership. Nationalism and communism provided popular ideologies, which challenged perceived American imperialism that many Vietnamese believed had replaced French colonialism. There was considerable popular support for the insurgency, and the Viêt Công provided the military forces necessary to wage the conflict. Washington, however, considered the NLF and COSVN to be directed and controlled by the Democratic Republic of Vietnam (DRV), supported by its larger Soviet and PRC patrons. Mass support for the insurgency was thought to be based somewhat on Communist and nationalist sympathies, but largely forced by Viêt Công fear tactics and terrorism. Finally, the military forces necessary to wage the war did not come solely from the South

Vietnamese population but were in main provided by North Vietnamese People's Army of Vietnam (PAVN) regulars, especially after the 1968 Têt Offensive.

—Arthur T. Frame

References: Gaddis, John Lewis. *Russia, the Soviet Union, and the United States: An Interpretive History.* New York: John Wiley & Sons, 1978.
Herring, George C. *America's Longest War: The United States and Vietnam, 1950–1975.* 2d ed. New York: Alfred A. Knopf, 1986.
Lewy, Gunther. *America in Vietnam.* New York: Oxford University Press, 1978.
See also: Containment Policy; COSVN (Central Office for South Vietnam or Trung Ương Cục Miên Nam); Counterinsurgency Warfare; Domino Theory; Khrushchev, Nikita Sergeyevich; National Front for the Liberation of South Vietnam (NFLSV).

Warships, Allied and Democratic Republic of Vietnam

Excluding submarines, virtually every type of modern combat vessel, from the largest aircraft carriers to the smallest river patrol boats, were used in the Vietnam War. Warships of several lesser navies took part in the conflict, but all were overshadowed by those of the U.S. Navy.

Australia The Australian destroyer HMS *Hobart* of the U.S. Navy Charles F. Adams class provided gunfire support for Allied forces in South Vietnam.

Democratic Republic of Vietnam (DRV or North Vietnam) In 1964 the DRV Navy was a coastal force composed of small combatants acquired from the larger Communist powers. Most numerous were the tiny Swatow-class motor gunboats, a Chinese-made version of the Soviet P-6. Displacing 80 tons, these steel-hulled vessels were powered by diesel engines, had a top speed of 28 knots, and were armed with four 37-mm cannon and depth charges. Swifter were the 12 P-4 motor torpedo boats with their two torpedo tubes. Although their stepped hull made possible a speed of 42 knots, their stability at high speeds was marginal. Three of these vessels were involved in the August 1964 Tonkin Gulf incidents.

During the ensuing Vietnam War the DRV Navy received reinforcements in 1967 in the form of four P-6 gunboats. Against these modest additions must be counted the loss of approximately 33 Swatows and P-4s to air strikes during Operation PIERCE ARROW.

Republic of Vietnam (RVN, or South Vietnam) The South Vietnamese Navy, as with its foe to the north, was built up from obsolescent small craft donated by its major ally. In 1964 it numbered 44 seagoing vessels and over 200 lesser craft. The best-armed of these warships were five escort patrol craft (PCEs) and 12 motor gunboats (PGMs). As fighting accelerated, the United States transferred to the RVN seven Coast Guard cutters of the Barnegat class and two Edsall-class frigates. By 1972 when Vietnamization had been completed, the RVN Navy numbered about 1,000 craft of varying types. Twenty-seven of its seagoing vessels carried 18,000 refugees to Subic Bay in the Philippines following the final 1975 Communist offensive.

United States Throughout the conflict, the United States possessed the strongest navy in the world. Its backbone was the attack aircraft carrier, the largest type of warship ever constructed. For instance, the USS *Enterprise,* the first nuclear-powered carrier, displaced almost 90,000 tons at full load and was armed with an air group of 90 aircraft.

Escorting the carriers were the Navy's newest surface warships: guided missile cruisers and frigates. Keeping pace with the *Enterprise* was the cruiser *Long Beach.* At 16,602 tons, she was equipped with one Talos and two Terrier missile launchers; her nuclear power plant drove her at 30 knots. While on station in the Tonkin Gulf in May 1968, this ship scored the first hit ever made on an enemy aircraft with guided missiles. In 1972 the cruiser *Chicago,* an 18,777-ton ship converted from a gunship, scored a similar success while providing cover for planes mining Hai Phòng Harbor.

Also operating in the South China Sea were the Navy's new frigates, including the nuclear-powered *Bainbridge.* Usually displacing close to 8,000 tons at full load, these fast ships (over 30 knots) were armed with one or two Terrier missile launchers and often a 5-inch gun. The newest ships of the Belknap class were fitted with the Naval Tactical Data System that allowed them to track hundreds of aircraft simultaneously. On 19 July 1972 one of these vessels, the *Biddle,* while on station in the Gulf of Tonkin, engaged five MiGs and shot down two. Another Belknap-class frigate, the USS *Sterett,* in an action of 19 April 1972, claimed two MiGs, a Styx antiship missile, and two PT boats. In his action report the commanding officer of the *Sterett* concluded that "combatant ships with the size, speed and weapons capabilities of a Guided Missile Frigate are an entity unto themselves, having the capability to defend against multiple air/surface/subsurface threats from any direction."

Gunnery support duties fell to the Navy's senior surface warships, some older than many of their crewmen. In 1964 only a few gun cruisers remained in commission, but, beginning in 1965, they supported friendly troops in South Vietnam and, starting the next year, bombarded North Vietnamese military forces north of the Demilitarized Zone (DMZ). Especially valuable in this role were the 8-inch gun cruisers *Newport News* and *St. Paul,* the latter a veteran of World War II and Korea. So scarce were major-caliber rifles on the gun line that the Navy's first guided missile cruisers *Boston* and *Canberra* remained in commission for their two 8-inch forward mounts even when their missile batteries aft were removed. The Cleveland-class missile cruiser conversions were valued more for their 6-inch guns than for their Terrier batteries. These older gunships shot off far more ammunition than they had during World War II; in fact, the *Boston* fired so many missions during Operation SEA DRAGON that the rifling in her gun barrels was worn virtually smooth. Also reinforcing the bombardment force was the battleship *New Jersey,* brought out of retirement in 1967.

Destroyers, both veterans of World War II and newer ships of the Forrest Sherman and Charles F. Adams classes, also performed in the gunnery role, as did newer destroyer escorts of the Claud Jones, Garcia, and Brooke classes. And as with the cruisers, the destroyer types engaged in lengthy fire missions: The *Towers,* for instance, expended 3,266 5-inch shells in July 1966 alone. These extensive bombardments revealed defects in ammunition of the new 5-inch/54-caliber gun, with several ships suffering in-bore explosions. Off Vietnam, the destroyer types also performed plane guard and search-and-rescue duties; radar picket destroyer escorts helped enforce the MARKET TIME patrols.

Smaller warships undertook a host of missions off South Vietnam's coasts and on her rivers. These smaller craft were as varied as Coast Guard cutters, Asheville-class patrol gunboats, minesweepers, hydrofoils, Swift boats, and Boston Whalers.

Essential to the Navy's power projection duty were the fleet's amphibious ships: assault ships, dock landing ships, infantry landing ships, inshore fire support ships, tank and infantry landing ships, transport docks, and others. Backing up the fighting forces was an armada of support craft with designations as varied as aircraft ferry, attack transport, ammunition ship, barracks ship, cargo ship, fleet tug, floating crane, floating dry dock, harbor tug, hospital ship, hydrographic survey ship, net-layer, oiler, open lighter, provision ship, refrigerator ship, repair ship, salvage ship, seaplane tender, stores ship, tanker, and transport.

—Malcolm Muir, Jr.

References: Friedman, Norman. *U.S. Small Combatants*. Annapolis, MD: Naval Institute Press, 1987.
Gardiner, Robert, ed. *Conway's All the World's Fighting Ships 1947–1982, Part 1: The Western Powers; Part 2: The Warsaw Pact and Non-Aligned Nations.* Annapolis, MD: Naval Institute Press, 1983.
Jane's Fighting Ships. New York: McGraw Hill, various editions.
U.S. Naval History Division. *Dictionary of American Naval Fighting Ships.* 8 vols. Washington, DC: U.S. Government Printing Office, 1959–1981.
See also: Aircraft Carriers; Australia; MARKET TIME, Operation; *New Jersey* (BB-62); PIERCE ARROW, Operation; SEA DRAGON, Operation; United States: Navy; Vietnam, Republic of: Navy (VNN).

Washington Special Actions Group (WSAG)

Contingency-planning crisis management board established and chaired by Henry Kissinger. The Washington Special Actions Group (WSAG) was composed of personnel responsible for national security, including the deputy secretaries of the State and Defense Departments, the director of the Central Intelligence Agency (CIA), the chairman of the Joint Chiefs of Staff (JCS), and the assistant to the president for National Security Affairs. In the spring of 1969 it became National Security Advisor Henry Kissinger's vehicle for crisis management. When a North Vietnamese–Pathet Lao offensive threatened the Laotian capital of Vientiane, the WSAG developed measures to support Royal Lao forces. The Communist offensive was halted and the North Vietnamese retreated beginning on 1 April 1970 after a Lao government counteroffensive supported by Thai volunteers.

The WSAG worked on various programs designed to harass North Vietnamese troops in the Cambodian border areas, including the employment of both air attacks and raids by South Vietnamese forces. When Prince Norodom Sihanouk was overthrown, the United States had to decide whether or not to support the Lon Nol government, which was under attack by North Vietnamese forces trying to isolate Phnom Penh by seizing provincial capitals.

In this crisis the WSAG—now augmented by the addition of various staff personnel and sending its documents through formal channels—approved the shipment of 3,000 captured Communist weapons from South Vietnam to Lon Nol's forces, and on 15 April 1970 arranged the transfer of $5 million for the purchase of arms. More important, the WSAG supported President Richard Nixon's subsequent decision to launch the incursion against Communist sanctuaries in Cambodian border areas, and one of its members, U. Alexis Johnson, prepared a detailed list of tasks for departments to perform.

The WSAG met almost daily during the 1972 North Vietnamese Easter Offensive, supporting Nixon's decision to mine Hai Phòng Harbor just before the May 1972 Nixon-Brezhnev summit in Moscow. As Washington moved toward the Paris Accords with the North Vietnamese, the WSAG worked on Operation ENHANCE PLUS in an effort to supply the Republic of Vietnam with sufficient equipment to defend itself when all U.S. troops were withdrawn. The WSAG thus played a key role in planning, implementing, and advising the chief executive on matters related to the national security during the Nixon presidency.

—Claude R. Sasso

References: Johnson, U. Alexis. *Right Hand of Power*. Englewood Cliffs, NJ: Prentice-Hall, 1984.
Kalb, Marvin, and Bernard Kalb. *Kissinger*. Boston: Little, Brown, 1974.
Kissinger, Henry. *White House Years*. Boston: Little, Brown, 1979.
See also: Cambodia; Cambodian Incursion; ENHANCE PLUS, Operation; Johnson, U. Alexis; Kissinger, Henry Alfred; Nixon, Richard Milhous; Sihanouk, Norodom.

Watergate

Term given to a vast array of abuses of power during the administration of President Richard M. Nixon (1969–1974). Watergate is generally accepted to have begun with the order given by National Security Advisor Henry Kissinger, with the approval of Nixon, to tap the telephone of William Beecher, reporter for the *New York Times*, to try to locate the source of Beecher's story on the secret bombing of Cambodia. White House paranoia over internal leaks to the news media reached a peak with the 1971 release to the press of the Pentagon Papers, a top-secret study on the conduct of the war, by one of the study's Defense Department authors.

Although nothing in the Pentagon Papers compromised his administration, Nixon was incensed by this breach of security and ordered his staff to find the source of the leak. The formation of the group commonly known as the "Plumbers" soon followed. Their efforts led directly to the 23 June 1972 attempted burglary at the Watergate Hotel complex in Washington, D.C., an attempt by the Plumbers to obtain information from the offices of the Democratic National Committee that might be of use in the upcoming presidential campaign. The attempt to cover up both the genesis of this crime and the existence of others committed by the administration caused the downfall of the Nixon administration and led to the resignation of the president on 8 August 1974.

To many Americans, the Vietnam War and Watergate represented the origins of what had gone wrong with American politics in the 1960s. Many would agree with historian Arthur M. Schlesinger, Jr. that the American presidency had become "imperial" in nature and that the same causes that had led to the abuse of the presidential war-making power in Vietnam—with Presidents John F. Kennedy, Lyndon Johnson, and Nixon committing troops to an undeclared war without adequate advice and consent from Congress—had led to a presidency that could commit gross abuses of power against its own citizenry, as occurred in Watergate. This feeling contributed greatly to the passage of the 1973 War Powers Act, which limited the president's ability to commit troops in times of military crisis without explicit reporting to Congress.

Watergate did, however, play an indirect role in the end of the Vietnam War in 1975. During the negotiations that led to the 1973 cease-fire and withdrawal of U.S. troops from Vietnam, Nixon secretly promised Republic of Vietnam President Nguyên Văn Thiêu that, if the North violated the peace, the United States would reenter the conflict and protect Sài Gòn. This promise, more than anything else, led Thiêu to accept the cease-fire. However, thanks to the new mood of congressional oversight toward the presidency caused largely by Watergate, new President Gerald R. Ford was unable to keep Nixon's promise. Despite the rather frantic entreaties of Thiêu after the fall of Ban Mê Thuôt in March 1975, Ford could not get Congress to appropriate significant funds. Recognizing the volatility of the political situation, Ford never asked for the troops that Thiêu requested.

—John Robert Greene

References: Greene, John Robert. *The Limits of Power: The Nixon and Ford Administrations.* Bloomington, IN: University of Indiana Press, 1992.
Kutler, Stanley I. *The Wars of Watergate: The Last Crisis of Richard Nixon.* New York: Alfred A. Knopf, 1990.
Schlesinger, Arthur M., Jr. *The Imperial Presidency.* Boston: Houghton Mifflin, 1973.
See also: Ellsberg, Daniel; Ford, Gerald R.; Kissinger, Henry Alfred; Mitchell, John Newton; Nixon, Richard Milhous; Pentagon Papers and Trial; United States: Department of Justice; War Powers Act.

Weathermen

Radical faction of the Students for a Democratic Society (SDS) that advocated violent means to alter American society. In January 1960 student activists organized the SDS to promote civil rights and protest the nuclear arms race. By 1965, however, the group had shifted its primary focus to the Vietnam War. Its protest activities included petition drives and draft resistance training. These efforts were successful in raising opposition to the war but not successful in changing government policy. As a result the SDS began to radicalize. During its national convention at Ann Arbor, Michigan, in December 1968 delegates split into opposing camps, some of which wanted to adopt revolutionary violence as a political tactic, first to end the draft and then to end the war. After the convention the radical factions began to encourage and engage in violent protests against what would become America's longest war. The Weathermen were one of the most violent of these factions.

The Weathermen specifically grew out of an SDS national "war council" held in Austin, Texas, in March 1969. This council resolved to promote "armed struggle" as the only way to transform American society. Members of the Weathermen agreed with the council's conclusions and in October organized over 600 people to engage in violent protests in Chicago. The protests became known as the "Days of Rage" and earned the Weathermen sufficient notoriety to catch the attention of the Federal Bureau of Investigation (FBI), particularly because of their reliance on arson and bombings to assault the federal government.

The philosophical foundations of the Weathermen were Marxist in nature: Militant struggle was the key to striking out against the state and building a revolutionary consciousness among the young, particularly the white working class. The message was antiracist and anti-imperialist; the goal was a radical counterculture that provoked arguments and incited fights within itself and with its opponents.

The Weathermen thought that perpetual criticism would force America's youth to continually question the political establishment and reverse the corruption of once-democratic American ideals. The radicals believed that most Americans understood their political message and the reasons they considered violent tactics necessary. In fact, an overwhelming number of Americans regarded the Weathermen's activities as criminal and supported efforts by federal law enforcement agencies to end their activities in the early 1970s.

—Tracy R. Szczepaniak

References: Gitlin, Todd. *The Sixties: Years of Hope, Days of Rage.* New York: Bantam Books, 1987.
Jacobs, Harold. *The Weathermen.* Berkeley, CA: Ramparts Press, 1971.
Miller, James. *Democracy Is in the Streets: From Port Huron to the Siege of Chicago.* New York: Simon & Schuster, 1987.
O'Neill, William L. *Coming Apart: An Informal History of America in the 1960s.* New York: Times Books, 1971.
Viorst, Milton. *Fire in the Streets: America in the 1960s.* New York: Simon & Schuster, 1979.
See also: Antiwar Movement, United States; Students for a Democratic Society (SDS); University of Wisconsin Bombing.

Westmoreland, William Childs

(1914–)

U.S. Army general; commander of American forces in Vietnam from June 1964 to June 1968. William Westmoreland was born in rural Spartanburg County, South Carolina, on 26 March 1914. Military service was traditional on both sides of young Westmoreland's family. His father, a textile plant manager, had attended the Citadel, and Westmoreland did so for one year before entering the U.S. Military Academy at West Point in 1932, where he became cadet first captain.

Commissioned a lieutenant of artillery in 1936, Westmoreland served in various posts in the United States. In 1942 he became a major and commanded an artillery battery in Tunisia and Sicily, distinguishing himself in the February 1943 Battle of Kasserine Pass. He then served in France with the 9th Infantry Division, where he was promoted to colonel and became division chief of staff. He fought with the division in Germany and after the war commanded a regiment in occupation duties. In 1946, after completing parachute training, he commanded the 504th Parachute Infantry Regiment. From 1947 to 1950 Westmoreland was chief of staff of the 82d Airborne Division. He then taught at the Army Command and Staff School and the Army War College. In August 1952 he commanded the 187th Airborne Regimental Combat Team in Korea, and that November he was promoted to brigadier general. For the next several years he served on the General Staff and was promoted to major general in 1956, after which he commanded the 101st Airborne Division at Fort Campbell, Kentucky. From 1960 to 1963 he served as superintendent at West Point. Promoted to lieutenant general in 1963, Westmoreland returned to Fort Campbell to command the XVIII Airborne Corps. He was then ordered to Vietnam as deputy commander, U.S. Military Assistance Command, Vietnam (MACV).

Westmoreland arrived in Vietnam on 27 January 1964, and in June he was named to succeed General Paul D. Harkins as commander of MACV. Westmoreland judged the South Vietnamese to lack a "sense of urgency." His own approach to command in Vietnam was to be one of action, not of contemplation. Secretary of Defense Robert McNamara noted in his memoirs that "Westy possessed neither Patton's boastful flamboyance nor LeMay's stubbornness but shared their determination and patriotism." In August Westmoreland was promoted to full general; it was now Westmoreland's war.

One characteristic that President Lyndon B. Johnson looked for in his new commander in Vietnam was mental agility and flexibility to adapt to unforeseen events. Few would disagree that Westmoreland brought abundant energy and impeccable standards to his command, but some have criticized his choice of tactics and timing.

The military strategy of search and destroy seemingly was consistent with the political character of limited war in Vietnam, where the United States and South Vietnam were partners in contesting a Communist insurgency that threatened the viability of the Republic of Vietnam. Search-and-destroy operations were designed to deny to the Viêt Công (VC) and the People's Army of Vietnam (PAVN) the cover and concealment of their jungle bases and to bring their military units to battle. Allied units would enter jungle sanctuaries, search methodically during the day, and occupy strong night defensive positions, daring the Communists to attack. MACV's approach depended on superior intelligence data and sufficient airmobile combat units to reach the decisive location in time to exploit the opportunity. Search-and-destroy operations were predicated on the assumption that combat in Vietnam had moved from insurgency/guerrilla actions to larger-unit actions.

General Bruce Palmer, Jr., who served as commander of II Field Force, Vietnam, and later of U.S. Army, Vietnam, concludes in his book The 25-Year War that the chosen American style of war "was tough, risky business, for our troops, moving into and searching a hostile area, were exposed to enemy ambush, mines, and booby traps." Moreover, he points out, this approach surrendered the initiative to the Communists, forcing the Allies "to react

and dance to the enemy's tune." Both Palmer and Andrew F. Krepinevich, Jr., have written that MACV's assumption that large-unit warfare had supplanted the Communists' small-unit guerrilla-style "hit-and-run" tactics after 1965 was invalid. In 1967 Westmoreland believed that the initiative had firmly switched to the Allies, noting that the VC and the PAVN had lost control over large areas and populations.

It may be that the flaw in the U.S. phase (1965–1973) of the war in Vietnam was a poorly conceived grand strategy. Neil Sheehan in A Bright Shining Lie says that in prosecuting a war of attrition, "The building of the killing machine had become an end in itself." Grand strategy—the sum of political, economic, military, and other component strategies—is designed to accomplish the purpose of the war. In the most striking way, the chosen military strategy of attrition did not lead directly and resolutely to the political end of the conflict. It is not surprising that General Westmoreland and the MACV staff sought a strategic solution to the growing VC/PAVN capability through the application of U.S. technology and firepower. What is surprising is that they believed that an American-style quick fix could win a protracted war. In many ways, the "other war," pacification, was the more important stepping stone to an Allied victory. American strategists discovered too late that carrying the war to the Communists at the same time as they were attempting to strengthen the South Vietnamese toward national self-sufficiency was like pulling on both ends of a rope simultaneously.

VC/PAVN forces were fighting the Americans and their allies like a seasoned boxer, willing to go the distance by slipping punches when possible and absorbing them with minimum damage when necessary. But through it all the Communists had their eyes on the objective—to frustrate and damage the Americans' will to continue the war. General Westmoreland's warriors had four years in the ring with General Võ Nguyên Giáp's unsophisticated but numerous and dedicated troops. Instead of being weakened by attrition, the VC/PAVN seemed to gain in strength and audacity after suffering enormous losses in their 1968 Têt Offensive.

Explaining that American intelligence had forecast a Viêt Công attack, General Westmoreland said "I made a mistake; I should have called a press conference and made known to the world that we knew this attack was coming." It was clear that after the Têt Offensive, the U.S. government, reflecting the impatience and confusion of the American people, began withdrawing the essential moral support and then the resources necessary for victory. It was not entirely Westmoreland's fault, only his misfortune to be the responsible official on the ground in Vietnam. In that regard Harry Summers is probably right that it is unfair to compare General Westmoreland with General Giáp because the PAVN commander enjoyed a unity of command that in the American system of war-fighting was distributed among many civilian and military authorities.

In July 1968 President Johnson recalled Westmoreland from Vietnam and appointed him U.S. Army chief of staff. As his former deputy, General Creighton Abrams, carried on with the gradual hands-off of the war to the unready and sometimes unwilling South Vietnamese, Westmoreland set his professional skills to work on issues such as the all-volunteer force. In July 1972 Westmoreland retired from the Army after more than 36 years of service. In 1976 he published his memoirs, *A Soldier Reports.*

In January 1982 the Columbia Broadcasting System (CBS) and its journalist Mike Wallace aired a television documentary that accused General Westmoreland and his staff of fudging Communist casualty figures to give the appearance of progress and eventual success in Vietnam. As the general put it in his December 1994 interview, "They accused me of basically lying. . . . If there is anything that I cherish, it's character." Westmoreland brought a libel suit against CBS that resulted in a two-and-a-half-month trial and ended with an out-of-court settlement on 18 February 1985. CBS stood by its documentary but issued a statement that it did not mean to impugn General Westmoreland's patriotism or loyalty "in performing his duties as he saw them." Following his retirement, Westmoreland made a brief, unsuccessful foray into politics in search of the Republican nomination for governor of South Carolina. He has been a frequent speaker at patriotic events.

—John F. Votaw

References: Furgurson, Ernest B. *Westmoreland: The Inevitable General.* Boston: Little, Brown, 1968.
Herring, George C. "Westmoreland, William Childs." In *Dictionary of American Military Biography,* edited by Roger Spiller. Vol. 3. Westport, CT: Greenwood Press, 1984, pp. 1179–1183.
Sheehan, Neil. *A Bright Shining Lie: John Paul Vann and America in Vietnam.* New York: Random House, 1988.
Webster's American Military Biographies. Springfield, MA: G. & C. Merriam, 1978, pp. 471–472.
Westmoreland, Gen. William C. Interview with the author at Cantigny, Wheaton, Illinois, 21 December 1994.
————. *A Soldier Reports.* Garden City, NY: Doubleday, 1976.
————. "Vietnam in Perspective." In *Vietnam: Four American Perspectives,* edited by Patrick J. Hearden. West Lafayette, IN: Purdue University Press, 1990.
Zaffiri, Samuel. *Westmoreland: A Biography of General William C. Westmoreland.* New York: William Morrow, 1994.
See also: Abrams, Creighton; Attrition; COWIN Report; Manila Conference; McNamara, Robert S.; Media and the War; Military Assistance Command, Vietnam (MACV); Order of Battle Dispute; Search and Destroy; Sheehan, Cornelius Mahoney (Neil); Têt Offensive: Overall Strategy; Têt Offensive: The Sài Gòn Circle; United States: Army; United States: Involvement in Vietnam, 1965–1968.

Weyand, Frederick C.

(1916–)

U.S. Army general; commander II Field Force, Vietnam; last commander of Military Assistance Command, Vietnam (MACV). Born in Arbuckle, California, on 15 September 1916, Frederick Weyand graduated from the University of California at Berkeley in 1939 and received a Reserve Officers' Training Corps (ROTC) commission. In 1940 he was called to active duty and assigned to the 6th Artillery.

During World War II Weyand served as an intelligence officer in Burma. After the war he transferred to the infantry. In the Korean War he was a battalion commander in the 7th Infantry and operations officer of the 3d Infantry Division.

In 1964 Weyand assumed command of the 25th Infantry Division in Hawaii. He took the division to Vietnam in 1966 and commanded it during Operations CEDAR FALLS and JUNCTION CITY. In March 1967 he became deputy commander of II Field Force and then its commander from July 1967 to August 1968.

As commander of II Field Force, Weyand controlled combat operations inside the "Sài Gòn Circle" during the 1968 Têt Offensive. In the months leading up to Têt, Weyand's maneuver battalions were increasingly sent to outlying border regions in response to increased Viêt Công (VC) attacks in those areas. But Weyand and his civilian political advisor, John Paul Vann, were uncomfortable with the operational patterns they were seeing. Weyand did not like the increase in Communist radio traffic around Sài Gòn, and his units were making too few contacts in the border regions.

On 10 January 1968 Weyand visited with General William Westmoreland and convinced him to let Weyand pull more U.S. combat battalions back in around Sài Gòn. As a result there were 27 battalions (instead of the planned 14) in the Sài Gòn area when the Têt attacks came. Weyand's shrewd analysis and subsequent actions unquestionably altered the course of the Têt fighting to the Allies' advantage. During the battle itself Weyand controlled U.S. forces from his command post at Long Bình, some 15 miles east of Sài Gòn.

Weyand left Vietnam in 1968 and served as the Army's chief of the Office of Reserve Components until 1969. In 1969 and 1970 he was a military advisor to the Paris peace talks. In April 1970 Weyand returned to Vietnam as deputy commander of MACV, succeeding General Creighton Abrams as MACV commander in July 1972. Weyand presided over the U.S. military withdrawal from Vietnam and folded MACV's flag on 29 March 1973.

After he left Vietnam, Weyand became commander in chief, U.S. Army Pacific, later becoming vice-chief of staff of the Army later in 1973 and chief of staff in October 1974. Just before the fall of the Republic of Vietnam (RVN), President Gerald Ford sent Weyand to Sài Gòn to assess the situation. Weyand arrived there on 27 March 1975 and delivered the message to President Nguyên Văn Thiêu that although the U.S. government would support the RVN to the best of its ability, America would not fight in Vietnam again. Upon his return to Washington, Weyand reported—to no avail—that the military situation could not be improved without direct U.S. intervention.

Weyand retired from the U.S. Army a full general (four-star rank) in October 1976. During his 36-year career, he spent almost 6 years in Vietnam and another 10 in Asia and the Pacific. He was one of America's most experienced and capable commanders of the Vietnam War.

—David T. Zabecki

References: Bell, William G. *Commanding Generals and Chiefs of Staff: 1775–1983.* Washington, DC: U.S. Army Center of Military History, 1983.
Oberdorfer, Don. *Tet!* New York: Doubleday, 1971.
Palmer, Bruce, Jr. *The 25-Year War: America's Military Role in Vietnam.* Lexington, KY: University Press of Kentucky, 1984.
Zabecki, David T. "Battle for Saigon." *Vietnam* (Summer 1989): 19–25.

See also: Abrams, Creighton; Ford, Gerald R.; Military Assistance Command, Vietnam (MACV); Nguyên Văn Thiêu; United States: Army; Vann, John Paul; Westmoreland, William Childs.

Wheeler, Earle G.

(1908–1975)

U.S. Army general; chief of staff (1962–1964); chairman of the Joint Chiefs of Staff (JCS) (1964–1970). Born in Washington, D.C., on 13 January 1908, Earle "Bus" Wheeler enlisted in the District of Columbia National Guard at age 16 and reached the rank of sergeant before entering the U.S. Military Academy. He graduated from West Point in 1932 and was commissioned in the infantry. He served with the 15th Infantry in Tianjin, China, from 1937 to 1938.

In 1940 Wheeler returned to West Point as a mathematics instructor. During the first half of World War II, he trained infantry units in the United States. In December 1944 he went to Europe as chief of staff of the 63d Infantry Division. Wheeler was selected to lead an assault regiment against Hitler's headquarters in the Bavarian Alps, but the war ended just as the operation was to begin.

A protégé of General Maxwell Taylor, Wheeler was a full general by 1962. That March he became deputy commander in chief of the U.S. European Command, and seven months later he was named chief of staff of the Army. When Taylor retired as chairman of the JCS in June 1964 to become ambassador to the Republic of Vietnam, Wheeler succeeded him.

Wheeler had good political relations with Congress, particularly with Senators John Stennis and Henry Jackson. He was fairly close to President Lyndon Johnson, and he had a reputation as a skillful player of the Pentagon's game under Secretary of Defense Robert S. McNamara's rules. Nonetheless, as the war progressed, Wheeler was increasingly overshadowed by McNamara and his systems analysis "whiz kids." As chairman, Wheeler worked hard to smooth over dissenting opinions or "splits" in JCS recommendations. He believed these opened the door for interference by McNamara and his assistants, resulting in civilians making military decisions they were not qualified to make. Even though there was a wide difference of opinion within the JCS on the air war strategy, Wheeler convinced all the chiefs to go along with it on the basis that they all agreed it was at least worth a try. Wheeler's approach did not work. Unanimity did not produce greater JCS influence, and McNamara increasingly made military decisions to a far greater degree than any of his predecessors.

General Earle G. Wheeler issues orders to halt bombing runs over North Vietnam, 31 October 1968. As chairman of the Joint Chiefs of Staff (JCS), Wheeler worked hard to smooth over dissenting opinions or "splits" in JCS recommendations.

As American involvement in the war grew, the JCS recognized the widening discrepancy between the total force needed to meet worldwide U.S. commitments and the manpower base the political leadership was willing to support. In August 1965 Wheeler and the chiefs proposed an overall strategy for American military operations in Vietnam that centered around three tasks: (1) forcing Hà Nôi to "cease and desist" in the South; (2) defeating the Viêt Công in the South; and (3) deterring China from intervening. To support the strategy and to rebuild the depleted strategic reserve at home, the JCS urged at least a limited call-up of reserve forces.

The chiefs continually pressed for the adoption of this overall strategy throughout the war, but their recommendations were never fully accepted. On the other hand, they could clearly see where McNamara's strategy of piecemeal force and graduated response would lead. Wheeler once commented, "Whatever the political merits of [graduated response], we deprived ourselves of the military effects of early weight of effort and shock, and gave the enemy time to adjust to our slow quantitative and qualitative increase of pressure."

As the American war effort grew, seemingly without end, frustration also grew among the JCS. In the fall of 1967 the chiefs even considered resigning en masse in protest over the reserve mobilization issue. Despite their frustration, however, Wheeler and the other chiefs failed in one of their most important responsibilities. Even though their own strategy recommendations were being ignored, they never once directly advised the president that the ad hoc strategy being pursued was sure to fail. Explaining (but not excusing) this glaring failure, General Bruce Palmer suggested that the chiefs were too imbued with the military's characteristic "can-do" attitude, and they did not want to appear disloyal or to be openly challenging civilian authority.

The 1968 Têt Offensive and the siege of Khe Sanh brought about the psychological turning point of the war. They also marked a historical low point in the relations between America's military leaders and their civilian superiors. President Johnson became obsessed with Khe Sanh. Haunted by the specter of Điên Biên Phu, he had a terrain model of the Khe Sanh base constructed for the White House situation room. Johnson spent evenings, sitting in his bathrobe, reading teletype traffic from the field and studying aerial photographs. In one of the most demeaning demands ever placed on military leaders by a U.S. president, Johnson insisted that Wheeler and the chiefs sign a formal declaration of their belief in General William Westmoreland's ability to hold Khe Sanh. In making his demand, the president told Wheeler, "I don't want any damn Dinbinphoo."

Immediately after the Têt Offensive, Westmoreland remained confident. Wheeler, however, strongly encouraged the Military Assistance Command, Vietnam (MACV) commander to request more troops. Wheeler apparently hoped that another large commitment of forces to Vietnam would finally force Johnson to mobilize the reserves. At that point in the war, the members of the JCS were alarmed over America's worldwide strategic posture. The only combat-ready division outside of Vietnam was the 82d Airborne Division—and even one of its three brigades was on its way to Vietnam. The once-proud Seventh Army in Europe had been re-

duced to little more than a replacement holding pool. The chiefs believed the reserve call-up was necessary to restore the military's global strategic posture.

On 23 February 1968 Wheeler flew to Sài Gòn to confer with Westmoreland. He informed the MACV commander of McNamara's impending departure. Wheeler also overstated the likelihood that Westmoreland's long-standing requests to attack Communist sanctuaries in Laos and Cambodia would be approved. The two generals developed a request for an additional 206,000 troops. Once back in Washington, however, Wheeler presented the proposal as if Westmoreland were on the verge of defeat unless he was rapidly reinforced. When a member of the White House staff leaked the story to the *New York Times,* it was presented in just those terms. Unfortunately, Wheeler, who had actually maneuvered Westmoreland into making the request in the first place, did little to set the record straight.

From that point on, Wheeler's influence declined even more. Although he continued to attend all high-level White House meetings on Vietnam, his advice was virtually ignored. Oddly enough, Johnson in July 1968 requested and received congressional approval to extend Wheeler's tenure as JCS chairman for another year. When Richard Nixon became president, he too requested another one-year extension. Nixon, however, also did not heed the military advice of Wheeler and the chiefs.

Wheeler retired on 2 July 1970 after an unprecedented six years in office. The stress and frustration of those years led to several heart attacks and ruined his health. Wheeler died in Frederick, Maryland, on 18 December 1975.

One positive legacy of the Wheeler years was the lesson of JCS unanimity. Under one of the provisions of the much-heralded 1986 Goldwater-Nichols Defense Reorganization Act, the chairman of the JCS is now required to report all dissenting opinions to the president, and the dissenting service chief is both allowed and obligated to state his views.

—David T. Zabecki

References: Bell, William G. *Commanding Generals and Chiefs of Staff: 1775–1983.* Washington, DC: U.S. Army Center of Military History, 1983. Halberstam, David. *The Best and the Brightest.* New York: Random House, 1972.
Palmer, Bruce, Jr. *The 25-Year War: America's Military Role in Vietnam.* Lexington, KY: University Press of Kentucky, 1984.
Sheehan, Neil, et al. *The Pentagon Papers.* Chicago: Quadrangle Books, 1971.
Webb, Willard J., and Ronald Cole. *The Chairmen of the Joint Chiefs of Staff.* Washington, DC: Historical Division, Joint Chiefs of Staff, 1989.
Wheeler, Earle G. *Addresses.* Washington, DC: U.S. Government Printing Office, 1970.
See also: Johnson, Lyndon Baines; Joint Chiefs of Staff; Khe Sanh, Battles of; McNamara, Robert S.; Military Assistance Command, Vietnam (MACV); Palmer, Bruce, Jr.; Stennis, John Cornelius; Taylor, Maxwell Davenport; Têt Offensive: Overall Strategy; Têt Offensive: The Sài Gòn Circle; Westmoreland, William Childs.

WHEELER/WALLOWA, Operation

(September 1967–November 1968)
Division-sized Army task force in Quang Nam and Quang Tín Provinces in I Corps from November 1967 until November 1968. Op-

Helmets, rifles, and jungle boots tell a grim tale of the fight waged by and against the U.S. 1st Brigade, 101st Airborne paratroopers in Operation WHEELER near Chu Lai. This battlefield memorial honored the GIs killed during the offensive.

eration WHEELER/WALLOWA followed Task Force Oregon (TFO), a multibrigade Army force deployed in April 1967, to southern I Corps to blunt an offensive by the People's Army of Vietnam (PAVN) 2d Division and to enable units of the 3d Marine Task Force to relocate to Quang Tri Province. Organized by Maj. Gen. William Rosson, TFO was composed of the 196th Light Infantry Brigade, the 1st Brigade of the 101st Airborne Division, and the 3d Brigade of the 25th Infantry Division (later designated the 3d Brigade, 4th Infantry Division). Shortly after the launching of Operation WHEELER on 11 September, Brig. Gen. Samuel W. Koster assumed command, and on 25 September U.S. Military Assistance Command, Vietnam (MACV) announced that TFO would be reconstituted as the Americal Division (23d Infantry), consisting of the 196th, 198th, and 11th Light Infantry Brigades, and would be headquartered at Chu Lai. The latter two brigades, however, would not arrive in South Vietnam until 22 October and 20 December, respectively, and only the 198th would join successor operations to WHEELER early in 1968.

Operation WHEELER had barely begun when the 1st Brigade, 1st Airborne and two battalions of the 3d Brigade, 4th Infantry returned to their parent divisions. These units were effectively replaced by the 3d Brigade and Troop B, 1st Squadron, 9th Cavalry of the 1st Cavalry Division (Airmobile), which on 3 October launched Operation WALLOWA in the northern sector of the Americal Division's area of operation (AO). On 11 November Operations WHEELER and WALLOWA were combined as WHEELER/WALLOWA under the command of Koster, who by that time was a major general.

WHEELER/WALLOWA became the code name for a series of sweeping operations throughout Quang Nam and Quang Tín Provinces, from Hôi An south to Tam Kỳ along Route 1, and west into the Quê Sơn and Hiệp Đức Valleys, areas never previously under Allied control. Communist strength proved much greater than anticipated, as four independent PAVN battalions reinforced the PAVN 2d Division.

Until mid-January 1968 the 1st Cavalry's highly mobile 3d Brigade and the 196th Brigade continuously engaged a determined Communist force, which managed to bring down dozens of helicopters in the Hiệp Đức Valley and mount regimental-sized attacks against three firebases in the Quê Sơn Valley. By 31 January WHEELER/WALLOWA claimed 1,718 Việt Công and 1,585 PAVN troops killed, and more than 600 weapons captured, at a cost of more than 200 American lives.

Just days after the 3d Brigade joined another 1st Cavalry brigade already deployed to Quang Tri Province the PAVN launched the Têt Offensive, during which the most intensive fighting in the WHEELER/WALLOWA area occurred at the provincial capital of Tam Kỳ. In February and March 1968 the 3d Brigade of the 82d Airborne Division also came under operational control of the Americal Division, and in late April the 198th Light Infantry Brigade assumed primary responsibility for the remaining six months of the operation. The 198th's 1st Battalion, 6th Infantry distinguished itself in successive battles against the 60th and 70th Main Force Việt Công (VC) Battalions at Lo Giang and Op Banh and in 22 days of consecutive fighting against the entire 3d Regiment of the 2d PAVN Division.

Ending on 11 November 1968, one year after it began, WHEELER/WALLOWA claimed 10,020 VC/PAVN killed and 2,053 captured weapons. U.S. casualties were 682 killed and 2,548 wounded. Nevertheless WHEELER/WALLOWA only temporarily halted the threat of the PAVN 2d Division. Quang Nam and Quang Tín defied pacification as thousands of fresh PAVN and VC replacements appeared during 1969.

—John D. Root

References: McCoy, J. W. *Secrets of the Viet Cong.* New York: Hippocrene Books, 1992.
Stanton, Shelby L. *The Rise and Fall of an American Army: U.S. Ground Forces in Vietnam, 1965–1973.* New York: Dell, 1985.
See also: Têt Offensive: Overall Strategy; Têt Offensive: The Sài Gòn Circle; United States: Army; Vietnam, Democratic Republic of: Army (People's Army of Vietnam [PAVN]).

White Star

Special Forces teams in Laos. The U.S. military aid program in Laos from 1955 to 1961 was managed by an office attached to the economic aid mission in Vientiane known as the Programs Evaluation Office (PEO). The PEO provided equipment to the Royal Laotian Armed Forces and trained Laotians in its use and maintenance. PEO personnel wore civilian clothes to avoid violating the ban on foreign military advisors (except for a small French military mission) in Laos. In April 1961, however, the PEO was converted into a full-scale Military Assistance and Advisory Group (MAAG) by presidential decision, and its members were allowed to wear uniforms. At this time a number of U.S. Army Special Forces teams were sent to Laos under the MAAG and were called White Star teams.

The July 1962 Geneva Agreement confirmed the neutrality of Laos. As early as 23 June the United States set the tone for compliance with Geneva Protocol provisions regarding the withdrawal of foreign troops by pulling out the White Star teams. Thereafter, the number of U.S. military advisors in Laos was steadily reduced, with the last of them gone by the 7 October 1962 deadline.

—Arthur J. Dommen

References: Castle, Timothy N. *At War in the Shadow of Vietnam. U.S. Military Aid to the Royal Lao Government, 1955–1975.* New York: Columbia University Press, 1993.
Dommen, Arthur J. *Conflict in Laos. The Politics of Neutralization.* New York: Praeger, 1964.
See also: Laos; United States: Special Forces.

Williams, Samuel T.

(1896–1984)

U.S. Army general and commander, U.S. Military Assistance and Advisory Group (MAAG), Vietnam, 1955–1960. Born in Denton, Texas, on 25 July 1896, Samuel Williams volunteered for the Texas National Guard, served in World War I and World War II, and commanded a division in Korea. He stressed discipline, scorned unfitness and negligence, and received his descriptive name "Hanging Sam" when he demanded a harsh penalty for a convicted child rapist.

When Williams replaced General John W. O'Daniel as the senior U.S. army officer in Vietnam on 24 October 1955, he eliminated "Indo-China" from the mission title, renaming it the Military Assistance and Advisory Group, Vietnam.

Williams had a close relationship with Republic of Vietnam President Ngô Đình Diêm and enjoyed the trust of that government's top-ranking officers. Williams defended Diêm without qualification and attested to the president's popularity nationwide. His determination to operate MAAG independent of the U.S. Embassy led to difficulties when Ambassador G. Frederick Reinhardt was superseded by Elbridge Durbrow, who exercised greater control. Personality differences between the two men made the clash bitter.

Under Williams the MAAG prepared for a conventional war. Influenced by their own experiences, Williams and his staff saw a strong similarity between the Korean and Vietnamese situations that caused them to concentrate on the possibility of a conventional attack by the Democratic Republic of Vietnam (DRV). Williams tended to downgrade the threat posed by the DRV.

Williams was critical of the organization of the Army of the Republic of Vietnam (ARVN), and he favored the elimination of territorial regiments and light units and the creation of division-size organizations able to cope with a cross-border invasion or internal insurgency. His accompanying defensive strategy, CINCPAC (commander in chief, Pacific) Operation Plan 46A, perceived an enemy drive through the Mekong Valley with the Central Highlands area as the decisive center of operations.

Williams was not alarmed by increasing guerrilla activity in the South. Believing that internal security was not the ARVN's principal responsibility, he advocated upgrading militia forces. Williams also doubted the value of the Michigan State University Advisory Group police and public administration advisors assisting the training of local security personnel. Williams preferred instruction by MAAG personnel.

At the time of his departure from Vietnam in 1960, Williams expressed confidence in an early American withdrawal. He retired from the service in August 1960 while in Vietnam and was replaced by General Lionel C. McGarr in September. Williams died at Fort Sam Houston, Texas, on 25 April 1984.

—Rodney J. Ross

References: Arnold, James R. *The First Domino: Eisenhower, the Military and America's Intervention in Vietnam.* New York: William Morrow, 1991.
Meyer, Harold J. *Hanging Sam: A Military Biography of General Samuel T. Williams, from Pancho Villa to Vietnam.* Denton, TX: University of North Texas Press, 1990.
Spector, Ronald H. *Advice and Support: The Early Years, 1941–1960.* Washington, DC: U.S. Army Center of Military History, 1983.
See also: Durbrow, Elbridge; Military Assistance and Advisory Group (MAAG), Vietnam; Ngô Đình Diêm; Reinhardt, George Frederick; United States: Involvement in Vietnam, 1954–1965.

Wilson, Harold

(1916–1995)

British prime minister, 1964–1970 and 1974–1975. Born at Huddersfield, England, on 11 March 1916, Harold Wilson was educated at Oxford, where he taught economics briefly. He served as director of economics and statistics for the Ministry of Fuel and Power from 1943 to 1944. The following year he entered Parliament, where he became the Labour Party's chief spokesman on economic issues and held a variety of secretarial posts. In 1963 Wilson became Labour Party leader on the death of Hugh Gaitskell. Labour won the 1964 parliamentary elections by just four seats. In 1966, however, Wilson led the party to a convincing victory when it secured a 97-seat majority. Most of Wilson's time in power as prime minister, between 1964 and 1970, was spent trying to keep Britain economically viable. In 1966 the government carried out a consolidation of steel companies into the British Steel Corporation; in 1967 it enacted legislation that created a decimal currency. With a widening trade deficit the government was forced into increasing austerity measures. Ultimately the pound sterling was devalued to $2.40 to the dollar.

Austerity also meant military retrenchment. Labour further reduced the size of the Royal Navy and gave up trying to maintain a sizable military force "East of Suez." The government also announced the closure of the great British base at Singapore and its intention to withdraw from the Persian Gulf.

Wilson was unable, and possibly unwilling, to influence U.S. policies in Vietnam. Both the Labor and Conservative Parties supported U.S. bombing of North Vietnam following the 1964 Gulf of Tonkin incidents, but privately Wilson wanted both an end to the bombing and a negotiated end to the war, and he so informed President Lyndon Johnson. Wilson was constrained from criticizing U.S. policy publicly both by the long-standing special relationship between the two countries and because of Washington's role in supporting the pound sterling.

In 1965 Wilson attempted several Vietnam peace initiatives, all of which failed. In early 1966 he endeavored to act as intermediary in setting up talks between Washington and Moscow regarding Vietnam. A halt in U.S. bombing of North Vietnam, in return for which the Democratic Republic of Vietnam (DRV) would stop infiltrating men into the South, collapsed when U.S. military leaders insisted that the DRV provide proof rather than promises. When Soviet Premier Aleksei Kosygin submitted this demand to DRV officials, they rejected it. In his memoirs Wilson noted Moscow's inability to "exert any real pressure on Hanoi in the face of continuing militant Chinese pressure."

In the 1970 British elections, Wilson squandered a huge lead and lost. The Conservatives returned to power with Edward Heath as prime minister, but Labour won the 1974 elections and Wilson again became prime minister. He retired unexpectedly in 1976 and James Callaghan took over. In 1983 he was made a life peer. He died in London on 24 May 1995.

—Spencer C. Tucker

References: Frankel, Joseph. *British Foreign Policy, 1945–1973.* New York: Oxford University Press, 1975.
Great Britain, Foreign Office. *Recent Exchanges Concerning Attempts to Promote a Negotiated Settlement of the Conflict in Viet-Nam.* London: H. M. Stationery Office, 1965.
Wilson, Harold K. *A Personal Record: The Labour Government, 1964–1970.* Boston: Little, Brown, 1971.

See also: de Gaulle, Charles André Marie Joseph; Great Britain; Johnson, Lyndon Baines; Kosygin, Aleksei Nikolayevich; SUNFLOWER, Operation.

Wilson, Thomas Woodrow

(1856–1924)

President of the United States, 1913–1921. Born on 28 December 1856 in Staunton, Virginia, Woodrow Wilson graduated from Princeton University in 1879. He then studied law at the University of Virginia but failed in the practice of law. In 1886 Wilson obtained a Ph.D. in History and Political Science under Herbert Baxter Adams at Johns Hopkins University. After holding several teaching positions, in 1890 Wilson joined the faculty at Princeton. In 1902 he became president of Princeton; he carried out a number of educational reforms and became nationally known as a leader of Democratic conservatism.

In 1910 Wilson was elected on the Democratic ticket as governor of New Jersey, beginning his meteoric rise to the presidency. Elected president in 1912, Wilson headed the nation during World War I and led negotiations at Paris following the end of the conflict. In that role Wilson had influence on developments in Southeast Asia.

Wilson advanced his plan for international peace in the Fourteen Points. In addition, in his call for a peacekeeping organization, the League of Nations, he set forth the principle of self-determination of peoples in the redrawing of the map of postwar Europe. Ironically, considering the later U.S. role in Vietnam, Wilson's rhetoric inspired the nationalist leader Hô Chí Minh to submit a statement to the 1919 Paris Peace Conference, noting that "all subject peoples are filled with hope by the prospect that an era of right and justice is opening to them." Hô did not demand independence for the French colony but asked for a constitutional government, democratic freedoms, and economic reforms. Although Hô did not gain an audience with Wilson, who seemed concerned only with Europe, this became the first step in his long campaign to gain Indo-Chinese self-determination.

The U.S. Senate later rejected Wilson's internationalism, including the Treaty of Versailles and membership in Wilson's cherished League of Nations. Wilson died in Washington, D.C., following a lengthy illness on 3 February 1924.

—Brenda J. Taylor

References: Ferrell, Robert H. *Woodrow Wilson and World War I: 1917–1921.* New York: Harper & Row, 1985.
Karnow, Stanley. *Vietnam: A History.* New York: Viking Press, 1983.
See also: Hô Chí Minh.

"Wise Men"

Senior advisors to President Lyndon Baines Johnson on Vietnam policy. Hoping to upgrade his foreign affairs credentials, deflect political criticism, and forge ties with America's foreign policy leadership, Johnson established an informal body of senior advisors that became known as the "Wise Men." They met for the first time in July 1965. Some participants, both past and current officials, had played significant roles in post–World War II policy making, including the establishment of the containment strategy. The group comprised establishment notables: Dean Acheson, George W. Ball, McGeorge Bundy, Douglas Dillon, Cyrus Vance, Arthur Dean, John J. McCloy, General Omar Bradley, General Matthew Ridgway, General Maxwell Taylor, Robert Murphy, Henry Cabot Lodge, Jr., Abe Fortas, and Arthur Goldberg.

The "Wise Men" assembled again on 2 November the day after Secretary of Defense Robert S. McNamara delivered a personal memorandum to Johnson urging an end to the bombing of North Vietnam and the curtailment of U.S. military operations in the Republic of Vietnam. He urged an examination of ground actions aimed at cutting U.S. losses and placing a greater burden on the South Vietnamese. To McNamara's disappointment, Johnson did not share this memorandum with the "Wise Men" who, with the notable exception of Ball, urged Johnson to press ahead with his current program, rejecting both de-escalation of the war and a Joint Chiefs of Staff proposal for a widened ground war and intensified bombing campaign.

In the wake of the 1968 Tết Offensive, President Johnson, prompted by Acheson, again summoned the "Wise Men" to the State Department. Briefed on 25 March 1968 the group was shocked to learn the extent of damage that the Communist attacks had done to security and pacification programs in the Vietnamese countryside. Following questions about the killed-to-wounded ratio and the remaining force capacity of the National Front for the Liberation of South Vietnam, the gathering was predisposed to admit the war had taken an unfortunate turn.

The next day at the White House the "Wise Men" met for the last time; the president, Vice-President Hubert H. Humphrey, General Earle G. Wheeler, Taylor, and Lodge were the only administration figures present. Acheson stated that he no longer believed that the United States could reach its goal by military methods. Instead, he favored measures to facilitate a U.S. withdrawal. Acheson's viewpoint, Bundy told a disappointed Johnson, was held by Dean, Vance, Dillon, and Ball. Only Bradley, Taylor, and Murphy thought the administration should take the counsel of the military leadership. Since a majority warned against further escalation, recourse to nuclear weapons, or expansion of the war, disengagement became the unquestioned alternative, a decision Johnson acknowledged only grudgingly.

—Rodney J. Ross

References: Berman, Larry. *Lyndon Johnson's War: The Road to Stalemate in Vietnam.* New York: W. W. Norton, 1989.
Herring, George C. *LBJ and Vietnam: A Different Kind of War.* Austin, TX: University of Texas Press, 1994.
Isaacson, Walter, and Evan Thomas. *The Wise Men.* New York: Simon & Schuster, 1987.
McNamara, Robert S., with Brian VanDeMark. *In Retrospect. The Tragedy and Lessons of Vietnam.* New York: Times Books, 1995.
See also: Acheson, Dean G.; Ball, George W.; Bradley, Omar Nelson; Bundy, McGeorge; Fortas, Abe; Goldberg, Arthur Joseph; Johnson, Lyndon Baines; Lodge, Henry Cabot, Jr.; McCloy, John Jay; McNamara, Robert S.; Murphy, Robert D.; Ridgway, Matthew B.; Taylor, Maxwell Davenport; Vance, Cyrus Roberts; Wheeler, Earle G.

Women in the War, U.S.

Estimates of the number of U.S. military women serving in Vietnam have varied from as low as 7,000 to as high as 21,000, de-

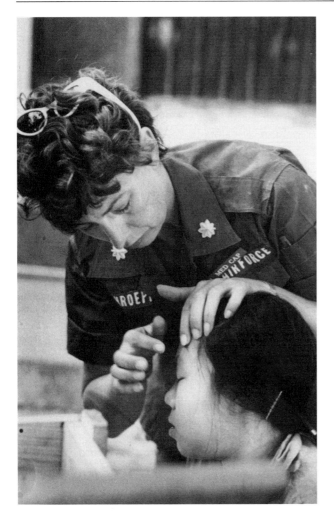

A U.S. Air Force nurse treats a blind girl with a head injury at Cui Loi Or-phanage in Cam Ranh Bay, South Vietnam. She is part of an Air Force Medical Civic Action Program MEDCAP team.

ties were administration (including clerical), personnel, intelligence, information, security, supply, transportation, data processing, training, special services, and law enforcement.

The first detachment of Army line women arrived in Sài Gòn in 1967. By midyear approximately 160 enlisted women were stationed in Sài Gòn and Long Bình, and the number would remain approximately constant at that level throughout the war. In the same year the first Navy and Marine women arrived. Not until 1969, however, were Air Force women assigned to Korat and Takhli in Thailand, and it was only in the following year, 1970, that enlisted Air Force women were assigned to Vietnam itself, at Tân Sơn Nhứt Air Base, although Air Force officers were already in place in Sài Gòn. In fact, the proportion of female Air Force officers serving in Southeast Asia, as a percentage of the total officer force, was nearly equal to that of male officers: 7 percent of female officers as compared with 8 percent of male officers.

Eight U.S. military women died in the line of duty during the war, and their names are inscribed on the Vietnam Veterans Memorial in Washington, D.C. The last of these female names on the Wall is that of an Air Force flight nurse who died during Operation BABYLIFT, the evacuation of children from South Vietnam in April 1975 as North Vietnamese forces began their final drive on Sài Gòn. Significantly for the varying estimates of female force strength, this flight nurse was not physically stationed in Vietnam but was assigned to the 57th Aeromedical Evacuation Squadron at Clark Air Base, the Philippines. Many other women were stationed outside the area normally considered the combat theater and yet participated to varying degrees in war operations, either as flight nurses, as medical and line personnel at hospitals receiving casualties in such places as Okinawa and Japan, or as line personnel for units whose male personnel were regularly deployed into the theater. Medical evacuation squadrons, for example, operated out of the Philippines, Guam, and as far away as Alaska.

Ironically, some female personnel in such units were awarded unit decorations such as the Outstanding Unit Award and Presidential Unit Citation for being part of combat units, but never received campaign ribbons and were therefore ineligible for official "Vietnam veteran" status or even membership in the Veterans of Foreign Wars.

In addition to military women, a large number of civilian women served in Vietnam and Thailand as headquarters staff workers as well as employees of U.S. government agencies, civilian charitable and relief organizations, and civilian corporations. Red Cross workers served in units based at 28 locations within Vietnam, and United Services Organization (USO) units maintained almost as many centers in-country, peaking at 17 centers during the years 1967 to 1969.

In November 1993 the Vietnam Women's Memorial was dedicated in Washington, D.C., depicting three nurses and a wounded soldier. The statue, honoring all the women who served during the Vietnam War, forms part of a triangle of memorials that incorporates the now-famous Wall and a statue of three male soldiers.

—Phoebe S. Spinrad

pending on what the compilers of statistics consider "serving in Vietnam" to mean, as well as on compilation methods. Counting only those service members stationed physically in Vietnam and Thailand, Maj. Gen. Jeanne Holm, in her 1982 book *Women in the Military,* estimates the total number at 7,500, although her individual service tallies do not seem to add up to this number: nurses and medical specialists, between 5,000 and 6,000; Army nonmedical personnel, 500; Air Force, 600 (more than half officers); Marines, under 36; and Navy, under 50 (all officers).

A small group of Army and Navy nurses had been serving in Vietnam and Thailand before 1965, primarily as advisors and trainers of local medical staffs. But after the beginning of active U.S. military engagement, larger numbers were deployed to field medical units in combat areas of Vietnam. Air Force nurses were added to the complement in medical evacuation units, as well as in major hospitals at Cam Ranh Bay and other Air Force installations in Vietnam and Thailand.

Among line (nonmedical) personnel, U.S. military women served in many different specialties. The most common special-

References: Holm, Maj. Gen. Jeanne (USAF, Ret.). *Women in the Military: An Unfinished Revolution.* Rev. ed. Novato, CA: Presidio Press, 1992.

Seeley, Charlotte Palmer, et al., eds. *American Women and the U.S. Armed Forces: A Guide to the Records of Military Agencies in the National Archives Relating to American Women.* Washington, DC: National Archives and Records Administration, 1992.

Walker, Keith. *A Piece of My Heart: The Stories of Twenty-Six American Women Who Served in Vietnam.* New York: Ballantine Books, 1985. (See especially the Appendices for lists of military units and civilian agencies in which women served.)

See also: BABYLIFT, Operation; Medevac; United States: Nurses; United States: Red Cross Recreation Workers; Vietnam Veterans Memorial.

Women in the War, Vietnamese

Vietnamese history is filled with strong women playing heroic roles in times of national crisis. This includes the celebrated Trưng sisters, who between 39 and 42 led a revolt against the Chinese. The two women are revered in Vietnamese history as the Hai Bà Trưng (the Two Trưng Ladies or the Trưng Sisters). There was also Triêu (Bà Triêu), who in 248 also led a popular revolt.

The Chinese victory in 42 established a family and bureaucratic system based on Confucian ideas and relegated women to a subordinate position. Thus twentieth-century Communist leaders could successfully appeal to women as a potential revolutionary class because laws and customs in Vietnam treated all women as inferior to all men.

When the Viêt Nam Quôc Dân Đang (VNQDD) was established in 1927, it admitted a large number of women who shared along with their male comrades experiences of torture and other hardships under the French security service. Nguyên Thi Giang and her sister Nguyên Thi Bắc inspired generations of Vietnamese women to become activists and soldiers in patriotic movements.

In 1930 the Indo-Chinese Communist Party (ICP) organized the Women's Union as the party organization responsible for political mobilization, education, and representation of Vietnamese women. The Women's Union became an important part of the Viêt Minh, the united front coalition formed in 1941 to combat the Japanese and French. The Viêt Minh constitution for Vietnam supported women's equality and suffrage. Hà Thi Quê, who became a member of the Central Committee of the Vietnamese Communist Party, formed the first all-woman guerrilla unit in 1945 to fight the French. Estimates in the early 1950s during the Indo-China War suggest that over 800,000 female guerrillas operated in the northern half of the country and about 140,000 in the South. More commonly, many women participated through community mobilization, intelligence gathering, and transportation of war material.

After the 1954 partition of Vietnam, both northern and southern governments sought the support of women's groups. Madame Nhu, sister-in-law of Republic of Vietnam (RVN) President Ngô Đình Diêm, formed the Women's Solidarity Movement to oppose public and private immorality—dancing, prostitution, and gambling. Her volunteer Paramilitary Girls provided training in firearms and first aid, and moral instruction for high school–age women. As with other groups formed to mobilize popular support by the Diêm regime, neither of Madame Nhu's women's groups

was very effective. Since both the French colonial administration and the RVN governments that followed supported the traditional Vietnamese cultural inferiority of women, village women had more incentive to back the revolutionary movement.

The "long-haired army" consisted of women who organized protest demonstrations, rallies, and strikes challenging first the French and then the RVN government. On 17 January 1960 a series of demonstrations by peasant women began in Bên Tre Province. Led by Madame Nguyên Thi Đinh, the women protested killing and looting by government troops. They forced the removal of government troops from a large area of Vĩnh Bình Province and equated Madame Đinh with the Trưng Sisters as a leader against invading or occupying foreigners.

Women formed a significant portion of the National Liberation Front (NLF), a coalition of forces dominated by the Communists that opposed the Diêm regime. About 40 percent of regimental commanders were women. Nguyên Thi Đinh was a general and was second in command of the southern insurgents. The women's "Movement to Drive Out the American Aggressors" set fire to the U.S. library in Sài Gòn, and the same group began a campaign to make life dangerous for GIs on Sài Gòn streets. Women served as spies, gaining access to U.S. military bases as laundresses, peddlers, servants, and secretaries, and they targeted locations for attack. They also participated in the 1968 Tết Offensive.

But female fighting forces represented only a small portion of southern women who supported the Communist movement. In March 1961 the Women's Liberation Association (WLA) was formed. Claiming that women possessed the characteristics of good revolutionaries—endurance, patience, sacrifice—the association portrayed women as "the water buffalo of the revolution." The WLA conducted extensive letter-writing campaigns urging RVN soldiers to desert, led village indoctrination sessions, raised and delivered food to guerrilla bands, made spiked foot traps, carried ammunition, and dug roadblocks. In 1965 the WLA claimed a membership of 1.2 million. In addition, the NLF retained the old Viêt Minh practice of organizing older women in villages into "Foster Mother Associations," whose members served as surrogate mothers to young guerrillas away from home. This "Children of the People" strategy added another traditional Vietnamese female cultural symbol to that of the heroic female leader—that of the nurturing mother.

The pre-1954 Vietnamese National Army employed young women in its Women's Auxiliary Personnel Corps. Its members served in clerical and medical jobs of various army units and agencies. It lasted until 1956. Women also staffed the small Social Assistance Service. Both had a hierarchical system and pay scale similar to that of the military. The latter organization helped care for soldiers' dependents with activities such as kindergarten teaching, and medical care in clinics and maternity rooms.

Women also participated in the formal armies of both the RVN and the Democratic Republic of Vietnam (DRV). The RVN established the Women's Armed Forces Corps in 1964. Its strength increased as the armed forces expanded. The social assistance branch was a separate service. Its members wore the

A U.S. Marine carries a blindfolded woman suspected of Viêt Công activities during the joint Vietnamese-U.S. Operation MALLARD near Đà Nẵng.

same uniforms and were under the administrative management of the Center for Training and Management of the Women's Armed Forces Corps. Other military service women served in many military branches and large units, including a women's parachutist team.

Part of the Army of the Republic of Vietnam (ARVN), the Women's Armed Forces Corps had an initial complement of 1,800 women. They served mainly in medical or clerical capacities, and their numbers remained small. Three women, however, reached the rank of full colonel.

Although these women were not supposed to fight, many proved their bravery under fire. But the mostly unknown fighting women were the wives of Popular Forces personnel. Many stood by their husbands, supplying them with ammunition, giving them first aid, and even—when the men were killed—using radio to direct and adjust artillery fire to repel Viêt Công (VC) attackers.

There were also woman officers in the Police Special Group, known as the "Thiên Nga" (the Swans). They ran intelligence nets and infiltrated into VC and underground organizations in RVN-controlled areas.

In the DRV the "Three Responsibilities Movement" set defense as a primary task for women, and they responded by forming self-defense teams in factories, schools, and villages. Many women became skilled with antiaircraft weapons and took credit for downing many U.S. aircraft. Although all women in the DRV received military training, including hand-to-hand combat, women were not subject to the draft and few joined the People's Army of Vietnam (PAVN). Those who did served primarily in support roles as medics, bomb defusers, or supply personnel. Most female members of the PAVN were young women without children.

Government propaganda in the DRV portrayed women as heroic revolutionaries in the manner of the Trưng Sisters as well as honoring women's traditional roles. Its willingness to recognize the contributions of women was one reason for the large number of Vietnamese women actively supporting the revolutionary movement.

—Elizabeth Urban Alexander

References: Eisen, Arlene. *Women and Revolution in Viet Nam.* London: Zed Books, 1984.
Mai Thi Tu. *Women in Vietnam.* Hà Nôi: Foreign Languages Publishing House, 1978.
Pike, Douglas. *Viet Cong: The Organization and Techniques of the National Liberation Front of South Vietnam.* Cambridge, MA: MIT Press, 1967.
Tetreault, Mary Ann. *Women and Revolution in Viet Nam.* East Lansing, MI: Michigan State University, 1991.
See also: Lao Đông Party; Ngô Đình Nhu, Madame (Trân Lê Xuân); Nguyên Thi Đinh; Trưng Trăc and Trưng Nhi.

Women Strike for Peace (WSP)

U.S. antiwar organization. Among the most active dissenting organizations during the Vietnam War, Women Strike for Peace's moderate approach effectively communicated the antiwar message to mainstream Americans. Founded by Dagmar Wilson as a nuclear disarmament group in November 1961, WSP achieved notoriety in December 1962, when several of its members deflected red-baiting tactics in testimony before the House Un-American Activities Committee.

Though operating primarily as informal local chapters, beginning in February 1965 WSP frequently lobbied Washington officials to end the war, sometimes drawing thousands of people for a single effort. WSP also participated in antiwar coalition activities and by 1967 became increasingly involved in draft counseling. Some of its members visited the Democratic Republic of Vietnam (DRV) and helped establish communications between American prisoners of war and their families.

Tactically, WSP appealed primarily to the nurturing role of traditional motherhood in challenging America's militaristic foreign policy, although especially during the Richard Nixon presidency that was not its sole thrust. Members avoided divisive radical rhetoric and supported amnesty for all war resisters, yet refused to criticize soldiers and veterans. The election of WSP's legislative chairperson Bella Abzug to the House of Representatives in 1970 marked its greatest electoral victory. The organization's influence faded with the war's conclusion.

—Mitchell K. Hall

References: Alonso, Harriet Hyman. *Peace as a Women's Issue: A History of the U.S. Movement for World Peace and Women's Rights.* Syracuse, NY: Syracuse University Press, 1993.
Swerdlow, Amy. *Women Strike for Peace: Traditional Motherhood and Radical Politics in the 1960s.* Chicago: University of Chicago Press, 1993.
See also: Antiwar Movement, United States; Draft; Prisoners of War, Allied.

X

Xuân Lôc, Battle of

(9–23 April 1975)

The last stand of the South Vietnamese military during the People's Army of Vietnam's Hô Chí Minh Campaign. The battle took place in April 1975 at the capital of Long Khánh Province, approximately 40 miles northeast of Sài Gòn. Xuân Lôc, located on National Route 1 near the junction with National Route 20, was a strategic location protecting the Biên Hòa–Long Bình–Sài Gòn area. During the height of the war, the city had been the headquarters of the 11th Armored Cavalry, commanded by Col. George Patton, Jr., and later it was the forward headquarters of the 199th Infantry Brigade. The American units worked there with the Army of the Republic of Vietnam (ARVN) 18th Infantry Division, considered the worst unit in South Vietnam's army. However, after the Paris Accords, General Lê Minh Đao converted the 18th Division into the most important unit in the Sài Gòn defense forces.

On 9 April the People's Army of Vietnam (PAVN) IV Corps, behind a heavy artillery barrage, pushed into the city. Brutal fighting for control of the town lasted for days. The North Vietnamese had cut Route 1, which meant that reinforcements for the 18th Division had to be helicoptered in, but men of the 1st Airborne Brigade, released from the direct defense of Sài Gòn, were pinned down as they landed at a rubber plantation east of the city. Two more PAVN divisions joined the siege.

Under General Đao's inspired leadership, the 18th ARVN Division and its supporting elements fought courageously against incredible odds. Their performance was probably the best of any South Vietnamese unit during the long war, but without reinforcements, their fate was sealed. With the Communist forces moving in for the kill, on 21 April an evacuation began. President Nguyên Văn Thiêu resigned on the same day. By 23 April the evacuation was complete, and the Battle of Xuân Lôc was over. The 18th Division suffered casualties of 30 percent in the fighting, and their Regional and Popular Forces allies were virtually decimated. During the fighting around Xuân Lôc and the evacuation, RVN air support effectively employed huge 750-pound cluster bombs (CBUs) and 15,000-pound "daisy cutter" bombs against PAVN troop concentrations. In a final act, a CBU-55 B asphyxiation bomb, the most powerful nonnuclear weapon in the American arsenal, was dropped on Xuân Lôc. This bomb, which had never before been employed, ate up the oxygen over a two-acre area and literally sucked air out of the lungs of its victims. More than 250 North Vietnamese were killed by the bomb. With the fall of Xuân Lôc, the march into Sài Gòn was merely days away.

—Joe P. Dunn

References: Butler, David. *The Fall of Saigon.* New York: Simon & Schuster, 1985.

Cao Van Vien, General. *The Final Collapse.* Washington, DC: U.S. Army Center of Military History, 1983.

Dawson, Alan. *55 Days: The Fall of South Vietnam.* New York: Prentice-Hall, 1977.

Le Gro, William E. *Vietnam from Cease Fire to Capitulation.* Washington, DC: U.S. Army Center of Military History, 1981.

Warner, Denis. *Certain Victory: How Hanoi Won the War.* Kansas City, MO: Sheed Andrews and McMeel, 1978.

See also: Bombs, Dumb; Hô Chí Minh Campaign; Nguyên Văn Thiêu; Vietnam, Democratic Republic of: Army (People's Army of Vietnam [PAVN]); Vietnam, Republic of: Army (ARVN).

Xuân Thuy

(1912–1985)

Vietnamese revolutionary; foreign minister, Democratic Republic of Vietnam (DRV) (1963–1965); headed Hà Nôi's delegation at the Paris peace talks (1968–1970). From 1970 to 1973 Xuân Thuy served as Lê Đưc Tho's chief deputy in Paris; he ultimately signed the Paris Peace Accords in 1973. Born on 2 September 1912 in Hà Đông Province, Xuân Thuy joined the Thanh Niên, or Revolutionary Youth Association, at age 16 and was a founding member of the Indo-Chinese Communist Party. In 1930 the French arrested Thuy and jailed him on the prison island of Poulo Condore. Released in 1935 he was rearrested by the French in 1939. He served six years in prison but was released in time to play a pivotal role in the August Revolution of 1945. Throughout that year Thuy served as editor for an official and important Communist Party newspaper, *Cửu Quôc* (National Salvation). His writings in *Cửu Quôc* crystallized the movement and offered a clear theoretical voice to the revolution.

Shortly after the creation of the Democratic Republic of Vietnam (DRV) in 1946 Thuy joined the National Assembly. From this vantage point he exercised considerable influence on the DRV's wartime diplomatic strategies.

Thuy rose within the diplomatic corps and by 1963 had become the DRV's foreign minister. Once the Paris peace talks opened in the spring of 1968, Thuy became the key spokesperson for the DRV. He insisted on four conditions for peace: a unilateral U.S. withdrawal, recognition of the National Front for the Liberation of South Vietnam, dissolution of the government of the Republic of Vietnam, and the reunification of Vietnam. The United States, on the other hand, demanded that the DRV end its support of the southern insurrection and withdraw its troops north of the 17th parallel. In one interesting development, President Richard Nixon had U.S. negotiator Henry Kissinger warn Thuy that refusal to compromise on these key issues would lead to increased air attacks against northern targets. Kissinger also initiated secret meetings with Thuy, away from the spotlights in Paris.

On 4 August 1969 Kissinger and Thuy met secretly outside of Paris, but the talks broke down after Thuy refused to accept American conditions and Nixon's ultimatum. The failure of the Kissinger-Thuy secret meeting was symbolic of the difficulties of previous negotiations; neither side was prepared to compromise. Ultimately, Nixon resorted to the policy of "Vietnamization," initiated by the Johnson administration, to extricate the United States from Vietnam. In addition, the White House expanded the air war over North Vietnam and neighboring Cambodia in further attempts to force a settlement.

In 1970 the DRV sent Lê Đức Tho to Paris to replace Thuy. Some scholars have suggested that Hô Chí Minh's death in September 1969 and the diplomatic stalemate in Paris created conditions for his replacement. Thuy accepted the demotion and served as Tho's chief deputy until signing the final accord in January 1973.

After the Vietnam War, at the Fourth Party Congress in 1976, Thuy became the secretary of the Central Committee, a position he held for seven years. He died in Hà Nôi on 18 June 1985 at the age of 73.

—Robert K. Brigham

References: Herring, George C., ed. *The Secret Diplomacy of the Vietnam War: The Negotiating Volumes of the Pentagon Papers.* Austin, TX: University of Texas Press, 1983.
Kalb, Marvin, and Bernard Kalb. *Kissinger.* Boston: Little, Brown, 1974.
Karnow, Stanley. *Vietnam: A History.* New York: Penguin Books, 1984.
Porter, Gareth. *A Peace Denied: The United States, Vietnam, and the Paris Agreement.* Bloomington, IN: Indiana University Press, 1975.
Thies, Wallace J. *When Governments Collide: Coercion and Diplomacy in the Vietnam Conflict, 1964–1968.* Berkeley, CA: University of California Press, 1980.
See also: Kissinger, Henry Alfred; Lê Đức Tho; National Front for the Liberation of South Vietnam (NFLSV); Nixon, Richard Milhous; Paris Negotiations; Paris Peace Accords; Poulo Condore (Côn Sơn).

Y

Yankee Station

Fixed point in international waters off the coast of North Vietnam in the South China Sea (17 degrees 30 minutes north, 108 degrees 30 minutes east). Yankee Station was the staging area for the U.S. Navy's Seventh Fleet Attack Carrier Strike Force (Task Force 77), from which Navy pilots conducted strikes on the Democratic Republic of Vietnam. The carrier force had two primary goals: control of the sea and projection of power ashore.

From Yankee Station, strikes were mounted on specific targets such as railyards or major bridges. From 1965 to 1968 these strikes were part of Operation ROLLING THUNDER. Target times were assigned to both the U.S. Air Force and the Seventh Fleet to facilitate the initial ROLLING THUNDER operation. The strategy became difficult to coordinate, and U.S. planners replaced it by dividing North Vietnam into geographical areas known as "route packages." With the new structure, interference between Task Force 77 and the Seventh Air Force was lessened; in addition, it became possible to assign responsibility to each service for target development and analysis, intelligence, and data collection in its own area.

The geographic point in the Gulf of Tonkin selected as the headquarters of operations for Task Force 77 received the code name Yankee Station. For other strike zones (those in Cambodia, Laos, and South Vietnam), Task Force 77 attacks were flown from the carriers of Dixie Station, established in May 1965, 100 miles southeast of Cam Ranh Bay.

Part of the so-called Tonkin Gulf Yacht Club, Yankee Station served as a crucial staging area and helped maintain both U.S. air and naval superiority during the Vietnam War. However, three of the four deployed carriers, one at Dixie Station and two at Yankee Station, had to spend a grueling and unacceptable 80 percent of the time at sea, with little time for rest and maintenance.

—J. Nathan Campbell

References: Marolda, Edward J., and G. Wesley Pryce, III. *A Short History of the United States Navy and the Southeast Asia Conflict, 1950–1975.* Washington, DC: Naval Historical Center, 1984.
Nichols, John B., and Barrett Tillman. *On Yankee Station.* Annapolis, MD: Naval Institute Press, 1987.
Polmar, Norman. "Support by Sea for War in the Air." *Aerospace International* 3 (July–August 1967): 29–31.
See also: Air Power, Role in War; Aircraft Carriers; ROLLING THUNDER, Operation; United States: Navy.

YELLOWSTONE, Operation

(8 December 1967–24 February 1968)
Military operation in the northwest section of War Zone C. In November 1967 the U.S. Military Assistance Command, Vietnam (MACV) received intelligence that Communist forces were massing on both sides of Vietnam's Cambodian border. MACV decided to launch offensive operations to seal off the area and prevent the Communists from penetrating into the III Corps Tactical Zone. In Operation YELLOWSTONE, which began on 8 December 1967, the 2d and 3d Brigades of the 25th Infantry ("Tropic Lightning") Division were deployed in War Zone C, principally in the northern half of Tây Ninh Province, with orders to locate and destroy Việt Cộng (VC) installations.

Since their arrival from Hawaii in October 1965, units of the 25th Division had maintained a continuous presence in the three-province area west and northwest of Sài Gòn, which included Tây Ninh, Bình Dương, and Hâu Nghĩa. During the first month of YELLOWSTONE, several battalions of the 25th Division initially encountered frequent mortar attacks on their temporary positions, but ground contact with the elusive VC was sporadic. The operation demonstrated, however, that War Zone C was still being used as a major VC and People's Army of Vietnam (PAVN) logistical base. The most intensive action occurred the night of 1 January 1968, when units of the 271st and 272d VC Regiments mounted a massive assault on the 3d Brigade's principal fire support base, known as Burt. Following a barrage of machine gun, recoilless rifle, and rocket grenade fire, VC soldiers charged the base and blasted their way into the perimeter. The result was a savage battle in which the defenders were forced to fire "beehive" artillery rounds and call for close-in aerial napalm strikes. Simultaneously, reserves were rushed from other sides of the perimeter. The attack was repelled by dawn. The VC left behind more than 300 dead, but U.S. casualties also were heavy, totaling 29 killed and 159 wounded.

Throughout January the 2d Brigade was involved in continuous heavy fighting along the Cambodian border south of Tây Ninh City. The 1968 Tết Offensive erupted while more than half of the 25th Division's maneuver battalions were tied down in YELLOWSTONE and thus unable to provide immediate support to the division's 1st Brigade and Army of the Republic of Vietnam (ARVN) units that became heavily engaged in the area between Sài Gòn and Cu Chi. During and after Tết, intense small-unit fighting continued throughout Tây Ninh Province, and YELLOWSTONE did not officially end until 24 February 1968. Known Communist casualties during Operation YELLOWSTONE totaled 1,254.

—John D. Root

References: Bergerud, Eric M. *The Dynamics of Defeat: The Vietnam War in Hau Nghia Province.* Boulder, CO: Westview Press, 1991.
Stanton, Shelby L. *The Rise and Fall of an American Army: U.S. Ground Forces in Vietnam, 1965–1973.* Novato, CA: Presidio Press, 1985.

Youth International Party ("Yippies")

Antiwar group founded by Jerry Rubin, Abbie Hoffman, Dick Gregory, and Paul Krassner. The Youth International Party ("Yippies") was formed during a 1967 New Year's Eve party in Hoffman's New York City apartment. The name Yippie is credited to Krassner, the editor of an underground newspaper, *The Realist.* According to Rubin the Yippies were conceived as a joke to scare Americans over the age of 30, but when the authorities began to take the movement's outlandish rhetoric and frivolous behavior seriously, so did Rubin. The movement supposedly sought to create a new myth of the dope-taking, freedom-loving, and politically committed activist.

Hoffman and Rubin promoted the Yippie movement in the underground press, and its existence was soon noted by the conventional media. At the same time they began planning a Festival of Life to coincide with the August 1968 Democratic National Convention in Chicago. In preparation, they held their first "Yip-in" on 22 March 1968 at New York City's Grand Central Station. Called to celebrate the spring equinox, over 6,000 young people attended. Acts of vandalism, the hanging of antiwar and antiestablishment banners, and the chanting of slogans prompted New York policemen to break up the gathering with considerable violence. Rubin and Hoffman were among those injured in what some called a "police riot."

Rubin predicted that the Chicago festival would be a blending of pot and politics, a cross-fertilization of the hippie and New Left philosophy. Ultimately, they hoped to attract 50,000 young people to the city to launch a demonstration that would end the war. Like other groups, however, they were not given a permit to stay in Lincoln Park because of delays imposed by Mayor Richard Daley, who promised that attempts to disrupt the convention would be met with the full power of local, state, and federal agencies.

In spite of Yippie predictions, at no time during convention week were there more than 5,000 protestors on the streets—out of an estimated 10,000 total demonstrators in the city. Trouble began for the Yippies on Sunday, 25 August 1968, when the police refused to allow a flatbed truck into Lincoln Park for a scheduled rock concert. Tensions rose until police moved against an estimated 1,000 people at midnight, causing scores of injuries. Three days later, on 28 August, 4,500 Yippies, radical members of the Spring Mobe (Spring Mobilization to End the War in Vietnam) and supporters of presidential candidate Eugene McCarthy gathered in Grant Park, across from the Hilton Hotel, where the Democratic Party leadership was staying. Within hours violence erupted as Chicago police again used massive force to break up the gathering. In March 1969 both Hoffman and Rubin were indicted for their activities during the Democratic convention and stood trial as members of the "Chicago Seven." Convicted of crossing state lines to riot and slapped with numerous contempt charges, Hoffman, Rubin, and three others saw their convictions overturned on appeal.

The Yippies began a gradual decline after 1968, an eclipse furthered by American troop withdrawals from Vietnam that made the antiwar movement increasingly irrelevant. Yippies were present during the 1972 Democratic National Convention at Miami Beach but did not repeat the demonstrations of 1968. Ironically, both Rubin and Hoffman were expelled from the Yippie movement after the 1972 election because of their ages and establishment tendencies.

—Clayton D. Laurie

References: Gitlin, Todd. *The Sixties: Years of Hope, Days of Rage.* New York: Bantam Books, 1987.
Matusow, Allen J. *The Unraveling of America.* New York: Harper & Row, 1984.

Z

Zhou Enlai (Chou En-lai)

(1898–1976)

Chinese Communist leader and diplomat. Born on 5 March 1898 to a scholarly, upper-class family in Zhejiang Province, Zhou Enlai attended private schools in Mukden, Tianjin, and Japan. After participating in the 1919 May Fourth Movement, Zhou went on a work-study program to France. It was in Europe where Zhou first met Hô Chí Minh. Because Hô was already a "mature Marxist" when Zhou first began to study Marxism, Zhou later referred to Hô as "my big brother." During July 1922 Zhou joined the Chinese Communist Party and helped found an overseas branch of the party among Chinese students studying in Europe.

Zhou Enlai, a close colleague of Mao Zedong, was from 1927 to 1976 a member of the Chinese Communist Party's Politburo. In 1935 Zhou backed Mao's guerrilla tactics over more conventional military tactics advocated by the Moscow-based Communist International. With Zhou's support, Mao became chairman of the Chinese Communist Party in 1935.

Zhou Enlai later became premier of the People's Republic of China (PRC), a post he held from 1949 until 1976. Zhou was widely regarded as China's most experienced and best-known diplomat. During World War II Zhou was the liaison officer with the Chinese Nationalist Party (Guomindang); in 1950 he traveled to Moscow with Mao to sign the Sino-Soviet Friendship Treaty, and in 1955 he participated in the Bandung Conference of nonaligned nations. U.S. Secretary of State Dean Acheson once described Zhou as "the ablest diplomat in the world, not excepting Mr. Churchill."

Zhou was instrumental in shaping the PRC's policy of recognizing Hô Chí Minh's Democratic Republic of Vietnam (DRV) in 1950. In 1954 Zhou attended the Geneva Conference, during which he supported the continued existence of Cambodia and Laos. The PRC did not want Vietnam to control all of Southeast Asia and preferred instead to work with several smaller—and weaker—states.

DRV Premier Pham Văn Đông was furious that Zhou had supported the West against Vietnam. Zhou was quoted later as complaining that he had been "had" at Geneva: "We thought the Americans would support the decision of the conference. But we were wrong." Between 18 and 22 November 1956 Zhou visited the DRV and told Hô Chí Minh that the PRC would increase its support. In a joint communiqué issued after this meeting, the PRC government promised to expand economic, cultural, and technical exchanges with the DRV. Zhou also promised to send Chinese technical experts to North Vietnam.

During the early 1960s PRC relations with the Soviet Union worsened. In 1965 Zhou Enlai tried to convene an Afro-Asian conference to oppose the USSR. Zhou even undertook an extensive tour of Africa to organize developing countries there. His efforts failed, however, and the PRC's international diplomacy became increasingly isolated.

Faced with renewed border tensions with the USSR, Zhou quietly probed American officials to see whether improving Sino-American relations might be used to offset the Soviet Union. Henry Kissinger later described these Chinese inquiries as an "intricate minuet." Upon receiving positive signs from Washington, on 21 April 1971 Zhou invited Kissinger to visit Beijing.

Kissinger's visit quickly led to President Richard Nixon's historic trip to China the following year. As a result of Zhou's diplomatic skills, the PRC and the United States signed the "Shanghai Communiqué" on 28 February 1972. This document not only opened formal diplomatic relations between the United States and the People's Republic of China, but it also helped lead to the end of the Vietnam War.

Zhou Enlai died in Beijing on 8 January 1976.

—Bruce Elleman

References: Chai, Winberg. *The Foreign Relations of the People's Republic of China.* New York: Capricorn Books, 1972.
Fairbank, John King. *The Great Chinese Revolution, 1800–1985.* New York: Harper & Row, 1986.
Kissinger, Henry. *White House Years.* Boston: Little, Brown, 1979.
Lee, Chae-jin. *Zhou Enlai, The Early Years.* Stanford, CA: Stanford University Press, 1994.
MacFarquhar, Roderick. *The Politics of China, 1949–1989.* New York: Cambridge University Press, 1993.
Wilson, Dick. *Zhou Enlai, a Biography.* New York: Viking Press, 1984.
See also: China, People's Republic of (PRC); Geneva Conference and Geneva Accords; Hô Chí Minh; Kissinger, Henry Alfred; Knowland, William F.; Mao Zedong (Mao Tse-tung); Nixon, Richard Milhous; Pham Văn Đông; Union of Soviet Socialist Republics (USSR) (Soviet Union).

Zorthian, Barry

(1920–)

Public affairs officer, U.S. Embassy, Sài Gòn; director, Joint U.S. Public Affairs Office (JUSPAO), Sài Gòn. Born in Turkey in 1920, Barry Zorthian emigrated to the United States with his Armenian parents in 1923. He received a B.A. from Yale in 1941 and an LL.B. from New York University in 1953. After working for the Voice of America from 1948 to 1961, Zorthian served as station chief in India for the U.S. Information Agency (USIA) until 1964.

From 1965 to 1968 Barry Zorthian was the "czar" of information in Sài Gòn. He was the embassy public affairs officer in Sài Gòn when Ambassador Maxwell Taylor named him to head a new Joint U.S. Public Affairs Office (JUSPAO), with responsibility for all psychological warfare operations as well as relations with the news media. Answerable only to the ambassador, Zorthian was able to marshal whatever powers he needed to present the positive side of the Vietnam story. Although the Johnson administration and the Military Assistance Command, Vietnam (MACV) preferred a system of press censorship, Zorthian's view prevailed that censorship was neither necessary, acceptable, nor workable. Zorthian instead established a set of voluntary guidelines, and, even as the number of accredited correspondents grew to more than 600 by Tết 1968, there were few serious violations of security.

In addition to initiating the notorious "Five O'Clock Follies," the daily briefings given by the MACV Office of Information at the JUSPAO center in downtown Sài Gòn, Zorthian provided weekly "backgrounders" to selected members of the media. Peter Braestrup recalled that while Zorthian had a tendency to "stroke" reporters, he was careful not to mislead them and resisted the administration's "all's well" syndrome. Less shrewdly, says Neil Sheehan, Zorthian believed that General William Westmoreland was correct in his assessment of the war, and it was he who pressed for the fall 1967 expeditions of Westmoreland, Ellsworth Bunker, and Robert Komer to publicize progress being made in Vietnam.

Under Zorthian, civilian and military information operations grew into a large, extremely effective system that provided the American media with what they wanted, especially hard news about military activity. After leaving government service in 1969, Zorthian noted that at the beginning of the U.S. buildup there was no accepted doctrine for dealing with the media, and that a government and military accustomed to withholding information was slow to learn that the media provided an opportunity to educate the public. "Without public support," noted Zorthian, "Vietnam could not continue. And public support was ultimately lost." He added that communication with the media must be candid and correspond to reality, something too often not done in Vietnam. In retrospect, Zorthian felt that the public was well served by the press, which, more often than not, was more accurate than the government in their coverage of Vietnam, "at least up until Tết." Zorthian's post-Vietnam prediction that "the open war is here to stay" was made before Grenada, Panama, and the Gulf War.

From 1968 to 1975 Zorthian was president of Time-Life Broadcasting, and from 1975 until his retirement in 1980 he served as vice-president for Washington affairs for Time Incorporated.

—John D. Root

References: Braestrup, Peter. *Big Story.* Abridged from 1977 edition. New Haven, CT: Yale University Press, 1978.
Hammond, William M. *Public Affairs: The Military and the Media, 1962–1968.* Washington, DC: U.S. Army Center of Military History, 1988.
Wyatt, Clarence R. *Paper Soldiers: The American Press and the Vietnam War.* Chicago: University of Chicago Press, 1993.
Zorthian, Barry. "The Press and the Government." In *Vietnam Reconsidered: Lessons from a War,* edited by Harrison Salisbury. New York: Harper & Row, 1984.
See also: Bunker, Ellsworth; Civilian Operations and Revolutionary Development Support (CORDS); Joint U.S. Public Affairs Office (JUSPAO); Komer, Robert W.; Media and the War; Psychological Warfare Operations (PSYOP); Westmoreland, William Childs.

Zumwalt, Elmo R., Jr.

(1920–)

U.S. Navy admiral; commander of U.S. riverine warfare units in South Vietnam (1968–1970). Born 20 November 1920 in San Francisco, Elmo Zumwalt graduated from the U.S. Naval Academy in 1942. His extensive World War II service included combat off Guadalcanal and the Philippines. Over the next two decades Zumwalt saw further action during the Korean War, served shore tours at the Naval and National War Colleges, and took command in 1959 of the Navy's first ship designed to carry guided missiles, the frigate *Dewey.* By 1964 Zumwalt was senior aide to Secretary of the Navy Paul Nitze and shared his chief's skepticism about the growing U.S. commitment to the war in Southeast Asia. Both viewed the Soviet armaments buildup as more challenging to America's vital interests. In 1965 Zumwalt became the youngest rear admiral in the Navy's history; the next year, he headed up the newly created Division of Systems Analysis.

In September 1968 Zumwalt was detailed to the post of commander, U.S. Naval Forces in Vietnam and the Naval Advisory Group, Vietnam, a position often viewed as a dead-end job—a "brown-water" post in a "blue-water" navy. Zumwalt was tasked with interdicting Communist waterborne logistics traffic in the Mekong Delta, cooperating with Allied ground troops in the area, and turning over the burden of the naval war to the South Vietnamese.

Zumwalt moved with vigor to execute all three charges. To cut Communist logistical support, Zumwalt supplemented the existing MARKET TIME patrols with strikes by small craft (Operation GIANT SLINGSHOT) against supplies coming down the backwaters from Cambodia. To assist Allied soldiers, Zumwalt provided shallow-draft landing craft in support of the U.S. Army's 9th Infantry Division. To execute his command's role in Vietnamization, Zumwalt organized a program dubbed ACTOV (Accelerated Turnover to the Vietnamese), with special emphasis on cooperation between American and South Vietnamese naval personnel. He set a personal example by his close relationship with Commodore Trần Văn Chơn, the head of the Republic of Vietnam Navy.

Zumwalt's performance in this demanding position was so impressive that his Vietnamese tour ended abruptly on 12 April 1970, when he was summoned to Washington to begin a four-year assignment as chief of naval operations (CNO). Sworn in on 1 July 1970, Zumwalt became the youngest officer to hold the Navy's top job and the rank of full admiral.

In his new position Zumwalt perforce turned to larger issues, such as the reform of personnel policies and the Navy's fading ability to confront a rapidly expanding Soviet fleet. Still, as CNO, Zumwalt continued to exert an influence on the Vietnamese struggle, especially during the Easter Offensive of 1972, when he strongly advocated the mining of Hai Phòng Harbor. Following the war, Zumwalt became involved as a private citizen in humanitarian concerns related to the Vietnam struggle, managing, for instance, to secure the release from captivity of Trần Văn Chơn, but most conspicuously in serving as a spokesman for U.S. servicemen suffering from exposure to the herbicide Agent Orange.

—Malcolm Muir, Jr.

References: Friedman, Norman. "Elmo Russell Zumwalt, Jr." In *The Chiefs of Naval Operations,* edited by Robert W. Love, Jr. Annapolis, MD: Naval Institute Press, 1980.

Reynolds, Clark G. *Famous American Admirals.* New York: Van Nostrand Reinhold, 1978.

Zumwalt, Elmo, Jr. *On Watch: A Memoir.* New York: Quadrangle Books, 1976.

Zumwalt, Elmo, Jr., Elmo Zumwalt, III, and John Pekkanen. *My Father, My Son.* New York: Macmillan, 1986.

See also: MARKET TIME, Operation; Mobile Riverine Force; Nitze, Paul Henry; Riverine Craft; Riverine Warfare; United States: Navy; Vietnam, Republic of: Navy (VNN); Vietnamization.

Nonfiction Works: A Selected Bibliography

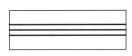

Alvarez, Everett, Jr., and Anthony S. Pitch. *Chained Eagle.* New York: Donald I. Fine, 1989.

Anderson, Charles B. *The Grunts.* San Rafael, CA: Presidio Press, 1976.

Anderson, David L., ed. *Shadow on the White House: Presidents and the Vietnam War, 1945–1975.* Lawrence, KS: University Press of Kansas, 1993.

Anderson, William C. *Bat–21.* Englewood Cliffs, NJ: Prentice-Hall, 1980.

Andrade, Dale. *Trial by Fire.* New York: Hippocrene Books, 1995.

Appy, Christian. *Working-Class War: American Combat Soldiers and Vietnam.* Chapel Hill, NC: University of North Carolina Press, 1993.

Arlen, Michael. *The Living Room War.* New York: Viking Press, 1969.

Arnett, Peter. *Live from the Battlefield, from Vietnam to Baghdad: 35 Years in the World's War Zones.* New York: Simon & Schuster, 1994.

Baker, Mark. *Nam: The Vietnam War in the Words of the Men and Women Who Fought There.* New York: William Morrow, 1981.

Balaban, John. *Remembering Heaven's Face: A Moral Witness in Vietnam.* New York: Poseidon Press, 1991.

Ball, George W. *The Past Has Another Pattern.* New York: W. W. Norton, 1982.

Baritz, Loren. *Backfire: A History of How American Culture Led Us into Vietnam and Made Us Fight the Way We Did.* New York: William Morrow, 1985.

Barrett, David. *Uncertain Warriors: Lyndon Johnson and His Vietnam Advisors.* Lawrence, KS: University Press of Kansas, 1993.

Bass, Thomas A. *Vietnamerica: The War Comes Home.* New York: Soho Press, 1996.

Beidler, Philip D. *American Literature and the Experience of Vietnam.* Athens, GA: University of Georgia Press, 1982.

Bergerud, Eric M. *Red Thunder, Tropic Lightning: The World of a Combat Division in Vietnam.* Boulder, CO: Westview Press, 1993.

Berman, Larry. *Planning a Tragedy: The Americanization of the War in Vietnam.* New York: W. W. Norton, 1982.

Berman, William C. *William Fulbright and the Vietnam War.* Kent, OH: Kent State University Press, 1988.

Bigeard, Gen. Marcel. *Pour une parcelle de gloire.* Paris: Plon, 1976.

Bigler, Philip. *Hostile Fire: The Life and Death of First Lieutenant Sharon Lane.* Arlington, VA: Vandamere Press, 1996.

Billings-Yun, Melanie. *Decision against War: Eisenhower and Dien Bien Phu.* New York: Columbia University Press, 1988.

Bilton, Michael, and Kevin Sim. *Four Hours in My Lai.* New York: Viking Press, 1992.

Blair, Anne E. *Lodge in Vietnam: A Patriot Abroad.* New Haven, CT: Yale University Press, 1995.

Bodard, Lucien. *The Quicksand War: Prelude to Vietnam.* Boston: Little, Brown, 1967.

Bowman, John S, ed. *The World Almanac of the Vietnam War.* New York: Pharos Books, 1985.

Brace, Ernest C. *A Code to Keep: The True Story of America's Longest-Held Civilian Prisoner of War.* New York: St. Martin's Press, 1988.

Braestrup, Peter. *Big Story: How the American Press and Television Reported and Interpreted the Crisis of Tet 1968 in Vietnam and Washington.* Boulder, CO: Westview Press, 1977.

Broughton, Jack. *Going Downtown: The War against Hanoi and Washington.* New York: Orion Books, 1988.

Browne, Malcolm W. *Muddy Boots and Red Socks: A Reporter's Life.* New York: Times Books, 1993.

————. *The New Face of War.* Indianapolis, IN: Bobbs-Merrill, 1965.

Broyles, William. *Brothers in Arms: A Journey from War to Peace.* New York: Alfred A. Knopf, 1986.

Bryan, C. D. B. *Friendly Fire.* New York: Putnam, 1976.

Bùi Diêm, with David Chanoff. *In the Jaws of History.* Boston: Houghton Mifflin, 1987.

Burchett, Wilfred G. *The Furtive War: The United States in Vietnam and Laos.* New York: International Publishers, 1963.

Butler, David. *The Fall of Saigon: Scenes from the Sudden End of a Long War.* New York: Simon & Schuster, 1985.

Buttinger, Joseph. *The Smaller Dragon: A Political History of Vietnam.* New York: Praeger, 1968.

Buzzanco, Robert. *Masters of War: Military Dissent and Politics in the Vietnam Era.* New York: Cambridge University Press, 1996.

Cable, Larry E. *Conflict of Myths: The Development of American Counterinsurgency Doctrine and the Vietnam War.* New York: New York University Press, 1988.

Cady, John F. *The Roots of French Imperialism in Eastern Asia.* Ithaca, NY: Cornell University Press, 1954.

Cao Van Viên and Ðông Văn Khuyên. *Reflections on the Vietnam War.* Indochina Monographs. Washington, DC: U.S. Army Center of Military History, 1980.

Capps, Walter H., ed. *The Vietnam Reader.* New York: Routledge, 1991.

Caputo, Philip. *A Rumor of War.* New York: Holt, Rinehart and Winston, 1977.

Chandler, David. *The Tragedy of Cambodian History.* New Haven, CT: Yale University Press, 1991.

Chanoff, David, and Doan Van Toai. *Portrait of the Enemy.* New York: Random House, 1986.

Chapuis, Oscar. *A History of Vietnam. From Hong Bang to Tu Duc.* Westport, CT: Greenwood Press, 1995.

Charlton, Michael, and Anthony Moncrief. *Many Reasons Why: The American Involvement in Vietnam.* New York: Hill & Wang, 1978.

Charton, Pierre. *Indochine 1950. La Tragédie de l'évacuation de Cao Bang.* Paris: Société de production littéraire, 1975.

Chen, King C. *China's War with Vietnam, 1979: Issues, Decisions, and Implications.* Stanford, CA: Hoover Institute Press, 1987.

Chomsky, Noam. *Rethinking Camelot: JFK, the Vietnam War, and U.S. Political Culture.* Boston: South End Press, 1993.

Clayton, Anthony. *Three Marshals of France: Leadership after Trauma.* London: Brassey's, 1992.

Clifford, Clark, with Richard C. Holbrooke. *Counsel to the President: A Memoir.* New York: Random House, 1991.

Coedès, Georges. *The Making of South East Asia.* Translated by H. M. Wright. Berkeley, CA: University of California Press, 1966.

Colby, William E. *Honorable Men: My Life in the CIA.* New York: Simon & Schuster, 1978.

Colby, William E., with James McCargar. *Lost Victory: A Firsthand Account of America's Sixteen Year Involvement in Vietnam.* Chicago: Contemporary Books, 1989.

Coleman, J. D. *Pleiku: The Dawn of Helicopter Vietnam.* New York: St. Martin's Press, 1988.

Conboy, Kenneth, and James Morrison. *Shadow War: The CIA's Secret War in Laos.* Boulder, CO: Paladin, 1995.

Cummings, Dennis J. *The Men behind the Trident. Seal Team One in Vietnam.* Annapolis, MD: Naval Institute Press, 1997.

Currey, Cecil B. *Edward Lansdale: The Unquiet American.* Boston: Houghton Mifflin, 1988.

_____. *Self-Destruction: The Disintegration and Decay of the United States Army during the Vietnam Era.* New York: W. W. Norton, 1981.

_____. *Victory at Any Cost: The Genius of Viet Nam's Gen. Vo Nguyen Giap.* Washington, DC: Brassey's, 1997.

Cutler, Thomas J. *Brown Water, Black Berets: Coastal and Riverine Warfare in Vietnam.* Annapolis, MD: Naval Institute Press, 1988.

Dalloz, Jacques. *The War in Indo-China, 1945–54.* Translated by Josephine Bacon. Savage, MD: Barnes and Noble, 1990.

Đăng Văn Viêt. *Highway 4, the Border Campaign (1947–1950).* Hà Nôi: Foreign Languages Publishing House, 1990.

Davidson, Phillip B. *Vietnam at War: The History, 1946–1975.* Novato, CA: Presidio Press, 1988.

Dawson, Alan. *55 Days: The Fall of South Vietnam.* Englewood Cliffs, NJ: Prentice-Hall, 1977.

De Benedetti, Charles, and Charles Chatfield. *An American Ordeal: The Antiwar Movements of the Vietnam Era.* Syracuse, NY: Syracuse University Press, 1990.

de Folin, Jacques. *Indochine, 1940–1955: La fin d'un rêve.* Paris: Perrin, 1993.

de Gaulle, Charles. *The War Memoirs of Charles de Gaulle.* Vol. 3. *Salvation, 1944–1946.* Translated by Richard Howard. New York: Simon & Schuster, 1960.

DeForest, Orrin, and David Chanoff. *Slow Burn: The Rise and Bitter Fall of American Intelligence in Vietnam.* New York: Simon & Schuster, 1990.

Denton, Jeremiah A. *When Hell Was in Session.* New York: Reader's Digest Press, 1976.

Devillers, Philippe. *Histoire du Viêt-Nam de 1940 à 1952.* Paris: Editions du Seuil, 1952.

Dommen, Arthur J. *Conflict in Laos. The Politics of Neutralization.* New York: Praeger, 1964.

Đông Văn Khuyên. *The RVNAF.* Washington, DC: U.S. Army Center of Military History, 1980.

Donovan, David. *Once a Warrior King: Memories of an Officer in Vietnam.* New York: McGraw-Hill, 1985.

Dooley, Thomas A. *Deliver Us from Evil: The Story of Viet Nam's Flight to Freedom.* New York: Farrar, Straus & Cudahy, 1956.

Duiker, William J. *The Communist Road to Power in Vietnam.* 2d ed. Boulder, CO: Westview Press, 1996.

_____. *Historical Dictionary of Vietnam.* Metuchen, NJ: Scarecrow Press, 1989.

_____. *The Rise of Nationalism in Vietnam, 1900–1911.* Ithaca, NY: Cornell University Press, 1976.

_____. *Vietnam: Revolution in Transition.* 2d ed. Boulder, CO: Westview Press, 1995.

Duncanson, Dennis J. *Government and Revolution in Vietnam.* New York: Oxford University Press, 1968.

Edelman, Bernard, ed. *Dear America: Letters Home from Vietnam.* New York: W. W. Norton, 1985.

Ellsberg, Daniel. *Papers on the War.* New York: Simon & Schuster, 1972.

Elwood-Akers, Virginia. *Women War Correspondents in the Vietnam War, 1961–1975.* Metuchen, NJ: Scarecrow Press, 1988.

Emerson, Gloria. *Winners and Losers: Battles, Retreats, Gains, Losses, and Ruins from the Vietnam War.* New York: Random House, 1976.

Engelmann, Larry. *Tears before the Rain: An Oral History of the Fall of South Vietnam.* New York: Oxford University Press, 1990.

Esper, George, and the Associated Press. *The Eyewitness History of the Vietnam War: 1961–1975.* New York: Ballantine, 1983.

Fall, Bernard B. *Hell in a Very Small Place: The Siege of Dien Bien Phu.* Philadelphia, PA: J. B. Lippincott, 1967.

_____. *Last Reflections on a War.* Garden City, NY: Doubleday, 1967.

_____. *Street without Joy.* Harrisburg, PA: Stackpole, 1961.

_____. *The Two Viet Nams.* Rev. ed. New York: Praeger, 1964.

_____. *Vietnam Witness, 1953–66.* New York: Praeger, 1966.

Férier, Gilles. *Les trois guerre d'Indochine.* Lyon, France: Presses Universitaires de Lyon, 1993.

FitzGerald, Frances. *Fire in the Lake: The Vietnamese and the Americans in Vietnam.* Boston: Little, Brown, 1972.

Franklin, H. Bruce. *M.I.A., or Mythmaking in America.* Brooklyn, NY: Lawrence Hill Books, 1992.

Freeman, James M. *Hearts of Sorrow: Vietnamese-American Lives.* Stanford, CA: Stanford University Press, 1989.

Gaiduk, Ilya. *The Soviet Union and the Vietnam War.* Chicago: Ivan R. Dee, 1996.

Garnier, Francis. *Voyage d'exploration en Indochine.* Paris: Editions la Découverte, 1985.

Glasser, Ronald J. *365 Days.* New York: G. Braziller, 1971.

Goff, Stanley, Robert Sanders, and Clark Smith. *Brothers: Black Soldiers in the Nam.* Novato, CA: Presidio Press, 1982.

Goldman, Peter, and Tony Fuller. *Charlie Company: What Vietnam Did to Us.* New York: William Morrow, 1983.

Gottlieb, Sherry Gershon. *Hell No, We Won't Go!: Resisting the Draft during the Vietnam War.* New York: Viking Press, 1991.

Gould, Lewis L. *1968: The Election That Changed America.* Chicago: Ivan R. Dee, 1993.

Grant, Zalin. *Survivors.* New York: W. W. Norton, 1975.

Gras, Yves. *Histoire de La Guerre d'Indochine.* Paris: Editions Denoël, 1992.

Greene, Bob. *Homecoming: When the Soldiers Returned from Vietnam.* New York: Putnam, 1989.

Groom, Winston, and Duncan Spencer. *Conversations with the Enemy: The Story of Pfc. Robert Garwood.* New York: Putnam, 1983.

Gruner, Elliott. *Prisoners of Culture: Representing the Vietnam POW.* New Brunswick, NJ: Rutgers University Press, 1993.

Guilmartin, John F. *A Very Short War: The Mayaguez and the Battle of Koh Tang.* College Station, TX: Texas A&M University Press, 1995.

Gustainis, J. Justin. *American Rhetoric and the Vietnam War.* New York: Praeger, 1993.

Hackworth, David H., and Julie Sherman. *About Face: The Odyssey of an American Warrior.* New York: Simon & Schuster, 1989.

Halberstam, David. *The Best and the Brightest.* New York: Random House, 1972.

_____. *Ho.* New York: Random House, 1971.

_____. *The Making of a Quagmire: America and Vietnam during the Kennedy Era.* Rev. ed. New York: Alfred A. Knopf, 1988.

Hamilton-Merritt, Jane. *Tragic Mountains: The Hmong, the Americans, and the Secret Wars for Laos, 1942–1992.* Bloomington, IN: Indiana University Press, 1993.

Hammel, Eric. *Fire in the Streets: The Battle for Hué, Tet, 1968.* Chicago: Contemporary Books, 1991.

_____. *Khe Sanh: Siege in the Clouds: An Oral History.* New York: Crown, 1989.

Hammer, Ellen J. *A Death in November: America in Vietnam, 1963.* New York: E. P. Dutton, 1987.

_____. *The Struggle for Indochina.* Stanford, CA: Stanford University Press, 1954.

Hammond, William M. *Public Affairs: The Military and the Media, 1962–1968.* Washington, DC: U.S. Army Center of Military History, 1988.

_____. *Public Affairs: The Military and the Media, 1968–1973.* Washington, DC: U.S. Army Center of Military History, 1996.

Hayslip, Le Ly, and Jay Wurts. *When Heaven and Earth Changed Places: A Vietnamese Woman's Journey from War to Peace.* New York: Doubleday, 1989.

Head, William, and Lawrence E. Grinter, ed. *Looking Back on the Vietnam War: A 1990's Perspective on the Decisions, Combat, and Legacies.* Westport, CT: Greenwood Press, 1993.

Heineman, Kenneth J. *Campus Wars: The Peace Movement at American State Universities in the Vietnam Era.* New York: New York University Press, 1993.

Hellman, John. *American Myth and the Legacy of Vietnam.* New York: Columbia University Press, 1986.

Hemingway, Albert. *Our War Was Different: Marine Combined Action Platoons in Vietnam.* Annapolis, MD: Naval Institute Press, 1994.

Herr, Michael. *Dispatches.* New York: Alfred A. Knopf, 1977.

Herring, George C. *America's Longest War: The United States and Vietnam, 1950–1975.* 2nd ed. New York: Alfred A. Knopf, 1986.

_____. *LBJ and Vietnam: A Different Kind of War.* Austin, TX: University of Texas Press, 1994.

Herrington, Stuart A. *Silence Was a Weapon: The Vietnam War in the Villages: A Personal Perspective.* Novato, CA: Presidio Press, 1982.

Hersh, Seymour. *Cover-Up: The Army's Secret Investigation of the Massacre at My Lai 4.* New York: Random House, 1972.

_____. *My Lai 4: A Report on the Massacre and Its Aftermath.* New York: Random House, 1970.

Higham, Charles. *The Archaeology of Mainland Southeast Asia.* New York: Cambridge University Press, 1989.

Hoffmann, Stanley. *Primacy or World Order: American Foreign Policy since the Cold War.* New York: McGraw-Hill, 1978.

Holm, Tom. *Strong Hearts, Wounded Souls: Native American Veterans of the Vietnam War.* Austin, TX: University of Texas Press, 1996.

Hooper, Edwin B., Dean C. Allard, and Oscar P. Fitzgerald. *The United States Navy and the Vietnam Conflict.* Vol. 1. *The Setting of the Stage to 1959.* Washington, DC: U.S. Navy, Naval History Division, 1976.

Hubbell, John G. *P.O.W.: A Definitive History of the American Prisoner-of-War Experience in Vietnam, 1964–1973.* New York: Reader's Digest Press, 1976.

Hunt, Richard A. *Pacification: The American Struggle for Vietnam's Hearts and Minds.* Boulder, CO: Westview Press, 1995.

Huỳnh, Jade Ngoc Quang. *South Wind Changing.* St. Paul, MN: Graywolf Press, 1994.

Isaacson, Walter. *Kissinger: A Biography.* New York: Simon & Schuster, 1992.

Jensen-Stevenson, Monika, and William Stevenson. *Kiss the Boys Goodbye: How the United States Betrayed Its Own POWs in Vietnam.* New York: E. P. Dutton, 1990.

Johnson, Lyndon. *The Vantage Point: Perspectives of the Presidency, 1963–1969.* New York: Holt, Rinehart and Winston, 1971.

Kahin, George McT. *Intervention: How America Became Involved in Vietnam.* New York: Alfred A. Knopf, 1986.

Kane, Rod. *Veteran's Day.* New York: Orion Books, 1989.

Karnow, Stanley. *Vietnam: A History.* New York: Viking Press, 1983.

Katsiaficas, George N., ed. *Vietnam Documents: American and Vietnamese Views of the War.* New York: M. E. Sharpe, 1992.

Kimball, Jeffrey P., ed. *To Reason Why: The Debate about the Causes of Involvement in the Vietnam War.* Philadelphia: Temple University Press, 1990.

King, Peter, ed. *Australia's Vietnam: Australia in the Second Indochina War.* Boston: Allen & Unwin, 1983.

Kirk, Donald. *Wider War.* New York: Praeger, 1971.

Kissinger, Henry. *White House Years.* Boston: Little, Brown, 1979.

_____. *Years of Upheaval.* Boston: Little, Brown, 1982.

Kolko, Gabriel. *Anatomy of a War: Vietnam, the United States, and the Modern Historical Experience.* New York: Pantheon, 1985.

Kovic, Ron. *Born on the Fourth of July.* New York: McGraw-Hill, 1976.

Krohn, Charles A. *The Lost Battalion: Controversy and Casualty in the Battle of Huê.* Westport, CT: Praeger, 1993.

Kutler, Stanley I, ed. *Encyclopedia of the Vietnam War.* New York: Charles Scribner's Sons, 1996.

Lacouture, Jean. *Ho Chi Minh: A Political Biography.* New York: Random House, 1968.

Lane, Mark. *Conversations with Americans.* New York: Simon & Schuster, 1970.

Lang, Daniel. *Casualties of War.* New York: McGraw-Hill, 1969.

Lansdale, Edward Geary. *In the Midst of Wars: An American's Mission to Southeast Asia.* New York: Harper & Row, 1972.

Larson, Stanley Robert, and James Lawton Collins, Jr. *Allied Participation in Vietnam.* Department of the Army, Vietnam Studies. Washington, DC: U.S. Government Printing Office, 1975.

Larzelere, Alex. *The Coast Guard at War. Vietnam, 1965–1975.* Annapolis, MD: Naval Institute Press, 1997.

Le Gro, William E. *Vietnam from Ceasefire to Capitalism.* Washington, DC: U.S. Army Center of Military History, 1981.

Lê Thành Khôi. *Histoire du Viet Nam des Origines à 1858.* Paris: Sudestasie, 1981.

Lifton, Robert Jay. *Home from the War: Vietnam Veterans, Neither Victims nor Executioners.* Boston: Beacon Press, 1992.

Lý Quí Chung, ed. *Between Two Fires: The Unheard Voices of Vietnam.* New York: Praeger, 1970.

Macdonald, Peter. *Giap: The Victor in Vietnam.* New York: W. W. Norton, 1993.

Maclear, Michael. *The Ten Thousand Day War, Vietnam: 1945–1975.* New York: St. Martin's Press, 1981.

MacPherson, Myra. *Long Time Passing: Vietnam and the Haunted Generation.* Garden City, NY: Doubleday, 1984.

Maneli, Mieczyslaw. *The War of the Vanquished.* New York: Harper & Row, 1969.

Mangold, Tom, and John Penycate. *The Tunnels of Cu Chi.* New York: Random House, 1985.

Marolda, Edward J. *By Sea, Air, and Land: An Illustrated History of the U.S. Navy and the War in Southeast Asia.* Washington, DC: Naval Historical Center, 1994.

Marolda, Edward J., and Oscar P. Fitzgerald. *The United States Navy and the Vietnam Conflict.* Vol. 2. *From Military Assistance to Combat.* Washington, DC: Naval Historical Center, 1986.

Marr, David G. *Vietnam 1945: The Quest for Power.* Berkeley, CA: University of California Press, 1996.

Marshall, Kathryn. *In the Combat Zone: An Oral History of American Women in Vietnam, 1966–1975.* Boston: Little, Brown, 1987.

Marshall, S. L. A. *Ambush.* New York: Cowles, 1969.

_____. *Battles in the Monsoon: Campaigning in the Central Highlands, Vietnam, Summer 1966.* New York: William Morrow, 1967.

_____. *Bird: The Christmastide Battle.* New York: Cowles, 1968.

_____. *West to Cambodia.* New York: Cowles, 1968.

Mason, Robert. *Chickenhawk.* New York: Viking Press, 1983.

Mauer, Harry. *Strange Ground: Americans in Vietnam, 1945–1975. An Oral History.* New York: Henry Holt, 1989.

McCarthy, Mary. *The Seventeenth Degree.* New York: Harcourt Brace Jovanovich, 1974.

McCloud, Bill. *What Should We Tell Our Children about Vietnam.* Norman, OK: University of Oklahoma Press, 1989.

McConnell, Malcolm. *Inside the Hanoi Secret Archives: Solving the MIA Mystery.* New York: Simon & Schuster, 1995.

McMaster, H. R. *Dereliction of Duty: Jonhson, McNamara, the Joint Chiefs of Staff, and the Lies That Led to Vietnam.* New York: HarperCollins, 1997.

McNamara, Robert S., with Brian VanDeMark. *In Retrospect, the Tragedy and Lessons of Vietnam.* New York: Times Books, 1995.

McNeill, Ian. *To Long Tan: The Australian Army and the Vietnam War, 1950–1966.* St. Leonards, NSW, Australia: Allen & Unwin/Australian War Memorial, 1993.

Michel, Marshall. *Clashes. Air Combat over North Vietnam 1965–1972.* Annapolis, MD: Naval Institute Press, 1997.

Moise, Edwin E. *Tonkin Gulf and the Escalation of the Vietnam War.* Chapel Hill, NC: University of North Carolina Press, 1996.

Moore, Harold G., and Joseph L. Galloway. *We Were Soldiers Once . . . And Young.* New York: Random House, 1992.

Morgan, Joseph G. *The Vietnam Lobby. The American Friends of Vietnam, 1955–1975.* Chapel Hill, NC: University of North Carolina Press, 1997.

Morrison, Wilbur H. *The Elephant and the Tiger: The Full Story of the Vietnam War.* New York: Hippocrene Books, 1990.

Moss, George. *Vietnam: An American Ordeal.* 2nd ed. Englewood Cliffs, NJ: Prentice-Hall, 1994.

Moyar, Mark. *Phoenix and the Birds of Prey. The CIA's Secret Campaign to Destroy the Viet Cong.* Annapolis, MD: Naval Institute Press, 1997.

Murphy, Edward F. *Dak To.* Novato, CA: Presidio Press, 1993.

Murphy, John. *Harvest of Fear: A History of Australia's Vietnam War.* Boulder, CO: Westview Press, 1994.

Neilands, J. B., et al. *Harvest of Death: Chemical Warfare in Vietnam and Cambodia.* New York: Free Press, 1972.

Newman, John, with Ann Hilfinger. *Vietnam War Literature: An Annotated Bibliography of Imaginative Works about Americans Fighting in Vietnam.* 3rd ed. Lanham, NJ: Scarecrow Press, 1996.

Newman, John M. *JFK and Vietnam: Deception, Intrigue, and the Struggle for Power.* New York: Warner Books, 1992.

Ngô Quang Trưởng. *Territorial Forces.* Washington, DC: United States Army Center of Military History, 1981.

Nguyên Cao Kỳ. *Twenty Years and Twenty Days.* New York: Stein & Day, 1976.

Nguyên Khăc Viên. *The Long Resistance, 1858–1975.* Hà Nôi: Foreign Languages Publishing House, 1975.

_____. *Vietnam: A Long History.* Hà Nôi: Gioi Publishers, 1993.

Nguyên Tiên Hưng, and Jerrold L. Schlecter. *The Palace File.* New York: Harper & Row, 1986.

Nichols, John B., and Barrett Tillman. *On Yankee Station: The Naval Air War over Vietnam.* Annapolis, MD: Naval Institute Press, 1987.

Nixon, Richard M. *No More Vietnams.* New York: Arbor House, 1985.

_____. *The Real War.* New York: Warner Books, 1980.

_____. *RN: The Memoirs of Richard Nixon.* New York: Grosset & Dunlap, 1978.

Nolan, Keith William. *Battle for Hué: Tet, 1968.* Novato, CA: Presidio Press, 1983.

Nolting, Frederick. *From Trust to Tragedy: The Political Memoirs of Frederick Nolting, Kennedy's Ambassador to Diem's Vietnam.* New York: Praeger, 1988.

O'Ballance, Edgar. *The Wars in Vietnam, 1954–1980.* Rev. ed. New York: Hippocrene Books, 1981.

Oberdorfer, Don. *Tet!* Garden City, NY: Doubleday, 1971.

O'Brien, Tim. *If I Die in a Combat Zone.* New York: Delacorte Press, 1973.

Olson, James S., ed. *Dictionary of the Vietnam War.* New York: Greenwood Press, 1988.

Olson, James S., and Randy Roberts. *The Vietnam War: Handbook of the Literature and Research.* Westport, CT: Greenwood Press, 1993.

_____. *Where the Domino Fell: America and Vietnam, 1945–1990.* New York: St. Martin's Press, 1991.

An Outline History of the Vietnam Workers' Party, 1930–1975. Hà Nôi: Foreign Languages Publishing House, 1978.

Palmer, Bruce. *The 25-Year War: America's Military Role in Vietnam.* New York: Simon & Schuster, 1984.

Palmer, Dave R. *Summons of the Trumpet: U.S.-Vietnam in Perspective.* San Rafael, CA: Presidio Press, 1978.

Palmer, Laura. *Shrapnel in the Heart: Letters and Remembrances from the Vietnam Memorial.* New York: Random House, 1987.

Patti, Archimedes L. A. *Why Viet Nam? Prelude to America's Albatross.* Berkeley, CA: University of California Press, 1980.

Pedroncini, Guy, and Gen. Philippe Duplay, eds. *Leclerc et l'Indochine.* Paris: Albin Michel, 1992.

Personalities of the South Vietnam Liberation Movement. New York: Commission for Foreign Relations of the South Vietnam National Front for Liberation, 1965.

Peterson, Michael E. *The Combined Action Platoons; the U.S. Marines' Other War in Vietnam.* New York: Praeger, 1989.

Pham Cao Dưởng. *Lich Su Dan Toc Viet Nam, Tap I: Thoi Ky Lap Quoc* (History of the Vietnamese People, Vol. I: The Formation of the Nation). Fountain Valley, CA: Truyen Thong Viet, 1987.

Phillips, William R. *Night of the Silver Stars. The Battle of Lang Vei.* Annapolis, MD: Naval Institute Press, 1997.

Pike, Douglas. *A History of Vietnamese Communism, 1923–1978.* Stanford, CA: Hoover Institute Press, 1978.

_____. *Viet Cong: The Organization and Techniques of the National Liberation Front of South Vietnam.* Cambridge, MA: MIT Press, 1966.

Pisor, Robert. *The End of the Line: The Siege of Khe Sanh.* New York: W. W. Norton, 1982.

Porch, Douglas. *The French Foreign Legion: A Complete History of the Legendary Fighting Force.* New York: HarperCollins, 1991.

Prados, John, and Ray W. Stubbe. *Valley of Decision: The Siege of Khe Sanh.* Boston: Houghton, Mifflin, 1991.

Pratt, John Clark, ed. *Vietnam Voices: Perspectives on the War Years, 1941–1982.* New York: Viking Press, 1984.

Prochnau, William. *Once upon a Distant War: Young War Correspondents and the Early Vietnam Battles.* New York: Random House, 1995.

Puller, Lewis B., Jr. *Fortunate Son: The Autobiography of Lewis B. Puller, Jr.* New York: Grove Weidenfeld, 1991.

Randle, Robert F. *Geneva 1954: The Settlement of the Indochinese War.* Princeton, NJ: Princeton University Press, 1969.

Robbins, Christopher. *Air America.* New York: Putnam, 1979.

Rotter, Andrew, ed. *Light at the End of the Tunnel: A Vietnam War Anthology.* New York: St. Martin's Press, 1991.

Rowe, John Crowe, and Rick Berg, eds. *The Vietnam War and American Culture.* New York: Columbia University Press, 1991.

Roy, Jules. *The Battle of Dienbienphu.* New York: Harper & Row, 1965.

Rusk, Dean, Richard Rusk, and Daniel S. Papp. *As I Saw It.* New York: W. W. Norton, 1990.

Sack, John. *M.* New York: New American Library, 1966.

Safer, Morley. *Flashbacks: On Returning to Vietnam.* New York: Random House, 1990.

Sainteny, Jean. *Histoire d'une Paix Manquée: Indochine, 1945–1947.* Paris: Amiot-Dumont, 1953.

_____. *Ho Chi Minh and His Vietnam: A Personal Memoir.* Chicago: Cowles, 1972.

Salisbury, Harrison E., ed. *Vietnam Reconsidered: Lessons from a War.* New York: Harper & Row, 1984.

Santoli, Al, ed. *Everything We Had: An Oral History of the Vietnam War by Thirty-Three American Soldiers Who Fought It.* New York: Random House, 1981.

_____. *To Bear Any Burden: The Vietnam War and Its Aftermath in the Words of Americans and Southeast Asians.* New York: E. P. Dutton, 1985.

Schell, Jonathan. *The Military Half.* New York: Alfred A. Knopf, 1968.

_____. *The Village of Ben Suc.* New York: Alfred A. Knopf, 1967.

Scholl-Latour, Peter. *Death in the Ricefields: An Eyewitness Account of Vietnam's Three Wars, 1945–1979.* New York: St. Martin's Press, 1985.

Schreadley, R. L. *From the Rivers to the Sea: The United States Navy in Vietnam*. Annapolis, MD: Naval Institute Press, 1992.

Scruggs, Jan C., and Joel L. Swerdlow. *To Heal a Nation: The Vietnam Veterans Memorial*. New York: Harper & Row, 1985.

Sevy, Grace, ed. *The American Experience in Vietnam: A Reader*. Norman, OK: University of Oklahoma Press, 1989.

Shapley, Deborah. *Promise and Power: The Life and Times of Robert McNamara*. Boston: Little, Brown, 1993.

Sharp, U. S. G. *Strategy for Defeat: Vietnam in Retrospect*. Novato, CA: Presidio Press, 1986.

Shawcross, William. *Sideshow: Kissinger, Nixon, and the Destruction of Cambodia*. New York: Simon & Schuster, 1979.

Shay, Jonathan. *Achilles in Vietnam: Traumatic Stress and the Undoing of Character*. New York: Atheneum, 1994.

Sheehan, Neil. *A Bright Shining Lie: John Paul Vann and America in Vietnam*. New York: Random House, 1988.

Sheppard, Don. *Riverine: A Brown-Water Sailor in the Delta, 1967*. Novato, CA: Presidio Press, 1992.

Showalter, Dennis E., and John G. Abert, eds. *An American Dilemma: Vietnam, 1964–1973*. Chicago: Imprint Publications, 1993.

Simpson, Howard R. *Dien Bien Phu: The Epic Battle America Forgot*. Washington, DC: Brassey's, 1994.

_____. *Tiger in the Barbed Wire: An American in Vietnam, 1952–1991*. Washington, DC: Brassey's, 1992.

Smith, Winnie. *American Daughter Gone to War: On the Front Lines with an Army Nurse in Vietnam*. New York: William Morrow, 1992.

Snepp, Frank. *Decent Interval: An Insider's Account of Saigon's Indecent End*. New York: Random House, 1977.

Solis, Gary D. *Son Thang. An American War Crime*. Annapolis, MD: Naval Institute Press, 1997.

Spector, Ronald H. *Advice and Support: The Early Years, 1941–1960*. The U.S. Army in Vietnam Series. Washington, DC: U.S. Army Center of Military History, 1983.

_____. *After Tet: The Bloodiest Year in Vietnam*. New York: Free Press, 1993.

Stanton, Shelby L. *Green Berets at War*. Novato, CA: Presidio Press, 1985.

_____. *The Rise and Fall of an American Army: U.S. Ground Forces in Vietnam 1965–1973*. Novato, CA: Presidio Press, 1985.

_____. *U.S. Army and Allied Ground Forces in Vietnam Order of Battle*. Washington, DC: U.S. News Books, 1981.

Stevens, Fitzgerald. *The Trail*. New York: Garland, 1993.

Stockdale, James B. *A Vietnam Experience: Ten Years of Reflection*. Stanford, CA: Hoover Institute Press, 1984.

Summers, Harry G. *Historical Atlas of the Vietnam War*. Boston: Houghton Mifflin, 1995.

_____. *On Strategy*. Novato, CA: Presidio Press, 1982.

Taylor, John M. *General Maxwell Taylor: The Sword and the Pen*. New York: Doubleday, 1989.

Taylor, Keith Weller. *The Birth of Vietnam*. Berkeley, CA: University of California Press, 1983.

Taylor, Maxwell D. *Swords and Plowshares*. New York: W. W. Norton, 1972.

Terry, Wallace. *Bloods: An Oral History of the Vietnam War by Black Veterans*. New York: Random House, 1984.

Thompson, Virginia. *French Indo-China*. New York: Octagon Books, 1968.

Tourison, Sedgwick D. *Project Alpha: Washington's Secret Military Operations in North Vietnam*. New York: St. Martin's Press, 1997.

_____. *Talking with Victor Charlie: An Interrogator's Story*. New York: Ivy Books, 1991.

Trujillo, Charley, ed. *Soldados: Chicanos in Viet Nam*. San Jose, CA: Chusma House, 1990.

Trường Như Tang, with David Chanoff and Doan Van Toai. *A Vietcong Memoir*. New York: Harcourt Brace Jovanovich, 1985.

Tuchman, Barbara W. *The March of Folly: From Troy to Vietnam*. New York: Alfred A. Knopf, 1984.

Turley, G. H. *The Easter Offensive: Vietnam 1972*. Novato, CA: Presidio Press, 1985.

U.S. Department of State. *Aggression from the North. The Record of North Viet-Nam's Campaign to Conquer South Viet-Nam*. Washington, DC: U.S. Government Printing Office, 1965.

Valentine, Douglas. *The Phoenix Program*. New York: William Morrow, 1990.

Valette, Jacques. *La Guerre d'Indochine, 1945–1954*. Paris: Armand Colin, 1994.

Van Devanter, Lynda. *Home before Morning: The Story of an Army Nurse in Vietnam*. New York: Beaufort Books, 1983.

VanDeMark, Brian. *Into the Quagmire: Lyndon Johnson and the Escalation of the Vietnam War*. New York: Oxford University Press, 1991.

Võ Nguyên Giáp. *"Big Victory, Great Task." North Viet-Nam's Minister of Defense Assesses the Course of the War*. Introduction by David Schoenbrun. New York: Praeger, 1968.

_____. *Dien Bien Phu*. 5th ed., revised and supplemented. Hà Nôi: Gioi Publishers, 1994.

_____. *The Military Art of People's War. Selected Writings of Vo Nguyen Giap*. Edited with an introduction by Russell Stetler. New York: Monthly Review Press, 1970.

_____. *People's War, People's Army. The Viet Cong Insurrection Manual for Underdeveloped Countries*. Forward by Roger Hilsman. New York: Praeger, 1962.

_____. *Unforgettable Months and Years*. Ithaca, NY: Cornell University, 1975.

_____. *Viet Nam People's War Has Defeated U.S. War of Destruction*. Hà Nôi: Foreign Languages Publishing House, 1969.

Walt, Lewis W. *Strange War, Strange Strategy: A General's Report on Vietnam*. New York: Funk & Wagnalls, 1970.

Warr, Nicholas. *Phase Line Green. The Battle for Hue, 1968*. Annapolis, MD: Naval Institute Press, 1997.

Wells, Tom. *The War Within: America's Battle over Vietnam*. Berkeley, CA: University of California Press, 1994.

Westmoreland, William C. *A Soldier Reports.* Garden City, NY: Doubleday, 1976.

Wexler, Sanford. *The Vietnam War: An Eyewitness History.* New York: Facts on File, 1992.

Wheeler, John. *Touched with Fire: The Future of the Vietnam Generation.* New York: Franklin Watts, 1984.

Wilcox, Fred A. *Waiting for an Army to Die: The Tragedy of Agent Orange.* New York: Random House, 1983.

Willbanks, James H. *Thiet Giap! The Battle of An Loc, April 1972.* Fort Leavenworth, KS: Combat Studies Institute, 1993.

Willenson, Kim. *The Bad War: An Oral History of the Vietnam War.* New York: New American Library, 1987.

Williams, Reese. *Unwinding the Vietnam War: From War into Peace.* Seattle, WA: Real Comet Press, 1987.

Williams, William Appleman, ed. *America in Vietnam: A Documentary History.* Garden City, NY: Anchor/Doubleday, 1985.

Winters, Francis X. *The Year of the Hare. America in Vietnam, January 25, 1963–February 15, 1964.* Athens, GA: University of Georgia Press, 1997.

Wirtz, James J. *The Tet Offensive: Intelligence Failure in War.* Ithaca, NY: Cornell University Press, 1991.

Wittman, Sandra M. *Writing about Vietnam: The Literature of the Vietnam Conflict.* Boston: G. K. Hall, 1989.

Wolff, Tobias. *In Pharaoh's Army: Memories of the Lost War.* New York: Alfred A. Knopf, 1994.

Wyatt, Clarence. *Paper Soldiers: The American Press and the Vietnam War.* 2nd ed. Chicago: University of Chicago Press, 1995.

Young, Marilyn B. *The Vietnam Wars, 1945–1990.* New York: HarperCollins, 1991.

Zaffiri, Samuel. *Hamburger Hill, May 11–20, 1969.* Novato, CA: Presidio Press, 1988.

_____. *Westmoreland: A Biography of General William C. Westmoreland.* New York: William Morrow, 1994.

Zaroulis, N. C., and Gerald Sullivan. *Who Spoke Up? American Protest against the War in Vietnam 1963–1975.* Garden City, NY: Doubleday, 1984.

Zumwalt, Elmo, III, and Elmo R. Zumwalt, Jr. *My Father, My Son.* New York: Macmillan, 1986.

Zumwalt, Elmo R., Jr. *On Watch: A Memoir.* New York: Quadrangle/Times Books, 1976.

—Compiled by Sandra M. Wittman with Spencer C. Tucker

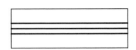
Alexander, David. *When the Buffalo Fight.* New York: Bantam Books, 1987. Originally published in Richmond, Victoria, Australia: Hutchinson of Australia, 1980.

Anderson, Kent. *Sympathy for the Devil.* Garden City, NY: Doubleday, 1987.

Baber, Asa. *Land of a Million Elephants.* New York: William Morrow, 1970.

Balaban, John. *Coming Down Again.* San Francisco: Harcourt Brace Jovanovich, 1985.

Balfour, Vivian Vie. *The Perimeter of Light.* Minneapolis, MN: New Rivers Press, 1992.

Bao Ninh. *The Sorrow of War.* New York: Pantheon, 1995.

Barry, Jan, and W. D. Ehrhart, eds. *Demilitarized Zones.* Perkasie, PA: East River Anthology, 1976.

Bosse, Malcolm J. *Incident at Naha.* New York: Simon & Schuster, 1972.

Brown, Larry. *Dirty Work.* Chapel Hill, NC: Algonquin Books, 1989.

Bunting, Josiah, III. *The Lionheads.* New York: G. Braziller, 1972.

Burdick, Eugene, and William Lederer. *The Ugly American.* New York: W. W. Norton, 1958.

Butler, Robert Olen. *The Alleys of Eden.* New York: Horizon Press, 1981.

———. *Good Scent from a Strange Mountain.* New York: Henry Holt, 1992.

———. *On Distant Ground.* New York: Alfred A. Knopf, 1985.

Casey, Michael. *Obscenities.* New Haven, CT: Yale University Press, 1972.

Cassidy, John. *A Station in the Delta.* New York: Charles Scribner's Sons, 1979.

Coleman, Charles. *Sergeant Back Again.* New York: Harper & Row, 1980.

Cramer, Lenox. *Slow Dance on the Killing Field.* Medina, OH: Alpha Publications of Ohio, 1990.

Crumley, James. *One to Count Cadence.* New York: Random House, 1969.

Currey, Richard. *Fatal Light.* New York: Dutton/Seymour Lawrence, 1988.

Dann, Jean Van Buren, and Jack Dann, eds. *In the Fields of Fire.* New York: Tor, 1987.

Danziger, Jeff. *Rising like the Tucson.* New York: Doubleday, 1991.

Davis, George. *Coming Home.* New York: Random House, 1971.

Del Vecchio, John. *The 13th Valley.* New York: Bantam Books, 1981.

DiFusco, John, et al. *Tracers.* New York: Hill & Wang, 1986.

Dodge, Ed. *Dau: A Novel of Vietnam.* New York: Macmillan, 1984.

Doolittle, Jerome. *The Bombing Officer.* New York: E. P. Dutton, 1982.

Duong Thu Huong. *Novel without a Name.* New York: William Morrow, 1995.

Durden, Charles. *No Bugles No Drums.* New York: Viking Press, 1976.

Eastlake, William. *The Bamboo Bed.* New York: Simon & Schuster, 1969.

Ehrhart, W. D., ed. *Carrying the Darkness: American Indochina, the Poetry of the Vietnam War.* New York: Avon Books, 1985.

———. *Unaccustomed Mercy: Soldier-Poets of the Vietnam War.* Lubbock, TX: Texas Tech University Press, 1989.

Farish, Terry. *Flower Shadows.* New York: William Morrow, 1992.

Ford, Daniel. *Incident at Muc Wa.* Garden City, NY: Doubleday, 1967.

Fuller, Jack. *Fragments.* New York: William Morrow, 1984.

Giovannitti, Len. *The Man Who Won the Medal of Honor.* New York: Random House, 1973.

Gray, Anthony. *Saigon.* Boston: Little, Brown, 1982.

Greenburg, Martin, and Augustus Richard Norton, eds. *Touring Nam: The Vietnam Reader.* New York: William Morrow, 1985.

Greene, Graham. *The Quiet American.* New York: Viking Press, 1955.

Groom, Winston. *Better Times than These.* New York: Summit Books, 1978.

Halberstam, David. *One Very Hot Day.* Boston: Houghton Mifflin, 1967.

Haldeman, Joe W. *The Forever War.* New York: Holt, Rinehart and Winston, 1972.

———. *War Year.* New York: Holt, Rinehart and Winston, 1972.

Hardesty, Steven. *Ghost Soldiers.* New York: Walker, 1986.

Hasford, Gustav. *The Short-Timers.* New York: Harper & Row, 1979.

Heinemann, Larry. *Close Quarters.* New York: Farrar, Straus & Giroux, 1977.

———. *Paco's Story.* New York: Farrar, Straus & Giroux, 1986.

Hempstone, Smith. *A Tract of Time.* Boston: Houghton Mifflin, 1966.

Herzog, Toby. *Vietnam War Stories: Innocence Lost.* New York: Routledge, 1992.

Huggett, William. *Body Count.* New York: Putnam, 1973.

James, Allston. *Attic Light.* Santa Barbara, CA: Capra Press, 1979.

Just, Ward. *Stringer.* Boston: Little, Brown, 1974.

Kaiko, Takeshi. *Into a Black Sun.* New York: Kodansha International, 1980.

Kalb, Bernard, and Marvin Kalb. *The Last Ambassador.* Boston: Little, Brown, 1981.

Karlin, Wayne. *Lost Armies.* New York: Henry Holt, 1988.

Karlin, Wayne, Basil T. Paquet, and Larry Rottmann, eds. *Free Fire Zone: Short Stories by Vietnam Veterans.* Coventry, CN: 1st Casualty Press, 1973.

Klinkowitz, Jerome, and John Somer. *Writing under Fire: Stories of the Vietnam War.* New York: Dell, 1978.

Kolpacoff, Victor. *The Prisoners of Quai Dong.* New York: New American Library, 1967.

Larson, Wendy, and Tran Thi Nga. *Shallow Graves: Two Women and Vietnam.* New York: Random House, 1986.

Lartequy, Jean. *The Centurions.* New York: E. P. Dutton, 1961.

_____. *Presumed Dead.* New York: E. P. Dutton, 1965.

Little, Loyd. *The Parthian Shot.* New York: Viking Press, 1975.

Malo, Jean-Jacques, and Tony Williams, eds. *Vietnam War Films.* Jefferson, NC: McFarland, 1994.

Mason, Bobbie Ann. *In Country.* New York: Harper & Row, 1985.

Mayer, Tom. *The Weary Falcon.* Boston: Houghton Mifflin, 1971.

McAfee, John. *Slow Walk in a Sad Rain.* New York: Warner Books, 1993.

McDonald, Walter. *A Band of Brothers: Stories from Vietnam.* Lubbock, TX: Texas Tech University Press, 1989.

Miller, Kenn. *Tiger, the Lurp Dog.* Boston: Little, Brown, 1983.

Moore, Gene D. *The Killing at Ngo Tho.* New York: W. W. Norton, 1967.

Moore, Robin. *The Green Berets.* New York: Crown, 1965.

Morris, Jim. *War Story.* Boulder, CO: Sycamore Island Books, 1979.

Myers, Thomas. *Walking Point: American Narratives of Vietnam.* New York: Oxford University Press, 1988.

Newhafer, Richard. *No More Bugles in the Sky.* New York: New American Library, 1966.

Nguyen Thanh T., and Bruce Weigl. *Poems from Captured Documents.* New York: Vantage, 1994.

O'Brien, Tim. *Going after Cacciato.* New York: Delacorte Press, 1978.

_____. *In the Lake of the Woods.* Boston: Houghton Mifflin, 1994.

_____. *The Things They Carried.* Boston: Houghton Mifflin, 1990.

Pelfrey, William. *The Big V.* New York: Liveright, 1972.

Phillips, Jayne Anne. *Machine Dreams.* New York: Dutton/Seymour Lawrence, 1984.

Pratt, John Clark. *The Laotian Fragments.* New York: Viking Press, 1974.

Proffitt, Nicholas. *Gardens of Stone.* New York: Carroll & Graf, 1983.

Rabe, David. *The Basic Training of Pavlo Hummel and Sticks and Bones.* New York: Viking Press, 1969.

_____. *Streamers.* New York: Alfred A. Knopf, 1977.

Riggan, Rob. *Free Fire Zone.* New York: W. W. Norton, 1984.

Rottmann, Larry. *Voices from the Ho Chi Minh Trail: Poetry of America and Vietnam, 1965–1993.* Desert Hot Springs, CA: Event Horizon Press, 1993.

Rottmann, Larry, Jan Barry, and Basil T. Paquet, eds. *Winning Hearts and Minds.* Brooklyn, NY: 1st Casualty Press, 1972.

Rowe, John. *Count Your Dead.* Sydney: Angus & Robertson, 1968.

Rubin, Jonathan. *The Barking Dog.* New York: G. Braziller, 1974.

Scarborough, Elizabeth. *The Healer's War.* Garden City, NY: Doubleday, 1988.

Schaeffer, Susan Fromberg. *Buffalo Afternoon.* New York: Alfred A. Knopf, 1989.

Sloan, James Park. *War Games.* Boston: Houghton Mifflin, 1971.

Stone, Robert. *Dog Soldiers.* Boston: Houghton Mifflin, 1974.

Straub, Peter. *Koko.* New York: E. P. Dutton, 1988.

Tran Van Dinh. *Blue Dragon, White Tiger: A Tet Story.* Philadelphia, PA: TriAm Press, 1983.

Walsh, Patricia L. *Forever Sad the Hearts.* New York: Avon Books, 1982.

Webb, James. *Fields of Fire.* Englewood Cliffs, NJ: Prentice-Hall, 1978.

Weber, Joe. *Rules of Engagement.* Novato, CA: Lyford Books, 1991.

Weigl, Bruce. *Song of Napalm.* New York: Atlantic Monthly Press, 1988.

Werder, Albert. *A Spartan Education.* Brooklyn Heights, NY: Beekman Publishers, 1978.

Williams, John A. *Captain Blackman.* Garden City, NY: Doubleday, 1972.

Wilson, William. *The LBJ Brigade.* Los Angeles, CA: Apocalypse, 1966.

Wright, Stephen. *Meditations in Green.* New York: Charles Scribner's Sons, 1983.

—Compiled by Sandra M. Wittman

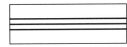

Chronology of Events Touching Vietnam through April 1975

2879 B.C.
Establishment of the kingdom of Văn Lang by Hùng Vương, or King Hùng (of the Hông Bàng dynasty, 2879–258 B.C.), considered by Vietnamese as the founder of Vietnam.

258 B.C.
King Thuc Phán of neighboring Tây Âu invades Văn Lang, annexes it to his own territory, and establishes a new kingdom, Âu Lac, with himself as ruler.

207 B.C.
Chinese warlord Triêu Đà (Chao To), who has broken with the Ch'in emperor, defeats King An Dưởng Vương and conquers Âu Lac. Triêu Đà combines it with previously held territory to form the new kingdom of Nam Viêt (Nan Yueh) or "southern country of the Viet," with its capital at Phiên Ngung (later Canton, today Guangzhou).

111 B.C.
Han expeditionary force conquers Nam Viêt and adds it to Chinese empire. For the next 1,000 years, present-day northern Vietnam is, save for a few brief but glorious rebellions, a Chinese province.

39–42
Vietnamese, led by Trưng Trăc, daughter of the Lac lord of Mê-Linh Chân, assisted by her sister Trưng Nhi, revolt against Chinese. The two women are revered in Vietnamese history as the Hai Bà Trưng (the Two Ladies Trưng, or the Trưng Sisters).

42
Battle of Láng Bac. Chinese General Ma Yüan (Mã Viên), commanding an invading army, defeats Trưng Trăc's forces and reestablishes direct Chinese rule.

192
Indianized kingdom of Champa established in vicinity of present-day city of Huê.

248
Unsuccessful Vietnamese revolt led by Bà Triêu, Lady Triêu.

542
Revolt by Lý Bôn, defeated in the Battle of Điên-Triêt Lake (546).

931
Dưởng Đình Nghê, ruler of Ái and Hoan (present-day Hà Trung and Thanh Hóa), drives Chinese forces from Giao Chi and wins recognition from them as military governor there.

938
Ngô Quyên defeats Chinese in Battle of the Bach Đăng River. After more than 1,000 years of Chinese control, the Vietnamese are again independent. Vietnamese now control all territory from foothills of Yunnan to the 17th parallel.

939
Ng ô Quyên takes title of king of now independent Nam Viêt.

966
Bo Linh declares himself emperor, naming his realm Dai Co Viêt.

982
Lê Hoàn, or Lê Đai Hành, defeats Sung invasion, preserving national independence, and also launches victorious southern expedition against kingdom of Champa.

1069
Lý Thánh Tông seizes Cham capital of Indrapura and imprisons its king, who wins release by ceding the districts of Đia Lý, Ma Ling, and Bô Chính. These subsequently become the Vietnamese provinces of Quang Bình and Quang Tri.

April 1288
Second Battle of Bach Đăng River. Vietnamese, led by Trân Hưng Đạo, defeat invading Mongols.

Early fourteenth century
Two more Cham districts, the Ô and the Rí, given to Dai Viêt in exchange for Vietnamese Princess Huyên Trân in marriage. In the fifteenth century Chams cede all territory north of the present province of Quang Nam. These fourteenth- and fifteenth-century additions became future Thưa Thiên Province with its imperial capital of Huê.

1407–1427
Ming dynasty briefly reestablishes Chinese control over Vietnam.

1418

Lê Lợi (Lê Thái Tô), proclaiming himself King Binh Đinh Vường, begins insurrection against the occupying Ming, defeating them in 1427. Lê Lợi establishes the Lê dynasty, which lasts until 1788, when it is ended by the Tây Sơn Rebellion.

1471

Vietnamese take the second Cham capital of Vijaya. This provides permanent Vietnamese foothold south of Hai Vân Pass. In seventeenth century the remnants of the old kingdom of Champa are definitively absorbed.

1481

Vietnamese government creates the Đôn Điên agricultural settlements as a means of absorbing lands to the south.

1527

Mac Đăng Dung, governor of Thăng Long (present-day Hà Nôi), overthrows the Lê dynasty and by 1527 is king in all but name, prompting southern feudal lord Nguyên Kim to set up a government in exile in Laos to support a Lê descendant.

1535

First lasting contact between Vietnam and Europe, resulting from arrival of Portuguese explorer and sea captain Antônio da Faria.

1545

Supporters of Mac murder Nguyên Kim, and Vietnam dissolves into long civil war lasting the next two centuries.

1615

First permanent Catholic mission established in Vietnam at Tourane (present-day Đà Năng).

1626

French priest Alexandre de Rhodes arrives in Vietnam. He is generally credited with the creation of *quôc ngư,* written Vietnamese language that uses the Latin alphabet and diacritical marks.

1630s

Nguyên rulers in the south build a wooden wall across narrow waist of Vietnam at Đông Hơi, ironically not far from the 1954 division of the 17th parallel. Reportedly the wall is 20 feet high and six miles long. For next 150 years, Vietnam is divided along that fortified line. The Trinh lords ruled the north and the Nguyên family the south. Each family claims to rule in the name of the powerless Lê king.

1636

Dutch establish a trading post at Hà Nôi.

1658

By this date the Vietnamese have taken all of South Vietnam north of Sài Gòn (then the fishing village of Prey Kor).

1658

Vietnamese troops invade Cambodia to settle a succession struggle. Two years later Cambodia begins paying regular tribute to Vietnam.

1672

Sài Gòn falls to Vietnamese control.

1680

French establish their first regular trading post in Vietnam at Phô Hiên.

1714–1716

Civil war in Cambodia and Vietnamese intervention.

1739–1749

War between Cambodia and Vietnam in which Cambodians are defeated and lose additional territory in the Mekong River region to Vietnam.

1755–1760

Continued Vietnamese expansion into Cambodia.

1769–1773

War between Vietnam and Siam over Cambodia, with Siam regaining control.

1773

Tây Sơn Rebellion begins, named for Nguyên Nhac, Nguyên Lư, and Nguyên Huê, three brothers from the village of Tây Sơn in present Bình Đinh Province.

19 January 1785

Battle of Rach Gâm–Xoài Mút. Nguyên Huê defeats invading Siamese army.

25–30 January 1789

Victory of Ngoc Hôi–Đông Đa, greatest military achievement in modern Vietnamese history. In lightning five-day campaign, King Quang Trung (Nguyên Huê) defeats Chinese expeditionary force commanded by Sun Shi-yi, assisted by General Xu Shi-heng, and supporting Lê King Chiêu Thông as king of An Nam.

1789–1802

Reign of Quang Trung.

1802

Nguyên Ánh, having captured all three Tây Sơn capitals, reunites Vietnam from the Linh Giang River to Gia Đinh. That same year, Nguyên Ánh crowns himself emperor with the name of Gia Long, establishing the Nguyên dynasty. He rules during the period 1802–1820.

1803

Official name of Vietnam established when Nguyên envoys travel to Beijing (Peking) to form diplomatic relations.

1820–1841
Reign of Emperor Minh Mang.

1841–1845
Vietnamese-Siamese Wars over Cambodia ending with joint rule over Cambodia by the two invaders.

1841–1847
Reign of Emperor Thiêu Tri.

15 April 1847
Incident at Tourane (Đà Năng) in which French warships sink three Vietnamese ships.

1848–1883
Reign of Emperor Tư Đức.

1856
French warship *Catinat* shells Tourane (Đà Năng).

1858
31 August
Arrival off Tourane (Đà Năng) of Adm. Rigault de Genouilly's squadron of 14 vessels with 3,000 troops. The latter, including 300 Filipinos sent by Spain, land the next day, storming Tourane's forts after only perfunctory Vietnamese resistance, taking forts and port, and inaugurating the first phase of the French conquest of Indo-China.

1859
17 February
French shift their operations south, and on this date take the fishing village of Sài Gòn, selected because of its proximity, its promise as a deepwater port, and that it could be important in controlling southern rice trade.

1860–1861
March 1860–January 1861
Siege of Sài Gòn, garrisoned by 1,000 French troops, against force of 12,000 Vietnamese. Raised by arrival of French relief expedition.

1862
Emperor Tư Đức forced to sign a treaty with France providing for 20 million franc indemnity, three treaty ports in Annam and Tonkin, and French possession of the eastern provinces of Cochin China including Sài Gòn.

1866–1867
French Navy Lt. Francis Garnier leads an expedition up the Mekong River that determines that the river is not navigable past the waterfalls at the Lao-Cambodian border.

1867
French forces have conquered all of Cochin China and also occupied three western provinces of Cambodia.

1870s
French turn attention to northern Vietnam, where Emperor Tư Đức's hold is weak.

1873
November
Francis Garnier and a force of some 180 men in three small ships seize citadel at Hà Nôi. Although Garnier is killed the next month while endeavoring to take all of Tonkin, and Paris repudiated his actions, Emperor Tư Đức's prestige suffers irreparably.

1874
March
Emperor Tư Đức recognizes French control of Cochin China and grants concessions in Hà Nôi and Hai Phòng.

1882–1885
Black Flag, or Tonkin Wars, between France and Vietnam/China.

1884–1885
December 1884–3 March 1885
Chinese siege of Tuyên Quang, raised by the French.

1885
9 June
Treaty of Tientsin between China and France, resulting from French military operations against China. As consequence of this treaty, China relinquishes nominal suzerainty over Vietnam.

1885–1913
Brief rebellion by Vietnamese nationalists acting in the name of Emperor Hàm Nghi against French rule. Betrayed to the French, Hàm Nghi is captured in 1888 and sent into exile in Algeria. Resistance to the French in Tonkin continues, led by Đê Thám.

1887
Paris forms its conquests into French Indo-China.

1893
Laos added to French Indo-China. Technically only Cochin China is an outright colony; Annam, Tonkin, Cambodia, and Laos are merely "protectorates." French leave emperor at Huê as symbol of Vietnamese unity, although French governor general is in overall control, responsible to the minister of colonies in Paris.

1896
Col. Joseph Galliéni leads an effort against Vietnamese guerrilla leader Đê Thám, with only partial success. By 1905 Đê Thám has expanded his activities and established the Nghĩa Hưng Party. During the next eight years, his forces inflict serious losses on the French.

1904–1905
Russo-Japanese War; for the first time in modern history, an Asian power defeats a European state.

1913

March

Đê Thám assassinated by an associate, a Vietnamese working for the French. Although his followers try to continue the struggle, the nationalist movement soon collapses.

1914–1918

The First World War. U.S. President Woodrow Wilson raises Vietnamese nationalist hopes by calling for the self-determination of peoples.

1920

Hô Chí Minh, foremost exponent of modern Vietnamese nationalism and member of the French Socialist Party, votes with the majority at the party conference at Tours to form the French Communist Party, becoming its expert on colonial affairs.

1927

25 December

Nguyên Thái Hoc and comrades establish the Viêt Nam Quôc Dân Đang (VNQDĐ, or Vietnam National Party) as the first well-organized nationalist revolutionary party in Vietnam.

1930

3 February

In Hong Kong, Hô Chí Minh helps to carry out a fusion of three Vietnamese Communist parties into what becomes the Indo-Chinese Communist Party (ICP), by World War II the dominant nationalist force in Indo-China.

1930–1931

Vietnamese nationalist uprisings, most notably at Yên Bái. Easily crushed by the French, these are led by moderate nationalists who take as their model the Chinese Nationalists. Their organization, the Viêt Nam Quôc Dân Đang (Vietnam National Party, or VNQDĐ), seeks an end to French rule and establishment of a republican form of government.

1930

30 April

Communist cadres lead hundreds of peasants in protests in many districts of Nghê An Province. Sporadic smaller-scale protests continue to the end of the year. Some 100 peasants are killed, but the events are not widely known and do not have the impact of the Yên Bái revolt.

1940

24 September

Under the threat of force, French Governor General of Indo-China Adm. Jean Decoux grants Japan the right to build three airfields and to station 6,000 men in Tonkin.

1940–1941

War between France and Thailand, ending in a Japanese-brokered peace treaty whereby France transferred to Thailand three Cambodian and two Laotian provinces, some 42,000 square miles of territory on the right bank of the Mekong River. These are regained by France after the Second World War.

1940

Indo-Chinese Communist Party stages revolt in southern Vietnam crushed by the French military.

1941

May

Hô Chí Minh and lieutenants form Viêt Nam Đôc Lâp Đông Minh Hôi (Vietnam Independence League), commonly known as the Viêt Minh.

July

Japan moves into southern Indo-China, placing long-range bombers within striking distance of Malaya, the Dutch East Indies, and the Philippines. Alarmed by this development and endeavoring to force Japan to withdraw, the United States, Great Britain, and the Netherlands impose an embargo on scrap iron and oil on Japan. With this decision, Tokyo opts for war against the United States.

1945

9 March

Japanese stage coup d'état against French and seize power directly in Vietnam.

11 March

Tokyo grants Vietnam its independence, proclaimed by Bao Đai, for the previous decade the French-controlled emperor of Annam who had spent the war years at Huê.

June

Provisional President of the French Republic Charles de Gaulle appoints General Jacques-Philippe Leclerc to command French Expeditionary Corps to restore French sovereignty in Indo-China.

July–August

Potsdam Conference produces agreement regarding disarmament of Japanese forces in Indo-China. Chinese Kuomintang (Nationalist) forces will take surrender of Japanese troops north of the 16th parallel; and British, south of that line.

15 August

Charles de Gaulle appoints monk-turned-admiral Georges Thierry d'Argenlieu as high commissioner for Indo-China, with instructions to restore French sovereignty in Indo-China.

16 August

In Hà Nôi, Hô Chí Minh declares himself president of the provisional government of a "free Vietnam."

19 August

Viêt Minh seize power in Hà Nôi.

24 August
In Sài Gòn, Viêt Minh leader Trân Văn Giàu declares the insurrection under way in the South.

25 August
Emperor Bao Đai abdicates, becoming First Citizen Vinh Thuy.

27 August
Hô Chí Minh convenes his first cabinet meeting at Hà Nôi.

2 September
Hô Chí Minh publicly announces formation of a "Provisional Government of the Democratic Republic of Vietnam" (DRV) with its capital at Hà Nôi.

13 September
In accordance with the Potsdam Agreements, 5,000 troops of the 20th Indian Division, commanded by General Douglas Gracey, arrive in southern Indo-China. Gracey, who detests the Viêt Minh, subsequently rearms some 1,400 French soldiers imprisoned by the Japanese.

14 September
Chinese nationalist troops enter North Vietnam to disarm Japanese troops north of the 16th parallel.

16–22 September
DRV government organizes *Tuân Lê Vàng* (Gold Week), appealing to the people to turn in gold and other valuables so that the government might purchase arms from the Chinese. Much of the money goes to bribe Chinese commander Lư Hán to secure his support and end aid to the nationalist parties.

22 September
French troops return to Vietnam.

26 September
Office of Strategic Services Lt. Col. A. Peter Dewey is killed in Sài Gòn by the Viêt Minh.

5 October
General Leclerc arrives in Sài Gòn.

25 October
Leclerc begins the reconquest of Indo-China for France, predicting it would take about a month for "mopping-up operations."

11 November
In a bid to widen his base at home and win Western support abroad, Hô Chí Minh dissolves the Indo-Chinese Communist Party.

1946
6 January
Elections in northern Vietnam. Although elections are not free, there is no doubt that Hô Chí Minh has won. The government is

Communist-dominated, but includes anti-Communist nationalists because Hô still hopes for U.S. recognition and aid.

28 February
Franco-Chinese Accords secure Chinese withdrawal from North in return for France yielding certain concessions in China. Chinese leave northern Vietnam the next month.

6 March
Hô Chí Minh signs agreement with French representative Jean Sainteny to set future relationship between the DRV and France. DRV agrees to a French military presence in the North: 15,000 French and 10,000 Vietnamese troops under unified French command to protect French lives and property, although Paris promises to withdraw 3,000 of them each year. All are to be withdrawn by the end of 1951, with the possible exception of those guarding bases. In return, France recognizes the DRV as a "free state with its own government, parliament, army and finances, forming part of the Indo-Chinese Federation of the French Union." In key provision, France also agrees to a referendum in South to see if it wanted to join DRV in a unified state, although no date for the vote is specified. Paris also agrees to train and equip units of the new Vietnamese Army.

27 March
General Leclerc in a report to Paris kept secret from French people says there will be no solution through force in Indo-China.

3 April
France and the DRV (Võ Nguyên Giáp for the DRV and General Raoul Salan for France) reach agreement on stationing of French troops in DRV.

1 June
Shortly after Hô Chí Minh's departure for France to meet with French government officials, High Commissioner d'Argenlieu torpedoes Sainteny's work by proclaiming in Sài Gòn the establishment of "Republic of Cochin China."

6 July–14 September
Fontainebleau Conference between DRV delegation and French officials fails to resolve the issue of Cochin China. The sum of its work is a draft accord reinforcing France's economic rights in northern Vietnam.

20 November
Armed clash between Vietnamese and French troops, escorting a commission to Lang Sơn to investigate French dead at the hands of the Japanese. French lose six men and each side accuses the other of responsibility. This is overshadowed by another and more ominous event the same day. French Navy has virtually blockaded Tonkin's principal port of Hai Phòng, when a French patrol vessel seizes a Chinese junk attempting to smuggle contraband. Vietnamese soldiers on the shore fire on the French

vessel, and shooting also breaks out in the city itself. A subsequent agreement between French and Vietnamese officials brings fighting to an end by the afternoon of 22 November.

22 November
D'Argenlieu, then in Paris and determined to teach the Vietnamese a lesson, cables General Etienne Valluy, his deputy in Sài Gòn, who in turn orders General Morlière, commander in the North, to use force against Vietnamese. In vain Morlière points out that the situation in Hai Phòng has stabilized and that any imprudent act might lead to general hostilities.

23 November
Valluy telegraphs Col. Pierre-Louis Dèbes, commander of French troops at Hai Phòng, ordering him to "give a severe lesson to those who have treacherously attacked you. Use all the means at your disposal to make yourself complete master of Hai Phòng and so bring the Vietnamese army around to a better understanding of the situation." Dèbes delivers ultimatum to the Vietnamese at Hai Phòng, ordering them to withdraw from the French section of the city, the Chinese quarter, and the port. He gives them only two hours to reply. The French then subject Vietnamese military positions to air, land, and sea bombardment, the bulk of the firepower from the French Navy cruiser *Suffren*. Casualty figures of from 200 to 20,000 are cited. Fighting in the port city continues into 28 November.

19 December
General Morlière demands the disarmament of the Tự Vê, the Viêt Minh militia that has been sniping at French troops in Hà Nôi. That night, fear and mistrust, fueled by bloodshed and broken promises, finally erupt into full-scale fighting. The Indo-China War has begun.

1947
11 May
France proclaims Laos an independent state within the French Union.

12 May
Paul Mus, personal advisor to French High Commissioner Emile Bollaert, meets with Hô Chí Minh to present a plan, drawn up by General Valluy and approved by Socialist Premier Paul Ramadier, calling on Viêt Minh to refrain from hostilities, lay down some arms, permit French troops freedom of movement, and return prisoners, deserters, and hostages. Hô rejects this as tantamount to surrender.

7 October
French begin Operation LEAA. Directed by General Raoul Salan, it involves some 12,000 men during three-week period over some 80,000 square miles of nearly impenetrable terrain in the northeast Viêt Băc region.

20 November.
French launch Operation CEINTURE ("Belt"), designed to crush enemy forces in a quadrangle northwest of Hà Nôi and capture the DRV leadership, who escape.

1948
15–16 January
Indo-Chinese Communist Party Central Committee decides to shift the fighting from the defensive to contention stage.

1949
8 March
Paris concludes the Elysée Agreements with former Emperor Bao Đai. These create State of Vietnam, with Paris conceding Vietnam is in fact one country.

1 July
State of Vietnam formally established by Bao Đai decrees.

October
Communists defeat Nationalists in China.

4 November
Hô Chí Minh decrees mobilization for all adult males between 16 and 55.

1950
14 January
Hô Chí Minh declares DRV as only legal government of Vietnam.

18 January
People's Republic of China formally recognizes the DRV and agrees to furnish it military assistance.

30 January
Soviet Union extends diplomatic recognition to the DRV.

7 February
Great Britain and United States extend full diplomatic recognition to State of Vietnam.

21 February
Hô Chí Minh declares general mobilization in DRV.

6 March
U.S. mission arrives in Sài Gòn to study economic assistance to State of Vietnam.

8 May
United States announces plans to extend economic and military aid to French in Indo-China.

30 May
U.S. economic mission established in Sài Gòn.

27 June
President Harry S Truman sends U.S. troops to Korea. Truman also announces "acceleration in the furnishing of military assistance to the forces of France and the associated states in Indo-China and dispatch of a military mission to provide close working relations with those forces."

30 June
Eight C-47 transports arrived in Sài Gòn with first direct shipment of U.S. military equipment.

26 July
President Truman signs legislations providing $15 million in aid to the French war effort in Indo-China.

7 October
French garrison evacuating Cao Băng and relief column from Thât Khê destroyed by the Viêt Minh at Đông Khê.

10 October
U.S. Military Assistance and Advisory Group (MAAG) established in Sài Gòn.

17 October
French evacuate Lang Sơn.

23 December
United States signs mutual defense assistance agreement with France, Vietnam, Cambodia, and Laos.

1951
January
Viêt Minh Operation TRÂN HƯNG ĐAO, "general counteroffensive" by large conventional units against main French defensive line in Red River Delta. Giáp's goal is to take Hà Nôi.

11–19 February
Second National Communist Party Congress, which changes the name to the Vietnamese Workers' Party.

March
Operation HOÀNG HOA THÁM, in which Viêt Minh again try to secure Red River Delta and are again defeated.

May–June
Operation HÀ NAM NINH, third Viêt Minh offensive to try to secure the Red River Delta. These attacks, centered in the southeastern part of the Delta, are again blunted by the French.

7 September
United States signs agreement with State of Vietnam to provide economic assistance.

November–February 1952
Battle of Hòa Bình, initiated by French commander General Jean de Lattre de Tassigny. Casualty totals suggest a French victory but the battle is actually something of a stalemate.

1952
July
President Truman upgrades the American legation in Sài Gòn to embassy status.

October
Over the next several months, Viêt Minh forces undertake conquest of Thai Highlands in northwestern Vietnam in what becomes known as the Northwest Campaign.

October–November
Operation LORRAINE. General Raoul Salan, de Lattre's replacement, employs 30,000 troops in largest French military operation of war. Salan hoped that by striking Giáp's base areas he could compel Giáp to return divisions to their defense and cause him to abandon effort to conquer the Thai Highlands. Operation is largely unsuccessful.

1953
April
Viêt Minh and Communist Pathet Lao troops seize much of northern Laos.

July 27
Armistice signed in Korea.

July
Operation HIRONDELLE ("Swallow"), 2,000-man paratroop operation initiated by new French commander General Henri Navarre to destroy supplies at the important Viêt Minh base of Lang Sơn.

30 September
President Eisenhower approves $385 million in military aid for the French in Indo-China.

October
Paris grants full independence to the Kingdom of Laos.

20 November
Operation CASTOR, 2,200 French paras drop into the valley north and south of village of Điên Biên Phu in northwestern Tonkin to defeat the Viêt Minh garrison there, create a new airhead, and draw Giáp into pitched battle.

25 December
French Union forces evacuate Thakhek on the Mekong River.

December
The Viêt Minh begin a drive that overruns much of southern and central Laos against only light resistance.

1954

January
Operation ATLANTE, 15-battalion mainly Vietnamese National Army (VNA) land assault northward from Nha Trang with amphibious landing near Tuy Hòa. Giáp anticipates this and orders his forces not to give battle but merely harass attacking units. VNA performs poorly with whole units deserting. ATLANTE bogs down and peters out.

13 March
Siege of the French entrenched positions at Điên Biên Phu officially begins with heavy Viêt Minh bombardment.

March
In a series of raids, Viêt Minh commandos attack French air bases at Gia Lâm, near Hà Nôi, and Đô Sơn and Cát Bì airfields, near Hai Phòng, destroying 22 aircraft vital to the French effort at Điên Biên Phu.

26 April
International conference to discuss range of Asian issues, including Indo-China, opens in Geneva.

29 April
President Eisenhower announces United States will not intervene militarily in Indo-China.

7 May
Last French troops surrender at Điên Biên Phu, officially ending the battle.

8 May
Indo-China phase of the Geneva Conference begins.

17 June
Pierre Mendès-France becomes French premier and foreign minister.

18 June
From his chateau in Cannes, France, Bao Dai selects Ngô Đình Diêm as new premier of State of Vietnam.

20 June
Mendès-France imposes 30-day timetable for an Indo-China agreement, promising to resign if one is not reached.

26 June
Ngô Đình Diêm returns to Sài Gòn.

June
French Groupe Mobile 100 destroyed by two Viêt Minh regiments along Route 19. French control in the Central Highlands is now limited to small area around Ban Mé Thuôt and Dalat.

7 July
Ngô Đình Diêm officially forms his new government, which claims to embrace all of Vietnam.

21 July
Geneva Conference issues three cease-fire agreements and one final declaration. Vietnam is temporarily divided into northern and southern zones pending nationwide elections to be held in 1956.

8 September
Southeast Asia Collective Defense Treaty and Protocol signed in Manila. Southeast Asia Treaty Organization (SEATO) member states—the United States, France, Britain, New Zealand, Australia, Pakistan, the Philippines, and Thailand—pledge themselves to "act to meet the common danger" in the event of aggression against any signatory state. Separate protocol extends treaty's security provisions to Laos, Cambodia, and the "free territory under the jurisdiction of the State of Vietnam."

9 October
French forces complete their evacuation of Hà Nôi.

24 October
U.S. President Dwight Eisenhower writes to Diêm and promises direct assistance to his government, now in control of South Vietnam.

8 November
Former Army Chief of Staff General J. Lawton Collins arrives in Sài Gòn. Appointed by Eisenhower as special ambassador with authority over all U.S. government agencies in Vietnam, Collins assures Diêm of U.S. support in his test of wills with Army Chief of Staff General Nguyên Văn Hinh, who at the end of the month goes into exile.

1955

1 January
Washington begins channeling its aid directly to the Diêm government.

12 February
U.S. Military Assistance and Advisory Group takes over responsibility from the French for training and organizing the State of Vietnam Army.

March and April
Fighting between State of Vietnam Army units loyal to Diêm and the Bình Xuyên.

10 May
Diêm formally requests U.S. military advisors.

19 July
DRV government proposes to the State of Vietnam government the naming of representatives for the conference to negotiate general elections as called for in 1954 Geneva Agreement.

20 July
South Vietnam rejects DRV request on grounds that elections in North would not be free.

9 August
South Vietnamese government declares it will not enter into negotiations with DRV on elections as long as Communist government continues in North.

31 August
Secretary of State John Foster Dulles supports position of government of Vietnam regarding refusal to hold national elections to reunify two Vietnam states.

23 October
After Emperor Bao Dai, still in France, tries to remove him as premier, Ngô Đình Diêm organizes a referendum, held on this date. Carefully managed by Diêm, it results in an announced 98 percent vote in his favor.

26 October
Using referendum results as justification, Diêm proclaims Republic of Vietnam (RVN), with himself as president.

1956
11 January
Diêm's government issues Ordinance No. 6, allowing arrest and detention of anyone "considered dangerous to national defense and common security."

4 March
South Vietnamese elect a 123-member national legislative assembly.

6 April
RVN again declares that it is a "non-signatory to the Geneva Agreements" and "continues not to recognize their provisions."

26 April
France officially abolishes its high command in Indo-China.

11 May
DRV government again proposes convening the Consultative Conference on elections called for in 1954 Geneva Agreement.

22 May
RVN government, in note to the British government, again rejects talks on countrywide elections.

20 July
Deadline set by the 1954 Geneva Conference for free elections. The date passes without elections being held. Diêm claims that lack of freedom in North makes it impossible to hold elections.

14 September
Last French troops leave Sài Gòn.

26 October
New RVN constitution, heavily weighted toward control by executive, goes into effect. RVN is divided into 41 provinces, then subdivided into districts and villages. These apparent reforms are largely a sham, as Diêm increasingly subjects South to authoritarian rule.

November
DRV land reform leads to outright revolt. People's Army of Vietnam (PAVN) 325th Division is called out to crush rebels in Nghê An Province. Some 6,000 farmers are deported or executed.

1957
3 January
International Control Commission (ICC) report accuses both DRV and RVN of failing to fulfill obligations under the 1954 Geneva Agreements during the period December 1955 to August 1956.

9 February
DRV requests that ICC investigate detention of 1,700 former Viêt Minh by RVN authorities at Hôi An, Quang Nam Province.

5–19 May
President Diêm visits United States, addressing a joint session of Congress.

1958
10 August
Some 400 raiders attack large Michelin rubber plantation north of Sài Gòn, easily defeating security force and capturing more than 100 weapons and 5 million piasters (approximately $143,000).

22 December
DRV Premier Pham Văn Đông writes Diêm and repeats proposals for mutual force reductions, economic exchanges, free movement between zones, and end to hostile propaganda.

1959
January
Lao Đông Party Central Committee issues Resolution 15, supporting armed insurrection in the South, although it should remain secondary to the "political struggle." This position is formalized at May Fifteenth Party Plenum.

6 February
ICC concludes that RVN authorities had subjected to reprisal former Viêt Minh in Quang Nam Province.

4 April
President Eisenhower, speaking at Gettysburg College, commits United States to maintain South Vietnam as separate national entity.

30 April
In Sài Gòn, 18 prominent opposition politicians, calling themselves Committee for Progress and Liberty, issue an open letter to Diêm protesting governmental abuses. They are promptly arrested.

6 May
RVN National Assembly passes law "10/59," an internal security measure that empowers government to try suspected terrorists by roving tribunals that could impose death penalty.

May
U.S. military advisors are assigned at the regimental level in the Army of the Republic of Vietnam (ARVN).

DRV forms 559th (for the fifth month of 1959) Transportation Group to move supplies south through eastern Laos, beginning the Hồ Chí Minh Trail complex.

At Diêm's invitation, three training teams of ten men each from 77th Special Forces Group on Okinawa arrive in Vietnam and set up training schools at Đà Nẵng, Nha Trang, and Sông Mao.

8 July
Two U.S. servicemen killed in a Communist attack on Biên Hòa, the first Americans to die in the Vietnam War.

July
DRV organizes Group 759 to oversee movement of supplies to the South by sea.

26 September
2d Liberation Battalion ambushes two companies of the ARVN 23d Division, killing 12 men and capturing most of their weapons. This attack leads RVN government and U.S. officials to begin referring to the rebels as "Việt Công," pejorative for "Vietnamese Communist."

September
At the Third Vietnamese Workers' Party Congress, held in Hà Nội, leadership goes on public record as supporting establishment of United Front and approving program of violent overthrow of Diêm government. There were now two preeminent tasks: carrying out a "socialist revolution" in the North and "liberating the South."

31 December
Some 760 U.S. military personnel in South Vietnam.

1960
16 January
Uprising in Bên Tre Province some 100 miles from Sài Gòn in Mekong Delta, largely in reaction to Diêm repression.

Late January
Communist forces attack a regiment of the ARVN 21st Infantry Division at Trang Sup, Tây Ninh Province, securing several hundred weapons.

5 February
RVN government requests that Washington double U.S. Military Assistance and Advisory Group strength from 342 to 685.

April
DRV imposes universal military conscription.

May
Thirty instructors from U.S. 7th Special Forces Group deploy to South Vietnam.

11–12 November
In Sài Gòn, three battalions of ARVN paratroopers and Marines under command of Col. Nguyên Văn Thái and Lt. Col. Vương Văn Đông surround the presidential palace in effort to force Diêm to institute reforms, a new government, and more effective prosecution of the war. Diêm outmaneuvers them by agreeing to a long list of reforms—including freedom of the press, a coalition government, and new elections—until he can bring up loyal units. Most ARVN officers participating in the coup flee to Cambodia, returning only after Diêm is overthrown.

November
DRV leadership calls for intensified struggle in the South and establishment of a "broad national united front."

20 December
Hà Nội establishes the National Front for the Liberation of South Vietnam, usually known as the National Liberation Front (NLF). Designed to replicate Việt Minh as an umbrella nationalist organization, it reaches out to all those disaffected with Diêm. From the beginning, NLF is completely dominated by the Lao Đồng Party Central Committee and is the North's shadow government in South.

31 December
Some 900 U.S. military personnel in South Vietnam.

1961
19 January
Outgoing President Eisenhower tells incoming President John F. Kennedy that Laos is "the key to the entire area of Southeast Asia" and that situation there may require U.S. armed intervention.

9 April
Diêm reelected RVN president with 89 percent of the vote.

15 May
U.S. State Department informs its allies it will increase U.S. Military Assistance and Advisory Group personnel beyond the Geneva limit, citing as justification North Vietnamese violations of the Geneva Agreement.

9–15 May
U.S. Vice-President Lyndon Johnson visits Sài Gòn. Although expressing private reservations about Diêm, he publicly hails him the "Winston Churchill of Southeast Asia." Less than a week after Johnson's return to Washington, Kennedy agrees to increase ARVN from 170,000 to 270,000 men.

June
Fourteen-nation conference convenes in Geneva and over the next year works out tripartite coalition government for Laos.

June–July
U.S. fact-finding mission under Dr. Eugene Staley in South Vietnam. Staley's findings, reported to Kennedy in August, stress that RVN needs self-sustaining economy and that military action alone will not work. Only with substantial social and political reform can favorable results be achieved. Staley's recommendations center on protection of civilian population. He advocates substantial increases in the size of ARVN, the Civil Guard, and local militias, and he seeks improved arms and equipment at the local level. Finally, he calls for construction of a network of strategic hamlets, based on Diêm's earlier Agroville program.

18 October
President Diêm declares a state of national emergency.

October
President Kennedy's chief military advisor General Maxwell D. Taylor and Special Assistant for National Security Affairs Walt W. Rostow lead second fact-finding trip to RVN. They see situation primarily in military terms and recommend to Kennedy a change in U.S. role from advisory only to "limited partnership" with the RVN. They urge increased U.S. economic aid and military advisory support to include intensive training of local self-defense forces and large increase in airplanes, helicopters, and support personnel. Secret appendix recommends deployment of 8,000 American combat troops that might be used to support ARVN in military operations.

16 November
President Kennedy announces decision to increase South Vietnamese military strength but not commit U.S. combat forces there.

22 November
National Security Action Memorandum No. 111 authorizes U.S. commitment of additional helicopters, transport planes, and

warplanes, as well as personnel to carry out training and actual combat missions.

6 December
U.S. Joint Chiefs of Staff authorize Operation FARM GATE. U.S. personnel and aircraft may undertake combat missions providing at least one Vietnamese national is carried on board strike aircraft for training purposes.

8 December
Washington issues a report accusing North Vietnam of aggression against the South and warning of a "clear and present danger" of Communist victory.

11 December
U.S. Navy vessel *Core* arrives at Sài Gòn with first U.S. helicopter units and 400 air and ground crewmen.

16 December
First FARM GATE mission flown.

31 December
Some 3,200 U.S. military personnel in South Vietnam.

1962
12 January
Operation RANCH HAND—the spraying of defoliant herbicides in South Vietnam—begins.

4 February
First U.S. helicopter shot down in Vietnam while ferrying ARVN troops into battle.

6 February
U.S. Military Assistance Command, Vietnam (MACV) established, commanded by General Paul D. Harkins, to direct U.S. war effort.

11 February
First FARM GATE casualties. Nine U.S. and South Vietnamese crewmen are killed in SC-47 crash near Sài Gòn.

14 February
President Kennedy authorizes U.S. military advisors in Vietnam to return fire if fired upon.

27 February
Diêm survives another coup attempt when Republic of Vietnam Air Force pilots Lieutenants Pham Phú Quôc and Nguyên Văn Cư try to kill him and his brother Ngô Đình Nhu by bombing and strafing presidential palace. Dozens of Diêm political opponents disappear, and thousands more are sent to prison camps. Lieutenant Quôc is arrested after his AD-6 crash lands in Nhà Bè, near Sài Gòn. Lieutenant Cư flees to Cambodia, where he remains until November 1963.

15 May
President Kennedy announces dispatch of U.S. troops to Thailand, at Thai government request, because of Communist offensive in Laos and movement of Communist forces toward Thai border.

May
Communist forces gain control of a large area of Laos as several thousand Royal Lao Army troops flee into Thailand.

2 June
Canadian and Indian members of the ICC find DRV guilty of violating the Geneva Agreements in carrying out "hostile activities, including armed attacks" against RVN armed forces and administration. All three members of ICC (Canada, India, and Poland) find the RVN guilty of violation of the Geneva Agreements by receiving additional military aid and entering into a "factual military alliance" with United States.

23 July
Declaration and protocol on the neutrality of Laos signed by 14-nation conference in Geneva. Tripartite coalition government that it establishes proves short-lived.

31 December
Some 11,300 U.S. military personnel in South Vietnam.

1963
2 January
ARVN forces suffer major defeat in the Battle of Ấp Bắc, located some 40 miles southwest of Sài Gòn.

26 February
U.S. helicopter crews escorting ARVN troops ordered to shoot first in encountering enemy soldiers.

8 May
Buddhist riots in Huê protesting RVN government ban on flying multicolored flag of World Fellowship of Buddhists. RVN riot police kill eight demonstrators, including some children, leading to widespread Buddhist demonstrations throughout South Vietnam.

11 June
Elderly Buddhist monk Thích Quang Đưc publicly burns himself to death to protest RVN government policies.

17 July
In Sài Gòn, RVN police break up Buddhist protest demonstration against alleged religious discrimination.

20 August
President Diêm declares martial law.

21 August
RVN Special Forces loyal to Diêm's brother Ngô Đình Nhu attack Buddhist pagodas. Many are damaged and over 1,400 Buddhists are arrested.

22 August
Henry Cabot Lodge replaces Frederick Nolting as U.S. ambassador to the RVN.

24 August
State Department cable to Lodge acknowledges Nhu responsibility for raids on Buddhist pagodas and says generals should be told that Washington is prepared to discontinue economic and military aid to Diêm.

2 September
President Kennedy, in CBS interview, says war in South Vietnam cannot be won "unless the people support the effort," adding "in my opinion, in the last two months, the Government has gotten out of touch with the people."

2 October
Washington decides to suspend economic subsidies for RVN commercial imports, freeze loans for developmental projects, and cut off financial support of Nhu's 2,000-man Vietnamese Special Forces. This is clear signal to those planning a coup against Diêm.

1 November
Military coup led by Major Generals Dương Văn Minh, Tôn Thât Đính, and Trân Văn Đôn overthrows Diêm government.

2 November
Both Diêm and Nhu, whom U.S. leaders assumed would be given safe passage out of the country, are murdered. Coup leaders set up provisional government, suspend the constitution, and dissolve National Assembly.

4 November
Washington recognizes new RVN provisional government.

14 November
In Sài Gòn, U.S. Army Major General Charles Timnes announces 1,000 Americans will be returning home by end of December.

22 November
President Kennedy assassinated in Dallas, Texas. He is succeeded by Vice-President Lyndon Johnson.

23 November
President Johnson reaffirms Washington's commitment to South Vietnam and to the defeat of Communists there.

21 December
U.S. Defense Secretary Robert McNamara reports to Johnson that the situation in South Vietnam is "very disturbing" and that

"current trends, unless reversed in the next 2–3 months, will lead to neutralization at best or more likely to a Communist-controlled state."

31 December
Some 16,300 U.S. military personnel in South Vietnam.

December
DRV leadership decides to send PAVN regulars to the South.

1964

16 January
President Johnson authorizes covert operations against North Vietnam (OPLAN 34A), recommended by U.S. Marine Corps Major General Victor H. Krulak to the Joint Chiefs of Staff. Such operations, to be conducted by South Vietnamese forces supported by United States, would gather intelligence and conduct sabotage to destabilize DRV regime. OPLAN 34A operations begin in February.

30 January
Major General Nguyên Khánh ousts RVN government headed by Dương Văn Minh. U.S. officials, caught by surprise, promptly hail Khánh as the new leader because he promises to rule with a strong hand.

March
Secretary of Defense McNamara visits the RVN and vows U.S. support for Khánh. McNamara barnstorms country, describing Khánh in memorized Vietnamese as the country's "best possible leader."

April
DRV commences infiltration of regular PAVN units south.

15 May
Khánh signs decree removing Diêm regime restrictions against Buddhists and granting them same rights as those enjoyed by Catholics.

9 June
In response to Communist Pathet Lao/PAVN Spring Offensive in Laos, United States begins Operation BARREL ROLL, bombing campaign to support Royal Laotian Army and Central Intelligence Agency–trained Hmong irregular forces led by General Vang Pao.

20 June
General William C. Westmoreland replaces General Harkins as MACV commander. Both Westmoreland and Ambassador Henry Cabot Lodge favor vigorous action to stiffen Khánh's resolve.

7 July
General Maxwell Taylor arrives in South Vietnam as new U.S. ambassador to the RVN.

25 July
Moscow calls for reconvening Geneva Conference on Laos.

30–31 July
RVN naval forces, using American "swift boats," carry out commando raid on Hòn Me and Hòn Nhiêu Islands, 12 and 4 kilometers off the North Vietnamese coast. DRV accuses United States and RVN of "extremely serious" violation of 1954 Geneva Agreement.

2 August
North Vietnamese torpedo boats attack U.S. destroyer *Maddox* on patrol in international waters some 28 miles from DRV coast.

3 August
DRV endorses call for reconvening of Geneva Conference "to preserve the peace of Indochina and Southeast Asia."

4 August
U.S. destroyers *Maddox* and *C. Turner Joy* claim they are attacked by North Vietnamese patrol boats. President Johnson orders U.S. air strikes against "gunboats and certain supporting facilities in North Vietnam."

7 August
Congress passes Tonkin Gulf Resolution, authorizing "all necessary steps, including the use of armed force" in Southeast Asia. Senate passage comes with only two dissenting votes; House vote is unanimous.
    In RVN Nguyên Khánh declares "state of emergency."

16 August
Khánh, elected president by the Military Council, ousts Dương Văn Minh as chief of state and installs new constitution, which U.S. Embassy helped draft.

21–25 August
Student demonstrations against Khánh and RVN military government, which then turn into riots.

27 August
New constitution withdrawn and Revolutionary Council dissolved. "Triumvirate" of Khánh, Minh, and General Trân Thiên Khiêm created.

29 August
Nguyên Xuân Oánh, former professor at Trinity College in Connecticut, named acting premier, says Khánh has suffered mental and physical breakdown.

5 September
DRV renews appeal to Geneva Conference cochairmen to reconvene the conference.

13 September
In RVN, bloodless coup by Brigadier General Lâm Văn Phát is aborted.

26 September
Provisional legislature ("High National Council") inaugurated in Sài Gòn.

30 September
First major antiwar demonstrations in United States, at University of California, Berkeley.

U.S. presidential advisor William Bundy says bombing North Vietnam would cut down threat to the RVN within months.

September
General Westmoreland initiates HOP TAC, pacification operation in six provinces around Sài Gòn.

31 October
Trân Văn Hương named RVN premier.

1 November
Communist forces attack Biên Hòa Air Base, killing five U.S. military personnel and destroying six B-57 bombers.

5 December
First Medal of Honor awarded to U.S. serviceman during the Vietnam War given to Capt. Roger Donlon.

8–20 December
Student and Buddhist demonstrations threaten military-supported Trân Văn Hương government.

14 December
U.S. aircraft begin bombing Hô Chí Minh Trail in Laos.

20 December
Khánh and generals dissolve the High National Council, arrest oppositionists, and conduct purge of military leadership, despite opposition by Ambassador Taylor.

24 December
Two Americans killed when Viêt Công sappers bomb U.S. billets in Sài Gòn.

Ambassador Taylor tells press Khánh has outlived his usefulness.

31 December
Some 23,300 U.S. military personnel in South Vietnam.

1965
4 January
In State of the Union address, President Johnson reaffirms U.S. commitment to the RVN.

7 January
Armed Forces Council and Khánh restore civilian government under Trân Văn Hương.

19–24 January
Buddhist demonstrations erupt in Sài Gòn and Huê. These include sacking of U.S. Information Service building. Demonstrators demand military ouster of the Hương government.

27 January
Armed Forces Council ousts the Hương government and reinstalls General Khánh in power.

7 February
Communists attack U.S. installations at Pleiku, killing 8 and wounding 109 U.S. servicemen and destroying or damaging 20 aircraft. In retaliation, U.S. aircraft strike targets in North Vietnam (Operation FLAMING DART).

9 February
U.S. Marine Corps Hawk air defense missile battalion deployed to Đà Nẵng.

15 February
People's Republic of China threatens to enter the war if United States invades North Vietnam.

18 February
South Vietnamese army and Marine units oust Khánh in a bloodless coup.

20 February
After forces loyal to the Armed Forces Council regain control, Armed Forces Council demands Khánh's resignation.

27 February
U.S. State Department issues report detailing North Vietnamese "aggression."

28 February
U.S. and RVN officials declare that President Johnson has decided to begin reprisal attacks against North Vietnam to secure a negotiated settlement.

2 March
Operation ROLLING THUNDER begins with first air mission against the North when 100 U.S. Air Force and Republic of Vietnam Air Force sorties strike the Xóm Bang Ammunition Depot 35 miles north of the Demilitarized Zone (DMZ).

8 March
United Nations Secretary-General U Thant proposes a preliminary conference to include United States, Soviet Union, Great Britain, France, China, and North and South Vietnam.

U.S. 9th Marine Expeditionary Brigade, deployed from Okinawa, begins arriving at Đà Nẵng.

9 March
Washington rejects U Thant's proposal until North Vietnam ends war in South.

2 April
United States announces it will send several thousand additional troops to South Vietnam.

7 April
President Johnson, speaking at Johns Hopkins University, announces that United States is willing to hold "unconditional discussions" with DRV and suggests inducement of a $1 billion economic aid program for Southeast Asia.

8 April
DRV Premier Pham Văn Đồng rejects President Johnson's offer and announces four-point position on peace, including settlement of South Vietnam's internal affairs "in accordance with the program of the National Liberation Front of South Vietnam, without any foreign interference."

April
U.S. begins STEEL TIGER air interdiction campaign over the Hồ Chí Minh Trail in the northern panhandle of Laos.

13–18 May
Six-day U.S. bombing pause over North Vietnam.

May
U.S. Navy begins Operation MARKET TIME to interdict Communist surface traffic in South Vietnamese coastal waters.

8 June
U.S. State Department reveals that U.S. troops are authorized to participate in direct combat, if so requested by ARVN.

11 June
RVN National Directorate comprised of ten military leaders forms a war cabinet headed by Air Marshal Nguyên Cao Kỳ as premier.

16 June
U.S. Secretary of Defense McNamara announces new troop deployments to South Vietnam, bringing U.S. troop strength there to 70,000 men.

18 June
ARC LIGHT campaign begins as B-52 bombers strike Communist targets within South Vietnam.

8 July
Henry Cabot Lodge reappointed as U.S. ambassador to the RVN, succeeding Maxwell Taylor.

11 September
1st Cavalry Division (Airmobile) begins arriving in South Vietnam.

15–16 October
Student-run National Coordinating Committee to End the War in Vietnam sponsors nationwide demonstrations in some 40 U.S. cities.

27 November
March for peace in Vietnam draws 15,000 to 35,000 marchers in Washington, D.C.

24 December
United States begins second pause in bombing of North Vietnam in effort to get DRV to negotiate.

31 December
Some 184,300 U.S. military personnel in South Vietnam.

December
U.S. Air Force strikes against targets in southern panhandle of Laos, Operation TIGER HOUND, begins, and ARC LIGHT campaign by B-52s is extended to Laos.

1966
31 January
U.S. air strikes resume against North Vietnam.

1 February
UN Security Council meets to consider U.S. draft resolution calling for an international conference to bring about peace in South Vietnam and Southeast Asia.

2 February
DRV Foreign Ministry formally rejects UN action on Vietnam.

4 February
U.S. Senate Foreign Relations Committee opens formal televised hearings on the war.

6–9 February
President Johnson holds talks in Honolulu with RVN Premier Nguyên Cao Kỳ.

12 March
Buddhists and students begin demonstrations in Huê and Đà Nẵng to protest ouster of ARVN I Corps Commander General Nguyên Chánh Thi and to demand elections for a new national assembly.

16–20 March
Mass Buddhist protests in Sài Gòn against RVN government.

23 March
General strikes in Đà Nẵng and Huế.

1 April
Communist sappers set off explosives in a Sài Gòn hotel, killing three Americans and four South Vietnamese.

2–5 April
Kỳ threatens troops to quell the antigovernment rebellion in Đà Nẵng, then flies two Ranger battalions there.

11 April
U.S. B-52s bomb North Vietnam for the first time.

12–14 April
RVN National Directorate promises elections for a constituent assembly within three to five months. Buddhists demonstrations come to an end.

15 May
Kỳ airlifts 1,000 RVN Marines to Đà Nẵng.

1 June
Students burn the U.S. cultural center and consulate in Huế.

19 June
RVN National Directorate schedules assembly elections for September.

23 June
RVN troops seize chief Buddhist stronghold in Sài Gòn.

29 June
U.S. aircraft carry out first strikes against oil installations in Hà Nôi and Hai Phòng areas.

8 July
South Vietnamese Chief of State Lieutenant General Nguyên Văn Thiêu states that the allies should invade North Vietnam, if necessary, to end the war.

30 July–5 August
U.S. aircraft for the first time intentionally strike targets in the DMZ.

11 September
South Vietnamese elect a 117-member constituent assembly from among officially approved anti-Communist slates. Buddhists denounce the election as "completely crooked."

25 October
Meeting in Manila of United States and five other nations assisting South Vietnam. They offer to withdraw their troops from South Vietnam six months after Hà Nôi disengages from the war.

26 October
President Johnson visits U.S. troops in South Vietnam.

October
U.S. Navy begins Operation SEA DRAGON, interdiction of Communist supply vessels in coastal waters off North Vietnam.

5 November
Defense Secretary McNamara announces that number of U.S. troops in South Vietnam will continue to grow in 1967 but at a lower rate than in 1966.

30 November
Polish ICC representative Janusz Lewandowski formulates a ten-point peace position on which basis DRV would negotiate seriously with United States.

2 December
U.S. State Department decides to contact DRV representative in Warsaw regarding secret talks.

2–5 December
U.S. bombers raid truck depots, rail yards, and fuel dumps in immediate vicinity of Hà Nôi.

9 December
Lewandowski informs Ambassador Lodge that no contact can take place in Warsaw in the face of escalation of bombing.

14–15 December
Further U.S. air strikes very close to Hà Nôi.

26 December
Responding to reports by Harrison Salisbury of the *New York Times,* officials admit that U.S. planes have "accidentally struck civilian areas while attempting to bomb military targets."

31 December
Some 385,300 U.S. military personnel in South Vietnam.

1967
10 January
President Johnson in course of State of the Union address asks for a 6 percent surcharge on income taxes to support the war.

January
U.S. Navy establishes Mekong Delta Mobile Riverine Force.

7 February
President Johnson sends proposal to British Prime Minister Harold Wilson for a DRV "assured stoppage" of infiltration in

return for a bombing halt and no further augmentation of U.S. forces in South Vietnam.

United States begins a six-day bombing pause.

10 February
Washington insists that formula for talks, presented by British Prime Minister Wilson to Soviet Premier Aleksei Kosygin, requires that North Vietnamese infiltration stop before a bombing halt, not afterward, as Wilson had suggested orally.

21 March
Hà Nội releases the February Johnson-Hồ exchange in which Hồ rejected peace talks unless United States unconditionally halted bombing and all other acts of war against North Vietnam.

15 April
Massive antiwar demonstrations in cities across United States.

20 April
U.S. aircraft strike power plant in Hà Nội for the first time.

24 April
U.S. aircraft attack two DRV air bases in North for first time.

1 May
Ellsworth Bunker replaces Henry Cabot Lodge as U.S. ambassador to the RVN.

13 May
Premier Kỳ says he might react "militarily" if a civilian with whose policies he disagreed is elected president.

14 May
Chief of State Thiệu says he believes that 50,000 U.S. or Allied troops will be needed in South Vietnam for 10 to 20 years after the end of the war.

30 June
Following three days of meetings of the ruling Armed Forces Council, Kỳ withdraws from presidential race and agrees to be vice-presidential candidate on Thiệu ticket.

16 July
Washington admits in a diplomatic note to the USSR that U.S. aircraft may have bombed the Soviet ship *Mikhail Frunze* in Hai Phòng Harbor on 29 June.

18–19 July
RVN Constituent Assembly approves 11-candidate slates for the upcoming presidential election, but rejects peace candidate Âu Trường Thanh on trumped-up charge of links to Communists and exiled General Dương Văn Minh.

31 August
U.S. Senate Preparedness Subcommittee declares that McNamara has "shackled" the air war against North Vietnam and calls for "closure, neutralization, or isolation of Hai Phòng."

3 September
Nguyễn Văn Thiệu and Nguyễn Cao Kỳ elected president and vice-president, respectively, of RVN. Thiệu-Kỳ slate secures 35 percent of the vote.

11 September
Heavy U.S. air strikes on Hai Phòng and suburbs in effort to isolate this port from Hà Nội.

29 September
President Johnson declares in a speech in San Antonio that the United States will stop the bombing of North Vietnam if this "will lead promptly to productive discussions."

12 October
Secretary of State Dean Rusk says Vietnam War is test of Asia's ability to withstand the threat of "a billion Chinese . . . armed with nuclear weapons."

12–14 October
Heavy U.S. Navy strikes against Hai Phòng shipyards and docks.

21–23 October
Some 50,000 Americans rally against the war in Washington, D.C., and march on Pentagon, protected by 10,000 troops.

21 November
General Westmoreland declares in a speech at National Press Club in Washington that the war has reached point when "the end begins to come into view."

29 November
President Johnson announces that Secretary of Defense McNamara will resign to become president of World Bank.

30 December
RVN government announces a 36-hour Lunar New Year (Tết) truce.

31 December
Some 485,600 U.S. military personnel in South Vietnam.

1968
1 January
DRV Foreign Minister Nguyễn Duy Trinh announces for first time that North Vietnam "will hold talks with the United States" after it has "unconditionally" halted bombing and "other acts of war" against North Vietnam.

21 January
Communist forces begin siege of U.S. Marine base at Khe Sanh near the DMZ.

25 January
Clark Clifford, President Johnson's nominee as secretary of defense, tells the Senate Armed Services Committee that the "no advantage" clause of the San Antonio speech means North Vietnam could continue to transport the "normal" level of goods and men into South after bombing halt.

30 January
First, premature, attacks in Communist Têt Offensive at Đà Nẵng, Pleiku, Nha Trang, and nine other cities in central South Vietnam.

31 January
Major attacks in Communist Têt Offensive. Offensive includes Sài Gòn and Huê, five of six autonomous cities, 36 of 44 provincial capitals, and 64 of 245 district capitals. The attacks—in both timing and magnitude—catch Allies off guard. Militarily, Têt Offensive is a tactical disaster for the Communists. By end of March 1968 they have not achieved a single one of their objectives. More than 58,000 Viêt Công and PAVN troops die in the offensive. U.S. forces suffer 3,895 dead; ARVN loses 4,954; non-U.S. Allies lose 214; more than 14,300 South Vietnamese civilians die.

7 February
PAVN troops overrun U.S. Army Special Forces camp at Làng Vei, southwest of Khe Sanh.

20 February
U.S. Senate Foreign Relations Committee begins hearings on the 1964 Gulf of Tonkin incident. Senators Fulbright and Morse charge Defense Department with withholding information on U.S. naval activities in the Gulf that might have provoked DRV.

25 February
ARVN and U.S. forces recapture Huê after 25 days of occupation by Communist troops.

Westmoreland states that additional U.S. troops "will probably be required" in Vietnam.

26 February
Allied troops discover first mass graves in Huê. From 1 to 25 February occupying Communist forces have massacred some 2,800 people identified with the RVN. One authority estimates that Communists may have killed in Huê as many as 5,700 people.

16 March
A platoon from Company C, 1st Battalion, 20th Infantry, 11th Infantry Brigade (Light) of the 23d (Americal) Division, commanded by Lt. William Calley, massacres between 200 and 500 unarmed civilians in hamlet of My Lai, a cluster of hamlets

making up Sơn My village, of Sơn Tinh district in coastal lowlands of Quang Ngãi Province, I Corps Tactical Zone.

22 March
President Johnson announces that General Westmoreland will be returning to Washington as chief of staff of the U.S. Army and be replaced as commander of MACV by General Creighton Abrams.

31 March
In the course of a televised address, President Johnson announces a bombing halt over North Vietnam except for "the area north of the demilitarized zone." He calls on DRV to agree to peace talks and announces he is withdrawing from presidential race.

3 April
DRV offers to send representatives to meet with U.S. officials "with a view to determining with the American side the unconditional cessation of the U.S. bombing raids and all other acts of war against the Democratic Republic of Vietnam so that talks may start." President Johnson agrees.

26 April
Massive antiwar demonstrations occur on college campuses across United States, including some 200,000 protesters in New York City.

3 May
After some haggling over site, Johnson announces U.S. acceptance of DRV suggestion that preliminary peace talks be held in Paris.

5–13 May
Second large-scale Communist offensive of year. Although it is smaller than Têt, Communists strike some 119 Allied targets. U.S. and ARVN forces defeat all attacks.

12 May
U.S.-DRV preliminary peace talks open in Paris.

25 May–4 June
Third widespread Communist offensive of the year, also defeated by Allied forces.

27 June
U.S. troops withdraw from their base at Khe Sanh after 77-day siege.

3 July
General Creighton Abrams formally replaces Westmoreland as commander of MACV.

31 October
President Johnson announces end to ROLLING THUNDER—the complete cessation of "all air, naval, and artillery bombardment of North Vietnam" as of 1 November.

1 November
The DRV delegation at Paris announces that a meeting to include representatives of DRV, South Vietnam National Front for Liberation, United States, and RVN will be held in Paris after 6 November.

2 November
RVN President Thiêu states that his government will not attend Paris negotiations.

12 November
U.S. Defense Secretary Clifford threatens that United States might proceed with Paris negotiations without participation of RVN government.

27 November
RVN government announces it will take part in Paris peace talks—after United States reiterates its nonrecognition of the NLF as a separate entity.

23 December
NLF representative in Paris Trân Bửu Kiêm rejects direct negotiations between NLF and RVN and insists on talks only with Washington.

31 December
Some 536,000 U.S. military personnel in South Vietnam.

1969
16 January
After protracted negotiations, United States and DRV announce agreement on round conference table format for the Paris peace talks.

25 January
Four-party peace talks begin in Paris.

23–24 February
Communist forces launch mortar and rocket attacks on some 115 targets in South Vietnam, including the cities of Sài Gòn, Đà Nẵng, Huê, and U.S. base at Biên Hòa.

18 March
Operation MENU, secret U.S. air strikes inside Cambodia by B-52 bombers, begins. It continues until 26 May 1970.

19 March
Secretary of Defense Melvin Laird proclaims "Vietnamization" of the war.

26 March
Women Strike for Peace, the first big anti–Vietnam War rally during the Nixon administration, occurs in Washington, D.C.

27 March
In Paris, Ambassador Henry Cabot Lodge and RVN Delegation Chief Pham Đăng Lâm declare that a peace settlement must include withdrawal of all North Vietnamese "regular and subversive forces" from Laos, Cambodia, and South Vietnam.

5–6 April
Weekend of antiwar protests in number of U.S. cities.

7 April
RVN President Thiêu says he would ask allies to remove their military forces after North Vietnamese withdrawal of regular troops and "auxiliary troops and cadres."

30 April
Peak U.S. military strength in South Vietnam reached, with 543,400 personnel there.

8 May
NLF delegate in Paris Trân Bửu Kiêm demands unconditional U.S. troop withdrawal and settlement of remaining military and political issues among Vietnamese parties to exclude RVN President Thiêu.

12 May
Communist forces launch largest number of attacks throughout South Vietnam since 1968 Têt Offensive.

14 May
In first major speech on Vietnam, President Richard Nixon proclaims eight-point peace proposal that calls for simultaneous withdrawal of U.S. troops and "all non–South Vietnamese forces" from South Vietnam.

8 June
President Nixon announces that United States will withdraw 25,000 troops from South Vietnam by August.

10 June
Provisional Revolutionary Government of the Republic of South Vietnam formed by NLF and other pro-NLF, anti-RVN organizations and individuals.

11 July
RVN President Thiêu offers internationally supervised elections and Communist participation in an "electoral commission," but on provision they first renounce violence. RVN would oversee election.

25 July
In Guam, President Nixon makes foreign policy statement, later dubbed the "Nixon Doctrine." The United States would have primary responsibility for defense of its allies against nuclear attack, but non-Communist Asian states would bear the brunt of

their conventional defense as well as be responsible for their own internal security.

4 August
U.S. National Security Advisor Henry Kissinger meets secretly in Paris with DRV representative Xuân Thuy.

2 September
DRV President Hô Chí Minh dies in Hà Nôi. DRV officials announce his death the next day.

16 September
President Nixon announces withdrawal from South Vietnam of an additional 35,000 U.S. troops.

15 October
National Moratorium antiwar demonstrations across United States involving hundreds of thousands of people.

16 October
Secretary of Defense Melvin Laird announces U.S. plans to keep a "residual force" of some 6,000 to 7,000 troops in South Vietnam after hostilities end there.

3 November
In major address on Vietnam, Nixon appeals to the "silent majority" of Americans and argues that "precipitate withdrawal" would lead to a "disaster of immense magnitude."

15 November
Antiwar demonstration at Washington Monument, largest in that city to date, drawing some 250,000 people.

16 November
U.S. Army announces investigation into charges that U.S. forces shot more than 100 Vietnamese civilians in My Lai village in March 1968.

24 November
U.S. Army Lt. William Calley, Jr. ordered to stand trial for premeditated murder of 109 Vietnamese civilians.

1 December
First military draft lottery since 1942 held at Selective Service headquarters.

4 December
Louis Harris survey reports 46 percent of those polled indicate sympathy with goals of the November Moratorium demonstrations; 45 percent disagreed.

15 December
President Nixon announces third reduction in U.S. troop strength in Vietnam: 50,000 troops to leave by 15 April 1970.

31 December
Some 475,200 U.S. military personnel in South Vietnam.

1970
28 January
Gallup poll shows 65 percent of those interviewed approved of President Nixon's handling of Vietnam War, his highest approval rating to date.

21 February
National Security Advisor Henry Kissinger begins Paris talks with DRV representative Lê Đức Tho.

13 March
With Prince Norodom Sihanouk abroad, leadership of Cambodia demands that Vietnamese Communist troops withdraw from the country immediately. Cambodians sack DRV embassy in Phnom Penh.

17 March
Cambodian troops attack Vietnamese Communist sanctuaries along the Cambodia-Vietnam border, supported by ARVN artillery.

18 March
Cambodian National Assembly deposes Prince Sihanouk, declaring General Lon Nol interim chief of state. RVN President Thiêu announces hope of working with new Cambodian government to control Communist border activity.

23 March
In Beijing, Sihanouk announces that he will form "national union government" and "national liberation army." DRV and Pathet Lao declare support.

27–28 March
ARVN forces, supported by United States, launch their first major attack against Communist base areas in Cambodia.

28 March
Washington announces that U.S. troops will be permitted, on judgment of field commanders, to cross into Cambodia in response to enemy threats. Washington insists this does not mean widened war.

4 April
Largest pro-U.S. involvement in Vietnam War to date is held in Washington, D.C.

5 April
Two ARVN battalions push more than ten miles into Cambodia, this time without U.S. air support.

8 April
Vietnamese Communist troops drive back Cambodian government forces in heavy fighting some nine miles from the South Vietnamese border.

11 April

Cambodian government troops begin the massacre of several thousand Vietnamese civilians living in southeast Cambodia; some 40,000 Vietnamese in Phnom Penh are sent to concentration camps.

Gallup poll shows that 48 percent of Americans polled approve of President Nixon's Vietnam policy; 41 percent disapprove.

20 April

President Nixon announces in televised speech his intention to withdraw 150,000 U.S. troops over the next year.

21 April

ARVN troops cross the Cambodian border for third time in one week to attack Communist base areas.

30 April

In nationally televised address, President Nixon announces that U.S. troops are attacking Communist sanctuaries in Cambodia, with one objective being Communist Central Office of South Vietnam headquarters in Fishhook area some 50 miles northwest of Sài Gòn. Widespread antiwar protests erupt on U.S. college campuses.

3 May

Pentagon confirms that the United States has conducted heavy bombing of targets in North Vietnam, the first major bombing of the North since November 1968 bombing halt. Pentagon calls these "protective reaction" strikes.

4 May

Ohio National Guardsmen fire on antiwar student demonstrators at Kent State University, killing 4 and wounding 11.

6 May

Some 200 college campuses across the United States shut down to protest the war and events at Kent State.

9 May

Some 75,000 to 100,000 people gather in Washington, D.C., in hastily organized protest against the U.S. invasion of Cambodia.

12 May

RVN Vice-President Nguyên Cao Kỳ reveals that on 9 May RVN and U.S. Navy warships began blockade of some 100 miles of Cambodian coastline to prevent Communist resupply there by sea.

20 May

Some 100,000 people demonstrate in New York City in support of President Nixon's Indo-China policy.

21 May

RVN Vice-President Kỳ announces that ARVN troops will remain in Cambodia after U.S. troops withdraw from that country.

26 May

Operation MENU, U.S. bombing of Cambodia, ends.

3 June

President Nixon declares in a televised speech that Allied invasion of Cambodia is the "most successful operation" of the war, enabling him to resume U.S. troop withdrawals.

7 June

Secretary of State William Rogers says no U.S. troops will assist Lon Nol's government, even if its existence should be threatened by Communist forces.

24 June

U.S. Senate repeals the Tonkin Gulf Resolution in vote of 81 to 10.

30 June

U.S. forces end two months of operations inside Cambodia; some ARVN forces remain there.

U.S. Senate approves (58 to 37) Cooper-Church Amendment aimed at limiting future presidential action in Cambodia by prohibiting military personnel to serve in either combat or advisory roles and prohibiting direct air support of Cambodian forces. This step, first limitation ever voted on the powers of a president as commander in chief during a war, nevertheless allows strategic bombing.

1 September

U.S. Senate rejects (55 to 39) McGovern-Hatfield Amendment setting a deadline of 31 December 1971 for complete withdrawal of U.S. forces from South Vietnam.

17 September

Provisional Revolutionary Government of South Vietnam (PRG) delegation in Paris proposes an eight-point peace plan, calling for complete U.S. withdrawal from South Vietnam by 30 June 1971 and political settlement between the PRG and interim government excluding Thiêu, Kỳ, and Premier Trân Thiên Khiêm.

26 September

Gallup poll finds that 55 percent of those surveyed favor Hatfield-McGovern Amendment to cut off funds for continued U.S. military activities in Indo-China unless there is a declaration of war; 36 percent are opposed.

7 October

President Nixon announces five-point proposal to end the war, based on cease-fire in place in South Vietnam, Laos, and Cambodia. He proposes eventual withdrawal of U.S. forces, unconditional release of prisoners of war (POWs), and political solution reflecting will of South Vietnamese people.

8 October
Communist delegations in Paris reject President Nixon's proposal, insisting instead on unconditional withdrawal of U.S. forces from Indo-China.

20–21 November
U.S. forces raid Sơn Tây prisoner-of-war compound 25 miles from Hà Nôi, but find no U.S. personnel there.

10 December
President Nixon warns the DRV that he will resume bombing North Vietnam if fighting in South Vietnam intensifies.

31 December
Some 334,600 U.S. military personnel in South Vietnam.

1971
1 January
Congress forbids the use of U.S. ground troops in Laos and Cambodia, although not airpower there.

8 February
ARVN forces invade southern Laos. Dubbed Operation LAM SỞN 719, its goal is the disruption of Communist supply and infiltration network. Operation is supported by U.S. airpower and artillery.

6 March
120 U.S. Army helicopters, protected by helicopter gunships and U.S. Air Force fighter-bombers, lift two ARVN battalions into Tchépone, Laos—one of LAM SỞN 719's objectives.

24 March
LAM SỞN 719 ends precipitously. ARVN captures extensive Communist supplies but sustains heavy casualties. Many U.S. helicopters are also lost.

29 March
At Ft. Benning, Georgia, U.S. Army court finds Lieutenant Calley guilty of premeditated murder of 22 Vietnamese civilians at My Lai 4. He is sentenced to life in prison, later reduced to ten years. (In 1974 Calley is paroled.)

7 April
President Nixon, in televised address, states in reference to Operation LAM SỞN 719, "Tonight I can report Vietnamization has succeeded." Nixon announces withdrawal from South Vietnam of additional 100,000 U.S. troops.

16 April
President Nixon announces that a residual U.S. force will remain in Vietnam as long as it is needed in order for the South Vietnamese "to develop the capacity for self-defense."

24 April
More than 200,000 people participate in Washington rally to protest the war.

31 May
In Paris, United States secretly proposes to the DRV a deadline for withdrawal of all American troops in return for repatriation of American prisoners and cease-fire.

13 June
The New York Times begins publication of Pentagon Papers, heretofore secret Pentagon analysis of the three-decades-long U.S. involvement in Indo-China.

26 June
DRV offers to release American prisoners at same time as civilian prisoners and withdrawal of U.S. forces, but insists United States also abandon support of RVN President Thiêu.

30 June
U.S. Supreme Court rules Pentagon Papers may be published.

1 July
The PRG delegation in Paris proposes plan whereby it would negotiate with a neutral coalition government excluding Thiêu, Kỳ, and Khiêm.

15 July
President Nixon announces he will visit Beijing.

20 August
Retired ARVN General Dưởng Văn Minh, only opposition candidate in RVN presidential election, withdraws from race, charging that it is rigged in Thiêu's favor.

3 October
RVN President Thiêu elected to another four-year term.

11 October
Washington proposes free elections in South Vietnam to be organized by independent body representing all political forces in the South, with Thiêu resigning one month before elections.

12 November
President Nixon announces the withdrawal from South Vietnam of additional 45,000 U.S. troops.

26–30 December
U.S. aircraft resume bombing of North Vietnam, mounting heavy attacks; Washington again characterizes these as "protective reaction" strikes.

31 December
Some 156,800 U.S. military personnel in South Vietnam.

1972

2 January
President Nixon announces that U.S. forces will continue to withdraw from South Vietnam, but that 35,000 U.S. troops will remain until the release of all U.S. POWs.

13 January
President Nixon announces that 70,000 U.S. troops will leave South Vietnam over next three months, reducing U.S. troop strength there by 1 May to 69,000 troops.

25 January
President Nixon reveals the details of Kissinger's secret trips to Paris and text of 11 October 1971 U.S. peace proposal.

26 January
Radio Hà Nôi announces DRV rejection of latest U.S. peace proposal.

3 February
In Paris, PRG delegation presents revised version of July 1971 peace proposals, calling for RVN President Thiêu's resignation in exchange for immediate discussion of political settlement, specific date for total U.S. withdrawal from South Vietnam and release of all military and civilian prisoners, and end to Sài Gòn's "warlike policy."

16 February
Gallup poll finds that 52 percent of those interviewed approve of President Nixon's handling of the war; 39 percent disapprove.

21–16 February
President Nixon visits People's Republic of China.

23 March
Washington announces indefinite suspension of Paris peace talks until Communists agree to "serious discussions" of predetermined issues.

30 March
PAVN forces launch Spring, or Easter, Offensive, largest Communist military action since 1968.

6 April
U.S. resumes heavy bombing of North Vietnam.

7 April–18 June
Battle of An Lôc.

15 April
United States resumes bombing of military targets in vicinity of Hà Nôi and Hai Phòng, the first such strikes in four years.

15–20 April
Widespread antiwar demonstrations across United States.

22 April
Antiwar demonstrators hold marches and rallies throughout the United States to protest renewed bombing of North Vietnam.

26 April
President Nixon announces the withdrawal of 20,000 troops over next two months, reducing U.S. troop strength in South Vietnam by 1 July to 49,000 troops.

27 April
Paris peace talks resume.

30 April
President Nixon warns North Vietnamese that they are "taking a very great risk if they continue their offensive in the South."

1 May
ARVN forces and U.S. advisors abandon Quang Tri, northernmost provincial capital of South Vietnam, following five days of heavy fighting.

4 May
Citing a "complete lack of progress," the United States and RVN announce indefinite halt to the Paris peace talks.

8 May
President Nixon announces the mining of all North Vietnamese ports, interdiction of rail and other communications, and air strikes against military targets in North Vietnam (Operation LINEBACKER), until return of U.S. POWs and establishment of internationally supervised cease-fire throughout Indo-China.

8–12 May
Wave of antiwar protests across United States.

28 June
President Nixon announces that no more draftees will be sent to Vietnam unless they volunteer for such duty.

June
General Fred Weyand replaces General Abrams as commander, MACV, with Abrams becoming Army chief of staff.

13 July
Formal peace talks resume in Paris.

28 August
President Nixon announces end to military draft by July 1973.

11 September
PRG announces that any settlement in South Vietnam must reflect "reality" of "two administrations, two armies and other political forces."

15 September
ARVN forces retake Quang Tri.

26–27 September
Kissinger holds additional secret talks in Paris with DRV representative Lê Đức Tho.

8 October
DRV representative in Paris Lê Đức Tho presents draft peace agreement proposing that two separate administrations remain in South Vietnam and negotiate general elections.

19–20 October
Kissinger meets with RVN President Thiêu in Sài Gòn. Thiêu opposes draft treaty provisions that allow North Vietnamese troops to remain in place in the South.

President Nixon announces halt in bombing of North Vietnam above the 20th parallel. He also sends message to DRV Premier Pham Văn Đông confirming that the agreement is complete and pledging that it would be signed by the two foreign ministers on 31 October, but seeks clarification on several points.

23 October
U.S. message to Hà Nôi requests further negotiations, citing difficulties with Sài Gòn.

26 October
Radio Hà Nôi announces that secret talks in Paris had produced tentative agreement to end the war.

Kissinger says "Peace is at hand," and that only one additional meeting is needed to complete the agreement.

1 November
RVN President Thiêu publicly objects to provisions in draft agreement permitting North Vietnamese troops to remain in South and providing for a three-segment "administrative structure" to preside over political settlement and elections.

16 November
President Nixon sends letter to President Thiêu pledging to press DRV for changes demanded by Thiêu.

20–21 November
Kissinger and Lê Đức Tho begin another round of secret negotiations near Paris.

13 December
Paris peace talks deadlock.

16 December
Kissinger holds a press conference and publicly blames the DRV for stalemate in negotiations.

18–29 December
United States renews bombing of Hà Nôi–Hai Phòng area (Operation LINEBACKER II also known as the "Christmas bombing"), using B-52s as well as fighter-bombers.

22 December
Washington announces that bombing of North Vietnam will continue until Hà Nôi agrees to negotiate "in a spirit of good will and in a constructive attitude."

30 December
Washington announces that negotiations between Kissinger and Lê Đức Tho will resume on 2 January and an end to bombing north of the 20th parallel.

31 December
Approximately 24,000 U.S. military personnel in South Vietnam.

1973
8–12 January
Kissinger and Tho resume private negotiations in Paris.

15 January
President Nixon announces end to all U.S. offensive military action against the DRV.

17 January
President Nixon warns RVN President Thiêu in private letter that his refusal to sign agreement would render it impossible for United States to continue assistance to RVN.

20 January
President Nixon sends an ultimatum to President Thiêu regarding signing peace agreement, demanding an answer by 21 January.

23 January
Kissinger and Lê Đức Tho initial peace agreement in Paris in which a cease-fire would begin on 27 January and all POWs would be released within 60 days.

25 January
Foreign ministers of United States, DRV, RVN, and PRG formally sign two-party and four-party versions of the peace agreement.

27 January
"Cease-fire" goes into effect, although both sides violate it. RVN forces continue to take back villages occupied by Communists in the two days before the cease-fire deadline.

U.S. Secretary of Defense Melvin Laird announces end to military draft.

1 February
In secret letter to DRV Premier Pham Văn Đông, President Nixon pledges to contribute to "postwar reconstruction in North Vietnam" in "range of $3.25 billion" over five years.

12 February
Release of U.S. POWs begins in Hà Nôi.

16 February
Four-Party Joint Military Commission appeals to both sides in South Vietnam to respect cease-fire. It reaffirms prohibition on air combat missions.

17 February
Washington and Hà Nôi issue joint communiqué following four-day visit by Henry Kissinger to Hà Nôi. They announce agreement to establish a Joint Economic Commission to develop economic relations, particularly U.S. contribution to "healing the wounds of war" in North Vietnam.

21 February
Peace agreement signed in Laos. United States halts bombing there.

15 March
President Nixon threatens to take unilateral action to force the DRV to suspend or reduce use of Hô Chí Minh Trail network to move military equipment into South Vietnam.

28 March
President Nixon again warns DRV leaders that they "should have no doubt as to the consequences if they fail to comply with the agreement."

29 March
Last 67 American prisoners of war held by DRV leave Hà Nôi.
    Last U.S. troops leave South Vietnam and MACV headquarters disestablished.

3 April
Joint communiqué from Presidents Nixon and Thiêu charges Communist violations of cease-fire agreement by infiltration and warns that continued violations "would call for appropriately vigorous reactions." U.S. Defense Secretary Elliot Richardson says United States will not renew bombing unless there were a "flagrant" violation of the agreement, such as full-scale invasion of the South.

24 April
United States and RVN publish texts of DRV and U.S. notes accusing each other of violations of peace agreement.

25 April
RVN and PRG delegations to talks in Paris offer incompatible proposals for political settlement.

10 May
U.S. House of Representatives passes second supplemental appropriations bill with amendment deleting authorization for transfer of $430 million by the Defense Department for bombing

of Cambodia. Another amendment prohibits use of funds for combat activities in or over Cambodia by U.S. forces.

9 June
Although Kissinger and Lê Đức Tho negotiate new agreement for implementation of Paris peace agreement, fighting in South Vietnam reaches highest level since mid-February.

13 June
Signatories to Paris agreement issue joint communiqué on its implementation that calls for resumption of processes interrupted in April, including meetings of the U.S.-DRV Joint Economic Commission. Kissinger notes a "satisfactory conclusion" on points of concern to United States.

20 June
Declassified Defense Department documents show that in seven years of war 3.2 million tons of bombs have been dropped on South Vietnam, 2.1 million on Laos, and 340,000 tons on North Vietnam.

29 June
U.S. House of Representatives passes compromise bill with 15 August deadline to halt all bombing of Cambodia and adds North and South Vietnam to areas included in ban on combat activities. President Nixon reluctantly signs bill into law on 1 July.

26 July
U.S. House of Representatives passes Foreign Assistance Bill after agreeing to amendment prohibiting use of authorized funds to aid in reconstruction of North Vietnam unless specifically authorized by Congress.

14 August
U.S. bombing of Cambodia ends, bringing to a halt all U.S. military activity in Indo-China.

10 September
RVN protests construction of air bases in the PRG zone on basis that it has control of all air space over South Vietnam.

1 October
RVN President Thiêu declares that Communists are planning a spring 1974 "general offensive" and calls for "preemptive attacks."

3–7 October
RVN Air Force planes carry out heavy raids against the PRG zone in Tây Ninh Province, beginning bombing campaign throughout Third Military Region.

15 October
Leadership of Communist forces in South Vietnam issues order to begin counterattacks of RVN bases and other points of its choosing in retaliation for Sài Gòn's earlier offensive operations.

16 October
U.S. Secretary of State Kissinger and DRV diplomat Lê Đức Tho are awarded the Nobel Prize for Peace. Kissinger accepts, but Tho declines the award until such time as "peace is truly established" in Vietnam.

October
DRV leaders decide on a new offensive in the South with projected final victory in 1976.

7 November
U.S. Congress overrides President Nixon's veto of War Powers Act limiting president's power to commit U.S. armed forces abroad without congressional approval.

15 November
Congress passes Military Procurement Authorization bill that prohibits funds for any U.S. military action in any part of Indo-China.

31 December
Approximately 50 U.S. uniformed military personnel in South Vietnam.

1974
4 January
RVN President Thiệu announces that "as far as the armed forces are concerned, I can tell you the war has restarted."

February
RVN forces launch major offensive operations against PRG areas in Quang Ngãi Province and Cu Chi–Trang Bàng area west of Sài Gòn.

22 March
In last major political initiative by either side in the war, PRG offers to hold elections within one year of establishment of National Council of National Reconciliation and Concord.

March
Communist Party's Central Military Committee passes resolution that, if United States and RVN "do not implement the agreement," it must "destroy the enemy and liberate the South." This month sees heaviest fighting in South Vietnam since cease-fire.

4 April
U.S. House of Representatives rejects Nixon administration request to increase military aid to RVN.

11 April
ARVN evacuates Ranger base at Tống Lê Chân, surrounded by Communist troops since cease-fire.

12 April
RVN representatives withdraw from Paris talks on political reconciliation with the PRG.

16 April
RVN government withdraws diplomatic "privileges and immunities" of PRG delegation to Joint Military Commission.

10 May
PRG delegation walks out of Joint Military Commission, refusing to return until privileges and immunities are restored.

13 May
PRG delegation suspends its participation in Paris political talks, citing earlier suspension of the conference by Sài Gòn, withdrawal of diplomatic privileges for PRG delegation in Sài Gòn, and RVN "land grabbing" operations.

July–August
Communist forces regain major areas of Quang Nam and Quang Ngãi Provinces in first major offensive in the lowlands.

6 August
U.S. House of Representatives cuts military aid appropriations for RVN from $1 billion to $700 million in vote of 233 to 157.

9 August
Under threat of impeachment, Nixon resigns presidency and is succeeded by Vice-President Gerald R. Ford.

20 August
U.S. Congress reduces aid to RVN from $1 billion to $700 million.

8 October
PRG calls on public figures and organizations in South Vietnam to work for overthrow of Thiệu government and establishment of new regime in Sài Gòn.

October
Communist political and military leadership in Vietnam concludes that United States is unlikely to intervene and could not save Thiệu regime even if it did.

13 December
PAVN General Trân Văn Trà and Communist Central Office for South Vietnam head and political commissar for Communist forces in South Pham Hùng order 7th Division and newly formed 3d Division to attack and seize Phước Long Province north of Sài Gòn.

31 December
Approximately 50 U.S. uniformed military personnel in South Vietnam.

1975
1 January
Khmer Rouge in Cambodia begin final offensive against besieged Phnom Penh.

6 January
Communist forces take Phước Bình, capital of Phước Long Province.

8 January
Communist forces seize Phước Long Province. United States does not intervene with airpower.

10 March
Communist forces attack and seize Ban Mê Thuôt in Central Highlands, opening their Spring Offensive.

12 March
Ban Mê Thuôt falls to Communist forces.

U.S. Congress turns down President Ford's request for $300 million in military aid for RVN.

14 March
RVN President Thiêu orders precipitous withdrawal of ARVN forces from Central Highlands.

15 March
ARVN forces begin retreat from Kontum and Pleiku, which soon becomes debacle. ARVN 23d Division is savaged before remnants reach the coast.

19 March
Communist forces attack and capture Quang Tri City. ARVN withdrawal from Đà Nẵng turns into rout and 1st Division disintegrates.

25 March
DRV Politburo revises its timetable for ending war, deciding that Sài Gòn should be taken before beginning of mid-May rainy season. Communist commander of the offensive General Văn Tiên Dũng asks permission to call this the Hồ Chí Minh Campaign, in the hope of achieving victory before Hồ's 19 May birthday anniversary. The Politburo agrees.

26 March
Huê falls to Communist troops. Đà Nẵng, flooded with refugees, is already under rocket attack.

30 March
Đà Nẵng falls to the Communists. Hà Nội orders General Văn Tiên Dũng to push toward Sài Gòn in the Hồ Chí Minh Campaign.

1 April
Cambodian President Lon Nol abdicates and flees Cambodia.

9–22 April
Battle for Xuân Lôc, capital of Long Khánh Province and strategically important to the defense of Sài Gòn. ARVN fights well in this, its only major stand of the Communist offensive.

10 April
President Ford requests additional $722 million in military aid to the RVN. Congress refuses.

12 April
Operation EAGLE PULL, evacuation of U.S. personnel from Phnom Penh.

16 April
President Ford orders all "unneeded" Americans to leave South Vietnam.

17 April
Khmer Rouge forces take Phnom Penh.

21 April
President Thiêu resigns. Vice-President Trân Văn Hưởng becomes president.

26 April
Final Communist assault on Sài Gòn begins.

28 April
President Hưởng resigns. Dưởng Văn Minh, who helped overthrow President Diêm in 1963, becomes president.

29 April
U.S. Ambassador to the RVN Graham Martin orders full evacuation. Fearing its negative impact on morale, he has delayed too long. Operation FREQUENT WIND takes place in chaotic circumstances as helicopters and U.S. Marines evacuate 395 Americans and 4,475 Vietnamese. Only a minority of Vietnamese thought to be at risk are evacuated or manage to escape by other means.

30 April
Communist forces capture Sài Gòn, for all practical purposes bringing the Vietnam War to a close.

—Spencer C. Tucker

Glossary

AAA—Antiaircraft artillery (also AA).

ACAV—Armored cavalry assault vehicle: M113 armored personnel carrier modified with two additional 7.62-mm machine guns and shielding for its main .50-caliber machine gun.

Agent Orange—Herbicide widely used in the defoliation of Vietnamese forests and jungles.

AID—See USAID.

AK47—Russian-designed assault rifle, Automat Kalashnikov, manufactured throughout the Communist bloc and considered to be one of the most successful infantry weapons of the twentieth century.

AO—Area of operations.

AOA—Amphibious objective area.

AOR—Area of responsibility.

APC—Armored personnel carrier.

Arc Light—Code name for B-52 bombing program within South Vietnam.

ARG/SLF—Amphibious ready group/special landing force.

ARVN—Army of the Republic of Vietnam.

ASEAN—The Association of South East Asian Nations, founded in 1967 to oppose the threat of feared Communist expansionism. Members include Brunei, Myanmar (Burma), the Philippines, Indonesia, Laos, Malaysia, Singapore, Thailand, and Vietnam (admitted in July 1995).

AWCC—Air Warning Control Center, established to broadcast warnings of artillery fire to friendly aircraft in the vicinity.

AWOL—Absent without leave.

Ba Mười Ba—A Vietnamese brand of beer (Vietnamese for "33").

Battalion—An army and marine corps organizational unit of three or more companies, normally commanded by a lieutenant colonel.

Battery—An army or marine corps artillery unit of approximately 100 soldiers led by a captain.

BDA—Bomb damage assessment.

Beehive ammunition—Antipersonnel weapon used by U.S. forces. Designed to be used against a massed infantry attack, beehive rounds were fired from howitzers and recoilless rifles and delivered thousands of small metal arrowlike projectiles (flechettes) that exploded in a 30-degree arc.

Berm—Built-up dirt wall; used as a barrier against attack.

Big Red One—Nickname for the U.S. Army 1st Infantry Division.

Black Horse—Nickname for the U.S. Army 11th Armored Cavalry Regiment.

BLT—Battalion landing team. Marine amphibious group.

BMEO—Brigade Marine l'Extreme Orient. French Far East Naval Brigade, the first French riverine unit.

Boonies—Slang for enemy territory; also called "Indian country" or "Apache country."

Brigade—In the U.S. Army in Vietnam, a division was grouped into three brigades, each commanded by a colonel. The number of soldiers would vary according to the purpose of a particular mission. There were also separate infantry brigades.

Bug out—Slang for departing an area quickly.

CAC—Combined action company. Organized by the U.S. Marines beginning in August 1965, the CACs were composed of a Vietnamese Popular Forces platoon, a Marine rifle squad, and a medical corpsman. (See also CAP.)

Cai táng—Vietnamese practice of ancestor veneration. Traditionally, especially before 1954, about three to five years after they had been temporarily buried, the remains of a dead relative would be exhumed, washed with scented alcohol, and reburied in a permanent grave. They might even be moved to another grave, at a site believed to bring success and luck to the dead person's descendants.

CAP—Combined action platoon. Organized in February 1967 by the U.S. Marines to wage "the other war," the CAPs combined a Marine rifle squad of 14 men and one Navy corpsman with three ten-man Popular Forces (PF) militia squads and a five-man platoon headquarters into a combined platoon of 50 American and Vietnamese soldiers to provide security at the local level and initiate civic action programs as part of the pacification effort. (See also CAC.)

CAS—Close air support.

CBU—Cluster bomb unit.

CG—Commanding general.

Charlie—One of the many slang names for Communist troops; military communications code word for the letter C; a shortened form of Victor Charlie (VC, for Việt Cộng).

Chicken plate—Bulletproof breastplate worn by helicopter crews.

CHICOM—Chinese Communist.

CHNAVADVGRP—Chief, Naval Advisory Group Vietnam (U.S. Navy).

Chogey—Slang term meaning to leave an area: "cut a chogey." Originally a Korean War term that was also used in Vietnam.

CIA—U.S. Central Intelligence Agency.

CIB—Combat Infantryman's Badge.

CIDG—Civilian Irregular Defense Group. Central Intelligence Agency project that combined self-defense functions with economic programs to win the support of the civilian population. Carried out among Montagnards by U.S. Army Special Forces.

CINCPAC—Commander in Chief, Pacific Command. Commander of U.S. forces in the Pacific, including Southeast Asia.

Claymore—U.S. M18 antipersonnel mine. Light, easily transported, and highly directional. Spraying over 100 steel balls in a 40-degree arc, it could be hand-detonated or emplaced to fire electronically (command detonated).

Clear and hold—Military operation used by U.S. and Republic of Vietnam troops in the pacification program in which troops encircled, captured, and searched an area, clearing it of Communist forces; South Vietnamese troops then usually held the area.

CO—Conscientious objector.

Company—Basic military unit of two or more platoons. Permanent companies usually have alphabetic names (e.g., Company A, Company B, Company C or, more colloquially, "Alpha Company," "Bravo Company," "Charlie Company").

COMUSMACV—Commander, U.S. Military Assistance Command, Vietnam.

CORDS—Civilian Operations and Revolutionary (later changed to Rural) Development Support. Organized all civilian agencies in Vietnam within the military chain of command. Successor to the Office of Civilian Operations (OCO).

Corps—Group of two or more divisions responsible for a military region.

COSVN—Central Office for South Vietnam (Trung Ưởng Cuc Miên Nam). Communist military headquarters representing the Democratic Republic of Vietnam Lao Đông Party Central Committee in South Vietnam.

CTZ—Corps Tactical Zone, a military region. Vietnam was divided into four military regions, I through IV.

DEROS—Date of estimated return from overseas service; date eligible to return from overseas. Điên cái đầu ("dinky dau")— Vietnamese for "crazy," widely used by GIs and by the Vietnamese to describe Americans in Vietnam.

Dinassauts—French integrated tactical units composed of naval and army forces for riverine warfare during the Indo-China War.

DIVARTY—Division artillery.

Division—An organizational and tactical unit of 15,000 to 20,000 men, made up of two to three brigades. Used for sustained combat.

DMZ—Demilitarized Zone. The five-mile-wide buffer zone along the demarcation line, just below the 17th parallel, that was established in the 1954 Geneva Accords to provisionally divide North and South Vietnam pending elections that were to have been held in 1956. According to the Geneva Accords, there were to be no military forces, supplies, or equipment within the zone during its "temporary" existence.

Đôc lâp—Vietnamese for "independence."

DOD—U.S. Department of Defense.

Donut dollies—Nickname for workers in the American Red Cross Supplemental Recreation Activities Overseas (SRAO) program in Vietnam, which provided a variety of recreational activities for American troops. The women were so named because they often dispensed donuts and coffee to the troops, especially in the field. They also assisted in hospitals and provided games and conversation in the field.

Door-gunner—Soldier who fired from the open door of a helicopter, a hazardous position usually filled by volunteers.

DRV—Democratic Republic of Vietnam (North Vietnam), established on 2 September 1945.

Dustoff—Helicopter evacuation of wounded.

Eagle Flight—Special U.S. helicopter assault force used to observe Communist positions, react to emergencies, and conduct raid and ambush missions.

ELINT—Electronic intelligence. Intelligence derived from electronic means.

FAC—Forward air controller. Low-flying spotter planes identified Communist positions and called the FAC, who in turn ordered air strikes against these positions.

FADAC—The U.S. Army's first digital fire direction computer.

FDC—Fire direction center.

FDO—Fire direction officer.

Firebase—A small artillery base used for patrol and to support ground operations, usually temporary.

Firefight—A brief and violent exchange of small-arms fire between two opposing units, rather than combat action between two larger forces during an assault.

First Team—Nickname for the U.S. Army 1st Cavalry Division (Airmobile). Also referred to as "Aircav," "1st Horse," or "1st Aircav."

FISCOORD—Fire support coordinator for artillery at company, battalion, or brigade level. Usually the senior artilleryman present who prepared fire plans and integrated all indirect-fire weapons.

Flashback—A strong recurrence of memory, usually a symptom of post-traumatic stress disorder (PTSD).

Flight—Basic air force organizational and tactical unit; a group of three to five aircraft used together in a common mission.

FMF—Fleet Marine Force.

FMFPAC—Fleet Marine Force, Pacific Command.

FO—Forward observer. A field artillery lieutenant assigned to an infantry or armor company for the purposes of calling for and adjusting artillery fire on a target.

FOB—Forward operating base.

Force Recon—The U.S. Marine Corps' elite reconnaissance element.

Frag—Fragmentation hand grenade. Also a fragmentary order. Also to kill or attempt to kill one's own officers or noncommissioned officers, usually with a fragmentation grenade.

Freedom Birds—Nickname given to the airplanes taking U.S. soldiers home after their tour of duty.

Free-fire zone—An area in which targets could be engaged at any time with any and all available weapons systems.

FSB—Fire support base.

GCMA—Groupement de commandos mixtes aéroportés. French Special Forces that conducted long-range penetration missions and clandestine raids into Viêt Minh territory.

GM—Groupe mobile. French military unit equivalent to a U.S. regimental combat team or a light separate brigade.

Going downtown—Slang for flying an air strike mission against Hà Nôi.

GPES—Ground Proximity Extraction System. A system whereby a long hook attached to cargo in a C-130 cargo plane would catch an arrest wire on the runway. Pulling the cargo from the plane. Used during air resupply to land loads, as during the siege of Khe Sanh.

Group—A command unit of two or more battalions used for combat service and support and usually commanded by a colonel; subordinate to a brigade. Also, an artillery unit consisting of three of more battalions commanded by a colonel and used for general support within a designated area.

Grunt—Slang term for an infantry soldier. Also "boonie rat," "11 bang-bang," "bush buster."

H&I—Harassment and interdiction fire: random rounds fired at "suspected or likely" enemy locations and routes.

Headhunters—Nickname for the 1st Squadron, 9th Cavalry, 1st Cavalry Division (Airmobile); also known as the "Blues." The element of the 1st Cavalry Division designated to perform reconnaissance missions. Their mission was to "fix and hold" Communist forces until the rest of the division could engage.

Hearts and minds—In 1965 President Lyndon B. Johnson said, "So we must be ready to fight in Vietnam, but the ultimate victory will depend on the hearts and minds of the people who actually live out there." The U.S. government tried to win the loyalty and trust of the Vietnamese through various pacification programs that included the provision of civic improvements and security from Viêt Công harassment with the objective of encouraging villagers to fight against the Communists.

HEAT—High-explosive antitank artillery ammunition.

Hô Chí Minh Trail—Network of roads and trails leading from North Vietnam through Laos and Cambodia to South Vietnam. Used by the Democratic Republic of Vietnam to transport troops and supplies.

Hootch—Slang for a soldier's shelter.

Hợp Tác—Vietnamese for "cooperation." Name of an unsuccessful 1964 pacification program concentrated around Sài Gòn.

HQ—Headquarters.

IADS—Integrated air defense system.

ICC—International Control Commission. (See ICSC.)

ICSC—International Commission for Supervision and Control. Established at the 1954 Geneva Conference to supervise implementation of the Geneva Accords, it consisted of delegates from three countries not involved in the conflict but nonetheless representing the different points of view: India (neutralist), Canada (Western), and Poland (Communist).

Later Indonesia replaced India in a revamped version of the ICSC known as the International Commission of Control and Supervision (ICCS) mandated by the 1973 Paris Peace Accords.

IGLOO WHITE—Code name for sensor operation in Laos.

IPSD—Infantry Platoon (Scout Dog). See entry for Canines (K-9 Corps).

IVS—International Voluntary Services. A private, nonprofit organization that served as a model for the Peace Corps and that first came to the Republic of Vietnam (RVN) in 1957. Funded primarily by the U.S. Agency for International Development (USAID), support also came from the RVN government during the early years. IVS workers were required to study Vietnamese and received instruction in Vietnamese culture. They signed up for a two-year stay in-country, with assignments at the village level ranging from agricultural development to the teaching of English. IVS saw its function as humanitarian and divorced from USAID political objectives. Sài Gòn ceased approving IVS projects in 1971.

JCS—Joint Chiefs of Staff. Heads of the U.S. military branches, consisting of a chairman, the Army chief of staff, the chief of naval operations, the Air Force chief of staff, and the Marine commandant (ex officio). Advises the president, the secretary of defense, and the National Security Council on military matters.

JUSPAO—Joint U.S. Public Affairs Office; created in 1965 to take charge of both relations with the news media and psychological warfare operations.

JUWTF—Joint Unconventional Warfare Task Force; composed of unconventional warfare personnel from the U.S. Air Force, U.S. Army, U.S. Marine Corps, and U.S. Navy.

KIA—Killed in action.

Killer Junior—A close-in artillery technique, in which shells are fired 30 meters above the ground at ranges of 200 to 2,000 meters with minimum time fuzes, set to arm within three to five seconds after the projectile has cleared the tube. Primarily employed by 155-mm artillery; used by U.S. firebases against ground assaults.

Kit Carson Scouts—Former Viêt Công or People's Army of Vietnam soldiers who were used as scouts by U.S. units.

KKK—Khmer Kampuchea Krom. Anti-Communist faction, loosely allied with the Khmer Serai, seeking autonomy for Khmer Krom people living in the Mekong River Delta of South Vietnam in return for military services. During the 1960s Khmer Krom soldiers made up numerous ethnic regular and irregular force battalions within the Army of the Republic of Vietnam (ARVN).

LAAGER—(also Lager) Slang term originating in the Boer War that denotes preparing a defensive position, usually at night (see also NDP). This term was most commonly used in U.S. armored or mechanized infantry units.

LAW—Light antitank weapon (M66).

Lima sites—Primitive airstrips in Laos used by U.S. forces for covert actions.

LLDB—Lực Lượng Đặc Biệt. Army of the Republic of Vietnam Special Forces.

LOCs—Lines of communication.

LOH—Light observation helicopter (pronounced LOOCH).

LP—Listening post.

LZ—Landing zone (for helicopters).

M14—See M16.

M16—U.S. assault rifle, primary infantry weapon of the war. Incurred great controversy, as early models tended to jam in combat. Troops initially preferred the M14, a magazine-fed Garand-action, U.S. rifle issued from 1957 until 1967.

M79—U.S. 40-mm grenade launcher. Also called "thumper" or "elephant gun."

MAAG—Military Assistance and Advisory Group.

MAC—Military Airlift Command.

MACV—Military Assistance Command, Vietnam.

MACV-SOG—Military Assistance Command, Vietnam, Studies and Observation Group.

Mad minute—Strategy used by U.S. forces in an effort to force or "trip" a Việt Công or People's Army of Vietnam ambush or assault. Just prior to daybreak, all forces within a position would open fire into the area surrounding the position, utilizing all weapons.

MAF—Marine Amphibious Force.

MARKET TIME—Code name for interdiction efforts against North Vietnamese seaborne infiltration.

MATS—Military Air Transport Service.

MAW—Military Airlift Wing.

MEB—Marine Expeditionary Brigade.

MEDCAPs—Medical civic action program that brought military doctors and medics to rural villages and hamlets.

Medevac—Acronym combining the words "medical" and "evacuation"; term applied to the movement of casualties from the battlefield to more secure locations for immediate medical attention.

MIA—Missing in action.

Montagnard—French term for indigenous Vietnamese mountain people. Often shortened to "Yard."

MOS—Military occupational specialty.

MRF—Mobile Riverine Force.

MSC—Military Sealift Command.

MUSSEL SHOALS—Code name for electronic sensor operations in the Demilitarized Zone.

MUST—Medical Unit Self-contained, Transportable.

NAG—Naval Advisory Group. Former U.S. Navy section in the Military Assistance and Advisory Group, Vietnam (until May 1964). In April 1965 it became an operational naval command.

Napalm—Incendiary chemical used by both France and the United States in Vietnam. A jellylike substance, it adheres to surfaces while it burns.

NATO—North Atlantic Treaty Organization.

NDP—Night defensive position.

NLF—National Liberation Front; officially National Front for the Liberation of South Vietnam (NFLSV) (Việt Công).

No-fire line—U.S. fire control measure. A designated point on a map beyond which no indirect-fire weapons or air assets could be employed without permission from the sector commander.

NSA—National Security Agency. U.S. agency responsible for the centralized coordination, direction, and performance of American signals intelligence.

Nung—Chinese ethnic group. Often served as mercenaries for the United States.

NVA—North Vietnamese Army. U.S. designation for People's Army of Vietnam (PAVN).

OCO—Office of Civilian Operations. Predecessor to CORDS (Civilian Operations and Revolutionary Development Support). The OCO organized all U.S. civilian agencies in the Republic of Vietnam under the jurisdiction of the U.S. Embassy.

Opcon—Operation control (e.g., the 196th Light Infantry Brigade, American Division was under the Opcon of the 3d Marines).

OPLAN—Operation plan.

OPORD—Operation order.

OSS—U.S. Office of Strategic Services; forerunner of the Central Intelligence Agency.

PAO—Public Affairs Officer.

Pathfinder—Airborne term for specially trained soldiers inserted ahead of the main body of troops to mark a landing zone.

PAVN—People's Army of Vietnam. Army of the Democratic Republic of Vietnam (North Vietnam).

PCS—Permanent change of station.

PIRAZ—"Positive Identification Radar Advisory Zone": U.S. destroyers, frigates, and cruisers operating in the Gulf of Tonkin providing support for Allied war planes.

Platoon—Basic infantry unit of 22 to 40 men (two or more squads) commanded by a lieutenant.

POL—Designation for petroleum, oil, and lubricants.

POW—Prisoner of war (also PW).

PSYOPS—Psychological warfare operations.

PSYWAR—Psychological warfare.

Puff (Puff the Magic Dragon)—Nickname for C-47 aircraft mounting a bank of electrically driven 7.62-mm Gatling guns.

Punji stake—A sharpened bamboo stake covered with feces or poison and placed at the bottom of a pit, underwater, or along a trail to be stepped on by troops; an effective physical and psychological weapon.

PX—Post exchange (U.S. Army); in the U.S. Air Force and Navy it was referred to as the Base Exchange (BX).

R&R—Rest and recuperation.

RDF—Radio direction finding. RDF provided essential information about command structure and unit deployment. It and associated signals intelligence activities were utilized by all major Indo-China antagonists.

Recon—Short for reconnaissance. Small recon patrols were used to get information about enemy troop strengths, movements, etc.; also called recce.

Regiment—Once a basic organizational unit in the U.S. Army, larger than a battalion, smaller than a brigade; now used only for armored cavalry units. In the Marine Corps, a regiment is a basic organizational unit of three infantry battalions.

Restricted fire line—U.S. fire control measure. A designated point on a map beyond which targets could be engaged only with indirect-fire weapons or air assets with permission from tactical headquarters or when direct contact was in progress.

RFs, PFs—South Vietnamese Regional Forces and Popular Forces. Locally recruited South Vietnamese forces not counted as part of the regular military establishment. The RFs were organized in company and battalion-size units, and some in battle groups of two or three battalions. RFs were the organic forces of the provinces and were under the command and control of the provincial military headquarters. Armed with light weapons, they were equipped, trained, and held ranks similar to the regular army. The PFs belonged to the villages and operated in separate platoons. They were to defend their villages and prevent infiltration by the Việt Cộng.

Rome plow—A bulldozer used for clearing forest, jungle, and brush; manufactured by the Rome (Georgia) Caterpillar Company.

RON—Remain overnight.

RPG—U.S. designation for a communist rocket-propelled grenade.

RR—Recoilless rifle.

RT—Reconnaissance team.

RTAFB—Royal Thai Air Force Base.

RTO—Radio (telephone/voice) operator.

Ruff-Puffs—U.S. slang term for Vietnamese Regional Forces and Popular Forces (RFs/PFs), which had a maximum strength of nearly 525,000 men. (See RFs, PFs.)

RVN—Republic of Vietnam (South Vietnam).

RVNAF—Republic of Vietnam Armed Forces.

Saigon commando—Derogatory slang term given by combat troops to soldiers assigned to rear areas. Often soldiers assigned to these billets wore the popular "boonie hats" and camouflage uniforms denied to frontline forces.

Saigon tea—Nonalcoholic drink that could be soda, cold tea, or colored scented water. Bar girls would ask GIs, "Buy me Saigon tea." Often the prices were prohibitive.

Saint-Cyr—French military academy.

Sapper—Specially trained Communist demolition commando, expert at penetrating enemy defenses to destroy equipment and fortifications; often part of suicide missions.

SAR—Search and rescue.

SCT—Sea Commando Team.

Seabees—U.S. Navy construction battalion.

SEAL—Sea Air Land. Elite U.S. Navy unconventional warfare teams.

SF—U.S. Army Special Forces.

SHINING BRASS—Code name for U.S.-led reconnaissance operations into Laos (October 1965 to March 1967).

Short-timer—A person coming to the end of his assignment in Vietnam.

SLAM—Search, Locate, Annihilate, and Monitor.

SLF—Special Landing Force. Each 2,000-man SLF was composed of a Marine Battalion Landing Team (BLT) and a helicopter squadron.

Slick—Transport helicopter; lacking guns, it had a "slick" exterior.

SOD—Special Operations Detachment.

SOG—Studies and Observations Group. Operating out of the Military Assistance Command, Vietnam, this organization carried out clandestine operations, such as road watch teams in Laos, in conjunction with the Central Intelligence Agency.

Sortie—One mission by one aircraft.

SP—Self-propelled (artillery).

Squad—A basic fighting unit of eight to ten men commanded by a sergeant, grouped for drill, inspection, and other purposes; part of a platoon.

Squadron—A battalion-sized army air or armored cavalry unit commanded by a lieutenant colonel. In the Navy or Air Force, a squadron is two or more flights of aircraft.

SRV—Socialist Republic of Vietnam. North and South Vietnam reunified in 1975.

TAC—Tactical Air Command.

TAOR—Tactical area of responsibility.

TDY—Temporary duty; usually a six-month assignment.

Toe poppers—Slang for Communist antipersonnel mines designed to maim (break a foot or blow off toes).

Tour of duty—The 365 days a soldier in the U.S. Army spent in Vietnam; for Marines the period was 13 months.

Track—Slang for armored vehicle.

Tunnel rat—U.S. soldier, usually slight in stature, detailed to go into tunnels used by Communist forces armed with only a pistol and a flashlight. This was extremely hazardous duty, as the men frequently encountered booby traps, poisonous snakes, and flooded tunnels. Psychological stress was profound.

USAF—U.S. Air Force.

USAID—U.S. Agency for International Development. Administered U.S. aid to the Republic of Vietnam.

USIA—U.S. Information Agency. Agency responsible for disseminating information about the United States overseas.

USMC—U.S. Marine Corps.

USN—U.S. Navy.

USOM—U.S. Operations Mission. USAID field agency in the Republic of Vietnam that administered the USAID program there.

VC—Viêt Công, derived from the term Công San Viêt Nam, which means Vietnamese Communist. Term used by the U.S. military to designate Communist forces in South Vietnam (the North Vietnamese military being known as the NVA). To the South Vietnamese, anyone—wherever and of whatever rank—who was in or who served the Communist military and public security forces was Viêt Công.

Victor Charlie—Military communications code words for VC (Viêt Công). (See Charlie.)

Viêt Minh—Common name for the Viêt Nam Dôc Lâp Dông Minh Hôi. Communist front organization founded in 1941 to resist French colonial rule and Japanese occupational forces. It fought the French in the Indo-China War.

VNAF—Vietnamese Air Force (Republic of Vietnam).

VNN—Vietnamese Navy (Republic of Vietnam).

VVAW—Vietnam Veterans Against the War.

WIA—Wounded in action.

Willy Pete—White phosphorus shell round used for screening, signaling, and incendiary action; illumination. Also known as "Wilson Pickett."

Wing—A major organizational Air Force unit in which aircraft fly in a side-by-side formation; it includes one primary mission group plus support.

"Wise Men"—A select group of senior advisors to President Lyndon Johnson.

"The World"—Slang for the continental United States. Also "land of the big PX."

Yankee Station—An operating area off the Vietnamese coast in the South China Sea used by the U.S. Navy's Seventh Fleet Attack Carrier Strike Force (Task Force 77). Air strikes against the Democratic Republic of Vietnam were launched from Yankee Station; code name for the Gulf of Tonkin.

ZOA—Zone of action.

—David Coffey, Stan McGowen, J. A. Menzoff, Harve Saal, Spencer C. Tucker, and Sandra Wittman

Illustration Credits

1	National Archives	266	UPI/Corbis-Bettmann
3	National Archives	267	National Archives
6	National Archives	270	National Archives
12	National Archives/Corbis	277	AP/Wide World
13	UPI/Corbis-Bettmann	282	National Archives
19	National Archives (top)	286	Hulton-Deutsch Collection/Corbis
19	Naval Historical Center (bottom)	290	Archive Photos
27	UPI/Corbis-Bettmann	296	National Archives
30	National Archives	297	Lyndon Baines Johnson Library
31	UPI/Corbis-Bettmann	300	National Archives
32	Archive Photos	303	National Archives
34	National Archives	324	National Archives
51	National Archives	333	John F. Kennedy Library
55	Tim Page/Corbis	335	UPI/Corbis-Bettmann
58	National Archives	341	UPI/Corbis-Bettmann
59	UPI/Corbis-Bettmann	347	National Archives
73	Hulton-Deutsch Collection/Corbis	365	AP/Wide World
75	National Archives	376	National Archives
92	UPI/Corbis-Bettmann	388	UPI/Corbis-Bettmann
93	National Archives	397	National Archives
106	National Archives	404	National Archives
119	National Archives	406	UPI/Corbis-Bettmann
125	Lyndon Baines Johnson Library	407	UPI/Corbis-Bettmann
129	National Archives	415	John F. Kennedy Library
130	National Archives	419	National Archives
132	National Archives	421	National Archives
137	National Archives	423	National Archives
140	UPI/Corbis-Bettmann	424	UPI/Corbis-Bettmann
143	UPI/Corbis-Bettmann	426	National Archives
145	UPI/Corbis-Bettmann	428	UPI/Corbis-Bettmann
155	Archive Photos	443	Center of Military History
158	UPI/Corbis-Bettmann	447	National Archives
163	UPI/Corbis-Bettmann	451	National Archives
164	UPI/Corbis-Bettmann	454	Naval Historical Center
167	UPI/Corbis-Bettmann	456	Lyndon Baines Johnson Library
177	National Archives	459	UPI/Corbis-Bettmann
190	Archive Photos	462	UPI/Corbis-Bettmann
201	National Archives	466	National Archives
207	Naval Historical Center	468	UPI/Corbis-Bettmann
216	UPI/Corbis-Bettmann	472	UPI/Corbis-Bettmann
221	National Archives	477	UPI/Corbis-Bettmann
224	National Archives	478	UPI/Corbis-Bettmann
227	UPI/Corbis-Bettmann	481	UPI/Corbis-Bettmann
232	UPI/Corbis-Bettmann	490	AP/Wide World
243	National Archives	496	Lyndon Baines Johnson Library
253	National Archives	500	National Archives
259	UPI/Corbis-Bettmann	502	UPI/Corbis-Bettmann

509	National Archives	707	National Archives
511	UPI/Corbis-Bettmann	710	National Archives
512	National Archives	716	National Archives
513	National Archives	719	UPI/Corbis-Bettmann
514	National Archives	728	National Archives
545	National Archives	733	UPI/Corbis-Bettmann
546	National Archives	735	UPI/Corbis-Bettmann
553	UPI/Corbis-Bettmann	736	UPI/Corbis-Bettmann
555	Naval Historical Center	737	National Archives
563	National Archives	738	UPI/Corbis-Bettmann
566	UPI/Corbis-Bettmann	743	Corbis
574	National Archives	750	National Archives
578	UPI/Corbis-Bettmann	759	National Archives
581	UPI/Corbis-Bettmann	762	UPI/Corbis-Bettmann
603	National Archives	766	National Archives
609	National Archives	768	UPI/Corbis-Bettmann
610	National Archives	777	UPI/Corbis-Bettmann
621	National Archives	778	National Archives
643	National Archives	779	National Archives
662	National Archives	783	National Archives
670	National Archives	791	UPI/Corbis-Bettmann
676	National Archives	800	National Archives
679	UPI/Corbis-Bettmann	801	AP/Wide World
680	National Archives/Corbis	817	Lyndon Baines Johnson Library/Corbis
681	National Archives	819	UPI/Corbis-Bettmann
685	National Archives	823	AP/Wide World
687	AP/Wide World	825	UPI/Corbis-Bettmann